THE AHLA/BVR GUIDE TO HEALTHCARE VALUATION

2010 EDITION

MARK O. DIETRICH, CPA/ABV
EDITOR

Business Valuation Resources, LLC
1000 SW Broadway, Suite 1200
Portland, OR 97205
(503) 291-7963 Fax • (503) 291-7955 • www.BVResources.com

What It's Worth

Copyright © 2010 by Business Valuation Resources, L.L.C. (BVR). All rights reserved. Printed in the United States of America.

No part of this publication may be reproduced, stored in a retrieval system or transmitted in any form or by any means, electronic, mechanical, photocopying, recording, scanning or otherwise, except as permitted under Sections 107 or 108 of the 1976 United States Copyright Act, without either the prior written permission of the Publisher or authorization through payment of the appropriate per copy fee to the Publisher. Requests for permission should be addressed to the Permissions Department, Business Valuation Resources, LLC, 1000 SW Broadway St., Suite 1200, Portland, OR, 97205, (503) 291-7963, fax (503) 291-7955.

Information contained in this book has been obtained by Business Valuation Resources from sources believed to be reliable. However, neither Business Valuation Resources nor its authors guarantee the accuracy or completeness of any information published herein and neither Business Valuation Resources nor its authors shall be responsible for any errors, omissions, or damages arising out of use of this information. This work is published with the understanding that Business Valuation Resources and its authors are supplying information but are not attempting to render business valuation or other professional services. If such services are required, the assistance of an appropriate professional should be sought.

Editor: Mark Dietrich
Managing Editor: Colin Murcray
Publisher: Doug Twitchell
Chair and CEO: David Foster
President: Lucretia Lyons
Customer Service Manager: Stephanie Crader
ISBN: 978-1-935081-41-8

Table of Contents

Introduction 1

Chapter 1: Healthcare 'Reform' 21
By Mark O. Dietrich, CPA/ABV

Chapter 2: The Healthcare Economy
National Health Expenditures Projections: 2009-2019 41
By Mark O. Dietrich, CPA/ABV

Chapter 3: Healthcare Market Structure and its Implication for Valuation of Privately Held Provider Entities—An Empirical Analysis 93
By Mark O. Dietrich, CPA/ABV

Chapter 4: Brief Summaries of Medicare and Medicaid 123
Prepared by Earl Dirk Hoffman, Jr., Barbara S. Klees, and Catherine A. Curtis

Chapter 5: Valuation Standards 153
By Edward J. Dupke, CPA/ABV

Chapter 6: Overview of Cost of Capital Models 173
By James Harrington, MBA

Chapter 7: The Anti-Kickback Statute and Stark Law: Avoiding Valuation of Referrals 195
By James Pinna, JD and Matt Jenkins, JD

Chapter 8: Tax-Exempt Healthcare Organization Valuation Issues Related to Excess Benefits, Private Inurement, and Intermediate Sanctions 211
By Robert F. Reilly

Chapter 9: Tax-Exempt Hospitals Under the Microscope— How Much Charity Care are You Providing? 239

By Robert Wolin, Susan Feigin Harris, Jason Pinkall and Edward Beckwith

Chapter 10: Why Boards of Directors Need to Understand Valuation Issues 253
    By Eleanor Bloxham, MBA

Chapter 11: Factors in Forecasting Cashflow and Estimating Cost of Capital in Healthcare 261
    Carol Carden, CPA/ABV, ASA, Mark O. Dietrich, CPA/ABV

Chapter 12: Choosing and Using the Right Valuation Methods for Physician Practices. 271
    By Mark O. Dietrich, CPA/ABV

Appendix to Chapter 12: A Heathcare Appraiser Reviews a Judge-Appraiser's 'Report'. 323
    By Mark O. Dietrich, CPA/ABV

Chapter 13: Fair Market Value **Requires** the Demonstration of Income to a Hypothetical Owner 335
    Mark O. Dietrich, CPA/ABV & Todd Sorensen, AVA

Chapter 14: Critical Condition—A Coding Analysis for a Physician Practice Valuation. 343
    By Mark O. Dietrich, CPA/ABV, and Frank Cohen, CMPA

Chapter 15: Why Transaction Structure Affects Value and Other Nuances of Valuing Medical Practices 351
    By Mark O. Dietrich, CPA/ABV

Chapter 16: Understanding and Using the Technical and Professional Component of Ancillary Revenue when Valuing Medical Practices 361
    By Mark O. Dietrich, CPA/ABV, and Kathie L. Wilson, CPA, CVA

Chapter 17: Deal Structure and Tax Considerations in Asset and Stock Transactions 367
By Scott Miller, CPA/ABV, CVA

Chapter 18: Converting Physician Practices to Tax-Exempt Status: Is There an Upside to the Downturn? 385
Mark O. Dietrich, CPA/ABV

Chapter 19: Identifying and Measuring Personal Goodwill in a Professional Practice 393
By Mark O. Dietrich, CPA/ABV

Chapter 20: Identifying and Measuring Personal Goodwill in a Professional Practice—Part II: Using the Single Period Capitalization Model 405
By Mark O. Dietrich, CPA/ABV

Chapter 21: Lost Profits for Physician Practices 409
By Mark Dietrich, CPA/ABV

Chapter 22: Designing a Chart of Accounts to Meet the Needs of Physician Practices 427
By David N. Gans, M.S.H.A., FACMPE and Steven Andes, PhD, CPA

Chapter 23: Benchmarking Practice Performance 435
By Gregory S. Feltenberger, MBA, CACMPE, FACHE, CPHIMS, and David N. Gans, MHSA, FACMPE

Chapter 24: Understanding and Using MGMA Data to Normalize Physician Compensation and Perform Financial Statement Benchmarks 455
By David Fein, MBA

Chapter 25: The CPA's Role in Mergers and Acquisitions Due Diligence Assistance to PPMCs and Private Equity Firms. . 483
By Ronald D. Finkelstein, CPA, and Lydia Glatz, CPA

Chapter 26: When the Marriage is Over, What is the Practice Worth? 499
    By Stacey D. Udell, CPA/ABV/CFF, ASA, CVA

Chapter 27: Jurisdictional Issues in Physician Practice Divorce Valuation: California. 515
    By Kathie Wilson, CPA, CVA and Tracy Farryl Katz, Esq., CPA

Chapter 28: Valuation of Physician On-Call and Coverage Arrangements 527
    By Greg Anderson, CPA, ABV, CVA

Chapter 29: Evaluating RVU-Based Compensation Arrangements 551
    By Mark O. Dietrich, CPA/ABV, and Gregory D. Anderson, CPA/ABV, CVA

Chapter 30: Valuing Medical Director Services 555
    By Andrea M. Ferrari, JD, MPH and Timothy R. Smith, CPA/ABV

Chapter 31: Valuing Management Services Contracts between Physicians and Hospitals 575
    By Randy Biernat, CPA

Chapter 32: Valuating Clinical Co-Management Arrangements 589
    By Greg Anderson, CPA, ABV, CVA and Scott Safriet, AVA, MBA

Chapter 33: Fair Market Value: Ensuring Compliance within the Life Sciences Industry 613
    By Ann S. Brandt, PhD, Jason Ruchaber, CFA, ASA, and Timothy R. Smith, CPA/ABV

Chapter 34: The Valuation of Hospitals 637
    By Don Barbo, CPA/ABV, and Robbie Mundy, CPA/ABV, CVA

Chapter 35: Valuing Joint Ventures & 'Under Arrangements' . 651
    By Carol Carden, CPA/ABV, ASA, CFE

Chapter 36: Ambulatory Surgery Centers 659
By Todd Sorensen, MBA, AVA

Chapter 37: Valuation Considerations Specific To Diagnostic Imaging Entities 691
By Doug Smith

Chapter 38: Valuing Dialysis Clinics 709
By Carol Carden, CPA/ABV, ASA, CFE

Chapter 39: Home Health Care Services 717
By Alan B. Simons, CPA/ABV, CMPE, DABFA

Chapter 40: What is to be Learned From Caracci? 735
By Mark O. Dietrich, CPA/ABV, and Kenneth W. Patton, ASA

Chapter 41: Quality Performance and Valuation: What's The Connection? 749
By Alice G. Gosfield, JD

Chapter 42: Fairness Opinions: Is the One You Receive Beyond Dispute?. 759
By Cain Brothers

Chapter 43: Valuation of S Corporations 783
by Nancy Fannon, CPA/ABV, ASA, MCBA and Laura Pfeiffenberger

Chapter 44: Buy-Sell Agreements: An Overview 799
By Chris Mercer

Appendix: Teleconference Transcript: Healthcare Reform and Its Impact on Valuation. 835
Presenters:
Mark O. Dietrich, CPA/ABV
Don Barbo, CPA/ABV
C. Elliott Jeter, CFA, CPA/ABV

Introduction

Healthcare is the single largest segment of the economy, the financial aspects of which are perhaps the least well understood. The March, 2010 Federal Healthcare Reform legislation will contribute to that lack of understanding as appraisers, attorneys and industry members probe the plethora of new regulations implementing the Reform for knowledge. The Second Edition of AHLA/BVR's *Guide to Healthcare Valuation* brings together the country's top healthcare industry experts in a reprise of the First Edition's comprehensive undertaking aimed at providing both preparers and users of valuation reports with an in-depth understanding of individual industry subsectors. From physician practices to home health care agencies, valuation across the continuum of medical care venues is addressed.

First and foremost, each member of the panel of valuation experts provides guidance consistent with the mandatory regulatory constraints on valuation assumptions and methodologies in the healthcare industry. Specific risks under the Stark Law and Anti-kickback statute are addressed in a separate Chapter along with *real* advice on how to deal with them in a valuation engagement. The import of the nonprofit hospital sector is addressed in another chapter on inurement and tax exemption issues.

As will be clear to experienced healthcare appraisers and other readers alike, no valuation task can be accomplished without a thorough understanding of the market area in which the entity being valued operates. Despite the significance of national trends and the federal Medicare program in the valuation of healthcare enterprises, local differences in provider reimbursement by health insurers and individual state Medicaid programs lead to significant differences in operating results and value.

Notably, each of the valuation chapters provides keen insights on the significance of understanding the revenue cycle. The manner in which healthcare providers – such as physicians, hospitals, imaging or ambulatory surgery centers – are paid or reimbursed for their services varies radically. As such, an assumption about inflation or growth in per unit reimbursement appropriate for one of these sectors may be wholly inappropriate for another.

Leading off the valuation chapters is a new chapter on Cost of Capital in the Healthcare Industry, one of the more complex financial issues confronting appraisers. The largest number of provider entities and the most frequent valuation engagement involves physician practices and the Guide reflects this. In addition to a detailed chapter on valuation methods for physicians, the Guide includes chapters on the newly extant use of the Cost Approach, personal and enterprise goodwill and noncompete agreements, how to analyze CPT™ codes, damages and the use of MGMA data. Two chapters address the tax aspects of transactions, which can have a significant affect on the manner in which a valuation method is approached. Where a medical practice valuation is the most common form of healthcare valuation, the most common reason for that valuation is a divorce. Two chapters on the unique issues of divorce valuation are also included.

Introduction

Physician business relationships with Hospitals and other provider entities are perhaps the major driving force in the healthcare industry today and the Guide devotes six separate chapters to valuation issues in this growing market segment. I am certain the heretofore unseen scale of these comprehensive works will stand as a major contribution to the healthcare community's Body of Knowledge.

As Editor and Technical Editor for this Second Edition of the Guide, I was particularly appreciative of the willingness of my friends and colleagues in the healthcare valuation discipline to share their vast knowledge, without reservation, in their specialty areas. The separate chapters devoted to Ambulatory Surgery, Imaging, Dialysis, Home Health and Hospitals offer the valuation analyst and legal communities information and insight usually obtainable only through hours of study and years of experience.

The Guide is rounded out with contributions from thought leaders in the broader healthcare community addressing such diverse areas as private equity, globalization, quality of care and issues to be addressed by an organization's Board of Directors. In addition, readers and users will benefit from discussions of the Cost of Capital and Valuation Standards by industry leaders. Finally, a number of chapters include checklists to aid the valuation analyst in the performance of the engagement.

On behalf of Business Valuation Resources and the American Healthcare Lawyers Association, our thanks to all of the contributors for their hard work on behalf of their healthcare industry colleagues, who we are certain will find *The AHLA/BVR Guide to Healthcare Valuation* an important and valuable addition to their professional library.

Mark O, Dietrich, CPA/ABV
August, 2010

Introduction

About the Editor

Mark O. Dietrich, CPA/ABV is a *summa cum laude*, Beta Gamma Sigma graduate of Boston University where he also earned an MBA with high honors; he holds a Master in Taxation degree from Bentley College as well. He is Editor, Technical Editor and Contributing Author to the **American Health Lawyers' Association/Business Valuation Resources** *Guide to Healthcare Valuation 2d Edition*, Editor and Principal Author of Business Valuation Resources *Guide to Physician Practice Valuation*, author of the *Medical Practice Valuation Guidebook*, co-author of PPC's *Guide to Healthcare Consulting* and nearly 100 articles on valuation, taxation, managed care and the healthcare regulatory environment. A regular speaker at state and national conferences on healthcare valuation, managed care and other healthcare industry topics including Reform, Mark has also lectured in the United Kingdom on Managed Care, and on Valuation of Medical Practices to Her Majesty's Revenue and Customs. He is a member of the Editorial Board of *Financial Valuation and Litigation Expert* and the AICPA's Healthcare Expert Panel (through 2010) and National Healthcare Industry Conference Committee. Mark has also served on the AICPA's ABV Credential Committee and ABV Exam Review Course Task Force.

In addition to more than 200 valuation engagements in the healthcare industry, Mark's career experience includes serving as partner-in-charge of the annual audit of an 80 physician tax-exempt faculty group practice; representation of tax exempt and taxable entities in Internal Revenue Service field audits; participation in the development of a 250 physician independent Network and negotiation of their managed care contracts with health insurers including capitated Medicare plans; consulting in the formation of numerous group practices; and issues of reasonable compensation, healthcare markets, regulatory planning and defense, personal and enterprise goodwill and noncompete agreements. Mark has served as an expert witness in shareholder disputes, marital dissolution and *qui tam* matters.

Contributing Authors

Gregory D. Anderson, CPA, ABV, CVA is a partner in Health Care Services with HORNE, a CPA and business advisory firm headquartered in the southeastern United States. He concentrates his practice in the design, implementation and valuation of hospital/physician employment and other compensation arrangements; financial analysis and consulting on compensation plans for physician group practices; and valuation of medical practices, hospitals, diagnostic facilities, ambulatory surgery centers and other healthcare facilities. Mr. Anderson serves as the director of the firm's healthcare valuation services group.

Mr. Anderson presents programs to healthcare attorneys and other healthcare organizations on issues related to the fair market value of physician compensation arrangements, medical practice valuation issues and the Stark law. In addition to authoring articles in regional and national publications, he co-authored the book, *Valuation of a Medical Practice* (John Wiley & Sons, Inc., 1999).Mr. Anderson is a Certified Public Accountant Accredited in Business Valuation and a Certified Valuation Analyst.

Introduction

Don Barbo, CPA, ABV is a Director with Deloitte Financial Advisory Services LLP in the Life Science & Health Care industry team. He specializes in healthcare business valuations involving mergers and acquisitions, divestitures, partnership transactions, leasing arrangements, divorces, commercial damages and financial reporting. His extensive healthcare valuation engagements have included hospitals, physician practices, ambulatory surgery centers, diagnostic imaging centers, pathology and clinical labs, cancer treatment centers, dialysis centers, and management services agreements.

Don has spoken extensively to various legal and valuation organizations and has published articles regarding business valuation issues. He also serves as an expert witness in litigated matters for his clients, including testifying before the U.S. Tax Court.

Don has been performing healthcare valuations since 1998. Prior to his valuation career, he served as the chief financial officer for a physician practice management company that provides management services to a variety of physician practices. Additionally, Don has served as the controller/financial officer for various emerging companies, and began his professional career as an auditor with an international accounting firm. He was recognized by Nightingale's Healthcare News as 1 of 10 recipients on their 2010 "People to Watch in Healthcare Transactions in the Southwest."

Edward J. Beckwith, Baker & Hostetler, LLP, is nationally recognized in the legal and administrative specialties which concern establishing and guiding the operations of charitable and educational organizations, healthcare institutions and trade associations. His advice is often sought with respect to the maintenance of the tax-exempt status of such organizations and the tax aspects of contributions and other financial support programs. Mr. Beckwith also advises affluent families with respect to the accumulation, management, and distribution of their personal wealth. These clients rely upon his extensive experience in several legal areas including business, tax and property law. A significant aspect of his practice involves the application of the tax laws to family and business financial arrangements, including the preparation of related documents to conserve and transfer wealth, the administration of such arrangements, and the representation of clients before legislative, judicial and regulatory branches of government at all levels.

Mr. Beckwith is active in the American and the District of Columbia Bar Associations, as well as the American Law Institute. He is a Fellow of the American Bar Foundation. He also is a Fellow and a Regent of the American College of Trust and Estate Counsel where he has served as the State Chair in the District of Columbia as well as the Chair of the College's Philanthropy Study Committee and its Committee on Charitable Planning and Exempt Organizations. He lectures throughout the United States and has written extensively, including articles and speeches for the American Law Institute/American Bar Association Committee on Continuing Professional Education and the Council on Foundations. Mr. Beckwith is the Founder and Chair of the Advanced Estate Planning Institute sponsored annually by the Georgetown University Law Center. In addition, he is an adjunct tax professor at the Georgetown University Law Center where he teaches graduate seminars in Advanced Estate Planning and Charitable Organizations and Planned Giving.

Introduction

Randy Biernat, a Manager in Katz, Sapper & Miller's Healthcare Resources Group, has been with the firm since 2004. Randy provides business valuation, fair market value analyses, expert testimony and general consulting services for a wide variety of healthcare clients.

Randy is experienced in performing healthcare appraisals and fair market value analyses in nearly all segments of the healthcare service industry. He is responsible for the planning and supervision of projects and the development of appropriate approaches and methodologies, and assists in the performance of technical research and writing with respect to emerging issues, including regulatory issues.

Randy obtained his Bachelor of Science degree in Finance with highest distinction, from the Kelley School of Business at Indiana University-Purdue University Indianapolis (IUPUI). He also completed a Masters of Professional Accountancy also from the Kelley School of Business at IUPUI.

Randy is a member of the American Institute of Certified Public Accountants (AICPA), the Business Valuation, Forensic, and Litigation Support Section of the AICPA, and is a member of the Indiana CPA Society.

Eleanor Bloxham is the Founder and Chief Executive Officer of The Value Alliance Company and the Corporate Governance Alliance, a senior executive and Board education, information and advisory firm. She is recognized internationally as an authority on strategic and corporate governance and valuation. She is the author of two books, Value-led Organizations and Economic Value Management: Applications and Techniques (published by John Wiley and Sons). In addition, she is the author of the governance chapter of The Investor Relations Guide (published by Kennedy) and many articles in director, business and financial publications.

She has been the featured and keynote speaker at major director and investor conferences as well as private forums of directors, CEOs, and investors. She has also been an invited guest lecturer and speaker at numerous universities as well as numerous public and private conferences and seminars across the globe, where she has chaired and spoken on the topics of corporate governance, performance, value, compensation and risk.

Prior to founding The Value Alliance, she headed a global practice for KPMG and before that, spent nearly twenty years in financial services holding executive positions at Prudential Financial Services and at Bank One (now JP Morgan Chase), where she managed strategic, financial, operations, technology, risk assessment and compliance functions. She holds an MBA in Finance from New York University's Stern School of Business (where she was a Stern Scholar). Other academic honoraries include Phi Beta Kappa, Phi Kappa Phi, and Beta Gamma Sigma.

Ann S. Brandt, PhD is a Manager at HealthCare Appraisers. Dr. Brandt has over twenty-five years of healthcare experience and focuses on compensation arrangements involving hospitals, physician groups, pharmaceutical companies and medical device companies. Prior to joining HealthCare

Introduction

Appraisers, she served as a senior consultant specializing in healthcare information technology and process redesign at a Fortune 15 technology and consulting company. Dr. Brandt has extensive experience in physician/hospital partnerships as well as in operational restructuring, information management and clinical transformation. In addition, she has owned and operated several healthcare-related businesses including a home healthcare agency and a comprehensive outpatient rehabilitation facility (CORF) development and management company. Dr. Brandt is a licensed psychologist and experienced presenter, and has authored several articles on healthcare valuation topics.

Cain Brothers is an employee-owned investment banking and financial advisory firm that focuses exclusively on the medical services and medical technology industries and their related businesses. Cain Brothers has one of the largest teams dedicated to the health care industry on Wall Street, with 58 bankers and traders who possess experience in all facets of the industry. Cain Brothers is all about ideas and direct senior banker involvement with the firm's clients. Our philosophy is to roll up our sleeves and work side by side with our clients to produce innovative, market driven solutions for the many opportunities and challenges they face.

The firm's client base is primarily composed of nonprofit and investor-owned health care service providers, third-party payors, medical technology companies, and companies that provide services to the health care industry such as information technology and real estate companies. The firm was formed in 1982 based on the belief that health care organizations have unique needs that can be best addressed by professionals with a focus on the health care delivery system as a whole. The firm has grown to become one of the nation's preeminent investment banking and advisory firms to the health care industry, with personnel in New York, Chicago, Houston, San Francisco, Long Beach, Indianapolis, St. Louis, Atlanta, and Sarasota.

Carol Carden, CPA/ABV, ASA, CFE, is a shareholder with ValuePoint Consulting Group, a specialized practice of Pershing Yoakley & Associates, P.C., and provides business valuation and related consulting services to a wide variety of business organizations, primarily in the healthcare industry. Ms. Carden's primary areas of expertise are in finance, valuation, managed care and revenue cycle operations for healthcare organizations. She has performed appraisals of businesses and securities for a wide variety of purposes such as mergers, acquisitions, joint ventures, management service agreements and other intangible assets. In addition to being a Certified Public Accountant, she has also earned the Accredited in Business Valuation (ABV) credential from the American Institute of Certified Public Accountants, the Accredited Senior Appraiser (ASA) credential from the American Society of Appraisers and the Certified Fraud Examiner (CFE) credential from the Association of Certified Fraud Examiners. For more information regarding ValuePoint's services, please see www.valuepointconsulting.com.

Frank Cohen, MPA is the Senior Analyst for MIT Solutions, Inc., developers of analytical and Decision Support tools and systems for healthcare organizations. He is a certified Six Sigma Black Belt and Lean instructor. His areas of expertise include data mining and analysis, applied statistics and decision support. For the past 30 years, he has worked as a health care data analyst, knowledge engineer and consultant.

Introduction

Mr. Cohen is the author of several books, including *A Practical Guide to Reengineering the Medical Practice, The Physician CEO, Coding for the Non Coder, Mastering RBRVS, The Complete Guide to E/M Utilization* and *Total Practice Improvement: A Lean Approach for Medical Practices.*

Mr. Cohen has participated in and published numerous articles and studies and trained thousands of CPAs, physicians, administrators and other healthcare professionals in the techniques used to conduct comprehensive medical practice analyses.

His consulting experience includes hospitals, large and small medical practices, medical and professional associations, legal and accounting professionals, government agencies and other health care professionals.

Edward J. Dupke, CPA/ABV, is a Senior Consultant in the Valuation and Forensic Services Division of Clifton Gunderson LLP, the 13th largest CPA and consulting firm in the United States. He is based in the firm's Phoenix, Arizona office. He holds the AICPA specialty designation of Accredited in Business Valuation (CPA/ABV). Mr. Dupke is a former chairman of the AICPA Business Valuation Committee and a past chairman of the Michigan Association of CPAs.

Ed has over 35 years of professional experience in Public Accounting and Business Valuation Practice, has been qualified as an expert witness in both State and Federal courts and is a regular instructor in Business Valuation at both the State and National level. He is a co-author of the text Financial Valuation: Applications and Models (Hitchner), John Wiley & Sons, New York, (Second Edition) 2006. He is licensed as a CPA in Michigan, Illinois, Kentucky and Arizona. Mr. Dupke is a past member of the AICPA Board of Directors and Chair of its Strategic Planning Committee.

He is a past member of the AICPA Forensic and Litigation Committee, and he Currently is a member of the AICPA Joint Trial Board, the Business Valuation / Forensic and Litigation Services Executive Committee and Chairs the AICPA Task Force writing the Business Valuation Standards for CPAs. In 1998, Mr. Dupke was awarded the Distinguished Service Award from the Michigan Association of CPAs and in 1999 was inducted into the AICPA Business Valuation Hall of Fame. In 2002, he received the AICPA "Business Valuation Volunteer of the Year" award. In 2005, he received the "Special Recognition" award from both the Michigan Association of CPAs and the American Institute of CPAs for his work on the AICPA Business Valuation Standards. Mr. Dupke holds a Bachelor's of Science in Business Administration from Wayne State University in Detroit.

Nancy J. Fannon, ASA, CPA•ABV, MCBA is the owner of Fannon Valuation Group, a business valuation and litigation support services firm located in Portland, Maine. She is an Accredited Senior Appraiser (ASA) with the American Society of Appraisers, holds the AICPA specialty designation of Accredited in Business Valuation (ABV), and is a Master Certified Business Appraiser (MCBA) with the Institute of Business Appraisers. Ms. Fannon has over 20 years of professional valuation experience. She has been qualified as an expert witness in

Introduction

State and Federal Court. She is a nationally known expert on lost profits damages, pass-through entity valuation, and the transaction databases, and has presented dozens of speeches and authored numerous papers on these and other areas of business valuation. She is the author of *Fannon's Guide to the Valuation of Subchapter S Corporations* and *The Comprehensive Guide to the Transaction Databases*, which she co-authored with Heidi Walker. She currently is in production on a text on lost profits damages, due for publication in 2008. She is a co-author of *Financial Valuation—Applications and Methods*, and was a contributing author for both *The Business Appraiser and Litigation Support* and *Business Valuation and Taxes: Procedure, Law, and Perspective* textbooks, has been a technical reviewer on several other textbooks including the fifth edition of Shannon Pratt's seminal textbook, *Valuing a Business*, published in 2008. Ms. Fannon has a Bachelor of Business Administration in Accounting from the University of Massachusetts. Ms. Fannon was a member of the AICPA Business Valuation Subcommittee, the ABV Credential Committee, and has chaired the AICPA Business Valuation Conference. She is a member of the Editorial Advisory Boards of *CPA Expert*, *Business Valuation Update*, and *Valuation Examiner*, and is on the Panel of Expert for the *Litigation and Consulting Expert*. In 2007, Ms. Fannon was inducted into the AICPA's Business Valuation "Hall of Fame", awarded for substantial contributions to the advancement of the business valuation profession.

David Fein, MBA is the CEO and president of ValuSource, which for over twenty years has been the leading provider of business valuation software, data and report writers for CPAs, M&A professionals and business owners. Founded in 1985, ValuSource had managed a track record of 50 percent year-over-year growth by 1994 with no external funding. Its products were used nationwide by more than a thousand satisfied customers. In 1994, seizing the opportunity to leverage ValuSource products into worldwide distribution channels, Mr. Fein managed the sale of the company John Wiley & Sons, Inc. (JWA), the billion dollar global publishing firm.

In 2004 it became clear that ValuSource needed the freedom to continue its growth and Mr. Fein joined with a group of investors and bought back the company. Once again privately held, ValuSource is in a position to leverage its technology, partnerships, and expertise.

Since 1997, Mr. Fein has partnered with the Medical Group Management Association (MGMA) to develop the MGMA's interactive survey CDs, which provide data and benchmarking tools on physicians' compensation, business costs, and coding practices. ValuSource has crucial technology and data for anyone that needs to benchmark or value a medical practice.

Mr. Fein's mission is to create state-of-the-art technology to automate and standardize complex financial analysis and reporting tasks. He has a bachelor's degree in computer science and an MBA.

Gregory S. Feltenberger, MBA, FACMPE, FACHE, CPHIMS, has over 15 years of operational health care experience and is an active duty Medical Service Corps officer (health services administrator) in the United States Air Force. Currently, he is the Chief of Information Project Management at the Office of the Air Force Surgeon General, Air Force Medical Support Agency, Decision Support Branch in Falls Church, Virginia. Greg has

Introduction

been a Chief Information Officer, Chief of Information Management, and Group Practice Manager. In addition, Greg was competitively selected and completed a 10-month fellowship in Survey Development, Analysis, and Performance Measurement at the Medical Group Management Association (MGMA).

Greg has extensive experience in the use of bivariate and multivariate statistics, sampling methodologies, quantitative and qualitative research methods, and statistical software. He is a PhD student at Old Dominion University in the Health Services Research program. Greg has a MBA in information systems from Kent State University, a BA in specialized studies (summa cum laude), and an associate degree in engineering technology in biomedical equipment technology from Edinboro University of Pennsylvania. He is a Fellow in the American College of Medical Practice Executives (ACMPE), the standard-setting and certification body of the MGMA; a Fellow in the American College of Healthcare Executives; a Certified Medical Practice Executive in the American College of Medical Practice Executives; and a Certified Professional in Healthcare Information and Management Systems in the Healthcare Information and Management Systems Society. Greg has taught many online courses, authored several research posters and articles, and presented at national and military health care management conferences. And he is principal and co-founder of SmHart, Inc. (www.SmHart.net), an education, training, and organizational improvement consulting firm. Finally, Greg co-authored a book titled, "Benchmarking Success: The Essential Guide for Medical Practices" with David N. Gans, published by the Medical Group Management Association in March 2008.

Andrea M. Ferrari, JD, MPH joined HealthCare Appraisers from the health law practice group of a major international law firm. Ms. Ferrari has experience structuring, negotiating, reviewing and executing many types of healthcare transactions, including mergers and acquisitions, hospital-physician joint ventures, physician recruitment arrangements, compensated on-call coverage arrangements, physician employment arrangements, medical director and physician consulting arrangements, clinical trial and research sponsorship agreements, and billing and other service arrangements. Ms. Ferrari has provided counsel and representation to various types of clients in the healthcare industry, including hospitals, physicians, and physician groups, and pharmaceutical and medical device vendors, distributors and manufacturers.

Ms. Ferrari has previously served as associate general counsel of a sizeable public health system, and in the in-house legal department of a major academic medical center. Prior to becoming an attorney, Ms. Ferrari oversaw clinical trials and quality research for nearly seven years.

Ms. Ferrari is a member of the Florida Bar and a Florida Licensed Healthcare Risk Manager.

Ronald Finkelstein, CPA, is a partner in the Accounting and Tax services department at Morrison, Brown, Argiz & Farra, LLP where he directs the firm's Health Care Services Group. MBAF is independently ranked as one of the top 45 public accounting and consulting firms in the nation and as the largest Florida-based CPA firm in the State.

Introduction

Ron has extensive experience in assisting healthcare providers with merger and acquisition transactions. Ron has been a frequent lecturer both locally and nationally on a wide variety of health care accounting and practice management topics. Clients include ambulatory surgery centers, imaging centers, anatomic and clinical laboratories, home health providers, hospitals, and physician group practices.

A contributing editor to the quarterly publication "Practice Management Advisor," Ron is a member of the Steering Committee of the AICPA National Healthcare Industry Conference and past president of the National CPA Health Care Advisor's Association. In addition, Ron is a member of the Healthcare Financial Management Association, the Medical Group Management Association, and the American Health Lawyers Association. Ron graduated with a Bachelor of Accounting from Concordia University in Montreal, Canada.

David N. Gans, MHSA, FACMPE, is Vice President of Practice Management Resources at the Medical Group Management Association (MGMA) in Englewood, Colorado, where he is the MGMA staff expert on medical group practice management. He is an educational program speaker, author of a monthly column in *MGMA Connexion*, and he provides technical assistance to the association's staff and members on topic areas of benchmarking, use of survey data, financial management, cost efficiency, physician compensation and productivity, managerial compensation, the resource based relative value scale, employee staffing, cost accounting, medical group organization, and emergency preparedness. He is a retired Colonel in the United States Army Reserve. Dave earned an undergraduate degree in government at the University of Notre Dame, a master's degree in education from the University of Southern California, and a master's degree in health administration from the University of Colorado. He is a Fellow in the American College of Medical Practice Executives and a Certified Medical Practice Executive in the American College of Medical Practice Executives.

Lydia Glatz, CPA is a manager in the Accounting and Tax services department at Morrison, Brown, Argiz & Farra, LLP. Lydia has twelve years of experience planning and providing assurance services for clients in the healthcare field.

Her expertise involves accounting and tax planning for physician groups, including performing due diligence procedures for mergers, acquisitions and buyouts, analyzing receivables, payer mix and benchmark reviews of group practices. She also has experience in planning and implementing accounting systems and internal accounting controls for new start-up businesses. Lydia graduated with a Bachelor of Science in Accounting from Florida Atlantic University.

For more information about Morrison, Brown, Argiz & Farra, LLP, please visit the website: www.mbafcpa.com

Alice G. Gosfield, Esq.'s entire legal career has been restricted to health law with an emphasis on representation of physicians and their group configurations and a focus on non-institutional reimbursement including Medicare; managed care; fraud and abuse compliance and avoidance; medical staff issues and utilization management and quality issues. A graduate of Barnard

Introduction

College and New York University School of Law, since 1973 her varied health law career has ranged from an OEO ("War on Poverty") and then DHEW funded research program to develop a consumer-oriented analysis of the PSRO law, to drafting codes of regulations for state health care agencies, and since 1978 to include the private practice of law.

Ms. Gosfield served as Chairman of the Board of Directors of the National Committee for Quality Assurance, reelected to serve five terms from 1998 through 2002. She served on the Board for twelve years from1992 through 2003. In the public policy arena, she has served on four committees of the Institute of Medicine of the National Academy of Sciences studying issues involving utilization management and clinical practice guidelines and has served as an advisor to the Agency for Health Care Policy and Research in both evaluating one of their first three clinical practice guidelines and in developing methodologies to translate guidelines into medical review criteria, performance measures and standards of quality.

She is currently participating as an Advisory Board Member of a small group convened by the American College of Physicians to serve for three years in developing an approach to pay for performance. She is the first Chairman of the Board of PROMETHEUS Payment, Inc. a notfor-profit, national, multi-stakeholder project to develop a new provider payment model (PROMETHEUS Payment) that will base provider payment on the cost of delivering guidelines based care as measured in a comprehensive scorecard. Ms. Gosfield served as President of the American Health Lawyers Association (formerly the National Health Lawyers Association), from 1992-1993 and chaired their Physician and Physician Organizations Institute from 2001 through 2006.

James P. Harrington is an accomplished financial writer and analyst, and is Director of Business Valuation Research in Morningstar's Individual Investor Unit. Mr. Harrington heads up the team that produces the widely used and cited Ibbotson SBBI Classic and Valuation Yearbooks, Ibbotson Cost of Capital Yearbook, the Ibbotson Beta Book, and various international and domestic cost of capital reports. Mr. Harrington is leading the effort to expand Morningstar's investment in valuation research, and in 2009 Morningstar will launch new web-based valuation and cost of capital tools based on this new research. Prior to joining Morningstar in early 2006, Mr. Harrington was a product manager in the financial communications group at Ibbotson Associates in Chicago. Before that, he was a bond and bond portfolio analyst, worked at the Chicago Board of Trade in the bond options pit for a filling group, managed inbound and outbound dock workers at a large trucking firm, and was even a Teamster for a year.

Mr. Harrington holds a bachelor's degree in marketing from Ohio State University, and a Masters of Business Administration (MBA) in both finance and economics from the University of Illinois at Chicago, where he graduated at the top of his class.

Susan Feigin Harris is a partner in the Baker Hostetler Healthcare Practice Group. Ms. Harris focuses her practice on providing comprehensive legal services to health industry clients, including hospitals and hospital systems, physicians and physician group practices, academic medical centers, rehabilitation facilities, ambulatory surgery centers and dialysis providers. Ms. Harris is

Introduction

board certified in Health Law by the Texas Board of Legal Specialization. Ms. Harris has advised clients with respect to unique reimbursement issues affecting healthcare providers and suppliers, including Medicare and Medicaid reimbursement, managed care, discount programs for the uninsured, issues of special significance to children's hospitals and academic medical centers. She has experience in drafting and negotiating managed care arrangements from the provider's perspective. She has represented physicians, provider networks and hospital systems in managed care contract negotiations and has developed comprehensive managed care contracts for clients. In addition, Ms. Harris has been involved in disputes over managed care contract matters on behalf of providers.

Ms. Harris is a former Vice President of the Texas Medical Center Legal Department. She is a member of the American Health Lawyers Association and currently serves as the Vice-Chair of its In-House Counsel practice group and formerly co-chaired its Children's Hospital Affinity Group. She is a member of the American and Houston Bar Associations and is a founding member of the HBA Health Law Section. Ms. Harris has served as an adjunct professor at the University of Houston Law Center and currently serves on the Board of Directors for Texans Care for Children. She served as a director of The Texas Lyceum and is a senior fellow of the American Leadership Forum: Medical Class 2. Ms. Harris has been listed in The Best Lawyers in America in healthcare law since 2006 and was been named a Texas Super Lawyer for 2007 and 2008.

Matthew D. Jenkins, JD is a partner in the Richmond, Virginia office of Hunton & Williams LLP and heads the firm's Health Law Group. He has worked extensively with hospitals and multi-hospital systems on regulatory, corporate, governance and transactional matters. He has led a number of non-profit entities through conversion transactions resulting in the creation of substantial community foundations. His work also involves legislative matters and practice before administrative agencies. Mr. Jenkins is a member of the American Bar Association's Health Law Section where he serves as a vice-chair of the Transactional & Business Interest Group. He served two terms as a governor's appointee on the Special Advisory Commission on Mandated Health Insurance Benefits for the Commonwealth of Virginia. He is a past chair of the Health Law Section of the Virginia State Bar. Mr. Jenkins earned his J.D. in 1984 from the University of Virginia and his B.A, Summa cum laude, in 1979 from the University of Richmond, where he was Phi Beta Kappa.

Tracy Farryl Katz, Esq., CPA is a partner at Gursey | Schneider, LLP, in the firm's Litigation Services Department, specializing in the area of forensic accounting in family law and civil litigation matters. She has performed a wide range of litigation accounting services including: business appraisals, determination of gross cash flow available for support, determination of celebrity goodwill, net spendable evaluations, pension plan allocations, stock option apportionments, characterization of assets, analysis of reimbursement claims, lifestyle analyses, and contract and royalty analyses in the film, television and music industries.

Chris Mercer is the founder and CEO of Mercer Capital, one of the leading business appraisal and investment banking firms in the nation. Chris has been valuing businesses—and helping people buy and sell them—for more than 30 years. He has served on the boards of directors

Introduction

of several private companies as well as one public company. He currently is an outside member of the board of directors of Klumb Lumber Company, Fair Hope, AL. Chris is also a prolific author and noted authority on business valuation.

Chris started Mercer Capital in 1982 after several years working for a regional bank and an investment banking firm, where he was the bank stock analyst. Chris has written eight books and more than one hundred articles. His two latest books, Business Valuation: An Integrated Theory, 2nd Edition (with Travis W. Harms, CFA, CPA/ABV) and Buy-Sell Agreements: Ticking Time Bombs or Reasonable Resolutions? highlight the breadth of his knowledge and experience, ranging from densely theoretical to highly practical.

Scott D. Miller, CPA/ABV, CVA, is President and founder of Enterprise Services, Inc., a Delafield, WI firm providing financial consulting services to private business, specializing in management buyouts, business valuations, fairness opinions and Employee Stock Ownership Plans. An entrepreneur himself, Scott understands closely held and family-owned businesses, serving as officer and principal in several businesses. Since founding ESI, he has helped hundreds of business owners through transition planning, valuations, and other strategic financial issues, including mergers and acquisitions.

A nationally recognized authority on business transitions and valuations, Scott publishes in professional journals and authors seminars for professional organizations and industry groups, including the National Society of Certified Public Accountants. His undergraduate degree is from Kenyon College and he holds an MBA from Cornell University Johnson Graduate School of Management.

Robert M. Mundy, CPA/ABV, CVA is the Manager of Healthcare Valuation Services for Hill Schwartz Spilker Keller, LLC (www.hsskgroup.com). HSSK is a full service business valuation and litigation consulting services firm consisting of approximately 20 professionals with offices in Dallas and Houston.

Robert has a broad background in business valuation engagements for matters involving estate and gift tax, mergers and acquisitions, dissenting shareholder actions, divorce and partnership transactions. He has performed valuations on over 300 closely-held businesses in many different industries including healthcare, retail, manufacturing, professional services, and wholesale distribution. His healthcare valuation experience includes hospitals, imaging centers, cancer treatment centers, ambulatory surgery centers, and physician practices. His business experience includes business valuation and auditing positions in a regional public accounting firm.

He holds an undergraduate degree in accounting from Bob Jones University. He is also a Certified Public Accountant (CPA), is Accredited in Business Valuations (CPA/ABV), and is a Certified Valuation Analyst (CVA).

James M. Pinna, JD is an associate in the Richmond, Virginia office of Hunton & Williams LLP and practices with the firm's Health Law Group. He works primarily with hospitals and

Introduction

multi-hospital systems on regulatory, transactional, corporate, governance and matters. He is a member of the American Health Lawyers Association and the American Bar Association's Health Law Section. Prior to attending law school, he was the Business Development Analyst for National Nephrology Associates, a privately owned dialysis company based in Nashville, Tennessee. Mr. Pinna earned his J.D. in 2006 from the University of Virginia and his B.A. in 2000 from Duke University.

Robert Reilly is a managing director of Willamette Management Associates, a valuation consulting, economic analysis, and financial advisory firm with regional offices in San Francisco, Chicago, Atlanta, New York City, Portland, Oregon, and Washington, D.C. Robert holds a BS in economics and an MBA in finance, both from Columbia University. He is a certified public accountant, certified management accountant, chartered financial analyst, accredited senior appraiser, certified business appraiser, certified review appraiser, and state certified general real estate appraiser. He is a member of the American Economic Association, National Association of Business Economists, American Society of Appraisers, Institute of Business Appraisers, American Bankruptcy Institute, Institute of Property Taxation, and several other professional organizations.

He is co-author of the following six textbooks: Valuing a Business: The Analysis and Appraisal of Closely Held Companies, The Handbook of Advanced Business Valuation, Valuing Intangible Assets, Valuing Small Businesses and Professional Practices, Valuing Accounting Practices, and Valuing Professional Practices: A Practitioners Approach. He is a frequent speaker to professional groups on topics related to business valuation, security pricing analysis, intellectual property valuation and transfer pricing, and economic damages/lost profits analysis.

Jason Ruchaber, CFA, ASA is a Manager in the Colorado office of HealthCare Appraisers, Inc. Mr. Ruchaber has over 11 years of finance and valuation experience, the last eight of which have been spent exclusively in business valuation and litigation consulting. Prior to joining HealthCare Appraisers, Mr. Ruchaber was a Principal in Cogence Group, P.C., a business valuation and litigation support firm located in Portland, Oregon. Mr. Ruchaber has also worked in Standard & Poor's Corporate Value Consulting practice where he focused on intellectual property valuation and damages calculations, as well as corporate planning roles with Dell Computer and Fluor Daniel.

Mr. Ruchaber received a degree in Finance from the University of Texas at Austin, has earned the Chartered Financial Analyst (CFA) designation, and is an Accredited Senior Appraiser (ASA). He is a member of the CFA Institute, the Portland Society of Financial Analysts, the American Society of Appraisers, and the Licensing Executives Society International.

Scott Safriet, AVA, MBA is a Principal of HealthCare Appraisers. Mr. Safriet has over five years of fulltime healthcare valuation experience, focusing primarily on any type of agreement or compensation arrangement which may have Stark and/or Anti-Kickback implications. Prior to becoming a partner at HealthCare Appraisers, Mr. Safriet served as Vice-President of Sales and Business Development for a national in-home care services organization. During his tenure

Introduction

there, he was responsible for all sales, contracting and strategic alliance / M&A activities, resulting in an increase in revenues from $35 million to $95 million. Before this, Mr. Safriet was a senior executive with a national healthcare consulting firm whose emphasis was on strategy, business planning and acquisitions/mergers and joint ventures.

Mr. Safriet is an Accredited Valuation Analyst (AVA) and holds a Masters of Business Administration in Corporate Finance. Mr. Safriet is a frequent speaker and author on healthcare valuation topics.

Alan B. Simons, **CPA/ABV, CFF, CMPE DABFA**, is the principal-in-charge of LarsonAllen's national health care valuation practice and the business valuation and litigation support practice for the Philadelphia office.

Alan has prepared hundreds of health care business valuations in conformity with IRS Revenue Ruling 59-60 and the Uniform Standards of Professional Appraisal Practice (USPAP). He has been engaged by health care providers to determine fair market value for transactions involving the Stark law, the Anti-Kickback statute, Internal Revenue Code section 4958 (intermediate sanctions) and transactions among for-profit and nonprofit organizations. In addition, Alan has prepared numerous opinions as to the reasonableness of compensation or payments paid to clinical, administrative, managerial, and executive physicians to support a rebuttable presumption of reasonableness with respect to IRS private inurement (private benefit) issues. His experience also includes providing consulting services related to business operations, information technology, compensation, and employee recruitment, primarily for health care businesses.

Alan is proficient in the valuation (appraisal) of health care businesses (physicians, medical practices, hospitals, senior care facilities, home health, and ancillary facilities such as imaging centers, dialysis centers, surgical centers, and radiation oncology treatment centers). He has represented clients in shareholder disputes, divorce, estate and gift tax valuations, mergers and acquisitions, and damage claims.

Alan is a certified public accountant (CPA, Commonwealth of Pennsylvania), accredited in Business Valuation (ABV) and certified in financial forensics (CFF) through the American Institute of Certified Public Accountants (AICPA). He is a certified medical practice executive (CMPE) through the American College of Medical Practice Executives, and he is a diplomate of the American Board of Forensic Accounting (DABFA) of the American College of Forensic Examiners. He received his Bachelor of Business Administration degree, majoring in accounting with a minor in economics, from Temple University. Alan is an active member of the Healthcare Financial Management Association (HFMA), the Medical Group Management Association (MGMA), the American Health Lawyers Association (AHLA), the American Society of Appraisers (ASA candidate), the Institute of Business Appraisers (IBA), the American Institute of Certified Public Accountants (AICPA), the Pennsylvania Institute of Certified Public Accountants (PICPA), and the Forensic and Valuation Services Division of the AICPA. Alan has written a number of articles and has made numerous presentations on business valuation topics. He was formerly an instructor for Continuing Professional Education, Inc. (CPE, Inc.), and taught a full-day course titled "How to Value a Business" to other certified public accountants.

Introduction

Douglas G. Smith is President, Barrington Lakes Group, LLC, a health care consulting firm specializing in Integrated Imaging Strategy Development, Strategic Action Planning, Imaging Center Development & Management, and Profit Improvement Initiatives for Radiology Group Practices, hospitals & health systems and other diagnostic imaging related organizations. Barrington Lakes Group is one of the leading Chicago-based Radiology-specific Business Consulting Firms, and is a leading Diagnostic Imaging Business Consulting and Outsourced Oversight Management firm. Barrington Lakes Group enjoys an outstanding reputation for assisting clients in the development and operation of effective and profitable healthcare organizations.

Mr. Smith has an extensive background and expertise in no-nonsense Strategic Action Planning and operations profit improvement for both large and small healthcare entities. He brings over 30 years of demonstrated professional experience as an operations improvement specialist, business strategist, business turnaround facilitator, merger and acquisition specialist, and operations executive to the healthcare market.

Following over 20 years in the Defense business sector as Vice President of Imaging Technology and Business Development, Imaging Systems Division, and six years as President of a Health Care Consulting Group, a division of a large CPA Firm, Mr. Smith founded Barrington Lakes Group as a unique niche consulting firm with specialized expertise and unique consulting firm business model. Barrington Lakes Group celebrated its 11th anniversary in 2010.

His specialized professional background and experience includes Management Operations & Oversight, Managed Care Contract Strategy Development, Physician/Hospital & Physician/Specialist Joint Venture Development, Health System Integrated Imaging Strategy Development, Strategic Business Action Planning and Federal Government and International Legislative and Policy Liaison.

Doug is a graduate of Ohio University, graduate of the Crosby Quality College Executive Program, and has been repeatedly elected into *Who's Who in National Healthcare*. He is a member of several professional associations including, Healthcare Financial Management Association (HFMA), Medical Group Management Association (MGMA), the Radiology Business Managers Association (RBMA) and the National Health Lawyers Association (NHLA). He also serves as a member of the Federal Affairs Committee of the RBMA.

He is an accomplished professional speaker and lecturer to local, national and international audiences and has authored and co-authored articles and business publications on a variety of profit enhancement processes and practices. Mr. Smith has been a featured speaker for the American Medical Association, Healthcare Financial Management Association, Washington G-2 Diagnostic Imaging Leadership Forum, International Business Conferences on Radiology Practice Management, Radiology Business Managers Association, American Healthcare Radiology Administrators, Congress of Imaging Administrators, and the American Institute of Certified Public Accountants.

Introduction

Mr. Smith is a contributing author to the recently published *Business Valuation Resources Complete Guide to Healthcare Valuation,* authoring the section on the specific and unique consideration required when valuing diagnostic imaging entities, and is Executive Editor and publisher of Radiology Leaders' Advisor.

Timothy R. Smith, CPA/ABV is the Director of Professional Practice with HealthCare Appraisers, Inc., where he specializes in the valuation of physician employment arrangements. He is a noted speaker and author on valuation and fair market value (FMV) issues in the healthcare industry. Prior to HealthCare Appraisers, Mr. Smith worked for more than 14 years at Hospital Corporation of America, Inc. (HCA), the nation's largest hospital company. During his tenure at HCA, he performed regulatory compliance reviews and evaluations on hundreds of third-party appraisals that were prepared by nearly two dozen appraisal firms for business and asset acquisitions and divestitures, service contracts, leasing agreements, and other forms of compensation arrangements. Mr. Smith also oversaw HCAs program for using third party appraisers. His HCA experience also included managing contractual negotiations, due diligence, and the outside appraisal process for hundreds of physician practice acquisitions and divestitures. He holds the Accredited in Business Valuation (ABV) certification from the American Institute of Certified Public Accountants (AICPA).

Todd Sorensen, MBA is a Partner with VMG HEALTH. He specializes in providing valuation and transaction advisory services to the firm's healthcare clients. He has acted as financial advisor in transactions with physician groups, acute care hospitals, health maintenance organizations, preferred provider organizations, diagnostic centers, ambulatory surgery centers, home health agencies, physical and operational therapy centers, institutional pharmacies, retail pharmacies and rural health clinics.

Prior to joining VMG Health, Mr. Sorensen was with the financial advisory group of Ernst & Young. Mr. Sorensen played an integral role in the development of healthcare valuation services. Mr. Sorensen completed his graduate studies (Masters of Business Administration) at Baylor University and undergraduate studies (Bachelor of Science – Business Administration / Finance) at Liberty University.

VMG Health is recognized by leading healthcare systems as one of the most trusted valuation and transaction advisors in the U.S. Unlike most valuation firms, which generally serve a wide variety of industries, healthcare is VMG Health's only area of focus, and their client list includes virtually every type of healthcare service provider, in markets across the country – from hospitals and healthcare networks to standalone facilities and ancillary service providers.

Stacey D. Udell, CPA/ABV/CFF, ASA, CVA, a partner in the public accounting firm of Gold Gocial Gerstein LLC, has been in public accounting since 1996 after spending three years in industry. She is a Certified Public Accountant (CPA) licensed in New Jersey and holds numerous credentials related to business valuations and litigation support; including Accredited in Business Valuation (ABV) and Certified in Financial Forensics (CFF) issued by the American Institute of Certified Public Accountants; Certified Valuations Analyst (CVA) issued by

Introduction

National Association of Certified Valuation Analysts (NACVA), and the Accredited Senior Appraiser (ASA) issued by the American Society of Appraisers (ASA).

Ms. Udell specializes in business valuation, forensic accounting, economic damages, and litigation support for a wide range of businesses and professional practices for purposes such as estate and gift tax planning and compliance, divorce, business succession planning, mergers and acquisitions, shareholder litigation, and bankruptcy proceedings.

Additionally, she provides accounting and tax services for closely-held and family businesses including financial statement preparation, business and personal income tax planning and compliance, estate and business succession planning.

Ms. Udell is a 1993 graduate of the University of Delaware where she received a Bachelor of Science in Accounting. She is a member of the AICPA, NJSCPA, NACVA, and ASA. She serves on the Executive Board of the New Jersey State NACVA Chapter and serves on the planning committees for both New Jersey and National NACVA conferences. She is the co-chair for the Matrimonial Track for the NACVA 2010 and 2011 Annual Consultants' Conferences. Ms. Udell is an instructor for the NACVA Matrimonial Litigation Support Workshop and is on the Litigation Forensics Board of NACVA. Ms. Udell will be the Chairperson of the NACVA Litigation Forensics Board. Additionally, Ms. Udell is on the CFF examination development committee.

Ms. Udell has presented on numerous topics on business valuation and litigation support as well as having been published. In 2008, she was a contributing author to Chapter 16 in the *Business Valuation Resources Healthcare Industry Valuation Guide* related to the valuation of medical practices for divorce purposes. She is also a contributing author to the *Family Law Services Handbook* which will be published in 2010 by John Wiley & Sons, Inc.

Kathie L. Wilson, CPA, CVA specializes in medical practice accounting and valuation. Formerly with Dietrich & Wilson, PC where she was the partner responsible for quality control of the firm's valuation, tax and accounting work, she returned to the West Coast in 2006. Kathie spent two years at Gursey|Schneider in Los Angeles in the family law litigation department, specializing in medical practice valuation and forensic accounting. Kathie currently resides in the San Francisco Bay Area and consults with accountants and attorneys on medical practice valuation and family law litigation issues. She can be reached at kwilson@cpa.net.

Robert Wolin, as a member of Baker & Hostetler's Healthcare team, maintains an active healthcare and business practice with an emphasis on counseling clients in the healthcare industry. These clients include dialysis providers, long term care providers, assisted living facilities, home health agencies, ancillary service providers, IDTFs, physicians, joint ventures, hospitals, pharmaceutical distributors, pharmacies, medical device distributors and manufacturers and healthcare related aviation service providers. Mr. Wolin has advised clients regarding a variety of business and regulatory issues, ranging from corporate structuring to compliance with the complex regulatory scheme facing clients in the healthcare industry.

Introduction

Mr. Wolin has served as lead counsel in many complex and substantial business transactions in several states, including the acquisition of First American Home Health, which involved negotiating one of the largest OIG fraud and abuse settlements in history on behalf of First American Home Health Care of Georgia, Inc. and its owner, Integrated Health Services, Inc., for $215 million and has negotiated several other OIG and Department of Justice healthcare compliance agreements. In addition, he has acted as lead counsel in many healthcare institution acquisition and disposition transactions, including hospitals, nursing homes and HMOs, and has provided regulatory, fraud and abuse advice to numerous healthcare providers. Mr. Wolin has also represented national distributors of healthcare products in connection with product distribution, group purchasing organization agreements, manufacturer representation agreements and business purchase agreements. Mr. Wolin has advised clients regarding the organization and structure of healthcare entities and joint ventures, including surgery centers, imaging centers and renal dialysis facilities.

Chapter 1

Healthcare 'Reform'

By Mark O. Dietrich, CPA/ABV

Introduction

The title of this chapter includes a word that is a matter of subjective determination: "Reform." The 2010 legislation does contain some elements of reform, particularly in terms of basic terms and benefits that a health insurance policy must contain. The legislative language proposing to compensate providers, in part, on the basis of quality and *not* to compensate them for errors in care might also be seen as reform if they ever come to pass. That said, much of the legislation reflects the traditional lobbying clout or lack thereof of various segments of the industry and leaves in doubt what reforms will ultimately be realized and, more importantly, what the effect of that realization will be.

From the standpoint of the valuation of healthcare enterprises, what is called reform in this legislation suggests the following financial factors:

1. Consolidation;

2. Higher volumes at lower rates;

3. Higher emphasis on payment for quality;

4. Lower volume providers will be at risk;

5. Cost shifts from older and sicker to younger and healthier;

6. Cost shifts to small business; and

7. Cost shifts to individuals from their health insurance.

In the Appendix, readers will find the transcript of the June 10, 2010, BVR webinar on the reform legislation which contains a discussion of the changes and their impact on valuation.

The following is a brief overview of where we were before those changes, followed by a summary of the significant elements of the reform legislation.

Chapter 1: Healthcare 'Reform'

A Brief Overview of the Healthcare Insurance Industry

Health insurance is a low-margin business when viewed over the time period known as the underwriting cycle. As in the business cycle for any industry, health insurance companies will experience periods of high profits, low profits, and outright losses. In loss periods, insurers tend to shed unprofitable lines of business, which often include the sick and dying or those businesses that employ disproportionate numbers of such individuals. In profitable periods, risk-taking tends to increase and expansion of market share is sought, which often results in marginal new business. The chart below illustrates the historical underwriting cycle and the periods of earnings before interest and taxes.[1] Interestingly, managed care companies tend to do well in times of weaker economic growth.

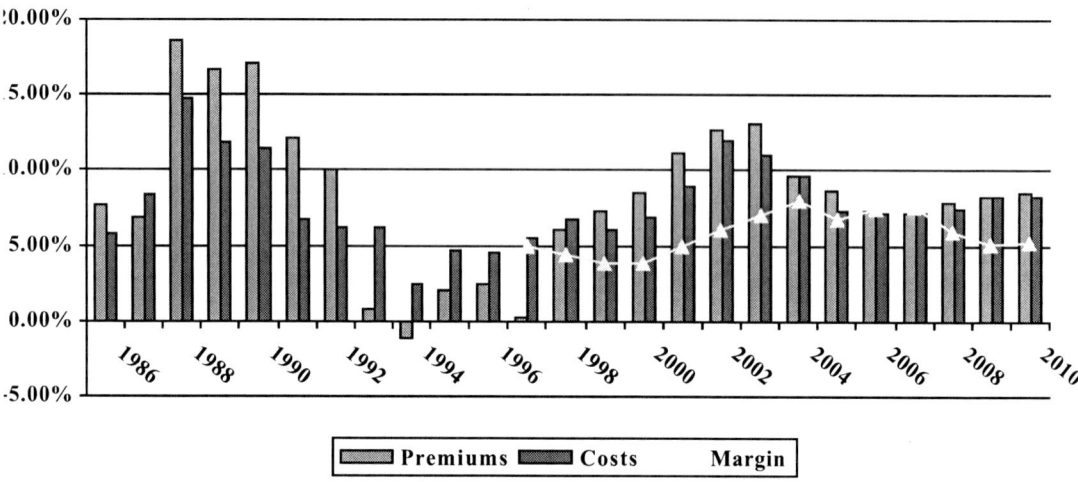

During the profitable period of the underwriting cycle, insurers also earn investment returns on their cash reserves, further enhancing profitability; in down periods, the lack of investment returns exacerbates losses.

Medicare National Coverage Determinations (NCDs)

Medicare has been and will remain the most important program in the healthcare delivery system. A critical feature of both the pre-reform and post-reform healthcare system is Medicare's National Coverage Determinations:

> An NCD sets forth the extent to which Medicare will cover specific services, procedures, or technologies on a national basis. Medicare contractors are required to follow NCDs. If an NCD does not specifically exclude/limit an indication or circumstance, or if the item or service is not mentioned at all in an NCD or in a Medicare manual, it is up to the Medicare contractor to make the coverage decision (see LMRP). Prior to an NCD taking effect, CMS must first issue a Manual Transmittal, CMS ruling, or

Chapter 1: Healthcare 'Reform'

Federal Register Notice giving specific directions to our claims-processing contractors. That issuance, which includes an effective date and implementation date, is the NCD. If appropriate, the Agency must also change billing and claims processing systems and issue related instructions to allow for payment. The NCD will be published in the Medicare National Coverage Determinations Manual. An NCD becomes effective as of the date listed in the transmittal that announces the manual revision.[2]

In English, that means the Centers for Medicare and Medicaid Services or CMS determines what is and is not covered by Medicare. That, of course, has a dramatic impact on what type of care and services Medicare beneficiaries can receive and, notably, what services *anyone* receives, something that is not widely understood. Some classic examples include the rapid approval by CMS (then HCFA) of drug-eluting stents for treatment of coronary artery disease, which led to the explosive growth in interventional cardiology back in the 1990s and a dispute that rages today between the cardiac surgery community and the interventional cardiology community about the efficacy of coronary artery bypass surgery as opposed to stents.

Medicare NCDs have significant influence across all insurance and delivery venues. Absent Medicare approval, it is rarely financially feasible to implement a new technology, since the elderly receive a large amount of healthcare services. Many insurers peg their coverage and payment rates to Medicare as well.

A more recent example is the type of procedures for which PET (positron emission tomography) scanners are approved. PET is used in conjunction with CT, and both are very expensive technologies; therefore they represent expensive services to provide to beneficiaries. The combination of PET and CT is used primarily for cancer treatment planning and effectiveness evaluation. Not all potential usages have been approved.

Incidentally, there are also Local Coverage Decisions (LCDs) where the Medicare intermediary (the contractor retained by the government to pay Medicare claims on its behalf) for a given area may approve a service that has not been subject to a NCD.

Reform Components

The legislation contains four basic sections listed below.

1. Tax increases;

2. Insurance market changes and expansion;

3. Medicare changes; and

4. Medicaid expansion and changes.

Chapter 1: Healthcare 'Reform'

Tax Increases

Tax increases are generally outside the scope of this chapter. Most of the tax increase revenue ($210 billion) comes from expanding the Medicare payroll tax to investment income and increasing the tax rate on the upper middle class and "wealthy." Other smaller but significant increases are the Cadillac Plan tax ("Cadillacs" and "Chevys" are discussed later), penalty taxes for failure to have health insurance coverage, a tax on tanning parlors, penalty taxes on tax-exempt hospitals for not meeting community benefit standards, and a number of reductions in the tax-favored treatment of medical expenditures.

Tax-Exempt Hospitals

Scrutiny of the tax exempt healthcare sector has been ongoing for a number of years now, and proponents of that scrutiny used the reform legislation to expand the monitoring of tax-exempt hospitals. The community benefit standard that formed the basis of the federal tax exemption has now been codified, and hospitals are required to conduct a periodic community health needs assessment using a broad section of community members and then adopt an implementation strategy. Failure to undertake the assessment and implementation can result in a $50,000 excise tax penalty.

Exempt hospitals are also required to adopt and make available a financial assistance policy for those unable to fully pay for care. For these individuals, no more than the lowest amounts charged to patients who have insurance covering such care are allowed.

Notably, the annual tax return, Form 990, which has undergone major expansions in the level of required disclosure—particularly with respect to compensation arrangements for key employees—will now be expanded once again. Now required are the community needs assessment and implementation report described above as well as a copy of the hospitals' audited financial statements. This latter provision may have significant implications in the valuation community due to the volume of physician practice acquisitions, many of which include arguably questionable amounts for goodwill and intangible assets (see Chapter 13). Under the provisions of Financial Accounting Standard 164, annual impairment testing of acquired goodwill and intangibles is required, and if there is no value found by the auditors, it must be written off. Clearly, the write-off of recently acquired intangible assets will give regulators and other users of the financial statements cause for concern.

Cadillac Tax

Perhaps the most peculiar feature of the reform in its final iteration, the nondeductible 40% excise tax on high cost plans is not effective until 2018; whether it survives until then is an open question. The threshold levels for what constitutes a high cost plan in 2018 are already established: $10,200 for a single plan and $27,500 for a family plan. In high-cost areas of the country such as New England, Minnesota, Indiana, and Alaska, these levels are likely to be exceeded for typical policies long before 2018.

Chapter 1: Healthcare 'Reform'

The chief actuary at CMS had the following comment in his April 22, 2010, *Estimated Financial Effects of the "Patient Protection and Affordable Care Act," as Amended*:

> Because plan benefit values will generally increase faster than the threshold amounts for defining high-cost plans (which, after 2019, are indexed by the CPI), additional plans would become subject to the excise tax over time, prompting many of those employers to scale back coverage.

Thus, it seems counterintuitive that a proposal designed to expand coverage, sold in part on the basis that individuals would be able to keep their present coverage and doctors, is expected to cause significant cutbacks in coverage in "Chevy" plans. One interpretation is that the level of insurance enjoyed by various segments of the population will become more egalitarian. Another implication is that increasing amounts of costs will be borne out of pocket by individuals, creating a disincentive to use the healthcare system.

Massachusetts: The Model for Reform

Given the size and diversity of the United States, it is fascinating that the model chosen for the entire nation is taken to a high degree of precision from a model developed for one of its smallest states. That state is unique in the way its healthcare delivery system works, particularly given the urban concentration of its population and the dominance of high-cost teaching hospitals in the provision of healthcare.

Massachusetts Feature	Federal Feature?
Individual mandate	Yes
Penalty for lack of coverage thru tax system • $52 each month, $624 for year for individuals aged 18-26. • $89 each month, $1068 for year for individuals 27 or older	Yes, but much lower
No lifetime limits, waiting periods or barriers for pre-existing medical conditions	Yes
Subsidies based on Federal Poverty Limit (FPL)	Yes
State has own "health connector" insurance exchange	Yes
Children eligible to age 26	Yes
Employer penalty	Yes
Benefit tiers (platinum, gold, silver, bronze)	Yes
Medicaid expansion	Yes
Merging the individual and small group markets	Allowed
Targeted primary care recruitment	Yes
Insurance market and rating rules	Yes
Rating variation in the individual and the small group market and the exchanges based *only* on • age (limited to 3 to 1 ratio), • premium rating area, • family composition, and • tobacco use (limited to 1.5. to 1 ratio)	Yes
Lack of Antitrust Reform	Yes

Chapter 1: Healthcare 'Reform'

A Summary of Massachusetts Reform Results

1. Highest rate of insured residents in the nation, 97.4%;

2. Highest premiums in nation;

3. Many mandated benefits, e.g., IVF;

4. Highest rate of healthcare cost increase in nation;

5. Antitrust issues—DOJ now investigating;

6. Second-highest unemployment rate in New England;

7. Self-insured employers increasing to avoid merged individual/small group market premium increases

8. Premium gap between small group market and self-insured large group market growing.

The Massachusetts Division of Healthcare Finance & Policy maintains quarterly reports that contain extensive data about the changes in health insurance premiums and healthcare costs. On September 2, 2010 the Center for Studying Health System Change released its report on the Massachusetts reform (available to online subscribers of this Guide).

Insurance Market Changes and Expansion

Certain healthcare insurance plans are exempt from all but a few of the new insurance market requirements, although these few could be expensive to those otherwise exempt plans and their insureds. Exempt plans include grandfathered plans and government plans.

Grandfathering as of March 23, 2010 (including renewals)

The legislation permits individual and employer-sponsored insurance plans to remain basically the same. However, the following provisions from the legislation apply to those otherwise grandfathered plans: Must extend dependent coverage to age 26; eliminate annual limits on coverage; eliminate lifetime limits on coverage by 2014; prohibit rescission of coverage; and eliminate waiting periods for coverage of greater than 90 days.

Interim regulations issued June 22, 2010, make the preservation of grandfathered status questionable as a number of common changes one might expect disqualify the plan from grandfathered status:

1. Entering into a new policy, certificate, or contract of insurance after March 23, 2010, including simply changing the insurer;

Chapter 1: Healthcare 'Reform'

2. Eliminating all or substantially all benefits to diagnose or treat a particular condition (for example, eliminating all benefits for in vitro fertilization);

3. Increasing the fixed-amount and percentage cost-sharing by more than specified amounts to reflect medical inflation;

4. Changes that decrease the employer contribution rate for coverage by more than 5%, such as decreasing the employer-paid share of premium from 75% to 65%; or

5. Changes that impose a new or modified annual limit on benefits.

As the introduction would suggest, the insurance market is where there is arguably some real reform, although one's reaction to that reform will likely depend upon how well one understands what it means in dollars and cents to the affected populations. The reforms include:

1. Rating rules;

2. Mandatory provisions with respect to coverage and prohibitions against certain other provisions;

3. Medical Loss Ratio (MLR) requirements; and

4. Minimum coverage requirements.

Rating Rules

Health plan premiums will be allowed to vary based on age (by a 3 to 1 ratio), geographic area, tobacco use (by a 1.5 to 1 ratio), and the number of family members. These are generally effective in 2014.

Mandatory provisions with respect to coverage and prohibitions against certain other provisions

Health insurers will be prohibited from imposing lifetime limits on coverage and will be prohibited from rescinding coverage, except in cases of fraud, starting generally in 2011. Young adults will be allowed to remain on their parents' health insurance up to age 26 starting September 23, 2010 (see IRS Notice 2010-38). Waiting periods for coverage will be limited to 90 days starting in 2014.

Medical Loss Ratio (MLR) requirements

MLR refers to the portion or percentage of the premium spent on actual healthcare costs for insured individuals, although regulations need to be issued to define MLR for purposes of the reform legislation. These provisions will become effective from 2011 through 2013 with the following provisions:

Chapter 1: Healthcare 'Reform'

    1. Large group plans must spend 85% of premium;

    2. Small group/individual plans must spend 80% of premium; and

    3. Excess not spent on actual healthcare costs must be rebated in some fashion.

(This may have implications for insurance costs in areas dominated by for-profit HMOs as it is not unusual to see those insurers spending 75% of premium on healthcare.)

Increases in health plan insurance premiums will also be subject to review.

Minimum Coverage Requirements

Insurance policies not subject to the grandfather rules will be required to provide the following *minimum essential coverage*:

    1. Ambulatory patient services;

    2. Emergency services;

    3. Hospitalization;

    4. Maternity and newborn care;

    5. Mental health and substance use disorder services, including behavioral health treatment;

    6. Prescription drugs;

    7. Rehabilitative and habilitative services and devices;

    8. Laboratory services;

    9. Preventive and wellness services and chronic disease management; and

    10. Pediatric services, including oral and vision care.

In addition, the deductible in the small group market will be limited to $2,000 for an individual and $4,000 for family. "First dollar" coverage will be required for primary care, meaning there can be no cost-sharing (deductible, co-pay) for primary care services.

Chapter 1: Healthcare 'Reform'

Analysis

One of the most perplexing aspects of the reform debate is the lack of focus on the near-term and long-term impact on both the cost of insurance and the coverage provided by that insurance. In simple terms, annual and lifetime benefit caps, for example, keep the underlying expense to the insurer both lower and more predictable. Insurance premiums are, in large part, a function of probability-adjusted or actuarial-computed expected outlays, with administrative costs and profit added on, as shown in the following table:

	Annual Cost	Percent
MLR	9,360	85%
Administration	1,101	10%
Profit	551	5%
	11,012	100%

The following illustration shows what might happen to total costs included in the MLR when the limits on pre-existing conditions and annual limits are removed.

PRE-REFORM	Number	Cost	Total
Standard Insured	9,000	2,000	18,000,000
Pre-existing conditons	500	2,000	1,000,000
Annual Limits	10	200,000	2,000,000
Total Costs		9,510	21,000,000
Cost per Insured:	2,208		

POST-REFORM	Number	Cost	Total
Standard Insured	9,000	2,000	18,000,000
Pre-existing conditons	500	10,000	5,000,000
Annual Limits	10	500,000	5,000,000
Total Costs		9,510	28,000,000
Cost per Insured:	2,944		
Percent Increase:	33.33%		

Expected cost in a large population insured for healthcare is typically a function of the statistical normal distribution as shown in the classic bell curve type distribution, illustrated below for 50,000 insured lives, with illustrative[3] costs per member per month. The average cost per member per month (PMPM) is $780.

Chapter 1: Healthcare 'Reform'

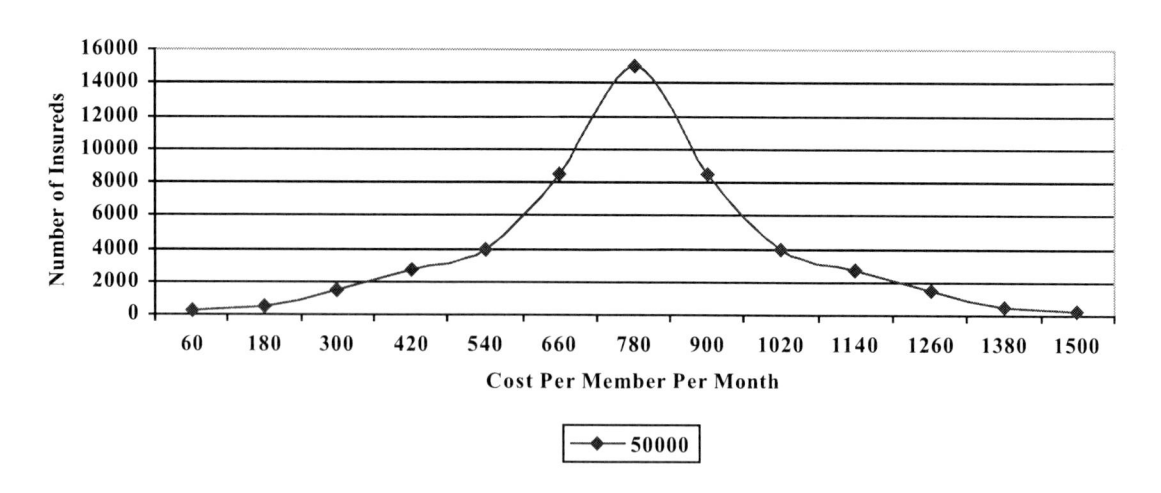

[Chart: Bell curve showing Number of Insureds vs. Cost Per Member Per Month, for population of 50000, peaking at approximately 15000 insureds at $780 PMPM]

In the bell curve above, high-cost individuals are shown at the extreme right, while low-cost individuals are shown at the extreme left. The clustering in the center is where most individuals' cost experience will lie. Naturally, to the extent that an insurer could cause its insureds to fall into the center and left of the curve, its costs would be less. If it charged a premium commensurate with the entire curve, it would expect to make a considerable profit. Thus, one stated goal of the reform was to institute safeguards against this sort of "cherry-picking" of healthy people, and to prevent dropping of unhealthy people from coverage when the cherry-picking failed to work.

Smaller populations are more unpredictable than large populations, of course. This is summed up in the commonly used phrase, "the law of large numbers," which, again, simply means that the aggregate behavior of a large population is more predictable—here in terms of the cost of their healthcare—than the behavior of a small population. This could be shown as a hypothetical sample smaller population of 10,000 compared to the 50,000.

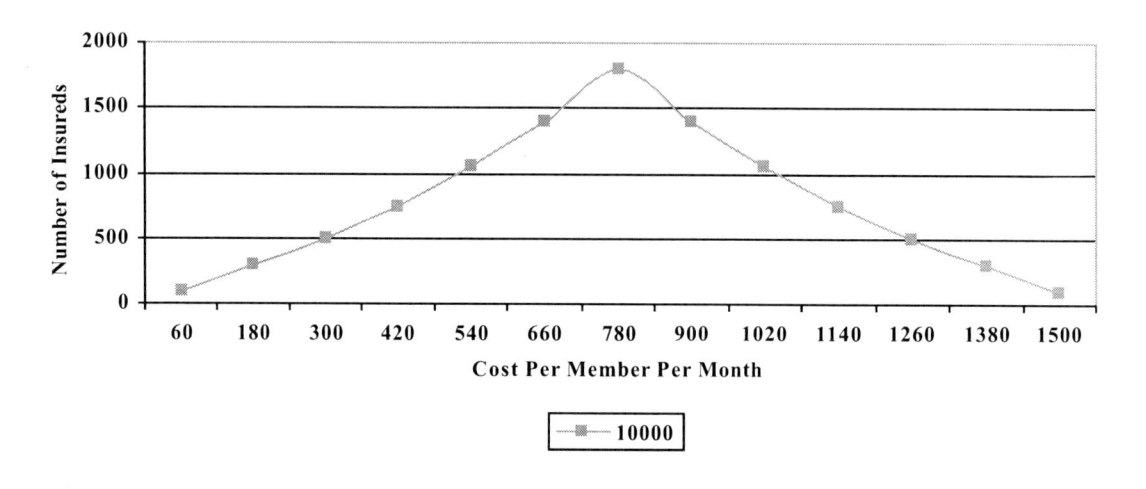

[Chart: Bell curve showing Number of Insureds vs. Cost Per Member Per Month, for population of 10000, peaking at approximately 1800 insureds at $780 PMPM]

The average cost PMPM is $780 in both cases, but the variability from the average is greater in the smaller population: 64% of the larger population has an expected cost PMPM between $660 and $900, while only 46% of the smaller population lies in that range.

Chapter 1: Healthcare 'Reform'

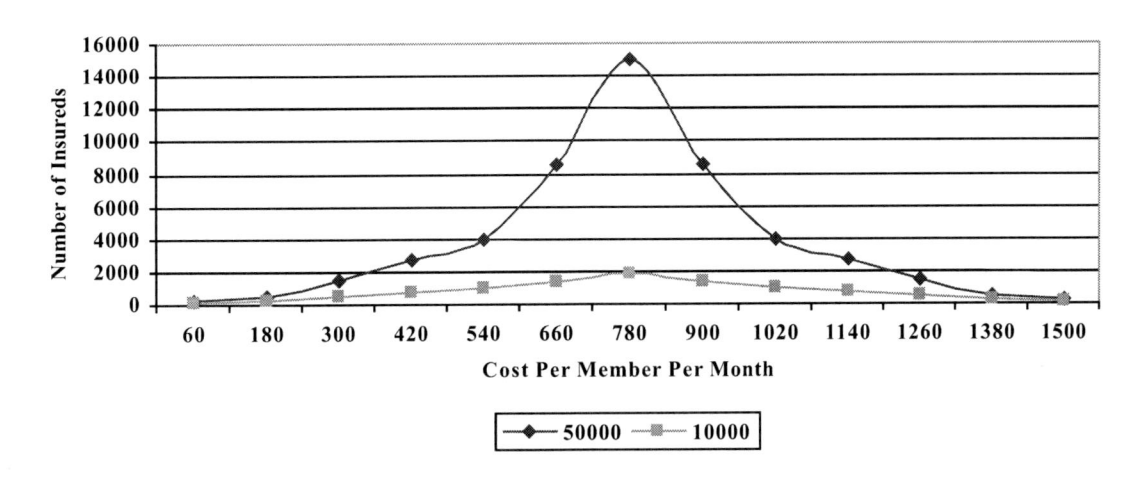

Here is an example of what we call in the industry "adverse selection" or a population of individuals who are less healthy than the "normal" aggregate population reflected in the original bell curve. The cost of providing healthcare for the individuals is much greater on a per capita basis than in the aggregate population. Thus, the cost of providing health insurance to such a group would be higher. The average cost PMPM is $886.20, nearly 14% higher than the larger groups.

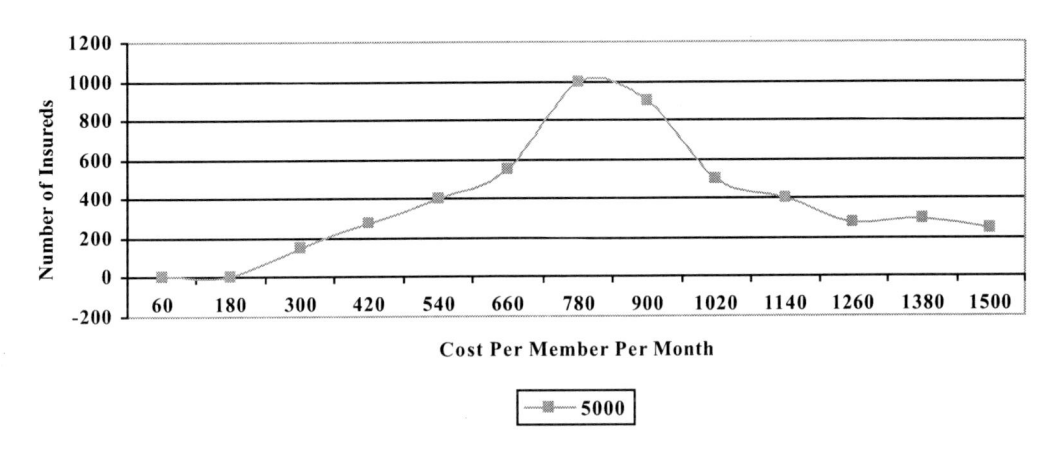

The insurance industry carves out the aggregate population into three distinct components with relativistic designations:

1. Large group market, *typically* more than 50 insureds;

2. Small group market, *typically* less than 50 insureds; and

3. Individual market, one person, as the name suggests.

"Large" is a subjective term, of course. It can then be divided into those employers, including government entities, who are large enough to self-insure and those who are not.

The AHLA/BVR Guide to Healthcare Valuation

Chapter 1: Healthcare 'Reform'

Self-Insured Groups

In light of the above discussion, another aspect of the reform debate that would be perplexing, were it not for the fact that the debate took place in the political arena, is lack of discussion of how the self-insured escaped much of the cost burden of the changes in rating and coverage requirements contained in the reform legislation. This is perhaps the single largest failure of the so-called reform, as it precludes the lowest aggregate cost per capita from being realized for all individuals contained in the aggregate population, therefore shifting those costs to the small group market. Cherry-picking of healthy people is still possible for the self-insured. This will be described in greater detail below.

How Insurance Works for a Large Group

As described in simple terms above, insurance premiums are in large part a function of probability-adjusted expected outlays, with administrative costs and profit added on. Those costs are more predictable for large populations than for small populations, and therefore the cost of actuarial uncertainty (risk) reflected in the premium charged is also less. From an administrative standpoint, it is cheaper to insure, say, 200 people under a single contract than it is to insure 40 groups of five people each under 40 contracts or 200 individuals.

Another key aspect for a large group desiring to self-insure is negotiating leverage. The larger an entity is, the more premium dollars it can bring to an insurer. As previously noted, the provision of health insurance is a low-margin business. A large employer contract can contribute disproportionately to the bottom line of the insurer, if appropriately priced in terms of premiums, because of the effect of spreading the insurer's relatively high fixed costs over more insureds.

To summarize, larger entities have lower premiums due to:

1. Predictability of cost;

2. Lower administrative costs; and

3. Potential contribution to profitability of the insurer.

Self-insured Employers

Depending on the makeup of the employees of a given employer in terms of demographics and healthcare status, an employer may decide to take advantage of the positive actuarial stability of a large group. In this case, the employer insures itself and is directly responsible for the dollar amount of those claims. It utilizes the health insurance company for its provider network (physicians, hospitals, etc.) and claims processing. This line of business is known as "ASO" (administrative services only) in the trade. The employee may carry an insurance card with the name of an insurance company on it, but the risk associated with the "insurance" is assumed by

Chapter 1: Healthcare 'Reform'

the employer. The employer makes monthly "premium" payments to the insurance company based on the insurer's estimate of the costs associated with the insured group.

Given the importance of demographics, it frequently is advantageous for larger employers with a prevalence of young employees to self-insure. Industries attracting younger employees, such as technology, can realize substantial savings through self-insurance versus being insured by the insurance company.

Self-insuring is not without risk; to guard against catastrophic losses if the costs of one or more employees fall outside the expected range, the employer purchases stop-loss insurance. A combination of actuarial input and gumption are used to determine the level at which the stop-loss insurance becomes effective. For example, an employer might decide to be at-risk for the first $50,000 of healthcare costs for an employee. Once the costs exceed that level, the stop-loss coverage cuts in and pays a negotiated percentage of the excess cost, generally 90% with the risk-bearing employer liable for the remaining 10%.

Medicare Changes

All told, reductions in the Medicare program are supposed to pay approximately $500 million of the cost of the reform legislation, less the costs associated with closing the so-called "donut hole" in the Medicare Part D Prescription Drug program.

Changes to the 'Market Basket' Update for Healthcare Facilities

The "market basket" refers to the annual healthcare inflation index that has historically been used to increase the fees paid by Medicare for acute hospital services. For both inpatient and outpatient services, acute care hospitals will be subject to reductions in the market basket update according to the following schedule:

> FY 2010-2011: market basket update reduced by 0.25% (effective April 1, 2010);
> FY 2012-2013 market basket update reduced by 0.10%;
> FY 2014 market basket update reduced by 0.30%;
> FY 2015-2016 market basket update reduced by 0.20%; and
> FY 2017-2019 market basket update reduced by 0.75%.

A similar reduction applies to inpatient rehabilitation facilities.

Hospital Productivity Adjustment

Hospitals will also be subject to a new Productivity Adjustment Based starting in 2012 on economy-wide productivity changes and the 10 year moving average in GDP, similar to a major component in the Medicare formula for the physician fee schedule update. This provision has

Chapter 1: Healthcare 'Reform'

created a good deal of concern in the hospital community. The chief actuary at CMS had the following comment in his April 22, 2010, *Estimated Financial Effects of the "Patient Protection and Affordable Care Act," as Amended*:

> It is important to note that the estimated savings shown in this memorandum for one category of Medicare provisions may be unrealistic. The PPACA introduces permanent annual productivity adjustments to price updates for most providers (such as hospitals, skilled nursing facilities, and home health agencies), using a 10-year moving average of economy-wide private, non-farm productivity gains. While such payment update reductions will create a strong incentive for providers to maximize efficiency, it is doubtful that many will be able to improve their own productivity to the degree achieved by the economy at large.[4] Over time, a sustained reduction in payment updates, based on productivity expectations that are difficult to attain, would cause Medicare payment rates to grow more slowly than, and in a way that was unrelated to, the providers' costs of furnishing services to beneficiaries. Thus, providers for whom Medicare constitutes a substantive portion of their business could find it difficult to remain profitable and, absent legislative intervention, might end their participation in the program (possibly jeopardizing access to care for beneficiaries). Simulations by the Office of the Actuary suggest that roughly 15 percent of Part A providers would become unprofitable within the 10-year projection period as a result of the productivity adjustments.[5] Although this policy could be monitored over time to avoid such an outcome, changes would likely result in smaller actual savings than shown here for these provisions.

There are also a number of additional provisions with respect to quality that take place starting in 2013 including payment reductions for preventable hospital readmissions; a "bundling" pilot program that is designed to pay a single fee for physician and hospital services; value-based purchasing (VBP) where institutions with proven positive outcomes would be preferred by the Medicare program. Ultimately, as much as 6% of the DRG (diagnosis related group) payment to a hospital may be at risk for quality factors.

Participants in the Disproportionate Share Hospital (DSH) programs receive additional Medicare payments to compensate them for providing care to the indigent. In 2014, DSH will be subject to reductions of 15%, since many of the indigent they now treat should be eligible for Medicaid coverage as described below.

Ambulatory Surgery Centers (ASCs)

ASCs compete directly with hospital outpatient departments for outpatient surgical cases, and they will be subject to a productivity adjustment factor as well. For example, if the reform legislation had been in effect in 2010, rather than receiving a 1.2% increase, ASCs would have seen a 0.1% decrease as a result of the 1.3% productivity adjustment.

Chapter 1: Healthcare 'Reform'

Medicare Advantage

Medicare Advantage is the program that privatizes Medicare coverage for beneficiaries who choose to opt out of the traditional Medicare program. It underwent major revisions in the 2003 Medicare Modernization Act aimed at halting the decline in enrollment that resulted from changes made in the 1997 Omnibus Budget Reconciliation Act (OBRA). OBRA had made major cuts in the payments to health insurers participating in what was then Medicare + Choice.

Approximately 24% of all Medicare beneficiaries are enrolled in Medicare Advantage Plans but they are most prevalent in a few states, including Florida, California, Arizona, Massachusetts, and Washington. Despite being targeted for elimination in earlier versions of the reform legislation, the cutbacks in the payments from the government to private insurers are not as draconian as might have been expected and are summarized as follows:

1. 2010 and 2011 rates will remain the same, *unadjusted for inflation*.

2. 2012 rates will be 96.5% of the current rate.

3. 2013 rates will be 98% of the current rate.

4. 2014 rates will be 100% of the current rate.

In effect, the inflation adjustment previously allowed is eliminated and further cuts are then made with reference to the baseline rate from 2009.

These cuts are particularly significant to HMOs and their participating physician groups who employ risk-based payment mechanisms. These types of arrangements represent large profit streams in Florida, Massachusetts, and California, to name three.

Generically, the changes in setting the capitation rate are described in the following from the Kaiser Family Foundation:

> [The legislation] Restructure[s] payments to Medicare Advantage (MA) plans by setting payments to different percentages of Medicare fee-for-service (FFS) rates, with higher payments for areas with low FFS rates and lower payments (95% of FFS) for areas with high FFS rates. Phase-in revised payments over 3 years beginning in 2011, for plans in most areas, with payments phased-in over longer periods (4 years and 6 years) for plans in other areas. Provide bonuses to plans receiving 4 or more stars, based on the current 5-star quality rating system for Medicare Advantage plans, beginning in 2012; qualifying plans in qualifying areas receive double bonuses. Modify rebate system with rebates allocated based on a plan's quality rating. Phase-in adjustments to plan payments for coding practices related to the health status of enrollees, with adjustments equaling 5.7% by 2019.

Chapter 1: Healthcare 'Reform'

Cap total payments, including bonuses, at current payment levels. Require Medicare Advantage plans to remit partial payments to the Secretary if the plan has a medical loss ratio of less than 85%, beginning 2014. Require the Secretary to suspend plan enrollment for 3 years if the medical loss ratio is less than 85% for 2 consecutive years and to terminate the plan contract if the medical loss ratio is less than 85% for 5 consecutive years.[6]

Accountable Care Organizations

The federal legislation similarly looks to physicians and hospitals to establish Accountable Care Organizations. According to a white paper from the Deloitte Center for Health Solutions:

> Accountable care organizations (ACOs) are a method of integrating local physicians with other members of the health care system and rewarding them for controlling costs and improving quality. ... Similar to physicians in integrated health care delivery systems, such as the Mayo Clinic, Geisinger Health System, and Intermountain Healthcare, ACO physicians are accountable for the outcomes and expenditures of their assigned population and are tasked with collaboratively improving care to reach cost and quality targets set by the payor.[7]

The legislation contains specific language that there should be a focus of primary care physicians:

> (D) The ACO shall include *primary care ACO professionals* that are sufficient for the number of Medicare fee-for-service beneficiaries assigned to the ACO under subsection (c). At a minimum, the ACO shall have at least 5,000 such beneficiaries assigned to it under subsection (c) in order to be eligible to participate in the ACO program.[8] [Emphasis added.]

Key to this focus is the concept of the Medical Home, which is defined in the legislation as follows:

(2) support patient-centered Medical Homes, defined as a mode of care that includes—

(A) personal physicians;

(B) whole person orientation;

(C) coordinated and integrated care;

(D) safe and high-quality care through evidence-informed medicine, appropriate use of health information technology, and continuous quality improvements;

(E) expanded access to care; and

(F) payment that recognizes added value from additional components of patient-centered care.[9]

Chapter 1: Healthcare 'Reform'

Primary Care Physicians (PCPs)

PCPs are among the big winners in the reform, at least for the near term, including the increased emphasis from the ACO and Medical Home provisions described above. PCPs are defined as physicians specializing in family medicine, internal medicine, geriatric medicine, and pediatric medicine if at least 60% of total Medicare Allowed Charges are for office, skilled nursing facility (SNF), home, rest home, and other visits specified by CPT Codes. For 2011 through 2015, eligible PCPs will receive a bonus equal to 10% of Medicare payments[10] for these services.

The relevant CPT codes are as follows:

1. 99201 through 99215 (the most common codes)

    a. Office - New and Established Patients visits

2. 99304 through 99340

    a. Nursing facility visits

3. 99341 through 99350

    a. Home visits

Other Physician Changes

General surgeons practicing in a health provider shortage area (HPSA) will also receive a 10% bonus in their Medicare payments. Physicians will be subject to/able to participate in the bundling pilots. There will also be a physician quality incentive program.

Medicaid

Of the 34 million uninsured who are supposed to receive coverage from the reform, 20 million are the result of the expansion of Medicaid, the program for low income individuals, the cost of which is shared between the federal and state governments.[11] Other than in a few states with very expansive benefits, Medicaid in the past did not cover adults who have no children; the expansion also picks up a large category of low income families previously ineligible. This is the single largest cost item in the reform, representing more than $450 billion over the first 10 years, most of which is picked up by the federal government through increased deficit spending, as suggested in the following quote from the aforementioned report of the CMS Chief Actuary:

> [W]e assume that employers and individuals would take roughly 3 to 5 years to fully adapt to the new insurance coverage options and that the enrollment of additional

individuals under the Medicaid coverage expansion would be completed by the third year of implementation. Because of these transition effects and the fact that most of the coverage provisions would be in effect for only 6 of the 10 years of the budget period, the cost estimates shown in this memorandum do not represent a full 10-year cost for the new legislation.

At present, those covered under Medicaid vary significantly from state to state, with states including Massachusetts, Arizona, Delaware, Hawaii, Maine, New York, and Vermont having the richest benefits. The reform legislation establishes a minimum uniform standard for Medicaid coverage in all states—those under age 65 with income up to 133 percent of the federal poverty limit—with the federal government paying most of the costs. The states providing more than the minimum coverage are required to maintain it, thus missing out on the subsidies.

Primary Care Physicians (PCPs)

For 2013 and 2014, PCPs treating Medicaid patients will be reimbursed at a rate equal to 100% of the Medicare rate.

Summary

The principal expansion of insurance coverage and the principal cost of the reform is the Medicaid program, while, aside from tax increases, the principal offsets of the cost are reductions in Medicare spending. Providers who lose through reduced Medicare spending hope to benefit from increased Medicaid spending.

Conclusions

If the experience of the model state, Massachusetts, is any indicator, small group premiums will skyrocket in those states that merge the small group and individual markets. States with health insurance premiums above the median are likely to find many of the insurance policies subject to the excise tax on Cadillac plans, which will in turn lead to cutbacks in benefits designed to avoid the excise. Assuming such a plan has survived as a grandfathered plan up to the point of the benefit cuts, it will then lose grandfathered status and be subject to the entire array of the reform's rules.

It is possible that businesses will increase their migration from high-cost states to low-cost states or even move operations overseas, exacerbating already difficult domestic employment opportunities. On the other hand, it is possible that some equalization of healthcare costs in existing lower-cost states may decrease their competitive advantage. To the extent the excise tax applies in high cost states, there will be a redistribution of income from those states to lower cost, lower income states.

Chapter 1: Healthcare 'Reform'

The primary care physician shortage will be exacerbated by the rise in the number of insured individuals and the mandated "first dollar" coverage for primary care services. Where the physicians to fill this gap will come from remains to be seen, despite the enhanced payments for primary care services and the attempt to refocus residency slots on primary care.

Perhaps the largest impact will come from Medicaid expansion. Already the leading budget buster in virtually every state in the Union, when the federal government subsidies for the expansion expire, states will be confronted with a need for enormous tax increases. Whether Reform-driven Medicaid expansion is ultimately added to the list of unfunded federal government mandates will have to wait until the turn of the next decade.

Sources of Information

CMS Chief Actuary
http://s3.amazonaws.com/thf_media/2010/pdf/OACT-Memo-FinImpactofPPACA-Enacted.pdf

Massachusetts Division of Healthcare Finance and Policy
http://www.mass.gov/Eeohhs2/docs/dhcfp/r/pubs/10/key_indicators_feb_10.ppt
http://www.mass.gov/Eeohhs2/docs/dhcfp/cost_trend_docs/presentations/2010_03_16_dianna_welch_trends.ppt

Commonwealth Fund
Paying the Price: How Health Insurance Premiums Are Eating Up Middle-Class Incomes; August 2009
http://www.commonwealthfund.org/Content/Publications/Data-Briefs/2009/Aug/Paying-the-Price-How-Health-Insurance-Premiums-Are-Eating-Up-Middle-Class-Incomes.aspx

Kaiser Family Foundation
Kaiser Fast Facts. Data Source: accessed on May 8, 2010;
  http://facts.kff.org/chartbook.aspx?cb=56

Sonnenschein, Nath, and Rosenthal, LLP
  http://www.sonnenschein.com/docs/Health_Care_Reform_Side-by-Side.pdf

Kaiser Family Foundation on Reform
  http://healthreform.kff.org/ (generally)
  http://www.kff.org/healthreform/upload/8061.pdf

Kaiser Family Foundation Subsidy Calculator
  http://healthreform.kff.org/Subsidycalculator.aspx

Kaiser Family/Alliance for Health Reform Podcast on Private Insurance Changes
  http://www.kff.org/healthreform/ahr043010video.cfm

Chapter 1: Healthcare 'Reform'

AHLA Tax and Finance Practice Group Members Briefing March 24, 2010 on Changes for Tax-Exempt Hospitals

McDermott, Will & Emory, *Health Care Reform: Legislation Affects Ambulatory Surgery Centers*, April 2, 2010

Deloitte Center for Health Solutions, Paul H. Keckley, Ph.D., Executive Director: *Accountable Care Organizations: A new model for sustainable innovation*

---

1. Data source: Health Care—Managed Care, January 7, 2010, Barclays Capital.
2. http://questions.cms.hhs.gov/cgi-bin/cmshhs.cfg/php/enduser/std_adp.php?p_faqid=2652&p_created=1079978647.
3. Note: This is not intended to be an actuarially valid model but rather to illustrate the concepts.
4. The provision of most health services tends to be very labor-intensive. Economy-wide productivity gains reflect relatively modest improvements in the service sector together with much larger improvements in manufacturing. Except in the case of physician services, we are not aware of any empirical evidence demonstrating the medical community's ability to achieve productivity improvements equal to those of the overall economy. The Office of the Actuary's most recent analysis of hospital productivity highlights the difficulties in measurement but suggests that such productivity has been small or negligible during 1981 to 2005.
5. The simulations were based on actual fiscal year 2007 Medicare and total facility margin distributions for hospitals, skilled nursing facilities, and home health agencies. Provider revenues and expenditures were projected using representative growth rates and the Office of the Actuary's best estimates of achievable productivity gains for each provider type, and holding all other factors constant. A sensitivity analysis suggested that the conclusions drawn from the simulations would not change significantly under different provider behavior assumptions.
6. Summary of New Health Reform Law. Last Modified: April 8, 2010.
7. Deloitte Center for Health Solutions, Paul H. Keckley, Ph.D., Executive Director: *Accountable Care Organizations: A new model for sustainable innovation.*
8. Patient Protection and Affordable Care Act.
9. Ibid.
10. Since Medicare pays 80% of the Allowed Charge and the beneficiary the other 20%, this results in an 8% overall increase.
11. 50% to 76% is paid for by the federal government.

Chapter 2

The Healthcare Economy
National Health Expenditures Projections: 2009-2019

By Mark O. Dietrich, CPA/ABV

The following material is based upon annual data from the Centers for Medicaid and Medicare Office of the Actuary released in February 2010, before the federal Reform legislation was passed. That office prepares annual projections of National Health Expenditures using an established model that incorporates three separate factors: actuarial, econometric and judgmental.[1]

The forecast for the decade through 2019 is as follows, with healthcare spending reaching 19% of GDP by that time, driven in part by a large jump in the GDP-share in 2009 due to the recession:

> In 2009, NHE is projected to have reached $2.5 trillion and grown 5.7 percent, up from 4.4 percent in 2008, while the overall economy, still in recession, is anticipated to have fallen 1.1 percent. The expected acceleration in growth for 2009 was due in part to projected faster growth in the use of services as many sought treatment for the H1N1 virus and in part to expected increases in subsidized coverage provided through the Consolidated Omnibus Budget Reconciliation Act (COBRA). As a result of NHE growth outpacing GDP growth in 2009, the health share of GDP is expected to have increased from 16.2 percent in 2008 to 17.3 percent in 2009, which would represent the largest one-year increase in history.
>
> In 2010, NHE growth is expected to decelerate to 3.9 percent while GDP is anticipated to rebound to 4.0 percent growth. Much of the projected slowdown in NHE growth is attributable to a deceleration in Medicare spending growth (1.5 percent in 2010, from 8.1 percent in 2009) that is driven by a 21.3-percent reduction in Medicare physician payment rates called for under current law's Sustainable Growth Rate (SGR) provisions. Under a scenario whereby physician payment rates are held at 2009 levels, total health spending is projected to grow 4.7 percent, 0.8 percentage point faster than under current law. (Medicare growth under this scenario would be 5.1 percent in 2010.) Private spending in 2010 is projected to grow just 2.8 percent, related to both declining private health insurance enrollment tied to sustained high rates of unemployment and the expiration of Federal subsidies associated with COBRA coverage.
>
> Over the projection period (2009-2019), average annual health spending growth (6.1 percent) is anticipated to outpace average annual growth in the overall economy (4.4 percent). By 2019, national health spending is expected to reach $4.5 trillion and comprise 19.3 percent of GDP. Public spending is projected to grow faster on average than

Chapter 2: The Healthcare Economy

private spending (7.0 percent versus 5.2 percent, respectively) for 2009 through 2019. As a result of more rapid growth in public spending, the public share of total health care spending is expected to rise from 47 percent in 2008, exceed 50 percent by 2012, and then reach nearly 52 percent by 2019.

The projected health spending share of GDP for 2018 (18.9 percent) is 1.4 percentage points lower than the share for 2018 from last year's projection (20.3 percent). Approximately two-thirds of this difference comes from a higher GDP projection (0.5 percentage point) and historical revisions to estimates of health spending (0.4 percentage point). The remaining difference results from somewhat slower projected spending for Medicaid, Medicare, and private payers.

After a brief respite due to the shift of prescription drug costs to Medicare Part D, Medicaid spending had exploded due to the recession; most of the newly insured contemplated by the Reform legislation would also be covered by expanding Medicaid:

> Opposite trends in spending growth for Medicare and Medicaid are projected to have occurred in 2009. Medicare spending ($507.1 billion) is projected to have increased 8.1 percent in 2009, down from 8.6 percent in 2008, partly due to slower growth in hospital spending. Medicaid spending ($378.3 billion) is projected to have increased 9.9 percent in 2009, up from 4.7 percent in 2008, due largely to rapidly increasing Medicaid enrollment during the recession. From 2009 through 2019, Medicare and Medicaid spending growth are projected to average 6.9 percent and 7.9 percent, respectively.

Hospital spending trends were described as follows. The Reform legislation contemplates paying for the expansion in significant part through cutbacks in hospital spending; however, the Chief Actuary of CMS[2] does not believe many of those savings can be realized:

> Hospital spending growth is expected to have increased 5.9 percent in 2009, up from 4.5 percent in 2008, and reached $760.6 billion. This acceleration was driven in part by higher Medicaid spending growth and increased demand for services associated with treating persons who contracted the H1N1 virus offset by the impact of reductions in demand for non-emergency procedures due to the recession. In 2010, hospital spending growth is projected to slow to 3.7 percent driven by slower growth in Medicare, Medicaid, and private payers. Hospital spending growth is projected to accelerate after 2010 and reach a high of 7.0 percent in 2016, mainly driven by faster private spending growth as projected incomes increase more rapidly. After 2016 and related to the shift of the eldest baby boomers into Medicare, public and private hospital spending trends are expected to diverge. By 2019, public spending growth for hospital services is projected to accelerate to 7.3 percent by 2019 while private spending growth is projected to slow to 4.8 percent.

The government researchers found that physician spending growth increased in 2009 in per unit terms. Although recent history suggests otherwise, the physician spending growth rate was

Chapter 2: The Healthcare Economy

forecast to decline in 2010 due to projected cuts under both Medicare's Sustainable Growth Rate formula (see discussion infra) and if that formula is suspended by Congressional action. The alternative growth calculation without those cuts is 4.1 percentage points.

> Physician and clinical services spending growth is expected to have increased 6.3 percent in 2009, up from 5.0 percent in 2008, and reached $527.6 billion mostly due to higher Medicaid spending and care associated with the H1N1 virus. Under current law, physician and clinical spending growth is expected to be 1.5 percent in 2010, driven by the projected 6.1-percent decrease in Medicare spending resulting from the SGR-mandated 21.3-percent Medicare physician payment rate reduction. Under the 0-percent SGR illustration, total physician and clinical spending growth is still projected to slow in 2010, but only to 4.1 percent. Driven largely by the improving economy, physician and clinical spending growth is expected to begin accelerating in 2011 and reach 6.6 percent by 2017. With similar factors influencing this sector as was projected to influence hospital spending, the public and private physician and clinical services spending growth trends diverge for the last three years of the projection, averaging 7.6 percent and 6.1 percent, respectively, for 2017 to 2019.

One of the principal drivers of the increase in health expenditures is prescription drug costs. It is important to understand the underlying components of the increase because the general growth rate in health expenditures will not serve as a valid proxy for the industry's individual subsets, which often have different rates of growth.

> Prescription drug spending growth is expected to have increased 5.2 percent in 2009, up from 3.2 percent in 2008, and reached $246.3 billion because of higher use of antiviral drugs, as well as faster price growth for brand-name prescription drugs. By 2011, drug spending growth is expected to accelerate to 5.6 percent, corresponding to an upward trend in use that is due to projected improving economic conditions. In 2012 and 2013, accelerating drug spending growth is expected to exhibit a temporary pause as many top-selling brand-name drugs lose patent protection. Prescription drug spending growth is anticipated to accelerate through 2019, reaching 7.7 percent with increases in drug prices are expected to account for about half of this growth.

Figure 1 plots the increase in total national expenditures (left axis) using projected data for the years 2006-2018 against those for prescription drugs (right axis). Note that there was a flattening of prescription growth commencing in 2006 followed by an upturn in the rate of increase commencing in 2009. Factors contributing to this rapid increase in prescription drug spending include consumer advertising and new product development along with increased reliance on clinical pharmacology.

The trend can be seen comparatively with other components in the following data based on the 2009 Milliman Medical Index, with pharmacy costs outstripping all others except for Outpatient; the latter is growing at the expense of Inpatient services:[3]

Chapter 2: The Healthcare Economy

Figure 1
National Health Expenditures and Prescription Drugs

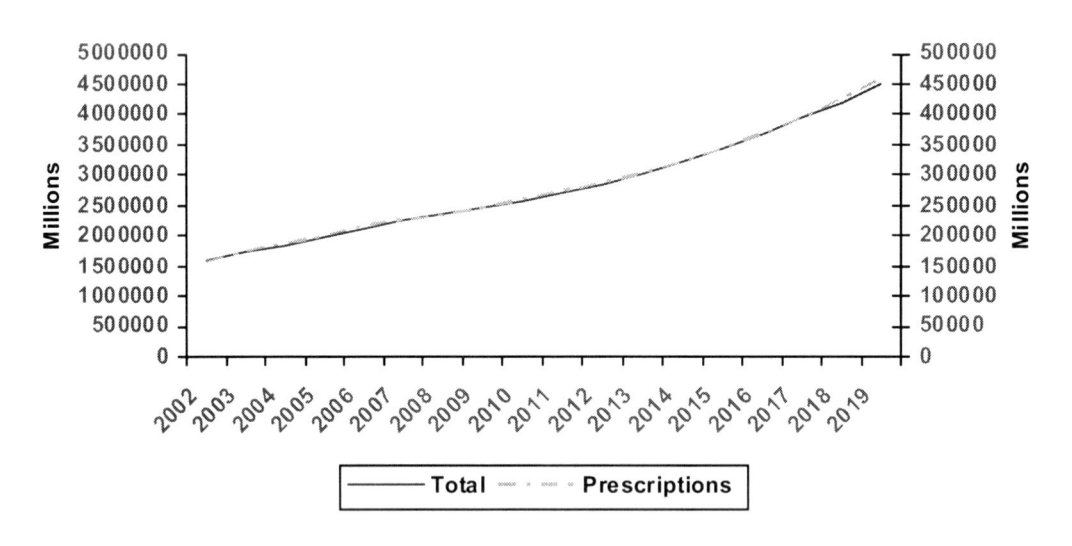

Annual Increase by Category

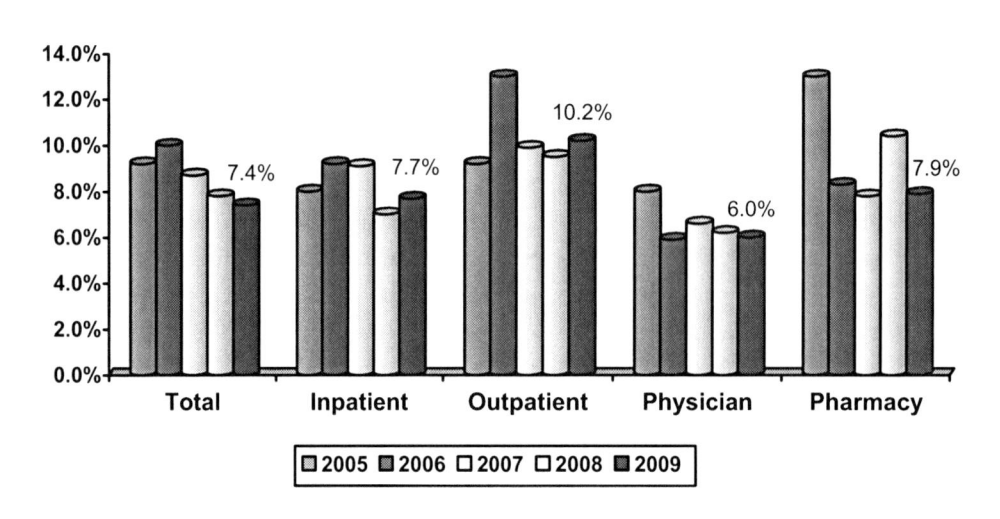

Prescription drug spending is important for a variety of reasons. Physicians increasingly rely upon pharmaceuticals to treat various conditions, often as a substitute for surgery or other procedures (e.g., coronary artery disease). The new Medicare prescription drug benefit was effective in 2006.

In contrast to prescription drugs, Medicare spending (Figure 2, right axis, purple line) was increasing at slightly more than the national rate before Part D. Note the extraordinary effect that the new Medicare Drug Benefit has on Medicare Spending by comparing the current projection to the prior projection as reflected in the red line. Shifting prescription drug spending to Medicare has caused the rate of growth in Medicare and overall spending to come close together. [The decline from 1997 to 2000 reflects the success of the Balanced Budget Act

Chapter 2: The Healthcare Economy

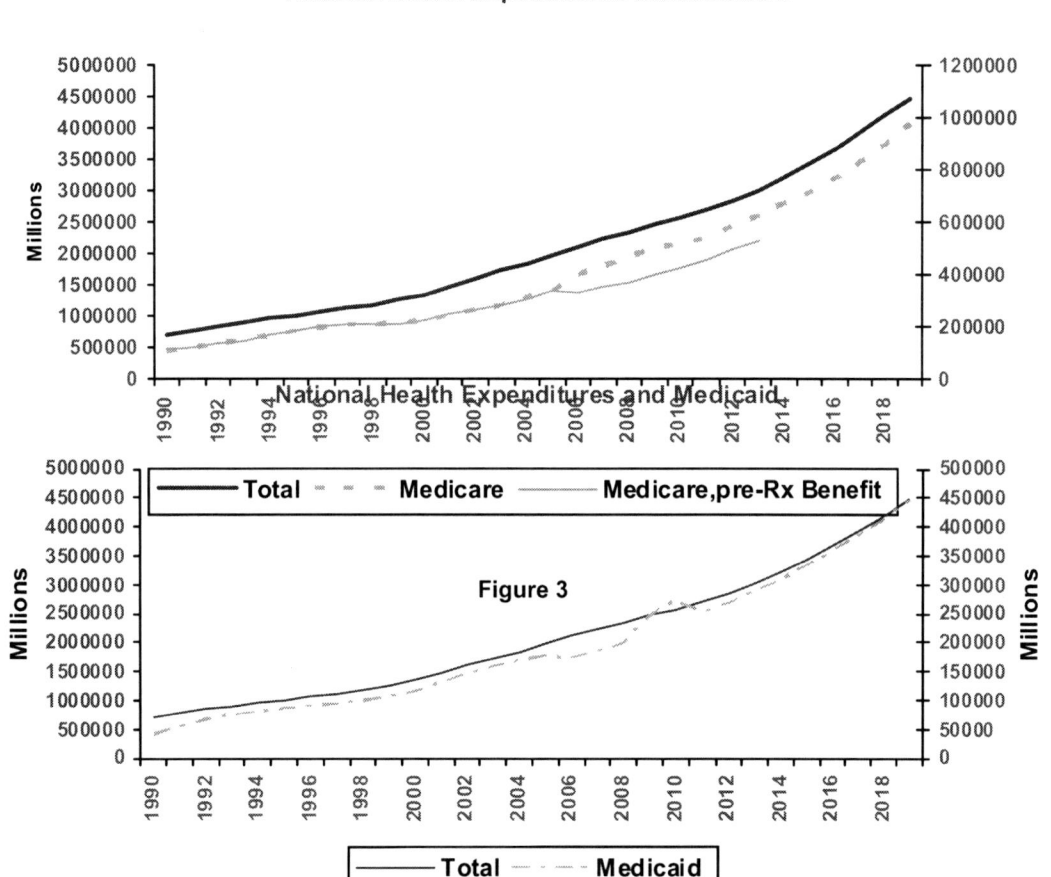

Figure 2
National Health Expenditures and Medicare

Figure 3
National Health Expenditures and Medicaid

(BBA) of 1997 in slowing Medicare spending increases, which was recently cited by the Chief Actuary of CMS in his analysis of the Healthcare Reform legislation.

Medicaid (Figure 3) is a program shared between the federal and state government that covers the poor and, more significantly, nursing home costs for lower income seniors. Program spending slows in 2006 due to the advent of the Medicare Prescription Drug benefit as described above and then resumes growth at a higher rate. This pattern is also reflective of the aging population, slower economic growth post 9-11, and immigration patterns. Where Medicaid spending was expected to outstrip Medicare spending in 2005, the Medicare Drug Benefit has changed that. Medicaid is one of, if not the, principal deficit driver in state budgets and generally speaking is the largest line item in those budgets.

Finally, the actual and projected trends for Hospital and Physician expenditures are plotted (Figure 4, right axis) against National Health Expenditures. As noted elsewhere in this report, physician expenditures are projected to grow more slowly for a variety of reasons, including present Medicare reimbursement limitations.

Chapter 2: The Healthcare Economy

Figure 4
National Health Expenditures, Hospital and Physician Costs

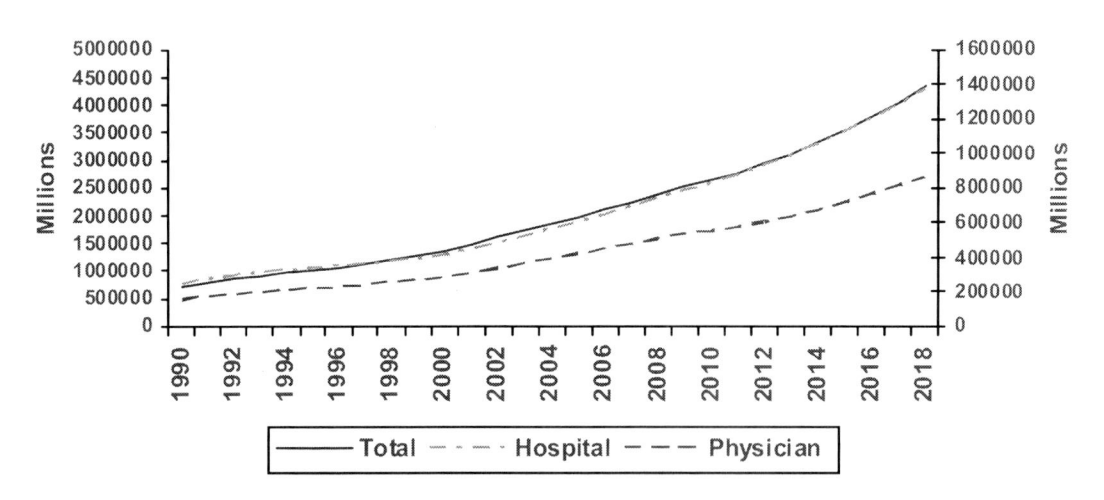

Healthcare spending is expected to continue to outstrip growth in GDP, exacerbated in the Recesssion, as shown in the illustration from MedPAC's 2010 Report to Congress on the followng page..

Quarterly Health Care Indicators

Note: CMS ceased reporting Quarterly utilization data in the third quarter of 2004.

Utilization

The following discussion is based in part upon an analysis of second and/or third quarter 2005 data from the Centers for Medicare and Medicaid Health Care Indicators released in June 2006.[4]

As in the case of price increases within any other segment of the economy, price increases for healthcare consist of both increases in purchases (utilization) and price (inflation and other increases). The analysis below reports increases in utilization and compares the increases in healthcare spending to both the Consumer Price Index (CPI) as a proxy for inflation and to gross domestic product (GDP), as a proxy for overall economic activity,[5] related to both purchase or volume of activity increases and price increases.

When a patient is admitted to the hospital, the character of the treatment is based upon the diagnosis reflected in the patient's medical record at the time of discharge from the hospital. Hospital discharges per 1000 population decreased to 123 in the third Quarter of 2004, reflecting an apparent decline in utilization.

Chapter 2: The Healthcare Economy

Health care spending has grown more rapidly than GDP

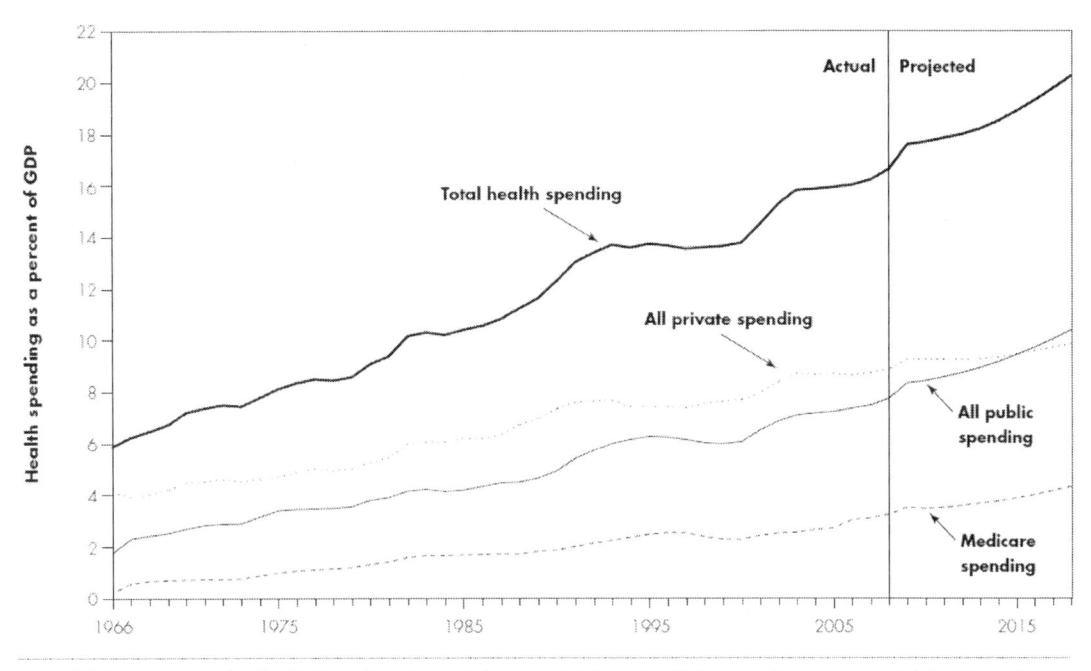

Note: GDP (gross domestic product). Total health spending is the sum of all private and public spending. Medicare spending is one component of all public spending.

Source: CMS, Office of the Actuary, National Health Expenditure Accounts, 2009.

Overall, inpatient admissions (or discharges) for the over age 65 (Medicare) population continue to grow based upon data from MedPAC's 2010 Report to Congress even though the rate of inpatient admissions per 1000 population has grown less dramatically (Figure 6). More and more services take place in the Outpatient department of hospitals as well.

This type of analysis is significant in valuing medical practices that have material earnings from hospital services. This would include the surgical specialties and consultative medical specialties, such as cardiology and particularly invasive cardiology. It also is connected to the trend to move surgical cases to Ambulatory Surgery Centers, one of the most significant trends of the last decade.

Costs

Costs per inpatient admission had increased relatively slowly until mid-2001, while displaying a seasonality factor (Figure 7). This pattern is consistent with other data discussed herein indicating that hospitals are seeing large revenue increases after years of pricing pressure. Overall data (Figure 8) on hospital costs per day show a steady increase each year.

Chapter 2: The Healthcare Economy

Figure 5
Quarterly Hospital Discharges and Trendline: All ages

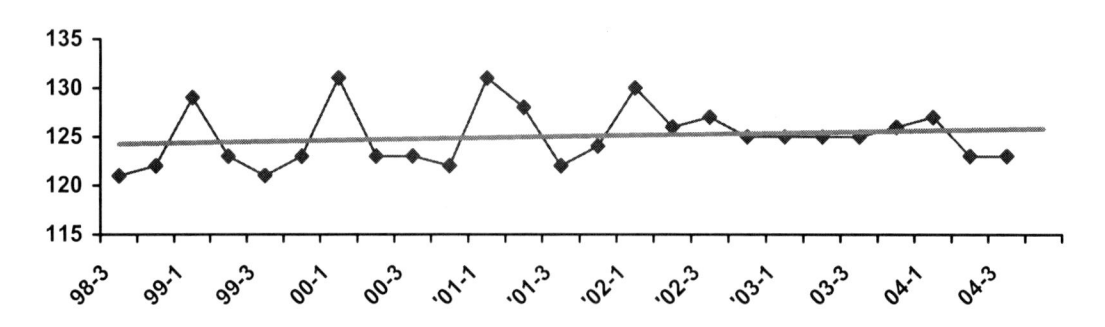

Figure 6
Medicare outpatient services grew while hospital inpatient discharges per FFS enrollee were fairly constant from 2003 to 2008

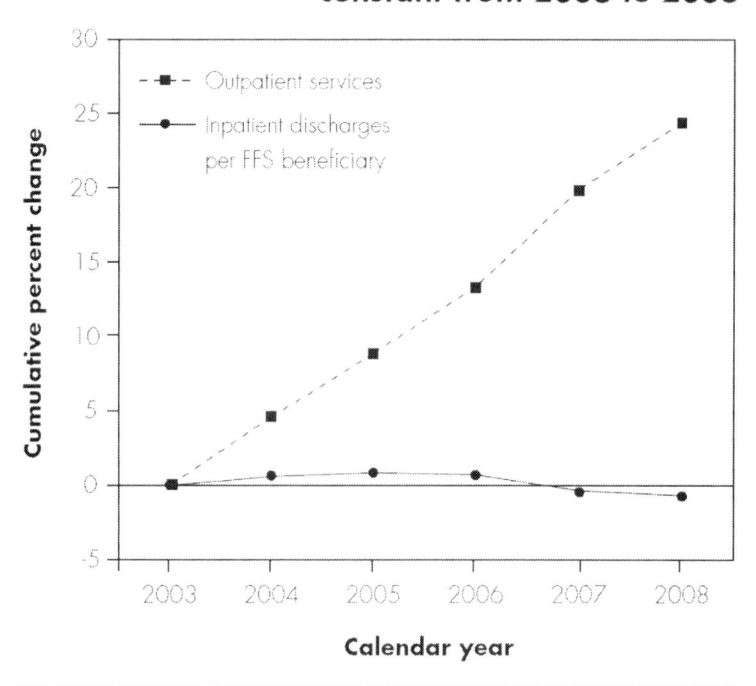

Note: FFS (fee-for-service). Data are for short-term general and surgical hospitals, including critical access and children's hospitals.

Source: MedPAC analysis of Medicare Provider Analysis and Review and hospital outpatient claims data from CMS.

Chapter 2: The Healthcare Economy

Figures 7, Inpatient Cost Trend
Quarterly Inpatient Cost per Admission

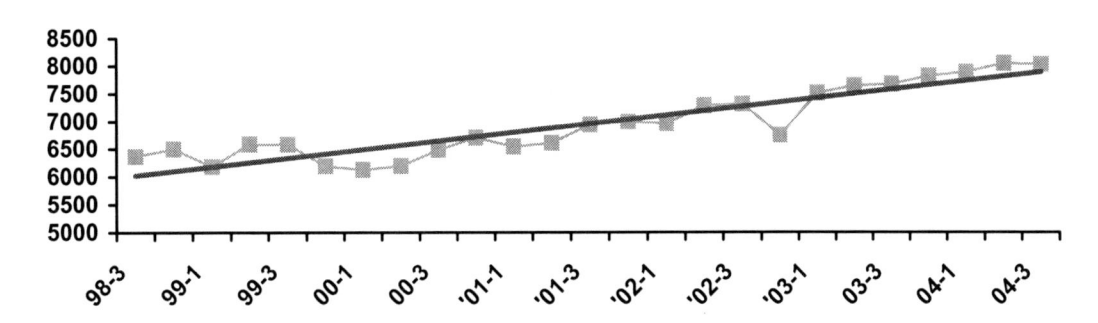

Figure 8 [6]
U.S. Trend in Cost & Rate of Increase per Inpatient Day

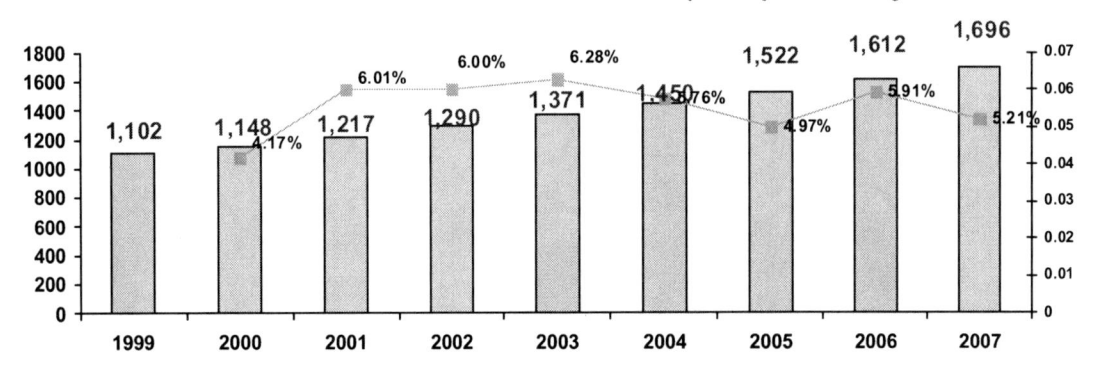

In contrast to hospital inpatient costs, outpatient visit costs had been increasing at a steadier rate as the uptrend continue through the second quarter of 2004 (Figure 9). Hospitals have been progressively moving volume to, and expanding the services of, outpatient settings where the government had historically been less successful in controlling utilization and price. Hospital inpatient services have for many years been paid a fixed rate per discharge diagnosis (DRG) (known as a Prospective Payment System, or PPS[7]) that varies principally based upon the number of admissions, rather than the number of days in the hospital. Until comparatively recently, outpatient services were not paid under a PPS. This was changed by the BBA and implemented in August of 2000. Such changes, of course, are very significant in attempting to forecast future outpatient revenues based upon historical results.

CMS ceased tracking Quarterly cost trend data but the following graph indicates that the rate of growth in per unit costs has slowed even though total costs continue to increase.

Finally, outpatient visit growth has slowed to near zero while actual inpatient days per 1000 continue to decline. [8]

Chapter 2: The Healthcare Economy

Figure 9, Outpatient Cost Trend
Quarterly Hospital Outpatient Cost per Visit

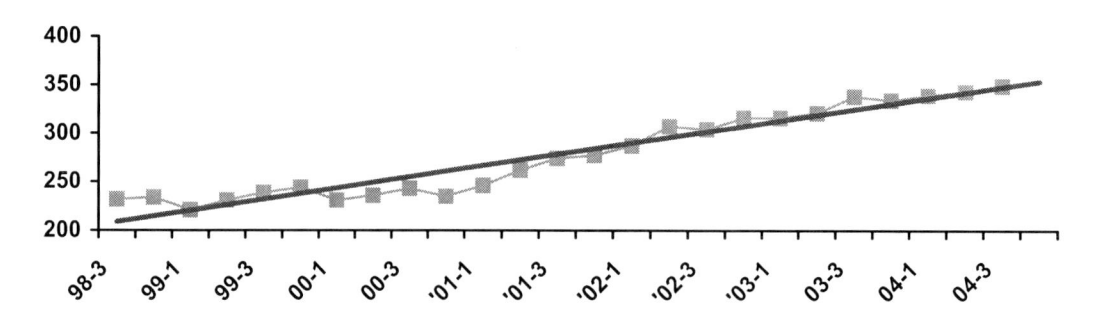

Consumer Price Index and Producer Price Index for Hospital Services, Percent Change from Same Period of Previous Year, 2000-2007

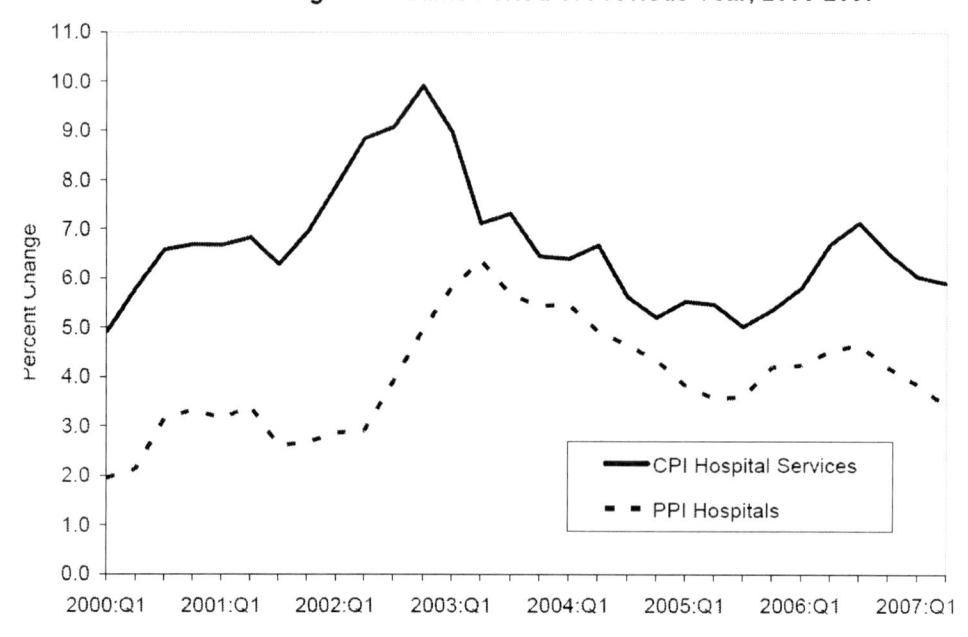

Figure 10
U.S. Trend Outpatient Visits vs Inpatient Days per 1000 Population

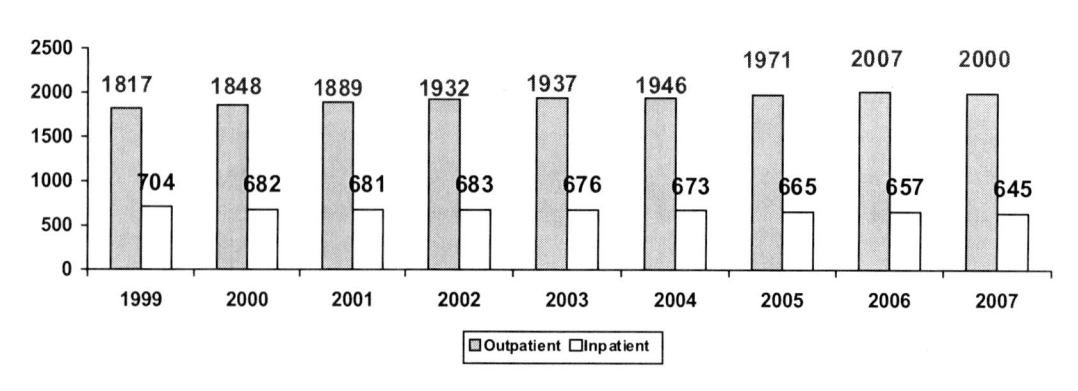

Year	Outpatient	Inpatient
1999	1817	704
2000	1848	682
2001	1889	681
2002	1932	683
2003	1937	676
2004	1946	673
2005	1971	665
2006	2007	657
2007	2000	645

50   The AHLA/BVR Guide to Healthcare Valuation

Chapter 2: The Healthcare Economy

Medical expense inflation continued to outstrip the overall CPI, with hospital inflation leading the way, showing a rapid acceleration throughout 2002 and then declining in 2003, consistent with the Inpatient costs per admission in Figure 8. Physician costs, in contrast, are increasing at a rate less than that of the Medical CPI and significantly less than hospital costs and GDP (Figure 11). Hospital costs had risen at a rate slightly less than GDP reflecting the downward pressure on costs and utilization from HMOs and limited government payment increases. As the economy entered recession in 2008, healthcare expenditures continued to increase even increasing during 2009 when the GDP and CPI otherwise declined, leading to concerns about deflation elsewhere in the economy. Once again, the healthcare segment proved to be more or less indifferent to the broad economy, an important factor to consider when conducting the valuation of healthcare entities. [9,10]

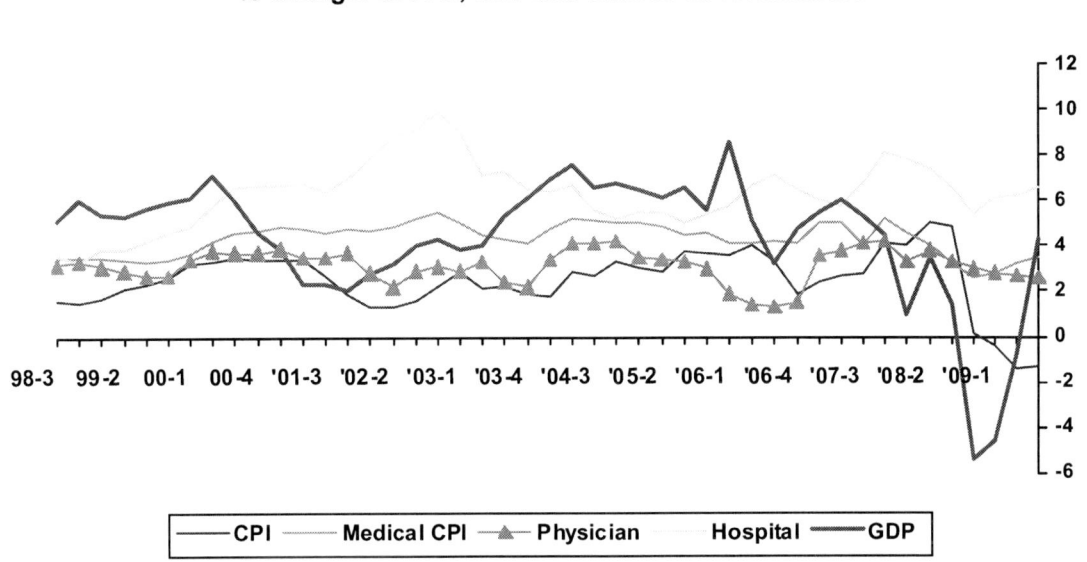

Figure 11, CPI Trend
% Change: CPI-All, GDP and various CPI-Healthcare

(Rates shown in Figure 11 represent the Percent Change from Same Period of Previous Year.)

A comparison of the CPI and Medical Care CPI with a trend line for Medical Care is shown below. The Recession has flattened the cost trend in the Medical CPI.

More telling, perhaps, is the CPI for Medical Care Services (Physicians and Hospitals) versus that of Physicians alone, indicating that Hospital costs are the main driver of healthcare inflation.[11]

Revised data indicates that Physician Practice Expenses are increasing at a higher rate than Physician Earnings including fringe benefits,[12] although both are less than the Medical CPI as shown in Figure 12. Physician Wages & Salaries data is no longer presented, although it showed considerably lower growth then the reported Earnings number through the last data point in

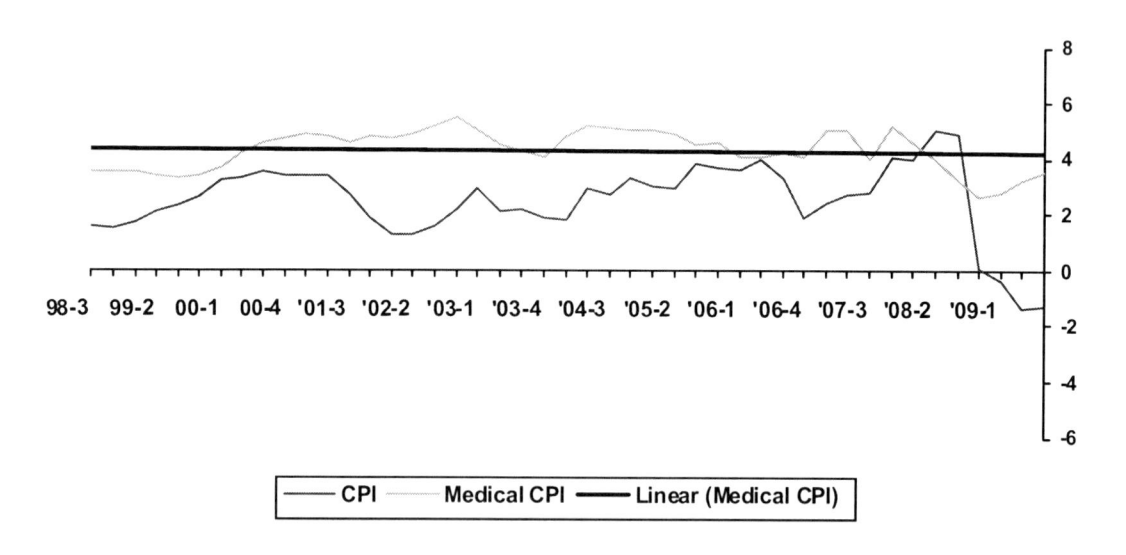

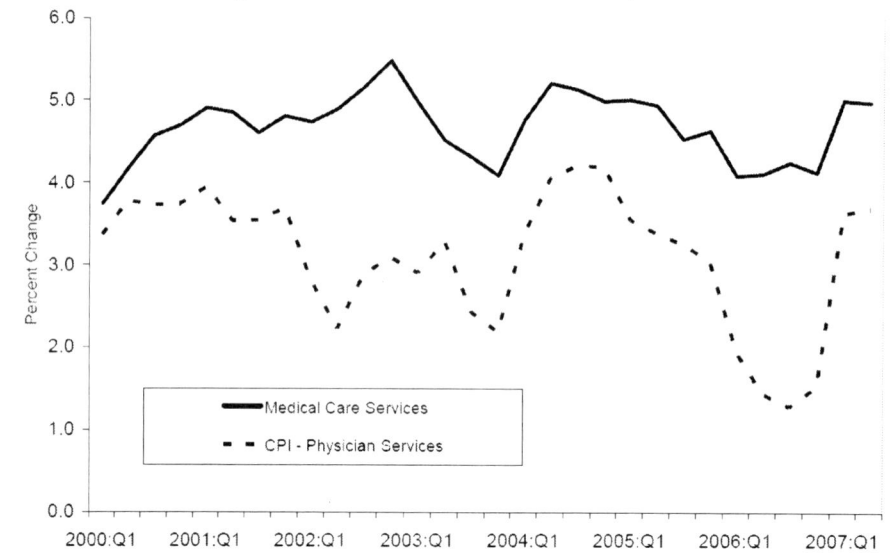

Chapter 2: The Healthcare Economy

% Change: CPI-All, GDP and various CPI-Healthcare

CPI Physician Services and CPI Medical Care Services, Percent Change from Same Period of Previous Year, 2000-2007

2004. Benefit growth accounts for significant part of the reported increase. The values are also productivity adjusted using Bureau of Labor Statistics non-farm multifactor productivity, a generic workforce measure that does not reflect physician practices. Historically, projections of practice expense growth declining to the rate of earnings growth do not, in fact, materialize; however, they continue to appear in the forecast! 2007 represents an exception due to the significant rate increases for physicians, offsetting years of accelerating costs without increases in per unit fees.

Chapter 2: The Healthcare Economy

The CMS forecast of physician earnings through 2005 reflected the passage by Congress of a 1.5% increase in Medicare reimbursement for 2004 and 2005 overriding mandated cuts, although significant cuts continue to be threatened by failure to repeal the Sustainable Growth Rate formula discussed elsewhere herein in the absence of legislative change. This is a result of the artificial constraints placed upon increases in physician reimbursement by the Medicare program, which have not been present for any other class of provider (e.g., hospitals or home health care). (See discussion infra) However, the Reform legislation imposes requirements for productivity gains on hospitals which, notably, the Chief Actuary of CMS says are likely unobtainable.

Figure 12, MD Earnings and Practice Expense Trend[13][14]
Physician Earnings and Practice Expenses, Base Year 2000 Forecast to 2019

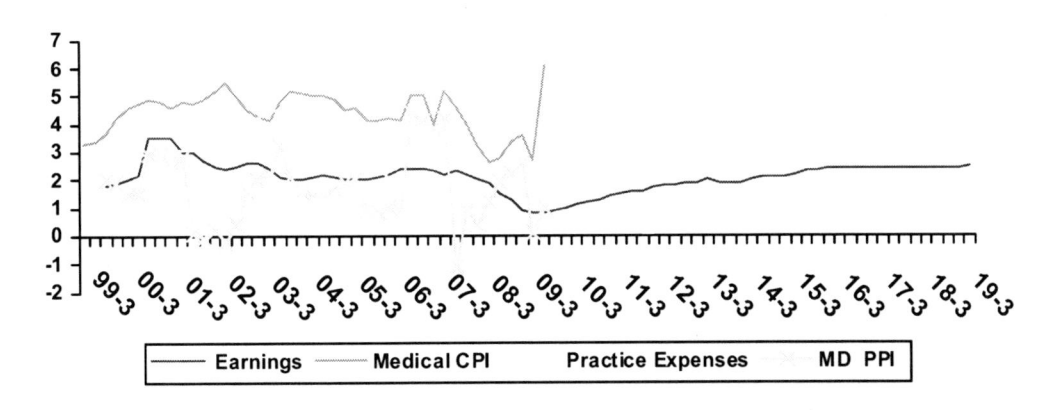

This PPI for physicians has steadily maintained a compound rate of growth of approximately 2%, although the year-to-year changes are quite volatile and particularly so in 2007. In fact, the compound rate of growth in physician fees during this 15-year period was only 1.94%.

Figure 13, Producer Price Index, Physician Services
BLS PPI-Physician Services, Annual

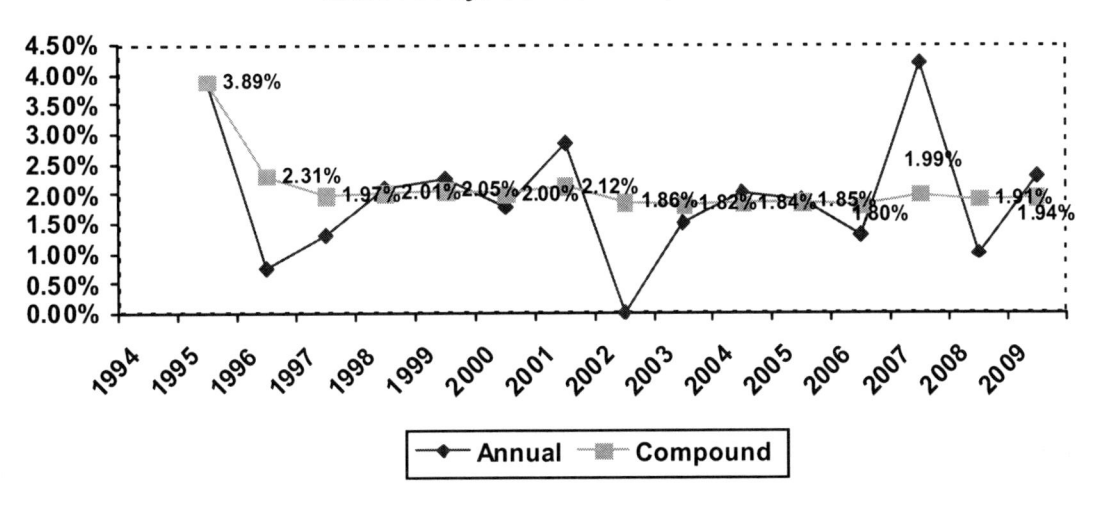

The AHLA/BVR Guide to Healthcare Valuation

Chapter 2: The Healthcare Economy

Trends in Physician Supply and Demand and Utilization

The Table below illustrates the breakdown of patient office visits by individual physician specialties from the National Center for Health Statistics.[15] General and family practice, internal medicine and pediatrics accounted for 51% of all patient office visits in 2006, down from 2005.

SPECIALTY	2006 % of visits	2005 % of visits	2004 % of visits	2003 % of visits	2002 % of visits	2001 % of visits	2000 % of visits
General Practice Family Practice	23.1	22.4	22.8	24.6	24.2	23.9	24.1
Internal Medicine	13.9	17.4	16.1	15.6	17.6	15.3	15.2
Pediatrics	13.6	13.4	12.8	10.4	13.5	12.6	12.6
All others	13.0	12.1	13.5	13.1	11.7	11.0	11.7
Obstetrics/Gynecology	7.7	6.7	7.2	8.8	7.9	7.9	7.9
Ophthalmology	6.4	6.1	5.2	5.4	5.6	6.1	5.2
Orthopedic Surgery	5.3	4.8	4.8	4.8	4.3	5.3	5.6
Dermatology	2.8	3.4	3.7	3.3	3.6	4.3	4.2
Cardiovascular	2.9	2.8	2.5	2.8	2.3	3.2	2.6
Psychiatry	2.8	2.9	3.4	3.2	2.4	3.1	3.5
General Surgery	1.6	2.5	2.1	2.2	1.9	2.2	2.1
Otolaryngology	1.9	2.3	2.2	2.4	1.9	2.0	2.0
Urology	2.0	2.0	2.0	2.0	1.9	1.9	2.3
Neurology	1.4	1.4	1.6	1.4	1.1	1.2	1.0

This Table shows expected office visits per patient per year from the same NCHS report and is valuable for estimating patient volume in an office setting, particularly where capitation may be involved.

Total Office Visits Per Patient Per Year for All Physician Specialties

Age	All	Female	Male
<1	2.60		
1–4	3.18		
5–14	1.86		
<15	2.60	2.57	2.56
15–24	1.75	2.43	1.09
25–44	2.26	2.95	1.55
45–64	3.45	3.92	2.96
65–74	6.45	6.00	5.54
>75	7.19	7.25	7.09
Total	3.07	3.55	2.56

Chapter 2: The Healthcare Economy

Figure 14 takes the data from the Table above and depicts all specialties accounting for more than 4% of patient visits. It is important to note that these specialties are predominantly primary care, or specialties such as Ophthalmology and Ob/Gyn that have primary care-like features, i.e., the need to be seen by many patients on a regular basis. Only orthopedics and ophthalmology among the non-primary care specialties have significant patient volume.

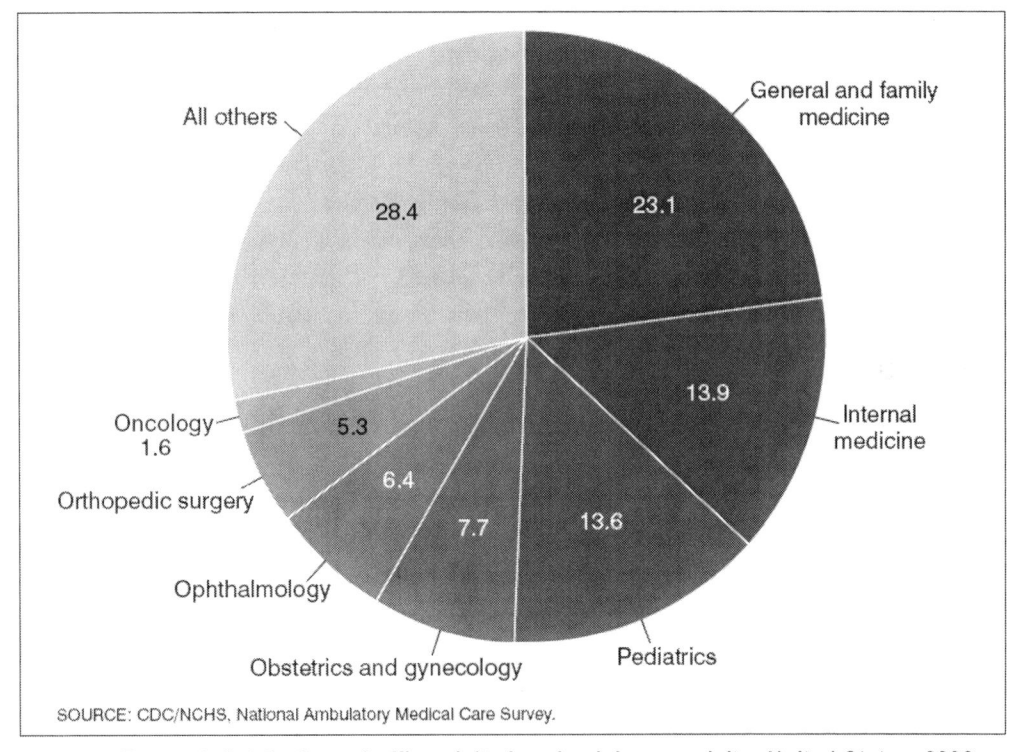

Figures 14, Concentration of Visits/Physicians by Specialty

- General and family medicine: 23.1
- Internal medicine: 13.9
- Pediatrics: 13.6
- Obstetrics and gynecology: 7.7
- Ophthalmology: 6.4
- Orthopedic surgery: 5.3
- Oncology: 1.6
- All others: 28.4

SOURCE: CDC/NCHS, National Ambulatory Medical Care Survey.

Percent distribution of office visits by physician specialty: United States, 2006

The Kaiser Family Foundation breaks down Primary Care Physicians as follows:

United States	Percent	0% - 100%
Internal Medicine	35%	
Family Practice	29%	
Pediatrics	18%	
Obstetrics/Gynecology	12%	
General Practice	6%	
Total Primary Care	100%	

Chapter 2: The Healthcare Economy

In interpreting the relative number of office visits among the various specialties illustrated, readers should bear in mind that the surgical specialties in particular perform many of their services in hospital settings. In addition, the medical specialties, such as cardiology and nephrology, for example, have many encounters in the hospital as well, such as for consultations requested by other physicians.[16]

The physician recruiting firm Merritt Hawkins released its annual report in May 2009. Data on annual recruiting engagements indicates that the specialties in highest demand include family medicine, internal medicine, hospitalist, orthopedic surgery, OB/Gyn and cardiology. Hospitals or existing practices looking to recruit such physicians typically find the starting salary very high and the structure of a future buy-in on the table from the outset.

Primary care physicians in Internal Medicine and Family Practice are in high demand, bucking the specialist trend, making it difficult or impossible in many markets to sell an interest in a practice at a significant price. Some speculate that the shortage of specialists is driving the demand for Internists and Family Practitioners, who may provide higher level adult medical care when specialists like cardiologists are not available.

Figure 15 reflects the growth of the various specialties from 1996 to 2006.[17]

A serious shortage of physicians and particularly primary care (generalist) physicians is expected in the next several decades. This has negative implications for practice value as new suppliers ease of entry to the market is enhanced when there is unmet, excess demand for services.[18]

Medicare-participating physicians by specialty and region are shown in the following tables from the publication 2009 CMS Statistics.[19] The regional data is of particular note given the differing concentrations of physicians per 100000 population around the country.

Chapter 2: The Healthcare Economy

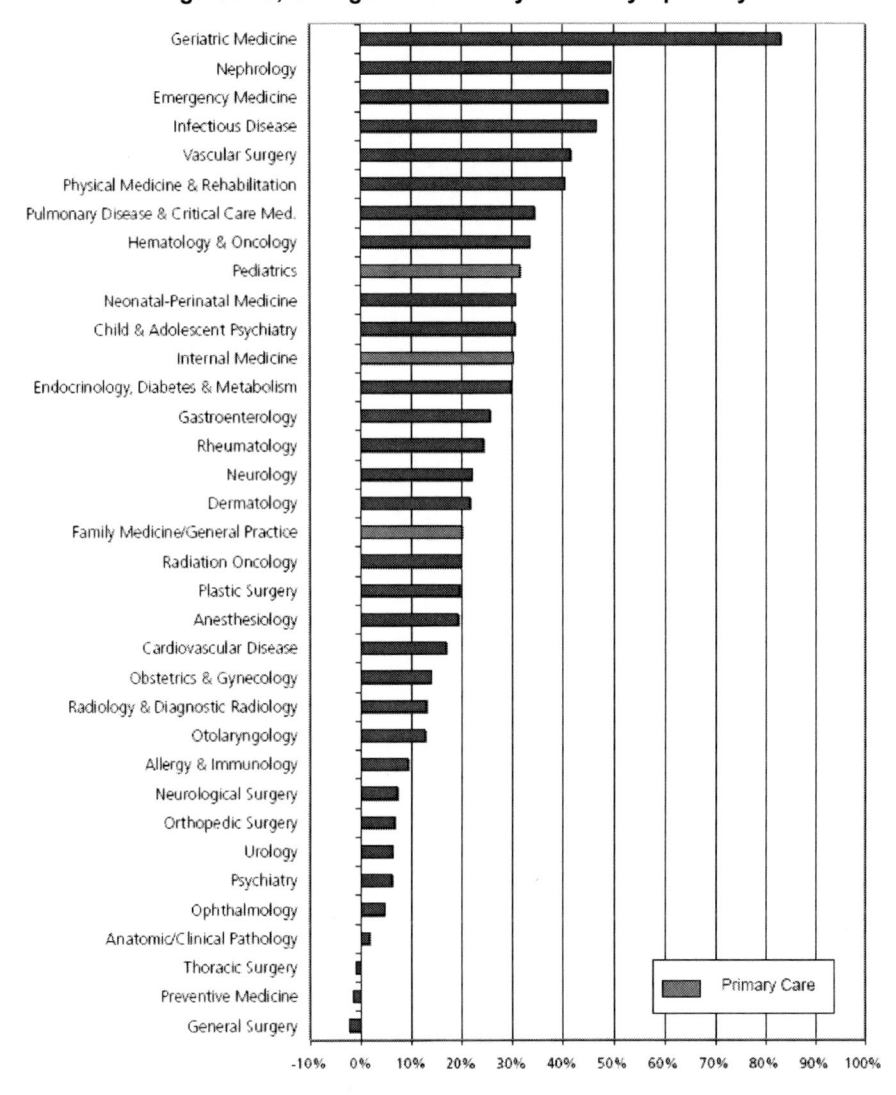

Figures 15, Change in Active Physicians by Specialty

Specialty	Change
Geriatric Medicine	~85%
Nephrology	~50%
Emergency Medicine	~49%
Infectious Disease	~46%
Vascular Surgery	~42%
Physical Medicine & Rehabilitation	~40%
Pulmonary Disease & Critical Care Med.	~35%
Hematology & Oncology	~33%
Pediatrics	~31%
Neonatal-Perinatal Medicine	~30%
Child & Adolescent Psychiatry	~30%
Internal Medicine	~29%
Endocrinology, Diabetes & Metabolism	~28%
Gastroenterology	~25%
Rheumatology	~23%
Neurology	~22%
Dermatology	~21%
Family Medicine/General Practice	~20%
Radiation Oncology	~20%
Plastic Surgery	~19%
Anesthesiology	~18%
Cardiovascular Disease	~16%
Obstetrics & Gynecology	~13%
Radiology & Diagnostic Radiology	~12%
Otolaryngology	~11%
Allergy & Immunology	~9%
Neurological Surgery	~7%
Orthopedic Surgery	~6%
Urology	~6%
Psychiatry	~5%
Ophthalmology	~4%
Anatomic/Clinical Pathology	~2%
Thoracic Surgery	~0%
Preventive Medicine	~-1%
General Surgery	~-2%

Legend: Primary Care

Chapter 2: The Healthcare Economy

Part B practitioners/CMS region

	Active practitioners	Practitioners per 100,000 population
All regions	1,245,003 [1]	413
Boston	96,484	676
New York	147,395	527
Philadelphia	133,101	459
Atlanta	221,727	374
Chicago	211,442	410
Dallas	118,319	323
Kansas City	62,890	469
Denver	46,248	444
San Francisco	151,680	325
Seattle	55,717	449

[1] Includes non-Federal physicians, limited licensed and non-physician practitioners. Practitioners with multi-State practices are duplicated in the enumeration for each State in which they operate.

NOTES: Physicians as of July 2007. Civilian population as of July 1, 2007. Resident population for outlying areas and the Virgin Islands are not available.

SOURCES: CMS, ORDI, and the Bureau of the Census.

Table II.8
Part B practitioners active in patient care/selected years

	July 2007 Number	Percent
All Part B Practitioners	1,087,845	100.0
Physician Specialties	667,340	61.3
Primary Care	246,314	22.6
Medical Specialties	108,694	10.0
Surgical Specialties	108,031	9.9
Emergency Medicine	36,644	3.4
Anesthesiology	38,358	3.5
Radiology	37,595	3.5
Pathology	13,984	1.3
Obstetrics/Gynecology	38,515	3.5
Psychiatry	38,921	3.6
Other and Unknown	284	0.0
Limited Licensed Practitioners	126,006	11.6
Non-physician Practitioners	294,499	27.1

NOTES: Specialty code is self-reported and may not correspond to actual board certification. Totals do not necessarily equal the sum of rounded components. Reflect unduplicated counts.

SOURCE: CMS, Office of Research, Development, and Information.

Chapter 2: The Healthcare Economy

Trends in Health Insurance Coverage

According to the Census Bureau's 2008 survey,[20] "The percentage of people without health insurance in 2008 was not statistically different from 2007 at 15.4 percent. The number of uninsured increased to 46.3 million in 2008, from 45.7 million in 2007. The number of people with health insurance increased to 255.1 million in 2008—up from 253.4 million in 2007. The number of people covered by private health insurance decreased to 201.0 million in 2008—down from 202.0 million in 2007. The number of people covered by government health insurance increased to 87.4 million—up from 83.0 million in 2007. The percentage of people covered by private health insurance was 66.7 percent in 2008—down from 67.5 percent in 2007. The percentage of people covered by employment-based health insurance decreased to 58.5 percent in 2008, from 59.3 percent in 2007. The number of people covered by employment-based health insurance decreased to 176.3 million in 2008, from 177.4 million in 2007."

Figure 16 indicates the percentages of the United States population covered by insurance during 2007 and 2008. The figures in the accompanying table add to more than 100% because some individuals were covered by more than one form of insurance during the year.

Summary

The preceding review indicates that healthcare spending is advancing at a rate in excess of that of inflation and exceeds GDP growth. Present trends indicate that the success of managed care in controlling medical costs has come to an end, resulting in a focus on new insurance products putting the consumer at increased risk for their decisions. Overall trends in healthcare spending, however, are neither indicative nor predictive of trends in specific subsectors of the industry. Physician incomes generally are increasing at a rate less than the Medical CPI, even as their operating expenses increase at a greater rate. Hospital expenses have consistently grown faster than the CPI and recently, at a rate faster than GDP, particularly in the Recession. This latter trend reflects increases in both utilization and unit price increases.

Chapter 2: The Healthcare Economy

Figure 16

Coverage by Type of Health Insurance: 2007 and 2008
(Percent)

Legend: 2007, 2008

Private insurance
- Any private plan: 67.5 / 66.7*
- Employment-based: 59.3 / 58.5*
- Direct-purchase: 8.9 / 8.9

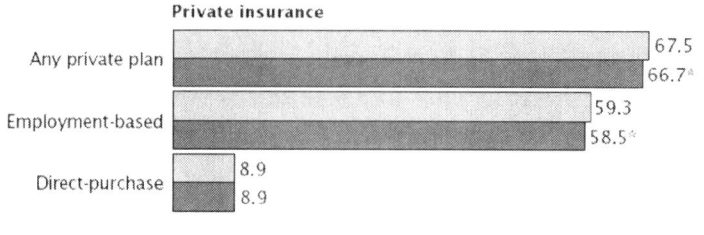

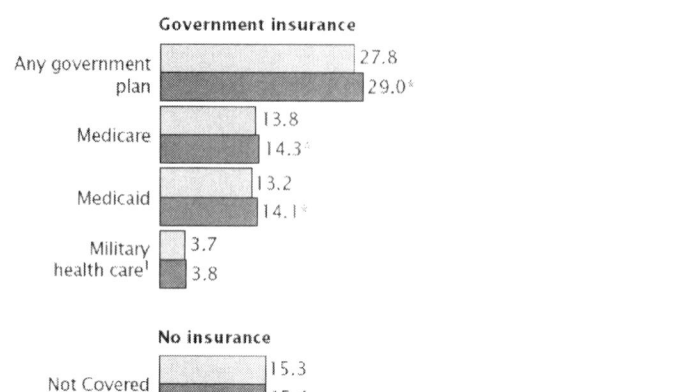

Government insurance
- Any government plan: 27.8 / 29.0*
- Medicare: 13.8 / 14.3*
- Medicaid: 13.2 / 14.1*
- Military health care[1]: 3.7 / 3.8

No insurance
- Not Covered: 15.3 / 15.4

* Statistically different at the 90 percent confidence level.
[1] Military health care includes Tricare and CHAMPVA (Civilian Health and Medical Program of the Department of Veterans Affairs), as well as care provided by the Department of Veterans Affairs and the military.

Note: The estimates by type of coverage are not mutually exclusive; people can be covered by more than one type of health insurance during the year.

Source: U.S. Census Bureau, Current Population Survey, 2008 and 2009 Annual Social and Economic Supplements.

Concentration of Market Share

As can be seen in the following Table, based upon a Government Accounting Office Study, the provision of health insurance is significantly state-specific. Most markets are dominated by a few insurance companies; many are dominated by a single company. This fact results in strikingly different market conditions from state to state and virtual oligopolistic or monopolistic valuation of physician services.

Lehman Brothers notes:

> Comparing the present data with a previous GAO study shows evidence of consolidation in the small group health insurance market. When looking at the 37 states which were included in both GAO studies, the number of licensed carriers declined by an average rate of 8.2%, or by more than five carriers in each state, in the three years since the last GAO study was made. Membership has consolidated even more rapidly within

Chapter 2: The Healthcare Economy

the largest carriers, with an 842-basis-point increase in the market share held by the five largest carriers to 83.9%, from 75.5%. The largest carrier now has an average of 43.7% of total market share, up 605 basis points from the prior study.[21]

	Number of Licensed Carriers	Largest Carrier	Market Share of Largest Carrier	Market Share of 5 Largest Carriers	Rank of Largest BCBS carrier	Market Share of all BCBS carriers
Alabama	NA	BCBS of Alabama	78.00%	NA	1	NA
Alaska	12	Premera Blue Cross	66.00%	100.00%	1	66.00%
Arizona	53	United of AZ	29.00%	66.00%	2	19.00%
Colorado	27	United	24.00%	72.00%	3	13.00%
Connecticut	25	Anthem BCBS of CT	NA	NA	1	NA
Delaware	16	BCBS of Delaware	58.00%	99.00%	1	58.00%
District of Columbia	13	Group H&M BCBS	43.00%	97.00%	1	65.00%
Florida	29	United of FL	22.00%	78.00%	3	31.00%
Georgia	75	BCBS of GA	27.00%	65.00%	1	41.00%
Idaho	16	BCBS Idaho	45.00%	97.00%	1	87.00%
Illinois	51	NA	NA	NA	NA	NA
Iowa	60	Wellmark BCBS	56.00%	91.00%	1	68.00%
Kansas	28	BCBS of KS	NA	NA	1	NA
Kentucky	10	Anthem BCBS	43.00%	93.00%	1	43.00%
Louisiana	35	Louisiana BCBS	29.00%	85.00%	1	54.00%
Maine	12	Anthem BCBS	48.00%	98.00%	1	63.00%
Maryland	16	CareFirst	43.00%	90.00%	1	59.00%
Massachusetts	25	BCBS MA	32.00%	86.00%	1	39.00%
Michigan	45	BCBS of MI	62.00%	78.00%	1	69.00%
Minnesota	11	BCBSM	45.00%	98.00%	1	45.00%
Missouri	38	Health Alliance Life	46.00%	87.00%	3	8.00%
Montana	13	BCBS of MT	36.00%	85.00%	1	36.00%
Nevada	35	Health Plan of NV	NA	NA	NA	NA
New Jersey	16	Aetna Health	37.00%	86.00%	2	27.00%
New York	29	Oxford	21.00%	63.00%	2	36.00%
North Carolina	32	BCBS of NC	54.00%	89.00%	1	54.00%
North Dakota	9	Noridian/BCBS	93.00%	99.00%	1	93.00%
Ohio	63	Community BCBS	32.00%	79.00%	1	32.00%
Oklahoma	36	Group Health BCBS	30.00%	71.00%	1	49.00%
Oregon	12	Lifewise (Premera)	25.00%	79.00%	5	14.00%
Rhode Island	3	BCBS RI	NA	NA	1	NA
South Carolina	29	BCBS of SC	49.00%	87.00%	1	49.00%
Tennessee	41	BCBS of TN	49.00%	85.00%	1	49.00%
Texas	58	United	19.00%	59.00%	3	17.00%
Utah	22	Regence BCBS	40.00%	93.00%	1	40.00%
Vermont	12	BCBS of VT	73.00%	100.00%	1	84.00%
Virginia	45	Anthem BCBS	NA	NA	1	NA
Washington	12	Premera Blue Cross	57.00%	92.00%	1	85.00%
West Virginia	33	BCBS	43.00%	77.00%	1	43.00%
Wisconsin	50	United of WI	20.00%	49.00%	3	6.00%
Wyoming	15	BCBS of WY	40.00%	74.00%	1	38.00%
Average	**29.05**		**43.30%**	**83.70%**	**1**	**46.50%**

Source: GAO Private Health Insurance Study

Chapter 2: The Healthcare Economy

Reflective of the GAO study, an independent study was conducted in January of 2008 by Mark Dietrich[22] (published in the Summer, 2008 edition of Business Valuation Review) of the distribution of for profit and nonprofit health insurers and providers in a number of specific markets in the United States. The findings are summarized as follows:

The degree of revenue and profit for healthcare provider entities varies significantly from state to state and even within different regions of individual states. As a threshold matter, areas with high healthcare spending and particularly high Medicare[23] spending tend to offer the greatest opportunity for profit. The elderly, of course, receive the bulk of medical care. Given that high localized spending is the primary driver of profit, the other factors contributing to the pattern of location of larger for-profit providers include:

- The presence and market strength of Blue Cross plans,

- The degree of market strength of local nonprofit hospitals versus for-profit hospitals,

- The degree of market strength of local nonprofit health insurers versus for-profit health insurers,

- Certificate of Need laws and

- Other local demographic and economic factors.

The State of Managed Care

In its Health Care- Managed Care, January 7, 2010, Barclays Capital stated:

> 1) We believe that our 2010 commercial margin projections, which represent trough levels, are conservative and believe that there is actually a higher likelihood of margin expansion than contraction in the next year.
>
> 2) After little progress in 2009, we believe that 2010 will show an incrementally improved commercial spread environment. At this point, we expect commercial premiums yields to at least match medical cost trends in the coming year.
>
> 3) While many of the companies are projecting an increase in medical cost trend (and overall earnings guidance), we see several data sets that would contradict that acceleration. We believe that our 2010 commercial margin projections, which represent trough levels, are conservative and believe that there is actually a higher likelihood of margin expansion than contraction in the next year.
>
> 4) It is hard to see how yields on short-term interest rates will create any additional pressure on earnings for the managed care industry.

Chapter 2: The Healthcare Economy

5) The managed care industry enters 2010 with more available capital than seen in previous years, a function of cautious deployment towards share repurchases in the past year.

6) Through two areas of consolidation, corporate and carrier, we expect the aggregation of market share among the largest plans to accelerate over the next 12 to 18 months.

7) We believe that one corollary benefit from the passage of reform will be a more constructive tone from the management's of the managed care companies.

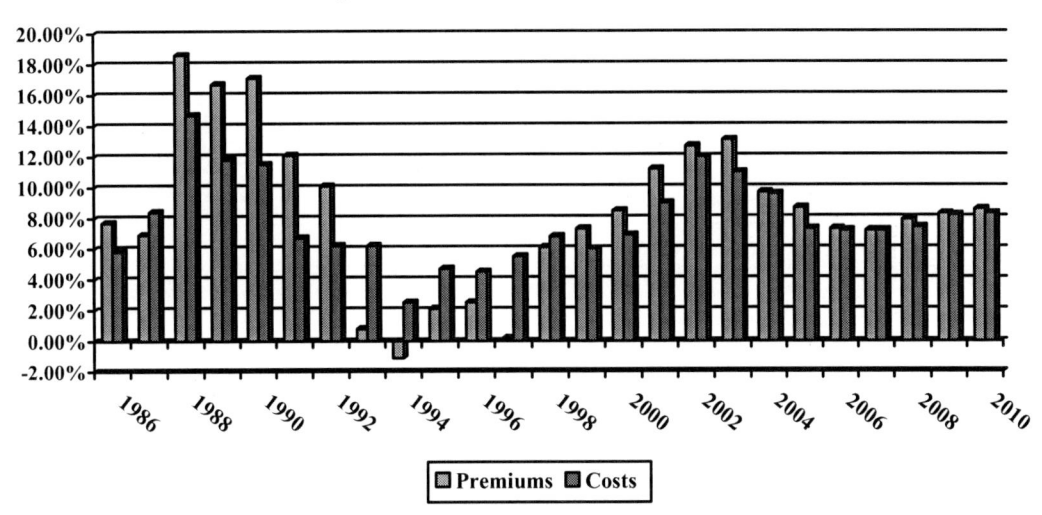

Figure 17, Premium and Cost Trends[24]

An important trend influencing health insurance premium growth is the use of so-called "buy-downs" or cost shifting to employees via cost-sharing for premiums, deductibles and co-pays for care. To elaborate, "cost-sharing of premiums" refers to the practice of having the employer pay less than 100% of the cost of insurance. "Deductible" refers to the practice of requiring the employee to pay a certain amount, say $1,000, out-of-pocket before insurance takes over. A "co-pay" refers to the amount that an employee must pay for each medical encounter, such as $25 for an office visit, or $250 per hospital visit. Another increasingly common buy-down is to charge a higher co-pay on prescriptions for name-brand drugs versus generics (referred to as a tiered formulary). Clearly, cost sharing by the consumers of the cost of their health care substantially influences the volume of consumption.

Each of these devices reduces the premium charged by the health insurer for coverage and also reduces the health insurers' medical costs. Thus, when we read that premiums are increasing by 12%, the overall cost of medical care – including that now borne by the consumer – is likely increasing at a higher rate. This is also reflected in the fact that most health insurers are experiencing a decrease in their medical costs (the Medical Loss Ratio or MLR).

Chapter 2: The Healthcare Economy

Recent trends in the MLR for various companies in the industry are shown below. As the MLR declines, profits are likely to increase (data source: Health Care- Managed Care, January 7, 2010, Barclays Capital, based on company documents):

As noted elsewhere herein, one of the most significant issues affecting the healthcare economy and therefore the forecast of future cashflow is the underwriting cycle. In part, that cycle of premium increases and decreases reflects the relationship between the costs of provider payments and the premium charged. The Chart below reflects both seasonality as well as overall decreases.

Trend in MLR

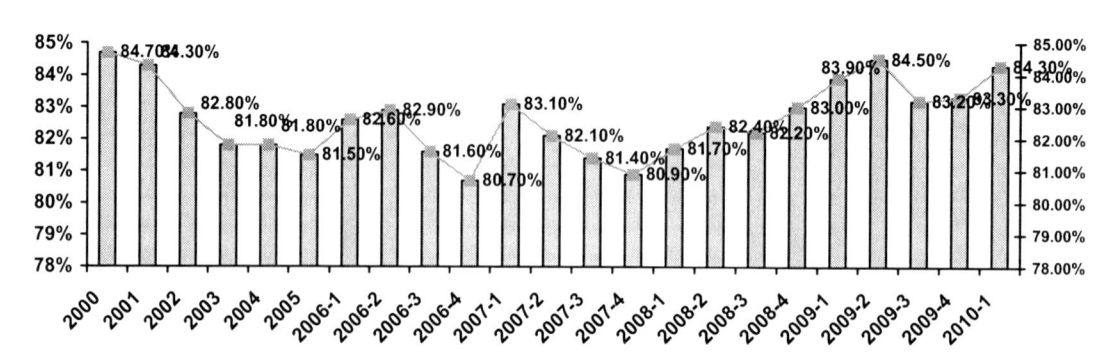

Period	MLR
2000	84.70%
2001	84.30%
2002	82.80%
2003	81.80%
2004	81.80%
2005	81.50%
2006-1	82.60%
2006-2	82.90%
2006-3	81.60%
2006-4	80.70%
2007-1	83.10%
2007-2	82.10%
2007-3	81.40%
2007-4	80.90%
2008-1	81.70%
2008-2	82.40%
2008-3	82.20%
2008-4	83.00%
2009-1	83.90%
2009-2	84.50%
2009-3	83.20%
2009-4	83.30%
2010-1	84.30%

Medical costs included in the MLR consist of four distinct components: inpatient, outpatient, physician and pharmacy. Inpatient costs refer to hospital and other facilities while outpatient includes such things as ambulatory surgery, imaging and lab work.

Managed care insurers at one time were actually engaged in taking risk for the cost of care of their insureds. Due to the catastrophic losses of the 1990s, which forced many, particularly smaller, competitors out of business, the industry has increasingly turned to providing self-funded or self-insured plans to employers. Under these arrangements, the insurer acts as the administrator[25] on behalf of the employer, and the employer (and its employees via any cost-sharing) assume the risk of their care. The insurer charges a fee for providing access to its provider network, paying claims, and providing "stop loss" or excess limits coverage.[26] Typical stop loss levels vary with the size of the insured group and the resultant actuarial risk, but may be as little as $10,000 or as high as $100,000 or more.

Premium Trend

The rapid increase in medical insurance premiums continues to slowing, consistent with the Underwriting Cycle. According to the Kaiser Family Foundation and Health Research and Educational Trust (HRET) 2008 Employer Health Benefits Survey released in September 2009:

> The key findings from the 2009 survey, conducted from January through May 2009, provide a mixed, but relatively stable story compared to 2008. In 2009, there was an increase in the average family premium, the percentage of covered workers with a

Chapter 2: The Healthcare Economy

deductible of $1,000 or more for single coverage, office visit copayments, and the percentage of large firms offering wellness programs. The average premium for single coverage did not significantly increase, breaking a long-standing trend.[27]

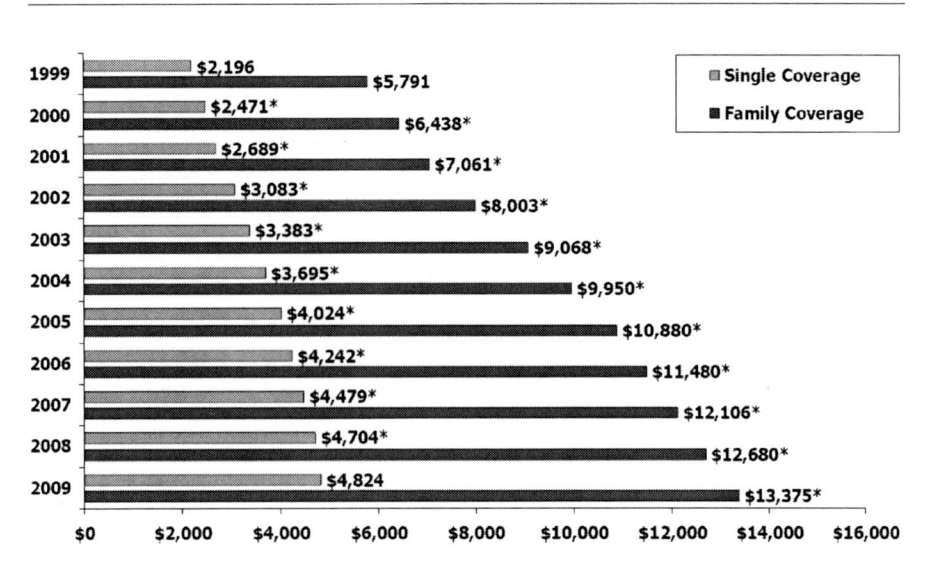

Average Annual Premiums for Single and Family Coverage, 1999-2009

Year	Single Coverage	Family Coverage
1999	$2,196	$5,791
2000	$2,471*	$6,438*
2001	$2,689*	$7,061*
2002	$3,083*	$8,003*
2003	$3,383*	$9,068*
2004	$3,695*	$9,950*
2005	$4,024*	$10,880*
2006	$4,242*	$11,480*
2007	$4,479*	$12,106*
2008	$4,704*	$12,680*
2009	$4,824	$13,375*

Product Trend

Another significant trend is the move away from HMO (tightly restricted) products and into PPO (preferred provider organization) and POS (point of service) products. In a PPO,[28] insureds pay lower costs when seeing a Provider who is "in-network" while deductibles, co-pays and even overall benefit limits may apply when seeing out of network providers.

A POS plan is one in which the insured typically has to choose an in-network primary care physician, but may be allowed to self-refer to specialists (in or out of network) again with deductibles, co-pays and perhaps overall benefit limits. In some cases, insurers have attempted to place capitated provider groups at-risk for out of network care in POS plans.

The dramatic shift away from HMO products in the managed care business in recent years is indicated in the following Chart. It is important to note that managed care companies referred to generically as "HMOs" may in fact offer PPO and POS products. This is certainly true of Blue/Cross Blue Shield Plans, Aetna/US Healthcare and United Health, to name a few.

The 2009 Kaiser Family Foundation /HRET Survey found that HMO enrollment continued to decline, although at a slower pace than previous years, with PPOs holding the largest market share by a considerable margin and high deductible plans showing a spike.

Chapter 2: The Healthcare Economy

Figure 18[29]

Distribution of Health Plan Enrollment for Covered Workers, by Plan Type, 1988-2009

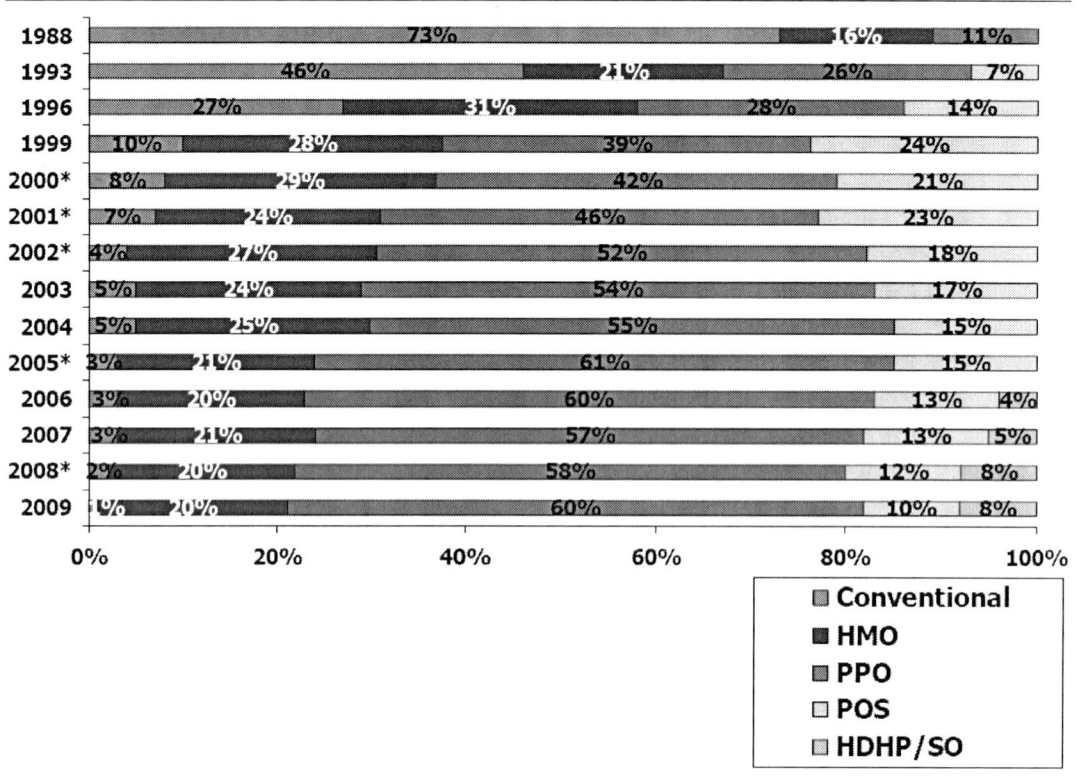

Year	Conventional	HMO	PPO	POS	HDHP/SO
1988	73%	16%		11%	
1993	46%	21%	26%	7%	
1996	27%	31%	28%	14%	
1999	10%	28%	39%	24%	
2000*	8%	29%	42%	21%	
2001*	7%	24%	46%	23%	
2002*	4%	27%	52%	18%	
2003	5%	24%	54%	17%	
2004	5%	25%	55%	15%	
2005*	3%	21%	61%	15%	
2006	3%	20%	60%	13%	4%
2007	3%	21%	57%	13%	5%
2008*	2%	20%	58%	12%	8%
2009	1%	20%	60%	10%	8%

As a result of the major financial losses of the 1990s, there has been both a reduction in the number of managed care companies and greater enrollment growth in those who survived, as insureds were forced to find solvent insurers. CMS reports that the number of HMOs has declined from a peak of 652 in 1997 to 490 in 2002, with further losses in 2003 and 2004. The Kaiser Family Foundation indicates the current number of HMOs as of July 2008 is 577, down from 602 in the previous year. This has resulted in growth in enrollment and premiums for the major players, despite an overall decrease in the number of individuals covered by managed care, as noted above in Trends in Health Insurance Coverage.

Perhaps a more significant trend in markets dominated by the national health insurance companies is the move to Consumer Directed Health Plans or CDHPs. Rather than simply making the consumption of healthcare services more costly and therefore painful, CDHPs seek to change the attitude of the consumer about healthcare spending, focusing on cost-effective purchasing. These types of plans are based upon the consumer having a budget for healthcare and choosing how that budget is to e spent. For example, a $5,000 budget from an employer may be used for health insurance premiums, uninsured medical expenses or even health club memberships. Health Savings Accounts (HSAs) are one variant of this type of plan.

Chapter 2: The Healthcare Economy

Summary

Managed Care Plans remain in a neutral segment of the underwriting cycle, with premiums increasing about as rapidly as costs, but it appears that this trend peaked in 2004. Employers are shifting more of the costs of healthcare onto employees via benefit buy-downs. The backlash against the tightly managed care characteristic of HMOs has resulted in a rapid growth of PPO and POS plans, both of which feature higher consumer costs. Current indications are that Consumer Directed Plans including HSAs are likely to be the growth product in the foreseeable future.

Acute Care Hospitals: Average Length of Stay

Medicare patients ALOS

Average length of stay (ALOS) is a measurement of the average number of days a patient stays in the hospital for each discharge. Earlier in this report it was noted that the number of admission/discharges is showing an up-trend. In contrast, ALOS had steadily declined from 1992 until 2004 (The following Chart presents the most recent year for which data is available). The 2007 and 2008 ALOS, however, was the same and declines appear to have bottomed out. [30]

Figure 19
US Medicare Average Lengths of Stay-Short Stay Hospitals-Trend

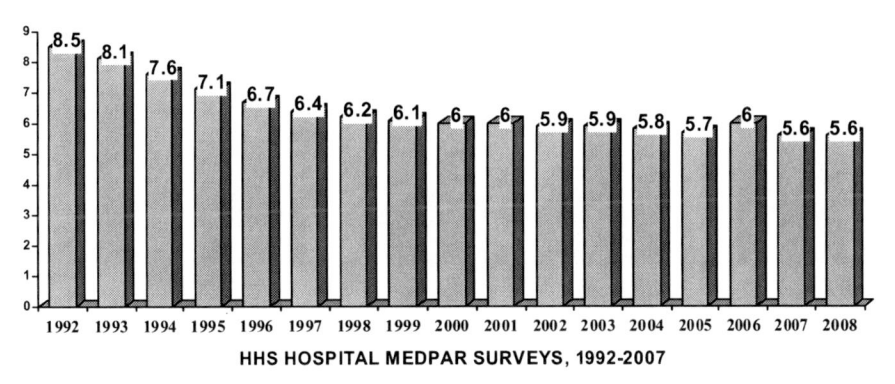

Year	1992	1993	1994	1995	1996	1997	1998	1999	2000	2001	2002	2003	2004	2005	2006	2007	2008
ALOS	8.5	8.1	7.6	7.1	6.7	6.4	6.2	6.1	6	6	5.9	5.9	5.8	5.7	6	5.6	5.6

HHS HOSPITAL MEDPAR SURVEYS, 1992-2007

This trend is very significant for hospitals, which, as noted earlier, are paid a fixed amount per discharge. Under such a payment system, there is a financial incentive to get the patient out of the hospital sooner, as costs tend to be correlated with days in the hospital and revenues are fixed based on the admission/discharge (and its character). Therefore, the hospital is likely to lose money on a long stay, and make money on a short stay. The inability to drive length of stay down still farther accounts in part for the strong adverse reaction from the hospital industry to cuts mandated by the BBA and later mitigated by the Balanced Budget Revision Act of 1999 and the Benefits Improvement and Protection Act of 2000.

Chapter 2: The Healthcare Economy

All patients ALOS

Average Length of Stay (ALOS) is one of the key factors for evaluating the cost-adjusted clinical efficiency of hospital-based treatment. 2006 ALOS for the population taken as a whole was 4.8 days, identical to the 2005 Survey result. Males had an average length of stay of 5.2 days compared with 4.5 days for females. The 2006 and 2005 Hospital Discharge Survey from the Centers for Disease Control[31] (released in July 2008 and July 2007, respectively) found that hospitalization average length of stay (ALOS) per admission was highest in the Northeast at 5.3 days, followed by the South at 4.9, the West at 4.6 days and Midwest at 4.2, similar to 2005. This data is for all admissions, as opposed to the Medicare data, which is for Medicare patients only.

Figure 20, Data by Region

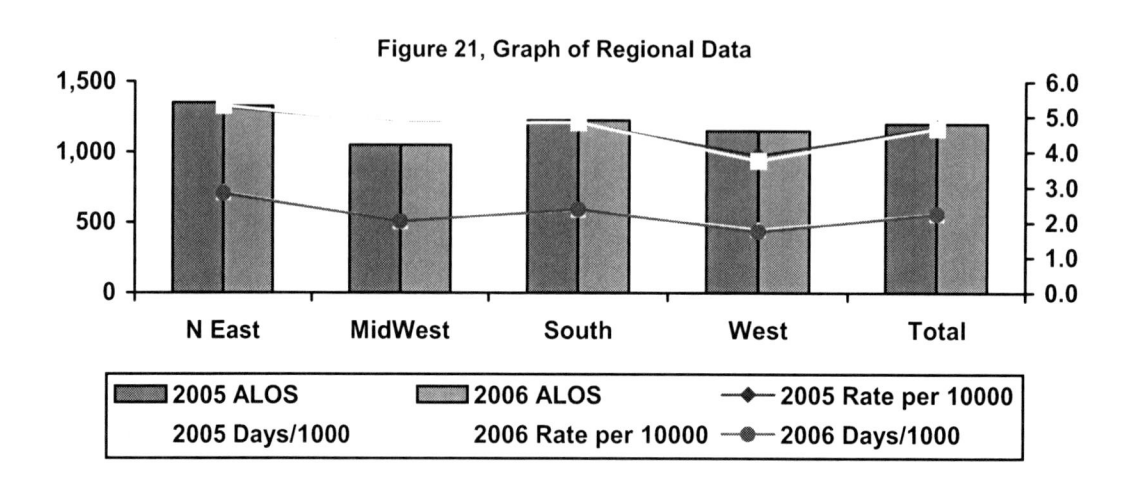

	2005 Rate per 10000	2005 ALOS	2005 Days/1000	2006 Rate per 10000	2006 ALOS	2006 Days/1000
N East	1,317.60	5.4	711.5	1,330.7	5.3	705.3
MidWest	1,206.20	4.2	506.6	1,202.3	4.2	505.0
South	1,208.30	4.9	592.1	1,212.0	4.9	593.9
West	975.1	4.6	448.5	940.2	4.6	432.5
Total	1,174.40	4.8	563.7	1,168.7	4.8	561.0

Figure 21, Graph of Regional Data

The comparison of data by age group (or cohort) for 2006 and 2005 shows little change, with ALOS holding steady.

Chapter 2: The Healthcare Economy

Figure 22, Data by Age Cohort

	2005 Rate per 10000	2005 ALOS	2005 Days/1000	2006 Rate per 10000	2006 ALOS	2006 Days/1000
<15	400.5	4.7	188.2	378.2	4.8	181.5
15-44	853.3	3.7	315.7	861.2	3.7	318.6
45-64	1,147.0	5.0	573.5	1,161.2	5.0	580.6
65	3,595.6	5.5	1,977.6	3,507.9	5.5	1,929.3

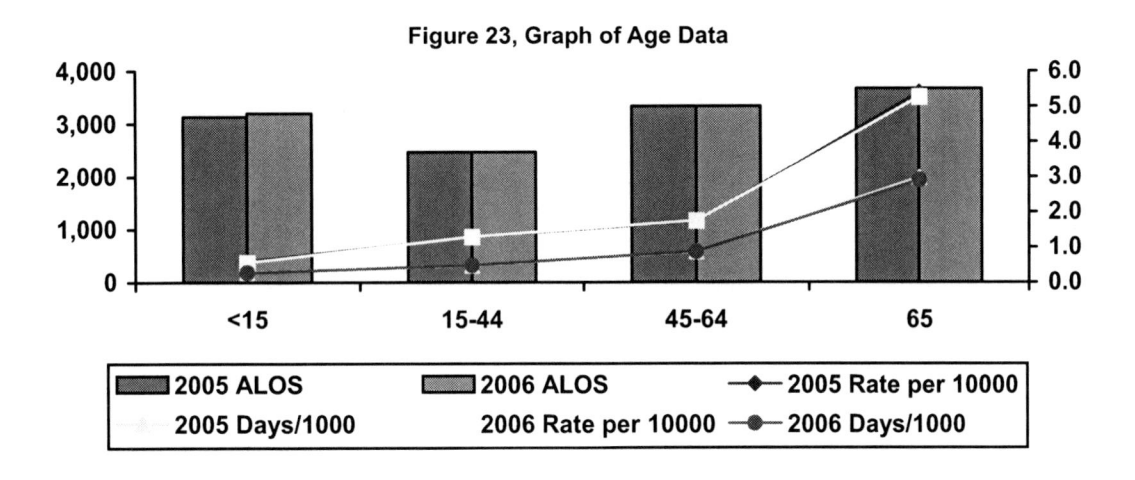

Figure 23, Graph of Age Data

Principal Reason for Admission

Heart Disease diagnoses represent 22% of all admissions for males, with cardiac catheterization the most frequent procedure; 11% for females. Thus, coronary artery bypass surgery, cardiac catheterization and angioplasty are main revenue drivers in acute care hospitals, followed by digestive procedures of the type principally done by general surgeons.

Costs per stay

Hospital costs vary significantly from state to state reflecting differences in wage scales, living costs and real estate, to name a few. Representative data for 2007 and 2006 from the American Hospital Association finds that costs are generally highest on the coasts and lowest in the mountain states and increasing almost everywhere.[32]

Acute Care Hospital Payments

Medicare inpatient hospital payments from the federal government are based upon a statutory formula pegged to a "market basket" of economic inputs. The actual update is usually less than the market basket for budgetary reasons.[33] Figure 25 show the history for hospitals since 1988, with the substantial declines after the Balanced Budget Act of 1997. The 2010 increase is described as follows:

Chapter 2: The Healthcare Economy

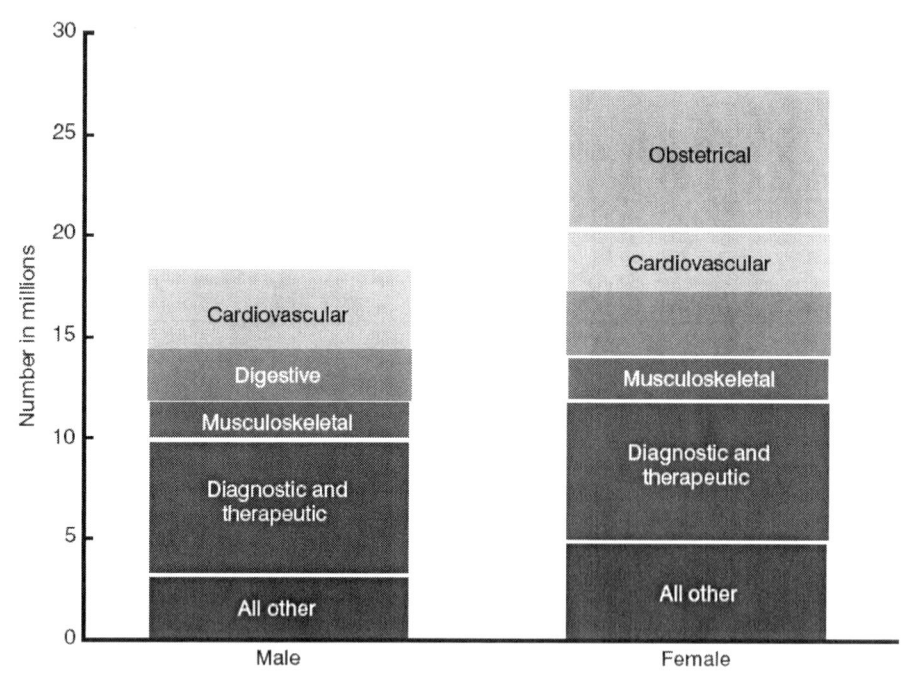

SOURCE: CDC/NCHS, National Hospital Discharge Survey.

Figure 24
Cost per Inpatient Hospital Day, 2007 v 2006

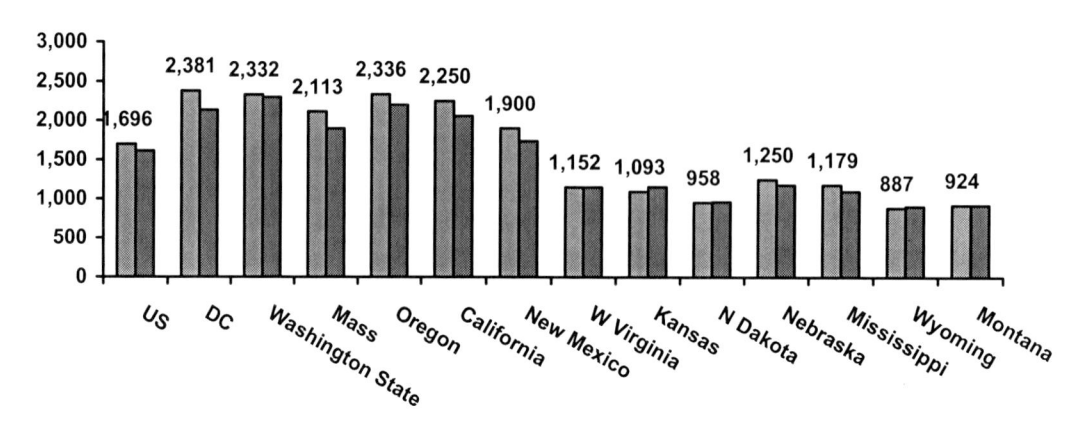

Location	2007	2006
US	1,696	
DC	2,381	
Washington State	2,332	
Mass	2,113	
Oregon	2,336	
California	2,250	
New Mexico	1,900	
W Virginia	1,152	
Kansas	1,093	
N Dakota	958	
Nebraska	1,250	
Mississippi	1,179	
Wyoming	887	
Montana	924	

The Centers for Medicare & Medicaid Services (CMS) today announced that acute care hospitals will receive an inflation update in their payment rates of 2.1 percent in fiscal year 2010. Earlier this year, CMS had proposed to reduce payments to account for the effect of increases in aggregate payments due to changes in hospital coding practices that do not reflect increases in patient's severity of illness.[34]

One of the key financial components of paying for the new federal Healthcare Reform legislation is a cutback in the Market Basket update, in part through required adjustments for productivity using a 10-year moving average of economy-wide private, non-farm productivity gains, somewhat analogous to one element of the physician Sustainable Growth Rate calculation discussed elsewhere herein.

Chapter 2: The Healthcare Economy

The Market Basket update for 2009 was 3.6%. "In this final [2009] rule, CMS completes the transition so that its payment rates are 100 percent cost-based. In addition, CMS is making changes to hospital cost reports that will allow Medicare to distinguish between high and low cost supplies and devices and to further refine and improve our cost-based payments." [35]

> The final rule updates IPPS rates by a market basket of 3.6 percent for inflation (1.6 percent for hospitals that do not submit quality data). However, CMS estimates that the new MS-DRGs will result in improvements in coding and documentation that increase spending without a real change in patient severity of illness. CMS estimates that Medicare spending for inpatient hospital services in FY 2009 will increase 1.8 percent as a result of changes in coding and documentation. However, rather than reducing IPPS rates by 1.8 percent in FY 2009 for budget neutrality, the law requires CMS to reduce the IPPS rates by 0.9 percent for FY 2009. If based on a retrospective review of FY 2008 and FY 2009 claims, CMS determines that improvements in documentation and coding from adopting the MS-DRGs led to an increase in total Medicare spending for inpatient hospital services, the law requires CMS to apply further adjustments to Medicare's IPPS rates in FY 2010 and later years to recoup this increased spending.[36]

For 2008, most hospitals saw an increase of 3.5%, although changes (moving towards hospital costs rather than charges) being made gradually by CMS to the DRG system could result in some hospitals seeing actual decreases.

> Payments to all hospitals will increase by an estimated average of 3.5 percent for FY 2008 when all provisions of the rule are taken into account, primarily as a result of the 3.3 percent market basket increase. Payments to specific hospitals may increase more or less than this amount depending on the patients they serve. For instance, urban hospitals generally treat more severely ill patients and are estimated to receive a 3.8 percent increase in payments.[37]

Figure 25
Inpatient PPS Update-Urban

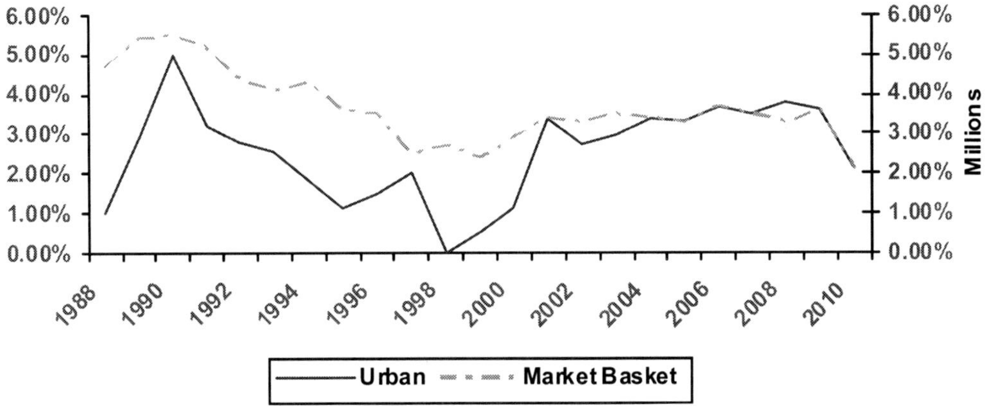

Chapter 2: The Healthcare Economy

Hospitals with a large percentage of Medicare admissions are confronted with revenues rising at less than operating costs, the latter reflected in the "market basket." Principal areas for rising costs include prescription drugs, labor (including a severe shortage of nursing staff) and liability insurance. The principal factors driving hospital revenue, besides the Medicare market basket, include the aging population's demand for more services, increase in market share and the success of negotiations with insurers.

Physician Reimbursement

Medicare pays physicians under the Resource-Based Relative Value Scale ("RBRVS") where each Current Procedural Terminology code ("CPT" Ô and five-digit codes © American Medical Association) is assigned a certain number of relative value units ("RVUs"). These RVUs are then multiplied by a conversion factor to set the fee Medicare pays. Prior to the BBA, there were three such conversion factors: One for surgery, one for primary care and one for other nonsurgical services. The BBA substituted a single conversion factor based upon the primary care factor for the three prior conversion factors. The effect has been a broad cutback in reimbursement for surgical services.

Resource-Based Relative Value Scale

The number of Relative Value Units is based upon the consumption of three types of resources in the delivery of physician services:

Physician work

The principal factors comprising this component are time, technical skill and physical effort, mental effort and judgment, and the stress on the physician of certain patient risk factors.

Practice Costs

This component looks at the cost of delivering services by physician type, for example family medicine versus cardiac surgery. Physician practice costs per dollar of revenue tend to be much higher in primary care then surgery.

Malpractice Insurance Cost

Surgical specialties, and particularly obstetrics, neurosurgery and cardiac surgery, tend to have the highest malpractice insurance. This is the least important of the three components.

Chapter 2: The Healthcare Economy

Geographic Adjustment

There is an additional adjustment for the geographic location of the practice based upon various government studies, including the census, HUD data, and others.[38]

The changeover to RBRVS mandated by the BBA resulted in a substantial increase in the RVUs assigned to office-based CPT codes. A significant portion was related to the practice expenses component described above, due to the fact that office-based physicians have higher operating costs per dollar of revenue than do hospital-based physicians. In addition, HCFA (CMS) believed that the prior reimbursement system over-compensated hospital-based surgeons and similar physicians because the Medicare program paid the hospital separately for the cost of its facilities which had been used by the surgeons.

The Evaluation and Management Codes

In the office-based specialties, primary care and consultative medicine, RBRVS is particularly significant in how office visits and other evaluation and management services are to be coded and reimbursed. RBRVS requires that physicians code according to a three-factor test:

1. History of the patient and complaint;

2. Examination of the patient necessary, and

3. Complexity of medical decision-making.

Each of these three factors has four levels of intensity associated with it. For example, a Level III office examination or CPT 99213 requires the second level of intensity in each of the History, Exam and Decision making components. A level IV exam or CPT 99214 requires the third level of intensity in two of the three components. Under RBRVS reimbursement systems, such as Medicare, the patient's chart must document the level of service for each component.[39]

The graph below (Figure 26, using the pre-BBA 1997 schedule and the 2009 National Physician Fee Schedule demonstrates how increasing levels of service, as reflected in the CPT codes, result in increasing levels of payment under Medicare RBRVS, as well as the cumulative effect in reimbursement of the changes described herein.[40] Note: The Chart is not updated for 2010 rates as the final rates continue to be n doubt due to pending Congressional action.

RBRVS is also typically used by HMOs and large national insurers like United, which therefore tend to pay higher rates for primary care services, since such services are key to the provision of healthcare to members.

Chapter 2: The Healthcare Economy

Figure 26

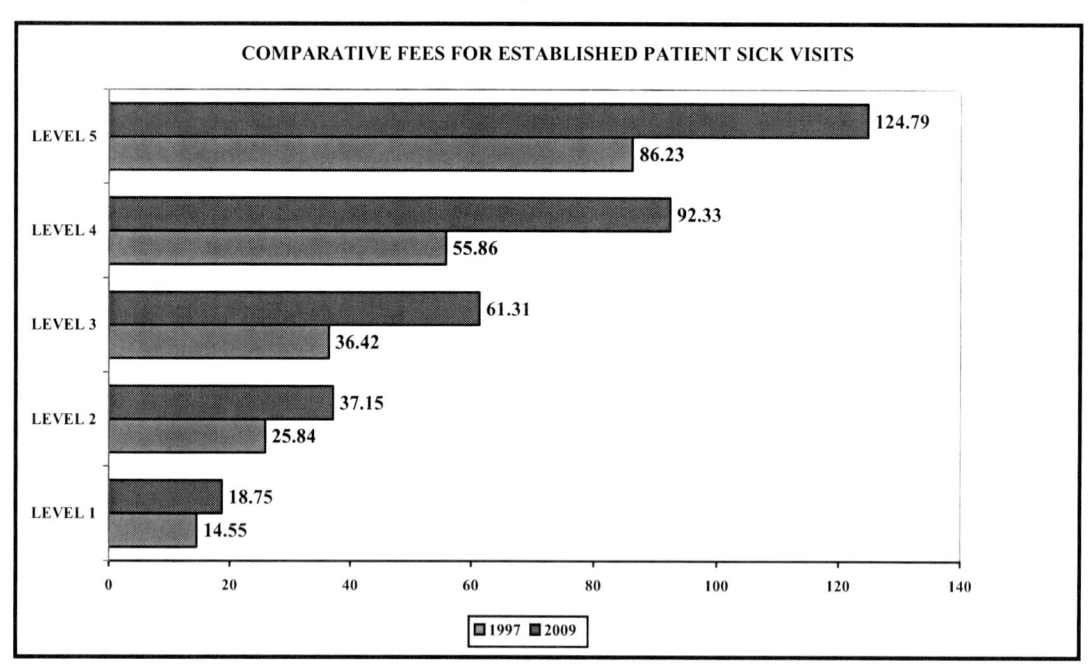

COMPARATIVE FEES FOR ESTABLISHED PATIENT SICK VISITS

Level	1997	2009
LEVEL 5	124.79	86.23
LEVEL 4	92.33	55.86
LEVEL 3	61.31	36.42
LEVEL 2	37.15	25.84
LEVEL 1	18.75	14.55

There has been a marked shift in the use of these five codes over the last several years as indicated in the following Chart taken from the annual letter from CMS to the Medicare Payment Advisory Commission dated April 7, 2006.

Distribution Across Levels of Office Visits for Established Patients

Codes	1998	1999	2000	2001	2002	2003	2004	2005
99211	5%	5%	5%	6%	6%	6%	5%	5%
99212	18%	17%	17%	16%	15%	13%	12%	12%
99213	52%	53%	54%	54%	54%	53%	53%	52%
99214	21%	21%	21%	21%	22%	24%	26%	28%
99215	4%	4%	3%	3%	3%	3%	3%	3%

2007 increases in the value of E&M Services

In the June 29, 2006 Federal Register, CMS announced its intent to increase the Relative Values of E&M services in 2007, following closely on the heels of a suggestion by MedPAC in its March 2006 report that these services had declined in value, in large part to the benefit of high tech imaging services. The final rule was released November 2, 2006 and adopted the proposed rule in large part.

> The work component for RVUs associated with an intermediate office visit [99213], the most commonly billed physician's service, will increase by 37 percent. The work component for RVUs for an office visit requiring moderately complex decision-making

Chapter 2: The Healthcare Economy

and for a hospital visit also requiring moderately complex decision-making will increase by 29 percent and 31 percent respectively. Both of these services rank in the top 10 most frequently billed physicians' services out of more than 7,000 types of services paid under the physician fee schedule.

The 99213 code presently has a fully implemented work RVU value of .67. Under the final rule, the value rises to .92 RVUs. This represents an increase in the value of nearly 18%. Significantly, because of the budget neutrality provisions of the existing Part B system, the increased cost associated with the increased RVUs has to come from reduction in the value of other services and CMS reduced all work RVUs by 10.1 percent to meet the budget neutrality provisions. CMS is also changing the Practice Expense component of the RVUs to be phased in over 4 years through 2010.

The following discussion tracks the history of changes in physician reimbursement since the enactment of the BBA and demonstrates the significant and often unpredictable changes:

Medicare Conversion Factor

Overview of the Problem

In March of each year, CMS releases its preliminary estimate (the final calculation is released in September) of the Sustainable Growth Rate (SGR) and the Conversion Factor for the following year. For example, the annual computation had estimated that Medicare physician reimbursement would drop by (5.7%) in 2003, as a result of two errors in 1998 and 1999 that affected the statutory limit on allowed expenditures for physician services. These errors carried forward to all future years, resulting in a lower overall limit on physician spending of approximately 6.4%. The compound rate of increase in the annual physician fee schedule update from 1998 through 2005 was only .3%! The Consolidated Appropriations Resolution of 2003 permitted CMS to correct the 1998 and 1999 errors, resulting in an increase in the fee schedule for 2003 rather than the prior decrease. Annual declines in the vicinity of 4% - 5% are generally expected under existing law. The Medicare Modernization Act of November 2003 overrode the scheduled decreases in the 2004 and 2005 Conversion Factors with 1.5% increases.

The pattern since 2006 has been for Congress to belatedly suspend the statutory cutbacks in the Conversion Factor. The 2007 Conversion Factor of $35.9848 initially reflected a decrease of 5.0% and was subsequently overturned by Congress left equal to the 2006 factor. The 2008 factor was scheduled to drop by 10.1% until the end of December 2007 when the Medicare, Medicaid, and SCHIP Extension Act of 2007 legislation updated the conversion factor by 0.5% to $38.0870. In July 2008, Congress extended the $38.09 conversion factor for the balance of 2008 over the President's veto and put a 1.1% increase in place for 2009. As of November 2009, Congress had not acted to repeal the scheduled cut for 2010, although a bill had passed the House of Representatives. NOTE: See the discussion regarding the calculation of the 2010 and 2009 later herein as the following Graph cannot be understood absent that discussion.

Chapter 2: The Healthcare Economy

Figure 27
Medicare Conversion Factor

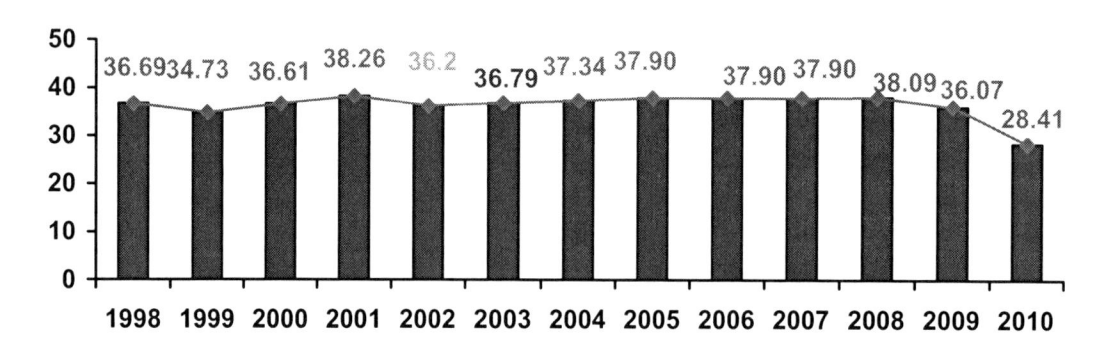

Year	Value
1998	36.69
1999	34.73
2000	36.61
2001	38.26
2002	36.2
2003	36.79
2004	37.34
2005	37.90
2006	37.90
2007	37.90
2008	38.09
2009	36.07
2010	28.41

Figure 28 below traces the growth rate in real GDP (in 1996 dollars) and the Medicare Sustainable Growth Rate (SGR), Medicare Economic Index (MEI) and the actual Conversion Factor Update. CMS made critical mistakes in computing the 2000 and 2001 conversion factors resulting in excess payments that were being paid back prior to the February 2003 legislative change. Note that the two are regain parity in 2005.[41] The red line plots what spending would have been based upon inflation in physician practice expenses, similar to that used to set fees for other sectors of the healthcare industry such as hospitals.

Figure 28
% Change in Real GDP and Physician Spending

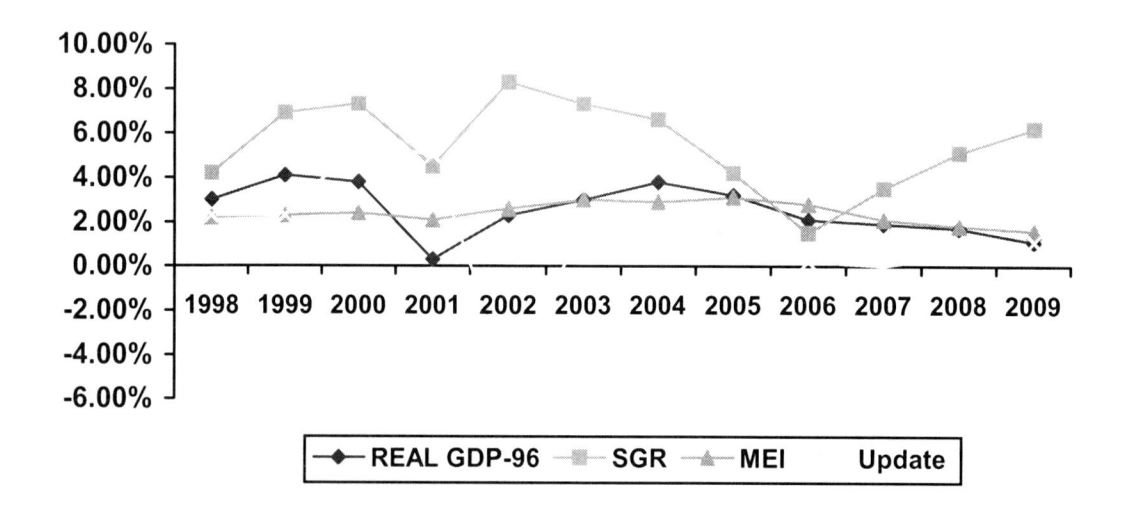

Legend: REAL GDP-96, SGR, MEI, Update

The following graph demonstrates that despite the SGR attempt to limit growth in physician spending, Actual spending is considerably higher.

Chapter 2: The Healthcare Economy

Quarterly SGR "Allowed" vs. Actual Expenditures

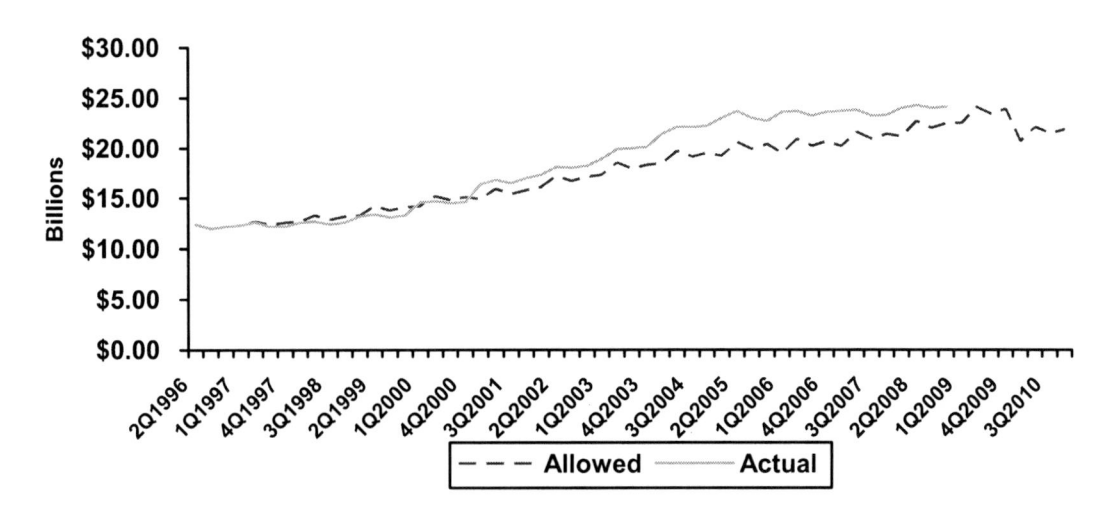

Determining the Conversion Factor

CMS first determines the Medicare Economic Index ("MEI"), which measures the weighted average price change for various inputs involved with producing physicians' services. The MEI is then multiplied by the update adjustment factor, which is based upon a statutory formula that limits annual expenditures for physician services (see Sustainable Growth Rate above). The MEI is similar in concept to the Market Basket update for hospitals described elsewhere herein.

> The MEI is a fixed-weight input price index, with an adjustment for the change in economy-wide labor productivity. This index, which has 1996 base weights, is comprised of two broad categories--physician's own time and physician's practice expense.[42]

A review of these factors for 2003 as a representative year illuminates in part the underlying mathematical rationale. For example, the increase in non-physician salaries and benefits was computed at 4.2% and given a weight in the overall computation of 16.8%. In effect, the MEI is an inflation adjustment factor for the cost of delivering physician services, including the estimated effect of productivity growth based on broad factors in the economy - not in physician offices. The update is equal to the product of 1 plus the percentage increase in the Medicare Economic Index (MEI) (divided by 100) and 1 plus the update adjustment factor.

The Update Adjustment Factor is designed "to reflect success or failure in meeting the expenditure target that the law refers to as "allowed expenditures." Allowed expenditures are equal to actual expenditures in a base period updated each year by the SGR.

The SGR is based upon the following:

1. The estimated change in fees for physicians' services.

Chapter 2: The Healthcare Economy

2. The estimated change in the average number of Medicare fee-for-service beneficiaries.

3. The estimated projected growth in real GDP per capita, which CMS estimated at 2.8% for 2004. The Medicare Modernization Act changed the GDP factor to a 10 year average growth, but it had little effect on the computation of the conversion factor, and in fact, due to the rapid growth of the economy in the last two years before the 2008 recession has actually made the situation worse rather than better!

4. The estimated change in expenditures due to changes in law or regulations.

The base period allowed expenditures roll forward from an initial fiscal year ending March 31, 1997. The formula reduces or increases for the current and future years by any excess or deficient expenditure in prior years. This is the critical point that a valuator or consultant must understand: Physician expenses under the Medicare Program cannot exceed a limit established by a pre-determined, statutory formula, built off of historical expenditures and real GDP.

Recap of the annual computation

To recap, the MEI is basically an inflation factor based upon physician compensation and physician office expenses; the annual allowed expenditures are based upon FY March, 1997 expenditures increased by the SGR; and the Update Adjustment Factor, which forces the projected expenditures for the upcoming year to be no more than a pre-determined limit.

Overview of Year by Year Changes in the Conversion Factor

Commencing with the phase-in of the changes mandated by the BBA, 1998 saw substantial increases in fee-for-service revenue for physicians in office-based medical specialties such as Internal Medicine, Family Medicine, and Cardiology. Much of this rise stemmed from increases in the Relative Value of the Evaluation and Management Codes. Radiology and Pathology also saw significant increases.

In contrast, hospital-based surgical specialties such as Orthopedics and Cardiac Surgery saw dramatic reductions in reimbursement.

CMS continued to refine its implementation of the BBA changes. The 1999 change generally provided moderate increases for the office-based medical specialties, ranging from 2% for internal medicine to 7% for family practice. The variability in the level of increase can be explained by the different utilization of individual CPT codes among the various specialties.

Cardiac Surgery and Neurosurgery received significant cutbacks from the 1999 changes, and Radiology suffered a cut of 10%, undoing the increase received under the 1998 changes. Similarly, Pathology reimbursement was cut by 13%. Cardiology practices saw reimbursement cut by 9% as fees for invasive procedures such as cardiac catheterization and balloon

Chapter 2: The Healthcare Economy

angioplasty received significant cuts. The conversion factor was set at $34.73, a significant decrease (5.3%) from the 1998 factor of $36.69.

As a result of intensive lobbying by the profession, CMS undertook a major revision in the assessment of the practice expense component of the RBRVS in 2000. The conversion factor was set at $36.6137, an increase over 1999 of 5.4%, which basically recaptured the 1999 decrease of 5.3%. Some of the practice specialties that had previously received dramatic cuts found those cuts mitigated, while others found no such relief.

Notably, a highly successful lobbying effort by its trade association resulted in a dramatic turnaround for Pathology, with reimbursement increases of 9% over three years partially offsetting the prior year's 13% decline.

The changes in the practice expenses component of services provided by the various specialties must be revenue neutral under the law. As such, to the extent that any specialty received more reimbursement, other specialties received less. Cardiology, Cardiac Surgery and Gastroenterology received reimbursement cuts, primarily due to decreases in the RVUs associated with procedures performed by these physicians, such as echocardiography.

In November 2000 CMS issued the scheduled updates to the RBRVS for 2001. The update reflected changes mandated by the BBA and subsequent legislation. The 2001 physician fee schedule conversion factor was $38.2581 per RVU, an increase of 4.5% over the 2000 factor of $36.6137.

Changes in 2002 basically followed the legislative formula, with the RVU changes of the BBA now phased in fully. The 2002 physician fee schedule conversion factor was $36.1992, a 5.4% decrease from the 2000 factor of $38.2581 per RVU. This reflected primarily decreased growth in per capita GDP as well as the cumulative effect of various errors made in prior computations of the Sustainable Growth Rate that resulted in it being set at too high a level.

The annual physician fee schedule update is difficult to predict with any certainty until the annual measurement date (September 1) occurs. After a cut in the 2003 Conversion Factor of –4.4% was announced belatedly at the end of 2002, Congress modified the conversion factor in mid-February to eliminate the cumulative effect of prior errors that had overstated earlier conversion factors.

"The update is equal to the product of 1 plus the percentage increase in the Medicare Economic Index (MEI) (divided by 100) and 1 plus the update adjustment factor. For CY 2002, the MEI is equal to 3.0 percent (1.030). The update adjustment factor is equal to –1.1 percent (0.989). … the Act requires an additional -0.2 percent (0.998) reduction to the update for 2003. Thus, the product of the MEI (1.030), the update adjustment factor (0.989), and the statutory adjustment factor (0.998) equals the CY 2003 update of 1.0166 [1.6%]."

Applying the 1.0162 factor (adjusted for Budget Neutrality) to the 2002 conversion factor of $36.1992 results in the 2003 conversion factor of $36.7856.

Chapter 2: The Healthcare Economy

Prior to yet another legislative "fix" in the Medicare Modernization Act (Act) of 2003, the 2004 update was to be equal to the Following: the product of 1 plus the percentage increase in the Medicare Economic Index (MEI) (divided by 100) and 1 plus the update adjustment factor (UAF). For CY 2004, the MEI is equal to 2.9 percent (1.029). The UAF is −7.0 percent (0.930). Section 1848(d)(4)(F) of the Act requires an additional -0.2 percent (0.998) reduction to the update for 2004. Thus, the product of the MEI (1.029), the UAF (0.930), and the statutory adjustment factor (0.998) would have resulted in a CY 2004 update of −4.5 percent (0.9551). The calculation for 2005 would have produced an update of approximately −3.3 percent. The Act set the increase at 1.5%% for 2004 as well as 2005. Thus, the 2004 physician fee schedule conversion factor will be $37.3374 and the 2005 conversion factor is $37.8975.

As of November 2, 2005, CMS announced the final rule for the Conversion Factor in 2006 of $36.1770, a decrease of -4.4%, which was subsequently revised in February of 2006 by the Deficit Reduction Act to maintain the 2005 conversion factor is $37.8975. The 2007 Conversion Factor - $37.8975 - is identical to 2006 as a result of the repeal of the scheduled decrease in the Tax Relief and Health Care Act of 2006, thus there was no increase for 3 years. A 10.1% cut was due to be implemented in 2008, but was (again) suspended at the last minute by Congress and an increase of .5% (one-half or one percent) was adopted or $38.09. The 2009 Medicare physician fee schedule final rule on October 30, 2008 which provides for the statutorily mandated 1.1% update for calendar year 2009; however, the budget neutrality adjustment to the Conversion Factor associated with the review and reallocation of RVUs was a negative 6.41%, resulting in a rate of $36.07.

2010 Changes

The Centers for Medicare and Medicaid Services (CMS) issued the 2010 Medicare physician fee schedule final rule on October 30, 2009 which provides for the statutorily mandated -21.2% negative update for calendar year 2010; however, the Budget Neutrality Adjustment is included in the Conversion Factor now where historically it was applied to a reduction of RVUs for each CPT code. This makes the apparent conversion factor lower than it might otherwise have been. As noted elsewhere herein the cut in the Conversion Factor has not been implemented as of May 2010. Even if that cut is not implemented, the practice expense RVU changes shown below on the 2010 Summary of Changes by Principal Affected Practice Specialty.

2010 Changes in Individual CPT© Code Reimbursement

CPT[1]/ HCPCS	MOD	Description	Facility 2009 ($)	Facility 2010 ($)	Percent Change	Non-facility 2009 ($)	Non-facility 2010 ($)	Percent Change
11721		Debride nail, 6 or more	27.77	20.74	-25%	40.39	31.25	-23%
17000		Destruct premalg lesion	48.69	40.90	-16%	69.97	57.95	-17%
27130		Total hip arthroplasty	1359.71	1082.84	-20%	NA	NA	NA
27244		Treat thigh fracture	1144.39	917.52	-20%	NA	NA	NA

Chapter 2: The Healthcare Economy

CPT[1]/HCPCS	MOD	Description	Facility 2009 ($)	Facility 2010 ($)	Percent Change	Non-facility 2009 ($)	Non-facility 2010 ($)	Percent Change
27447		Total knee arthroplasty	1456.37	1158.40	-20%	NA	NA	NA
33533		CABG, arterial, single	1892.05	1534.21	-19%	NA	NA	NA
35301		Rechanneling of artery	1067.93	868.66	-19%	NA	NA	NA
43239		Upper GI endoscopy, biopsy	165.55	134.08	-19%	323.16	257.08	-20%
66821		After cataract laser surgery	251.38	216.45	-14%	266.53	228.67	-14%
66984		Cataract surg w/iol, 1 stage	638.74	549.09	-14%	NA	NA	NA
67210		Treatment of retinal lesion	561.56	478.93	-15%	580.67	493.98	-15%
71010		Chest x-ray	NA	NA	NA	24.16	18.18	-25%
71010	26	Chest x-ray	9.02	7.10	-21%	9.02	7.10	-21%
77056		Mammogram, both breasts	NA	NA	NA	107.48	82.95	-23%
77056	26	Mammogram, both breasts	44.36	34.66	-22%	44.36	34.66	-22%
77057		Mammogram, screening	NA	NA	NA	81.15	61.64	-24%
77427		Radiation tx management, x5	188.27	153.11	-19%	188.27	153.11	-19%
78465	26	Heart image (3d), multiple	78.99	62.21	-21%	78.99	62.21	-21%
88305	26	Tissue exam by pathologist	37.15	28.97	-22%	37.15	28.97	-22%
90801		Psy dx interview	128.04	100.27	-22%	152.92	121.01	-21%
90862		Medication management	45.08	35.79	-21%	55.18	44.31	-20%
90935		Hemodialysis, one evaluation	66.36	53.12	-20%	NA	NA	NA
92012		Eye exam established pat	45.80	38.35	-16%	70.69	58.80	-17%
92014		Eye exam & treatment	70.33	58.80	-16%	103.15	85.79	-17%
92980		Insert intracoronary stent	847.93	644.53	-24%	NA	NA	NA
93000		Electrocardiogram, complete	20.92	NA	NA	20.92	15.62	-25%
93010		Electrocardiogram report	9.02	7.10	-21%	9.02	7.10	-21%
93015		Cardiovascular stress test	100.27	73.00	-27%	100.27	73.00	-27%
93307	26	Echo exam of heart	49.77	38.35	-23%	49.77	38.35	-23%
93510	26	Left heart catheterization	248.86	185.21	-26%	248.86	185.21	-26%
98941		Chiropractic manipulation	30.30	24.15	-20%	33.90	27.27	-20%
99203		Office/outpatient visit, new	68.17	57.38	-16%	91.97	76.98	-16%
99213		Office/outpatient visit, est	44.72	38.06	-15%	61.31	51.70	-16%
99214		Office/outpatient visit, est	69.25	58.80	-15%	92.33	77.55	-16%
99222		Initial hospital care	122.63	100.27	-18%	NA	NA	NA
99223		Initial hospital care	180.33	147.14	-18%	NA	NA	NA

Chapter 2: The Healthcare Economy

CPT[1]/ HCPCS	MOD	Description	Facility 2009 ($)	Facility 2010 ($)	Facility Percent Change	Non-facility 2009 ($)	Non-facility 2010 ($)	Non-facility Percent Change
99233		Subsequent hospital care	95.58	77.83	-19%	NA	NA	NA
99236		Observ/hosp same date	207.38	166.18	-20%	NA	NA	NA
99239		Hospital discharge day	96.30	77.83	-19%	NA	NA	NA
99243		Office consultation	97.38	Discontinued	Discontinued	124.79	Discontinued	Discontinued
99244		Office consultation	154.00	Discontinued	Discontinued	184.30	Discontinued	Discontinued
99253		Inpatient consultation	114.69	Discontinued	Discontinued	NA	NA	NA
99254		Inpatient consultation	165.55	Discontinued	Discontinued	NA	NA	NA
99283		Emergency dept visit	61.31	48.57	-21%	NA	NA	NA
99284		Emergency dept visit	114.33	91.18	-20%	NA	NA	NA

2010 Summary of Changes by Principal Affected Practice Specialty

	(A) Specialty	(B) Allowed Charges (mil $)	(C) Impact of Work RVU Changes	(D) Impact of PE RVU Changes** Full	(E) Impact of PE RVU Changes** Tran	(F) Impact of MP RVU Changes	(G) Combined Impact Full	(H) Combined Impact Tran
1	TOTAL	77,796	0%	0%	0%	0%	0%	0%
2	ALLERGY/IMMUNOLOGY	173	0%	-1%	0%	0%	-2%	0%
3	ANESTHESIOLOGY	1,744	0%	4%	1%	0%	3%	0%
4	CARDIAC SURGERY	373	-1%	-1%	0%	2%	1%	1%
5	CARDIOLOGY	7,158	-1%	-10%	-5%	-1%	-13%	-8%
6	COLON AND RECTAL SURGERY	130	-1%	4%	1%	1%	4%	1%
7	CRITICAL CARE	223	-1%	2%	1%	1%	3%	1%
8	DERMATOLOGY	2,520	1%	1%	1%	1%	3%	3%
9	EMERGENCY MEDICINE	2,416	0%	2%	1%	0%	3%	1%
10	ENDOCRINOLOGY	374	-1%	3%	0%	0%	2%	0%
11	FAMILY PRACTICE	5,094	2%	5%	2%	1%	7%	4%
12	GASTROENTEROLOGY	1,792	-2%	0%	0%	1%	0%	-1%
13	GENERAL PRACTICE	727	1%	4%	1%	0%	6%	3%
14	GENERAL SURGERY	2,227	-1%	3%	1%	1%	4%	1%
15	GERIATRICS	170	1%	6%	2%	1%	8%	3%
16	HAND SURGERY	89	-1%	3%	1%	-1%	2%	-1%
17	HEMATOLOGY/ONCOLOGY	1,897	0%	-5%	-1%	0%	-6%	-1%
18	INFECTIOUS DISEASE	554	-1%	3%	0%	1%	3%	0%
19	INTERNAL MEDICINE	10,133	1%	4%	1%	1%	5%	2%
20	INTERVENTIONAL PAIN MANAGE.	356	-2%	3%	-1%	0%	0%	-3%
21	INTERVENTIONAL RADIOLOGY	225	-1%	-9%	-2%	0%	-10%	-3%
22	NEPHROLOGY	1,803	-1%	2%	0%	1%	2%	1%
23	NEUROLOGY	1,414	-3%	4%	1%	0%	1%	-2%
24	NEUROSURGERY	591	-1%	2%	0%	0%	1%	-1%
25	NUCLEAR MEDICINE	74	-5%	-15%	-10%	-2%	-23%	-18%
26	OBSTETRICS/GYNECOLOGY	624	0%	0%	-1%	0%	0%	-1%
27	OPHTHALMOLOGY	4,758	0%	11%	3%	2%	13%	5%
28	ORTHOPEDIC SURGERY	3,261	0%	3%	1%	-1%	2%	0%
29	OTOLARNGOLOGY	933	-1%	1%	-1%	0%	0%	-2%

Chapter 2: The Healthcare Economy

	(A) Specialty	(B) Allowed Charges (mil $)	(C) Impact of Work RVU Changes	(D) Impact of PE RVU Changes** Full	(E) Impact of PE RVU Changes** Tran	(F) Impact of MP RVU Changes	(G) Combined Impact Full	(H) Combined Impact Tran
30	PATHOLOGY	994	0%	-1%	1%	-1%	-3%	-1%
31	PEDIATRICS	65	1%	3%	1%	0%	4%	2%
32	PHYSICAL MEDICINE	824	-1%	6%	2%	0%	5%	1%
33	PLASTIC SURGERY	284	0%	4%	1%	1%	5%	2%
34	PSYCHIATRY	1,095	0%	2%	1%	1%	3%	2%
35	PULMONARY DISEASE	1,765	-1%	2%	0%	1%	2%	0%
36	RADIATION ONCOLOGY	1,809	0%	-3%	0%	-2%	-5%	-1%
37	RADIOLOGY	5,056	0%	-14%	-3%	-2%	-16%	-5%
38	RHEUMATOLOGY	493	0%	-1%	0%	0%	-2%	-1%
39	THORACIC SURGERY	389	-1%	0%	0%	2%	1%	1%
40	UROLOGY	1,993	-1%	-8%	-3%	0%	-10%	-4%
41	VASCULAR SURGERY	656	-1%	-3%	-2%	0%	-3%	-2%
42	AUDIOLOGIST	36	-1%	-16%	-9%	-7%	-23%	-17%
43	CHIROPRACTOR	713	0%	3%	1%	1%	4%	2%
44	CLINICAL PSYCHOLOGIST	544	0%	-8%	-2%	0%	-8%	-2%
45	CLINICAL SOCIAL WORKER	362	0%	-7%	-1%	0%	-7%	-1%
46	NURSE ANESTHETIST	681	0%	4%	1%	0%	4%	1%
47	NURSE PRACTITIONER	1,018	1%	5%	1%	1%	6%	3%
48	OPTOMETRY	848	1%	10%	3%	1%	12%	5%
49	ORAL/MAXILLOFACIAL SURGERY	36	-1%	4%	1%	0%	3%	0%
50	PHYSICAL/OCCUPATIONAL THERAPY	1,883	0%	9%	3%	-1%	8%	2%
51	PHYSICIAN ASSISTANT	757	0%	4%	1%	0%	5%	2%
52	PODIATRY	1,682	1%	6%	2%	-1%	6%	2%
53	DIAGNOSTIC TESTING FACILITY	923	-1%	-29%	-7%	-4%	-34%	-12%
54	INDEPENDENT LABORATORY	970	0%	-5%	0%	-1%	-7%	-1%
55	PORTABLE X-RAY SUPPLIER	87	0%	8%	3%	-1%	7%	2%

2009 Changes

The Centers for Medicare and Medicaid Services (CMS) issued the 2009 Medicare physician fee schedule final rule on October 30, 2008 which provides for the statutorily mandated 1.1% update for calendar year 2009; however, the budget neutrality adjustment to the Conversion Factor associated with the review and reallocation of RVUs was a negative 6.41%, resulting in a rate of $36.07 (last year, the budget neutrality adjustment was accomplished by applying an across the board reduction to Work RVUs of 10%). As described below, an additional 4% in payment incentives for adopting electronic prescribing and reporting on certain quality measures was part of the final rule; thus, any forecast of 2009 and subsequent cashflows would have to consider the likelihood of qualifying for the incentive.

> ...the reporting period for the 2009 PQRI [Physician Quality Reporting Initiative] is defined as the entire year, or January 1, 2009 through December 31, 2009. Therefore, for the 2009 PQRI, eligible professionals who satisfactorily report data on quality measures for covered professional services furnished between January 1, 2009 through December 31, 2009 will receive an incentive payment equal to 2.0 percent of the total estimated allowed charges submitted by no later than February 28, 2010 for all covered professional services furnished between January 1, 2009 and December 31, 2009.

Chapter 2: The Healthcare Economy

Specifically, for 2009, in accordance with section 1848(m)(2) of the Act, as added by section 132(a) of the MIPPA, a "successful electronic prescriber" as defined by MIPPA and further discussed below, is eligible to receive an incentive payment equal to 2.0 percent of the total estimated allowed charges submitted not later than 2 months after the end of the reporting period for all covered professional services furnished during the 2009 reporting period. This new E-prescribing Incentive Program is separate from and in addition to any incentive payment that eligible professionals may earn through the PQRI program discussed above.[43]

2009 Changes in Individual CPT© Code Reimbursement

Despite the apparent cut in the 2009 conversion factor, the increase in RVUs for many office-based procedures results in a fairly significant increase for the two most commonly used codes, 99213 and 99214, as well as the consultation codes and hospital inpatient codes. As seen in the Table which follows this one, those increases are being paid for by diagnostic imaging providers.

Figure 29

CODE	MOD	DESCRIPTION	Facility (e.g., HOPD) 2008	2009	Change	Non-Facility (MD Office) 2008	2009	Change
11721		Debride nail, 6 or more	27.42	$27.77	1%	39.61	40.39	2%
17000		Destruct premalg lesion	46.47	$48.69	5%	67.41	69.97	4%
27130		Total hip arthroplasty	1,336.09	$1,359.71	2%	NA	NA	NA
27244		Treat thigh fracture	1,077.10	$1,144.39	6%	NA	NA	NA
27447		Total knee arthroplasty	1,435.12	$1,456.37	1%	NA	NA	NA
33533		CABG, arterial, single	1,854.84	$1,892.05	2%	NA	NA	NA
35301		Rechanneling of artery	1,045.11	$1,067.93	2%	NA	NA	NA
43239		Upper GI endoscopy, biopsy	156.92	$165.55	5%	329.07	323.16	-2%
66821		After cataract laser surgery	$253.53	$222.81	-12%	$270.97	$237.80	-12%
66821		After cataract laser surgery	249.47	$251.38	1%	266.23	266.53	0%
66984		Cataract surg w/iol, 1 stage	626.15	$638.74	2%	NA	NA	NA
67210		Treatment of retinal lesion	545.79	$561.56	3%	567.88	580.67	2%
71010		Chest x-ray	NA	NA	NA	25.52	24.16	-5%
71010	26	Chest x-ray	8.76	$9.02	3%	8.76	9.02	3%
77056		Mammogram, both breasts	NA	NA	NA	104.74	107.48	3%
77056	26	Mammogram, both breasts	41.9	$44.36	6%	41.9	44.36	6%
77057		Mammogram, screening	NA	NA	NA	82.65	81.15	-2%
77057	26	Mammogram, screening	33.9	$35.71	5%	33.9	35.71	5%
77427		Radiation tx management, x5	177.1	$188.27	6%	177.1	188.27	6%
78465	26	Heart image (3d), multiple	74.27	$78.99	6%	74.27	78.99	6%
88305	26	Tissue exam by pathologist	36.18	$37.15	3%	36.18	37.15	3%

Chapter 2: The Healthcare Economy

CODE	MOD	DESCRIPTION	Facility (e.g., HOPD) 2008	2009	Change	Non-Facility (MD Office) 2008	2009	Change
90801		Psy dx interview	125.31	$128.04	2%	147.02	152.92	4%
90862		Medication management	43.8	$45.08	3%	52.18	55.18	6%
90935		Hemodialysis, one evaluation	65.13	$66.36	2%	NA	NA	NA
92012		Eye exam established pat	43.04	$45.80	6%	70.08	70.69	1%
92014		Eye exam & treatment	66.27	$70.33	6%	101.69	103.15	1%
92980		Insert intracoronary stent	806.3	$847.93	5%	NA	NA	NA
93010		Electrocardiogram report	8.38	$9.02	8%	8.38	9.02	8%
93015		Cardiovascular stress test	103.98	$100.27	-4%	103.98	100.27	-4%
93307	26	Echo exam of heart	47.23	$49.77	5%	47.23	49.77	5%
93510	26	Left heart catheterization	241.09	$248.86	3%	241.09	248.86	3%
98941		Chiropractic manipulation	28.57	$30.30	6%	33.14	33.9	2%
99203		Office/outpatient visit, new	65.51	$68.17	4%	91.03	91.97	1%
99213		Office/outpatient visit, est	41.9	$44.72	7%	59.8	61.31	3%
99214		Office/outpatient visit, est	65.51	$69.25	6%	89.89	92.33	3%
99223		Initial hospital care	171.77	$180.33	5%	NA	NA	NA
99231		Subsequent hospital care	35.42	$37.15	5%	NA	NA	NA
99232		Subsequent hospital care	63.22	$66.72	6%	NA	NA	NA
99233		Subsequent hospital care	90.65	$95.58	5%	NA	NA	NA
99236		Observ/hosp same date	200.34	$207.38	4%	NA	NA	NA
99239		Hospital discharge day	92.93	$96.30	4%	NA	NA	NA
99243		Office consultation	92.93	$97.38	5%	122.26	124.79	2%
99244		Office consultation	145.49	$154.00	6%	179.01	184.3	3%
99253		Inpatient consultation	108.55	$114.69	6%	NA	NA	NA
99254		Inpatient consultation	156.54	$165.55	6%	NA	NA	NA
99283		Emergency dept visit	59.03	$61.31	4%	NA	NA	NA
99284		Emergency dept visit	108.93	$114.33	5%	NA	NA	NA
99291		Critical care, first hour	204.15	$212.07	4%	250.99	253.91	1%
99292		Critical care, addll 30 min	102.45	$106.04	3%	111.98	114.69	2%
99348		Home visit, est patient	NA	NA	NA	76.17	79.35	4%
99350		Home visit, est patient	NA	NA	NA	155.78	160.86	3%
G0008		Admin influenza virus vac	NA	NA	NA	20.57	20.92	2%
G0317		ESRD related svs 4+mo 20+yrs	$283.09	$245.29	-13%	$283.09	$245.29	-13%

2009 Summary of Changes by Principal Affected Practice Specialty

The following table shows CMS' estimate of the impact on payments in 2009 from both the Work and Practice Expense RVU changes described in the previous section and the Conversion Factor. Note that imaging providers are primarily bearing the brunt of the changes in RVUs.

Chapter 2: The Healthcare Economy

Figure 30

Specialty	Allowed Charges -mil	RVU Changes*	Budget Neutrality	Statutory 1.1%	Total***
Total	81,669	0%	0%	1%	1%
Allergy/Immunology	184	1%	-3%	1%	-1%
Anesthesiology	1,966	-1%	3%	1%	3%
Cardiac Surgery	400	0%	1%	1%	2%
Cardiology	7,775	-2%	-1%	1%	-2%
Colon And Rectal Surgery	136	0%	1%	1%	2%
Critical Care	224	0%	2%	1%	3%
Dermatology	2,557	2%	-2%	1%	1%
Emergency Medicine	2,451	0%	3%	1%	4%
Endocrinology	385	0%	0%	1%	2%
Family Practice	5,354	0%	0%	1%	2%
Gastroenterology	1,883	2%	1%	1%	3%
General Practice	842	0%	0%	1%	2%
General Surgery	2,408	1%	1%	1%	3%
Geriatrics	175	0%	2%	1%	3%
Hand Surgery	88	-1%	-1%	1%	-1%
Hematology/Oncology	2,019	-1%	-2%	1%	-1%
Infectious Disease	561	1%	2%	1%	4%
Internal Medicine	10,662	0%	1%	1%	2%
Interventional Radiology	228	-1%	0%	1%	0%
Nephrology	1,840	-1%	1%	1%	2%
Neurology	1,489	0%	0%	1%	1%
Neurosurgery	620	-1%	0%	1%	0%
Nuclear Medicine	79	-1%	-2%	1%	-1%
Obstetrics/Gynecology	654	0%	0%	1%	0%
Ophthalmology	5,026	0%	0%	1%	0%
Orthopedic Surgery	3,454	0%	0%	1%	0%
Otolarngology	984	-1%	-1%	1%	-1%
Pathology	1,007	0%	0%	1%	1%
Pediatrics	72	1%	0%	1%	2%
Physical Medicine	850	0%	1%	1%	1%
Plastic Surgery	288	0%	0%	1%	1%
Psychiatry	1,169	1%	2%	1%	4%
Pulmonary Disease	1,828	1%	1%	1%	3%
Radiation Oncology	1,854	-1%	-3%	1%	-3%
Radiology	5,554	0%	-1%	1%	0%

Chapter 2: The Healthcare Economy

Specialty	Allowed Charges -mil	RVU Changes*	Budget Neutrality	Statutory 1.1%	Total***
Rheumatology	521	0%	-1%	1%	-1%
Thoracic Surgery	431	0%	1%	1%	2%
Urology	2,146	0%	-1%	1%	0%
Vascular Surgery	685	0%	-1%	1%	1%
Audiologist	33	-9%	-2%	1%	-10%
Chiropractor	768	-1%	2%	1%	2%
Clinical Psychologist	571	-2%	3%	1%	2%
Clinical Social Worker	378	-1%	3%	1%	3%
Nurse Anesthetist	846	0%	4%	1%	5%
Nurse Practitioner	963	1%	1%	1%	3%
Optometry	867	0%	-1%	1%	0%
Oral/Maxillofacial Surgery	38	1%	-1%	1%	1%
Physical/Occupational Therapy	1,772	2%	0%	1%	3%
Physician Assistant	711	0%	1%	1%	2%
Podiatry	1,727	1%	-1%	1%	1%
Diagnostic Testing Facility	1,186	-2%	-5%	1%	-6%
Independent Laboratory	878	5%	-4%	1%	2%
Portable X-Ray Supplier	87	2%	-4%	1%	-2%

* PE changes are CY 2009 third year transition changes. For fully implemented CY 2010 PE changes, see CMS-1403-FC.
** Prior to the application of the OPPS imaging caps under DRA 5102
***Components may not sum to total due to rounding

2008 Changes in Individual CPT© Code Reimbursement

NOTE: The following Table reflects CMS calculation of fee schedule changes[44] BEFORE the repeal of the 10.1% cut in the 2008 conversion factor; a revised table was not issued. You can estimate the changes for each code by adding .5% to the 2007 numbers shown in conjunction with the RVU Changes by Principal Affected Practice Specialty which follows this one.

Figure 31

CODE	MOD	DESCRIPTION	Facility 2007	Facility 2008	Change	Non-Facility (MD Office) 2007	Non-Facility (MD Office) 2008	Change
11721		Debride NAil, 6 or more	$28.80	$24.53	-15%	$39.03	$35.43	-9%
17000		Destruct premalg lesion	$44.72	$41.56	-7%	$63.29	$60.30	-5%
27130		Total hip arthroplasty	$1,360.52	$1,194.77	-12%	NA	NA	NA
27244		Treat thigh fracture	$1,100.92	$963.11	-13%	NA	NA	NA
27447		Total knee arthroplasty	$1,464.74	$1,283.35	-12%	NA	NA	NA
33533		CABG, arterial, single	$1,908.52	$1,658.44	-13%	NA	NA	NA
35301		Rechanneling of artery	$1,071.74	$934.49	-13%	NA	NA	NA

Chapter 2: The Healthcare Economy

CODE	MOD	DESCRIPTION	Facility 2007	Facility 2008	Change	Non-Facility (MD Office) 2007	Non-Facility (MD Office) 2008	Change
43239		Upper GI endoscopy, biopsy	$155.00	$140.36	-9%	$325.16	$294.01	-10%
66821		After cataract laser surgery	$253.53	$222.81	-12%	$270.97	$237.80	-12%
66984		Cataract surg w/iol, 1 stage	$641.98	$560.08	-13%	NA	NA	NA
67210		Treatment of retiNAl lesion	$556.34	$487.86	-12%	$580.59	$507.96	-13%
71010		Chest x-ray	NA	NA	NA	$26.15	$22.83	-13%
71010	26	Chest x-ray	$8.72	$7.84	-10%	$8.72	$7.84	-10%
77056		Mammogram, both breasts	NA	NA	NA	$97.40	$93.35	-4%
77056	26	Mammogram, both breasts	$41.31	$37.48	-9%	$41.31	$37.48	-9%
77057		Mammogram, screening	NA	NA	NA	$81.86	$73.93	-10%
77057	26	Mammogram, screening	$33.35	$30.32	-9%	$33.35	$30.32	-9%
77427		Radiation tx maNAgement, x5	$176.22	$158.42	-10%	$176.22	$158.42	-10%
78465	26	Heart image (3d), multiple	$73.14	$66.43	-9%	$73.14	$66.43	-9%
88305	26	Tissue exam by pathologist	$37.90	$32.36	-15%	$37.90	$32.36	-15%
90801		Psy dx interview	$129.99	$112.08	-14%	$145.15	$131.50	-9%
90862		Medication maNAgement	$44.72	$39.18	-12%	$50.40	$46.67	-7%
90935		Hemodialysis, one evaluation	$67.46	$58.26	-14%	NA	NA	NA
92012		Eye exam established pat	$34.11	$38.50	13%	$61.77	$62.69	1%
92014		Eye exam & treatment	$55.71	$59.28	6%	$91.33	$90.96	0%
92980		Insert intracoroNAry stent	$795.85	$720.88	-9%	NA	NA	NA
93000		Electrocardiogram, complete	$24.63	$20.78	-16%	$24.63	$20.78	-16%
93010		Electrocardiogram report	$8.34	$7.50	-10%	$8.34	$7.50	-10%
93015		Cardiovascular stress test	$104.22	$93.01	-11%	$104.22	$93.01	-11%
93307	26	Echo exam of heart	$46.99	$42.24	-10%	$46.99	$42.24	-10%
93510	26	Left heart catheterization	$242.92	$215.31	-11%	$242.92	$215.31	-11%
98941		Chiropractic manipulation	$28.80	$25.55	-11%	$33.35	$29.64	-11%
99203		Office/outpatient visit, new	$67.08	$58.60	-13%	$91.71	$81.42	-11%
99213		Office/outpatient visit, est	$42.07	$37.48	-11%	$59.50	$53.15	-11%
99214		Office/outpatient visit, est	$66.32	$58.60	-12%	$90.20	$80.40	-11%
99222		Initial hospital	$119.00	$104.59	-12%	NA	NA	NA
99223		Initial hospital	$173.57	$153.65	-11%	NA	NA	NA
99231		Subsequent hospital care	$35.62	$31.68	-11%	NA	NA	NA
99232		Subsequent hospital care	$63.67	$56.55	-11%	NA	NA	NA
99233		Subsequent hospital care	$90.95	$81.08	-11%	NA	NA	NA
99236		Observ/hosp same date	$205.40	$179.20	-13%	NA	NA	NA
99239		Hospital discharge day	$94.74	$83.13	-12%	NA	NA	NA
99243		Office consultation	$93.23	$83.13	-11%	$122.41	$109.36	-11%
99244		Office consultation	$145.91	$130.14	-11%	$179.26	$160.12	-11%
99253		Inpatient consultation	$108.77	$97.09	-11%	NA	NA	NA
99254		Inpatient consultation	$156.52	$140.02	-11%	NA	NA	NA
99283		Emergency dept visit	$60.64	$52.81	-13%	NA	NA	NA
99284		Emergency dept visit	$110.28	$97.44	-12%	NA	NA	NA
99291		Critical care, first hour	$208.82	$182.61	-13%	$256.19	$224.17	-12%
99292		Critical care, addïl 30 min	$104.60	$91.64	-12%	$114.45	$100.16	-12%
99348		Home visit, est patient	NA	NA	NA	$66.32	$68.14	2%
99350		Home visit, est patient	NA	NA	NA	$150.83	$139.34	-8%
G0008		Admin influenza virus vac	NA	NA	NA	$18.95	$18.40	-3%
G0317		ESRD related svs 4+mo 20+yrs	$283.09	$245.29	-13%	$283.09	$245.29	-13%

Chapter 2: The Healthcare Economy

2008 Summary of RVU Changes by Principal Affected Practice Specialty

The following table shows CMS' estimate of the impact on payments in 2008 from *only* the Work and Practice Expense RVU changes described in the previous section *without* either the suspended cut in the Conversion Factor *or* the .5% increase. It should offer a rough estimate of the relative positions of the specialties for 2008. Note the winners and losers, particularly Anesthesiology.

Figure 32

Specialty	Percent Change	Specialty	Percent Change
Total	0%	Otolaryngology	1%
Allergy/Immunology	2%	Pathology	-2%
Anesthesiology	14%	Pediatrics	0%
Cardiac Surgery	-2%	Physical Medicine	-1%
Cardiology	-2%	Plastic Surgery	-1%
Colon And Rectal Surgery	0%	Psychiatry	0%
Critical Care	-1%	Pulmonary Disease	-1%
Dermatology	2%	Radiation Oncology	0%
Emergency Medicine	-2%	Radiology	0%
Endocrinology	-1%	Rheumatology	-1%
Family Practice	0%	Thoracic Surgery	-2%
Gastroenterology	0%	Urology	-1%
General Practice	0%	Vascular Surgery	-1%
General Surgery	-1%	Audiologist	12%
Geriatrics	3%	Chiropractor	-2%
Hand Surgery	-2%	Clinical Psychologist	-3%
Hematology/Oncology	-1%	Clinical Social Worker	-3%
Infectious Disease	-1%	Nurse Anesthetist	22%
Internal Medicine	0%	Nurse Practitioner	2%
Interventional Radiology	-2%	Optometry	4%
Nephrology	-3%	Oral/Maxillofacial Surgery	-1%
Neurology	-1%	Physical/Occupational Therapy	0%
Neurosurgery	-2%	Physicians Assistant	2%
Nuclear Medicine	4%	Podiatry	0%
Obstetrics/Gynecology	-1%	Diagnostic Testing Facility	3%
Ophthalmology	1%	Independent Laboratory	2%
Orthopedic Surgery	-1%	Portable X-Ray Supplier	0%

Chapter 2: The Healthcare Economy

(Endnotes)

1. A detailed description of the methodology is located at http://www.cms.hhs.gov/NationalHealthExpendData/downloads/projections-methodology-2006.pdf and the data is at http://www.cms.hhs.gov/NationalHealthExpend-Data/03_NationalHealthAccountsProjected.asp.
2. http://s3.amazonaws.com/thf_media/2010/pdf/OACT-Memo-FinImpactofPPACA-Enacted.pdf
3. http://www.milliman.com/expertise/healthcare/products-tools/mmi/
4. http://www.cms.hhs.gov/MedicareProgramRatesStats/03_HlthCrInds.asp#TopOfPage
5. Both *nominal* and *real* (less inflation) GDP growth is reported.
6. http://www.statehealthfacts.kff.org/cgi-bin/healthfacts.cgi?action=profile, 2007 data
7. http://www.cms.gov/providers/
8. http://www.statehealthfacts.kff.org/cgi-bin/healthfacts.cgi?action=profile, 2007 data
9. http://www.bls.gov/cpi/#tables
10. http://www.bea.gov/newsreleases/national/gdp/gdpnewsrelease.htm
11. http://www.cms.hhs.gov/MedicareProgramRatesStats/03_HlthCrInds.asp#TopOfPage
12. http://www.cms.hhs.gov/MedicareProgramRatesStats/04_MarketBasketData.asp
13. http://www.bls.gov/schedule/archives/ppi_nr.htm
14. http://www.bls.gov/cpi/#tables
15. http://www.cdc.gov/NCHS/data/nhsr/nhsr003.pdf National Health Statistics Reports Number 3 August 6, 2008. Note that not all of the possible physician specialties were separately tracked in the NCHS study. 2009 Report has been delayed.
16. http://www.cdc.gov/nchs/fastats/docvisit.htm
17. 2008 Physician Specialty Data, AAMC Center for Workforce Studies
18. Will Generalist Physician Supply Meet Demands Of An Increasing And Aging Population? Jack M. Colwill, James M. Cultice, and Robin L. Kruse; *Health Affairs*, 29 April 2008
19. http://www.cms.gov/ResearchGenInfo/02_CMSStatistics.asp
20. http://www.census.gov/hhes/www/hlthins/hlthin08.html, issued September 2009
21. Health Care – Managed Care, June 22, 2006
22. Healthcare Market Structure And Its Implication For Valuation Of Privately Held Provider Entities: An Empirical Analysis; *Business Valuation Review*, Summer 2008; included in Chapter 3 of this guide with permission
23. Medicare spending varies considerably from region to region with states such as Florida, Texas, California and Tennessee having high per capita and total dollar spending and many for-profit providers.
24. Based on *Health Care- Managed Care*, January 7, 2010, Barclays Capital, sourced from Milliman, CMS and Company Documents
25. Also known as **ASO** or Administrative Services Only business.
26. See the Glossary at the end of this Report.
27. http://ehbs.kff.org/
28. See the Glossary at the end of this Report.
29. PPO - Preferred Provider Organization, POS – Point of Service plan, HDHP (High Deductible Health Plan)
30. http://www.cms.hhs.gov/MedicareFeeforSvcPartsAB/03_MEDPAR.asp#TopOfPage, last updated January 20, 2010
31. http://www.cdc.gov/nchs/products/pubs/pubd/nhsr/nhsr.htm#nhsr005 July 30, 2008; current version not released as of November 2009
32. http://www.statehealthfacts.kff.org/cgi-bin/healthfacts.cgi?action=profile, 2007 data
33. A CMS explanation of the Medicare inpatient and other payment formulas is located at http://www.cms.gov/reports/hcimu/hcimu_04292002_append.pdf.

Chapter 2: The Healthcare Economy

34. http://www.cms.hhs.gov/apps/media/press/release.asp?Counter=3482
35. http://www.cms.hhs.gov/apps/media/press/factsheet.asp?Counter=3223
36. http://www.cms.hhs.gov/apps/media/press/factsheet.asp?Counter=3223
37. http://www.cms.hhs.gov/apps/media/press/release.asp?Counter=2335
38. The fee schedule for each geographic area can be located at http://www.cms.gov/providers/pufdownload/carrcrst.asp
39. Various versions of the documentation guidelines can be located at http://www.cms.gov/medlearn/emdoc.asp
40. The National Physician Fee Schedule is here http://www.cms.gov/providers/pufdownload/
41. Data from www.cms.hhs.gov/NationalHealthExpendData/Downloads/proj2007.pdf and http://www.cms.hhs.gov/SustainableGRatesConFact/01_overview.asp
42. Federal Register Vol. 66, No. 212, November 1, 2001
43. CMS-1403-FC
44. CMS-1385-FC.pdf, http://www.cms.hhs.gov/PhysicianFeeSched/

Chapter 3

Healthcare Market Structure and its Implication for Valuation of Privately Held Provider Entities—An Empirical Analysis

By Mark O. Dietrich, CPA/ABV

This article first appeared in the Summer 2008 Edition of Business Valuation Review. *Reprinted with permission.*

Introduction

The explosion in healthcare transactions after a 10-year hiatus has created a booming market for appraisal and valuation services. One of the peculiar aspects of the healthcare industry is that many if not most transactions must be supported by an independent appraisal due to governmental regulatory concerns. As such, failure of appraisers or valuation analysts to understand healthcare markets and government regulations can lead to transactions taking place at prices inconsistent with both economic reality and, as discussed later herein, regulatory parameters. These transactions can then find their way into databases relied upon by other appraisers resulting in further transactions based upon suspect opinions of value.

The degree of revenue and profit for healthcare provider entities varies significantly from state to state and even within different regions of individual states. As a threshold matter, areas with high healthcare spending and particularly high Medicare[1] spending tend to offer the greatest opportunity for profit. The elderly, of course, receive the bulk of medical care. Given that high localized spending is the primary driver of profit, what other factors contribute to the pattern of location of larger for-profit providers?

- The presence and market strength of Blue Cross plans,

- The degree of market strength of local nonprofit hospitals versus for-profit hospitals,

- The degree of market strength of local nonprofit health insurers versus for-profit health insurers,

- Certificate of Need laws and

- Other local demographic and economic factors.

Chapter 3: Healthcare Market Structure and its Implication for Valuation

As discussed later herein with respect to Blue Cross Plans and nonprofit hospitals, these primary indicators reflect prevailing attitudes in different areas of the nation about the appropriateness of "profit" motivation in the provision of healthcare. In turn, the presence or lack thereof of these larger for-profit providers and insurers has a substantial impact on the acquisition/sales value of provider entities. This impact can be traced to at least two specific factors: the likelihood that for-profit entities will be acquirers of providers in a given area and the revenue and profit growth potential inherent in such acquisitions.

Growth potential in the form of acquisition growth is typically only available to publicly-traded companies whose stock prices are in large part driven by expected growth rates. High growth rates typically result in high valuation multiples due to low capitalization rates. Economies of scale from acquisitions which affect future "same store" profit growth also contribute to localized valuation differences. As such, all things being equal, a growth-driven public company is able to pay a higher value for a given business because the stock market rewards growth.[2]

The Stark laws contain restrictions on the use of "comparable" market data, much of which is pegged to local market conditions. As far back as 1994, published statements of the Internal Revenue Service focused on local factors that determined the character of a market. The factors discussed in this paper suggest that the government agencies' views of "fair market value" should be seriously considered by appraisers and analysts in their own opinions of fair market value.

This study offers appraisers and valuation analysts a foundation for comparing market conditions in different areas of the country. In turn, it provides a basis for determining whether market data in the form of merged and acquired companies or guideline companies is comparable to a given subject company that is being valued.

Data Sources and Impact on Analysis

Sources of data utilized in this study include that maintained by The Kaiser Family Foundation (KFF). KFF maintains data on the breakdown of for-profit and not-for-profit hospitals for each of the 50 states along with Medicare and Medicaid enrollment, spending, length of stay and other detailed statistical data, some of which is described and utilized in this article. Detail of the market share of each state's HMO and PPO enrollment is available from each state's division or department of insurance or, for example, from Lehman Brothers' *Managed Care Guidebook*.[3] Often times, states will provide detail at the county level as well. Data on local Medicare spending from the Centers for Medicare and Medicaid (CMS) was also utilized along with information taken directly from the SEC filings of the public companies discussed.

Local market conditions can lead to dramatic differences in provider revenue, profitability and related acquisition demand. This affects both the relevance of transaction data in determining fair market value as well as the perceived risk of provider entities in a given market area, which in turn affects the discount rate and value determined under the income approach.

Chapter 3: Healthcare Market Structure and its Implication for Valuation

As will be seen from the analysis throughout this paper, for-profit public companies engaged in the healthcare industry tend to concentrate their activities in certain states, notably Texas and Florida, which have specific characteristics discernible from the data sources. The analysis considers presence and dominance of the following companies and certain of their competitors:

- Ambulatory Surgery: AmSurg (AMSG)

- Hospitals: HCA, Tenet, HMA, Vanguard

- Health Insurers: United Healthcare (United), as well as Aetna, Cigna, Humana and Health Net, collectively referred to later as "Other Public"

- Imaging: RadNet

Public Healthcare Insurers

One key to understanding the strategy of provider entities such as AMSG discussed later is to examine the presence of the for-profit health insurers in a given state as well as the concentration of market power by those companies along with Blue Cross plans and local HMOs. The more concentrated a market is in terms of health insurers, the less likely a healthcare services provider will be able to negotiate favorable contracts. This is because market control over pricing is then held by those few insurers.[4] That, of course, leads to an expectation of lower profits.

There are a number of large publicly-traded companies engaged in providing health insurance primarily in a managed care format. These include United Healthcare, Aetna, Cigna, Humana and Health Net.[5] There has been a spate of consolidation in the industry stemming back to the late 1990s when a number of smaller entities got burned at the bottom of the so-called *Underwriting Cycle*.[6] Aggressive setting of premiums over multi-year contracts in order to build market share resulted in bankruptcy or near-bankruptcy for such companies as Oxford when the costs increased more rapidly than expected. The consolidation trend continues today, driven in part by Medicare Advantage contracts as reflected in the acquisition of Pacificare – the originator of Secure Horizons, the oldest Medicare HMO in the country - by United. Given the present backlash against managed care, Medicare HMOs are the principal source of growth for these public health insurers.

For purpose of this analysis, using data from Lehman Brothers *2007 Managed Care Guidebook*, the market shares of each of the 50 states was divided into sub-groupings based upon 1) Blue Cross plans, 2) United (the largest public health insurer), 3) Aetna, Cigna, Health Net and Humana, and 4) local HMOs with strong market presence, e.g., Harvard Pilgrim and Tufts in Massachusetts. After eliminating States[7] where for-profit insurers had small market share, where for-profit providers had little or no market presence and/or rural states were eliminated. 35 states were left in the sample.

Chapter 3: Healthcare Market Structure and its Implication for Valuation

The remaining states were then ranked by the concentration of market power in the hands of those insurers as well as by the number of insurers[8] operating in each market. Concentration percentages were as high as 98% in Alaska where the Blue Cross plan had a 49% share and the named public companies collectively had a 49% share as well. Rhode Island's market consolidation ratio was 97%, with 58% in the Blue plan and 26% in United. The lowest concentrations were in Wisconsin and Kansas. The latter market is highly stratified, however, as described later herein.

Market Share

Figures 1, 2, and 3 summarize the analysis for eight states, divided into those where public for-profit providers are principally present (Florida, Texas, California and Tennessee) and those where they have little or no presence (New York, North Carolina, Massachusetts and Michigan). Market Concentration is defined here as the total market share of the Blue Plans, Public Health Insurers and large local health insurers. Average is the Market Concentration divided by the number of insurers included in the Market Concentration total. Blue Plans are discussed in the next section.

Figure 1 lists the above larger states where for profit providers are prevalent. Although market concentration varies, these states generally have smaller Blue plans and a large market presence of for profit health insurers (shown as United and Other Public). Tennessee is the only state in the top half of market concentration[9] where for-profit providers are prevalent - and it is the location of the headquarters of many of those companies.

Figure 1

Insurance Market Concentration in States Where For-Profit Providers are Prevalent

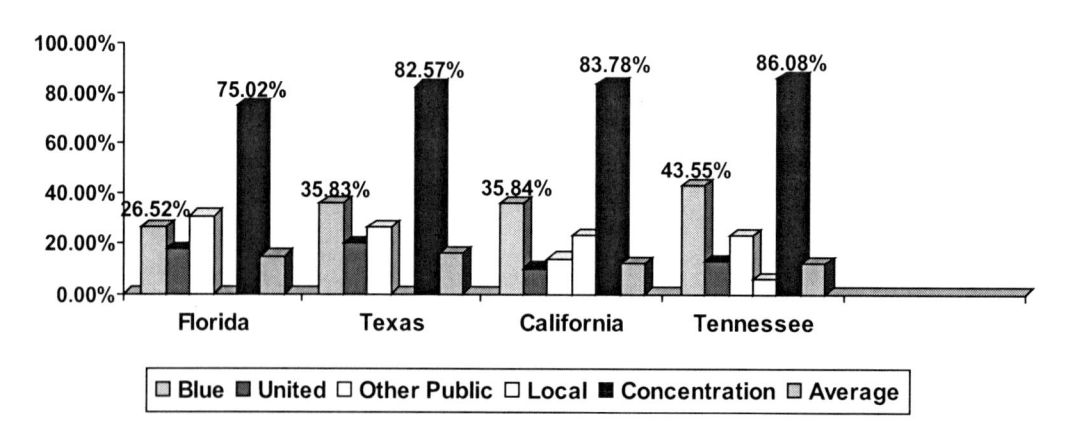

State	Blue	Concentration
Florida	26.52%	75.02%
Texas	35.83%	82.57%
California	35.84%	83.78%
Tennessee	43.55%	86.08%

☐ Blue ■ United ☐ Other Public ☐ Local ■ Concentration ☐ Average

Notes
In California, Kaiser has a market share of 23.40% and there are two Blue plans.
In Tennessee, John Deere Health (owned by United) and Cariten have significant market share. Even at that, much of Cariten's market is in eastern Tennessee, where Deere and the Blue plan have significant market share as well.

Chapter 3: Healthcare Market Structure and its Implication for Valuation

Figure 2 is of representative larger states where for profit providers are not prevalent. Although market concentration again varies, these states generally have very large Blue plans and a small market presence of for profit health insurers.

Figure 2

Insurance Market Concentration States Where For-Profit Providers are not Prevalent

[Bar chart showing data for New York, North Carolina, Massachusetts, and Michigan with categories: Blue, United, Other Public, Local, Concentration, Average. Key values shown: New York — 38.26%, 74.27%; North Carolina — 60.48%, 94.84%; Massachusetts — 58.33%, 86.65%; Michigan — 61.15%, 79.01%.]

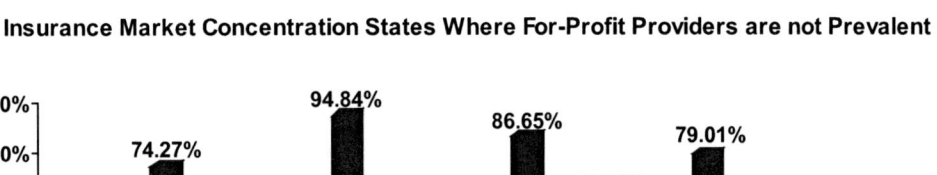

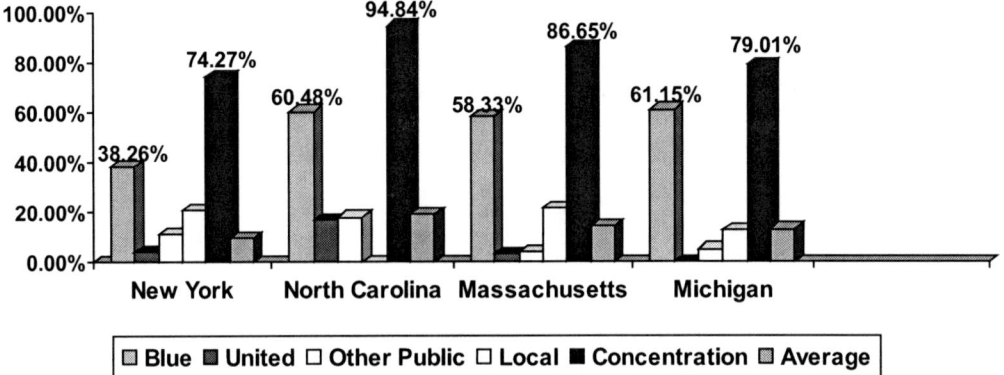

History of Blue Plans

The history of Blue Cross plans plays an important part in the structure of today's health insurance and provider markets. Blue Cross plans expanded rapidly during the Second World War's period of wage and price controls as union sought enhanced benefits to supplement their members' limited incomes. At one point there were more than 100 Blue plans, the majority of which were located in the industrialized states primarily north of the Mason-Dixon Line in what is sometimes called the Rust Belt. There were certain of these plans that refused to contract with for-profit hospitals, thus serving as an effective barrier to market entry. Blue plans also enjoyed a tax-exempt status[10] for many years and protection from anti-trust action in many states.

As will be seen below, this type of insurance market analysis is one critical element in understanding why public healthcare companies locate in some states and not others. In turn, the acquisition transactions of those public companies are likely only relevant in such states. Further, if an analyst or appraiser is considering the Guideline Publicly-Trade Company method, it is likely only relevant in those states where the purported Guideline Companies are active.

Figure 3 combines the earlier two Charts to compare Blue, For Profit (the combined United and Other Public companies' share) and Market Concentration. In markets where for-profit insurers are prevalent (Florida, Texas, Calif and Tenn), Blue plans are less so and for-profit hospitals also tend to be more prevalent, as seen in the next section.

Chapter 3: Healthcare Market Structure and its Implication for Valuation

Figure 3
Comparative Insurance Market Consolidation

State	Blue	All Public	Concentration
Florida			75.02%
Texas			82.57%
Calif			83.78%
Tenn			86.08%
NY			74.27%
N Carolina			94.84%
Mass			86.65%
Mich			79.01%

Public Hospital Companies

As a basis for the analysis of four[11] public, for-profit hospital providers, extracts from their 2006 Form 10Ks follow below. From these extracts, the primary state locations and the extent of concentration can be observed as well as the rationale for locating there (see Tenet and Vanguard Health below). Two other hospital chains not discussed below are Lifepoint and Community Health. Lifepoint,[12] based in Brentwood, Tennessee, has operations primarily in the rural South and border states including Alabama, Louisiana, Kentucky, Tennessee and Virginia. Community Health,[13] based in Franklin, Tennessee, has many of its facilities in Texas, Alabama, Tennessee, northeastern Illinois and southeastern Pennsylvania.

HCA (now privately held)

> We operated 173 hospitals at December 31, 2006, and 73 of those hospitals are located in Florida and Texas. Our Florida and Texas facilities' combined revenues represented approximately 51% of our consolidated revenues for the year ended December 31, 2006. This concentration makes us particularly sensitive to regulatory, economic, environmental and competition changes in those states.

Tenet

> As of December 31, 2006, the largest concentrations of licensed beds in our general hospitals were in California (23.6%), Florida (22.8%) and Texas (18.3%). Strong concentrations of hospital beds within market areas help us contract more successfully with managed care payers, reduce management, marketing and other expenses, and more efficiently utilize resources. However, such concentrations increase the risk that, should any adverse economic, regulatory, environmental or other development occur in these areas, our business, financial condition, results of operations or cash flows could be materially adversely affected.

Chapter 3: Healthcare Market Structure and its Implication for Valuation

HMA Health Management Associates, Inc.

As of December 31, 2006, we operated 60 hospitals with a total of 8,589 licensed beds. During the year ended December 31, 2006, we operated facilities in Alabama, Arkansas, Florida, Georgia, Kentucky, Mississippi, Missouri, North Carolina, Oklahoma, Pennsylvania, South Carolina, Tennessee, Texas, Virginia, Washington and West Virginia.

Our facilities are heavily concentrated in Florida and Mississippi, which makes us sensitive to regulatory, economic and competitive changes in those states, as well as the harmful effects of hurricanes and other severe weather activity in such states. We operated 61 hospitals on February 23, 2007, with 29 of those hospitals in Florida and Mississippi. Such geographic concentration of our hospitals makes us particularly sensitive to regulatory, economic, environmental and competitive changes in those states. Any material changes therein in Florida or Mississippi could have a disproportionate effect on our business.

Vanguard Health

Our ability to negotiate favorable contracts with health maintenance organizations, insurers offering preferred provider arrangements and other managed care plans significantly affects the revenues and operating results of our hospitals. Revenues derived from health maintenance organizations, insurers offering preferred provider arrangements and other managed care plans, including Medicare and Medicaid managed care plans, accounted for approximately 52% of our net patient revenues for the year ended June 30, 2007. Managed care organizations offering prepaid and discounted medical services packages represent an increasing portion of our admissions, a general trend in the industry which has limited hospital revenue growth nationwide and a trend that may continue if the Medicare Modernization Act increases enrollment in Medicare managed care plans. In addition, private payers are increasingly attempting to control healthcare costs through direct contracting with hospitals to provide services on a discounted basis, increased utilization review, including the use of hospitalists, and greater enrollment in managed care programs such as health maintenance organizations and preferred provider organizations. Additionally, the trend towards consolidation among private managed care payers tends to increase their bargaining prices over fee structures.

Approximately 35% of our net patient revenues for the year ended June 30, 2007 came from Medicare and Medicaid programs, excluding Medicare and Medicaid managed plans. In recent years, federal and state governments have made significant changes in the Medicare and Medicaid programs. Some of those changes adversely affect the reimbursement we receive for certain services. In addition, due to budget deficits in many states, significant decreases in state funding for Medicaid programs have occurred or are being proposed.

Historically, we have concentrated our operations in markets with high population growth and median income in excess of the national average.

Chapter 3: Healthcare Market Structure and its Implication for Valuation

At first glance, Vanguard may represent a partial anomaly in the public companies discussed herein. 17% of its hospital beds are located in Massachusetts, with approximately half of those in Framingham/Natick[14] and the other half in Worcester, 20 miles west. The Framingham/Natick facilities were acquired from Tenet after that entity's difficulties stemming from a federal government investigation of its Alvaredo facility in San Diego, California; Tenet had acquired them in 1999 from the predecessor of HCA after that entity encountered regulatory problems leading to a fine of nearly $1 billion. Prior to that, Columbia/HCA acquired the facilities as a result of financial difficulties experienced by the local nonprofit institutions in competing with larger nonprofit entities.

Vanguard is a much smaller entity than either HCA or Tenet as can be seen from the Graph below of the total number of beds each entity has and therefore is less significant to the analysis. It is clear once again that Florida and Texas are primary locations for for-profit hospital providers.

Figure 4
Number of Beds by State

On a percentage basis, HCA and Tenet each have more than 40% of their hospital beds in Florida and Texas.

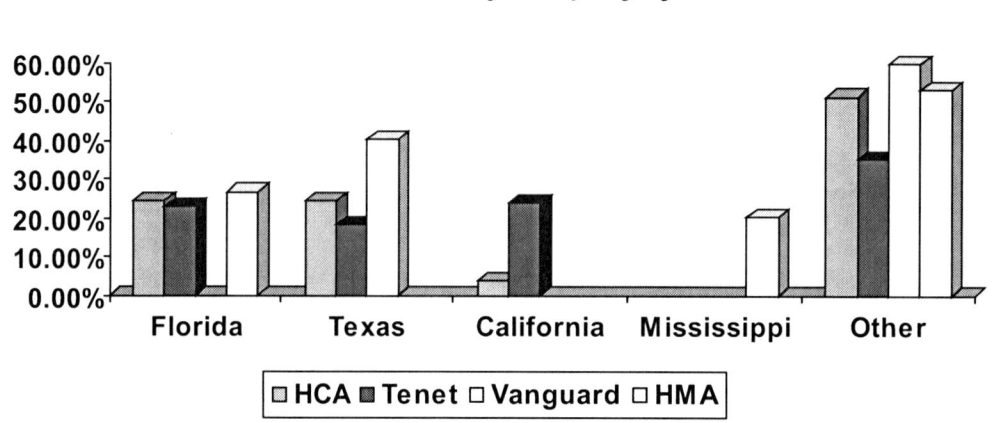

Figure 5
Percent of Beds by Company by State

Chapter 3: Healthcare Market Structure and its Implication for Valuation

For the valuation of an individual Hospital in a state other than Florida, Texas or California, what is the relevance of transactions by one of these publicly-traded entities? As the author and Reed Tinsley, CPA, CVA noted in a co-authored article in the December 2006 American Bar Association's *The Heath Lawyer*:

> What does [out of market] transaction data say or reveal about the value of a hospital with EBITDA of $1.0 million located in North Carolina? Does it tell a valuator that it could be worth the median [multiple] value of $5 million or the [average multiple] value of $7.5 million – the average being 50% greater than the median? Could it be worth [the highest multiple value of] $18.2 million? Given the Stark regulations requirement that comparable transactions be in a particular market at the time of acquisition, can any of these [out of market] multiples be used?

Medicare Part A Spending

Medicare divides providers into two general groupings, Part A Hospital Insurance which is paid for by the combined employer-employee 2.9% Medicare tax and Part B Physician Insurance which is paid for out of general federal revenues, after a nominal premium contribution by beneficiaries withheld from Social Security checks. Medicare Advantage, the risk-based Medicare HMO program, publishes per capita rates county by county across the country split into Part A and Part B components. There are more than 3200 counties including Puerto Rico and Guam with published rates. Because these rates are one proxy for local county Medicare spending,[15] they provide useful insight into a public healthcare provider's location strategy.

Medicare spending is driven by two principal factors: utilization or volume of service, typically expressed in per beneficiary measures, and price or rate per unit of service. Although beyond the scope of this article, utilization data is readily available from such sources as the Medicare Payment Advisory Commission's (MedPAC) 2007 report *Assessing Alternatives to SGR*.[16] While price or rate is a function of statutory formulas and local cost of service differences, utilization is a function of medical practice styles. The differences in utilization are dramatic and warrant study by an appraiser looking to use out of market valuation multiples.

The previous sections discussion on location of for-profit hospitals is consistent with high levels of Medicare spending. Of the top 50 counties, five are in Florida (which has 9 of the top 100), four in Texas (which has 15 of the top 100 and another 22 in the next 200) and one in California (which also has 9 of the top 100). Two of the top 10 counties (Dade and Okeechobee) are in Florida. The location of individual facilities in other states, such as Louisiana, is typically driven by high localized spending as reflected in Medicare Part A or B statistics.

For total Medicare spending, both Part A and Part B, the pattern is similar but more dramatic for Florida and California:

Chapter 3: Healthcare Market Structure and its Implication for Valuation

Figure 6

# of Top 200 Counties for Part A Per Capita Spending

- Florida, 9
- California, 9
- Texas, 37
- Other, 145

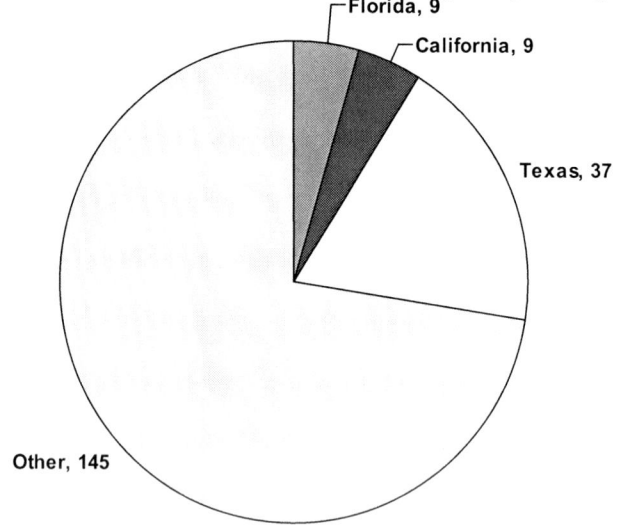

Figure 7

# of Top 200 Counties for Part A & B Total Spending

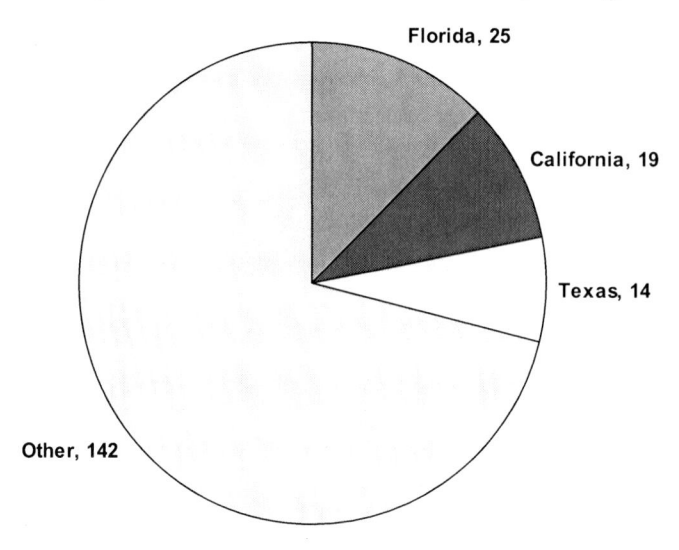

- Florida, 25
- California, 19
- Texas, 14
- Other, 142

The counties shown in Figure 8 have the largest total dollar Medicare spending. Two counties—Maricopa County, AZ and Middlesex County, MA—which appear elsewhere in the article where the presence of public for-profit providers was not explained by other factors are clearly explained in this Chart. Despite the high levels of Medicare spending, there are no significant for-profit hospitals present in Cook County (Chicago) or the various boroughs of New York City,[17] for example. These are counties where unions have historically been very strong.

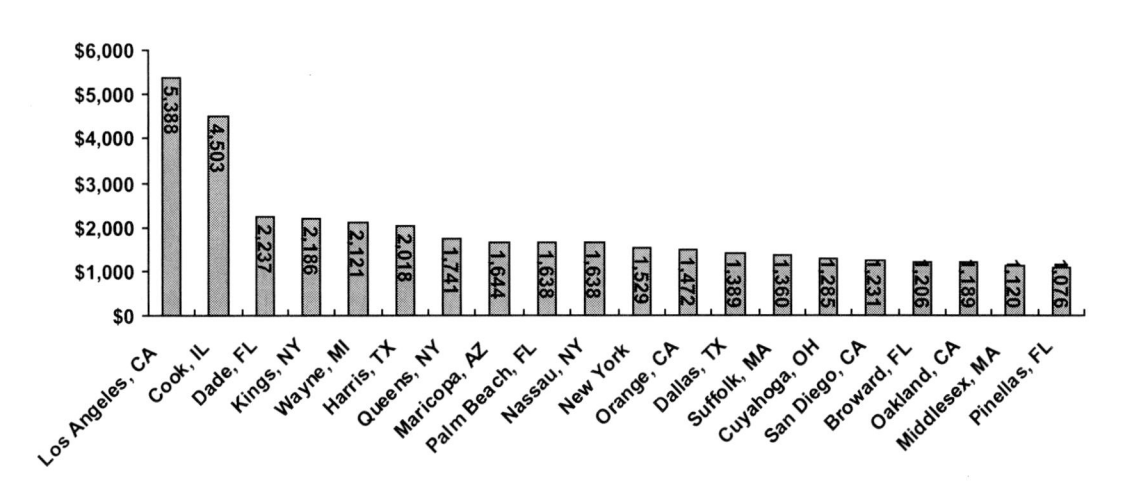

Chapter 3: Healthcare Market Structure and its Implication for Valuation

Figure 8
20 Largest Counties for 2005 Medicare Spending ($Billions)

County	$Billions
Los Angeles, CA	5,388
Cook, IL	4,503
Dade, FL	2,237
Kings, NY	2,186
Wayne, MI	2,121
Harris, TX	2,018
Queens, NY	1,741
Maricopa, AZ	1,644
Palm Beach, FL	1,638
Nassau, NY	1,638
New York	1,529
Orange, CA	1,472
Dallas, TX	1,389
Suffolk, MA	1,360
Cuyahoga, OH	1,285
San Diego, CA	1,231
Broward, FL	1,206
Oakland, CA	1,189
Middlesex, MA	1,120
Pinellas, FL	1,076

Other Hospital Market Factors

Perhaps the most difficult factor to quantify without local market knowledge or study is the presence of not for profit hospitals and particularly large, wealthy teaching hospitals. These institutions tend to be present in large urban markets. Examples include the Harvard-Affiliated Partners Health System in Boston which includes the Massachusetts General and Brigham & Women's Hospitals; Baylor Health Care System in Dallas,[18] Texas; Yale-New Haven Hospital in New Haven Connecticut; any number of institutions in New York City including Mt. Sinai Hospital, Beth Israel Medical Center and NYU Medical Center; The University of Chicago Health System and Northwestern Memorial Hospital and Health System in Chicago; and Johns Hopkins Hospital and Health System in Baltimore. These institutions frequently have market power not only in terms of hospital volume but also in terms of physician affiliations, managed care contracts and political influence.

Another example of nonprofit hospitals are the multi-state religious health systems such as Ascension Health. Many times these institutions are located in underserved areas where access to healthcare is limited by income considerations. They may also be small institutions located in rural areas where providing multi-discipline and emergency care is unprofitable and requires charitable support.

There is nothing that precludes the reporting of acquisitions by not for profit hospitals of other hospitals, physician practices, surgery centers and the like. However, there is often no requirement of reporting and it is certainly less common than reporting by the public for-profit companies described herein.[19] Some transactions may warrant reporting under GAAP and/or GAAS and many states require not for profits to file financial statements with the state Attorney

Chapter 3: Healthcare Market Structure and its Implication for Valuation

General's office; fairness opinions may also be required. Analysts and appraisers need to keep in mind that single-state or single-locale not for profit transactions[20] likewise reflect only that local market's considerations and are equally suspect as value indicators in other markets.

Valuation Imperative

Appraisers and analysts should bear in mind that in addition to the Stark Laws and Anti-Kickback Statute that apply to all healthcare providers, nonprofit/tax-exempt providers are subject to the requirements of the Internal Revenue Code including anti-inurement and intermediate sanctions provisions.

Example

One common business strategy that Hospitals utilizes in acquiring physician-owned entities such as Ambulatory Surgery Centers and Imaging Centers include converting them to hospital outpatient billing or so-called "provider-based billing."[21] This typically results in a higher revenue stream for the same services as both government and nongovernmental insurers frequently have different payment levels for the same service based upon the type of provider submitting the bill, i.e., higher revenue for hospital entities than physician entities. Notwithstanding the business strategy, including the enhanced revenue in a valuation where the standard is fair market value raises serious if not fatal concerns. Since physicians cannot access this billing routine when they own the entity outright, including the enhanced revenue available to a hospital owner creates issues under both the Stark law and Anti-Kickback statute as well as anti-inurement issues for tax exempt entities.

Surgery Centers

After medical practice purchases, surgery center transaction are perhaps the most common form of healthcare transaction. As a result of private equity deals, Amsurg is one of the few remaining public companies in this line of business. Due to the importance of acquisitions to the value of this company and to the valuation of individual surgery centers, the article addresses AMSG in detail. Although the primary location of its facilities is Florida followed by Tennessee and California, it does, in fact, have locations in many other states which make it a particularly interesting subject for analysis. A number of these other locations are examined for consistency with the factors discussed elsewhere herein.

A review of AMSG's December 31, 2006 10K filing with the SEC revealed the following statements:

> Practice-based ASCs, such as those in which we own a majority interest, depend upon third-party reimbursement programs, including governmental and private

Chapter 3: Healthcare Market Structure and its Implication for Valuation

insurance programs, to pay for services rendered to patients. We derived approximately 35%, 35% and 37% of our revenues in the years ended December 31, 2006, 2005 and 2004, respectively, from governmental healthcare programs, primarily Medicare. The Medicare program currently pays ASCs and physicians in accordance with predetermined fee schedules.

At December 31, 2006, 30 of the 156 surgery centers we operated were located in the State of Florida. This concentration makes us particularly sensitive to adverse weather conditions and other factors that affect the State of Florida.

Ninety-two percent of our centers specialize in gastroenterology or ophthalmology procedures. These specialties have a higher concentration of older patients than other specialties, such as orthopedic or [gastro]enterology. We believe the aging demographics of the U.S. population will be a source of procedure growth for these specialties. We target these medical specialties because they generally involve a high volume of lower-risk procedures that can be performed in an outpatient setting on a safe and cost-effective basis.

We begin our acquisition process with a due diligence review of the target center and its market. We use experienced teams of operations and financial personnel to conduct a thorough review of all aspects of the center's operations, including the following:

- market position of the center and the physicians affiliated with the center;

- payor and case mix;

- growth opportunities;

- staffing and supply review; and

- equipment assessment.

In presenting the advantages to physicians of developing a new practice-based ASC in partnership with us, our development staff emphasizes the proximity of a practice based surgery center to a physician's office, the simplified administrative procedures, the ability to schedule consecutive cases without preemption by inpatient or emergency procedures, the rapid turnaround time between cases, the high technical competency of the center's clinical staff that performs only a limited number of specialized procedures and the state-of-the-art surgical equipment. We also focus on our expertise in developing and operating centers. In addition, as part of our role as the manager of our surgery center limited partnerships and limited liability companies, we market the centers to third-party payors.

Chapter 3: Healthcare Market Structure and its Implication for Valuation

The 10K also reveals that 105 of the 156 centers are gastroenterology, 4 multi-specialty, 40 ophthalmic and 7 orthopedic. Appraisers and analysts should consider the prospects for these service lines versus other (*non*-gastroenterology—also called endoscopy—or ophthalmology) medical service lines when contemplating using AMSG acquisition multiples. It is critical to understand precisely what types of procedures a facility is performing as part of the assessment of market data's relevance.

Figure 9 displays AMSG's historical cumulative acquisitions of surgery centers (103, or 66% of the total)) followed by cumulative total centers (156) to emphasize the importance of acquisition growth to the value of the company.

Figure 9
AMSG Cumulative Acquisitions

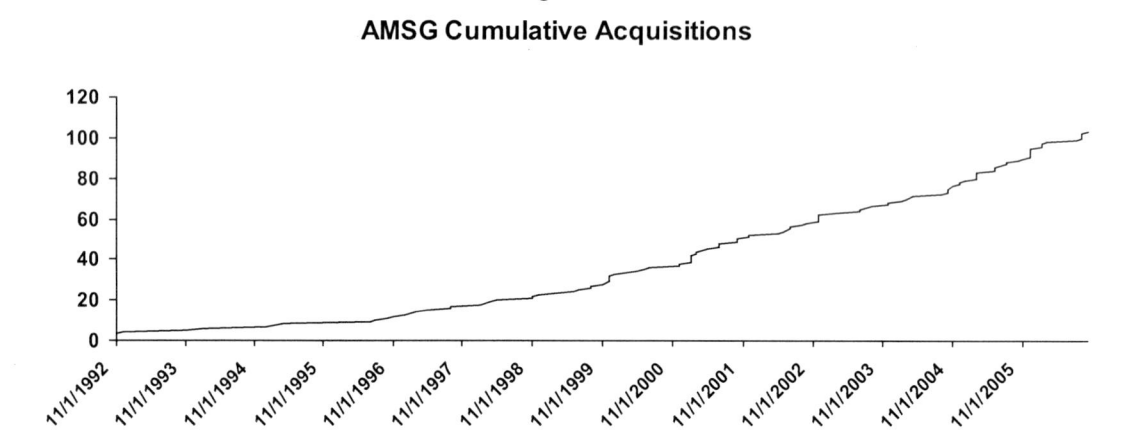

Figure 10
AMSG Cumulative Centers

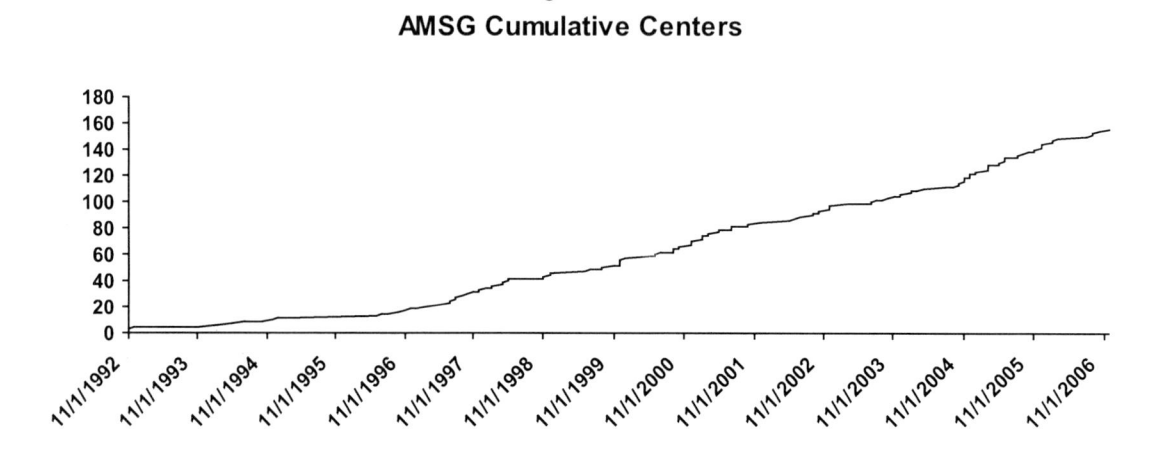

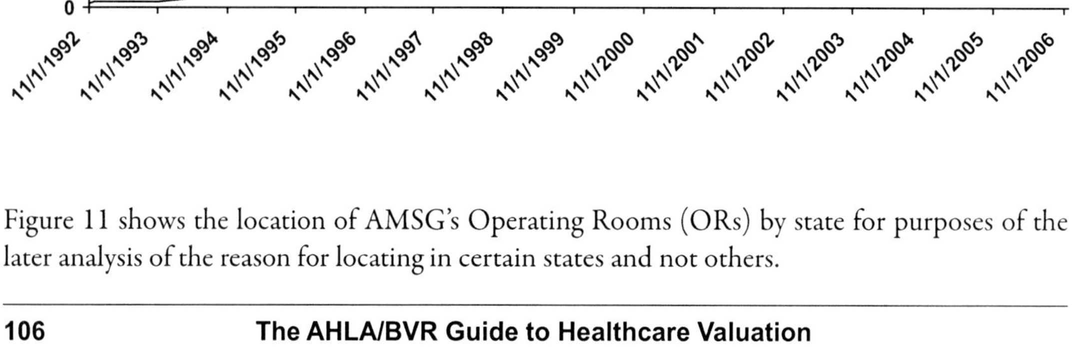

Figure 11 shows the location of AMSG's Operating Rooms (ORs) by state for purposes of the later analysis of the reason for locating in certain states and not others.

Chapter 3: Healthcare Market Structure and its Implication for Valuation

Figure 11
AMSG ORs by State

- Florida 19%
- Tennessee 9%
- California 7%
- Maryland 6%
- Ohio 6%
- Arizona 5%
- Texas 5%
- New Jersey 4%
- Pennsylvania 4%
- Kansas 3%
- Other (23 states) 32%

Figure 12
# of Top 200 Counties for Part B Per Capita Spending

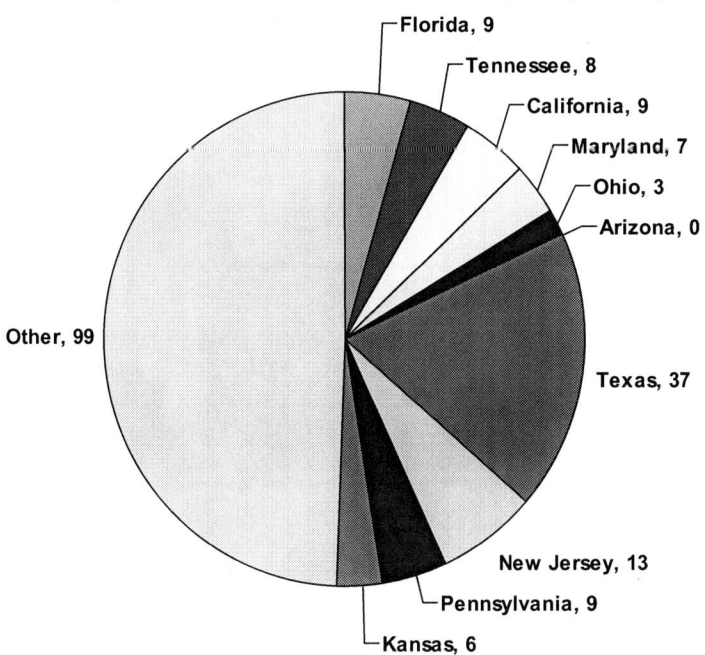

- Florida, 9
- Tennessee, 8
- California, 9
- Maryland, 7
- Ohio, 3
- Arizona, 0
- Texas, 37
- New Jersey, 13
- Pennsylvania, 9
- Kansas, 6
- Other, 99

Chapter 3: Healthcare Market Structure and its Implication for Valuation

Medicare Part B Spending

The states in which AMSG is located consistently have the highest rates for Part B physician spending – and that is where such transaction are or may be relevant depending upon further analysis. Of the 200 counties with the highest Part B Medicare Advantage rates, half (101) are located in the 10 states in which AMSG has most of its facilities. Of the top 50 counties, five are in Florida, four in Texas (which has 15 of the top 100 and another 22 in the next 200) and six in New Jersey. Two of the top 10 counties (Dade and Okeechobee) are in Florida. Only Arizona does not appear in the top 200.

Prevalence of For Profit Hospitals

Earlier, the presence of for-profit hospitals and health insurers was examined. Figure 13 shows the percentage of for-profit hospitals[22] for each of the 10 states where AMSG has the largest number of ORs, with the largest states at the left. Florida, Tennessee and California have 35% of AMSG's capacity. Florida has the second highest percentage of for-profit hospitals in the country with Tennessee seventh.

Pennsylvania is below the national average but the activity in this state could be explained in part by a strong state government commitment to rating outpatient surgery facilities including going so far as to require extensive financial disclosure[23] on top of clinical quality.

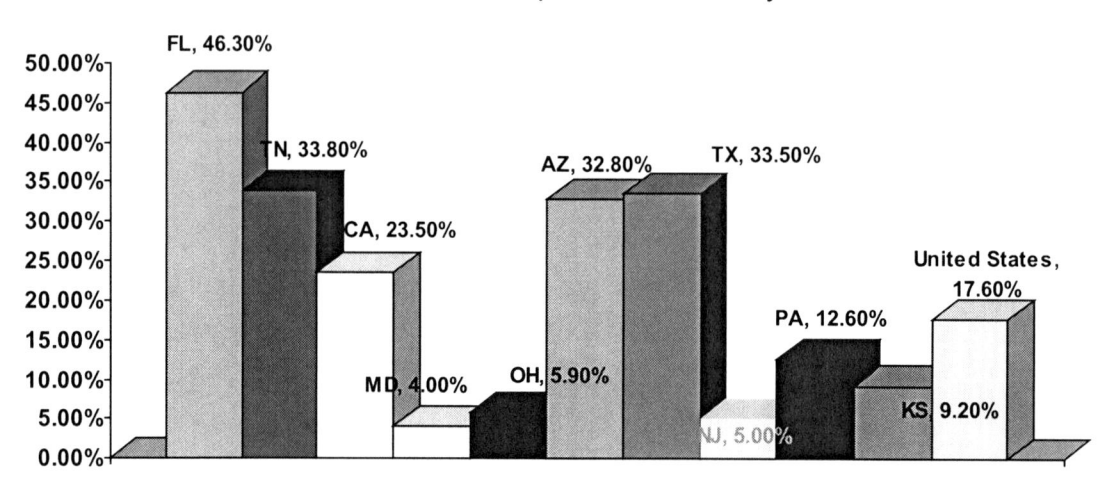

Figure 13
Prevalence of For Profit Hospitals For AMSG's Major States

State	Percentage
FL	46.30%
TN	33.80%
CA	23.50%
MD	4.00%
OH	5.90%
AZ	32.80%
TX	33.50%
NJ	5.00%
PA	12.60%
KS	9.20%
United States	17.60%

Another manner to evaluate for-profit presence is by the number of hospital **beds** as opposed to the number of hospitals. Both data sets are relevant as there are a number of specialty hospitals, such as cardiac and orthopedic, that may have relatively few beds but extremely high profitability. Cardiac and orthopedic care is at the core of most hospitals' profitability. Appraisers

Chapter 3: Healthcare Market Structure and its Implication for Valuation

seeking to value a hospital should be certain to understand the underlying case mix of both the purported comparables and the subject. A specialty orthopedic hospital transaction is likely of little use in valuing a general hospital.

Figure 14
Prevalence of For Profit Beds For AMSG's Major States

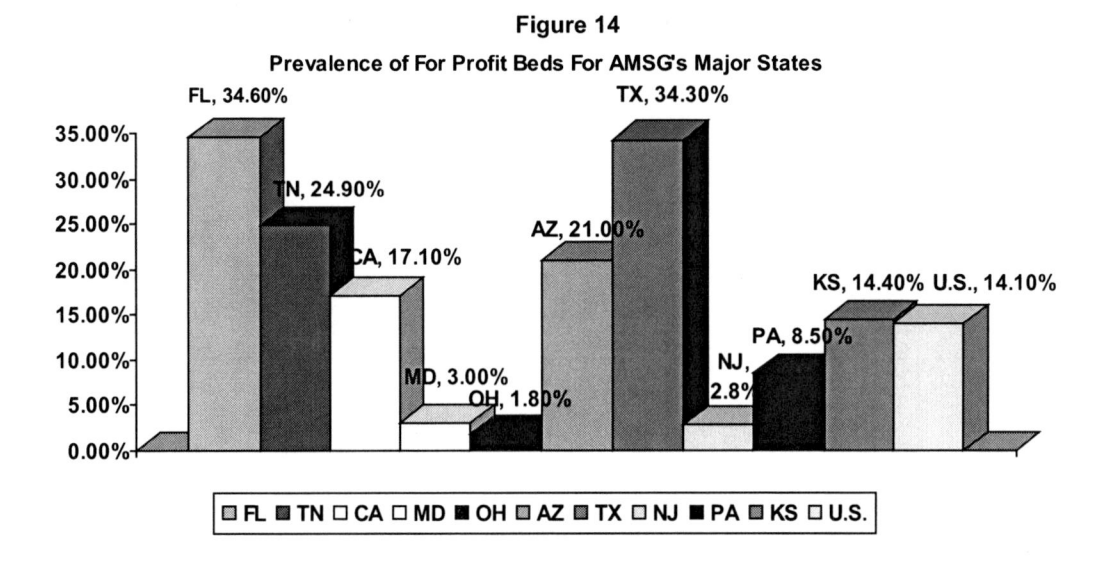

State	Percentage
FL	34.60%
TN	24.90%
CA	17.10%
MD	3.00%
OH	1.80%
AZ	21.00%
TX	34.30%
NJ	2.8%
PA	8.50%
KS	14.40%
U.S.	14.10%

Table 1 summarizes criteria which impact the desirability of locating a surgery center in a given state based upon the 10 states above. Bold items are those which appear partially determinative. For example, Florida has the third highest number of for-profit hospital beds in the country, is ranked 4th in overall healthcare spending, sixth in the concentration of population in metropolitan areas, 9th in spending on physician services and 19th in per capita healthcare spending. The percentage of overall spending in the state on physician services is more than 3% greater than the national average.

For certain of the principal states in which AMSG does business, the listed factors do not appear to readily explain the desirability. For example, Kansas is ranked 8th in overall physician spending as a percent (31.50%) of healthcare expenses but otherwise does not appear attractive based on the criteria. This is where individual local market conditions become important.

Kansas is a largely rural state with population centers in larger cities. The list below is the location of the AMSG facilities. Overland Park and Shawnee are part of suburban Kansas City (the metropolitan area includes the larger Kansas City, Missouri) while Hutchinson is a suburb of Wichita. Thus, the ranking of Kansas as a rural state is misleading with respect to the location of the AMSG facilities.

- Hutchinson, Kansas
- Shawnee, Kansas
- Wichita, Kansas
- Overland Park, Kansas
- Topeka, Kansas

Chapter 3: Healthcare Market Structure and its Implication for Valuation

Similarly, Arizona has only high total spending for healthcare as a positive criteria in the analysis. Arizona, however, has a very high percentage of Medicare-eligible retirees and as noted earlier, Medicare is a key source of revenue for AMSG. Below is a listing of AMSG's Arizona locations.

- Mesa, Arizona
- Peoria, Arizona
- Phoenix, Arizona
- Sun City, Arizona
- Sun City, Arizona
- Sun City, Arizona
- Yuma, Arizona

Table 1

Top 10 AMSG States	For-Profit Beds %	MD Spending%	For-Profit Beds (Rank)	Total Healthcare $Spending (Rank)	Metropolitan Pop (Rank)	MD Spending (Rank)	Per Capita (Rank)
Florida	**34.60%**	31.50%	**3**	4	6	9	19
Tennessee	**24.90%**	31.40%	**10**	15	26	**10**	21
California	17.10%	33.40%	18	1	2	3	44
Maryland	3.00%	28.70%	34	19	7	20	18
Ohio	1.80%	26.80%	39	7	25	35	15
Arizona	**21.00%**	33.00%	15	21	14	5	50
Texas	**34.30%**	30.80%	**4**	3	11	11	45
New Jersey	2.80%	28.20%	35	9	1	27	13
Pennsylvania	8.50%	26.60%	28	5	22	38	11
Kansas	14.40%	31.50%	22	31	35	8	24
United States	14.10%	28.20%	NA	NA	NA	NA	

Explanations
For-Profit Beds %: The percentage of all hospitals beds owned by for-profit hospitals
MD Spending %: The portion of the state's healthcare spending that goes to physician services

Rankings
For Profit Beds: The rank based on total for-profit beds, with 1 being highest,
Total Healthcare Spending: The rank based upon total dollars spent
Metropolitan Population: The rank based upon the percentage of the states population located in Metropolitan areas (as opposed to rural)
MD Spending: The rank based upon total dollars spent
Per Capita: The rank based upon per capita income

Chapter 3: Healthcare Market Structure and its Implication for Valuation

Sun City, Mesa and Peoria are part of greater Phoenix (Maricopa County, described earlier herein), one of the fastest growing metropolitan areas in the nation with Sun City a prime locale for retirees. Maricopa County has the third highest total Medicare spending in the country at *$1.64 billion*. Yuma is near the Mexican border and an even more localized market analysis would be in order.

New Jersey is a particularly interesting case in point where the criteria do not appear to explain the presence of AMSG. Fortunately, the Center for Studying Health System Change[24] which tracks development in 12 markets nationally includes Northern New Jersey, where three of the faculties are located. This is an area where specialist physicians—which would include gastroenterology and ophthalmology, have been terminating provider agreements with insurers to compel higher fees as "out of network" providers. Ambulatory surgery centers are being developed as part of this strategy to shift revenue from hospitals to physicians.

Characteristics of areas with no AMSG locations

AMSG has no facilities in Vermont, Massachusetts, Maine, New Hampshire and Rhode Island and a single one in Connecticut. Thus, the New England area, for example, would not appear to be a target market. These states have comparatively few for-profit beds (Rhode Island and Vermont have none) and high Market Concentration of insurers. Maine, New Hampshire, Connecticut and Vermont have more than 94% Market Concentration as defined earlier herein and the largest insurer in each market is a Blue plan, with 67%, 38%, 33% and 60% Blue Market Share, respectively.

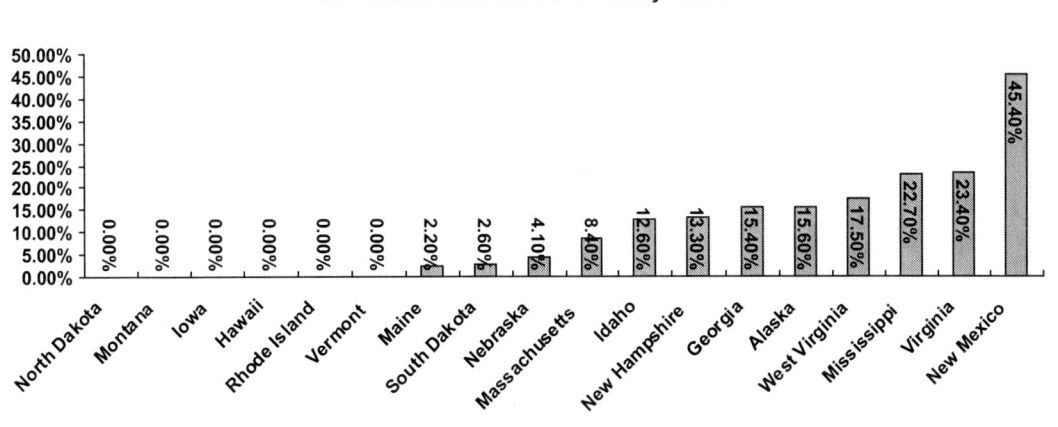

Figure 15
For Profit Beds in AMSG's No Facility States

State	%
North Dakota	0.00%
Montana	0.00%
Iowa	0.00%
Hawaii	0.00%
Rhode Island	0.00%
Vermont	0.00%
Maine	2.20%
South Dakota	2.60%
Nebraska	4.10%
Massachusetts	8.40%
Idaho	12.60%
New Hampshire	13.30%
Georgia	15.40%
Alaska	15.60%
West Virginia	17.50%
Mississippi	22.70%
Virginia	23.40%
New Mexico	45.40%

Chapter 3: Healthcare Market Structure and its Implication for Valuation

Valuation Imperative

An appraiser or analyst should also consider the requirement or lack thereof for a *Certificate of Need* (CON) in each state[25] where a purported comparable operates and in the state where the valuation subject is located. Florida, Texas, Pennsylvania and California do not require a CON for an ASC! Lack of a CON makes it easier to establish an ASC – although actually having a difficult to obtain CON in a state that requires them is generally deemed to be a valuation positive, assuming the CON is transferable. Some states waive a CON for expenditures below a specified level, e.g., $1 million for an MRI in Missouri.

Radnet

The one large publicly-traded[26] provider of fixed location imaging services, Radnet – which acquired its principal competitor Radiologix in the fall of 2006 – has the majority of its facilities in three of the same states (CA, MD and FL) listed above, with a concentration in California. An appraiser or analyst should consider the requirement or lack thereof for a Certificate of Need in each state[27] where a purported comparable operates and in the state where the valuation subject is located.

Figure 16 reflects total units of equipment (e.g., MRI, CT etc.).

Figure 16
Radnet, Units by State

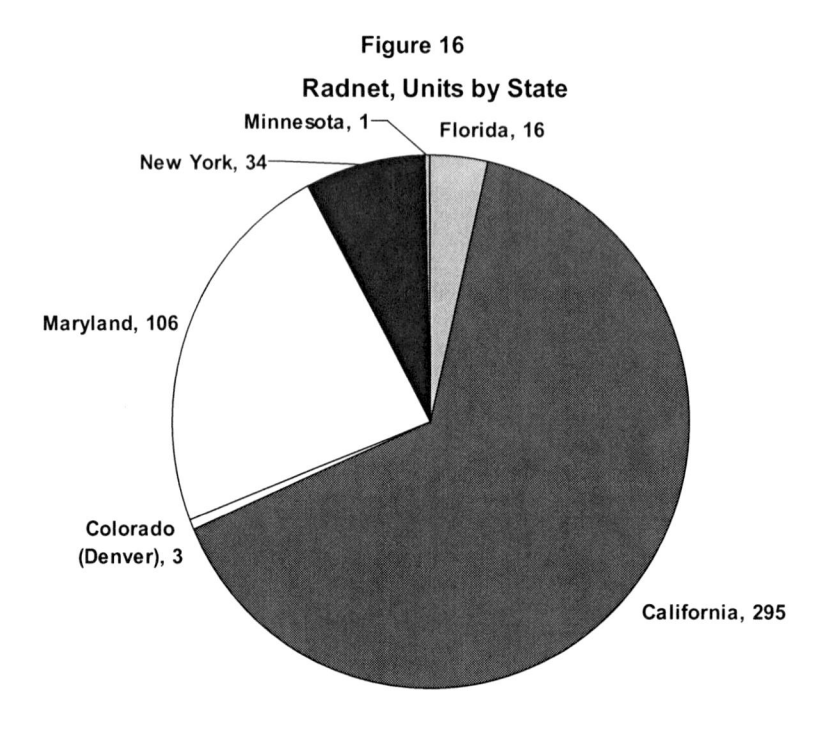

- Minnesota, 1
- Florida, 16
- New York, 34
- Maryland, 106
- Colorado (Denver), 3
- California, 295

Chapter 3: Healthcare Market Structure and its Implication for Valuation

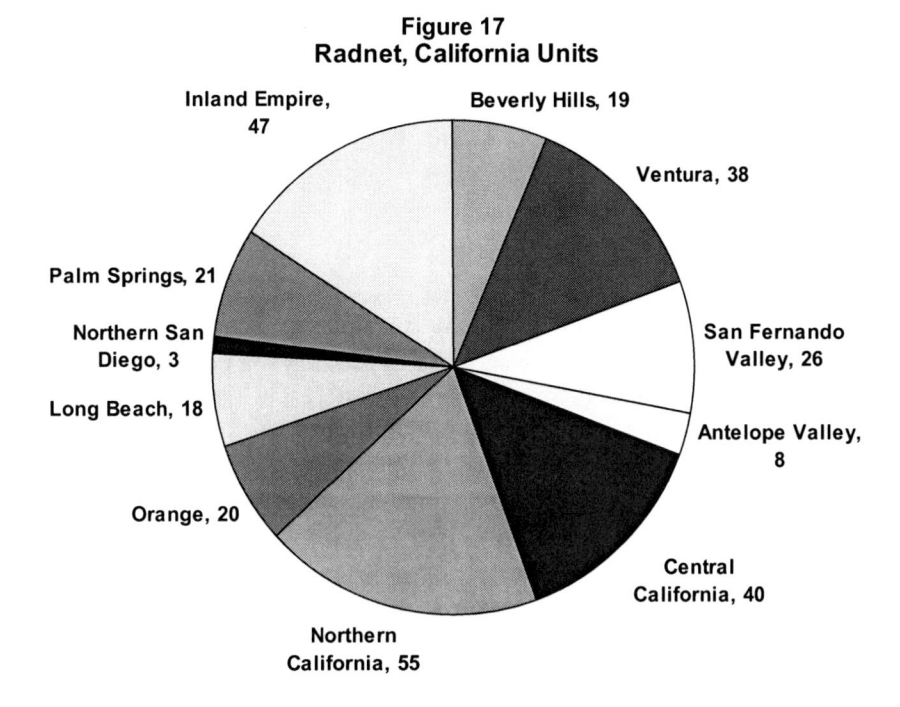

**Figure 17
Radnet, California Units**

- Inland Empire, 47
- Beverly Hills, 19
- Ventura, 38
- San Fernando Valley, 26
- Antelope Valley, 8
- Central California, 40
- Northern California, 55
- Orange, 20
- Long Beach, 18
- Northern San Diego, 3
- Palm Springs, 21

Certainly, a substantive argument could be made that the multiples paid by RadNet for imaging centers in California would be relevant to the valuation of an imaging center located in California. It seems questionable, particularly in light of regulatory considerations, that those transactions would be relevant in New Mexico or Georgia, for example. At best, the multiples might provide some insight, especially if the effect of acquisition growth could be eliminated.

Acquisition vs. Same Store Growth

One of the most important and fundamental differences between a single location valuation subject and a large multi-location, multi-market alleged comparable is the availability of acquisition growth to enhance value through the earnings or cashflow capitalization rate[28] or to offset a decline in same store revenue and profit growth. Consider the following statement from Lehman Brothers analyst Adam Feinstein about AMSG in anticipation of the announcement of the Final Rule by the Centers for Medicare and Medicaid with respect to the adoption of a new revenue model for ASCs that would contain significant cutbacks for endoscopy:

> In regards to an LBO, AMSG has noted that it believes that the overhang created by the proposed changes in Medicare reimbursement (with a final rule expected sometime this summer [*2007*] and the changes expected to take effect on January 1, 2008) reduces the likelihood that a financial sponsor would be interested in acquiring the company (due to the anticipated negative impact in 2008 and 2009). In addition, we get the sense that the company is not interested in going private since *the company has*

Chapter 3: Healthcare Market Structure and its Implication for Valuation

noted that it believes it needs to undertake 12-15 acquisitions per year in 2008 and 2009 in order to generate the same cash flow in those years as it will in 2007 (with the anticipated negative impact from the changes in Medicare reimbursement being offset by the cash flow the company acquires).[29] (Emphasis added)

Valuation Imperative

One observation about the valuation implication of AMSG's statement regarding new acquisitions is that in order for those acquisitions to be accretive to earnings – a necessity if the stock price is to be maintained – acquisition multiples are likely to drop! This is a key test that the appraiser or analyst should employ as part of the reality check for an ultimate valuation conclusion if the merged and acquired company method is being used: would the acquisition be accretive to earnings?

Another observation is that a single location endoscopy center, for example, is unlikely to be in a position to respond to per unit revenue cutbacks by acquiring other endoscopy centers; at best, it might hope to attract additional providers to its facility assuming it had excess capacity.

How would the plan by a public surgery center consolidator to offset per unit revenue declines impact the transaction price for a single location provider? Unless that provider is located in a state that the consolidator is active in or likely to become active in, there would be no impact. The universe of hypothetical buyers under the fair market value standard or even for strategic value does not include buyers who are not present in the market. Figure 18 presents AMSG 35 most recent centers by state.

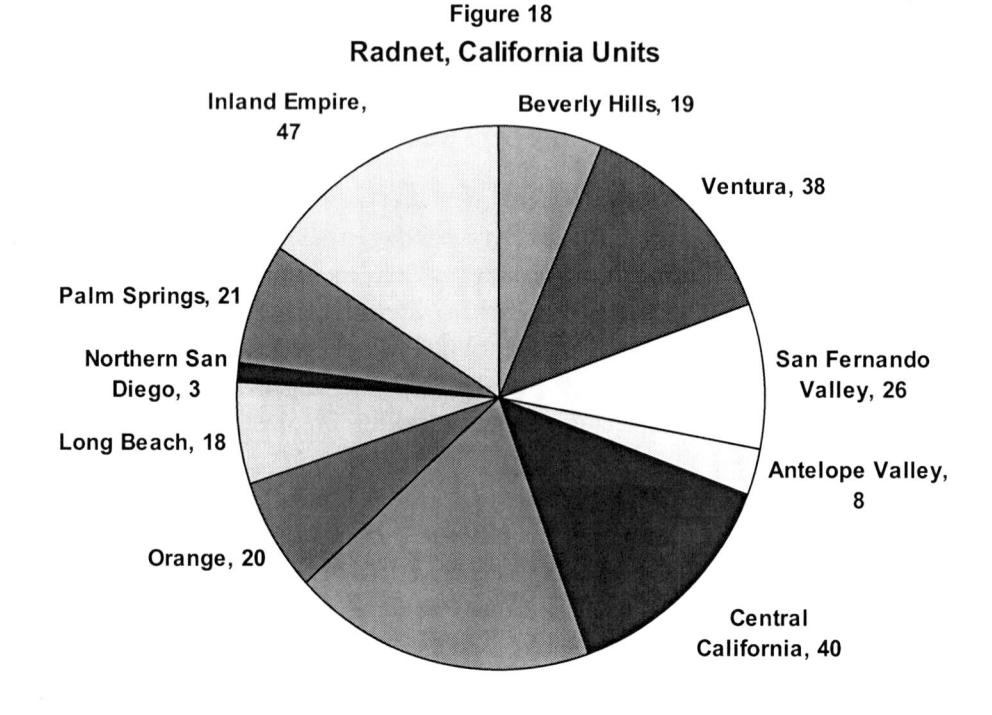

Figure 18
Radnet, California Units

- Inland Empire, 47
- Beverly Hills, 19
- Ventura, 38
- San Fernando Valley, 26
- Antelope Valley, 8
- Central California, 40
- Orange, 20
- Long Beach, 18
- Northern San Diego, 3
- Palm Springs, 21

Chapter 3: Healthcare Market Structure and its Implication for Valuation

Implications for Valuation of Private Healthcare Providers

Follow the Money

The old adage "Follow the Money" is employed in many professions. As the analysis in this article demonstrates, to some extent you can find large for-profit providers by looking at high local rates of healthcare spending. Or perhaps it is more accurate to say you will *not* find those providers where there is low healthcare spending. Factors in addition to total and per capita spending play a significant role in the desirability of a particular location for larger for-profit entities and highlight the importance of understanding local market conditions, including:

- Income levels of population

- Health insurance coverage statistics, including coverage by Medicaid

- Hospital spending per capita and in total

- Physician spending per capita and in total

- Competing nonprofit providers including whether the entities have established integrated healthcare networks

- Identity and Market Share of health insurers; in large states, regional market concentration should be considered along with state-wide data; HMO penetration (reported by KFF) versus indemnity and other types of health insurance should also be considered

- Competing for-profit local providers, e.g., Shields MRI in Massachusetts

All Healthcare is Local

Healthcare markets are highly localized. When seeking to apply comparable transactions under the Merged and Acquired Company method or the Guideline Publicly Traded Company method, it is incumbent on the appraiser or analyst to establish that an acquirer or public company is likely to be active in the market of the valuation subject. Failure to establish that limits the usefulness of the Market Data and may, in fact, lead to an erroneous conclusion of value.

Other relevant local market factors:

- The concentration of the population in urban versus rural areas; urban areas provide easier access

Chapter 3: Healthcare Market Structure and its Implication for Valuation

- In rural areas, the extent and quality of road systems enabling access to healthcare providers; barriers to access such as bridges or ferries from peninsula or island communities

- Age distribution of population

Earlier, portions of public hospital company 10-Ks were cited which described the economies of scale and negotiating leverage with managed care insurers that was obtained through concentrating activities in a given state. It stands to reason that acquisition multiples in that state could properly reflect the inherent value from the economies of scale, but it is difficult to see how that acquisition multiple could be applied to a valuation subject in another state.

Another element to consider is localized supply and demand for a particular healthcare provider. Hospitals often compete to acquire physician practices, seeking to increase or defensively maintain inpatient admissions and referrals for tests. Nonetheless, there are regulatory prohibitions against considering such admissions and referrals in the purchase price and any demand-driven increase in value is limited to factors not precluded by law. Many times, it is difficult to appropriately include even factors such as reduced cost of capital or economies of scale due to the need to rely upon the fair market value standard.

Other Uses of Market Data

There is an arbitrage effect when private company cashflows are moved into the public markets via acquisition, as described earlier with respect to evaluating whether a particular acquisition would be accretive to earnings. If possible, an appraiser or analyst might attempt to extract acquisition growth from valuation multiples to obtain an indication of market value when acquisition-driven market data is used to value a subject in a market where no such buyer is present. This would require analyzing the out of market acquirer's stock and EBITDA valuation multiples and extracting that portion representing acquisition-driven growth. A fundamental analysis can also be performed on the subject to derive discounts from the public company's value for size and growth, for example.[30]

Valuation Imperative

Of course, not all transaction data represents activity of publicly traded companies. However, it is reasonable to believe that privately-held or nonprofit buyers of healthcare entities in markets dominated by public for-profits find acquisition prices driven by what the public for-profit is willing to pay, *even if* the nonprofit cannot match the growth rate. There are many policy and economic implications beyond the scope of this article with respect to the availability of tax-exempt bonds to lower a nonprofit's cost of capital.

Chapter 3: Healthcare Market Structure and its Implication for Valuation

Regulatory Issues

At the outset of the article, it was stated "that the government agencies' views of "fair market value" should be seriously considered by appraisers and analysts in their own opinions of fair market value." The core of the Stark Regulations limitations on use of market data in establishing fair market value can be found in the following extract:

> Usually the fair market price is the price at which bona fide sales have been consummated for assets of like type, quality, and quantity in a particular market at the time of acquisition...[31]

The presence of this statement, drafted at the Department of Health and Human Services which operates the Medicare program, likely reflects that agency's intimate familiarity with differences in local healthcare spending and local healthcare providers.

Appraisers conforming to USPAP and other standards frequently cite those standards as the basis for employing certain methods even in the face of apparent government rejection, typically in Tax Court or other tax-oriented proceedings. For example, USPAP Standards Rule 9-4 provides in part that

> An appraiser must, when necessary for credible assignment results, analyze the effect on value, if any, of: ... sales of capital stock or other ownership interests in similar business enterprises.

However, the Jurisdictional Exception Rule provides

> If any part of USPAP is contrary to the law or public policy of any jurisdiction, only that part shall be void and of no force or effect in that jurisdiction.

Appraisers and analysts should not assume that government's views of fair market value are inconsistent with the usage of that term in the appraisal profession and do well to remember that the Law always trumps professional standards. Improper use of market data in the face of the above regulation could result in unlawful conduct.

Conclusion

The results of this study are critically important to appraisers and analysts working in the healthcare industry. Healthcare markets are highly localized and use of out-of-market data for the valuation of a healthcare business requires a detailed analysis of conditions in the source market as well as the subject market. Regulatory restrictions on the use market data in the Stark laws cannot be dismissed as there are fundamental economic reasons for those restrictions as well as professional standards which require they be respected.

Chapter 3: Healthcare Market Structure and its Implication for Valuation

Markets in which larger for-profit provider entities are present will have transactions that reflect not only the local market conditions but the revenue and earnings growth inherent in the motivation of public companies. Public healthcare providers, such as AMSG, are consolidators driven by acquisition growth. Even those nonprofit markets where healthcare spending and insurer concentration are *otherwise* similar to for-profit markets may have very different values for local entities than is indicated by consolidator-driven multiples. Thus, methods under the Market Approach have to be used with considerable skill and intensive analysis.

There are few absolutes in valuation in general and healthcare valuation in particular. However, terms such as "north," "south," "Rust Belt" and "Mason Dixon Line" seem to have consequential importance. Finally, there is an abundance of readily available and often free data on local healthcare markets that enable the appraiser or analyst to accomplish the tasks necessary for the appropriate application and weighting of the Market Approach.

My thanks to Barry Sziklay, James Rigby, Michael Crain, Nancy Fannon, Don Barbo, Kevin Yeanoplos and Carol Carden who contributed to the review of this paper, but may or may not agree with its conclusions.

CHECKLIST OF FACTORS TO CONSIDER WHEN EVALUATING SIGNIFICANCE OF OUT OF MARKET TRANSACTIONS

Factor	Subject Market	Comparable Market	Data Source(s) *
Economic & Demographic Factors			
Medicare Part A Spending total & per capita			1, 2
Medicare Part B Spending total & per capita			1, 2
Pending or anticipated per unit revenue changes			3, 4
Hospital spending per capita and in total			1
Physician spending per capita and in total			1
Per capita income levels of population			1
Age distribution of population			1
The concentration of the population in urban versus rural areas			1
In rural areas, the extent and quality of road systems enabling access to healthcare providers; barriers to access such as bridges or ferries from peninsula or island communities			
Health insurance coverage statistics, including coverage by Medicaid			1

Chapter 3: Healthcare Market Structure and its Implication for Valuation

CHECKLIST OF FACTORS TO CONSIDER WHEN EVALUATING SIGNIFICANCE OF OUT OF MARKET TRANSACTIONS			
Factor	Subject Market	Comparable Market	Data Source(s) *
Presence of Medicare Advantage plans			2
Medicaid spending and crisis status (Medicaid is typically the single largest line item in a state budget)			1
Health Insurer factors			
Identity and Market Share of health insurers; in large states, regional market concentration should be considered along with state-wide data; HMO penetration versus indemnity and other types of health insurance should also be considered			1, 5, 6, 7
Whether or not Insurers use Network Fee Schedules or Individually Negotiated Fee Schedules			
Utilization Factors			
Hospital length of stay			1
Hospital days per 1000			1
Hospital cost per day			1
Imaging per capita, rate of increase			3
Inpatient v. Outpatient Surgery			1
Market Competition Factors			
Presence of publicly held provider entities			6
Competing for-profit local providers			
Competing not for profit providers			
The percentage of all hospitals beds owned by for-profit hospitals			1
The rank by state based on total for-profit beds			1
Presence of Integrated Hospital Systems			
Presence of Integrated Delivery Systems with physician networks			
Potential economies of scale resulting from multiple locations in terms of costs, negotiating strength, marketing, etc.			

The AHLA/BVR Guide to Healthcare Valuation

Chapter 3: Healthcare Market Structure and its Implication for Valuation

\multicolumn{4}{c	}{**CHECKLIST OF FACTORS TO CONSIDER WHEN EVALUATING SIGNIFICANCE OF OUT OF MARKET TRANSACTIONS**}
Factor	Subject Market	Comparable Market	Data Source(s) *
Whether or not Insurers use Network Fee Schedules or Individually Negotiated Fee Schedules (again)			
Intensity of market competition for acquisitions			6
Impact of acquisition growth on stock price			
Legal Factors			
For physician practices, enforceability of noncompete laws including judicial precedent			
Certificate of Need laws for various provider entities			8
Federal Regulatory Status			9
Anti Kickback Stark Laws False Claims Act CMS Administrative Sanctions Enforcement Trends, e.g., Big Pharma is current target			
State Regulatory Status			
Political Factors			
Lobby strength of state Hospital Association, Medical Society, Imaging, ASC, Chiropractic, etc.			
Board Representation on Provider Entities, particularly Exempt Hospitals and Teaching Hospitals			

*Data Sources:
1. http://www.statehealthfacts.org/
2. http://www.cms.hhs.gov/MedicareAdvtgSpecRateStats/
3. www.medpac.gov
4. Centers for Medicare & Medicaid generally
5. Lehman Brothers analysis
6. SEC filings
7. State Insurance Commissioner
8. http://www.ncsl.org/programs/health/cert-need.htm
9. http://www.cms.hhs.gov/home/regsguidance.asp

---

1. Medicare is a federal program primarily for the elderly and is distinct from Medicaid, a state-determined program for the poor which is funded 50% by federal funds and 50% by state funds.
2. See "Understanding the Difference between Strategic Value and Fair Market Value in Consolidating Industries" *Business Valuation Review*, June 2002, by the author
3. Used in this study's market analysis.

Chapter 3: Healthcare Market Structure and its Implication for Valuation

4. The Federal Trade Commission and Department of Justice Anti-Trust Division favor insurers over providers
5. Wellpoint is a large public company however it owns Blue plans, including Anthem, which are otherwise addressed.
6. This is the Business Cycle for the insurance industry and refers generally to the annual gap between premium increases and cost increases and the Medical Loss Ratio, that portion of the premium expended on medical costs
7. Hawaii, Idaho, Iowa, Maine, Montana, Nebraska, Nevada, New Mexico, North Dakota, Oklahoma, South Dakota, Utah, Vermont, West Virginia.
8. For example, New York has multiple Blue Cross plans.
9. The median is 85% versus 86% for Tennessee
10. Repealed in the Tax Reform Act of 1986
11. HCA has since been taken private in one of the largest LBOs ever.
12. LifePoint Hospitals operated 50 hospitals in 19 states as of May, 2007.
13. As of December 31, 2006, it owned, leased, or operated 77 hospitals, with an aggregate of 9,117 licensed beds in 22 states
14. The author lives in Framingham and formerly resided in Natick, a bordering community; located in Middlesex county, which has the 19th highest total Medicare spending in the nation.
15. At least for the high cost counties; low cost counties have artificially higher rates than their fee-for-service equivalents as a means of inducing Medicare Advantage Plans to offer coverage
16. Utilization and utilization growth is very high in Florida, for example, and low in mature managed care markets like San Francisco and Portland, Oregon.
17. Less than 3.2 % and 1% of hospital beds in Illinois and New York, respectively, are for-profit according to the Kaiser Family Foundation
18. A highly competitive market with both for-profit and nonprofit hospitals.
19. For competitive reasons and regulatory fear, among others.
20. For example, North and South Carolina not-for-profit integrated healthcare system Novant Health's acquisition of imaging provider MQ Associates
21. Medicare requires eligible healthcare providers to bill services in two parts: one for the facility or technical fee to the Hospital or facility for owning the building and equipment and employing nonphysician staff and one for physicians for interpreting/performing the test or procedure known as the professional fee; a hospital-owned facility may be able to bill under higher hospital rates.
22. Kaiser Family Foundation State Health Facts, http://www.statehealthfacts.kff.org/
23. Pennsylvania Health Care Cost Containment Council, http://www.phc4.org
24. www.hschange.org
25. http://www.ncsl.org/programs/health/cert-need.htm, a CON is basically a form of state-issued license.
26. Alliance is the other with primarily mobile imaging and locations in many states. It has recently turned its attention to development of PET/CT. The revenue prospects for different types of imaging can vary dramatically.
27. http://www.ncsl.org/programs/health/cert-need.htm
28. Defined as the discount rate less the long-term or perpetual growth rate
29. Lehman Brothers Health Care Facilities: March Qtr Review: "Buyouts Rule The Day", May 18, 2007
30. See, e.g., Goeldner, "Adjusting Market Multiples of Public Guideline Companies for the Closely Held Business," ASA 18th Annual BV Conference, October 1999
31. 420 CFR 411.351

Chapter 4

Brief Summaries of Medicare and Medicaid

Title XVIII and Title XIX of The Social Security Act as of November 1, 2007

Prepared by Earl Dirk Hoffman, Jr., Barbara S. Klees, and Catherine A. Curtis
Office of the Actuary, Centers for Medicare & Medicaid Services, 7500 Security Blvd., Baltimore, MD 21244. The authors wish to express their gratitude to Mary Onnis Waid, who originated these summaries and diligently prepared them for many years prior to her retirement.
—Reprinted with permission.

NOTE: The following are brief summaries of complex subjects. They should be used only as overviews and general guides to the Medicare and Medicaid programs. The views expressed herein do not necessarily reflect the policies or legal positions of the Centers for Medicare & Medicaid Services (CMS) or the Department of Health and Human Services (DHHS). These summaries do not render any legal, accounting, or other professional advice, nor are they intended to explain fully all of the provisions or exclusions of the relevant laws, regulations, and rulings of the Medicare and Medicaid programs. Original sources of authority should be researched and utilized.

Introduction

Since early in the 20th century, health insurance coverage has been an important issue in the United States. The first coordinated efforts to establish government health insurance were initiated at the State level between 1915 and 1920. However, these efforts came to naught. Renewed interest in government health insurance surfaced at the Federal level during the 1930s, but nothing concrete resulted beyond the limited provisions in the Social Security Act that supported State activities relating to public health and health care services for mothers and children.

From the late 1930s on, most people desired some form of health insurance to provide protection against unpredictable and potentially catastrophic medical costs. The main issue was whether health insurance should be privately or publicly financed. Private health insurance, mostly group insurance financed through the employment relationship, ultimately prevailed for the great majority of the population.

Private health insurance coverage grew rapidly during World War II, as employee fringe benefits were expanded because the government limited direct wage increases. This trend continued after the war. Concurrently, numerous bills incorporating proposals for national health insurance, financed by payroll taxes, were introduced in Congress during the 1940s; however, none was ever brought to a vote.

Chapter 4: Brief Summaries of Medicare and Medicaid

Instead, Congress acted in 1950 to improve access to medical care for needy persons who were receiving public assistance. This action permitted, for the first time, Federal participation in the financing of State payments made directly to the providers of medical care for costs incurred by public assistance recipients.

Congress also perceived that aged individuals, like the needy, required improved access to medical care. Views differed, however, regarding the best method for achieving this goal. Pertinent legislative proposals in the 1950s and early 1960s reflected widely different approaches. When consensus proved elusive, Congress passed limited legislation in 1960, including legislation titled "Medical Assistance to the Aged," which provided medical assistance for aged persons who were less poor, yet still needed assistance with medical expenses.

After lengthy national debate, Congress passed legislation in 1965 establishing the Medicare and Medicaid programs as Title XVIII and Title XIX, respectively, of the Social Security Act. Medicare was established in response to the specific medical care needs of the elderly, with coverage added in 1973 for certain disabled persons and certain persons with kidney disease. Medicaid was established in response to the widely perceived inadequacy of welfare medical care under public assistance.

Responsibility for administering the Medicare and Medicaid programs was entrusted to the Department of Health, Education, and Welfare—the forerunner of the current Department of Health and Human Services (DHHS). Until 1977, the Social Security Administration (SSA) managed the Medicare program, and the Social and Rehabilitation Service (SRS) managed the Medicaid program. The duties were then transferred from SSA and SRS to the newly formed Health Care Financing Administration (HCFA), renamed in 2001 to the Centers for Medicare & Medicaid Services (CMS).

National Health Care Expenditures

Historical Overview

Health spending in the United States has grown rapidly over the past few decades. From $27.5 billion in 1960, it grew to $912.6 billion in 1993, increasing at an average rate of 11.2% annually. This strong growth boosted health care's role in the overall economy, with health expenditures rising from 5.2% to 13.7% of the gross domestic product (GDP) between 1960 and 1993.

Between 1993 and 1999, however, strong growth trends in health care spending subsided. Over this period health spending rose at a 5.6-percent average annual rate to reach nearly $1.3 trillion in 1999, and the share of GDP going to health care stabilized, with the 1999 share measured at 13.7%. This stabilization reflected the nexus of several factors: the movement of most workers insured for health care through employer-sponsored plans to lower-cost managed care; low general and medical-specific inflation; excess capacity among some health service providers, which boosted competition and drove down prices; and GDP growth that matched slow health spending growth.

Chapter 4: Brief Summaries of Medicare and Medicaid

Between 1999 and 2002, growth picked up again, increasing 7.0% in 2000, 8.6% in 2001, and 9.1% in 2002. Though growth slowed after 2002 (8.1% in 2003, 7.2% in 2004, and

6.9% in 2005), U.S. health spending still reached almost $2.0 trillion by 2005. Over this period health spending as a share of GDP increased sharply, from 13.8% in 2000 to 16.0% in 2005. For the 297 million people residing in the United States, the average expenditure for health care in 2005 was $6,697 per person.

Health care is funded through a variety of private payers and public programs. Privately funded health care includes individuals' out-of-pocket expenditures, private health insurance, philanthropy, and non-patient revenues (such as revenue from gift shops and parking lots), as well as health services that are provided in industrial settings. For the years 1974-1991, these private funds paid for 59.3 to 58.4% of all health care costs. By 1996, however, the private share of health costs had declined further to 54% of the country's total health care expenditures, due primarily to the falling share of out-of-pocket spending, and remained relatively stable at 54-56% between 1996 and 2005. The share of health care provided by public spending increased correspondingly during the 1992-1996 period and stabilized during the period 1997-2005.

Public spending represents expenditures by Federal, State, and local governments. Of the publicly funded health care costs for the United States, each of the following accounts for a small percentage of the total: the Department of Defense health care program for military personnel, the Department of Veterans' Affairs health program, non-commercial medical research, payments for health care under Workers' Compensation programs, health programs under State-only general assistance programs, and the construction of public medical facilities. Other activities that are also publicly funded include maternal and child health services, school health programs, subsidies for public hospitals and clinics, Indian health care services, migrant health care services, substance abuse and mental health activities, and medically related vocational rehabilitation services. The largest shares of public health expenditures, however, are made by the programs run by the Centers for Medicare & Medicaid Services (CMS)—Medicare, Medicaid, and the State Children's Health Insurance Program (SCHIP).

Together, Medicare, Medicaid, and SCHIP financed $661 billion in health care services in 2005— one-third of the country's total health care bill and almost three-fourths of all public spending on health care. Since their enactment, both Medicare and Medicaid have been subject to numerous legislative and administrative changes designed to make improvements in the provision of health care services to our nation's aged, disabled, and disadvantaged.

Projected Expenditures

The latest update of the annual projections of national health spending consists of projections from 2006 through 2016. These projections are based on National Health Expenditure (NHE) historical data through 2005, which were released by CMS in January 2007. The Medicare

Chapter 4: Brief Summaries of Medicare and Medicaid

and Medicaid projections and economic and demographic assumptions are based on the 2006 Medicare Trustees Report and the 2006 Old-Age and Survivors Insurance and Disability Insurance Trustees Report, updated with available information through November 2006. As did last year's projections, this forecast includes the effects associated with the introduction in 2006 of Medicare Part D. This new prescription drug benefit resulted in a substantial shift in funding from Medicaid and the private sector to Medicare in 2006.

National health expenditures are projected to reach $4.1 trillion in 2016, up from $2.0 trillion in 2005. From 2005 through 2016, health care spending is projected to grow at an average annual rate of 6.9%, roughly 2.1 percentage points faster than the GDP rate. As a percentage of GDP, national health spending is expected to reach 19.6% by 2016, up from 16.0% in 2005. After increasing 6.9% in 2005, NHE growth is projected to be 6.8% in 2006 and 6.6% in 2007.

Private personal health care spending growth is expected to decelerate from 6.5% in 2005 to 3.7% in 2006, as private prescription drug spending for Medicare beneficiaries shifts due to the implementation of Medicare Part D. Growth is expected to accelerate to 6.9% by 2009 and then to gradually fall to 6.0% in 2016. Much of this overall trend is ascribed to an expected lagged response of health spending to changes in income.

Growth in private health insurance premiums per enrollee peaked at 11.0% in 2002 and by 2006 is projected to decelerate to 4.4%. Private health insurance benefits per enrollee are also projected to slow—from 7.2% in 2005 to 4.4% in 2006. The current phase of the underwriting cycle is one in which premium growth is similar to benefit growth, unlike in 2002 and 2003, when premium growth was faster than benefit growth.

With the exception of 2006, out-of-pocket (OOP) spending growth is expected to edge higher over the projection period, in comparison to the previous decade, and to continue toward a convergence with overall private growth, largely due to efforts by employers and insurers to share costs with employees. However, the growth rate of total health spending is still expected to be higher than the growth rate of OOP spending, causing the OOP share of total health expenditures to fall from 12.5% in 2005 to 10.7% in 2016.

Growth in spending on hospital care, the largest health care sector in 2005, is expected to decelerate to 6.6% in 2006. Slowing growth in hospital care is driven by an expected deceleration in both Medicare and Medicaid growth. This slowdown is projected to be short-lived, as hospital spending is expected to modestly rebound in 2007 to 7.0% and to increase at an average annual rate of 7.2% over the course of the forecast period.

Prescription drug spending growth is projected to rebound modestly in 2006, attributable, in part, to increased utilization of certain classes of drugs, including cardiovascular, endocrine, diabetes, and central nervous system drugs. Increases in utilization among Medicare beneficiaries covered by Medicare Part D are expected to be offset by slowing price growth, due to larger-than-anticipated

Chapter 4: Brief Summaries of Medicare and Medicaid

discounts secured by the private plans participating in the program. Aggregate prescription drug spending growth is expected to remain relatively steady over the projection horizon, with an average annual growth rate of 8.6%, despite the additional Medicare drug spending.

Medicare: A Brief Summary

Overview of Medicare

Title XVIII of the Social Security Act, designated "Health Insurance for the Aged and Disabled," is commonly known as Medicare. As part of the Social Security Amendments of 1965, the Medicare legislation established a health insurance program for aged persons to complement the retirement, survivors, and disability insurance benefits under Title II of the Social Security Act.

When first implemented in 1966, Medicare covered most persons age 65 or over. In 1973, the following groups also became eligible for Medicare benefits: persons entitled to Social Security or Railroad Retirement disability cash benefits for at least 24 months, most persons with end-stage renal disease (ESRD), and certain otherwise non-covered aged persons who elect to pay a premium for Medicare coverage. Beginning in July 2001, persons with Amyotrophic Lateral Sclerosis (Lou Gehrig's Disease) are allowed to waive the 24-month waiting period. (This very broad description of Medicare eligibility is expanded in the next section.)

Medicare originally consisted of two parts: Hospital Insurance (HI), also known as Part A, and Supplementary Medical Insurance (SMI), which in the past was also known simply as Part B. Part A helps pay for inpatient hospital, home health, skilled nursing facility, and hospice care. Part A is provided free of premiums to most eligible people; certain otherwise ineligible people may voluntarily pay a monthly premium for coverage. Part B helps pay for physician, outpatient hospital, home health, and other services. To be covered by Part B, all eligible people must pay a monthly premium.

A third part of Medicare, sometimes known as Part C, is the Medicare Advantage program, which was established as the Medicare+Choice program by the Balanced Budget Act (BBA) of 1997 (Public Law 105-33) and subsequently renamed and modified by the Medicare Prescription Drug, Improvement, and Modernization Act (MMA) of 2003 (Public Law 108-173). The Medicare Advantage program expands beneficiaries' options for participation in private-sector health care plans.

The MMA also established a fourth part of Medicare, known as Part D, to help pay for prescription drugs not otherwise covered by Part A or Part B. Part D initially provided access to prescription drug discount cards, on a voluntary basis and at limited cost, to all enrollees (except those entitled to Medicaid drug coverage), and, for low-income beneficiaries, transitional limited financial assistance for purchasing prescription drugs and a subsidized enrollment fee for the discount cards. This temporary plan began in mid-2004 and phased out during 2006. In 2006 and later, Part D provides subsidized access to prescription drug insurance coverage on a voluntary basis, upon payment of premium, for all beneficiaries, with premium and cost-sharing subsidies for low-income enrollees.

Chapter 4: Brief Summaries of Medicare and Medicaid

Part D activities are handled within the SMI trust fund, but in an account separate from Part B. It should thus be noted that the traditional treatment of "SMI" and "Part B" as synonymous is no longer accurate, since SMI now consists of both Parts B and D. The purpose of the two separate accounts within the SMI trust fund is to ensure that funds from one part are not used to finance the other.

When Medicare began on July 1, 1966, approximately 19 million people enrolled. In 2007, over 44 million people are enrolled in one or both of Parts A and B of the Medicare program, and almost 8 million of them have chosen to participate in a Medicare Advantage plan.

Entitlement and Coverage

Part A is generally provided automatically, and free of premiums, to persons age 65 or over who are eligible for Social Security or Railroad Retirement benefits, whether they have claimed these monthly cash benefits or not. Also, workers and their spouses with a sufficient period of Medicare-only coverage in Federal, State, or local government employment are eligible beginning at age 65. Similarly, individuals who have been entitled to Social Security or Railroad Retirement disability benefits for at least 24 months, and government employees with Medicare-only coverage who have been disabled for more than 29 months, are entitled to Part A benefits. (As noted previously, the waiting period is waived for persons with Lou Gehrig's Disease. It should also be noted that, over the years, there have been certain liberalizations made to both the waiting period requirement and the limit on earnings allowed for entitlement to Medicare coverage based on disability.) Part A coverage is also provided to insured workers with ESRD (and to insured workers' spouses and children with ESRD), as well as to some otherwise ineligible aged and disabled beneficiaries who voluntarily pay a monthly premium for their coverage. In 2006, Part A provided protection against the costs of hospital and specific other medical care to about 43 million people (36 million aged and 7 million disabled enrollees). Part A benefit payments totaled $189.0 billion in 2006.

The following health care services are covered under Part A:

- *Inpatient hospital* care coverage includes costs of a semi-private room, meals, regular nursing services, operating and recovery rooms, intensive care, inpatient prescription drugs, laboratory tests, X-rays, psychiatric hospitals, inpatient rehabilitation, and long-term care hospitalization when medically necessary, as well as all other medically necessary services and supplies provided in the hospital. An initial deductible payment is required of beneficiaries who are admitted to a hospital, plus copayments for all hospital days following day 60 within a benefit period (described later).

- *Skilled nursing facility* (SNF) care is covered by Part A only if it follows within 30 days (generally) of a hospitalization of 3 days or more and is certified as medically necessary. Covered services are similar to those for inpatient hospital but also include rehabilitation services and appliances. The number of SNF days provided under Medicare is limited to

Chapter 4: Brief Summaries of Medicare and Medicaid

100 days per benefit period (described later), with a copayment required for days 21-100. Part A does not cover nursing facility care if the patient does not require skilled nursing or skilled rehabilitation services.

- *Home health agency* (HHA) care is covered by both Parts A and B. The BBA transferred from Part A to Part B those home health services furnished on or after January 1, 1998 that are unassociated with a hospital or SNF stay. Part A will continue to cover the first 100 visits following a 3-day hospital stay or a SNF stay; Part B covers any visits thereafter. Home health care under Part A and Part B has no copayment and no deductible. HHA care, including care provided by a home health aide, may be furnished part-time by a HHA in the residence of a home-bound beneficiary if intermittent or part-time skilled nursing and/or certain other therapy or rehabilitation care is necessary. Certain medical supplies and durable medical equipment (DME) may also be provided, though beneficiaries must pay a 20-percent coinsurance for DME, as required under Part B of Medicare. There must be a plan of treatment and periodical review by a physician. Full-time nursing care, food, blood, and drugs are not provided as HHA services.

- *Hospice* care is a service provided to terminally ill persons with life expectancies of 6 months or less who elect to forgo the standard Medicare benefits for treatment of their illness and to receive only hospice care for it. Such care includes pain relief, supportive medical and social services, physical therapy, nursing services, and symptom management. However, if a hospice patient requires treatment for a condition that is not related to the terminal illness, Medicare will pay for all covered services necessary for that condition. The Medicare beneficiary pays no deductible for the hospice program, but does pay small coinsurance amounts for drugs and inpatient respite care.

An important Part A component is the benefit period, which starts when the beneficiary first enters a hospital and ends when there has been a break of at least 60 consecutive days since inpatient hospital or skilled nursing care was provided. There is no limit to the number of benefit periods covered by Part A during a beneficiary's lifetime; however, inpatient hospital care is normally limited to 90 days during a benefit period, and copayment requirements (detailed later) apply for days 61-90. If a beneficiary exhausts the 90 days of inpatient hospital care available in a benefit period, he or she can elect to use days of Medicare coverage from a non-renewable "lifetime reserve" of up to 60 (total) additional days of inpatient hospital care. Copayments are also required for such additional days.

All citizens (and certain legal aliens) age 65 or over, and all disabled persons entitled to coverage under Part A, are eligible to enroll in Part B on a voluntary basis by payment of a monthly premium. Almost all persons entitled to Part A choose to enroll in Part B. In 2006, Part B provided protection against the costs of physician and other medical services to about 40 million people (34 million aged and 6 million disabled enrollees). Part B benefits totaled $165.9 billion in 2006.

Chapter 4: Brief Summaries of Medicare and Medicaid

Part B covers certain medical services and supplies, including the following:

- Physicians' and surgeons' services, including some covered services furnished by chiropractors, podiatrists, dentists, and optometrists. Also covered are the services provided by these Medicare-approved practitioners who are not physicians: certified registered nurse anesthetists, clinical psychologists, clinical social workers (other than in a hospital or SNF), physician assistants, and nurse practitioners and clinical nurse specialists in collaboration with a physician.

- Services in an emergency room, outpatient clinic, or ambulatory surgical center, including same-day surgery.

- Home health care not covered under Part A.

- Laboratory tests, X-rays, and other diagnostic radiology services.

- Certain preventive care services and screening tests.

- Most physical and occupational therapy and speech pathology services.

- Comprehensive outpatient rehabilitation facility services, and mental health care in a partial hospitalization psychiatric program, if a physician certifies that inpatient treatment would be required without it.

- Radiation therapy, renal (kidney) dialysis and transplants, heart, lung, heart-lung, liver, pancreas, and bone marrow transplants, and, as of April 2001, intestinal transplants.

- Approved DME for home use, such as oxygen equipment and wheelchairs, prosthetic devices, and surgical dressings, splints, casts, and braces.

- Drugs and biologicals that are not usually self-administered, such as hepatitis B vaccines and immunosuppressive drugs (certain self-administered anticancer drugs are covered).

- Certain services specific to people with diabetes.

- Ambulance services, when other methods of transportation are contraindicated.

- Rural health clinic and federally qualified health center services, including some telemedicine services.

To be covered, all services must be either medically necessary or one of several prescribed preventive benefits. Part B services are generally subject to a deductible and coinsurance (see next section). Certain medical services and related care are subject to special payment rules, including

Chapter 4: Brief Summaries of Medicare and Medicaid

deductibles (for blood), maximum approved amounts (for Medicare-approved physical, speech, or occupational therapy services performed in settings other than hospitals), and higher cost-sharing requirements (such as those for outpatient treatments for mental illness). The preceding description of Part B-covered services should be used only as a general guide, due to the wide range of services covered under Part B and the quite specific rules and regulations that apply.

Medicare Advantage (Part C) is an expanded set of options for the delivery of health care under Medicare. While all Medicare beneficiaries can receive their benefits through the original fee-for-service program, most beneficiaries enrolled in both Part A and Part B can choose to participate in a Medicare Advantage plan instead. Organizations that seek to contract as Medicare Advantage plans must meet specific organizational, financial, and other requirements. Following are the primary Medicare Advantage plans:

- Coordinated care plans, which include health maintenance organizations (HMOs), provider-sponsored organizations (PSOs), preferred provider organizations (PPOs), and other certified coordinated care plans and entities that meet the standards set forth in the law.

- Private, unrestricted fee-for-service plans, which allow beneficiaries to select certain private providers. For those providers who agree to accept the plan's payment terms and conditions, this option does not place the providers at risk, nor does it vary payment rates based on utilization.

These Medicare Advantage plans are required to provide at least the current Medicare benefit package, excluding hospice services. Plans may offer additional covered services and are required to do so (or return excess payments) if plan costs are lower than the Medicare payments received by the plan.

Beginning in 2006, a new regional Medicare Advantage plan program was established that allows regional coordinated care plans to participate in the Medicare Advantage program. There are 26 regions (statute required that between 10 and 50 regions be established), and plans wishing to participate must serve an entire region. There are provisions to encourage plan participation, and a fund was established that is used to encourage plan entry and limit plan withdrawals. Enrollment began in late 2005.

For individuals entitled to Part A or enrolled in Part B (except those entitled to Medicaid drug coverage), the new Part D initially provided access to prescription drug discount cards, at a cost of no more than $30 annually, on a voluntary basis. For low-income beneficiaries, Part D initially provided transitional financial assistance (of up to $600 per year) for purchasing prescription drugs, plus a subsidized enrollment fee for the discount cards. This temporary plan began in mid-2004 and phased out in 2006.

Beginning in 2006, Part D provides subsidized access to prescription drug insurance coverage on a voluntary basis, upon payment of a premium, to individuals entitled to Part A or enrolled

Chapter 4: Brief Summaries of Medicare and Medicaid

in Part B, with premium and cost-sharing subsidies for low-income enrollees. Beneficiaries may enroll in either a standalone prescription drug plan (PDP) or an integrated Medicare Advantage plan that offers Part D coverage. Enrollment began in late 2005. In 2006, Part D provided protection against the costs of prescription drugs to about 28 million people. Part D benefits totaled $47.1 billion in 2006.

Part D coverage includes most FDA-approved prescription drugs and biologicals. (The specific drugs currently covered in Parts A and B remain covered there.) However, plans may set up formularies for their prescription drug coverage, subject to certain statutory standards. Part D coverage can consist of either standard coverage (defined later) or an alternative design that provides the same actuarial value. For an additional premium, plans may also offer supplemental coverage exceeding the value of basic coverage.

It should be noted that some health care services are not covered by any portion of Medicare. Non-covered services include long-term nursing care, custodial care, and certain other health care needs, such as dentures and dental care, eyeglasses, and hearing aids. These services are not a part of the Medicare program unless they are a part of a private health plan under the Medicare Advantage program.

Program Financing, Beneficiary Liabilities, and Payments to Providers

All financial operations for Medicare are handled through two trust funds, one for HI (Part A) and one for SMI (Parts B and D). These trust funds, which are special accounts in the U.S. Treasury, are credited with all receipts and charged with all expenditures for benefits and administrative costs. The trust funds cannot be used for any other purpose. Assets not needed for the payment of costs are invested in special Treasury securities. The following sections describe Medicare's financing provisions, beneficiary cost-sharing requirements, and the basis for determining Medicare reimbursements to health care providers.

Program Financing

The HI trust fund is financed primarily through a mandatory payroll tax. Almost all employees and self-employed workers in the United States work in employment covered by Part A and pay taxes to support the cost of benefits for aged and disabled beneficiaries. The Part A tax rate is 1.45% of earnings, to be paid by each employee and a matching amount by the employer for each employee, and 2.90% for self-employed persons. Beginning in 1994, this tax is paid on all covered wages and self-employment income without limit. (Prior to 1994, the tax applied only up to a specified maximum amount of earnings.) The Part A tax rate is specified in the Social Security Act and cannot be changed without legislation.

Part A also receives income from the following sources: (1) a portion of the income taxes levied on Social Security benefits paid to high-income beneficiaries; (2) premiums from certain persons who are not otherwise eligible and choose to enroll voluntarily; (3) reimbursements from the general

Chapter 4: Brief Summaries of Medicare and Medicaid

fund of the U.S. Treasury for the cost of providing Part A coverage to certain aged persons who retired when Part A began and thus were unable to earn sufficient quarters of coverage (and those Federal retirees similarly unable to earn sufficient quarters of Medicare-qualified Federal employment); (4) interest earnings on its invested assets; and (5) other small miscellaneous income sources. The taxes paid each year are used mainly to pay benefits for current beneficiaries.

The SMI trust fund differs fundamentally from the HI trust fund with regard to the nature of its financing. As previously noted, SMI is now composed of two parts, Part B and Part D, each with its own separate account within the SMI trust fund. The nature of the financing for both parts of SMI is similar, in that both parts are primarily financed by contributions from the general fund of the U.S. Treasury and (to a much lesser degree) by beneficiary premiums.

For Part B, the contributions from the general fund of the U.S. Treasury are the largest source of income, since beneficiary premiums are generally set at a level that covers 25% of the average expenditures for aged beneficiaries. The standard Part B premium rate will be $96.40 per beneficiary per month in 2008. While this will be the amount paid by most Part B beneficiaries, there are three provisions that can alter the premium rate for certain enrollees. First, penalties for late enrollment (that is, enrollment after an individual's initial enrollment period) may apply, subject to certain statutory criteria. Second, beginning in 2007, beneficiaries whose income is above certain thresholds are required to pay an income-related monthly adjustment amount, in addition to their standard monthly premium. Following are the 2008 Part B income-related monthly adjustment amounts and total monthly premium amounts to be paid by beneficiaries who file either individual tax returns (and are single individuals, heads of households, qualifying widows or widowers with dependent children, or married individuals filing separately who lived apart from their spouses for the entire taxable year) or joint tax returns:

Beneficiaries who file individual tax returns with income:	Beneficiaries who file joint tax returns with income:	Income-related monthly adjustment amount	Total monthly premium amount
Less than or equal to $82,000	Less than or equal to $164,000	$0.00	$96.40
Greater than $82,000 and less than or equal to $102,000	Greater than $164,000 and less than or equal to $204,000	$25.80	$122.20
Greater than $102,000 and less than or equal to $153,000	Greater than $204,000 and less than or equal to $306,000	$64.50	$160.90
Greater than $153,000 and less than or equal to $205,000	Greater than $306,000 and less than or equal to $410,000	$103.30	$199.70
Greater than $205,000	Greater than $410,000	$142.00	$238.40

The income-related monthly adjustment amounts and total monthly premium amounts to be paid by beneficiaries who are married and lived with their spouses at any time during the taxable year, but who file separate tax returns from their spouses, are as follows:

Chapter 4: Brief Summaries of Medicare and Medicaid

Beneficiaries who are married and lived with their spouses at any time during the year, but who file separate tax returns from their spouses:	Income-related monthly adjustment amount	Total monthly premium amount
Less than or equal to $82,000	$0.00	$96.40
Greater than $82,000 and less than or equal to $123,000	$103.30	$199.70
Greater than $123,000	$142.00	$238.40

Finally, a "hold-harmless" provision, which prohibits increases in the standard Part B premium from exceeding the dollar amount of an individual's Social Security cost-of-living adjustment, lowers the premium rate for certain individuals who have their premiums deducted from their Social Security checks.

For Part D, as with Part B, general fund contributions account for the largest source of income, since Part D beneficiary premiums are to represent, on average, 25.5% of the cost of standard coverage. The Part D base beneficiary premium for 2008 will be $27.93. The actual Part D premiums paid by individual beneficiaries equal the base beneficiary premiums adjusted by a number of factors. Premiums vary significantly from one Part D plan to another and seldom equal the base beneficiary premium. As of this writing, it is estimated that the average enrollee premium for basic Part D coverage, which reflects the specific plan-by-plan premiums and the actual number of beneficiaries in each plan, will be about $25 in 2008. Penalties for late enrollment may apply. (Late enrollment penalties do not apply to enrollees who have maintained creditable prescription drug coverage.) Beneficiaries meeting certain low-income and limited-resources requirements pay substantially reduced premiums or no premiums at all.

In addition to contributions from the general fund of the U.S. Treasury and beneficiary premiums, Part D also receives payments from the States. With the availability of prescription drug coverage and low-income subsidies under Part D, Medicaid is no longer the primary payer for prescription drugs for Medicaid beneficiaries who also have Medicare, and States are required to defray a portion of Part D expenditures for those beneficiaries.

During the Part D transitional period that began in mid-2004 and phased out during 2006, the general fund of the U.S. Treasury financed the transitional assistance benefit for low-income beneficiaries. Funds were transferred to, and paid from, a Transitional Assistance account within the SMI trust fund.

The SMI trust fund also receives income from interest earnings on its invested assets, as well as a small amount of miscellaneous income. It is important to note that beneficiary premiums and general fund payments for Parts B and D are redetermined annually and separately.

Payments to Medicare Advantage plans are financed from both the HI trust fund and the Part B account within the SMI trust fund in proportion to the relative weights of Part A and Part B benefits to the total benefits paid by the Medicare program.

Chapter 4: Brief Summaries of Medicare and Medicaid

Beneficiary Payment Liabilities

Fee-for-service beneficiaries are responsible for charges not covered by the Medicare program and for various cost-sharing aspects of both Part A and Part B. These liabilities may be paid (1) by the Medicare beneficiary; (2) by a third party, such as an employer-sponsored retiree health plan or private "Medigap" insurance; or (3) by Medicaid, if the person is eligible. The term "Medigap" is used to mean private health insurance that pays, within limits, most of the health care service charges not covered by Parts A or B of Medicare. These policies, which must meet federally imposed standards, are offered by Blue Cross and Blue Shield and various commercial health insurance companies.

For beneficiaries enrolled in Medicare Advantage plans, the beneficiary's payment share is based on the cost-sharing structure of the specific plan selected by the beneficiary, since each plan has its own requirements. Most plans have lower deductibles and coinsurance than are required of fee-for-service beneficiaries. Such beneficiaries, in general, pay the monthly Part B premium. However, some Medicare Advantage plans may pay part or all of the Part B premium for their enrollees as an added benefit. Depending on the plan, enrollees may also pay an additional plan premium for certain extra benefits provided (or, in a small number of cases, for certain Medicare-covered services).

For hospital care covered under Part A, a fee-for-service beneficiary's payment share includes a one-time deductible amount at the beginning of each benefit period ($1,024 in 2008). This deductible covers the beneficiary's part of the first 60 days of each spell of inpatient hospital care. If continued inpatient care is needed beyond the 60 days, additional coinsurance payments ($256 per day in 2008) are required through the 90th day of a benefit period. Each Part A beneficiary also has a "lifetime reserve" of 60 additional hospital days that may be used when the covered days within a benefit period have been exhausted. Lifetime reserve days may be used only once, and coinsurance payments ($512 per day in 2008) are required.

For skilled nursing care covered under Part A, Medicare fully covers the first 20 days of SNF care in a benefit period. But for days 21-100, a copayment ($128 per day in 2008) is required from the beneficiary. After 100 days of SNF care per benefit period, Medicare pays nothing for SNF care. Home health care has no deductible or coinsurance payment by the beneficiary. In any Part A service, the beneficiary is responsible for fees to cover the first 3 pints or units of non-replaced blood per calendar year. The beneficiary has the option of paying the fee or of having the blood replaced.

There are no premiums for most people covered by Part A. Eligibility is generally earned through the work experience of the beneficiary or of his or her spouse. However, most aged people who are otherwise ineligible for premium-free Part A coverage can enroll voluntarily by paying a monthly premium, if they also enroll in Part B. For people with fewer than 30 quarters of coverage as defined by the Social Security Administration (SSA), the 2008 Part A monthly premium rate will be $423; for those with 30 to 39 quarters of coverage, the rate will be reduced

Chapter 4: Brief Summaries of Medicare and Medicaid

to $233. Penalties for late enrollment may apply. Voluntary coverage upon payment of the Part A premium, with or without enrolling in Part B, is also available to disabled individuals for whom coverage has ceased due to earnings in excess of those allowed.

For Part B, the beneficiary's payment share includes the following: one annual deductible ($135 in 2008); the monthly premiums; the coinsurance payments for Part B services (usually 20% of the remaining allowed charges, with certain exceptions noted below); a deductible for blood; certain charges above the Medicare-allowed charge (for claims not on assignment); and payment for any services that are not covered by Medicare. For outpatient mental health services, the beneficiary is liable for 50% of the approved charges. For services reimbursed under the outpatient hospital prospective payment system, coinsurance percentages vary by service and currently fall in the range of 20-50%. For certain services, such as clinical lab tests, home health agency services, and some preventive care services, there are no deductibles or coinsurance.

For the standard Part D benefit design, there is an initial deductible ($275 in 2008). After meeting the deductible, the beneficiary pays 25% of the remaining costs, up to an initial coverage limit ($2,510 in 2008). The beneficiary is then responsible for all costs until an out-of-pocket threshold is reached. (The 2008 out-of-pocket threshold will be $4,050, which is equivalent to total covered drug costs of $5,726.25.) For costs thereafter, there is catastrophic coverage, which requires enrollees to pay the greater of 5% coinsurance or a small defined copayment amount ($2.25 in 2008 for generic or preferred multi-source drugs and $5.60 in 2008 for other drugs). The benefit parameters are indexed annually to the growth in average per capita Part D costs. Beneficiaries meeting certain low-income and limited-resources requirements pay substantially reduced cost-sharing amounts. In determining out-of-pocket costs, only those amounts actually paid by the enrollee or another individual (and not reimbursed through insurance) are counted; the exception to this "true out-of-pocket" provision is cost-sharing assistance from the low-income subsidies provided under Part D and from State Pharmacy Assistance programs. Many Part D plans offer alternative coverage that differs from the standard coverage described above. In fact, the majority of beneficiaries are not enrolled in the standard benefit design but rather in plans with low or no deductibles, flat payments for covered drugs, and, in some cases, partial coverage in the coverage gap. The monthly premiums required for Part D coverage are described in the previous section.

Payments to Providers

For Part A, before 1983, payments to providers were made on a reasonable cost basis. Medicare payments for most inpatient hospital services are now made under a reimbursement mechanism known as the prospective payment system (PPS). Under the PPS for acute inpatient hospitals, each stay is categorized into a diagnosis-related group (DRG). Each DRG has a specific predetermined amount associated with it, which serves as the basis for payment. A number of adjustments are applied to the DRG's specific predetermined amount to calculate the payment for each stay. In some cases the payment the hospital receives is less than the hospital's actual cost for providing the Part A-covered inpatient hospital services for the stay; in other cases it is more. The hospital absorbs the loss or makes a profit. Certain payment adjustments exist for extraordinarily costly

Chapter 4: Brief Summaries of Medicare and Medicaid

inpatient hospital stays and other situations. Payments for skilled nursing care, home health care, inpatient rehabilitation hospital care, long-term care hospitals, and hospice are made under separate prospective payment systems. A prospective payment system for inpatient psychiatric hospitals has been implemented and is in a transition period, with payments reflecting blends of the old reasonable cost basis payment system and the new prospective payment system.

For Part B, before 1992, physicians were paid on the basis of reasonable charge. This amount was initially defined as the lowest of (1) the physician's actual charge; (2) the physician's customary charge; or (3) the prevailing charge for similar services in that locality. Beginning January 1992, allowed charges are defined as the lesser of (1) the submitted charges, or (2) the amount determined by a fee schedule based on a relative value scale (RVS). (In practice, most allowed charges are based on the fee schedule.) Payments for DME and clinical laboratory services are also based on a fee schedule. Most hospital outpatient services are reimbursed on a prospective payment system, and home health care is reimbursed under the same prospective payment system as Part A.

If a doctor or supplier agrees to accept the Medicare-approved rate as payment in full (takes assignment), then payments provided must be considered as payments in full for that service. The provider may not request any added payments (beyond the initial annual deductible and coinsurance) from the beneficiary or insurer. If the provider does not take assignment, the beneficiary will be charged for the excess (which may be paid by Medigap insurance). Limits now exist on the excess that doctors or suppliers can charge. Physicians are "participating physicians" if they agree before the beginning of the year to accept assignment for all Medicare services they furnish during the year. Since Medicare beneficiaries may select their doctors, they have the option to choose those who participate.

Medicare Advantage plans and their precursors have generally been paid on a capitation basis, meaning that a fixed, predetermined amount per month per member is paid to the plan, without regard to the actual number and nature of services used by the members. The specific mechanisms to determine the payment amounts have changed over the years. Under the new regional plan program, which began for Medicare Advantage in January 2006, capitated payment rates are based on a competitive bidding process.

For Part D, each month for each plan member, Medicare pays Part D drug plans (stand-alone PDPs and the prescription drug portions of Medicare Advantage plans) their risk-adjusted bid (net of estimated reinsurance), minus the enrollee premium. Plans also receive payments representing premiums and cost-sharing amounts for certain low-income beneficiaries for whom these items are reduced or waived. Under the reinsurance provision, plans receive payments for 80% of costs in the catastrophic coverage category.

To help them gain experience with the Medicare population, Part D plans are protected by a system of "risk corridors," which allow Medicare to assist plans with unexpected costs and to share in unexpected savings. The risk corridors become less protective after 2007.

Chapter 4: Brief Summaries of Medicare and Medicaid

Under Part D, Medicare provides certain subsidies to employer and union prescription drug plans that continue to offer coverage to Medicare retirees and meet specific criteria in doing so.

Medicare Claims Processing

Medicare's Part A and Part B fee-for-service claims are processed by non-government organizations or agencies that contract to serve as the fiscal agent between providers and the Federal government. These claims processors are known as intermediaries and carriers. They apply the Medicare coverage rules to determine the appropriateness of claims.

Medicare intermediaries process Part A claims for institutional services, including inpatient hospital claims, SNFs, HHAs, and hospice services. They also process outpatient hospital claims for Part B. Examples of intermediaries are Blue Cross and Blue Shield (which utilize their plans in various States) and other commercial insurance companies. Intermediaries' responsibilities include the following:

- Determining costs and reimbursement amounts.
- Maintaining records.
- Establishing controls.
- Safeguarding against fraud and abuse or excess use.
- Conducting reviews and audits.
- Making the payments to providers for services.
- Assisting both providers and beneficiaries as needed.

Medicare carriers handle Part B claims for services by physicians and medical suppliers. Examples of carriers are the Blue Shield plans in a State, and various commercial insurance companies. Carriers' responsibilities include the following:

- Determining charges allowed by Medicare.
- Maintaining quality-of-performance records.
- Assisting in fraud and abuse investigations.
- Assisting both suppliers and beneficiaries as needed.
- Making payments to physicians and suppliers for services that are covered under Part B.

Chapter 4: Brief Summaries of Medicare and Medicaid

Claims for services provided by Medicare Advantage plans (that is, claims under Part C) are processed by the plans themselves.

Part D plans are responsible for processing their claims, akin to Part C. However, because of the "true out-of-pocket" provision discussed previously, the Centers for Medicare & Medicaid Services (CMS) has contracted the services of a facilitator, who works with CMS, Part D drug plans (stand-alone PDPs and the prescription drug portions of Medicare Advantage plans), and carriers of supplemental drug coverage, to coordinate benefit payments and track the sources of cost-sharing payments. Claims under Part D also have to be submitted by the plans to CMS, so that certain payments based on actual experience (such as payments for low-income cost-sharing and premium subsidies, reinsurance, and risk corridors) can be determined.

Quality improvement organizations (QIOs; formerly called peer review organizations, or PROs) are groups of practicing health care professionals who are paid by the Federal government to generally oversee the care provided to Medicare beneficiaries in each State and to improve the quality of services. QIOs educate other health care professionals and assist in the effective, efficient, and economical delivery of health care services to the Medicare population. The ongoing effort to combat monetary fraud and abuse in the Medicare program was intensified after enactment of the Health Insurance Portability and Accountability Act of 1996 (Public Law 104-191), which created the Medicare Integrity Program. Prior to this 1996 legislation, CMS was limited by law to contracting with its current carriers and fiscal intermediaries to perform payment safeguard activities. The Medicare Integrity Program provided CMS with stable, increasing funding for payment safeguard activities, as well as new authorities to contract with entities to perform specific payment safeguard functions.

Administration

The Department of Health and Human Services (DHHS) has the overall responsibility for administration of the Medicare program. Within DHHS, responsibility for administering Medicare rests with CMS. SSA assists, however, by initially determining an individual's Medicare entitlement, by withholding Part B premiums from the Social Security benefit checks of most beneficiaries, and by maintaining Medicare data on the master beneficiary record, which is SSA's primary record of beneficiaries. The MMA requires SSA to undertake a number of additional Medicare-related responsibilities, including making low-income subsidy determinations under Part D, notifying individuals of the availability of Part D subsidies, withholding Part D premiums from monthly Social Security cash benefits for those beneficiaries who request such an arrangement, and, for 2007 and later, making determinations as to the amount of the individual's Part B premium if the income-related monthly adjustment applies. The Internal Revenue Service (IRS) in the Department of the Treasury collects the Part A payroll taxes from workers and their employers. IRS data, in the form of income tax returns, play a role in determining which Part D enrollees are eligible for low-income subsidies (and to what degree) and, for 2007 and later, which Part B enrollees are subject to the income-related monthly adjustment amount in their premiums (and to what degree).

Chapter 4: Brief Summaries of Medicare and Medicaid

A Board of Trustees, composed of two appointed members of the public and four members who serve by virtue of their positions in the Federal government, oversees the financial operations of the HI and SMI trust funds. The Secretary of the Treasury is the managing trustee. The Board of Trustees reports to Congress on the financial and actuarial status of the Medicare trust funds on or about the first day of April each year.

State agencies (usually State Health Departments under agreements with CMS) identify, survey, and inspect provider and supplier facilities and institutions wishing to participate in the Medicare program. In consultation with CMS, these agencies then certify the facilities that are qualified.

Data Summary

The Medicare program covers 95% of our nation's aged population, as well as many people who are on Social Security because of disability. In 2006, Part A covered about 43 million enrollees with benefit payments of $189.0 billion, Part B covered about 40 million enrollees with benefit payments of $165.9 billion, and Part D covered about 27.9 million enrollees with benefit payments of $47.1 billion. Administrative costs in 2006 were under 1.6%, 1.9%, and 0.7% of expenditures for Part A, Part B, and Part D, respectively. Total expenditures for Medicare in 2006 were $408.3 billion.

Medicaid: A Brief Summary

Overview of Medicaid

Title XIX of the Social Security Act is a Federal/State entitlement program that pays for medical assistance for certain individuals and families with low incomes and resources. This program, known as Medicaid, became law in 1965 as a cooperative venture jointly funded by the Federal and State governments (including the District of Columbia and the Territories) to assist States in furnishing medical assistance to eligible needy persons. Medicaid is the largest source of funding for medical and health-related services for America's poorest people.

Within broad national guidelines established by Federal statutes, regulations, and policies, each State establishes its own eligibility standards; determines the type, amount, duration, and scope of services; sets the rate of payment for services; and administers its own program. Medicaid policies for eligibility, services, and payment are complex and vary considerably, even among States of similar size or geographic proximity. Thus, a person who is eligible for Medicaid in one State may not be eligible in another State, and the services provided by one State may differ considerably in amount, duration, or scope from services provided in a similar or neighboring State. In addition, State legislatures may change Medicaid eligibility, services, and/or reimbursement at any time.

Title XXI of the Social Security Act, known as the State Children's Health Insurance Program (SCHIP), is a program initiated by the Balanced Budget Act (BBA) of 1997 (Public Law 105-33).

Chapter 4: Brief Summaries of Medicare and Medicaid

In addition to allowing States to craft or expand an existing State insurance program, SCHIP provides more Federal funds for States to expand Medicaid eligibility to include a greater number of children who are currently uninsured. With certain exceptions, these are low-income children who would not qualify for Medicaid based on the plan that was in effect on April 15, 1997. Funds from SCHIP also may be used to provide medical assistance to children during a presumptive eligibility period for Medicaid. This is one of several options from which States may select to provide health care coverage for more children, as prescribed within the BBA's Title XXI program.

Medicaid Eligibility

Medicaid does not provide medical assistance for all poor persons. Under the broadest provisions of the Federal statute, Medicaid does not provide health care services even for very poor persons unless they are in one of the groups designated below. Low income is only one test for Medicaid eligibility for those within these groups; their financial resources also are tested against threshold levels (as determined by each State within Federal guidelines).

States generally have broad discretion in determining which groups their Medicaid programs will cover and the financial criteria for Medicaid eligibility. To be eligible for Federal funds, however, States are required to provide Medicaid coverage for certain individuals who receive federally assisted income-maintenance payments, as well as for related groups not receiving cash payments. In addition to their Medicaid programs, most States have additional "State-only" programs to provide medical assistance for specified poor persons who do not qualify for Medicaid. Federal funds are not provided for State-only programs. The following enumerates the mandatory Medicaid "categorically needy" eligibility groups for which Federal matching funds are provided:

- Limited-income families with children, as described in section 1931 of the Social Security Act, are generally eligible for Medicaid if they meet the requirements for the Aid to Families with Dependent Children (AFDC) program that were in effect in their State on July 16, 1996.

- Children under age 6 whose family income is at or below 133% of the Federal poverty level (FPL). (As of January 2007, 100% of the FPL has been set at $20,650 for a family of four in the continental U.S.; Alaska and Hawaii's FPLs are substantially higher.)

- Pregnant women whose family income is below 133% of the FPL. (Services to these women are limited to those related to pregnancy, complications of pregnancy, delivery, and postpartum care.)

- Infants born to Medicaid-eligible women, for the first year of life with certain restrictions.

- Supplemental Security Income (SSI) recipients in most States (or aged, blind, and disabled individuals in States using more restrictive Medicaid eligibility requirements that pre-date SSI).

Chapter 4: Brief Summaries of Medicare and Medicaid

- Recipients of adoption or foster care assistance under Title IV-E of the Social Security Act.

- Special protected groups (typically individuals who lose their SSI payments due to earnings from work or from increased Social Security benefits, but who may keep Medicaid for a period of time).

- All children under age 19, in families with incomes at or below the FPL.

- Certain Medicare beneficiaries (described later).

States also have the option of providing Medicaid coverage for other "categorically related" groups. These optional groups share characteristics of the mandatory groups (that is, they fall within defined categories), but the eligibility criteria are somewhat more liberally defined. The broadest optional groups for which States will receive Federal matching funds for coverage under the Medicaid program include the following:

- Infants up to age 1 and pregnant women not covered under the mandatory rules whose family income is no more than 185% of the FPL. (The percentage amount is set by each State.)

- Children under age 21 who meet criteria more liberal than the AFDC income and resources requirements that were in effect in their State on July 16, 1996.

- Institutionalized individuals eligible under a "special income level." (The amount is set by each State—up to 300% of the SSI Federal benefit rate.)

- Individuals who would be eligible if institutionalized, but who are receiving care under home and community-based services (HCBS) waivers.

- Certain aged, blind, or disabled adults who have incomes above those requiring mandatory coverage, but below the FPL.

- Aged, blind, or disabled recipients of State supplementary income payments.

- Certain working-and-disabled persons with family income less than 250% of the FPL who would qualify for SSI if they did not work.

- TB-infected persons who would be financially eligible for Medicaid at the SSI income level if they were within a Medicaid-covered category. (Coverage is limited to TB-related ambulatory services and TB drugs.)

- Certain uninsured or low-income women who are screened for breast or cervical cancer through a program administered by the Centers for Disease Control. The Breast and Cervical Cancer Prevention and Treatment Act of 2000 (Public Law 106-354) provides these women with medical assistance and follow-up diagnostic services through Medicaid.

Chapter 4: Brief Summaries of Medicare and Medicaid

- "Optional targeted low-income children" included within the SCHIP program established by the BBA.

- "Medically needy" persons (described below).

The medically needy (MN) option allows States to extend Medicaid eligibility to additional persons. These persons would be eligible for Medicaid under one of the mandatory or optional groups, except that their income and/or resources are above the eligibility level set by their State. Persons may qualify immediately or may "spend down" by incurring medical expenses that reduce their income to or below their State's MN income level.

Medicaid eligibility and benefit provisions for the medically needy do not have to be as extensive as for the categorically needy, and may be quite restrictive. Federal matching funds are available for MN programs. However, if a State elects to have a MN program, there are Federal requirements that certain groups and certain services must be included; that is, children under age 19 and pregnant women who are medically needy must be covered, and prenatal and delivery care for pregnant women, as well as ambulatory care for children, must be provided. A State may elect to provide MN eligibility to certain additional groups and may elect to provide certain additional services within its MN program. As of 2004, thirty-five States plus the District of Columbia have elected to have a MN program and are providing at least some MN services to at least some MN beneficiaries. All remaining States utilize the "special income level" option to extend Medicaid to the "near poor" in medical institutional settings.

The Personal Responsibility and Work Opportunity Reconciliation Act of 1996 (Public Law 104-193)— known as the "welfare reform" bill—made restrictive changes regarding eligibility for SSI coverage that impacted the Medicaid program. For example, legal resident aliens and other qualified aliens who entered the United States on or after August 22, 1996 are ineligible for Medicaid for 5 years. Medicaid coverage for most aliens entering before that date and coverage for those eligible after the 5-year ban are State options; emergency services, however, are mandatory for both of these alien coverage groups. For aliens who lose SSI benefits because of the new restrictions regarding SSI coverage, Medicaid can continue only if these persons can be covered for Medicaid under some other eligibility status (again with the exception of emergency services, which are mandatory). Public Law 104-193 also affected a number of disabled children, who lost SSI as a result of the restrictive changes; however, their eligibility for Medicaid was reinstituted by Public Law 105-33, the BBA.

In addition, welfare reform repealed the open-ended Federal entitlement program known as Aid to Families with Dependent Children (AFDC) and replaced it with Temporary Assistance for Needy Families (TANF), which provides States with grants to be spent on time-limited cash assistance. TANF generally limits a family's lifetime cash welfare benefits to a maximum of 5 years and permits States to impose a wide range of other requirements as well—in particular, those related to employment. However, the impact on Medicaid eligibility has not been significant. Under welfare reform, persons who would have been eligible for AFDC under the AFDC

Chapter 4: Brief Summaries of Medicare and Medicaid

requirements in effect on July 16, 1996 are generally still eligible for Medicaid. Although most persons covered by TANF receive Medicaid, it is not required by law.

Medicaid coverage may begin as early as the third month prior to application—if the person would have been eligible for Medicaid had he or she applied during that time. Medicaid coverage generally stops at the end of the month in which a person no longer meets the criteria of any Medicaid eligibility group. The BBA allows States to provide 12 months of continuous Medicaid coverage (without reevaluation) for eligible children under the age of 19.

The Ticket to Work and Work Incentives Improvement Act of 1999 (Public Law 106-170) provides or continues Medicaid coverage to certain disabled beneficiaries who work despite their disability. Those with higher incomes may pay a sliding scale premium based on income.

The Deficit Reduction Act (DRA) of 2005 (Public Law 109-171) refined eligibility requirements for Medicaid beneficiaries by tightening standards for citizenship and immigration documentation and by changing the rules concerning long-term care eligibility—specifically, the look-back period for determining community spouse income and assets has been lengthened from 36 months to 60 months, individuals whose homes exceed $500,000 in value are disqualified, and the States are required to impose partial months of ineligibility.

Scope of Medicaid Services

Title XIX of the Social Security Act allows considerable flexibility within the States' Medicaid plans. However, some Federal requirements are mandatory if Federal matching funds are to be received. A State's Medicaid program must offer medical assistance for certain basic services to most categorically needy populations. These services generally include the following:

- Inpatient hospital services.

- Outpatient hospital services.

- Pregnancy-related services, including prenatal care and 60 days postpartum pregnancy-related services.

- Vaccines for children.

- Physician services.

- Nursing facility services for persons aged 21 or older.

- Family planning services and supplies.

- Rural health clinic services.

Chapter 4: Brief Summaries of Medicare and Medicaid

- Home health care for persons eligible for skilled-nursing services.

- Laboratory and x-ray services.

- Pediatric and family nurse practitioner services.

- Nurse-midwife services.

- Federally qualified health-center (FQHC) services, and ambulatory services of an FQHC that would be available in other settings.

- Early and periodic screening, diagnostic, and treatment (EPSDT) services for children under age 21.

States may also receive Federal matching funds to provide certain optional services. Following are some of the most common, currently approved optional Medicaid services:

- Diagnostic services.

- Clinic services.

- Intermediate care facilities for the mentally retarded (ICFs/MR).

- Prescribed drugs and prosthetic devices.

- Optometrist services and eyeglasses.

- Nursing facility services for children under age 21.

- Transportation services.

- Rehabilitation and physical therapy services.

- Hospice care.

- Home and community-based care to certain persons with chronic impairments.

- Targeted case management services.

The BBA included a State option known as Programs of All-inclusive Care for the Elderly (PACE). PACE provides an alternative to institutional care for persons aged 55 or older who require a nursing facility level of care. The PACE team offers and manages all health, medical, and social services and mobilizes other services as needed to provide preventive, rehabilitative,

Chapter 4: Brief Summaries of Medicare and Medicaid

curative, and supportive care. This care, provided in day health centers, homes, hospitals, and nursing homes, helps the person maintain independence, dignity, and quality of life. PACE functions within the Medicare program as well. Regardless of source of payment, PACE providers receive payment only through the PACE agreement and must make available all items and services covered under both Titles XVIII and XIX, without amount, duration, or scope limitations and without application of any deductibles, copayments, or other cost sharing. The individuals enrolled in PACE receive benefits solely through the PACE program.

Amount and Duration of Medicaid Services

Within broad Federal guidelines and certain limitations, States determine the amount and duration of services offered under their Medicaid programs. States may limit, for example, the number of days of hospital care or the number of physician visits covered. Two restrictions apply: (1) limits must result in a sufficient level of services to reasonably achieve the purpose of the benefits; and (2) limits on benefits may not discriminate among beneficiaries based on medical diagnosis or condition.

In general, States are required to provide comparable amounts, duration, and scope of services to all categorically needy and categorically related eligible persons. There are two important exceptions:

(1) Medically necessary health care services that are identified under the EPSDT program for eligible children, and that are within the scope of mandatory or optional services under Federal law, must be covered even if those services are not included as part of the covered services in that State's Plan; and

(2) States may request "waivers" to pay for otherwise uncovered home and community-based services (HCBS) for Medicaid-eligible persons who might otherwise be institutionalized. As long as the services are cost effective, States have few limitations on the services that may be covered under these waivers (except that, other than as a part of respite care, States may not provide room and board for the beneficiaries). With certain exceptions, a State's Medicaid program must allow beneficiaries to have some informed choices among participating providers of health care and to receive quality care that is appropriate and timely.

Payment for Medicaid Services

Medicaid operates as a vendor payment program. States may pay health care providers directly on a fee-for-service basis, or States may pay for Medicaid services through various prepayment arrangements, such as health maintenance organizations (HMOs). Within federally imposed upper limits and specific restrictions, each State for the most part has broad discretion in determining the payment methodology and payment rate for services. Generally, payment rates must be sufficient to enlist enough providers so that covered services are available at least to the extent that comparable care and services are available to the general population within that geographic

Chapter 4: Brief Summaries of Medicare and Medicaid

area. Providers participating in Medicaid must accept Medicaid payment rates as payment in full. States must make additional payments to qualified hospitals that provide inpatient services to a disproportionate number of Medicaid beneficiaries and/or to other low-income or uninsured persons under what is known as the "disproportionate share hospital" (DSH) adjustment. During 1988-1991, excessive and inappropriate use of the DSH adjustment resulted in rapidly increasing Federal expenditures for Medicaid. Legislation that was passed in 1991 and 1993, and again within the BBA of 1997, capped the Federal share of payments to DSH hospitals. However, the Medicare, Medicaid, and SCHIP Benefits Improvement and Protection Act (BIPA) of 2000 (Public Law 106-554) increased DSH allotments for 2001 and 2002 and made other changes to DSH provisions that resulted in increased costs to the Medicaid program.

States may impose nominal deductibles, coinsurance, or copayments on some Medicaid beneficiaries for certain services. The following Medicaid beneficiaries, however, must be excluded from cost sharing: pregnant women, children under age 18, and hospital or nursing home patients who are expected to contribute most of their income to institutional care. In addition, all Medicaid beneficiaries must be exempt from copayments for emergency services and family planning services. Under the DRA, new cost sharing and benefit rules provide States the option of imposing new premiums and increased cost sharing on all Medicaid beneficiaries except for those mentioned above and for terminally ill patients in hospice care. The DRA also established special rules for cost sharing for prescription drugs and for non-emergency services furnished in emergency rooms.

The Federal government pays a share of the medical assistance expenditures under each State's Medicaid program. That share, known as the Federal Medical Assistance Percentage (FMAP), is determined annually by a formula that compares the State's average per capita income level with the national income average. States with a higher per capita income level are reimbursed a smaller share of their costs. By law, the FMAP cannot be lower than 50% or higher than 83%. In fiscal year (FY) 2007, the FMAPs varied from 50% in twelve States to 75.89% in Mississippi, and averaged 56.8% overall. The BBA permanently raised the FMAP for the District of Columbia from 50% to 70%. For children covered through the SCHIP program, the Federal government pays States a higher share, or "enhanced" FMAP, which averages about 70% for all States.

The Federal government also reimburses States for 100% of the cost of services provided through facilities of the Indian Health Service, for 100% of the cost of the Qualifying Individuals (QI) program (described later), and for 90% of the cost of family planning services, and shares in each State's expenditures for the administration of the Medicaid program. Most administrative costs are matched at 50%, although higher percentages are paid for certain activities and functions, such as development of mechanized claims processing systems.

Except for the SCHIP program, the QI program, and DSH payments, Federal payments to States for medical assistance have no set limit (cap). Rather, the Federal government matches (at FMAP rates) State expenditures for the mandatory services, as well as for the optional services that the individual State decides to cover for eligible beneficiaries, and matches (at the appropriate administrative rate) all necessary and proper administrative costs.

Chapter 4: Brief Summaries of Medicare and Medicaid

Medicaid Summary and Trends

Medicaid was initially formulated as a medical care extension of federally funded programs providing cash income assistance for the poor, with an emphasis on dependent children and their mothers, the disabled, and the elderly. Over the years, however, Medicaid eligibility has been incrementally expanded beyond its original ties with eligibility for cash programs. Legislation in the late 1980s assured Medicaid coverage to an expanded number of low-income pregnant women and poor children and to some Medicare beneficiaries who are not eligible for any cash assistance program. Legislative changes also focused on increased access, better quality of care, specific benefits, enhanced outreach programs, and fewer limits on services.

In most years since its inception, Medicaid has had very rapid growth in expenditures. This rapid growth has been due primarily to the following factors:

- The increase in size of the Medicaid-covered populations as a result of Federal mandates, population growth, and economic recessions.

- The expanded coverage and utilization of services.

- The DSH payment program, coupled with its inappropriate use to increase Federal payments to States.

- The increase in the number of very old and disabled persons requiring extensive acute and/or long-term health care and various related services.

- The results of technological advances to keep a greater number of very low-birth-weight babies and other critically ill or severely injured persons alive and in need of continued extensive and very costly care.

- The increase in drug costs and the availability of new expensive drugs.

- The increase in payment rates to providers of health care services, when compared to general inflation.

As with all health insurance programs, most Medicaid beneficiaries incur relatively small average expenditures per person each year, and a relatively small proportion incurs very large costs. Moreover, the average cost varies substantially by type of beneficiary. National data for 2004, for example, indicate that Medicaid payments for services for 28.6 million children, who constituted 52% of all Medicaid beneficiaries, averaged about $1,615 per child (a relatively small average expenditure per person). Similarly, for 13.5 million adults, who comprised 24% of beneficiaries, payments averaged about $2,400 per person. However, certain other specific groups had much larger per-person expenditures. Medicaid payments for services for

Chapter 4: Brief Summaries of Medicare and Medicaid

4.7 million aged, who constituted 8% of all Medicaid beneficiaries, averaged about $13,295 per person; for 8.8 million disabled, who comprised 16% of beneficiaries, payments averaged about $13,320 per person. When expenditures for these high- and lower-cost beneficiaries are combined, the 2004 payments to health care vendors for 55.6 million Medicaid beneficiaries averaged $4,640 per person.

Long-term care is an important provision of Medicaid that will be increasingly utilized as our nation's population ages. The Medicaid program paid for over 41% of the total cost of care for persons using nursing facility or home health services in 2004. National data for 2004 show that Medicaid payments for nursing facility services (excluding ICFs/MR) totaled $42.1 billion for more than 1.7 million beneficiaries of these services—an average expenditure of $24,475 per nursing home beneficiary. The national data also show that Medicaid payments for home health services totaled $4.6 billion for 1.1 million beneficiaries—an average expenditure of $3,975 per home health care beneficiary. With the percentage of our population who are elderly or disabled increasing faster than that of the younger groups, the need for long-term care is expected to increase.

Another significant development in Medicaid is the growth in managed care as an alternative service delivery concept different from the traditional fee-for-service system. Under managed care systems, HMOs, prepaid health plans (PHPs), or comparable entities agree to provide a specific set of services to Medicaid enrollees, usually in return for a predetermined periodic payment per enrollee. Managed care programs seek to enhance access to quality care in a cost-effective manner. Waivers may provide the States with greater flexibility in the design and implementation of their Medicaid managed care programs. Waiver authority under sections 1915(b) and 1115 of the Social Security Act is an important part of the Medicaid program. Section 1915(b) waivers allow States to develop innovative health care delivery or reimbursement systems. Section 1115 waivers allow statewide health care reform experimental demonstrations to cover uninsured populations and to test new delivery systems without increasing costs. Finally, the BBA provided States a new option to use managed care without a waiver. The number of Medicaid beneficiaries enrolled in some form of managed care program is growing rapidly, from 48% of enrollees in 1997 to 65% in 2006.

More than 55.6 million persons received health care services through the Medicaid program in FY 2004 (the last year for which beneficiary data are available). In FY 2006, total outlays for the Medicaid program (Federal and State) were $319.6 billion, including direct payment to providers of $219.2 billion, payments for various premiums (for HMOs, Medicare, etc.) of $65.9 billion, payments to disproportionate share hospitals of $13.7 billion, administrative costs of $19.1 billion, and $1.8 billion for the Vaccines for Children Program. Outlays under the SCHIP program in FY 2006 were $7.9 billion. With no changes to either program, expenditures under Medicaid and SCHIP are projected to reach $478.0 billion and $7.5 billion, respectively, by FY 2012.

Chapter 4: Brief Summaries of Medicare and Medicaid

The Medicaid-Medicare Relationship

Medicare beneficiaries who have low incomes and limited resources may also receive help from the Medicaid program. For such persons who are eligible for full Medicaid coverage, the Medicare health care coverage is supplemented by services that are available under their State's Medicaid program, according to eligibility category. These additional services may include, for example, nursing facility care beyond the 100-day limit covered by Medicare, prescription drugs, eyeglasses, and hearing aids. For persons enrolled in both programs, any services that are covered by Medicare are paid for by the Medicare program before any payments are made by the Medicaid program, since Medicaid is always the "payer of last resort."

Certain other Medicare beneficiaries may receive help with Medicare premium and cost-sharing payments through their State Medicaid program. Qualified Medicare Beneficiaries (QMBs) and Specified Low Income Medicare Beneficiaries (SLMBs) are the best-known categories and the largest in numbers. QMBs are those Medicare beneficiaries who have financial resources at or below twice the standard allowed under the SSI program, and incomes at or below 100% of the FPL. For QMBs, Medicaid pays the Hospital Insurance (HI, or Part A) and Supplementary Medical Insurance (SMI) Part B premiums and the Medicare coinsurance and deductibles, subject to limits that States may impose on payment rates. SLMBs are Medicare beneficiaries with resources like the QMBs, but with incomes that are higher, though still less than 120% of the FPL. For SLMBs, the Medicaid program pays only the Part B premiums. A third category of Medicare beneficiaries who may receive help consists of disabledand-working individuals. According to the Medicare law, disabled-and-working individuals who previously qualified for Medicare because of disability, but who lost entitlement because of their return to work (despite the disability), are allowed to purchase Medicare Part A and Part B coverage. If these persons have incomes below 200% of the FPL but do not meet any other Medicaid assistance category, they may qualify to have Medicaid pay their Part A premiums as Qualified Disabled and Working Individuals (QDWIs).

For Medicare beneficiaries with incomes above 120% and less than 135% of the FPL, States receive a capped allotment of Federal funds for payment of Medicare Part B premiums. These beneficiaries are known as Qualifying Individuals (QIs). Unlike the QMBs and SLMBs, who may be eligible for other Medicaid benefits in addition to their QMB/SLMB benefits, the QIs cannot be otherwise eligible for medical assistance under a State plan. The QI benefit is 100% federally funded, up to the State's allotment. The QI program was established by the BBA for FY 1998 through FY 2002 and has been extended several times. The most recent extension expired at the end of FY 2007.

The Centers for Medicare & Medicaid Services (CMS) estimates that, in 2006, Medicaid provided some level of supplemental health coverage for about 8.0 million Medicare beneficiaries.

Starting January 2006, a new Medicare prescription drug benefit provides drug coverage for Medicare beneficiaries, including those who also receive coverage from Medicaid. In addition,

Chapter 4: Brief Summaries of Medicare and Medicaid

individuals eligible for both Medicare and Medicaid receive the low-income subsidy for the Medicare drug plan premium and assistance with cost sharing for prescriptions. Medicaid no longer provides drug benefits for Medicare beneficiaries.

Since the Medicare drug benefit and low-income subsidy replace a portion of State Medicaid expenditures for drugs, States will see a reduction in Medicaid expenditures. To offset this reduction, the Medicare Prescription Drug, Improvement, and Modernization Act of 2003 (Public Law 108-173) requires each State to make a monthly payment to Medicare representing a percentage of the projected reduction. For 2006 this payment was 90% of the projected 2006 reduction in State spending. After 2006 the percentage will decrease by 1-2/3% per year to 75% for 2014 and later.

Notes

National Health Expenditure (NHE) historical estimates and projections are from the National Health Statistics Group in the Office of the Actuary (OACT), the Centers for Medicare & Medicaid Services (CMS). Refer also to:

- "National Health Spending in 2005: The Slowdown Continues," by Aaron Catlin et al., *Health Affairs*, January/February 2007, Volume 26, Number 1, pages 142-153, http://www.healthaffairs.org/.

- "Health Spending Projections through 2016: Modest Changes Obscure Part D's Impact," by John Poisal et al., *Health Affairs*, Web Exclusive, February 21, 2007, pages w242–w253, http://content.healthaffairs.org/cgi/content/abstract/26/2/w242.

- "National Health Expenditure Data" http://www.cms.hhs.gov/NationalHealthExpendData/

Medicare enrollment data are based on estimates prepared for the 2007 annual report of the Medicare Board of Trustees to Congress (available on the Internet at www.cms.hhs.gov/ReportsTrustFunds/). Medicare benefits, administrative costs, and total disbursements for 2006 are actual amounts for the calendar year, as determined from financial statements provided by the Department of the Treasury and CMS.

Medicaid data are based on the projections of the Mid-Session Review of the President's Fiscal Year 2008 Budget and are consistent with data received from the States on the Forms CMS-2082, MSIS, CMS-37, and CMS-64.

Chapter 5

Valuation Standards

By Edward J. Dupke, CPA/ABV

Medical practice valuation, like most market segments in valuation, is impacted as to form and content by the valuation standards followed by the valuation practitioner.

The discussion of business valuation standards is distinguished from the concept of "Standard of Value." The standard of value for a given valuation could be fair market value, fair value—state courts, fair value—financial reporting, investment value, intrinsic value, book value, liquidation value or others. Discussion of these standards of value will be covered elsewhere in this book.

This chapter is devoted to the valuation standards prepared by and adopted by the American organizations that have issued standards. These organizations include the American Institute of Certified Public Accountants (AICPA), the Appraisal Foundation (AF), the American Society of Appraisers (ASA), and the National Association of Certified Valuation Analysts (NACVA). Omitted from this listing is the Institute of Business Appraisers (IBA) which has combined its future direction with NACVA.

Each of these organizations has addressed its standards to serve the needs of its members. For Example, the American Institute of Certified Public Accountants is an organization of CPAs. Its standards are written from the perspective of CPA practice.

The Appraisal Foundation has authored the Uniform Standards of Professional Appraisal Practice (USPAP) for the benefit of appraisers. This set of standards is the only set that is multi-disciplinary. There are 10 USPAP Standards. Standards 1 through 6 apply to real estate appraisers. Standards 7 and 8 apply to personal property (equipment) appraisers and Standards 9 and 10 apply to business valuation appraisers. Recently, the application of Standard 3 dealing with the review of the report of another appraiser was extended to cover business valuation and equipment valuation applications as well as real estate valuation.

The NACVA Standards are written to serve the needs of its members, most of whom are CPAs.

The ASA Standards are written to serve the needs of business valuation appraisers. ASA also requires that its members conform to USPAP.

The business valuation standards of each of these organizations are dynamic documents in that they are constantly being reevaluated and changed as the valuation profession changes. The practitioner should check with the respective organization to gather the most recent information and data related to the standards of a particular organization.

Chapter 5: Valuation Standards

Impact of the Daubert and Kuhmo Tire decisions

Those who choose to spend their professional life as expert witnesses in the litigation arena have been impacted by these two decisions of the US Supreme Court. From the early 1920's forward, expert testimony has been governed by the *Frye* test. These criteria resulted from the *Frye v. United States* case decided in 1923. The opinion of the *Frye* court stated that scientific expert testimony was admissible only if the scientific methodology on which it was based was generally accepted within the scientific community. This "generally accepted methodology" doctrine has governed expert testimony from the 1920's until the *Daubert* decision.

In the *Daubert v. Merrill Dow Pharmaceuticals* case, the issue centered around the scientific knowledge of the expert witnesses and their ability to assist the trier of fact in understanding the scientific nuances of the case. The *Daubert* court opined that the court had a "gate keeping" function. This function requires that the court first determine whether the witness qualifies as an expert in the stated field identified and second the court must make a determination whether the proposed testimony is, in fact, scientific knowledge that will assist the trier of fact to understand or decide a fact that is at issue. The *Daubert* court further suggested that there are four factors that must be considered in making the gate keeping decision. These factors are:

Whether the theory can be (or has been) tested.

Whether the theory or technique has been subjected to peer review or publication.

The theory's potential rate of error.

The theory's general acceptance in the scientific community, as described in *Frye*.

The *Daubert* court did not abandon the principles of *Frye*, but expanded them. The *Daubert* court further opined that the inquiry into whether expert testimony was reliable should be "flexible".

In the *Kuhmo Tire* case, the Supreme Court held that the "gate keeping" role it outlined in *Daubert* applied to all expert testimony, not just scientific testimony. The court gave a qualified "yes" to the four *Daubert* factors.

For business valuation experts, the documents that establish generally accepted valuation procedures that have been tested by the peer group are standards. The AICPA business valuation standards have undergone three exposures to the peer group including two public exposures. The USPAP standards have a public exposure each time the standards are to be changed. The ASA and NACVA all circulate their standards among the member group each time there is to be a significant change. Clearly, the standards of each of these organizations satisfy the *Daubert* test of peer review.

Chapter 5: Valuation Standards

In healthcare valuation, a further standard is implicit in expert testimony: an understanding of the specific regulatory factors affecting the underlying assumptions used in a valuation engagement.

AICPA Business Valuation Standard

The American Institute of Certified Public Accountants issued its Statement on Standards for Valuation Services No. 1, *Valuation of a Business, Business Ownership Interest, Security or Intangible Asset* in June, 2007 effective for engagements entered into after January 1, 2008. This is a principle based standard rather than a primer on how to do business valuation.

The standard endorses the concept that in performing the valuation, the valuation practitioner is to take into consideration information and data that was "known or knowable" as of the valuation date. It suggests that the practitioner is generally not to take into consideration information or data becoming "known or knowable" after the valuation date. The standard also endorses the concept that each business valuation report is restricted the client and to any others who may be identified in the report and the report is to be used only for the purpose specified in the report. It may not be used by the client for any other purpose and may not be used by others for any purpose.

The standard applies to all AICPA members and to all CPAs licensed to practice in states that have adopted the AICPA standards as part of their respective states' accountancy laws. All of the AICPA Ethics pronouncements apply to those who are bound by this standard.

The standard applies to all engagements to estimate value in which the valuation practitioner applies valuation approaches and methodology and exercises professional judgment in the process. There are a number of exceptions to the standard related directly to activity of CPAs on behalf of their clients. A key focus is the maintenance of the CPA's independence to perform an attest function.

The standard adheres to existing AICPA principles of ethics that document ethical conduct for all client engagements and further document when and how audit independence is impaired. For publicly traded companies, the Sarbanes Oxley legislation is controlling and forbids the CPA or the CPA firm from performing any valuation work on behalf of its audit clients. For closely held companies, the AICPA Ethics rules are slightly more flexible. Audit independence for closely held companies is impaired if the valuation performed by the individual CPA or the CPA firm is material to the financial statements undergoing an attest function. If the valuation is not material to the financial statements, there is no audit impairment.

The exceptions to the standard come generally under the headings of audit exception, members in industry exception, economic damages litigation exception, two tax exceptions and an exception when the valuation in question is provided to the valuation practitioner by the client or a third party. We will not discuss these in detail here as they are clearly explained in the standard.

Chapter 5: Valuation Standards

There is also a jurisdictional exception provided in this standard that if any part of this standard differs from published governmental, judicial, or accounting authority, or such authority specifies valuation development procedures or reporting procedures, then the valuation practitioner should follow the applicable published authority or stated procedures with respect to that part applicable to the valuation in which the practitioner is engaged. All other parts of the standard remain in effect. A classic example of the jurisdictional exception is the tax regulations on transfer pricing. These regulations specify exactly how the calculation of the transfer pricing adjustments are to be made and exactly how these calculations are to be reported in the tax return. These regulations super cede the business valuation standard for this type of calculation and are to be followed as prescribed in the regulations. In the healthcare area, the Stark regulations with respect to consideration of the market approach to valuation are another example of the Jurisdictional exception.

Editor's Note: When the standard of value is Fair Market Value, as it generally is for a healthcare transaction or valuation engagement, The Market Approach needs to be considered within the light of these definitions found in the Stark regulations.

> Fair market value means the value in arm's-length transactions consistent with general market value. 'General market value' means the price that an asset would bring as the result of bona fide bargaining between well-informed buyers and sellers who are not otherwise in a position to generate business for the other party; or the compensation that would be included in a service agreement as a result of bona fide bargaining between well-informed parties to the agreement who are not otherwise in a position to generate business for the other party, on the date of acquisition or at the time of the service agreement. Usually the fair market price is the price at which bona fide sales have been consummated for assets of like type, quality, and quantity in a particular market at the time of acquisition ... (420 CFR 411.351)
>
> Moreover, the definition of "fair market value" in the statute and regulation is qualified in ways that do not necessarily comport with the usage of the term in standard valuation techniques and methodologies. For example, the methodology must exclude valuations where the parties to the transactions are at arm's length but in a position to refer to one another." (69 Fed. Reg. 16053)

The jurisdictional exception should also be considered with respect to the types of normalization adjustments that are considered in the Income Approach, given the above statement that the well-informed buyers and sellers are not otherwise in a position "to generate business for the other party."

A simple example of this can be seen in a comparison of a generic commercial lease with a commercial lease subject to Stark. A Dunkin Donuts store located inside a Home Depot would expect to pay rent based upon the customer traffic in the Home Depot. Typical leases provide for a percentage of revenues in such a circumstance. In stark contrast (pun intended), a lease of space for an MRI and CT Scan Center in a medical office building occupied by neurologists and orthopedic surgeons could

Chapter 5: Valuation Standards

not consider the fact that those two medical specialties are the highest users of such testing. The lease would have to reflect only the real estate value, not the patient referrals from the physicians, and a percentage of revenue certainly could not be charged.

One additional exemption provided in the AICPA Business Valuation Standard is an exemption from the reporting section of the standard for litigation or for certain controversy proceedings. As such, a valuation performed for a matter before a court, an arbitrator, a mediator or other facilitator, or a matter in a governmental or administrative proceeding is exempt from the reporting provisions of the standard. The developmental provisions of the statement still apply.

There are two types of engagements permitted under the AICPA business valuation standard. These are the valuation engagement and the calculation engagement.

Under a valuation engagement, the valuation practitioner is free to apply any and all valuation approaches and methods deemed appropriate in the circumstances. This engagement is said to be unrestricted. The result of the engagement is expressed as a conclusion of value and may be either a single amount or a range.

Under a calculation engagement, the valuation practitioner and the client agree on the valuation approaches and methods and the extent of the procedures the practitioner will perform in the process of calculating the value of the subject interest. The result of the calculation engagement is expressed as a calculated value and may be either a single amount or a range. It is important to note that a calculation engagement does not include all of the procedures that would be required in a valuation engagement.

The developmental provisions of the Standard cover the three most common approaches to valuation, namely the income based approach, the asset based approach and the market based approach.

The reporting provisions of the standard permit flexibility in reporting. Under the valuation engagement, the provided written reports may either be a detailed report or a summary report. The detailed written report is structured to provide sufficient information to permit intended users to understand the data, the reasoning, and the analysis underlying the valuation practitioner's conclusion of value. The standard provides items that are to be included in the detailed report. A summary report is an abridged version of a detailed report. It is not intended to provide all of the detail but will still convey a description of the work done and the conclusions of value reached.

Under a calculation engagement, a calculation report is permitted. The calculation report is intended to convey an understanding of the approaches and methodology used in the calculation and to identify the calculated value.

Regardless of the type of engagement, each report is required to contain a valuation analyst's representation, a summary of assumptions and limiting conditions and a statement of qualifications of the valuation analyst.

Chapter 5: Valuation Standards

Oral reports are permitted for both valuation engagements and calculation engagements.

The AICPA business valuation standard also included 4 appendices. One appendix includes an illustrative list of Assumptions and Limiting Conditions, a second includes the International Glossary of Business Valuation Terms, a third includes a supplemental glossary of business valuation terms from the CPA's perspective and the fourth appendix includes Interpretation No. 1-01 which contains questions and answers related to practice issues dealing with the Standard. The Interpretation carries the same force and effect as the Standard and has sections related to General areas of practice, tax engagements, personal financial planning engagements and other engagements.

The Valuation Standards subcommittee of the AICPA Business Valuation committee monitors the standard and from time to time issues updates and questions and answers related to the standard and practice under the standard. The standard can be downloaded from the AICPA Web Site at aicpa.org.

In a memorandum released May 13, 2008, the AICPA Valuation Standards subcommittee ruled that SSVS do not apply to the following valuation engagements:

- Professional/Executive Compensation

- Rental rate on equipment or real estate

- Contractual price for professional or other services

- Transfer price for goods and services between a for profit entity and a not for profit entity

The subcommittee made this decision on the basis that the above were not intangible assets. It is important to point out that a valuation analyst could be engaged to value a specific Intangible Asset such as an Employment Contract or an Equipment Lease as opposed to expressing an opinion on the market value of services and/or goods. Such valuation of intangible assets would be subject to SSVS.

USPAP Standards

The Uniform Standards of Professional Appraisal Practice (USPAP) are a product of the Appraisal Standards Board of the Appraisal Foundation. The Appraisal Foundation was formed as part of the FIRREA Act in the late 1980's. It was part of Congress' response to the Savings & Loan crisis of the 1980's.

The Appraisal Foundation has a central Board and two standing Boards, the Appraiser Qualifications Board and the Appraisal Standards Board. The Appraiser Qualifications Board

Chapter 5: Valuation Standards

was primarily responsible for authoring the regulations used by the states in the early 1990's in the process of registering real estate appraisers.

The Appraisal Standards Board is primarily responsible for publishing the Uniform Standards of Professional Appraisal Practice (USPAP) and for providing periodic updates to these standards.

There are 10 USPAP Standards and a number of published advisory opinions. Of the 10 original Standards, Standards number 1 – 6 relate to real estate appraisal, Standards number 7 – 8 relate to development and reporting of a personal property appraisal and standards number 9 – 10 relate to development and reporting of a business valuation. In recent years, the application of Standard 3, Appraisal Review development and reporting, has been extended beyond real estate appraisal to personal property appraising and to business valuation. Standard 3 contains the work to be done in evaluating the work and the report of another appraiser and issuing a report thereon.

Of the USPAP standards, standard 9 deals with the development of a business appraisal and standard 10 deals with reporting the result of the business appraisal. Within each standard, USPAP utilizes what it terms "Rules" to expand on the standard itself. For example, in Standard 9, the standard proper states:

> In developing an appraisal of an interest in a business enterprise or intangible asset, an appraiser must identify the problem to be solved, determine the scope of work necessary to solve the problem, and correctly complete the research and analysis necessary to produce a credible appraisal.

This generic statement is followed by "rules" that provide the specifics. The rules, for example, require that the appraiser "be aware of, understand, and correctly employ those recognized approaches, methods and procedures that are necessary to produce a credible appraisal; not commit a substantial error of omission or commission that significantly affects an appraisal; and not render appraisal services in a careless or negligent manner, such as by making a series of errors that, although individually might not significantly affect the results of an appraisal, in the aggregate affect the credibility of those results."

Like the AICPA standards, the USPAP standards identify the intended user and the intended use of the appraisal and determine the scope of the work necessary to produce a credible appraisal and then requires the appraiser to perform the appraisal in conformity with the scope of work so determined.

Chapter 10 covers business appraisal reporting. Again, the standard begins with a generic paragraph describing what needs to be done:

> In reporting the results of an appraisal of an interest in a business enterprise or intangible asset, an appraiser must communicate each analysis, opinion, and conclusion in a manner that is not misleading.

Chapter 5: Valuation Standards

The generic standard is followed by "rules" that provide the detail related to the standard. These rules provide for a written or oral report that must: "clearly and accurately set forth the appraisal in a manner that is not misleading; contain sufficient information to enable the intended user(s) to understand the report; and clearly and accurately disclose all assumptions, extraordinary assumptions, hypothetical conditions, and limiting conditions used in the assignment." Other rules discuss the content to be included in the appraisal report and the limitations on its use.

Editor's Note: The aforementioned Stark restrictions on the market approach often make it inapplicable. Standards Rule 10-2 requires that any exclusion of an approach be explained.

Standard 3 covers "Appraisal Review, development and reporting." The generic description used in Standard 3 is:

> In performing an appraisal review assignment, an appraiser acting as a reviewer must develop and report a credible opinion as to the quality of another appraiser's work and must clearly disclose the scope of the work performed.

The rules for Standard 3 provide the detail procedures for performing and reporting a review of another appraiser's work.

In addition to the respective rules for each standard, the Appraiser Standards Board of the Appraisal Foundation from time to time issues Advisory Opinions. These advisory opinions do not establish new standards or interpret standards. They illustrate specific situations and offer advice from the Appraisal Standards Board.

The USPAP standards are the only American standards that cover multiple disciplines. They contain standards for real estate appraising, personal property appraising and business valuation. One of the criticisms leveled at these standards is that they are multidisciplinary and so real estate and personal property appraisers who are members of the Appraisal Standards Board are voting and deciding on standards for appraising that is not in their area of expertise (business valuation for example). The USPAP standards must be followed when preparing appraisal reports for certain governmental agencies who have adopted USPAP. The Internal Revenue Service is not an agency that has adopted USPAP. The American Society of Appraisers (ASA) is the only business valuation credentialing organization whose members are required to follow USPAP.

American Society of Appraisers Business Valuation Standards

The American Society of Appraisers business valuation standards are prepared by the business valuation standards committee of the ASA. The chairmanship of this committee moves on a two year rotating basis. Although the ASA is a multidisciplinary organization, the business valuation standards are prepared by business valuation practitioners. This differs from USPAP where

Chapter 5: Valuation Standards

preparation of the standards is the responsibility of the Appraisal Standards Board. Members of this board may be from any of the three appraisal disciplines and may vote on the standards designed for any of the other disciplines.

There are eight sections to the Introduction to the ASA business valuation standards. These include:

Section 1 – Introduction

1. Describes ASA as a multidisciplinary organization

2. Defines Appraisal practice and Property

    i. Appraisal practice applies to any of the following four items:

    - "Determination of the value of property;

    - Forecasting of the earning power of property;

    - Estimation of the Cost of:

        - Production of a new property;

        - Replacement of an existing property by purchase or production of an equivalent property;

        - Reproduction of an existing property by purchase or production of an identical property.

        - Determining non-monetary benefits or characteristics that contribute to value."

    ii. The term Property is used to describe the rights to the future benefits of something owned or possessed to the exclusion of others.

3. Notes that the Principles of Appraisal Practice and the Code of Ethics are promulgated to:

    i. Inform those who use the services of appraisers what, in the opinion of the ASA, constitutes competent and ethical appraisal practice.

    ii. Serve as a guide to ASA members in achieving competency and adhering to ethical standards.

    iii. To aid in accomplishing the purposes of the ASA which include:

Chapter 5: Valuation Standards

- Fosterage of appraisal education

- Improvement and development of appraisal techniques.

- Encouragement of sound professional practices.

- Establishment of criteria of sound performance for use of employers of staff appraisers.

- Epitomize those appraisal practices that experience has found to be effective in protecting the public against exploitation.

Section 2 of the introduction describes the objectives of appraisal work, including:

1. The various kinds of objectives of Appraisal work

2. The objective character of the results of an appraisal engagement.

Section 2 focuses on the objectivity required of the appraiser and of the final result.

Section 3 of the introduction details the appraiser's primary duties and responsibilities generally. These include:

1. The Appraiser's obligation to determine and to describe the Apposite Kind of Value or Estimated Cost.

2. The Appraiser's obligation to determine numerical results with whatever degree of accuracy the particular objectives of the engagement necessitate.

3. The Appraiser's obligation to avoid giving a false numerical result.

4. The Appraiser's obligation to attain competency and to practice ethically.

5. The professional character of appraisal practice.

6. The Appraiser's fiduciary relationship to third parties.

Section 4 of the introduction section restates the appraiser's obligations to his/her client. These include:

1. The confidential character of an appraisal engagement.

2. The appraiser's obligation to provide competent service.

Chapter 5: Valuation Standards

3. The appraiser's obligation relative to giving testimony.

4. The appraiser's obligation to document appraisal testimony.

5. Clarification of the appraiser's obligation to serving more than one client in the same matter.

6. Discussion of a written contract for appraisal services.

Section 5 of the introduction covers the appraiser's obligation to other appraisers and to the American Society of Appraisers. These include:

1. Protecting the professional reputation of other appraisers.

2. The appraiser's obligation relative to the ASA's disciplinary actions.

Section 6 discusses various appraisal practices and methods including:

1. Various kinds of value

2. Selection of the appraisal method

3. Fractional appraisals

4. Contingent and limiting conditions affecting an appraisal

5. Hypothetical Appraisals

6. Appraisals in which access to pertinent data is denied

7. Ranges of value or estimated cost and reliability estimates

8. Values or estimated costs under different hypotheses

9. Inspection, Investigation, analysis, and description of the subject property

10. Collaboration between appraisers and utilization of the services of members of other professions

Section 7 discusses unethical and unprofessional appraisal practices including:

1. Contingent fees deemed to be unethical

2. Percentage fees based on the amount of the value

Chapter 5: Valuation Standards

3. Disinterested appraisal – the appraiser has no vested interest

4. Responsibility connected with signatures to appraisal reports

5. Non-advocacy

6. Unconsidered opinions and preliminary reports

7. Advertising and solicitation

8. Misuse of membership designations

9. Causes for disciplinary action by the ASA

Section 8 discusses the items to be included in a quality appraisal report including:

1. Description of the property which is the subject of an appraisal report

2. Statement of the objectives of the Appraisal work

3. Statement of the contingent and limiting conditions to which the appraisal finding are subject

4. Description and explanation of the appraisal method used

5. Statement of the appraiser's disinterestedness

6. Appraiser's responsibility to communicate each analysis, opinion and conclusion in a manner that is not misleading

7. Mandatory recertification statement

8. Signatures to appraisal reports and the inclusion of dissenting opinions.

In the general preamble to the Standards, the ASA business valuation standards take the following action:

1. The principles of Appraisal Practice and the Code of Ethics of the ASA and the USPAP standards are incorporated by reference

2. There is an affirmative statement that these standards represent the minimum criteria to be followed by business appraisers in developing and reporting the valuation of a business, business ownership interest and securities.

3. Deviation from the standard should not create any assumption that a legal duty has been breached.

Having put all of this information on the record, the ASA moves to the eight BVS Standards which include:

- BVS I – General requirements for developing a business valuation

  1. Preamble

  2. Appropriate definition of the assignment

  3. Information collection and analysis

  4. Approaches, methods and procedures

  5. Documentation and retention

  6. Reporting

BVS I describes the general requirements for developing a business valuation and includes the items the appraiser must identify and define, the scope of the work, and the types of appraisals that are available under the ASA standards. These would include the appraisal, the limited appraisal and calculations. The information collection and analysis section generally follows the guidelines in Revenue Ruling 59-60.

- BVS II – Financial Statement Adjustments

  1. Preamble

  2. Conceptual framework

  3. Documentation of adjustments

BVS II describes the potential adjustments to the financial statements. It defines the adjustments as modifications to the financial information that are relevant and significant to the appraisal process. The standard notes that all adjustments should be fully described and supported.

- BVS III – Asset-Based Approach to Business Valuation

  1. Preamble

  2. The asset-based approach

Chapter 5: Valuation Standards

BVS III generally describes the asset approach to business valuation as the value of the assets less the value of the liabilities. The standard makes the affirmative statement that the asset-based approach should not be the sole appraisal approach for an operating company unless this approach is customarily used by buyers and sellers.

- BVS IV – Income Approach to Business Valuation

1. Preamble

2. The income approach

3. Anticipated benefits

4. Conversion of anticipated benefits

BVS IV generally describes the income approach to business valuation. It notes that both the capitalization of benefits and the discounted future benefits methods are acceptable. It describes the process of converting a stream of anticipated benefits to value.

- BVS V – Market Approach to Business Valuation

1. Preamble

2. The market approach

3. Reasonable basis for comparison

4. Selection of valuation ratios

5. Rules of thumb

BVS V generally describes the market approach to business valuation. It notes that this method includes both the guideline public company method and the analysis of prior transactions in the ownership of the subject company method. It emphasizes that the valuation ratios should be meaningful given all of the relevant factors.

- BVS VI – Reaching a Conclusion of Value

1. Preamble

2. General

3. Selection and weighting of methods

Chapter 5: Valuation Standards

4. Additional factors to consider

BVS VI describes the process the appraiser should use in determining a conclusion of value following completion of the appraisal work. The selection and reliance on the methods used will depend on the facts and circumstances of the case. The appraiser will use informed judgment to determine the relative weight to be accorded to each valuation method used.

- BVS VII – Valuation Discounts and Premiums

1. Preamble

2. The concepts of discounts and premiums

3. The application of discounts and premiums

BVS VII covers modification of the computed appraised value through the use of discounts or premiums as appropriate. It attaches significant importance to the conceptual basis underlying the application of a discount or premium. It emphasizes that discounts and premiums come into play when there is a difference between the base value and value of the subject interest. When discounts and premiums are appropriate, the rationale accompanying them should be thoroughly explained.

- BVS VIII – Comprehensive Written Business Valuation Reports

1. Preamble

2. Signature and certification

3. Assumptions and limiting conditions

4. Definition of the valuation assignment

5. Business description

6. Financial analysis

7. Valuation methodology

8. Comprehensive written business valuation report format

9. Confidentiality of the report

BVS VIII covers the written business valuation report. Similar to USPAP and the AICPA business valuation standards, it requires that the report contain the listing of assumptions and limiting conditions and that the certification (representation in the AICPA standards) be signed by at least one individual responsible for the valuation conclusion. The standard goes on to describe generally the items to be included in the written report including items 4 through 8 above. It concludes with a comment on the confidentiality of the report which is similar to the restricted use provisions of the AICPA and USPAP standards.

- BVS IX – Intangible Asset Valuation

  1. Preamble

  2. Principles

  3. Valuation methodology

  4. Factors

BVS IX covers the methodology to be followed in all valuations of intangible assets by ASA members. "This standard applies to appraisals and may not necessarily apply to limited appraisals and calculations as defined in BVS-1 ...." The Standard describes the valuation approaches that should be considered in valuing intangible assets including the Income approach, the Market Approach and the Cost Approach. It also defines certain factors that the appraiser should consider in the valuation of an intangible asset.

Appendix A to BVS-IX provides definitions and examples of intellectual property including Patents, Trade Secrets, Trademarks and Copyrighted Works. It also provides additional factors the appraiser should consider with each category of intellectual property.

The nine Standards are followed and embellished by a glossary and two Statements on Business Valuation Standards; one on the Guideline Company Valuation Method and one on the Merger and Acquisition market method. These two statements have the full effect of standards.

Lastly, the ASA standards have advisory opinions and procedural guidelines that supplement the information contained in the standards.

National Association of Certified Valuation Analysts

The National Association of Certified Valuation Analysts is an organization of Certified Public Accountants and other valuation professionals who perform valuation services. It is based in Salt Lake City, Utah and provides business valuation and consulting technical education to its membership. Because many of its members are CPAs, the business valuation standards committee of NACVA conformed its standards to the AICPA Standards when the AICPA standards became effective. Although structured in a slightly different manner, the underlying principles and their impact on valuation practitioners is very similar to that of the AICPA Standards.

Chapter 5: Valuation Standards

The NACVA Standards consist of 6 standard sections and an appendix. The appendix contains the International Glossary of Business Valuation Terms which was a collaborative effort among a number of business valuation credentialing organizations including the American Institute of CPAs (AICPA), the American Society of Appraisers (ASA), the National Association of Certified Valuation Analysts (NACVA), the Institute of Business Appraisers (IBA) and the Canadian Institute of Chartered Business Valuators (CICBV).

Section 1 – Preamble and General and Ethical Standards

1. Preamble – All members shall comply with these standards.

2. General and ethical standards – Members shall perform their work in compliance with the code of professional conduct which includes:

    i. Integrity and Objectivity

    ii. Professional competence

    iii. Due professional care

    iv. Understandings and communications with Clients

    v. Planning and supervision

    vi. Sufficient relevant data

    vii. Confidentiality

    viii. No commission of acts discreditable to the profession

    ix. Client Interest

    x. Financial interest in the property being valued (if any)

Section one is the overview section and identifies the general and ethical standards that NACVA members are required to observe.

Section 2 – Member Services

1. Valuation services

    i. Valuation engagement

    ii. Calculation engagement

2. Other services

Chapter 5: Valuation Standards

Section two describes the two types of valuation services that a NACVA member may perform; a valuation engagement and a calculation engagement. It further describes that a member may perform other services including consulting, fraud and damage determinations and other non-valuation services.

Section 3 – Development Standards

1. General

2. Expression of value

3. Identification of the assignment and the scope of the work

4. Fundamental analysis

5. Scope limitations

6. Use of Specialist

7. Valuation approaches and methods

8. Rules of thumb

9. Financial statement adjustments

10. Earnings determination

11. Capitalization/Discount rate

12. Marketability, control, and other premiums and discounts

13. Documentation

Section three presents the development standards and represents the key developmental elements. Similar to the AICPA standards, the NACVA standards indicate that the value may be represented as a single value or as a range of values.

Section 4 – Reporting Standards

1. General

2. Form of report

Chapter 5: Valuation Standards

   3. Contents of report

      i. Summary reports

      ii. Detailed reports

      iii. Calculation reports

      iv. Statement that the report is in conformity with NACVA standards

   4. Litigation engagement reporting standards

Section four describes the reporting standard. It specifies that the report may be written or oral and should be appropriate for the circumstances of the engagement. The standard suggests that the wording used in the report should effectively communicate important thoughts, methods and reasoning, and identify supporting documentation in a simple and concise manner. This section provides an exemption from the reporting portion of the standard for certain controversy proceedings including matters before a court, an arbitrator, a mediator or other facilitator, or a matter in a governmental or administrative proceeding.

Section 5 – Other Guidelines and Requirements

   1. Other organizations whose guidelines may require compliance

      i. Department of Labor (DOL)

      ii. Internal Revenue Service (IRS)

      iii. Applicable Court Rules

      iv. Federal and State Laws

      v. The Appraisal Foundation (USPAP)

      vi. Financial Accounting Standards Board (FASB)

   2. International Glossary of business valuation terms

Section five alerts the NACVA member to other organizations whose rules and regulations may require compliance depending upon the nature of the assignment.

Chapter 5: Valuation Standards

Section 6 – Effective Date

1. Effective Date

Section 6 indicates that these standards are effective for engagements accepted on or after January 1, 2008.

Conclusion

While each of these standards contains certain idiosyncrasies, the differences relate primarily to the differing membership to whom they are addressed. For example, the AICPA standards are directed toward CPAs. Many of the NACVA members are also CPAs and both of these standards are written with language and understanding common to CPAs. The business valuation section of USPAP and the ASA business valuation standards are written within the context of an appraiser. The language and the references are directed in that manner.

Overall, there may be differences in terminology, but the thrust of each of these standards is clear. They are directed toward assisting the members of each of the respective organizations in performing a credible business valuation and accurately reporting the results of their work to clients and to other appropriate parties.

Chapter 6

Overview of Cost of Capital Models

By James Harrington, MBA
Copyright, 2008 by Morningstar, Inc. Reprinted with permission.

Introduction

Valuation

Valuation is the act of placing a value or worth on an asset.[1] An asset's value is, in its simplest form, the present value of the expected future benefits of the asset. To determine present value, analysts can develop a "cost of capital" to use as a rate in discounting expected (future) cash flows, or alternatively, can look at the values of similar entities and make an assumption that the value of the subject entity should be similar. In either case, the value arrived at is intended to be the present value of the future benefits of the investment.

In practice, analysts seek to determine the value of businesses based on earnings outlook, analysis of financial statements, comparisons to other similar entities, and a plethora of other economic variables. Public companies are typically easier to value because of the availability of data; however, the methodologies discussed here may be used to value private as well as public companies.

Cost of Capital

The cost of capital is the discount rate that should be used to derive the present value of an asset's future cash flows.[2] The cost of capital is also commonly referred to as the expected rate of return, required rate of return, or a hurdle rate. From the demand side, it is the rate an investor requires to justify investing; from a supply side, it is the rate a firm must offer to attract capital.

The cost of capital is used as a discount rate to determine the present value of expected future cash flows. It is an "opportunity cost"—the benefits of one investment foregone versus the benefits of another investment. For example, say you were presented with an investment that is expected to return a cash flow of $1.00 in one year's time, while alternative investments of similar risk are returning 15% annually. The present value of this investment is:

$$\$1.00 / (1+0.15) \approx \$0.87$$

To look at this from another angle, you could alternatively have invested ≈$0.87 *today* to receive $1.00 *in one year*:

Chapter 6: Overview of Cost of Capital Models

$$\$0.87 \times (1+0.15) \approx \$1.00$$

It is important to note that "the cost of capital is a function of the investment, not the investor."[3] For example, if two investors with different capabilities borrow money to purchase a business, this does not mean that the investor who can borrow at a lower rate of interest should use a lower discount rate in assessing the investment (or, conversely, that the investor who can only borrow at a higher rate of interest should use a higher discount rate in assessing the investment). The cost of capital is purely an *opportunity cost,* and is therefore a function of the "next best" investment alternative and is *not* a function of the capabilities or other characteristics of the investor.

Standard of Value

Although various standards of value may be used based upon the situation, "fair market value" is the most commonly used standard in business valuation. Fair market value is defined in IRS Ruling 59-60 as:

> ...the price at which the property would change hands between a willing buyer and a willing seller when the former is not under any compulsion to buy and the latter is not under any compulsion to sell, both parties having reasonable knowledge of relevant facts.

Ownership Interest

The analyst should identify whether a "minority" or a "controlling" interest is being valued, as the nature of the ownership interest will most likely have a bearing on overall value. For instance, a controlling interest usually entails control over both the equity and debt of the company, hiring and firing, the acquisition or disposition of assets, entry into or retreat from markets or business lines, and so on. A minority interest may have very little say in these types of management and policy decisions, and therefore may be less valuable than a controlling interest.

Valuation Date

IRS Ruling 59-60 states that valuation is a forward-looking process but must be based on facts available as of the required date of appraisal.[4] The logic embedded in Ruling 59-60 is based on the process by which the market values a business. First, the value of a business depends on expected *future* benefits, not benefits received in the past (although past benefits can be, and in most cases should be, used as a gauge of future benefits). Second, a company's value is reflective of the collective actions and perceptions of all market participants based upon the information known *at the time*. If information other than what was actually available at the time is used, a different value may be reached—potentially under- or overvaluing the business as of the valuation date.

Think about it this way: If the three bedroom houses on a particular street in 1990 sold for an average of $100,000 and three-bedroom houses on the same street are selling for an average of

Chapter 6: Overview of Cost of Capital Models

$200,000 in 2008, it wouldn't make much sense to try to argue in 2008 that the value of one of these houses "as of" 1990 is $200,000 because that's what they are trading for in 2008 (or vice-versa).

Commonly Used Approaches to Valuation

The three most common approaches to valuation, each having its own reasoning and instances of best practice, include: income-, market-, and asset-based approaches. This overview will primarily concentrate on cost of capital methods stemming from the development of discount rates used in an income-based approach, but an overview of all three approaches is included.

Income-Based Approach

The income-based approach projects a company's cash flows into the future, and then discounts these future expected cash flows by an appropriate cost of capital rate to determine the present value of the company. The discount rate—or cost of capital—should mirror the level of risk inherent in the cash flow being valued.[5]

In the field of business valuation, the appropriate cash flows used in the equation are the free cash flows generated by the entity that is being valued. Free cash flow represents a company's after-tax cash once adjustment is made for non-cash accounting entries and capital expenditures required to maintain the company as a going concern. As stated in the *2008 Ibbotson SBBI Valuation Yearbook*:

"Free cash flow represents the total amount of cash that can potentially flow to the shareholders and long-term interest bearing debt holders of the company; it is thus the free cash flow that drives the value for all equity and debt holders of the entity."[6]

Free cash flow can be determined by the following formulas[7]:

<u>Cash Flow Formula</u>
EBIT x (1-t)
+ Depreciation and Amortization
+ Deferred Taxes
− Capital Expenditures
<u>− Changes in Working Capital</u>
= Free Cash Flow

where:
t = tax rate

<u>Alternate Cash Flow Formula</u>
Net Income
+ Depreciation and Amortization
+ Deferred Taxes
− Capital Expenditures
− Changes in Working Capital
<u>+ Interest Expense x (1-t)</u>
= Free Cash Flow

Chapter 6: Overview of Cost of Capital Models

It is important to note that:

1) free cash flow is an *after-tax* concept,

2) pure accounting adjustments (depreciation, deferred taxes) must be added back, and

3) cash flows necessary to keep the company's operations going (capital expenditures, changes in working capital) must be subtracted.

Also note that we start with tax-adjusted EBIT because we want to focus on cash flows independent of capital structure. Alternatively, we tax-adjust interest expenses to take into account the effect of the tax shield on interest expense.

The two most commonly used methods for applying the income approach are the capitalization method and the discounted cash flow (DCF) model. The capitalization of earnings method may be used when a company's current operations are indicative of its future operations; the DCF method is used when a company's future operations are expected to be substantially different from current operations. A more detailed discussion of these concepts is found in the section on the discounted cash flow method of estimating cost of equity.

Market-Based Approach

The market-based approach to valuation uses transaction and/or financial data from comparable "guideline" companies to develop measures of value for a subject company. This data may include the prices at which similar businesses have been bought and sold, or the comparison of the stock price of a company to various accounting measures of fundamental data.

For example, if family medical practices of a certain size in a certain city at a certain time are trading at (sold or bought for) $1,000,000, one could argue that the value of a practice with the same characteristics could also be expected to have a value of around $1,000,000.

Alternatively, we could form a group of our subject company's peers and calculate an "industry average" of the relationship that equity price has with an accounting measure. A familiar valuation multiple is the price/earnings ratio, or P/E ratio. Say we determine that our subject company's peers have, on average, a price/earnings ratio of 20. We could argue that our subject company has a similar P/E ratio, and derive an equity price if we knew the subject company's earnings to be, say, $80,000:

$P/E_{\text{(Peer Group Average)}} = \$1,000,000/\$50,000 = 20$

$P/E_{\text{(Subject Company)}} \approx P/E_{\text{(Peer Group Average)}}$

$P/E_{\text{(Subject Company)}} = P_{\text{(Subject Company)}}/\$80,000 \approx 20$

$P_{\text{(Subject Company)}} \approx \$80,000 \times 20 \approx \$1,600,000$

Chapter 6: Overview of Cost of Capital Models

This is only one of many valuation multiples that can be used in a market-based approach to equity valuation; other ratios include price to sales, price to cash flow, and price to shareholders' equity. In cases where a market-based approach is used to determine the value of all invested capital (both debt and equity), commonly used multiples include market value of invested capital (MVIC) to sales, MVIC to earnings before interest and taxes (EBIT), or MVIC to earnings before interest, taxes, and depreciation and amortization (EBITDA).

Asset-Based Approach

The asset-based approach requires a comprehensive evaluation of a company's tangible and intangible assets and liabilities. This approach is typically used when valuing holding companies, family limited partnerships (FLPs), or entities in bankruptcy proceedings.

On the upside, the format of the asset-based approach to valuation is naturally adapted to a familiar "balance sheet" format, and is also conducive to identifying specific sources of value. On the downside, the asset-based approach is time-consuming and expensive, as this approach may require more involvement of the subject company's management team, may require the analyst to have extensive accounting knowledge, and may involve paying outside experts to value certain types of assets and liabilities that are outside the expertise of the analyst.

Estimating the Cost of Capital

As previously discussed, cost of capital is "the discount rate that should be used to derive the present value of an asset's future cash flows." Cost of capital is the expected or required return from an investment, an opportunity cost, or a "hurdle" rate. The cost of capital is a forward-looking concept. The *Ibbotson Stocks, Bonds, Bills, and Inflation (SBBI) Valuation Yearbook*[8] says it best in this regard:

"While the past performance of an investment and other historical information can be good guides and are often used to estimate the required rate of return on capital, the *expectations of future events are the only factors that actually determine the cost of capital.* An investor contributes capital to a firm with the expectation that the business's future performance will provide a fair return on the investment. If past performance were the criterion most important to investors, no one would invest in start-up ventures."[9] (emphasis added).

A confusion that sometimes arises among people just becoming familiar with cost of capital concepts is the difference between "cost of capital," "cost of equity," "cost of debt," and "weighted average cost of capital"— terms that at times are used interchangeably, and sometimes incorrectly. Cost of equity and cost of debt are specific types of cost of capital. Cost of debt is the return expected from investing in debt (lending), and cost of equity is the return expected from investing in equity (ownership). Weighted average cost of capital (WACC) is the weighted average of both cost of debt and cost of equity. WACC is the rate that is appropriately used

Chapter 6: Overview of Cost of Capital Models

when discounting free cash flow, as free cash flow represents the cash-flow stream from the entire entity. WACC can be represented by the following formula:

Equation 1

$$WACC = W_D k_D (1-t) + W_E k_E$$

Where:

- W_D = weight of debt in the capital structure;
- k_D = cost of debt capital;
- t = effective tax rate for the company;
- W_E = weight of equity in the capital structure; and
- k_E = cost of equity capital

The weights are calculated as follows:

Equation 2

$$W_D = \frac{D}{D+E} \quad W_E = \frac{E}{D+E}$$

Where:

- W_D = weight of debt in the capital structure;
- W_E = weight of equity in the capital structure;
- D = the market value of debt outstanding; and
- E = the market value of equity outstanding

Yield to maturity (or yield to call, when appropriate) on similar debt is the best approximation for the cost of debt. Unlike cost of equity, the cost of debt can be directly observed in the marketplace. For this reason, entire books are written about developing cost of equity, but not as much is written about developing the cost of debt. The rest of this chapter will focus on models that are commonly used to develop cost of equity.

Also, note that the cost of debt is multiplied by 1 minus the tax rate. Interest payments are generally an expense, and therefore not taxed. The cost of debt is thus adjusted downward by the tax rate to take into account this tax "shield" benefit. For example, say a company has a 35% tax rate and is paying $8 to service $100 in debt, (which implies a cost of debt of 8%). That $8 is deducted from net income as an expense, reducing taxes by $2.80, and effectively making our cost of debt 5.2% (8% x (1-0.35).

The following sections briefly discuss three popular models for estimating the cost of equity: the capital asset pricing model (CAPM), the buildup method, and the discounted cash flow model (DCF). Other models exist, but these three are among the most widely used.

Chapter 6: Overview of Cost of Capital Models

Capital Asset Pricing Model (CAPM)

The capital asset pricing model (CAPM) is a result of the work of Nobel Prize recipients Harry M. Markowitz, James Tobin, and William F. Sharpe, and has grown to become one of the most commonly utilized techniques to estimate cost of equity. The CAPM can be represented by the following formula:

Equation 3

$$k_s = r_f + (\beta_s \times ERP)$$

Where:
- k_s = the cost of equity for company **s**;
- r_f = the expected return of the riskless asset;
- β_s = the beta of the stock of company **s**; and
- ERP = the expected equity risk premium, or the amount by which investors expect the future return on equities to exceed that of the riskless asset.

Risk versus Return

The principal insight of the CAPM is that risk-taking is rewarded. The model assumes that there is a riskless rate of return that can be earned on a hypothetical investment with returns that do not vary.[10] All things held the same, an investor presented with two investments—one having absolute certainty of returns (returns that do not vary); the other having uncertainty of returns (returns that vary)—will prefer the former investment, which is riskless. What would entice our hypothetical investor to choose to invest in the second, riskier investment? More reward—a risk "premium," so to speak.

The CAPM distinguishes two types of risk (variability of returns): unsystematic risk and systematic risk. Unsystematic risk is company-specific risk (a strike of the company's employees, for instance). Unsystematic risk can be diversified away, and because it is avoidable under the assumptions of the CAPM, it is *not* rewarded. Systematic risk, on the other hand, pervades (to a greater or lesser degree) every asset (or claim on assets) in the economy. Systematic risk, also known as "market" risk, *cannot* be diversified away, and because it is unavoidable under the assumptions of the CAPM, it *is* rewarded proportionally, and in a linear fashion, to the amount of systematic risk taken.

This relationship between expected return and systematic risk can be represented graphically in the form of the security market line, as shown in graph.

Chapter 6: Overview of Cost of Capital Models

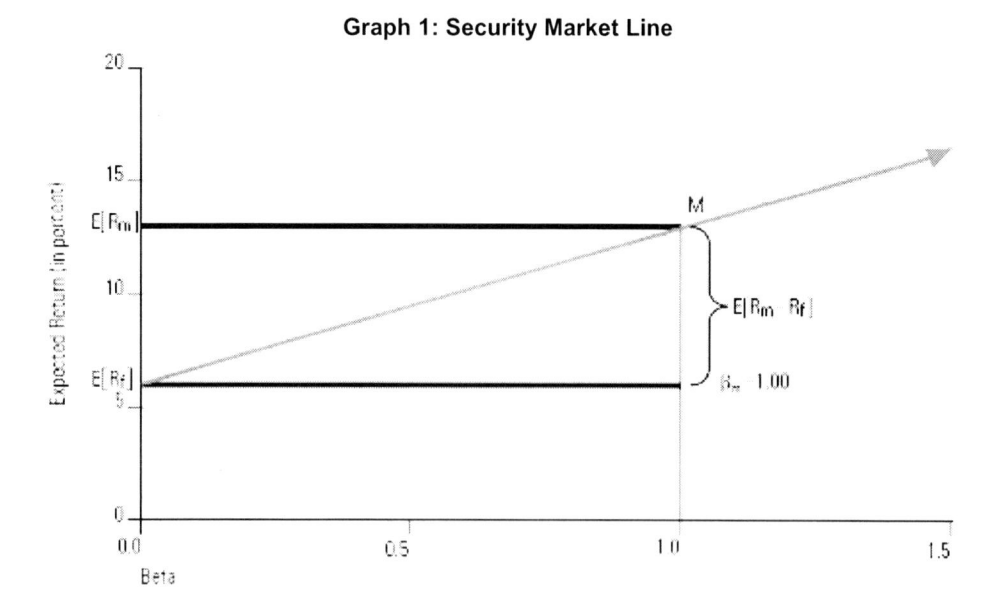

Graph 1: Security Market Line

There are only three variables needed in the CAPM equation—a risk-free rate, a beta (β), and an equity risk premium—making the CAPM easy to understand and easy to work with.

Risk-Free Rate

The risk-free rate is the return on a riskless investment; it is the rate of return an investor gets for investing in an asset for which there is no variability in returns (as measured by standard deviation). There is no uncertainty as to what the investor will get out of the investment as far as return is concerned. Typically, the yield on a U.S. government Treasury security is chosen as a proxy for the riskless asset because U.S. government obligations are virtually default free. The maturity of the chosen Treasury security should match the time frame of whatever is being valued. If a company is being valued under the assumption that it is a going concern, the risk-free asset should be a long-term Treasury, regardless of the investor's intended holding period. Remember: "The cost of capital is a function of the investment, not the investor." The standard that Ibbotson Associates uses for its long-term risk-free asset is a Treasury of approximately 20 years to maturity.

Equity Risk Premium (ERP)

The equity risk premium can be defined as the additional return an investor expects to receive to compensate for the additional risk associated with investing in equities as opposed to investing in riskless assets. It is an essential component in several cost of equity estimation models, including the buildup method, the capital asset pricing model (CAPM), and the Fama-French three-factor model (not discussed here). It is important to note that the expected equity risk premium, as it is used in discount rates and cost of capital analysis, is a forward-looking concept. That is, the equity risk premium that is used in the discount rate should be reflective of what investors think the risk premium will be going forward.[11]

Chapter 6: Overview of Cost of Capital Models

Ibbotson's long-term historical equity risk premium is based upon the historical differences of the returns of stocks and bonds, and is defined as large company stock total returns minus long-term government bond income returns. For example, in the *2008 Ibbotson SBBI Valuation Yearbook*, the historical long-horizon expected arithmetic equity risk premium was calculated (using annual returns) as the difference between the average annual U.S. large company stock total return over the 1926–2007 period (12.26 %) and the average annual U.S. long-term government bond income return over the 1926–2007 period (5.21 %), or 7.05 %.

It is important to note that the income return on the appropriate horizon Treasury security, rather than the total return, is used in the calculation of equity risk premia. Total return is comprised of three return components: income return, capital appreciation return, and reinvestment return. Bond prices generally change in reaction to unexpected fluctuations in yields, adding a degree of uncertainty (risk) to capital appreciation returns. Unexpected changes in yield also add a degree of uncertainty to the rate we will receive on reinvestment of income payments. Income return is thus used in the estimation of the equity risk premium because it represents the truly riskless portion of the return.

The original data source Ibbotson uses for the time series comprising the equity risk premium is the Center for Research in Security Prices (CRSP) at the University of Chicago. CRSP chose to begin its analysis of market returns with 1926 for two main reasons. CRSP determined that the time period around 1926 was approximately when quality financial data became available. It also made a conscious effort to include the period of extreme market volatility from the late twenties and early thirties; 1926 was chosen because it includes one full business cycle of data before the market crash of 1929. These are the two most basic reasons why our equity risk premium calculation window starts in 1926.

Choice of Market Benchmark

The market benchmark that is chosen can have significant impact on equity risk premia estimation. The market benchmark should be broad and varied enough to be representative of the market as a whole. For instance, the Dow Jones Industrial Average contains thirty securities and may not appropriately reflect a market of over 10,000 securities. In the Ibbotson SBBI Yearbook series, large stocks are represented by the Standard & Poor's 500, which is an unmanaged group of securities and considered to be representative of the stock market in general.

Arithmetic versus Geometric Returns

In general, arithmetic estimates are typically used in mean-variance analysis (or asset allocation) and business valuation practices, while geometric estimates are typically used to derive the median or the average accumulated wealth over a period of time in wealth forecasting or simulation.

For use as the expected equity risk premium in either the CAPM or the buildup method approach, the arithmetic mean or the simple difference of the arithmetic means of stock market

Chapter 6: Overview of Cost of Capital Models

returns and riskless rates is the relevant number. This is because both the CAPM and the buildup method approaches are additive models, in which the cost of capital is the sum of its parts. The geometric average, however, is more appropriate for reporting past performance, as it represents the compound average return. A basic rule of thumb, then, is: If you are describing past performance, use a geometric (compound) rate; if you are formulating a best guess as to future performance, use an arithmetic average.

Historical versus Supply-Side Equity Risk Premia (ERP) Models

In 2004, Ibbotson began publishing a long horizon equity risk premium estimate based on a "supply-side" model in the *Ibbotson SBBI Valuation Yearbook's* "Key Variables in Estimating the Cost of Capital" table. Supply-side models use fundamental information such as earnings, dividends, or overall economic productivity to estimate expected equity risk premia.

Diermeier, Ibbotson, and Siegel (1984) proposed a supply-side approach to link the return of aggregate financial assets to the overall growth of economic productivity. This early paper provides the foundation for the supply models later developed by Ibbotson and Chen (2003)[12], where a model was developed to estimate a forward-looking long-term equity risk premium using a combination of the historical and the supply-side approaches. In Ibbotson and Chen's 2003 study, the historical equity return was broken into four components, with only three historically being supplied by companies: inflation, income return, and the growth in real earnings per share. The fourth component, growth in the P/E ratio, is a reflection of investors' changing predictions of future earnings growth and their willingness to pay for these earnings. This model assumes that the growth in P/E ratio that is embedded in historical returns is not sustainable, so this component is subtracted from the forecast.

Since 2004, the long-horizon equity risk premium estimated using the supply-side approach has only been slightly lower than the pure historical return estimate, and the two seem to be converging. These results confirm Ibbotson Associates' belief that these two models are not in conflict, and that both methods are valid when used to estimate expectational equity risk premia. These results also confirm that the historical equity risk premium estimate is a very solid estimate, and should continue to serve as a starting point for applying the equity risk premium in portfolio optimization and business valuation.

Beta

Beta is estimated by regressing a security's excess returns against a market benchmark's excess returns. The slope of the regression equation is the beta and is a measure of the security's sensitivity to the market, and thus is a measure of systematic (market) risk. A beta of 1.00 indicates that the security has the same level of systematic risk as the market, a beta of 2.00 indicates that the security's systematic risk is twice that of the market, and a beta of less then 1.00 indicates that the security's systematic risk is than that of the market.

Chapter 6: Overview of Cost of Capital Models

Note that in Graph 1, an investor is "rewarded proportionally, and in a linear fashion, to the amount of systematic risk taken." The equity risk premium is expressed as $E[R_m-R_f]$, the difference in return between the market and a risk-free asset. How much of the equity risk premium does the investor get? Under the CAPM, if a security's systematic risk is half that of the market (a beta of 0.5), then the investor expects to get half the equity risk premium: if systematic risk is twice as risky as the market (a beta of 2.00), then he expects to get twice the equity risk premium, and if there is no systematic risk (a beta of 0.00), he expects to get *none* of the equity risk premium (In this case he would expect to get the same return as the risk-free asset provides.)

Example: CAPM

For example, say we have a risk-free rate of 4.5%, an equity risk premium of 7.05%, and security with a beta of 1.2. Plugging these values into the CAPM would result in an expected return of 12.96%:

Equation 4

$$k_s = r_f + (\beta_s \times ERP)$$

$$k_s = 4.5 + (1.2 \times 7.05) = 12.96\%$$

CAPM + Size Premium (Modified CAPM)

One of the most remarkable discoveries of modern finance is that of a relationship between firm size and return. The relationship cuts across the entire size spectrum but is most evident among smaller companies, which have higher returns on average than larger ones.[13] The need for a size premium when using the CAPM arises because, although the betas of small companies tend to be greater than those of large companies, these higher betas do not fully account for all of the risks faced by those who invest in small companies. The "modified CAPM" formula addresses this by adding an adjustment in expected return based upon size.

The difference in the actual return of small company stocks over the risk-free rate versus the return of small company stocks over the risk-free rate as predicted by the CAPM is called a "size premium." Rearranging the basic CAPM equation enables us to isolate the "estimated return in excess of the risk-free rate" as beta times the equity risk premium:

$$k_s = r_f + (\beta_s \times ERP)$$

$$k_s - r_f = (\beta_s \times ERP)$$

Chapter 6: Overview of Cost of Capital Models

As of the *2008 Ibbotson SBBI Valuation Yearbook*, micro-cap[14] stocks had a historical arithmetic mean return (1926–2007) of 17.75%, 13.25% higher than the long-term risk-free rate at that time (4.5%) micro-caps had a beta of 1.36, and the historical equity risk premia was 7.05%, so within the context of CAPM the estimated return in excess of the risk-free rate was

(β_s × ERP) = 1.36 × 7.05 = 9.59%.

The size premium for micro-cap stocks at year end 2007 is thus calculated as 3.65% as follows:

Realized return in excess of the risk free rate (13.25%)
(–) CAPM-evaluated return in excess of the risk free rate (9.59%)
= 3.65% (difference due to rounding).

This concept is demonstrated in Graph 2. As previously discussed, the relationship between expected return and systematic risk can be represented graphically in the form of the security market line (SML). The SML is the line that would result if we did the calculations as shown in Example 1 over and over, varied the beta (0 beta, 0.2 beta, 0.4 beta, etc.), and then drew a line connecting the points.

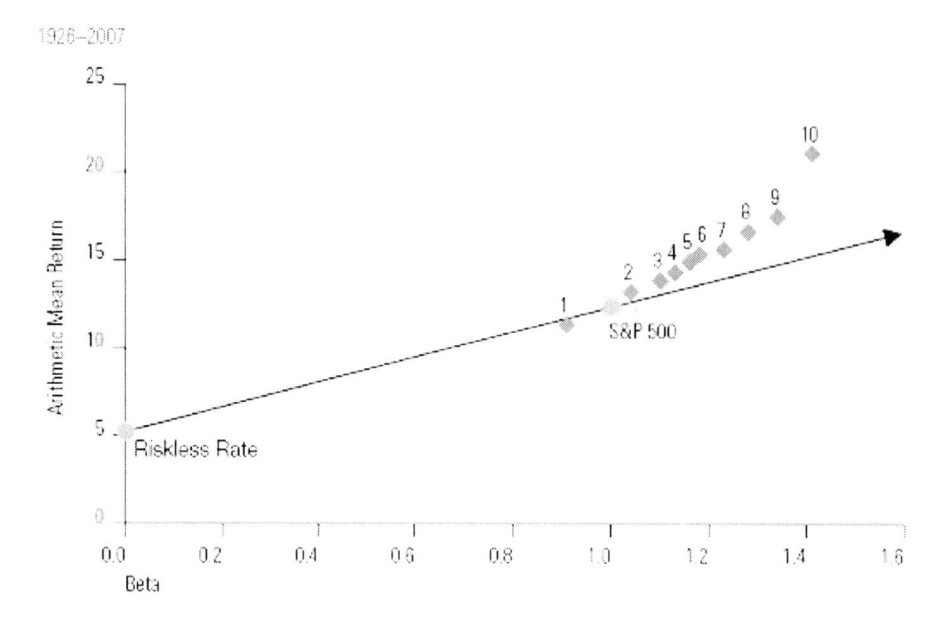

Graph 2: Security Market Line versus Size-Decile Portfolios of the NYSE/AMEX/NASDAQ

The actual returns for CRSP deciles 1–10 of the NYSE/AMEX/NASDAQ[15] are also shown in Graph 2. Decile 1 contains the largest stocks; decile 10 contains the smallest stocks. Note that deciles 2–10 lie above the SML, indicating that these deciles have had returns in excess of what

Chapter 6: Overview of Cost of Capital Models

their systematic risk (as measured by beta) would predict within the context of the CAPM. Each decile's distance from the SML is its respective beta-adjusted size premium.[16]

Beta-Adjusted versus Non-Beta-Adjusted Size Premia

"Beta-adjusted" size premia just means that the portion of excess return attributed to beta is "controlled for," or removed. Looking again at Graph 2, note that the size premia for each decile is that portion of return that lies *above the SML*, while the excess return attributed to beta lies *on the SML line*. The distance between the individual points and the SML therefore isolates the excess return due to size, and excludes the excess return due to systematic risk.

We could calculate a non-beta-adjusted small stock premium by subtracting the arithmetic mean return of large company stocks from the arithmetic mean return of the small company stocks. The problem with using a non-beta adjusted small stock premium is that in doing so one assumes that the company being valued has the same systematic risk (or beta) as the portfolio of small stocks used in the calculation of the size premium. This ignores much of the information that we have regarding market returns—primarily, that different industries tend to have different levels of systematic risk.

Since the beta-adjusted size premium isolates the excess return due to size, it can be applied to a company without making any assumptions regarding the company's systematic risk. For example, utilities tend to be less risky than, say, oil exploration companies. If we have a utility company and an oil exploration company of equal size, we can apply the same beta-adjusted size premium to each, regardless of the companies' differing systematic risk. In the context of CAPM, the systematic risk is measured by beta, and using a non-beta-adjusted size premium may constitute a double counting of this risk.

Beta-adjusted size premia are appropriately used as an adjustment to the CAPM, and also appropriately used as an adjustment in the buildup method, as discussed in the next section.

EXAMPLE: CAPM + Size Premium (Modified CAPM)

In Example 1, we developed an expected return of 12.96% using the basic CAPM formula

$$k_s = r_f + (\beta_s \times ERP).$$

Assuming that our subject company falls in the micro-cap category,[17] a modified CAPM estimate of expected return is:

$$k_s = r_f + (\beta_s \times ERP) + SP_s$$

$$k_s = 4.5 + (1.2 \times 7.05) + 3.65 = 16.61\%$$

where:

k_s = the cost of equity for company **s**;
r_f = the expected return of the riskless asset;
β_s = the beta of the stock of company **s**; and
ERP = the expected equity risk premium, or the amount by which investors expect the future return on equities to exceed that of the riskless asset.
SP_s = size premium for company **s**.

The Buildup Method

The buildup method is an additive model in which the return on an asset is estimated as the sum of a risk-free rate and one or more risk premia. Each premium represents the reward an investor receives for taking on a specific risk. The building blocks are summed arithmetically to form an estimate of the cost of capital:[18]

> Risk-Free Rate
> + Equity Risk Premium
> + Firm Size Premium
> + Industry Risk Premium
> + ?
> = Cost of Equity

While the risk-free rate, the equity risk premium, a size premium, and an industry premium are common "building blocks" in the buildup method, the analyst may make other adjustments as he or she sees fit.

Risk-Free Rate

Any risky asset should earn at least as much as an asset that is risk free, so expected return of the appropriate riskless asset is an appropriate starting point for use in the buildup model. Usually the yield on a U.S. Treasury security that has a maturity that matches whatever is being valued is used. In the case of a business being valued as a going concern, a long-term bond yield is appropriate (Ibbotson uses a 20-year Treasury.)

Equity Risk Premium

After determining the appropriate risk-free rate, several premia can be added to the buildup model. The most common of these is an equity risk premium. The equity risk premium can be defined as the additional return an investor expects to receive to compensate for the additional risk associated with investing in equities as opposed to investing in riskless assets. For additional discussion of the equity risk premium, please see the section on the CAPM model.

Chapter 6: Overview of Cost of Capital Models

Size Premia

A small stock or size premium may also be added in the buildup method to account for the additional risk inherent in investing in small company stocks. It is important to use a "beta-adjusted" size premium since the beta-adjusted size premium isolates the excess return due to size, and it can therefore be applied to a company without making any assumptions regarding the company's systematic risk. For additional discussion of size premia, please see the section on the CAPM model.

Industry Premia

To incorporate a measure of systematic risk into a cost of equity estimate in the context of the buildup model, Ibbotson developed an industry risk premium (IRP) methodology based upon a full information beta estimation process.[19]

The full information beta estimation process includes the proportionate risk of all companies that participate in a given industry. This approach seeks to include data from all companies participating in a given industry in the formation of an industry premium. While the full information approach is a complex cross-sectional regression, it is most important to note that company data is sales weighted so that its effect on the formation of an IRP estimate is only to the degree in which the firm participates in that industry. The reason that adding an industry risk premium to the buildup method is fairly straightforward:

Recall that a modified CAPM (includes a size adjustment) cost of equity estimate is expressed as follows:

$$k_s = r_f + (\beta_s \times ERP) + SP_s$$

Also recall that a basic buildup method (also including a size adjustment) cost of equity estimate is expressed as follows:

$$k_s = r_f + ERP + SP_s$$

where:

- k_s = the cost of equity for company **s**;
- r_f = the expected return of the riskless asset;
- β_s = the beta of the stock of company **s**;
- ERP = the expected equity risk premium, or the amount by which investors expect the future return on equities to exceed that of the riskless asset;
- SP_s = size premium for company **s**.

Chapter 6: Overview of Cost of Capital Models

Note that while the CAPM equation includes a measure of systematic (market) risk in the form of beta, the buildup equation does not include a measure of systematic risk. So, to reintroduce a measure of systematic risk in the buildup method, an industry risk premia (IRP) can be added:

$$k_s = r_f + ERP + SP_s + IRP_i$$

Industry Risk Premia Derivation

Ibbotson's industry risk premium estimation methodology classifies industries by SIC (Standard Industrial Classification) and utilizes the following equation:

$$IRP_i = (\beta_i \times ERP) - ERP$$

where:

IRP_i = the expected industry risk premium for industry i, or the amount by which investors expect the future return of the industry to exceed the market as a whole;

β_i = the full information beta for industry i;

ERP = the expected equity risk premium

An IRP of 0 implies that the industry has the same risk as the market, an IRP greater than 0 implies that the industry is riskier than the market, and an IRP less than 0 implies that the industry is less risky than the market. For example, if SIC 806, "Hospitals", has a full information beta of 0.67, and using Ibbotson's historical equity risk premium as of the end of 2008 (7.05%), the industry risk premia of Industry A would be calculated as −2.34% (difference due to rounding):

$$IRP_i = (\beta_i \times ERP) - ERP$$
$$-2.34\% = (0.67 \times 7.05) - 7.05$$

Using Industry Risk Premia

As of December 2007, the *2008 Ibbotson SBBI Valuation Yearbook's* "Key Variables in Estimating the Cost of Capital" table listed the long-term rate as 4.5%, the historical equity risk premium as 7.05%, and the size premium for companies that fall in the micro-cap category as 3.65%.

Assume that our subject company is classified in SIC 806, "Hospitals", which, as discussed above, had an industry risk premium of −2.34% as of December 31, 2007. Plugging these values in to the buildup method equation results in an expected return of 12.86%:

$$k_s = r_f + ERP + SP_s + IRP_s$$
$$12.86\% = 4.5 + 7.05 + 3.65 + (-2.34)$$

Chapter 6: Overview of Cost of Capital Models

Remember, industry premia are appropriate for use in the buildup method, but should *not* be added to a CAPM estimate. The CAPM model already includes a measure of systematic risk in the form of beta; including an industry premia may constitute double counting.

The framework used in this example is conceptually correct in that it allows for the introduction of a measure of systematic (market) risk into a buildup model. The cost of equity arrived at in the preceding example used an intentionally general categorization, "hospitals", in order to highlight that specific situations require specific inputs, and such a general categorization may not be as narrow as most situations require.

First and foremost, it is critical that the analyst carefully consider the merits of each valuation on a case-by-case basis. One of the main purposes of this book is to discuss and educate the reader on the situation-specific factors that must be taken into account when valuing businesses–especially businesses as varied as those found in the health care arena. In addition, the analyst needs to fully understand the methodology and data utilized to formulate any published premia and make an informed decision as to whether the information applies to the specific situation at hand as a starting point, an end point, or something in between (or not at all).

For instance, if we make an assumption that the adjustment that we have made for market risk is defensible, we would then consider making additional adjustments insofar as the subject company differs from the other companies used to formulate the industry adjustment. These additional adjustments could include payer mix, specialty-specific variables, provider-specific variables, dependence on technology, etc.

Discounted Cash Flow Model

The discounted cash flow (DCF) model, or income method, was developed by John Burr Williams and elaborated by Myron J. Gordon and Eli Shapiro.[20] DCF models can be constructed in many forms, but the most general form can be written as follows:

Equation 5

$$PV_s = \frac{CF_1}{(1+k_s)^1} + \frac{CF_2}{(1+k_s)^2} + \ldots + \frac{CF_i}{(1+k_s)^i}$$

PV_s = the present value of the expected cash flows for company **s**;
CF_i = the dividend or cash flow expected to be received at the end of period I; and
k_s = the cost of equity capital for company **s**.

The two most commonly used methods for applying the income approach are the capitalization method and the discounted cash flow (DCF) model. The capitalization method *is* a form

Chapter 6: Overview of Cost of Capital Models

of discounting, and a "capitalization rate" *is* a discount rate minus a growth rate, but we use the terms to differentiate between 1) calculating a present value for all future cash flows based upon a single period's cash flow and an assumed constant expected growth rate, and 2) calculating a present value for future cash flows that cannot all be derived from a single period's cash flow and an assumed expected growth rate (DCF).

The capitalization of earnings method may be used when a company's current operations are indicative of its future operations; the DCF method is used when a company's future operations are expected to be substantially different from current operations.

A capitalization rate and a discount rate are equal in the one instance when all expected cash flows can be derived from a single period's cash flow and an expected constant growth rate. This "single period" is usually the first period (usually year) following the valuation date. For example, if expected cash flows are the receipt of $100 in the first year, growing at a constant 5% each year thereafter, we can derive all future cash flows from this information. For example, in Year 1 we would anticipate receiving $100 x 1.05, or $105; in Year 2 we would anticipate receiving $100 x 1.05^2, or $110.25, and so on.

If we replace each cash flow in Equation 1 with:

$$CF = CF_i(1+g)^{i-1}$$

where:

CF_i = the dividend or cash flow expected to be received at the end of period i; and

g = the expected cash flow growth rate into perpetuity.

This allows us to simplify Equation 1 to:

Equation 6

$$PV_s = CF_1/(k-g)$$

Equation 6 is known as the single-stage growth model or the Gordon Growth Model.

The capitalization of earnings method takes the same expected discount rate (expected return or cost of capital) that the DCF uses, but subtracts the company's expected annual growth rate. In other words, the relationship between a discount rate and a capitalization rate can be expressed as:

Chapter 6: Overview of Cost of Capital Models

Equation 7

$$c = k - g$$

where:

c = capitalization rate
k = discount rate
g = growth rate

This relationship allows us to restate Equation 2 as:

Equation 8

$$PV_s = CF_1/c$$

So, if:

- We expect to receive cash flow of $100 at the end of period 1, and

- All subsequent periods' cash flows are expected to grow at a constant rate of 7%, and

- Our discount rate (expected or required return) is 15% per period; it follows that our capitalization rate is then (15% – 7%) = 8%

then the present value (PV) of receiving $100 growing at a constant rate of 7% per period (forever) is $1,250:

$$PV_s = CF_1/c$$

$$PV_s = \$100 / (0.08) = \$1,250$$

where:

PV_s = the present value of the expected cash flow to be received at the end of the following period (usually year) for company **s**;
CF_1 = the expected cash flow to be received at the end of the following period (usually year);
c = the capitalization rate.

A shortcoming of using the single-stage model is that it does not allow the growth rate to exceed the cost of equity. If g > r, then the model returns a negative present value. It is entirely possible that growth could exceed the cost of equity in some firms, like in the case of a fast-growing start-up.

Chapter 6: Overview of Cost of Capital Models

A solution to this limitation is to use a multi-stage model. Employment of a multi-stage model allows growth to be greater than the cost of equity in all stages except the last stage. Since expected growth rates for a business (or new product) usually decline over time, the chances of growth exceeding the cost of equity in the final stage are lowered. In the *Ibbotson Cost of Capital Yearbook,* [21] a three-stage DCF employs growth rates that decline over time to the expected industry average, and finally to the expected growth rate of the economy as a whole.

Two-Stage DCF Model

$$PV_s = \sum_{i=1}^{n} \frac{CF_0(1+g_1)^i}{(1+k_s)^i} + \frac{\frac{CF_n(1+g_2)}{(k_s - g_2)}}{(1+k_s)^n}$$

k_s = the cost of equity for company **s**;
PV_s = the current market value of company **s**;
i = a measure of time (in this example the unit of measure is a year);
n = the number of years in the first stage of growth;
CF_0 = the dividend or cash flow amount (in $) in year 0;
CF_n = the expected dividend or cash flow amount (in $) in year n;
g_1 = the expected dividend or cash flow rate from year 1 to year n; and
g_2 = the expected perpetual dividend or cash flow growth rate starting in year (n + 1).

Three-Stage DCF Model

$$PV_s = \sum_{i=1}^{n1} \frac{CF_0(1+g_1)^i}{(1+k_s)^i} + \sum_{i=n1+1}^{n2} \frac{CF_{n1}(1+g_2)^{i-n1}}{(1+k_s)^i} + \frac{\frac{CF_{n2}(1+g_3)}{(k_s - g_3)}}{(1+k_s)^{n2}}$$

k_s = the cost of equity for company **s**;
PV_s = the current market value of company **s**;
i = a measure of time (in the is example the unit of measure is a year);
$n1$ = the number of years in the first stage of growth;
$n2$ = the last year in the second stage of growth;
CF_0 = the dividend or cash flow amount (in $) in year 0;
CF_{n1} = the expected dividend or cash flow amount (in $) in year n_1;
CF_{n2} = the expected dividend or cash flow amount (in $) in year n_2;
g_1 = the expected dividend or cash flow rate from year 1 to year n; and
g_2 = the expected dividend or cash flow rate from year (n_1 + 1) to year n_2; and
g_3 = the expected perpetual dividend or cash flow growth rate starting in year (n + 1)

Chapter 6: Overview of Cost of Capital Models

Discounted cash flow models are generally used in two ways:

1. to estimate cost of capital (usually the cost of equity capital) if expected cash flows, expected growth rates, and the present value of expected cash flows (the stock price, for instance) are known. In this case, an iterative process can be used to solve for the cost of equity, k_s. In an iterative process, a series of values for k_s is used, each progressively yielding a better result. In the case of a DCF model, the iteration would continue until the right hand side of the equation matched the value of the left hand side of the equation (the stock price).

2. to calculate present value, assuming that expected cash flows are known and a cost of capital (developed using CAPM, buildup method, etc.) is known.

Conclusion

In its purest form, valuation is the present value of expected future benefits. Valuation is a forward looking process, and is estimated within the context of IRS Ruling 59-60. Ruling 59-60 states that valuation is a forward-looking process, but must be based on facts available as of the required date of appraisal.[22] The logic embedded in Ruling 59-60 is based on the process by which the market values a business. Market value is reflective of the collective actions and perceptions of all market participants based upon the information known *at the time.*

The cost of capital is the rate used to discount expected future cash flows to present value cost of capital is also referred to as the expected rate of return, required rate of return, or a hurdle rate. The cost of capital is purely an *opportunity cost,* and is therefore a function of the "next best" investment alternative and is *not* a function of the capabilities or other characteristics of the investor. The value of an investment is not a function of an investor's intended length of ownership or ability to acquire funds.

The three most common approaches to valuation are income-, market-, and asset-based approaches. Each approach has its own reasoning and instances of best practice; however, this overview has concentrated on the income-based valuation approach, which values free cash flow – an after-tax concept – via capital asset pricing, buildup, discounted cash flow, and other models.

Although each of these approaches can provide an excellent framework relevant to healthcare valuation, it is critical that the analyst account for factors unique to each valuation assignment, especially with businesses as varied and complex as those found in the health care arena. For instance, additional adjustments may need to be made for payer mix, specialty-specific variables, provider-specific variables, dependence on technology, etc. In addition, the analyst needs to fully understand the methodology and data utilized to formulate any published premia and make an informed decision as to whether the information applies to the specific situation at hand as a starting point, an end point, or something in between (or not at all).

Chapter 6: Overview of Cost of Capital Models

1. *2008 Ibbotson SBBI Valuation Yearbook*, pg 9
2. Ibid. at. 265
3. A quote widely attributed to Roger Ibbotson, founder, advisor and former chairman of Ibbotson Associates (Ibbotson Associates is now a Morningstar Company). Professor Ibbotson is Professor in the Practice of Finance at Yale University and Chairman and CIO of Zebra Capital Management, LLC, a quantitative equity hedge fund manager.
4. *2008 Ibbotson SBBI Valuation Yearbook*, pg 11
5. Ibid. at 12
6. Ibid. at 13
7. Ibid. at 13
8. The *Ibbotson Stocks, Bonds, Bills, and Inflation (SBBI) Yearbook* is now published by Morningstar, Inc.
9. *2008 Ibbotson SBBI Valuation Yearbook*, pg 23
10. Ibid. at. 57
11. Ibid at. 71
12. Ibbotson, Roger G., and Peng Chen, "Long-Run Stock Returns: Participating in the Real Economy." *Financial Analysts Journal*, January/February, vol. 59, no. I, 2003, pp.88-98
13. *2008 Ibbotson SBBI Valuation Yearbook*, pg. 129
14. Micro-cap stocks are defined here as the portfolio of stocks comprised of the 9–10th deciles of the New York Stock Exchange, including similar-sized AMEX and NASDAQ companies. Source of underlying returns and breakpoints for NYSE/AMEX/NASDAQ deciles: ©200807 CRSP, Center for Research in Security Prices. Graduate School of Business, The University of Chicago used with permission. All rights reserved. www.crsp.chicagogsb.edu.
15. Source of underlying returns and breakpoints for NYSE/AMEX/NASDAQ deciles: ©2008 CRSP, Center for Research in Security Prices. Graduate School of Business, The University of Chicago used with permission. All rights reserved. www.crsp.chicagogsb.edu.
16. Morningstar publishes "Key Variables in Estimating Cost of Capital" in the annual *Ibbotson SBBI Valuation Yearbook*, which includes updated yield, equity risk premium, and size premium data.
17. As of December 31, 2007, Ibbotson defined micro-cap companies as those that are less than $723,258,000 in market cap.
18. *2008 Ibbotson SBBI Valuation Yearbook*, pg. 37
19. Kaplan, Paul D., and James D. Peterson. "Full-Information Industry Betas," *Financial Management*, Summer 1998. Ibbotson first published industry risk premia (IRP) estimates in the *2000 Ibbotson SBBI Valuation Yearbook*.
20. *2008 Ibbotson SBBI Valuation Yearbook*, pg. 37
21. Ibid. at. 64
22. Ibid. at. 11

Chapter 7

The Anti-Kickback Statute and Stark Law: Avoiding Valuation of Referrals

By James Pinna, JD and Matt Jenkins, JD

The federal Anti-Kickback Statute, 42 U.S.C. § 1320a-7b(b), sets forth the general principle that health care providers cannot exchange remuneration in return for referrals of federal health care program business. The federal Stark Law, 42 U.S.C. § 1395nn, and the regulations promulgated thereunder by the Centers for Medicare and Medicaid Services incorporate a similar principle, providing exceptions to the general prohibition on physician self-referrals for designated health services only when physicians are not compensated based upon the volume or value of their referrals. The fundamental prohibition on remuneration in return for referrals exemplified in these two statutes has important consequences in the valuation context and requires that health care providers and their advisors be careful to avoid ascribing value to prior or anticipated referrals when structuring transactions involving business ventures providing services to beneficiaries of federal health care programs. This Chapter explores the framework created by the Anti-Kickback Statute and the Stark Law and some of the specific contexts in which health care providers and their advisors should be careful to avoid attributing value to referrals.

Anti-Kickback Statute

The Anti-Kickback Statute prohibits the knowing and willful offer, payment, solicitation, or receipt of "any remuneration (including any kickback, bribe, or rebate) directly or indirectly, overtly or covertly, in cash or in kind," to induce or reward referrals of items or services reimbursable by a federal health care program.[1] In addition to criminal penalties, violations of the Anti-Kickback Statute can lead to the imposition of civil sanctions and/or administrative exclusion from participation in federal health care programs (which carries a lower burden of proof than that which is required to sustain a criminal conviction). In order to prove a violation of the Anti-Kickback Statute, the government must show that an entity: "(a) knowingly and willfully; (b) with the intent to induce the referral of federal health care program business; (c) solicited, received, offered, or paid remuneration."[2] Courts have interpreted the Anti-Kickback Statute to prohibit arrangements if one purpose of the arrangement is the inducement of referrals of Medicare or Medicaid patients, regardless of whether there are other appropriate purposes for the arrangement.[3]

Health care providers should be careful to properly structure investment and compensation arrangements with each other to avoid ascribing value to referrals of federal health care program business. Several courts, as well as the Office of Inspector General, have indicated that certain facts and circumstances in such arrangements, such as paying greater than fair market

Chapter 7: The Anti-Kickback Statute and Stark Law

value for services or items, can support an inference that improper remuneration is being paid to induce referrals.[4] In order to appropriately structure and evaluate investment and compensation arrangements, health care providers and their advisors should look to guidance provided by the Office of Inspector General and federal court decisions to determine what could be considered remuneration for referrals and the key steps for avoiding such problematic remuneration.

Remuneration. In order to avoid remuneration for referrals, health care providers should first understand what could be considered improper remuneration under the Anti-Kickback Statute. In plain English, the term "remunerate" is defined as "to pay an equivalent for."[5] Congress used the term "any remuneration" in the Anti-Kickback Statute to more broadly capture various forms of value that may be traded in exchange for referrals in order to strengthen the capability of the government to detect, prosecute and punish fraudulent activities under the Medicare and Medicaid programs.[6] The language "directly or indirectly, overtly or covertly, in cash or in kind" makes clear that the form or manner of the payment includes indirect, covert, and in kind transactions. The statutory exception for discounts further demonstrates that the statutory language is intended to address transactions, even where there is no direct payment at all from the party receiving referrals. Federal courts have held that remuneration encompasses both traditional kickback payments, where no actual service was performed, as well as payments for which some service was performed.[7]

Even the mere opportunity to earn money may constitute remuneration to induce a person to channel potential Medicare patients toward a particular recipient.[8] For instance, giving a person the opportunity to generate consulting fees through a consulting contract, even if those fees were the result of actual services provided, could potentially constitute improper remuneration if coupled with an improper intent to induce referrals.[9] The Office of Inspector General has noted that the opportunity to split a global surgical fee may constitute something of value to a referring party apart from any payment for the referral. An example used by the Office of Inspector General is where an optometrist/ophthalmologist network refers patients for cataract surgery only to ophthalmologists who agree to split the global surgical fee by referring patients back to the optometrist for post-operative care.[10] Another illustration of where the ability to generate a fee could potentially constitute improper remuneration is when an existing supplier of a health care service (e.g. laboratory services) contracts to supply those services to a provider in a position to refer business (e.g. physician group) who can then bill and collect fees for business typically provided by the existing supplier.[11] Additionally, the Office of Inspector General has taken the position that the mere opportunity to invest in a joint venture (and consequently receive profit distributions) may in certain circumstances constitute improper remuneration if offered in exchange for past or future referrals.[12]

As indicated by the examples discussed above, health care providers should bear in mind that potentially problematic remuneration may take many forms, including: (i) payments or kickbacks for referrals, where no services are performed in return; (ii) payments for which some services or items was were provided in return; (iii) discounts or rebates off the price of an item or service received; or (iv) the opportunity to make a profit by generating fees or receiving distributions from a joint venture.

Chapter 7: The Anti-Kickback Statute and Stark Law

Fair market value. One of the key ways to ensure there is no remuneration for referrals is to make sure that the parties pay or receive fair market value in exchange for the items or services provided under the particular arrangement. Some of the most commonly cited instances of potentially improper remuneration are providing goods or services to another party for more or less than fair market value, or providing an inappropriate discount or premium to the fair market value purchase price of an investment interest. For example, in the context of purchasing physician practices, federal courts have held that "to the extent that a payment exceeds the fair market value of the practice, or the value of the services, it can be inferred that the excess amount paid over fair market value is intended as payment for the referral of program-related business."[13] Conversely, it may be argued that when the amount paid for services, items or investment interests is fair market value, there is a presumption that there is no remuneration in exchange for referrals because the amount paid is directly attributable to the service, item or investment interest provided.[14] Note, however, that the Office of Inspector General has not chosen to provide safe harbor protection to all arrangements that are consistent with fair market value, but rather only a small subset of such arrangements, and it takes the approach that fair market value alone will not insulate an arrangement from violating the Anti-Kickback Statute.[15]

When considering the question of fair market value in the context of health care providers, traditional methods of economic valuation may not always comport with the prescriptions of the Anti-Kickback Statute. To be sure, compensation that attributes value to previous or expected referrals of federal health care program business must be excluded from consideration. Additionally, parties should be careful in evaluating comparable market data. Merely because another buyer is willing to pay a particular price does not mean the price is fair market value; especially if the price offered reflects the value of referrals likely to result from the purchase.

To illustrate these differences, consider the context of physician practice acquisitions. Parties unfamiliar with the limitations imposed by the Anti-Kickback Statute might normally expect the acquisition price paid by a hospital to a physician practice to account for potential revenues from anticipated future referrals by the selling physician to the hospital for non-physician services. However, because the Anti-Kickback Statute prohibits remuneration as an inducement for referrals, anticipated future referrals to the hospital must be excluded from any calculation of fair market value and may not be considered in determining the acquisition price.[16] This departure from what might otherwise seem appropriate under traditional methods of economic valuation is also made clear in the safe harbor provisions under the Anti-Kickback Statute which provide that for purposes of determining the value of space or equipment rentals, "fair market value" is specifically defined to exclude the additional value one party would attribute to the property or equipment as a result of its proximity or convenience to sources of referrals or business otherwise generated, such as the added value a hospital places on having referring physicians located in a medical building the hospital owns on its property.[17]

Investment arrangements. The Office of Inspector General has provided guidance on investment arrangements by creating safe harbors that protect certain types of investment interests and provide that the corresponding distributions related to such investment interests will not

Chapter 7: The Anti-Kickback Statute and Stark Law

constitute "remuneration" under the Anti-Kickback Statute when all of the enumerated requirements are satisfied.[18] These safe harbors contain two common requirements that are important to consider in the valuation context: (i) terms on which an investment interest is offered to an investor must not be related to previous or expected volume of referrals, and (ii) payment to an investor in return for the investment interest must be directly proportional to the amount of capital investment of that investor.[19]

The Office of Inspector General has provided further guidance on investment arrangements in its Special Fraud Alerts that identifies a number of factors it views as indicators of potentially unlawful activity, which separately or taken together may result in a business arrangement that violates the Anti-Kickback Statute.[20] In the Office of Inspector General's view, these improper investment arrangements are not intended "to raise investment capital legitimately to start a business, but to lock up a stream of referrals from the physician investors and to compensate them indirectly for these referrals."[21] Two significant "questionable features" identified by the Office of Inspector General as potential indicators of a "suspect joint venture" are: (i) the amount of capital invested by the physician is "disproportionately small" and the returns on investment may be "disproportionately large" when compared to a typical investment in a new business enterprise, and (ii) investors may be paid what the Office of Inspector General terms "extraordinary returns" on the investment in comparison with the risk involved, often well over "50 to 100 % per year."[22] In a recent advisory opinion, the Office of Inspector General has also identified concerns in the context of a hospital's purchase of investment interests in a surgery center when: (i) the investment appears unrelated to enhancing the operations of the surgery center, but instead allows specific physician investors to realize a gain on their investment; and (ii) only selected physicians are selling ownership interests, raising the possibility that the hospital's investment is intended to influence the referrals of those selected physicians.[23]

Compensation arrangements. The Office of Inspector General has provided guidance as to the appropriate characteristics of compensation arrangements in its safe harbor regulations under the Anti-Kickback Statute. The safe harbors for space rentals, equipment rentals, and personal services and management contracts generally include the following characteristics: (i) the aggregate compensation paid over the term of the agreement is set in advance, is consistent with fair market value in arms-length transactions and is not determined in a manner that takes into account the volume or value of any referrals or business otherwise generated between the parties for which payment may be made in whole or in part under a federal health care program, and (ii) the aggregate services contracted for do not exceed those which are reasonably necessary to accomplish the commercially reasonable business purpose of the services.[24] Additionally, the Office of Inspector General has specifically noted that per patient, per order, per click and percentage based compensation arrangements are disfavored under the Anti-Kickback Statute because these types of payment inherently vary based on the volume and value of business generated between the parties.[25] In its Supplemental Compliance Guidance to Hospitals, the Office of Inspector General encouraged hospitals to review their physician compensation arrangements to assess the risk of fraud and abuse by analyzing, among other things: (i) whether the items and services obtained from a physician are legitimate, commercially

Chapter 7: The Anti-Kickback Statute and Stark Law

reasonable, and necessary to achieve a legitimate business purpose of the hospital (apart from obtaining referrals); (ii) whether the remuneration takes into account, directly or indirectly, the value or volume of any past or future referrals or other business generated between the parties; and (iii) whether physicians were selected to participate in the arrangement in whole or in part because of their past or anticipated referrals.[26]

Stark Law

The Stark Law prohibits physicians having a direct or indirect "financial relationship" with an "entity" from referring patients to such entity for certain "designated health services" paid under a federal healthcare program, unless such financial relationship meets one of the exceptions enumerated under the statute or the regulations promulgated thereunder.[27] The Stark Law also prohibits any entity from billing any individual, Medicare, or other payor for designated health services furnished pursuant to a prohibited referral. Any payments (including co-payments) received in violation of this prohibition must be promptly refunded. A financial relationship regulated under the Stark Law can take the form of a direct or indirect ownership interest or compensation arrangement. The Stark Law and the regulations promulgated thereunder define a referral to mean the request by a physician for, or ordering of, or the certifying or recertifying of the need for, any designated health service for which payment may be made under Medicare, but not including any designated health service personally performed or provided by the referring physician.[28]

Fair Market Value. The Stark Law generally requires that remuneration under any compensation arrangement with a referring physician be: (i) set in advance, (ii) consistent with fair market value, and (iii) not determined in a way that takes into account the volume or value of referrals or other business generated.[29] The Centers for Medicare and Medicaid Services have noted that the definition of "fair market value" under the Stark Law is qualified in ways that do not necessarily comport with the usage of the term in standard valuation techniques and methodologies. In particular, the Stark Law requires that the methodology for analyzing fair market value exclude valuations where the parties to the transactions are at arm's length but in a position to refer to one another, and modifying the definition of fair market value depending on the type of transaction: leases or rentals of space and equipment cannot take into account the intended use of the rented item or the value of proximity or convenience to the lessor.[30]

The Stark Law definition of "general market value" means the price that an asset would bring as the result of bona fide bargaining between well-informed buyers and sellers who are not otherwise in a position to generate business for the other party, or the compensation that would be included in a service agreement as the result of bona fide bargaining between well-informed parties to the agreement who are not otherwise in a position to generate business for the other party, on the date of acquisition of the asset or at the time of the service agreement.[31] The Stark Law regulations generally define "fair market price" as the price at which bona fide sales have been consummated for assets of like type, quality, and quantity in a particular market at the time of acquisition, or the compensation that has been included in bona fide service agreements with comparable terms at the time of the agreement, where the price or compensation has not been determined in any manner that takes into account the volume or value of anticipated or actual referrals.[32] Note that this language reflects that the particular market in which a transaction occurs is important in assessing the relevance of comparable transactions.

With respect to space and equipment rentals, the Stark Law regulations specifically define "fair market value" as the value of rental property for general commercial purposes (not taking into account its intended use, provided that costs incurred by the lessor in developing or upgrading the property or maintaining the property or its improvements may be considered), and in the case of a space rental, this value may not be adjusted to reflect the additional value the prospective lessee or lessor would attribute to the proximity or convenience to the lessor when the lessor is a potential source of patient referrals to the lessee.[33]

Per-unit and percentage compensation. The exceptions to the Stark Law permit per-unit and percentage based compensation in certain limited circumstances. Unlike the safe harbors under the Anti-Kickback Statute, compensation is considered to meet the Stark Law requirement of being "set in advance" so long as the aggregate compensation, a per-unit of service amount, or a specific formula for calculating the compensation is: (i) set forth in the written agreement between the parties, (ii) set forth in sufficient detail so that it can be objectively verified, and (iii) may not be changed or modified during the course of the agreement in any manner that takes into account the volume or value of referrals or other business generated by the referring physician.[34] Per-unit compensation is deemed not to take into account "the volume or value of referrals" or "other business generated between the parties" if the compensation is fair market value for services or items actually provided and does not vary during the course of the compensation arrangement in any manner that takes into account referrals or other business generated by the referring physician.[35] However, in its 2009 Hospital Inpatient Prospective Payment System Final Rule the Centers for Medicare and Medicaid Services prohibited, effective October 1, 2009, the use of per-unit payments in space and equipment rentals when the per-unit charge reflects services provided to patients referred by the lessor to the lessee.[36] This prohibition applies regardless of whether the referring physician is the lessor or whether the lessor is an entity in which the referring physician has an ownership interest. The prohibition also applies when the lessor is an entity providing designated health services that refers patients to a physician lessee or a physician organization lessee. In its commentary to the 2009 Hospital Inpatient Prospective Payment System Final Rule, the Centers for Medicare and Medicaid Services specifically noted that it did not consider an agreement to be at fair market value if the lessee is paying a physician substantially more for equipment than it would have to pay a non-physician owned company and had serious questions as to the commercial reasonableness of an agreement if the lessee is performing a sufficiently high volume of procedures such that it would be economically feasible to purchase the equipment rather than lease it.[37] In the view of the Centers for Medicare and Medicaid Services, these types of per-unit arrangements raised the question of whether the lessee is paying more than what it would have to pay another lessor (or if the lessee purchased the equipment) in order to avoid losing referrals from the lessor.[38]

Chapter 7: The Anti-Kickback Statute and Stark Law

Percentage compensation arrangements can also meet the set in advance requirement under the Stark Law when the percentage compensation does not vary based upon the volume or value of referrals, such as compensation for personally performed services of a physician.[39] However, in its 2009 Hospital Inpatient Prospective Payment System Final Rule the Centers for Medicare and Medicaid Services prohibited, effective October 1, 2009, the use of compensation formulae based on a percentage of revenue raised, earned, billed, collected or otherwise attributable to the services performed or business generated in determining rental charges for the lease of office space or equipment.[40] In its commentary to the 2009 Hospital Inpatient Prospective Payment System Final Rule, the Centers for Medicare and Medicaid Services specifically mentioned its concern that fluctuating rental payments determined using a percentage based formula may not result in fair market value payments (even when the formula is arguably reasonable).[41] Although the Centers for Medicare and Medicaid Services did not extend the prohibition on percentage based compensation to arrangements for non-professional services (such as management or billing services), it reiterated its intent to continue to monitor these types of compensation arrangements.[42]

Valuation Contexts

The following examples of valuation contexts are intended to identify some of the specific situations in which health care providers and their advisors should be careful to avoid attributing value to referrals of federal health care program business.

Compensation arrangements. Any remuneration flowing under a compensation arrangement between health care providers in a position to make referrals to each other should be at fair market value for actual and necessary items furnished or services rendered based upon an arm's-length transaction and should not take into account, directly or indirectly, the value or volume of any past or future referrals or other business generated between the parties. Otherwise, the parties may be subject to the inference that some portion of the remuneration flowing under the compensation arrangement could be attributed to the volume or value of referrals between the parties. Compensation that is entirely set in advance is more effective in avoiding any inference that there is remuneration in exchange for referrals because there is no opportunity for variance in compensation based upon referrals. Nevertheless, parties should be careful when resetting compensation under an agreement (that may be set in advance for each term or year of an agreement) to make sure that the compensation is fair market value for the items or services provided and is not adjusted in a manner that provides incentives based on increases or decreases in business or revenue generated.

Percentage and per-unit compensation arrangements have a greater likelihood of being viewed as tied to the volume or value of business or revenue generated. This is especially true when the party receiving compensation has an ability to influence referrals of federal health care program business in some way, whether as a physician, another health care provider who refers business, or someone who conducts marketing-related activities. For instance, a management fee based on a percentage of revenue would be of less concern when the manager is not owned by physicians or other health care providers in a position to refer business and does not conduct marketing activities in an effort to drive referrals to the managed entity.

Percentage or per-unit arrangements involving physicians or physician owned entities should be reviewed carefully to ensure that such arrangements meet the Stark Law requirements that the compensation is fair market value for services or items actually provided and does not vary during the course of the arrangement in any manner that takes into account referrals or other business generated. Beginning October 1, 2009, per-unit compensation methodologies may no longer be used in equipment or space rentals when the per-unit charge reflects services provided to patients referred by the lessor to the lessee. Additionally, after October 1, 2009, percentage based formulae may not be used in determining rental charges for office or space rentals. Following the guidance from the Centers for Medicare and Medicaid Services under the 2009 Hospital Inpatient Prospective Payment System Final Rule, percentage compensation arrangements with physicians are generally reserved only for personally performed services under the Stark Law. Note that even if a percentage compensation arrangement fits within a Stark Law exception, there is no equivalent provision protecting such arrangements with safe harbor status under the Anti-Kickback Statute.

Physician practices. Hospitals acquiring physician practices cannot attribute value to the prior or anticipated referrals, as clarified below, from physician owners in calculating the purchase price for the physician practice. This means that the hospital cannot calculate the purchase price for the physician practice based on the anticipated revenues from referrals from physician owners to the hospital or its affiliates for non-physician services. These revenues are wholly unrelated to the going concern value of the business being acquired. This does not mean, however, that the hospital has to disregard revenues of the physician practice attributable to: (i) professional services of the physician owners, as these services would not constitute a referral to another person or entity for reimbursable services or items, or (ii) other revenue of the practice, to the extent this revenue is reflective of the going concern value of the practice's business. Value may be also be attributed to the physical assets (including patient records) as well as the goodwill and other intangible assets of the practice, provided that these values accurately reflect fair market value for the respective asset and do not relate in any way to prior or anticipated referrals from the physician practice.

Non-competition agreements. Agreements not to compete from physician owners may be attributed a fair market value price to the extent that these non-competes are necessary and important to preserve the value of a business by prohibiting the detrimental effect of a physician owner competing with the business. The value of a non-compete is related to the avoidance of having a competitor in the marketplace that could take away business and should not be construed as requiring referrals from a physician. Thus, the value of a non-compete should be based on the potential negative impact on cash flows from allowing a physician owner to establish a competitive entity and not the volume of referrals attributable to the physician owner because the physician owner could refer business to another entity regardless of the presence

Chapter 7: The Anti-Kickback Statute and Stark Law

of a non-compete. The value of a non-compete should also take into account the reasonable ability of a physician owner to engage in competitive activity. For example, a physician might be able to establish a surgery suite or inexpensive imaging equipment in his or her office relatively easily, but going out and establishing a full-scale surgery hospital may be a distant reality. Note, however, that for non-competes related to the acquisition of a physician practice, the potential negative impact on cash flows would be due to the ability of a physician to provide physician services on behalf of another entity in the market and therefore would be based upon the scope of physician services provided by the specific physician.

When the valuation of a business or physician practice owned by physicians is based upon historical cash flows (including the cash flows that could be negatively impacted by a physician competing in the market), the value of a non-compete would be part of the enterprise value and not in addition to it. A non-compete may have independent value, however, when a physician is not receiving consideration based on historical cash flows. For example, if a group of physicians has set up a laboratory or imaging facility but not yet generated cash flows on which to base a valuation, a purchaser might pay a fair market value price for the equipment and other assets as well as a fair market value price for a non-compete from the physicians. In such case, the value of the non-compete would be based upon the reasonable ability of the physicians to impact the projected future cash flows of the laboratory or imaging business by setting up a competing facility in the market.

Another example that sometimes arises is when physicians want to invest in a joint venture that will own a surgery center or surgical hospital (whether a to-be-developed facility or a facility contributed by a hospital), and the physicians desire to receive consideration for contributing an agreement not to compete. This situation is decidedly different from the previous example discussed above because the physicians have not demonstrated a reasonable ability to compete with the proposed joint venture by establishing a facility on their own. Moreover, the establishment of a surgery center or surgical hospital is a very capital and expertise intensive endeavor. A physician may be able to set up a surgery suite in his or her office relatively easy, in which case there may be some value to the physician agreeing not to do so, however, a valuator should carefully consider what value is properly attributable to a non-compete in the context of the development of a surgery center or surgical hospital.

Investment interests in de novo joint ventures. In valuing investment interests in a de novo (new) joint venture that includes investors in a position to make referrals to the joint venture, the Anti-Kickback Statute generally requires that anticipated referral volumes from such investors, which might otherwise be taken into account in a normal commercial setting, must be disregarded in determining the value of the joint venture. In the context of a de novo joint venture, there is no existing business to be valued and the price per unit of investment interest would be based solely upon the equity capital required to start up the business. The price per unit of investment interest in a de novo joint venture should not reflect anticipated revenues based upon anticipated referrals from investors, as this could be construed as attributing value to future referrals. Notably, in a de novo joint venture, if one party is contributing assets or selling assets comprising all or part of an ongoing business enterprise, it is essential that such assets be fairly valued and that the contributing or selling party receive fair market value in exchange. However, the valuation of those assets should not assign any value to anticipated referrals by either party to the de novo joint venture.

The purchase price for units of investment interests in a de novo joint venture should not vary between individual investor, as this variance could be considered remuneration for anticipated referrals. One of the key principles enunciated in the guidance on investment arrangements from the Office of Inspector General is that the amount of payment to each investor must be directly proportional to capital invested. The Office of Inspector General has explicitly indicated its concern when investors who are potential referral sources for the investment entity are permitted to obtain their investment interests at insider prices or at prices more favorable than those available to the general public.[43] This does not, however, prohibit investors from contributing capital in the form of pre-operational services or sweat equity, provided that the sweat equity is not related to referrals, and the investment interests received in return are fair market value for the sweat equity contributed.[44]

Investment interests in existing joint venture with operating history. Just as with de novo joint ventures, the value of investment interests in an existing joint venture that includes investors in a position to make referrals to the joint venture also should not attribute value to anticipated referrals from such investors. In contrast to a de novo joint venture, an existing joint venture typically has some going concern value that may be affected by revenues stemming from referrals made by investors. Additionally, the inflow and outflow of investors actively involved in providing services in connection with a joint venture (which may actually be required for safe harbor protection in the case of ambulatory surgery centers) could potentially impact the future revenues of the joint venture. In these circumstances, it is important that the value of investment interests is determined using projected cash flows based upon the prior operating history of the joint venture, as opposed to the projected future referrals by investors. When a business is valued using projected cash flows based upon historical operations, the value of the business is not tied to anticipated referrals from investors, but rather the ability of the business to continue to operate in a profitable manner. Potential outflows of investors and losses in revenue could be reflected in the discount premium applied to the cash flows of the joint venture (reflecting a higher risk with respect to future operations), however potential inflows of investors and additional revenues attributable thereto should not be reflected in the purchase price because this could be construed as attributing value to future anticipated referrals.

For example, if a physician owner of a surgery center is retiring and selling his or her ownership interests to a new physician, and the new physician performs procedures that receive higher reimbursement than the retiring physician, the valuation of the ownership interests in the surgery center should not reflect any anticipated increase in reimbursement from the activity of the new physician at the surgery center because this would reflect the value of anticipated referrals. In contrast, if a surgery center invests in a new piece of high technology equipment enabling it to perform certain cutting edge procedures that receive higher reimbursement, the

Chapter 7: The Anti-Kickback Statute and Stark Law

valuation of the surgery center should reflect the projected revenues from this new equipment. The important distinction here is that in the latter case the valuation is appropriately based upon the projected ability of the business to perform new procedures and is not based on projections of anticipated referrals from a particular physician investor.

In valuing an existing joint venture that has a measurable operating history, it is also important that an appropriate discount premium is applied so that the amount of capital invested by new investors is not disproportionately small compared to disproportionately large returns that an enforcement authority might assert to be "extraordinary returns" in comparison with the risk involved.[45] Assuming that a joint venture has a significant operating history and a relatively stable risk profile that allows for the application of an appropriate discount premium, the mere purchase of an investment interest should avoid any inference of improper remuneration to the purchaser, the seller, or other investors so long as the purchase is not targeted towards certain investors in return for their referrals, and the purchase price is fair market value. The logical argument that can be made here is that if the price paid for an investment interest is fair market value, then the value of the purchase price consideration is equivalent to the value of the investment interest exchanged and there could be no additional remuneration in exchange for referrals.

The above described situation is distinguishable from the two advisory opinions from the Office of Inspector General announcing that even the mere opportunity to investment (and consequently receive profit distributions) may in certain circumstances constitute illegal remuneration.[46] The potentially problematic factors mentioned by these advisory opinions applied to joint ventures where: (i) there was no stable operating history or risk profile, (ii) one or several investors in a joint venture control a sufficiently large stream of referrals to make the venture's financial success highly likely, (iii) one investor has an established track record with similar ventures, or (iv) the financial investment required is so small that the investors have little or no real risk.[47] By contrast, in an established joint venture where the operations and risk profile are unlikely to change significantly, individual investors purchasing or selling interests at fair market value are less likely to be in position to make the joint venture succeed or fail on their own. In such a situation, the purchase price paid for investment interests should be equivalent value, and absent extenuating circumstances linking the ability to invest to referrals by investors (such as targeting of certain high volume investors), it arguable that there is no improper remuneration that could be attributed to anticipated referrals.

Investment interests in existing joint venture with limited operating history. Sometimes investors may purchase ownership in a joint venture following the initial syndication of ownership interests and the formation of the business entity, but before the business actually begins operations. In other instances, investors may purchase ownership in a joint venture that has just begun operations but still has a very limited operating history. These types of situations present unique challenges for valuation professionals. The valuation of investment interests in an existing entity with a limited operating history should be careful to avoid (i) underestimating the value that has been created by the formation of the business or (ii) overestimating the value that has been created by the formation of the business by ascribing certainty to referrals from physician investors.

To be sure, there is some value created by the syndication of ownership interests and the formation of a business entity. This value is likely to increase as the business entity reaches additional milestones such as obtaining additional financing, constructing a facility, purchasing equipment, obtaining licenses and other regulatory approvals, and commencing operations. Until those milestones are reached, the risk that they might not be met likely warrants some discount. The attainment of certain milestones means that the value of ownership units in the business likely is no longer based solely upon the equity capital required to start up the business. If, following syndication and formation of the business entity, the fair market value of a minority ownership interest in the business has increased, then it would no longer be appropriate to sell units to physician investors at the initial offering price if this price is less than the current fair market value of the business.

On the other hand, a business entity with a limited operating history has significantly higher risks than an existing business with stable, continuing operations, and there is less certainty that a startup business will be able to meet projected cash flow levels.[48] When there is no operating history upon which to base cash flow projections, valuators may be relying principally on their analysis of management's preliminary projections for future cash flows. Management's future cash flow projections, in an attempt to be more accurate, may likely incorporate an analysis of the procedures expected to be performed in the business' facility by physician owners and other physicians in the community. This analysis might be particularly relevant in the context of ambulatory surgery centers, where the Anti-Kickback Statute safe harbor affirmatively requires that physician owners perform at least one-third of their procedures in the surgery center.

To prevent attributing value to the referrals of physician owners, the valuation of a business with a limited operating history should avoid ascribing certainty to referrals from physician investors. Therefore, an analysis of projected cash flows should include an appropriate discount rate to reflect, among the many other business risks, that physician owners are not required to make referrals to the facility (except to the extent to meet regulatory requirements under the ambulatory surgery center safe harbor or the whole hospital exception to the Stark Law) and there can be no assurance that the business will meet revenue targets in its cash flow projections.

---

1. 42 U.S.C. § 1320a-7b(b). A "federal health care program" includes any plan or program that provides health benefits, whether directly, through insurance, or otherwise which is funded directly, in whole or in part by the federal government. 42 U.S.C. § 1320a-7b(f).

2. *Hanlester Network v. Shalala*, 51 F.3d 1390, 1397-1400 (9th Cir. 1995).

3. *United States v. Greber*, 760 F.2d 68 (3d Cir. 1985), cert. denied, 474 U.S. 988 (1985).

4. *See United States v. Lipkis*, 770 F.2d 1447 (9th Cir. 1985) (noting that the fair market value of services provided under an arrangement was substantially less than the compensation received, and there is no question that there was payment for the referrals as well as the described services); *United States ex rel. Constantino Perales v. St. Margaret's Hospital*, 243 F. Supp. 2d 843, 851 (C.D. Ill. 2003) (indicating that payment in excess of fair market value for a physician practice may create an inference of improper remuneration); *United States ex rel. Obert-Hong v. Advocate Health Care*, 211 F. Supp. 2d 1045, 1049 (N.D. Ill. 2002) (indicating that payment in excess of fair market value for a physician practice may create an inference of improper remuneration); *OIG Special Fraud Alert: Arrangements for the Provision of Clinical Laboratory Services* (issued

Chapter 7: The Anti-Kickback Statute and Stark Law

October 1994), republished at 59 Fed. Reg. 65372 (Dec. 19, 1994) (Whenever a laboratory offers or gives to a source of referrals anything of value not paid for at fair market value, the inference may be made that the thing of value is offered to induce the referral of business. The same is true whenever a referral source solicits or receives anything of value from the laboratory. By "fair market value" we mean value for general commercial purposes. However, "fair market value" must reflect an arms length transaction which has not been adjusted to include the additional value which one or both of the parties has attributed to the referral of business between them); Letter from D. McCarty Thornton, Associate General Counsel, OIG to T.J. Sullivan, Technical Assistant, Office of the Associate Chief Counsel, Employee Benefits and Exempt Organizations dated December 22, 1992 (available at http://oig.hhs.gov/fraud/docs/safeharborregulations/acquisition122292.htm) (indicating that payment in excess of fair market value may create an inference of improper remuneration); *OIG Supplemental Compliance Program Guidance for Hospitals*, 70 Fed. Reg. 4858, 4866 (January 31, 2005) (Arrangements under which hospitals (i) provide physicians with items or services for free or less than fair market value, (ii) relieve physicians of financial obligations they would otherwise incur, or (iii) inflate compensation paid to physicians for items or services pose significant risk. In such circumstances, an inference arises that the remuneration may be in exchange for generating business).

5. Merriam-Webster Online Dictionary (2008).

6. *See* H.R. Rep. No. 95-393, Pt. II, 95th Cong., 1st Sess. 53 *reprinted in* 1977 U.S.C.C.A.N. 3039, 3056; *Medicare and State Health Care Programs: Fraud and Abuse; OIG Anti-Kickback Provisions*, 56 Fed. Reg. 35952, 35958 (July 29, 1991) (Congress's intent in placing the term "remuneration" in the statute in 1977 was to cover the transferring of anything of value in any form or manner whatsoever. The statute's language makes clear that illegal payments are prohibited beyond merely "bribes," "kickbacks," and "rebates," which were the three terms used in the original 1972 statute); *Hanlester Network*, 51 F.3d at 1398 (Noting that the phrase "any remuneration" was intended to broaden the reach of the law which previously referred only to kickbacks, bribes, and rebates); *Greber*, 760 F.2d at 71 (Indicating that Congress included "any remuneration" to make it clear that even if the transaction was not considered to be a "kickback" for which no service had been rendered, payment could nevertheless violate the statute).

7. *Greber*, 760 F.2d at 71; *United States v. Bay State Ambulance and Hospital Rental Service, Inc.*, 874 F.2d 20, 30 (1st Cir. 1989).

8. *Bay State Ambulance*, 874 F.2d at 29.

9. *See Id.* (Court rejected defendant's argument that consulting fees had to be of substantially more value than services performed in order to constitute illegal remuneration and upheld jury instruction indicating that payments could be illegal remuneration if they were made with improper purpose).

10. *Medicare and State Health Care Programs: Fraud and Abuse; Clarification of the Initial OIG Safe Harbor Provisions and Establishment of Additional Safe Harbor Provisions Under the Anti-Kickback Statute*, 64 Fed. Reg. 63518, 63548 (November 19, 1999).

11. *OIG Special Advisory Bulletin on Contractual Joint Ventures*, 68 Fed. Reg. 23148 (April 30, 2003); see also OIG Advisory Opinion No. 04-17 (December 10, 2004); OIG Advisory Opinion No. 08-10 (August 19, 2008) (noting that arrangement where intensity-modulated radiation therapy facility block leases time to urologists who then bill Medicare for the professional and technical components could potentially result in problematic remuneration to the urologists in the form of the difference between the fees collected and the fixed amounts to be paid to the facility under the block lease arrangement).

12. *OIG Advisory Opinion No. 98-19* (December 14, 1998); OIG Advisory Opinion No. 97-5 (October 6, 1997).

13. *Perales*, 243 F. Supp. 2d at 849; *Obert-Hong*, 211 F. Supp. 2d at 1049.

14. *See e.g.* Letter from D. McCarty Thornton (noting the importance of fair market value in the context of physician practice acquisitions and stating that "it is necessary to consider the amounts paid for the practice or as compensation to determine whether they reasonably reflect the fair market value of the practice or the services rendered, in order to determine whether such items in reality constitute remuneration for referrals"); *United States ex rel. Goodstein v. McLaren*, 202 F. Supp. 2d 671 (E.D. Mich. 2002) (holding that a lease for medical office space was based on fair market value and not remuneration for referrals of Medicaid patients to the defendant based on applying the statutory allowances for lessee and lessor relationships); *U.S. ex rel. Obert-Hong*, 211 F. Supp.2d at 1049 (holding that "the Anti-Kickback Act does not prohibit hospitals from acquiring medical practices, nor does it preclude the seller-doctor from making future referrals to the buyer-hospital, provided there are no economic inducements for those referrals. To comply with the statute, the hospital must simply pay fair market value for the practice's assets").

15. 70 Fed. Reg. at 4864 (Neither a legitimate business purpose for the arrangement, nor a fair market value payment, will legitimize a payment if there is also an illegal purpose (i.e., inducing federal health care program business).

Chapter 7: The Anti-Kickback Statute and Stark Law

16. *Obert-Hong*, 211 F. Supp.2d at 1049.
17. 42 C.F.R. 1001.952(b) and (c); 56 Fed. Reg. at 35971-73.
18. 42 C.F.R. § 1001.952(a) and (r).
19. *Id.*
20. *OIG Special Fraud Alert: Joint Venture Arrangements* (issued August 1989), republished in 59 Fed. Reg. 65372 (December 19, 1994).
21. *Id.*
22. *Id.*
23. OIG Advisory Opinion No. 07-05 (June 12, 2007).
24. 42 C.F.R. § 1001.952(b), (c) & (d).
25. *See* 56 Fed. Reg. at 35973 (noting that percentage or per-unit agreements between health care providers in a position to refer Medicare or Medicaid business threaten to violate the statute because the payments in these arrangements are directly tied to the volume of business or amount of revenue generated, providing an improper incentive to refer); OIG Advisory Opinion 03-8 (April 3, 2003) (noting that that "per patient", "per order", "per click" and similar payment arrangements with referral sources are disfavored); OIG Advisory Opinion 06-02 (March 21, 2006) (noting that percentage-based compensation was inherently problematic from a fair market value perspective because the compensation necessarily relates to the volume and value of business generated between the parties).
26. 70 Fed. Reg. 4866-67.
27. 42 U.S.C. § 1395nn. Designated health services include clinical laboratory services; physical therapy, occupational therapy, and speech-language pathology services; radiology and certain other imaging services; radiation therapy services and supplies; durable medical equipment and supplies; parenteral and enteral nutrients, equipment, and supplies; prosthetics, orthotics, and prosthetic devices and supplies; home health services; outpatient prescription drugs; inpatient and outpatient hospital services. 42 U.S.C. § 1395nn(h)(6); 42 C.F.R. § 411.351.
28. 42 U.S.C. § 1395nn(h)(5); 42 CFR § 411.351.
29. *See* 42 C.F.R. § 411.357(a) (rental of office space), (b) (rental of equipment), (c) (employment), (d) (personal services), (f) (isolated transactions), (i) (payments by physician) and (l) (fair market value).
30. *Medicare Program; Physicians' Referrals to Health Care Entities With Which They Have Financial Relationships (Phase II); Interim Final Rule*; 69 Fed. Reg. 16054, 16107 (March 26, 2004).
31. *Id.*
32. *Id.*
33. *Id.*
34. 42 C.F.R. § 411.354(d).
35. *Id.*
36. *See Medicare Program; Changes to the Hospital Inpatient Prospective Payment Systems and Fiscal Year 2009 Rates*; 73 Fed. Reg. 48434 (August 19, 2008).
37. *Id.* at 48714.
38. *Id.*
39. See 69 Fed. Reg. at 16066-70 (indicating that percentage compensation arrangements can meet the set in advance requirement, but must also meet the volume or value and other business generated requirement).
40. *See* 73 Fed. Reg. 48434.
41. *Id.* at 48710.
42. *Id.* Note that in its 2009 Hospital Inpatient Prospective Payment System Proposed Rule, the Centers for Medicare and Medicaid Services originally proposed to limit percentage compensation arrangement only to personally performed services. *Medicare Program; Proposed Changes to the Hospital Inpatient Prospective Payment Systems and Fiscal Year 2009 Rates*, 73 Fed. Reg. 23528, 23694 (April 30, 2008).
43. 64 Fed. Reg. at 63522.

Chapter 7: The Anti-Kickback Statute and Stark Law

44. *See* 56 Fed. Reg. at 35970.

45. Note that the Office of Inspector General has stated that "a reasonable return can be appropriately measured only in light of the risk of the investment. An investor would surely expect a much higher return from an investment in an expensive piece of diagnostic equipment that might soon become obsolete than from an investment in a relatively inexpensive piece of equipment that can be expected to generate a steady profit stream for the foreseeable future." 56 Fed. Reg. at 35970.

46. *OIG Advisory Opinion No. 98-19; OIG Advisory Opinion No. 97-5.*

47. *Id.*

48. In contrast to a business with historical continuing operations, a business with limited operations has significantly higher risks depending on its ability to, among other things, obtain additional financing, complete construction and equipment purchases, obtain licensure and regulatory approvals, ramp-up operations, and meet revenue and expense targets. Beyond such risks over which a startup business may be able to exert some control, there are the additional risks confronted by any startup, such as competition, obsolescence, regulatory changes and adverse reimbursement changes.

Chapter 8

Tax-Exempt Healthcare Organization Valuation Issues Related to Excess Benefits, Private Inurement, and Intermediate Sanctions

By Robert F. Reilly

Introduction

This discussion focuses on the regulatory reasons why tax-exempt healthcare organizations retain valuation analysts to perform transaction valuations, reasonableness of compensation analyses, and similar fair market value analyses. This discussion will not present a "how to" explanation of valuation approaches, methods, and procedures for the valuation analyst. Such "how to" procedural explanations are presented elsewhere in this text (and in numerous principles and advanced valuation texts). Rather, this discussion will summarize the regulatory considerations that the valuation analyst (and all parties to a proposed transaction) should be aware of with respect to the valuation of a tax-exempt healthcare organization.

With regard to most tax-exempt organization transactions, the principal parties (and the valuation analyst) should be concerned with at least three potential regulatory challenges: (1) Medicare fraud and abuse challenges, (2) Internal Revenue Service private inurement issues, and (3) Stark laws compliance issues. This discussion will focus on the second potential regulatory challenge: federal income tax issues related to private inurement allegations and the related intermediate sanctions excise tax penalties. In particular, this discussion focuses on: what type of transaction price or structure may result in a private inurement, what parties are subject to the private inurement considerations, what types of transactions are encompassed in the spectrum of private inurement considerations, what the Internal Revenue Service looks for in its consideration of private inurement issues, and how the intermediate sanctions penalties work in instances of alleged private inurement.

The first half of this discussion will summarize the tax-related regulatory issues related to tax-exempt healthcare organization transactions. The valuation analyst should be generally aware of these issues in the fair market value analysis of any transaction involving (1) a tax-exempt entity and a for-profit entity or (2) a tax-exempt entity and any "disqualified person." The second half of this discussion will present a sample illustrative valuation analysis and report related as a hypothetical purchase of a tax-exempt healthcare entity by a newly-formed for-profit healthcare entity. As will be presented, that hypothetical transactional valuation is prepared to provide the hypothetical transaction participants (who are created to be "disqualified persons") with professional assurance related to any private inurement aspects of the proposed transaction.

Chapter 8: Tax-Exempt Healthcare Organization Valuation Issues

Valuation Issues

It is noteworthy that the private inurement and excess benefit issues related to tax-exempt healthcare entities encompass two types of transactions: (1) the transfer of property and (2) the transfer for services. Both of these types of tax-exempt organization transactions involve valuation issues and fair market value valuations. Both of these types of transactions are analyzed by valuation analysts who estimate a fair market value related to a proposed or consummated transaction. And, the term fair market value is defined the same way for both types of transactions. According to Treasury Regulation Section 53.4958-(b)(1)(i):

> Fair market value is defined as the price at which property, or the right to use property, would change hands between a willing buyer and a willing seller, neither being under any compulsion to buy, sell, or transfer property or the right to use property and both having reasonable knowledge of relevant facts.

Many valuation analysts are more familiar with valuations related to the transfer of property-type transactions. This type of transaction occurs when the tax-exempt entity buys or sells a business, a business ownership (equity) interest, or operating assets. Some common examples exclude when the tax-exempt healthcare entity buys or sells a hospital, clinic, physicians' practice, MRI center, urgent care center, HMO, home healthcare agency, medical equipment provider, or any other healthcare delivery organization. And, these transactions encompass the purchase or sale of either assets or equity interests.

Many valuation analysts may be less familiar with valuations related to the transfer of services-type transactions. This type of transaction occurs when the tax-exempt entity hires employees or contracts for professional services. Some common examples include when the tax-exempt healthcare entity compensates a CEO (or other executives), pays a medical director (or other physician professionals), hires a physician group to manage the emergency room or operating room, rents office or professional space to/from staff physicians, leases equipment to/from staff physicians, provides billing or other administrative services to staff physicians, or generally enters into any joint venture or related contractual agreement with staff physicians. In order to analyze such services-type transactions for concerns of private inurement, valuation analysts are often asked to opine on the fair market value of the services transfer transaction.

Other Regulatory Considerations

In addition to Internal Revenue Service and taxation considerations, tax-exempt healthcare entities should comply with numerous other federal and state regulations regarding the transfers of property and services. This section provides a very brief summary of some of these other regulatory considerations that the valuation analyst should be aware of.

Chapter 8: Tax-Exempt Healthcare Organization Valuation Issues

The Medicare fraud and abuse statutes make it illegal to pay, offer, or induce any remuneration in exchange for patient referrals. For example, a hospital cannot pay a staff physician in exchange for his or her patient referrals to that hospital. Accordingly, in a physician practice acquisition transaction, a hospital cannot pay any purchase price related to the physician's current or expected patient referrals. Therefore, tax-exempt acquirers (and any other healthcare industry acquirers) should not structure a transaction that appears to involve either (1) a "kickback" payment for physicians' patient referrals or (2) a "lock up" of physicians' patent referrals.

The Stark laws prohibit physicians with a financial relationship with an entity from referring patients to the entity for "designated health services" covered by either Medicare or Medicaid programs.

The Medicare anti-kickback laws prohibit the giving or receipt of anything of value in order to induce the referral of medical business reimbursed under the Medicare or Medicaid programs. Unlike the Stark laws, summarized next, the Medicare anti-kickback law is an "intent-based" statute. In addition, the Medicare anti-kickback law statutes make it clear that the healthcare entity payments for any property or services should be based on fair market value (and should not be variable, based on patient volume or patient referrals).

The Stark II statute became effective on January 1, 1995. Like the Stark I statute, Stark II was intended to curb abuses inherent in physician self-referral arrangements. Like Stark I, Stark II prohibits physicians who have a financial relationship with a healthcare entity (whether tax-exempt or for-profit) from referring their patients to the entity for "designated health services" covered by either Medicare or Medicaid programs.

A financial relationship consists of an ownership or investment interest in the healthcare entity or a compensation arrangement with the healthcare entity. If the physician (1) does not own any portion of the healthcare entity and (2) does not pay the entity or receive any kind of payment from the entity for the referral or for anything else, then there is no financial relationship. Under the Stark legislation, a financial relationship can exist between a physician and a healthcare entity even if that relationship does not involve designated health services or the Medicare or Medicaid programs.

For example, a compensation arrangement is defined in the Stark II statute as any arrangement involving any remuneration between (1) a physician (or family member) and (2) a healthcare entity. This remuneration can involve payments for anything, such as payments for rent, payments for nonmedical services, or payments for housing or travel expenses. Accordingly, the Stark statutes would interpret the purchase of a physician's practice by a hospital (and the related payment to the selling physicians) as a financial arrangement.

Section 1877(e)(6) of the Stark II regulations provides that an isolated transaction, such as a one time sale of a property or a practice, is not considered to be a compensation arrangement for purposes of the prohibition on patient referrals. This is true if the following conditions are met:

Chapter 8: Tax-Exempt Healthcare Organization Valuation Issues

- The amount of remuneration for the one time transaction sale is consistent with fair market value and is not determined, directly or indirectly, in a manner that takes into account the volume or the value of the physician's patient referrals.

- The remuneration is provided under an agreement that would be commercially reasonable even if no patient referrals are made to the acquirer healthcare entity.

- The arrangements meets any other requirements the Secretary may impose by regulation as needed to protect against Medicare program or patient abuse.

It is noteworthy that the term "isolated transaction" is defined as a transaction involving a single payment between two or more persons. A transaction that involves long-term or installment payments is not considered to be an isolated transaction.

In order to comply with the Stark laws, a healthcare entity's property or practice purchase transaction (1) should be priced at fair market value and (2) should be structured with a purchase price that is not paid in installments.

In order to comply with the Stark laws related to the payment for services, the healthcare entity purchase transaction should be structured as follows:

1. There should be a written agreement signed by parties which specifies the services to be covered under the arrangement.

2. The term of the agreement should be at least one year.

3. The aggregate services contracted for should not exceed those that are reasonable and necessary for the legitimate business purpose of the subject arrangement.

4. The compensation to be paid by the healthcare entity over the term of the agreement should be:

- defined in advance

- not in excess of fair market value

- not determined in a manner which takes into account patient volume or the value of any patient referrals or other business generated by the parties.

Chapter 8: Tax-Exempt Healthcare Organization Valuation Issues

Definitions

This section will summarize the definitions of certain terminology that is associated with the tax-related regulation (and valuation) of healthcare organization transactions.

1. Tax-exempt organization

First, a non-profit entity is not the same as a tax-exempt organization. And, a tax-exempt entity is not the same as a charitable institution. There are many types of tax-exempt organizations:

- Section 501(c)(4) – civic leagues and social welfare organizations
- Section 501(c)(5) – labor, agricultural and horticultural organizations
- Section 501(c)(6) – business leagues
- Section 501(c)(7) – social and recreational clubs
- etc.

This discussion focuses on the tax regulation with regard to Section 501(c)(3) "charitable organizations." The requirements to be a Section 501(c)(3) organization include:

- the organization is organized and operated exclusively for exempt purposes
- the net earnings of the organization do not inure to the benefit of individuals
- the organization is without substantial lobbying activity
- the organization is without any political activity
- examples of Section 501(c)(3) organization include schools, churches, and hospitals

Again, the focus of this discussion is on Section 501(c)(3) public charity healthcare organizations.

There are numerous advantages of Section 501(c)(3) status, including:

- exemption from most federal and state income taxes
- exemption from most state sales taxes
- exemption from certain payroll taxes

Chapter 8: Tax-Exempt Healthcare Organization Valuation Issues

- state and local property tax benefits

- preferred U.S. postal service mailing rates

- charitable contribution deductions are allowed for its donors

- eligibility for tax-exempt bond financing

To maintain its Section 501 (c)(3) status, the healthcare organization is required to operate "exclusively" for exempt purposes. However, the term "exclusively" doesn't mean exclusively—it means "primarily."

2. Disqualified person
This term (which is also used in the private foundation tax statutes) refers to the person or persons who have a close relationship with a tax-exempt organization.

3. Excess benefit transaction
This is the type of property transfer or services transfer transaction that is at the heart of the intermediate sanctions rules. It is an impermissible transaction between (1) a tax-exempt organization and (2) a disqualified person.

4. Excess benefit
An excess benefit is the impermissible aspect of a tax-exempt organization transaction that constitutes an excess benefit transaction. It is the amount that is used to compute one or more of the intermediate sanctions excise tax penalties.

5. Revenue-sharing transaction
This is a transaction between a tax-exempt organization and a disqualified person, where the benefit flowing to the disqualified person is based, in whole or in part, on the revenue flow of the tax-exempt organization.

6. Initial contract exception
This is one broad exception to the concept of the excess benefit transaction. Based on the initial contract exception, the transaction created by the initial relationship between the tax-exempt organization and the disqualified person is exempted from the intermediate sanctions excise tax penalties.

7. Initial tax
This is the tax that is initially levied on an excess benefit amount. This tax is also referred to as a first-tier tax.

8. Additional tax
This is the tax that can be imposed on an excess benefit amount, if the initial tax is not timely paid.

Chapter 8: Tax-Exempt Healthcare Organization Valuation Issues

9. Correction

A correction is the process that is required to undo an excess benefit transaction and return the parties to the economic position they were in before the excess benefit transaction was entered into.

Tax-Exempt Organization Transactions—Private Inurement and Excess Benefits

Tax-exempt organizations are exempt from federal income tax as organizations described in Section 501(c)(3) only if they are organized and operated exclusively for charitable purposes within the meaning of the statute. However, such tax-exempt organizations are subject to certain restrictions with regard to acquisition, professional services, employee compensation, and other types of transactions.

The Internal Revenue Code, the Service, and many state attorneys general view tax-exempt organizations as charitable trusts for the benefit of the public. The regulatory scheme of Section 501(c)(3) is designed to:

1. ensure the furtherance of public purposes, and

2. prevent the diversion of charitable assets into private hands.

Accordingly, the tax law includes two important types of restrictions (or prohibited activities) related to tax-exempt organization transactions.

Private Inurement

The first type of restriction relates to private inurement. For Section 501(c)(3) tax-exempt organizations, no part of the net earnings may inure to the benefit of any private shareholder or individual. This means that an individual can't receive the tax-exempt organization's funds, except as reasonable payment for goods or services. There is no minimum threshold related to the private inurement restriction, and there is no de minimis exception.

The private inurement restriction applies only to "private shareholders or individuals," commonly referred to as "insiders" (i.e., those having a personal and private interest in or opportunity to influence the activities of the organization from the inside). It is noteworthy that the term "insider" does not appear in the Internal Revenue Code or regulations. However, it is widely used in the related legal, accounting, and valuation literature.

The intermediate sanctions provisions of Section 4958 were added to the Internal Revenue Code in 1996 and (as discussed below) uses the terms "excess benefits transaction" and "disqualified person." The legislative history of Section 4958 states that "[t]he Committee intends that physicians will be considered disqualified persons only if they are in a position to exercise substantial influence over the affairs of an organization." The tax-exempt organization's payment of excessive or greater than reasonable compensation to an insider, such as a healthcare entity officer or director, is a prime example of prohibited private inurement.

Private Benefit

The second type of restriction relates to private benefit. Section 501(c)(3) tax-exempt organizations should be organized and operated to serve public rather than private interests. Unlike the private inurement transaction restrictions, the private benefit transaction restrictions are not absolute. To be a permissible transaction, a private benefit transaction should be incidental to (or a necessary concomitant of) accomplishment of the public benefits involved. Private benefit should be balanced against the public benefit. And, the Service has issued regulations that provide examples illustrating the test for serving a public rather than a private interest.

The private benefit prohibition is not limited to insiders. For example, some incidental private benefit is always present in hospital-physician relationships (e.g., when a private practice physician uses a tax-exempt hospital facilities to treat his or her paying patients).

Any private inurement or too much (i.e., other than incidental) private benefit could cause a tax-exempt hospital to lose its tax exemption. Until 1995, the revocation of the organization's tax exemption was the only sanction available to the Service. However, with regard to both private inurement and excess private benefit, the service now relies principally on the imposition of Section 4958 intermediate sanctions excise tax penalties.

Excess Benefit

Section 4958, enacted as part of the 1996 Taxpayer Bill of Rights, allows the Service to impose penalty excise taxes on certain "excess benefits transactions" between "disqualified persons," and tax-exemption organizations described in Sections 501(c)(3) or 501(c)(4).

Excess benefit transactions include:

1. a transaction priced at other than fair market value (FMV) in which a disqualified person (a) pays less than FMV to the tax-exempt organization or (b) charges the tax-exempt organization more than FMV for a good or service,

2. an unreasonable compensation transaction, in which a disqualified person receives greater than a FMV level of compensation from the tax-exempt organization, and

3. a prohibited revenue sharing transaction, in which a disqualified person receives payment based on the revenue of the tax-exempt organization in an arrangement specified in Section 4958 regulations that violates the inurement prohibition under current law.

Chapter 8: Tax-Exempt Healthcare Organization Valuation Issues

Disqualified Persons

Section 4958 defines certain people to be "disqualified persons" with respect to a tax-exempt organization, including:

1. voting members of the tax-exempt organization's governing board,

2. persons who have or share ultimate responsibility for implementing the decisions of the governing body or for supervising management, administration, or operation of the tax-exempt organization (such as president, CEO, COO, treasurer, and CFO unless demonstrated otherwise), and

3. persons with a material financial interest in a provider-sponsored organization.

The Section 4958 regulations clarify that this category of disqualified persons can include organizations such as management companies.

Section 4958 identifies other parties as not being a disqualified person:

1. all organizations described in Section 501(c)(3) (although the Pension Protection Act of 2006 appears to have created on exception for supporting organizations),

2. with respect to Section 501(c)(4) organizations, other Section 501(c)(4) organizations, and

3. full-time or part-time employees receiving total direct and indirect economic benefits in an amount less than the amount of compensation necessary to be highly compensated, as defined in Section 414(q)(1)(B)(i) (i.e., $100,000 in 2007), who are not substantial contributors within the meaning of Section 507(d)(2) (taking into account certain adjustments) or otherwise within the definition of "disqualified person."

In all other cases, the Section 4958 regulations indicate that a "disqualified person" is (1) any person who was, at any time during the previous five years, in a position to exercise substantial influence over the affairs of the organization, (2) certain family members (lineal descendents, brothers and sisters, whether by whole or half-blood, and spouses of any of them), or (3) an entity 35% or more of which is controlled by such persons.

The legislative history of Section 4958 recognizes that a non-employee, such as a management company or the employee of a subsidiary (even a taxable subsidiary), could be in a position to exercise substantial influence. The Section 4958 regulations provide that, in the case of multiple organizations affiliated by common control or governing documents, the determination of whether a person does or does not have substantial influence is made separately for each applicable tax-exempt organization.

Chapter 8: Tax-Exempt Healthcare Organization Valuation Issues

The Pension Protection Act of 2006 added several new classifications of disqualified persons. Any disqualified person with respect to a Section 509(a)(3) supporting organization is a disqualified person with respect to the supported organization. Any substantial contributor to a donor advised fund is a disqualified person with respect to the donor advised fund. Any investment advisor to an organization sponsoring a donor advised fund is a disqualified person with respect to he sponsoring organization.

The Initial Contract Rule

The Section 4958 regulations establish an "initial contract rule" to protect from intermediate sanctions liability certain "fixed" payments for the provision of services or the sale of property made under a binding written contract. The initial contract only applies to persons who were not disqualified persons immediately before entering into the initial contract. Fixed payments are defined to include an amount of cash or other property that is either (1) specified in the contract or (2) determined using a fixed formula specified in the initial contract. And, payments that include a variable component (such as achieving certain levels of revenue or business activity) may qualify as a fixed payment as long as the components are calculated pursuant to a pre-established, objective formula.

Section 4958 Penalty Excise Taxes

Under Section 4958, a disqualified person is liable for (1) an initial 25% penalty excise tax on the amount of the excess benefit and (2) an additional penalty tax of 200% on the amount of the excess benefit if the transaction is not timely corrected. A tax-exempt organization manager who knowingly, willfully, and without reasonable cause participates in an excess benefit transaction is personally liable for a 10% penalty tax (up to a maximum of $20,000) on the amount of the excess benefit.

It is noteworthy that no Section 4958 penalties are assessed on the tax-exempt organization itself. Of course, a tax exemption revocation remains an option of the Service in extreme cases.

Intermediate Sanctions

The purpose of the intermediate sanctions tax law is to prevent wrongdoing by persons who have a special relationship with tax-exempt organizations, particularly charitable entities. Before the enactment of the intermediate sanctions laws, the Internal Revenue Service, when faced with one of these inappropriate transactions, had essentially two choices:

1. apply the private inurement doctrine or the private benefit doctrine and revoke the tax-exempt status of the subject organization, or

2. ignore the matter (and perhaps informally attempt to influence the behavior of the parties involved on a going-forward basis).

From the Service's standpoint, these two options were not sufficient. Accordingly, the Treasury and the Internal Revenue Service urged Congress to enact the intermediate sanctions legislation.

Revocation of an organization's tax-exempt status is a particularly harsh consequence. Moreover, the loss of the subject organization's tax-exempt status does not necessarily resolve the underlying problem—the party that obtained the inappropriate benefit still has it. Often, the only individuals truly punished in these situations are the beneficiaries of the tax-exempt organization's programs.

Intermediate sanctions are penalties imposed on the person or persons who engage in the inappropriate transaction with the tax-exempt organization. These sanctions are called "intermediate" because they fall between (1) the revocation of tax-exempt status and (2) inaction on the part of the Service. Also, the sanctions are not applied to the tax-exempt organization that was abused. Rather, the sanctions are imposed on the person or persons who improperly benefited from the subject property or services transfer transaction.

It is noteworthy that the intermediate sanctions law does not replace either (1) the private inurement doctrine or (2) the private benefit doctrine. Rather, the Service now has a range of taxpayer penalty options. The Service can impose the sanctions alone. The Service can impose both the sanctions and the private inurement doctrine. Or, the Service can find the sanctions do not apply and nonetheless invoke the private benefit doctrine.

Intermediate Sanction Taxes

The intermediate sanctions are, in fact, federal excise taxes. These federal excise taxes are applied to the amount involved in the impermissible transaction—i.e., the excess benefit. The person who pays for intermediate sanctions tax (again, not the tax-exempt organizations) is referred to as a disqualified person.

The first intermediate sanctions tax is an "initial tax." The initial tax is 25% of the amount of the excess benefit. Also, the excess benefit property or services transaction must be reversed. This reversal or refund of the excess benefit transaction is intended to put the parties in the same economic position they were in before the excess benefit transaction was entered into. This process is referred to as correction of the transaction.

If (1) the initial tax is not timely paid and (2) the offending transaction is not timely and properly corrected, then an "additional tax" may be imposed. This intermediate sanctions tax is 200% of the amount of the excess benefit. In some instances, the trustees, directors, or officers with the tax-exempt organization may also be required to pay a tax of 10% of the amount of the excess benefit.

Chapter 8: Tax-Exempt Healthcare Organization Valuation Issues

Under certain circumstances, the intermediate sanctions tax may be abated. Generically, the Section 4958 intermediate sanctions excise taxes are referred to as "penalties."

Intermediate Sanctions and Applicable Tax-Exempt Organizations

The Section 4958 intermediate sanctions statute and associated regulations apply with respect to public charities and tax-exempt social welfare organizations. These entities are called "applicable tax-exempt organizations" for this Section 4958 purpose.

Applicable tax-exempt organizations include any organization described in either of these two categories of tax-exempt organizations at any time during the five-year period ending on the date of the property sale or services transfer transactions. Accordingly, public charities can be:

1. churches, integrated auxiliaries of churches, and associations and conventions of churches

2. colleges, universities, and schools

3. hospitals, other providers of healthcare, and medical research organizations

4. foundations supportive of governmentally operated colleges and universities

5. units of government

6. publicly supported charitable, educational, religious, scientific, and like organizations

7. organizations that are supportive of other types of public charities

Tax-exempt social welfare organizations include entities that are: (1) civic in nature, (2) assist a community in various ways, and/or (3) engage in more advocacy (usually lobbying) than is allowed for charitable organizations. Therefore, an entity qualifies as an applicable tax-exempt organization if it operated as either type of tax-exempt organization at any time in the five-year period before the excess benefit transaction occurred. This five year period rule is referred to as the "lookback rule." And, this five-year period is referred to as the "lookback period."

Section 4958 provides for no exemptions from these rules (e.g., for small organizations or religious entities). That is, all domestic public charities and all social welfare organizations are applicable tax-exempt organizations. However, a foreign organization that is tax-exempt, by determination of the Service or by treaty, as a charitable or social welfare entity is not an applicable tax-exempt organization if it receives substantially all of its support from sources outside the United States.

The Section 4958 definition of the term "applicable tax-exempt organization" encompasses the concept of recognition of the entity's tax-exempt status. Most categories of tax-exempt

Chapter 8: Tax-Exempt Healthcare Organization Valuation Issues

organizations are tax exempt because they satisfy one or more federal tax law definitions of the term. However, to be recognized as tax exempt, some organizations (1) must file notice with the Service to that effect and (2) have their exempt status recognized by the Service. This recognition is accomplished by the Service's issuing of a determination letter or private ruling.

For an organization to be a tax-exempt charitable organization, it typically files a notice with, and has its tax-exempt status recognized by, the Service. Some charitable organizations, such as churches and certain other religious organizations and small organizations, are exempt from this requirement of recognition. For a charitable organization to be recognized as an applicable tax-exempt organization, it should be in compliance with the recognition requirements.

To be tax exempt, social welfare organizations do not need to have their exempt status recognized by the Service. An organization can qualify as an applicable tax-exempt organization by reason of being an exempt social welfare organization in the following four ways:

1. The organization has applied for and received recognition from the Service as an exempt social welfare organization.

2. The organization has filed an application for recognition with the Service, seeking exempt social welfare status.

3. The organization has filed an annual information return as an exempt social welfare organization.

4. The organization has otherwise held itself out as an exempt social welfare organization.

A governmental unit or an affiliate of a governmental unit will not be recognized as an applicable tax-exempt organization if the governmental unit is (1) exempt from or not subject to taxation without regard to the general statutory basis for tax exemption or (2) relieved from the requirement of filing an annual information return. A governmental entity may be recognized as tax-exempt as an integral part of the state: (1) by reason of the doctrine of intergovernmental immunity or (2) because its income is excluded from federal taxation.

An entity qualifies as a governmental unit if it is:

1. a state or local governmental unit as defined in the rules providing an exclusion from gross income for interest earned on bonds issued by these units,

2. entitled to receive deductible charitable contributions as a unit of government, or

3. an Indian tribal government or a political subdivision of this type of government.

Chapter 8: Tax-Exempt Healthcare Organization Valuation Issues

Intermediate Sanctions and Individual Executives and Professionals

Under the Section 4958 intermediate sanctions law, excise taxes are imposed on excess benefit transactions that occur on or after September 14, 1995. The Section 4958 excise taxes do not apply to any transaction made pursuant to a written contract that was binding on September 13, 1995, and continued in force through the time of the subject transaction.

An excess benefit transaction is any transaction in which a Section 501(c)(3) or 501(c)(4) organization provides an economic benefit to a disqualified person that has a greater value than what it receives from that person. An excess benefit transaction would include: (1) providing compensation to a person in excess of the value of the services rendered or (2) selling or renting property to a person for less than the property's sale or rental value. The excess benefit is measured as the difference of (1) the fair market value of the benefit provided to the person over (2) the fair market value of the consideration received by the tax-exempt organization.

As summarized above, there are two types of Section 4958 excise taxes. The first type of excise tax is imposed on the disqualified person who receives an excess benefit. That tax is equal to 25% of the amount of excess benefit. There is an additional excise tax equal to 200% of the amount of the excess benefit if it is not corrected before (1) the date that the Services' deficiency notice is mailed for the 25% tax or (2) the date that the 25% tax is assessed, whichever comes first. The second type of excise tax is imposed on "organizational managers" who knowingly, willfully, and without reasonable cause or participate in the excess benefit transaction. This Section 4958 excise tax is equal to 10% of the amount of the excess benefit, but no more than $20,000.

A disqualified person is defined in Section 4958 as someone who, at any time during the five year preceding an excess benefit transaction, was in a position to exercise "substantial influence" over the affairs of the tax-exempt organization. If an individual is considered to be a disqualified person, then certain related parties are also considered disqualified persons. These related parties include: spouses, brothers or sisters, spouses of brothers or sisters, direct ancestors, direct descendants and their spouses, and corporations, partnerships and trusts in which the disqualified person has more than a 35% interest.

Certain individuals within a tax-exempt organization are automatically identified as disqualified persons. These individuals include: (1) any individual who serves as a voting member of the governing body of the tax-exempt organization, (2) any individual who has the power or responsibilities of the president, chief executive officer, or chief operating officer of the tax-exempt organization, and (3) any individual who has the power or responsibilities of treasurer or chief financial officer of the tax-exempt organization.

An employee of a tax-exempt organization is not considered a disqualified person if he or she: (1) receives less than $100,000 of direct or indirect benefits from the tax-exempt organization for the year (adjusted for inflation), (2) is not a member of a specifically included category above, and (3) is not a substantial contributor of the organization.

Chapter 8: Tax-Exempt Healthcare Organization Valuation Issues

The Service looks at specified facts and circumstances to indicate whether a person has "substantial influence" over the subject tax-exempt organization. In particular, the Service often considers the following factors in deciding if an individual has "substantial influence" over the tax-exempt organization:

1. the person founded the tax-exempt organization,

2. the person is a substantial contributor,

3. the person's compensation is based on the revenue derived from the activities of the tax-exempt organization,

4. the person has authority to control or determine a significant portion of the organization's capital expenditures, operating budget or compensation for employees, or

5. the person has managerial authority or serves as a key adviser to a person with managerial authority.

The following types of facts and circumstances would indicate to the Service that a person does not have "substantial influence" over the tax-exempt organization:

1. the person has taken a bona fide vow of poverty,

2. the person is an independent contractor (e.g., an attorney) who would not benefit from a transaction aside from the receipt of professional fees, or

3. the person is a donor who receives no more preferential treatment than other donors making comparable contributions as part of a solicitation intended to attract a substantial number of contributions.

An individual can be liable for the 10% excise tax penalty on organization managers if he or she is an officer, director, or trustee of the tax-exempt organization, or is a person with powers or responsibilities similar to those of officers, directors, or trustees. Attorneys, accountants, and investment advisers acting as independent contractors are typically not considered to be organizational managers. Any person who has authority merely to recommend particular administrative or policy decisions, but not to implement them without approval of a superior, is also excluded.

A tax-exempt organization's manager will be considered to have "participated" in an excess benefit transaction not only by affirmative steps, but also by silence or inaction. That would be the case when the organization's manager does not exercise a duty to speak or take action. However, the tax-exempt organization manager will not be considered to have participated in a transaction when he or she opposed it in a manner consistent with that manager's responsibilities to the tax-exempt organization.

Chapter 8: Tax-Exempt Healthcare Organization Valuation Issues

Tax-exempt organization managers can avoid the 10% penalty if they can show that they did not act willfully or knowingly. Tax-exempt organization managers can meet this requirement if, after disclosing all facts to an attorney, they receive a reasoned written legal opinion that a transaction does not provide an excess benefit. This procedure will protect the manager even if a transaction is later determined to be an excess benefit transaction.

Compensation to an organization's management for services rendered will not be considered an excess benefit if it is an amount that would ordinarily be paid for similar services in a similar situation. For purposes of this Section 4958 excise tax, compensation includes, but is not limited to: salary, fees, bonuses, severance payments, and all forms of deferred compensation that are earned and vested, whether paid under a tax-qualified plan or not. If deferred compensation is paid to a manager in one year for services performed by the manager in two or more years, then that compensation will be allocated to the years in which the services are performed.

Compensation also includes all benefits, whether or not included in income for federal tax purposes. For example, such benefits include: medical, dental, life insurance, and disability benefits, and both taxable and nontaxable fringe benefits (other than job-related fringe benefits and fringe benefits of inconsequential value).

An economic benefit will not be treated as reasonable compensation unless the tax-exempt organization clearly indicates its intention to treat it as compensation at the time it is provided. For example, if the tax-exempt organization fails to include compensation or other payments to disqualified persons on a Form W-2 (for employees) or Form 1099 (for board members and other non-employees) and does not treat the payments as compensation on its Form 990, then the payments will be considered an excess benefit.

A special rule applies to arrangements that compensate a disqualified person in proportion to the revenue generated by the tax-exempt organization. Such compensation may be considered an excess benefit even if it does not exceed the fair market value of the services provided. This result can occur if, at any point, the arrangement permits a person to receive additional compensation without providing proportional benefits to the tax-exempt organization. Whether such compensation is an excess benefit will depend on the facts of the individual case. The Service will consider such factors as: (1) the relationship between the size of the benefit provided and the quality and quantity of the services provided and (2) the ability of the party receiving the compensation to control the activities that generate the revenue.

To avoid the above-mentioned 200% excise tax, the excess benefit must be undone to the extent possible. In addition, other procedures may be necessary to place the tax-exempt organization in the same position that it would have been in if the excess benefits transaction was made under the highest fiduciary standards. An excess benefit can be corrected if the disqualified person repays the tax-exempt organization an amount equal to: (1) the excess benefit plus (2) an interest element for the period the excess benefit was outstanding. A correction may also be accomplished, in some situations, by: (1) returning the transferred

Chapter 8: Tax-Exempt Healthcare Organization Valuation Issues

property to the tax-exempt organization and (2) making any additional procedures necessary to make the tax-exempt organization whole.

Excess Benefit Transaction Presumption of Reasonableness

There is an important "presumption of reasonableness" that every tax-exempt organization subject to the intermediate sanctions law may endeavor to take advantage of. That presumption is in favor of the tax-exempt organization that a compensation arrangement or property sale or rental is not an excess benefit. To qualify for this presumption of reasonableness, the tax-exempt organization must meet the following three requirements:

1. The compensation arrangement or property sale or rental must be approved by the tax-exempt organization's governing body or a committee of the governing body composed entirely of individuals who do not have a conflict of interest with respect to the subject transaction,

2. The governing body or its committee must have obtained and relied on "appropriate data" as to comparability prior to making its decision, and

3. The governing body or its committee must have "adequately documented" the basis for its decision at the time it was made.

These three presumption of reasonableness requirements are summarized below.

Conflict of Interest

A member of a tax-exempt organization governing body or its committee will be treated as not having a conflict of interest if he or she:

1. is not (a) the disqualified person benefiting from the subject transaction or (b) a person related to the disqualified person,

2. is not an employee subject to the control or direction of the disqualified person,

3. does not receive compensation or other payments subject to approval of the disqualified person,

4. has not financial interest affected by the subject transaction, and

5. will not receive any economic benefit from another transaction in which the disqualified person must grant approval.

Appropriate Data

The category of "appropriate data" includes such information and documents as: (1) the compensation levels actually paid by similarly situated organizations, both for-profit and tax-exempt, for similar positions, (2) independent compensation surveys compiled by independent consulting firms, (3) actual written offers from similar organizations competing for the services of the disqualified person, and (4) independent appraisals of the fair market value of the to-be-transferred property. There is a special "appropriate data" relief provision for tax-exempt organizations with annual gross receipts of less than $1 million. Such a tax-exempt organization will be automatically treated as satisfying the appropriate data requirement if it has data on the level of compensation actually paid by five comparable organizations in similar communities for similar services.

Adequate Documentation

To meet the "adequate documentation" requirement, the tax-exempt organization governing body or its committee must have written or electronic records showing (1) the terms of the transaction and the date it was approved, (2) the members of the tax-exempt organization governing body or committee who were present during debate on the transaction and the names of those who voted on it, (3) the comparability data obtained, and (4) what was done about the members who had a conflict of interest. For a decision to be documented concurrently, the records must be prepared by the next meeting of the governing body or committee occurring after the final action is taken. Also, the records must be reviewed and approved by the governing body or committee as reasonable, accurate, and complete within a reasonable time period thereafter.

For purposes of this presumption of reasonableness exclusion, a tax-exempt organization governing body is: (1) a board of directors, (2) a board of trustees, or (3) an equivalent controlling body of the tax-exempt organization. A committee of the tax-exempt organization governing body (1) may be composed of any individuals permitted under state law to serve on such a committee and (2) may act on behalf of the governing body to the extent permitted by state law. The tax-exempt organization should note that if a committee member is not on the governing board and the presumption of reasonableness if relied upon, then the committee member becomes an "organization manager" for purposes of the 10% excise tax penalty. In other words, the committee member is treated like a member of the tax-exempt organization governing body if the presumption of reasonableness relied upon is rebutted by the Service. Also, a person will not be treated as a member of the governing body or its committee if he or she (1) meets with other members only to answer questions and (2) is not present during debate and voting on the transaction.

In addition, a tax-exempt organization subject to the intermediate sanctions law should note that this presumption of reasonableness is only a presumption. The Service can rebut the

Chapter 8: Tax-Exempt Healthcare Organization Valuation Issues

presumption of reasonableness if there is information indicating that (1) the compensation was not reasonable or (2) the property transfer was not at a fair market value price. However, these three requirements should go a long way toward helping a tax-exempt organization avoid the Section 4958 intermediate sanctions penalties.

Valuation Analyst Considerations Regarding Private Inurement

This section will summarize a "top ten" list of valuation analyst considerations with regard to valuations performed for tax-exempt healthcare organizations. These valuations include both (1) fair market value appraisals of property (business interests or assets) bought and sold by the healthcare organization and (2) fair market value appraisals of the services paid for by the healthcare organization (paid as either employee compensation or vendor fees).

These considerations may not affect the valuation approaches, methods, and procedures that the valuation analyst selects and performs. And, these considerations may not affect the valuation analyst's conclusions regarding the fair market value of the subject property or services. However, these are ten factors related to the intermediate sanctions law and regulations that the valuation analyst should be aware of during the conduct of the tax-exempt healthcare organization valuation.

1. Tax-exempt Healthcare Organizations

The Internal Revenue Code grants a tax exemption for non-profit hospitals and other healthcare organizations provided that their net earnings do not inure (1) to the benefit of private shareholders or (2) to individuals with a "personal and private" interest in the healthcare entity's activities.

2. Criteria to be Recognized as a Tax-exempt Organization

To meet the statutory criteria to be recognized as a tax-exempt healthcare entity, the organization must comply with the following rules:

- Physicians cannot be "in a position to exercise substantial influence over the affairs of (the hospital)."

- The total compensation must be "reasonable" and the incentive arrangement may not be a disguised distribution of profits.

- The compensation arrangements must be negotiated or established in the context on an arm's-length relationship.

- There is a ceiling or reasonable maximum compensation level.

Chapter 8: Tax-Exempt Healthcare Organization Valuation Issues

3. No Inurement

No portion of a tax-exempt healthcare organization's income or assets may inure to the benefit of "insiders." For purposes of this consideration, the term "insiders" may be defined as someone with decision power (e.g., board members, officers, founders, selected physicians, etc.). Examples of such private inurement may include:

- excessive employee/subcontractor compensation

- compensation based on the "net earnings" of the tax-exemption organization

- any transfer of property or services at less than a fair market value price

4. Penalty for Private Inurement

There are taxation-related penalties for any violation of this no inurement rule. The Service may apply a broad spectrum of remedies, including:

- revocation of the subject healthcare entity's tax-exempt status

- settlement of the amount of the inurement

- the Section 4958 intermediate sanctions excise taxes

5. Purpose of Intermediate Sanctions

The objective of the Section 4958 intermediate sanctions law is to curb potential abuses by penalizing participating parties (both those that benefit from the abuse and those that knowingly authorize the abuse). The intermediate sanctions law applies if there is an "excess benefit" transaction with a "disqualified person." An excess benefit transaction occurs when the economic benefit given in a transaction is greater than the consideration received by the healthcare tax-exempt organization. A disqualified person is any person having the ability to exercise influence over the affairs of the tax-exempt organization.

6. Imposition of Penalty Excise Taxes

Section 4958 imposes excise tax penalties on:

1. the disqualified person who has to correct the excess amount (i.e., pay it back to the tax-exemption healthcare organization) plus pay a penalty tax of 25%, and

2. the organization manager who has to pay a tax equal to 10% of the excess benefit amount (not to exceed $20,000 per transaction).

Chapter 8: Tax-Exempt Healthcare Organization Valuation Issues

7. Rebuttable Presumption of Reasonableness

There is a rebuttable presumption of reasonableness with regard to the tax-exempt healthcare organization entering into property or services transfer transactions when:

1. the transaction is approved in advance by an independent, authorized body of the tax-exempt organization,

2. the decision was based on the appropriate comparability data, and

3. the decision is adequately and timely documented (i.e., written down by the later of the next meeting or 60 days).

8. Excess Benefit Transaction

An excess benefit transaction is any transaction in which an economic benefit is provided by the tax-exempt healthcare organization directly or indirectly to or for the use of any "disqualified person" if the fair market value of the benefit exceeds the fair market value of the consideration.

9. Disqualified Persons

For purposes of the Section 4958 intermediate sanctions rules, a "disqualified person" includes:

1. a voting member of a board of the tax-exempt organization

2. the CEO, COO, treasurer, or CFO

3. any person, at any time during the previous five years, in a position to exercise substantial influence over the affairs of the organization

4. identified family members of the above

5. a 35% controlled entity

10. Not Disqualified Person

For purposes of the Section 4958 intermediate sanctions rules, the following "persons" are not disqualified persons:

1. organizations described in Section 501(c)(3); this exception was created by the Pension Protection Act of 2006.

2. other Section 501(c)(4) organizations (applicable for Section 501(c)(4) organizations only).

3. employees receiving less than $100,000 a year in compensation.

Reasonableness of Tax-Exempt Organization Compensation

One of the current controversy areas related to the intermediate sanctions requirements relates to the reasonableness of compensation. This is particularly true with regard to healthcare industry tax-exempt organizations. This reasonableness of compensation issue appears to be the current focus of Internal Revenue Service scrutiny with regard to tax-exempt healthcare entities. To alleviate concerns regarding intermediate sanctions, the tax-exempt healthcare entity should establish that its executives and physician employees are not paid more than a fair market value level of compensation.

Related to this reasonableness of compensation issue, many tax-exempt healthcare entities are considering the formation of a dedicated compensation committee. Such a compensation committee would:

1. adopt a written charter

2. be comprised of independent directors

3. be authorized to approve the organization's executive compensation

And, such a compensation committee would likely adopt a written compensation policy.

When considering the reasonableness of tax-exempt healthcare organization compensation, the Service looks to how the organization determined and documented the comparability of its executive compensation to other similarly situated organizations. In particular, the valuation analyst can assist the tax-exempt healthcare organization with the following:

1. compensation levels paid by similarly situated organizations, both taxable and tax-exempt,

2. independent compensation surveys compiled by independent consulting firms,

3. actual written offers from similar institutions, and

4. independent appraisals of the fair market value of the subject executive compensation.

The valuation analyst can assemble compensation data and/or prepare a compensation appraisal that considers the following:

Chapter 8: Tax-Exempt Healthcare Organization Valuation Issues

1. make sure that any compensation consultant relied on is independent and has no incentive to support higher pay/benefits

2. use data for the same or the closest functional position, and support these data in the board minutes

3. use data for organizations with a similar level of annual revenue, or show that the compensation data was "normalized" to fit organizations of a similar size

In the preparation of a fair market value compensation appraisal (i.e., a reasonableness of compensation study), the valuation analyst should note the following:

1. for-profit entity compensation data is permitted, but do not rely exclusively on for-profit entity compensation data

2. include compensation data related to prevalence and the value of significant employee benefits

3. make sure that every element is considered, and make sure that the total compensation is assessed for reasonableness (and approved by an authored body of the tax-exempt healthcare organization)

The approving body of the tax-exempt healthcare organization is protected in relying on the valuation analyst's written reasoned analysis, if the valuation analyst certifies that he or she:

1. holds themselves out to the public as a compensation consultant,

2. performs this type of compensation valuation regularly, and

3. is qualified to perform such compensation valuations.

Such a written certification should be included in every type of compensation appraisal performed by the valuation analyst.

Recent Developments

Effective March 28, 2008, the Treasury issued final Section 501(c)(3) regulations regarding applicable tax-exempt organizations and excess benefit transactions. These new regulations clarify the substantive requirements for tax exemption under Section 501(c)(3). These new regulations also clarify the relationship between the substantive requirements for tax exemption under Section 501(c)(3) and the imposition of Section 4958 excise taxes on excess benefit transactions.

Chapter 8: Tax-Exempt Healthcare Organization Valuation Issues

These new regulations discuss both (1) the imposition of the Section 4958 intermediate sanctions excise taxes and (2) the possible revocation of a tax-exempt organization's exemption status. Regulation 1.501(c)(3)-1 adds a new paragraph F that includes in part:

> (ii) *Determination of whether revocation of tax-exempt status is appropriate when section 4958 excise taxes also apply.* In determining whether to continue to recognize the tax-exempt status of an applicable tax-exempt organization (as defined in Section 4958(e) and Section 53.4958-2) described in Section 4958(c)3 that engaged in one or more excess benefit transactions (as defined in Section 4958(c) and Section 53,4958-4) that violate the prohibition on inurement under Section 501(c)(3), the Commissioner will consider all relevant facts and circumstances, including, but not limited to, the following—

> (A) The size and scope of the organization's regular and ongoing activities that further exempt purposes before and after the excess benefit transaction or transactions occurred;

> (B) The size and scope of the excess benefit transaction or transactions (collectively, if more than one) in relation to the size and scope of the organization's regular and ongoing activities that further exempt purposes;

> (C) Whether the organization has been involved in multiple excess benefit transactions with one or more persons;

> (D) Whether the organization has implemented safeguards that are reasonably calculated to prevent excess benefit transactions; and

> (E) Whether the excess benefit transaction has been corrected (within the meaning of Section 4958(f)(6) and Section 53-4958-7), or the organization has made good faith efforts to seek correction from the disqualified person(s) who benefited from the excess benefit transaction.

> (iii) All factors will be considered in combination with each other.

In addition, the new regulations provide several examples regarding private inurement and the application of the Section 4958 intermediate sanctions penalty taxes. While it is not related to a healthcare industry organization, the following example is included in the March 28, 2008, regulations and is relevant to this intermediate sanctions discussion:

> *Example 1.* (i) O was created as a museum for the purpose of exhibiting art to the general public. In Years 1 and 2, O engages in fundraising and in selecting, leasing, and preparing an appropriate facility for a museum. In Year 3, a new board of trustees is elected. All of the new trustees are local art dealers. Beginning in Year 3 and continuing to the present, O uses a substantial portion of its revenue to purchase art solely from its

Chapter 8: Tax-Exempt Healthcare Organization Valuation Issues

trustees at prices that exceed fair market value. O exhibits and offers for sale all of the art it purchases. O's Form 1023, "Application for Recognition of Exemption," did not disclose the possibility that O would purchase art from its trustees.

(ii) O's purchases of art from its trustees at more than fair market value constitute excess benefit transactions between applicable tax-exempt organization and disqualified persons under section 4958. Therefore, these transactions are subject to the applicable excise taxes provided in that section. In addition, O's purchase of art from its trustees at more than fair market value violate the proscription against inurement under section 501(c)(3) and paragraph (c)(2) of this section.

The following example from the March 28, 2008 regulations is also relevant to this discussion of private inurement, excess benefits transactions, and the Section 4958 intermediate sanctions penalties:

Example 4. (i) O conducts activities that further exempt purposes. O uses several buildings in the conduct of its exempt activities. In Year 1, O sold one of the buildings to Company K for an amount that was substantially below fair market value. The sale was a significant event in relation to O's other activities. C, O's Chief Executive Officer, owns all of the voting stock of Company K. When O's board of trustees approved the transaction with Company K, the board did not perform due diligence that could have made it aware that the price paid by Company K to acquire the building was below fair market value. Subsequently, but before the IRS commences an examination of O, O's board of trustees determines that Company K paid less than the fair market value for the building. Thus, O concludes that an excess benefit transaction occurred. After the board makes this determination, it promptly removes C as Chief Executive Officer, terminates C's employment with O, and hires legal counsel to recover the excess benefit from Company K. In addition, O promptly adopts a conflicts of interest policy and new contract review procedures designed to prevent future recurrences of this problem.

(ii) The sale of the building by O to Company K at less than fair market value constitutes an excess benefit transaction between an applicable Tax-exempt organization and a disqualified person under section 4958 in Year 1. Therefore, this transaction is subject to the applicable excise taxes provided in that section. In addition, this transaction violates the proscription against inurement under section 501(c)(3) and paragraph (c)(2) of this section.

Revocation of Tax-Exempt Status

As indicated in the recently issued Section 501(c)(3) regulations, the Service still possesses its ultimate weapon with regard to tax-exempt healthcare organizations—i.e., the revocation of the organization's tax exempt status. With regard to healthcare industry entities and other tax-exempt organizations, the valuation analyst should be aware that the Service may seek revocation—in addition to the provision of the Section 4958 intermediate sanctions excise taxes.

Chapter 8: Tax-Exempt Healthcare Organization Valuation Issues

The Service has made it clear that it will consider a list of facts and circumstances in determining when the level of excess benefit transactions will jeopardize a healthcare organization's tax exemption. These factors include, but are not limited to, the following:

1. the size and scope of the tax-exempt organization's regular and ongoing activities that further exempt purposes before and after the excess benefit transaction or transactions occurred,

2. the size and scope of the excess benefit transaction or transactions (collectively, if there are more than one) in relation to the size and scope of the tax-exempt organization's regular and ongoing activities that further exempt purposes,

3. whether the tax-exempt organization has been involved in repeated excess benefit transactions,

4. whether the tax-exempt organization has implemented safeguards that are reasonably calculated to prevent future violations, and

5. whether the excess benefit transaction has been corrected or the tax-exempt organization has made good faith efforts to seek correction from the disqualified persons who benefited from it.

In other words, both the valuation analyst and the tax-exempt organization board should be aware that the imposition of the Section 4958 excise taxes are the Service's "intermediate" weapon. Revocation of the tax-exempt organization's exemption status is still the Service's ultimate weapon.

Summary and Conclusion

The valuation analyst should be aware of the Section 4958 relationship with other federal tax laws and with other federal and state regulations. There are three general sets of federal laws that are intended to achieve the same objective: prevent persons who have a close relationship with a tax-exempt healthcare organization form manipulating the flow of income or assets to them for their private benefit. These federal laws include the Stark legislation, the Medicare fraud and abuse statutes, and the tax-exempt organization provisions of the Internal Revenue Code.

All of these federal laws (and many corresponding state laws) are directly influenced by the following three legal concepts:

1. the private inurement doctrine

Chapter 8: Tax-Exempt Healthcare Organization Valuation Issues

2. the private benefit doctrine

3. the self-dealing rules

The valuation analyst should be aware that the private inurement doctrine directly influences the Section 4958 intermediate sanctions rules. In many ways, the Section 4958 rules are a codification of the private inurement legal doctrine. The legal concepts of private inurement and excess benefit transactions are essentially identical. The same is true with respect to the legal concepts of the insider and the disqualified person. In the case of the private inurement doctrine, the ultimate sanction is the Service's revocation of tax-exempt status. The Service can apply the private inurement doctrine either (1) in lieu of the intermediate sanctions excise tax penalties or (2) in addition to the Section 4958 excise tax penalties.

The valuation analyst should be aware that the private benefit doctrine is applicable only to charitable organizations. That is, this legal doctrine is not applicable to other types of tax-exempt organizations, including social welfare organizations. The private inurement doctrine is applicable to both public charities and private foundations. In many ways, the legal concepts of private benefit and private inurement are essentially the same. That is, every transaction that is a private inurement is also a private benefit. The ultimate sanction, too, is the same: the Service's revocation of the organization's tax-exempt status.

The two principal differences between these legal doctrines are: (1) a private benefit transaction does not require an insider and (2) the tax law recognizes the idea of incidental private benefit. Therefore, the private benefit doctrine can apply even where the private inurement doctrine and/or the Section 4958 intermediate sanctions tax penalties cannot apply.

The valuation analyst should be aware that the rules concerning self-dealing and the Section 4958 intermediate sanctions rules do not overlap. This is because the legal rules concerning self-dealing apply to charitable organizations only with respect to private foundations. In contrast, the Section 4958 intermediate sanctions tax rules apply only with respect to public charities. Nonetheless, the self-dealing rules are still significant within the intermediate sanctions context. This is because the Section 4958 intermediate sanctions rules are patterned largely on the private foundation rules.

The valuation analyst should be aware that most healthcare industry professional advisers consider the Section 4958 intermediate sanctions rule to be a good idea. The Section 4958 provisions place the sanction—i.e., the excise tax penalties—where it should be: on the persons who inappropriately extracted a benefit from charitable and social welfare organizations and not on the tax-exempt healthcare organization itself. The intermediate sanctions rules—based on a standard of reasonableness—are an improvement over the unnecessarily stringent private foundation rules. Those rules effectively prohibit transactions with foundations and disqualified persons with respect to them.

Chapter 8: Tax-Exempt Healthcare Organization Valuation Issues

The valuation analyst who practices in the healthcare industry should be aware of the various regulatory requirements with regard to property transfer fair market value appraisals and compensation for services fair market value appraisals. The valuation analyst should be familiar with the regulatory environment with regard to private inurement, excess benefit transactions, intermediate sanctions excise tax penalties, and other tax-exempt organization regulatory issues. The valuation analyst should be aware of these issues in order to provide valuation services to tax-exempt healthcare organizations that will help them address these regulatory concerns.

Chapter 9

Tax-Exempt Hospitals Under the Microscope— How Much Charity Care are You Providing?

By Robert Wolin, Susan Feigin Harris, Jason Pinkall and Edward Beckwith
Copyright 2008 by Baker & Hostetler, LLP. Reprinted with permission.

The IRS, Congress, and several states have all been looking extensively at whether the benefits received by communities from tax-exempt hospitals justify the tax breaks they receive from federal, state and local governments. Most recently, the IRS issued new proposed revisions to Form 990 and late last week, the Senate Committee on Finance – Minority Staff (Minority Staff) issued a report which, if implemented, would dramatically change health care financing in the U.S.

Evolving Tax Exemption Standards

Historically, hospitals have been considered charitable institutions, entitled to tax exemption because they provided relief to the poor. In 1956, the IRS published Revenue Ruling 56-185, 1956-1 C.B. 202, which established the criteria a hospital must satisfy to be recognized as tax-exempt. The Revenue Ruling required, that to the extent financially able, a hospital must provide services to those unable to pay and must not refuse to accept patients in need of hospital care who cannot pay. With the advent of the Medicare and Medicaid programs, access to health care increased substantially. As a result, the IRS relaxed the criteria for hospital tax exemption in 1969, instituting a flexible "community benefit" standard to reflect the perceived diminished need for charitable care. Revenue Ruling 69-545, 1969-2 C.B. 117.

The community benefit standard generally considers the following factors in determining whether a hospital qualifies for tax exemption:

- Whether the hospital's governing body is composed of independent members of the community;

- Whether medical staff privileges are available to all qualified physicians in the area, consistent with the size and nature of the facilities;

- Whether the hospital operates a full-time emergency room open to all regardless of ability to pay;[1]

Chapter 9: Tax-Exempt Hospitals Under the Microscope

- Whether the hospital admits patients able to pay for care, either themselves or through third-party payers or government programs such as Medicare;

- Whether the hospital provides free or below cost services to the poor; and

- Whether the hospital's excess funds are generally applied to expansion and replacement of existing facilities and equipment, amortization of indebtedness, improvement in patient care, and medical training, education, and research.[2]

Under current law, a hospital need not satisfy every factor to be considered tax-exempt. Under the community benefit test, the IRS generally considers all of the hospital's circumstances in determining and evaluating its exemption.

As the number of uninsured and underinsured individuals in the U.S. has risen (that is, those individuals who do not otherwise qualify for the Medicare or Medicaid programs), Congress and others have begun to question whether the current community benefit standard adequately assures tax-exempt hospitals will meet their obligation to provide benefits to the poor.[3]

Community Benefits Currently Provided by Tax-Exempt Hospitals

In an effort to understand and quantify the contributions made by tax-exempt hospitals to their communities, the IRS sent detailed questionnaires to nearly 500 tax-exempt hospitals last year. Recently, the IRS issued an interim report summarizing its preliminary findings. The report concluded:

- No uniform definition of what constitutes "uncompensated care" exists and measurement of the value of uncompensated care is difficult because no common measurement standard exists (e.g., costs, charges, etc.). This makes assessment difficult;

- There is significant variation among hospitals in the level of expenditures in furtherance of community benefit;

- Hospitals use a wide range of income and asset criteria to establish eligibility for uncompensated care;

- Community benefits averaged 9% of hospital revenues, but vary widely. The median community benefit expenditure, however, was 5% of hospital revenues. On average, uninsured patients accounted for 7% of the total patients seen by nonprofit hospitals; and

- Community benefits generally included uncompensated and discounted care (56% of total community benefits); medical education and training; research; community programs; studies of unmet community health needs; immunization programs; programs to improve access to health care; and health promotion programs.

Chapter 9: Tax-Exempt Hospitals Under the Microscope

The survey findings highlighted for the IRS and Senate Finance Committee how difficult it is for policy makers to accurately measure whether the community contribution by tax-exempt hospitals and whether the cost of the tax exemption to the community can be justified by the benefit to the community.

Exempt Organization Compliance and Revision of IRS Form 990

On June 14, 2007, the IRS released a draft Form 990[4] designed to provide greater transparency and reporting consistency among tax-exempt charitable organizations.[5] For more information on the changes made to the IRS Form 990 see Baker Hostetler's Health Law Update, dated July 18, 2007.[6] After the release of the draft Form 990, members of the Senate Finance Committee urged the IRS to focus its efforts on gathering more detailed information from tax-exempt organizations and to pay particular attention to the operational complexities of nonprofit hospitals.[7]

Chairman Baucus and ranking member Grassley of the Senate Finance Committee affirmed the Committee's views in a letter to the Secretary of the Treasury, following issuance of the draft Form 990. The letter stated "that transparency and openness are pillars in encouraging our nation's charities to be responsive to the needs of the community and to act in accordance with the principles and goals for which they were established and that they seek contributions from the public." The letter urged the IRS to focus its efforts on the following areas for nonprofit compliance activities:

- Executive compensation, both the source and amount;
- Endowment management and utilization;
- Related organizations;
- Joint ventures;
- Governance;
- Dollars raised v. dollars for charity;
- Community benefit reporting;
- Disclosure of billing and debt collection policies; and
- Disclosure of a hospital's charity care policy.

Chapter 9: Tax-Exempt Hospitals Under the Microscope

Although the information derived from the revised Form 990 may allow the IRS to reconsider whether Revenue Ruling 69-545 and its progeny should be modified in a new Revenue Ruling, it is unclear whether Congress will wait for the IRS to promulgate the form, receive returns and analyze the data before acting on its own.

In response to an inquiry from Senator Grassley, the Tax-Exempt and Government Entities Division of the IRS[8] outlined the IRS' top exempt organization compliance concerns, some of which were addressed in the proposed Form 990. Some of the other issues, however, await further action by the IRS, Congress or both. The compliance issues identified in the letter applicable to health care facility operations include:

- The blurring of distinctions between tax-exempt hospitals and nursing homes as compared to for-profit facilities;

- Unrelated business income (UBI) compliance issues related to (i) distinguishing related from unrelated activities; (ii) allocation of expenses and income between related and unrelated activities; and (iii) losses incurred in unrelated activities;

- Executive compensation reporting;

- Loans to executives and disqualified persons;

- Political activities; and

- Tax-exempt bond issues

- Illegal arbitrage;

- Overpricing of certain financial products; and

- Record retention issues.

Congressional impatience was demonstrated this week when, shortly after the IRS released the preliminary results of its survey and the revised Form 990, Sen. Grassley publicly released a Minority Staff discussion draft on hospital tax-exemption reforms. The discussion draft suggests a number of reforms to help assure tax-exempt hospitals provide meaningful contributions to their communities.

Senate Finance Committee Minority Staff Proposed Cures

The Minority Staff Discussion Draft of Non-profit Hospital Reforms[9] is not legislation. However, it does provide insight into approaches Congress may take to change tax-exempt hospital organizational reporting and additional requirements it may impose on tax-exempt hospitals.

Chapter 9: Tax-Exempt Hospitals Under the Microscope

The Minority Staff believes that "the present community benefit standard is extraordinarily vague and does not correlate with the federal tax benefits received by" tax-exempt hospitals. Discussion Draft at 3. The Minority Staff also suggests that legislative mandates are likely necessary. Discussion Draft at 4. Voluntary efforts are, according to the Minority Staff, likely to fail as "many non-profit hospitals . . . say the right words but too often fail to do the right thing when it comes to providing for low-income families." Id.

The Discussion Draft suggests a two-tiered approach to nonprofit hospital community benefit obligations. Hospitals exempt under Internal Revenue Code (the Code) § 501(c)(3) would have a higher community benefit obligation than hospitals organized under Code §501(c)(4)[10] because the benefits of exemption under Code § 501(c)(3) are greater. In particular, contributions to Code §501(c)(4) organizations are generally not deductible as charitable donations and Code §501(c)(4) organizations are generally not eligible for tax-exempt bond financing. The requirements proposed in the Discussion Draft are detailed below and are in addition to the requirements presently imposed for tax exemption.

1. Proposed Additional Standards Applicable to 501(c)(3) Exempt Hospitals

   a. Written Charity Care Policy. Hospitals would be required to develop a written charity care policy in plain language. The policy would set forth eligibility requirements, procedures for obtaining free or discounted care, and identify where a patient could obtain additional information on accessing such care. The policy would be publicized and the Discussion Draft suggests that it would be available on hospital websites, available at all times in emergency rooms and admission areas, and available upon request to members of the public, the IRS and HHS. Finally, the Discussion Draft urges that the availability of charity care be widely posted in the institution.

   b. Charitable Care Eligibility Criteria. The Discussion Draft suggests setting the patient financial eligibility threshold for hospital uncompensated care at a level no less than 100% of the federal poverty level (FPL) for uncompensated medically necessary in- and outpatient hospital services and urges policymakers to consider imposing eligibility levels above the FPL. Hospitals would, however, have considerable flexibility in how they determined patient eligibility.

   c. Minimum Actual Annual Amounts of Charitable Care. The Discussion Draft recommends that each exempt hospital, after a transition period, annually provide charitable care in an amount equal to no less than the greater of: (i) 5% of annual patient operating expenses, or (ii) revenues. The 5% test was based on other current charitable care standards and the fact that the IRS had utilized a similar standard prior to implementing Revenue Ruling 69-545. The Discussion Draft recommends that critical access hospitals (CAH) be exempt from this requirement. Minority Staff considered a net income charitable care requirement, but concluded that such a measure was too easy to manipulate.

Chapter 9: Tax-Exempt Hospitals Under the Microscope

Charitable Care Defined. Perhaps most important, the Discussion Draft offered a definition of charity care and its measurement. Charity care would be defined as: (i) care provided "without expectation of payment from or on behalf of" the patient; (ii) the amount of revenue expected to be written off, prior to patient billing, as a result of a patient's inability to pay; (iii) uncompensated medical care provided through free clinics, community medical clinics and other mechanisms designed to serve vulnerable populations; and (iv) grants to other charities to provide free medical care to vulnerable populations. Bad debt was specifically excluded from the definition of charity care.

To assure uniformity in measurement, the value of charity care provided would be determined at the lower of: (i) the rate that would be paid by Medicaid for the services; (ii) the rate that would be paid by Medicare for the services; or (iii) the hospital's actual unreimbursed cost for such services.

d. Joint Venture Requirements. The Discussion Draft expressed concern that joint ventures between exempt organizations and for-profit entities may divert surplus funds away from charitable care and hospital services that are less profitable. In response, the Discussion Draft proposed that whole hospital joint ventures between exempt organizations and for-profit entities must: (i) implement a charity care policy; (ii) meet the charity care policy proposed for 501(c)(3) hospitals; and (iii) have a board controlled by the exempt hospital(s).

In the case of ancillary service joint ventures between exempt organizations and for-profit entities involving patient care services, the Discussion Draft proposed that the joint venture must: (i) implement a charitable care policy that is controlled by the exempt member hospital(s) that meets the charity care requirements applicable to the exempt member hospital(s) themselves; (ii) have a board including at least one representative of each exempt member hospital; and (iii) provide that no decision may be made by the joint venture's board that affects the charity care policy without approval by the exempt member hospital(s). Charity care provided through the joint venture would be applied to member tax-exempt hospital's charitable care obligations based upon the hospital's pro rata ownership interest in the joint venture relative to total exempt hospital ownership interests in the joint venture.[11]

Under this formulation, exempt hospitals likely would be given credit for the value of charitable care services well in excess of their pro rata interest in the joint venture for purposes of computing their annual charitable care obligations, even though the cost of the charitable care was largely imposed upon their for-profit joint venture partners.[12] These charitable care obligations and related costs, however, could make it more difficult for exempt hospitals to participate in joint ventures with for-profit entities.[13]

The Discussion Draft also recommends that the protection available to exempt organizations under the initial contract exception and the rebuttable presumption of reasonableness of compensation for Code §4958 excess benefit transactions[14] be eliminated with respect to joint ventures between for-profit entities and tax-exempt hospitals. In addition, the

Chapter 9: Tax-Exempt Hospitals Under the Microscope

Discussion Draft recommends expanding the definition of disqualified person for purposes of the excess benefit transaction rules to include any person that participates in a joint venture between an exempt hospital and a for-profit entity where: (i) such person receives an excess financial benefit; or (ii) the exempt hospital suffers a disproportionate financial detriment. Finally, the Discussion Draft proposes that a manager of any exempt hospital who knowingly participates in or authorizes an excess benefit transaction should be subject to an excise tax in an amount equal to 25% of the excess benefit.

e. Community Needs Assessment. The Discussion Draft also recommends that every three years exempt hospitals conduct a community needs assessment, reviewed and approved by their boards, with a particular emphasis on vulnerable populations (i.e., populations with barriers to care: financial, transportation, disability, language, etc.) in consultation with local advocates and representatives for vulnerable populations as well as state and local Department of Health officials.

f. Community Wellness / Outreach Services. The Discussion Draft urges policymakers to consider whether exempt hospitals also should be required to provide other community benefits, such as education and outreach, training or research, health protection and health promotion for vulnerable populations.

2. Proposed Additional Standards Applicable to Both 501(c)(3) And 501(c)(4) Exempt Hospitals

a. Charges to Medically Indigent Patients. The Discussion Draft recommends charges to medically indigent patients who are uninsured or under-insured should be limited to the lower of: (i) the lowest rate that would be paid by Medicaid for the services; (ii) the lowest rate that would be paid by Medicare for the services; or (iii) the hospital's actual cost for the services. The Discussion Draft suggests that medically indigent patients should be defined to include patients with incomes of not more than 200% of the FPL.[15]

b. Governance.

i. Board Composition. Members of hospital boards would be required to represent the "broad interests of the community," including public officials, individuals with special knowledge or expertise in community health care, community leaders and advocates or representatives of those benefiting (or potentially benefiting) from charity care and discounted care for the medically indigent. Under the proposal not more than 25% of an exempt hospital's board voting interests could be held by members who are employed by the hospital or who would benefit financially, directly or indirectly, from the organization's activities (other than through the receipt of reasonable directors' fees). In addition not more than 25% of a hospital's board or committee membership would be comprised of physicians and/or hospital management, except for committees responsible for quality of care, credentialing, determining medical staff privileges and the like.

ii. Conflict of Interest Policies. Hospitals would be required to implement detailed conflict of interest policies that fully describe covered persons and arrangements (including all officers and directors and joint venture arrangements for-profit entities and other partnering arrangements with for-profit entities), the procedures for addressing an actual or potential conflict of interest, and the consequences of conflict of interest policy violations. At least annually boards would be required to review these policies and the potential conflicts reviewed thereunder.

iii. Board Responsibility for Charitable Care. Hospital boards would be required to determine the following: (i) criteria for charity care; (ii) policies related to discounts for low-income or uninsured patients who have the ability to pay a small portion of their bill; (iii) policies regarding eligibility determinations when there is insufficient information provided by the patient to fully evaluate all the eligibility criteria, and the ability to pay cannot be reliably determined; (iv) policies regarding the extent of verification necessary for charity care eligibility determinations; (v) policies regarding the time frame within which patients are eligible for charity care; and (vi) related issues.

iv. Other Board Responsibilities. Hospital boards would be expected to review the IRS Form 990 tax return and related schedules filed on behalf of the hospital.

v. IRS Exempt Organization Governance Proposals. In February 2007, the IRS issued draft good governance standards.[16] The standards are generally consistent with the Discussion Draft's proposals. Under the proposed standards, an exempt organization's board would:

1. Adopt a clearly articulated mission statement;

2. Implement ethical standards throughout the organization, including the adoption of: (a) a code of ethics; (b) internal complaint reporting policy; and (c) confidential whistleblowing policy;

3. Assure that board members exercise due diligence and receive accurate information to make informed decisions;

4. Assure that board members fulfill their duty of loyalty, that the organization has an effective conflict of interest policy, and that directors and staff annually disclose, direct and familial, business relationships with the organization;

5. Make complete, full and accurate information about the organization's mission, activities and finances public, including on the organization's web site;

6. Assure that fund-raising activities (a) are undertaken in compliance with applicable laws, (b) are undertaken in an accurate, truthful and candid manner, and (c) have reasonable costs;

Chapter 9: Tax-Exempt Hospitals Under the Microscope

7. Assure financial responsibility through the use of annual budgets, timely financial statements and review of the IRS Form 990, auditor's letters and committee reports;

8. Assure that compensation not exceed reasonable amounts for services rendered and not compensate directors in most cases; and

9. Develop a document retention policy, including standards for retaining electronic files.

> The IRS stated that the board should be composed of persons who are informed and active in overseeing the exempt organization's operations and finances. Successful governing boards, according to the IRS draft, should include individuals not only knowledgeable and passionate about the organization's programs, but also those with expertise in critical areas involving accounting, finance, compensation, and ethics. The IRS also stated that transparency was critical because charitable assets are more likely to be misused in a climate of secrecy or neglect.
>
> In a subsequent letter to Senator Grassley, the IRS questioned whether it was appropriate to require adoption of a core set of "good governance principles" as a condition to an organization's exemption from tax.[17] More concerning, the IRS also questioned whether exempt organizations should be required to demonstrate that (1) they are efficiently using their resources; (2) their expenses are reasonable; and (3) they are not accumulating resources beyond the organization's needs.[18]
>
> c. Billing and Collection Practices. Exempt and public hospitals would be required to comply with the Fair Debt Collection Practices Act (FDCPA) prohibitions against unfair and deceptive collection practices. Normally, the FDCPA is applicable only to third party debt collectors and attorneys who regularly collect debts. The Minority Staff specifically requested comments on debt collection practices that should be prohibited.
>
> d. Reporting and Transparency Requirements. The following information would be reported annually to the IRS and the public by exempt and public hospitals: (i) composition of board of directors; (ii) total patient operating expenses and revenues for the year; (iii) total amount of charity care provided, number of people receiving such care, and number of people who applied to receive such care; (iv) the total amount of community benefits provided disaggregated by type of community benefit provided and the total number of persons who benefited; (v) amounts reimbursed by private and governmental insurers; (vi) amounts paid to the hospital from special indigent funds, such as charitable care pools; and (vii) the purpose of each joint venture, copy of any charity care or community benefits policy of each joint venture, number of persons benefiting under such policies, and a description of the composition of the board. In addition, the exempt organization would be required to make publicly available the comparables survey on which it relied to establish the salaries of executives. These disclosure proposals are consistent with recent legislation enacted as Code §6104(d)(1)(A)(ii) (§1225 of

the Pension Protection Act of 2006) which requires organizations that file unrelated business income tax returns (Form 990-T) to also make the UBI returns available for public inspection and copying.[19]

e. Conversion of Exempt Organization to For-Profit Status – Termination Tax. Exempt hospitals, may, in some cases, convert their assets for use by a taxable entity through a sale of assets, joint venture, merger, and change in form of the corporation or a reorganization of the entity. According to a report prepared by the staff of the Joint Committee on Taxation,[20] the conversion of public charities, especially of hospitals and other health care providers, has resulted in significant amounts of charitable assets being converted to for-profit uses. The Discussion Draft proposes imposing a termination tax on the liquidation or conversion of a charitable organization in an amount equal to the value of the organization's net assets that will not be dedicated to charitable purposes after the liquidation or conversion transaction. The termination tax would be paid from assets other than the exempt organization's remaining charitable assets.

f. Executive Compensation. The Discussion Draft recommends that Congress consider prohibiting the provision of certain executive perks, including payments for country club fees, spousal travel, private airplanes (unless for provision of medical services), and loans to executives and it would place significant restrictions on first class travel. Recently, the IRS also has examined exempt organization executive compensation and found that significant reporting issues exist.[21] The IRS found that 25 exempt organizations studied paid excessive compensation to 40 employees. As a result, the IRS imposed $21 million in excise taxes. Based upon the IRS' recent study of 500 exempt hospitals, the IRS has begun investigation of more than 20 hospitals. The IRS expects to review executive compensation in all future compliance initiatives.[22] Consequently, exempt organization executive compensation is likely to remain a prominent issue for reform.

The Discussion Draft also proposes eliminating the exception to the excess benefits transaction rules for initial employment contracts of hospital affiliated personnel. Current law excepts a disqualified person's first written employment agreement with an exempt organization from the excess benefit transaction rules, if the person prior to entering into the contract was not a "disqualified person" as to the exempt hospital, if the contract calls for a fixed amount of compensation.

3. Proposed Additional Standards Applicable Only to 501(c)(4) Exempt Hospitals

a. Community Needs Assessment. Every three years, hospitals exempt under Code § 501(c)(4) would be required to conduct a community needs assessment with a particular emphasis on vulnerable populations. It is unclear whether these assessments would be required to meet all of the requirements associated with those performed by hospitals exempt under Code § 501(c)(3).

Chapter 9: Tax-Exempt Hospitals Under the Microscope

b. Community Benefits / Outreach. Hospitals exempt under Code § 501(c)(4) would be required to dedicate a minimum of 5% of their annual patient operating expenses or revenues to the provision of community benefits. The Discussion Draft would exempt critical access hospitals from this requirement.

The following services, under the proposal, would be deemed per se community benefits: (1) charity care; (2) an emergency room open to all, regardless of ability to pay; (3) burn units; (4) trauma centers; (5) health profession education and training programs; (6) health research; and (7) activities conducted in response to issues raised by a community needs assessment. Under the proposal, the IRS would have authority to designate additional items and services as per se community benefits. Other community benefit activities would be subject to written approval by the IRS. The Minority Staff suggests that the Catholic Health Association's "Community Benefit Categories and Standard Definitions—Hospitals" could serve as a template for defining community benefits.[23]

4. Proposed Sanctions for Non-Compliance

a. Excise Tax. An excise tax would be imposed on hospitals that fail to meet the proposed applicable quantitative requirements in an amount at least equal to twice the hospital's shortfall. However, the IRS would be authorized to be flexible in measuring compliance. In addition, smaller fines could be imposed if a hospital could demonstrate that it had met the requirements over a period of years (e.g., 4 out of 5 years) and that the shortfall was due to a lack of demand for services by medically indigent persons.

b. Revocation of Exempt Status. Under the proposals, the IRS also would be able to revoke a hospital's exempt status if it failed to meet any of the foregoing requirements. Repeated violations of the charity care requirement also could result in ineligibility to raise additional tax-exempt bonds, ineligibility to raise tax deductible charitable contributions and a recapture of tax benefits relating to such subsidies.

c. Revocation of Medicare Provider Status. The Discussion Draft also suggests that consideration be given to terminating an exempt hospital's Medicare provider status if it fails to meet the foregoing requirements over time. However, the Discussion Draft recognizes the harm that could result from such an action and suggests that the decision be weighed carefully.

Looking Ahead

While the proposals discussed herein are still formative, it is clear reforms and additional requirements for tax-exempt hospitals will be a topic of keen interest in Washington in the coming months. The Senate Finance Committee has stated that it is "clear [Congress] need[s] to do more work."[24] It is also likely that the IRS will advocate that the reforms be based, to the extent possible, on bright line tests to help relieve the IRS of its current "difficult and fact intensive" exemption administration requirements.[25] The standards proposed in the Discussion Draft go beyond the pre-Medicare I.R.S. standards and may be impossible for many exempt hospitals to meet, especially if they are implemented in a rigid quantitative bright line manner.

In addition, many states are carefully redefining charitable care and requiring the provision of minimal levels of care and/or reporting of charitable care by exempt hospitals. See, e.g., Tex. Health & Safety Code §311.041 et seq., California Health & Safety Code §127340 and Minnesota H.R. No. 1078 (legislation that would establish a minimum charity care requirement of 6% that hospitals must satisfy in order to qualify for property tax exemption). As states grapple with how best to treat the growing uninsured population, it is likely that more states will make mandatory exempt hospital charitable care obligations and subject the requirement to specific definitions and limitations. Moreover, states are encouraging consumers to take advantage of charitable care provided by hospitals.[26] More frequently, states are seeking to revoke ad valorem tax exemptions for hospitals that fail to provide sufficient charitable care. For example, the Illinois Department of Revenue ruled in 2006 that Provena Covenant Medical Center and, later, that Richland Memorial each failed to prove that it provided enough free medical care to the needy to qualify for a tax exemption and revoked its ad valorem tax exemption. While the Illinois Circuit Court of Sangamon County recently reversed the Provena decision and restored the ad valorem exemption, the state's objective may have been served because Provena Covenant expanded its charity care guidelines to provide more uncompensated care.[27]

Being Proactive

All exempt hospitals should review their organizational and governance structures, as well as policies and procedures, to assure they can reasonably comply with the new evolving federal and state standards. In addition, exempt hospitals should start planning actions to ameliorate the impact of these proposals and should consider preparing comments to these proposals.

The Minority Staff has requested comments on the proposals in the Discussion Draft, and the IRS has requested comments on the new Form 990. It is critical that hospitals provide substantive comments on both proposals to assure that their interests are properly considered. Baker Hostetler's Health Industry team will be collaborating with the firm's Legislative and Tax-Exempt teams to assure clients are able to make these critical evaluations of their infrastructures and are well represented as these matters are considered by Congress and the IRS as well as regulators at the state level.

---

1. Revenue Ruling 83-157, 1983-2 C.B. 94 provides that a hospital can qualify for tax exemption even if it does not operate an emergency room under certain circumstances.
2. Revenue Ruling 98-15, 1998-1 C.B. 718 and subsequent court decisions have permitted hospital joint ventures with for-profit companies to receive tax-exemption.

Chapter 9: Tax-Exempt Hospitals Under the Microscope

3. For example, in a well publicized case, the Los Angeles city attorney's office recently settled false-imprisonment and dependent-care-endangerment charges against Kaiser Permanente for allegedly "dumping" patients on skid row. See http://www.lacity.org/atty/index/attyindex56045233_05152007.pdf. See also Sicko (Michael Moore 2007).

4. The IRS Form 990 is the return for organizations exempt from federal income tax (other than private foundations) and provides the information required by Code § 6033. The IRS Form 990 is subject to public disclosure.

5. For tax years ending on or after December 31, 2006, exempt organizations (other than private foundations) with $10 million or more in total assets ($100 million in 2005) are required to file their IRS Form 990 electronically if the organization files at least 250 returns in a calendar year, including income, excise, employment tax and information returns. The electronic returns will increase transparency and public access to the data. See June 28, 2007 IRS Letter to Senator Grassley at page 27. This requirement may be expanded to smaller exempt organizations in the future. Id.

6. Available at http://www.bakerlaw.com/PublicDocs/News/Newsletters/HEALTH%20LAW%20UPDATE/2007/15%20July%2018.pdf.

7. See Senate Finance Committee Statement on Redesigned Form 990 for tax-exempt organizations at http://www.senate.gov/~finance/press/Bpress/2007press/prb061407b.pdf.

8. Letter dated June 28, 2007 and made public on July 23, 2007. The letter is available at http://www.senate.gov/~finance/press/Gpress/2007/prg072307a.pdf.

9. The Discussion Draft is available at: http://finance.senate.gov/press/Gpress/2007/prg071907a.pdf.

10. Code § 501(c)(4) organizations are entities that are operated exclusively for the promotion of social welfare and primarily engaged in promoting in some way the common good and general welfare of the community. The Minority Staff was unaware of any hospitals that are currently exempt under Code § 501(c)(4).

11. For example, if two nonprofit hospitals own 10% of a joint venture entity each and a for-profit entity owns the remaining 80% interest in the joint venture, each exempt member hospital would be allowed to count 50% of the joint venture's total charity care toward its minimum charity care requirement. However, an exempt hospital, according to the Discussion Draft, would not be allowed to include as charity care: (a) any portion of a joint venture's charity care if exempt members do not control the joint venture's charity care policy or (b) charity care that is provided by another separate entity taxed as a corporation.

12. For example, an exempt hospital with a 10% interest in a joint venture would be allowed to count 100% of the charity care provided by the joint venture towards its charity care requirement, even though 90% of the cost was imposed upon the for-profit joint venture partner.

13. The Minority Staff are also considering whether it is appropriate to tax an exempt joint venture member hospital on income derived from any non-medically necessary services (such as certain cosmetic surgery) performed by a joint venture as unrelated business income.

14. Excess benefit transactions are generally defined as transactions with a disqualified person in which the economic benefit provided by the exempt organization, directly or indirectly, exceeds the value of the consideration received by the exempt organization.

15. Hospitals exempt under Code § 501(c)(3) are, however, also required to provide free care for families below 100% of the FPL.

16. Available at http://www.irs.gov/pub/irs-tege/good_governance_practices.pdf.

17. See June 28, 2007 IRS Letter to Senator Grassley at page 27 made public on July 23, 2007. The letter is available at http://www.senate.gov/~finance/press/Gpress/2007/prg072307a.pdf.

18. Id at 28.

19. See IRS Notice 2007-45. Available at http://www.irs.gov/pub/irs-drop/n-07-45.pdf.

20. Options to Improve Tax Compliance and Reform Tax Expenditures prepared by the Staff of the Joint Committee on Taxation, January 2005 at page 230. Available at: http://www.house.gov/jct/s-2-05.pdf

21. Report on Exempt Organizations Executive Compensation—Compliance Project--Parts I and II, March 2007. Available at: http://www.irs.gov/pub/irs-tege/exec._comp._final.pdf.

22. See June 28, 2007 IRS Letter to Senator Grassley at page 18.

Chapter 9: Tax-Exempt Hospitals Under the Microscope

23. Available at: http://www.chausa.org/NR/rdonlyres/68057062-B902-420D-BB04C5B1597E64BB/0/CBCategories_Hospitals.pdf <http://www.chausa.org/NR/rdonlyres/68057062-B902-420D-BB04-C5B1597E64BB/0/CBCategories_Hospitals.pdf> . The Catholic Health Association defines community benefits in general as "programs or activities that provide treatment and/or promote health and healing as a response to identified community needs. They are not provided for marketing purposes. A community benefit must meet at least one of the following criteria: (i) Generates a low or negative margin; (ii) Responds to needs of special populations, such as persons living in poverty and other disenfranchised persons; (iii) Supplies services or programs that would likely be discontinued—or would need to be provided by another not-for-profit or government provider—if the decision was made on a purely financial basis; (iv) Responds to public health needs; or (v) Involves education or research that improves overall community health." Community Benefit Categories and Standard Definitions—Hospitals, Catholic Health Association of America.

24. See Senate Finance Committee Memorandum dated July 23, 2007. Available at: http://www.senate.gov/~finance/press/Gpress/2007/prg072307.pdf.

25. See IRS June 28, 2007 Letter to Senator Grassley at 26.

26. See e.g. Texas Senate Bill 1731 (effective September 2007) – which provides that the Texas Department of State Health Services shall include information in its consumer guide to advise consumers that "the consumer, if uninsured, may be eligible for a discount on facility charges based on a sliding fee scale or a written charity care policy established by the facility."

27. Provena Covenant Medical Center v. Illinois Department of Revenue, Ill. Cir. Ct., No. 2006-MR-597, 7/20/07.

Chapter 10

Why Boards of Directors Need to Understand Valuation Issues

By Eleanor Bloxham, MBA

Whether tax-exempt or not, all boards of directors are charged with overseeing the organization, in the best interest of the organization itself, and *all* its capital providers and other stakeholders, including customers, suppliers, employees and others.

For boards, valuations are like heart rate monitors, giving them assessments of the organization's pulse, and the pulse of the organization's capital providers and stakeholders.

Although most often used during times of major change or crisis, boards need to recognize that valuations are more than that. Boards should make sure that valuations are not just used at specific times but rather valuation should be part of the board's regular oversight of the organization's health and fitness.

This chapter will outline the reasons boards of directors need to understand valuation issues and the questions they need to ask in assessing the validity of the valuation models they review.

In understanding why directors need to understand valuation issues, it is important to understand:

1. The ways in which directors should use valuations.

2. The pre-requisites of a good valuation for directors and questions directors need to address in this regard.

3. Key issues directors will need to sort through in assessing and using valuations.

Valuation issues are at the heart of the board's oversight responsibilities.

The questions directors should address with valuations are many. Valuations, the right ones, can help boards make decisions about major transactions, provide essential input for oversight of strategy, and perform effective ongoing monitoring and oversight functions. Exhibit A is a partial list of some of the key topics directors should use valuations to address.

It is critical here to recognize that there are many kinds of valuations. Some examples include valuations to determine a fair sales price, valuations that reflect the intrinsic value creation of an

Chapter 10: Why Boards of Directors Need to Understand Valuation Issues

ongoing concern, valuations that describe a liquidation value in a crisis situation, valuations that describe the value of stock or other securities to their owners, and valuations that describe the value the organization has provided to the community.

Valuations should be used by boards to carry out many of their duties and functions. Other chapters in this book describe responsibilities specific to boards of non-profit hospitals and other non-profit healthcare entities, as well as boards of for-profit healthcare organizations. Specific issues addressed in other chapters of this book include community benefit, intermediate sanctions, fairness opinions, Stark issues, private inurement, fair value of physician services, and other issues. Valuation is important in each of these areas.

Board nominations and board governance. In determining the qualifications for future nominations to the board, and the right board composition, the board should use valuations as one measure to assess their own current strengths and weaknesses. For example, given the board's key role in overseeing the organization, in the best interest of the organization itself, and *all* its capital providers and other stakeholders, including customers, suppliers, employees and others, should ask the question: what improvements, in adding value from these perspectives, have occurred (or not) during the directors' tenures? This is an important element in assessing the efficacy of the current board. Boards should use valuations, not just of the organization as a whole, but on all these dimensions to assess how they, as directors, are doing. For example, how has the organization contributed to shareholder wealth, if a stock company? Or how has the organization contributed to the community, especially if tax exempt?

Exhibit B outlines a question guide boards can use to apply valuation information to assess their own performance. Given this information, boards can then assess their own strengths and weaknesses, and use that information to improve their board governance – and to develop a succession plan for the board that shores up their weaknesses and provides the organization with the board composition needed for the future.

Compensation, management oversight and succession. Given the board's key role in oversight of management, answering the question of management competence and contribution to value is also a key way that boards should use valuations. In addition, performance driven compensation requires an understanding of an executive's performance which valuations can provide. Similarly, valuations provide boards with insights into succession and hiring decisions. Do candidates have a track record of adding value to their organizations? In what ways? In addition, making a regular practice of using valuations can strengthen the financial literacy of executives and allow directors to assess executives' current level of development. Exhibit C summarizes some of the key areas where valuations should inform directors in their oversight roles.

Strategic oversight. Given the board's role in approving strategy, valuations should be used by boards to ascertain:

- The outcomes that may be achieved with different strategic choices

Chapter 10: Why Boards of Directors Need to Understand Valuation Issues

- The likelihood that those outcomes will be achieved

- Whether the promised outcomes are, in fact, being achieved and how or what the organization should do to make mid-course corrections

Stakeholder relations. Valuations should also be used by boards to address matters of stakeholder relations. Directors should understand valuation issues to help them better assess the need for stakeholder disclosures and to understand the information that should be provided to stakeholders about the organization's risks and opportunities, its operations, products and services, and future direction.

Directors should also understand valuation issues to help them assess the competence of a key stakeholder: valuation providers. Without that ability, boards are at the mercy of management and/or service providers in situations which may be conflicted. For example, major mergers and acquisitions require board oversight and approval. Directors are often unable to solely rely on management or investment bank analyses because both of those parties may have a conflict of interest in the transaction, and often do. Directors that do rely on those sources without adequate assessments put themselves at risk.

Similarly, even non-conflicted service providers must be able to be judged by directors as qualified and acting in the interests the directors serve i.e. the best interest of the organization itself, and *all* its capital providers and other stakeholders, including customers, suppliers, employees and others. If directors cannot make this determination, they have neglected their own duties by delegating the information for their decision making to those who are not acting in those best interests. In other words, at the very least, boards need to be able to determine if a good valuation has been obtained.

Key issues directors will need to sort through in assessing and using valuations. Exhibit D provides the pre-requisites of a good valuation for directors and the questions directors need to address in this regard. Because the purposes for which directors may use valuations are many, directors need to ensure that the valuations they use suit the job and address the particular purpose for which they are using the valuation. They also need to ask probing questions so they can understand the strengths and weaknesses of any given model.

For directors, the list of valuations issues they need to address in making the assessment and using valuations is long.

Mathematical models are used in developing valuations. Directors need to understand these models, their applicability to the specific purpose or question being addressed, and to recognize their benefits and limitations. This is important to ensure that the models are being used correctly and any inherent assumptions in the models will not distort the valuation's results. As noted earlier, this knowledge can also help the directors in other ways. By understanding valuation issues in-depth, they can better assess needs for executive development and the overall state of management's financial literacy.

Chapter 10: Why Boards of Directors Need to Understand Valuation Issues

What might directors want to understand about mathematical models? One example is this. Some valuations contain mathematical models that assume a variable (such as dividends or growth) will remain constant or contain a positive value over time. Directors need to evaluate whether those assumptions hold in a particular analysis and if not, they need to ask for other models that more properly represent a fair valuation for the issue being addressed.

Directors also need to understand the assumptions in the model and to ask probing questions about those assumptions. Valuations (as is the case with any model) are only as good as the math and the data used in those models. Interest rate assumptions, time horizon assumptions and other parameters can make a significant difference in valuation results.

Directors need to understand and probe these issues. As an example of the kinds of questions directors should ask, Exhibit E provides a list of questions for one assumption in valuations which directors should probe.

In sum, directors need to understand valuations issues:

- To fulfill their duties as directors
- To determine areas for organizational improvement
- To monitor and improve their own performance

From strategic development to specific decisions, valuations are the heart monitors of the organization. Directors need to use them to take the pulse often, understanding the issues inherent in their readings, and act with this knowledge in mind.

Bibliography and References

Many of the comments in this chapter are expanded upon in the following works which can be used by the reader as reference works to understand the concepts and details discussed in this chapter in greater depth.

Books:

1. Bloxham, Eleanor *Value-led Organizations*, Copyright 2002, John Wiley and Sons.

2. Bloxham, Eleanor, *Economic Value Management: Applications and Techniques*, Copyright 2003, John Wiley and Sons.

Articles:

Chapter 10: Why Boards of Directors Need to Understand Valuation Issues

1. Bloxham, Eleanor *Five Key Principles: Protecting Yourself and Your Board*, April 10, 2007, *Corporate Board Member*. Copyright 2007, The Value Alliance Company.

2. Bloxham, Eleanor *Model Risk and Accountability*, February 15, 2008, *Accountability Central*. Copyright 2008, The Value Alliance Company.

3. Bloxham, Eleanor *Behind the Boardroom Door with Eleanor Bloxham: Valuation: A Discipline and a Science*, August 2008, *IR Update*. Copyright 2008, The Value Alliance Company.

4. Bloxham, Eleanor *Improving Governance: Solutions for the Healthcare Sector*, August 2008 (Volume 27, Number 3) *New Perspectives on Healthcare Risk Management, Control and Governance*. Copyright 2008, Association of Healthcare Internal Auditors, Inc.

5. Bloxham, Eleanor *Behind the Boardroom Door with Eleanor Bloxham: Annual Reports: An Important Boardroom Conversation*, September 2008, *IR Update*. Copyright 2008, The Value Alliance Company.

Exhibit A

For Directors, valuations have multiple uses:

- Decisions on major transactions:
    - Sale (whole organization or part)
    - Purchase (whole organization or part)
    - Capital expenditure
    - Securities offering
- Strategy development
- Ongoing monitoring:
    - Organization's operational health
    - Organization's financial health and capitalization requirements
    - Stakeholder health and well-being: including benefits provided to and from capital providers, customers, employees, suppliers, communities, etc.

Chapter 10: Why Boards of Directors Need to Understand Valuation Issues

- Health of particular initiatives and the outcome of particular transactions

- Key risk areas for the organization

Exhibit B

Self-assessment and assessment by governance experts is critical for good board governance.

Valuations can address specific questions related to the value the board is adding.

Directors need to probe and obtain answers to the following:

- Has the organization's valuation increased, decreased or remained unchanged during our tenure?

- How have we as a board contributed to this?

- Has the organization increased the value it provides to key stakeholders during our tenure?

- Have we provided an increase in value to customers? How have we, as a board, contributed to this?

- Have we provided an increase in value to shareholders (if shareholder funded)? How have we, as a board ,contributed to this?

- Have we provided an increase in value to the community (whether or not but especially if community funded/tax-exempt)? How have we, as a board, contributed to this?

- Have we provided an increase in value to employees? How have we, as a board, contributed to this?

Exhibit C

For directors, valuations help them better assess:

- Management's financial literacy

- Management's competence (true organizational results)

- CEO candidates' competence in past assignments (external or internal) for succession planning and advancement purposes

Chapter 10: Why Boards of Directors Need to Understand Valuation Issues

- Compensation which should be awarded to key executives

Exhibit D

For Directors, good valuations:

- Address answers to specific questions (no one size fits all).
  Directors need to probe and obtain answers to the following:

    - What is the reason this valuation is being performed?

    - Who will use it?

    - How will it be used?

    - What questions are we answering and what questions are not being answered by looking at this valuation?

    - Does this valuation fully address our question?

    - What other information do we need?

    - How will this valuation influence our current and future decisions and behaviors?

    - Are there other questions we should be addressing as well?

- Are neither overly complex or overly simplistic
  Directors need to probe and obtain answers to the following questions:

    - Does the valuation address all the important variables for the question we are attempting to address?

    - Does it ignore any important variables?

    - Does it include variables that make little difference?

    - What would be the outcome (in terms of results, decisions and behaviors) if the valuation were less complex? Were less simplistic?

    - How can we monitor the ongoing impact of the variables used and the variables ignored?

Chapter 10: Why Boards of Directors Need to Understand Valuation Issues

- Use as few assumptions as possible and those that are used are disclosed
  Directors need to probe and obtain answers to the following questions:

  - What is the genesis for the choice of valuation model(s) being used?

  - What are the inherent assumptions in that model?

  - Do those assumptions really apply to our situation or the question we are addressing?

  - Would those assumptions apply and apply consistently in the future?

  - To what extent is it likely that any assumption would not apply?

  - How much will that assumption influence the valuation as well as the decisions we will make? How much will that assumption influence future behavior?

  - What decision or behavior is likely to result from the use of that assumption?

  - How can we monitor the ongoing impacts of the assumption on our valuation outcomes and adjust our modeling as required?

Exhibit E

For Directors, understanding valuation model assumptions and parameters is critical:

- For example, assumptions regarding capital adequacy
  Directors need to probe and obtain answers to the following:

  - What are the capital assumptions built into the valuation model?

  - What capital adequacy modeling has been performed in making these assumptions?

  - Have the capital assumptions been tested?

  - Have the tests included alternative market, competitive, political, inflationary, regulatory and other conditions?

  - Why have the capital assumptions been chosen?

  - Have different valuations been developed with other alternative capital assumptions?

Chapter 11

Factors in Forecasting Cashflow and Estimating Cost of Capital in Healthcare

Carol Carden, CPA/ABV, ASA, Mark O. Dietrich, CPA/ABV

It is critical when undertaking the valuation of any company to have a good understanding of the risks associated with the future cash flows. In today's environment in the healthcare industry, it has never been more important or more difficult to appropriately assess risk and correctly apply discount or capitalization rates. It is equally difficult in the uncertain healthcare environment to develop revenue forecasting assumptions that are reasonable and reflective of likely trends in the various healthcare industry sectors. This article offers some guidance on the myriad of factors which impact the cost of capital/risk assessment and cash flow forecasting for healthcare industry transactions.

What Comprises the "Healthcare Industry?"

Before delving into a discussion about the risk and uncertainty associated with the healthcare industry, it is important to first establish the different types of organizations included under this broad umbrella. At 17% of the US economy, healthcare is the single largest segment. The treatment of "Healthcare" as a single industry obscures the fact that it is really a complex set of separate subsections that are to one extent or another interrelated and may have very different prospects at different points in time.

Primary components of the industry include physicians, facilities, pharmaceutical and life sciences, medical equipment manufacturers and technology, and home health care. As a further division, facilities include acute care hospitals, long-term care hospitals, skilled nursing facilities, freestanding ambulatory surgery centers (ASCs) and senior housing. These are all dramatically different businesses. Acute care hospitals compete with ASCs for outpatient surgery, for example, but ASCs are paid only 60% of what a hospital outpatient department receives for the same case. Therefore, even two businesses that provide essentially the same service have very different risk characteristics and future revenue prospects.

In the physician sector, hospital-based physicians such as anesthesiologists or neonatal intensive care unit (NICU) physicians favored by private equity investors are very different from one another and from other types of practices that typically have much greater overhead than hospital-based physicians

Chapter 11: Factors in Forecasting Cashflow and Estimating Cost of Capital

Each of these sectors is likely to have a very different risk profile. That risk, to a large extent, is a function of the relative success or failure of industry lobbyists in winning support for their subsection from government payors such as Medicare and Medicaid. As such, identifying trends in future government program revenue is one key to the accurate assessment of risk as well as the forecasting of future cashflow.

Governmental influence

No other segment of the economy is so closely tied to the action of federal and state governments. Governmental influence flows from the executive branch through regulatory authorities such as the Office of the Inspector General, Federal Trade Commission, Anti-Trust Division of the Department of Justice (DOJ), States' Attorneys General, DOJ Civil and Criminal Division, Centers for Medicare & Medicaid Services (CMS) and numerous others. Each of these agencies plays a critical role in the prospects for the various components of the healthcare industry.

The legislative branch plays a less frequent but often dramatic role in subsector prospects as discussed in greater detail later in this article. At the state level, the Medicaid program for low income and indigent individuals is a significant factor for many individual companies within each subsector but may not be significant to others who do not service that population. Reform legislation at the state level- such as universal coverage in Massachusetts- can have a highly localized effect. It is critical in assessing the risk and cash flows associated with a healthcare company that you have a good understanding of the potential impact of governmental action or inaction on your particular healthcare subsector.

Identifying Factors That Contribute to Risk

One of the great challenges of business valuation is quantification of future changes in cash flow through the forecast or through the discount rate. Due to the high level of regulation and government influence in healthcare, the forecasting of revenue growth assumptions is much more difficult than a similar undertaking for a less regulated industry. On the other hand, there are a number of sources for near term trend analysis for the healthcare industry as well as longer- term crystal ball gazing to assist in this undertaking.

Near Term Forecasting and Risk Assessment

Each year in March, the Medicare Payment Advisory Commission (MedPac) issues their report to Congress regarding Medicare Payment Policy. While the MedPac report is not authoritative, it has proven to serve as a good indicator of potential areas of Medicare payment action as well as which sectors are likely to be targeted for significant reimbursement changes or industry re-structure. Many times, recommendations from the MedPac report will be included in the proposed Physician Fee Schedule as discussed below.

Chapter 11: Factors in Forecasting Cashflow and Estimating Cost of Capital

CMS publishes each year proposed - and after a comment period - final regulations announcing rates for the subsequent calendar year. For example, the proposed Medicare Physician Fee Schedule (MPFS) Rule is typically published in July or August and the final rule in early November. While labeled "physician fee schedule", the MPFS also contains proposed fees for outpatient, physician-based healthcare entities such as ASCs. There is approximately three months notice about what is likely to occur in the next calendar year. There have also been instances, such as when the ASC fee schedule was completely revamped in 2005, where fee changes are so significant that they will be phased in over a number of years providing a reliable revenue assumption forecasting tool for the short term.

Notably, since 2003, massive cuts in the physician fee schedule have been announced in the Proposed Rule only to be overturned by Congress in late December before a January 1st effective date and replaced with small increases in the range of .5% to 1.5% due to the Sustainable Growth Rate (SGR) Formula. It is beyond the scope of this article to discuss the SGR in detail, but in summary, the premise of the SGR is that budget neutrality is intended related to changes in the MPFS, but has historically not been achieved. Therefore, to place the MPFS back in "balance" would require a significant single year reduction across the board in physician fees. As such, when dealing with a valuation date that falls after the Proposed Rule but before the Final Rule is issued, application of revenue assumptions from the Proposed Rule must be tempered based upon the likelihood of implementation in the analyst's professional judgment.

The Proposed and Final Rules are closely watched by management and by industry analysts, although seemingly less so by investors given the lag in some stock's price response. For example, Alliance Imaging (AIQ) is a provider of magnetic resonance imaging (MRI), positron emission tomography/computed tomography (PET/CT) and radiation therapy, primarily on an outpatient basis. Approximately 80% of its revenue comes from contracts with hospitals and much of that is subject to the HOPPS or Hospital Outpatient Prospective Payment System. Nonetheless, it has a significant exposure to the MPFS.

The following graph plots AIQ's stock price and volume for the period June through November of 2009. As can be seen, there was some reaction to the MPFS Proposed Rule on July 1 which called for significant cuts in the payment rates for MRI and radiation therapy, particularly intensity-modulated radiation therapy (IMRT), an expensive form of radiation therapy. Thereafter, the stock recovered much of the loss in value following the announcement, only to plunge following the company's earnings conference call when management quantified the loss in net revenue (and effectively operating income) at more than $5.5 million. From an appraiser's standpoint in looking at a comparable company, one would have to believe that the impact of the proposed cuts (which were in large part adopted as part of the Final Rule on October 31) was subject to calculation and therefore reasonably knowable at the beginning of July.

The drop of about 30% in the stock's price on July 31 is a function of three factors: 1) expected/known reduction in future cashflow; 2) increased risk of cashflows; and 3) selling pressure due

Chapter 11: Factors in Forecasting Cashflow and Estimating Cost of Capital

to high trading volume. Note that despite the quantification of the loss in cashflow, the stock's price recovers after the downward price pressure of the selloff is gone. When the Proposed Rule is finalized at the end of October, the stock's price declines again. Investor reaction appears more immediate since the reductions under the Proposed Rule announced July 31 are confirmed on October 31 and "all hope is lost."

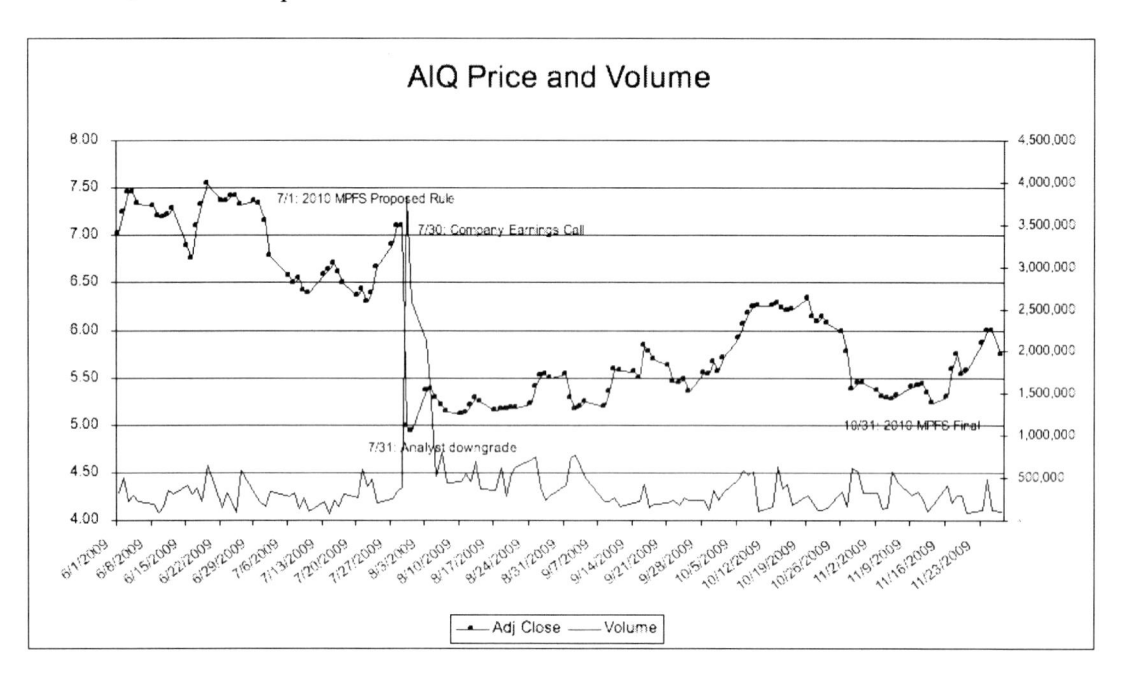

Point: The response of public market investors as reflected in stock prices often times lags knowledge of likely or pending reimbursement changes. Aside from the tendency to view bad news about one's investment in the most favorable light, the lag may be due to awaiting the assessment of professional industry analysts, e.g. Joshua Raskin & Adam Feinstein of Barclays Capital.

Identifying Reimbursement Trends that are not Sustainable

Perhaps the single largest error made in forecasting cashflows for a medical practice or other entity that relies on the MPFS is failure to evaluate the likely direction that reimbursement for that particular sector is headed using the tools just discussed. Additionally, as a general rule, no single location, single market or single service line healthcare entity will have reimbursement growth rate assumptions greater than 3% over the long-term. Growth of this magnitude is possible in the discrete periods of the forecast, but given the complexity of the regulations just discussed, it is highly unlikely, and quite likely impossible, for any sector to grow at a rate greater than 2 ½% to 3% over the long-term. The key to identifying and addressing risk and future cashflows is that frequently utilized, high cost procedures and tests will be targeted for dramatic cutbacks. It is not a matter of if, but of when, the cuts will be implemented.

Chapter 11: Factors in Forecasting Cashflow and Estimating Cost of Capital

As an Example:

Current Procedural Terminology (CPT™) Code 78465,[1] Heart image (3d) multiple, is a single photon emission computed tomography (SPECT) code for myocardial infusion and represented a staggering 10.3% ($2,072,176,147) of charges for Cardiovascular physicians billing Medicare in 2007, the highest single code in terms of charges as well as frequency of billing.[2] CPT™ Code 78465 also represented 10.4% ($2,017,599,660) of charges in 2006 and 10.4% ($1,863,154,763) of charges in 2005. The following Chart depicts the growth in Allowed Charges (left axis) – those that Medicare actually approves for payment as opposed to those that are submitted - from 2003 to 2008 and Billed Charges (right axis) – those actually submitted by providers – from 2005 to 2007.

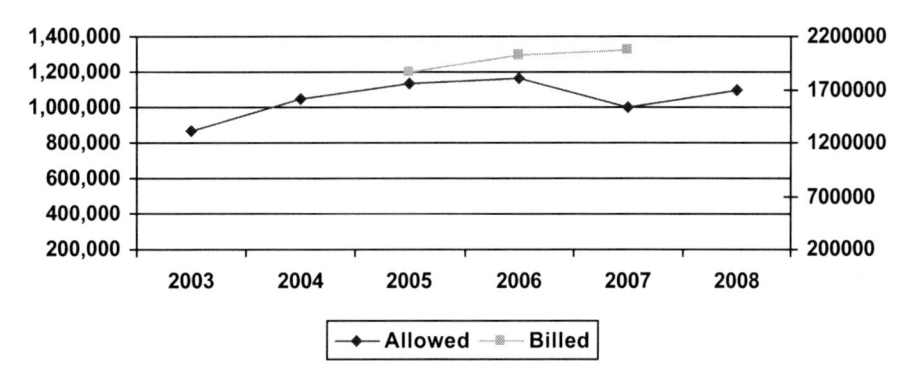

The technical component or TC paid in connection with ownership of the equipment, employment of a technician and provision of supplies and other overhead is approximately 85% of the global fee for CPT™ Code 78465. The Medicare program sets fees by assigning a value factor in terms of Relative Value Units (RVU) to each code and multiplying that by a dollar rate called a Conversion Factor.[3] Thus, the fee paid for a code is proportional to the RVU value assigned to it.

RVU values are based upon three principal factors: The cost of providing the service known as the Practice Expense component; the Physician Work associated with providing the service or interpreting the results of a test and the cost of Malpractice Insurance. Therefore, the more resources a particular service consumes in terms of physician time and effort, as well as operating costs, the higher the RVU assignment will be, and therefore, the higher the associated payment will be. The TC consists of a Practice Expense component and a small Malpractice component.

In 2007, the TC had an RVU value of 11.51. That declined to 11.26 in 2008 and 10.73 in 2009. The Final Rule published in November of 2009 set the RVUs for the TC at 8.32, a drop of 22%. This illustrates one of the critical insights that experienced healthcare industry appraisers possess: **expensive procedures will be targeted for dramatic cutbacks eventually. As stated previously, it is not a matter of if, but when, this will occur.**

Other notable examples of such cuts include the Deficit Reduction Act of 2005 that dramatically reduced the explosive growth in spending on high tech imaging (e.g., MRI and CT), perhaps the most significant of the past decade, part of a continuing trend highlighted by the earlier discussion of AIQ. Another example is the Medicare Modernization Act of 2003 (MMA) that changed the methodology for paying for physician office chemotherapy drugs from one based on published list prices (Average Wholesale Price) to one based on *actual* Average Selling Price. The scale of the cuts was such that many physicians were unable to continue in-office chemotherapy and incomes of affected specialties such as oncologists dropped dramatically. The MMA also expanded the Medicare Advantage program in a manner that proved to be highly questionable from a cost-benefit standpoint, causing MedPAC to devote an entire chapter in its 2009 *Report to Congress* on the problems therewith. This is a likely target for near-term cuts.[4]

A final example and one that garnered much attention due to the Tax Court case *Caracci*,[5] involved home health agencies and the changeover from a cost-based payment system to a prospective payment system (PPS) in the late 1990s.

Point: If a healthcare service or procedure reflects dramatic profits, it probably is going to change, change soon and change in a significant, negative fashion.

Understanding the Impact of Payor Relationships

To this point in the article, we have focused much of our discussion on understanding the direction that governmental payors, such as Medicare and Medicaid, are headed. However, it is critical that the appraiser also gain an understanding regarding the composition and reimbursement trends for the remaining payors. Many times, commercial payors tend to follow the direction of Medicare albeit with a lag of one or more years. Therefore, the analyst should review and be familiar with the reimbursement terms for the most significant commercial contracts held by a healthcare organization to effectively forecast cash flows.

An often overlooked but important consideration is whether or not the company has a significant amount of out of network business. In this situation, the company does not hold a contract with the commercial payor, but treats patients of the payor nonetheless. In the early periods of this practice, it can be a lucrative arrangement for the healthcare company as they may receive fees that are higher than would be included in a contract. However, over the long term, this tactic will generally fail, resulting in a decrease in fees, if not in the complete elimination of a portion of the company's patient base. Therefore, when determining the level of revenues to forecast as well as the associated risk, it is critical to understand whether the company has exposure in this area and to factor such risks into the assessment of the discount/capitalization rate.

Additionally, as with any company being appraised, it is critical to assess concentration of risk when determining the appropriate discount rate/cost of capital. The tool used to assess concentration of risk for a healthcare company is the "payor mix." The payor mix is a reflection of the proportionate level of revenues attributable to the various payors such as Medicare and Medicaid as well as significant commercial health insurers such as BlueCross/BlueShield or

Chapter 11: Factors in Forecasting Cashflow and Estimating Cost of Capital

United Healthcare. If the appraiser determines that the healthcare company has a concentration with a particular payor, it would likely increase the assessment of risk related to the cash flows. Additionally, it would make it imperative that the appraiser gain a very thorough understanding of the direction of reimbursement trends for that particular payor to ensure the revenue forecast is achievable.

Another important factor to analyze in terms of payor mix is the proportion of patients who are self-pay or any significant changes in the proportion of self-pay patients. A significant increase in self-pay patients can trigger the appraiser to the fact that the company has lost an important commercial insurance contract or that the geographic location of the company has been harder hit by economic changes than anticipated. Generally speaking, the collections rate on self-pay patients will be extremely low and most collections will happen very early in the process if at all.

Point: You cannot assess the risk and discount rate or estimate future cashflow without a knowledge of the underlying revenue sources. The risk of Medicare and Medicaid revenues is substantially different and both of these may be very different from those of non-governmental payors, those individuals with insurance, co-pays and deductibles and uninsured individuals.

Using Guideline Company Data to Forecast Cash Flows and Assess Risk

To the extent that a public company's operations are representative of a given valuation subject's risk and prospects, it can provide insight into both the discount rate and forecast of cash flow. However, there are several critical limitations on the use of this data in a healthcare industry context that are often overlooked.

There have been two significant trends in the broader healthcare industry that affect the availability of guideline data and its usefulness. The first of these is consolidation within the payor industry. Consolidation of health insurers was possible due to their long-standing antitrust waiver. This has in turn led to an ongoing and dramatic consolidation trend amongst providers. The practical outcome of these two interrelated and parallel trends has been to create a situation in many markets where providers pass increasing costs back to insurers who then pass those costs back to employers and insureds through their premiums. Consolidation has also led to a declining number of guideline companies. The remaining companies are larger, more diverse in their revenue sources and therefore less exposed - or risky - to changes in a given market area.

Point: Future cash flow depends upon the relative market power of a company.[7] Market risk is a function of many factors, and in the healthcare industry, size and diversity and particularly diversity as to revenue sources and number of distinct geographic market areas in which the company operates are drivers of market or negotiating power.[8]

Chapter 11: Factors in Forecasting Cashflow and Estimating Cost of Capital

Additionally, the detail regarding the guideline's payor contracts will likely not be known to the appraiser. Therefore, it is impossible for the appraiser to make the necessary adjustments to make the guideline truly "comparable."

As discussed previously, commercial insurance contracts can have a dramatic impact on the risk assessment as well as the revenue forecast. Therefore, even if the guideline operates in only one industry segment that coincides with the subject company, the guideline can still have a much different revenue outlook and cost of capital due to interaction with commercial insurance payors across different geographic markets. To illustrate, if you are appraising a healthcare company that operates in the state of Alabama where BlueCross/BlueShield is by far the most dominant commercial payor, application of revenue trends from a guideline would have very little, if any, relevance to determining the revenue forecast or risk assessment of the company.

As an example, much of the consolidation of physician practices by hospital buyers is driven by the ability of a larger, integrated entity to obtain better contracts and rates from insurers. Many times, independent physician practices will be unable to obtain the higher rates available to physicians who are part of a hospital-physician entity. Certain affiliation structures leave the physician practices as freestanding entities which obtain their insurer contracts through the affiliation structure but otherwise are independent. These practices will earn better incomes and therefore have higher values, all things equal. The relevance of market transactions of these practices to those without such payor contracts is limited or nonexistent.

Smaller, privately held companies with one or a few locations are typically less diverse and more exposed to local market conditions. Therefore, to extrapolate reimbursement trends from a guideline to a local healthcare company is a recipe for disaster! A guideline may be able to achieve higher growth rates over a longer period of time related solely to the fact that the guideline has a diversified revenue base which insulates the guideline from the impact of significant changes to any one segment of its business. In contrast, the local healthcare company typically has "all its eggs in one basket" and can be significantly benefitted or harmed from changes to one industry segment. Additionally, using the cost of capital of a guideline for purposes of assessing the risk of a local healthcare company, again ignores the impact of size and diversity on the assessment of risk and would likely result in an overvaluation of the local healthcare company.

Point: You cannot assess the relevance of revenue-based market multiples to a valuation subject without knowing the underlying quality of the payor contracts of both comparable and subject.

Point: In healthcare, only pureplay comparable companies are typically appropriate. Even a pureplay may have limits due to geographic diversity or difference in markets served, revenue sources and localized trends.

Because public stock prices do not react as one might "expect" them to or it might be better said "when" one expects them to, attempting to draw conclusions about cost of capital and trends using guideline companies becomes even more difficult in a healthcare industry context. This

Chapter 11: Factors in Forecasting Cashflow and Estimating Cost of Capital

fact, combined with the limitations just discussed, makes determination of discount rates/cost of capital and revenue forecasting assumptions using a guideline company approach a virtual exercise in futility for a healthcare company. Therefore, the appraiser is better served to rely upon a build-up or capital asset pricing model for purposes of assessing risk for healthcare companies. Comparisons can be made to guideline companies benchmarks, but this approach is better suited as a pressure test rather than a primary method.

Conclusion

It is critical in any valuation assignment to develop a cash flow projection that is reasonable and achievable and to then estimate value based on a realistic assessment of risk related to those cash flows. In the healthcare industry in particular, these tasks are complicated by the myriad of regulations which govern healthcare companies and impact their ability to achieve projected results. Add to this complication, significant potential changes in how healthcare is delivered and reimbursed in the US, and the result is an assignment that is extremely complex and requires a substantial amount of experience to accomplish successfully. This article discussed various factors which contribute to the risk of a healthcare company as well as provided guidance regarding means by which a business appraiser can go about doing the necessary research to appropriately forecast cash flows and assess cost of capital.

---

1. Codes are Copyright, American Medical Association. This code was "cross-walked" or changed to 78452 in the period between the 2010 proposed and final rules. One more complication that emphasizes the import of understanding CPT codes.
2. Current data can be downloaded at http://www.cmpasupport.com/download/files/Top10Procs_2008.zip and historical data is available at http://www.cms.hhs.gov/MedicareFeeforSvcPartsAB/04_MedicareUtilizationforPartB.asp#TopOfPage
3. The concept of RVUs is analogous to billable hours while the Conversion Factor is analogous to a billing rate per hour. For example, if a Code has an RVU value of 10 and the Conversion Factor is $50, it would have a fee of $500.
4. Such cuts did, in fact, occur in the March 2010 Reform Legislation.
5. 118 T.C. No. 25, Sta-Home Health Agency, et al. v. Commissioner, Case No. 02-60912 (5th Cir.), July 11, 2006
6. Such cuts did, in fact, occur in March 2010 reform legislation.
7. For a detailed analysis of health insurer/payor market strength see *Competition in Health Insurance, comprehensive study of U.S. markets, 2007 update*, American Medical Association
8. For further healthcare industry risk factors, see Chapter 3: Healthcare Market Structure and Its Implication for Valuation of Privately Held Provider Entities: An Empirical Analysis; origininally published in *Business Valuation Review*, Summer 2008, Mark O. Dietrich, CPA/ABV

Chapter 12

Choosing and Using the Right Valuation Methods for Physician Practices

By Mark O. Dietrich, CPA/ABV

The Market in 2008-10

The volume of activity in healthcare industry transactions has certainly recovered from the late 1990s when the failure of the MedPartners/Phycor merger marked the end of that period of consolidation. One of the notable differences between today's market and that of the 1990s is that there is recognition in most quarters of the need to carefully tie physician compensation to the forecast used to value the practice. Another is that physician compensation is typically linked to productivity and not fixed, the latter practice having led to low patient volumes and large operating losses. These changes were re-emphasized in the 2008 Tax Court case *Derby*, cited in numerous places herein. Nonetheless, as described in other chapters, the message has failed to reach certain valuation firms and hospitals with respect to cardiology practices.

The consensus today, including that of many of the contributors to this Guide, is that future physician compensation is typically a more significant element of a transaction than is the value of the practice. In many circumstances, hospitals and Integrated Delivery Systems have superior contracts with insurers that in turn permit physicians to receive better compensation for the same amount of work. Over the course of 5 or more years, compensation is typically more valuable than sales proceeds to a physician, given the range of valuation multiples. Readers should note that it is not appropriate to value the practice using the buyer's better insurer contracts as that is inconsistent with fair market value, although those contracts *should* be considered in determining fair market compensation as discussed in Chapter 29 on RVU-based compensation agreements.

As a final observation, practices with intensive investment in ancillaries are likely to be more valuable all things being equal. Given the Stark laws restrictions or prohibition on post-transaction compensation with respect to the technical component of ancillary services in different employment and independent contractor settings, there is not the usual tradeoff between future compensation and current value.

Introduction

Simply stated, valuation models require two major components: future cashflows and a discount or capitalization rate. All valuation results are a function of the interaction between these

Chapter 12: Choosing and Using the Right Valuation Methods

two factors. Once the valuation analyst has gained a sufficient knowledge of the marketplace, regulatory environment and the subject practice as described elsewhere in this Guide, the actual measuring of value can begin.

Other Chapters to review in this *Guide*:

1. Factors in Forecasting Cashflow and Estimating Cost of Capital in Healthcare

2. Fair Market Value Requires the Demonstration of Income to a Hypothetical Owner

3. Critical Condition: A Coding Analysis for a Physician Practice Valuation[1]

4. The Anti-Kickback Statute and Stark Law: Avoiding Valuation of Referrals

5. Understanding Healthcare Markets

6. Tax-Exempt Healthcare Organization Valuation Issues Related to Excess Benefits, Private Inurement, and Intermediate Sanctions

7. The CPA's Role in Mergers and Acquisitions: Due Diligence Assistance to PPMC's and Private Equity Firms

Many experienced valuation analysts new to healthcare will be familiar and (perhaps) more comfortable with the Guideline Publicly Traded Company (Guideline) method or the Market Approach based upon databases such as those maintained by the IBA or *Pratt's Stats*™. When considering the Merged and Acquired Company method, bear in mind that the historical data available regarding the "acquisition" of practices via management services agreements with Physician Practice Management Companies (PPMCs), is generally not relevant.[2] A PPMC transaction is fundamentally different from an outright purchase of the practice and therefore should not be used for such a valuation without various adjustments, including those to cash-equivalent consideration and compensation. Finally, my experience is that physicians focus on cash returns in the form of additional compensation when they buy practices and regulators expect hospitals to focus on cash returns from within the practice.

This chapter is organized with a discussion of rules of thumb presented first, in the expectation that someone new to medical practice valuation will benefit from a frame of reference when studying the actual methods. Bear in mind that such rules are not methods and merely provide an oft-suspect means of a reality check.

A presentation of a discounted cashflow valuation is beyond the scope of the Chapter but considerable detail about the differences in DCFs for physician practices is provided. A discussion of the build-up method for determining discount and capitalization rates then follows.

Chapter 12: Choosing and Using the Right Valuation Methods

The chapter explains in detail the use of the excess earnings method and the capitalization of cashflows (CCF). The focus of this Chapter is on asset purchases, not stock purchases, since the vast majority of physician practice transactions, aside from buy-ins, are assets only.

The excess earnings method is presented in its traditional physician-to-physician transaction approaches, using *pre-tax* excess earnings and a discount and capitalization rate applicable to *pre-tax* earnings for a hypothetical physician buyer.

Insight and Analysis

A notable aspect of valuing a physician practice is the need to get into the detail behind operating expenses for normalization purposes in order to identify discretionary expenses available to the owner of the practice in lieu of taking taxable compensation. A General Ledger is a basic element of a Data Request—like it or not! Prior to commencing the actual quantitative valuation analysis, I review in detail the normalized operating results and compare them to statistical norms from the Medical Group Management Association or other sources.[3] You need to ask "How would the practice look if operated by the typical buyer or seller?" Bear in mind that the hypothetical buyer of a physician practice is interested primarily in what the cash return of the practice will be, not what anecdotal or "market" data says the practice might be bought or sold for.

For perhaps the best analysis of the general limitations of market data in valuation see Business Valuation Resources The Comprehensive Guide to the Use and Application of the Transaction Databases *by Nancy Fannon, CPA/ABV and Heidi Walker, CPA/ABV.*

Alleged Comparative Practice Sales Method

Medical practices, like most businesses, have rules of thumb for valuation. These are commonly expressed as a percentage of the practice's receipts. The most common source of such information is *The Goodwill Registry*, published annually by The Health Care Group of Plymouth Meeting, Pennsylvania. This consulting firm's figures are cited in such trade publications as *Medical Economics* and *Physicians Management* widely read by physicians. The *Registry* contains information on practice sales, valuations, and divorce settlements accumulated by The Health Care Group from its own activities, as well as others who submit data to it. The data is usually (and abusedly) cited as an average percentage of revenues ostensibly paid for "Goodwill."

Insight and Analysis

It is a commonplace principle of research in the scientific community that "The plural of anecdote is not data." Valuation analysts do well to remember this when using rules of thumb.

Chapter 12: Choosing and Using the Right Valuation Methods

Rules of Thumb and Market Date: Understanding Comparatives

A comparative is only as useful as the underlying analysis of the subject practice. For example, if you decide to purchase a four-bedroom home, you cannot go to a Realtor's office and get a standard price for a home. The price will vary with numerous factors, such as the age of the house, the size of the rooms, the number of bathrooms, the quality of the kitchen, the size of the lot, and so on. A medical practice is no different. It is not possible to value any practice by taking a percentage of its receipts. Further, just because Practice A is valued at 60% of receipts, it does not mean that Practice B is worth 60%. It may be worth 10%—or nothing.

Insight and Analysis

These "rules" originate from physician-to-physician transactions and have always been of limited use in a market area in which physician practice management companies operate or for purchases by hospitals or integrated delivery systems; in the latter circumstance, serious regulatory issues are raised from such use. In addition, during the buying frenzy of the mid-1990s, the market value (as reflected by actual transactions) often exceeded these levels. Like any rules of thumb, they need to be considered within the context of market conditions at the time a valuation is performed. I do not endorse use of such "Rules" as valuation methods and caution against their use even as reality checks, especially where regulatory factors govern.

Use of the Goodwill Registry to Determine Intangible Value

If one were to accept the premise that the *Goodwill Registry* constitutes a valid source of market data on the intangible value of medical practices, it is necessary to understand precisely what that "valuation method" includes.

The *Goodwill Registry* contains the following definition of "Goodwill:"

> As we see it, professional practice "goodwill" is a combination of practice intangibles varying, on a case by case basis, as to existence and value. That combination might include location, use of a practice's or an *individual's name*, patient information (embodied in the clinical record), a favorable leasehold, *a covenant not to compete, compensation for past (or future) management and entrepreneurial services, payments made for referral to an associate or recommendation of a successor*, patient lists, credit records, patient care and or employee contracts, as well as assignments of future income. (*Emphasis added* to identify those items denoting personal goodwill rather than practice goodwill and therefore not divisible property.)[4]

Thus, the reported values in the *Goodwill Registry* clearly *include,* for example, nondivisible personal goodwill via a noncompete, which is relevant in many jurisdictions for marital dissolution purposes. The entries also include **control** and **noncontrol** transactions, valuations which did not result in a transaction and final divorce settlements, which are Court decisions, not transactions. In order for "market data" to be valid, it must represent actual transactions.

Chapter 12: Choosing and Using the Right Valuation Methods

Valuation Community Professional Standards

Besides my own views of the limitations of Rules of Thumb, the broad valuation profession holds a similar view. A Rule of Thumb is a means of estimating what a transaction value might be, using a "deal" price rather than cash-equivalents. Valuation analysts use Rules of Thumb to gauge or reality check the results of valuation methods under the three approaches to valuation. Rules of Thumb are widely disparaged as valuation *methods* in the professional literature:

> Formula values are not substitutes for careful consideration of other appropriate valuation methods that are applicable to the business being appraised.[5]

> Sometimes called 'rules of thumb,' the industry method can prove to be a valuable tool but should *never* be relied upon by itself for the valuation of an appraisal subject. ... If enough transactions take place using a particular method, the end result is that *there is market data that will support the use of that method*. However, if these formulas are the only methods used, *an inappropriate valuation may result*.[6] (*Emphasis added*)

> Rule of Thumb—a mathematical relationship between or among variables based on experience, observation, *hearsay*, or a combination of these, usually applicable to a specific industry.[7] (*Emphasis added*)

More importantly, Rules of Thumb do not represent *cash-equivalent values*, which is a key requirement of the definition of fair market value. Cash-equivalent value might well include proceeds attributable to a *stock* sale, not an *asset* sale. Rules of Thumb represent the value of assets, not stock. There is a substantial difference between valuing the *stock* of an entity, which is sometimes the relevant task such as in marital dissolution, and valuing the *assets*. The purchaser of *assets* obtains *tax benefits* consisting of 1) the basis step-up in fixed assets (e.g., equipment and furniture) and the resultant additional depreciation deduction and 2) the basis attributable to intangible assets and the resultant amortization deduction (IRC §197 allows the purchase price of intangibles to be written off over 15 years generating substantial tax savings). Rules of thumb are "deal" prices representing the "value" of *assets*.

There is no data provided in the Goodwill Registry to determine whether or not the values reflected are cash-equivalent values, a necessary prerequisite for its use in determining fair market value.

Levin Associates' Health Care Acquisition Report

One source used widely during the consolidation era of the 1990s for "market" data was Irving Levin Associate's *Health Care Acquisition Report*. This Report includes the location of the acquired practice, a brief description, the "price" paid (which may or may not represent cash-equivalent value, a prerequisite for fair market value), a brief summary of deal terms, the

Chapter 12: Choosing and Using the Right Valuation Methods

number of "units" (physicians) acquired, price paid divided by revenue and price paid divided by "income" are the data points available; few are actually reported since the information is not publicly available. This Report led to the questionable practice of valuing physicians based upon the number working for the acquired practice—something akin to the method during the Stock Market Bubble of valuing software companies with large accumulated deficits based on the number of engineers and programmers.

Pratt's Stats™[8]

Pratt's Stats™, perhaps the most comprehensive and justifiably highly-regarded of the databases, has data entry points for state, city, firm and individual submitting the report of the transaction, 14 Income Statement items, 13 balance sheet items, actual transaction data based upon equity, market value of invested capital, allocation to noncompete agreement and other assets and dozens of yes or no questions about the transaction as well as ratios computed from the core financial data. Often, however, not all of the data is submitted for each transaction and there are very few medical practices. Regionalization is also critical to assessing the usefulness of this market data. For example, in November 2004, nearly 90% of 96 items identified as general dentistry were from three states: Pennsylvania, Arizona and Oregon. 50 of the entries were submitted by one brokerage firm and 20 by another. As the investigations of Wall Street investment bankers indicates, a few individuals' views of the market value of a business can distort the picture. Even broadly held views of market value, such as those that preceded the bursting of the Stock Market Bubble in March 2000, can be based upon a *lack* of "reasonable knowledge of relevant facts."

A closer look at regional economics and the market data presents an even greater challenge. Managed care and its limitations on services and pricing are most prevalent in urban areas, where population density and employers make attractive insurance markets. Rural areas have less managed care and fewer patients per square mile. The profitability of a practice per unit of service is likely to be better in areas with less managed care. For example, an analysis of mean physician salaries from the Medical Group Management Association (MGMA) *Physician Compensation and Production Survey* for 2004 indicates that incomes were greatest for 69 of the 108 specialties in the sample in the Southern Region, where population density is lowest. The greater incomes are a function of several factors, including lower managed care, higher unit fees and lower operating costs. This greatly limits the common use of "goodwill percentage" averages paid for all practices of a particular specialty from the *Goodwill Registry*. Valuation is, after all, a function of cashflow from profit not cashflow from revenue!

Guideline Publicly Traded Companies

With very rare exception, a physician practice should not be valued based upon public company multiples. It is very difficult indeed to find a public company, even in SIC 801, which is comparable to a physician practice. Pediatrix Medical Group, Inc. (NYSE: PDX) and IntegraMed America, Inc. (NASDAQ: INMD) could be relevant in limited circumstances depending upon the nature of the transaction.

Chapter 12: Choosing and Using the Right Valuation Methods

Insight and Analysis

Always look at the underlying components of any SIC data to be certain you understand what the companies actually do. The result is often amazing.

Current Recruiting Data

Data on annual recruiting engagements from such firms as Merritt Hawkins[9] and Delta Medical indicates that the specialties in highest demand include internists, family medicine, orthopedic surgery, gastroenterology, dermatology, interventional and general radiology, and interventional cardiology. Hospitals or existing practices looking to recruit such physicians typically find the starting salary very high and the structure of a future buy-in on the table from the outset. It is not uncommon for a well-informed physician exiting residency to base his or her employment decision on competing buy-in opportunities—and the lower the better. For example, orthopedic surgeons are often looking for practices with Ambulatory Surgery Centers, which offer significantly enhanced incomes and better working conditions, and the buy-in opportunity has to be affordable.

Recruiting data is another application of the Market Approach in that it represents Market Data on physician income. Income is what the investor in a physician practice is buying. There is a substantive question of whether a hypothetical buyer will pay for an asset that generates less income to that buyer than a position as a noninvestor employee. Thus, it is important to compare the earnings available from the practice being valued to that offered in the recruiting market.

A serious shortage of physicians and particularly primary care (generalist) physicians is expected in the next several decades. This has negative implications for practice value as new suppliers ease of entry to the market is enhanced when there is unmet, excess demand for services.[10]

The ratio of physician to population varies quite significantly from state to state and from urban to suburban and rural areas. Medicare-participating physicians by specialty and region can be found in the publication *2010 CMS Statistics*.[11] This in turn affects the value of practices as well as the incomes available in recruitment settings.

Value of Transactions in another Market Area

There are regional differences in what sellers will pay for physician practices, much of which are or were driven by the presence or lack of presence of for-profit buyers, as well as such items as the enforceability of noncompetes and enhanced income opportunities. These factors along with the Stark regulations' requirement that data in a "particular market" be used for determining fair market value make the data for one region of questionable relevance to another in the absence of appropriate correlation. What should drive price differentials from market to market are differences in the availability of cash profits and ease of entry of competitors.

Chapter 12: Choosing and Using the Right Valuation Methods

Insight and Analysis

For those circumstances in which government regulations such as the Stark laws or the Anti-Kickback Statute (AKS) are implicated, regionalized market data is further suspect. In recognition of the seeming abuses—intentional or unintentional—of market data, the Stark II regulations specifically define "fair market value" as "the price at which bona fide sales have been consummated for assets of like type, quality, and quantity in a particular market at the time of acquisition"[12] (emphasis added).

During the period of the 1990's consolidation, the vast majority of purchases were in the South and Southwest, although the available market data was widely used in all regions. The Stark II regulations create a critical limitation on market data when the valuation is being undertaken for regulatory purposes, unless the valuation analyst can demonstrate that data from one region or state is somehow relevant to another.

The *IRS Exempt Organizations Continuing Professional Education Technical Instruction Program Textbook* for 1995[13] states the following in a section entitled Establishing Comparability under the Market Approach: "Factors affecting comparability include markets served; practice and specialty type; competitive position; profitability; growth prospects; risk perceptions; financial composition (capital structure); physician compensation; physician age, health and reputation; physician productivity; average revenues per physician; cost structure; and average revenue per visit or covered life to revenue to revenue mix (capitated versus fee for service)" citing *Financial Valuation: Businesses and Business Interests*. I know of no database with such information!

Empirical Study of Healthcare Markets

My article "Healthcare Market Structure and Its Implication for Valuation of Privately Held Provider Entities: An Empirical Analysis" was published in the Summer 2008 *Business Valuation Review* and is included as Chapter 3 of this guide. The idea for that article came from a Government Accounting Office study of market share of health insurers in various states and my experience that pricing and profit differed significantly across the country. I reasoned that this Insurer Market Share and related Market Power would be one key element defining a Market and set out to find out how it and other factors contributed. This, in turn, would define Comparability for purposes of the Market Approach to valuation.

Here is a summary of my findings as to the key elements defining a Market:

1. Total Medicare spending and Medicare spending per capita,

2. The presence and market strength of Blue Cross plans,

3. The degree of market strength of local nonprofit hospitals versus for-profit hospitals,

Chapter 12: Choosing and Using the Right Valuation Methods

4. The degree of market strength of local nonprofit health insurers versus for-profit health insurers,

5. Certificate of Need laws, and

6. Other local demographic and economic factors.

These factors contribute to the fact that most (certainly not all) larger for-profit healthcare providers are primarily located in Florida, Texas, California and Tennessee. They also confirm the underlying rationale for the Stark Laws restrictions on the use of out of market data as "comparable." The "Checklist of Factors to Consider when Evaluating the Significance of Out-of-Market Transactions" included in this *Guide* provides a means for undertaking this analysis as well as links to websites where the underlying data is located.

As I observed with my friend Reed Tinsley in a 2006 article for the American Bar Association's Health Law Section

> If the acquirer is a public company, an important dynamic is in effect. Public companies' stock prices or valuation multiples are heavily based upon their earnings growth. The higher the earnings growth, the higher the valuation multiple and the higher the value of the company. Thus, that growth needs to continue or the stock's price will decline. There is an arbitrage effect when the earnings of private companies are placed in the public equity markets through acquisition that can enable a public company to afford a higher price than a private company, all other things being equal.[14] Although fair market value in a given market area may be driven by the economics of public companies, the Stark requirement that comparable transactions be in a particular market at the time of acquisition addresses this if public companies are not active acquirers in a given market area.[15]

Other common Pitfalls in the Market Approach

Valuation analysts frequently prefer the market approach to valuing a business. As a colleague observed "Appraisers are market observers not market makers."[16] Courts tend to understand easily that if businesses of a certain type sell for 3 times earnings, then a given business is likely worth three times earnings. Valuation analysts tend to be comfortable for the same reason; there is less judgment[16] in the market approach than in the income approach, if a good database of transactions for a type of business exists.

Medical practices present a unique challenge for proper use of the market approach. As we will see in the analysis that follows, the market data often does not contain sufficient data to determine precisely what the multiples in a given transaction were.

Chapter 12: Choosing and Using the Right Valuation Methods

Example

Assume that a representative transaction in a database contains the following information:

Date of Transaction: July 1, 1997
Type of Practice: Ophthalmology
Subject Revenues: 1,000,000
Owner compensation: 450,000
Earnings after taxes: 2,000
Purchase Price: 540,000
Debts assumed: -0-
Working Capital Included: Yes

Multiples:
Owner's Discretionary Comp: 1.20
Revenues: .54

What does this tell us about the value of this practice, or about the practice we are trying to value today? Painfully little, unfortunately.

Analysis

1997 represented the last "big year" of buying by the PPMC industry, which collapsed and died following the failed merger between MedPartners and Phycor at the end of that year. We do not know if the above transaction was a purchase by a PPMC, but it is likely that it was, since very few other transactions in medical practices were disclosed.[17]

PPMC's purchased practices based upon a multiple of earnings contracted to the PPMC. The contracted earnings typically were 15% to 20% of the earnings of the physician. In the above sample transaction, the purchase price of 540,000 could have been based upon a multiple applied to an earnings stream between 67,500 (15% of 450,000) and 90,000 (20% of 450,000). As such, the correct valuation multiple to be garnered from this transaction could be as little as 6.0 (540,000 divided by 90,000) or as much as 8.0 (540,000 divided by 67,500). Generally, such multiples ranged between 4.0 and 7.0, but we cannot tell what the multiple was from the transaction. The purchase price included working capital, intangibles and fixed assets. The illustrated multiples of 1.20 times Owner's Discretionary cashflow and .54 of revenues are not meaningful if this is a PPMC transaction. The PPMC was not buying 100% of the physician's earnings, nor was it buying the revenues—it was buying a portion of the practice's earnings before physician compensation.

If this was a physician to physician transaction, of course, the valuation multiples would be more meaningful. One clue that this is *NOT* a physician to physician transaction, however, is that accounts receivable were included—that is rarely the case in physician to physician deal, while it was normally the case in a PPMC transaction. This, of course, is critical to the valuation analyst attempting to use the data to develop a market conclusion of value.

Chapter 12: Choosing and Using the Right Valuation Methods

Particular problems for hospital buyers

It is critical from a regulatory standpoint that the hospital receives an accurately determined fair market value for the practice. Using "market" data from the 1990s which includes a class of buyers (PPMCs) no longer present for most physicians, even if normally reasonable to general business valuation analysts, is a serious mistake from a regulatory standpoint. Besides the problems with using such data outlined above, equally important is the fact that the market conditions today are no longer what they were in 1990s.

Use of the *Goodwill Registry* "rule of thumb" based on a percentage of collected revenues is risky from a regulatory standpoint.

> Using the *Goodwill Registry* to value a practice for purchase by a hospital would be a critical mistake as there would be no way of determining if the hospital was receiving an appropriate return on its investment without a disciplined application of the Income Approach described earlier. This is because an asset that has or will generate no cash flow has no value to the hypothetical buyer of the fair market value standard.[19]

When confronted with this type of valuation engagement, a valuation analyst can also consider a *replication cost* approach, looking at such intangible assets as workforce-in-place and going concern value, in addition to fixed assets such as equipment and furniture. At a minimum, one might think, the practice should be worth the cost to a physician buying it of establishing a similar practice, including the quantification of the reduced revenue during the start-up period. Nonetheless, there is a substantive question for a Hospital as to whether replication cost is appropriate because a hypothetical investor will likely not invest in something which lacks cash return.

> The key question, of course, is whether or not the hypothetical buyer of the fair market value standard would incur a value based upon replication cost if there was no return on the investment. Most experienced healthcare appraisers would likely answer no in the absence of some additional mitigating factors. It is worth noting that, at least in this author's view, a hospital employing a physician post-transaction should evaluate the practice value differently than a physician buying a practice from another physician, where the seller retires or otherwise ceases to practice in the service area.

> Tax-exempt hospitals generally are subject to a standard of providing community benefit for the costs they expend. Thus, one potential mitigating factor in utilizing replication cost would be where the acquiring hospital met the community benefit standard. This might occur where the service area of the target physician was underserved and/or the physician serving that area planned to leave for a better opportunity.[20]

Chapter 12: Choosing and Using the Right Valuation Methods

Note should be taken as well of any contractual relationships between the hospital and the physician in the proposed transaction documents, including a covenant not to compete held by the hospital, and any guaranteed rights under an employment contract held by the physician. Valuing such contractual rights can be an important part of a proper fair market value determination when a transaction is being consummated or unwound. This was a critical issue in *Derby v. Commissioner*[21] which involved valuation issues associated with the donation of the intangible value of a medical practice to a tax-exempt Hospital.[22]

Conclusion

Old market data in particular is only relevant if the market conditions today are the same as when the comparable transaction took place. We cannot sell 100 shares of a NASDAQ market index future today for the same price that we would have gotten in March of 2000. Similarly, we cannot sell a physician practice today for a market multiple, or even to the same class of buyers, as we could have during the period 1990 through 1997. Care needs to be taken to understand the market conditions and terms when using databases of market transactions.

Understanding Physician Practice Discount and Capitalization Rates

Insight and Analysis

What is a Discount Rate? One of the most difficult concepts to grasp in valuation is the relationship between stock market returns and discount rates for businesses. A discount rate is the percentage of cash return an investor expects to receive for an investment of given risk. In the stock market—from where we derive discount rates used in all valuation engagements—the cash return consists of dividends plus capital appreciation on the stock. In a medical practice, the return consists of enhanced compensation and perhaps dividends, if the practice is an S Corporation or LLC, or if the entity is an Ambulatory Surgery Center or Imaging Center. There *may* also be capital appreciation at the time the practice is sold, although most physicians realize the bulk of the net present value of their investment through annual earnings, not from a business sale. When a business distributes all or most of its cash profits, it tends to have a lower rate of appreciation than a business which reinvests its cash.

The terms discount rate, expected rate of return and cost of equity[23] all mean the same thing. It is important to note that the *actual* return in a given year is not likely to be equal to the *expected* return—that is what risk is all about! Over a long period of time, for investments in physician practices with the same risk profile, the actual return should equal the expected return—much the same way that stocks go up and down and have good years and bad years, but are known to outperform bonds and money market funds over the long haul.

A capitalization rate is obtained, of course, by subtracting the expected long-term (perpetual) growth rate in net cashflows from the discount rate. Growth rates are discussed in detail below.

Chapter 12: Choosing and Using the Right Valuation Methods

Practice Risk Premium: Being Objective with the Subjective?

The actual unsystematic risk premium—RP_u—or the medical practice premium will depend upon whether your build-up method approach uses 1) the microcap premium or 2) the 10th decile premium. For example, a significant amount of the unsystematic risk of a physician practice is accounted for in the 10th decile premium, considering that the healthcare industry is *less* risky than the broad market (S&P 500) from which the equity risk premium for large companies is derived. This can be seen by examining the industry risk premium data for healthcare companies contained in the Valuation Edition of the Morningstar Yearbook, bearing in mind that excessive reliance on the Industry Risk Premium leads to errors as well. As I stated in a 2007 article on the *Delaware Open MRI* case, better known for its S Corporation tax-effecting scheme:

> Perhaps the most fundamental valuation mistake in the health care industry is failure to differentiate the risk of a small entity operating in a single state (Delaware) in a single line of business (MRI) with a few dominant health insurers from the risk of large public entities operating in multiple states in multiple lines of business with multiple health insurers paying for the cost of services. Use of the Industry Risk Premium in the Build-up Method compounds this typical error.[24]

The risk premium for the medical practice being valued (i.e., unsystematic risk) is a highly subjective number and one that is heavily dependent upon the knowledge and skill of the valuation analyst. Some valuation analysts use a list of risk factors with a range of premium percentages assigned to each factor, while others use a single percentage and justify the additional premium in their written report. The following is a nonexhaustive listing of some of the factors that should be considered in developing the practice risk premium.

1. Specialty
2. Presence or lack of a repeat patient (customer) base
3. Reliance upon individual skills and referrals from other physicians
4. Profitability
5. Total Receipts
6. Payor Mix and Quality of Contracts
7. Coding (!)
8. Age/Gender of Provider
9. Quality of Staff, particularly billing staff
10. Longevity of Staff

Chapter 12: Choosing and Using the Right Valuation Methods

11. Number of Active Patients
12. Number of Competitors
13. Ease of Entry to the Market
14. Current Recruiting Salaries
15. Risk of Reimbursement Changes
16. Available Market Strategies
17. Underwriting Cycle for Health Insurance Industry (see discussion below)

Additional Risk Factors for Markets or Practices with Capitation:

1. Likely Transition to Capitation
2. Presence of Medicare Capitation
3. Experience with Capitation
4. Covered Lives
5. Reserves for capitated referrals or risk pools
6. The Underwriting Cycle for Health Insurance Industry is particularly important here

The following Chart appeared in the article "Medical Practices: A BV Rx" in the November 2005 *Journal of Accountancy*.

Hierarchy of Risk Premums in Medical Practices

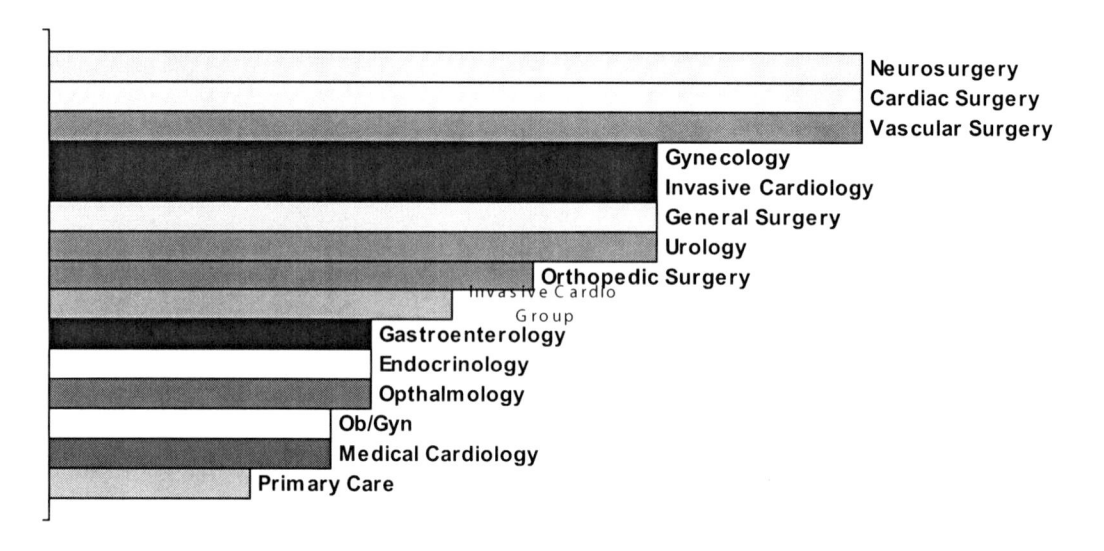

Neurosurgery
Cardiac Surgery
Vascular Surgery
Gynecology
Invasive Cardiology
General Surgery
Urology
Orthopedic Surgery
Invasive Cardio Group
Gastroenterology
Endocrinology
Opthalmology
Ob/Gyn
Medical Cardiology
Primary Care

Chapter 12: Choosing and Using the Right Valuation Methods

Weighted Average Cost of Capital (WACC)

Another commonly overlooked fact of valuation is the Accounting Equation, something that was emphasized by the Fifth Circuit Court of Appeals when overturning the Tax Court's decision in *Caracci*.[25] If equity and long-term debt (including the current portion of long-term debt) are the *Right Side* of the accounting equation used in the Market Value of Invested Capital, the *Left Side* of the equation includes tangible assets, such as furniture and equipment and working capital assets (such as accounts receivable and prepaid items), and intangible assets such as personal and enterprise or practice goodwill, as well as the value of any noncompete agreement or Enterprise Value (EV). In computing the value of the business enterprise, working capital is reduced by accounts payable and accrued items to arrive at net working capital (NWC). Note that a valuation model that measures EV will include the entire value of the operating assets: tangible, intangible, and net working capital.

If the goal of a valuation engagement is to value MVIC/EV (the invested capital or operating assets of the practice, again, both equity and long-term debt), then use of the WACC is appropriate. If the goal of the valuation is to value a controlling interest in the practice, as is common for hospital buyers or transfers of solo practices to a new physician, the WACC can be used and the ratio of debt and equity can be based upon the optimum mix of debt and equity for the hypothetical any willing buyer or seller. This is because a control buyer has the ability to alter the capital structure to the optimal ratio and debt is cheaper than equity, all things being equal. (The optimum capital structure of a specific buyer should not be used, as this is in the nature of a strategic adjustment inconsistent with fair market value.)

The discounted cashflow method when applied to an asset purchase/sale of a controlling interest should use a weighted average cost of capital, consisting of the result of the risk-adjusted equity rate above, and the after-tax cost of debt. If a control interest is being purchased, such as 100% of the practice, the percentage of debt utilized should, again, represent the optimum obtainable in the marketplace, and the cost of debt should reflect that of the hypothetical owner. If a minority interest is being valued, the percentage and cost of debt should generally be the present level in the practice since a minority owner cannot alter them—but be certain to read the discussion of excessive debt later in this chapter.

Insight and Analysis

The interest rate for debt used in computing this weighted average cost of capital, as well as the percentage of debt to equity available, must also consider those circumstances where a lender is looking to the personal guarantees of the owner(s), as well as the assets of the practice as collateral. In my view, a valuation analyst should consider adding a premium to the interest rate cost of debt for the value of the guarantees.[26]

Chapter 12: Choosing and Using the Right Valuation Methods

Valuation Tip

The percentage of debt should be a function of the underlying assets and the normal financing pattern for medical practices. Fixed assets are often financed, accounts receivable less frequently so. Equipment intensive practices like radiology, dentistry, ophthalmology or sports medicine (with physical therapy) have greater percentages of debt than, for example, primary care practices or general surgery.

We know as well from the Capital Asset Pricing Model that, all other things being equal, the more debt a company has versus an Industry Norm, the higher its cost of equity will be! The implications of this are profound because it demonstrates a *dynamic relationship* between the percentage of debt in the WACC and the cost of equity, which is part of the WACC. Therefore, although mathematically a valuation analyst can lower the WACC by increasing the percentage of debt in that computation, the CAPM—and relevering of Beta—tells us that the cost of equity must be simultaneously adjusted. If the percentage of debt in the capital structure goes up, the cost of equity goes up as well. If the percentage of debt in the capital structure goes down, the cost of equity goes down as well. The example in this Chapter's "In-Depth Review of the Excess Earnings Method" explores the impact of excessive debt as well. Medical practices with more debt than other practices of the same size and specialty have greater risk and therefore greater equity discount rates.

Growth Rate

As noted earlier, the cap rate is determined by subtracting the growth rate from the discount rate. The growth rate should reflect the long-term prospects for the practice's growth. The growth can come from increases in reimbursement for services, whether fee-for-service or capitation, or addition of providers or ancillary services, such as lab and imaging. Generally, this expansion is forecasted during the first five years. It is important to remember that the terminal growth rate is a growth rate into *perpetuity*[27] and must be sustainable. Very few businesses can sustain growth rates in excess of the inflation rate forever.

Insight and Analysis

There is a great opportunity for influencing the ultimate valuation conclusion via the growth rate, either deliberately or through an error of judgment. I recall one situation in a specialty practice where the independent valuation analyst used a cap rate on after-tax earnings of 13%, without first developing a discount rate, although this discount rate must have been at least 22%, implying a long-term growth rate into perpetuity of 9%—almost inconceivable!

I generally use the current estimate of the long-term rate of inflation as a *ceiling* on the growth rate; a reasonable range in my view in the absence of contradictory evidence is 2.0% to 2.5%. You can obtain the current rate of inflation estimate at the Philadelphia Federal Reserve Bank's website at http://www.philadelphiafed.org/index.cfm. I should emphasize that in my view, it is

Chapter 12: Choosing and Using the Right Valuation Methods

wholly inappropriate to use the nominal growth rate in GDP (real growth plus inflation) as a long-term growth rate.

General Price per Unit of Service

What about increases in fees per unit of service? From 1994 to 2009 or 13 years, the compound rate of increase was only 1.99%, based on data from the Bureau of Labor Statistics Producer Price Index for Physician Services.

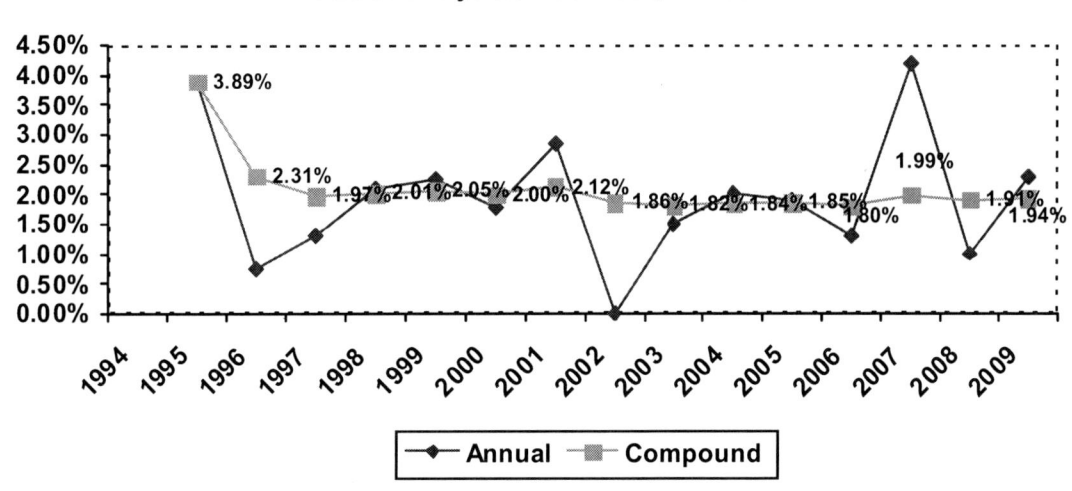

BLS PPI-Physician Services, Annual

Medicare Price per Unit of Service

Clearly, there is no evidence that unit reimbursement is growing at that GDP rate, and the capacity to provide units of service in a small practice is limited. Under federal law, the Medicare Sustainable Growth Rate, or SGR, Medicare expenditures for physician services are limited by a complex formula that considers the change in fees, the number of beneficiaries, growth in GDP per capita, and the impact of new laws. The SGR is then applied to the Medicare Economic Index (MEI), which measures the weighted average price change in physician services. The MEI[28] is a physician practice-specific measure of inflation and generally is in the range of 3.5%. The Medicare Payment Advisory Commission or MedPAC website has the data each March (www.medpac.gov). For 2008, the scheduled increase of .5% (19 cents) was a result of legislation temporarily overturning the SGR methodology which would have resulted in a 10.5% decrease in the conversion factor used to set the fee schedule. The compound rate of increase from 1998 to 2009 amounted to only 0.43%!

Chapter 12: Choosing and Using the Right Valuation Methods

Medicare Conversion Factor

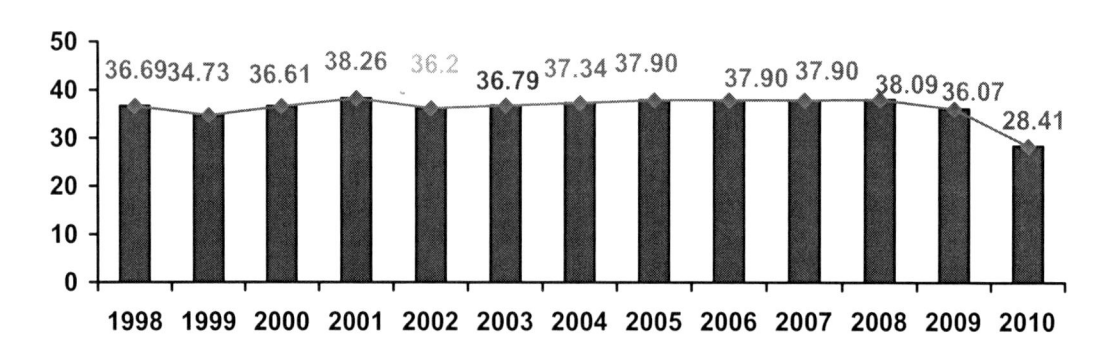

[Bar chart showing Medicare Conversion Factor values by year:
1998: 36.69; 1999: 34.73; 2000: 36.61; 2001: 38.26; 2002: 36.2; 2003: 36.79; 2004: 37.34; 2005: 37.90; 2006: 37.90; 2007: 37.90; 2008: 38.09; 2009: 36.07; 2010: 28.41]

As I observed in the 2006 article for the American Bar Association's Health Law Section:

> In the valuation community, much of the potential inaccuracy in growth rates stems from a poor understanding of the impact of growth on value and of the limitations in the growth of per unit revenue under the current reimbursement system. For example, the Medicare Conversion Factor which represents the value per Relative Value Unit or RVU of services provided under Part B has increased less than .5% in the last 9 years; the compound rate of growth—which would be used to compare it to inflation, for example—is virtually zero, while annual inflation has been in the 3% range. What drives Part B revenue in general is utilization along with intensity of service as reflected in coding.[29]

Underwriting Cycle

One of the primary influences on the forecast of future cashflow is the underwriting cycle in the health insurance industry. The Chart below reflects the historical cycle of premium increases and cost[30] increases. Note that in recent years, the rate of increase in premiums and costs has been equal. However, you can also see at the end of the 1990s a period of aggressive premium cutting in the face of mounting costs when the Industry tried to buy market share. This led to the failure of many smaller insurers and the consolidation that affects the ability of providers to negotiate fees today.[31]

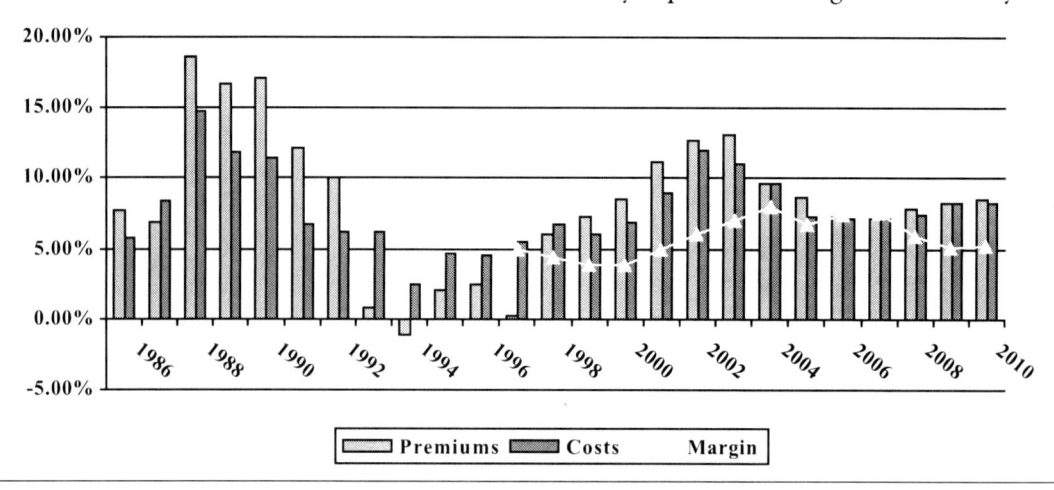

[Chart showing Premiums, Costs, and Margin from 1986 to 2010, with values ranging from -5.00% to 20.00%]

288 The AHLA/BVR Guide to Healthcare Valuation

Chapter 12: Choosing and Using the Right Valuation Methods

Medical Loss Ratio

In part, that cycle of premium increases and decreases reflects the relationship between the costs of provider payments and the premium charged. The Chart below reflects both seasonality as well as overall changes in the Medical Loss Ratio or MLR which represents the portion of the health insurance premium dollar spent on medical care on insured individuals. As the percentage goes down, less money is paid to providers of healthcare and insurance company profits increase.[32]

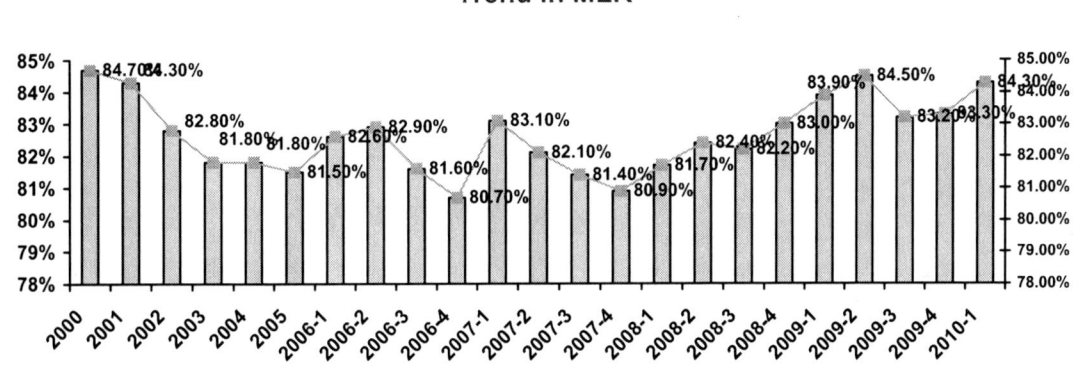

Trend in MLR

[Chart showing MLR percentages from 2000 to 2010-1, with values including: 2000: 84.70%, 2001: 84.30%, 2002: 82.80%, 2003: 81.80%, 2004: 81.80%, 2005: 81.50%, 2006-1: 82.60%, 2006-2: 82.90%, 2006-3: 81.60%, 2006-4: 80.70%, 2007-1: 83.10%, 2007-2: 82.10%, 2007-3: 81.40%, 2007-4: 80.90%, 2008-1: 81.70%, 2008-2: 82.40%, 2008-3: 82.20%, 2008-4: 83.00%, 2009-1: 83.90%, 2009-2: 84.50%, 2009-3: 83.20%, 2009-4: 83.30%, 2010-1: 84.30%]

Growth in Units of Service

On a more practice-specific level, look at the impact of various units of service volume growth rates on a practice currently seeing 4500 patient encounters a year.

	Base Year	1	2	3	4	5	6	7	8
Visits	4,500								
Growth Rate	4.00%	4,680	4,867	5,062	5,264	5,475	5,694	5,922	6,159
Growth Rate	5.00%	4,725	4,961	5,209	5,470	5,743	6,030	6,332	6,649
Growth Rate	6.00%	4,770	5,056	5,360	5,681	6,022	6,383	6,766	7,172
Growth Rate	7.00%	4,815	5,152	5,513	5,899	6,311	6,753	7,226	7,732
Growth Rate	8.00%	4,860	5,249	5,669	6,122	6,612	7,141	7,712	8,329
Growth Rate	9.00%	4,905	5,346	5,828	6,352	6,924	7,547	8,226	8,967
Growth Rate	10.00%	4,950	5,445	5,990	6,588	7,247	7,972	8,769	9,646

If this were a solo primary care practice, the maximum number of encounters is going to top out at between 4500 and 5500, depending upon whether it is adult, pediatric, or a mix of both![33]

Chapter 12: Choosing and Using the Right Valuation Methods

Conclusion of Growth Rate Discussion

External evidence of the growth rate may be obtained by reviewing government data on the healthcare segment of the economy.[34] Historically, this segment grows by well in excess of the inflation rate. However, the growth is driven in large part by the aging population and new technology, and is generally spread over more physicians, not focused on existing physicians. Therefore, the long-term growth rate for a given practice is much less than that for the industry as a whole. Only very large entities involved in a substantial cross section of the healthcare delivery system have an opportunity to match the industry growth rate.

> Perhaps the greatest risk of overestimating value and implicating Stark or the AKS stems from improper or unrealistic assumptions as to future growth in cashflow or profits.[35]

Discounted CashFlow (DCF)

Development of Assumptions

Underlying the discounted cashflow method is the necessity of developing a five-year forecast of financial operations. The normalization of earnings process described above typically provides the base year for the financial forecast. Various assumptions about the increases in revenues, expenses, numbers of patients, penetration of capitation, and capitation rates then need to be made. The acquiring entity should play a crucial role in this process, as the ability to achieve the forecast will depend in large part on the actions taken by the acquirer's management after the acquisition. If the valuation is conducted by a CPA, a representation letter signed by the acquirer, and perhaps the seller acknowledging development of the assumptions used in the model, should be considered.

Where the capitalization of excess earnings methods tend to focus on normalized historical results and assumes those results will continue (often an incorrect assumption), the discounted cashflow method requires that future results be forecasted, and the cashflows there from be discounted. The future results are forecasted, of course, based upon an analysis of the historical results. Future physician earnings must be forecasted as well. Note: This method is typically used in larger transactions and for regulatory purposes. It is rarely used in a buy-in or sale of a small practice.

Expense Growth

In addition to the discussion about Growth Rates in Revenues in the previous section, as the number of patients and encounters increases, underlying operating costs must increase as well. Items such as nonphysician salaries and fringe benefits, supplies, and telephone will typically vary as a function of volume. Rent may be a function of the underlying lease, and depreciation will be a function of capital expenditures. The cash cost of purchases must be at least equal to the depreciation expense in the terminal period calculation—in order to continue to have deprecation expense, you have to continue to buy fixed assets!

Chapter 12: Choosing and Using the Right Valuation Methods

An excellent source of expected increases in physician operating costs is the MedPAC Annual Report to Congress released each March. Here is a Table from that Report.

Forecasted input price increases and weights for physician services for 2009

Input component	Price increases for 2009	Category weight
Total	2.6%	100.0%
Physician work	2.7	52.5
Wages and salaries	2.4	42.7
Fringe benefits (nonwage compensation)	3.5	9.7
Physician practice expense	2.4	47.5
Nonphysician employee compensation	2.9	18.7
Wages and salaries	2.9	13.8
Fringe benefits (nonwage compensation)	2.8	4.8
Office expense	2.1	12.2
Professional liability insurance	2.3	3.9
Medical equipment	0.7	2.1
Drugs and supplies	3.0	4.3
Pharmaceuticals	1.7	2.3
Medical materials and supplies	3.9	2.0
Other professional expense	2.1	6.4

Note   Forecasted price changes for individual components are calculated by multiplying the component's weight (as listed in the Medicare Economic Index) by its price proxy. Forecasted price changes are not adjusted for productivity. Numbers may not total exactly due to rounding.

Source: Unpublished estimates from CMS, dated December 4, 2007.

Of course, local economic conditions have to be considered as well.

Cashflow Adjustments

This is a forecast of cashflow, not earnings! Valuation analysts unfamiliar with the deep discounts experienced by physicians from their usual charges for services frequently make major mistakes if they attempt to take "accrual" revenues and apply a "bad debt" allowance. It is not uncommon for physicians to have a 40% or greater difference between gross revenues and net revenues. (See discussion of Accounts Receivable *infra*) The various payors, such as Medicare or HMOs, determine what physicians are paid, and the physicians have little or no control. As a general rule, the discount rate applied to earnings is higher than that applied to cashflow due to the lag between generating earnings and collecting the cash.

Only the excess earnings method typically requires a separate measure of the value of tangible personal property, while the discounted cashflow method calculation includes both the tangible and intangible value of the practice in MVIC. Nonetheless, in a practice with large amounts of equipment such as that used in MR or CT Imaging, Radiation Oncology or a Blood Chemistry Lab, a separate measure of fixed assets is important to determine the depreciation expense that goes into the DCF and reduces income tax expense, thereby increasing value. Bear in mind that healthcare transactions are usually of assets not equity and therefore the basis step-up in the hands of the acquirer is relevant. The same rationale applies to amortizing any intangible value under IRC section 197.

Chapter 12: Choosing and Using the Right Valuation Methods

MVIC includes net working capital (NWC) as well, although NWC is often backed out of the valuation model as buyers typically do not acquire it in an asset purchase. The upshot is that it is very difficult to value the operating assets of a healthcare enterprise without allocating MVIC (the right hand side of the accounting equation) to the assets on the left-hand side.

Insight and Analysis

The reason NWC is not acquired is the difficulty of measuring the collectible value of accounts receivable, as well as a general desire not to assume liabilities. Even when it is acquired, retroactive adjustments to the purchase price are typically made based upon the ultimate receivable collections and actual payments of liabilities.

Physician Compensation

This is the most critical component of the model as it is generally the single largest expense. The compensation should be based upon some reasonable measure, *such as the employment agreement expected to be entered into as part of the transaction or some other measure consistent with the standard of value in the transaction, if the sellers will continue as employees post-acquisition.*[36] For example, if the physicians will have an incentive equal to 35% of any increase in net revenues, this should be reflected as part of the model. If additional providers will be added during the forecast period, the cost of salary and fringe benefits should be added.

Insight and Analysis

In fact, the valuation submitted in connection with the Friendly Hills transaction in 1991, cited in *Derby* and therefore relevant today, contains a letter signed by the managing partner stating that the partners recognized they were selling a portion of their earnings and that their future incomes would be less by virtue of that sale. In relevant part he states,

> . . . It has been clearly stated to the partners that, in the past, their compensation reflected not only the value of their medical services, but also the profits attributable to their ownership of the Network; that the latter element will be replaced by a cash payment, which they can invest . . . that the Medical Group's income will thereafter be derived from arms-length contract for medical services; and that these rates will necessarily be significantly lower than the total historical income they have been receiving . . . (Friendly Hills Valuation Report).

Relative Value Units

RVU-based compensation models are increasingly common when hospitals acquire physician practices. Medicare and other payors pay physicians under the Resource-Based Relative Value Scale (RBRVS) where each Current Procedural Terminology code is assigned a certain

Chapter 12: Choosing and Using the Right Valuation Methods

number of Relative Value Units (RVUs). These RVUs are then multiplied by a dollar-value Conversion Factor to set the fee Medicare pays.

The number of Relative Value Units is based upon the consumption[37] of three types of resources in the delivery of physician services:

Physician work

The principal factors comprising this component are time, technical skill and physical effort, mental effort and judgment, and the stress on the physician of certain patient risk factors.

Practice Costs

This component looks at the cost of delivering services by physician type, for example family medicine versus cardiac surgery. Physician practice costs per dollar of revenue tend to be much higher in primary care than surgery.

Malpractice Insurance Cost

Surgical specialties, and particularly obstetrics, neurosurgery and cardiac surgery, tend to have the highest malpractice insurance. This is the least important of the three components.

Geographic Adjustment

There is an additional adjustment for the geographic location of the practice based upon various government studies, including the census, HUD data, and others.

Physician Work RVUs or wRVUs are used in RVU-based models because they measure the work effort of the physician and avoid regulatory risks inherent in using broader measures of RVUs. For example, a cardiologist interpreting the result of a Stress Test ordered on a patient may be allocated the wRVU from the Professional Component of the Global Fee in a productivity-based compensation system, but not the practice expense RVUs associated with the Technical Component of the Global Fee. To illustrate the impact of wRVUs, CPT code 93015—cardiac stress testing—has a wRVU weight of .75, whereas CPT code 33206—insertion of a cardiac pace maker—has a weight of 7.31. Obviously, the work effort involved in the more invasive insertion of a pace maker will be rewarded with a higher level of compensation in a wRVU based compensation model.

Insight and Analysis

This is one of the most difficult assumptions in a forecast as the acquirer may not have any idea what the incentive portion of a physician's compensation will be or what the outcome of a wRVU-based model will be. Although not advisable for a variety of regulatory reasons, the compensation

Chapter 12: Choosing and Using the Right Valuation Methods

arrangement is sometimes negotiated after the purchase price determined by the valuation has been agreed to by the parties to the transaction. My standard report advises the client that they should consider revisiting the valuation if the compensation ultimately negotiated differs from that in the valuation model. (See also *Derby v. Commissioner*)[38] Whatever the amount used, bear in mind that "The accepted interpretation of reasonable compensation under the fair market value standard is the salary necessary to hire a nonowner replacement physician of equal experience."[39]

If the client does not specify a compensation formula (subject to its meeting an overall test of reasonableness for the valuation model), I will either work with them to develop a formula that meets the fair market value criteria I am opining on or suggest retention of an independent compensation consultant. Many acquirers now use Work RVUs as a basis for measuring productivity and compensation is a function of those RVUs and a payment rate. One of the many reasons I obtain data by CPT code when valuing a practice is that it is frequently not possible for the client to determine compensation without that data.

As a final observation, because compensation and value of the practice are opposite sides of the same coin—as compensation goes up value goes down—the question often arises about changing compensation to make the value different, while maintaining the required mathematical relationship between the two. All valuation models are DYNAMIC. You cannot properly change one assumption without considering the impact on all the others. One simple example: if you were to decrease compensation payable post-transaction to generate a higher value, you would have to consider the impact on the physician's productivity which would then effect all the revenue and variable expense assumptions!

Insight and Analysis

Notwithstanding the following discussion, I want to emphasize that I regard the MGMA data as the most useful in performing valuations. The key to using it is to use it expertly.

Using the MGMA Compensation and Cost Data

As noted elsewhere herein, statistical data cannot be used blindly. The valuation analyst needs to understand the data in order to use it effectively in the valuation process. One of the most commonly used sources of data on compensation is the MGMA Compensation and Production Survey. The document contains numerous tables listing compensation, including means, medians, 75th percentile, single specialty, multi-specialty, regional data, and a host of others. Which ones are relevant? [See also Chapter 14 in this Guide]

Table 1.1, for example, in the MGMA data represents all physicians included in the survey by specialty. It is therefore the largest database and arguably the means, medians, and other data items are the most representative: Without commenting on Statistical Science, the larger the population sampled, the more meaningful the data.[40]

Chapter 12: Choosing and Using the Right Valuation Methods

The data is then broken down by single specialty and multi-specialty practices. A single specialty practice would represent a group practice reporting to MGMA that employs only physicians of a specific specialty, such as hematology/oncology or cardiology. The multi-specialty groups include the physicians of more than one specialty—how many more, we do not know. Multi-specialty practices could simply include cardiology and gastroenterology, for example. The combination of these two types of groups should equal the data contained in the combined data.

The data by geographic section or region breaks the combined data down into East, West, South, and Midwest. Looking at the tables, you should note that the sample size is, of course, smaller for each region than the total. The regional data is then broken down by single specialty and multi-specialty practices, with even smaller sample sizes. There may be as few as only several dozen sample items, and perhaps fewer.

The problem is even more pronounced in the Cost Survey for specific physician practice specialties. The sample sizes for each of these practice types are quite small—and remember that those are number of physicians, not numbers of reporting practices. The data for multi-specialty practices, which constitute a large sample size, are more meaningful. Nonetheless, this data is commonly cited and is the best available. It is most wisely used when its limitations are understood.

Accounts Receivable

In many valuation engagements, the valuation analyst may not need to be overly concerned with intangible value but may need to reach a conclusion of value on such assets as accounts receivable. Many small businesses and virtually all professional practices use the cash method of accounting. Under this method, accounts receivable are not reflected on the tax returns (or financial statements, if they exist), and the valuation analyst will need to reflect them.

Introduction

In the absence of accrual accounting, measuring the accounts receivable becomes in large part the responsibility of the valuation analyst. (And even if accrual accounting is in place, the accounts receivable warrant careful attention.) In many medical practice valuation engagements, it may be the largest single asset. Some common examples include:

- A divorce where intangible assets such as goodwill are not marital property

- A hospital-based practice where the patient base and other intangibles are owned by the hospital and not by the practice

- A practice buy-in where goodwill is being excluded

- Any practice where the intangible value is small

Chapter 12: Choosing and Using the Right Valuation Methods

- In a liquidation scenario

Like many aspects of valuation, valuing medical accounts receivable is as much an art, as it is a science. However, there are a number of key factors that must be evaluated if the valuation analyst is to generate a meaningful estimate of value.

Characteristics of Medical Accounts Receivable

Unlike manufacturing or most service businesses, medical accounts receivable tend to consist of a large number of accounts with relatively small balances. Oil dealerships[41] are analogous in some ways, but they typically are selling a single product—oil, and perhaps some service and repair contracts.

Although some medical specialties, such as cardiac surgery, may have relatively large balances from a particular patient for procedures, there are typically additional smaller balances for office visits and similar services. In an Internal Medicine or Family Medicine practice, the typical charge may consist of a $75 office visit plus additional small charges such as $15 to draw blood and $20 for a rapid strep test. Each of the charges that originate with a single visit must be separately billed and accounted for. When (if) it is paid, the payment, if made by an insurer, will specify both the date the service was provided and the specific service that is being paid. Not all of the services will necessarily be paid and the percentage that is paid will not necessarily be the same for each service—and it is a rare instance indeed where 100% of the charge for any service is paid.

The payment of medical charges raises another significant issue: the majority of such charges are not paid for by the patient individually, but rather by the third party insurance company that provides the patient's insurance, or by a government program such as Medicare or Medicaid (hereinafter collectively referred to as payors). Further, these payors typically pay by a fee schedule that they set and it often bears little or no resemblance to the fee that the physician charges. As a result, each charge that is processed by the physician's billing department reflects both a payment and an *adjustment*, or *contractual allowance*. There may be multiple payments for a particular service, such as when the patient has a deductible or co-pay due after the insurer pays its share or where the patient has a secondary insurance that covers any balance not paid by the primary insurance. The term "*write-off*" is generally limited to those situations involving a bad debt from an uninsured patient, or where a payor refuses to pay for a service due to any of a host of reasons described below.

Situations in which write-offs may occur

The following is a nonexhaustive listing of the causes of write-offs or "bad debts" in a medical practice. These factors are also significant for normalizing revenue and determining the specific risk premium.

1. Uninsured patient fails to pay.

2. Office personnel fail to collect co-pays at the time of treatment.

Chapter 12: Choosing and Using the Right Valuation Methods

3. Practice fails to meet payor's contractual deadline for submitting a "clean claim." A clean claim is one in which all of the necessary information appears on the claim, including the patient's name, insurance number, the procedure provided by CPT™ (or Current Procedural Terminology) code, the diagnosis by ICD (or International Classification of Disease) code, consistency of the CPT™ and ICD codes, the date of service and other requirements specified by the payor. Typical periods for submission of clean claims are 60 days; thereafter, the payor is not obligated to pay the claim (although a denial can be appealed).

4. Failure to meet any requirements for pre-authorization of the service by the insurer or a primary care physician, for example.

5. Failure to obtain correct insurance information from the patient.

6. Failure to submit additional information with the claims, such as operative reports for certain surgical procedures.

7. Failure to timely appeal denial of claims.

8. Billing for uncovered services (those that are not covered by the patient's insurance).

9. Billing incorrectly for services, which are considered part of a package or "bundle" of services, such as pre-operative and post-operative visits considered part of the global fee paid for the surgery.

There are a host of others. One conclusion the valuation analyst should draw from this discussion is that the billing process in a medical practice is very complex, both in generating the charges and in recording the payment and adjustments for write-offs. This complexity leads to a variety of errors in all but the best-run practices. These errors result in otherwise collectible balances not being collected, uncollectible balances not being written off, uncovered services being paid, and the same service being paid more than once (a credit balance). Office staff involved in the process may be poorly educated, inadequately assisted or supervised, overwhelmed, or simply irresponsible.

The Process of Valuing Accounts Receivable

Generally speaking, the valuation of accounts receivable consists of two distinct components: identification of those charges that include *some* collectible amount, and determination of the portion of those charges that is ultimately collectible. We will examine each of these two components in the paragraphs that follow.

Identification of (Partially) Collectible Balances vs. Uncollectible Balances

The first step is to obtain an aged accounts receivable by payor. This report typically consists of a listing of the various payors that the practice does business with and the total due from

Chapter 12: Choosing and Using the Right Valuation Methods

each of those payors by aging category: current, greater than 30 days, greater than 60 days, greater than 90 days, and greater than 120 days. The "# Days" is the number of days gross charges in accounts receivable.

Payor	Current	> 30	> 60	>90	>120	Total	# Days
A	7,000	8,000	5,000	5,000	15,000	40,000	72
B	1,000	4,000	5,000	10,000	20,000	40,000	144
Total	8,000	12,000	10,000	15,000	35,000	80,000	96
	10.0%	15.0%	12.5%	18.8%	43.7%	100.0%	

Table 1

Analysis of this report provides the valuation analyst with a significant amount of the information necessary needed to determine what steps will be necessary to properly measure the accounts receivable. The first step is to compare the percentage of receivables in each aging category to statistical norms or to the valuation analyst's own experience. (Statistical norms are typically obtained from the Medical Group Management Association's Cost Survey). If the aging falls within accepted parameters, the valuation analyst may employ simple "short-cut" computations to estimate the collectible value. If not, a more complex computation may be required.

The most common indicator that a short-cut approach will not work is where the percentage of receivables in the greater than 120 day category is more than the expected level. The larger the variance, the more complex the computation required to determine the true collectible value.

Example

Assume that the MGMA norm for the greater than 120 days category is 20% and the valuation subject has 44% of its receivables in that category. This is an almost certain indication that uncollectible balances are not being written off. These balances more often than not consist of the unpaid portion of a charge representing the contractual allowance—that being the amount that the payor is not obligated to pay under the terms of its contract with the physician. Another common component is uncollectible "self-pay" or uninsured balances. These balances accumulate because it often takes a lot of work to identify such balances, and to get approval for having them written off. In the typical medical office, time tends to be spent on collecting collectible balances rather than on writing-off uncollectible ones.

The fact pattern of the example will require, at a minimum, that the valuation analyst separate the aged accounts receivable into two distinct groups: those greater than 120 days old and those less than 120 days old. Each of the two groups will then need to be valued separately.

Chapter 12: Choosing and Using the Right Valuation Methods

The balances should be analyzed by payor. For example, it may be that certain payors have unusual aging distributions while others do not. Another common occurrence is where the practice's *largest* payor has an aging distribution different than that of the remaining payors.

Example

In a valuation of a large healthcare facility where the cost approach was important, the entity's single largest payor was in serious financial difficulty. The aging of receivables from that payor was significantly worse than for the balance of the receivables. Although there was an audited financial statement, it was on the income tax method of accounting and therefore did not reflect an allowance for uncollectible accounts. A substantial reduction in the audited accounts receivable balance was required to reach fair market value of the receivables.

Measuring the portion of charges that are collectible

A standard analysis that should be done in any medical practice valuation is to compute charges, collections (payments) and adjustments for each of the practices principal insurers. It is important to perform this analysis by payor because the contractual payment rate is likely to vary (and often significantly) for each payor that the practice contracts with.

Example

For simplicity, assume that a practice has contracts with two payors. Data from the billing system indicates that Payor A reimburses the practice at a rate equal to 50% of charges, while Payor B reimburses at a rate equal to 60% of charges, as shown in Table 2 below.

\multicolumn{6}{c}{Table 2}
Payor	Charges	Payments	Adjustments	Collection Rate	Realization Rate
A	200,000	100,000	100,000	50%	50%
B	100,000	60,000	36,000	60%	62.5%

The collection rate *is equal to current payments divided by current charges.*

The realization rate *is equal to current payments divided by current payments plus current adjustments.*

If the billing system is working properly and adjustments are being recorded properly at the time payments are received, the realization rate is the best measure of the true collectible value. This is due to the fact that it reflects *both* elements of the charge relief activity: the payment and the contractual allowance or adjustment. If the adjustments are not being

Chapter 12: Choosing and Using the Right Valuation Methods

recorded properly however, the realization rate is inaccurate and the collection rate may be a better measure. The collection rate may understate collectibility when unpaid claims are inadequately reviewed and overstate collectibility when, for example, charges to a payor in the current period decline from prior periods.

A "short-cut" valuation of receivables would appear as follows (Table 3):

Table 3			
Payor	Receivable	Collection Rate	Collectible
A	40,000	50%	20,000
B	40,000	60%	24,000
	80,000	55%	44,000

Or, (Table 4) using the realization rate approach:

Table 4			
Payor	Receivable	Collection Rate	Collectible
A	40,000	50%	20,000
B	40,000	62.5%	25,000
	80,000	56.25%	45,000

The problem with either of these approaches should be obvious: Payor B constitutes only 33% of charges while it constitutes 50% of receivables. This is a clear clue that something may be "wrong" with the Payor B receivables. A further analysis is likely to reveal one of several generic causes: Payor B pays more slowly than Payor A, there are completely uncollectible balances included in the Payor B receivables meeting one or more of the criteria discussed earlier, there has been a contract issue or termination, or an unusual decline in charges to Payor B patients.

If the valuation analyst suspects or determines that the collection rate and realization rate approach are inaccurate, the earlier approach described of dividing receivables into two distinct groups of those greater than 120 days old and those less than 120 days old should be followed. (Refer to this approach as the "detailed" method.) In the next example (Table 5) below, the valuation analyst determines that the Payor B receivables greater than 120 days will yield only 40 cents on the dollar rather than the collection rate of 60 cents. (It should not be seen as unusual for insured receivables in the greater than 120 day category to be worth substantially less than the historical collection rate for a particular payor.)

Chapter 12: Choosing and Using the Right Valuation Methods

Table 5							
Payor	<120 Days	Factor	Collectible	>120 Days	Factor	Collectible	Total
A	30,000	50%	15,000	10,000	50%	5,000	20,000
B	20,000	60%	12,000	20,000	40%	8,000	20,000
	80,000		30,000			11,000	40,000

Recap of Methodologies

	Collection Rate	Realization Rate	Detail
Value	45,000	44,000	40,000

The recap indicates that the choice of approach to valuing receivables can generate very different results. If you are not convinced, multiply each of the values in the Recap by 10.

Gaining insight into the aging

Depending upon the sophistication of the practice's billing software, the importance of the receivables to the overall valuation, and the budget for the engagement, it may be desirable to obtain a *detailed aging by individual account* of the greater than 120 day balances.

Insight and Analysis

In a litigation engagement, the greater than 120-day balances were 3.5 times the MGMA norm. My investigation indicated that a host of problems existed in the recording (or lack thereof) of contractual allowances. The review, for example, of several annual detailed agings demonstrated that the same balances appeared year after year and there was a clear failure to write them off. Inquiries of management disclosed that the largest payor had negotiated a fixed weekly payment (or capitated arrangement) for services and that the difference between the practice's charges to that payor and the capitated payment were never written off. The uncollectible balances in this case amounted to multiple seven figures and resulted in a dramatic reduction in the valuation.

Credit balances

This is one of the most difficult potential problems to identify and resolve when valuing medical accounts receivables. Credit balances *may* represent overpayments on a particular account, or they may be payments posted to an account which could not be matched with a particular service and service date. For example, assume that a patient has four distinct services recorded. A check is received from the patient's insurer that does not specify which services are being paid. The data entry person posts the payment to the patient's account but does not apply it to any particular

Chapter 12: Choosing and Using the Right Valuation Methods

service. The detailed aging will typically reflect the credit separately from the individual charges. In this case, the credit balance is not a true credit, but rather requires a journal entry. As another example, assume that the insurer mistakenly pays the claim twice, creating a true credit balance. Finally, a common source of credit balances exists where the patient has insurance, but the practice has not contracted to accept direct payment from the insurer. As a courtesy, the practice may submit a bill to the insurer for the patient, but expects the patient to pay the bill directly. If the insurer subsequently pays the practice as well, a true credit balance will result.

Because credit balances are generally considered lost property under most states' law and must be "escheated"[42] back to the state, the seriousness of this problem should not be overlooked. Further, failure to refund overpayments from government programs may subject the practice to civil or criminal sanctions. Certain state laws may provide for civil or criminal sanctions for non-governmental payors as well.

Tax Effecting

The question frequently arises whether "zero basis" accounts receivable (as they are known for tax purposes where the taxpayer uses the cash method) should be tax-effected or reduced for the estimated income taxes that will be due when they are collected. If the standard of value is Fair Market, many valuation analysts believe the adjustment is appropriate; some jurisdictions would not allow tax-effecting if the tax would never, in fact, be paid. This is of particular significance if the ultimate value of the business will be offset against property received by the other spouse in a divorce. For example, if the spouse is to receive cash of $100,000 (previously taxed by definition) and the business owner is to receive a like amount of accounts receivable that have not yet been taxed, there will clearly be an inequitable result.

In valuing a corporate professional practice with zero basis receivables, they would typically be offset by a claim for future compensation due to the owner. Arguably, therefore, the balance sheet accounts receivable and liability for deferred compensation would offset and reflect no increase in equity. However, the deferred compensation would be an individual asset of the practice owner. This asset should, again, be offset for the taxes expected to be paid when the receivables are paid out of the corporation as salary. In addition, it should be considered whether these same receivables, when collected, will be subject to a claim for alimony and whether there should not be some adjustment for this as well. Because receivables are the source of future income typically subject to alimony, counting them as both an asset and as income is seen as "double counting" in some Courts and by some valuation experts.

Insight and Analysis

If the standard of value for divorce in your state is fair market value on a going concern basis, reducing the receivables by collection costs is an inappropriate modification to collectible value. Going concern means that after the valuation date (hypothetical sale date) the practice will continue to operate in the ordinary course. If the standard of value were liquidation value, collection costs would be considered.

Chapter 12: Choosing and Using the Right Valuation Methods

Conclusion

In order to properly measure accounts receivable of a medical practice, the valuation analyst requires a considerable knowledge of what information to request and how to interpret and use it. Even if relying primarily on an income approach or market approach, failure to properly estimate net working capital can expose the valuation to a serious possibility of overstatement. If the valuation engagement is to measure asset value, the individual components thereof—fixed assets, net working capital and intangible value—must be known to compute the tax benefit from depreciation of fixed assets and amortization of the intangible value. It is difficult to escape the need to apply the cost approach in valuing a medical practice, at least as far as net working capital is concerned.

An In-Depth Review of the Correct Use of the Excess Earnings Method

Insight and Analysis

This section is based upon material I use in my continuing education courses for both basic business valuation and medical practice valuation. The premise is that the excess earnings method is a very useful tool, but one that has been maligned due to its misuse, rather than any inherent weakness in the method itself. Be certain to read this ENTIRE section to avoid drawing incorrect conclusions about the examples—the initial example contains a deliberate error. Bear in mind that "When weighted capitalization rates for tangible- and intangible-asset cash flows are used to derive a single capitalization rate for all cash flows, CEE [capitalized excess earnings] will generate the same result as CCF [capitalization of cashflows]."[43]

Net Tangible Assets

Though there is no uniform agreement as to what the term "Net Tangible Assets" means. It is important that the choice of a return on those net assets, however defined, is consistent (i.e., properly paired) with the definition being used—and there is no disagreement about that.

One definition of Net Tangible Assets is the sum of Net Working Capital and Fixed Assets (See example 1: Historical Balance Sheet, option 1). These values should be stated at fair market value, although typically the book value of fixed assets is used unless the valuation analyst is comfortable *estimating* their fair market value or has a separate appraisal.

Example 1: Historical Balance Sheet	
Net working capital	80,000
Fixed assets	290,000
"Net Tangible Assets"—Option 1	370,000
Long-term debt	300,000
Equity or "Net Tangible Assets"—Option 2	70,000

Chapter 12: Choosing and Using the Right Valuation Methods

The correct computation of the required return on Net Tangible Assets using this definition is shown in Example 1: Weighted Average Cost of Capital. Here, we have assumed that the pre-tax cost of debt is 6%, based upon a borrowing rate of 9% less long-term growth rate of 3%. The cap rate for equity is 34%, determined by the 37% pre-tax discount rate less long-term growth rate of 3%. We know from the Historical Balance Sheet that there is $300,000 of debt and that the Equity is equal to the Net Tangible Assets of $70,000. Doing the calculations results in a required return on Net Tangible Assets of 11.30%.

Valuation Tip

The components of the build-up of a discount rate below are hypotheticals for a *hypothetical* valuation date. You need to use the correct components based upon the *actual* valuation date from Morningstar's SBBI Yearbook and other sources.

Long Treasury Bond	5.80%
Equity Risk Premium, S&P 500	7.50%
Base Equity Rate	**13.30%**
10th Decile Risk Premium, S&P 500	4.60%
Practice Risk Premium	5.50%
After-Tax Discount Rate	**23.40%**
Less: Growth Rate	-3.00%
Capitalization Rate, Subsequent Year	**20.40%**
Pre-Tax Cap Rate	**34.00%**
Plus: Growth Rate	3.00%
Pre-Tax Discount Rate	**37.00%**

Example 1: Cap Rate from the Weighted Average Cost Of Capital

Debt	6.00%	300,000	81.08%	4.86%
Equity	34.00%	70,000	18.92%	6.43%
		370,000	100.00%	11.30%

In the next portion of Example 1, we illustrate the calculation of the value of the business enterprise using the Excess Earnings method. Normalized 2002 earnings are based upon cashflows to invested capital (debt-free cashflows), which includes both long-term debt and equity, as should be clear from Example 1—Option 1.[44] $270,000 is the fair market value of the owner/employee physician's services. For simplicity, we assume that the required return on intangibles is equivalent to the required return on equity of 34%. In an actual engagement the valuation analyst should, of course, consider whether the intangibles require a higher rate of return than the "generic" return on equity.[45]

Chapter 12: Choosing and Using the Right Valuation Methods

Example 1: Net Tangible Assets Based On Net Working Capital (NWC) Plus Fixed Assets				
Normalized 2002 earnings			375,000
Fair market earnings			-270,000
Excess earnings			105,000
"Net tangible assets"	370,000	11.30%	-41,800
Excess earnings attributable to intangibles			63,200
Capitalization rate			34.00%
Intangible Value			185,882
Practice Tangibles			370,000
Business Enterprise Value			555,882

The second definition of Net Tangible Assets (Example 2: Historical Balance Sheet, Option 2) is the sum of Net working Capital and Fixed Assets, less Long-term Debt. If book values are used for all of these factors, "Net Tangible Assets" in this circumstance will equal stockholders' equity, unless there are excluded assets or liabilities.[46]

Example 2: Historical Balance Sheet	
Net working capital	80,000
Fixed assets	290,000
"Net Tangible Assets"—Option 1	370,000
Long-term debt	300,000
Equity or "Net Tangible Assets"—Option 2	70,000

Recall that Normalized 2002 earnings are based upon cashflows to invested capital (debt-free cashflows), which includes both long-term debt and equity. There are two critical aspects of correctly performing the calculation when using this (Option 2) definition of Net Tangible Assets. The first is to recognize that the return on the $300,000 of debt ($18,000) must be subtracted from the Normalized 2002 earnings. This is necessary because the $18,000 is not available to equity.

The second critical aspect is that there is no need to compute a weighted average return because the Net Tangibles Assets are equal to equity only. As such, the required return on the 70,000 is 34%, or 23,800.

Chapter 12: Choosing and Using the Right Valuation Methods

Example 2: Net Tangible Assets Based On NWC Plus Fixed Assets Less Long-Term Debt			
Normalized 2002 earnings			375,000
Interest on debt			-18,000
Fair market earnings			-270,000
Excess earnings			87,000
"Net tangible assets"	70,000	34.00%	23,800
Excess earnings attributable to intangibles			63,200
Capitalization rate			34.00%
Intangible Value			**185,882**
Practice Tangibles			**370,000**
Business Enterprise Value			**555,882**

The proof that the two calculations have been handled correctly is that the valuation result—$555,882—is exactly the same in both Options! I highly recommend that valuation analysts using the excess earnings method structure their spreadsheet models to perform the calculation using both Option 1 and Option 2. In this manner, you have an automatic proof of the correct application of the method.

The Balance Sheet based upon the fair market value calculation is shown below. The Business Enterprise Value of $555,882 would be the price a buyer would pay for the assets while the $255,883 would be the value of the equity (stock) of the company.[47]

Fair Market Balance Sheet			
	Historical Cost	Adjust	Fair Market
Net working capital	80,000		80,000
Fixed assets	290,000		290,000
	370,000		370,000
Intangibles		185,882	185,882
Business enterprise value	370,000	185,882	555,882
Long-term debt	300,000		300,000
Equity	70,000	185,882	255,882

Insight and Analysis

Bear in mind that the above example contains (what may be) a deliberate error in the concluded value—see the discussion under the caption Cost of Capital later in this Chapter.

Chapter 12: Choosing and Using the Right Valuation Methods

The Use of the Capitalization of Cashflows in Conjunction with the Excess Earnings Method

A common user error is the failure to consider, or properly assess, whether the *overall* (weighted average) capitalization rate that results from the *separate* rates on tangibles and intangibles is reasonable. Computing the weighted average capitalization rate, and using it to determine the practice's value under the capitalization of cashflows method, can prevent this pitfall.

Table 1 revisits the example from the previous section. In Table 2, we have determined that the *pre-tax*[48] cost of debt is 6% and the pre-tax cost of equity is 34%. The cost of equity will apply to the tangibles not financed by debt as well as to the intangibles.[49]

Table 2: Historical Balance Sheet	
Net working capital	80,000
Fixed assets	290,000
"Net Tangible Assets"	370,000
Long-term debt	300,000
Equity or "Net Tangible Assets"	70,000

Table 3: WACC Cap Rate for Tangible Assets				
Debt	6.00%	300,000	81.08%	4.86%
Equity	34.00%	70,000	18.92%	6.43%
		370,000	100.00%	11.30%

Table 3 is the calculation of the value of the practice using the excess earnings method from the previous section. The return on the tangibles of 11.30% is based upon the weighted average of the return on debt and the return on equity reflected in Table 2.

Chapter 12: Choosing and Using the Right Valuation Methods

Table 4: Excess Earnings Method			
Normalized 2002 earnings			375,000
Fair market earnings			(270,000)
Excess earnings			105,000
"Net tangible assets"	370,000	11.30%	(41,800)
Excess earnings attributable to intangibles			63,200
Capitalization rate			34.00%
INTANGIBLE VALUE			185,882
PRACTICE TANGIBLES			370,000
BUSINESS ENTERPRISE VALUE			555,882

It is important to understand that the excess earnings method is nothing more (or less) than a *two-stage* capitalization of cashflows: the first stage is "reversed" in that we determine the value of the tangible assets *first*,[50] and then apply a pre-determined rate of return to that value. In the second stage, we determine the value of the intangible assets by capitalizing the remaining cashflow by the pre-determined rate of return for intangibles. In effect, the excess earnings method says that there are two returns on equity to the owner of the practice: one on tangibles and one on intangibles. The reasonable compensation is a return on labor.

How do we know that the rate of return on the earnings after reasonable compensation—earnings attributable to both tangibles and intangibles-—is itself reasonable? The only way to confirm this is to compute the weighted average return based upon the values determined in the excess earnings method and then apply it to the total earnings in excess of reasonable compensation. This computation is shown in Table 4.

Table 5: WACC Cap Rate for Entire Practice				
Tangibles	370,000	66.56%	11.30%	7.52%
Practice Intangibles	185,882	33.44%	34.00%	11.37%
Weighted Average Cost Of Capital	555,882	100.00%		18.89%

Thus, we see that the choice of a 6% pre-tax cap rate for debt and a 34% pre-tax cap rate for equity results in a WACC cap rate of 18.89% applied to the pre-tax earnings or cashflow of the practice, after the payment of reasonable compensation for labor. The analysis of whether or not this is reasonable requires the valuation analyst's assessment of the reasonableness of the separate costs of equity (34%) and debt (6%). It can also be viewed in the conventional fashion of the weights of equity and debt, rather than the weights of tangibles and intangibles, as shown in Table 5.

Chapter 12: Choosing and Using the Right Valuation Methods

Table 6: Conventional WACC Cap Rate for Entire Practice				
Debt	6.00%	300,000	53.97%	3.24%
Equity	34.00%	255,882	46.03%	15.65%
		555,882	100.00%	18.89%

What Table 5 demonstrates is that the high percentage of debt is making the WACC quite low. The valuation analyst should consider whether this is a reasonable degree of debt for an engagement to value a controlling interest—the excess earnings method should only be used to value a controlling interest.

Finally, we can "prove" the computation of the WACC for the entire practice and the excess earnings method by valuing the practice using the traditional capitalization of cashflows method. This "proof" does not confirm the reasonableness of the 18.89% cap rate, only that it has been computed correctly.

Table 7: Capitalization of Cashflows	
Normalized 2002 Earnings	375,000
Fair Market Earnings	(270,000)
Cashflow After Reasonable Compensation	105,000
Capitalization Rate	18.89%
	555,882

The value is exactly the same—as it should be!

Table 7 indicates the most common mistake: assuming that all of the tangible assets can be financed with debt, or at a low rate of return, based upon the IRS excess earnings method. Table 8 is the calculation of the value under the Excess Earnings method. This silly result is based upon a case study presented in my course on business valuation.[51]

Table 8: WACC Cap Rate for Tangible Assets				
Debt	0.00%	0	0.00%	0.00%
Equity—Tangibles	10.00%	1,000,000	100.00%	10.00%
		1,000,000	100.00%	10.00%

Chapter 12: Choosing and Using the Right Valuation Methods

Table 9: Excess Earnings Method			
Normalized 2002 Earnings			375,000
Fair Market Earnings			(270,000)
Excess Earnings			105,000
"Net Tangible Assets"	1,000,000	10.00%	(100,000)
Excess Earnings Attributable To Intangibles			5,000
Capitalization Rate			34.00%
INTANGIBLE VALUE			14,706
PRACTICE TANGIBLES			1,000,000
BUSINESS ENTERPRISE VALUE			1,014,706

Table 9 will clue the valuation analyst into the *FACT* that a mistake has been made: a pre-tax return of 10.35% for a medical practice is not reasonable in any event! If we do a short-cut conversion of this rate to an after-tax rate by multiplying by 1 minus the tax rate (40%) or 60%, we get a return we can compare to standard costs of equity from Morningstar. 10.35% times 60% = 6.21% (a cap rate). Adding the growth rate of 3% gives us an after-tax discount rate of 9.21%. This is *less than* the required rate of return on the S&P 500, which represents the risk of an equity investment in the broad market, the standard of comparison. Simply put, it is ridiculous.

Table 10: Conventional WACC Cap Rate for Entire Practice				
Tangibles	1,000,000	98.55%	10.00%	9.86%
Practice Intangibles	14,706	1.45%	34.00%	0.49%
Weighted Average Cost Of Capital	1,014,706	100.00%		10.35%

Notwithstanding the mistake in the selection of the return on the $1,000,000 of tangibles, Table 10 demonstrates that this method agrees with Table 8's Excess Earnings method.

Table 11: Capitalization of Cashflows	
Normalized 2002 Earnings	375,000
Fair Market Earnings	(270,000)
Cashflow After Reasonable Compensation	105,000
Capitalization Rate	10.35%
	1,014,706

Chapter 12: Choosing and Using the Right Valuation Methods

Conclusion

Failure to test the reasonableness of the two rates of return used in the excess earnings method by computing a single rate of return for the cashflow attributable to both tangibles and intangibles (capitalization of cashflows method) can lead to serious mistakes, such as that shown in Tables 7 through 10. The valuation analyst should structure spreadsheets to perform this test *automatically*. The key element is whether the combined pre-tax cap rate (or the return in the practice's assets) is reasonable when compared to proper external benchmarks, such as those developed from Morningstar data under the Capital Asset Pricing Model or Build-up Method.

Control Adjustments to the Excess Earnings Valuation Model?

Introduction

The Excess Earnings Method generally produces a control value. The technical reason for this is that the Tangible Asset measurement requires the cost approach, which always produces a control value. It *is* mathematically possible to adjust the assumptions in an Excess Earnings model to generate a noncontrol value, just as it is possible—and common—to vary the assumptions in a Capitalization of Cashflows model to produce a control or a noncontrol value. Medical practices are somewhat unusual in that the Excess Earnings method—properly applied, of course—could be used to determine a noncontrol value. This is in large part because the distribution of cash is generally governed by employment contracts and other ownership rights via a stockholders agreement, and because the tangible assets are not typically material when compared to the intangible assets.

Control Adjustments

In order to apply control premiums to reach a control value, you must first have used a method which determines a *noncontrol* value. In addition, the valuation community has moved towards the position that most "control" premiums actually represent strategic considerations not consistent with fair market value. Use of control premiums when using the Excess Earnings method is therefore inappropriate, or stated more frankly, *wrong*.

Equally risky is use of the Excess Earnings method to determine a *non*control value. Lack of control or minority discounts should be *considered* when the excess earnings method is used to produce a noncontrol value. Better yet, *eliminate the control adjustments*. Perhaps the most frequently overlooked fact of medical practice valuation is that if all cash distribution is contractual, i.e., via a compensation plan and employment contracts, and the tangible value is low, using the excess earnings method for a physician practice buy-in is acceptable (and common), providing the noncontrol elements are properly considered.

Chapter 12: Choosing and Using the Right Valuation Methods

Reasonable compensation

In valuing medical practices using the excess earnings method, the most important adjustment is the one for reasonable compensation. As noted earlier in the Chapter, determining the reasonable compensation for a physician requires more than merely looking at a statistical source and choosing the mean or median. The valuation analyst needs to first compare the physician's productivity or work effort to statistical norms and then base the reasonable compensation on that productivity. You cannot expect to pay a hypothetical buyer of the practice a 35 hour wage for 50 hours of work.[52]

It is equally important to focus on where the income in the practice is coming from. Practices which own laboratories or imaging equipment, e.g., x-ray, ultrasound, CT Scan or MRI, may have significant profits from such operations. These profits need to be determined to correctly perform the valuation. They are not part of the physician work effort. Moreover, they may not be part of personal or professional goodwill in a divorce context and should be factored out of that debate in those jurisdictions where personal goodwill is not a divisible asset.

The "compensation" needs to be considered in its broader sense of fringe benefits, retirement plan contributions and other perquisites. For example, the compensation in the MGMA data includes only W-2 compensation; retirement plan benefits are reported separately. As such, when figuring reasonable compensation in a valuation model, if the valuation analyst adds back the retirement plan contribution to available earnings, he/she then needs to add the MGMA retirement plan contribution to whatever (W-2) earnings are selected from the MGMA data.

Cost of capital

In the first part of this section, we saw that there was substantial debt in the practice used to finance tangible assets. This debt drove down the required rate of return on the tangibles, which in turn increased the amount of excess earnings available for intangible assets. This, of course, apparently increases the value of the practice. In short, the more debt one adds to the capital structure, the lower the cost of capital goes and the higher the value goes—*unless* one understands the CAPM and Betas! This suggests that the analysis of the percentage of debt in the capital structure is critical to a correct valuation, although simply adding debt to lower the cost of capital is not acceptable since it increased debt also increases the cost of equity.

Variations in the percentages of debt and equity that a hypothetical control owner of a practice would make need to be thought through carefully. In the real world, the debt of a medical practice is limited to some portion of the fixed assets and the accounts receivable in the practice. Rarely does one see the intangible value financed with debt. As such, it would generally be inaccurate to assume that the intangible value would be financed with debt in the absence of some peculiar set of circumstances.

Figure 1 is the computation of the Pre-tax Cap rate and Discount rate for this example.

Chapter 12: Choosing and Using the Right Valuation Methods

Insight and Analysis

The components of the build-up of a discount rate are *hypotheticals* for a hypothetical valuation date. You need to use the correct components based upon the actual valuation date from Ibbotson's Yearbook and other sources.

Figure 1	
Long Treasury Bond	5.80%
Equity Risk Premium, S&P 500	7.50%
Base Equity Rate	13.30%
10th DECILE RISK PREMIUM, S&P 500	4.60%
Practice Risk Premium	5.50%
After-Tax Discount Rate	23.40%
Less: Growth Rate	-3.00%
Capitalization Rate, Subsequent Year	20.40%
Pre-Tax Cap Rate	34.00%
Plus: Growth Rate	3.00%
Pre-Tax Discount Rate	37.00%

Figure 2 highlights the presumed hypothetical optimal mix of debt and equity used for the (same) practice that was presented in the first two parts of this article.

Figure 2 WACC Cap Rate for Tangible Assets			
Pre Tax Discount Rate		37.00%	
Equity Percentage		75.00%	
			27.75%
Cost Of Debt	9.00%		
Tax-Rate	0.00%		
After-Tax Cost Of Debt		9.00%	
Debt Percentage		25.00%	
			2.25%
Weighted Avg Cost of Capital			30.00%
Less: Growth Rate			-3.00%
Cap Rate, Subsequent Year			27.00%

Chapter 12: Choosing and Using the Right Valuation Methods

Figure 3 is the calculation of the value of the practice using the excess earnings method from the previous section.

Figure 3: Excess Earnings Method			
Normalized 2002 earnings			375,000
Interest on debt			(5,550)
Fair market earnings			(270,000)
Excess earnings			99,450
"Net tangible assets"	277,500	34.00%	(94,350)
Excess earnings attributable to intangibles			5,100
Capitalization rate			34.00%
Intangible value			15,000
Practice tangibles			370,000
Business enterprise value			385,000

Figure 4 is the Cap rate determined in the earlier example, followed by the cap rate based on Figure 2:

Figure 4: WACC Cap Rate for Tangible Assets				
Old Debt	6.00%	300,000	53.97%	3.24%
Equity	34.00%	255,882	46.03%	15.65%
		555,882	100.00%	18.89%

Figure 5: WACC Cap Rate for Tangible Assets				
Here, debt is 25% of the tangible assets of $385,000, or $92,500.				
New Debt	6.00%	92,500	24.03%	1.44%
Equity	34.00%	292,500	75.97%	25.83%
		385,000	100.00%	27.27%

Insight and Analysis

Note the substantial difference in the weighted average cost of capital when the debt level is adjusted to 24% from the nearly 54% in the original example. Since "the lower the cap rate the higher the value," we know that the value of the practice with 25% debt—Figure 5—will be much less than with 54% debt—Figure 6.

Chapter 12: Choosing and Using the Right Valuation Methods

Figure 6: Capitalization of Cashflows—New	
Normalized 2002 Earnings	375,000
Fair Market Earnings	(270,000)
Cashflow After Reasonable Compensation	105,000
Capitalization Rate	27.27%
Asset Value	385,000
Less: Long-term Debt	300,000
Equity Value	85,000

Figure 7: Capitalization of Cashflows—Old	
Normalized 2002 Earnings	375,000
Fair Market Earnings	(270,000)
Cashflow After Reasonable Compensation	105,000
Capitalization Rate	18.89%
Asset Value	555,882
Less: Long-term Debt	300,000
Equity Value	255,882

Which of these two answers is correct? This decision requires that most difficult of skills: judgment. Part of the answer lays in the conversion of the two cap rates to after-tax discounts rates (Figure 7) that can be compared to Morningstar's return on capital. Bear in mind that the cap rates are being applied to *invested capital* whereas the Morningstar data determines a cost of *equity* that then needs to be used in a computation of a weighted average cost of capital capitalization rate. The valuation analyst needs to ask the question: Is 19.36% (14.33%) a reasonable return[53] on invested capital for a medical practice? In point of fact, 14.33% would be quite low by both current and historical standards. At the peak of acquisition activity in the mid-1990s when perceived risk was lowest, the weighted average cost of capital for the best physician practices was rarely less than 16%. Today, practices are considered much more risky. The 19.36% is a more reasonable rate of return.

Figure 8		
Cap Rate-Pre-tax	27.27%	18.89%
1 less the Tax rate	60.00%	60.00%
Cap Rate-After-tax	16.36%	11.33%
Growth rate	3.00%	3.00%
Discount rate-After-tax	19.36%	14.33%

Chapter 12: Choosing and Using the Right Valuation Methods

Insight and Analysis

One question I have often been asked: If using a hypothetical mix of debt and equity in the WACC, what is subtracted from the result to determine the actual equity of the practice—actual debt or hypothetical debt? The answer, of course, is the actual debt. The assumption is that the hypothetical owner would use an optimal mix of debt and equity, which in turn is what drives the Enterprise Value in the valuation. From the *seller's* standpoint, they get the entire Enterprise Value and then pay off *whatever debt they have, if any*. Think about a scenario in which the optimal debt-equity mix is 25%-75%, but the seller has 50% debt—clearly, the equity is less than if they had 25% debt. It is useful to prepare FMV balance sheet—allocating to working capital, fixed assets and intangibles—from the model so you can see what the actual assets, debt and equity look like.

What about a noncontrol value?

Lawyers, judges and some valuation analysts[54] like the excess earnings method for valuing physician practices. Many of the members of that subset of professionals do not really understand how it works, however. The most frequent mistake in a transactional setting is using the excess earnings method to value a *non*control interest.

For example, let's assume that the practice in Figures 3 and 6 consisted of one owner and one employee physician. The owner is paid $250,000 per year and the employee is paid $125,000. The valuation analyst determines that reasonable compensation for the owner is $140,000 and for the employee $130,000. The employee is going to buy 50% of the practice. Since the value is a control value and you do not get control with 50%, this should be your first clue that the value of the 50% interest is *not* one-half of $385,000 or $192,500. Since the employee does not get control, he cannot reduce the current owner's salary to $140,000 per year and therefore cannot get 50% of the excess earnings of $105,000. If he doesn't get that 50%, what is the practice worth? It is only worth the excess earnings that the employee receives capitalized at 27.27%. If the owner continues to get paid $250,000, there are not any excess earnings *and the practice is worth nothing to the employee.*

In point of fact, valuing a practice for buy-in purposes really requires that the terms of the buy-in be known. The 2008 *Derby* Tax Court case indicates that the actual terms must be known for a sale to a Hospital. As can be seen from the simple example above, *the value to the buyer depends upon what the buyer's income will be after the purchase.* If it doesn't change, there is no value. If the income does not change for a number of years, the excess earnings method (or CCF method) is not a correct choice, as both of these methods assume that there is level cashflow throughout the period of ownership which grows at a fixed rate each year. The correct method in such a circumstance is the Discounted Cashflow (DCF) method which permits the valuation analyst to specifically match the year of the cashflow with the appropriate discount factor for that year.

Chapter 12: Choosing and Using the Right Valuation Methods

A noncontrol owner could not alter the cost of capital either. Therefore, one generally would not make this adjustment in determining a value for noncontrol purposes. However, if the capital structure contains *excessive* debt, the noncontrol buyer should not be willing to pay the inflated value resulting from the apparently lower WACC—since the lower WACC likely does not accurately reflect the true cost of equity. *Remember that fair market value will generally not exceed the amount determined on a control basis for the hypothetical buyer.* If the level of debt exceeds that hypothetical amount, the value will exceed fair market value. If fair market is the standard of value, then a lower level of debt would have to be assumed in the valuation model.

Chapter Summary

In this chapter, we reviewed the nuts and bolts of applying the commonly accepted valuation methods to physician practices. The key points for most readers are as follows:

The discount rate for a valuation measures the expected return on investment based upon the risk involved. The greater the risk, the higher the discount rate a hypothetical investor will demand. The discount rate consists of a risk free rate, a large company equity risk premium, a small company equity risk premium plus a specific practice risk premium. The latter is subjective and highly contingent upon the skill, knowledge, and experience of the valuation analyst. The capitalization rate is derived from the discount rate by subtracting the expected growth rate in cashflows during the terminal period from the discount rate.

The discounted cashflow method is the most commonly accepted valuation method for physician practices subject to regulatory scrutiny and should be used with after-tax earnings. It measures enterprise value (EV), which includes tangible assets such as equipment and working capital plus intangible assets. Use of the method requires considerable effort and skill on the part of the valuation consultant.

Physician compensation expense in the valuation model should be based upon what is to be paid if the transaction takes place because a hypothetical investor would not pay for a cashflow return that was, in fact, being paid out to a physician employee. Valuation analysts may wish to advise clients that actual compensation negotiated in a transaction that differs from that used in the valuation suggests revisiting the valuation.

The excess earnings method is in the author's opinion the best method for small-scale transactions between physicians, and can be performed using pre-tax or after-tax cash earnings, so long as the discount and capitalization rates are adjusted appropriately.

For experienced valuation consultants new to physician practice valuation, the factors for selecting the specific practice risk premium should be considered, along with the requirements of regulatory authority outlined in this chapter and throughout this Guide.

Chapter 12: Choosing and Using the Right Valuation Methods

This Chapter was edited by Carol Carden, CPA/ABV, ASA of Pershing Yoakley Associates.

The Thornton Letter

This letter is one of the seminal events in physician practice valuation 'lore and legend.' Although 15 years later it is generally accepted that a physician practice may be valued based upon its own internal revenue streams, there are still those who feel—or fear—that the letter is relevant.

November 2, 1993
John E. Steiner, Jr., Esquire
Assistant General Counsel
American Hospital Association
840 North Lake Shore Drive
Chicago, Illinois 60611
Dear John:

I am responding to your letter of July 20, 1993, requesting assistance in interpreting the scope of prohibited referrals under the Medicare and Medicaid anti-kickback statute with respect to the acquisition of physician practices. The focus of your inquiry was the position taken in my December 22, 1992 letter to T. J. Sullivan at the Internal Revenue Service that payments for intangible assets or goodwill were open to question under the anti-kickback statute, and my subsequent oral comments on this issue.

In particular, in your letter you presented two specific situations involving the acquisition of a physician's practice. The first situation involved the purchase of a physician practice by another physician or a group practice. I have assumed the acquiring practice is not in a position to benefit from referrals by the acquired practice. After reaching agreement on the price for the hard assets, the parties proceed to value the remainder of the practice and assign a value for the expectation of future patronage by patients to the practice being acquired. The total price negotiated for the practice includes an amount for both the hard assets and the intangible assets. You described this situation as involving a "one-step" referral, a situation where the patients "self-refer" because of word of mouth about the physician or because another unrelated physician refers to the practice.

The second situation involves the acquisition of the same or a similar physician practice, except that the purchaser is a hospital, which is in a position to benefit from referrals by the acquired practice. The same valuation method is used to determine the purchase price. Even though the hospital can be expected to receive admissions and referrals from the practice, the value of these referrals are not used in the valuation of the practice. Only the expected future patronage to the practice is included and the hospital does not pay more for the practice than would another physician. This situation is described as involving a "two-step" referral process, one to the practice and a second one to the hospital.

Chapter 12: Choosing and Using the Right Valuation Methods

You sought an opinion clarifying whether the payments made in either or both of these situations would be allowable under the anti-kickback statute. As you know, the Medicare and Medicaid anti-kickback statute, section 1128B(b) of the Social Security Act, 42 U.S.C. 1320a-7b(b), makes it a criminal offense to knowingly and willfully offer, pay, solicit, or receive remuneration to induce, or in return for, the referral of business covered by Medicare or Medicaid.

For a number of reasons, we are not in a position to issue advisory or interpretive opinions on whether a particular practice or arrangement violates the anti-kickback statute. One reason is that since section 1128B(b) is a criminal statute, the Department of Justice has exclusive authority to initiate a criminal prosecution or decline to do so under the statute. Another reason is that the statute requires proof of knowing and willful intent, and it is generally impossible to evaluate intent on the basis of a paper submission. Finally, in reviewing a particular arrangement, we cannot be sure that we have all the necessary information concerning the nature of the arrangement or practice and how it operates in order to make a proper decision concerning its legality or illegality.

I would like to emphasize that the position I articulated in the December 22, 1992 letter to T. J. Sullivan remains the same. I did not state that payments for intangible assets are illegal per se. Nor have I indicated approval of any particular acquisition practices or valuation methodologies. Since payments for items other than the hard assets of a physician practice could be a payment to induce referrals or could be in return for future referrals, any such payments are subject to scrutiny to determine whether they violate the anti-kickback statute. The fact that the parties may identify the purpose of the payment as something other than a payment for referrals is not determinative.

Similarly, the fact that two different parties may offer to pay the same price for a particular or a comparable physician practice or may use a similar approach in "valuing" the practice does not mean that both will be afforded the same treatment under the anti-kickback statute. The intent of the parties is the critical element in the determination of a violation under the anti-kickback statute, and different parties may have different purposes and reasons for seeking to acquire a particular physician practice and for paying a particular price. Finally, the facts and circumstances involved in each situation are likely to be different as will be the nature of the relationship between the parties. Consequently, each particular situation must be judged on its own merits and based on its own facts and circumstances.

Turning to the two situations described above, we believe the first situation is far less problematic than the second. However, either situation could constitute a violation of the anti-kickback statute, depending on the intent of the parties, the nature of the intangible assets, the amounts paid for the intangible assets, and the past and future relationship of the parties, etc. One major factor is where the seller becomes or remains

Chapter 12: Choosing and Using the Right Valuation Methods

affiliated with the buyer. In such a case, the terms of that continued affiliation as well as the remuneration paid to the seller for services rendered would also need to be taken into account in determining whether a violation exists.

With respect to the second situation involving the purchase of the practice by a hospital, anytime an entity is acquiring a practice where the entity is in a position to benefit from referrals from the practice, there is always a question that a portion of the amount paid for the practice is attributable to the future referrals. As indicated above, it is the intent of the parties and the facts and circumstances of the particular acquisition that are relevant. Accordingly, the fact that a hospital purchases a physician practice for the same amount that another physician might pay does not insulate the hospital from liability under the anti-kickback statute. For example, another physician may offer a high price based on the savings in administrative costs and overhead which could be realized by combining practices. However, a hospital may not have that motivation at all; its offer of the same price could be motivated by a desire to pay for future referrals.

We hope this information is helpful and regret that we are unable to provide further guidance. Thank you for your interest in this matter.

Sincerely,

/s/
D. McCarty Thornton
Associate General Counsel
Inspector General Division

---

1. In my view, you cannot value a physician practice without doing a Coding Analysis
2. This Guide's Chapter on *The CPA's Role in Mergers and Acquisitions Due Diligence Assistance to PPMC's and Private Equity Firms* suggests there are limited circumstances such as Anesthesia and Pathology where these types of transactions remain relevant.
3. *The CPA's Role in Mergers and Acquisitions Due Diligence Assistance to PPMC's and Private Equity Firms* provides details and a Checklist on how to approach gaining an understanding of a practice.
4. *Goodwill Registry*, Explanatory Notes
5. Glenn Desmond, *Handbook of Small Business Valuation Formulas*, as quoted in *The Lawyers' Business Valuation Handbook*, ibid, page 189
6. *Understanding Business Valuation*, 2d Edition, Gary R. Trugman, American Institute of CPAs, 2002, page 255
7. International Glossary of Business Valuation Terms
8. Edited portions of this discussion appeared in *Medical Practices: A BV Rx, Journal of Accountancy,* November 2005 by the author
9. http://www.merritthawkins.com/
10. *Will Generalist Physician Supply Meet Demands Of An Increasing And Aging Population?* Jack M. Colwill, James M. Cultice, and Robin L. Kruse; *Health Affairs*, 29 April 2008

Chapter 12: Choosing and Using the Right Valuation Methods

11. http://www.cms.gov/ResearchGenInfo/02_CMSStatistics.asp
12. 420 CFR 411.351
13. http://www.irs.gov/pub/irs-tege/
14. See, e.g., *Understanding the Difference between Strategic and Fair Market Value in Consolidating Industries, Business Valuation Review*, May 2002, by the author
15. *Identifying Appropriate Business Valuation Approaches under Stark and the AKS*, the author with Reed Tinsley, CPA, CVA, *The Health Lawyer*, American Bar Association, December, 2006
16. Perhaps not the first to say it, but I heard it from Steve Bravo, CPA/ABV, ASA
17. My opinion
18. At least in my review of the databases, many if not most of the transactions pre-date 1998 and fall into the PPMC era.
19. *Identifying Appropriate Business Valuation Approaches under Stark and the AKS*, the author with Reed Tinsley, CPA, CVA, *The Health Lawyer*, American Bar Association, December, 2006
20. *Regulatory Issues in using Replication Cost for Valuing Physician Practices, Financial Valuation and Litigation Expert*, February/March 2007 by the author
21. *Charles A. And Marian L. Derby, Et Al., Petitioners v. Commissioner, Respondent*, T.C. Memo. 2008-45, GALE, Judge
22. *What Goes Around Comes Around:* Derby v. Commissioner, *CPA Expert*, Fall 2008 by the author
23. As seen later herein, the same terms can apply to Debt or the Cost of Capital
24. See, e.g., *A Healthcare Appraiser Reviews a Judge-Appraiser's "Report" Business Valuation Review*, Summer, 2007, by the author
25. *What Is To Be Learned From* Caracci? Ken Patton, ASA and the author, *CPA Expert*, Fall 2007 included elsewhere in this Guide
26. See, e.g., *Valuing Small Businesses and Professional Practices*, Chapter 27
27. As I am fond of saying, forever is a long time.
28. This is similar to the Market Basket used for Hospitals described in that Chapter.
29. *Identifying Appropriate Business Valuation Approaches under Stark and the AKS*, the author with Reed Tinsley, CPA, CVA, *The Health Lawyer*, American Bar Association, December, 2006
30. Cost here is the amount paid by the health insurers for the care of their insureds.
31. Data source: Lehman Brothers *2008 Managed Care Guidebook* February 20, 2008, based on company documents.
32. Date source: Lehman Brothers *2008 Managed Care Guidebook* February 20, 2008, based on company documents.
33. See, e.g., *Computing The Growth Rate In Physician Practice Revenue, CPA Expert*, Winter 2005 by the author
34. The Wall Street firm Lehman Bros. has some of the best industry analysis available.
35. *Identifying Appropriate Business Valuation Approaches under Stark and the AKS*, the author with Reed Tinsley, CPA, CVA, *The Health Lawyer*, American Bar Association, December, 2006
36. *Charles A. And Marian L. Derby, Et Al.,1 Petitioners V. Commissioner, Respondent*, T.C. Memo. 2008-45, GALE, Judge
37. It is worth observing that the process of allocating RVUs is highly politicized; see www.medpac.gov for the Medicare Payment Advisory Commission discussion of this and related issues.
38. *Charles A. And Marian L. Derby, Et Al.,1 Petitioners V. Commissioner, Respondent*, T.C. Memo. 2008-45, GALE, Judge
39. *Medical Practices: A BV Rx, Journal of Accountancy*, November 2005 by the author
40. In a truly random sample, which the MGMA is not, a sample as small as 30 or 32 drawn from a population can be statistically relevant to one extent or another, depending upon the presence of outliers. What the MGMA *does* tell us is how the physician population included in that Data fares from year to year.
41. At least before the $145 a barrel prices seen in 2008!

Chapter 12: Choosing and Using the Right Valuation Methods

42. The term is commonly believed to be based on the fact that the 'S'tate ["Es"] "cheats" the consumer or business out of the money but actually is a term originating in feudal England and Wales when land was owned by the King and granted in "fiefs" to royalty and would revert to the King upon certain occurrences.

43. *Medical Practices: A BV Rx, Journal of Accountancy,* November 2005 by the author

44. Read this two or three times—it is the key to understanding how to do the calculation correctly!

45. In fact, the return on equity of the entire business should be a separate weighted average of the required equity rates of return on tangibles partially financed by debt and intangibles financed by equity.

46. An example of excluded assets in valuing the business enterprise would be marketable securities not part of required working capital which are considered a nonoperating asset. Another example would typically be a loan receivable from an officer of the company.

47. If the goal of the valuation is to value assets, the valuator should consider adding the present value of the tax benefit of amortizing the intangible value under Internal Revenue Code 197.

48. We use pre-tax rates of return since that is what is commonly done for medical practices.

49. It is (also) correct to have a *higher* cost of equity for the intangibles and a *lower* cost of equity for the tangibles under the theory that intangibles are more risky and therefore demand a higher rate of return.

50. This is why the method is thought of as a hybrid method: in effect, you have to use the cost approach to determine the value of the tangibles.

51. This is a case study based upon actual mistakes I have seen made by other "experts."

52. See, e.g., *Medical Practices: A Bv Rx, Journal of Accountancy*, November 2005 by the author

53. Net of growth

54. Including the author for physician to physician transactions

Appendix to Chapter 12

A Heathcare Appraiser Reviews a Judge-Appraiser's 'Report'

By Mark O. Dietrich, CPA/ABV

This article first appeared in the Summer 2007 Edition of Business Valuation Review. Reprinted with permission.

Introduction

The decision in *Delaware Open MRI Radiology Associates, PA (majority) v. Kessler et al (minority)*[1] has created a great deal of commotion in the valuation community for a variety of reasons. Not the least of these is that Vice Chancellor Strine (hereinafter "Judge") of the Delaware Chancery Court adopted an S Corp tax effecting scheme based on the difference between the after-tax dividend cashflow in the hands of an S shareholder versus that of a C shareholder, the later taxed at 15%. There is also a replication of a DCF model based upon the Judge's changes in the underlying assumptions and an oft scathing critique of the majority's valuation expert. This article does not focus on those issues but rather the failures in the application of the Income Approach, including a discussion of the use of the Industry Risk Premium in lieu of CAPM's beta in the Build-up method.

When using the Income Approach in any business valuation engagement, the appraiser's most critical task is to perform a reasoned analysis of the future revenue and profit prospects for the valuation subject. Industry expertise is required for many valuation engagements in various industries. In the valuation of healthcare entities in general and the MRI facilities that were the subject of this case in particular, studying industry trends commonly used by the peer group of healthcare industry valuation specialists is required. As will be seen from the analysis which follows, either the experts failed to address known industry trends in their reports, legal counsel failed to bring it out in testimony or the Judge ignored it. Healthcare industry knowledge can be readily obtained from sources such as the Medicare Payment Advisory Commission described below.

Timeline of the Case

The merger giving rise to the lawsuit in this matter occurred in January of 2004. This date is critical as the Medicare Payment Advisory Commission (MedPAC) had already identified high tech imaging like MRI as a problem spending area in 2003. The first lawsuit was filed in February of 2004.

Appendix to Chapter 12: A Heathcare Appraiser Reviews a Judge-Appraiser's 'Report'

The Court's Findings on Revenue Growth are directly contradictory to foreseeable changes – foreseen by the majority expert (Mr. Reed), whose testimony was dismissed in the following extract from the Opinion. If, in fact, Mr. Reed failed to cite external sources to give his revenue reduction forecast credibility, it is indeed unfortunate since he had it right.

> I also find that Mitchell (minority expert) made reasonable assumptions regarding the revenues that Delaware Radiology would receive for doing scans. Mitchell began by using the same base reimbursement rates as Reed for Delaware I ($601 per scan) and Delaware II ($571 per scan). Mitchell used those reimbursement rates because they were the numbers the Broder Group provided to Reed for the purpose of performing a valuation, and Mitchell found them reasonable. *Mitchell* [minority expert] *held these rates constant throughout his projection period*. Reed, by contrast, assumed reductions in reimbursement rates of 9% for Delaware I and II in year two, or 2005, and then increased them at 3%, the rate of inflation, annually. Essentially, the basis for Reed's reduction was speculation by Carr, and Reed's own opinion that Delaware reimbursement rates were high relative to neighboring states and that they were likely to fall. But the record is devoid of information from more objective sources to substantiate that viewpoint, which, like other elements of Reed's and Carr's testimony, fits with the self-interest of the Broder Group.

History of MedPAC's Identification of High-Tech Imaging Expense Trends

"The Medicare Payment Advisory Commission (MedPAC) is an independent federal body established by the Balanced Budget Act of 1997 to advise the U.S. Congress on issues affecting the Medicare program."[2] This is the most easily identifiable and readily obtainable source of insight into future healthcare industry reimbursement. Although it applies specifically to Medicare payments to healthcare providers, many health insurers link their payment levels to Medicare.

Revenue, of course, is a function of the number of units of service provided and the rate per unit paid. Consider the following from the March 2003 MedPAC Report to Congress, highlighting the rapid growth in MRI services provided to the Medicare population.

> Relatively high growth rates for imaging services were concentrated in several specific categories, all of which involve technology of one kind or another. For instance, nuclear medicine grew by 13.0%, computerized automated tomography (CAT) of parts of the body other than the head grew by 15.3%, *magnetic resonance imaging (MRI) of parts of the body other than the brain grew by 15.9%, and MRI of the brain grew by 14.6%*. It is noteworthy, however, that none of these technologies are new. Instead, *it appears that use of well-established technologies is increasing*. CAT, for example, was introduced in the 1970s. MRI began to diffuse as a new technology in the 1980s. Thus, the indications for use of these technologies may be changing. (*Emphasis added*)

Appendix to Chapter 12: A Heathcare Appraiser Reviews a Judge-Appraiser's 'Report'

Change in per capita use of physician services by beneficiaries in traditional Medicare, by selected type of service, 1999-2002

Type of service	Per capita service use 1999	2000	2001	2002	Average annual percent change 1999-2001	2001-2002	Percent of total service use
All services	663.4	691.8	707.9	738.5	3.3%	4.3%	100.0%
Evaluation and management	353.6	359.4	361.9	372.5	1.2	2.9	50.4
Office visits—established patient	127.6	131.2	130.3	133.3	1.1	2.3	18.1
Hospital visit—subsequent	65.0	64.6	64.7	66.7	-0.2	3.1	9.0
Consultations	39.8	41.5	42.6	44.5	3.5	4.4	6.0
Emergency room visit	18.1	19.0	20.1	21.4	5.3	6.5	2.9
Specialist—psychiatry	18.5	18.3	18.2	18.5	-1.0	2.1	2.5
Specialist—ophthalmology	15.9	16.8	17.5	18.1	4.9	3.5	2.4
Hospital visit—initial	17.6	17.4	17.2	17.2	-1.2	0.3	2.3
Office visits—new patient	15.4	15.5	14.9	14.9	-1.4	-0.2	2.0
Imaging	81.1	88.2	96.1	105.1	8.9	9.4	14.2
Echography—heart	12.6	13.8	14.9	16.5	8.8	10.8	2.2
Standard—nuclear medicine	10.0	11.7	13.6	15.4	16.5	13.0	2.1
Advanced—CAT: other	9.3	10.7	12.3	14.1	14.8	15.3	1.9
Advanced—MRI: other	6.4	7.9	9.4	10.9	21.3	15.9	1.5
Standard—musculoskeletal	8.5	8.8	9.2	9.5	3.9	2.9	1.3
Advanced—MRI: brain	5.1	5.8	6.5	7.4	12.6	14.6	1.0
Standard—chest	6.7	6.5	6.3	6.3	-3.3	0.4	0.9
Advanced—CAT: head	2.7	2.8	2.9	3.0	3.2	4.5	0.4
Imaging/procedure—heart, including cardiac catheterization	1.9	2.1	2.4	2.4	10.4	-0.4	0.3

Use of physician services in fee-for-service Medicare, for selected services, 1999-2002

Type of service	Percent change in units of service per beneficiary Average annual 1999-2001	2001-2002	Percent change in volume per beneficiary Average annual 1999-2001	2001-2002	Percent of total volume
All services	3.8%	5.1%	4.9%	5.6%	100.0%
Evaluation and management					
Office visit—established patient	2.2	2.8	2.7	4.0	18.3
Hospital visit—subsequent	1.9	2.6	2.1	4.0	8.5
Consultation	4.6	4.2	5.8	6.0	5.9
Emergency room visit	4.1	2.8	6.9	6.6	2.7
Hospital visit—initial	0.3	1.1	0.4	1.8	2.2
Office visit—new patient	0.4	1.2	0.1	0.9	2.1
Nursing home visit	-0.8	1.2	0.3	3.5	1.8
Imaging					
Echography—heart	9.2	9.8	11.0	13.1	2.0
Standard—nuclear medicine	14.7	12.1	18.0	17.1	1.9
Advanced—CT: other	14.5	13.8	16.4	16.5	1.8
Advanced—MRI: other	18.5	15.3	22.3	17.4	1.5
Standard—musculoskeletal	3.5	3.7	5.5	6.5	1.2
Advanced—MRI: brain	19.2	12.3	16.1	13.8	1.0
Standard—chest	-0.4	1.9	-1.1	1.2	0.8
Advanced—CT: head	5.6	5.6	4.9	5.3	0.4
Imaging and procedure—heart, including cardiac catheterization	6.9	3.2	8.8	6.4	0.3

Appendix to Chapter 12: A Heathcare Appraiser Reviews a Judge-Appraiser's 'Report'

The March 2004 MedPAC Report to Congress repeated the observation.

> Among broad categories of services—major procedures, evaluation and management, other procedures, imaging, and tests—growth rates vary, but all are positive. Imaging and tests grew the most. *From 2001 to 2002, the imaging growth rate is 9.4%,* and the growth rate for tests is 11.1%.
>
> Within these categories, some services grew much faster than others (Table 3B-3). From 2001 to 2002, we see the highest growth in volume—*approaching 20%*—of nuclear medicine, computed tomography, *magnetic resonance imaging,* laboratory tests, and minor procedures which include outpatient rehabilitation. (*Emphasis added*)

And yet again in the March 2005 MedPAC Report to Congress. At this time MedPAC formally advised Congress to implement strategies for reducing the volume of MRI and other high-tech imaging. These reductions were announced in August 2005 by CMS[3] and were scheduled to be implemented over two years starting in January of 2006. The Deficit Reduction Act signed in 2006 brought further dramatic reductions to MRI reimbursement in 2007.

Use of selected physician services per beneficiary in fee-for-service Medicare, 1999-2003

Type of service	Percent change in units of service per beneficiary — Average annual 1999-2002	2002-2003	Percent change in volume per beneficiary* — Average annual 1999-2002	2002-2003	Percent of total volume*
All services	4.3%	3.6%	5.2%	4.9%	100.0%
Evaluation and management	2.3	2.2	3.4	3.9	42.1
Office visit—established patient	2.4	2.5	3.2	3.9	18.1
Hospital visit—subsequent	2.2	1.8	2.8	3.5	8.4
Consultation	4.5	3.3	5.9	5.0	5.9
Emergency room visit	3.7	1.9	6.8	4.8	2.7
Hospital visit—initial	0.6	1.3	0.9	2.1	2.1
Office visit—new patient	0.7	-1.9	0.4	-1.2	2.0
Nursing home visit	-0.1	1.8	1.4	4.0	1.8
Imaging	5.4	4.2	10.1	8.6	14.8
Echography—heart	9.4	6.2	11.8	7.6	2.1
Standard—nuclear medicine	13.8	9.1	17.8	13.2	2.2
Advanced—CT: other	14.3	12.9	16.6	14.6	2.0
Advanced—MRI: other	17.4	15.9	19.5	16.5	1.6
Standard—musculoskeletal	3.6	3.6	5.9	4.5	1.3
Advanced—MRI: brain	16.9	8.0	15.5	8.6	1.0
Standard—chest	0.4	0.5	-0.3	0.1	0.7
Advanced—CT: head	5.6	4.6	5.1	4.2	0.4
Imaging/procedure—heart, including cardiac catheterization	5.6	1.6	8.0	4.6	0.3

> Imaging services have been growing much more rapidly than other services paid under the physician fee schedule. We examined per-beneficiary growth in the volume and intensity, or complexity, of fee schedule services. Between 1999 and 2002, the per-beneficiary average annual growth rate in the use of fee schedule imaging services was twice as high as the growth

Appendix to Chapter 12: A Heathcare Appraiser Reviews a Judge-Appraiser's 'Report'

rate for all fee schedule services (10.1% vs. 5.2%) (Table 2B-4, p. 80).5 Use of the following types of imaging services increased by 15% to 20% per year: magnetic resonance imaging (MRI) of parts of the body other than the brain, nuclear medicine, computed tomography (CT) of parts of the body other than the head, and MRI of the brain.

Between 2002 and 2003, the per beneficiary growth rate for imaging services moderated to 8.6% but was still much higher than the growth rate of all fee schedule services (4.9%). Although imaging services paid under the fee schedule have been shifting from facilities, such as hospitals, to physician offices, about 80% of the increase in the volume and intensity of these services between 1999 and 2002 was unrelated to this shift in setting (MedPAC 2004a).

The Secretary should improve Medicare's coding edits that detect unbundled diagnostic imaging services *and reduce the technical component payment for multiple imaging services performed on contiguous body parts. (Emphasis added)*

To reiterate, *one place valuation analysts are sure to find insight into future changes in Medicare reimbursement is in the annual MedPAC report released in March of each year.*

The Medicare Conversion Factor

Valuation firms have work codes and rates per hour (unit of service) for their services. Similarly, healthcare providers have work codes (CPT™ codes or Current Procedural Terminology[4]) for their services. The Medicare program and most health insurers pay for services included in Medicare Part B based upon a unit of service called a Relative Value Unit or RVU (see discussion later herein) assigned to services under the Resource-Based Relative Value Scale (RBRVS). The rate per RVU from Medicare is known as the Medicare Conversion Factor.

The lack of growth in the Medicare Conversion Factor is separate and distinct from this foreseeable response to the enormous growth in imaging utilization and expenditures, which has risen from $36.69 in 1998 to $37.90 in 2007 – a compound growth rate of virtually zero. For non-Medicare services, the compound rate of growth for the last 11 years based upon the Bureau of Labor Statistics Producer Price Index for physician services is 1.85%.

The Gordon Growth model used in the discounted cashflow models of the two experts and the Judge assumed perpetual growth in cashflow to equity (3% for one the majority expert and 4% for the minority expert, the Judge choosing 4%). Cashflow to equity is revenue *less* expenses! There is no evidence in available industry data to suggest that a 4% perpetual growth rate could be sustained.

The recent history of the relationship between physician practice expenses and the physician producer price index demonstrates that practice expenses are rising much more rapidly than fees (CMS data).

Appendix to Chapter 12: A Heathcare Appraiser Reviews a Judge-Appraiser's 'Report'

As the facts demonstrate, expenses were and are rising more rapidly than per unit costs. This is called an Eroding Profit Margin. The only way to maintain an overall profit would be to do more and more services at a lower and lower margin – *precisely* what the MedPAC analysis from 2003 forward indicated was happening and precisely what the government moved to put an end to in 2005!

The graph below shows the recent history of Medicare payments for an MRI Scan of the chest (CPT code 71552) one of the most frequently performed MRI services. Note that the bottom drops out in 2007. No future increases could be expected to offset such a dramatic drop so as to generate a 4% terminal growth rate.

The decreases in another common MRI procedure were less dramatic, but nonetheless wholly inconsistent with a 4% terminal growth rate.

The following graphs are the *per unit* of service payments only. They do *not* illustrate the effect of the implemented recommendation from MedPAC in its 2005 Report that the "*payment for multiple imaging services performed on contiguous body parts*" be reduced, which had a dramatic effect on many MRI providers.[5]

Medicare Payment for Chest MRI

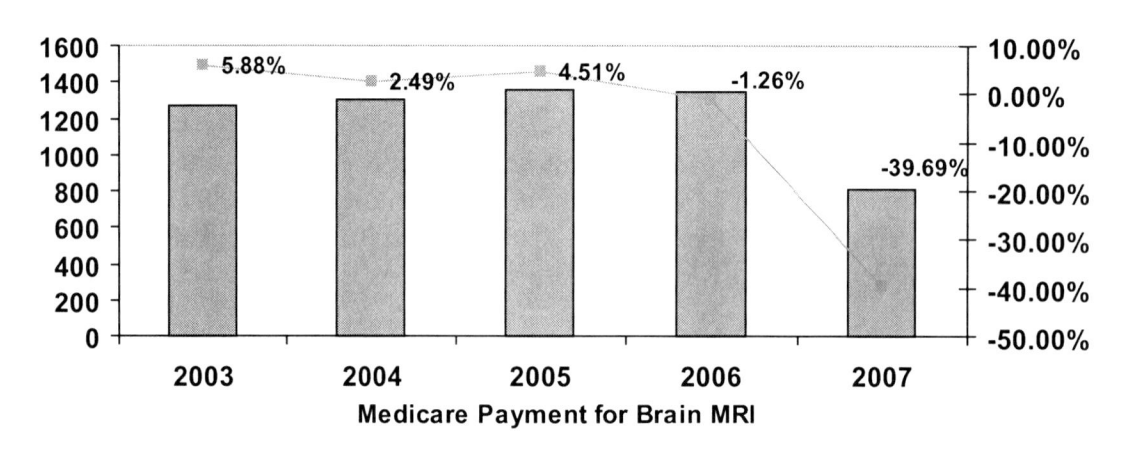

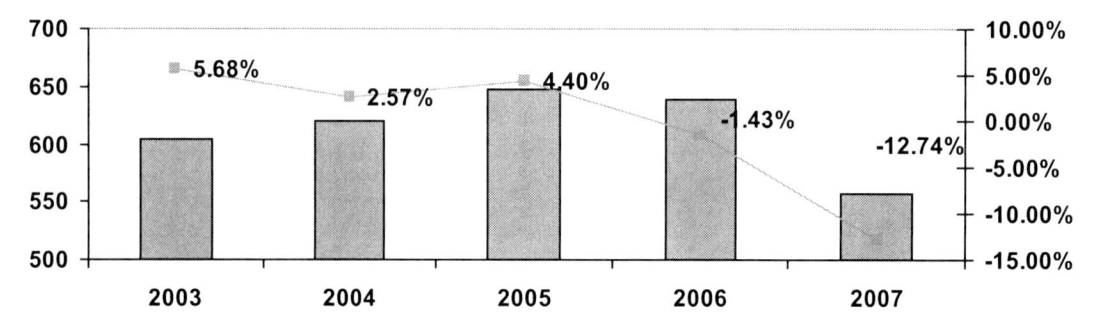

Medicare Payment for Brain MRI

Appendix to Chapter 12: A Heathcare Appraiser Reviews a Judge-Appraiser's 'Report'

Reduction in the Relative Value of MRI Services

As if this is not compelling enough evidence that explosive growth in service volume leads to forceful counter-measures, on June 29, 2006 CMS published in the Federal Register notice of a plan to re-value physician services under the Resource-Based Relative Value Scale; the plan was adopted in August 2006. Less one think this only affects Medicare, many insurers follow Medicare's lead – particularly when it gives them an excuse to cut expenses. The changes followed closely on the heels of a suggestion by MedPAC in its March 2006 report that Evaluation and Management services (typically, face to face physician-patient encounters) had declined in value, in large part to the benefit of high tech imaging services. The changes would cut radiology reimbursement 5% as of January 2007.

A Quantitative Analysis of the Court's Excessive Terminal Growth Rate

Returning to the Court's conclusion that the terminal growth in cashflow (profit) should be pegged at 4%, the following sort of quantitative analysis must have been missing from the experts' reports.

The first table presents a "base case" scenario with no growth in volume of services. A 'profit margin' of 44% (close to that determined by the Court) is used in the illustration. Note that the Compound Growth rate in cashflow continues to decline at an ever increasing amount.

Year	0	1	2	3	4	5
Revenue	100	101	102	103	104	105
Expense	56	58	60	62	64	67
Cashflow	44	43	42	41	40	39
Compound Growth in Cashflow		-2.18%	-2.27%	-2.37%	-2.48%	-2.59%
Revenue Growth		1.00%	1.00%	1.00%	1.00%	1.00%
Expense Growth		3.50%	3.50%	3.50%	3.50%	3.50%

The second table presents what the growth in annual volume would have had to have been to maintain the constant 4% growth rate in cashflow through the fifth year as determined by the Court. The key assumption is that total unit expenses grow as rapidly as the units provided. The lower the profit margin, the greater the annual growth in units of service to maintain the 4% cashflow growth rate. By Year 5, growth in units of service would have to be 7.26%. By year 15, to maintain a constant growth rate of 4%, the units of service would have to grow more than 13.00% per annum – and that rate would *increase* in each subsequent year *into perpetuity*. Clearly, this is an unrealistic assumption that violates professional standards as well as common sense.

Appendix to Chapter 12: A Heathcare Appraiser Reviews a Judge-Appraiser's 'Report'

Year	0	1	2	3	4	5
Revenue	100	107	116	125	135	146
Expense	56	62	68	75	83	92
Cashflow	44	46	48	49	51	54
Compound Growth in Cashflow		4.00%	4.00%	4.00%	4.00%	4.00%
Revenue Growth per Unit		1.00%	1.00%	1.00%	1.00%	1.00%
Revenue Growth Units		6.32%	6.52%	6.74%	6.99%	7.26%
Expense Growth per Unit		3.50%	3.50%	3.50%	3.50%	3.50%
Expense Growth Units		6.32%	6.52%	6.74%	6.99%	7.26%
Constant Growth Per Court		4.00%	4.00%	4.00%	4.00%	4.00%
Target Growth in Cashflow		46	48	49	51	54

The Broader Revenue Picture in the Healthcare Industry

The cutback in imaging is not an isolated occurrence. The same thing happened with outpatient physical, occupational and speech therapy, on which Medicare has imposed an annual limitation per beneficiary of only $1,790 (with some limited exceptions). This was done to rein in explosive growth in the cost of outpatient physical therapy in particular, as noted in this quote from a December 30, 2004 MedPAC letter to the Vice President of the United States.

Amount of medically unnecessary PT services

The Office of Inspector General (OIG) of the Department of Health and Human Services examined the provision of outpatient physical and occupational therapy services provided in skilled nursing facilities (SNFs) and found considerable and widely varying shares of medically unnecessary services. One study found that from 5 to 26% of services was unnecessary, depending on the patient diagnosis. Another OIG study found that three quarters of the contractors hired to review and process claims for payment commonly found medically unnecessary and excessive therapy claims. The services were medically unnecessary because:

- the services were not skilled,

- the treatment goals were too ambitious for the patient's condition, and

- the frequency of the service provision was excessive given the patient's condition.

The appropriateness of care provided at CORFs[6] and ORFs[7] has also prompted examination. In its study of ORFs, the OIG found that about 40% of the claims reviewed were for services that were not reasonable and medically necessary for the conditions of the patient. The Government Accountability Office (GAO) examined CORFs in

Appendix to Chapter 12: A Heathcare Appraiser Reviews a Judge-Appraiser's 'Report'

Florida and found that on a per patient basis, Florida CORFs' payments were two to three times higher than payments to other facility-based therapy providers and that the differences were not explained by patient characteristics such as diagnosis. These studies indicate that unnecessary therapy is frequently provided and that the current requirements alone do not eliminate unnecessary service provision, even in settings supervised by physicians, such as SNFs and CORFs. The studies may also reflect low levels of physician oversight provided in some institutional settings. It is possible that unnecessary services are provided more frequently in settings where there even less physician supervision. Finally, the findings may illustrate a poor understanding of Medicare coverage by physicians and physical therapists.

Another recent case of significance in the healthcare valuation arena—*Caracci*—found the 5th Circuit[8] throwing out the Tax Court's decision that a home health care agency that had never made a profit had an asset value well in excess of its liabilities. The Tax Court had acknowledged that the government was planning a changeover to a Prospective Payment System (PPS)[9] at the time the *Caracci* case arose, but rather than focusing on the Income Approach to value the taxpayer, the Tax Court used the IRS' expert's *Market* Approach, primarily based upon Guideline Public Companies that were in dissimilar lines of business. The changeover to the PPS resulted in Total Medicare spending on home health falling by 52% in two years! It is difficult indeed to see how a business losing money (i.e., expenses in excess of revenues) could make more money if revenues dropped by 52%.

There are numerous examples across all sectors of the healthcare industry to conclusively prove that the government and private insurers will move to defeat excessive utilization and cost. In the hospital sector, outlier payments for inpatient services – those where the patient's length of stay exceeded a defined limit for the underlying Diagnosis Related Group (DRG) - were a major cost problem for the government. In a June 29, 2006 press release, the Department of Justice Civil Division and U.S. Attorney for the Central District of California in Los Angeles announced that Tenet Healthcare Corporation, the nation's second largest hospital chain, had agreed to pay a fine of more than $900 million for "alleged unlawful billing practices." "Of the $900 million settlement amount, the agreement requires Tenet to pay: more than $788 million to resolve claims arising from Tenet's receipt of excessive "outlier" payments (payments that are intended to be limited to situations involving extraordinarily costly episodes of care) resulting from the hospitals' inflating their charges substantially in excess of any increase in the costs." A fine of nearly $250 million was levied against the University of Medicine and Dentistry in New Jersey for similar outlier issues—and that is a tax exempt State-owned institution.

An Observation on the Industry Risk Premium

An analysis of *Ibbotson Stocks Bonds Bill and Inflation Industry Premia Company List Report for 2003* would indicate that the companies used in the determination of the Industry Risk Premium

Appendix to Chapter 12: A Heathcare Appraiser Reviews a Judge-Appraiser's 'Report'

are not comparable to an MRI operator. The SIC codes of some of these companies were likely assigned at a point in their history when they were engaged in some other line of business.

SIC CODE 801	
Amsurg Corp	Surgery Center Operator
Coventry Health Care	Managed care products
Health Grades Inc	Provides ratings of hospitals, physicians etc.
Integramed America	National network of fertility/infertility clinics
Metropolitan Hlth Ntwrks Inc	Provides healthcare benefits to Medicare Advantage members in Florida
Novamed Eyecare Inc	Surgery Center Operator
Sight Resource Corp	Manufactures, distributes, sells eyewear and related products

An analysis of *Ibbotson Stocks Bonds Bill and Inflation Industry Premia Company List Report for 2004*[10] in SIC Code 807 would indicate that only three of the companies (Alliance, Primedex, Miracor) used in the determination of the Industry Risk Premium is arguably comparable to an MRI operator. The betas of these stocks would have been a better indicator of industry risk.[11]

Outside the community of healthcare appraisers, there seems to be an assumption that all providers are paid in a similar fashion. Nothing could be more factually inaccurate. This leads to such errors as the use of inappropriate and irrelevant comparables for obtaining Betas and market transactions. Physicians, non-hospital-based imaging providers such as Delaware Open MRI, podiatrists and a host of others, for example, are paid from Medicare Care Part B using the RBRVS as described above. Hospitals are paid from Medicare Part A using a methodology based upon Diagnoses Related Groups (DRGs) which bundle hospital services based upon an expected length of stay for the patient's diagnosis. Home health care agencies are paid in yet another fashion, as are surgery centers and skilled nursing facilities. Most private health insurers follow a similar construct, but the rates of payments vary radically from state to state and even market areas within states.

Perhaps the most fundamental valuation mistake in the healthcare industry is failure to differentiate the risk of a small entity operating in a single state (Delaware) in a single line of business (MRI) with a few dominant health insurers[13] from the risk of large public entities operating in multiple states in multiple lines of business with multiple health insurers paying for the cost of services. Use of the Industry Risk Premium in the Build-up Method compounds this typical error.

Conclusions

As Valuation Experts, we can only fault the Court if a) we do not provide adequate compelling evidence, b) legal counsel does a poor job on direct and/or cross-examination or c) the Court decides to ignore the evidence and rule on some other basis, the expert testimony notwithstanding. Like newspaper reporters trying to write stories on complex economic matters without adequate

Appendix to Chapter 12: A Heathcare Appraiser Reviews a Judge-Appraiser's 'Report'

SIC CODE 807	
Alliance Imaging Inc	Medical diagnostic imaging
Array Biopharma Inc	Biopharmaceutical company
Bio Imaging Technologies Inc	Medical image management for clinical trials
Bio Reference Labs	Clinical laboratory in the greater New York
Enzo Biochem Inc	R&D, MFR, biotechnology and molecular biology
Labone Inc	Medical Laboratory operator (now part of Quest)
Laboratory Cp of Amer	Medical Laboratory operator
Medcath Corp	Cardiac hospital operator
Medtox Scientific Inc	Specialty laboratory testing services
Miracor Diagnostics Inc	Medical diagnostic imaging
National Dentex Corp	Dental Laboratory operator
Orchid Biosciences Inc	DNA testing
Primedex Health Systems Inc	(Now part of Radnet: Diagnostic imaging services)
Psychemedics Corp	Detection of abused substances
Quest Diagnostics Inc	Medical Laboratory operator
Sagemark Companies Ltd[12]	Management, and operation of PET imaging
Specialty Laboratories Inc	Medical Laboratory (now part of Ameripath)

research, Judges need lots of input in understandable terms which must be coupled with a desire and willingness to be educated when making decisions on healthcare valuation. Most of the traditional valuation rules fail in healthcare because of the substantive and repetitive interference by government regulators that make historical performance nothing more than yesterday's news.

A unit growth analysis is a critical part of the determination of the reasonableness of a perpetual growth rate for a healthcare entity. Due to the statutory construct of Medicare Part B reimbursement, providers drawing revenue from that program face fixed or declining per unit revenue even as costs increase more rapidly than the generic rate of inflation. Entities limited to a single service line—such as *Delaware Open MRI*—have no ability to respond by expanding services, unlike large healthcare entities which operate in multiple lines of business. Even those large entitles face numerous problems, as witnessed by the fines levied against Tenet.

---

1. Since the case involved suit and countersuit, "majority" and "minority" is more descriptive than plaintiff and defendant
2. 2003 Report to Congress
3. Centers for Medicare and Medicaid Services of the Department of Health and Human Services
4. Copyrighted by the American Medical Association
5. Medicare estimated the cuts at 8% of revenue for the affected scanning procedures.

Appendix to Chapter 12: A Heathcare Appraiser Reviews a Judge-Appraiser's 'Report'

6. Comprehensive Outpatient Rehabilitation Facility
7. Outpatient Rehabilitation Facility
8. Correctly in the author's view
9. *Simply* stated, a PPS establishes a standard fee schedule for services, rather than basing the fee on a retrospective settlement, such as one based upon the actual cost of providing those services.
10. The only match for the -4.51% negative risk premium cited in the case is SIC 807 in Ibbotson's 2004 yearbook, which post-dates the merger/valuation date of January 2004.
11. An interesting exercise is to plot the prices of these stocks against the S&P 500 in this time period; they are quite volatile!
12. Unlike MRI, Positron Emission Tomography or PET was not covered by the Stark laws at this time (although it now is) giving it a much different cashflow profile.
13. See, e.g., Government Accounting Office *Private Health Insurance: Number and Market Share of Carriers in the Small Group Health Insurance Market.*

Chapter 13

Fair Market Value *Requires* the Demonstration of Income to a Hypothetical Owner

A Review of Established Valuation Theory and the Regulatory Environment

Mark O. Dietrich, CPA/ABV & Todd Sorensen, AVA

Introduction

Fair market value is a Standard of Value, defined generally as the value to a hypothetical buyer and seller where neither is under compulsion and both have reasonable knowledge of relevant facts. Other Standards of Value include Investment Value, the value to a *specific* buyer[1] and Fair Value, either a financial reporting standard under the rules of the Financial Accounting Standards Board or a shareholder rights standard under state corporate law. To apply a Standard of Value, the appraiser must then have a Premise of Value. The four Premises of Value, of which Going Concern is the most commonly employed, are discussed below.

Premises of Value

There are four accepted premises of value in the professional literature:[2]

1. Value in continued use as part of a going concern

2. Value in place, as part of mass assemblage of assets[3]

3. Value in exchange in an orderly disposition

4. Value in exchange in a forced liquidation

Value as a Going Concern is defined as "Value in continued use, as a mass assemblage of *income-producing assets*, and as a going concern enterprise."[4] (*Emphasis added*) Appraisers are required to consider orderly disposition if the underlying assets have more value when not employed as a going concern. This typically occurs where, for example, real estate used in an operating business is worth more in a sale for a different purpose than as part of the existing business.

The standard of value in healthcare appraisal under the Stark law, Anti-Kickback Statute, and the Internal Revenue Code[5] is "fair market." To understand fair market value, the appraiser[6] must first look to the established literature from which the definition of fair market value is

Chapter 13: Fair Market Value Requires the Demonstration of Income

taken. Then, the appraiser must consider the modifications and constraints on the term specified in the Stark regulations and implied by the Anti-Kickback Statute and advisory opinions of the OIG.

Stark Regulations

Section 1877(h)(3) of the Social Security Act defines fair market value for purposes of Stark as the value in an arm's-length transaction, consistent with general market value. The Stark I regulations (420 CFR 411.351) state

> Fair market value means the value in arm's-length transactions consistent with general market value. *'General market value' means the price that an asset would bring as the result of bona fide bargaining between well-informed buyers and sellers who are not otherwise in a position to generate business for the other party*; or the compensation that would be included in a service agreement as a result of bona fide bargaining between well-informed parties to the agreement who are not otherwise in a position to generate business for the other party, on the date of acquisition or at the time of the service agreement. Usually the fair market price is the price at which bona fide sales have been consummated for assets of like type, quality, and quantity in a particular market at the time of acquisition, or the compensation that has been included in bona fide service agreements with comparable terms at the time of the agreement.

The Stark II regulations elaborated on the modifications or limitations on the traditional use of fair market value:

> *Moreover, the definition of "fair market value" in the statute and regulation is qualified in ways that do not necessarily comport with the usage of the term in standard valuation techniques and methodologies.* For example, the methodology must exclude valuations where the parties to the transactions are at arm's length but in a position to refer to one another. In addition, the definition itself differs depending on the type of transaction: leases or rentals of space and equipment cannot take into account the intended use of the rented item; and in cases where the lessor is in a position to refer to the lessee, the valuation cannot be adjusted or reflect the value of proximity or convenience to the lessor. Our Phase I discussion made clear that we will consider a range of methods of determining fair market value and that the appropriate method will depend on the nature of the transaction, its location, and other factors. *While good faith reliance on a proper valuation may be relevant to a party's intent, it does not establish the ultimate issue of the accuracy of the valuation figure itself.* (Emphasis added)

Chapter 13: Fair Market Value Requires the Demonstration of Income

Commercially reasonable

Phase 2 of the Stark II regulations elaborated on the earlier use of the term "commercially reasonable:"

> Comment: In the preamble of the January 1998 proposed rule (63 FR 1700), we indicated our intent to interpret the "commercially reasonable" requirement for purposes of all exceptions that require commercial reasonableness to mean that an arrangement was a sensible, prudent business arrangement from the perspective of the particular parties involved, even in the absence of potential referrals. In the commenter's view, this interpretation injected an unwarranted subjective element into the test.
>
> Response: An arrangement will be considered "commercially reasonable" in the absence of referrals if the arrangement would make commercial sense if entered into by a reasonable entity of similar type and size and a reasonable physician (or family member or group practice) of similar scope and specialty, even if there were no potential DHS referrals.[7]

If the standard of value is Fair Market Value and the premise of value is Going Concern, it cannot be "commercially reasonable" to pay a price for goodwill or other intangible assets if the buyer has no expectation of income. As *defined* above from the literature, the Going Concern premise of value *requires* that the assemblage of assets be *income producing*. In addition, it cannot be said that the Stark definition of General Market Value is met if there is no expectation of income *other than that* which results because the parties are "informed buyers and sellers ... in a position to generate business for the other party."

The Cost Approach

Technically, when a buyer is interested in Liquidation or Replication, the latter a "Make or Buy" Decision, the Cost Approach would be appropriate. The Cost Approach is often considered when the buyer and seller are both physicians, the scenario contemplated by the so-called Thornton Letter of 1992. In the recent Tax Court case *Bergquist*,[8] the Cost Approach prevailed because the practice was not a going concern, as suggested by the premise of value definition *Value in exchange in an orderly disposition or liquidation*. Thus, this very basic principle of valuation has been recognized in a recent Tax Court decision involving physicians and hospitals.

The Cost Approach basically involves identifying discrete tangible and intangible assets, valuing each one separately, and then aggregating the individual values of those assets. General categories of assets seen valued in a physician practice when using the Cost Approach include the following, with the last item being a recent addition to the list.

Chapter 13: Fair Market Value Requires the Demonstration of Income

1. Furniture & Equipment

2. Accounts Receivable

3. Leasehold Improvements

4. Telephone Numbers

5. Staff Workforce in Place

6. Patient Charts

7. Trade Name

8. Physician Workforce in Place

There has been a trend in certain segments of the appraisal community engaged in healthcare transactional valuation to express conclusions of enterprise going concern fair market value based solely on the Cost Approach. Disputes among appraisers are commonplace, of course. Among other things, Revenue Ruling 59-60 states that "Valuation of securities is, in essence, a prophesy as to the future;" and "... an appraiser will find wide differences of opinion as to the fair market value of a particular stock." There are no Prophets in the appraisal community, only the Profits subject to valuation under the Income Approach. This said, there is no support in the professional literature of valuation and appraisal for exclusive reliance on the Cost Approach, as can be seen in the quotes from various authoritative sources below.

Revenue Ruling 59-60

Revenue Ruling 59-60 sits at the very core of the appraisal profession, defining fair market value, the approaches to valuation and which approaches are appropriate for what types of entities. Now 51 years old, this Ruling has withstood the test of time. Medical practices, surgery centers and hospitals, for example, are in the business of "selling services to the public" and should be valued using the earnings as can be seen in the following quote:

> In the final analysis, goodwill is based upon earning capacity. The presence of goodwill and its value, therefore, rests upon the excess of net earnings over and above a fair return on the net tangible assets.
>
> Earnings may be the most important criterion of value in some cases whereas asset value [Cost Approach] will receive primary consideration in others. *In general, the appraiser will accord primary consideration to earnings when valuing stocks of companies which sell products or services to the public*; (*Emphasis added*)

Chapter 13: Fair Market Value Requires the Demonstration of Income

Valuation Literature

The most well-known and frequently cited textbook on business valuation is *Valuing a Business*, originally written by Dr. Shannon Pratt:

> For an intangible asset to have a quantifiable value, it should possess certain additional attributes such as….It should generate measurable amount of economic return to its owner. This economic benefit could be in the form of an income increment or a cost decrement. This economic income may be measured in any of several ways, including present value of net income, net operating income, net cash flows, and so on.[9]

Note that whether an income increment or cost decrement, it must be measurable in the present value of net income, operating income or cash flow.[10]

Another well-known valuation text with contributions from leading valuation experts is *Financial Valuation*, edited by James Hitchner, CPA/ABV, ASA:

> Although the asset approach can be used in almost any valuation, it is seldom used in the valuation of operating companies. The time and costs involved in valuing individual tangible and intangible assets typically is not justified, because there is little if any, increase in the accuracy of the valuation. The value of all tangible and intangible assets is captured, in aggregate, in the proper application of the income and market approaches.[11]

The 1996 Internal Revenue Service Exempt Organization's Division Continuing Professional Education Text – the predecessor 1994 Text was cited by the Court in the *Derby* case below - made it clear that sole reliance on the Cost Approach is not appropriate for intangibles if there is no intangible value under the Income Approach:

> The value of goodwill can be allocated to specific intangible assets; *the value of the latter is limited to the value of the former, as calculated under the income approach.* For example, if the total value of the individual intangible assets exceeds the total value of the medical practice net of the aggregate fair market value of the tangible assets, the amount of value that can be allocated among the intangible assets is more limited. *Also, it is important to note that intangible value may not always be present in a medical practice.*[12] (*Emphasis added*)

The last statement in that paragraph is of particular note since, again, the expectation of income is required for the presence of intangible assets.

Chapter 13: Fair Market Value Requires the Demonstration of Income

Hospital acquisitions of physician practices

Hospitals expect that the acquisition of a practice whose physicians are already on its staff will prevent loss of referrals and that a physician practice whose physicians are not on its staff will generate new referrals. The Hospital cannot, of course, pay for either expectation. In addition, either expectation is at risk under the AKS[13] as well as the Stark law. Given the definition of Fair Market Value as modified by those two provisions (as discussed previously) it is incumbent upon the appraiser to document an expectation or rationale for the acquisition aside from referrals *via a fair market value opinion under a disciplined application of the Income Approach*. It is often overlooked that the Appraiser's role is to serve as both hypothetical buyer and seller in reaching his or her conclusion of value.

Replication Cost

Why would a Hospital want to "replicate" that practice if a physician is already in a Hospital's catchment area and/or on its staff?

Seemingly, this very question was addressed in Phase 2 of the Stark II regulations[14] which allows only a very narrow exception for retention payments in Health Professional Shortage Areas (HPSAs).

> Response: We are sympathetic to the problems faced by hospitals and other entities in certain rural and inner city areas in retaining sufficient numbers of qualified physicians in the community. *On the other hand, we are concerned about, among other things, protecting payments to physicians in bidding wars between hospitals.* The commenter's suggested standard of a reasonable and documented belief that a physician may terminate his staff privileges would not adequately address this potential abuse. We are persuaded that a narrow retention exception for some remuneration paid to physicians with practices in HPSAs to retain them in the community is appropriate and consistent with the statutory scheme.[15] (Emphasis added)

A payment for physician workforce-in-place would seem to be a retention payment under this provision of the Stark law and therefore not permitted unless it was in a HPSA, at which point it would have to meet various other regulatory parameters.

The Derby Tax Court case of 2008

Taken together with *Bergquist*, *Derby*[16] is perhaps the most significant Tax Court for the appraisal of physician practices ever decided. The case originated with a Sutter Health physician acquisition transaction in 1992 and took 16 years to wind its way through the Internal Revenue Service and judiciary. At issue were the same fundamental concepts and issues that

Chapter 13: Fair Market Value Requires the Demonstration of Income

confront appraisers in the healthcare transaction market today, including expected post-transaction physician compensation in the valuation model; allocating enterprise or invested capital value among working capital, fixed assets, and intangible assets; studying transaction documents to discern the character and extent of any intangibles being transferred or not being transferred; and the IRS Continuing Professional Education Technical Instruction Program Manuals of the 1990s on hospital-physician transactions.

Notably, the Court observed in its decision that the Dutcher Appraisal submitted by the physicians did not consider the **actual transaction** that took place, the reference below being specifically within the context of a discussion of 1) the use of using Survey-based median compensation in the valuation model under the Income Approach rather than actual, negotiated compensation and 2) the actual intangibles that the physicians received in the transaction:

> More fundamentally, the Dutcher appraisal takes no account of the various contractual rights and other intangible benefits that petitioners and the other SWMG physicians sought and obtained in the transaction with SMF, such as avoiding signing noncompete agreements and obtaining preferred working conditions. Because it does not fully account for the benefits that petitioners received in the transaction with SMF, the Dutcher appraisal does not establish that petitioners contributed property to SMF that exceeded the values of the benefits they received in return.

Returning to the example of paying for physician workforce, even if one can meet the fair market standard and going concern premise and not be precluded from making such a payment under the Stark anti-retention payment rule, how much value would one assign if the underlying employment contracts have a 90 day voluntary termination provision exercisable by the physician? Here the *Derby* rule would step in and require the actual transaction provision to be valued.

Merging with other Regulatory Venues?

The Healthcare Reform legislation requires that tax-exempt hospitals submit their audited financial statements along with their From 990 to the Internal Revenue Service. This will bring to the regulatory forefront the recently adopted Financial Accounting Standards Board Statement 164 that applies to the not for profit sector the impairment testing of goodwill and other intangible assets previously adopted in FAS 141 and 142 for profit-making enterprises.[17] Acquired physician practice goodwill that does not have value under FAS 164 will have to be written off and disclosed in the audited financial statements.

Chapter 13: Fair Market Value Requires the Demonstration of Income

Conclusion

Debate contemplates the debaters having reasonable knowledge of the relevant facts of established valuation theory, in the same fashion as the hypothetical buyer and seller of the fair market value standard must have reasonable knowledge of the relevant facts concerning the business to be transacted. In the healthcare industry, reasonable knowledge also includes an in-depth familiarity with and understanding of the regulatory environment, including the Stark Law, Anti-Kickback Statute and anti-inurement and Intermediate Sanctions provisions of the Internal Revenue Code. As suggested by *Bergquist*, sole reliance on the Cost Approach can be appropriate when the premise of value is orderly disposition or liquidation. Exclusive reliance on the Cost Approach in valuing physician practices when there is little or no value under the Income Approach is inconsistent with the fair market value standard and the going concern premise of value, as well as Revenue Ruling 59-60, the professional literature and the authors' understanding of the regulatory modifications to fair market value, including commercial reasonableness.

---

1. In deliberate and striking contrast to a hypothetical buyer.
2. See generally, *Valuing a Business*, Shannon Pratt, 5th Ed, Ch 14, Asset-Based Approach
3. Certain intangibles, such as workforce-in-place, are not included under this premise, since the assets are not part of a going concern and that assumption is necessary if employees are going to get paid!
4. *Valuing a Business*, Shannon Pratt, 5th Ed, page 47
5. Section 501(c)(3)'s prohibition of inurement and the Intermediate Sanctions Provisions
6. As well as users of the appraisal opinion including buyer and seller and their representatives.
7. 42 CFR Parts 411 and 424,
8. 131 T.C. No. 2
9. 5th Ed, Ch 14, Asset-Based Approach, page 366
10. For a given amount of revenue, a decrease in cost would increase profit, net income, cashflow, etc.
11. Financial Valuation, 2d Ed, Asset Approach, Ch 7
12. http://www.irs.gov/pub/irs-tege/eotopicq96.pdf
13. (see, e.g., *Greber*)
14. These were issued after the litigation over Tenet's Alvarado San Diego's Heart Hospital payment to existing physicians on staff for hosting newly recruited physicians.
15. CMS-1810-IFC, page 2
16. T.C. Memo. 2008-45
17. Financial Accounting Standard 164 requires testing of goodwill and other intangible for impairment.

Chapter 14

Critical Condition—A Coding Analysis for a Physician Practice Valuation

By Mark O. Dietrich, CPA/ABV, and Frank Cohen, CMPA

This article first appeared in the Fall 2006 Edition of CPA Expert. *Reprinted with permission.*

INTRODUCTION

At the outset, we should emphasize that a coding analysis is not always feasible. In a number of circumstances, the data may not be available because of poor information systems or a refusal to provide the data. Depending upon the nature of the engagement, the analyst may want to consider the implications of the lack of availability or a refusal to supply data. That said, this article focuses on the significance of a coding analysis. Basic coding analysis is within the reach of the valuation analyst using the approaches and tools described herein.

ESTABLISHED PATIENT OFFICE VISITS

The most commonly used codes in the Medicare database are the established patient office visits, which are designated 99211 through 99215. The codes are copyrighted by the American Medical Association (AMA). Of these five codes, 99212, 99213, and 99214 are the most frequently used; 99214 pays about 60% more than a 99213; and more than 220% of 99212. Clearly, incorrect or improper coding can dramatically affect the normalized revenues of a practice. For this reason alone, a coding analysis is critical.

In the last five years, there has been a steady rightward shift of the historical bell curve coding pattern, with a decrease in 99212 codes and an increase in the 99214 codes.

This shift has not gone unnoticed. The Department of Health and Human Services (DHHS), Office of Inspector General (OIG) produced Medicare Fee for Service (FFS) error rates from 1996 to 2002. This process, known as the Comprehensive Error Rate Testing (CERT) program revealed that payers were reimbursing practices erroneously for procedures that were not documented properly and/or did not meet medical necessity tests. A focus of this study has been a select group of procedure codes that have historically had very high levels of improper payment, the least of which has been the aforementioned code 99214. Medical reviews of 4,436 lines for the period between January 1, 2004, and December 31, 2004, disclosed that 648 lines, or 14.6%, were in error. Based on the application of these results, CMS estimates that improper payments

Chapter 14: Critical Condition—A Coding Analysis for a Physician Practice Valuation

of $234,489,004 were made to physicians for this code alone. For medical practices, this means that these codes are under greater scrutiny from payers and other outside investigative agencies.

Evaluation and management (E/M) coding in particular is dependent on a series of guidelines that require the physician to consider 1,600 unique decision points during a typical patient visit. In determining the code to be assigned, there are two major players with respect to validating the use of the E/M code, namely, documentation and medical necessity.

Documentation is simply the process of recording or writing down a detailed summary of the visit, including the chief complaint, past family and social history, results of the physical exam, and information that would indicate the level of complexity of decision making during the examination. This process is analogous to the working papers of the valuation analyst or certified public accountant (CPA).

Medical necessity is a process used by Medicare and private payers to determine whether they should pay for goods or services billed by the physician. Medical necessity is defined as including that which is reasonable and necessary to diagnose or treat illness or injury, or improve the function of a malformed body member. Medicare has a number of policies, including national coverage determinations (NCDs) and local medical review policy (LMRP), also known as local coverage determinations (LCDs), which outline what is and is not covered. In a small number of cases, Medicare may even determine whether a method of treating a patient should be covered on a caseby- case basis. Even if a service is accepted as reasonable and necessary, coverage may be limited if the service is provided more frequently than allowed under standard policies or standards of care.

In almost every case, these two tests dominate the decision to reimburse the provider for the procedure submitted on the claim. It is a complicated process because there is no effective relationship between documentation and medical necessity even though both medical necessity and documentation are tied to the procedure code. Submitting a claim for a service or procedure binds the practice to a highly complex and complicated series of laws, policies, rules, and regulations, any violation of which could result in substantial civil and criminal penalties.

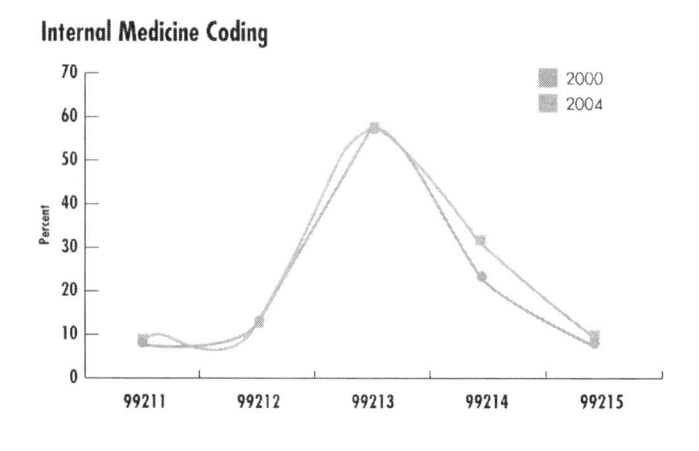

Internal Medicine Coding

Chapter 14: Critical Condition—A Coding Analysis for a Physician Practice Valuation

OTHER EXAMPLES

Many medical specialists such as cardiologists, infectious disease specialists, and pulmonologists earn a substantial amount of their income from consultations. A consultation is specifically defined as a request from another physician. The AMA's Current Procedural Terminology defines a consultation as "a type of service provided by a physician whose opinion or advice regarding evaluation and management of a specific problem is requested by another physician or other appropriate source." There are three parts to a consultation, namely, a request for review and/or an opinion; the rendering of the opinion; and the documentation in the patient's chart, and the report provided to the referring physician. A recent OIG study suggests that billions of dollars in improper consultations were being billed to Medicare, placing these procedures, along with established office visits and subsequent hospital visits, high on the OIG's hit list.

SOURCES OF DATA

Certain data can be downloaded from the CMS Web site at www.cms.hhs.gov/PhysicianFeeSched/01_Overview.asp#TopOfPage.

Copies of the CERT report, updated definitional information on consults, the physician fee schedule database (PFSDB) and other files related to this article may be downloaded for free by going to www.cpahealth.com and clicking on the download tab.

IDENTIFYING PROBLEMATIC CODING

A major area of utilization analysis involves the use of the E/M codes. This kind of analysis involves looking at the use of codes within specific categories and between specific categories and comparing the utilization of each category to the global use of E/M codes. Performing a complete E/M utilization analysis can be complex and time-consuming; however, it is the category that most frequently accounts for the resource utilization and/or financial revenue of the practice. The use of E/M codes is under considerable scrutiny from outside reviewers and special attention should be paid to this area.

In the valuation practice of Mark Dietrich, one of the coauthors of this article, the Top 50 code spreadsheets by specialty are used extensively to identify potential issues that warrant further inquiry. These data are extracted from the Medicare Master Database and summarized by CPT code and frequency of use. A complete set of tables for all specialties can be purchased by contacting info@cpahealth.com.

For example, the spreadsheet for infectious disease (ID) indicates that the most frequently billed consult code is 99254, initial inpatient consult, which is 52% of all inpatient consults. The most frequently billed code is 99232, subsequent hospital care. The ratio of all consultations (both office and hospital) to all patient visits is 12%.

Chapter 14: Critical Condition—A Coding Analysis for a Physician Practice Valuation

Rank in Top 50	CPT Code	Service Description	Count	Percent of Inpatient Consults
7	99254	Initial inpatient consult	337,300	52.31%
13	99255	Initial inpatient consult	204,283	31.68%
21	99253	Initial inpatient consult	103,218	16.01%
				100.00%

Rank in Top 50	CPT Code	Service Description	Count	Percent of Top 50
35	99291	Critical care, first hour	37,849	0.68%
45	99238	Hospital discharge day	24,241	0.44%
26	99262	Followup inpatient consult	61,413	1.11%
34	99263	Followup inpatient consult	39,668	0.71%
39	99223	Initial hospital care	26,367	0.48%
7	99254	Initial inpatient consult	337,300	6.08%
13	99255	Initial inpatient consult	204,283	3.68%
21	99253	Initial inpatient consult	103,218	1.86%
33	99312	Nursing fac care, subsequent	40,830	0.74%
43	99311	Nursing fac care, subsequent	24,467	0.44%
46	99244	Office consultation	22,299	0.40%
6	99213	Office/outpatient visit, established	339,957	6.13%
10	99214	Office/outpatient visit, established	247,192	4.45%
24	99212	Office/outpatient visit, established	67,810	1.22%
29	99215	Office/outpatient visit, established	49,383	0.89%
31	99211	Office/outpatient visit, established	47,594	0.86%
2	99232	Subsequent hospital care	2,367,869	42.67%
3	99231	Subsequent hospital care	840,012	15.14%
4	99233	Subsequent hospital care	704,910	12.70%
			5,586,662	100.00%

Note that the remaining Top 50 services in this subspecialty represent injections or tests. In reviewing the coding of an ID practice as part of a valuation, the Medicare data can easily be compared to those of the practice.

Another benchmark is to statistically analyze the incidence of related procedures, such as office visits and outpatient consults. In performing this intercategory analysis, we could take the total number of outpatient consults (99241 to 99245) compared to the total volume of new office visits (99201 to 99205). For example, the ratio of office consults to new office visits for cardiology is 4.3 to 1, meaning that for every new patient office visit, the average cardiovascular (CV) doctor or cardiologist reports about four consults. In our example, let's say that, for the practice, the ratio was 2 to 1. This might indicate that the practice is shifting what should be consults to new office visits. These kinds of aberrant practices could result in financial and/or compliance problems.

Chapter 14: Critical Condition—A Coding Analysis for a Physician Practice Valuation

For example, significant excessive numbers of consults, no matter how they are measured, can help frame the interview questions used to assess whether there is something particular to the practice. The interview of an Infectious Disease doctor might take place as follows:

Analyst:

"Dr. Smith, I noted in my review of your coding data that the volume of office consultations you report is significantly higher than that of your peer group. I generally see physicians in your specialty seeing consults in the hospital. Can you tell me about the unique aspects of your practice that might explain the difference?"

Dr. Smith:

Answer A: "Since my office is here on campus, many patients simply come here rather than wait for me to see them in the hospital."

Answer B: "You'll note that many of my patients have communicable diseases and, in this area, I receive most of the referrals to confirm or rule out a particular diagnosis."

Answer C: "I didn't realize there was a difference."

Answer D: "When I see patients for the first time, I charge for a consult. It pays more than a new patient visit."

ANALYSIS

Answer A would require the analyst to know whether a particular medical condition typically requires hospitalization before an ID consult. Answer B might be a perfectly acceptable answer if, for example, Dr. Smith practices in an inner city, where tuberculosis is often a public health problem. Answer D is a red flag and a tacit admission of incorrect coding. Obviously, Answer C is of no assistance to the analyst.

MODIFIERS

The same sort of analysis applies to the use of modifiers. Over- or underuse of certain modifiers may raise a flag with carriers, payers, and other outside reviewing agencies. For example, if modifier 25 (used to describe *separate, distinctly identifiable* services from other services or procedures rendered during the same visit) is used at a level greater than 10% of a particular E/M category, it may cause a carrier to perform a review of the practice's billing and coding patterns. These flags are most often the source of focused reviews and audits. Most recently, OIG published two separate reports, one on modifier 59 and one on modifier 25. According to the reports, violations

Chapter 14: Critical Condition—A Coding Analysis for a Physician Practice Valuation

in the way these codes are reported by providers resulted in hundreds of millions of dollars in inappropriate payments. These reports are also available at www.cpahealth.com by clicking on the download tab.

UTILIZATION OF TESTS

One process is the ranking of procedure codes within the practice compared to national averages. For example, we might rank the codes within our practice by frequency and dollar volume, and compare this result with the top 50 codes for that specific specialty based upon the national average. This analysis identifies areas in which there may be patterns of over or under use. A subset of this analysis is the utilization of tests in the physician's office, and many of the Top 50 CPT codes consist of such tests. Some of this variation can be traced to the ancillary capabilities of the practice, such as whether it has a blood chemistry lab, x-ray, or other imaging technology. Comparisons between the practices with and without this equipment are not possible; therefore, it is important to ascertain the practices' capabilities before attempting a utilization analysis.

SURGICAL PRACTICES

For surgical practices, the utilization of procedure codes is more complex and can involve a number of different kinds of analysis, many of which are likely beyond the purview of the valuation analyst. However, certain simple analyses can rule out or identify common problems. It may also be helpful to identify the revenue potential associated with procedures that are not being provided by the practice but that are being performed or reported by other practices within the same specialty. In specialty practices, such as ophthalmology, physicians trained in the most recently developed surgical techniques may have greater earning power than the current practitioners who are relying on less advanced techniques.

Another utilization issue concerns the use and reporting of the postoperative code 99024. Medicare pays for all surgery on the basis of a global fee that includes *both* preoperative and postoperative care. For example, a practice reports 5,250 global surgical procedures that have either a 10- or 90-day follow-up period. In performing a utilization analysis, it is found that they reported the 99024 code (surgical followup) 1,025 times. The resulting ratio of .195 to 1 indicates that only one in five surgical procedures was followed! This conclusion could raise troubling questions about the quality of care, as well as compliance and *the potential for reimbursement.* Even though the relevant codes are considered bundled codes for Medicare, it is important to ensure that all postoperative visits that fall within the global period, i.e., are recorded for reasons relating to the global procedure, and accurately documented as such. For each global surgical code, there is a preservice, intraservice, and postservice component that represents both the resource consumption and fee allocation for that procedure. For example, for procedure code 28190 (the removal of a foreign body from the foot), the preoperative portion

Chapter 14: Critical Condition—A Coding Analysis for a Physician Practice Valuation

is 10%, the surgical portion is 80%, and the postoperative portion is 10%. If adequate followup is not reported, the insurer could reduce the postservice payment portion (by 10%), indicating that the follow-up portion was not satisfied based upon the utilization statistics.

The use of global fees for surgery is a critical consideration in valuation or litigation. For example, assume a surgeon has left the group practice and the geographic area and is seeking additional compensation or other benefits. The group practice has the responsibility and lost revenue associated with providing postoperative care, including the repair of complications, for any patients of that departed surgeon. This must be considered in any damages calculation.

BEWARE CHANGES IN THE VALUE OF CODES

For example, in June 2006, CMS announced its intent to increase the Relative Values of E&M services in 2007, following closely on the heels of a suggestion by MedPAC in its March 2006 report that these services had declined in value, in large part to the benefit of high-tech imaging services.

The work component for RVUs [Relative Value Units] associated with an intermediate office visit [99213], the most commonly billed physician's service, will increase by 37%. The work component for RVUs for an office visit requiring moderately complex decision-making and for a hospital visit also requiring moderately complex decision-making will increase by 29% and 31% respectively. Both of these services rank in the top 10 most frequently billed physicians' services out of more than 7,000 types of services paid under the physician fee schedule.

The 99213 code presently has a fully implemented work RVU value of .67. Under this proposal, the value would rise to approximately .92 RVUs. With a conversion factor of $37.90, this would represent an increase in the fee of nearly $10 or 18%, to about $62.15 from the present level of $52.68 on the National Physician Fee Schedule.

Significantly, because of the budget neutrality provisions of the existing Part B system, the increased cost associated with the increased RVUs has to come from a reduction in the value of other services and CMS proposes "to establish a budget neutrality adjustor that would reduce all work RVUs by an estimated 10% to meet the budget neutrality provisions." For example, CMS estimated that the proposed changes would increase reimbursement for internal medicine by 5% in 2007 while decreasing the reimbursement for radiologists by the same amount. The Federal Register notice contains the details of estimated changes for all specialties.

CMS is also proposing changes to the Practice Expense component of the RVUs to be phased in over four years through 2010, which will result in further revenue shifts.

Chapter 14: Critical Condition—A Coding Analysis for a Physician Practice Valuation

CONCLUSION

Valuation analysts are not coding consultants. Nevertheless, given regulatory issues and the impact of coding on the future cashflow being valued, it is necessary that analysts have some basic knowledge of the subject and conduct a basic review. Relatively simple processes can be implemented using readily available data from the Internet or vendors such as MIT Solutions, Inc. (www.mitsi.org) to incorporate a basic assessment of coding into the valuation process. This results in a valuation conclusion that reflects the risk, if any, of unusual coding patterns and may identify potential lost revenues available to a hypothetical or other owner of the practice. In the latter instance, the analyst can bring additional value to the valuation.

Chapter 15

Why Transaction Structure Affects Value and Other Nuances of Valuing Medical Practices

By Mark O. Dietrich, CPA/ABV

A Review of Complex Tax Issues

Defining the standard and premise of value, such as Fair Market Value on a going concern basis; the interest being valued, such as Market Value of Invested Capital (MVIC) or Equity; and the level of value, control or noncontrol, is not the end of the story. Substantial differences in the concluded value of an interest should result when the transaction contemplated by the engagement is an asset transaction or a stock transaction. Further, some apparent stock transactions should be treated as if they were asset transactions due to requirements of the Internal Revenue Code and there are a variety of other Code provisions that influence the ultimate valuation result. Finally, the Cost Approach for the valuation of intangible assets is not appropriate for the valuation of a medical practice for transfer to a tax-exempt hospital if the intangible have less or no value under the Income Approach.

Fair Market Value?

Many times, appraisers feel that the specifics of a transaction are outside the scope of their assignment, citing the "hypothetical" buyer and seller as a rationale such that looking at the specific terms of the transaction would represent strategic value. This represents a misunderstanding of the term "hypothetical" within the context of an actual transaction. The hypothetical refers to the buyer and seller and their price motivations being consistent with fair market value. It does NOT refer to the specific interest being valued. For example, a hypothetical buyer and seller would pay two different prices for a business where one contemplated transaction included a noncompete from a seller capable of competing post-transaction and the other excluded such a noncompete. Thus, the specific transaction terms for a business result in different values under the fair market value standard.

In healthcare appraisal and transaction, Fair Market Value is modified by the statutory and regulatory constraints of the Stark laws, the Anti-Kickback Statute, anti-inurement provisions of the Internal Revenue Code and, as is described below, other tax statutes and regulations. Proper application of the government restrictions on the underlying motivations of the buyer and seller and the resultant price that can be paid for a business must of necessity be part of the consideration of Fair Market Value; the law always trumps *perceived* differences with appraisal standards. Certainly, a hypothetical buyer subject to fair market value would not pay anything for an illegal cocaine dealership recognizing that law enforcement officials could confiscate not only all the assets of the business but any assets

Chapter 15: Why Transaction Structure Affects Value and Other Nuances

acquired from income generated by the business – to say nothing of sending the owner to prison. The Anti-Kickback Statue coupled with the False Claims Act works in much the same way.

Stock and Asset Transactions

The principal difference between an asset transaction and a stock transaction, of course, is that in an asset transaction the buyer obtains a basis step-up in fixed assets and if intangible value is present, a code section 197 asset which can be amortized over 15 years. These added depreciation and amortization deductions create additional value[1] in an asset transaction because they reduce future taxable income and taxes, thus making after-tax cashflow higher. In contrast, when valuing an equity interest, only the pre-existing basis of depreciable and any intangible assets is used for purposes of computing future depreciation and amortization deductions. Thus, after-tax cashflow is lower and value is lower.

Unlike the generic Market Value of Invested Capital or right-hand side of the balance sheet approach to valuation, medical practices and other healthcare enterprises should also be viewed from the Asset or left-hand side.[2] In structuring a discounted cashflow model for an asset transaction, it is advisable for the appraiser to, at the least, estimate the value of underlying assets using the residual method of allocation under section 338; otherwise, the necessary depreciation and amortization deductions cannot be incorporated into the valuation model. This method first allocates value to cash, than receivables and inventory, fixed assets, various intangibles and finally goodwill. It is comparatively easy to estimate the value of Cash and Receivables, of course. An appraiser with industry experience can often obtain sufficient knowledge of the fixed assets from studying the depreciation schedule and other records of historic acquisitions and inquiries of management to estimate that value. Good examples of where this is possible include ophthalmology and optometry practices, imaging centers and dental practices.

For tax purposes, code section 1060 requires buyer and seller to file a statement with their tax returns for the year of sale (Form 8594) indicating the allocation of the transaction value to the underlying assets. Many times this may seem outside the scope of the typical asset transaction appraisal, but to reiterate, the depreciation and amortization deductions directly affect the concluded value, creating the equivalent of an algebraic simultaneous equation: the total value of the assets cannot be known until allocation of that value to each class of assets is known.

Healthcare transactions in particular

"Where ignorance is bliss, 'tis folly to be wise"[3] seemingly defines the state of appraisal engagements in the healthcare industry, with methodologies debunked in the 1990s reappearing and lessons learned then forgotten or overlooked.

Chapter 15: Why Transaction Structure Affects Value and Other Nuances

Cash-Basis Taxpayers

One advantage that CPAs often have over competing appraisers is their familiarity with tax law as a result of providing tax services in addition to performing business valuations. Medical practices are a peculiar beast in this regard.

IRC section 441 permits "qualified personal service corporations" (PSCs) of practically any size to utilize the cash method of accounting. The price paid for this flexibility is that PSCs are subject to a flat 35% federal corporates tax rate and cannot use the graduated rates available to other (small) businesses. For CPAs or other appraisers unfamiliar with cash-basis taxpayers, the cash-method creates some interesting issues to be addressed in valuation, particularly when addressing "normal" working capital.

Year-End Tax Planning

Many valuations take place at the end of a company's fiscal year. For a closely-held accrual method taxpayer, IRC section 267 may require any bonuses to stockholder-management and family members as well as related entity transaction to be settled via a cash payment, but unrelated trade payables and (many[4]) accrued expenses can be deducted irrespective of whether they have been paid in cash.

For a cash-method taxpayer, virtually all expenses have to have been paid in cash by the end of the year to be deducted in computing taxable income for that year. The primary exception is the deduction for qualified retirement plan contributions, which can be deducted for a given year if paid over to the plan before the due date (including extensions) of the tax return – which is the 15th day of the third month after the tax year closes, or if a valid extension is filed, the 15th day of the 9 month after the tax year closes.

As a result of the differences in tax planning between a cash-method and accrual method taxpayer, there may be significant differences in the historical working capital levels for a cash-basis taxpayer at the end of a taxable year versus an accrual method taxpayer. One thing that is common to cash-basis medical practices is paying all available trade payables at year end, before paying out "bonuses" as part of "zeroing out" taxable income. Many practices, in fact, pay bonuses only once a year at year-end such that during the year, there may be significant accumulations of cash – resulting in *apparent* excess working capital when looking at a cash-basis balance sheet since accrued bonuses will not be reflected. Depending upon the reason for the valuation, this excess can be addressed in several different manners.

1. Treat as excess wording capital and add back to operating asset value.

2. Accrue a bonus to extent of apparent excess cash less outstanding trade payables, based upon historic practice.

Chapter 15: Why Transaction Structure Affects Value and Other Nuances

3. Normalize working capital to industry levels for an accrual taxpayer and reassess the presence of excess working capital.

Observation

When preparing a discounted cashflow method valuation under the income approach, there is likely to be a significant difference between the historical working capital and the "normal" working capital for a hypothetical nonphysician practice buyer. As such, if possible, a thorough analysis of current and prior year's balance sheets should be made and each year should be converted to a "full" accrual basis. Besides obvious accruals that are typically made for accounts receivable, there may be inventories and prepaid items on the asset side that the valuation analyst or appraiser will have to identify through inquiry or analysis.[5] On the liability side, there is often little readily available historical data for payables or accruals. The lack of historical data can make conversion of prior year balance sheets problematic.

Working capital is, of course, equal to current assets less current liabilities. If accruals for inventories and prepaids are not made, current assets will be understated and existing working capital understated.[6] This could, in turn, lead to a failure to properly calculate any excess working capital. Similarly, if accounts payable or accrued items are not reflected – considered in light of cash balances not reduced by early payment of these items – working capital could be overstated along with any excess working capital - or a deficit in working capital could be understated. In the assessment of normal working capital, cash balances and accounts payable are closely tied for the typical medical practice.

Section 448

Less well-known than the nuances of cash-basis tax planning and working capital is the requirement under section 448 that the acquisition of 80% of more of the stock of a cash-method taxpayer by an accrual method taxpayer requires the cash-method taxpayer to convert to the accrual method as of the transaction date if the combined entities' receipts exceed $5 million. For purposes of section 448, the two entities are treated as one under Section 448(c)(2)'s aggregation rules. This typically occurs because the acquirer (a hospital or related entity, private equity entity or public company) is not eligible for PSC status and the cash-basis of accounting is only available generally to entities with less than $5 million in gross receipts.

Section 337

Prior to the Tax Reform Act of 1986, C corporations could liquidate and not incur a tax at the corporate level on any appreciated assets distributed in the liquidation. Since that legislation, any liquidation of a C corporation generally subjects the liquidating corporation to tax on the difference between the fair market value of its assets and their tax basis. An election is available to avoid any tax by the acquiring entity electing to take a carryover tax basis in the assets.

Chapter 15: Why Transaction Structure Affects Value and Other Nuances

Since many hospital-buyers of physician practices are tax-exempt, it may appear that this is not an issue. However, hospital buyers of the stock of a physician practice in jurisdictions where the corporate practice of medicine doctrine[7] permits same often plan to convert the for-profit practice to tax exempt status. *Section 337(d)(4) specifically treats the conversion to tax-exempt status as if an asset sale had taken place, resulting in a gain at the corporate level.* The IRS has long taken[8] two significant positions with respect to acquisition of a taxable healthcare corporation's stock by a tax-exempt entity: 1) that continuing to operate the acquired corporation as a taxable entity is not an efficient use of the acquirer's tax-exempt status and 2) that the conversion tax must be taken into account by the appraiser in opining on the fair market value of the stock. It is directly analogous to the Built-in Gains tax in valuing S Corporations. Whether and to what extent the tax can be discounted may be open to question in the appraisal community but it is not clear that the IRS would entertain such a discount if the conversion is contemplated at the time of the sale of the stock.

If the hospital purchases the C Corporation's stock, the corporate level tax is borne while the corporation is owned by the exempt hospital, and does not reduce the proceeds available to the selling physician-shareholders. However, in an arm's-length purchase, the buyer would pay less for the stock than it would for the net assets because the buyer assumes the burden of the corporate level tax on the assets built-in appreciation. Thus, the hospital's failure to make a downward adjustment to the fair market value of the stock, as determined by an independent appraisal, to reflect the corporate level tax might be viewed as a private benefit to the selling physicians.

> Under Reg. 1.337(d)-4, a taxable corporation that transfers substantially all its assets to a tax-exempt organization must recognize gain or loss at the time of the transaction. The corporate tax is imposed on the taxable corporation. The act of transferring is referred to as the Asset Sale Rule under Reg. 1.337(d)-4(a)(1). It is very important to understand that transferring assets includes liquidating the corporation's assets, which was previously a taxable event to the taxable corporation, *as well as transferring the taxable corporation's stock, which is considered an asset under IRC 1.337(d)-4.* [to wit, 1.337(d)-4(a)(2) states: "For example, if a State, a political subdivision thereof, or an entity any portion of whose income is excluded from gross income under section 115, acquires the stock of a taxable corporation and thereafter any of the taxable corporation's income is excluded from gross income under section 115, the taxable corporation will be treated as if it transferred all of its assets to a tax-exempt entity immediately before the stock acquisition." (**Note: The meaning of the italicized portion of this statement is not clear; however, it appears that the statement would be incorrect if the intent was to make the mere transfer of the stock an asset gain recognition event in the selling corporation. It is possible it refers to a subsequent transfer of the stock by the acquirer.**)
>
> Under Reg. 1.337(d)-4, if a taxable corporation converts to a tax-exempt organization the taxable corporation must pay the corporate taxes. The act of conversion is referred

Chapter 15: Why Transaction Structure Affects Value and Other Nuances

to as the Change in Status Rule under Reg. 1.337(d)-4(a)(2). Thus, the corporate level tax is borne while the taxable corporation's stock is owned by the selling physician/stockholders, which ultimately reduces their available proceeds.

Reg. 1.337(d)-4(a)(4)(b) provides that if an asset will be used partly or wholly in an exempt entity's IRC 511(a) activity, the taxable corporation will recognize an amount of gain or loss that bears the same ratio to the asset's built in gain or loss as 100 percent reduced by the percentage of use in the IRC 511(a) activity bears to 100 percent.

A taxable professional medical corporation, C, merges with a tax-exempt affiliate of hospital A or medical foundation B, created by A to operate C. After January 28, 1999, this "A" reorganization is subject to gain or loss recognition by C, and payment of corporate tax on gain by C.[9]

When valuing a medical practice for acquisition by an exempt entity, it is wise to consider whether section 337 has an impact similar to that of the rules for estate tax valuation (Chapter 14) and ESOP valuations. If, however, one ignores the statutory/regulatory construct, this raises two issues for the appraiser:

- Would the hypothetical buyer of the subject – whether it be a C Corporation, a tax-exempt or some other form of business enterprise – liquidate the target in order to obtain a basis step-up in the underlying assets to fair market value; and

- Would that hypothetical buyer insist on a discount equal to the tax incurred on liquidation.

If the answer to the first question is yes, then the expected basis step-up to be obtained in the liquidation has to be taken into account in the appraisal via the higher depreciation and amortization deductions described above! This will result in higher sales proceeds to the seller, partially compensating them for the loss of capital gains treatment. Thus, employing the proper approach to the appraisal – assets versus stock – is necessary.

If the answer to the first question is an unqualified no, the second question may be evaluated in the more traditional built-in gains tax approach. Typically, one would not expect a hypothetical buyer of a going concern operating company to insist on any built-in gain discount for the underlying operating assets inside a corporation. By the same token, a properly undertaken appraisal would not reflect any of the value associated with an asset acquisition, effectively building the discount into the price.

If the specific tax-exempt buyer does, in fact, intend to convert the target corporation to exempt status, buyer and seller may have an issue independent of the appraisal, depending upon the Appraiser's assessment of the hypothetical buyer and seller. This requires a more complex

Chapter 15: Why Transaction Structure Affects Value and Other Nuances

assessment of hypothetical buyer and seller driven by local market conditions and jurisdictional rules. For example, if a medical practice transaction takes place in a state where only a licensed physician or another professional corporation can own the stock, an asset transaction may effectively be the only way to consummate the sale. A variant on this circumstance may occur if the state permits the stock to be held through a so-called Friendly PC where a physician employed by the acquiring entity is the nominal owner of the stock but all the rights of that stock are effectively held by the acquirer. This suggests that an asset transaction is not mandated.

Another consideration for the Appraiser is the use of the Cost Approach or Asset Accumulation Method is used to determine Net Asset Value and the impact on the conclusion of value. If Net Asset Value is the concluded value, the Appraiser will have to evaluate whether the hypothetical buyer would liquidate the target to acquire the assets or is motivated by avoiding replication cost on a going-concern basis. This may involve consideration of the premise of value and or highest and best use of the assets.

Use of the Cost Approach

As enumerated in the CPE Texts cited above, longstanding IRS is that the use of the Cost Approach in valuing *intangible* assets of a medical practice is only appropriate if intangible value is first found to be present under the income approach. The 1996 CPE Text explains:

> The value of goodwill can be allocated to specific intangible assets; the value of the latter is limited to the value of the former, as calculated under the income approach. For example, if the total value of the individual intangible assets exceeds the total value of the medical practice net of the aggregate fair market value of the tangible assets, the amount of value that can be allocated among the intangible assets is more limited. Also, it is important to note that intangible value may not always be present in a medical practice. Thus, ascribing value to intangible assets is a matter of allocating value derived using the income approach to specific intangible assets.[10]

In other words, the total value of the individual intangible assets cannot exceed the total value of the medical practice under the Income Approach, net of the aggregate fair market value of the tangible assets.

The 2008 Tax Court case *Derby*[11] specifically makes mention of the 1994 CPE Text having to do with Integrated Delivery Systems and how institutions might acquire the assets of a physician practice, including outright purchase, donation or a combination of both. Irrespective of the means of transfer, the entire transaction is subject to Fair Market Value. Thus, the Court's commentary in the *Derby* opinion applies to Fair Market Value in general, not solely to the specific means of transfer present in the *Derby* matter, namely a charitable donation.

Chapter 15: Why Transaction Structure Affects Value and Other Nuances

In the following extracts from the Opinion, the Court highlights what are general principles of transactions: specific contractual rights are obtained in the exchange and it is those rights that are subject to valuation.

> More fundamentally, the Dutcher appraisal takes no account of the various contractual rights and other intangible benefits that petitioners and the other SWMG physicians sought and obtained in the transaction with SMF, such as avoiding signing noncompete agreements and obtaining preferred working conditions. Because it does not fully account for the benefits that petitioners received in the transaction with SMF, the Dutcher appraisal does not establish that petitioners contributed property to SMF that exceeded the values of the benefits they received in return.

> But when petitioners were offered the opportunity to affiliate with Foundation (and receive an outright cash payment for their intangibles), they collectively rejected the prospect in favor of an acquirer that offered them working conditions they preferred, greater economic security through multiple sources of payment, a "free to compete" provision whereby any of them could essentially "unwind" the transaction and retrieve his or her patients if he or she desired to terminate the relationship with the acquirer, a role in management, and other intangible benefits that were negotiated between the SWMG physicians and SMF. Viewed in this light, it is apparent that the intangible benefits that petitioners received in the transaction with SMF were of substantial value to them. Petitioners spurned a cash payment for their medical practice intangibles in order to obtain these benefits in a different transaction.[12]

Where the Derby Court states "…the Dutcher appraisal does not establish that petitioners contributed property to SMF that exceeded the values of the benefits they received in return" it is easy to foresee a circumstance in which a Court would similarly state "The Cost Approach Appraisal of intangible assets does not establish that Sellers transferred property to Buyer that exceeded the value of the tangible assets transferred by Sellers and the contractual employment benefits that Sellers received."

Conclusion

---

1. The wave of transactions in healthcare today mirrors that which took place during the 1990s, providing evidence that my late mentor, Jim Rigby, CPA/ABV, ASA, was correct when he advised that consolidation trends are cyclical every 10 years or so. It is wise for those new to healthcare appraisal as well as those who have been practicing in the sector since the last consolidation, to review the lessons and rules learned in the 1900s.
2. Generally, pre-tax proceeds are higher to both buyer and seller, but not after-tax for seller; for the buyer, individual asset components must be analyzed to determine the difference between pre- and after-tax value.
3. See the 5th Circuit of Appeals decision in *Caracci/Sta Home* for a good explanation of why
4. *Ode on a Distant Prospect of Eton College,* Thomas Gray's poem, 1742

Chapter 15: Why Transaction Structure Affects Value and Other Nuances

5. Accruals treated as "deferred compensation" such as those for uncompensated absences are one troublesome aspect.
6. Privately-held companies typically focus on tax minimization in their bookkeeping and tax filings. As such, "product" inventories such as chemotherapy drugs could be understated and supplies inventories such as x-ray film or MRI and CT contrast may not even be recorded.
7. This also has implications for the Net Asset Value or Asset Accumulation Approach.
8. An excellent if perhaps dated discussion is in the IRS Exempt Organizations CPE Text *Corporate Practice of Medicine* by Charles Kaiser III and Marvin Friedlander; another source is *Corporate Practice of Medicine Doctrine 50 State Survey Summary* by the firm Boerner Van Deuren s.c. in conjunction with the National Hospice and Palliative Care Organization (NHPCO) and the Center to Advance Palliative Care (CAPC)
9. 2000 Exempt Organizations CPE Text *Treas. Reg. Section 1.337(d)-4 and Exempt Organizations* by Charles Kaiser III and Thomas Miller
10. *Treas. Reg. Section 1.337(d)-4 and Exempt Organizations,* ibid
11. Charles F. Kaiser and Amy Henchey, IRS Exempt Organizations Continuing Professional Education Text for FY 1996, Topic Q, "Valuation of Medical Practices" (1996 EO CPE Text), available at www.irs.gov/pub/irs-tege/eo-topicq96.pdf
12. *Derby et al v Commissioner*, T.C. Memo. 2008-45
13. ibid

Chapter 16

Understanding and Using the Technical and Professional Component of Ancillary Revenue when Valuing Medical Practices

By Mark O. Dietrich, CPA/ABV, and Kathie L. Wilson, CPA, CVA

Introduction

Valuing any business requires an understanding of how revenue is generated: what products or services are sold, how much revenue comes from each, competing products or services and competing sellers. Valuing a medical practice is no different in that regard. It is important to understand that services sold by medical practices are commonly specified by CPT™ (Current Procedural Terminology) Codes and HCPCS (Healthcare Common Coding Procedure System or "Hickpicks") Codes. For example, CPT™ code 99213 is a level 3 office visit for an established patient. HCPCS codes can denote "Products" such as certain injectible drugs or chemotherapy which are specified by J codes or services and procedures which are specified by G codes. The HCPCS codes are alphanumeric and start with a letter. For example, J0133 is the code for an acyclovir injection; G0202 is the code for screening mammography. Thus, considerable background is required by an appraiser to understand the revenue lines in the variety of medical practice specialties.

Many of the more common specialties require more expertise than simply being familiar with the codes for seeing patients in the office. Of particular note is the differentiation between the Technical Component and Professional Component of ancillary services for practices such as radiology, cardiology, neurology and others. The technical component is paid in connection with ownership of equipment, provision of a technologist to operate the equipment, supplies and general overhead. The Professional Component is paid to the physician specifically for interpreting the results of the test or study, e.g., an imaging study like an x-ray or MRI. Revenue from the technical component, therefore, is related to the equipment investment of the practice, not the efforts of the physician.

This can be seen in the following quotes from the Centers for Medicare and Medicaid Medicare Physician Fee Schedule 2010 Final Rule:[1]

> Services with Technical Components (TCs) and Professional Components (PCs) Diagnostic services are generally comprised of two components: a professional component (PC) and a technical component (TC), both of which may be performed independently or by different providers. When services have TCs, PCs, and global components that can be billed separately, the payment for the global component equals the sum of the payment for the TC and PC. This is a result of using a weighted average of the ratio of indirect to

Chapter 16: Understanding and Using the Technical and Professional Component

direct costs across all the specialties that furnish the global components, TCs, and PCs; that is, we apply the same weighted average indirect percentage factor to allocate indirect expenses to the global components, PCs, and TCs for a service. (The direct PE RVUs for the TC and PC sum to the global under the bottom-up methodology.)

Modifier. A modifier is shown if there is a technical component (modifier TC) and a professional component (PC) (modifier -26) for the service. If there is a PC and a TC for the service, Addendum B contains three entries for the code. A code for: the global values (both professional and technical); modifier -26 (PC); and, modifier TC. The global service is not designated by a modifier, and physicians must bill using the code without a modifier if the physician furnishes both the PC and the TC of the service.

Within the RVU allocations are components for Physician Work, Practice Expense and Malpractice Insurance. As you might expect, the largest element in the TC is for Practice expense, whereas the largest element in the PC is typically for Physician Work, known as wRVUs. In some circumstances, these can be important in measuring the productivity for reasonable compensation purposes as defined later herein.[2]

Some Common Mistakes

Most appraisers determine reasonable compensation when valuing a medical practice by reference to the physician's (or physicians' aggregate) productivity benchmarked against statistical norms such as those from the Medical Group Management Association. The definition of collected revenue in the MGMA data is with the Technical Component of Ancillary Services excluded! MGMA does have some data that includes the technical component and nonphysician providers at two levels, greater than 10% or less than 10%, but that differentiation is generally not specific enough to be useful for reasonable compensation purposes.[3] Thus, in order to use the data appropriately it is necessary for the appraiser to separate the revenues associated with the professional component (related to the efforts of the physician) from those of the ancillary or technical component (related to the equipment investment).

Example

While valuing a four physician neurology practice with a single owner, the appraiser notes that the owner has collected revenue credited to him of more than twice the 90th percentile of MGMA. Upon investigation of the practice's reports of productivity by CPT (including HCPCS) code and the list of fixed assets, he determines that the practice owns an MRI unit in addition to other ancillary equipment. The Technical Component of the MRI services representing approximately 85% of the Global (or total) collected revenue has been credited to the owner physician as well as the professional component. In order to determine the owner's productivity consistent with the MGMA definition, the technical component of

Chapter 16: Understanding and Using the Technical and Professional Component

the MRI and other ancillaries will have to be backed out. This has a dramatic effect on the reasonable compensation determination: after the appropriate modifications are made, the owner physician's collections are only at the 75th percentile of MGMA. Failure to identify and appropriately adjust for the Technical Component collected revenue would have resulted in a dramatic understatement of the practice's value due to an overstatement of reasonable compensation for the services of the owner physician.

Jurisdictional Issues

Aside from the obvious effect on the reasonable compensation determination, the source of profit in a practice can be quite significant from a jurisdictional standpoint. For example, in marital dissolution valuation, many jurisdictions distinguish between personal goodwill and enterprise goodwill. In many circumstances, the revenue, profit and value resulting from the Technical Component of ancillary services may be included in enterprise goodwill and therefore considered marital property subject to division. Again, because it is not related to the personal efforts of the physician but to the investment in the equipment of the practice. In other circumstances, even the Technical Component element may be considered nondivisible if a noncompete agreement is required from the seller to maintain the related revenue and profit in the hands of a buyer. Absent a jurisdictional rule, that portion of the practice value connected to Technical Component revenue that would be present absent the seller is perhaps the clearest element of enterprise goodwill.

Transactions

In the current transaction market, differentiating reasonable compensation along with enterprise and personal goodwill can be equally important. After a physician practice is acquired by a hospital, a number of employment settings are possible, including employment by the hospital, by a hospital-controlled group practice, or by the physician practice itself, if the hospital purchases the stock. The Stark laws have different permitted compensation rules depending on the nature of the employment setting, which can impact how profits from the Technical Component of ancillaries are handled. This should, in turn, influence precisely what is being valued and how reasonable compensation is determined.

One of the most important practice types from a valuation and transaction standpoint in the present market is cardiology. Cardiologists employ a variety of ancillary testing equipment including SPECT[4] (or Single photon emission computed tomography, used for myocardial perfusion), Ultrasound (echocardiogram as distinct from an electrocardiogram or EKG), Coronary Computed Tomography Angiogram and Cardiac MRI. Despite some fairly dramatic cuts for SPECT and other nuclear medicine in the 2010 Medicare Physician Fee Schedule, these practices remain attractive for the Technical Component of tests as well as for the highly profitable admissions they generate for hospitals.

Chapter 16: Understanding and Using the Technical and Professional Component

Example

CPT™ Code 78465,[5] Heart image (3d) multiple, is a SPECT code for myocardial infusion and represented a staggering 10.3% ($2,072,176,147) of charges for Cardiovascular physicians billing Medicare in 2007, the highest single code in terms of charges as well as frequency of billing. CPT™ Code 78465 also represented 10.4% ($2,017,599,660) of charges in 2006 and 10.4% ($1,863,154,763) of charges in 2005. The following Chart charts are taken from the indicated Proposed and Final Rules and show the global, technical and professional component breakdown by RVU.

2010 Final Rule

CPT¹/ HCPCS	Mod	Status	Description	Physician Work RVUs[2,3,4]	Fully Implemented Non-Facility PE RVUs[2,4]	Year 2010 Transitional Non-Facility PE RVUs[2,4]	Fully Implemented Facility PE RVUs[2,4]	Year 2010 Transitional Facility PE RVUs[2,4]	Malpractice RVUs[2,4]	CPT¹/ HCPCS
78452		A	Ht muscle image spect. mult	1.62	8.84	8.84	NA	NA	0.06	XXX
78452	TC	A	Ht muscle image spect. mult	0.00	8.32	8.32	NA	NA	0.01	XXX
78452	26	A	Ht muscle image spect. mult	1.62	0.52	0.52	0.52	0.52	0.05	XXX

2009 Final Rule

STRESS LAB (P-K counted once)		UNITS	PERCENT	NET REVENUE	PERCEN
SPECT MYOCARDIAL PERF	78465	1,353	5.82%	1,488,000	24.00
MYOCARDIAL PERFUSION	78478	1,143	4.92%	248,000	4.00
MYOCARDIAL PERFUSION	78480-78481	517	2.22%	310,000	5.00
MYOCARDIAL PERFUSION	78483	860	3.70%	744,000	12.0
GENERATION AUTODATA-P	78490	1,240	5.33%	248,000	4.00
INFUSION	90765	559	2.40%	248,000	4.00
STRESS	93015	1,488	6.40%	372,000	6.00
OTHER		4,960	21.33%	248,000	4.00
SUBTOTAL		12,119	52.12%	3,906,000	63.00%

The following Table is sample data from a cardiology group practice with numerous subspecialties (service codes in addition to those for SPECT also shown). Net revenue (expected collections) from SPECT nuclear medicine tests is $2.8 million. Assuming for the sake of illustration that all payors use an 85% TC and 15% Professional Component split, nearly $2.4 million of net revenue has to be excluded from individual physician production to be comparable to MGMA data

In some practices the Professional Component and Technical Component may be billed separately either because of payor rules or because the practice, in fact, only provides one or the other. In this case, a modifier is used for billing and should appear in the billing system reports: 26 is the modifier used for the Professional Component only and TC is the modifier used for the Technical Component only. If the Billing is global (has no modifier), it is necessary to separate the Professional Component and Technical Component. The Checklist provides detail on how to accomplish this.

Chapter 16: Understanding and Using the Technical and Professional Component

---

What is "incident to" billing?

Many medical practices increase revenue through the use of nonphysician providers (NPP's). These are employees who provide separately billable services to patients, but are not physicians. Physician assistants (PA's), Nurse practitioners (NP's) and Midwives are examples of NPP's.

Although they provide separately billable services, there are options for how to bill these services. The services can be billed directly and, because they are not physicians, the reimbursement for these services is a portion of the physician's fee schedule (Medicare sets the rate for many services at 85% of the rate for a physician; non-Medicare payors may have different rules). Another option is to bill the services as "incident to" the services of a physician. If the requirements for incident to billing are met, the services are billed under the physician's provider number and reimbursement is at the full physician's fee schedule. The physician is required to participate in the services provided by the NPP (e.g., supervision, chart review, physical presence in the office suite when the services are provided, among others), but the bulk of the effort is provided by the NPP.

This becomes an issue in valuation because, like the technical component billing, the productivity related to the nonphysician providers' services could be included in the physician's productivity. Without identifying and segregating the production unrelated to the efforts of the physician from the productivity related to the efforts of the physician, the valuation analyst can end up with an inconsistent reasonable compensation calculation. In addition to understanding technical component revenue, understanding the use of nonphysician providers and the methodology for billing their services is important to developing reasoned valuation conclusions.

Individual Market Idiosyncrasies

In some poorly reimbursed markets, it may, in fact, be necessary for the Technical Component Income to supplement reasonable compensation for the physicians. For example, Rhode Island is notorious for the low levels of fees paid to physicians. This is due in large part to the fact that two insurers control nearly all of the health insurance market in that state and rates are artificially low as a result. As such, in order to attract and retain physicians, many practices have profitable ancillaries in place. In such a circumstance, it may be necessary to test the reasonable compensation analysis against an alternative measure of production such as compensation per RVU (Relative Value Unit), Work RVUs (wRVUs) or annual encounters. This is an example where the productivity data *including* Technical Component revenue may need to be evaluated as well.

Conclusion

Valuing medical practices requires an in depth understanding of the individual practice and the healthcare industry. This article highlights just one aspect of a myriad of issues unique to medical practice valuation and the determination of reasonable compensation (see sidebar

Chapter 16: Understanding and Using the Technical and Professional Component

regarding "incident to" billing). The environment that physicians work in, dominated by the Medicare system, changes frequently. Some of these changes can be anticipated, such as the annual Medicare fee schedule modifications. Other changes are less predictable, but can have a far greater impact, such as legislation. As any other highly regulated industry, it is critical that valuators remain current. The goal is always to have your valuation upheld, be it in court or in a settlement conference. Failure to understand the industry and its related terminology can undermine your authority as a valuation analyst and reduce the value of your opinion.

---

1. CMS-1413-FC
2. Not all, or even many, practices track wRVUs, however.
3. See the Rhode Island example later herein for an important exception.
4. Due to its ability to generate true 3-D images, it is gradually replacing traditional gamma (ray) cameras.
5. Codes are Copyright, American Medical Association. This code was "cross-walked" or changed to 78452 in the period between the 2010 proposed and final rules. This illustrates one more complication that emphasizes the import of understanding CPT™ codes.

Chapter 17

Deal Structure and Tax Considerations in Asset and Stock Transactions

By Scott Miller, CPA/ABV, CVA

This chapter is a survey of the most commonly encountered transactions likely to be found in the healthcare industry. We assume that most of the transactions will be between private or closely held entities, but this is not an absolute requirement. Publicly held corporations, due to their readily traded stock on established markets and sheer size, have inherent advantages over closely held corporations. We will organize the chapter materials first along taxable transactions and then tax preference transactions. Within these two broad categories, we shall consider such tax attributes as stock versus asset transactions, and the impact of being an S corporation (or pass through entity for tax purposes) or a C corporation.

Assumptions

Prior to our discussion of transaction structure and planning for the tax considerations, a few assumptions are outlined to provide an appropriate framework. First, the proposed transaction should make economic sense and provide a realistic return to investors. For our purposes, economic sense refers to transaction related valuations predicated more closely to traditional capital market models. This distinction is more clearly realized when compared to the unbridled speculation that accompanied the "dot.com" rise and subsequent bust. During that time in the late 1990s valuations of the dot.coms defied traditional capital market models and distorted the most commonly encountered historic deal structures.

We also assume that the proposed transactions have been justified on the basis of achieving organizational goals and objectives. In the healthcare industry we find a complex combination of both for-profit and non-profit organizations. Further, many for-profit entities are guided by mission or vision statements grounded on providing healthcare services and not necessarily providing the maximum return to investors. Correspondingly, we assume that there is solid economic or service justification for the transaction to proceed. The healthcare industry is often sensitive to organizations attaining economies of scale and therefore combinations and mergers are common.

When considering asset based transactions, we generally are not including real estate and land. The tax environment for those assets is often distinctive and substantially different than the tax exposure of more traditional business related assets such as inventories, receivables, equipment, goodwill and other intangible assets.

Chapter 17: Deal Structure and Tax Considerations in Asset and Stock Transactions

For ease of discussion, we assume there is a single seller (referred to as the Sell-side of the transaction or Seller) and a single buyer (referred to as the Buy-side of the transaction or Buyer).

Price and Terms

In our discussion of transactions, we want to emphasize that the playing field consists of myriad elements that will be negotiated between the parties. This negotiation process is dynamic and fluid. There may be an overall understanding of the approximate value of the "deal," but the precise shape of the transaction will be the result of the parties vigorously negotiating nearly every facet of the acquisition. Typically, the Buy-side will introduce measures intended to provide additional security should the due diligence fail to uncover or identify contingent or unknown liabilities. These measures are defined as transaction "terms," and assist the Buy-side in managing risk and provide a degree of post transaction financial security.

Terms may include items such as: implementation of an escrow or a hold back amount; seller financing; purchase agreement warranties and representations; contingent payment or "earn-out" provisions for the Seller; non-competition agreement; and consulting or employment agreement. These transaction provisions are there to protect the Buy-side interests for a period of time following the closing date. Depending on the circumstances, the combined impact of the terms may be significant and have a material impact on the proceeds received by the Sell-side. However, in health care transactions, earn-outs have a high risk of violating the Anti-kickback statute since they may be based on "future referrals." As a policy matter, an earn-out may encourage over-utilizing health services and therefore be a problem.

Although, the terms are crafted in a manner to protect the Buy-side, the final form of the documents will be a function of the relative negotiation strength of the parties. If the Sell-side has built an enviable and financially successful organization, considerable strength is already present and the terms of the ultimate agreement will reflect this fact. In certain instances, the Sell-side is so well prepared that an all cash transaction with few contingent provisions is possible. Contrast this to the Sell-side of an entity that is barely breaking-even financially and the owners are rapidly aging or in failing health. Those Sell-side attributes are so negative that the Buy-side will typically have a pronounced upper hand in structuring a transaction exceedingly favorable to its interests.

Taxable Transactions

This category, "taxable transactions," is a convenient classification of acquisitions for our purposes. Generally, the taxable transaction will be taxable to the Sell-side investors the extent to which there is a reportable taxable gain. We will consider asset and stock transaction sales in S corporations (or other pass through tax entities) and C corporations.

Chapter 17: Deal Structure and Tax Considerations in Asset and Stock Transactions

Overview Taxable Asset Sales

There is a belief that most transactions involving closely held companies are asset sales because asset sales enjoy two significant advantages. First, the ability of the buyer to receive a stepped-up basis in the assets being acquired is a significant advantage. This means that the Buy-side will be able to increase the basis of the assets being purchased to the amount of the purchase price subject to applicable regulations and tax guidelines. The second major advantage is the ability to selectively acquire only certain assets and restrict the assumption of unknown or contingent liabilities. Our tax code and the legal liability system tend to favor asset transactions based on this cursory introduction.

The advantages of asset based acquisitions are typically tilted in favor of the Buy-side. The Buy-side will gain the ability to receive a stepped-up basis in the assets being acquired, but with proper planning the purchase price will be allocated to the assets in the most efficient tax manner. The purchase price will be allocated for Federal reporting purposes according to Internal Revenue Code (IRC) Section 1060.

Briefly, IRC Section 1060 states that when assets are acquired, the purchase price will be allocated to one of seven (7) asset classes. The residual method of allocation applies, meaning the purchase price will be first allocated to the market value of the Class I assets until that value is reached; then the balance amount of the purchase price will be allocated to the market value of the Class II assets until that value is reached; and so on, until the final amount of unallocated purchase price will be by default allocated to Class VII.

Class I assets include cash and other general deposit amounts. Class II assets include actively traded personal property and certain other assets such as certificates of deposit, foreign currently and investments in publicly traded stock. Generally, these first two asset classes are infrequently used in actual transactions. Class III assets are "market to market" at least annually and include trade accounts receivable and other receivables. Buyers may or may not purchase the receivables depending on the certainty of collectability and quality. Class IV assets include inventories and other items held for resale, which are typically acquired by the Buy-side. Class V assets are understood to include assets subject to depreciation such as furniture and fixtures, machinery and equipment and buildings. Some multi-specialty practices, practices with high technology imaging equipment, or ambulatory surgery centers, can have significant value in Class V tangible assets. These assets are typically acquired by the Buy-side.

Class VI and Class VII assets both considered intangible assets. Generally, Class VI includes all IRC Section 197 intangible assets with the exception of goodwill and going concern which are specifically Class VII assets. In summary regarding the seven Classes of assets, once the purchase price has been allocated on the residual basis to the first six asset Classes, the balancing number will be allocated to Class VII, most commonly goodwill. When an asset based transaction is being completed in a medical practice for example, it is possible that goodwill is going to be the dominant item acquired. Some medical practices have few tangible assets. Many desirable

Chapter 17: Deal Structure and Tax Considerations in Asset and Stock Transactions

candidates have in place successful clinical management systems, loyal and well trained employees and practice development programs. The combination of few tangible assets and significant intangible assets may culminate in a practice achieving superior financial results, leading to a high percentage of goodwill.

For tax purposes goodwill is amortized over 15 years; as are most other IRC Section 197 intangible assets. For financial reporting purposes, however, goodwill is not amortized but is subject to annual impairment testing. The Buy-side typically has a vested interest in allocating the purchase price to the other asset categories with shorter recovery periods because most assets (with the primary exception of buildings) may be depreciated in less than 15 years. The Buyer typically stipulates in the asset purchase agreement that the Seller agrees to their allocation.

Following the transaction the Buyer and the Seller will report the transaction on IRS Form 8594. It is beneficial that both sides to the transaction agree to the purchase price allocation, as they both can file substantially identical IRS Form 8594. This will not raise concerns at the IRS about potentially abusive allocations.

Asset based transactions also require a distinction between capital assets (as understood in the IRC) and non-capital business assets. This distinction is particularly important for S corporation shareholders on the Sell-side because capital assets and non-capital assets are taxed to the S corporation shareholders at different rates (the S corporation itself pays no taxes as it is a pass through entity for tax purposes). At the time of this writing, gains on capital assets are taxed to the S corporation shareholders at Federal capital gain rates (currently 15%) plus any applicable taxes at the state and local level. Gains on non-capital assets are typically taxed to the S corporation shareholders at personal ordinary income tax rates, assumed for sake of discussion to be approximately an effective maximum of 35% plus any applicable state and local taxes. The effective Federal and state tax rate on gains of non-capital assets may be between 28% and +40%. Compare this to the Federal capital gain rate of 15% and the distinction between assets is material. We should also note that in most instances, accumulated depreciation on capital assets and depreciable assets is recoverable in the year of the transaction, and the full depreciation and amortization recovery (previously taken depreciation and amortization) is taxable as ordinary income to the Sell-side S corporation shareholders.

The distinction between capital and non-capital assets for a C corporation is not as critical as Congress has passed legislation that makes substantially all gains of sales of assets in a C corporation taxable to the corporation as ordinary income. This represents the first layer of taxes on the gain of sale in a C corporation. Following the sale of the assets, the after tax consideration received by the C corporation is now locked inside the corporation. When shareholders remove this liquidity from the corporation, typically in a liquidating distribution to avoid personal holding company issues, that distribution is taxable to the shareholders as capital gain representing a second level of taxes.

Chapter 17: Deal Structure and Tax Considerations in Asset and Stock Transactions

C Corporation Asset Sales

As mentioned in the prior section, gains on the sale of assets in a C corporation are exposed to double taxation. First the taxable gain on the sale of assets is taxed at the corporation's ordinary income tax rate for both the Federal government and state and local authorities. The second layer of taxes is administered when the shareholders remove the transaction proceeds from the corporation. Between these two layers of both Federal and state and local taxes, the gain on the sale may be effectively taxed at a combined rate of between 45% and 55%. Many, including this author, consider the combined effective tax rate to be confiscatory.

Clearly, the Sell-side of the transaction is not likely to be enthusiastic about the prospects of an asset sale due to the highly unfavorable tax exposure. The Buy-side in such transactions is often driving the deal structure, providing financing and the preparing the legal documents. In such a hostile tax environment for the Sell-side, the Buy-side will often consider or be compelled to pay a higher price to lessen the impact of the double taxation.

It is amazing to me how often closely held C corporations are encountered in our economy. It is a given fact all owners of closely held businesses will eventually leave the company. When that occurs, there is a strong chance the sale will be an asset based transaction subject to one of the most hostile tax environments in the IRC. This is often the price for failing to anticipate the future liquidity event; the sale of the business.

One item for selling C corporation shareholders to explore is the possibility of the existence of personal goodwill among the individual shareholders. If personal goodwill can be justified, the transaction proceeds may be allocated to the assets of the corporation and the individual's personal goodwill. Personal goodwill is an individual's capital asset and subject to capital gain taxes on any taxable gain. Personal goodwill is not taxable to the corporation; therefore there is just a single layer of capital gain taxes to the selling shareholder. This is classic tax rate arbitrage; the challenge being to justify personal goodwill taxed at only capital gain rates as opposed to an asset of the C corporation subject to double taxes.

S Corporation Asset Sales

Unlike the tax environment for C corporations, asset transactions in S corporations may not be as negatively taxed. Since the S corporation is a pass through entity for tax purposes, the asset sale proceeds are prorated to the shareholders according to applicable tax regulations. While it is beyond our scope to discuss the taxation of gains to S corporation shareholders in detail, a number of overall observations are applicable.

Gains on asset sales will be taxable to the Selling shareholders at effective tax rates applicable to certain categories of assets. Unlike C corporations, the distinction between capital and non-capital assets is very important for S corporations. Generally, gains on the sale of capital assets such as goodwill, gains on machinery and equipment in excess accumulated depreciation, and intangible assets such as licenses and patents when sold are taxed at capital gain rates. Currently the Federal capital gain rate is 15%, at an historic low point. Gains on non-capital assets including such items as inventory, accounts receivable, and depreciation recapture are taxable to the shareholders at their ordinary income tax rates, which can be +35% plus the tax liability at the state and local level.

The Sell-side of an S corporation asset transaction will want to allocate as much of the purchase price as possible to capital assets for the favorable capital gain tax exposure. Capital assets such as goodwill and other intangible assets are amortized for tax purposes over 15 years. The Buy-side of the transaction will typically favor allocating the purchase price to asset categories with much shorter depreciation lives for faster cost recovery. This process of allocating purchase price to asset Classes with the shortest cost recovery periods is referred to as depreciation rate arbitrage. This depreciation rate arbitrage is beneficial to the Buy-side, while putting the Sell-side at a disadvantage since assets with shorter depreciation and amortization periods are often taxed as non-capital assets. For example the Buyer may allocate more purchase price to inventories which promises a quick cost recovery but will be taxable to the Seller as ordinary income. Typically the Buyer will insist on their allocation of purchase price for the purposes of filing IRS Form 8594.

Clearly there are compelling advantages to C corporation shareholders faced with the likelihood of an asset sale to make an S corporation election and thereby end the exposure to a double layer of taxes. To optimize tax efficiency the election to the S corporation must be at least 10 years prior to the asset sale. During the entire 10 year period following the election to an S corporation, the C corporation shareholders are subject to a layer of taxes that in effect assumes the corporation is still a C corporation for the purposes of an asset sale. The tax exposure is referred to as the Built-in-Gain (BIG) liability. The BIG tax is hostile to C corporation shareholders, and it is a decided negative for many corporations remaining as a C. Owners should anticipate the day when they leave the business and appropriately consider the tax implications of selling.

Overview Taxable Stock Sales

A stock based transaction will favor the Sell-side because any gain will likely be subject to capital gain taxes since stock is a capital asset, assuming the applicable regulatory holding period is maintained. Additionally, a stock based transaction will mean that the Buy-side will be assuming unknown or contingent liabilities that may be realized in the future. This potential liability could be crippling in the case of such things as environmental damage or medical injury to people. The potential exposure to unknown liabilities is often the reason the Buy-side will insist on an asset transaction to limit the exposure.

Conversely, some reasons why the Buy-side may agree to a stock transaction includes an interest in the candidate business because of operations and the licensing already obtained in the name of the Seller. This is often the case in the healthcare industry where the candidate company has taken perhaps years to obtain the medical licenses to conduct business with the applicable

Chapter 17: Deal Structure and Tax Considerations in Asset and Stock Transactions

commonwealth or with medical reimbursement sources such as Medicare and Medicaid. However, many of these licenses cannot be transferred without specific consent of the applicable authority.

A stock based transaction may also be favored by private equity firms when most of the assets in the acquired company represent goodwill. The private equity firm, for example may have a relatively short time horizon for ownership of the target company because it will resell (or "flip") the business within say a 4-6 year period. In such a short time horizon, the amortization of intangible assets such as goodwill over a 15 year period with an asset purchase is not that attractive to the Buy-side. Of course, the willingness of the Buy-side to acquire stock is largely dependent on controlling potential unknown liabilities with insurance or the application of terms such as escrow accounts, seller financing and earn-outs.

Stock based transactions may also be found when the acquisition candidate is very well managed and the Sellers understand they have significant negotiating leverage. For example, a medical practice with an excellent local clinical reputation; state-of-art equipment; fully computerized patient and clinical records; and low employee turnover in high skill disciplines is an attractive acquisition candidate. Candidate Buyers may have to be willing to complete a stock transaction to make the acquisition sufficiently attractive to the Seller. However, unless a physician is buying the stock from another physician, this rarely happens due to the Corporate Practice of Medicine doctrine. The Corporate Practice of Medicine doctrine generally does not allow a business to practice medicine or employ a physician to provide professional medical services. The Corporate Practice of Medicine prohibitions may be found in state statutes or regulations or may develop from court decisions or state Attorney General Opinions. For these reasons, it is important to research these issues for each individual state.

C Corporation Stock Sales

The Sell-side often benefits from a stock sale because of tax environment for a C corporation asset sale, especially with a significant taxable gain. Avoiding the double layer of taxes on an asset sale is a high priority. Unless there is a compelling reason for the Buy-side to consider a stock sale, like licenses, they may resist a stock sale and press for an asset transaction. When there is an impasse, the Seller is often more flexible in the transaction price knowing that an asset sale is more beneficial to the Buyer from a tax deduction and liability standpoint. In such circumstance, the Sell-side may consider a discount from the anticipated sale proceeds for the benefits a stock transaction provides. Correspondingly, we have also witnessed many potential deals that unraveled and were not completed because the Buy-side insisted on an asset based transaction with terrible tax liabilities for the Sell-side that were ultimately deemed to be unacceptable.

In the world of transactions, it is wise for the Sell-side to remember that what is often the most important are the net proceeds after taxes and expenses following the sale available for distribution to the shareholders. The gross sale price may at first seem attractive, but the tax efficiency of the transaction has to be considered.

Chapter 17: Deal Structure and Tax Considerations in Asset and Stock Transactions

S Corporation Stock Sales

The circumstances surrounding an S corporation stock sale are somewhat different than a C corporation. The Seller will still favor a stock sale because virtually the entire transaction price is subject to capital gain taxes. An exception to stock sale preference is if the target company is comprised substantially of intangible assets such as goodwill. The goodwill would be taxable to the individual shareholders as a capital asset and be subject to capital gain. Therefore, there may be little tax exposure difference between a stock and an asset sale to the S corporation shareholders in this instance. However, if the underlying assets of the business are comprised of assets with significant accumulated depreciation or they are non-capital assets such as receivables and inventory, the Sell-side could be faced with exposure to substantial individual ordinary income taxes. In this case the shareholders may insist on a stock sale. For example, a larger ambulance and emergency transportation company may have decided to let its rolling stock of vehicles mature and become largely depreciated. An asset based transaction in this case would mean that substantial amounts of accumulated depreciation would be recaptured and become ordinary income to the Sellers.

Ultimately, whether the transaction is a stock based or asset based will often depend on the acquisition appetite of the Buy-side. If the Buy-side is aggressive and wants to expand the business with acquisitions, it may have to be flexible and be more accepting of stock based deals. If the Sell-side controls a highly desirable and profitable business, the sellers may be able to insist only on a stock transaction. The relative negotiating strength of the parties to the deal will typically have a substantial impact on the eventual deal structure.

Tax-Preference Transactions

This section refers to tax preference transactions. Generally the tax preference transactions relate to a section of the IRC that permits acquisitions and consolidations of business entities on exceedingly favorable tax terms. The acquisition or consolidation may proceed with little or nominal tax impact if applicable regulations are observed. Perhaps the best way to illustrate this is with a simple example. Assume that two separate corporations wish to combine operations without one company having to sell itself to the other and incur taxable gain to the Sell-side of the transaction. If the tax preference regulations are applied, the two companies may be combined in a manner to avoid a taxable gain to the shareholders. This is a compelling advantage as all applicable synergies are combined going forward without the payment of transaction based taxes. Of course at some point the shareholders may wish to liquidate their investment in the consolidated company, but that gain could be deferred for years and allowed to grow and compound.

In this section we are expanding our vocabulary to reference the acquisition aspects of the tax preference reorganization and the acquired vantage point. We are also considering the transactions involving the sale of stock to an Employee Stock Ownership Plan and Trust (ESOP) as a tax preference transaction. As we shall soon see, the IRC significantly favors employee ownership in our

Chapter 17: Deal Structure and Tax Considerations in Asset and Stock Transactions

market based capitalistic economy. This clear bias in favor of employee ownership is best evidenced by the tax incentives in place for corporations to install ESOPs and sell stock to its employees.

IRC Section 368 Tax Preference Reorganization

This part of the IRC allows corporate reorganizations on a tax preference basis. Generally tax preference reorganizations are discussed as part of IRC Sections 354-368. The more common reorganizations are discussed from IRC Sections 368(a)(1)(A) through (G), which includes seven (7) commonly incurred types of activities. Typically, these reorganizations are referred to by the capital letter that is part of the IRC. For example an IRC Section 368(a)(1)(A) reorganization is often referred to as "Type A" statutory merger or reorganization. The same similar letter designation follows for each of the seven letters A through G.

Common Attributes of Tax Preference Reorganizations

The first several types of reorganizations are often referred to as acquisitive. The reorganizations are typically used to acquire or consolidate entities. There are a number of common attributes of these acquisitive reorganizations which have evolved with time and are not necessarily part of the IRC, but part of the total regulatory proceedings regarding the tax preference reorganizations.

First, there must be a legitimate business purpose for the reorganization, (IRS Regulation 1.368-1(b) and (c)). Saving taxes is a worthwhile objective; it is not acceptable as a business purpose. Establishing a defensible business purpose is often an easy task as most reorganizations are negotiated between independent parties following numerous reasons for the transaction. Some examples of acceptable business purposes for the regulators: realizing cost savings, enhancing an acquisition, maintenance of corporate control, providing diversification, reducing market risks and an upcoming equity offering.

Regulations also require a tax preference reorganization to proceed under a plan of reorganization (IRC Sections 354 and 361). It is recommended that the plan be put into writing and filed with applicable tax returns. Often the purchase and sale agreement will incorporate wording to the effect that it includes the plan of reorganization. The purchase and sale agreement is usually sufficient evidence that there is a plan of reorganization.

There must also be a continuity of business enterprise. This standard may be achieved in one of two common forms: the business continuity test and the asset continuity test. The business continuity test basically means that the acquiring corporation will continue the business of the acquired company. There are few absolute rules regarding what constitutes the continuation of the acquired corporation's business, but generally the acquiring corporation must continue significant business lines of the target. The asset continuity test basically means that the acquiring

Chapter 17: Deal Structure and Tax Considerations in Asset and Stock Transactions

corporation will employ a significant portion of the assets of the acquired corporation following the reorganization, but those assets do not have to be in the same industry.

There is also a requirement for the continuity of interest, which is similar in concept to the continuity of business enterprise. The continuity of interest standard applies to the shareholders of the acquired corporation. Legislation in 1998 clarified this issue and is intended to insure that the shareholders of the acquired corporation have a significant and definite financial interest in the acquiring corporation. A material percentage of the total consideration paid to the shareholders of the target corporation must consist of stock in the acquiring corporation. For our purposes, if the shareholders receive at least half of the transaction consideration in the stock of the acquiring corporation, this will help meet the complex test. Even if these shareholders subsequently sell their stock in the acquiring corporation to a third party, say on a public stock exchange, this sale will still meet the continuity of interest requirement.

If the IRS suspects that the tax preference reorganization is merely a cleverly disguised taxable transaction accomplished in multiple steps in different years, the IRS may declare the existence of a "step transaction." The step transaction theory finds that multiple transactions are deemed to be related into a single event. If the IRS prevails the reorganization will be collapsed into a single taxable event with taxes and interest assessed accordingly.

This abbreviated overview of common attributes of acquisitive reorganizations suggests that the tax advantages of these transactions must be accompanied by a thoughtful plan of reorganization in compliance with the applicable regulations.

The Common Reorganizations Designated by Capital Letters

The Type A Statutory Reorganization, IRC Section 368(a)(1)(A), is often the most common because of the flexibility of the regulations governing this transaction. These Type A reorganizations must be completed in compliance with both state and Federal regulations, hence the reference to the term "Statutory." Typically in a Type A reorganization, stock in the acquiring corporation is exchanged for stock of the acquired corporation, but the transaction may also include the exchange of some cash or other consideration. If the shareholders of the acquired corporation receive stock and additional consideration, say cash, the cash is typically taxable to those shareholders (the cash is often referred to as "boot"). Historically, the Type A reorganizations are the most common because they are so flexible in meeting shareholder objectives.

The Type B Reorganization, IRC Section 368(a)(1)(B), is often referred to as a stock for stock transaction. Under the regulations the Type B reorganization is commonly understood to mean the exchange of stock in the acquired corporation for the voting stock of the acquiring corporation. Immediately following the reorganization the acquiring corporation must be in control of the acquired corporation, which is typically a subsidiary of the acquirer. The stock for stock requirement is a strict standard, and it means only stock may be exchanged between the parties. This is not nearly as flexible as a Type A reorganization. Following the reorganization the

Chapter 17: Deal Structure and Tax Considerations in Asset and Stock Transactions

acquiring corporation must have control of the target corporation. Control is generally understood to mean to include at least 80% of all of target's voting stock and at least 80% of all other classes of outstanding stock. Typically only publicly held corporations employ this type of reorganization due to the strict regulatory environment.

The Type C Reorganization, IRC Section 368(a)(1)(C), is often referred to as a stock for assets transaction. These transactions fall between the Type A and Type B reorganizations for the ease of application. Generally, in Type C reorganizations the acquiring corporation will exchange its voting stock for substantially all of the assets of the target corporation. There is no absolute test for the understanding of what constitutes "substantially" all the assets of the target corporation, but there is some guidance on this point from the regulations. Generally, substantially all assets include at least 90% of the fair market value of the net assets transferred, and at least 70% of the fair market value of the gross assets of the target corporation immediately before the reorganization. Typically following the C reorganization the target corporation is liquidated.

The Type D Reorganization (IRC Section 368(a)(1)(D) is generally a stock for assets transaction, but different from a Type C in that they are often categorized as divisive, in that a corporation is typically being divided into one or more corporations. Common terms such as spin-off, split-off, and split-up often apply to these transactions. The regulatory environment is exceedingly complex for Type D reorganizations and they are relatively rare. Most typically only a public corporation would employ a Type D reorganization.

The other reorganizations under IRC Section 368 are briefly mentioned, although they are not as applicable to our purposes as the other sections. The Type E Reorganization refers to corporate recapitalizations. One common application is the exchange of debt for preferred stock. The Type F Reorganization refers to corporate change in identify. Common applications include changing the corporate name, changing the corporate form (public to private corporation), and changing the place of organization such as changing the state of incorporation often to Delaware or Nevada. Finally, the Type G Reorganization is related to bankruptcy proceedings and is exceedingly complex.

The tax savings with acquisitive tax preference reorganizations are very attractive to two or more corporations wishing to combine operations. It must be emphasized that the tax preference reorganizations are often completed between co-operating entities and that following the combination the entities should work to make the process a financial and organizational success. With so many applications in the business world, theory falls short and the intended benefits of the combined entities are never realized or they are poorly misjudged.

Employee Stock Ownership Plan and Trusts (ESOP)

ESOPs are included in this section on tax preference transactions because the Federal government has passed significant legislation with substantial tax incentives to encourage employee

Chapter 17: Deal Structure and Tax Considerations in Asset and Stock Transactions

ownership of their employers. The tax incentives apply to both the Buy-side and the Sell-side of the sale of stock to the ESOP. Most importantly the ESOP, as the Buyer of stock from a selling shareholder, will be able to deduct the entire purchase price. The corporation will make tax deductible contributions to the ESOP in compliance with qualifying payroll regulations in an amount necessary to meet acquisition debt interest and principal obligations. In this manner, acquisition debt principal is deductible for taxes, the only part of the IRC where repaying debt principal is tax deductible. This is a significant advantage. For example, if the effective Federal and state income tax rate for an S corporation shareholders is 35%, a stock purchase by the ESOP in an amount of $1,000,000 will yield a tax benefit of $350,000 ($1,000,000 x 35% tax rate). Similar tax benefits exist for a C corporation.

From the Sell-side perspective, there are significant incentives for C corporations to consider ESOPs. If the shareholders sell at least 30% of the company equity in a single transaction to the ESOP, that transaction qualifies for tax treatment similar to the previously mentioned tax preference reorganizations. Under IRC Section 1042, the shareholders of the C corporation meeting the 30% test among other more minor regulations, will qualify to receive the funds from the sale of their stock tax free providing certain requirements are met. The funds will remain free of all taxes, most commonly federal and most state capital gain taxes, provided the shareholder has invested the money in qualified replacement property (QRP) within one year of the sale. As long as the shareholder remains invested in the QRP, the taxes are deferred. If at any time the QRP is sold prior to death, then a taxable event occurs and the QRP will be subject to gain based on the shareholders basis in the original stock. The deferral of transaction related taxes become permanent upon the death of the shareholder when the QRP is included in the decedent's estate, thereby avoiding any tax on the original sale of stock to the ESOP. At this point, the ESOP sale proceeds will not be subject to capital gain taxes, but the proceeds will be included in the estate of the Seller; the estate receives a step-up in basis; and is subject to estate taxes. Shareholder's in an S corporation selling to an ESOP are not eligible for the IRC Section 1042 election and will pay capital gain taxes on the transaction.

An ESOP, a qualified retirement plan under the Employee Retirement Income and Security Act when it holds a majority of its assets as stock of the plan sponsor or the company, is not subject to Federal income taxes. The most spectacular applications of ESOPs involve closely held S corporations that are 100% owned by the employees. Given an S corporation is a pass through entity for income tax purposes, the taxable income of the S corporation is passed through to its shareholders and is taxed on a prorated basis as ordinary income. Typically the S corporation will distribute cash to the shareholders in an amount sufficient for them to pay their taxes on the ordinary income allocated to them. When the S corporation is owned by the ESOP, the ESOP does not pay taxes. This means the company is a for-profit corporation without exposure to Federal and most state income taxes. Of course, a signature aspect of the ESOP is that the plan sponsor must make a market for the stock allocated into the accounts of all the employees as those employees leave the employment of the company over time. This market making mandate on the part of the company is generally referred to as the repurchase obligation, which is typically a significant long term financial obligation of the corporation to

Chapter 17: Deal Structure and Tax Considerations in Asset and Stock Transactions

its employees. This obligation is typically very manageable if the company is owned entirely or substantially by the ESOP. The deferral of paying taxes is a compelling attribute of 100% ESOP S corporations.

There has been a renaissance in ESOP installations just in the past few years. Effectively, prior to 1999 virtually all closely held company ESOPs were in C corporations, exposed to C corporation income taxes, with the combined challenge of the ESOP repurchase obligation and providing working capital to grow the business. The ability of S corporations to sponsor ESOPs has fundamentally changed the situation. ESOPs require compliance to complex Federal rules, but in the right circumstances they may be an option for shareholders. For example, one attractive application is home healthcare services. Such care providers are labor intensive and longer term success is a function of providing a high standard of service. An ESOP will reward the selling shareholders, but it will also provide an excellent benefit to the many employees on the front lines interacting with patients.

Public vs. Private Corporations

While we have assumed that most of the transactions you are likely to incur involve closely held entities, this is not always the case. There are a great many publicly held healthcare corporations that have been active in the mergers and acquisitions (M & A) arena. There are a number of key points to emphasize regarding the attributes and advantages of publicly held corporations.

Publicly traded corporations by definition have the discipline of complying with Federal listing rules and regulations. This is an exceedingly complex compliance environment requiring the most sophisticated accounting and financial reporting. These firms are typically of a size to justify the compliance expense with extensive resources.

Public companies often have a bias to favoring transactions that enhance revenue and earnings growth because their stock value is driven by both reported earnings and future anticipated results as evidenced by growth. Therefore, public companies often favor stock transactions and not asset based deals because they do not wish to incur the stepped-up basis through an allocation of purchase price to asset Classes. The higher basis in the assets in this case will lead to greater depreciation and amortization which depresses earnings. With a stock based transaction, depreciation and amortization will be at the same approximate level of the Seller just prior to the transaction. Often in the healthcare industry the target company may have considerable goodwill. From a public company financial reporting perspective, goodwill incurred from an asset purchase is not subject to amortization. Instead the goodwill is subject to annual impairment testing as part of the annual audit. Goodwill is amortized for tax reporting, creating deferred tax accounts on the books of the public corporation. Assuming the goodwill is not impaired going forward, there is no decrease in earnings due to amortization of the intangible asset.

Chapter 17: Deal Structure and Tax Considerations in Asset and Stock Transactions

Public companies also enjoy a significant advantage in financing transactions. Assume the public company is successful with a history of providing market returns to investors. The extent to which the company is able to identify acquisition candidates, it is able to pay for the acquisition in part or in whole by issuing more stock. The public company may not have to rely on debt markets as much as closely held companies. This is often a compelling advantage. If a public company finds substantial growth opportunities, it may more easily take advantage of those opportunities by being able to issue acquisition equity.

One major issue with public companies is that they typically must seek growth opportunities in revenue and profitability. In the healthcare industry there is often a fine line between obtaining profitability and faithfully providing the best possible health services. Indeed, maximizing profitability for the public company shareholders may conflict with the mission of many in the medical profession to provide the best possible care irrespective of "cost." The tension between profitability and providing healthcare services is not isolated to public corporations, but public companies are answerable to highly visible outside investors seeking a market driven competitive return on their investment.

One example of public companies flexing their considerable strengths is in the growth of retail healthcare clinics. CVS/Caremark has recently acquired Minute Clinic and Walgreens has completed the acquisition of Take Care clinics. If the acquiring public companies demonstrate the managerial competence to profitably expand this segment of revenue, they will be rewarded with access to additional financial resources to pursue the strategic plan. Public companies have a wide spectrum of acquisition options. Well managed companies will be able to attract new capital at the same time serving as a desirable acquirer. Due to the attributes of tax preference reorganizations, public companies may use their own authorized but unissued stock as transaction currency.

Conversely, there are also examples where public companies have used their strong acquisition attributes to grow too fast and irresponsibly. Regrettably, publicly held healthcare companies are subject to the growth expectations and demands of shareholders just like other public corporations. In recent years both PhyCor, Inc. and MedPartners proved to be unsustainable business models by growing too rapidly and creating unwieldy organizations.

Transaction Terms Overview

The focus here is on the most common types of business transactions. Generally, there are asset based and stock based transactions. We have divided the transactions into taxable events and tax preference transactions. The final form of the deal will be impacted by negotiations between the two sides on a wide range of terms. The Buy-side is often concerned with the time to accomplish the due diligence discovery, commonly just 2-3 months from the time a letter of intent is signed. There is a chance that something material may be missed exposing the Buy-side to unanticipated future costs, liabilities or losses. The Buyer would prefer that the Seller has some financial exposure following the close of the deal to protect against such unknown contingencies.

Chapter 17: Deal Structure and Tax Considerations in Asset and Stock Transactions

There are a number of common terms most frequently encountered in transactions. Most typically, the terms are protections for the Buy-side to manage transaction risk and have some recourse against the Sell-side if something goes wrong.

The Buyer will typically state that a certain amount of the transaction proceeds will be held in an escrow account, the "hold back" amount. The escrow is a stipulated amount agreed to by the parties that dictates a certain portion of the sale proceeds will be set aside in a designated account. This account is often maintained at a trust company or an institution independent of the parties to the transaction. This amount is withheld from payment to the Seller for a period of time, often in the range of 6 months to 1 year, although longer periods are used. When the passage of time permits distribution subject to the terms of the purchase agreement, the escrow funds are paid to the Seller. The purchase agreement typically will reference an escrow account which will have its own binding agreement. The escrow agreement should stipulate how claims are to be filed and paid to the Buy-side.

The Buy-side may ask for Sell-side financing for a percentage of the transaction amount. Sell-side financing is more common in smaller transactions as a method to help insure the Sell-side has a vested interest in the future success of the business. If Sell-side financing is requested, the Sell-side becomes a creditor to the Buy-side immediately following the transaction. It is a best practice for the Sell-side to complete a thorough credit check of the Buy-side to verify creditworthiness. It is also recommended that the Sell-side engage experienced counsel to draft the loan agreement and the note. The loan agreement must cover a wide range of contingencies such as a default on the note, acceleration of payments, calling the note, additional Sell-side rememdies, and loan guarantee. No one likes to think about loan default when the transaction is being entered and there is an upbeat mood. The Sell-side must think about the harsh reality of a default and be protected accordingly. If the Sell-side is asked to provide financing, it is critical to know if the position will be subordinate to a primary or senior lender. If that is the case, there is likely very little collateral in the company left to attach. By any other name, largely unsecured loans are often referred to a mezzanine debt, and that debt is priced to the borrower at interest rates and terms far in excess of the rates and terms extended by the primary lender. It is appropriate for the Sell-side to be compensated for the often unsecured or modestly secured credit exposure evidenced by the note.

Earn-outs and contingent payments are another example of helping insure the Sell-side has a vested interest in the company following the transaction. To make the transaction more appealing, the Buy-side may pay a future contingent payment to the seller based on operating results going forward following the transaction. From the Sell-side of the transaction, structuring a favorable contingent future payment is a function of terms. However, in health care transactions, earn-outs have a high risk of violating the Anti-kickback statute since they may be based on "future referrals." As a policy matter, an earn-out may encourage over-utilizing health services and therefore be a problem.

Once the target company is sold, the former owner is typically no longer in control, and not in charge of preparing the financial statements. The Sell-side is advised to accept an earn-out, if

Chapter 17: Deal Structure and Tax Considerations in Asset and Stock Transactions

allowed, predicated on easily verified financial information such as sales revenue or number of new accounts. Accepting an earn-out based on future profitability, with profitability determined by the new owner, is a dangerous situation. The new owner may have a vested interest in reducing or avoiding the earn-out payment as much as practicable. Clearly the Buy-side will want as much flexibility in the design and payment of the earn-out, if allowed. There are conflicting interests in such arrangements and the details need to be negotiated.

Another category of Buy-side risk management is to extend a consulting agreement or an employment agreement to the seller. From a tax standpoint, either type of financial arrangement will be ordinary income to the recipient and tax deductible to the buyer. One worthy suggestion is to insure that if there is a consulting agreement or employment agreement; services are in fact being provided for the compensation. The understanding may still be subject to offsets if something is later discovered to be misrepresented by the Sell-side. On the Sell-side a best practice is to negotiate the shortest term possible.

Non-competition agreements are typically listed in most asset and stock purchase agreements. In asset purchase agreements the non-competition clause may not be quantified. This is typically done because from the Buy-side perspective the non-competition agreement is considered an IRC Section 197 intangible asset for tax reporting purposes, and the agreement is capitalized and then amortized over a 15 year period. Even if the payouts are for a significantly shorter period of time, say 2-4 years, the agreement must still be capitalized producing a terrible cash flow timing problem for the Buy-side. Interestingly, some stock based transactions will specifically quantify the non-competition agreement, and may even err to the side of placing a significant value on the agreement. When the value of the non-competition agreement is deducted from the stock purchase price (often the case), then the value of the non-competition agreement is subject to the 15 year tax amortization regulations and the buyer will get to amortize a portion of the purchase price not available to cost recovery as part of a stock purchase.

The existence of transaction terms as those just discussed serve primarily as protections for the buyer. If the terms dictate that part of the sale proceeds will be received in succeeding years, those proceeds may qualify for installment sale treatment. Installment sale tax attributes are generally beneficial to the Seller as the transaction tax liability may be allocated to more than one fiscal year for a more balanced obligation. The installment sale potential is an example of one of the benefits that accrue to the Seller as a result of terms imposed by the Buyer.

Summary

Transactions do not just happen. They are aggressively negotiated, often by experienced personnel on both sides of the deal. Once a proposed transaction makes some sort of organic or economic sense, then the structure of the deal takes precedence to be as tax and cost efficient as possible. There is a wide array of planning techniques available to facilitate the completion of deals. As the transaction financial stakes rise, it is our experience that good professional help

Chapter 17: Deal Structure and Tax Considerations in Asset and Stock Transactions

pays, it is not a cost. The chances for an error are significant given the complexity of our rules, regulations and the market. This is one of those occasions that merits looking for the most experienced professionals with the strength of successfully completed transactions and the command the requisite resources to discharge obligations in a timely fashion.

Chapter 18

Converting Physician Practices to Tax-Exempt Status: Is There an Upside to the Downturn?

Mark O. Dietrich, CPA/ABV

Introduction

Historically, hospitals and physician practices have integrated for a variety of non-tax-related reasons. Integrated delivery systems provide hospitals with immediate direct revenues from an expanded patient base and offer the potential for substantial indirect revenues flowing from inpatient referrals. The physicians who sell their practice may benefit from having access to an established hospital and its attendant perks, such as superior managed care contracts and the ability to offer patients a wider range of services. Another particularly significant consideration, given the longstanding opposition of the Federal Trade Commission (FTC) and Department of Justice (DOJ) to physician joint-contracting efforts, includes qualification under the *Copperweld* doctrine,[1] where common legal control permits the negotiation of non-risk contracts in addition to risk-based and quality-based contracts.

Tax benefits play a role, however. When the acquiring hospital is tax-exempt, another benefit is the ability to operate the acquired physician practice on a tax exempt basis. The obvious incentive is the ability to retain the practice's profits free of income tax, but this strategy presents a variety of issues.

This article is concerned with the tax aspects of a physician practice's acquisition and conversion to tax-exempt status. Basis tax principles of the transaction are discussed first. The article then explains how to reduce the tax cost of the transaction through proper valuation techniques. The article concludes with a comment on how the current economic downturn may benefit acquiring hospitals and selling physicians by reducing their tax cost.

Basic Tax Consequences

A Section 501(c)(3)[2] hospital seeking to acquire a for-profit physician practice to operate on a tax-exempt basis typically structures the acquisition through a newly formed nonprofit corporation, of which the hospital is the sole member and ultimate governing authority. The newly formed entity purchases the practice's assets or stock if the practice is in corporate form. When the physician practice is organized as a subchapter C corporation, the selling physicians face an unavoidable "double tax" if they sell the corporation's assets to the hospital. First, the

Chapter 18: Converting Physician Practices to Tax-Exempt Status

corporation pays tax on any gain realized from the sale of its assets,[3] leaving only the after-tax proceeds available for distribution to the physician shareholders. The shareholders are then individually taxed on any distributions received from the corporation.[4] Reversing the two steps does not change the result; double taxation similarly applies if the corporation first distributes its assets to its shareholders, who then sell the assets to the hospital. The Internal Revenue Service (IRS) illustrated these principles in the following example in its 2000 Exempt Organizations Continuing Professional Education Text (EO CPE Text):

> In 1990, 10 physicians invested $50,000 each ($500,000 in total) in a C corporation to purchase land and construct a freestanding ambulatory surgery center. The ambulatory surgery center was constructed and has thrived. In 1999, the physician-owners decided sell the center to a local hospital. The hospital wanted to purchase the corporate assets instead of the stock because of liability concerns and to operate as a tax-exempt organization. Assume for this example that the C corporation's basis in its assets is $1 million and it has no liabilities. If it sells its assets to the hospital for $6 million, it will be taxed on its gain (35% x $5 million = $1.75 million), leaving $4.25 million for the physician/shareholders in liquidation. They will net about $2.57 million on the sale after paying individual tax (39.6% x $4.25 million = $1.68 million).[5]

The physician shareholders can avoid double taxation, however, by instead selling their stock in the C corporation. In a taxable stock purchase, the selling shareholders are still subject to one level of tax on the gain realized from the sale of their stock, but there is no corporate-level tax on the sale. The above example continues:

> In contrast, if the hospital buys the C corporation stock from the physicians, the physicians will be taxed $1.68 million on their gain on the stock, but the corporate tax, $1.75 million, will be deferred.[6]

The preceding example illustrates that the selling shareholders are theoretically able to increase their after-tax proceeds by $1.75 million by selling their stock in the C corporation rather than selling the corporation's assets. But, the 2000 EO CPE Text importantly points out that corporate-level tax is not eliminated; it merely shifts to the purchaser. Although the hospital could continue to defer the corporate-level tax as long as it operates the C corporation as a for-profit subsidiary, this is not an effective use of its tax-exempt status. If the hospital wishes to operate the physician practice on a tax-exempt basis, it must either convert the subsidiary to a tax-exempt organization or distribute the subsidiary's assets to itself—both options trigger taxable gain to the hospital.[7]

A hospital engaging in an arm's-length stock purchase should adjust the purchase price to account for the corporate-level tax it would eventually incur on the built-in gain. The failure to consider the tax could constitute a private benefit to the selling shareholders and implicate the anti-inurement or intermediate sanctions provisions of the Code.[8] Thus, the shareholders in the preceding example have not necessarily increased their after-tax proceeds by $1.75 million by selling stock rather than assets. An appraisal prepared in connection with such a stock transaction must consider this tax.

Chapter 18: Converting Physician Practices to Tax-Exempt Status

Valuing Intangible Assets

An arm's-length acquisition of a physician practice requires an independent appraisal, and thus a 1996 EO CPE Text discussing the valuation of medical practices has become a staple in the healthcare appraisal community.[9] Although instructional on the use of the discounted cash-flow method under the income approach, the document importantly establishes criteria for the allocation of intangible asset value that while basic to valuation theory, are often overlooked in valuing medical practices.

For example, the 1996 EO CPE Text explains that although the value of goodwill can be allocated to specific intangible assets, "the value of the latter is limited to the value of the former, as calculated under the income approach."[10] In other words, the total value of the individual intangible assets cannot exceed the total value of the medical practice net of the aggregate fair market value of the tangible assets.

The authors of the 1996 EO CPE Text also point out that intangible value is not always present in a medical practice, a fact appraisers all too frequently overlook. Rather, they mistakenly attribute value to certain intangible assets even when the discounted cash-flow method shows that the medical practice has no overall intangible value. This error often occurs with intangible assets that are typically valued using the cost method, such as medical records, assembled workforce, and trade name. Appraisers forget that using the cost method to value such intangible assets is only appropriate if the income approach first finds the presence of intangible value.

Personal vs. Enterprise Goodwill

Well-defined tax principles, originally enunciated by the United States Tax Court in *Martin Ice Cream*[11] and *Norwalk*,[12] and recently re-emphasized in *Derby*,[13] establish a framework for potentially reducing the value of corporate-level intangible assets, thus reducing the tax cost of converting a physician practice to tax-exempt status. These cases illustrate how to distinguish between personal goodwill, i.e., goodwill owned personally by the business' owners or employees, and goodwill owned by the corporation.

In *Derby*, a group of independent physicians decided to affiliate with a larger healthcare organization and sold the tangible assets of their practices to a tax-exempt medical foundation that was affiliated with multiple hospitals in an integrated delivery system. The acquiring organization, however, refused to purchase the goodwill or similar intangible assets associated with the physicians' practices, citing, in part, potential violation of the Medicare and Medicaid Anti-Kickback Statute. Instead, the physicians donated their intangibles to the tax-exempt foundation and claimed charitable contribution deductions. The Tax Court, however, denied the physicians' deductions, finding that the physicians received consideration for their intangible assets in the form of future employment with the medical foundation.

Chapter 18: Converting Physician Practices to Tax-Exempt Status

The *Derby* court observed that the terms of employment contracts—and particularly non-competition provisions—are a crucial factor in determining whether enterprise goodwill is present and whether a physician has assigned his or her professional goodwill to the practice, thereby making it a practice asset. However, many appraisers incorrectly believe that "fair market value" contemplates or requires the seller(s) agreeing to provide the buyer(s) with a non-compete agreement. This assumption is often blindly included in the valuation without confirmation, as was the case in *Derby*.

Appraisers must keep in mind that non-compete agreements can be independently valued, and that such agreements do not contain standard provisions. The nature of the included (or excluded) provisions drives the value of non-compete agreements. Moreover, different states have different statutory and judicial precedents on what is and what is not enforceable in such an agreement, and these also may have a consequential effect on value. It is more accurate to state that "fair market value" contemplates understanding the terms of the transaction and the laws that govern it before attempting to assign value to the whole or its component parts.

Derby also emphasized the necessity of using negotiated post-transaction compensation in the valuation model. Reasonable compensation is a critical aspect of determining whether and to what extent any enterprise goodwill (as distinct from personal goodwill) is present, and how much of that enterprise goodwill would be allocable to a non-compete agreement. A November 2005 article in the *Journal of Accountancy* articulated why an accurate valuation must incorporate compensation:

> If the selling physician(s) still will be employed by the practice after the sale, the cash flow the buyer is purchasing—the subject of the valuation— can't be known without including a realistic amount of post-sale compensation in the valuation model.[14]

The threshold question in such a valuation is relatively easy to state, if difficult to appraise or value: How much of the practice's value would be lost if the physicians competed/were able to compete with the practice following conversion. Importantly, this question applies *whether or not* the physicians have a pre-existing non-compete agreement, as it is the basis for the methodology used to value that non-compete agreement.

The valuation method's mechanics are beyond the scope of this article but can be summarized as follows:

1. Determine reasonable compensation under the fair market value standard for the physicians post-conversion.

2. Determine the value of the entity assuming that non-compete agreements are in place based on historical and forecasted entity cash-flows using the discounted cash-flow method.

3. Allocate that value first to working capital assets (cash, receivables, inventory), then to property and equipment, and finally any remainder to intangible assets in the manner contemplated by the Residual Method of Allocation described in the regulations under Section 338.

Chapter 18: Converting Physician Practices to Tax-Exempt Status

4. Allocate that intangible value first to any readily identifiable intangible assets, such as a below market lease on real property assumable by a purchaser, trade name, trained workforce, patient charts, or others that the buyer could retain if the seller(s) competed. (Trained workforce contemplates an enforceable non-solicitation provision; patient chart valuation requires an understanding of the extent to which a patient requesting transfer of their personal health information to a new practice entity could be charged).

5. Any remaining value is attributable to the sellers' non-compete agreement (an ordinary income component) and personal goodwill (a capital asset component).

6. Assess and quantify the entity cash-flows that would be lost if the seller(s) competed post-transaction.

7. Revisit any allocation in step three above to identifiable intangible assets.

8. Assess and quantify the probability that the seller(s) would, in fact, compete post-transaction.[15]

9. The quantified probability is applied to the forecasted cash-flow expected to be lost as a result of competition then discounted to present value to determine the non-compete's value. This step must consider the enforceability of a non-compete in the applicable jurisdiction.

10. The balance is a capital asset in the nature of personal goodwill of the seller(s).

Hypothetical Sale

Appraisers are often confused by the concept of the hypothetical buyer and seller in the fair market value standard. They mistakenly believe that it requires the use of hypothetical assumptions such as an enforceable non-compete agreement, even when the interest being valued has no such agreements in place.

Appraisers must understand that a valuation in an actual transaction is significantly different than a valuation based upon a hypothetical sale. Valuations accompanying an estate and gift tax reporting, litigation, or a property division for marital dissolution, unlike a business acquisition, lack transactional documents and do require the appraiser to make a variety of assumptions.

An interest in the assets or equity of a private company is a specific basket of legal and contractual rights and obligations and economic risks and rewards. Each of that basket's characteristics must be evaluated to determine at what price a member of the universe of hypothetical buyers and sellers would transact. The "hypothetical" aspect of the valuation in a real transaction is what buyer and seller would pay for the specific business or business interest being transacted *as reflected in the transaction documents.*

Chapter 18: Converting Physician Practices to Tax-Exempt Status

Understanding this difference is critical in a healthcare transaction because failure to do so may implicate the Anti-Kickback Statute, Stark Law, or other civil and criminal penalty provisions. It is perhaps easier to understand within the concept of post-closing adjustments in an actual transaction. A typical post-closing adjustment in the purchase of the stock or equity of a business would be an increase or decrease in the sales price based upon the actual measure of the liabilities assumed and paid; in an asset transaction, those liabilities would typically not be assumed. Another adjustment would be for any difference in the value of accounts receivable purchased versus ultimately collected, if they are purchased at all. Certainly, a hospital purchasing a physician practice for a value that includes the accounts receivable when they are not transferred would be placed in significant jeopardy. Paying an amount that assumes a non-compete is in place without obtaining one as part of the transaction should be viewed no differently.

Advantages of a Down Economy

The current troubled economic times may offer an unforeseen and counterintuitive benefit to hospitals and physicians seeking to integrate. Namely, the depressed economy may produce depressed valuations of physician practices. This might not sound like a reward, but lower valuations translate to reduced tax costs in converting physician practices to tax-exempt status.

One cause for lower valuations is that perceived risk is significantly higher in the current environment than any other time in recent memory. Risk and value are inversely related. Another factor is that access to capital is significantly more difficult. Despite heretofore unseen low interest rates, many entities are unable to borrow money at any rate. Inability to access debt capital in turn requires increasing amounts of more-expensive equity capital. But as the stock market indicates, that well has been reduced to a trickle.

An appraiser typically captures these factors in the valuation multiple through development of the discount rate or cost of capital. Traditional methods of developing that multiple, however, do not capture the current combination of increased risk and decreased availability of capital.

In addition to lower enterprise values, increased marketability discounts— including consideration of liquidity factors—may be available for conversions taking place now. As the economic depression reduces the pool of potential buyers, it is becoming more difficult to find a suitable acquirer. A smaller market thus warrants consideration of a larger valuation discount for lack of marketability.

Conclusion

The contractual agreements a physician practice entity has in place with its owner and non-owner physicians determine how much of the goodwill or intangible value is owned by the practice and how much is owned personally by the physicians. To the extent that the enforceability of a non-compete, non-solicitation, trade secrets, or other provision is limited or barred

Chapter 18: Converting Physician Practices to Tax-Exempt Status

by state law, that portion of the agreement will have less or conceivably no value. A practice owned by physicians that has no post-termination non-compete agreements does not contractually own the personal goodwill of those physicians and therefore should not recognize a taxable gain on that personal goodwill in a conversion to tax-exempt status.

---

1. *See Copperweld v. Independence Tube*, 467 U.S. 752 (1984).
2. Unless otherwise specified, all section references are to the Internal Revenue Code of 1986, as amended (Code).
3. Code Section 1001.
4. Code Sections 301 and 311.
5. Charles F. Kaiser III and Thomas Miller, IRS Exempt Organizations Continuing Professional Education Text for FY 2000, Topic U, "Treas. Reg. Section 1.337(d)-4 and Exempt Organizations" (2000 EO CPE Text), at p. 3 of the PDF, *available at* www.irs.gov/pub/irs-tege/eotopicu00.pdf.
6. *Id.* at p. 3 of the PDF.
7. Code Sections 311 and 337(b)(2); *see* Treas. Reg. Section 1.337(d)-4.
8. *See* 2000 EO CPE Text, *supra* note 5, at p. 2 of the PDF.
9. Charles F. Kaiser and Amy Henchey, IRS Exempt Organizations Continuing Professional Education Text for FY 1996, Topic Q, "Valuation of Medical Practices" (1996 EO CPE Text), *available at* www.irs.gov/pub/irs-tege/eotopicq96.pdf.
10. *Id.* at p. 22 of the PDF.
11. *Martin Ice Cream v. Commissioner*, 110 T.C. 189 (1998).
12. *Norwalk v. Commissioner*, T.C. Memo. 1998-279; *see Goodwill Requires Enforceable Covenant Not To Compete*, *CPA Expert* (Spring 1999).
13. *Derby v. Commissioner*, T.C. Memo. 2008-45.
14. *Medical Practices: A BV Rx*, J. ACCOUNTANCY (Nov. 2005).
15. For litigation, alternative damage causation theories may be relevant such as violation of fiduciary obligations or intent to defraud via the sale, among others.

Chapter 19

Identifying and Measuring Personal Goodwill in a Professional Practice[1]

By Mark O. Dietrich, CPA/ABV[2]

In many situations, most notably valuation for marital dissolution and allocation of purchase price for tax or financial reporting purposes, distinguishing personal goodwill from enterprise goodwill is a critical undertaking.

In the marital arena, personal goodwill is not a divisible asset in some jurisdictions, and the status is uncertain in many, and therefore cannot be awarded by the Court. Given this norm, it is curious that many valuation analysts fail to provide evidence as to the separate values of personal and enterprise goodwill.

In tax planning, particularly for C Corporations, allocating the proceeds of a sale of a business to personal goodwill and/or a noncompete agreement can reduce or eliminate the amount recognized as corporate gain and the related corporate level tax. In valuation for purposes of a sale of a business, properly attributing value to different intangible assets may be critical to both buyer and seller obtaining the proper measure of the bargain.

There are two fundamental issues in differentiating personal from enterprise goodwill:

1. Identifying which portions of cash flow are attributable directly to the individual's characteristics.

2. Identifying which cash flows attributable to otherwise enterprise-level tangibles and intangibles would be lost if the individual competed.

Illustrative Examples

1. Personal goodwill flowing from individual characteristics:

- A physician at a renowned medical center is well known for his skill in diagnosing complex diseases. His ability to do so is due to his intellectual skills, knowledge base, and experience in similar cases.

- An attorney has won several high profile cases because of her ability to relate to the jury and make complex issues understandable. In her current firm, she is also the principal "rainmaker."

Chapter 19: Identifying and Measuring Personal Goodwill in a Professional Practice

2. Enterprise goodwill flowing from individual characteristics:

- The same physician is part of a group practice. Subsequent to the diagnosis, other group physicians, some of whom are employed, may treat the patient. The employed physicians generate a profit in excess of their compensation that the practice owners share.

- The same attorney has attracted dozens of new cases and is unable to handle most of them, which are assigned to other partners or members of the growing staff. The "points system" in the law firm allocates profits based in large part upon who generated the underlying business.

> *Observation:* *The second set of examples is perhaps subject to some dispute in jurisdictions that treat personal goodwill as a non-divisible asset in marital dissolution. Some judges may treat any profit resulting from the personal goodwill of a marital litigant as non-divisible. For example, in a Florida appellate case (Weinstock v. Weinstock 634 So. 2d at 777), the Court ruled that a dental practice had no divisible goodwill because the expert testified that a noncompete agreement would be required in any sale of the practice as well as the dentist's continued presence for a six-month patient transition period. Valuation analysts need to obtain a clear understanding from legal counsel as to the proper interpretation of state law or precedent.*

Personal goodwill, then, is the asset that generates cash profits of the enterprise that are attributed to the business generating characteristics of the individual, and may include any profits that would be lost if the individual were not present.[3] The value of a noncompete with that individual is the value of those cash profits, adjusted for the probability of the individual competing in each future year where the potential of competition exists. Thus, the noncompete is a portion of the value of personal goodwill and cannot exceed that value. Unless the probability of competition is 100%, the personal goodwill will always exceed the value of the noncompete.

Enforceability of Noncompetes

How much is an unenforceable promise to pay worth? Or, better yet, how much will the hypothetical buyer pay for an unenforceable contract with a hypothetical seller? "Not much" would seem to be the answer. To illustrate the concepts involved in factoring enforceability into the value of a noncompete, the following section looks at the statutes and precedents of several states.

> *Observation:* *The enforceability of noncompetes is a volatile area of law. Courts in many states have moved to restrict enforceability when public policy is an issue, such as noncompetes that by their nature restrict the free access of a patient to his or her physician. Other states have liberally interpreted noncompetes, finding that separate consideration is not necessary.*

Chapter 19: Identifying and Measuring Personal Goodwill in a Professional Practice

Representative State: Texas

The Texas Business and Commercial Code, §§15.50 provides that in order for a noncompete to be enforceable, it must be "ancillary to or part of an otherwise enforceable agreement at the time the agreement is made." If there is only an at-will employment relationship, the covenant is not enforceable. The term "at-will" appears to be interpreted as one in which the agreement has no specific term. If the relationship is other than at-will, the limitations of the covenant in time, scope, and geographic area must be no more than necessary to protect the goodwill of the employer or other entity.

Noncompetes among physicians are subject to a special set of provisions. To be enforceable, the agreement must conform to the statutory provisions including not denying the physician access to a list of his patients whom he had seen or treated within one year of termination of the contract or employment and the covenant must provide for a buy out of the covenant by the physician at a reasonable price.

Therefore, the value of the covenant must exclude the value of that patient list.[4] The provision in subparagraph (C) would appear to require that the covenantor[5] receive an electronic copy of medical records if they are kept in that fashion. As a logical consequence, the enterprise value of a medical practice in Texas is different from an identical practice located in another state that has no limitations on the enforceability of a noncompete and does not require that the physician be given a patient list! Where fair market value is the standard, hypothetical buyers and sellers must be assumed to be familiar with the law in the state in which the transaction takes place—as should valuation analysts.

Representative State: Pennsylvania

It is likely that a November 2002 Pennsylvania Supreme Court decision has significantly altered the law as it applies to the transfer of a business including employment contracts. The case, Hess v. Gebhard & Co., Inc., involved the sale of an insurance agency. As an employee of the agency, Hess's employment contract contained a covenant not to compete within a 25-mile radius for a five-year post-employment term. Significantly, the contract contained no language regarding the transferability of the contract.

The related purchase and sale agreement allocated no value to the Hess employment contract. Hess did not continue employment with the purchaser4 and sought a position with another insurance agency. In the process, Hess solicited a customer of his former agency. As a result of threatened legal action, the new agency did not hire Hess. Hess then sued for interference with contractual relations.

The Pennsylvania Supreme Court ultimately held that the noncompete was not transferable to a subsequent purchaser absent a specific transferability provision: "We hold that a restrictive

Chapter 19: Identifying and Measuring Personal Goodwill in a Professional Practice

covenant not to compete, contained in an employment agreement, is not assignable to the purchasing business entity, in the absence of a specific assignability provision, where the covenant is included in a sale of assets." Perhaps a different result would have been reached if a sale of stock had been at issue.6 It seems that, in Pennsylvania at least, when valuing the assets of a business, the analyst should read any employment contracts to see if the noncompete is transferable.

> ***Observation:*** *Valuators should be aware that the various states might have one standard for enforcing covenants not to compete in an employment setting and another for enforcing a covenant in a purchase and sale of a business.*

Reasonable Compensation

In the typical valuation of any professional practice or small business, the analyst's key assumption relates to reasonable compensation for services—there will not be any excess earnings to capitalize or any cash profit to discount if the professional does not earn more than "reasonable compensation." The higher the reasonable compensation relative to the total compensation earned (of course) the lower the value of any goodwill.

Arguably, if there is no business/practice profit before normalization of the income statements, then some portion of the compensation earned must be coming from the return on tangible assets of the enterprise, namely net working capital and fixed assets. Later in this article, in the section titled "Mechanics of Valuation," we address the importance of this analysis. The analyst must understand not only how much compensation is earned, but also what the sources of that compensation are.

The other critical aspect of determining reasonable compensation is the work effort of the individual, typically referred to as "productivity." Many analysts determine reasonable compensation for their valuation models by taking the median or mean (average) compensation for a particular position, without considering the individual's productivity compared with the median or mean.

For example, the Medical Group Management Association (MGMA) data is commonly used for valuing physician practices. MGMA reports not only median and mean compensation, but also the 25th, 75th and 90th percentiles of compensation. It reports the same percentiles for productivity, as to both charges and collections for professional services. The analyst should ask, "Can I hire a replacement physician for this practice at a median salary if the practice owner is producing at the 75th percentile?"[7] Given that most medical practices, as well as accounting and law practices, compensate their senior associates and partners at a percentage of production, the answer is almost surely "NO." For those practices and businesses in which compensation is a function of piecework (patients seen, hours billed/collected, etc.), reasonable compensation must be a function of productivity.

Chapter 19: Identifying and Measuring Personal Goodwill in a Professional Practice

Proper compensation analysis is critical to the overall quest to value goodwill because an understatement of reasonable compensation will result in an overstatement of goodwill. To the extent that reasonable compensation is understated, the amount of personal goodwill included in total goodwill will be greater. Alternatively stated, some portion of the personal goodwill issue can often be minimized by properly addressing reasonable compensation.

Categories of Intangibles

Perhaps the most easily identified discreet intangible in a professional practice is the value of a trained workforce, or workforce-in-place. This asset is also one of the easiest to measure, typically being based upon a percentage of payroll reflecting longevity and skill, along with training and recruiting costs.[8] An initial analysis should be considered to determine if the practice owners can leverage junior or support staff such as associates (as in a law firm), staff (as in an accounting firm). For example, one of the reasons dental practices are readily saleable and at significant prices is that they afford the owner an opportunity to profit from providing cleaning (prophylaxis) through hygienists. Workforce-in-place should thus be divided into two components: one for direct revenue producers such as dental hygienists or staff accountants, and another for support personnel such as medical assistants, secretaries, and the like. Direct revenue producers can be valued similar to any other intangible using their associated profit stream, while support personnel can be valued in the conventional manner based upon costs of recruiting and training, as a percentage of payroll.

A Simplified Example[9]

The analyst determines that $45,000 of annual free cash flow is derived from profits on non-partner professional staff who are direct revenue producers, and that this profit stream will continue to grow at a constant rate.

Free cash flow from direct revenue producers	45,000
Cap rate from weighted average cost of capital	16.17%
Value	278,336

Often missed in the analysis of personal goodwill is the potential impact of the presence or lack of a nonsolicitation provision. Such a provision would preclude the signer from seeking to employ the practice's personnel after terminating. As such, a portion of the value of workforce-in-place can be attributable to the noncompete if it contains a nonsolicitation provision and the analyst believes that certain employees would leave if the covenantor were no longer with the business. This could result from the covenantor operating a competing business or simply no longer being associated with the sold enterprise. A standard Purchase and Sales document would typically contain both a noncompete and a nonsolicitation provision. Nonsolicitation provisions may also apply to the business's clients, patients, and customers.

Chapter 19: Identifying and Measuring Personal Goodwill in a Professional Practice

Mechanics of Valuation

It is critical that the analyst consider the three principal categories of assets included in business enterprise value (BEV) when assessing the profits attributable to the seller: net working capital (NWC), fixed assets, and intangible assets. Just as the right-hand side of the BEV equation has a rate of return or discount rate for each of equity and debt, the left-hand side has a return on each of the assets. It does not seem reasonable for the return on net working capital or fixed assets to be attributed in its entirety to a seller and therefore the noncompete.

Once the BEV is known, it is typically possible to calculate the value of NWC using the historical balance sheets; certainly, if a DCF is used, the working capital requirement needs to be estimated. Fixed assets can be valued by an appraisal. Once these two values are known, they are subtracted from the BEV to determine the aggregate value of the intangibles.

Constructing a noncompete DCF is best accomplished after estimating the value of each of the asset categories; it may also require calculating the value of certain individual components for each category, such as the workforce-in-place described above. This assists the analyst in gauging a reasonable total value for the noncompete. The analyst should also consider whether any portion of the value of fixed assets or working capital is attributable to the covenantor.

One approach to making this determination is to differentiate between the going concern value of these two categories of assets—which requires to one degree or another the continued presence or forbearance of the seller—and their liquidation or other value. For example, fixed assets are likely to have a significantly greater value in use as part of a going concern than as an assemblage not in a going concern or in liquidation. In liquidation, a buyer will not pay for the in-use value and is likely to consider the cost to transport and a mark-up to resell. The value of working capital may or may not be different in a going concern context depending upon the collectibility of receivables for example.

Estimating that value may also require establishing a discount rate for each asset and allocating the cash flow based upon the discount rate.[10] The weighted average of those discount rates must, of course, be equal to the weighted average cost of capital (WACC) determined from the right hand side of the BEV equation. Therefore, the analyst must also consider the portion of the value of each category that would be financed with debt.

> ***Observation:*** *Notwithstanding the disdain with which some in the valuation community regard the Excess Earnings method, it is the classic example of a left-hand side of the equation approach to capitalization rates, and, by adding the appropriate long-term growth rate, deriving discount rates. Unfortunately, users of the method rarely calculate the capitalization rate derived by weighting the respective returns on tangibles and intangibles and comparing it to the traditional WACC approach for reasonableness.*
>
> Note: *The weighted average cap rate based on assets should then be used in the Capitalization of Cash flows method.*

Chapter 19: Identifying and Measuring Personal Goodwill in a Professional Practice

Table 1 shows the result of a DCF valuation along with an allocation of fair market to the three major categories of assets and their percentage of total BEV.

Table 2 is the calculation of the WACC used in the DCF model; note that the WACC is based upon the fair market value of debt and equity, not book values.

Table 1		
	Value	% of Value
Fixed Assets	975,000	34.97%
Net Working Capital	1,064,217	38.17%
Intangible Value	749,141	26.87%
	2,788,358	**100.00%**

Table 2				
	Weight	Capital	Discount rate	WACC
Debt	25.00%	697,089	3.54%	0.89%
Equity	75.00%	2,091,268	23.71%	17.78%
		2,788,358		**18.67%**

Table 3 is the computation of the WACC, based on returns for the individual categories of Assets. Fixed assets are financed with 50% debt (the pre-tax rate is 6%, the after-tax rate is 3.54%, using a 41% tax rate) and 50% equity; net working capital is financed with the remainder of the debt and the balance with equity. Intangible assets are financed entirely with equity.

Table 3									
Category (Cat)	Value	%	Debt	Cost of Debt	Equity	Cost of Equity	Cat WACC	Return	Total WACC
Fixed Assets	975,000	34.97%	487,500	3.54%	487,500	17.25%	10.40%	101,351	3.63%
Net Working Capital	1,064,217	38.17%	209,589	3.54%	854,628	17.50%	14.75%	156,979	5.63%
Intangible Value	749,141	26.87%			749,141	35.00%	35.00%	262,199	9.40%
	2,788,358	100.00%	697,089		2,091,268			520,530	18.67%

Chapter 19: Identifying and Measuring Personal Goodwill in a Professional Practice

The analyst determines equity returns for each asset category. The aggregate weighting should agree with the WACC used in the original DCF.[11] The appropriate discount rates will vary from industry to industry and subject to subject. Bear in mind that intangible assets are generally the most risky and therefore have the highest expected rates of return.

Table 4 is a condensed version of the DCF from which the Table 3 values are determined.[12] The analyst has concluded that a net of 55% of the free cash flow is attributable to the seller and would be lost to the buyer in the event of competition.[13] This is approximately equal to that percentage of the total return represented by the intangibles as reflected in Table 3. This does not suggest, however, that only intangible value is relevant to the determination of cash flows attributable to the seller, since some of the workforce-in-place value might not be lost in the event of competition, and some of the fixed asset value might be lost. For example, if the valuation subject was a medical practice using medical equipment for diagnostic testing, the departure of a physician might lower the volume of tests and therefore the value in use of the equipment.[14] The analyst can also utilize these allocated cash flows to assess the reasonableness of the annual cash payment for a noncompete.

Tables 5, 6 and 7 show the calculation of the probability-adjusted lost cash profits assuming that competition begins in year 1 (Table 5), year 2 (Table 6) and year 3 (Table 7). In this example, if competition does not commence before the end of year 3, it is assumed never to commence.

			Table 5: Year 1			
Year	1	2	3	4	5	Terminal
PV Net Profits Attributed to Sellers	224,822	213,818	189,054	158,683	104,351	503,451
Net % Attributed To Seller	55.00%	55.00%	55.00%	55.00%	55.00%	55.00%
Net $Profit Attributed To Seller	123,652	117,600	103,980	87,275	57,393	276,898
Probability Of Competing	10.00%	10.00%	10.00%	10.00%	10.00%	10.00%
PV of Lost Profits by year	12,365	11,760	10,398	8,728	5,739	27,690
PV of Year 1 Lost Profits	**76,680**					

Chapter 19: Identifying and Measuring Personal Goodwill in a Professional Practice

Table 6: Year 2						
Year	1	2	3	4	5	Terminal
PV Net Profits Attributed to Sellers		213,818	189,054	158,683	104,351	503,451
Net % Attributed To Seller		55.00%	55.00%	55.00%	55.00%	55.00%
Net $Profit Attributed To Seller		117,600	103,980	87,275	57,393	276,898
Probability Of Competing		18.00%	18.00%	18.00%	18.00%	18.00%
PV Of Lost Profits		21,168	18,716	15,710	10,331	49,842
PV of Year 2 Lost Profits	115,766					

Table 7: Year 3						
Year	1	2	3	4	5	Terminal
PV Net Profits Attributed to Sellers			189,054	158,683	104,351	503,451
Net % Attributed To Seller			55.00%	55.00%	55.00%	55.00%
Net $Profit Attributed To Seller			103,980	87,275	57,393	276,898
Probability Of Competing			21.60%	21.60%	21.60%	21.60%
PV Of Lost Profits			22,460	18,851	12,397	59,810
PV of Year 3 Lost Profits	113,518					

Total: **$305,964**

Chapter 19: Identifying and Measuring Personal Goodwill in a Professional Practice

At first glance, Tables 5, 6 and 7 may appear to count the same cash flows multiple times.[15] The way to be certain that there is no double counting is to check the Joint Probability Table (see Table 8). The probability of possible outcomes must total exactly 100%. For example, adding the probability-adjusted present value of lost profits for year 3 from each of Tables 5, 6 and 7 totals $51,574, less than the total present value of year 3's profits attributable to the sellers of $103,980. Assuming the rest of the model is properly constructed, the probability check assures that there is no double counting.[16]

If the probability of competing were 100% at the beginning of year 1, the value of the noncompete (see Table 4) would be $766,798, slightly more than the total intangible value. This value could be compared to the value of workforce-in-place and any other discretely measured intangibles while considering the probability that the sellers would take some portion of the value of those intangibles with them if they competed, as well as any diminution in the value in use of fixed assets. The $766,798 represents all of the present value of future profits attributable to the seller and is therefore also the value of personal goodwill.[17]

	Table 8: Joint Probability Table							
	Year 1		Year 2		Year 3		Joint Probability
	Compete	Don't Compete	Compete	Don't Compete	Compete	Don't Compete	
Compete Year 1	10.00%						10.00%
Compete Year 2		90.00%	20.00%				18.00%
Compete Year 3		90.00%		80.00%	30.00%		21.60%
Never Compete		90.00%		80.00%		70.00%	50.40%
							100.00%

The distinction between the value of personal goodwill and the value of a noncompete is less important in equitable distribution than for tax purposes. For the latter, the noncompete is ordinary income to the covenantor while personal goodwill should be long-term capital gain.[18] It is prudent for the analyst to value both the noncompete and the personal goodwill where tax considerations are important.

In the following article, a single period capitalization model is explained and the author summarizes the key tasks for the valuation analyst.

Chapter 19: Identifying and Measuring Personal Goodwill in a Professional Practice

The author expresses his gratitude to Kevin R. Yeanoplos, CPA/ABV, ASA for his thoughtful critique of the concepts explored in this article, as well as for his corrections to my use of English language grammar.

---

1. Copyright 2005 by AICPA, reproduced with permission. Opinions of the authors are their own and do not necessarily reflect policies of the AICPA.
2. Mark O. Dietrich, CPA/ABV, is with Dietrich & Wilson, PC, Framingham, Massachusetts.
3. Subject to jurisdictional precedents.
4. Always ask: Would the hypothetical buyer pay for something they already own?
5. He was not offered a position he was interested in.
6. And, may I further add that this is but one dramatic difference between asset sales and stock sales, suggesting that a hypothetical buyer should pay a different price for assets than for stock.
7. Certainly, if one looks at Tax Court cases involving reasonable compensation, the Court always focuses on hours worked, responsibilities, etc. Why should it be any different in 'regular' valuation engagements?
8. See, for example, Financial Valuation, Hitchner et al; Medical Practice Valuation Guidebook, Mark O. Dietrich.
9. I use capitalization of cash flows here assuming the profit stream qualifies for capitalization.
10. This process is described in Financial Valuation as well as Valuation for Financial Reporting, Mard, Hitchner, Hyden, Zyla.
11. This is easier said than done using a DCF and individual WACCs for each asset category because discount rates (WACCs) are different for each category and there is not a linear relationship between discount rates and present value; the solution can only be found iteratively. It is comparatively easy to do using capitalization rates since the cash flow is fixed in the first period.
12. Note that the free cash flow in any year is not equal to the "return" shown in Table 3. As noted earlier, an iterative process is required in the actual reconciliation of the individual WACCs with the entity WACC, in part because year to year cash flows are, in fact, variable, as shown in Table 4.
13. As more fully explained in the original article, there may be a difference between the gross profits attributable to the sellers and what profits the buyer would lose if the sellers competed. This gives recognition to such intangibles as location.
14. The analyst could isolate the profit on the equipment and determine that profit's present value.
15. As noted by one reviewer, thereby prompting this explanation.
16. The second test, as discussed in the following paragraph, is to determine the value of the noncompete if the probability of competition is 100%; any probability less than 100% in year 1 should result in a lower value for the noncompete.
17. I caution that the example has personal goodwill in excess of total intangible value. I do not mean to imply or suggest that this is, or is not, the norm or that the analyst should not carefully consider the implications.
18. With respect to tax issues, see, e.g., Martin Ice Cream 110 TC 189 (1998) and Norwalk v. Commissioner TC Memo 1998-279. The full-text Court opinion of Martin is included online.

Chapter 20

Identifying and Measuring Personal Goodwill in a Professional Practice—Part II: Using the Single Period Capitalization Model[1]

By Mark O. Dietrich, CPA/ABV[2]

As noted in the footnotes to the discounted cash flow (DCF) model used in Part I of this article, it is very difficult to devise a weighted average cost of capital (WACC) for each asset category, allocate the cash flow to each category, and get a net present value that agrees to the enterprise-level cash flow discounted to present value. Although a single period capitalization model is not appropriate for those circumstances in which the future growth rate is not the same for all years, it is much easier to use and understand.

In this example, which might be representative of an approach in many jurisdictions for marital dissolution purposes, the following data were used.

Table 1: Calculation of WACC Cap Rate					
	WACC	Equity Only			
Discount Rate	41.86%	49.04%			
Growth Rate	2.50%	2.50%			
Capitalization Rate	**39.36%**	**46.54%**			

		FMV	Percent	Return	Weighted
Debt	4.00%	30,000	24.49%	0.98%	
Equity	46.54%	92,500	75.51%	35.14%	
Cap Rate: Tangibles		122,500	100.00%	36.12%	

Practice Intangibles	55,341	31.12%	46.54%	14.48%
Practice Tangibles	122,500	68.88%	36.12%	24.88%
Cap Rate—Weighted Average Cost Of Capital	**177,841**	100.00%		**39.36%**

Debt		30,000	16.87%	4.00%	0.67%
Equity		147,841	83.13%	46.54%	38.69%
Cap Rate—Weighted Average Cost Of Capital		**177,841**	100.00%		**39.36%**

Chapter 20: Identifying and Measuring Personal Goodwill in a Professional Practice—Part II

The WACC cap rate3 is based upon the fair market value (FMV) of the business enterprise. From the right-hand side of the balance sheet—debt and equity—the weighted average cap rate is based upon $30,000 of debt costing 4%, net of growth at 2.50%, with the balance of the capital structure consisting of equity. From the left-hand side of the balance sheet, the weighted average cap rate is based upon the pre-tax cap rates applicable to tangibles and intangibles. The result must be the same in both cases.

The capitalization of cash flows method reflects all pre-tax cash earnings in excess of reasonable compensation capitalized at the cap rate derived from the WACC of 39.36%. The excess earnings method capitalizes excess earnings on tangibles at the rates of return applicable to the portion financed with debt, $30,000, and the portion financed with equity, $92,500. These may be based upon the actual balance sheet of the valuation subject, or upon optimal mix of debt and equity, depending upon the analyst's assessment.

Table 2: Capitalization of Cashflows	
Normalized 2002 Earnings	460,000
Fair Market Earnings	390,000
Cashflow After Reasonable Compensation	70,000
Capitalization Rate	39.36%
Business Enterprise Value	**177,841**

Note that the two methods produce exactly the same value. If used correctly, the WACC cap rate derived from either the left- or right-hand side of the balance sheet when applied to all enterprise cash flows will yield the same value as the excess earnings method, which splits those cash flows into two components.

The excess earnings grow at a constant rate of 2.50% into perpetuity. Table II-4 values the noncompete assuming that the probability of competition is 100%, as it may be in many valuations for marital dissolution purposes. The base valuation reflects a DCF model with a uniform growth rate of 2.50%. Note that this DCF produces exactly the same value as the capitalization of cash flows and capitalization of excess earnings method.4

The section of Table 4 entitled "Noncompete Valuation–Using WACC" values the cash flows attributable to the seller using the WACC of 41.86%. This is less than the cost of equity of 49.04% and, therefore, results in a higher value. Use of the WACC would be appropriate if the analyst concludes that the cash flows attributable to the seller are a uniform blend of enterprise level cash flows from both tangibles and intangibles. The section of Table 4 entitled "Noncompete Valuation–Using Equity Discount Rate" values the cash flows attributable to the seller using the equity discount rate of 49.04%, and results in a lower value. This would be appropriate if the analyst concludes that the cash flows attributable to the seller are limited to those associated with intangibles. The value is identical to the value of intangibles previously determined. This is due to the probability of competition being 100%.

Chapter 20: Identifying and Measuring Personal Goodwill in a Professional Practice—Part II

Table 3: Capitalization of Excess Earnings

Normalized 2002 Earnings			460,000
Fair Market Earnings			390,000
Excess Earnings			70,000
Return On Practice Tangible Value: Debt Capital	30,000	4.00%	(1,200)
Return On Practice Tangible Value: Equity Capital	92,500	46.54%	(43,046)
	122,500		
Excess Earnings Attributable To Intangibles			25,754
Capitalization Rate			46.54%
Practice Intangible Value			55,341
Practice Tangibles			122,500
Business Enterprise Value			177,841

Probability of Competition

In addition to the factors discussed in the first part of this article, the analyst should consider how the noncompete is paid for. Payments are often made annually over the period of time that the covenant is in place as part of the inducement to the covenantor not to compete. Such a payment structure is likely to reduce the probability of competition.

Key Conclusions

Personal goodwill is the asset that generates cash profits of the enterprise that are attributed to the business generating characteristics of the individual and may include any profits that would be lost if the individual was not present.

Tasks for the Analyst

- Identify which portions of cash flow are attributable directly to the individual's characteristics and identify which cash flows attributable to otherwise enterprise-level intangibles would be lost if the individual competed.

Chapter 20: Identifying and Measuring Personal Goodwill in a Professional Practice—Part II

- Have a clear understanding from legal counsel of the proper interpretation of state law or precedent as to the value of a noncompete—and, therefore, the business itself. An unenforceable contract has little if any value. Even enforceable agreements are subject to "the hazards of litigation."5 Similarly, the analyst should read all contracts between the valuation subject and its employees or others that may have a bearing on "who owns what" and obtain clarification from counsel as appropriate.

- Conduct a proper reasonable compensation analysis because an understatement of reasonable compensation will result in an overstatement of goodwill.

- Estimate the fair-market value of the three principal categories of assets included in business enterprise value (BEV): net working capital (NWC), fixed assets and intangible assets.

- Consider the need to value individual intangible assets, such as workforce in place. Recognize that a portion of the value of the workforce in place could be attributable to the noncompete if the agreement contains a nonsolicitation provision.

- Construct a joint probability table to be certain that the sum of the probability of competing and not competing is exactly 100%.

---

1. Copyright 2005 by AICPA, reproduced with permission. Opinions of the authors are their own and do not necessarily reflect policies of the AICPA.
2. Mark O. Dietrich, CPA/ABV, is with Dietrich and Wilson, PC, Framingham, Massachusetts.
3. Technically, it is the capitalization rate derived from the WACC, the latter being the discount rate.
4. Using end of period cash flows. It will not produce the same result if the mid-period convention is used, since that convention results in a higher value.
5. A term of art used to explain why unwinnable cases are won and unlosable cases are lost.

Chapter 21

Lost Profits for Physician Practices

By Mark Dietrich, CPA/ABV

Unlike lost profits pertaining to other businesses, claims for lost profits in connection with physician practices are typically defined in terms of loss of compensation. As such, for the typical small practice, a lost profits analysis might look much the same as a physician's claim for lost earnings in a personal injury case, although the loss period is likely to be different.

Larger practices and/or those with ancillary testing capability such as imaging and laboratory services may have more traditional lost profits damages claims, as might those practices with greater leverage over non-owner physicians or physician extenders such as nurse practitioners and physician assistants. A good example would be a medical practice's claim for damages resulting from the alleged violation of a non-compete/non-solicitation agreement by a former employee. In this situation, the practice could lose profits related to ancillary testing revenues and from losing the violator's patients. It could also incur recruiting and training costs for replacing the lost employee(s), and losses due to the unabsorbed overhead that revenues from the violator formerly covered.[1]

Basic Factors to Consider

Basic compensation analysis

Physician profits and compensation are in large part driven by individual productivity and the rate-per-unit-of-service paid for the various services. Thus, any claim for lost profits should consider the historical pattern of work by the physician(s) and the local market area. A proper analysis would require, at a minimum, consideration of the following factors:

- Plaintiff's work hours in the office, hospital, or other venue

- Number of patients seen, surgeries performed, images read, etc.

- Use of physician billing codes

- Trends in reimbursement rates for the services provided

- Staffing and overhead rates for the practice

- Age of the physician(s)

Chapter 21: Lost Profits for Physician Practices

- Historical earnings of the physician(s)

- Presence of physician extenders

- Ancillary testing income, if any

- Ancillary driven differences in physician compensation

- Regional, localized, or practice-specific differences in payments by insurers for physician services

- Regional differences in physician compensation due to:

  - Supply and demand effects of a surplus (unlikely) or shortage of physicians

  - Cost of living

  - Utilization (clinical practice styles)[2]

- Collection rate for services performed versus charges for those services

- Payor mix; e.g., percentage of revenue generated from Medicare, Medicaid, private insurance plans, self-pay, etc

- Training and skill of the physician, such as surgical skills for a surgeon[3]

- Malpractice claim history

- Activities in developing the practice

- Competing practices

Of course, undertaking the analysis requires that the financial expert (through efforts by the attorney) successfully obtains the necessary data during the discovery process. Thus, it is wise to retain an expert early in such litigation to be certain the document request contains the appropriate information. Furthermore, review of *initial* documents produced invariably leads to additional requests for other documents, making early retention in the discovery phase even more critical.

Example

A member of a hospital medical staff brings a claim for lost income against the hospital after it terminated her staff privileges. In valuing her claim, the plaintiff's financial expert uses MGMA[4] national data for median physician earnings as a basis for the "but-for" earnings

Chapter 21: Lost Profits for Physician Practices

calculation (the income the physician would have earned, but for the defendant's alleged wrongful termination). The following are the particular areas that the expert should review for purposes of analyzing potential lost earnings..

General measures of productivity

Productivity measures in a physician practice include hours worked, patients seen, physician extenders (such as Nurse Practitioners and Physician Assistants) supervised, as well as charges and collections for services.

Hours worked is an important element to assess in conjunction with the number of patients seen during those hours. Industry sources such as MGMA, for example, provide data on the number of patients seen and hours worked. Looking at the relationship between the two can offer insight into the efficiency of the practice, an important driver of income.

Nurse Practitioners and Physician Assistants (referred to as Non-Physician Providers or "NPP" in the MGMA data) are frequently billed under the physician's provider number if the physician supervises their services, including reviewing the charts of patients seen.[5] In some instances, these extenders can also bill directly for their services without physician supervision. If extenders are included in the individual physician's productivity, then the analyst will need to separately identify the work that the particular physician actually performed versus the work that extenders did when using the MGMA benchmark data. *Tip*: All the MGMA data (see the chart later in this chapter) exclude the productivity associated with physician extenders. Thus, one all-too-frequent misuse of MGMA data is failing to adjust for physician extender revenues.

Physician Billing Codes

One of the most challenging aspects of measuring damages relative to a physician practice is to understand the revenue cycle, including CPT™[6] codes for billing. These are a series of 5-digit billing codes used for the vast majority of physician services, although there are also HCPCS (Healthcare Common Procedure Coding System) codes for certain testing, G[7] codes and J[8] codes, and a host of other esoteric terms that may be relevant in a particular engagement.

Example one

An orthopedic surgeon specializing in knee and shoulder arthroscopy brings a claim for lost wages against a practice for wrongful discharge. During his employment, the CPT™ codes associated with arthroscopy permitted the practice to use multiple codes to bill for certain procedures, resulting in enhanced payments. Subsequent to the alleged discharge and damaging event, these codes were combined into a required G code for billing, resulting in significantly lower payment levels for the same arthroscopic services. As a result, part of the physician's decline in income could be traced to specific reductions in payment for the services he provided, and the expected "but for" earnings could be lower.

Chapter 21: Lost Profits for Physician Practices

Example two

A primary care physician brings a claim for loss of income due to unlawful discharge from a medical practice. Prior to the discharge she was earning $150,000 per year and her use of billing codes was subject to review by the practice manager and compliance officer before their submission to insurance companies for payment; the physician did not properly educate herself in the use of codes.

Coding Distribution

Code Level	Distribution	Visits	Fee	Revenue
99211	5.00%	250	20	$5,000
99212	10.00%	500	40	$20,000
99213	50.00%	2,500	60	$150,000
99214	30.00%	1,500	80	$120,000
99215	5.00%	250	110	$27,500
	100.00%	5,000		$322,500

In her new practice, an inexperienced individual who does not understand physician codes manages the billing, and is concerned that patients may be overcharged. Although the physician sees the same number of patients with a similar set of clinical problems in the new practice as in the old, her income has dropped to $100,000.

Code Level	Distribution	Visits	Fee	Revenue
1	15.00%	750	20	$15,000
2	20.00%	1,000	40	$40,000
3	50.00%	2,500	60	$150,000
4	10.00%	500	80	$40,000
5	5.00%	250	110	$27,500
	100.00%	5,000		$272,500

As the two charts indicate, the entire $50,000 drop in income *could* be due to incorrect coding of services.

Physician Supply and Demand

The relevance of local versus national data on physician compensation depends on many factors, including supply and demand and the recruiting market. A nationwide shortage of a particular specialty can lead to relative equivalence in compensation expectation from one area to the next. Other factors are rates paid by particular insurers for services, cost of living differentials and such local factors as the relationship between a physician with significant

Chapter 21: Lost Profits for Physician Practices

influence and his or her hospital. The latter is a particularly important factor in hospital-based practice such as radiology, pathology and anesthesia.

Ancillary testing income

This item refers to physician practice profits or compensation contributed by testing equipment owned or leased by the practice. (The MGMA data refer to this revenue as "TC" or the technical component.[9] Clearly, if the practice does not have such equipment, the physician cannot partake in any such profits or compensation.

Collections for Services

Charges are generally considered a poor measure of productivity because the payment system controlled by health insurers is often indifferent to charges. Charges may be relevant as *one* productivity measure in a practice with little or no insured patients, such as a cosmetic plastic surgery practice or a walk-in clinic that does not accept insurance.

The following Table shows the representative data for collections available from the MGMA survey. Note that "NPP Excluded" is part of each subset of the sample data. Collections for practices with over 10% TC are significantly higher than those with less than 10% TC. The sample sizes also vary significantly.[10]

	Providers	Practices	Mean	Std. Dev.	25th %tile	Median	75th %tile	90th %tile
Overall TC/NPP Excluded	1,569	182	$345,779	$140,449	$258,320	$329,767	$403,896	$501,279
Eastern Region TC/NPP Excluded	369	40	$354,056	$133,686	$275,169	$346,302	$421,846	$514,994
Overall NPP Excluded, with 1-10% TC	601	85	$410,983	$166,632	$313,776	$386,401	$476,962	$564,883
Overall NPP Excluded, with over 10% TC	164	38	$474,743	$212,399	$344,813	$441,338	$582,429	$727,105

Data from Eastern Region are representative; other regions are reported[11]

Payor mix

Perhaps the most critical factor affecting a physician's income after productivity and coding is the practice's revenue per procedure, which is significantly influenced by the underlying payor mix. There is no uniformity among the ways that various government and private insurers pay for services. Although Medicare[12] might pay 60% of a particular charge, Medicaid[13] might pay only 25% and Blue Cross might pay 70%. Data from a Medicaid plan in one state will usually have no relationship to data from another, and the many Blue Cross and Blue Shield plans in the United States do not value physician services the same way. Medicare actually adjusts the fee schedule for each state to account for geographic differentials such as cost of living and wages.

The payor mix therefore constitutes a limitation on using national data, and an analysis of the mix is critical to assessing a plaintiff's future income prospects in a "but-for" earnings analysis.

Chapter 21: Lost Profits for Physician Practices

Financial experts should also bear in mind that the payor mix may have changed during the loss period which could impact the "but-for" damages analysis. In a given circumstance, assessing the payor mix over several years should be considered to see how any changes may impact the measurement of damages.

Example

A financial expert reviews the physician's productivity in terms of hours worked, patient encounters, and gross charges and finds that each figure is at or near the MGMA mean value. In examining the collections, however, the value is near the 25th percentile. Analysis of the payor mix indicates that the practice has a large Medicaid patient base and Medicaid is paying only 30% of the practice's charges. Conclusion: The "but-for" earnings prospects of this practice are not comparable to a mean MGMA value.

Compensation

One of the difficulties with MGMA compensation surveys is that they do not present the data in the same categories as the collections data; i.e., there are no categories for compensation with NPP excluded, or for TC included. Therefore, the financial expert must exercise judgment and adjust the compensation data as necessary to account for differences in the degree of NPP and TC (ancillary) revenues.

Competition

The financial expert should also assess the extent to which the alleged damages might be due to some factor other than the cause alleged by the plaintiff. This prescription applies regardless of which party, plaintiff or defendant, engages the expert.

Physicians compete on many factors. An adage among doctors says that practice success is driven by "availability, affability, and ability," in that order. Although the saying may be trite, this discussion has already identified hours as a key element in compensation. If at the time the alleged damages occurred, a competing practice extended its hours to evenings and weekends, this might have been a contributing factor in the plaintiff's loss of income. A financial expert would have to consider and measure the impact of this and other factors, since the plaintiff must prove that the defendant's actions proximately caused the damages.

Affability may be difficult to assess other than from a personal interview, which an expert for the defendant may not have access to; a change in affability contributing to a decline in the physician's income is also difficult to assess, if not altogether unusual. To the extent possible, legal counsel should make inquiries about the plaintiff's reputation with patients and colleagues as well as personal difficulties contributing to demeanor, such as a divorce or death in the family. Financial experts should expect cross-examination questions such as, "If Dr. Smith were known to raise his voice with employees, how would this affect your conclusion?" Or, "If patients had lodged complaints about Dr. Smith's hostile attitude during examinations, how would this affect your conclusion?" Defense counsel may very well depose various fact witnesses to assess a physician's comportment and professional as well as patient relationships. In addition to the physician's affability, that of the office staff, particularly the front desk and reception personnel, may also be critical. If a key employee was replaced at or near the time of the alleged damages, the financial expert should also consider its potential impact on the claimed damages. Public records, such as the state Boards of Registration in Medicine are generally good sources of information regarding prior complaints or disciplinary action involving the physician.

Ability is another factor that the attorney and financial expert should consider, particularly when the case involves specialists such as surgeons; however, assessing a physician's ability may require another expert with clinical expertise. Medicine is a dynamic practice area and new techniques and procedures are always being developed. These technical and procedural innovations can have consequences on the physician's income. If competing surgeons at a hospital, for example, have trained in a new, less invasive procedure with a lower complications rate and the plaintiff surgeon failed to train in it, then this lapse could lead to a gradual decline in referrals from other physicians, with a concomitant loss of income. An excellent example comes from the current rise of using interventional radiology in breast cancer biopsy as one example and certain gynecological surgeries versus traditional surgical intervention as another. Another example is the shifting tide of opinion about the effectiveness of coronary stents[14] placed by interventional cardiologists versus traditional coronary bypass surgery done by cardiac surgeons. The advent of drug eluting coronary stents[15] and their approval by Medicare led to dramatic declines in cardiac surgeon incomes and dramatic increases in interventional cardiologists incomes.

Other factors that financial experts may commonly overlook in their lost profits analysis include:

- An increase in the number of physicians practicing a particular specialty in a service area (known as a "catchment" area), resulting in decreased volume for existing physicians

- A decline or increase in population

- Poor economic conditions contributing to a rise in bad debts and a drop in patient insurance coverage, such as those present in 2008 through 2010

- Changes in health insurance that reduce a patient's benefits[16]

- Decreases (or increases) in the fee schedule paid by health insurers to the physician

- Competition among hospitals that affect the incomes of physicians on the staff of those hospitals, particularly when a hospital system is able to negotiate contracts superior to that of competing hospitals (common in many market areas)

Chapter 21: Lost Profits for Physician Practices

- Failure of the physician practice billing department to collect all otherwise collectible amounts (an absolute must-review in any damages analysis)

- Poor quality medical billing software or a failed attempt at changing to a new software program

In short, there are dozens of factors that can contribute to an observed change in physician income that both parties' financial experts should consider in assessing causality.

In-depth Look at Special Issues in Identifying Damages

Physician compensation systems

Unallocated Overhead

A physician who quits a group practice in violation of a non-compete agreement or a fiduciary responsibility may leave his former colleagues with a large amount of fixed overhead to pay out of what otherwise would have been their income. Physicians often share variable expenses based upon productivity; e.g., if one doctor produces 30% of the revenues, then she will be allocated 30% of the variable expenses.

Example one: fixed expense

A two-owner medical practice with four physicians relocates to new office space designed for the four physicians. But the two employed physicians leave the practice in violation of their non-compete agreements and open a competing practice nearby. Each physician's share of the rent was $50,000 per year, such that the remaining two physician/owners now face an additional out-of-pocket cost of $50,000 a piece. The expert's "but/for" lost profits analysis should consider fixed and variable expenses projected separately for the relevant period of time, depending upon the circumstances. Generally, one would expect variable expenses to trend down sooner as part of the mitigation process, and the fixed expenses to remain fairly constant for a longer period of time. Experts should, however, consider that even for fixed expenses, plaintiffs will likely be expected to mitigate their losses within a reasonable period of time.

Example two: variable expense

Assume further that this same practice spends $800,000 per year on staff wages and benefits, representing 25% of annual revenues of $3,200,000. The competing physicians recruited staff with a cost of $200,000. As part of their attempt to mitigate damages, the owners reduced staff by an additional $100,000. On a per capita basis, the two owners now have $50,000 of additional payroll costs to contend with, but depending on the compensation system, each may suffer a different degree of harm.

Chapter 21: Lost Profits for Physician Practices

For example, if Owner 1 generates 55% of the collections and Owner 2 generates 45%, Owner 1 suffers a loss of $55,000 while owner 2 suffers a loss of $45,000. This can be important if the financial expert is required to allocate the damages among the injured parties.

Large practices and integrated providers

Depending on the type of entity claiming the damages—e.g., a hospital or a large, integrated group practice with significant ancillary capability—the magnitude of the loss-types can be substantial. One ready source for assessing the magnitude of these potential revenue losses is the survey by Merritt Hawkins & Associates of hospital CFOs, although data specific to the litigation should be used in a damages calculation, if available:

> The 2010 Survey indicates that average net inpatient/outpatient revenue generated by physicians for their affiliated hospitals differed from the 2007 Survey based upon specialty. Average revenue generated by primary care physicians declined from $1,433,532 in 2007 to $1,385,775 in 2010. Specialist physician revenue increased from $1,509,910 in 2007 to $1,577,764 in 2010. Neurosurgery was the single largest contributor followed by Invasive [invasive is generally considered a cardiologist who performs cardiac catheterization while interventional is a cardiologist who inserts coronary stents] Cardiology, Orthopedics and General Surgery. [17]

Surgical specialties tend to generate the largest revenues. The largest and most profitable lines of business in the typical acute care hospital are cardiology and orthopedics. For example, an orthopedic surgeon who leaves a hospital position in violation of a non-compete and goes to work for a competing organization may cause the hospital to lose significant inpatient and outpatient surgery revenues. Orthopedic surgeons are large users of MRI and CT Scans, both of which represent significant revenue sources. Similarly, if the orthopedic surgeon leaves a position with a medical practice that provides an outpatient surgery center along with MRI and CT services, damages well in excess of the surgeon's annual income can result.

Growth rates in "but-for" and future earnings calculations

In the author's experience, this is the single most common and most serious error that occurs in physician damages calculations. In general, there are a variety of broad economic and Medicare-specific limitations on physician incomes.

Chapter 21: Lost Profits for Physician Practices

General price per-unit of service[18]

What about increases in fees per-unit of service? From 1994 to 2009—or for 15 years, the compound rate of increase for all physician services was only 1.94%, based on data from the Bureau of Labor Statistics Producer Price Index for Physician Services:

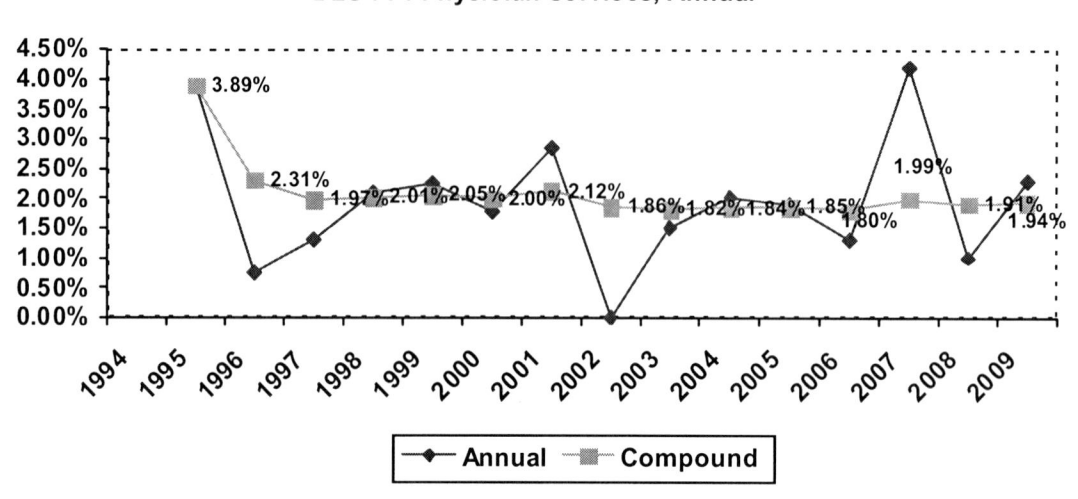

BLS PPI-Physician Services, Annual

Year	Annual	Compound
1995	3.89%	
1996		2.31%
1997		1.97%
1998		2.01%
1999		2.05%
2000		2.00%
2001		2.12%
2002		1.86%
2003		1.82%
2004		1.84%
2005		1.85%
2006		1.80%
2007		1.99%
2008		1.91%
2009		1.94%

Medicare Price per Unit of Service[19]

Clearly, there is no evidence that per unit reimbursement rates are growing at the GDP (Gross Domestic Product) rate or the Consumer Price Index rate, and a small practice's capacity to provide units of service is limited. Under the federal Medicare Sustainable Growth Rate (SGR) formula, Medicare expenditures for physician services are limited by a complex formula that considers the change in fees, the number of beneficiaries, growth in GDP per capita, and the impact of new laws. The SGR is then applied to the Medicare Economic Index (MEI), which measures the weighted average price change in physician services. The MEI is a physician practice-specific measure of inflation and generally is in the range of 3.5%. The Medicare Payment Advisory Commission (MedPAC) website publishes the updated, annual data each March.[20]

The pattern since 2006 has been for Congress belatedly to suspend the statutory cutbacks in the Conversion Factor. The 2007 Conversion Factor of $35.9848 initially reflected a decrease of 5.0% and was subsequently overturned by Congress and left equal to the 2006 factor. The 2008 factor was scheduled to drop by 10.1% until the end of December 2007 when the Medicare, Medicaid, and SCHIP Extension Act of 2007 legislation updated the conversion factor by 0.5% to $38.0870. In July 2008, Congress extended the $38.09 conversion factor for the balance of 2008 over the President's veto and put a 1.1% increase in place for 2009. Since November 2009, Congress has acted several times to delay the scheduled cut for 2010 to $28.41, having failed to include a fix in the Healthcare Reform legislation. **NOTE: The 2009 Medicare physician fee schedule final rule on October 30, 2008 provided for the statutorily mandated 1.1% update for calendar year 2009; *however*, the budget neutrality adjustment to the Conversion Factor associated with the review and reallocation of RVUs was a negative 6.41%, resulting in a rate of **$36.07**. The Budget Neutrality Adjustment is now included in the Conversion Factor where historically it was applied to a reduction of RVUs for each CPT code. As such, the 2009 rate and the precipitous drop in the 2010 rate below are not entirely comparable to the prior years.

Medicare Conversion Factor

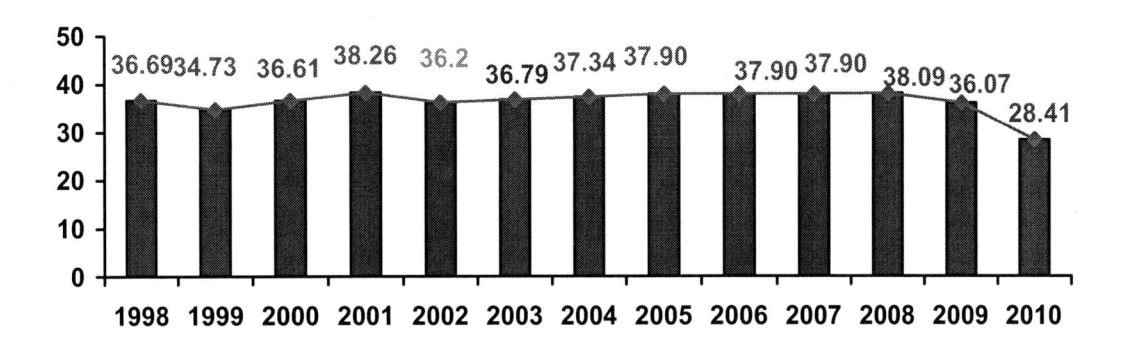

Year	Value
1998	36.69
1999	34.73
2000	36.61
2001	38.26
2002	36.2
2003	36.79
2004	37.34
2005	37.90
2006	37.90
2007	37.90
2008	38.09
2009	36.07
2010	28.41

These two items represent the broad picture for physician practices in general. For a physician practice of a specific specialty, an in-depth analysis of that particular specialty's income growth opportunities is necessary.

Example

Larger physician practices including cardiology, neurology, and orthopedics as well as multi-specialty practices frequently invest in high-tech imaging equipment such as MRI and CT scanners. A lost profits analysis that involves a practice with such equipment should account for the impact of the Deficit Reduction Act of 2005 on the payment for these services;[21] the changes in Independent Diagnostic Testing facilities qualification;[22] and the Stark IV regulations adopted as part of the 2009 Inpatient Payment System final rule.[23] MRI, CT and PET were all further negatively impacted by provisions of the federal 2010 Healthcare Reform legislation, with the utilization assumption[24] increased from 50% to 75% for diagnostic imaging equipment costing more than $1 million. This significantly reduces the Technical Component of Medicare Revenue and will spread to other payors.

Regulatory considerations

Healthcare may well be the most regulated industry in the country. Since it also represents the largest sector of the economy (+/- 17%) and drives federal and state budget concerns, regulatory and other government agencies conduct extensive enforcement activities in the healthcare sector. Many of the more common claims for damages may, in fact, be irrelevant in a physician practice analysis because the underlying rationale for the claim violates one or more federal or state laws. As such, the financial expert should make a threshold determination whether the conduct of the allegedly damaged entity is consistent with the law. Cases in which the plaintiff's and/or defense counsel may be experienced in civil litigation but unfamiliar with healthcare law can create considerable challenges for the expert.

Violations of non-compete agreements are one area that results in frequent litigation. In these cases, financial experts must carefully scrutinize the assumptions related to expected profit contributions from the covenanter.

Example

Assume that a hospital claims lost profits against a former physician employee (cardiologist) who violated a non-compete agreement by joining a competing practice. During the course of his former employment, the physician referred patients to the hospital for services such as catheterization and angioplasty as well as lab tests, CT Scans, stress testing, and cardiac ultrasound (collectively considered "ancillaries" for this example). After leaving the hospital, the physician's new practice has the same testing capabilities, and so he refers his patients there. The physician also joins the medical staff of a competing hospital to admit his patients.

Because federal law prohibits payment for patient referrals, there could be some concern that the hospital could not claim damages against the physician based on his historic referrals. Although this appears unlikely,[25] the financial expert needs to carefully examine the physician's historical utilization patterns for compliance with applicable laws before using these as the basis for the damages calculation. Even if otherwise permissible, the type of "hockey stick" assumptions seen in many damage claims are unlikely to pass regulatory muster, as it will likely be difficult to construct a permissible rationale for the physician referring ever-increasing amounts of business to the hospital.

Another common but perhaps fatal approach to calculating damages in this example would be to use the physician's *post*-employment utilization in his new practice as a basis for measuring the hospital's losses. If the physician becomes an owner in his new practice and shares in the profits generated by ancillary referrals, then utilization is likely to be higher than the physician historically incurred as an employee in the hospital, where the Stark laws precluded him from receiving a part of the ancillary profit.[26] A proper analysis would differentiate between growth in referrals due to an increase in the number of patients seen by the physician, which might have been foreseeable had he remained with the hospital, as opposed to growth motivated by his ability to profit from those referrals. Plaintiff's counsel could use the latter, of course, to attack the credibility of the defendant and his motives to violate the non-compete.

From the standpoint of the physician defendant, the scrutiny of the previous relationship may yield potential defenses and counterclaims. So-called *qui tam* or whistleblower cases in healthcare, along with their astounding fines—in which the whistleblowers often share—frequently result from wrongful termination or other lawsuits that the informants may have instigated against the *qui tam* defendants.[27] Surprisingly, perhaps, informants often escape penalties for whatever part they played in the alleged schemes because the government has a vested interest in whistleblowers coming forward.[28]

From the standpoint of the plaintiff, the discovery process directed against the new practice unit could uncover regulatory violations that would lead to settlement.

Typical physician practice claims that do not 'fly'

A typical claim for lost profits generally arises from the proximity of the parties to one another in a business relationship, and the resulting strategic advantages that they each enjoyed prior to a breach. For example, a small donut store located in a strip mall next to a major consumer retailer such as Home Depot or Loews would benefit from the customer flow to those stores. If the donut shop brings a claim against the landlord for failure to deliver the lease, for example, then a financial expert would certainly look at both the historical and future customer traffic flow to the home goods retailer as one basis for measuring the donut shop's lost profits.

By contrast, the Stark laws specifically prohibit market value from being based on the ability of strategic parties to refer patients to one another; similarly, the Anti-kickback statute prohibits payment for referrals.[29] Assume that the physician-owners of a medical office building lease space to a tenant who plans to construct an imaging center; assume further that the physicians-owners decide to construct their own center and force out the tenant. If one accepts the premise that claimed damages cannot be based on a possible violation of the law, then it would be incorrect to base the tenant's future profits on the potential referrals that would have been available from all physicians in the building. Further, with respect to referrals from the physician-owners, although they likely would have referred all of their business to their own center, they likely would not have referred all of their business to a tenant's independent center. Of course, the tenant may have alternative damages claims available, to preclude the physician-owners from unjustly profiting from their actions.

Conclusion

After reading this chapter, one might conclude that it focused primarily on factors that tend to reduce potential claims for lost profits related to physician practices. In fact, there are a host of potential damages theories that can apply to these and related cases, but because physician practices are one of the economy's most heavily regulated sectors, calculating damages based on these damages theories requires a body of knowledge that the typical damages expert may not generally have. More importantly, in litigation of this type, the opposing party is more likely than not to retain an expert to refute any damages claim, and any plaintiff's expert who does not appropriately consider the factors discussed in this chapter will likely be subject to attack. Accordingly, it is critical that any financial expert retained in this area of practice consider the following *areas of inquiry and evaluation for potential damage claims*:

Chapter 21: Lost Profits for Physician Practices

1. Loss of physician income in general

2. Loss of non-physician support staff

3. Loss of non-physician provider staff who perform billable services

4. Loss of physician staff (e.g., to a hospital)

5. Loss of practice value

6. Loss of ancillary revenue from laboratory, imaging, cardiac testing

7. Loss of inpatient admissions

8. Loss of skilled nursing facility admissions

9. Loss of outpatient surgical facility fees

10. Loss of home health agency revenue

11. Loss of durable medical equipment revenue

In an era when hospitals and larger practice entities are fiercely competing for physician specialties—including cardiology, cardiac surgery and orthopedics—events giving rise to potential damages claims are on the increase. Analysis of the expansive revenue and profit opportunities that plaintiffs have lost in such circumstances is where financial and damages experts should focus their attention.

Glossary of Terms

In many ways, the financial aspects of medical practices have a unique vocabulary. The following definitions will be helpful to financial experts and attorneys who may be new to the area.

- Ancillary – refers to a collection of testing equipment such as imaging (CT, MRI, Ultrasound, stress testing etc.).

- Payor – An industry term for the source of payment for services, such as Blue Cross, Medicare, Medicaid, an HMO, etc.

- Payor mix – the percentage of business done with various payors.

- Stark laws – Federal civil legislation comprised of three separate statutory provisions governing physician self-referral for Medicare and Medicaid patients.[30] Stark regulations contain an

Chapter 21: Lost Profits for Physician Practices

outright prohibition on physicians referring certain services to entities in which they have defined financial interests, for example. The statute is enforced with draconian fines.

- Anti-kickback statute - Federal criminal legislation that prohibits payment of anything of value to a healthcare provider for referring services provided to beneficiaries of federal programs including Medicare, Medicaid, and CHAMPUS (Civilian Health and Medical Program of the Uniformed Services).[31]

- Integrated provider – An entity that engages in a variety of services in the "continuum of care." For example, a large physician practice may have both primary care and specialist physicians, broad-based radiology/imaging capability, a freestanding ambulatory surgery center, and a laboratory.

- Integrated delivery system – An entity with hospital and physician components, usually both primary care and specialist care, in addition to such services as radiology/imaging, laboratory, skilled nursing facility, and home health care.

- Professional component (PC or "26") – The portion of a payment for a test or imaging (e.g., cardiac stress or a CT scan) that compensates the physician for interpreting the results of the test.

- Revenue Cycle – the process commencing with the preparation of a charge or bill (claim) for a service through the collection of all the payments for it. In healthcare, the process is complicated by different rates for the same service by different payors, partial payments by one or more payors for the same service and the need to collect from the patient after all insurance and government payors have weighed in on a claim. There are also complex documentation and coding rules as well as retrospective review of charges for claims already paid.

- Technical Component (TC) – The portion of a payment for a test or imaging (e.g., a cardiac stress test or a CT scan) that compensates the physician practice for owning the equipment, employing the technician (if any), providing supplies etc. (See also Professional Component, above)

- Global - The combination of the PC and TC for a service.

---

1. Note: Financial aspects of medical and physician practices involve unique terms and statutory regulations; for the reader's convenience, a glossary of such terms and legislative references is set forth in the final section (**Section G**) of this Chapter.

2. For example, certain areas of the country have high incidences of caesarean deliveries, use of advanced imaging like MRI, or surgical versus interventional treatment of coronary artery disease.

3. A decline in physician's income could be traced to failure to train in current surgical or clinical techniques, for example.

4. Medical Group Management Association; www.mgma.com.

5. Medicare allows this under the so-called "incident to" rules; other insurers may or may not follow Medicare guidelines.

Chapter 21: Lost Profits for Physician Practices

6. Current Procedural Terminology, trademarked by the American Medical Association.

7. G Codes apply to professional healthcare procedures and services that would be coded as CPT but for which no CPT code exists; insurers sometimes combine services that have separate CPT codes into a single G Code resulting in reduced payment. See,e.g., www.reimbursementcodes.com/hcpcs_codes_d.html.

8. J codes are used for injections and pharmaceuticals.

9. For an excellent discussion of Technical Component revenue and its implications in physician compensation see BVR's *Guide to Physician Practice Valuation*.

10. MGMA bases its data on a survey of medical group members as opposed to a random sample from a population; it includes more private practice groups than other surveys, something to consider.

11. Medical Group Management Association Physician Compensation and Production Survey, 2006 Report Based on 2005 Data

12. A federal program primarily for the elderly with a generally uniform benefit package but vastly different pay rates from area to area. Local coverage determinations by Medicare intermediaries can affect the benefit package.

13. A state-specific program of benefits that is funded partially by each of the state and federal government; which government pays what depends in part on state decisions as to benefits.

14. Another area under current debate is drug-eluting stents versus standard stents.

15. See 67 Fed. Reg. 49,983, 50,004 (Aug. 1, 2002) for advance approval of drug eluting stents by CMS even before their approval by the FDA.

16. This factor will be exacerbated by the 2010 federal Healthcare Reform, for example, which increases the economic burden of healthcare on insured patients, thereby discouraging utilization even as it expands coverage to the uninsured, trying to make room for them in the system

17. *2010 Physician Inpatient/Outpatient Revenue Survey*, Merritt Hawkins & Associates (Irving, TX); www.merritthawkins.com.

18. Mark Dietrich, "Choosing and using the Right Valuation Methods for Physician Practices," BVR's *Guide to Healthcare Valuation*, Business Valuation Resources (2009).

19. Ibid.

20. www.medpac.gov.

21. Pub.L. 109-171, 120 Stat. 4, February 8, 2006; see, e.g., Mark Dietrich, A Healthcare Appraiser Reviews a Judge-Appraiser's 'Report,'" *Business Valuation Review* (Summer 2007); Douglas Smith, "Valuation Considerations Specific to Diagnostic Imaging Entities," BVR's *Guide to Healthcare Valuation* (2009).

22. See generally 42 CFR 410.33, Independent Diagnostic Testing Facility (December 2005); http://cfr.vlex.com/vid/410-independent-diagnostic-testing-19805522.

23. 42 CFR Part 412, Medicare Program; Inpatient Rehabilitation Facility Prospective Payment System for Federal Fiscal Year 2009; Final Rule, *Federal Register*, Vol. 73, No. 154 (Friday, August 8, 2008); http://edocket.access.gpo.gov/2008/pdf/E8-17797.pdf.

24. The utilization assumption determines the expected number of units of service over which fixed expenses of operation are spread in establishing the fee that Medicare will pay. The higher the utilization assumption, the lower the expected fixed expense per unit of service and as a result, the lower the fee Medicare will pay.

25. "A requirement to refer to a specific provider is different from an agreement not to establish a competing business. In other words, a covenant not to compete might prevent a physician from setting up a private practice or offering services that compete with the entity that purchases his or her practice. If an agreement also included the requirement that the physician refer business to the purchaser, the Agreement would be suspect under the Antikickback Statute." 66 Fed. Reg. 879 (Jan. 4, 2001).

26. See generally 420 CFR 411.

27. The University of Medicine and Dentistry in New Jersey (UMDNJ) investigation is an excellent case in point. In December 2005, the DOJ entered into an agreement with UMDNJ, by which UMDNJ paid back nearly $5 million in double-billings to Medicaid and undertook certain operational reforms in return for deferred charges of healthcare fraud; see www.usdoj.gov/usao/nj/press/files/pdffiles/UMDNJFINALDPA.pdf.

Chapter 21: Lost Profits for Physician Practices

28. *McLeod Regional Medical Center to Pay U.S. Over $15 Million to Resolve False Claims Act Allegations*, DOJ Press Release (November 1, 2002); www.usdoj.gov/opa/pr/2002/November/02_civ_634.htm.

29. Arguably, even if the standard of value in physician lost profits is not fair market value, the outright prohibition on paying for referrals likely precludes the use of "strategic value" assumptions.

30. Stark legislation is codified at 42 U.S.C.S. §1395nn (§1877 of the Social Security Act) and 42 C.F.R. §411.350 through §411.389.

31. See CRIMINAL PENALTIES FOR ACTS INVOLVING FEDERAL HEALTH CARE PROGRAMS, 42 U.S.C. § 1320a-7b(b)(2000).

Chapter 22

Designing a Chart of Accounts to Meet the Needs of Physician Practices

By David N. Gans, M.S.H.A., FACMPE and Steven Andes, PhD, CPA

The Chart of Accounts is the basis for an organization's accounting system. Whether the organization is a public entity or a private business it needs a set of statements to record its financial condition. The chart of accounts is the starting point for every organization's financial records as it is the list of accounts used to record the organization's expenses and revenues as well as its assets and liabilities.

Businesses use accounting to record, monitor, and report their financial condition to managers, owners/shareholders, creditors, and governmental bodies. Accounting records describe an organization's current financial position as well as any changes. Managers require accurate and consistent financial information for both short term and strategic decision making. Creditors need the same information to decide the level of lending risk which is the basis for the amount of the loan and the interest rate that the organization is qualified to receive. Financial statements are also the basis for the tax return and other financial documents required by local, state and federal agencies.

To be useful to all the various users, accounting records need to reliable, relevant and consistent. Reliable means that the records are free from bias or error, faithfully represent the financial status of the organization, and must be verifiable, after the fact. Reliability means that financial records are neutral in their nature and can be verified by different accountants using the same objective data and measurement techniques. Accounting records must also be relevant, meaning that the records have the information that decision makers need and are sufficiently prepared and distributed in a timely manner. Additionally, accounting records should show consistency, meaning that there is comparability across organizations and with previous time periods.[1]

Financial accounting has standard rules, terms, and procedures that have been developed over time. These rules, terms, and procedures are classified as "generally accepted accounting practices" or GAAP. Until recently, a nongovernmental agency, the Financial Accounting Standards Board, was the ultimate authority for GAAP. Since the Sarbanes-Oxley Law of 2002 (Public Company Accounting and Investor Protection Act), the Public Company Accounting Oversight Board (PCAOB, www.pcaob.org) is now the final authority for GAAP, at least as it relates to publicly traded corporations. While the PACOB is also technically not a government agency, the Security and Exchange Commission, which is a governmental agency, appoints the chair and the members, and approves the budget.[2]

Chapter 22: Designing a Chart of Accounts

As stated before, the chart of accounts forms the basis for all accounting information recorded in the financial records. The chart of accounts lists each account with a corresponding number for the accounting system to track. The accounts in the chart of account determine the detail that financial transactions are recorded. Without a designated accounting code stated in the chart of accounts, it is impossible to track a revenue or expense item in the accounting records.

Therefore, the designation of an account code from the chart of accounts determines how an expense or revenue can be recorded into the financial records, and from there into the financial reports prepared for the organization.

All business and public entities have similar legal requirements to maintain accurate, representative accounting records that accurately show the financial status of the organization. All business and public entities have similar needs for reliable, relevant and consistent accounting information for managerial decision making. Health care organizations, in particular, have unique business requirements that dictate how financial information should be categorized. Health care entities need to understand their sources of revenue, how discounts and contracts are applied, how expenses are incurred and a detailed understanding of the costs incurred to provide services. These complexities make it necessary that health care organizations use a chart of accounts developed to meet their specific needs.

A healthcare manager must ensure that the chart of accounts has an account for every revenue and expense it needs to track. The number of separate accounts an organization needs in its chart of accounts depends somewhat on its size and organizational complexity. Generally, larger and more complex organizations need more accounts than smaller, less sophisticated entities. Managers need input from their organization's financial and legal advisors, as well as their creditors to identify particular revenues or expenses that must be tracked to meet specific legal and other reporting needs.

As stated earlier, a medical practice cannot track any revenue or expenses not listed in the chart of accounts. However, the more the accounts listed for recording various revenues and expenses, the more costly it is to maintain an accounting system. Additionally, if the accounting system records information in too much detail, the managerial uses of the information are handicapped by the inability to easily interpret financial records. The selection of the level of detail is an important aspect in the design of the organization's chart of accounts. Managers need to designate the accounts needed to generate the financial reports required for decision making, for lenders, and to meet the legal reporting and tax filing requirements of government. In general, smaller organizations usually need fewer accounts than larger, and all organizations will usually expand the number of accounts they use as managers find the need for more detailed accounting and financial record keeping.

To set up a chart of accounts, a manager needs to define the various financial accounts the organization will need. Each account will be given a unique number and similar financial activities should have numbers that have closely associated digits. Smaller, less complex organizations may find that all of their accounting needs can be accommodated using only three digits (potentially yielding

Chapter 22: Designing a Chart of Accounts

999 separate accounts). However, more digits may be needed in order to simplify how accounts are categorized and to provide room to add new accounts in the future. Complex organizations may have a chart of accounts with hundreds of categories with each category having multiple subclassifications. The chart of accounts for a large, complex organization can have thousands of different account numbers. Additionally, a chart of accounts can be set up to have multiple fields, allowing the organization to use the same accounting system for various legal entities and subordinates or to track the specific revenues or expenses for various responsibility centers within each entity.

Every chart of accounts is divided into five major categories:

1. assets,

2. liabilities,

3. equity, net assets, or fund balances,

4. revenues, and

5. expenses.

Each category will have a "block" of numbers assigned to show the general classification of each financial account and are generally presented in a standard order, beginning with the accounts presented in the Balance Sheet (also called the "Statement of Financial Position") and then the accounts that build the "Statement of Income" for the organization.

Assets are resources owned by the organization such as accounts receivable, equipment and property. Assets may be tangible, such as land, buildings, and equipment; a direct right to tangible property, such as amounts due from patient or insurance company payers, or assets can be intangible, such as good will, patents owned by the organization, licenses, and leaseholds. The chart of accounts will usually list assets in descending order of liquidity. Cash and other assets which are easily converted to cash are listed first, fixed assets such as property and equipment are listed next, and intangible assets are listed last. Asset accounts usually start with the number "1" and will be the first accounts listed in the chart of accounts.

Liabilities are debts or obligations owed by the organization to creditors, such as loans and accounts payable. These obligations come from the purchase of goods or services on credit or by obtaining a loan from a financial institution to finance the purchase of equipment or buildings. Current liabilities, the obligations which are due to be paid within one year, are generally listed first in the chart of accounts, with accounts payable, bank overdrafts payable and payroll obligations (tax, insurance, and retirement plan withholdings and accrued payroll amounts) will be listed before other payables such as rent or insurance. Long-term liabilities such as construction loans, long-term notes, and capital leases follow current liabilities. Deferred revenue, deferred compensation, and severance plan obligations will be listed last. Liability accounts usually start with the number "2."

Chapter 22: Designing a Chart of Accounts

Equity accounts (sometimes called "fund balance" in some nonprofit organizations) reflect the financial worth of the organization and represent the residual value of an entity's assets after deducting its liabilities. In a for-profit business enterprise, the equity will be the ownership interest and in a not for profit will represent the net financial worth of the organization. In for-profit organizations, equity generally is derived from two sources: contributed capital by the owner(s) or shareholders and retained earnings, the accumulated value of income, less expenses and owner's withdrawals. Typical equity accounts are contributed capital, preferred and common stock, dividends and distributions (unique to for-profit corporations), and not-for-profit equity accounts such as unrestricted assets, restricted assets and endowments. Net asset accounts usually start with the number "3."

The accounts used to create the Income Statement accounts follow the Statement of Position accounts. While there is general agreement in the general numbering system for the accounts used to create the Statement of Position, there is no such convention for the income statement accounts. Generally the accounts used to describe revenue will precede the expense accounts and the last accounts will reflect nonoperating revenue, expenses, and income taxes paid. This sequence enable the chart of accounts to follow the same sequence as the Statement of Position, with account numbers that start with a "4" reflecting revenue, operating expenses will start with a "5," "6," "7," or 8" and nonoperating revenue and expenses starting with a "9."

In 1979, the Medical Group Management Association (MGMA) published a chart of accounts that was specifically designed to record the financial information needed to manage a medical group practice. The MGMA Chart of Accounts is structured to accurately describe the revenue and expenses associated with a health care organization and its accounts flow logically into the financial statements a medical group practice has to produce. It classifies financial transactions into eight major categories and assigns a four digit coding number to each.[3]

The eight major categories used by the MGMA Chart of Accounts are ordered in the way they appear on the practice's financial statements. The major categories and their corresponding codes appear in the table on the following page.

The first three categories relate to the balance sheet or "Statement of Financial Position." The remaining categories relate to the Statement of Income and to the order in which they appear on the Statement of Income

There are two unique aspects of the MGMA Chart of Accounts that differ from most other charts of accounts. "Adjustments and allowances" is categorized as a 4000 series, the category for revenues, rather than a 6000 series expense because allowances and adjustments must be treated as offsets to revenue rather than as expenses in order to understand the effect of the discounts required by government and insurance payers and to easily gauge the net revenue associated with operations. Another difference is to categorize provider salaries and fringe benefits as an 8000 series account. The majority of medical groups are owned and operated by the physicians who practice in the medical group. The compensation of the physicians/owners is based

Chapter 22: Designing a Chart of Accounts

Account numbers	Description
1000	Assets
2000	Liabilities
3000	Owner's equity
4000	Revenues and adjustments to revenue
5000	Operating expenses – support staff salaries and fringe benefits
6000	Operating expenses – general and administrative
7000	Operating expenses – clinical and ancillary services
8000	Operating expenses – physician and nonphysician provider salaries and fringe benefits
9000	Nonoperating revenue and expenses

on the amount that remains from total net revenue after all expenses are subtracted. By organizing the MGMA Chart of Accounts with physician compensation and benefits as the last series of accounts, the logical flow of financial information is maintained. This sequence also allows management to logically present the financial situation of the practice in the same sequence as the chart of accounts.

The chart of accounts structure should allow the user to add subcategories in the future and to logically associate expenses with like costs. If the chart of accounts utilizes a four digit accounting system it can use the second digit of the account for a sub-categories of the eight major categories and can use the last two digits of the coding number to reflect specific elements. Using this logic, a chart of accounts subdivides each major category into as many as nine subcategories. The subcategories can, each, have nine more minor classifications. Each category can be "rolled up" to equal the total for that category, usually reflecting the "0" account in the series. For example, if account 7000 is used to reflect "Clinical Expense," account 7100 can address "Clinical Equipment, Supplies, and Services", account 7110 will record "Drugs and Medications," and 7111 will be "Vaccines" and 7112 will be used for "Chemotherapy Drugs." In this example, the general ledger for the organization will provide both detailed information (71111 shows only the cost of vaccines), while 7110 shows the costs of all drugs and medications for the organization, 7100 is the sum of all the subaccounts related to clinical equipment, supplies, and services, and 7000 will have the total costs of all clinical expenses for the organization.

A chart of accounts can also establish codes for specific revenues and expenses that relate to more than one of the categories. For example, the employee benefits section can categorize payroll taxes paid for employees as 5710 and payroll taxes—State Unemployment Insurance as 5713. The same chart of accounts can classify physician benefits as 8200 and nonphysician provider (nurse practitioner, physician assistants, etc.) benefits as 8400. In this organization, the cost of State Unemployment Insurance for physicians would be categorized as 8213 and the cost of State Unemployment Insurance for nonphysician providers would be categorized as 8413.

Chapter 22: Designing a Chart of Accounts

Different business types need to structure their chart of accounts using different sequences that, ideally, will meet their individual needs. However, this may not always be the situation for healthcare organizations. Often a healthcare organization is a legal subset of a government entity, university, or private business. In these instances, the healthcare organization may be required to use the chart of accounts of its parent organization, so its financial performance can easily aggregated into the parent organization's financial records.

When a healthcare organization has the flexibility to design a chart of accounts that can meet its specific information requirements, it has options well beyond the "basic field" of three or four digits that describe the specific asset, liability, revenue, or expense.

Through the use of additional single and multi-digit fields, the chart of accounts can be expanded to allow the reporting of financial information from multiple legal entities, to track revenues or expenses to a specific responsibility center, or to identify the revenue or costs attributed to a specific physician or nonphysician provider. Using a "multi-tiered" chart of accounts enables the organization to easily customize the information collected in its financial information system to meet management's need for accurate information for its major units or to allow a medical group practice to track the productivity of each of its physicians.

A complex healthcare organization often has separate legal entities that integrate their functions in what externally appears to be a seamless organization, but require separate financial statements. For example, a ambulatory care center may be part of a larger hospital-owned integrated delivery system, with a separate imaging center and ambulatory surgery center. If each organization uses the same chart of accounts, expenses can be easily tracked for each organization as can patient revenues. Using an "Entity Field" as the first digit of the chart of accounts allows each entity to use the same "Basic Field" that describes the actual asset, liability, entity, revenue and expense accounts, while keeping a separate set of financial records. The use of the same accounts, with a different entity field allows the parent organization to easily "roll" up the financial performance of its subordinate organizations to evaluate the performance of the entire enterprise.

Another often used field allows the organization to track costs by responsibility center, organizational units within the organization that have responsibility to generate revenue and/or expenses. Such a "Responsibility Center Field" simplifies the accumulation of revenue and expenses for a specific department or location. By tracking revenue and direct costs to each specific responsibility center, management can understand the relative contribution of the responsibility center to the organization. Additionally, if direct costs can be easily traced to a responsibility center, the organization can also allocate a fair share of the indirect costs incurred by other parts of the organization.

Some healthcare organizations need to track the amount of revenue produced by individual physicians and nonphysician providers, or the expenses associated with their use of fringe benefits such as continuing education tuition, travel, and lodging costs. Using a separate field that

Chapter 22: Designing a Chart of Accounts

identifies each physician or nonphysician provider, can enable the organization to easily prepare financial reports for each health care provider. Use of a provider field can be limited to recording only revenue, or to record revenue and only certain expenses, such as fringe benefits.

The use of multiple tiers or fields allows the organization the greatest flexibility in its accounting records. Simultaneously, the organization can record revenue or expenses for specific locations or clinics (responsibility centers) and for each physician practicing in the location or clinic (provider field).

In order to decide what to include in a chart of accounts, a manager needs to evaluate several issues:

- What reports does the organization want to prepare?

- What financial decisions, evaluations and assessments will be made on a regular basis?

- What level of detail is required in the financial reports?

- Will the organization compare its financial performance to other organizations and therefore need to collect financial data using agreed upon definitions?

- Does the organization report financial performance to national, state, or local governmental agencies?

- Does the accounting software used by the organization limit the design?

Designing a chart of accounts that meets all the needs of a health organization can be a complex task. While complex, the task is not impossible, and the benefits that the organization will obtain from a well designed chart of accounts and financial information system will far outweigh the costs associated with its design and implementation.

---

1. Chart of Accounts for Health Care Organizations. Neill F. Piland, Dr. P.H. and Kathryn P. Glass, MBA, MSHA, Center for Research in Ambulatory Health Care Administration, Englewood, CO p. 2-3

2. Wolper, Chapter. Accounting and Budgeting for Medical Practice Managers, Gans and Andes. P.

3. Chart of Accounts for Health Care Organizations. Neill F. Piland, Dr. P.H. and Kathryn P. Glass, MBA, MSHA, Center for Research in Ambulatory Health Care Administration, Englewood, CO p. 2

4. Management Accounting for Fee-for-Service/Prepaid Medical Groups, Eldon L. Schafer, PhD, CPA; Dwight J. Zulauf, PhD, CPA; Michael E. Gocke, MBA, CPA, Center for Research in Ambulatory Health Care Administration, Englewood, CO., 1985, pp. 5-17.

Chapter 23

Benchmarking Practice Performance

By Gregory S. Feltenberger, MBA, CACMPE, FACHE, CPHIMS, and David N. Gans, MHSA, FACMPE

Why benchmark? There are many reasons for benchmarking and most are related to a specific purpose (usually improvement). For example, a practice may want to determine how the billing office performance or physician productivity compares to other like practices. But in general, practices benchmark to gain a deeper understanding of where they are, where they want to go, and how to get there.

However, benchmarking when used in conjunction with trending—comparison to a standard over time—can be a powerful tool for assessing the past and present. And although the past cannot predict the future, it can be used to "suggest" the future. Therefore, benchmarking and trending can provide numerical insights into the past, present, and future "value" of an organization. And since the current state of healthcare—constantly changing and growing in complexity—dictates more elaborate and accurate methods of measurement, analysis, comparison, and improvement, long-term success has become directly related to a practice's ability to identify, predict, and adjust for changes.

Two key principles of benchmarking are (1) if you don't measure it, you can't manage it and (2) if you don't value it, you won't change it. These principles have been applied to non-healthcare industries for many years and are ideally suited for use in healthcare. It has been said, healthcare is the only service industry that doesn't treat itself like one. And although the healthcare industry appears to have gone to great lengths to separate itself from other business sectors, there are many more similarities than differences.

If You Don't Measure It, You Can't Manage It

In order to manage something, it's necessary to know what it is (description), where it is (comparison), and how it got there (context). This can be accomplished through measurement and benchmarking (see Exhibit 1.1). Proper practice management requires the use of subjective and objective measurement, analysis, comparison, and improvement.

If You Don't Value It, You Won't Change It

Driving change in a practice will affect every member of the organization and many will resist; therefore, the value (benefit) of instituting a change must outweigh the status quo or leaving things

Chapter 23: Benchmarking Practice Performance

"as-is". Measurement and benchmarking are not the final step in the process—they simply enable the process to evolve toward action. It is completely appropriate to measure and benchmark; however, this activity is in vain if something isn't done with the findings. Ideally, the results should be used to support change; however, they may be used to validate past changes or support the current status. And once a benchmarking process is finished, the practice can "pick-n-choose" the areas to focus its efforts, create buy-in (sell the change), and start the process of improvement (or repeat the entire benchmarking exercise, that is, continuous process improvement).

What can be done with the findings? There are many options: (1) drive and/or support change, (2) educate staff, (3) validate the past, (4) build buy-in, (5) conduct performance reviews, and (6) plan for the future.

When using the key benchmarking principles—"if you don't measure it, you can't manage it" and "if you don't value it, you won't change it," it is imperative to understand the interrelationship. First, proper management requires some degree of measurement to ensure the attribute of interest if fully understood (for example, is a FTE clearly defined?). Second, once measurement has taken place, management must decide whether the value of pursuing change is worth disrupting the practice in the quest for improvement. And third, if management feels the measures dictate a need to change and value can be realized by making the change, the most important step is to instill a sense of value in making the change with physicians and staff—without buy-in, the value (benefit) of change will never be fully realized.

Of special note, processes can easily be changed, but it's only with the support and buy-in of physicians and staff that real improvement can be achieved. It has been said, "if you take care of your people, your people will take care of you, but if you don't take care of your people, your people will take care of you."

What is benchmarking? Simply put, benchmarking is measurement and comparison for the purpose of improvement. In particular, medical practice benchmarking is a systematic, logical, and common-sense approach to measurement, analysis, comparison, and improvement (see Exhibit 8.1). Therefore, benchmarking is comparison to a standard. Benchmarking improves understanding of processes and clinical and administrative characteristics at a single point in time (snapshot) or over time (trend).[1] In addition, benchmarking is the continuous process of measuring and comparing performance internally (over time) and externally (against other organizations and industries). And finally, benchmarking is determining how the "best in class" achieve their performance levels. This consists of analyzing and comparing best practices to uncover what they did, how they did it, and what must be done to adopt it for your practice (process benchmarking).[1]

The 'Value' of Benchmarking

Proper benchmarking consists of more than simple comparison of two numbers. The true value of benchmarking lies in the numbers and through an understanding of the current state of the

Chapter 23: Benchmarking Practice Performance

Exhibit 8.1 What is Benchmarking?

- A systematic, logical, and common-sense approach to measurement, comparison, and improvement
- Copying the best, closing gaps/differences, and achieving superiority[1]
- "A positive, proactive process to change operations in a structured fashion to achieve superior performance. The purpose if to gain a competitive advantage."[1]
- Comparing organizational performance to the performance of other organizations[1]
- Continuous process of comparison with the best[5] or "the toughest competitors or companies renowned as leaders"[1]
- A method for identifying processes to new goals with full support of management[2]

practice, calculation of a difference between the current state and a new value or benchmark, knowing the context and background of the practice values when interpreting the results, deciding on a course of action and goal, and determining when the goal is achieved. For example, a comparison of average number of procedures per patient visit per physician to a known benchmark will only permit a mathematical analysis. However, what if one physician in the practice has been focusing on patients with simple medical issues that don't generate multiple procedures? The numbers alone would indicate this physician is underperforming and is below the others in procedural productivity; whereas, knowing the background, context, or other measures permit for a more detailed analysis. Perhaps this physician's focus is on acute care services and his/her average number of patient encounters per day is almost twice that of other physicians in the practice?

How to Benchmark[1]

There are several methods of benchmarking. A simple 10 step process might consist of the following:

1. Determine what is critical to your organization's success

2. Identify metrics that measure the critical factors

3. Identify a source for internal and external benchmarking data

4. Measure your practice's performance

5. Compare your practice's performance to the benchmark

6. Determine if action is necessary based on the comparison

7. If action is needed, identify the best practice and process used to implement it

8. Adapt the process used by other in the context of your practice

9. Implement new process, reassess objectives, evaluate benchmarking standards, and recalibrate measures

10. Do it again—benchmarking is an ongoing process and tracking over time allows for continuous improvement

Standardizing Data for Comparison[1]

Since the primary purpose of benchmarking is comparison, it is necessary to standardize data so organizations of different sizes can be compared. A common method for standardizing data is to convert measures to percentages, per unit of input, or per unit of output. For example, per unit of input can be presented as per full-time equivalent (FTE) physician, per FTE provider, or per square foot; whereas per unit of output can be presented on a per patient, per RBRVS unit, or per procedure level.

What's Our Baseline?

Benchmarking, like any activity involving comparison, requires an understanding of "where you are"—this is known as your baseline (see Exhibit 8.2). The baseline represents where you are today or where you've been and provides a point of origin or starting point. In addition, a baseline is an initial state that forms a logical basis for comparison.[5] For example, to determine whether physicians have increased the average number of procedures per patient visit, it is necessary to have two measurements – the old value or baseline and the new value. To calculate the delta (or difference) between the two values, a simple formula can be used: new value minus old value. Without the baseline, it would not be possible to perform this or many other calculations like percent change.

How Are We Doing?

This question can be answered by asking the question, "what is the difference between the baseline and current state (or where we are today)?" The baseline can be an internal benchmark (historical measure) from inside the practice, a benchmark across like practices from a MGMA Survey Report, or a benchmark from outside the industries like Disney or Wal-Mart. Additional insights can also be assessed by calculating the difference between current state and an established benchmark or industry average or median. To determine the difference there are several methods and statistical tools. For instance, the mathematical difference or delta consists of subtracting the baseline value from the current value. Whereas, percent change is a method for assessing changes over time or the proportion of one value in comparison to another. In addition to these methods, there are more statistically intense methods for determine difference that can be generalized across a group (see Exhibit 8.2).

Chapter 23: Benchmarking Practice Performance

Exhibit 8.2 What is the Difference?

- Mathematical Difference (Delta)
- New value minus Old value
- Current state minus Initial state
- Benchmark/Industry value minus Current state
- Percent Change
- Difference between three or more average

Interpretation of the difference is dependent on the method used. When using the delta, the difference will be a raw number, since the method consists of simple subtraction. Determining whether the difference is good or bad depends on the context, background, and what the values represent. For example, if medical revenue after operating cost per FTE family practice physician is $145,000 and the MGMA benchmark indicates a median of $214,377, then the delta is $69,377 ($214,377—$145,000). A delta of $69,377 may suggest poor practice performance, reduced physician productivity, a capital investment, or other practice deficiencies or large expenses. Whereas, the percent change method indicates this practice is only generating 67% of the median for similar types of practices (see Exhibit 8.4). Therefore, the result is different between delta and percent change and the interpretation may also be different.

Exhibit 8.4 Difference between Delta and Percent Change

Is the result positive or negative?	Delta	Percent Change
Positive value	New value (or benchmark) is *greater* than the old value. For example, $214,377 minus $145,000 equals a delta of $69,377	New value has *increased*. For example, $145,000 divided by $214,377 equals 0.67. This when multiplied by 100 equals 67%.
Negative value	New value is *less*.	New value has *decreased*.

Methods and Checklists

Failing to plan, it has been said, is planning to fail. Therefore, an integral component of the benchmarking process is the proper use of systematic methods, checklists, scales, and comparable measures. Systematic methods consist of formulas and ratios as found in this chapter. Checklists are a planning tool to ensure all variables and methods are used and considered—checklists ensure attention to detail and minimize the chance of missing steps in a process (see Exhibit 8.6). Scales provide the measuring stick—meaning they indicate whether your measures are high or low, good or bad, or where they are in comparison to others. And comparable measures are key to the heart and soul of benchmarking and provide a means for determining how your practice compares to others.

Chapter 23: Benchmarking Practice Performance

Exhibit 8.6 Example Checklist[3]

- ☐ The following checklist items can be used to increase the likelihood that a claim will be processed and paid when first submitted:
- ☐ Patient information is complete.
- ☐ Patient's name and address matches the insurer's records.
- ☐ Patient's group number and/or subscriber number is correct.
- ☐ Physician's social security number, provider number or tax identification number is completed and correct.
- ☐ Claim is signed by the physician.
- ☐ All necessary dates are completed.
- ☐ Dates for care given are chronological and correct – For example is the discharge date listed as before the admission date?
- ☐ Dates for care given are in agreement with the claims information form other providers such as the hospital, etc.
- ☐ Diagnosis is complete.
- ☐ Diagnosis is correct for the services or procedures provided.
- ☐ Diagnostic codes are correct for the services or procedures provided.
- ☐ CPT and ICD-9 codes are accurate.
- ☐ Diagnosis is coded using ICD-9-CM to the highest level of specificity.
- ☐ Fee column is itemized and totaled.
- ☐ All necessary information about prescription drugs or durable medical equipment prescribed by the physician is included.
- ☐ The claim is legible.

Small and Solo Practice Benchmarking

Small and solo practices share many similarities with their larger counterparts; however, the benefits and risks associated with the differences can have significant impact on a small practice's longevity and financial success.

Similarities with Larger Practices

There are many similarities small and solo practices share with larger organizations. For instance, all medical practices must operate in the same healthcare environment and deal with the same healthcare legislation, malpractice insurance, payers, collection challenges, patient needs and expectations, delivery/standards of care, and processes—just to name a few.

Also, the benchmarking methods used by large organizations are identical to those used by small and solo practices (see Exhibit 8.7). And the use of normalized metrics permits comparison regardless of organizational size. Common examples available in most benchmarking datasets consist of measures per FTE physician/provider, per square foot, per patient, per procedure, and per RVU.[3]

Chapter 23: Benchmarking Practice Performance

Exhibit 8.7 Similarities Regardless of Size or Type[4]

- Legislation can change payment (for example, Medicare/Medicaid reimbursement rates are determined through legislation)
- Costs are increasing greater than inflation (for example, medical supplies and equipment costs are increasing at a greater percentage than reimbursement rates)
- Expenses change
- Increases in physician compensation are from production (for example, much of physician compensation is based on physician production or the number of patients seen and the procedures performed)
- Health savings accounts will change patient behavior (for example, patients will treat medical care more like a product or service they pay for using the funds in their account)
- Hospitals are purchasing physician practices (again)
- Advances in medical care are changing care delivery
- Physicians are publicly rated for quality and outcomes
- Physicians are publicly rated for patient satisfaction

What's the Difference?

Small and solo practices are different from larger groups in several ways, some of which a beneficial, while others are not. For instance, smaller organizations are generally more flexible, can adapt/change quickly, and in general, tend to be more efficient. However, small and solo practices are more sensitive to the risks associated with costly mistakes, lack of alternative revenue generating methods, and the absence of (or antiquated condition of) robust information systems. For example, with only one or two physicians in a practice, what impact would a poor decision or loss of a physician (due to sickness or some other unforeseen event) have on the practice? Can a small practice afford to retain adequate earnings for contingencies? Does the existing information system compliment and add to the efficiency of the practice? And does it interface (communicate) with the information systems used by payers, hospitals, and other medical practices like referring practices/physicians?

Ultimately, the goals of smaller practices mirror those of larger groups—to have more satisfied patients, more fulfilling work environments for physicians and staff, and better economic outcomes.[2] However, the additional sensitivities of small and solo practices must be considered to ensure surprise events don't adversely impact the practice.

Practice Measurement

Measurement is the collection and organization of data. In many cases, measurement is a method of converting an array, group, list, or set of data into a single variable that describes the entire dataset. A mean or average is a calculation that summarizes the central tendency or mathematical

Chapter 23: Benchmarking Practice Performance

center of many data points, provided all data is of the same unit of measurement. In general, an average is the most common calculation used to analyze and compare data. It's the most common since most people understand the concept of an average and how to calculate it. For example, if we count the number of patients seen per month for the last 10 months for an eight provider family medical practice located in the suburbs, we have an array of data with 10 data points—one data point for each month (see Exhibit 3.1). If we also have a list with the number of patients seen per month for the last 10 months for an eight provider family medical practice located in a rural community, how can we easily compare these two practices? We can line up and organize the data points in ascending order, but what does this tell us? We might conclude the suburban practice sees a greater number of patients per month, but we can't accurately describe the difference or make a comparison. All we've done so far is arrange the data and guessed there was a difference by looking at or "eyeballing" the data—not the most accurate method. However, by calculating the average number of patients seen per month for the last 10 months for each practice, a single and accurate measure can be used to describe and compare the two groups.

Exhibit 3.1 Example of Measurement: Number of Patients Seen per Month

Month	Suburban Practice	Rural Practice
January	2,620	2,650
February	2,231	2,660
March	2,264	2,266
April	2,650	2,067
May	2,657	1,687
June	2,670	3,690
July	3,067	3,070
August	2,690	2,071
September	3,171	2,731
October	3,710	3,730
Sum of patients seen	**27,730**	**26,622**
Number of data points (months)	10	10
Average patients seen per month	**2,773**	**2,662**

Comparing these practices, the suburban practice, on average, sees more patients per month than the rural practice—111 more (average number of patients seen per month in the suburban practice minus average number of patients seen per month in the rural practice; 2,773 minus 2,662 = 111).

Art and Science of Benchmarking

Benchmarking, as it's related to measurement, is the art and science of comparison. The "art" takes place during the data gathering and interpretation phases and requires a method with some common sense; whereas, the "science" is the systematic and logical process of analysis. Once interpretation and

Chapter 23: Benchmarking Practice Performance

analysis have occurred, data is considered transformed into information that can be used for comparison and decision-making. That is, it is possible to determine whether the data is similar or different and by how much. Exhibit 3.2 represents several examples of metrics and associated benchmarks.

Exhibit 3.2 Examples of Benchmarks[1]

Encounters per FTE* physician	Mean	3,006	4,759	5,891	7,612	9,159
Total procedures per FTE physician	6,341	3,006	4,759	5,891	7,612	9,159
Physician work RVUs** per FTE physician	4,751	4,412	7,506	5,123	5,622	6,809
Physician compensation	4,751	1,426	3,684	5,123	5,622	6,809

Other topics associated with benchmarking are (1) continuous improvement (2) evaluation and assessment.[2] Continuous improvement refers to the need for repeated analysis using the same measures over time (trend). An evaluation is a subjective, personal judgment of the value (or worth) of something; whereas, an assessment is objective and quantifiable (or assigned a numeric value).[1]

Benchmarking Methods

Effective benchmarking consists of a systematic process; therefore, several methods have been developed to ensure the process is efficient (see Exhibit 3.3).

Proper measurement begins with selecting the right practice attribute, characteristic, property, dimension, or variable to be assessed.[5] In other words, what do we want to measure? For example, encounters per FTE physician, total procedures per FTE physician, and physician work RVUs per FTE physician are common examples of benchmarks and practice measures (see Exhibit 3.2). This book presents many practice attributes that have been operationally defined, that is, the attribute and measurement process have been clearly described in practice and literature as generally accepted. However, there may be practice attributes that are not typically measured or found in the literature. In these cases, it would be necessary to fully explore the characteristic before moving to the next step—this type of attribute could be called "homegrown." Of note, there are probably few instances when "homegrown" attributes are needed since the healthcare management field is sufficiently mature to have identified most, if not all, key practice characteristics.

Once a practice variable is selected, the next step is to decide on the appropriate method of measurement (or what metric should be used) and the intended purpose. There are two general categories of metrics: (1) informational and (2) actionable. Informational metrics provide a simple description and unlike actionable metrics, they don't clearly suggest ways of affecting change. For example, if we decide to measure the average number of patients seen per month in a suburban practice as a metric to describe monthly practice productivity, then this metric simply tells us the arithmetic mean;—it doesn't suggest anything more; whereas, actionable metrics are usually more complex, require an understanding of the context, and are compared to a benchmark or baseline. For instance, the formula to calculate average number of patients seen

Chapter 23: Benchmarking Practice Performance

Exhibit 3.3 Common Benchmarking Methods

Transfer Model[1]	Five Stages of Benchmarking[1]	5 Steps of Benchmarking[2]	10 Steps to Benchmarking[3]
1. Identification and documentation of best practices. 2. Validation and consensus of what to focus on and what are true best practices. 3. Transfer and develop buy-in; sell ideas to management and get commitment to performance assessments, identification of priorities, and establishment of a plan. 4. Implementation using team champions, selection of critical practices to support strategic initiatives.	1. Planning, selecting the processes to benchmark, and identification of customer expectations and critical success factors. 2. Form the benchmarking team from across the organization. 3. Collect the data from best practice organizations and identify own processes. 4. Analyze data for gaps. 5. Take action, identify what needs to be done to match best practice, and implement change.	1. Planning what to benchmark and what organization to benchmark against. 2. Analyze performance gaps and project future performance. 3. Set targets for change and communicate to all levels. 4. Develop action plans, implement plans, and adjust as necessary. 5. Achieve a state of maturity by integrating best practices into organization.	1. Determine what is critical to your organization's success. 2. Identify metrics that measure the critical factors. 3. Identify a source for internal and external benchmarking data. 4. Measure your practice's performance. 5. Compare your practice's performance to the benchmark. 6. Determine if action is necessary based on the comparison. 7. If action is needed, identify the best practice and process used to implement it. 8. Adapt the process used by others in the context of your practice. 9. Implement new process, reassess objectives, evaluate benchmarking standards, and recalibrate measures 10. Do it again, benchmarking is an ongoing process and tracking over time allows for continuous improvement.

Chapter 23: Benchmarking Practice Performance

per month (for the last 10 months) per provider for an eight- provider family medical practice is the sum of the number of patients seen per month for the last 10 months divided by the number of months divided by the number of providers (see Exhibit 8.1). If we use this formula as a metric to assess monthly practice productivity per provider and we want to improve productivity per provider, then this metric used in this context suggests, for example, we can affect change by working with individual providers whose average is below the practice's overall average to increase the number of patients seen per month by the provider of interest.

Several questions should be asked as part of preliminary measurement steps. For instance, what do you want to measure? Is it a generally accepted practice characteristic (typical practice factor) or is it a "homegrown" practice attribute (custom or self-defined factor or metric)? What metric should be used? What is the appropriate method for measurement? And finally, what type of metric do you wan to use and what is your intended purpose (information or action)?

Interpretation Pitfalls

Reliability is defined as repeatability and consistency. If given the same data set and using the same measure, someone else should be able to calculate, describe, and compare the data in the same way. For instance, if given the number of patients seen per month for the last 10 months in a suburban and rural practice and asked for the average number of patients seen per month for both practices, you would find the same average with the same comparison for each practice. Note that the same unit of measurement must be used, that is, all the data in your data set or data array should be the same unit of measurement (in the example above, all numbers are based on number of patients seen). Reliability cannot be achieved if the unit of measurement is different in any of the data used in the measurement. For example, you cannot calculate an average using 2650 patients seen in January, 2264 seen in February, 3265 seen in March, 2166 seen in April, 3167 seen in May, 1869 seen in June, 2771 seen in July, and 3171 appointments booked in August without first changing appointments booked to the number of patients seen in August.

Validity is meaningfulness within a generally accepted theoretical basis (see Exhibit 3.4).[1] Or simply stated, does it really mean what it's expected to mean or is it being interpreted accurately? How you interpret your data and measurements are as important as ensuring you have used a highly reliable method. Understanding what a particular measure is meant to describe is paramount to using data properly to support good decisions. For instance, averages (means) represent the mathematical center of an array of data or central tendency; whereas, the median is the 'actual' center-point of the array. In some cases, the average and median can be the same but often times, there is a difference. Therefore, knowing how a measure is used, collected, and how it's calculated will assist in supporting your decisions, that is, your conclusions and analysis will be more valid and meaningful. This is particularly important when presenting your findings to others since the better you understand the measures, why you selected them, and how to explain them to others—the value and usefulness of your results will add significant credibility to your recommendations and/or decisions.

Chapter 23: Benchmarking Practice Performance

Figure 3.4 Example of Meaningfulness

> It is important to understand the formulas used for measurement and how the measurement is collected and calculated. Using the data array from the previous example of number of patients seen per month (suburban practice):
> 2620 (Jan), 2231 (Feb), 2264 (Mar), 2650 (Apr), 2657 (May), 2670 (Jun), 3067 (Jul), 2690 (Aug), 3171 (Sep), 3710 (Oct)
> Average (mean) = Sum of all data divided by the number of data points
> Sum of all data = 27730
> Number of data points = 10
> Average = 2773
> Median = The data point in the center of the array (when arranged in order)
> Data array = 2231, 2264, 2620, 2650, 2657, 2670, 2690, 3067, 3171, 3710
> Center of array are two data points = 2657 & 2670
> Median = 2657 + 2670 divided by 2 = 2664
> NOTE: If the data array consisted of an odd number of data points, the median would be the true center data point

Another pitfall to avoid that is a common mistake is averaging averages, for example, presents a danger during measurement. Since any array of data points can be averaged (or measured using other methods), it's important to understand the limitations or implications of measuring calculated measures. The validity of the interpretation may be suspect (see Exhibit 3.5).

The extremely low and high values in all the practices are minimized or diluted (their effect is almost eliminated). The effects of the low productivity and high productivity practices almost eliminate one another which is why the average of the averages is near the average of the more balanced array (Family Practice 1).

Strength is related to validity and is the power, magnitude, or accuracy of your interpretation or how confident you are in your interpretation. For instance, if you want to describe the number of patients seen per month for three months (2231, 2264, and 2620), a mean is an ideal descriptive statistic (mean = 2372). This figure is somewhat descriptive of the lower months of 2231 and 2264, but a mean of 2372 is not descriptive of the higher months when 2620 patients were seen. Therefore, your confidence in a mean of 2372 patients seen per month provides a less accurate description of the average number of patients seen per month. However, if this array consisted of a large number of months, that is, a large dataset with many data points, the accuracy of this metric and your confidence in the descriptive power of the mean is much higher.

A final interpretation issue is related to the mutually exclusive and exhaustive nature of data. Mutually exclusive refers to a data point fitting into only one category.[2] For example, we decide months with 3,600 or more patients are categorized as high productivity, months with between 2,401 and 3,599 patients are medium or normal, and months with 2,400 or less patients are low. Therefore, each month 'fits' into only one category—that's mutually exclusive—a single month cannot be categorized as "high" and "medium." If a single month could be assigned to multiple categories, it would be difficult to accurately describe each month or interpret your findings.

Chapter 23: Benchmarking Practice Performance

Exhaustive refers to the description of the attribute, that is, does the definition encompass all collected attributes?[2] For example, since all the measurements taken consisted of the number of patients seen per month, this attribute was defined to be actual patient encounters with a provider and all collected measures were based on this definition. That is, patients seen only by a nurse were not included since these encounters didn't "fit" the definition (or criteria).

Management can use numbers to diagnose and treat practice deficiencies, plan improvements, and examine practice activities and processes. And because numbers are less susceptible to the effects of human variation (feelings and emotions), they are more appropriate for decision-making. The beauty of numbers comes from their brevity, clarity, and precision. For example, using the example array (list) of no-shows which shows the number of no-shows per day from last month, it is possible to quickly summarize the week or entire month regarding no-show activity (see Exhibit 4.3, Weekly Average and Total and Monthly Average and Total). These averages and totals provide a brief, clear, and precise picture describing no-show activity during each week or the entire month. There's little room for misinterpretation or confusion, provided a no-show is clearly defined, that is, a no-show is a patient who fails to show up within 15 minutes of an appointment rather than someone who fails to cancel 24 hours prior to his/her appointment.

Organizing a group of numbers is the cornerstone in the benchmarking process. An array or group of numbers only become valuable once they are organized; whereas, statistical methods and proper interpretation of the findings are necessary to uncover the useful information behind the numbers. A systematic approach is necessary and has been established through the use of averages (or means), medians, standard deviations, percentiles, quartiles, and percent change (see Exhibit 4.1). These techniques can be used to measure and benchmark all practice attributes. In addition, these methods are easy to use, understand, and communicate – most people are familiar with some, if not all methods.

There are a handful of key financial performance indicators understood and used by the majority of practices to measure financial operations. Many of these formulas are presented in this chapter as a comprehensive "starter set" of key performance indicators and financial metrics for benchmarking.

Key Financial Indicators

Benchmarks for many of the following formulas are available in the MGMA Cost Survey and Performance and Practices of Successful Medical Groups Reports.

Total net collections[1]

Net fee-for-service revenue + Capitation revenue – Provision for bad debt

Chapter 23: Benchmarking Practice Performance

Gross (unadjusted) collection ratio[1]

Definition: Indicates how much of what is being charged is actually collected.

Goal: Higher the better

$$\frac{Total\ net\ collections}{Total\ gross\ charges}$$

Note: In general, the goal of this measure is 'higher the better'; however, this metric will vary significantly depending on the fee schedule of the practice. For instance, a practice with a high fee schedule will have a lower gross collection ratio than a practice with a low fee schedule (setting a fee schedule too low can have a negative effect on net revenue). This metric is often used to measure billing office performance.

Gross collection ratio

Definition: Indicates a ratio of the amount of revenue "actually" collected over the amount charged.

Goal: Higher the better

$$\frac{Net\ FFS\ revenue\ or\ collections}{Gross\ FFS\ charges}$$

Adjusted (net) collection ratio[1]

Definition: Indicates how much of what is being charged (gross FFS charges) is actually collected after total adjustments to charges; does not include funds the practice should not receive (e.g., contractual allowances) and funds it will not receive (e.g., bad debt).

Goal: Higher the better

$$\frac{Net\ fee\text{-}for\text{-}service\ collections}{Net\ fee\text{-}for\text{-}service\ charges}$$

Average adjusted revenue per day[1]

Definition: Indicates the average amount of revenue generated per business day.

Goal: Higher the better

Chapter 23: Benchmarking Practice Performance

$$\frac{\textit{Adjusted charges for the last three months}}{\textit{Number of business days for the same time period}}$$

Note: It isn't required that the time period be three months; rather, it should be a recent period of time.

Days revenue outstanding[2]

Definition: Indicates how long it takes before claims/charges are paid.

Goal: Lower the better

Step 1: Calculate 'days revenue'

$$\frac{\textit{Total revenue for the last three months}}{\textit{Number of business days in the last three months}}$$

Step 2: Calculate 'days revenue outstanding'

$$\frac{\textit{Outstanding net A/R}}{\textit{Day's revenue}}$$

Days in A/R[3]

Definition: Indicates how long it takes before claims/charges are paid.

Goal: A net collection ratio (NCR) of 96% – 99% and 40 – 50 days in A/R (a days in A/R of 45 or less is ideal) indicate your practice is functioning efficiently and doing very well. If NCR is 93% – 95% and 50 – 60 days in A/R, there is some (little) room for improvement. And if 92% or less and 70 or more days in A/R, there is significant room for improvement in billing operations.[2]

$$\frac{\textit{Outstanding A/R}}{(\textit{Average monthly charges / 30})}$$

Note: Include at least the last three months to calculate the average monthly charges

Days in A/R[4] **(alternate calculation)**

Definition: Indicates how long it takes before claims/charges are paid.

Goal: Lower the better

Chapter 23: Benchmarking Practice Performance

$$\frac{Outstanding\ net\ A/R}{Average\ adjusted\ revenue\ per\ day}$$

Months revenue in A/R

Definition: Indicates the average number of months charges are outstanding for collection.

Goal: Lower the better

$$\frac{Total\ A/R}{(Annual\ adjusted\ FFS\ charges\ *\ 1/12)}$$

Expense to earnings[4]

Definition: Indicates the ratio of overhead (expenses) to revenue (collections).

Goal: Lower the better

$$\frac{Total\ operating\ expenses}{Total\ collections}$$

Average revenue per patient[4]

Definition: Indicates the average amount of revenue generated per patient seen. In addition, it can be used to determine the number of patients that must be treated to receive a predetermined amount of revenue (collections).

Goal: Higher the better

$$\frac{Total\ monthly\ collections\ for\ last\ month}{Total\ patient\ visits\ last\ month}$$

Average cost per patient[4]

Definition: Indicates the average cost of providing treatment per patient visit.

Goal: Lower the better

Chapter 23: Benchmarking Practice Performance

$$\frac{\textit{Total operating expenses}}{\textit{Total patient visits}}$$

Departmental or service ratio[4]

Definition: Indicates the expenses to revenues ratio for a specific department or service.

Goal: Lower the better

$$\frac{\textit{Total expenses for ancillary service for the last three months}}{\textit{Total net charges for all CPT codes related to ancillary service}}$$

Collections rate by payer[1]

Definition: Indicates different rates of reimbursement by payer.

Goal: Depends on many practice factors; should be proportional to the percentage of patients covered by each payer.

$$\frac{\textit{Net collections by payer}}{\textit{Total gross charges by payer}}$$

Note: Reimbursement received from a payer is based on the specific fee schedule established with a payer and is on a per procedure basis. Net collections is the sum of all reimbursement received from a payer; whereas, gross charges is what the practice billed the payer.

Volume and reimbursement by service line[1]

Definition: Indicates workload volume and revenue generated by service line; provides a method for identifying the relative contribution of each service line.

Goal: Depends on many practice factors; in most cases, volume should be directly related to revenue generated by service line.

Chapter 23: Benchmarking Practice Performance

Volume by service line:

$$\frac{\textit{Volume measurement (encounters/visits, RVUs, etc.) by service line}}{\textit{Volume measurement for total practice}}$$

Reimbursement by service line:

$$\frac{\textit{Revenue by service line}}{\textit{Total practice revenue}}$$

Surgical yield[14]

Definition: Indicates relative contribution of revenue generated from surgical or procedural workload to total practice revenue.

Goal: Depends on many practice factors; in most cases, volume should be directly related to revenue generated by service line.

$$\frac{\textit{Revenue derived from surgeries or procedures}}{\textit{Total practice revenue}}$$

Reimbursement per procedure code

Definition: Indicates average amount of revenue generated from procedures provided to patients.

Goal: Depends on many practice factors; in general, it will be higher if the procedures provided to patients are higher RVU procedures.

$$\frac{\textit{Net collections}}{\textit{Total number of procedures}}$$

Note: This metric can be adapted to show average reimbursement per procedure by payer using net collections by payer divided by total number of procedures charged to a payer.

Chapter 23: Benchmarking Practice Performance

In conclusion, benchmarking provides a means to measure performance in relation to a standard like the odometer (total mileage) in a car is used as one-of-many measures to assess value (future performance). For example, a car with 100,000 miles is probably worth less than the same type of car with 50,000 miles. And this can be determined by comparison (benchmarking) against a standard like the Kelly Blue Book values for a car or the Medical Group Management Association Surveys for medical practice performance. Trending, as it's related to benchmarking, can be used to compare practice measures against a standard over a period of time—this increases the "value" benchmarking by displaying past and present performance. And once benchmarks are complimented with trended data, it is possible to extend the measures into the future, thereby predicting the future. However, like any measure of a complex system or organization, a single measure studied in a vacuum, only provides a narrow view that's prone to error. Therefore, multiple benchmarks and trends should be evaluated to gain a richer, fuller, and more rewarding picture of the performance landscape and associated "value" of the organization.

---

1. E.W. Woodcock, "Practice Benchmarking," in Physician Practice Management: Essential Operations and Financial Knowledge (Sudbury, MA: Jones and Bartlett Publishers, 2005).
2. E.W. Woodcock, "Practice Benchmarking," in Physician Practice Management: Essential Operations and Financial Knowledge (Sudbury, MA: Jones and Bartlett Publishers, 2005).
3. DecisionHealth, "A/R Benchmarks," Part B News 20, no. 40 (October 16, 2006).
4. E.J. Pavlock, Financial Management for Medical Groups, 2nd ed. (Englewood, CO: MGMA, 2000).

Chapter 24

Understanding and Using MGMA Data to Normalize Physician Compensation and Perform Financial Statement Benchmarks

By David Fein, MBA

Overview

Valuation of a medical practice, as with any valuation, consists of quantifying earnings and risk. The drivers of earnings and risk in a medical practice, however, are unique. There is a tremendous amount of diversity in medical practices, with over 700,000 physicians in the US and over 470,000 working in over 40,000 group practices. There are single specialty, multi-specialty, hospital affiliated, non hospital affiliated, for profit, not for profit, and academic practices. Specifically, on the revenue side of a medical practice, the valuator must understand how encounters, procedures and surgeries (physician production/RVUs) drive gross charges and billings and how the collection process (which can be complicated in a medical practice) drives gross revenue. In addition, many medical practices operate on a cash basis and pay out dollars to physician owners before year-end earnings.

On the expenses side, a medical practice has significant physician and staff (e.g. business, front office, clinical, ancillary, contracted, etc.) costs as well as a number of unique general operating costs (e.g. medical supply, drug supply, lab, radiology/imaging, etc.). It's also very important to evaluate physician compensation in relationship to production, whereas in most businesses the relationship between compensation and production is disregarded. A medical practice can be managed by physician owners, a hospital, an HMO or MSO (Management Service Organization). Medical practices also exist within a complex regulatory environment which must also be evaluated in relationship to revenue and risk.

The diagram on the following page shows some of the revenue and expense drivers in a medical practice.

To accurately value a medical practice, the valuator must understand these distinct characteristics. Medical Group Management Association's (MGMA) data provides excellent information professional valuators rely on to normalize physician compensation and benchmark financial performance. It is also important to understand that valuation of physician compensation arrangements (particularly when paid by tax-exempt hospitals) is becoming an increasing focus of IRS and the Office of Inspector General scrutiny.

Chapter 24: Understanding and Using MGMA Data

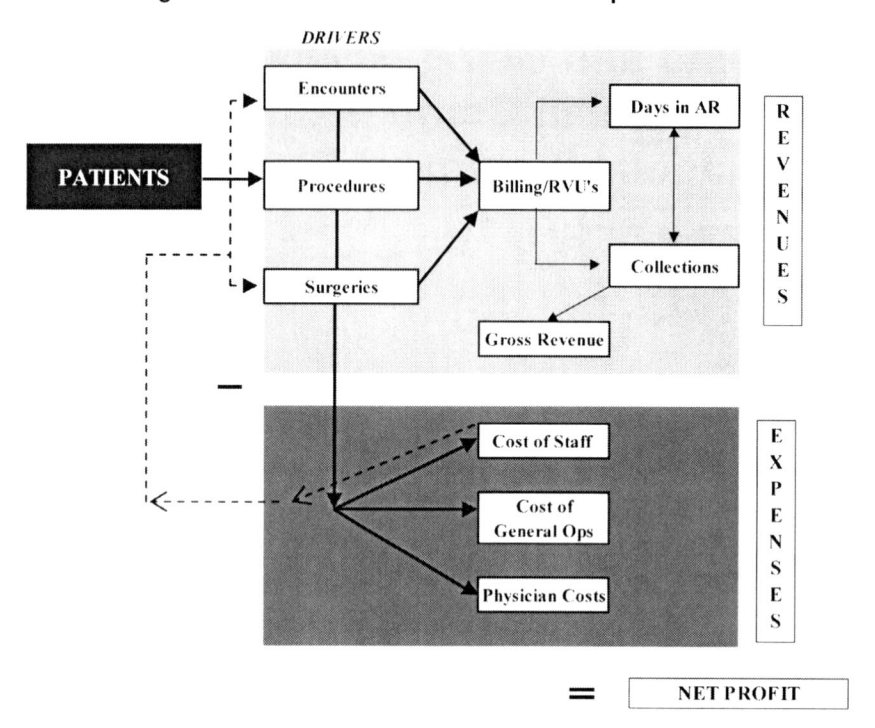

Figure 1: Medical Practice Revenue and Expense drivers

Founded in 1926, MGMA has nearly 21,000 members who manage and lead 12,500 practice organizations, representing 270,000 physicians. MGMA survey Interactive Reports provide the valuator with statistically robust data, as well as sophisticated, easy-to-use tools.

The MGMA is a premier source of benchmarking data, but valuators should consider other sources, as well. You can find benchmarking data from the following:

- MGMA offers a number of benchmarking tools as well as the comparative data

- CMS and state governments can provide some external data, but it may be limited

- Some specialty groups offer data, but it also may be limited

- Physician Compensation and Production Survey reports that can be used include:

- **Medical Group Management Association's** *Physician Compensation and Production Survey Report*

- **Sullivan-Cotter & Associates'** *Physician Compensation and Productivity Survey Report*

- **Hay Group's** *Physician's Compensation Survey Report*

Chapter 24: Understanding and Using MGMA Data

- **Hospital and Healthcare Compensation Services'** *Physician Salary Survey Report*

- **ECS Watson Wyatt's** *Hospital and Health Care Management Compensation Report*

- **American Medical Group Association's** *Medical Group Compensation & Financial Survey*

- **American Medical Association's** publications on physician statistics

MGMA data is specifically useful for valuators because:

- MGMA has conducted physician practice surveys for over 50 years

- Data is derived from group practices of all sizes, types and specialties (with major reporting categories separately portrayed)

- The 2007 Report on Physician Compensation observes more than 50,000 providers

- Distinguishes private and academic physicians

- The *2007 Cost Survey* observes more than 1,200 single and multi-specialty practices

- Cost surveys are individualized for some of the larger specialties

- Both tools use a census-style approach

- Built-in benchmarking tools are provided

As with any data, MGMA data has limitations you should understand. One limitation is the data may not be representative of all practices. Because participation in MGMA surveys is voluntary and all practices do not complete and return the survey questionnaires, respondents represent only a sample of medical practices. It's difficult, therefore, to determine if a sample is biased. Bias could occur if more professionally managed practices participate; with differences in region and size; with a lack of responses; and other characteristics.

It's important to use statistics correctly and understand both their strengths and weaknesses. There are a number of things to keep in mind when using statistics, including MGMA's:

- *Benjamin Disraeli* once said, "*Lies, damn lies and statistics.*" It's important to understand the data, how it was collected, what it truly represents, its strengths, limitations and appropriate application to avoid both misusing and misinterpreting statistics.

- Understand medians vs. means. Means include every data point; the median is the middle data point. Medians remove the impact of outliers and are a better representation of the midpoint than the mean.

- Skewness. The shape (or skewness) of sample can have a large impact on how you interpret the data. Understand not only the specific data points, but the overall response curve, as well. The shape of the curve is represented by the standard deviation, but having a good visual picture of what this represents can be very useful.

- Exercise your judgment. Understand the limitations of the data and do not read more into it than is warranted.

- Talk to your peers. They can validate your thinking and you can learn from them.

- Know the practice! Understand which MGMA data may not represent a particular practice due to specific characteristics of the practice.

- Consult other sources of information, such as specialty societies.

The Three Ps of Benchmarking

Before delving into the specifics of MGMA data, it's important to have a general feel for the kind of data the survey represents. MGMA data is best understood as a function of the three "Ps" of medical practice benchmarking. The three "Ps" are based on what the survey is observing or the "unit of observation." MGMA develops its survey products by sending out questionnaires to its members and asks questions about various aspects of physician and medical practice performance. The three major areas the surveys observe are the physician, the practice and the procedure. MGMA produces surveys covering each of these areas.

The first 'P' is for "Physician." Individual physicians are the focus of MGMA's *Physician Compensation and Production Survey,* which has over 50,000 responses from more than 100 specialties. This survey includes compensation and productivity (Compensation, RVUs, Collections, Gross Charges, etc.). This survey, in other words, revolves around what the physician is paid and what they produce. As a valuator, it's crucial to understand the relationship between physician compensation and production, and to normalize physician compensation in relationship to both of these metrics. The survey that relates to physician compensation and production,

The second 'P' represents the Practice. Based on the entire practice, the MGMA Cost survey measures more than 700 practice-wide variables, such as revenue, costs, staffing and A/R.

The third 'P' is Procedures. This survey is based on measuring individual procedures. There are more than 10,000 procedures physicians can perform and each has a unique CPT

Chapter 24: Understanding and Using MGMA Data

code. Think of procedures as the unique (mostly billable) tasks a physician performs when they see a patient. The CPT procedure codes are the basis for all medical practice billing and also are the basis for computing physician Work RVUs (more RVUs information to follow). Although there is a great number of complex analyses you can perform using procedure-based data, one of the most useful is understanding how physicians are coding (i.e., what CPT code they assign) office visits (CPT codes 99201 - 99205 and 99211 - 99215). Although this advanced benchmarking topic will not be covered in this chapter, it's a very useful analysis we encourage valuators to understand. The survey pertaining to procedures is the MGMA Coding Profiles Sourcebook.

The data we are going to examine in this chapter comes from two following MGMA Interactive Reports:

- *Physician Compensation and Production Survey*

- *Cost Survey*

This chapter will cover both compensation normalization and financial statement benchmarking, and how each of the Interactive Reports data and tools can be used effectively. The chapter is organized around some of the important steps in the valuation process and concepts unique to medical practice valuation. As these topics are discussed, I will explain more about the available data and relevant tools that provide the valuator a strong quantitative approach.

Benchmarking Basics

It's important to understand benchmarking basics to best use the MGMA Interactive Reports. Benchmarking means comparing the data from a practice to either internal or external standards. Internal standards can be based on either comparing to physicians within the practice or comparing to data from a different time period (i.e., this quarter vs last quarter). This chapter will focus on external benchmarking using the MGMA data as the external standard.

Benchmarking Checklist

To understand the general concepts and steps in benchmarking, let's review the benchmarking checklist from Consulting Training Institute's "Health Care Boot Camp." This checklist applies to both the Interactive Reports as well as the printed reports. The checklist takes you step-by-step through the benchmarking process:

Step 1: Determine what you are benchmarking (i.e., RVUs, Compensation, A/R aging, Cost per FTE, etc.).

Step 2: Determine what is the benchmark (i.e., the specific number you are benchmarking against. For example, median RVUs for Family Practice would be 4,073).

Step 3: What is the practice data? (If you are benchmarking RVUs, determine the physician's RVU data.)

Step 4: Determine how you compare to the benchmark.

- Is your performance better than the benchmark? ❏ Yes ❏ No

- Is your performance in an acceptable range? ❏ Yes ❏ No

- Is your performance worse than the benchmark? ❏ Yes ❏ No

- Is there any action we need to take? ❏ Yes ❏ No (This step can be ignored for valuation.)

Step 5: If the benchmark is not acceptable, estimate the economic benefit derived if the benchmark were achievable and quantify best-case potential. (This is a very valuable step for valuators to take.)

Note: Steps 6–9 can be ignored for valuation, but are included to provide the full benchmarking process.

Step 6: Assess potential changes if action needs to be taken.

Step 7: Quantify potential cost and estimate potential cost benefit of action/changes.

Step 8: What are the action items/responsibilities for the above action?

Step 9: How often will you review this benchmark and what progress do you expect?

On the following page is a diagram of the full benchmarking process. For the purposes of valuation, focus on the "Assess" phase of the process. If you consult with medical practices as well, you can provide a tremendous service to your clients by understanding and using the full benchmarking process.

How MGMA Interactive Report Can Help You Benchmark More Precisely

One important concept to understand is the difference between benchmarking against medians and using rankings. Medians (also called the 50th percentile) represent the midpoint of the data and are commonly used as the key measure to benchmark against. For example, the median compensation for a family practice physician (without OB) is $164,000. If the physician you are benchmarking is making $185,000, you would determine the difference as a percentage and use that as your benchmark. In this case, $185,000 is 13% greater than the median. If you have access

Chapter 24: Understanding and Using MGMA Data

to the entire curve of responses as you do in the Interactive Reports, however, you can quickly determine that $185,000 represents the 64th percentile. In other words, the compensation of $185,000 is larger than 64% of what the survey respondents reported as their compensation. Determining that your physician ranks at the 64th percentile is more precise than saying their compensation is 13% greater than the median.

Since response curves can have small or large standard deviations (i.e., be steep or shallow), it's difficult to quickly determine if the magnitude of the variation from the median is significant. MGMA Interactive Reports allow you to easily understand the shape of the response curve and exactly where your data is ranked.

Figure 2: This diagram shows the benchmarking process.

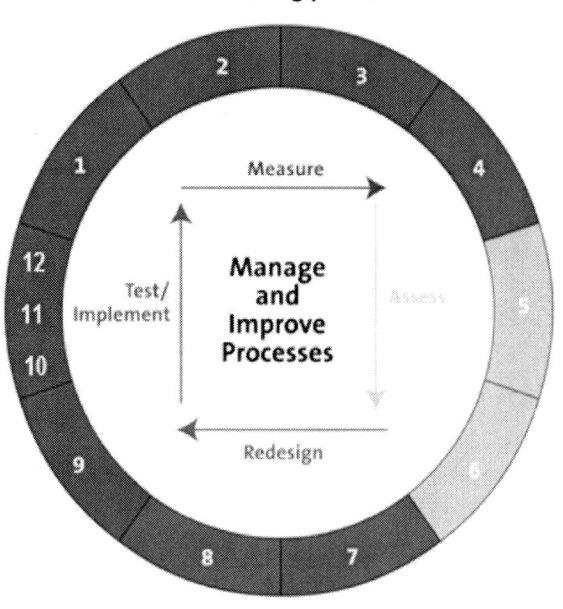

Figure 3 below shows two different response curves: One with a standard deviation of one, the other with a standard deviation of two. You can see that the number 2 on the x-axis represents the 99th percentile for the curve with a standard deviation of one; and the 62nd percentile for the curve with a standard deviation of two. The numerical difference from the median of zero is two for both curves, but this really represents vastly different situations. For the steeper curve, the data point 2 is extremely high, but for the flatter curve, the data point represents being slightly higher than the median.

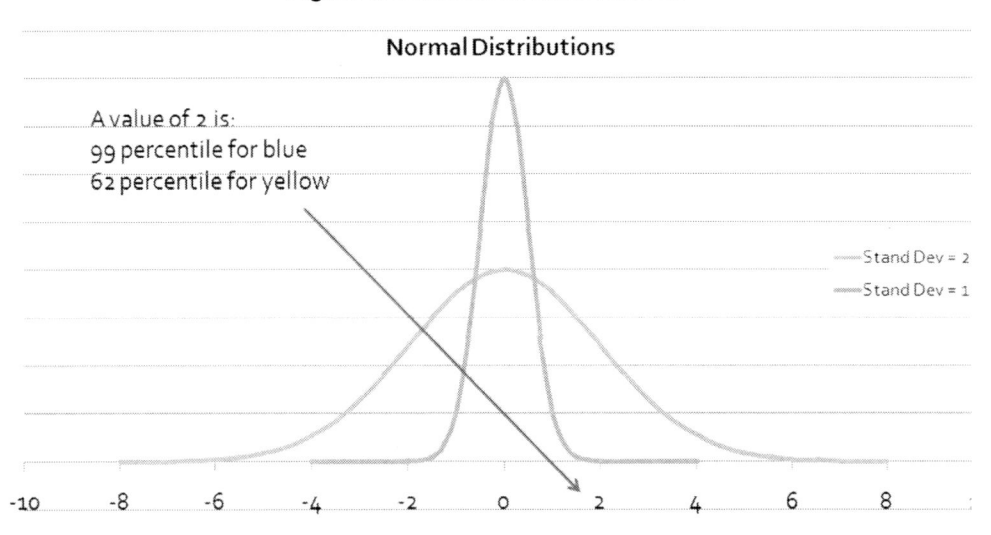

Figure 3: Standard deviation curves

Chapter 24: Understanding and Using MGMA Data

Normalizing Physician Compensation

MGMA's *Physician Compensation and Production Survey* Interactive Report provides a wide variety of data and tools to assist you in normalizing physician compensation for a medical practice valuation. The goal in normalizing physician compensation is to determine what is fair compensation for all owner/shareholder physicians and make an adjustment (normalize) for the excess compensation. For example, if there are three owner physicians in a family practice with each of them receiving more than fair compensation, you would make the following adjustments as shown in Figure 4:

Figure 4: Compensation normalization example

	Actual Compensation	Fair Compensation	Adjustment
Physician 1	190,000	174,000	16,000
Physician 2	209,000	174,000	35,000
Physician 3	234,000	174,000	60,000
Total	633,000	522,000	111,000

This example is simplified to show the concept of making adjustments for each physician based on fair compensation. However, in reality each physician's "Fair Compensation" will probably be different based on a number of factors including years in specialty, production, etc.

Your task in normalizing compensation is to develop a practice-wide compensation adjustment that will normalize the physician's compensation; it represents what owners would be earning if they were paid as non-owners. This means looking at each owner in a practice and determining the fair-market compensation for each of them. To accomplish this, you will have to look at each individual physician, taking into account all the various conditions that impact fair compensation, including specialty, years in the practice, production levels, etc.

It is possible to develop a practice-wide compensation adjustment by using metrics, such as overall compensation, as a percentage of revenue or average compensation on a per FTE (full time equivalent) basis. Using these practice-wide adjustments, however, is just an approximation and not nearly as accurate as evaluating each physician and making individual adjustments. It is recommended you develop normalization adjustments for each individual physician.

To understand physician compensation, you have to understand physician production. To understand production, you have to understand specific production metrics, including:

- **RVUs:** Relative Value Units, the value the Centers for Medicare and Medicaid Services (CMS) assigns to physician procedures.

- **Encounters:** Number of patients the physician treats

Chapter 24: Understanding and Using MGMA Data

- **Procedures:** Number of procedures the physician performs

- **Gross Charges:** How much the physician bills

- **Collections:** How much the physician actually collects

- **Hours Worked:** How many hours per week the physician works

Many valuators feel RVUs are the most appropriate measure for gauging production, but collections and charges are commonly used, as well. When using something other than RVUs as a productivity measure, you should compare RVU productivity to the measure being used. If both measures lead to the same conclusion about productivity, you can be more confident in the productivity measure. On the other hand, if RVUs provide a different productivity benchmark, you need to understand why. Collections can be used as a productivity measure, but a practice's billing procedures, payer mix and other variables make it more challenging to isolate physician production from collections data. Encounters are a very weak indicator of production because they measure how many patients a doctor sees rather than how much work they are performing. Therefore, attempting to gauge the amount of "work" a physician does based on encounters is not feasible. Gross charges can be a useful measure of productivity, but because there is wide variation in fee schedules, it's once again, difficult to isolate physician productivity from the data.

The relationship between compensation and production is an area where medical practice valuation is significantly different from general business valuation. In general business valuation, there is no standardized method to gauge "productivity," therefore compensation is analyzed without regard to productivity. An easy way to think about this is to consider physician compensation as based on the amount of work performed. The more work a physician performs, the more they are compensated. A physician who is making 50% more than another physician may be fairly compensated if they are working twice as hard (however you measure "work"). That is why only looking at compensation data, without considering production data, is not recommend for normalizing physician compensation.

What is an RVU?

Now that we understand that an RVU is a good measure of physician productivity, let us review what an RVU is and how it is calculated. There are a number of complexities in understanding RVUs, but this chapter will provide only the basics so you can use them as productivity measures to normalize physician compensation. For a fuller understanding of RVUs, we recommend *RVUs: Applications for Medical Practice Success*, 2nd edition, by Kathryn P. Glass, MBA, MSHA, PMP, available through the MGMA store.

RVUs were developed by CMS to provide a standardized method to measure the work performed by physicians, as well as provide the basis to reimburse physicians. RVUs were constructed to represent the relative intensity of resources required to care for a broad range of diseases and conditions and are associated with CPT codes. An RVU contains three components: malpractice, physician work (Work RVU or wRVU) and practice expenses. For our purposes, we will only use Work RVUs.

How are RVUs and CPT Codes Related?

When a physician provides any type of service to a patient, they must provide a billing code associated with that service to get paid. There are over 10,000 different CPT (Current Procedural Terminology) codes representing every possible service a physician can provide, from an office visit to brain surgery. Each CPT code has a corresponding RVU assigned to it; these values are the basis to determine how many RVUs a physician produces in a period of time

Let's look at an example to see how this works. The CPT for a new patient office visit is 99201; the associated work RVU is 0.45. The CPT code for removal of a brain lesion (brain surgery) is 61510; the associated work RVU is 28.41. This makes sense, because brain surgery requires more "work" from a physician than an office visit. The beauty of the RVU system is that for most specialties, it is a very reliable indicator of how hard a physician is working. However, if you are working with radiologists, anesthesiologists, pathologists or emergency room physicians, you will need to find a different productivity measure than RVUs, because RVUs do not accurately reflect the amount of work physicians in these specialties are performing.

For our neurosurgeon, let us take a very simple example calculating his RVU production for the year. We will assume he does only two procedures (new patient office visits and brain surgery). We need to determine how many of each of these procedures he performs, then calculate his total work RVU number for the year.

CPT Code	Frequency	Description	RVU Value	Total
99201	500	New patient office visit	0.45	225
61510	100	Removal of brain lesion	28.41	2841
Total				3066

Although this is a simplified example, the concept is exactly how you would calculate a physician's total work RVUs for a period of time. Take every procedure (i.e., CPT code) they perform, how many times they perform the procedure and multiply that frequency by the Work RVU value. Do this for every procedure, add them up and you have calculated the total number of work RVUs for the physician.

Remember, the MGMA data is based on annual data, so make sure your data also represents a full year. The MGMA data also represents a full-time physician, so make sure you normalize your physician data to one FTE. For example, if you have a physician that is working half time (i.e., 0.5 FTE), you will need to multiply their work RVUs by two, to calculate a one FTE equivalent.

Chapter 24: Understanding and Using MGMA Data

Luckily, most practice management systems have a built-in report that computes RVUs; just ask someone in the practice for the work RVU report. Make certain you specify "work RVUs" or you may get total RVUs, making your benchmarks meaningless because you will be comparing apples to oranges.

Using the Physicians Compensation and Production Interactive Report

The Interactive Report provides access to both data and tools to assist you in developing reasonable and defendable normalization adjustments for physician compensation. It also offers a wealth of data on more than 100 specialties and breaks the data down in a number of categories, including:

- By all providers
- Group type
- Region of the country
- Method of compensation
- Ownership

The metrics the survey reports on are as follows:

Compensation	Total compensation Retirement contribution
Productivity	Collections Gross charges Work RVUs Total RVUs Encounters Surgical cases Hours worked per week Weeks worked per year
Relationship of compensation to productivity	Compensation per $ of collections Compensation per $ of gross charges Compensation per work RVU Compensation per total RVU

Chapter 24: Understanding and Using MGMA Data

The Interactive Report also includes data based on individual characteristics:

- Specialty
- Years of experience
- Gender
- Partner/shareholder status

And organizational characteristics:

- Ownership
- Geographic location
- Percent of capitation contracts
- Compensation method
- Group type

There are two basic tasks the Interactive Reports will be used for: Opening tables and using the built-in benchmarking tools. When the Interactive Report starts, you'll see this startup dialog box in Figure 5:

Figure 5-Startup dialog in the Interactive Report

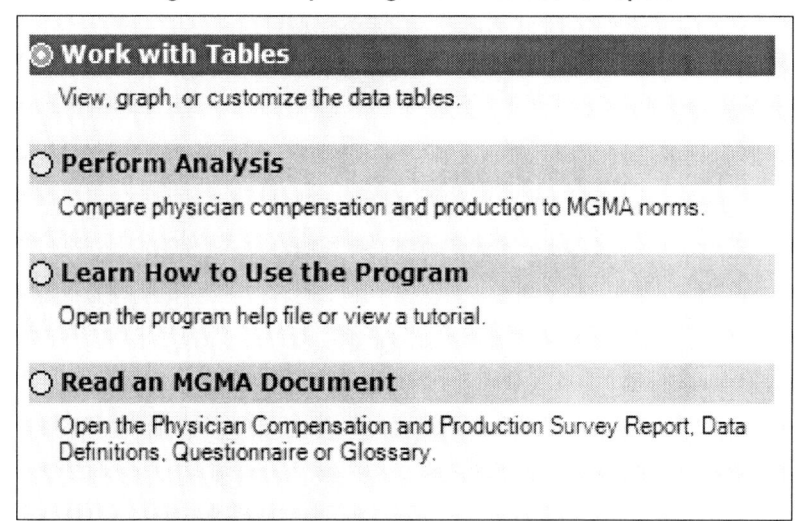

◉ **Work with Tables**
View, graph, or customize the data tables.

○ **Perform Analysis**
Compare physician compensation and production to MGMA norms.

○ **Learn How to Use the Program**
Open the program help file or view a tutorial.

○ **Read an MGMA Document**
Open the Physician Compensation and Production Survey Report, Data Definitions, Questionnaire or Glossary.

Chapter 24: Understanding and Using MGMA Data

From this dialog, you can perform all the major functions of the Interactive Report. We encourage you to read the MGMA documentation, particularly the Survey Data Definitions for a clear understanding of each metric in the survey. When you are collecting data from a practice, it is crucial you explain exactly what you are looking for. Otherwise, you may be provided data which does not match the MGMA definitions and your comparisons will be meaningless. For example, if you are seeking encounters, be sure the practice is not providing procedures.

To open a table, select the "Work with Tables" option or the "Open Tables" toolbar button from the main menu. You will see the following dialog (advanced mode is shown) in Figure 6:

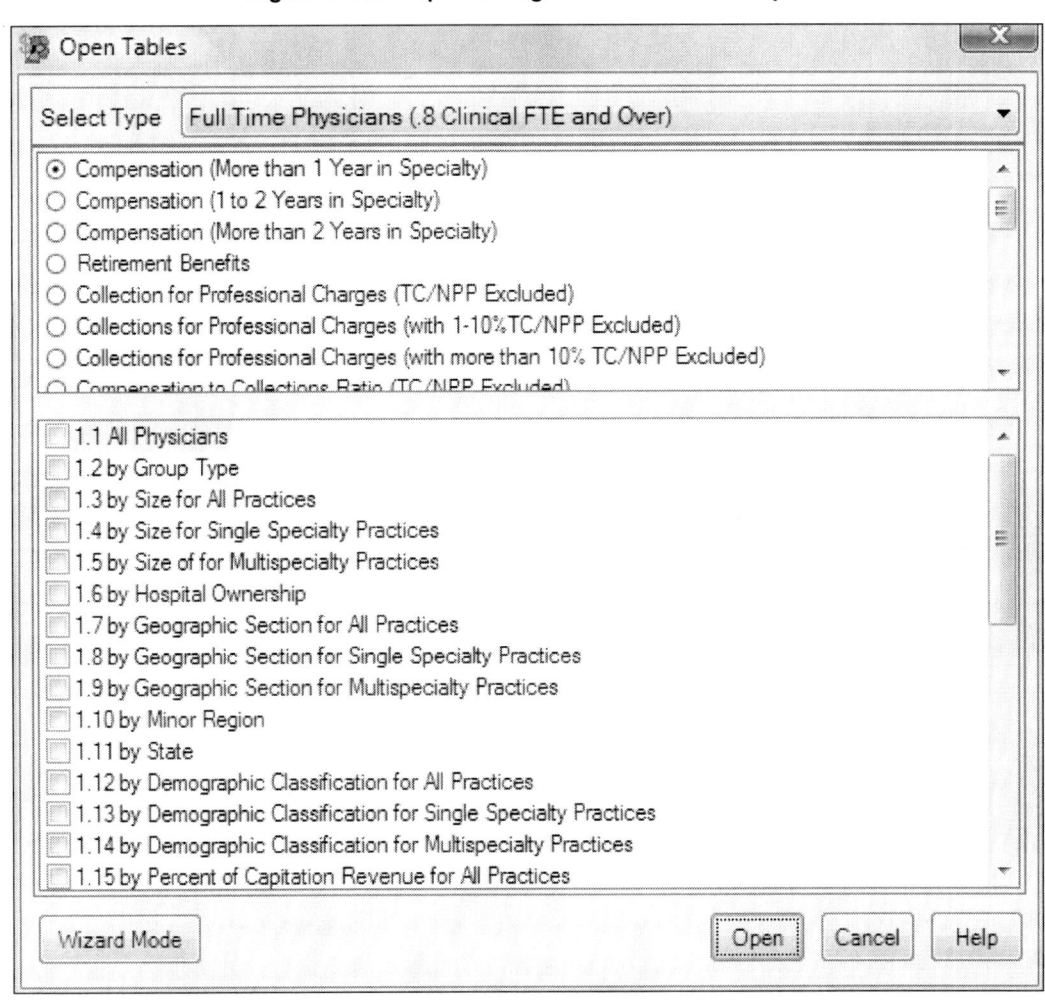

Figure 6-Table open dialog in the Interactive Report

Chapter 24: Understanding and Using MGMA Data

This dialog allows you to open any table on the Interactive Report. Note that for every metric (compensation, retirement benefits, collections, etc.) there are a number of tables available for view. Select the metric, then choose the table to open. For example the Compensation for All Physicians (Table 1.1) appears as below in Figure 7:

Figure 7-Table 1.1

Specialty	Providers	Practices	Mean	Std. Dev.	25th %tile	Median	75th %tile	90th %tile
Allergy/Immunology	175	85	$295,873	$136,255	$208,263	$267,688	$340,967	$539,160
Anesthesiology	3,903	184						
Anesthesiology: Pain Management	191	62						
Anesthesiology: Pediatric	105	10						
Cardiology: Electrophysiology	203	96						
Cardiology: Invasive	528	139						
Cardiology: Inv-Intvl	627	161						
Cardiology: Noninvasive	516	138						
Critical Care: Intensivist	97	20						
Dentistry	58	18						

Specialties are displayed on the left, with statistics shown in the columns. Be aware the Interactive Report will not display data unless there are at least 10 providers (physicians) and three unique practices. If you see blanks or stars in the data, it's because there are insufficient physicians or practices.

Since the Interactive Report contains every percentile from 10–90, you can customize the display to show more of the data. This is helpful to get a feel for what the entire MGMA curve looks like. The same table expanded to show deciles appears as below in Figure 8:

Figure 8-Table 1.1 expanded to show deciles

Specialty	Providers	Practices	Mean	Std. Dev.	10th %tile	20th %tile	30th %tile	40th %tile	Median	60th %tile	70th %tile	80th %tile	90th %tile
Allergy/Immunology	175	85	$295,873	$136,255	$161,624	$196,749	$218,202	$239,055	$267,688	$284,229	$320,976	$374,534	$539,160
Anesthesiology	3,903	184											
Anesthesiology: Pain Management	191	62											
Anesthesiology: Pediatric	105	10											
Cardiology: Electrophysiology	203	96											
Cardiology: Invasive	528	139											
Cardiology: Inv-Intvl	627	161											
Cardiology: Noninvasive	516	138											
Critical Care: Intensivist	97	20											
Dentistry	58	19											
Dermatology	361	128											

You can set the program defaults to always show more data so you do not have to customize each table. The Interactive Report allows you to open many tables at the same time to view multiple metrics or slices of the same table. All of the tables can be easily exported to Excel for custom analysis and charting. You also can chart any table by selecting the chart toolbar buttons.

Benchmarking Tools

One of the most important functions of the Interactive Report is the seven built-in benchmarking tools, which allow you to input data from a practice and have the benchmarks performed automatically.

Chapter 24: Understanding and Using MGMA Data

Physician Benchmarking Tool

This comprehensive benchmarking tool provides both internal (i.e., physician against physician) and external (i.e., against MGMA norms) benchmarking. You can input data monthly, quarterly or annually. It provides a ranking report both in table and graphic formats. You can automatically load data from a practice's IT system into this tool, without having to manually input data. This tool also produces a number of tables and charts, including the ranking report below in Figure 9, which you can export to Excel for custom analysis. Note each physician is ranked for each metric benchmarked; the rankings show exactly where the physician lies on the curve.

Figure 9-Ranking report section of the Physician Benchmarking Tool

Physician Ranking Compared to MGMA Data for Specialty Cardiology: Invasive				
	MGMA	Tyler Jones	Michael Cane	Sample Practice
Compensation	Median	3 to 7 years in Specialty	8 to 17 years in Specialty	Practice Average
Physician Compensation	$431,533	<10th %tile	68th %tile	30th %tile
Physician Retirement Benefits	$29,500	18th %tile	70th %tile	32nd %tile
Production				
Physician Collection for Professional Charges	$629,195	42nd %tile	45th %tile	42nd %tile
Physician Gross Charges	$1,497,479	13th %tile	58th %tile	34th %tile
Physician Total RVUs	18,419	12th %tile	31st %tile	20th %tile
Physician Work RVUs	9,256	27th %tile	48th %tile	38th %tile
Physician Ambulatory Encounters	2,257	31st %tile	43rd %tile	36th %tile
Physician Hospital Encounters	1,264	34th %tile	52nd %tile	43rd %tile
Physician Surgery/Anesthesia Cases	82	61st %tile	82nd %tile	71st %tile
Physician Clinical Hours Worked per Week	40	54th %tile	23rd %tile	53rd %tile
Physician Weeks Worked per Year	46	11th %tile	11th %tile	11th %tile

Physician Compensation Analysis Tool

This tool offers a quick method to determine compensation based on data from a number of tables. The output (Figure 10, following page) is a weighted average compensation that allows you to change the default weights and recalculate the weighted average compensation level.

Physician Compensation Estimator Tool

This tool provides a predictive statistical model based on the most significant compensation drivers. *Note: This tool should not be used to normalize physician compensation.*

Physician Pay-to-Production Plotter Tool

This is the single best (and statistically valid) method to get a comprehensive picture of how physician compensation and production (RVUs and Collections) are related. You can input the compensation and production values for your physicians, and they are plotted against the MGMA data. This is the only tool that allows you to see individual MGMA responses rather than statistics based on the responses. The Pay-to-Production Plotter Tool offers a significant

Chapter 24: Understanding and Using MGMA Data

Figure 10-Compensation Analysis Tool

Data Source	Compensation	Weight
Physician Compensation by All Physicians All Physicians	187,393	1
By Years in Specialty: 1 to 2 years	-	0
By Method of Compensation: 1-99% prod less allocated overhead	-	0
By Group Type: Single Specialty	187,396	1
By Geographic Location: Midwest	251,518	1
By Gender: Male	201,148	1
By Size of Practice: 10 FTE or fewer	212,785	1
Weighted Average Compensation Level	$ 208,048	

advantage to using compensation and production tables to correlate compensation and production, because the data is based on a sample population that responded to both the compensation and production questions. In this case, RVUs are along the x-axis, with compensation along the y-axis. You will see your physicians plotted as diamonds against the MGMA data (circles) in Figure 11 below:

Figure 11-Pay-to-Production plotter

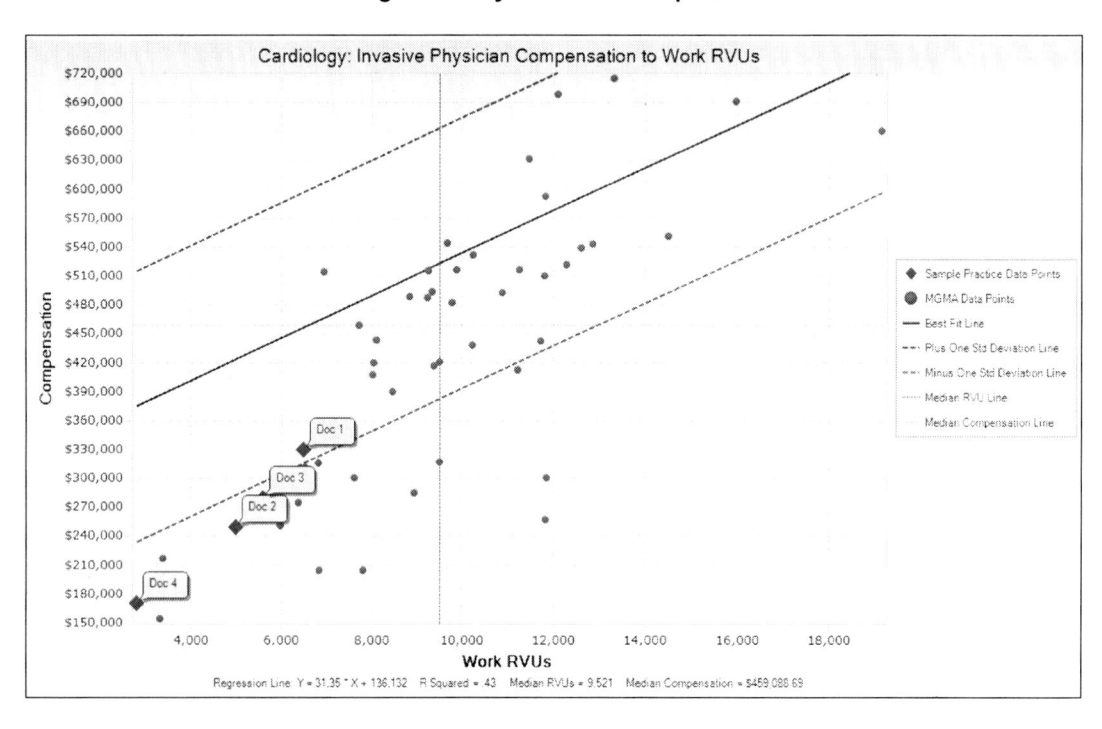

Chapter 24: Understanding and Using MGMA Data

Physician Dashboard Report Tool

This tool provides a 50,000-foot view of physician compensation and production in a dashboard format. The dashboard gauges provide rankings for compensation, charges, collections, RVUs, ambulatory encounters and hospital encounters. Because the dashboard presents the data in an easy-to-understand, green-yellow-red gauge format, the "benchmarking story" the gauges tell can be communicated to those who do not understand statistics, benchmarks or MGMA data. Figure 12 shows the dashboard:

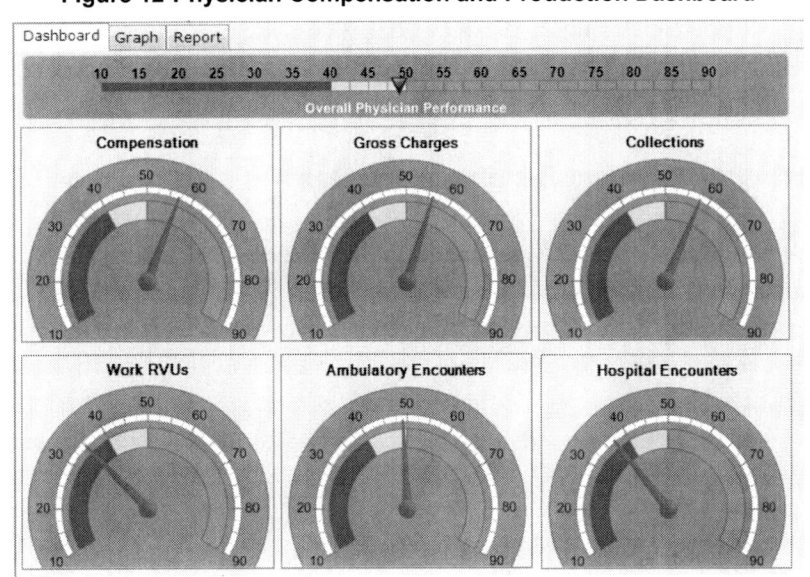

Figure 12-Physician Compensation and Production Dashboard

Management Summary Analysis Tables Tool

Provides summary tables for the management data that is included in an expanded version of the Physicians Compensation Interactive Report.

RVU 06-08 Conversion Utility Tool

This tool allows you to convert work RVUs from one year's values to another year's values. RVU values changed substantially between 2006 and 2007 and a little between 2007 and 2008. It's important the data you input into the benchmarking tools and the comparisons you make are based on the same year's RVU scale.

Chapter 24: Understanding and Using MGMA Data

Financial Statement Benchmarking

In the normal course of valuing a company, a financial statement benchmark often is performed to better understand how the company performs against industry norms. Performing this analysis assists the valuator is assessing ongoing cash flows, company risk and sustainable growth. One of the challenges of financial statement benchmarking, however, is there is no direct correlation between the results of benchmarking and drivers of business value (cash flows, risk and growth). In other words, there is no accepted valuation standard that allows the valuator to apply a formula or method to translate the results of financial statement benchmarking into something directly related to company value. Financial statement benchmarking will provide you a better understanding of the practices financial and operational dynamics and give you a quantitative approach to assist you in developing and defending your assumptions relating to value drivers.

Finding Financial Statement Benchmarking Data

In looking for financial statement benchmarking data for medical practices, the industry has relied on sources such as Risk Management Association (RMA), Integra and other general sources of benchmarking data. Although this general data provides some insight into how a medical practice is performing, a medical practice is substantially different from a general business. For example in RMA data, you'll find common size statements and general financial ratios for physician practices, but the underlying financial and operational drivers that are unique to a medical practice are ignored.

This is where the MGMA data provides a far superior set of data and tools to benchmark a medical practice. RMA provides approximately 45 metrics (i.e., data points) MGMA's *Cost Survey* has more than 700.

Medical Practice Benchmarking Basics

To understand financial statement benchmarking for medical practices you have to understand some of the value drivers in the practice. To understand these drivers, you have to understand the fundamental categories of group practice metrics including:

- **A/R:** Accounts receivable should be broken down per physician, as well as a percentage of total medical revenue. You should also review a standard A/R aging.

- **Gross Charges by Payer Type:** A practice's revenue can be significantly impacted by its payer mix (i.e. insurance companies).

- **Charges and Revenue:** Physician charges and revenue should be broken down per physician and as a percentage of total medical revenue.

Chapter 24: Understanding and Using MGMA Data

- **Operating Cost:** General operating costs should be broken down per physician, as well as a percentage of total medical revenue.

- **Provider Cost:** Provider costs (i.e., cost for anyone providing billable services including physicians, PA, RNs, etc.) should be broken down provider per physician, per provider along with as a percentage of total medical revenue.

- **Staff FTE Levels and Costs:** Staff costs should be broken down by FTE (i.e., how many FTE per position) and their associated costs. The data should be also broken down on a per FTE basis as well as a percentage of total medical revenue.

- **Procedures:** Procedures are broken down on a per FTE basis.

This data, as you can see, delves deeper into the dynamics of value in a medical practice than a general data set like RMA. As with the Physician Compensation data, it's important to understand the exact definition of each metric you use to obtain and interpret the data correctly. The *Cost Interactive Report* includes a definitions document we strongly encourage you read to be sure you are collecting data based on the same definitions that MGMA uses to collect it. There also are a number of complex formulas that go into calculating some of these metrics. By using the benchmarking tools in the Interactive Report, you are assured the calculations are performed correctly.

Using the Cost Interactive Report

The Cost Interactive Report is based on observing organizations, not individuals. The data is presented in 30 tables that cover the 700+ metrics. Each "slice" of data contains the exact same 30 tables. The 30 tables include the following:

Staffing and Practice Data

- Accounts Receivable Data, Collection Percentages and Financial Ratios

- Breakout of Total Gross Charges by Type of Payer

- Staffing, RVUs, Patients, Procedures and Square Footage per FTE Physician

- Charges and Revenue per FTE Physician

- Operating Cost per FTE Physician

- Provider Cost per FTE Physician

Chapter 24: Understanding and Using MGMA Data

- Net Income or Loss per FTE Physician

- Charges and Revenue as a % of Total Medical Revenue

- Operating Cost as a % of Total Medical Revenue

- Provider Cost as a % of Total Medical Revenue

- Net Income or Loss as a % of Total Medical Revenue

- Staffing, RVUs, Patients, Procedures and Square Footage per FTE Provider

- Charges, Revenue and Cost per FTE Provider

- Staffing, RVUs, Patients and Procedures per 10,000 Square Foot

- Charges, Revenue and Cost per Square Feet

- Staffing, Patients, Procedures and Square Footage per 10,000 Total RVU

- Charges, Revenue and Cost per Total RVUs

- Staffing, Patients, Procedures and Square Footage per 10,000 Work RVU

- Charges, Revenue and Cost per Work RVUs

- Staffing, Patients, Procedures and Square Footage per 10,000 Patients

- Charges, Revenue and Cost per Patient

- Activity Charges to Total Gross Charges Ratios

- Medical Procedure Data (inside the practice)

- Medical Procedure Data (outside the practice)

- Surgery/Anesthesia Procedure Data (inside the practice)

- Surgery/Anesthesia Procedure Data (outside the practice)

- Clinical Laboratory/Pathology Procedure Data

- Diagnostic Radiology and Imaging Procedure Data

Chapter 24: Understanding and Using MGMA Data

- Nonprocedural Gross Charge Data

The data is broken down by:

- Per FTE physician
- Per FTE provider
- Expense as a percentage of total medical revenue
- Per square foot
- Per total RVU
- Per work RVU
- Per patient

The key indicators for medical group practices include the following:

Financial	Revenue - Medical revenue, ancillaries, other revenue Expense - Support staff, general operating and provider expense
Operational	Staffing Process efficiency and quality Resource utilization Contracting Relationship management – referrals/marketing
Clinical	Profile Quality – outcomes, adverse events Patient satisfaction Compliance

Chapter 24: Understanding and Using MGMA Data

Individual	Productivity – work effort
	Income/Cost
	Clinical Profile – quality, procedure mix
	Job Performance
Environmental	Population
	Other Medical Groups – partners/competitors
	Payer Market
	Hospital Market
	Vendors

Depending on the nature of the engagement, you may have to understand and review one or more of these areas. The Interactive Report provides a robust benchmarking tool that allows you to quickly and easily perform a financial and operational benchmark.

The two basic tasks you will use the Interactive Report for are opening tables and using the built-in benchmarking tools. When the Interactive Report begins, you'll see the following startup dialog box in Figure 13:

Figure 13-Startup dialog in the Interactive Report

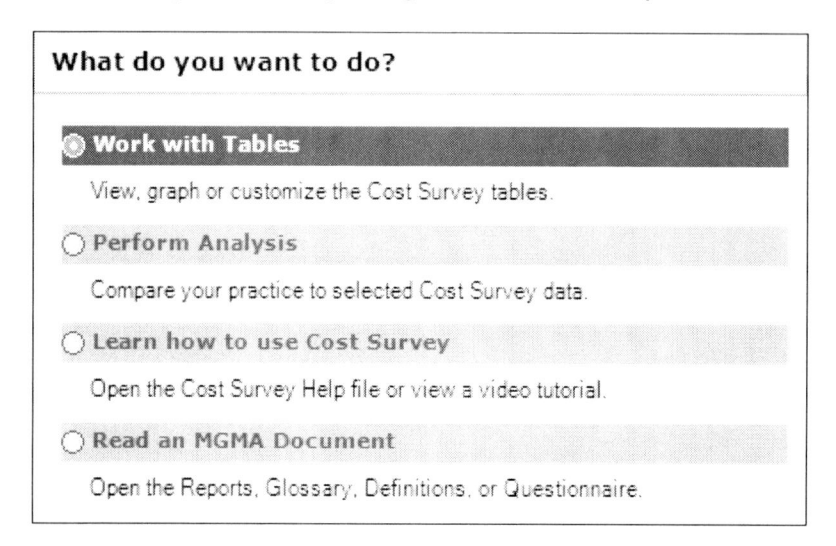

Chapter 24: Understanding and Using MGMA Data

To open a table, select the "Work with Tables" option or the "Open Tables" toolbar button from the main menu. You will see the following dialog (advanced mode is shown) in Figure 14:

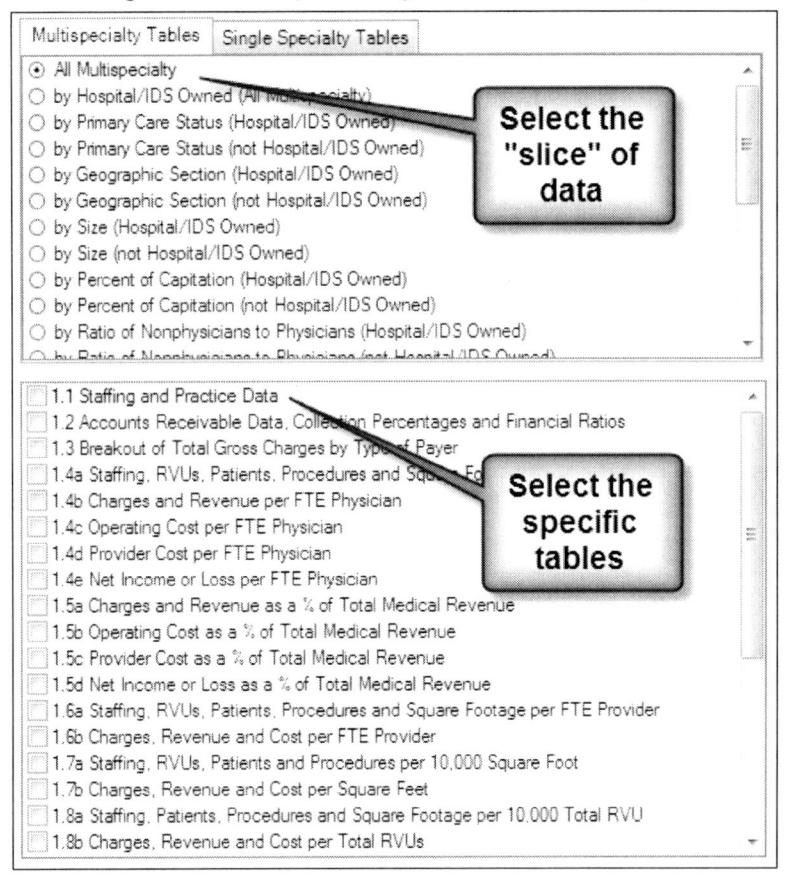

Figure 14-Table open dialog in the Interactive Report

The Interactive Report consists of both multispecialty and single-specialty tables. In each of these categories, you may select from a number of different data "slices," including All, Hospital Owned, Geographic Section, etc. The next step is to pick one of the tables (1.1 –1.11h) to display the specific data you are interested in. For all Multispecialty, Staffing and Practice Data, the table (1.1) appears as in Figure 15:

Figure 15-Table 1.1

Staffing and Practice Data	Practice Type							
	All Multispecialty							
	Count	Mean	Std. Dev.	10th %tile	25th %tile	Median	75th %tile	90th %tile
Total provider FTE	282	69.76	86.47	9.45	18.37	45.51	89.79	160.93
Total physician FTE	325	52.90						
Total nonphysician provider FTE	283	13.95						
Total support staff FTE	325	257.65						
Number of branch clinics	315	8.95						
Square footage of all facilities	279	110,946						

The AHLA/BVR Guide to Healthcare Valuation

Metrics are on the left; statistics are shown in the columns. As with the *Physician Compensation and Production* Interactive Report, the program will not show data unless there are at least 10 providers (physicians) and three unique practices. If there are see blanks or stars in the data, it is because there are insufficient physicians or practices.

Since the Interactive Report contains every percentile from 10–90, you can customize the display to show more data. This is helpful to get a feel for what the entire MGMA curve looks like. The same table expanded to show deciles appears as below in Figure 16:

Figure 16-Table1.1 expanded to show deciles

Staffing and Practice Data	Practice Type — All Multispecialty										
	Count	Mean	Std. Dev.	10th %tile	20th %tile	30th %tile	40th %tile	Median	60th %tile	70th %tile	80th %tile	90th %tile
Total provider FTE	282	69.76	86.47	9.45	15.84	21.95	29.12	45.51	55.48	71.42	102.78	160.93
Total physician FTE	325	52.90										
Total nonphysician provider FTE	283	13.95										
Total support staff FTE	325	257.65										
Number of branch clinics	315	8.95										
Square footage of all facilities	279	110,946										

In the Cost Interactive Report, there is data available for multispecialty and 18 single-specialty practices. If your specialty is not provided, you will either have to use the multispecialty data or select a single specialty you feel is representative of the specialty.

Benchmarking Tools

One of the most important functions of the Interactive Report are three built-in benchmarking tools, which allow you to input practice data and have the benchmarks performed automatically.

Dashboard Report Tool

This tool provides a 50,000-foot view of a medical group in a dashboard format. The dashboard gauges provide rankings for Total Medical Revenue per Physician, Total A/R per Physician, Total Operating Cost per Physician, Total General Operating Cost per Physician, Total Support Staff Cost per Physician and Total Medical Revenue after Operating Cost per Physician. Once again, because the dashboard presents the data in an easy-to-understand, green-yellow-red gauge format, the "benchmarking story" can be communicated to those who do not understand statistics, benchmarks or MGMA data. The following screen shows the dashboard in Figure 17.

Practice Performance Report Tool

This is the tool you want to use if you are a valuator. Once data is collected, you can perform a comprehensive income statement, staffing, A/R and ratio analysis in under an hour. As with all benchmarking tools, select the areas you want to benchmark and ignore the rest. Unless you

Chapter 24: Understanding and Using MGMA Data

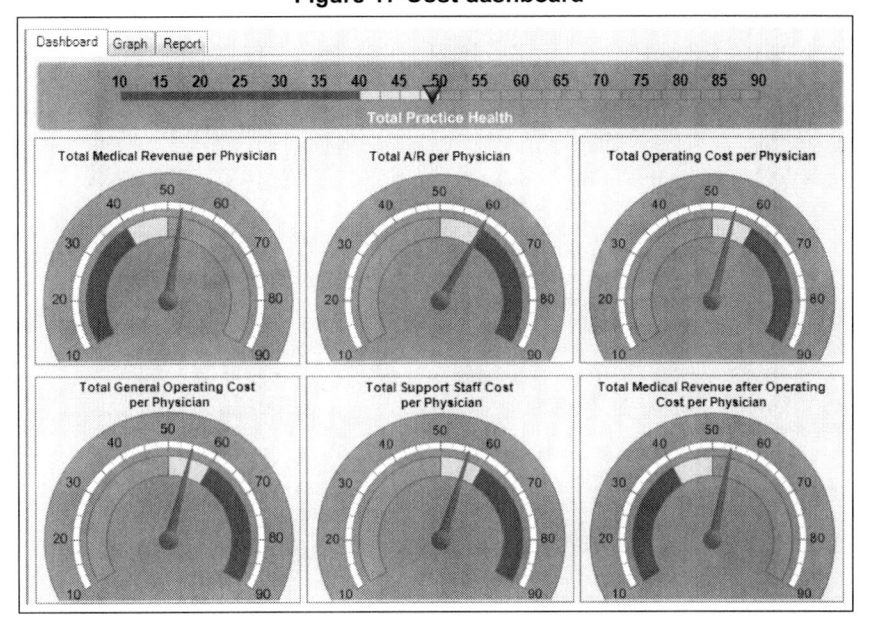

Figure 17-Cost dashboard

have the background to interpret staffing data (FTEs and Costs), stick with the other sections of this tool. Staffing levels and costs, however, are a significant driver of value in a medical practice; we encourage you to learn how this area impacts both financial performance and value. This tool is Excel-based, so you can export the entire tool to perform detailed analysis, roll-ups and other custom analyses. It is also possible to pre-populate the tool with data, so you do not have to type in each engagement's data. Figure 18 shows the first input screen from the tool.

Once you input data, the tool performs the rest of the calculations and benchmarks, including a ranking report. The following schedule shows the Revenue and Cost as a percentage of Total Medical Revenue, which is calculated based on the input screen. The last three columns show MGMA data, the differences between the practice and MGMA data, and the ranking of the practice. The ranking gives you a precise picture of how your practice compares to MGMA data, shown in Figure 19.

Advanced Benchmarking Report Tool

The Practice Performance Report provides an easy to input financial statement format benchmark report. However, it only provides benchmarking for a subset of the Cost Survey's 700+ metrics. If you need to benchmark anything that is not contained in the Practice Performance Report, use the Advanced Benchmarking Report. This tool will allow you to customize the report for exactly the metrics you are interested in Benchmarking.

Chapter 24: Understanding and Using MGMA Data

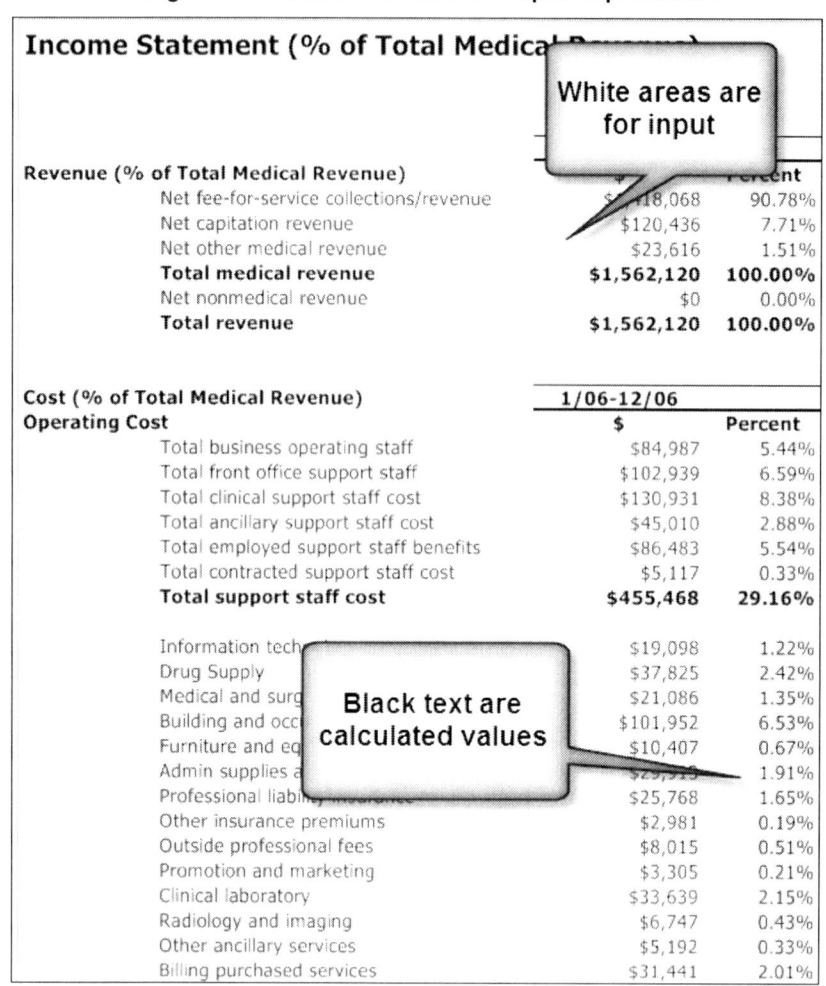

Figure 18-Practice Performance Report input screen

Income Statement (% of Total Medical Revenue)

White areas are for input

Revenue (% of Total Medical Revenue)	$	Percent
Net fee-for-service collections/revenue	$1,418,068	90.78%
Net capitation revenue	$120,436	7.71%
Net other medical revenue	$23,616	1.51%
Total medical revenue	**$1,562,120**	**100.00%**
Net nonmedical revenue	$0	0.00%
Total revenue	**$1,562,120**	**100.00%**

Cost (% of Total Medical Revenue) — 1/06-12/06

Operating Cost

	$	Percent
Total business operating staff	$84,987	5.44%
Total front office support staff	$102,939	6.59%
Total clinical support staff cost	$130,931	8.38%
Total ancillary support staff cost	$45,010	2.88%
Total employed support staff benefits	$86,483	5.54%
Total contracted support staff cost	$5,117	0.33%
Total support staff cost	**$455,468**	**29.16%**

Black text are calculated values

	$	Percent
Information tech	$19,098	1.22%
Drug Supply	$37,825	2.42%
Medical and surg	$21,086	1.35%
Building and occ	$101,952	6.53%
Furniture and eq	$10,407	0.67%
Admin supplies		1.91%
Professional liab	$25,768	1.65%
Other insurance premiums	$2,981	0.19%
Outside professional fees	$8,015	0.51%
Promotion and marketing	$3,305	0.21%
Clinical laboratory	$33,639	2.15%
Radiology and imaging	$6,747	0.43%
Other ancillary services	$5,192	0.33%
Billing purchased services	$31,441	2.01%

Summary

Since medical practices are unique, using MGMA and other medically based data will help you understand the unique drivers of value in a medical practice. This chapter was developed as a brief look at using MGMA data for valuing a medical practice; it does not provide a comprehensive discussion of these topics. If you are interested in getting more detailed information, we encourage you to check out the following resources:

- Join the MGMA (www.mgma.com)

- MGMA Physicians Compensation and Production Survey Interactive Report

- MGMA Cost Survey Interactive Report

Chapter 24: Understanding and Using MGMA Data

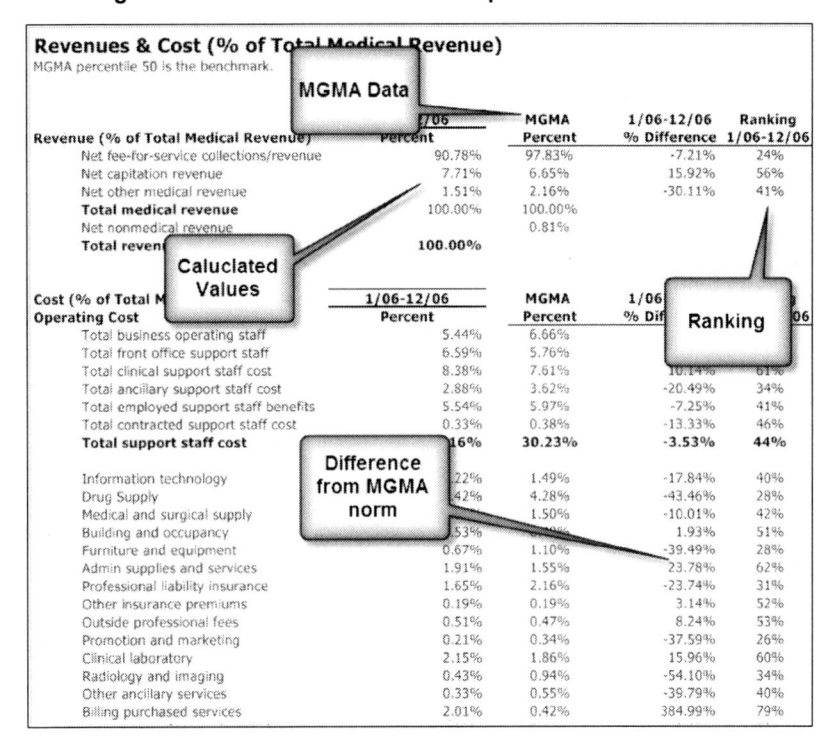

Figure 19- Practice Performance Report benchmark screen

Revenue (% of Total Medical Revenue)	1/06-12/06 Percent	MGMA Percent	1/06-12/06 % Difference	Ranking 1/06-12/06
Net fee-for-service collections/revenue	90.78%	97.83%	-7.21%	24%
Net capitation revenue	7.71%	6.65%	15.92%	56%
Net other medical revenue	1.51%	2.16%	-30.11%	41%
Total medical revenue	100.00%	100.00%		
Net nonmedical revenue		0.81%		
Total revenue	100.00%			

MGMA percentile 50 is the benchmark.

Callouts: MGMA Data, Calculated Values, Ranking, Difference from MGMA norm

Cost (% of Total Medical Revenue) Operating Cost	1/06-12/06 Percent	MGMA Percent	1/06-12/06 % Difference	Ranking 1/06-12/06
Total business operating staff	5.44%	6.66%		
Total front office support staff	6.59%	5.76%		
Total clinical support staff cost	8.38%	7.61%	10.14%	61%
Total ancillary support staff cost	2.88%	3.62%	-20.49%	34%
Total employed support staff benefits	5.54%	5.97%	-7.25%	41%
Total contracted support staff cost	0.33%	0.38%	-13.33%	46%
Total support staff cost	16%	30.23%	-3.53%	44%
Information technology	1.22%	1.49%	-17.84%	40%
Drug Supply	2.42%	4.28%	-43.46%	28%
Medical and surgical supply		1.50%	-10.01%	42%
Building and occupancy	1.53%		1.93%	51%
Furniture and equipment	0.67%	1.10%	-39.49%	28%
Admin supplies and services	1.91%	1.55%	23.78%	62%
Professional liability insurance	1.65%	2.16%	-23.74%	31%
Other insurance premiums	0.19%	0.19%	3.14%	52%
Outside professional fees	0.51%	0.47%	8.24%	53%
Promotion and marketing	0.21%	0.34%	-37.59%	26%
Clinical laboratory	2.15%	1.86%	15.96%	60%
Radiology and imaging	0.43%	0.94%	-54.10%	34%
Other ancillary services	0.33%	0.55%	-39.79%	40%
Billing purchased services	2.01%	0.42%	384.99%	79%

- RVUs: Applications for Medical Practice Success, 2nd edition by Kathryn P. Glass, MBA, MSHA, PMP

- Benchmarking Success: The Essential Guide for Group Practices by Gregory Feltenberger, MBA, FACMPE, FACHE, CPHIMS, and David Gans, MHSA, FACMPE

- Arrange a custom training session with ValuSource on these topics. You can reach ValuSource at 800-825-8763 or email sales@valusourcesoftware.com or visit our web site at www.valusourcesoftware.com.

- Participate in the Consulting Training Institute's (CTI) five-day healthcare boot camp (www.nacva.com)

- Read books and take webinars on these topics

Thanks

I would like to thank the MGMA, Laurie Foote, Bill Sipes and Robert Cimasi for their time, numerous conversations and outstanding comments and suggestions regarding material in this chapter.

Chapter 25

The CPA's Role in Mergers and Acquisitions Due Diligence Assistance to PPMCs and Private Equity Firms

By Ronald D. Finkelstein, CPA, and Lydia Glatz, CPA

Editor's Note: Many of the approaches and techniques described in this chapter are appropriate to a regular valuation engagement as well as to a due diligence engagement. The discussion of the reports to obtain from the medical practice's billing system, how to use them, and the nuances thereof is of particular value. Portions of the checklist can be adapted for a standard valuation engagement.

Introduction

Caveat emptor—let the buyer beware—and the term "due diligence" go hand in hand. Due diligence, or the process of investigating and providing financial analysis and assistance, can prove to be an invaluable tool during mergers and acquisitions (M&A) when planned and carried out properly. CPAs can assist their Physician Practice Management Company (PPMC) and Private Equity Firm (PEF) clients to properly structure M&A transactions to reach optimum financial results for both the acquiring and acquirer entity. This chapter will address the various types of due diligence assistance the CPA can provide as well as provide insightful information and guidance on carrying out the engagement.

Professional Reporting Standards

The first step in the M&A due diligence assistance process is for the CPA to determine the scope of the work and the type of reporting desired by the PPMC/PEF. Due diligence services performed by the CPA generally fall under the following professional engagement and reporting standards promulgated by the American Institute of Certified Public Accountants (AICPA) and the Financial Accounting Standards Board (FASB):

- Audit of financial statements – rendering an independent audit opinion in accordance with the Statement on Auditing Standards (SAS) by adhering to generally accepted auditing standards (GAAS) and applying generally accepted accounting principles (GAAP);

- Agreed-upon procedures – performing specific analytical testing agreed upon by the PPMC/PEF and the CPA and rendering a findings report in accordance with the Statement on Standards for Attestation Engagements (SSAE);

Chapter 25: The CPA's Role in Mergers and Acquisitions

- Forecasts and Projections – reporting on an entity's forecasted or projected financial position and operating results in accordance with the Statement on Standards for Attestation Engagements (SSAE);

- Pro forma financial information – reporting on the effects that an M&A transaction (proposed or consummated) would have on the historical financial information of an entity in accordance with the Statement on Standards for Attestation Engagements (SSAE);

- Financial analytics – review and analysis of key financial areas of a target entity that PPMC/PEF requests the CPA to perform in accordance with the Statement on Standards for Consulting Services (SSCS); and

- Calculation of value of intangible assets – rendering a calculation report on the calculated value of intangible assets in an M&A transaction in accordance with the Statement on Standards for Valuation Services (SSVS).

Engagement Planning

After the PPMC/PEF and CPA have agreed upon the scope and extent of the M&A work, the next important step is to develop a due diligence assistance program and related detailed document request list. The document request list is an invaluable tool in planning any due diligence engagement; it should be tailored to request sufficient information that the PPMC/PEF needs for the M&A transaction. The document request list should include requests for documentation that can be utilized to perform analytical procedures on the operational statistics of the target practice. The list should be sent to the target practice well in advance of any due diligence field work in order to provide the target practice ample time to gather the requested information.

For larger transactions that require a significant exchange of documents, the latest trend in due diligence document management is for a PPMC/PEF to set up a web–based data site, where designated parties to the M&A transaction can access and share stored information.

A sample document request list is attached as Appendix A.

A critical step the CPA must perform at the initial stage of engagement planning is to obtain and read the memorandum of understanding or, as it is commonly referred to, the letter of intent (LOI). The LOI will provide the CPA with information on the purchase price, the type of purchase for tax purposes (stock or asset purchase), the calculation of the purchase price and any related purchase price adjustments agreed upon by the parties. To the extent the purchase price is based on a multiple of earnings before interest, taxes, depreciation and amortization (EBITDA), the CPA may be required to report on EBITDA and calculate an adjusted or normalized EBITDA, as defined in the LOI.

Chapter 25: The CPA's Role in Mergers and Acquisitions

Operating Statistics

Physician practices maintain a plethora of historical data which can assist the CPA in analyzing the operational statistics of the practice. Historical data containing operational statistics may consist of:

- Reports produced from electronic data bases containing patient billing information;

- Insurance company contracts;

- Contracts for the provision of professional medical services with hospitals; ambulatory facilities, diagnostic facilities, third-party and related party contracts;

- Audited, compiled and/or internally produced financial statements;

- Filed tax returns; and

- Monthly bank statements.

Historical data from these sources can be utilized to extract and analyze various operational aspects of target practices, such as information relative to the number of patient encounters, types of procedures performed, charges billed, charges collected, accounts receivable, and reimbursement rates. Further, historical productivity data can be utilized to compare and analyze the operational results of the target practice with the operational results of other practices of similar size and specialty in the same geographic area. The target's historical performance measures can also be benchmarked to performance measures contained in published industry–wide data and various analytics and pro-forma calculations can be performed to compare the target's productivity to the performance measures of the PPMC/PEF.

The information gathered can prove to be invaluable at yielding answers to past and future trends, which, in turn, may be utilized by the acquiring and selling practices to arrive at mutually agreeable buy/sell transactions.

Patient Volume

When comparing a practice's operational results, patient volume is by far one of the leading indicators of revenue trends. Patient volume can be measured in terms of the number of patients seen by the physician providers in the office, inpatient hospital consults, and/or in the number of cases/procedures performed at outpatient diagnostic testing facilities. Patient volume also bears a direct relationship to practice size, number of physicians in the practice, number of midlevel providers, employees, and number of practice locations. In other words, when comparing patient volume, the CPA should not just look at medical billing reports, but should also compare the medical billing reports with other practice variables in order to verify the accuracy and reliability of the reports.

Chapter 25: The CPA's Role in Mergers and Acquisitions

The CPA should request that billing reports be generated by date of service and, at the very least, for two concurrent periods, such as for the immediate and previous calendar year. Comparing similar reports of differing periods can also prove to be invaluable at yielding answers to past and future trends.

Some sample patient volume comparisons may include comparing the number of patients seen in total by the practice and by the individual providers in the office, hospitals, diagnostic centers, and/or outpatient facilities during the current and prior year. Testing the reliability of the billing reports may include comparing the number of patients listed on the billing reports to the patient sign-in sheets and hospital admission or operating room case records.

Trends generated through this exercise can assist and provide the PPMC/PEF with an understanding of the productivity of the practice and of individual physicians within the group. It will also assist in addressing areas for improvement, pinpointing profitable and non-profitable practice centers, and determining the size of the personnel pool required to run and maintain the practice in an efficient manner. Further inquiry into this flux analysis will most certainly generate answers to questions that could improve physician productivity post acquisition and assist in crafting an incentive based productivity compensation arrangement. A sample table comparing patient volume by provider on a daily and weekly basis could be fashioned as follows:

Physician	Average Number Office Visits Daily	Average Number Office Visits Weekly	Average Number Surgeries Daily	Average Number Surgeries Weekly
Dr. 1	13	38	3	12
Dr. 2	31	94	4	12
Dr. 3	21	41	3	14
Dr. 4	38	76	6	19
Dr. 5	20	61	5	15
Dr. 6	20	61	3	11
Dr. 7	9	19	2	7
Total	152	390	26	90

Charges and Collections

Medical billing reports can be generated to provide historical physician practice productivity data related to charges billed and collections received. These reports can be customized to include numerous variables, such as total charges billed and collections received by provider, by CPT code, by payor source, and by practice location. And, as a caveat, the CPA should be cognizant during this exercise that medical billing systems have the capability of producing reports that match

Chapter 25: The CPA's Role in Mergers and Acquisitions

collections to actual charges based on date of service (accrual basis reporting) or in the alternative, that simply track collections received in a period to charges posted in the same period (cash basis reporting). Reports that match collections to actual charges by date of service are comparable to accrual financial statements; and vice versa, reports that match collections to charges posted in a period, are comparable to cash basis financial statements. Both types of reports contain valuable information but must be read with caution, as the data contained in each of the two reports may be misleading when not interpreted and applied to analytical procedures correctly.

The PPMC/PEF would be interested in the historical information these medical billing reports contain. For instance, the PPMC/PEF would want to know such information as the types of procedures the physicians perform, reimbursement rates, total charges and collections during specific periods, and the productivity of the various practice locations. Numerous analytical procedures can be performed utilizing the data in the medical billing reports. Analytical procedures may include summarizing and comparing total charges and collections received by procedure (CPT) code during the current year and comparing them to the previous year's total charges and collections; calculating gross and net collection percentages; calculating average charge and average collections by type of practice specialty; and determining the significance the practice's fee schedule plays on these calculations.

This type of information can be presented in the form of a table chart that highlights total charges and collections by CPT code, location, and provider. The table chart could also be expanded to include information relative to gross and net collection percentages. The CPA should utilize the "accrual" type billing reports for this exercise, in order to compare actual collections applied actual charges. Utilizing the "cash" type billing reports could skew the true collection percentage results.

Physician fee schedules play an important role in comparing a physician practice collection ratio to another practice of similar size and specialty. Since fee schedules can be fashioned utilizing numerous variables, prior to calculating a practice's gross and net collection percentages, the CPA should obtain the group's fee schedule and inquire how the fee schedule was developed and whether there were any changes to the fee schedule during the reporting periods. Was it based on Medicare allowable rates, a multiple of Medicare allowable, or some other benchmark? Lower fee schedules will produce higher gross collection percentages than will higher fee schedules. Preparing a chart which compares the practice's fee schedule to other fee schedules will assist the PPMC/PEF with its gross and net collection analysis. The table on the following page demonstrates the role a practice fee schedule plays when calculating gross and net collection percentages.

Assuming a Medicare reimbursement rate of $50, the following gross collection percentages can be calculated.

	Physician Fee Schedule	CPT Code 99242	Gross Collection %
Medicare x 2	$100	$50	50%
Medicare x 3	$150	$50	33%

Chapter 25: The CPA's Role in Mergers and Acquisitions

Total collections during specific periods can be verified to the total deposits per the bank statements. Further inquiry and analysis can be performed utilizing the "cash" basis billing reports to verify the validity of the receipts by tracing a sample of individual deposits from the bank statement to the supporting backup documentation. This exercise could be taken one step further by reconciling the previous year's net collections to financial statements and to the net revenues reported on the federal income tax returns.

Appendix B contains a list of the more commonly used ratios, including formulas for calculating gross collection and net collection ratios.

Payor mix

A payor mix analysis can provide valuable insight into understanding the target practice's reimbursement rates and who its key payors are. This type of analysis will highlight profitable and non-profitable payors. A payor mix analysis will assist the PPMC/PEF in planning and projecting future revenue growth trends and highlighting non-profitable payors whose contracts the PPMC/PEF may want to renegotiate.

Medical billing reports generated on the "accrual" basis to include total charges, collections and adjustments by payor will contain the information required to perform this analysis. Most medical billing software can export reports into Excel-formatted files, which allow the data to be sorted to achieve various results. The data should be sorted by total charges in descending order in order to segregate payor billings from largest to smallest. This type of analysis can be presented in a table which highlights the top 10 payors, along with charges, collections, adjustments, and gross and net collection percentages by payor.

A payor mix analysis could also be utilized by the PPMC/PEF to compare the practice's collection percentages with those of published industry-wide benchmarks and with its own collection percentages.

CPT Code Analysis

A practice's total charges and collections are a function of the number and type of procedures performed. CPT codes can be compared with payor reimbursement rates. For instance, a payor reimbursement matrix could be prepared to compare the fee charged by the practice for its top 10 procedures to the reimbursement rate of its top 10 payors.

A sample matrix is presented in the following format.

This type of analysis highlights reimbursement and collection percentages by payor and can lead to PPMC/PEF contract renegotiation and follow up.

Chapter 25: The CPA's Role in Mergers and Acquisitions

Top CPT Code	Fee Schedule	Payor 1	Payor 2	Payor 3	Payor 4	Payor 5
64483	$374	$77	$130	$104	$86	$271
64484	267	50	135	69	94	149
77003	120	27	19	40	23	21
99214	220	43	62	64	72	64
99215	355	73	92	95	97	91
	$1,336	$270	$438	$372	$372	$596
Collection%		20%	33%	28%	28%	45%

Accounts Receivable

Accounts receivable plays a vital role in the determining the practice's cash flow. How quickly charges are collected is determined by the efficiency and accuracy with which the practice's billing and collection department processes claims and makes subsequent timely collection follow-up. The practice's accounts receivable can be benchmarked with the Medical Group Management Association (MGMA) annual publications, which provide statistical comparisons for different specialty and size practices by geographic regions. Ratio analysis can also be performed to calculate the number of days it takes the practice to collect its receivables. Accounts receivable at the beginning of a period can be compared to accounts receivable at the end of the period, and cash collections can be analyzed to determine if significant differences have occurred as a result of increases or decreases in accounts receivable.

Cash to accrual conversion

Generally, most medical practices and other healthcare providers maintain their accounting records and financial statements on the cash basis of accounting. The PPMC/PEF usually requests the CPA to convert the financial statements from the cash to the accrual basis of accounting. This conversion process requires revenue and expense cutoff information for both the beginning and ending reporting periods in order to properly measure EBITDA under GAAP.

The following financial information can assist the CPA in preparing cash to accrual accounting conversion adjustments:

- Accounts receivable aging reports

- Charges, adjustments, and collections—by date of service

Chapter 25: The CPA's Role in Mergers and Acquisitions

- Accounts payable and accruals

- Cash disbursements cutoff data

- Payroll register for payroll period ending reporting

- For risk based providers—Incurred but not reported (IBNR) lag analysis

EBITDA Measurement

The LOI may define how the purchase price is calculated and specify certain agreed upon purchase price adjustments to EBITDA. The PPMC/PEF may request the CPA to report on EBITDA as of a certain period. This period(s) can be as of the most recent year and a subsequent stub period through the closing date of the transaction, or a trailing 12 month period. EBITDA measurement for purposes of the LOI is generally calculated as follows:

- GAAP EBITDA

- Purchase price adjustments for:

- Nonrecurring revenue and expenses

- Owner compensation and fringe benefits

- Assumption of certain debt

- Related party transactions

- Other agreed upon post acquisition expenses

Tax Matters

Depending on the type of M&A tax structure, the PPMC/PEF may require the CPA to assist in computing the tax consequences to both the buyer and seller. Typically, the PPMC/PEF buyer prefers an asset purchase whereby there is no assumption of seller related liabilities. Conversely, the selling entity's owners prefer a sale of stock in order to maximize its after tax sale proceeds by taking advantage of the lower capital gains tax rates.

A common tax strategy that may be agreed upon by both the buyer and seller is the Internal Revenue Code Section 338(h)(10) election. This code section is intended to make the tax benefits neutral with respect to acquisitions of corporate stock and acquisitions of corporate assets.

Chapter 25: The CPA's Role in Mergers and Acquisitions

Following a qualified stock purchase, and depending on the circumstances, the purchasing corporation could elect under Section 338(g) to step up the basis of the underlying acquired assets to their adjusted grossed-up basis (generally equal to FMV). In this scenario, the buyer obtains a tax benefit on depreciation/amortization deductions on the acquired tangible and intangible assets. To the extent the seller recognizes an incremental tax liability on the difference between the tax liability incurred on the sale of stock versus the tax liability incurred on the theoretical sale of assets, the CPA can assist the parties by computing the incremental gross up in income taxes required to be reported in the purchase agreement.

Unique structural considerations relating to healthcare entity buyouts include those designed to minimize the possibility that the transactions will constitute a change in ownership or "CHOW" for licensure or certification purposes, or trigger anti-assignment provisions in professional service or managed care contracts (which should be avoided if possible because the counterparties often use the consent process to renegotiate or extract additional consideration).

One way to minimize the regulatory and contractual approvals required is through a reverse triangular merger structure under Internal Revenue Code Section 368(a) (2)(D), in which a newly formed subsidiary of the acquirer merges with and into the parent of the target holding company. Often, the providers and facilities are organized as subsidiaries of the target holding company, and in many cases CHOW approvals will not be required using this approach. Similarly, this structure may limit (but not eliminate) the managed care and provider contract consents required. See Figure 1 below.

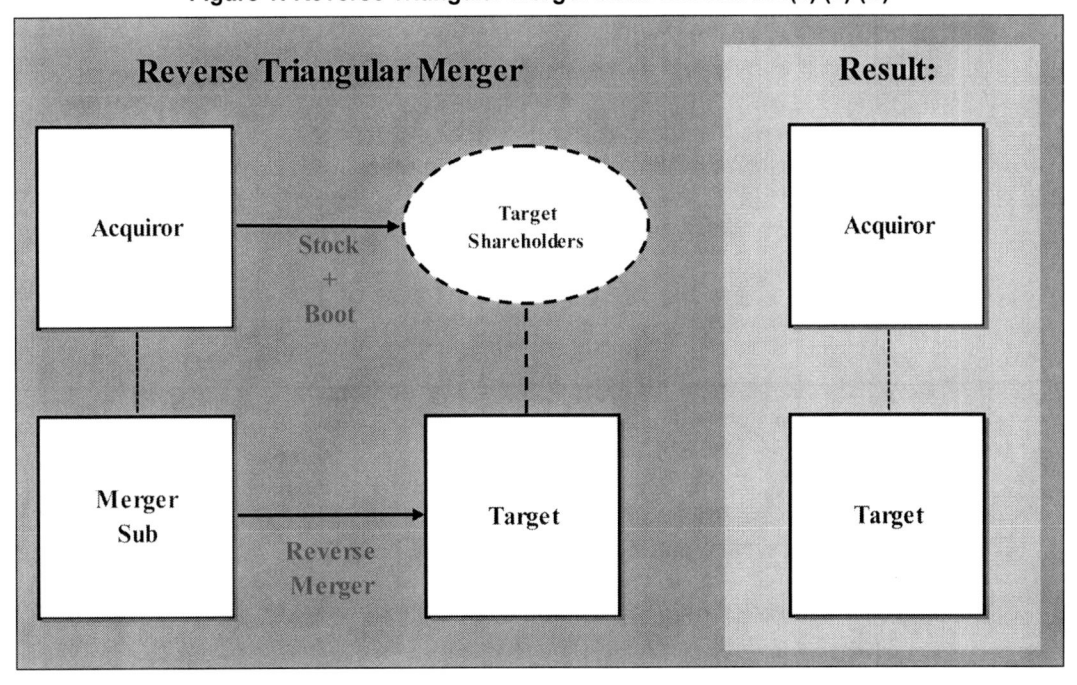

Figure 1: Reverse Triangular Merger Code Section 368(a) (2) (D)

Chapter 25: The CPA's Role in Mergers and Acquisitions

Appendix A: Sample Document Request

Due Diligence and Document Request

For the Acquisition of: _____

If you feel that any of the requested information does not apply or exist, please provide a statement to that effect for the applicable section.

Financial Data: **Comments**

_____ 1. Audited or compiled financial statements for six months ended June 30, 200_ and for the year ended December 31, 200_ and supporting detailed general ledger reports for both periods. _____

_____ 2. Accounts receivable aging report run at June 30, 200_ month-end closing and at December 31, 200_ month-end closing by patient and payor source, detailing charges, payments, adjustments, and credit balances. _____

_____ 3. All bank statements for the six month period ended June 30, 200_ and for the 12 months ended 200_. _____

_____ 4. Description of intercompany transactions, if any. _____

_____ 5. List of related parties and transactions with related parties. _____

_____ 6. List of suppliers and vendors and copies of any written purchase agreements or other contractual agreements. _____

_____ 7. Copies of debt or line of credit arrangements. _____

_____ 8. Copy of any operating budgets or forecasts of the Companies. _____

_____ 9. Income tax returns filed for federal, state, city and county for prior 3 years. _____

_____ 10. Copies of 200_ Form 940—Employer Annual Federal Unemployment Tax Return, Forms W-2 and W-3, and most recent federal and state quarterly payroll tax filings, Form 941. _____

_____ 11. Tangible personal property tax returns for prior three years. _____

Chapter 25: The CPA's Role in Mergers and Acquisitions

Corporate Documents:

_____ 1. Articles of Incorporation of the entities. _____

_____ 2. Bylaws of the entities and any other shareholder/partnership agreements. _____

_____ 3. Minutes of Board of Directors. _____

_____ 4. Copies of stock certificates including both sides and copy of stock transfer ledger. _____

_____ 5. Copies of any D/B/A and fictitious name filings. _____

_____ 6. Corporate organizational chart of entities and ownership. _____

_____ 7. List of states in which Company is qualified to do business and evidence that Company is qualified to do business in each state. _____

Physical Plant, Real Property and Other Property:

_____ 1. List of all real estate (owned and leased). _____

_____ 2. Instruments evidencing title to such real estate (e.g., deeds, title papers, title insurance policies and binders, title opinions, appraisals, and surveys). _____

_____ 3. Real property office leases. _____

_____ 4. Personal property leases, for example; copier lease, telephone equipment lease, computer equipment and software, etc. _____

_____ 5. Description of any property which is collateral under financing arrangements. _____

_____ 6. Detailed listing of furniture, fixtures, and medical equipment, and a general description of condition. _____

Environmental Matters:

_____ 1. Biomedical hazardous waste permits. _____

_____ 2. Description of the Company's generation, storage, handling, and disposal of all hazardous and infectious waste, including asbestos, chlordane, medical related waste and radioactive materials. _____

_____ 3. Copy of written agreement with any contracted waste disposal service. _____

Chapter 25: The CPA's Role in Mergers and Acquisitions

Risk Management:

_____ 1. Complete copies of professional liability insurance policies (malpractice) and commercial liability policies (property and office). Malpractice insurance policy and loss history (loss runs) as provided by malpractice insurance carrier, including claims status reports from the insurance carrier. Include status on any physicians for which there are no claims. Description of any claims or events which have not been reported to the insurance carrier. _____

_____ 2. Copies of letters from Company's outside legal counsel to independent accountants for the past three years regarding litigation in which the Company or an employed physician was involved. _____

_____ 3. Copies of correspondence relating to any federal or state governmental investigations or proceedings before any federal, state, or municipal department, board, bureau, agency, or other instrumentality and any citations received. _____

_____ 4. Copies of any documents related to payment denials, appeals, or other payment controversies between the Company and a nongovernmental third-party payor. _____

_____ 5. A description of any settled, pending, or threatened claim or action against the Company arising from its participation in a government program, including, without limitation, investigations or legal action arising under the federal healthcare program fraud and abuse laws. _____

_____ 6. Copies of internal investigation memoranda, assessment or audit reports, correspondence, review letters, or other documents relating to healthcare regulatory compliance audits and other activities. _____

_____ 7. Any correspondence regarding employees or personnel policies from any regulatory agency such as:
    The Department of Immigration and Naturalization
    Department of Labor
    National Labor Relations Board
    Internal Revenue Service _____

_____ 8. Identify any employment related claims, lawsuits, arbitrations, or other proceedings (including administrative and arbitrage proceedings and government agency investigations) which are pending or threatened. Furnish copies of any related documentation. _____

_____ 9. List all discrimination complaints against the Company or any predecessor during the last 5 years. Show date of claims, persons involved and actual or expected outcome. _____

Chapter 25: The CPA's Role in Mergers and Acquisitions

_____ 10. Description of workers' compensation program and copies of certificates of insurance. _____

Human Resources:

_____ 1. Copies of all employment or employment-related contracts, agreements, or understandings with current employees (inclusive of officers, directors, managers, physicians, nurses, technicians and any other allied healthcare professionals). Include agreements with former employees if employment-related commitments exist. _____

_____ 2. Listing of all current personnel, including title, date of hire, site location, classification (full-time, part-time, per diem), experience, certifications and education, compensation, bonus targets, and accrued benefits. Description of any special compensation arrangements or incentive programs and accrued but unpaid benefits. _____

_____ 3. Copies of all consulting agreements currently in effect. _____

_____ 4. Most recent payroll register. _____

_____ 5. Current internal organizational chart of officers and key management. _____

_____ 6. Provide a description of any of the following programs: bonus, company car or auto expense allowances, cellular phone, housing and relocation, deferred compensation arrangements, jury duty, bereavement leave, personal time off, educational assistance, tuition reimbursement, employee recognition, community service programs, service awards, and executive perquisites. Provide copies of all relevant documentation, including plan documents/communication to employees. If you have programs other than those listed above, please include. _____

_____ 7. Copies of employer policy manuals or statements. _____

_____ 8. To the extent not provided above, describe all vacation, sick pay, paid time off, and holidays. _____

_____ 9. Description of any employee loans or loans to directors or officers. _____

_____ 10. Description of group employee benefit plans, for example: (i) group health, (ii) pension and profit sharing, (iii) disability, (iv) life insurance, and (v) cafeteria plan and copies of invoices. _____

Chapter 25: The CPA's Role in Mergers and Acquisitions

_____ 11. Employee benefit plan documents for the above and 5500 filings for 200_ and 200_ for both 401k, money purchase pension plans, and cafeteria plans. The original adoption agreements, the plan document and any amendments, the summary plan descriptions, copies of fidelity bonds, most recent nondiscrimination testing results, external audit report if required, trust agreements, recent plan statements, any cafeteria plan documents, and IRS determination letters. _____

Contractual:

_____ 1. All hospital, ambulatory facility, diagnostic facility, or other contracts related to the provision of professional services. _____

_____ 2. Copies of operating policy and procedure manuals. _____

_____ 3. All written contracts and agreements, for example; postal meter agreements, biomedical waste agreements, maintenance agreements, telephone equipment, etc. _____

Billing and Collections:

_____ 1. Copies of current billing fee schedules. _____

_____ 2. Schedule of major payor contract rates. _____

_____ 3. All contracts, agreements and understandings with any party regarding the provision of medical services to patients, including all provider agreements with HMOs, PPOs, third party payors, IPAs, PHOs, MSOs, etc. Include all supporting schedules, amendments, addendums, referenced documents, etc. _____

_____ 4. Describe global or special arrangements with facility/providers (written and verbal). Provide copies of agreements. _____

_____ 5. Describe self-pay arrangements (written and verbal). _____

_____ 6. Description of any outsourced billing services and copies of agreements. _____

_____ 7. Medical Billing Systems generated reports (by date of service) for the six months ended June 30, 200_ and for the year ended December 31, 200_ detailing unit volume, charges, adjustments, and collections by:
    a. CPT Code
    b. CPT Code for major managed care providers
    c. Provider
    d. Location
    e. Payor source _____

Chapter 25: The CPA's Role in Mergers and Acquisitions

Credentialing:

_____ 1. Licensing and credentialing information for all physicians, other allied healthcare providers, and the P.A. These include medical licensure, curriculum vitae, occupational licenses, radiological licenses, bio-medical hazardous waste permits, and CLIA licenses. Note: Please see grid provided (Provider Information). _____

_____ 2. Listing of health care facilities in which good standing staff memberships are maintained by physicians ('privileges'). Note: This should be indicated on the grid above. _____

_____ 3. Listing of Medicare and Medicaid group and individual provider numbers and any other billing numbers pertinent to claim submission. Note: Please see grid provided (Government Plan Information). _____

Other:

_____ 1. Software and computer hardware licenses and agreements for services (please specify function software is used for, i.e. accounting, billing, payroll, etc). _____

_____ 2. Listing of other business interests of any owners, partners, or employees that represent a potential conflict of interest. _____

_____ 3. Provide copies of all government permits, clearances, and approvals for each clinic(s) held by the Company or its employees necessary to conduct business (e.g. HCC Clinic License for the State of _____). _____

Appendix B: Commonly Used Physician Practice Ratios

Gross Collection Ratio $= \dfrac{\text{Gross Collections}}{\text{Gross Charges}}$

Net Collection Ratio $= \dfrac{\text{Gross Collections}}{\text{Gross Charges} - \text{Adjustments} + \text{Refunds}}$

Days in Accounts Receivable $= \dfrac{\text{Average AR for the year x 365 days}}{\text{Net Collections for the year}}$

Overhead Expense % $= \dfrac{\text{Operational (nonphysician expenses)}}{\text{Net Collections}}$

Current Ratio $= \dfrac{\text{Current Assets}}{\text{Current Liabilities}}$

Debt Ratio $= \dfrac{\text{Total Liabilities}}{\text{Total Assets}}$

Total Asset Turnover $= \dfrac{\text{Total Net Medical Revenue}}{\text{Total Assets}}$

Chapter 26

When the Marriage is Over, What is the Practice Worth?

By Stacey D. Udell, CPA/ABV/CFF, ASA, CVA

When a physician gets divorced, the value of his or her ownership interest in the practice is likely to be included as an asset for property distribution purposes. Additionally, the income generated from the practice is likely to be utilized in the determination of support.

Valuation is an art, not a science, which makes the task of valuing a medical practice more difficult (and more likely to be disputed) than valuing the marital residence or a spouse's retirement plan. The value of a practice is based on the valuator's judgment applied to the specific facts and circumstances. Different assumptions lead to different conclusions of value, any of which may be reasonable.

Some of the major issues that must be considered are:

- Standard of Value

- Premise of Value

- Valuation Date(s)

- Buy/Sell Agreements

- Goodwill

- "Double dip"

Standard of value

The valuator must determine the appropriate standard of value applicable in the state or jurisdiction of the divorce. Standards of value differ among the various states and jurisdictions. Often, the family law attorney can inform the valuator of the appropriate standard of value. This standard may be based on state statute or case law. Reliance on an incorrect standard of value could lead to an incorrect value conclusion, your report and testimony being excluded as evidence and, more significantly, becoming the basis of a malpractice suit.

Chapter 26: When the Marriage is Over, What is the Practice Worth?

Arkansas[1] and Louisiana[2] have statues precisely defining the standard of value to be used in divorce. In other states, the standard of value is often left undefined. To confuse matters even more, many state statutes refer to "value" or "net value" without any further clarification or definition. To take it even further, many states inconsistently apply standards of value in order to arrive at an equitable result. We are not aware of any case law or statutes in Alabama or Georgia discussing the standard of value to be used in matrimonial litigation. Therefore, determining the appropriate standard of value can be a perplexing problem for the valuation expert to resolve.

The standards of value utilized in the valuation arena are fair market value, fair value, intrinsic value, and investment value.

Fair market value, which is used for estate and gift tax purposes, is defined as:

> the price, expressed in terms of cash equivalents, at which property would change hands between a hypothetical [emphasis added] willing and able buyer and a hypothetical [emphasis added] willing and able seller, acting at arms length in an open and unrestricted market, when neither is under compulsion to buy or sell and when both have reasonable knowledge of the relevant facts.[3]

While the foundation of fair market value considers a hypothetical sale, fair market value could be viewed as not contemplating one sale but a blend of potential sales.

In a marital dissolution, an actual sale of the practice is not usually contemplated. Often times in divorce, the term fair market value is used but the Court's definition may not conform to the definition for tax purposes as quoted above. Frequently, in application, a different standard of value is actually used, even though it is termed fair market value.

One derivation of fair market value is "net value," which is defined as the fair market value of the business minus any debts, liens, liabilities, or encumbrances. Net value is the standard of value used in Alaska,[4] Michigan,[5] Nevada,[6] North Carolina,[7] and West Virginia.[8]

Table 1 reflects the states that are considered fair market value states, either explicitly or by application. States that have utilized fair market value in addition to another standard of value are reflected in Table 2.

Discounts. As part of the determination of fair market value, it may be appropriate to apply discounts for lack of control and/or marketability. These discounts have historically been allowed in Alaska, Arkansas, Connecticut, Iowa, New Hampshire, New York, Oregon, Vermont, West Virginia, and Wisconsin.[9]

Fair value is a statutorily or judicially defined standard of value. Frequently used in oppressed minority shareholder actions, this standard assumes one owner is an unwilling participant in the transaction, generally the seller. To compensate, discounts (for lack of control and/or marketability) are often not applied or applied only under extraordinary circumstances.

Chapter 26: When the Marriage is Over, What is the Practice Worth?

Table 1—Fair Market Value States - Explicitly or by Application	
Arizona	Sample v. Sample, 731 P.2d 604, 606 (Ariz. Ct. App. 1986)
Arkansas	Ark. Code Ann. § 9-12-315 (2005)
Connecticut	Eslami v. Eslami, 591 A.2d 411, 416 (Conn. 1991)
Delaware	E.E.C. v. E.J.C., 457 A.2d 688, 694 (Del. 1983);
District of Columbia	McDiarmid v. McDiarmid, App. D.C., 649 A.2d 810 (1994)
Florida	Thompson v. Thompson, 576 So. 2d 267 (Fla. 1991)
Hawaii	Antolik v. Harvey, 761 P.2d 305, 319 (Haw. Ct. App. 1988);
Idaho	McAffee v. McAffee, 971 P.2d 734, 740 (Idaho Ct. App. 1994);
Illinois	In re Marriage of Grunsten, 709 N.E.2d 597, 602 (Ill. App. Ct. 1999);
Indiana	Trost-Steffen v. Steffen, 772 N.E.2d 500 (Ind. Ct. App. 2002);
Iowa	In re Marriage of Frett, No. 4-083/03-1305, 2004 LEXIS 694, at 7 (Iowa Ct. App. May 14, 2004) (unpublished);
Kansas	Bohl v. Bohl, 232 Kan. 557; 657 P.2d 1106; 1983 Kan. LEXIS 236
Kentucky	In Clark v. Clark, 782 S.W.2d 56, 58-59 (Ky. Ct. App. 1990);
Maine	Dargie v. Dargie, 778 A.2d 353, 357 (Me. 2001);
Maryland	Long v. Long, 743 A.2d 281, 291 (Md. Ct. Spec. App. 2000);
Massachusetts	Champion v. Champion, 764 N.E.2d 898, 901 (Mass. App. Ct. 2002); now replaced by *Bernier*
Minnesota	In re the Marriage of Berenberg, 474 N.W.2d 843 (Minn. Ct. App. 1991);
Mississippi	Singley v. Singley, No. 1999-CT-00754-SCT, 2003 LEXIS 283, at 20 (Miss. June 12, 2003);
Missouri	L.R.M v. R.K.M., 46 S.W.3d 24, 29 (Mo. Ct. App. 2001);
Montana	In re Marriage of Ortiz, 938 P.2d 1308, 1310 (Mont. 1997);
Nebraska	Gohl v. Gohl, 13 Neb. App. 685 (Ct. App. 2005), No. A-03-1102, 2005 LEXIS 143, at 30-31 (Neb. Ct. App. July 5, 2005);
New Hampshire	Rattee v. Rattee, 767 A.2d 415, 421 (N.H. 2001).
New Mexico	Trego v. Scott, 961 P.2d 168, 172-73 (N.M. Ct. App. 1998);
Oklahoma	Bond v. Bond, 916 P.2d 272, 275 (Okla. Ct. App. 1996);
Oregon	I/M/O the Marriage of Hanson, 86 P.3d 94, 98 (Or. Ct. App. 2004);
Pennsylvania	Traczyk v. Traczyk, No. 78435. 891 P.2d 1277. 1995 OK 22
Rhode Island	Moretti v. Moretti, 766 A.2d 925, 928 (R.I. 2001);
South Carolina	Dixon v. Dixon, 512 S.E.2d 539, 549 (S.C. Ct. App. 1999);
South Dakota	Fausch v. Fausch, 697 N.W.2d 748 (S.D. 2005), No. 23316, 2005 LEXIS 63, at 11, 13-14 (S.D. May 18, 2005);
Tennessee	Barbara Lee Bunce Kerce v. Stephen Paul Kerce, No. M2002-01744-COA-R3-CV (Tenn. Ct. App. August 29, 2003)
Texas	Zeptner v. Zeptner, 111 S.W.3d 727, 738 (Tex. Ct. App. 2003);
Utah	Sorenson v. Sorenson, 769 P.2d 820 (Utah App. 1989)
Vermont	Goodrich v. Goodrich, 613 A.2d 203 (Vt. 1992), 158 Vt. 587, 591-92 (1992);
Wisconsin	Frawley v. Frawley, 693 N.W.2d 146 (Wis. Ct. App. 2005), No. 03-2550, 2005 LEXIS 7, at 4 (Wis. Ct. App. Jan. 6, 2005);
Wyoming	Neuman v. Neuman, 842 P.2d 575, 581-82 (Wyo. 1992).
Primary source of data: Vuotto, Charles F., Jr., Esquire. "Fair Market Value - Everyone Else is Doing It, So Why Can't We?" *New Jersey Law Journal: Family Law Supplement* (2005), http://www.vuotto.com/new-jersey-divorce-articles/fair-market-value.htm	

Chapter 26: When the Marriage is Over, What is the Practice Worth?

State	Fair Market Value Case Law	Additional Standard of Value	Additional Standard Case Law
California	In re Cream, 16 Cal. Rptr. 2d 575, 579 (Ct. App. 1993)	Investment value	In re Marriage of Hewitson, 142 Cal. App. 3d 874 (Ct. App. 1983).
Michigan	Golden v. Golden, No. 218106, 2001 LEXIS 1057 (Mich. Ct. App. Mar. 20, 2001) (unpublished)	Investment value	Sutherland v. Sutherland, No. 240158, 2004 LEXIS 174, at 9 (Mich. Ct. App. Jan. 20, 2004) (unpublished)
New York	Morse v. Morse, 784 N.Y.S.2d 590, 591 (App. Div. 2004);	Investment value	O'Brien v. O'Brien, 66 N.Y.2d 576; 489 N.E.2d 712; 498 N.Y.S.2d 743
North Dakota	Heggen v. Heggen, 452 N.W.2d 96, 99 (N.D. 1990),	Fair Value	In Fisher v. Fisher, 568 N.W.2d 728, 732-33 (N.D. 1997).
Ohio	Cronin v. Cronin, 2005 Ohio 301 (Ct. App. 2005), No. 02-CA-110, 03-CA-75, 2005 LEXIS 268, at 5-6 (Ohio Ct. App. Jan. 28, 2005).	Intrinsic Value	Brookhart v Brookhart, No. 93 CA 1569, 1993 LEXIS 5586 (Ohio Ct. app. Nov. 18, 1003) (unpublished)

Table 2—States Utilizing More Than One Standard of Value

Primary source of data: Vuotto, Charles F., Jr., Esquire. "Fair Market Value - Everyone Else is Doing It, So Why Can't We?" *New Jersey Law Journal: Family Law Supplement* (2005), http://www.vuotto.com/new-jersey-divorce-articles/fair-market-value.htm

As reflected in the New Jersey case of *Brown v. Brown*, 348 N.J. Super. 466 (App. Div. 2002), New Jersey's standard of value for divorce purposes is fair value. In New Jersey, fair value reflects fair market value without discounts (for lack of control or marketability), barring extraordinary circumstances.[10] Unfortunately, what constitutes an extraordinary circumstance is undefined. Case law indicates that Indiana,[11] North Dakota,[12] Virginia,[13] and now Massachusetts[14] are also considered fair value states. North Dakota has also utilized fair market value, as reflected in *Heggen v. Heggen*, 452 N.W.2d 96, 99 (1990).

Intrinsic value is defined in the International Glossary of Business Valuation Terms as "the value that an investor considers, on the basis of an evaluation or available facts, to be the 'true' or 'real' value that will become the market value when other investors reach the same conclusion." In other words, for valuation purposes, intrinsic value represents the value that a securities analyst places on the investment based on his or her perception of the risk and returns inherent in the investment.

The term intrinsic value has been used rather liberally by the courts and appears to be defined by the facts and circumstances of the particular case. The only state specifically requiring the use of the intrinsic value standard is Virginia. In the Virginia case of *Howell v. Howell*, 31 Va. App. 332, 345-46, 523 S.E. 2d 514, 521 (2000), Mr. Howell was an owner in a family business started by his father. Mr. Howell's two sons worked in the business, with one likely to operate the business after him. The Court determined that since the sale of the business to

Chapter 26: When the Marriage is Over, What is the Practice Worth?

a third party was not contemplated, no discount for lack of marketability should be taken from the value of the stock. In its decision, the Court defined intrinsic value as "the value of the business interest to its current owner given the owner's current use of the interest, current resources, and current capabilities for economically exploiting the business interest." By application, this appears to be a fair value standard even though it is specifically identified as intrinsic value by the Virginia Court.

Investment value represents the value to a specific buyer, as opposed to the hypothetical buyer contemplated in the fair market standard of value. In his book Standards of Value: Theory and Applications, Jay Fishman aptly states that "Fair market value is impersonal, but investment value reflects the unique situation of a particular person or company."[15]

This standard of value allows the consideration of synergies available to the potential buyer. In the California case of *Golden v. Golden*, 270 Cal. App. 2d 401, 75 Cal. Rptr. 735, 1969 Cal. App. LEXIS 1538, the Court recognized the similarities between value to the holder and investment value.

Particularly in divorce matters, investment value is often referred to as "value to the holder" or "divorce value" because it recognizes that, in the context of a divorce, there is no hypothetical or actual sale of the practice and the physician owner will continue to receive benefits based on his or her ownership in the practice. Courts in California, Colorado,[16] Michigan, New York, and Washington[17] have adopted the investment value standard of value for marital dissolution purposes.

Premise of value

The International Glossary of Business Valuation Terms defines premise of value as "an assumption regarding the most likely set of transactional circumstances that may be applicable to the subject valuation."[18] The two recognized premises of value are going concern and liquidation.

The going concern value assumes the business will continue operating into the future. This results from having such things as "a trained work force, an operational plant, and the necessary licenses, systems, and procedures in place."[19] Unless otherwise excluded from the marital estate (by statute, for example), goodwill is included under the going concern premise of value.

Liquidation value can be defined as the amount that would be realized if the business was terminated. Liquidation can be either "orderly" or "forced." An orderly liquidation would generate higher proceeds and results when the business is terminated and the assets are sold piecemeal. In a forced liquidation, the assets are sold as quickly as possible and lower proceeds are usually generated. Liquidation value is applicable when a controlling interest is being valued because a minority (non-controlling) owner may not compel the sale of the business. Furthermore, the liquidation value would be pertinent only if it is greater than the value determined by an income or market approach.

Chapter 26: When the Marriage is Over, What is the Practice Worth?

In the North Dakota case of *Sommers v. Sommers*, 2003 N.D. 77, 660 N.W. 2d 586 (2003), when valuing an orthodontics practice, the Court stated "liquidation value is the least favored method of valuing any type of marital property in a divorce."

Valuation date

State law reflects the appropriate date to value the practice for divorce purposes. Fourteen states require the use of a date as close as possible to the date of trial. Fifteen states and the District of Columbia require the use of the date of complaint. Nineteen states suggest using the date of divorce. Two states mandate the use of the date of separation. When the use of a trial date or dissolution date is required, often the state laws suggest the use of a current date. Table 3 reflects each state's requirement.

Table 3—Property Valuation Date			
Trial	**Complaint**	**Divorce**	**Separation**
Alabama	Arizona	Arkansas	Hawaii
Alaska	Dist. of Columbia	Connecticut	North Carolina
California	Florida	Georgia	
Colorado	Indiana	Idaho	
Delaware	Kansas	Illinois	
Iowa	Maine	Kentucky	
Missouri	Michigan	Louisiana	
North Dakota	Mississippi	Maryland	
Oregon	New Hampshire	Massachusetts	
Pennsylvania	New Jersey	Minnesota	
Rhode Island	New York	Montana	
Tennessee	Ohio	Nebraska	
Vermont	Oklahoma	Nevada	
Virginia	South Carolina	New Mexico	
	West Virginia	South Dakota	
	Wyoming	Texas	
		Utah	
		Washington	
		Wisconsin	

Trial: as close as possible to date of trial
Complaint: date petition or complaint for divorce is filed
Divorce: as close as possible to date of dissolution
Separate: date of separation

Chapter 26: When the Marriage is Over, What is the Practice Worth?

Appreciation

What happens when a physician gets married and then divorced, all while owning a medical practice? Depending on the state, the appreciation in the value of the practice during the marriage may need to be determined. The appraiser must determine the value of the practice at the date of marriage and the date of complaint.

In re Marriage of Ackerman, 146 Cal. App. 4th 191 (Cal. App. *2006*), the husband was board certified in plastic and reconstructive surgery. He began his practice in 1987 and was married in 1991. The husband and wife signed a premarital agreement in which they stipulated to a value of the practice as of the date of marriage. In 2001, the couple separated. Therefore, only the increase in value from the date of marriage to the date of complaint was deemed community property subject to equitable distribution.

Clearly, when a value is not determined at the beginning of the marriage, the valuator has a difficult task ahead because often a significant amount of time has passed and/or records may not be available.

Buy/Sell agreements

Often physicians are party to a buy/sell agreement. These agreements are typically utilized in situations of death, disability, retirement, or withdrawal of a partner. While these agreements may set a value and be binding for transfers of an ownership interest, disagreements exist as to the use of these values or formulas in the context of marital dissolution because the non-physician spouse is not party to the agreement and no change in ownership is occurring.

The courts have recognized that often values included in these agreements contain artificially low values. However, some states consider the agreement value the sole indicator of value, concluding that the amount in the agreement is the only amount the owner will ever receive and it would be inequitable for the non-owner spouse to receive more than the owner spouse.

In the New Mexico case of *Hertz v. Hertz*, 99 N.M. 320, 325, 657 P.2d 1169, 1174 (N.M. 1983), the spouse was bound by the $1 value contained in the attorney husband's Restrictive Stock Agreement because, as the Court stated, "We hold that a non-shareholder spouse is bound to the same terms of a shareholder valuation agreement which affects the shareholder spouse. This insures that the non-shareholder spouse does not receive a *greater* value than that of the shareholder." The State Supreme Court, overturning the local district court's decision, noted that if the husband terminated his employment with the law firm, he would never realize the value of the goodwill that was awarded to the wife by the district court.

The New York case of *McDiarmid v. McDiarmid*, 649 A.2d 810, 815 (D.C. App. 1994) referenced the *Hertz* case and stated that goodwill of the medical practice was not includable as marital property since the buy/sell agreement specifically excluded it.

Chapter 26: When the Marriage is Over, What is the Practice Worth?

In *Weaver v. Weaver*, 72 N.C. App. 409, 324 S.E.2d 915 (1985) and *Stern v. Stern*, 66 N.J. 340, 331 A.2d 257 (1975), the courts indicated that when the terms of a partnership agreement are followed, the value of the interest calculated is only a presumptive value, which can be attacked by either plaintiff or defendant as not reflective of the true value. In *Stern v. Stern*, the Supreme Court of New Jersey stated that the value of a partnership interest determined by use of the partnership agreement should only be used "once it is established that the books of the firm are well kept and that the value of the partners' interests are in fact periodically and carefully reviewed…"

The majority of states follow West Virginia's ruling in the case of *Bettinger v. Bettinger*, 396 S.E.2d 709, 714 (W.Va. 1990), wherein the Court opined that the value pursuant to the Buy/Sell Agreement should be considered along with any other relevant evidence regarding the value and weighted accordingly.

Additionally, the physician's age may be a consideration. A value set by an agreement may be more relevant in the case of a 58 year old physician subject to mandatory retirement at age 60 who is nearing the end of his professional career than the case of a 38 year old physician subject to the same agreement when sale or retirement is not imminent.

Valuation approaches. Generally, the preferred approach for valuing a medical practice, like any other service business, is an income approach. This method considers the expected long term earnings stream that the physician can reasonably expect to receive until retirement.

In valuing medical practices, asset approaches are generally not favored because there is often value beyond the physical assets.

The market approaches, particularly the comparable transactions method, are often utilized, but many times sufficient details regarding the transactions are unknown, and the valuator may not be comparing apples to apples. Specifically, a valuator would not be aware of any synergies or other investment value characteristics that influenced the transaction.

There are situations where the market approach may be considered an indicator of value. For example, in recent years, AmSurg, a publicly traded hospital management company, has purchased a number of ambulatory surgical centers. The multiples used by AmSurg have been relatively consistent, so their application to the subject practice may be appropriate. The weakness in this approach, of course, is knowledge of the underlying characteristics of the comparable companies and the subject company.

The question arises as to whether it is fair to use a market approach when a transaction is not likely to occur. A market approach is often better used as a reasonableness check, rather than a primary or even secondary indicator of value.

Chapter 26: When the Marriage is Over, What is the Practice Worth?

Goodwill

In addition to the value of the tangible assets owned by a medical practice, the value is also comprised of intangible assets such as goodwill, patient lists, medical records, and covenants not to compete. The value of the intangible component is often greater than the value of the tangible component.

Goodwill is defined as "that intangible asset arising as a result of name, reputation, customer loyalty, location, products, and similar factors not separately identified."[20] It can be viewed as the ability to earn a return over and above the return earned on the tangible assets.

Once it has been determined that goodwill exists, it must be valued. Goodwill is often valued to compensate the non-physician spouse for his or her marital contribution.

There are two types of goodwill that may be associated with the value of a medical practice. Personal (or professional) goodwill is attached to the individual and his or her unique abilities and characteristics. Practice (or entity) goodwill is attached to the medical practice and is not associated with the physician's unique abilities and characteristics.

Personal goodwill presumes that a practice has a higher value as a result of the particular professional's knowledge, experience, and reputation. "Personal goodwill is that which would make a doctor's patients follow him even if he changed his location, staff, and phone number."[21] As such, personal goodwill is difficult to transfer, but it may be done with advance planning and cooperation between the buyer and the seller. However, would a hypothetical buyer pay anything for personal goodwill (under the fair market value standard of value)?

Practice goodwill is associated with the practice as a unit, including its location, systems, operating procedures and policies, staff, an established client base, and patient records. Another indicator of practice goodwill is a telephone number. Assume a family practice has a telephone number of 808-555-1212. As a patient of that practice needing an appointment, you will call that number and ask for an appointment with Dr. A. If Dr. A is not there, you still are likely to see whatever doctor is available at that telephone number.

A distinction must be made between personal goodwill and practice goodwill because the majority of states do not consider personal goodwill a marital asset (Table 4).

A minority of states have ruled that goodwill is never marital property, whether it is personal goodwill or practice goodwill (Table 5). Then, there are states that have ruled that all goodwill is marital property (Table 6). These three tables reflect cases specifically related to medical practices, unless noted otherwise. Of course, there are some states (Alabama, Georgia, Idaho, Iowa, South Dakota, and Vermont) that are undecided in this matter.

Chapter 26: When the Marriage is Over, What is the Practice Worth?

\multicolumn{2}{c}{**Table 4—Practice Goodwill is a Divisible Marital Asset**}	
\multicolumn{2}{c}{**Personal Goodwill is not a Divisible Marital Asset**}	
Alaska	Fortson v. Fortson, 131 P.3d 451 (Alaska 2006)
Arkansas	Wilson v. Wilson, 294 Ark. 194 (1987)
Connecticut	Eslami v. Eslami, 218 Conn. 801, 591 A.2d 411 (1991)
Delaware	E.E.C. v. E.J.C., 457 A.2d 688 (Del. 1983) (Law Practice)
District Of Columbia	McDiarmid v. McDiarmid, 594 A.2d 79 (D.C. 1991 (Law practice)
Florida	Young v. Young, 600 So.2d 1140 (Fla. App. 5 Dist. 1992).
Hawaii	Antolik v. Harvey, 761 P.2d 305, 319 (Haw. Ct. App. 1988)
Illinois	In re Marriage of Head, 273 Ill. App.3d 404, 652 N.E.2d 1246, 210 Ill. Dec. 270 (1995)
Indiana	Yoon v. Yoon, 711 N.E.2d 1265 (Ind. 1999)
Maine	Ahern v. Ahern, 2008 ME 1, (January 3, 2008)
Maryland	Skrabak v. Strabak, 108 Md. App. 633, 673 A.2d 732, 1996 Md. App. LEXIS 39
Massachusetts [1]	Goldman v. Goldman, 28 Mass. App. Ct. 603, 554 N.E.2d 860 (1990)
Minnesota	In re Marriage of Baker, 2007 Minn. App. A06-1252
Missouri	Hanson v. Hanson, 738 S.W.2d 429 (Mo. 1987)
Nebraska	Taylor v. Taylor, 222 Neb. 721, 386 N.W.2d 851 (1986)
New Hampshire	In re Watterworth, 149 N.H. 442, 821 A.2d 1107 (2003)
Oklahoma	Traczyk v. Traczyk, No. 78435. 891 P.2d 1277, 1995 OK 22
Oregon	Matter of the Dissolution of the Marriage of Goger, 27 Or. App. 729 (1976)
Pennsylvania	Gaydos v. Gaydos, 693 A.2d 1368 (Pa. Super. 1997)
Rhode Island	Gibbons v. Gibbons, 619 A.2d 432 (R.I. 1993))
Texas	Nail v. Nail, 486 S.W.2d 761 (Tex. 1972)
Utah	Sorenson v. Sorenson, 769 P.2d 820 (Utah Ct. App. 1989)
Virginia	Hoebelheinrich v. Hoebelheinrich, 2004 Va. App. LEXIS 376
West Virginia	May v. May, 214 W.Va. 394, 589 S.E.2d 536 (2003)
Wisconsin	Holbrook v. Holbrook, 103 Wis.2d 327, 309 N.W.2d 343 (1981)
Wyoming	Root v. Root, 2003 WY 36, 65 P.3d 41 (2003)

[1] Although *Goldman* is oft-cited as suggesting that personal goodwill is nondivisible, it has little sway in that it involved a neurosurgery practice where transferable enterprise goodwill would be hard to find. The sole statement in this Appellate decision is "The judge was warranted in accepting the husband's accountant's opinion that there was no goodwill in this one-man professional corporation." As a result of *Sampson* (62 Mass . App. Ct. 366 (2004), Massachusetts now considers the extent of any "Double Dip" in what is equitable; Double Dipping is not precluded, however, as it may be in other jurisdictions.

Chapter 26: When the Marriage is Over, What is the Practice Worth?

Table 5—Goodwill is a Divisible Marital Asset - Whether Personal or Practice	
Arizona*	Wisner v. Wisner, 129 Ariz. 333, 631 P.2d 115 (Ariz. Ap. 1981)
California*	In re Marriage of Foster, 42 Cal.App.3d 577 (1974)
Colorado	In re Marriage of Nichols, 43 Colo. App. 383 (1979)
Kentucky	Clark v. Clark, Ky.App., 782 S.W.2d 56 (1990)
Michigan	Kowalesky v. Kowalesky, 148 Mich. App. 151, 384 N.W.2d 12 (1986)
Montana	Marriage of Hull, 219 Mont. 480 (1986)
Nevada*	Ford v. Ford, 105 Nev. 672, 782 P.2d 1304 (1989)
New Jersey	Stern v. Stern, 66 N.J. 340, 331 A.2d 257 (1975) (Law practice)
New Mexico*	Hurley v. Hurley, 94 N.M. 641, 615 P. 2d 256 (1980)
New York	Nehorayoff v. Nehorayoff, 08 Misc. 2d 311; 437 N.Y.S.2d 584 (1981)
North Carolina	Poore v. Poore, 75 N.C. App. 414, 331 S.E.2d 266 (1985)
North Dakota	Sommers v. Sommers, 2003 ND 77, 660 N.W.2d 596 (2003)
Ohio	Kahn v. Kahn, 42 Ohio App.3d 61 (1987)
Washington*	In re Marriage of Fleege, 91 Wn.2d 324 (1979)
* Community Property State	

Table 6—Goodwill is Never a Divisible Marital Asset	
Kansas	Powell v. Powell, 231 Kan. 456, 648 P.2d 218 (1982)
Louisiana	Chance v. Chance, 694 So. 2d 613 (La. App. 1997)
Mississippi	Singley v. Singley, 1999-CT-00754-SCT (Miss. 6-12-2003)
South Carolina	Donahue v. Donahue, 299 S.C. 353, 384 S.E.2d 741 (1989)
Tennessee	Hazard v. Hazard, 833 S.W.2d 911 (Tenn.App. 1991)

Many court cases have detailed factors to consider in determining professional goodwill. *In re Marriage of Lopez*, 38 Cal.App.3d 93 (1974) identifies the following factors:

1. Practitioner's age and health

2. Demonstrated earning power

3. Reputation for judgment, skill, and knowledge

4. Comparative professional success

5. Nature and duration of practice, either as sole practitioner or as a contributing member of a partnership or professional corporation

Chapter 26: When the Marriage is Over, What is the Practice Worth?

The Pennsylvania case *Fexa v. Fexa*, 396 Pa. Super. 481, 578 A.2d 1314 (1990) addressed the distinction between personal goodwill and practice goodwill. The court reasoned that since:

> partners have bought in and been bought out and the practice has been maintained, there is a clear basis upon which to determine that the goodwill enjoyed by the practice was not entirely personal to the individual professionals involved. Likewise, where the professionals share clients within the corporation or partnership, there is a basis upon which to conclude that the goodwill is not purely personal.

In valuing a medical practice, many factors, such as those described following, must be evaluated that contribute to goodwill, whether it is personal or practice goodwill.

Age and health of practitioner. There is likely less goodwill in the case of an older or unhealthy practitioner, since expected future earnings are not expected to continue for long period of time.

Ancillary services. A medical practice that has a laboratory attached or in close proximity is likely to have greater practice goodwill and receive a greater return on its investment. Alternatively, however, a primary care physician with a single X-ray machine is not likely to earn excess profits by having that single machine.

Area of specialization. A cardiologist or neurologist is likely to have personal goodwill, while a radiologist is more likely to have practice goodwill; particularly because the patient may not even see the radiologist.

Cash flow/earnings ability. A physician's cash flow or earnings ability as compared to his or her partners is likely an indicator of personal goodwill, while the earning ability of the practice compared to its peers is likely an indicator of practice goodwill.

Changes in ownership. When physicians are entering and leaving the practice on a regular basis and there is little or no impact on the practice, it likely is an indicator of practice goodwill. On the other hand, if the practice disbands or suffers economically upon the termination of an individual; it was likely personal goodwill creating the value.

Location and competition. If the subject is the only local practice, it is likely that practice goodwill exists. However, if there are many physicians in town, personal goodwill is likely the driver.

Patient base. Where a practice has a large, established patient base that requires recurring care, practice goodwill is likely to exist. This could be the case with practices specializing in primary care, internal medicine, pediatrics, and family medicine, for example.

Patient visits. If a patient is shared among practice physicians, it likely represents the existence of practice goodwill. For example, in a group obstetrics practice, a pregnant woman is likely to visit various physicians. If she returns to the practice, she is likely continuing due to practice goodwill.

Chapter 26: When the Marriage is Over, What is the Practice Worth?

Referral base. Referrals made to the individual physician would likely indicate personal goodwill, while referrals to the practice in general would indicate practice goodwill. Some examples are that a patient is likely to get a referral to a specific cardiologist (personal goodwill) or may be referred to a certain radiology practice for X-rays (practice goodwill).

Relationships. Example: A pulmonologist is an owner of a group medical practice that provides inpatient services to various hospitals under contract. The physician also sees patients in the office one or two days per week, which are primarily follow up visits from hospital patients. This pulmonologist is likely to have practice goodwill because the practice receives the majority of its patients due to the follow up visits required as a result of the physician's relationship with the hospital, rather than the physician's individual reputation. However, one could argue that if a patient continues to visit this same pulmonologist after the initial follow up visit, then personal goodwill exists. [Editor's Note: Appraisers should also consider the underlying contracts with the Hospitals as part of this practice/personal goodwill analysis.]

Tangible assets/equipment owned. A practice with a significant investment in equipment is likely to have more practice goodwill than a physician, such as a family practitioner, that does not require the use of highly technical and expensive equipment.

Work habits. When comparing two physicians working the same amount of hours in the same specialty, for example, the physician that works more efficiently is likely to have more personal goodwill. Increased time spent per patient is also likely an indicator of personal goodwill.

Years in profession. The longer a physician has been in practice, the more likely he or she is to have personal goodwill.

Double dip

The "double dip" dilemma exists when the same income stream is used for multiple purposes—for example, when the income stream of a business is utilized to value a practice and that same earnings stream is used as the basis for support.

Normalized compensation is utilized in determining the value of a practice. It represents what the owner physician would have to pay another physician to come in and perform the same function as the owner physician, distinguishing between the return on labor and the return on equity—This is the key task for the appraiser of a professional practice. Often, the determination of reasonable compensation is the most disputed part of the valuation. Further discussion of reasonable compensation is located at the end of this chapter.

The actual compensation, which is usually greater than the normalized compensation, often includes discretionary personal expenses that are paid by the business, such as automobile expenses, dues and subscriptions, household expenses, meals and entertainment, retirement

Chapter 26: When the Marriage is Over, What is the Practice Worth?

plan contributions, telephone, and travel. The use of normalized compensation for valuation purposes increases the value of the practice. At the same time, actual compensation is often used as the basis for support.

For example, assume the following information for Dr. A:

	Actual	Normalized
Revenue	$800,000	$800,000
Operating Expenses	300,000	300,000
Operating Income before Physician Compensation	500,000	500,000
Physician Compensation	490,000	200,000
Pre-tax Income	10,000	300,000
Income taxes	4,000	120,000
Net income	$6,000	$180,000

Assuming a capitalization rate for net income of 20%, the value of the practice using normalized compensation is $900,000. The spouse's alimony is going to be calculated based on the physician's compensation of $490,000. Therefore, the spouse is receiving the double benefit from the normalized earnings utilized in determining the value of the practice and the actual compensation taken by the physician.

As is the case with determining the applicable standard of value, the states' treatment of the double dip varies.

Michigan[22] and New Jersey have implied that the double dip dilemma does not exist. In 2005, The New Jersey Supreme Court ruled in *Steneken v. Steneken*, 183 N.J. 290 (App. Div. 2005):

> The interplay between an alimony award and equitable distribution is subject to an overarching concept of fairness…The goal of a proper alimony award is to assist the supported spouse in achieving a lifestyle reasonably comparable to the one enjoyed during the marriage… Much of the controversy inherent in this appeal stems from the unspoken premise that because alimony and equitable distribution are interrelated, a credit on one side of the ledger must perforce require a debit on the other side; otherwise, defendant claims, the interplay between alimony and equitable distribution results in 'double counting.' We disagree…

In other words, in Michigan and New Jersey, it is acceptable to use a normalized compensation for purposes of valuing the business but actual compensation for determining support.

On the other side of the coin, in *Holbrook v. Holbrook*, 103 Wis. 2d 327, 309 N.W. 2nd 343 (Ct. App. 1981), a Wisconsin Appellate Court disallowed the double dip and stated that Mr. Holbrook's actual earnings could not be utilized for purposes of determining the value of the practice's goodwill.

Chapter 26: When the Marriage is Over, What is the Practice Worth?

New Hampshire[23] and New York have taken it a step further by stating that the double dip is not allowed for alimony but is allowable for child support. In *Holterman v. Holterman*, 3 N.Y. 3d 1; 814 N.E. 2d 765; 781 N.Y.S. 2d 458 (2004), the state reiterated that there is a value to a physician's medical license (or other advanced degrees, certifications, or celebrity status) for equitable distribution purposes. The Court also opined that the income stream utilized in valuing the license may not be used to determine spousal support but is allowed to be used in the determination of child support.

Reasonable compensation. The reasonable compensation adjustment is likely the biggest bone of contention in marital litigation because it is often the largest adjustment in terms of dollars. While this section is not designed to discuss the topic in its entirety, this discussion will provide an overview specifically for the purposes of medical practice valuation.

Often, surveys provide the best data for use in determining reasonable compensation, also called normalized compensation. Some of the most commonly referenced surveys are the following:

- American Medical Association's Physician's Socioeconomic Statistics surveys

- Medical Group Management Association Physician Compensation and Production Survey

- Merritt Hawkins Physician Compensation Surveys

- Sullivan Cotter and Associates, Inc. Physician Compensation Survey

Additionally, the Economic Research Institute has a database that provides compensation figures based on numerous classifications.

Rather than relying on any of the survey data blindly, as the appraiser or valuation analyst you must know and understand how and where the data is obtained. While the data itself may be reliable, common sense must also be utilized. In the California case of *In re Marriage of Ackerman* (2006), Cal. App. 4th, at issue was the reasonable compensation of a plastic surgeon located in Newport Beach. The experts utilized information contained in the Medical Group Management Association surveys and the American Medical Association surveys. The Court requested the husband's expert survey local plastic surgeons. In this particular case, the survey of local practitioners was given the greatest weight by the Court. The Court reasoned that plastic surgery used discretionary income, which is more available in Newport Beach than other areas that would have been included in the survey data.

In addition to the specialty and geographic area of a physician, the appraiser must consider, at a minimum, the duties, experience, efficiency, productivity, and hours worked. Often, the size of the practice has an impact on compensation, as does the profit distribution method. In addition to a physician's patient care duties, any administrative duties or hospital board duties should be evaluated.

Chapter 26: When the Marriage is Over, What is the Practice Worth?

Summation

Successful valuation engagements require sound judgment. You must be confident that the conclusions reached are reasonable based on the unique facts and circumstances of the case and that your value is reasonably defensible. With the majority of the issues discussed in this chapter, the courts have looked to previous decisions not only in their own state, but often in other states as well. As valuators, knowledge of the relevant case law would likely increase the value of your services to referring attorneys.

1. Arkansas Statute § 9-12-315 (4)
2. La. R.S. 9:2801.
3. International Glossary of Business Valuation Terms, 2001.
4. *McQueary v. McQueary*, 902 P.2d 1326, 1327 (Alaska 1995)
5. *Kowaleski v. Kowaleski*, 148 Mich. App. 151; 384 N.W.2d 112; 1986 Mich. App. LEXIS 2380
6. *Robison v. Robison*, 691 P.2d 451, 455 (Nev. 1984)
7. *Walker v. Walker*, No. COA03-998, 2004 LEXIS 1319, at 7-9 (N.C. Ct. App. July 20, 2004) (unpublished).
8. Alley, No. COA02-594, 2003 LEXIS 1986, at 8-10; *Durnell v. Durnell*, 460 S.E.2d 710, 717-18 (W. Va. 1995)
9. Fishman, Jay *Standards of Value: Theory and Applications* (Hoboken: John Wiley & Sons, Inc., 2007), 218.
10. *Brown v. Brown*, 348 N.J. Super. 466 (App. Div. 2002)
11. *Bobrow v. Bobrow*, 711 N.E.2d 1265:1999
12. *Fisher v. Fisher*, 568 N.W.2d 728, 732-33 (N.D. 1997).
13. *Gardner v. Gardner*, No. 0468-04-03, 2005 LEXIS 10, at *15 (Va. Ct. App. Jan. 11, 2005) (unpublished).
14. *Judith E. Bernier v. Stephen A. Bernier*, SJC-09836, September 14, 2007)
15. Fishman, Jay *Standards of Value: Theory and Applications* (Hoboken: John Wiley & Sons, Inc., 2007), 218.
16. *In re marriage of Huff*, 834 P.2d 244, 254 (Colo. 1992).
17. *Matter of Marriage of Fleege*, 588 P.2d 1136 (1979)
18. International Glossary of Business Valuation Terms, 2001.
19. International Glossary of Business Valuation Terms, 2001.
20. International Glossary of Business Valuation Terms, 2001.
21. Fishman, Jay E. *Standards of Value: Theory and Applications* (Hoboken, NJ: John Wiley & Sons, Inc., 2007), 203.
22. *McGregor v. McGregor*, 2004 Mich. App. Lexis 2560
23. *Rattee v. Rattee*, 767 A.2d, 415 (Sup. Ct. New Hampshire 2001)

Chapter 27

Jurisdictional Issues in Physician Practice Divorce Valuation: California

By Kathie Wilson, CPA, CVA and Tracy Farryl Katz, Esq., CPA

Family law courts are "courts of equity" and as such they can define and redefine concepts to achieve just results. The result in California has been a very fluid body of family law. A significant amount of the medical practice valuation methodology is not found in the Family Code or prior court cases, but is entirely up to the discretion of the Court. In recognition of this, the organization of this chapter is based upon the stability of the concepts. It starts with some concepts right from the Family Code and ends with an analysis of four recent court cases involving professional practice valuation issues. The discussion here is limited to concepts that appear to be unique to California. As you read through this chapter, you will get a flavor for the concepts that are routinely accepted by the courts and those concepts that are more situationally accepted. The fluidity of family law means that the effects of the four recent significant court cases, are still not completely known.

Family Code §771, Earnings and accumulations after date of separation are separate property

It is a relatively simple concept; what you earn after the date of separation, you get to keep. Once the community is irreparably broken, it no longer has an interest in either spouse's earned income or accumulations related to that earned income. This general rule impacts physician practice valuations in two key ways: date of value and permissible valuation methods.

Family Code §2552, Valuation date of assets and liabilities

The valuation date for the assets and liabilities of the community, under Family Code §2552, is "as near as practicable to the time of trial." As a general rule, this makes sense; the community retains its interest in the assets and liabilities until they are legally divided. Certainly a clear example of this is the valuation of a brokerage or retirement account that has no activity subsequent to the date of separation, and nothing affecting its value other than market forces. In this instance, the community either bears the risk or shares in the reward when the asset is ultimately divided at the time of trial.

It is the reconciliation of these two code sections that can affect the date of value of a physician's practice because the value of the practice is typically impacted by the efforts of the physician. If he or she is working less after the date of separation, all things being equal, the value of the

Chapter 27: Jurisdictional Issues in Physician Practice Divorce Valuation: California

practice would be expected to decrease. By the same token, an increase in efforts after the date of separation, all things being equal, should result in an increase in practice value. In both of these examples, the rise or fall in value after the date of separation is due to the efforts of the doctor. When post-separation efforts affect the practice value, an alternate valuation date (i.e., date of separation) may be available. An alternate valuation date is only available if it is requested and approved by the court. It does not apply automatically.

It follows that the community's interest in the physician practice is correctly determined at the date of separation as earnings and *accumulations* after the date of separation are separate property. This is not to say that all physician practices are greatly impacted by the efforts of the individual doctor. A large group practice or one with significant ancillary income, nonphysician providers, large capital investment and/or a compensation system less determined by individual productivity could arguably be correctly valued near the time of trial as an individual physician's efforts may not have a great impact on the practice value. In the case of *Aufmuth v. Aufmuth*, 89 Cal.App.3d 446 (1979), valuation at the date of separation was denied because the court determined that the efforts of the spouse, a young attorney with a 5% ownership interest in his firm, were not the reason for the increase in the value of the law firm between date of separation and time of trial. The Court concluded that the increase in the value of the law firm was related to the increase in the accounts receivable and that Mr. Aufmuth's efforts were not responsible for the increase in the accounts receivable.

The concept that earnings after the date of separation are separate property can also impact the valuation methodology. In the case of *Foster v. Foster*, 42 Cal.App.3d 577 (1974), the Court summarized permissible valuation methods for goodwill as follows:

> In sum, we conclude the applicable rule in evaluating community goodwill to be that such goodwill *may not be valued by any method that takes into account the post-marital efforts of either spouse* but that a proper means of arriving at the value of such goodwill contemplates any legitimate method of evaluation that measures its present value by taking into account some past result. Insofar as the professional practice is concerned it is assumed that it will continue in the future. [emphasis added]

The above quote seems to prohibit the use of any method of valuation that involves projecting income or cash flow into future periods, such as a discounted cash flow model. In practice, although discounted cash flow models are not used, capitalized excess earnings models are permitted (see case table at the end of this chapter). The growth rate used in a capitalization rate build up would seem to violate the prohibition against looking into the future. One can only surmise that the courts accept this form of projection because the long term growth rate is often presented and defended based on the expected rate of inflation, not actual practice growth and the efforts of the physician could hardly be deemed to influence rates of inflation. That being said, the use of build up models to achieve capitalization rates for medical practice valuations is less common in California than the use of rounded capitalization rates such as 40% or 50% (or the reciprocal multipliers, 2.5 or 2) which have not been built up.

Chapter 27: Jurisdictional Issues in Physician Practice Divorce Valuation: California

Premise of value

Investment value seems to be the premise of value for medical practice valuations in marital dissolutions in California. Investment value here means "value to the holder" as contrasted with fair market value which is the "willing buyer" standard. This principle does not come directly from the Family Code, but has been accepted and reaffirmed throughout the years. Numerous cases have used investment value rather than fair market value for professional practices, each making the statement slightly differently. For example, in 1962, *Brawman v. Brawman*, 199 Cal. App.2d 876 (1962), the Court said:

> In considering this value, consideration must be given to the fact that, on divorce and dissolution of the community, a professional practice goes automatically to the spouse licensed to practice it. He is not selling out or liquidating, but continuing the business. Effectually, it is the case of a silent partner withdrawing from a going business. And, if such partner is to receive fair compensation for her share, on her enforced retirement, it should be evaluated.

Another California case, *Golden v. Golden*, 270 Cal.App.2d 401 (1969), stated it slightly differently and contrasted divorce with the dissolution of a partnership:

> We believe the better rule is that, in a divorce case, the good will of the husband's professional practice as a sole practitioner should be taken into consideration in determining the award to the wife. Where as in *Lyon* (*Lyon v. Lyon*, 246 Cal.App.2d 519 (1966)), the firm is being dissolved, it is understandable that a court cannot determine what, if any, of the good will of the firm will go to either partner. But, in a matrimonial matter, the practice of the sole practitioner husband will continue, with the same intangible value as it had during the marriage. (case citation added)

In 1974, in *Foster*, the Court confirmed again:

> The value of community goodwill is not necessarily the specified amount of money that a willing buyer would pay for such goodwill. In view of exigencies that are ordinarily attendant a marriage dissolution the amount obtainable in the marketplace might well be less than the true value of the goodwill. Community goodwill is a portion of the community value of the professional practice as a going concern on the date of dissolution of the marriage.

Property can be characterized as separate, community, quasi community or a combination

California is a community property state. The rebuttable presumption is that property acquired during marriage is community. This means that the court presumes that all property acquired during marriage is community property unless that presumption is contested and proven

Chapter 27: Jurisdictional Issues in Physician Practice Divorce Valuation: California

otherwise. In the case of a medical practice started or joined during marriage, the value of the practice on the date of separation (or trial depending on whether the factors discussed above exist) is generally the value that will be divided. An interesting issue regarding the character of the practice arises when a practice is started or joined *before* marriage. Arguably, this practice would be both community and separate in nature. A portion of the value of the medical practice is the separate property of the spouse that owned it prior to marriage, and it therefore is not subject to division by the community. The portion of the practice fostered during marriage belongs to the community. Remember that earnings and accumulations after the date of separation are separate. Family Code §760 states "Except as otherwise provided by statute, all property, real or personal, wherever situated, acquired by a married person during the marriage while domiciled in this state is community property." The physician's efforts during marriage that increase the value of the practice benefit the community via his or her earned income and the increase in practice value.

How to apportion value between separate and community estates is the subject of two very old yet very significant, court cases, *Pereira v. Pereira*, 156 Ca.1, 103 (1909) and *Van Camp v. Van Camp*, 53 Cal.App 17 (1921). In the case of a typical medical practice, *Pereira*, decided in 1909, is the case most applicable. Under the *Pereira* methodology, as applied to a medical practice, valuations are performed as of the date of marriage and as of the date of separation. The value calculated as of date of marriage, which is the value of the separate property interest, is treated as if it had been "invested" during the marriage and earning interest. That value, grown by the interest factor, represents the separate property component of the valuation as of either the date of separation or trial. To derive the community's interest in the practice, the value as of date of marriage, grown by the interest factor, is subtracted from the value calculated as of either the date of separation or trial. The Court described this concept as follows:

> It appears, however, that the decision of the court was made upon the theory that all of his gains received after marriage, from whatever sources, were to be classed as community property, and that no allowance was made in favor of his separate estate on account of interest or profit on the fifteen thousand five hundred dollars invested in the business at the time of the marriage. This capital was undoubtedly his separate estate. The fund remained in the business after marriage and was used by him in carrying it on. The separate property should have been credited with some amount as profit on this capital.

Conversely, the *Van Camp* decision, in 1921, typically applies when the efforts of the spouse are farther removed from the overall success of a business. In other words, the business grew in value, but it did so as a result of the capital invested rather than the efforts of the owner spouse. The types of businesses that would be vulnerable to a Van Camp argument would be capital intensive with more than one investor, perhaps manufacturing concerns or very large companies. This is usually not an arguable case with medical practices, even large medical practices.

You can compare the Courts' statements in *Pereira* and *Van Camp* to understand the different views of the circumstances. In *Pereira*, where the husband owned and operated a saloon and cigar business, the Court states:

Chapter 27: Jurisdictional Issues in Physician Practice Divorce Valuation: California

> It is true that it is very clearly shown that the principal part of the large income was due to the personal character, energy, ability, and capacity of the husband. This share of the earnings was, of course, community property. But without capital he could have not carried on the business.

In *Van Camp*, where the husband was president of Van Camp Sea Food Company, the Court states:

> While it may be true that the success of the corporation of which defendant was president and manager was to a large extent due to his capacity and ability, nevertheless without the investment of his and other capital in the corporation he could not have conducted the business, and while he devoted his energies and personal efforts to making it a success, he was by the corporation paid what the evidence shows was an adequate salary, and for which another than himself with equal capacity could have been secured.

The significant difference between *Pereira* and *Van Camp* is that *Pereira* allows the community to obtain an interest in an otherwise separate property business. *Van Camp* does not. Even if the spouse in a *Van Camp*-type business receives inadequate compensation (i.e., below-market salary), all that the community can get is the value of the services provided. The community does not gain an interest in the separate property business.

Current Case Analysis

Rosen v. Rosen, 105 Cal.App.4th 808 (2002)

In 2002, in the *Rosen* case, the Court once again affirmed the use of excess earnings in the calculation of professional goodwill, but also concluded that Mr. Rosen did not have any professional goodwill. The Court had interesting discussions about a variety of issues surrounding goodwill calculations in the context of divorce. One of the primary issues was that Mrs. Rosen's expert used one year's net income to calculate goodwill. That single year was the most recent full calendar year at the time the valuation was performed, but it was also a high income year. The Court said:

> Further, it is obvious that using one year's net income (not coincidentally a high-income year) is not illustrative of Bruce's volatile income over a period of several years....Picking one year's net income, where income rises or falls from year to year is not a reasonable basis for determining value....Pat's expert admitted that had he averaged Bruce's income over any period of years he considered, goodwill value would be nominal or nothing.

The Court was also displeased with Mrs. Rosen's expert's use of national surveys for the calculation of reasonable compensation without applying the survey results against some kind of local measure:

Chapter 27: Jurisdictional Issues in Physician Practice Divorce Valuation: California

> Pat's expert testified he did not have any particular knowledge of lawyer compensation, other than what he had learned from valuations he had performed. He admitted he was not familiar with a law practice like Bruce's. He did not conduct a survey or perform any kind of study of lawyer compensation in Southern California. Rather, he relied entirely upon two surveys of compensation (the Altman Weil survey and the Robert Morris survey), neither of which dealt with a sole practitioner lawyer handling state-funded criminal appeals. The expert did not attempt to relate the information in the surveys to Bruce's law practice.

The surveys were deemed, by the Court, not representative of law practices like Mr. Rosen's. The Court also disliked the fact that Mrs. Rosen's expert used his own judgment in determining which reasonable compensation numbers to use. Her expert stated that he had no experience in the area of attorney reasonable compensation outside of preparing law practice valuations in the context of divorce.

> Pat's expert then used his own 'judgment' to come up with a compensation figure based upon the numbers in these two surveys, even though he admitted he did not have any particular knowledge about lawyer compensation and did not know of any attorney with a law practice like Bruce's. In essence, Pat's expert did nothing more than pick $100,000 because it was about halfway between $125,000 and $67,000. Those two numbers bear no particular materiality to the issue of reasonable compensation in this case.
>
> Our concern is that the surveys relied upon by Pat's expert were not relevant to Bruce's law practice and therefore were not useful in establishing compensation under either the 'average salaried person' standard of In re Marriage of Garrity and Bishton (181 Cal.App.3d 675) or the 'similarly situated professional' standard. We are also troubled by the fact that Pat's expert ultimately reached his determination of compensation by exercising his 'judgment' when the expert admitted he did not have any knowledge of a law practice like Bruce's (citation added).

In the end, the Court determined that Mr. Rosen's law practice had no goodwill without any expert testimony being offered by Mr. Rosen.

Iredale v. Cates, 121 Cal.App.4th 321 (2004)

Two years later, the Court affirmed and expanded a concept used in *Nichols v. Nichols*, 27 Cal. App.4th 661 (1994) that allowed a stock purchase agreement to determine the value of the community's interest in a corporate law firm. In *Nichols*, the Court allowed the limited use of the stock purchase agreement where the stockholder did not purchase accounts receivable or work in process upon joining and did not own any accounts receivable or work in process upon withdrawing. The Court was persuaded because the agreement was arm's length and entered into for an independent business purpose, not entered into in contemplation of divorce and

Chapter 27: Jurisdictional Issues in Physician Practice Divorce Valuation: California

resulted in a value similar to the value derived from other approaches. Although the stock purchase agreement also addressed the value of goodwill, the Court did not discuss goodwill valuation in the context of goodwill in the law firm as opposed to personal goodwill of the attorney, but ultimately decided that the attorney had personal goodwill. In *Iredale*, the Court followed the partnership agreement which stated that the partner (and therefore community) had no interest in certain assets (e.g., accounts receivable, work in progress and goodwill of the firm). The *Iredale* Court, while using *Nichols* as a basis to accept the values from the partnership agreement, took it one step further by discussing the partnership agreement's limitation on Ms. Iredale's interest in the firm's goodwill. The Court opined:

> Thus, the trial court was not evaluating Iredale's interest in PHJW at liquidation value rather than as a going concern as Cates claims, but instead was looking at the specific interest which Iredale holds in PHJW. That interest does not include an entitlement, at any time, to collect a portion of the accounts receivable, work in progress, or goodwill of the law firm. The trial court reasonably concluded that Iredale's interest was limited to the value of her capital account, which reflected the value of her interest in the hard assets of the firm, but not the firm's accounts receivable, work in progress or goodwill.

The Court did find goodwill for Ms. Iredale, not goodwill in her law firm, but, personal goodwill.

> After concluding that Iredale did not have an interest in a proportionate share of the goodwill of her law firm, the court determined that Iredale herself possessed goodwill and accepted the value of that goodwill offered by her expert, $42,318, finding her goodwill to be 'partially a community asset'.

In reviewing the goodwill calculation, the Court revisited the reasonable compensation issue. It adopted the "similarly situated professional" standard over the "average salaried person" standard. The Court stated:

> We conclude that the trial court's use of the 'similarly situated professional" standard to calculate goodwill was entirely reasonable and supported by substantial evidence. Cates's own expert had to concede that his method of comparing Iredale's compensation number to what it would cost to hire an associate (actually 1.4 associates) did not account for the nonbillable hours expended by Iredale, nor would an associate be likely to have a client base comparable to Iredale's. Comparing Iredale's compensation to that of similarly situated professionals, rather than to a salaried employee, was indeed a more rational and reasonable method by which to calculate the value of Iredale's goodwill in this case.

Iredale marks the end of using an "average salaried employee" in the calculation of reasonable compensation in favor of the "similarly situated professional". Use of the "similarly situated professional" usually mean a lesser value for goodwill; e.g. there are zero excess earnings when reasonable

Chapter 27: Jurisdictional Issues in Physician Practice Divorce Valuation: California

compensation mirrors actual compensation. Further, when relying on national surveys to obtain reasonable compensation, the valuator must consider adjustments to the compensation of the "similarly situated professional" that make the national survey data more relevant and applicable to their subject; i.e. for excessive hours worked. It also solidifies the use of agreements to limit the community's interest in a law firm's (or, logically, medical practice's) goodwill in certain situations.

McTiernan v. Dubrow, 133 Cal.App.4th 1090 (2005)

California's celebrity goodwill case was *McTiernan* and, unlike New Jersey, it was decided that celebrities do not generate divisable goodwill. The Court focused on the definition of goodwill found in the Business and Professions Code at §14102, "The good will of a business is property and is transferable." The Court also focused on the definition of a business, determining that it is "...a professional commercial or industrial enterprise with assets, i.e., an entity other than a natural person." The Court stated:

> Endowing 'a person doing business' with the capacity to create goodwill, as opposed to limiting goodwill to 'a business' has wide ramifications...all such persons who would have the 'expectation of continued public patronage' would possess goodwill. This would create a substantial liability, as in this case, without a guaranty that the liability would be funded. It is clear that, from an economic perspective, the 'goodwill' in this case is based on earnings, and that 'goodwill' is an expression of husband's earning capacity.*N7 However, there is no guaranty, especially in the arts that earnings will not decline or even dry up, even though expectations were to the contrary. In such an event, a person would find him- or herself saddled with a massive liability without the means of satisfying it. Putting it another way, endowing directly persons with the ability to create goodwill would create an 'asset' predicated on nothing other than predictions about earning capacity.

In the middle of that quote is a footnote reference, N7. That footnote reads as follows:

> While we acknowledge that the 'excess earning' method of valuing goodwill in a professional corporation is generally accepted, it is true that this method is not far removed from a prediction about future earnings. For good and sufficient reasons, the expectancy of future earnings may not be considered in determining goodwill. (See generally 11 Sitkin, Summary of Cal.Law, need cite, Community Property, §71.) Whether categorized as 'excess earnings' or 'future earnings,' the point is that this type of goodwill is an expression of earnings that have not yet been paid. Thus, when, as here, a person 'doing business' is found to have goodwill and the goodwill is measured by the excess earnings approach, the 'asset' that is credited is a prediction, not a fact. This is quite a distance from an established business enterprise with assets, and a clientele, that has generated goodwill in the traditional sense.

The Court makes the observation, more than once, that Mr. McTiernan's business activity is unlike doctors' or lawyers' practices.

Chapter 27: Jurisdictional Issues in Physician Practice Divorce Valuation: California

> The fact that husband's 'elite professional standing' is not transferable effectively refutes the trial court's conclusion that husband's 'practice' as a motion picture director is like the 'practice' of an attorney or physician. The practice of an attorney, physician, dentist or accountant is transferable, but husband's 'elite professional standing' is his alone, and not susceptible to being transferred or sold.

McTiernan opened the door for all professionals to craft arguments grounded in the case's dicta to try to subvert the traditional calculations of goodwill. Although the case specifically states that a film director is different from a doctor or lawyer, in stating that "elite professional standing" "is not a property interest", it has opened the door for any professional to make a claim of "elite professional standing". If a medical practice has to be transferable in order to generate goodwill, what about psychiatrists' practices? The characteristics of a physician that would allow the generation of significant excess earnings are the same characteristics that would allow a claim of "elite professional standing" and the corresponding claim that the practice is not transferable.

Judge Cooper concurred with the Court on all issues except the determination of goodwill. In his concurring and dissenting opinion, he states:

> The lead opinion's effort to limit goodwill to a 'business' as opposed to an individual is semantic. Any professional who independently practices his or her profession, for profit – be it lawyer, doctor computer consultant or film director – thereby conducts a business, with the lead opinion's own unattributed definition, as well as more traditional ones.

In discussing the issue of transferability, he says:

> As for whether this goodwill is transferable and therefore qualifies as property, the short answer is that the law has determined both question. Business and Professional Code section 14102 establishes, as a matter of law, that "The good will of a business is property and is transferable." That includes the goodwill of husband's business as a director. Whether or not a third party is willing to buy it is not material.

Judge Cooper's final statement on the case:

> In this case, the trial court properly determined the existence and extent of husband's goodwill, in accord with substantial evidence and with California law, as consistently expounded for half a century. Even under the majority's refashioning of that law, those determinations remain sustainable. I respectfully dissent.

The ramifications will become clear when *McTiernan* type arguments wind their way through the courts. So far, California has not distinguished between personal or professional goodwill and enterprise (practice) goodwill. *McTiernan* appears to identify a type personal goodwill that is not owned by the community. If McTiernan's excluded personal goodwill is combined with an *Iredale* agreement that excludes enterprise goodwill, it leads to a conclusion that the "court of equity" might not favor.

Chapter 27: Jurisdictional Issues in Physician Practice Divorce Valuation: California

Ackerman v. Ackerman, 146 Cal.App.4th 191 (2006)

Ackerman follows *Rosen* regarding the use of national surveys and their applicability locally to determine reasonable compensation. The addition in *Ackerman* was that Dr. Ackerman's attorney compared survey data from the American Medical Association to an informal local survey that he performed. In the end, the court determined the reasonable compensation for Dr. Ackerman, using neither expert's numbers, and applied the excess earnings method to determine goodwill.

The trial court once again rejected the "average salaried person" for the "similarly situated professional" standard saying:

> ...it just boggles the mind to think anyone making as much money as husband would work for an employer and receive a third of what he is actually making.

The above quote seems to indicate that using compensation statistics that do not correspond to productivity statistics would generate incorrect reasonable compensation assumptions.

Although *Ackerman* was decided after *McTiernan*, its proximity in date to *McTiernan*, meant that Dr. Ackerman, a plastic surgeon, would not have been able to make a claim of "elite professional standing". Future cases involving professional practices will be important in determining where California goes from here.

Conclusion

California's family law principles come from both the Family Code and court cases, but court decisions are the primary sources for most of the business valuation issues. The concrete concepts, such as, earnings after date of separation are separate, are fairly easily understood and have an impact on both the date of valuation and the methodology allowed. California, over the years, has recognized practice value using the "value to the holder" or investment value premise rather than the "willing buyer" or fair market value premise, although the *McTiernan* case could possibly signal a change in this area. A medical practice can consist of both community and separate property, necessitating multiple valuations. The date of marriage and date of separation are two of the most important pieces of information that are needed for any case. Finally, the valuation case decisions over the last few years signal that the Court may be changing its direction in the future. We await the first professional practice valuation case in the post-*McTiernan* period to see what that future holds.

Chapter 27: Jurisdictional Issues in Physician Practice Divorce Valuation: California

	Selected California Dissolution Cases Timeline	
Year	Case Name and Citation	Valuation Issues
1909	*Pereira v. Pereira* 156 Ca. 1, 103	Cigar store owner, separate and community property valuation and apportionment; theory based on efforts.
1921	*Van Camp v. Van Camp* 53 Cal.App 17	President of large seafood company, separate and community property valuation and apportionment; theory based on capital.
1969	*Golden v. Golden* 270 Cal. App.2d 401	Physician, goodwill exists in professional practice, valuation methodology not addressed.
1974	*Lopez v. Lopez* 38 Cal. App3d 93	Attorney, trial court erred in not determining the value of any goodwill in law practice. Discusses factors to be considered in determination of goodwill.
1974	*Foster v. Foster* 42 Cal. App.3d 577	Physician, goodwill value upheld, valuation methodology not specifically identified.
1976	*Fonstein v. Fonstein* 17 Cal.3d 738	Attorney, value determined by partnership agreement which called for compensation payments upon withdrawal from firm. Improper to take into account tax consequences in determining value unless the taxable event occurred during marriage or will occur as a result of the division of property. To be taken into account, a tax liability must be "immediate and specific", not speculative.
1979	*Aufmuth v. Aufmuth* 89 Cal.App.3d 446	Attorney, date of valuation should be date of trial because spouse's efforts were not responsible for increase in value after date of separation.
1986	*Garrity v. Bishton* 181 Cal. App.3d 675	Attorney, excess earnings method not sufficient to calculate practice value if it fails to take into account fixed assets, accounts receivable, costs advanced and work in process.
1986	*Slivka v. Slivka* 183 Cal. App.3d 159	Physician, no goodwill in case of partnership that services only Kaiser patients. Situation deemed similar to an employee with no ownership interest.
2002	*Rosen v. Rosen* 105 Cal. App.4th 808	Attorney, use of a single year's income in the excess earning method to calculate goodwill when historical income is highly volatile is incorrect. Reasonable compensation based on national surveys is incorrect unless related to local data.
2004	*Iredale v. Cates* 121 Cal. App.4th 321	Attorney, upheld use of partnership agreement to limit value of accounts receivable, work in process and partnership goodwill. Calculated personal goodwill using excess earnings.
2005	*McTiernan v. Dubrow* 133 Cal.App.4th 1090	Movie director, no goodwill, despite excess earnings. Elite professional standing deemed not transferable and therefore could not generate divisible goodwill.
2006	*Ackerman v. Ackerman* 146 Cal.App.4th 191	Physician, goodwill calculated using excess earnings method. Discussion of national surveys to determine reasonable compensation.

Chapter 28

Valuation of Physician On-Call and Coverage Arrangements

By Greg Anderson, CPA, ABV, CVA

Historical Perspectives

Senior physicians in today's market and their predecessors once recognized the importance of emergency department on-call coverage as a community service and as a means for building their practices. Indigent patients, tort system disrepair and declining reimbursement were not the daily reality for these physicians that they now are. Hospital medical staff bylaws required on-call coverage, and physicians once accepted this in the course of practicing medicine. Compensation for taking call was not the hotly contested issue that it is in many facilities today.

Market Forces Affecting Physician Availability

The growth in the trend toward payment for physician on-call services is a function of market factors affecting the need for the service and physician unwillingness to provide the service without separate compensation. These market forces impact physician reimbursement, quality of life and liability exposure, while hospitals, health systems and other medical facilities experience increased regulatory requirements and community demands for physician availability in the emergency department.

Uncompensated Care

The uninsured population in the United States continues to grow at alarming rates. Between 2005 and 2006, an additional 2.1 million people became uninsured.[1] With the growth in the uninsured population, physicians providing emergency and trauma care increasingly provide care to patients who are unable to pay their professional fees.

Tort Climate

Physicians are reluctant to furnish on-call services in an emergency setting because of the risk of malpractice claims. According to the American College of Surgeons, "a significant number of surgeons have been sued by patients first seen in the emergency department (ED)."[2] This stems from a condition of substantial disrepair that remains in many states. A survey by The Schumacher Group in 2005 identified malpractice concerns as the primary reason that surgeons are being discouraged to provide ED coverage.[3]

Fewer Emergency Departments and Increasing Utilization

Nationwide hospital closures or closures of emergency rooms have placed additional stresses on those that remain, while increasing problems with limited access to care for many Americans results in over-utilization of the nation's emergency services. This places additional stress on the system and on physicians working in hospital EDs, increases the intensity of on-call services and negatively impacts payer mix and, consequently, reimbursement for physicians' services.

Quality of Life for Physicians

Physicians see ED call as a detriment to their quality of life, because most ED calls occur on nights and weekends. Call duties also often interfere with the physician's private practice, requiring more time away from personal or more profitable activities and resulting in greater inconvenience.

Physician Shortages

Aside from physician shortages resulting from an aging population, other factors such as the following result in a decrease in the number of physicians in the call rotation, magnifying the difficulty and stress of those physicians who remain:

- Shortage of physician residents in certain specialties

- Desirability of location

- General economic factors affecting the ability of many communities to recruit and retain quality physicians

- Increasing sub-specialization of physicians has caused many physicians to limit the patients treated while on call

- Increasing numbers of physicians dropping out of call rotation because of age, lack of compensation, and rigorous schedules has exacerbated an already growing problem.

Chapter 28: Valuation of Physician On-Call and Coverage Arrangements

Other Reasons

In December 2005, the Missouri Hospital Association published a report[4] on the state of ED call coverage, which noted the following additional reasons, among others, for physician resistance to taking call:

- "It's not my responsibility"
- Resentment for not being paid for call
- Difficulty in enforcing medical staff bylaw requirements to take call

Observing this market dynamic in a community can be sobering for a hospital administrator. What begins as a request for on-call compensation by a single physician quickly escalates into broad and costly demands by many specialties, further spreading to other facilities in the market. Physician threats to drop out of the call schedule and demands for higher and higher payment, coupled with hospital concerns about regulatory compliance and fiscal responsibility, create an environment of distrust and emotionally charged tensions.

Regulatory Environment

Health care is viewed as one of the most heavily regulated industries in the United States, primarily due to the fact that the Federal government is the primary consumer of health care goods and services through health care programs such as Medicare. As such, the Federal government controls public policy as it relates to health care and is directly involved in nearly all aspects of the delivery of care. Many laws and regulations directly impact the financial relationships between health care providers, bringing compensation arrangements into the spotlight of regulatory agencies.

Stark Law

Physician self-referral legislation (Stark Law) is described in **Chapter 7** as a critical regulatory element that must be addressed in most physician compensation arrangements, because of its broad, strict liability implications and significant penalty provisions. To avoid violation of its general prohibitions on referrals of designated health services and billing for proscribed referrals, contractual arrangements with physicians for on-call services are generally designed in such a way as to comply with the provisions of the Stark exceptions for bona fide employment relationships[5] (for employer-employee arrangements) or personal service arrangements[6] (for independent contractor relationships). Among other requirements, the *bona fide* employment relationships exception requires that compensation be consistent with the fair market value (FMV) of the services, while the personal service arrangements requires that compensation not exceed FMV. As such, FMV is an important element of both exceptions, as well as several other Stark exceptions, and critical to compliance with the Stark Law's far-reaching scope.

Chapter 28: Valuation of Physician On-Call and Coverage Arrangements

Anti-Kickback Statute

The Federal anti-kickback statute makes it a criminal offense for individuals or entities to knowingly and willfully offer, pay, solicit or receive remuneration to induce the referral of business reimbursable under a Federal health care program.[7]

The anti-kickback statute contains safe harbor provisions to protect legitimate arrangements, including *bona fide* employment relationships[8] and personal services and management contracts.[9]

On September 20, 2007, the Office of Inspector General (OIG) of the Department of Health and Human Services issued Advisory Opinion 07-10[10] in response to a request for an opinion as to whether a physician on-call and uncompensated care arrangement constituted grounds for imposition of sanctions related to acts in violation of the Federal anti-kickback statute. This advisory opinion provides useful insight into the mindset of the OIG as it relates to the risk that payments for physician call on-call coverage could result in illegal remuneration and safeguards that the OIG believes reduce the risk that remuneration is intended to generate referrals of items or services reimbursable by Federal health care programs.

In the text of the advisory opinion, the OIG commented on the increasing compensation of physicians for hospital emergency department on-call coverage and the existence of legitimate reasons for such arrangements, including compliance with the Emergency Medical Treatment and Active Labor Act (EMTALA), physician shortages and access to trauma care. The OIG noted the risk that physicians may demand payment for on-call coverage when neither the services provided nor market conditions warrant payment and that hospitals may misuse payments to entice physicians to generate additional business for the hospital. The OIG further commented that covert kickbacks might take the form of payments in excess of FMV or payments for services not actually provided. Problematic compensation structures noted in the advisory opinion include payments that do not represent *bona fide* lost income, payments when no identifiable services are provided, aggregate payments that exceed the practice's regular medical practice income and payments for physician services when the physician actually receives separate reimbursement from insurers or patients (essentially double-paying the physician).

The OIG noted that the requestor engaged an independent consultant to advise on the reasonableness of the per diem rates paid under the arrangement, the report on which was provided to the OIG. The consultant's analysis incorporated both public and private data on pay rates at dozens of medical facilities, resulting in a set of benchmarks used by the consultant to opine on the FMV of the payment arrangements. The advisory opinion also noted several other features that the OIG considered useful in minimizing the risk of fraud and abuse, which the author believes should be considered by any organization entering into a physician on-call arrangement.

In the advisory opinion, the OIG concluded that it would not subject the requestor to administrative sanctions under the Social Security Act, although it noted that the opinion should not be construed as a requirement for a medical center or other facility to pay for on-call coverage.

Chapter 28: Valuation of Physician On-Call and Coverage Arrangements

Tax-Exempt Organizations

For organizations exempt from Federal income taxes under Internal Revenue Code Section (IRC) 501(c)(3), no part of the net earnings of the organization may inure to the benefit of any private shareholder or individual.[11] Doing so may jeopardize the tax-exempt status of the organization; however, an organization may pay reasonable compensation without violating the prohibition on private inurement. Section 4958 of the IRC also provides for a tax, known as Intermediate Sanctions penalties, on excess benefit transactions, defined as a transaction in which the economic benefit provided by an exempt organization exceeds the value of the consideration received for such benefit.[12]

Unreasonable compensation contributes to private inurement and to excess benefit transactions, which in the more egregious cases can jeopardize the organization's exempt status and, in less arrant cases, subject the exempt organization and the compensated individual to Intermediate Sanctions penalties. Reasonable compensation is the amount that would be ordinarily paid for like services by like organizations in like circumstances. IRC Section 162 guidance on reasonable compensation is often cited as a reference in reasonable compensation cases and in examinations of exempt organizations.

EMTALA

The Emergency Medical Treatment and Active Labor Act was created by Congress in 1986 to ensure access to care for emergency medical conditions, regardless of an individual's ability to pay. Sections 1866 and 1867 of the Social Security Act impose the requirements of EMTALA on hospitals and critical access hospitals that offer emergency services by imposing civil monetary penalties on hospitals and physicians for failure to appropriately screen or stabilize a patient needing emergency care or negligently transferring a patient.

Section 1866 of the Social Security Act requires that hospitals maintain a listing of on-call physicians to provide treatment to stabilize a patient with an emergency medical condition; however, EMTALA does not specify how frequently a hospital's on-call staff physicians are expected to be available.

In the preamble to the September 2003 final rule, CMS notes, "some physicians have in the past expressed a desire to refuse to be included on a hospital's on-call list but nevertheless take calls selectively. These physicians might, for example, respond to calls for patients with whom they or a colleague at the hospital have established a doctor-patient relationship, while declining calls from other patients, including those whose ability to pay may be in question. Such a practice would clearly be a violation of EMTALA."[13] Because the final rule did not mandate requirements for call coverage, hospitals have lost some leverage in requiring specialists to take call, a situation which has contributed, at least in part, to the growing demand for on-call compensation.

Chapter 28: Valuation of Physician On-Call and Coverage Arrangements

Common Structuring of Coverage and Compensation Arrangements

Restricted and Unrestricted Arrangements

As with many physician contractual arrangements, the type of on-call or physician coverage arrangement may vary dramatically from one contract to the next. In some cases, the physician specialty may dictate the type of arrangement. For example, anesthesiologists in a hospital setting are often required to remain in the OR department during specified weekday and weekend shifts. This allows for anesthesia coverage for scheduled and unscheduled surgical cases throughout the shift. In other cases, the needs of the facility may dictate the requirements for physician coverage. Consider the example of the cardiovascular surgeon, required by the hospital to remain on-site in a hospital's cardiac catheterization lab during normal operating hours to provide backup services to the cardiologists and their patients in the facility.

Unrestricted call. In an unrestricted call arrangement, the physician is not restricted to the facility but obligated to respond timely in accordance with medical staff by-laws or other contractual arrangements. This is essentially known as "beeper" call, with the physician carrying a pager or cell phone to ensure timely contact. Many arrangements require the physician to respond within 30 minutes. This arrangement is fairly common among a wide range of specialists who provide coverage to a hospital's emergency department and can include primary (first responder) call and secondary (backup) call.

Restricted call. In a restricted coverage arrangement, the physician is physically restricted to the facility during the restricted coverage period. This is often called "in-house" call and can apply to many different specialties, although hospital-based specialists are among the most commonly utilized in these agreements.

Blended Arrangements

When circumstances dictate, facilities may contract with physicians for an arrangement that includes more than one type of on-call coverage or service. These may take on the form of arrangements that include both unrestricted and restricted coverage during a specified period, or a blending of on-call and other personal services, such as clinical or administrative services.

Blended unrestricted call and restricted coverage. In some situations, the physician will have periods of both unrestricted and restricted call during the same shift. An example of this would include coverage by an independent hospitalist of a hospital's inpatient services, in which the physician is required to be on-site for a 12-hour shift, immediately followed by a 12-hour shift of unrestricted call.

Blended call with clinical service. In certain circumstances, the physician will have periods of unrestricted and/or restricted call, combined with clinical duties and responsibilities. In this

Chapter 28: Valuation of Physician On-Call and Coverage Arrangements

arrangement, the physician is also contracted to provide patient care, for which the employer or contracting entity bills for the physician's professional fees. Locum tenens firms often offer these arrangements to hospitals, mixing unrestricted call with two to four hours of patient care within a 24-hour shift. Another example would be a primary care physician who is contracted to work in a weekend community clinic for six hours on Saturday afternoons and remains on unrestricted call for the duration of the weekend.

Blended call with administrative service. Under an administrative service arrangement, the physician furnishes administrative or management services, such as a medical directorship, which is often combined with restricted/unrestricted arrangements, such as those found in an outsourcing of a hospital-based physician service. An example of this would be the outsourcing to a physician-owned group practice for emergency department (ED) physician coverage, including medical direction of the ED, restricted coverage (wherein the physician group bills for its professional fees) and unrestricted call.

Common Payment Arrangements

Hourly, shift or daily rates. Payment rates for physician on-call coverage consist of unrestricted rates, restricted rates, clinical services or administrative rates, and blended rates (such as per diem rates that include an assumed clinical time). Payment arrangements are most often based on hourly, shift, daily, monthly or annual rates, although many variations and combinations can be found. Among the more creative arrangements include the following:

- Hospital A only pays for shortage specialty ED coverage, such as when the physician is required to cover a call rotation vacated by a departing or retiring physician.

- Hospital B only pays physicians taking call who are otherwise excused from ED call coverage duties by virtue of the medical staff by-laws, such as those who are exempt from call based on age.

- Hospital C only pays for excessive call, basing the payment on the number of days in excess of a threshold number, such as 10 per month.

The appropriate payment mechanism for physician on-call coverage is affected by professional fee billing arrangements and physician compensation plan structure, as will be more fully described later in this chapter.

Activation fee. An activity-based payment, or activation fee, usually a flat fee, is initiated when the physician is actually called in while on-call. This is often combined with unrestricted call payments. An example of this can be found in a psychiatry weekend coverage arrangement, in which the physician was paid a fixed rate for weekend unrestricted coverage, and paid an additional $200 if the physician was called in during the weekend.

Chapter 28: Valuation of Physician On-Call and Coverage Arrangements

Group practice "tax" arrangements. Freestanding, physician-owned groups are not immune from the need to establish the value of physician participation in the on-call rotation. Many groups, faced with aging physicians interested in reducing or eliminating the burden of call coverage, use a variety of means to reduce the compensation of physicians dropping out of the rotation, often with a charge or "tax" levied against the physician, which is then credited to the other members of the group. Examples of this include multi-specialty group practices that charge the physician for accepting a reduced call schedule or OB/GYN practices that reallocate compensation to members who elect to drop out of the obstetric call rotation.

Stipend and subsidy arrangements. Fixed monthly or annual amounts may be necessary to make physician or group compensation levels representative of market values for services furnished, especially with respect to low/no-pay care (often effective with hospital-based physician groups and others dramatically impacted by the hospital's payer mix).

Subsidy for uncompensated care. Particularly when the physician bills for the professional fee, this is usually in an amount needed to bring net physician compensation to market levels and often based on market reimbursement levels for low/no-pay care (i.e., Medicare or Medicaid rate). Another example is the malpractice insurance premium subsidy, which serves as a means for providing limited relief toward premium costs incurred by medical staff. Additional examples include payments based on relative value units (RVUs) for uncompensated services and subsidized fee-for-service arrangements in which the physician assigns his benefit under Medicare, Medicaid or third-party payers to the hospital, the hospital bills and collects the professional fee, and the hospital remits a market-value fee-for-service payment or payment per RVU to the physician.

Deferred compensation. A new trend in on-call compensation involves the deferral of pay for on-call compensation until the occurrence of a specified event or certain period of time, such as milestone tenure on the medical staff or for years of participation in the on-call rotation. This method has proven effective in some circumstances in promoting physician loyalty.

Determining Fair Market Value of On-Call Compensation

The proliferation of health care regulations impacting physician compensation arrangements and the variety of physician on-call arrangements in the market lead to a significant and looming compliance risk for parties to on-call and coverage agreements, particularly when remuneration is exchanged. This necessitates consideration of whether the arrangements are within FMV constraints and the applicable statutory and regulatory exceptions and safe harbors.

Valuation Theory Applicable to On-Call Compensation

As with most compensation arrangements in the health care industry, there is a limited body of knowledge related to the theory of valuation of compensation for physician availability. While

Chapter 28: Valuation of Physician On-Call and Coverage Arrangements

business valuation and asset appraisal standards abound among credentialing organizations, only recently has the American Institute of Certified Public Accountants issued standards[14] related to business valuations, which does not include valuation of compensation arrangements. This absence of published standards on the subject has contributed to inconsistencies in how accountants, appraisers, and consultants approach the valuation of physician compensation arrangements such as on-call payments. The wide range of valuation methods extends from a simple reliance on historical compensation to complex analyses including algorithms and detailed market research.

The following three fundamental principles coexist in the theory of business valuation: the Principles of Substitution, Alternatives, and Future Benefits, and these can be transferred into the context of valuing service agreements. The Principle of Substitution states that an investor will pay no more for a service than for a substitute of equivalent economic utility. Under the Principle of Alternatives, each party to a contemplated contractual arrangement has alternatives to consummating the deal. The Principle of Future Benefits emphasizes that the value of an investment is based on the future benefits the investment will provide. These principles lay the foundation for the application of valuation methodology to developing a conclusion of FMV in compensation for physician availability.

Valuation Methodology

Several methods exist for determining value in a compensation arrangement. The justification for the use of a particular method or methods will often be dictated by the facts and circumstances of the contractual arrangement. These methods of valuation can be generally categorized into one of three broad approaches: Cost-Based, Income-Based and Market-Based. Within each valuation approach, numerous methods exist for determining value, the relevance and applicability of each depending on the circumstances and the analyst's considered judgment. Valuation analysts often think of this process as a funnel, with various valuation methods entering the top of the funnel, subsequently yielding a conclusion of value at the bottom.

Factors Impacting the Value of Call Coverage

The valuation of on-call and coverage compensation is significantly impacted by the specific requirements of the contractual arrangements and factors related to market conditions, physician specialty, and the frequency and intensity of the coverage. To properly analyze FMV, the valuation analyst should consider the following factors, and perhaps others, before employing the valuation methodology necessary to arrive at a conclusion of value.

Before undertaking the analysis of FMV in any on-call or coverage arrangement, it is crucial to understand what makes up the value of these arrangements, as distinct differences lie in whether the valuation results in a conclusion of value related to physician availability, the value of uncompensated care furnished by the physician, or a combination of the two. The burden of physician availability (i.e., the time spent away from family, sleep, and personal activities) carries with it an element of value to the physician as the seller of the service, as does the fact that the physician may be sacrificing time away from the private practice of medicine (clinical disruption) to provide his or her availability to the contracting facility. The physician also experiences foregone earnings from uncompensated care when providing ED coverage, particularly in the case of trauma and indigent care, not only in the facility, but also in follow-up care that may be necessary. Furthermore, the physician subjects himself or herself to heightened risk of malpractice claims in many instances, a situation which is further aggravated by a lack of compensation for that element of risk. In many situations, particularly in trauma center ED coverage, the physician experiences a combination of both inconvenience and uncompensated care. Some facilities address both issues in a single compensation arrangement (i.e., through a single payment for physician on-call shifts or hours) while others separately address the issues (i.e., through a combination of payments for availability only when beyond the norms and with special rates such as a percentage of Medicare or Medicaid allowables for uncompensated care). Understanding these nuances and appropriately considering the elements of risk and reward are key to a comprehensive and accurate analysis and conclusion of value.

Facility trauma level. A level-one trauma center contracting with the on-call physician will likely have a greater level of intensity, higher acuity and more frequent call than a facility with a lower trauma level. It is also likely that the facilities with higher trauma designations will have a larger proportion of no-pay or low-pay patients and a higher malpractice risk to the physician. In many cases, this translates into greater stresses and demands on the covering physicians and may result in market conditions that support higher compensation.

Physician supply and demand. Markets and facilities with an imbalance between the supply and demand of physicians may see variations in the levels and methods of compensation. For example, some hospitals pay only for on-call coverage when shortage specialties are involved, such as when the number of physicians in the community falls short of a predetermined level of active full-time equivalent (FTE) physicians. Others pay additional compensation to encourage senior physicians to rejoin the call rotation when the medical staff bylaws permit the physician to drop out of call upon reaching a certain age.

Payer mix. The payer mix of the community and the hospital can have a dramatic effect on the value of on-call payments. For example, facilities with high indigent patient volume often find physicians reluctant to participate in the call rotation without separate compensation, as physicians consider the risk of caring for the patient to outweigh the community benefit and professional fees received during the episode of emergency care and any follow-up care required.

Specialty-specific factors. The rigors of call coverage vary quite widely among specialties; therefore, the specific physician specialty should be carefully considered. For example, neurosurgery call may be substantially more complex than ENT coverage, necessitating higher compensation for the former to account for complexity and frequency. Most valuation analysts look directly at specialty-specific information when applying methodology to value on-call and coverage arrangements.

Chapter 28: Valuation of Physician On-Call and Coverage Arrangements

Unrestricted call or restricted coverage. The value of on-call and coverage arrangements relates to the value of physician availability and the value of care for indigent and low-paying patients. As an important element of value, physician availability increases in value as restrictions on the physician's movement are tightened. Because unrestricted call allows the physician to move about the community while accepting the responsibility to respond timely to calls, this carries a lower value in most cases than restrictions that bind the physician to remaining in the facility while on-call.

Time of day/week. It can be said that greater inconvenience for on-call arrangements translates to higher value for compensation, as more intrusive scheduling increases the level of difficulty in finding physicians willing to cover and raises concerns over quality-of-life issues.

Rotation. More frequent participation in the call rotation means more time away from practice and personal activities. It is important for the valuation analyst to consider the "normal" level of call for a particular specialty (i.e., 1-in-4 rotation) and evaluate whether the required rotation results in excessive commitment by the physician beyond the typical level experienced by peers. For example, one proprietary survey of a local market by the author indicated an average rotation of 1-in-4 for orthopedic surgery and an average of 1-in-3 for trauma surgery.

Length of shift. Clearly, longer hours of on-call time equate to higher value, particularly when considering the value of shifts less than 24 hours paid at per diem rates. More commonly, shift lengths differ among facilities as it relates to weekend coverage, when weekend shifts may range from 48 hours (7:00 p.m. on Friday to 7:00 p.m. on Sunday) to 63 hours (5:00 p.m. on Friday to 8:00 a.m. on Monday), which directly affects the level of shift compensation.

Intensity. The intensity level of physician coverage is an essential distinguishing factor in assessing the value of on-call and coverage. Physicians whose coverage results in care for cases of higher acuity experience higher levels of stress, greater risk of malpractice claims, and often an increased likelihood of non-payment. Intensity can also be measured in terms of the number of interactions during a call shift, such as the number of calls received or the number of times a physician has to physically respond to calls when on unrestricted call.

Frequencies of calls and call-ins. Higher call volume and more frequent in-person response to calls generally equates to less time for the physician to spend in his/her practice or in personal activities, thus increasing the degree of hardship and, consequently, the degree of resistance of many physicians to accepting the burden of call. In many situations, the sheer intensity of on-call and coverage and the volume of calls and call-ins have driven some physicians and groups to refuse coverage to facilities. Others have used this as rationale for demanding compensation for on-call and coverage arrangements, or in demanding higher compensation.

Concurrent call. Simultaneous coverage at multiple facilities is becoming a more important factor in determining the FMV of unrestricted on-call arrangements. In many markets, physicians in high-demand specialties agree to cover two or more facilities at the same time. This can become a significant issue, as the implications are far-reaching, given the following risks:

Chapter 28: Valuation of Physician On-Call and Coverage Arrangements

- Coverage at multiple facilities can result in a lapse of coverage when the physician is tied up on a case at one facility and another facility calls the physician.

- The need for secondary, or backup, coverage is paramount to avoid the lapse in coverage.

- Some groups have used multi-facility unrestricted call as a reason to request payment for secondary coverage when asked to supply a backup physician.

- Spreading physician call coverage across multiple facilities may dilute the value of the service provided to any one facility, yet physicians inevitably feel that each facility should pay the same rate as if exclusive coverage was furnished. However, some valuation analysts believe that some concurrency arrangements result in the diminution of value.

These and other elements pertinent to the specific situation should be given strong consideration when valuing concurrent call arrangements. Further analysis of the specific impact of these characteristics will follow in the discussion of valuation methodology.

Utilizing the Three Broad Approaches to Valuing On-Call Arrangements

Cost-based approach. Using the cost-based approach, the analyst seeking to reach a conclusion of FMV for compensation related to physician availability, such as an on-call or coverage arrangement, generally considers the cost of an substitute arrangement, such as the avoided cost to replace or recreate the subject service.

Avoided cost-to-replace method. In evaluating the avoided cost to replace physician availability with a substitute arrangement, consideration is often given to the costs of *locum tenens* or physician staffing firm coverage. In most cases, these represent short-term solutions to the problem of physician coverage, and the cost of obtaining this type of coverage can be high. In applying this method, the valuation analyst conducts research of firms to provide the requisite coverage, obtaining information about applicable rates for the level of coverage, considering time and shift requirements, the necessity for unrestricted or restricted coverage and the appropriate physician specialty, skill set, and experience requirements. It should be noted, however, that rates obtained from firms to provide physician coverage must often be adjusted, or *normalized*, to ensure comparability to the subject arrangement. For example, rates quoted by physician staffing firms most often include some allowance for the cost of malpractice insurance coverage associated with the physician service. However, if a hospital negotiates with an employed physician to assume extra unrestricted call for a shortage specialty, the compensation paid by the hospital (employer) to the physician (employee) does not include reimbursement for the physician's malpractice cost, as this cost is already borne by the hospital as employer. Therefore, a normalizing adjustment would be necessary to remove from the market research on staffing firm rates the portion of the rates attributable to malpractice coverage. Similar circumstances exist with respect to the payment of payroll taxes, employee fringe benefits and other costs that must be properly matched to the replacement arrangement.

Chapter 28: Valuation of Physician On-Call and Coverage Arrangements

Earlier in this chapter, discussion was given to the quantitative and qualitative elements of on-call and coverage arrangements. The valuation analyst gives consideration to these traits of an arrangement in an effort to arrive at a normalized analysis of the arrangements or data used in the determination of FMV. Using the cost-to-replace method, the analyst must ensure that the substitute arrangement (i.e., physician staffing firm) is comparable in terms of frequency, shift length, intensity and other factors. Simple comparison of a *per diem* rate to a 12-hour shift would be blatantly unrealistic, as would comparisons that improperly matched the physician specialty, restricted/unrestricted terms, and time of day or week. It is the responsibility of the analyst when performing market research to be certain that the substitute arrangement is comparable to the subject arrangement being valued, or to adjust the comparable data accordingly; otherwise, an incorrect result will be obtained.

Avoided cost-to-recreate method. Often, the FMV of compensation for physician availability can also be determined through the assessment of the avoided cost to recreate the subject arrangement. One effective use for this method is in the evaluation of avoided costs associated with subsidies tied to hospital-based physician coverage arrangements. In the example of a health system's contract with an anesthesia group to furnish surgery department, obstetrics and ambulatory surgery center anesthesia coverage, the avoided cost of directly employing anesthesiologists may represent a valid cost-to-recreate method. This analysis is quite complex and incorporates a great deal of assumptions regarding physician professional fees, overhead and physician costs, and, as a result, can be overly speculative.

This type of analysis is also heavily dependent upon the qualitative and quantitative factors specific to the subject arrangement being valued. For example, physician supply and demand issues, such as community need, will drive the determination of compensation necessary to retain physicians in an employment-alternative analysis, while payer mix issues have a measurable effect on physician professional fee reimbursement when projecting the expected revenues from the cost-to-recreate service with employed physicians.

Income-based approach. In valuing most unrestricted on-call and restricted coverage arrangements, the income-based approach is of little use usefulness in the valuation of physician availability. This is primarily attributable to the fact that, in and of itself, physician availability generates no income for the purchaser of the service. However, when considering the value of subsidized arrangements, such as in the case of outsourced anesthesia coverage, the income approach is often one of the most significant methods available to the valuation analyst.

While it is important to consider the economic benefit to both purchaser and seller under income-based approach methodology, it is widely accepted that the economic benefit to the seller of the service—the physician—is measured in the same way as under the market-based approach, using data relevant to evaluate physician earnings associated with the furnishing of availability.

Subsidy method. The valuation of subsidy arrangements using a methodology under the income-based approach can be fully applicable and of significant use to the analyst. Consider

Chapter 28: Valuation of Physician On-Call and Coverage Arrangements

the example of a hospital-based physician group, paid by a hospital for furnishing 24/7 coverage of a hospital department, such as an emergency physician group's contract with a hospital to furnish complete restricted and unrestricted coverage of the hospital's emergency department. Because a growing number of the group's patient encounters in the emergency department are unpaid, the hospital subsidizes the operation of the group by payment of a monthly subsidy. The valuation analyst may give strong consideration to a methodology that would quantify the shortfall experienced by the physician group, such as a measurement of the value of unpaid patient visits based on a percentage of Medicare allowables, as a proxy for the FMV of the service provided by the group.

Another method often used in valuing subsidies involves the analysis of compensation deficits experienced by the physician group. This method includes analysis of the financial statements and production information of the physician group for purposes of determining a normalized physician compensation level. Normalizing adjustments necessary for this analysis include, but are not limited to, the following adjustments to the financial statements of the physician group:

- Adjusting non-physician compensation levels to account for related party arrangements

- Adjusting occupancy costs to market levels, eliminated related party rental premiums or discounts

- Removing one-time or non-recurring expenses, such as legal fees or non-recurring physician recruitment costs

Physician compensation levels should also be adjusted to reflect market levels commensurate with the production levels of physicians in the group. This analysis results from benchmarking comparisons of various production measurements, as more fully described below, including patient encounters, surgical cases, work relative value units and others. For example, emergency room physician production in a group practice contracted by the hospital for emergency department coverage approximates median levels for emergency physicians in the market, yet actual physician compensation falls below median levels as a result of high indigent and trauma volume in the hospital's emergency department. The adjustment necessary to reflect market-level compensation is applied to arrive at normalized financial statements for the group, yielding a normalized operating deficit that represents a proxy for the FMV of the hospital subsidy.

Market-based approach. In the valuation of on-call and coverage arrangements, methods under the market-based approach are the most often applied, yet most often misapplied methods for determining FMV. Methodology under the market-based approach seeks to assess FMV by considering that the buyer of a service will not pay more than, and the seller will not accept less than, the value of a comparable service. Thus, the central focus of the market-based approach and its related valuation methods is to identify comparable services, and to do so within the context of the definition of FMV in the health care regulatory environment.

Chapter 28: Valuation of Physician On-Call and Coverage Arrangements

Published survey method. As an industry, health care is fortunate to have a plethora of information in the form of published survey data on physician compensation and productivity; however, as a subset of the various types of physician services and the related compensation methods, compensation survey data for on-call and coverage arrangements lags behind other market data in the following ways:

- Lack of surveys committed to obtaining on-call compensation information

- Low respondent numbers in surveys of on-call compensation

- Difficulty in comparability

- As will be discussed later, concerns that survey data may be tainted by the physician-hospital referral relationship

Despite these difficulties, competent surveys exist that are gaining in widespread acceptance and in the quality of data presented. An example is the Sullivan, Cotter and Associates, Inc. (SCA) Physician On-Call Pay Survey Report, which includes data on physician on-call pay rates and practices of 160 organizations from across the United States. State hospital associations, such as the Florida Hospital Association and the Missouri Hospital Association, also publish survey data on physician on-call market and compensation issues, while private companies and consultants also conduct proprietary surveys of local and regional market for data on compensation and other issues related to the growing need for data on these types of arrangements.

Surveys of physician on-call and coverage payment arrangements bring to light an important limitation when compared to other physician compensation surveys, particularly as it relates to the referral relationship that exists between the parties to the agreement. In the preamble to the Stark II Phase I Interim Final Rule, CMS notes concerns with the use of "comparables or market values involving transactions between entities that are in a position to refer"[15] and in the preamble to the Phase II Interim Final Rule, CMS notes, "For example, the methodology must exclude valuations where the parties to the transactions are at arm's length but in a position to refer to one another."[16]

Most survey products on physician compensation arrangements include compensation arrangements between hospitals, academic medical centers and other facilities and the physicians employed or contracted by the health care providers, where the physician has the opportunity to refer Federal health care program beneficiaries and other business to the employer or contracting facility. However, these surveys also contain compensation data submitted by respondents in solo or physician group practices, where fair market value and referral relationships take on less significance. This data, along with what are often large numbers of respondents, helps to mitigate the effects of any disguised payments for referrals that might be buried in the survey respondent data. On the other hand, physician on-call surveys (published surveys, local and regional surveys) are generally comprised of data furnished by parties to on-call payment arrangements for which

Chapter 28: Valuation of Physician On-Call and Coverage Arrangements

at least one party has the ability to refer Federal health care business to the other. Regardless of whether the payments are truly representative of disguised remuneration for referrals, this fact pattern presents unique challenges in the utilization of the data in determining the fair market value of on-call arrangements. For this reason, some valuation analysts do not give consideration to the results of survey methodology.

The market-based approach considers the value of the subject on-call or coverage arrangement based on comparable data as determined through various methods, several of which are described in the paragraphs that follow.

The published survey method considers the value of an on-call or coverage arrangement based on data reported by published surveys. As previously noted, SCA and various state medical associations publish surveys on compensation related to on-call arrangements. The SCA survey reports data on physician compensation in a variety of ways, including the following examples (assuming sufficient respondent data is available):

- By physician specialty
- Unrestricted and restricted rates
- Hourly and per diem rates
- Separate reporting for trauma and non-trauma coverage
- Mean, median, quartile and top decile data

State medical association reports typically contain less cross-tabulated information about physician payment arrangements, but include good discussions of the market dynamics impacting pay-for-call arrangements in the state. Some surveys include hourly and per diem rates for call coverage, yet only average, median or high-and-low ranges of data may be reported.

In the application of the published survey methodology, the valuation analyst performs research to gather information from published surveys to determine a broad range of market data on physician compensation, generally from the 10th or 25th percentile, depending on the survey product, to the 90th percentile. It is within this broad range of market rates that the valuation analyst refines the value of the subject arrangement by considering the comparability of the market data and by making normalizing adjustments to the data or by fine tuning the range of survey data to consider the qualitative and quantitative factors described earlier in this chapter.

At this point in the analysis, it is important to evaluate the quantitative and qualitative elements when valuing call. Some valuation analysts use information such as intensity, acuity, payer mix, frequency, need (i.e., supply and demand) and other defining elements of value to

Chapter 28: Valuation of Physician On-Call and Coverage Arrangements

determine where in the spectrum of value the conclusion of FMV should lie. For example, high levels of intensity or frequent participation in the call rotation may contribute a higher value for the on-call arrangement, while a good payer mix and low levels of uncompensated care may partially or completely mitigate the additional value. In many cases, these analysts use professional judgment and experience to determine how these issues impact the value of the arrangement. In one example, the valuation analyst determines that the qualitative and quantitative measures are such that high levels of inconvenience and uncompensated care yield a conclusion of value that ranges between the 75th and 90th percentile of market survey data, which the analyst concludes as FMV.

Other analysts employ proprietary methods, such as algorithms, to measure the effects on value. In these cases, the analysts input information on qualitative and quantitative measures into the algorithm from which the output aids in narrowing the range of value within the universe of possible values or provides normalizing adjustments to be applied to the survey market data to arrive at a conclusion of FMV. An example of such an algorithm would compute an intensity or severity index for on-call coverage, based on a points structure that awards varying levels of points to each specialty, then using patient admissions and visits data to arrive at the factor representing relative intensity or severity.

Percentage-of-compensation method. As valuation theory has been developed by valuation analysts and applied to the area of compensation for on-call arrangements, the percentage-of-compensation method has gained in acceptance and in practice. This method is grounded in the concept that the compensation of most physicians includes an element of compensation attributable to the requirement that physicians make themselves available to their patients and to the community at times other than clinic operating hours. In a more obvious example, in a free-standing, physician-owned group practice of obstetricians and gynecologists, it is understood that most, if not all, physicians in the group must take hospital OB call to handle deliveries that take place at nights and on weekends. Physicians who do not take call, whether because of age or because they have limited their practice to gynecology only, are typically penalized or "taxed" by the group for opting out of the group's call rotation. Hence, a portion of the compensation of those physicians who do take call is made up, to some degree, of compensation for taking call. The same is true for most physician specialties, particularly those with patient care obligations that go beyond the eight-to-five schedule. That said, it is reasonable to apportion some physician compensation to the act of "being available."

Valuation analysts who do a great deal of work in the area of on-call compensation have recognized this fact and have developed methodology to account for the fact that some portion of physician compensation is attributable to on-call duties and responsibilities. This analysis generally involves a review of survey data to compute the relationship of on-call pay to total physician compensation, first by specialty, and then in aggregate. First, the analyst accumulates survey data on on-call pay rates for available physician specialties, using tools such as the SCA survey of physician on-call compensation. From there, the analyst gathers data for those same specialties from surveys on physician compensation, such as the following:

Chapter 28: Valuation of Physician On-Call and Coverage Arrangements

- Medical Group Management Association (MGMA), *Physician Compensation and Production Survey.* The MGMA survey reports national and regional data for more than 2,300 group practices, primarily single specialty practices, representing more than 52,000 physicians and non-physician providers.

- American Medical Group Association (AMGA), *Medical Group Compensation and Productivity Survey.* The AMGA survey reports national and regional data for more than 220 group practices, primarily multi-specialty practices, representing more than 43,000 physicians.

- Sullivan Cotter and Associates, Inc. (SCA), *Physician Compensation and Productivity Survey Report.* The SCA survey reports national and regional data for 263 healthcare organizations and total compensation data for more than 39,000 physicians, PhDs, mid-level providers, residents, and medical group executives.

The data for physician aggregate compensation may be studied individually or as an average of the survey products. Once accumulated, the analyst computes a fraction, the numerator of which is the on-call pay rate and the denominator of which is the total compensation rate (converted to an hourly rate from annual compensation survey data), to arrive at an estimate of the portion of physician compensation attributable to on-call pay. This is most often done using median survey data for both numerator and denominator and, in many cases, results in a non-specialty-specific estimate of approximately 14 to 15% of physician compensation attributed to unrestricted on-call pay. A similar analysis can also be performed for restricted coverage.

Aside from its usefulness in determining the portion of physician compensation attributed to unrestricted and restricted call for the surveyed specialties, this methodology also has some other very important applications. For example, not all specialties have sufficient respondent volume to permit reporting of on-call pay for unrestricted and restricted arrangements. Using the fraction derived from this analysis on a non-specialty-specific basis allows the valuation analyst to estimate the value of on-call pay for the unreported specialty (although some degree of normalization may be necessary, depending upon the physician specialty).

Another critically important use of this methodology is in addressing the risk of tainting of on-call survey data, due to the referral relationship of parties to arrangements embedded in survey data. In a few cases, valuation analysts have sought to prove that survey data of specialties with referral relationships is not tainted by the possibility that respondent data is corrupted by any respondents that may have a compensation arrangement representing disguised remuneration in exchange for referrals of Federal health care program business. To accomplish this analysis, valuation analysts have considered only those specialties that are generally considered to not have the ability to refer business to the hospital with which they have an on-call compensation arrangement. [17]

As with the published survey data method, a critical element of analysis considers the quantitative and qualitative elements of the on-call or coverage arrangement. Similar to the

Chapter 28: Valuation of Physician On-Call and Coverage Arrangements

previous example, factors such as intensity, acuity, payer mix, frequency and community need will likely dictate the degree to which the valuation analyst's judgment indicates higher or lower values of compensation. In the percentage-of-compensation method, these elements of risk and intensity are often used in considering the base compensation to which the percentage-of-compensation fraction is applied. As a hypothetical example, trauma surgeons in the community are in short supply, and the market data from the analyst's research indicates compensation between the 75th and 90th percentiles for FMV compensation; thus, the analyst applies a computed fraction of 15% to these levels of compensation to determine the range of FMV compensation for on-call coverage. Additional normalizing adjustments may also be necessary in making determinations under this methodology, as the valuation analyst's research and judgment may indicate that the result obtained should be adjusted to reflect specific market conditions, possibly yielding a premium or discount to be applied to the calculated result to reach the conclusion of FMV.

Nurse call pay method. Another method gaining in popularity among valuation analysts is the nurse call pay method, which determines the FMV of physician on-call compensation through the application of a formula based on market rates of compensation for nurses for on-call services. This method is slightly limited in its applicability, as it generally relates only to unrestricted call arrangements and only to the inconvenience and time factor of on-call services, rather than to the uncompensated care element.

The application of this method involves research into the payment arrangements by the subject hospital and other facilities in the market that pay nurses for on-call services. For example, average nurses' salaries are $22 per hour, while the going rate for on-call pay is $3 per hour. The fraction resulting from this data is $3 divided by $22, or 13.6%, which is then applied to the range of compensation for the physician specialty to arrive at the range of comparable physician on-call compensation. This method is particularly useful when considering the FMV of on-call pay for physician-employees, as the element of uncompensated care is absent from the equation. Additionally, this methodology is useful in addressing the issue of referral-tainted survey data, as nurses are not considered referral sources for hospitals.

Methods Not Considered Valid

In the minds of many physicians, the equivalent of private practice earnings, or "opportunity cost," is the value of service in an on-call or coverage arrangement, stating that the foregone practice earnings are representative of the value the physician brings to the on-call arrangement, particularly when the on-call service removes the physician from his or her clinical practice for a time. CMS clearly warns against the consideration of opportunity cost in the preamble to the Stark Phase III regulations when referring specifically to the value of administrative compensation,[18] stating that the two values may differ. Further, the OIG in Advisory Opinion 07-10 identified "lost opportunity" payments as problematic, particularly when they do not reflect *bona fide* lost income.

Chapter 28: Valuation of Physician On-Call and Coverage Arrangements

A significant difference in the value of practice earnings and the value of physician availability is that physician availability is only a small component of a physician's earnings, and that the two are not interchangeable.

Synthesis of Valuation Methods

As in the application of general appraisal theory, valuation of service agreements, including the value of physician availability, is a result of the application of as many methods as are available and reasonably applied. Arriving at a conclusion of value is the result of careful application of all available methods and the synthesis and reconciliation of those methods. As this chapter describes, some methods may be more appropriately applied to the specific circumstances of the subject arrangement, while others may not. The reliability of methods also varies from one to another, as does the degree to which the valuation analyst places considered judgment in weighing the relevance, degree of subjectivity and overall applicability. The end result, which may be a single point value or a range, is the result of the analyst's judgment as to the relative weight of each method in contrast to the others available, or as to the methods that create the lower and upper boundaries of FMV.

Capping Physician Compensation

It is important with many physician compensation arrangements to ensure that variable compensation arrangements contain an aggregate limit, or cap, to avoid runaway compensation. In the area of compensation for physician unrestricted on-call and restricted coverage, the cap is quite often a function of the *per diem* or hourly rate and the maximum expected number of hours or days of coverage. However, determining a cap for stipend or subsidy arrangements may be exceedingly complex. In those cases, the upper end of the FMV range is most likely the level at which the valuation analyst will establish the cap. For example, the valuation analyst involved in an analysis of FMV for anesthesia coverage found that the range of stipend compensation for an anesthesiologist to furnish unrestricted on-call coverage to a hospital's obstetrical unit was $150,000 to $175,000, based on cost-, income- and market-approach methodology applicable to the proposed subsidy arrangement. In that instance, the upper limit or cap on physician compensation was determined to be $175,000.

Other Considerations

Stacked Arrangements

Ensuring that compensation for physician services represents FMV, both separately and in the aggregate, can be difficult in situations in which a physician is performing separate tasks under separate or "stacked" agreements. In some situations, a physician may receive compensation for clinical services under an employment agreement, but also receive compensation for providing

Chapter 28: Valuation of Physician On-Call and Coverage Arrangements

on-call coverage or other services. To accurately determine FMV for each service provided, careful consideration must be given to the data and methods used to determine FMV to ensure that compensation under each agreement accurately reflects compensation for the type and level of service actually provided.

When reviewing the FMV of each agreement as related to the services being provided, it is important to understand how the compensation for each was determined, including the sources and methodology considered to arrive at FMV for each agreement or component thereof. As already noted, one method of establishing the FMV of compensation for physician services is through the use of market data, including the use of published surveys. Due care must be taken in considering the types of payments likely included in compensation figures presented in physician compensation surveys.

Paying employed physicians for on-call availability presents its own unique challenges. For employed physicians, it is important for the analyst to consider the fact that compensation for call is likely included in the physician's compensation structure. In certain circumstances, it may be appropriate to pay an employed physician with an additional layer of compensation for call, but only when the call responsibility exceeds a level generally expected for the specialty. For example, to fill vacancies left by a departing physician, a specialist may be asked to temporarily assume an additional slot in the ED call rotation, essentially doubling his or her current call responsibilities. Further, a physician already taking call for the hospital-owned clinic in which he or she practices may also be asked to cover call for another hospital-owned clinic or other facility run by the hospital. In these and other situations, considering additional compensation means considering the additional value the services bring, how much beyond the norm the on-call services are, and how long the additional services will be required.

If a physician is employed and the employer is billing and collecting for the physician's professional services and the physician's compensation is not dependent on collections, the burden of uncompensated care falls on the employer, not the physician. In such a situation, incorporating compensation for uncompensated care into the call coverage arrangement (through the failure to consider its inclusion in survey data) results in a two-fold problem, as the employer ends up taking a loss on the care and compensates the physician for the loss, essentially doubling the loss to the employer and overpaying the physician.

Conclusion

To conclude, economic and market forces not experienced by earlier generations of physicians have caused today's physicians to rethink the former practice of accepting on-call responsibilities as an obligation to the community and a requirement of the active medical staff. This environment has resulted in reluctance on the part of physicians to take call and in demands for compensation associated with physician availability and for the risks assumed by physicians in caring for indigent and low-paying patients.

Chapter 28: Valuation of Physician On-Call and Coverage Arrangements

The uniqueness of the various types of on-call and coverage arrangements, along with the implications of violating important statutory and regulatory requirements applicable to tax-exempt entities and to providers caring for Federal health care program beneficiaries, makes payment for physician availability a costly and risky venture for many facilities. Crucial to this process is the valuation of the compensation arrangements, yet no formal guidance exists as to how to determine the fair market value of these payments. The various types of coverage arrangements and the difficulty in obtaining truly comparable data makes the science of valuating physician availability difficult at best. Regardless of the approaches and methods used by the valuation analyst, determining the fair market value of these types of agreements is a complex task. Only through a complete understanding of the specifics of the subject arrangement and in the proper application of widely accepted methodology and analyst judgment can a reliable and defensible conclusion of value be reached.

Bibliography

"A Growing Crisis in Patient Access to Emergency Surgical Care" *American College of Surgeons* (June 2006) www.facs.org.

O'Malley, Ann, Debra A. Draper and Laurie E. Felland. "Hospital Emergency On-Call Coverage: Is There A Doctor In The House?" *Center for Studying Health System Change* No.115 (November 2007): 1.

"Availability of On-Call Specialists" *American College of Emergency Physicians* (May 2005) www.acep.org.

Henzke, Leonard J. http://findarticles.com/p/articles/mi_m3257/is_1_61/ai_n17114335/. [Internet accessed May 9, 2008].

Rowland, Robert G. and Leonard J. Henzke. "What Boards Should Know about the Emerging Call Coverage Crisis" *American Governance Leader* Vol 3, no.4 (July 2003): 1.

"Report of the Board of Trustees: Report 14-I-06," *American Medical Association*

http://www.ama-assn.org/ama1/pub/upload/mm/475/bot14i06.doc. [Internet accessed on May 9, 2008].

Trugman, Gary R. CPA/ABV, MCBA, ASA, MVS. *Understanding Business Valuation* Second Edition. American Institute of Certified Public Accountants, Inc., 2002.

Broccolo, Bernadette M. Esq., et al. *Fundamentals of Health Law* Third Edition. American Health Lawyers Association. July 2004.

Chapter 28: Valuation of Physician On-Call and Coverage Arrangements

1. "The Uninsured and Their Access to Health Care." *Key Facts: October 2007.* The Henry J. Kaiser Family Foundation, Kaiser Commission on Medicaid and the Uninsured.
2. "A Growing Crisis in Patient Access to Emergency Surgical Care." American College of Surgeons, Division of Advocacy and Health Policy,
3. *2005 Hospital Emergency Department Administration Survey*, The Schumacher Group
4. Smith, M. et al, *Emergency Department On-Call Coverage: Issues and Solutions*. Missouri Hospital Association, December 2005.
5. 42 C.F.R. §411.357(c)
6. Ibid., §411.357(d)
7. 42.C.F.R. §1320a – 7b(b).
8. 42.C.F.R. §1001.952(i).
9. 42.C.F.R. §1001.952(d).
10. OIG Advisory Opinion 07-10, issued September 20, 2007 and posted September 27, 2007.
11. I.R.C. §501(c)(3).
12. I.R.C. §4958(c)(1).
13. 68 Fed. Reg. (September 9, 2003) p. 53255.
14. Statement on Standards for Valuation Services Number One. American Institute of Certified Public Accountants.
15. 66 Fed. Reg. (January 4, 2001), p. 944.
16. 69 Fed. Reg. (March 26, 2004), p. 16107.
17. In the author's analysis, the computation of this rate was found to exceed the rate obtained by analyzing all available physician specialties, which supports the theory that the volume of respondent data and other factors mitigate the risk that referral relationships taint the on-call compensation survey data.
18. 72 Fed. Reg. (September 5, 2007), p. 51016.

Chapter 29

Evaluating RVU-Based Compensation Arrangements

By Mark O. Dietrich, CPA/ABV, and Gregory D. Anderson, CPA/ABV, CVA

Relative Value Unit (RVU) based compensation arrangements are increasingly popular for compensating physicians. Where collected revenue-based systems—historically common in group practice, for example—reflect the individual physician's underlying payor mix, RVU systems are payor-mix neutral. A RVU system[1] is therefore attractive to a physician employed by a hospital that treats patients regardless of their ability to pay. However, RVU systems may be tainted by payor mix and other market conditions, requiring that the analyst understand and examine the effects of this issue when using compensation survey data to establish fair market value incentive compensation based on RVUs.

There are several RVU measurement systems associated with physician billing codes (Current Procedural Terminology or CPT™), but the most commonly used is the Resource-Based Relative Value Scale (RBRVS), which is also used by the Medicare program for establishing its physician fee schedule (MPFS). The RBRVS allocates RVUs to each procedure or service in the CPT™ based upon the amount of physician work, the cost of delivering the service, and the cost of malpractice insurance associated with the service. These RVUs are then multiplied by an amount known as a Conversion Factor and adjusted for geographic differences (the GPCI) to arrive at the fee for the service.

RBRVS has its weaknesses. The Medicare Conversion Factor suffers from a statutory construct, which attempts to peg overall Medicare physician spending to an annual limit that would seem to make that measurement unit meaningless in the present environment. Sitting at around $38 per RVU before geographic adjustment, the rate has been virtually flat for many years and does not maintain pace with inflation, which the Medicare Payment Advisory Commission (MedPAC) estimates at approximately 3.0% per annum in physician practices. Nonetheless, the vast majority of physicians continue to accept Medicare patients, suggesting, at least to government agencies such as MedPAC, that payment rate has some relevance in assessing value. RBRVS is also subject to government manipulation that manifests itself in instability. For example, legislative intervention into the formula used to account for the practice expense formula and statutory five-year adjustments to the physician work component of the RVU affect how RBRVS impacts physician payment.

Payment rates per RVU vary significantly from region to region, as well as from payor contract to contract. Providers and, particularly, provider-systems with negotiating strength may have payment rates per RVU well in excess of their competitors. Evaluating reasonable compensation for a physician therefore requires knowledge of the specific contract rates being paid for that

Chapter 29: Evaluating RVU-Based Compensation Arrangements

physician's services, as well as knowledge of the underlying payor mix. Consider the following example of how contract rates and payor mix impact physician compensation:

Example

Payor Mix	40.00%	10.00%	60.00%	
Payor	Medicare	Best	Non-Medicare Avg Including Best	Weighted Average
Total RVUs	10,000	10,000	10,000	10,000
Rate	38.00	55.00	48.00	44.00
Collections	380,000	550,000	480,000	440,000
Practice Expenses	250,000	250,000	250,000	250,000
Physician Income	130,000	300,000	230,000	190,000
Compensation per total RVU	13.00	30.00	23.00	19.00

Note: Payor Mix weights are used to determine the Weighted Average Rate per RVU. Each column indicates what the Physician would have earned if 100% of the services provided were for each of the Payor Columns shown. For purposes of the example, assume that none of the Total RVUs include Stark or other prohibited incentives.

In the example, the physician is earning $190,000 per year on collected revenue of $440,000. The physician's earnings would vary from $130,000 if the practice were entirely Medicare to $300,000 if it was entirely "marketbest," a difference of 230%. The key observation to be taken from the example is that because expenses are fixed for a given volume of services in each scenario, all of the additional revenue from better contracts drops to the bottom line as physician compensation. That in turn suggests that "reasonable compensation" for 10,000 RVUs of services could range from $130,000 to $300,000, depending upon the mix and strength of the underlying payor contracts.

Lest that seem unrealistic on its face, consider the view from the physician working in a private practice holding only "market-best" contracts. Certainly, he/she would not be willing to work for $130,000 per year as if seeing only Medicare patients. Similarly, a physician employed by a hospital or Integrated Delivery System (IDS) with strong contracts for physician services would expect to be compensated at a commensurate rate, rather than have the employing institution retain the excess as profit. Similarly, it is unlikely that the managed care companies and other payors would be paying premium rates per RVU, unless market conditions warranted it and made it necessary to attract physician providers into their networks.

The Non-Medicare Average value per RVU of $48 is an initial reference point for what "market" value for physician services is in this particular circumstance, assuming the Weighted Average

Chapter 29: Evaluating RVU-Based Compensation Arrangements

Conversion Factor, as described in the following paragraph. The Medicare Conversion Factor is not negotiated but is rather a legislatively imposed *force majeure* disconnected from market forces. As such, it has limited worth in assessing "market" value.

The compensation reported in Survey data such as that of the Medical Group Management Association will reflect the "Weighted Average" compensation or Rate per RVU of only those entities participating in the Survey. In the Example, this compensation would be $190,000. The actual Rate per RVU in a given practice may be more or less than the Survey result. If practices participating in the Survey have a better Payor and Rate mix than all practices in a given area, the compensation will be higher and conversely, if the participating practices have poorer rates, the Survey compensation will be less.

This type of analysis is critical to assessing the fair market value of compensation for hospitals employing physicians. In many markets, integrated provider networks that include both physicians and hospitals succeed in obtaining superior reimbursement from payors, which in turn results in superior compensation. The contracts may be a function of enhanced clinical quality from integration, market-based negotiating leverage, reduced administrative costs to payors due to single-signature contracting, or shifting of contract administration. Traditional analysis focusing solely on Compensation Surveys to determine fair market value may well fall short of the market value of services based upon actual negotiated contracts for providers with a strong market position.

Returning to the Example, assume that an IDS has managed care and other payor agreements that result in the following Payor Distribution and Revenue for a physician practice.

Payor Mix	35.00%	30.00%	35.00%	100.00%
	Medicare	Best	Other Payors	Weighted Average
Total RVUs	3,500	3,000	3,500	10,000
Rate	38.00	55.00	48.00	46.60
Collections	133,000	165,000	168,000	466,000
Practice Expenses	87,500	75,000	87,500	250,000
Physician Income	45,500	90,000	80,500	216,000
Compensation per total RVU	13.00	30.00	23.00	21.60

Note: This Example differs from the first in that the Payor Mix has been applied to the total RVUs of services performed to arrive at the actual compensation earned based upon the given payor mix.

In this case, the actual contracts in place generate physician compensation of $216,000 as compared to the "market" compensation described in the first example of $190,000, or about 14% greater. Solely relying on the Survey result would seem to understate what is "reasonable

Chapter 29: Evaluating RVU-Based Compensation Arrangements

compensation" for a physician employed in this particular provider entity. The determination of what is reasonable requires the valuation analyst and the employing provider to have keen insight into market conditions to arrive at an appropriate conclusion.

An appropriate alternative to sole reliance on survey data is to measure the value of compensation per RVU based on data from the practice on revenues and RVUs produced by major payor or payor group. Some analysts will benchmark the physician practice on a more global scale, analyzing collections per RVU to get an overall sense of favorable or unfavorable payor arrangements when the practice is compared against survey data. After this initial "litmus test" is interpreted, exploration of data by payor group, drilling down to compensation per RVU as in the example above, can give an indication as to whether and to what extent favorable or unfavorable payor contracts impact physician compensation. This, essentially the use of the income-based approach in analyzing physician compensation value, supplements the market-based approach conclusions derived from an interpretation of raw survey data.

What becomes clear to the analyst is that simple reliance on single survey data is not enough to yield a completely defensible conclusion of value for compensation under a RVU arrangement. Use of as many independently published surveys and as many different valuation methods as are reasonably available is certainly a prudent practice for those with the responsibility for determining compensation that must be defended as fair market value. Not only should the use of RVUs be considered, but other physician productivity benchmarks (i.e., encounters/visits for primary care, surgical cases for surgeons) may also be appropriate.

Finally, as an observation, physician practice acquisition value is often considered simultaneously with an employment decision and reasonable compensation analysis. In the practice valuation model, it is NOT appropriate to consider payor contracts held by a *particular* purchasing provider entity unless such contracts are common to the universe of potential purchasing entities in the market. This is because such an adjustment would be inconsistent with fair market value's requirement for "*any* willing buyer."

In contrast, compensation is a function of who employs you and what your services are worth at the time they are performed. From the standpoint of the hypothetical seller of services—i.e., the employed physician—being employed at a rate less than what the market is paying his or her employer currently for the physician's services would be inconsistent with the expected result in arms-length negotiation where reasonable knowledge is present. Thus, a physician practice may have a low value because there is little profit once the physician receives reasonable compensation for services based upon the practice's existing contracts. However, the physician may be better compensated in the future because his or her new employer holds better payor contracts.

---

1. It is important to note that most compensation systems focus on the physician Work RVU component (WRVU), which is but one component of the RBRVS measuring of total RVU values; the other two are practice expense and malpractice insurance cost. This allows for measurement of physician productivity using a measurement tool that essentially measures those areas of productivity that are under the control of the physician.

Chapter 30
Valuing Medical Director Services

By Andrea M. Ferrari, JD, MPH and Timothy R. Smith, CPA/ABV

Introduction

A wide variety of healthcare providers, including hospitals, long-term care facilities, and pharmaceutical and device manufacturers routinely engage physicians to provide administrative services. These arrangements are commonly termed "medical directorships," but numerous other descriptions (*e.g.*, "thought leadership agreements") are also frequently used. While medical directorships have been in widespread use for quite some time, the healthcare regulatory and valuation climate has evolved in the last decade or so to the point where the parties to a medical directorship face some significant hurdles and issues that did not exist before.

This chapter discusses the various and sometimes complex issues that should be considered when valuing medical directorships in the current regulatory environment. It addresses issues related to the valuation of medical directorships in the following order:

1. Legal and regulatory issues to consider when determining compensation for medical directorships.

2. Identifying and analyzing the scope of services covered by a medical directorship arrangement.

3. Selecting and applying the appropriate valuation methodology to determine the fair market value of medical director services.

4. Arriving at an FMV range based on consideration of all relevant facts and circumstances.

Legal and Regulatory Context for Valuing Medical Directorships

Understanding the application of healthcare laws and regulations to medical directorship arrangements is critical for establishing the scope of work for an appraisal assignment involving a medical directorship.[1] Healthcare laws and regulations will often dictate the intended use of the appraisal opinion (to the extent that, generally, when healthcare providers request the valuation of medical directorship agreements, their purpose in doing so is to ensure compliance with healthcare laws and regulations) as well as the definition of value to be used for the assignment. Healthcare laws and regulations require that certain types of agreements comply

Chapter 30: Valuing Medical Director Services

with specialized definitions of value that may differ from those used outside of the healthcare industry. For this reason and others, clients who engage appraisers to value health care arrangements will generally need the appraiser to understand the legal and regulatory context in which the arrangement is being entered, as well as any guidance from regulators concerning appropriate methods for valuing the subject services. Otherwise, the appraiser may provide a client with a value that is later found to be in violation of healthcare laws and regulations. The penalties for such violations can be significant and very costly to healthcare organizations.

Since healthcare laws and regulations may be complex and voluminous, it is advisable for appraisers to consult with the client and/or the client's legal counsel to ensure that the applicable regulations are followed when determining the value of medical director services. These laws and regulations may be subject to varying and complex interpretations. As such, regulatory interpretation and guidance most often requires the expertise of legal counsel rather than that of the appraiser. Consequently, the appraiser should generally consider any regulatory guidance given by the client's legal counsel as clarification with regard to the definition of value. In other words, legal counsel is articulating the regulatory definition of value for which the appraiser will provide an opinion of value. Such regulatory guidance is comparable to the legal direction given in litigation-related valuation assignments with respect to specialized, state law-based definitions of value, such as fair value in shareholder lawsuits or personal goodwill in divorce proceedings. The appraiser, however, should not subvert his or her judgment to that of the client or the client's counsel for matters that are properly the domain of the appraisal professional. Unfortunately, the distinction between legal issues related to regulatory matters and valuation issues may not always be clear. To help the intended users of the report understand how such regulatory and valuation issues were handled, the appraiser should disclose any such client-provided regulatory guidance in the appraisal report as part of the discussion of the scope of work for the assignment.

The three major categories of healthcare laws and regulations that should be considered by the appraiser are:

- the federal Anti-Kickback Statute and related regulations and advisory opinions (collectively, FAKS)

- the Stark Law and accompanying Stark Regulations (Stark)

- for not-for-profit entities, provisions of the Internal Revenue Code, and associated regulations and guidance promulgated by the IRS that prohibit private inurement in transactions with tax-exempt entities (Tax Regulations)[2]

By way of background information, prior to passage of the Stark Law[3] (*i.e.*, Stark), payments for medical directorships were subject to scrutiny under the federal Anti-Kickback Law[4] (*i.e.*, FAKS). Under the FAKS, an arrangement is illegal if even one purpose of the arrangement is to generate referrals between the parties.[5] Certainly, medical directorship arrangements involving no discrete services or questionable duties may be subject to scrutiny as potential violations of

Chapter 30: Valuing Medical Director Services

FAKS. Until recently, however, FAKS was not widely enforced (at least with regard to medical directorships) because prosecution under FAKS requires the government to prove that the parties possessed the intent to induce referrals at the time they entered into the arrangement.

The initial incarnation of the Stark, referred to as Stark I, was enacted in 1992 to regulate physician self-referrals for clinical laboratory services subject to Medicare reimbursement. In 1993, Stark II extended the physician self-referral restrictions to a wide variety of designated health services (aside from clinical laboratory services), and extended the reach of Stark enforcement activities to nearly all compensation arrangements between parties in a position to refer patients from federally-funded payment programs (*e.g.,* Medicare and Medicaid). Unlike FAKS, Stark is a *strict liability* statute. As such, enforcement of Stark does not require the government to prove any intent by the parties to induce referrals. In light of Stark, as well as increased vigor in enforcement of FAKS, payments to physicians for administrative services are now subject to considerable scrutiny.[6]

In their current form, FAKS and Stark generally prohibit payments to physicians for referrals of healthcare services. To ensure that remuneration flowing between physicians and providers of healthcare services are not disguised payments for referrals, FAKS and Stark generally require all arrangements between such physicians and providers to be consistent with *fair market value* and *commercially reasonable*. Additionally, for purposes of complying with tax regulations, not-for profit, tax-exempt entities will have to give special attention to assuring that compensation paid for medical director services is consistent with *fair market value*. Appraisers need to be aware that fair market value for purposes of complying with healthcare laws and regulations differs in some respects from the standard formulation of fair market value as understood by the appraisal profession.[7] For example, as defined by the International Glossary of Business Valuation Terms, the term *fair market value* is defined as the price, expressed in terms of cash equivalents, at which property would exchange hands between a hypothetical willing and able seller, acting at arms' length in an open and unrestricted market, when neither is under a compulsion to buy or sell and when both have reasonable knowledge of the relevant facts. In the context of healthcare transactions, *fair market value* is generally defined as the value in arm's length transactions, consistent with the general market value, where "general market value" means the compensation that would be included in a service arrangement as the result of *bona fide* bargaining between well-informed parties to an arrangement when neither party is otherwise in a position to generate business for the other party.[8]

Stark Exclusion of Market Comparables between Parties in a Position to Refer

Since it is a strict liability statute, Stark is generally the statute of greatest concern for parties entering into medical directorship arrangements. Over the years and through various phases of the Stark regulations, CMS and its predecessor agencies have provided guidance and commentary on the definition and determination of fair market value for purposes of complying with Stark. CMS has explicitly noted that fair market value as defined by Stark may differ from fair market value as determined through standard appraisal practices. One example of a critical difference in the valuation methodology prescribed by Stark and the valuation methodologies used

Chapter 30: Valuing Medical Director Services

in standard appraisal practice is that compliance with Stark requires certain limitations on the use of a market approach. [Editor's note: A critical point made in numerous other places in this Guide.] That is, the determination of fair market value for Stark purposes should not be based on market comparable transactions between referral-source physicians and providers of DHS.[9]

This is because guidance from CMS suggests that transactions between parties who are in a position to refer or generate other business for each other are not "arm's length" transactions. The prevalence of transactions between referral-source physicians and providers of health care services may distort pricing in the marketplace since, consciously or otherwise, the parties to such transactions may tend toward compensation that rewards referrals.[10] CMS has acknowledged that exclusion of such market comparables may prohibit the use of the market approach in valuing compensation arrangements in certain cases. In these cases, CMS advises the use of alternative approaches or valuation methods.[11] Applying this prohibition to the valuation of medical director services has critical consequences.[12] Market information on medical directorships between referral-source physicians and providers of DHS would appear to be excluded from the determination of fair market value for Stark compliance purposes. As a result, appraisers may be severely limited in the market information that can be used to establish fair market value for medical director services. Most medical director arrangements are between referral-source physicians and providers of DHS under Stark.

While many appraisers may take exception with this limitation on the use of the market approach, it is important to assess this prohibition within the larger context of business valuation body of knowledge. Most appraisers would exclude, discount, or treat cautiously any market comparables for transactions between family members, related parties, affiliated or sister companies, or parent-subsidiary companies. Such parties or entities would not be considered to be fully at arms-length, and therefore, any corresponding financial arrangements would also be viewed as not fully arms-length. In the case of the Stark Regulations, the potential for referrals is considered significant enough to warrant the required exclusion of arrangements between physicians and certain healthcare providers as sources of market data for purposes of determining fair market value under Stark.

Stark Distinction between Clinical Services and Administrative Services

In Stark regulations issued in September 2007 (the "Stark Phase III Regulations") CMS made an important distinction between the clinical and administrative work provided by physicians and the determination of fair market value for physician services. In its commentary to responses, CMS stated:

> A fair market value hourly rate may be used to compensate physicians for both administrative and clinical work, provided that the rate paid for clinical work is fair market value for the clinical work performed and the rate paid for administrative work is fair market value for the administrative work performed. We note that the fair market value of administrative services may differ from the fair market value of clinical services.[13]

Chapter 30: Valuing Medical Director Services

Given this guidance, an appraiser who is engaged to provide an opinion of value relating to medical director services should consider the distinction between clinical and administrative duties when appraising the services. Appraisals of medical director services obtained for Stark compliance purposes should address the distinction in clinical and administrative services and the corresponding levels of compensation for each type of service.

Understanding the Types of Services Provided by a Physician Medical Director

In valuing the compensation provided under a service arrangement, it is essential for the appraiser to understand the nature and scope of the services provided under the subject arrangement. The types, level, and extent of services provided are key factors in arriving at the compensation paid under a service contract. Another critical element in determining the compensation is the required qualifications of the service provider. This relationship between the services provided and amount of compensation should be self-evident to appraisers, who establish appraisal fees on a routine basis with clients based on the scope of the particular appraisal assignment. The level and extent of valuation services coupled with the qualifications of the appraisers providing those services generally determine the fees. In a similar manner, the scope of medical director services and the required qualifications of the individual providing those services are fundamental factors in determining the compensation for a medical director arrangement. The beginning point for valuing medical director services, therefore, is cataloging and analyzing the scope of services and the qualifications necessary for providing these services.

Many forms of arrangements include duties typical of a medical director, and such arrangements do not always come with a label that clearly identifies the services to the appraiser as a medical directorship. An arrangement for medical director services may be found on a generic form agreement labeled a "Professional Services Agreement," or may be a component of a complex management services arrangement, employment arrangement, or other service arrangement between healthcare providers.

Since medical directorships are diverse, comparison for purposes of either identification or valuation is not an easy task. Nonetheless, most medical directorships share at least a few common characteristics. To identify and appropriately appraise medical directorships, appraisers of healthcare relationships should have some understanding of the common as well as distinguishing characteristics of the subject medical director arrangements.

Medical Directorships Frequently Involve Specialized Physician Services

In basic terms, a medical directorship is an arrangement by which a physician is engaged to provide leadership, oversight, and planning services for a clinical program or department of a healthcare provider, healthcare entity, or healthcare facility. Generally, medical directorship services consist of duties that are most appropriately performed by a physician and often, by a physician of a particular specialty. Many medical director duties require the professional training, experience and peer-to-peer communication skills that only a physician (or in some cases, a physician of a particular specialty) is likely to possess. Examples of a medical director's responsibilities may include the following:

- Developing, leading and/or managing quality and efficiency initiatives for a particular clinical unit, department or program. Specifically, a medical director's duties may include developing clinical quality assessment and improvement programs, providing direct oversight of the care that is provided to patients by the clinical practitioners in the department or program, and selecting, procuring and/or directly providing clinical education for practitioners in the department or program.

- Identifying clinical equipment needs, and selecting appropriate equipment for purchase to meet those needs and assure that the department or program is able to maximize the quality, efficiency and safety of care.

- Communicating and securing "buy-in" for operational initiatives from clinical staff that are reluctant to take directives from non-physician managers.

The training, knowledge and communication skills of a physician are certainly an asset—if not a requirement—in effectively performing these types of tasks. Accordingly, general training as a physician is a requisite qualification for almost all medical directorships.

Training and experience in a particular specialty or subspecialty is a hallmark qualification for some types of medical directorships. For example, consider an internal medicine physician who has never personally performed or participated in a cardiac surgery. This individual would not reasonably be expected to develop clinical quality assessment and improvement programs, anticipate the equipment and staffing needs, or secure clinical practitioner "buy-in" for operational initiatives in a cardiovascular surgery program. There are a number of reasons why a training and practice in a specific specialty or subspecialty may be required to perform the required duties of a medical director position..

Understanding the Duties to be Performed by the Medical Director

An appraiser needs to analyze the nature of the duties to be provided in a medical director arrangement in order to assess the value of the services to be provided. Accordingly, an appraiser should seek to answer questions of *"who, what, when, where and how."* Although the nature of the arrangement will dictate the specific questions that should be asked, questions may generally be similar to those posed here:

1. *Who* will perform the duties required by the arrangement?

    - Do the duties require the expertise of a physician?

Chapter 30: Valuing Medical Director Services

- Do the duties require the expertise of a physician of a particular specialty (*e.g.*, pediatrics, cardiology, neurology or surgery)?

- Do the duties require the expertise of a physician of a particular subspecialty (*e.g.*, pediatric cardiology, stroke, or sports medicine)?

- Do the duties require the expertise of a physician with highly specialized training, experience or expertise (*e.g.*, joint replacement, fetal surgery, or neuroradiology)?

2. *What* are the specific duties to be performed under the arrangement?

    - Is the physician providing oversight of a department or program?

    - Is the physician developing or administering quality assessment or quality improvement programs for a particular department or program?

    - Is the physician assessing need for, selecting, developing and/or personally delivering education programs for staff in a department or program?

    - Is the physician selecting, purchasing, testing or developing protocols for the use of new equipment or supplies in a department or program?

    - Is the physician performing other duties related to leadership, oversight or planning of specific services, departments, facilities or clinical units?

3. *When* are the duties to be performed?

    - What is the term of the agreement under which the duties are to be performed?

    - What is the specific schedule or time interval over which the duties are to be performed (*e.g.*, a fixed or maximum number of hours per month, per year or per week)?

    - Can the duties be performed during regular work hours (*i.e.*, Monday through Friday during regular business hours)?

    - Does the physician have a greater or lesser burden as a result of the schedule (or lack thereof) for performing the duties?

4. *Where* will the duties be performed?

    - What is the geographic region where the services and related duties will be performed?

Chapter 30: Valuing Medical Director Services

- In which facility or service location will the physician perform the duties?

- What is the specific service center or unit within a facility where the physician will perform the duties?

5. *How* will the physician be compensated for performing the duties?

    - Will payment be hourly, based on hours worked and documented?

    - Will payment be a fixed fee or salary?

        —If compensation is with a fixed fee or salary payment, the valuator should discern whether the payment is based on:

        —The estimated time (hours) required to perform the duties;

        —The completion of discrete tasks or work products that have a measureable and discernible value; or

        —Other measurable and discernible measures of value.

Detailed answers to the questions of *"who, what, when, where and how"* assist the appraiser in specifically identifying the scope and level of contemplated medical director services. The appraiser then uses this information to determine the value of these services with greater accuracy and precision.

Medical Director Compensation: Hourly Rate or Fixed Fee Arrangements

Medical director services are often provided through independent contractor agreements that provide for hourly compensation to the physician based on time actually worked and documented. As noted previously, however, physician administrative services are sometimes included as a component of employment relationships, management arrangements, or independent contractor agreements wherein the physician receives fixed compensation at regular intervals (*e.g.*, weekly, monthly, or yearly). When a physician is compensated for medical director duties with a fixed fee, the appraiser must carefully consider: 1) the nature of the administrative duties that the physician performs, 2) the range of reasonable hourly compensation for performing such duties; and 3) the hours that are reasonably required and likely to be spent actually performing such duties. A more detailed discussion of valuation considerations for fixed fee arrangements is provided later in this chapter.

Chapter 30: Valuing Medical Director Services

Application of the Three Approaches to Value

While the conceptual framework for generally accepted appraisal practice was developed to value assets and business interests, the valuation principles and concepts supporting the three approaches to value can also be applied to the appraisal of compensation in services agreements, including the valuation of medical directorships. At the foundation of the three approaches to value are the fundamental appraisal principles of substitution, alternatives, and future benefits. The following section of this chapter seeks to demonstrate how these principles can be applied in valuing medical director services.

The Market Approach

The International Glossary Business Valuation Terms (the "International Glossary"), defines the market approach as *"a general way of determining a value indication of a business, business ownership interest, security, or intangible asset by using one or more methods that compare the subject to similar businesses, business ownership interests, securities, or intangible assets that have been sold."* In basic terms, the market approach uses comparable sales transactions that have occurred in the marketplace to determine the value a subject asset or business interest. The valuation principle of substitution is employed in the market approach as the concept that a buyer will not pay more for a subject asset than for substitute asset that provides the equivalent economic utility. As applied to service agreements, the market approach seeks to value the subject arrangement by referencing comparable arrangements in the marketplace.

The key to utilizing the market approach for valuing the compensation paid in service agreements is identifying and obtaining information on comparable agreements that can be used to establish the value of the subject contract. Yet, finding such information on comparable agreements with sufficient detail is often the greatest difficulty an appraiser experiences in applying the market approach to the valuation of service agreements. It should be noted, however, that an appraiser can often use market information from arrangements that are not fully similar to the subject arrangement, as long as the appraiser has sufficient information to make the appropriate adjustments to the market data and/or the subject arrangement in order to make them comparable for valuation purposes.

Use of the market approach in valuing medical director services underscores the need for the appraiser to identify and understand the scope of services provided in both the subject arrangement and the market comparables. Without such information, the appraiser may treat as comparable service arrangements that are essentially different as to the services provided and/or the qualifications required of the service provider. As a result, the appraiser may arrive at a range of value for the subject arrangement based on a fundamentally dissimilar mix of services or qualifications. In addition, the specific facts and circumstances of the service arrangement, such as the geographic locality and other characteristics of the local market in which the services are being provided, should be carefully analyzed and factored into the valuation. The understanding of the specific facts and circumstances of an arrangement is crucial to identifying appropriate market comparables, which is a key step in valuing the services using a market approach.

Chapter 30: Valuing Medical Director Services

Applying the Market Approach

In utilizing the market approach to value medical director services, the appraiser performs market research to accumulate information on medical director arrangements, including the scope of services provided, the required qualifications of the physician director, and the level of compensation paid. Multiple sources of published data exist relating to physician compensation for clinical services or for compensation from all sources, such as the MGMA, AMGA, or SCA physician compensation surveys described in detail below. There are few sources of published survey data, however, that are specific to physician compensation for specialized services such as medical directorships.[14] One potential source of market data for medical director compensation is the *Medical Director Survey* that is published annually by Integrated Healthcare Strategies (formerly Clark Consulting—Healthcare Group). The *Medical Director Survey* reports data on a comprehensive list of specialty medical directorships. It sorts the universe of medical directorships into a large number of specialty categories and reports compensation levels by hospital size. Other medical director surveys or information such as proprietary databases may be available to an appraiser as well.

Appraisers should be aware of the issues and limitations that may be encountered in using medical director compensation surveys or other market databases. Such surveys and other sources of market information on medical directorships often do not present survey compensation results in terms of the specific duties or services that are provided under the directorship arrangements included in the survey or database. As a result, comparisons between the subject medical directorship and those reported in the information source are difficult for purposes of valuation. In addition, labels and descriptors assigned to the categories of medical directorships in such information sources may lack precision or uniform definition. The valuation analyst should use caution in making comparisons based solely on such labels and descriptors.

Since the essence of the market approach is using comparable transactions in the marketplace to establish the value of the subject arrangement, sole or unqualified use of medical director surveys or information databases for establishing the fair market value of medical director services is problematic. Differences in the detailed scope of services distinguish medical directorships, even though agreements may appear to be similar on the surface. Significant differences in the *"who, what, when, where and how"* of the medical director's duties may have a material impact on the comparability of services and the valuation analysis. The valuation of medical directorships is not a "one size fits all" analysis. Unless information is available for the appraiser to determine comparability, survey results reported in a general or summary manner may not be adequate for establishing the value of medical director services. As stated previously, fair market value is ultimately a function of the specific facts and circumstances of the arrangement being analyzed.

A second layer of difficulty may be encountered in using medical director surveys to establish the value of medical director services. Most market information on medical directorships will come from physicians and healthcare providers who have referral relationships that implicate Stark or the

Chapter 30: Valuing Medical Director Services

FAKS. When, as is often the case, the valuation is requested for purposes of complying with healthcare laws and regulations, market comparables derived from physicians and providers with referral or potential referrals relationships may need to be excluded from consideration. Compensation to physicians under these types of arrangements may be skewed by the potential for referrals between the parties, and as such, may not be an appropriate benchmark for fair market value in these types of transactions. Even when the Stark limitation on the use of market comparables is not part of the valuation assignment scope of work, it may be advisable not to rely solely on market data concerning medical director compensation to establish the fair market value of medical director services. Simply put, some market data points may not represent arms-length transactions.

Compensation amounts for physician administrative (*i.e.,* non-clinical) or medical director services that are paid by entities that are not in a position to receive referrals from physicians are less likely to be distorted by an overcompensation bias. Accordingly, to the extent available, data concerning compensation paid by (as an example) an automotive manufacturing company to a physician who oversees the company's cardiovascular health program for employees may be a reliable supporting benchmark for valuation of hospital-based cardiovascular health medical directorship, assuming that the duties of the company and hospital-based programs are comparable.

For use of the market approach, additional comparability issues are encountered when service contracts for medical director duties are included with other service arrangements between the parties. On occasion, a candidate for a medical directorship may be a party to other (existing or contemplated) compensated service agreements with the contracting healthcare entity, such as professional services, management, or employment agreements. When this situation occurs, the appraiser must be attuned to possible overlapping duties in the various arrangements to which the physician and healthcare entity are parties. If appropriate, the appraiser should demonstrate that the physician is not compensated for the same duties through different arrangements, since multiple payment for a single set of duties would result in compensation to the physician that is *in excess of fair market value for the overall bundle of services*.[15]

The Cost Approach

The International Glossary defines the Cost Approach as *"a general way of determining a value indication of an individual asset by quantifying the amount of money required to replace the future service capability of that asset."* The cost approach looks to the replacement cost of an asset or business interest as the basis for valuing the subject asset or interest. In business valuation, the cost approach is categorized as the asset-based or build-up approach because the appraiser attempts to recreate the value of the subject business by accumulating the values of the individual assets that comprise the subject. The appraisal attempts to recreate the business one asset at a time, building up a business enterprise value based on the value of each asset. The cost/asset-based/build-up approach illustrates the valuation principle of alternatives: the idea that there are alternatives to acquiring the future service capacity of the subject asset or business interest.[16]

Chapter 30: Valuing Medical Director Services

The cost approach as applied to service contracts seeks to value the compensation for the subject arrangement by looking to the value of alternatives for those services in the marketplace. As applied to valuing medical director services, the cost approach seeks to value an arrangement between a healthcare entity and a medical director by considering the healthcare entity's costs in the alternative to contracting with a medical director. For example, such alternate cost might be based upon the employment of one or more physicians to provide the required medical director services. As a practical matter, however, the appraiser should keep in mind that most medical directorships are structured as independent contractor arrangements. The duties of a medical director require variable and often limited hours. As such, securing medical director services through an employment arrangement is generally less practical than through an independent contractor arrangement.

Applying the Cost Approach

In following the valuation principle of alternatives, an appraiser may look to physician compensation levels in the marketplace, whether from employment or private practice, as a basis for the alternative cost to procuring the physician services provided in medical directorship arrangements. There are several reliable and readily available sources of survey data for physician compensation in the marketplace. These sources include:

1. **Medical Group Management Association (MGMA),** *Physician Compensation and Production Survey.* This is an annually-published survey that typically reports compensation data from over 2,300 physician practices (predominantly, independent physician-owned organizations).

2. **Sullivan, Cotter and Associates, Inc. (SCA),** *Physician Compensation and Productivity Survey Report* (SCA). This is a compendium of data reported by 263 healthcare organizations (including medical centers, group practices, integrated delivery systems, and HMOs). The 2007 edition represents responses from 39,407 MDs, PhDs, midlevel providers, residents and medical group executives.

3. **Client & Healthcare Compensation Service (HCS),** *Physician Salary Survey Report* and *Client Salary & Benefits Report* The *Physician Salary* report incorporates data from 302 healthcare organizations (including group practice facilities and HMOs). The 2008 edition represents responses from 21,412 physicians. The "Client Salary" report incorporates data from 374 HCS clients, including responses from various Client executives, administrators, and non-physician and midlevel providers.

4. **American Medical Group Association (AMGA),** *Medical Group Compensation and Financial Survey.* The AMGA report discloses salary survey data obtained from medical groups, (predominantly large multi-specialty group practices). Second in size to only the MGMA survey, the AMGA survey is one of the most reliable sources of physician clinical compensation data.

Chapter 30: Valuing Medical Director Services

5. **Watson Wyatt Data Services (WW)**, *Client and Healthcare Management Compensation Report, 2007/2008 Survey Report*. The WW report incorporates data from 415 healthcare organizations representing 63,886 physicians, midlevel providers, and healthcare executives.

It is essential that appraisers understand how these various physician compensation surveys gather and report financial information on physician compensation. Such knowledge is needed for the valid use the survey data to determine physician compensation rates. An appraiser will need to address four critical issues in using the survey data to establish the fair market value of physician compensation for purposes of medical director services. These issues include:

1. The distinction between clinical services and administrative services and any corresponding differentiation in compensation levels for clinical versus administrative work.

2. The distinction between compensation for physician services and business owner compensation.

3. Determining the appropriate level of annual hours worked for purposes of computing an hourly rate for physician services.

4. Adjustment of employment compensation hourly rate to an independent contractor basis.

The appraiser's analysis and resolution of these critical issues may have a material impact on the valuation opinion for a subject medical directorship arrangement.

Compensation for Clinical versus Administrative Services

At noted in the section on the regulatory context for valuing medical director services, CMS recently indicated that it recognizes a distinction between clinical and administrative services with regard to physician compensation. According to the regulators, the fair market value for physician clinical services may differ from the fair market value of administrative services provided by a physician for Stark compliance purposes. Appraisers valuing medical director services for Stark compliance purposes should address this distinction between clinical and administrative duties when determining the fair market of those services. The salient point to this distinction appears to be that the value of clinical work may be greater than the value of administrative work. The presumption is that clinical services warrant higher levels of compensation than administrative services such as medical directorship services. Under this line of reasoning, clinical work is deemed to involve a higher degree of complexity and risk than administrative work. Clinical procedures involve the immediate health and well-being of patients, and in some specialties and cases the literal difference between life and death. While administrative functions and duties, such as those of a physician medical director, may require a skill set only found in physicians of a given specialty, these functions and duties do not generally entail the same level of complexity or risk as the provision of healthcare services to patients. As a result, the level of compensation paid for administrative services should be less than the compensation paid for the same amount of time spent performing clinical procedures. [Editor's Note: Readers should take note of this key point.]

An alternative line of reasoning derived from an opportunity cost analysis argues against the opinion that administrative services should be compensated at a level different from clinical work. It contends that physicians would not agree to provide services at a lower rate because of the opportunity cost for providing administrative services in comparison to clinical services. Compensation levels for clinical procedures are the indicator of the value of a physician's time. Physicians should be paid at clinical levels in order for them to agree to provide non-clinical types of services. Otherwise, physicians have no incentive to provide administrative services. [Editor's Note: And similarly, this point, as it is the key to understanding the hypothetical physician seller of services' opportunity cost.]

Whatever position an appraiser takes on this issue, appraisal opinions prepared for Stark compliance purposes should address the distinction and provide support and defense for the position taken on the issue. Failure to consider this question may constitute an inadequate scope of work for such appraisal assignments. In addition, appraisers may be given regulatory guidance by the client and/or the client's legal counsel that determines the approach to be taken by the appraiser in valuing administrative services. In such cases, the appraiser should document this regulatory guidance as part of definition of value applicable to the assignment.

The approach taken in comparing compensation for clinical and administrative work is critical in determining how physician compensation survey information is used in valuing medical director services. Physician compensation surveys generally report compensation from all sources. The primary source of income for a physician outside of an academic practice setting or a purely administrative role is clinical services. As a result, the compensation in most of the published surveys primarily represents clinical compensation. If an appraiser takes the position that administrative services should be compensated at a lower rate than clinical services, the appraiser may need to adjust the survey compensation levels or choose the lower percentiles from the survey to derive hourly physician compensation rates applicable to medical director services. On the other hand, appraisers who argue in favor of the opportunity cost basis for valuing medical director services will tend to use compensation levels from the published surveys without such adjustment or consideration of the lower percentiles.

Compensation for Physician Services versus Business Owner Compensation

The various published physician compensation surveys gather and publish data from a variety of physicians who practice in diverse settings. The surveys report compensation information in varying levels of detail corresponding to these diverse practice settings. The key compensation

Chapter 30: Valuing Medical Director Services

measures, however, tend to report total compensation received by the physician from all sources. This reporting of compensation from all sources may obscure the fact that certain forms of compensation received by physician may not relate to services provided directly or personally by the physician. Income received from ancillaries, employment of mid-level providers or physician extenders, leasing of space or equipment, or sharing in group practice earnings may relate more to ownership of a medical practice rather to physician services. In other words, business owner compensation is often reported along with compensation from physician services in the physician compensation tables in published surveys. Other forms of non-clinical income such as on-call pay stipends, medical directorship payments, expert testimony fees, and other forms may also be included in the physician compensation tables.

Appraisers seeking to find the market information on the value of physician services may need to adjust reported compensation levels to eliminate forms of compensation not related to physician services, such as business owner compensation. Quantifying these amounts, however, may be extremely difficult. Analysis of various financial, production, and operational metrics, ratios, and benchmarks reported in the surveys may be required for the appraiser to attempt to adjust for business owner compensation that is included in the survey-reported physician compensation tables. While there are clear practical difficulties to addressing this issue, appraisers valuing medical director services should be aware of disparate forms of income or compensation that are included in the published surveys and make adjustments to the valuation analysis where they deem appropriate and practicable. In other words, appraisers should not use compensation amounts from the published surveys in an uncritical or unqualified manner. Such use may lead to an overstatement of the cost of physician services for valuing medical director services.

The Annual Hours for Used in Computing Hourly Physician Compensation Rates

In using publish survey data on physician compensation to arrive at hourly rates for valuing medical director services, appraisers must select the number of annual hours to be used as the divisor for the published annual compensation amounts. Many appraisers use 2,000 or 2,080 hours as the best approximation of typical hours worked by physicians. While this convention may be appropriate and valid, appraisers should be aware of the reported levels of annual physician work hours as provided by certain of the surveys. For those surveys that do report physician work hour levels, reported levels may indicate a continuum of annual hours worked that deviates from the standard 40 hour work week less 10 holidays (*i.e.,* 2,000 hours). Indicated hours may be below or above the typical annual hours. The assumption of standard annual hours may have the greatest valuation impact when an appraiser uses the upper percentiles of the reported compensation levels to determine an hourly rate. In reality, physicians at these higher compensation levels may be working higher annual hours than assumed in the standard rates for annual hours worked. As a result, appraisers may need to perform additional research and analysis using survey information to arrive at the appropriate annual hours amount used for determine hourly physician compensation rates when relying on the upper percentiles of the compensation surveys.

Chapter 30: Valuing Medical Director Services

Adjustment of Hourly Physician Compensation to an Independent Contractor Basis

Because most medical directors serve as independent contractors to healthcare facilities, many appraisers argue that the hourly rates derived from physician compensation surveys should be grossed-up to include a provision for benefits. The theory supporting such gross-up is that independent contractors across all industries are generally paid at higher rates than employees. Such premium rates are intended to cover benefits and other costs incurred by contractors providing services. In the area of physician services, it is argued that one can observe such premiums in the rates paid to locum tenens physicians. Appraisers who value medical director services should be aware of this issue and provide the support and defense in the appraisal report for the position taken.

The Income Approach

The income approach may be the most difficult of the three approaches to value to apply to the valuation of service arrangements. This difficulty derives from the traditional definition in the business valuation body of knowledge. As defined by the International Glossary, the income approach is a "a general way of determining a value indication of a business, business ownership interest, security, or intangible asset using one or more methods that convert anticipated economic benefits into a present single amount." Converting the compensation under a service agreement to a "present single amount" often represents a conundrum for appraisers. How can such a statement of value be meaningful for a service contract? For valuing service agreements, the definition of the income approach may need to be adapted in terms of the valuation principle of future benefits as the basis for value, but without the conversion to a present value amount. With this adaptation, the income approach can be employed to calculate the future economic benefits to be received by each party to the service agreement.[17] These benefits are then evaluated in terms of investment levels, resources utilized, and services provided in comparison to market rates of return and profitability. Under this reformulation of the income approach, the appraiser seeks to value the services by ensuring that each party receives market returns or margins given the levels of investment, risk, and resource utilization attributable to either party to the service contract.

For valuing medical director services, use of the income approach may be limited or impracticable. An appraiser might attempt to isolate such benefits by borrowing the with-and-without competition technique commonly used in business valuation to arrive the value of a covenant not-to-compete. Under such a method, the appraiser would attempt to place a value on medical director services by showing the decrement in net cash flow to the healthcare entity by not contracting with a medical director. Isolating the specific amount of future benefits attributable to contracting with a medical director, however, is a difficult task. In addition, the appraiser would need to prepare projections of revenues and expenses related to the entity or service line in question. The cost of preparing such a pro forma statement appears to outweigh its benefit. Applying the income approach to the other party to the arrangement, *i.e.*, the physician, would require the appraiser to assess the future benefits to the physician in terms of market rates of compensation

Chapter 30: Valuing Medical Director Services

for physician services. This evaluation returns the appraiser to the analyses of the market and cost approaches. In general, the income approach appears to be the least relevant and applicable of the three approaches available for valuing medical director services.

Formulation of the Opinion of Value

After completing the applicable approaches to value, the appraiser engages in an evaluation and reconciliation process to determine the fair market value of the subject arrangement for medical director services. This process is ultimately based on the independent and professional judgment of the appraiser. Weight may given to a greater or lesser degree to the results of any particular valuation method or technique based on a variety of considerations, such as the reliability of data, extent of comparability, scope of information, regulatory guidance, and facts and circumstances unique to the subject arrangement. The opinion of value may be stated a specific dollar amount or a range. Whatever the conclusion of value determined, the appraiser should be prepared to support and defend the conclusion based on the relevant information and sound valuation methodology.

Evaluating the Method of Compensation: Hourly versus Fixed Fee Arrangements

Medical directorships may be independent contractor or employment relationships. In either case, the method of compensation for medical director services is most often hourly and paid in accordance with the number of hours actually worked and recorded by the physician on a time log. The alternative compensation structure is a fixed fee paid in weekly, monthly, or other time intervals, or upon the achievement of certain milestones or the completion of certain tasks.

Regardless of whether an arrangement provides for hourly or fixed fee payments, all payments should be based on a fair market value hourly rate. Accordingly, to evaluate fixed fee payments, the valuator must determine the hours reasonably required to perform the services provided and calculate an underlying hourly rate. Unfortunately, benchmark data to assist with the estimation of time requirements for medical director tasks is rarely available, forcing the valuator to rely upon rely upon his or her own best judgment, client representations, or the requirements specified in the arrangement.

In order to appraise and/or validate the fair market value of an arrangement involving a fixed fee payment for medical director services, a valuator must be able to compare the compensation derived from the arrangement to benchmark data from the marketplace. To permit such comparisons, values must be in comparable units *(i.e.,* they must have the same denominator). If all compensation values are reduced to and expressed in terms of dollars *per hour*, the valuator can freely make comparisons to benchmark data, as is required to validate an appraisal using a market data.

When asked to value a medical director arrangement that provides for fixed fee payments, the valuator may tie the fixed fee payment to an hourly rate using the following four step process:

Chapter 30: Valuing Medical Director Services

1. As specifically as possible, identify the duties that the medical director is required to perform.

2. Determine (from benchmark data) reasonable hourly compensation for performing such duties.

3. Determine the hours that are reasonably necessary (based on any available benchmark data, client representations, or the valuator's independent judgment) or that will actually be required under the arrangement to perform the duties.

4. Multiply the reasonable hourly compensation for performing the duties by the hours that are reasonably necessary or that will actually be required to perform the duties.

After applying this four step process, the fixed fee should reflect reasonable hourly compensation for the duties, based on a reasonable estimate of the time to be spent performing the duties as required under the arrangement.

Conclusion

Applying the three approaches in valuing medical directorship agreements requires the skill and analytical ability of an experienced and well trained healthcare appraisal professional. The appraiser must analyze and synthesize three areas of specialized knowledge in order to arrive at an opinion of value. First, the appraiser studies and evaluates the scope of services and the physician qualifications required to provide the medical director services in the subject agreement. Second, the appraiser completes research and analysis of market data and information to derive comparables for use of the market and cost approaches. Third, the appraiser must adjust and adapt the valuation analysis and the scope of work to comply with any regulatory guidance and specialized regulatory definitions of value. To arrive at an opinion of value, the appraiser evaluates the findings of the valuation process and arrives at a conclusion of fair market value for the subject agreement.

---

1. While the Uniform Standards of Professional Appraisal Practice (USPAP) do not formally apply to the valuation of compensation amounts under service arrangements, appraisers would do well to follow the broad outlines of USPAP's Scope of Work Rule in appraising such arrangements. Identifying key assignment elements, such as intended use and users of the appraisal opinion, definition of value, etc. are useful tools in providing clients with appraisal reports that meet their needs, especially in the healthcare regulatory context.
2. Detailed discussion of the IRS regulations and guidance is not provided herein, as many of the issues are similar or identical to the issues under Stark and FAKS.
3. The physician Self Referral Law (the "Stark Law") is codified at 42 U.S.C.S. §1395nn
4. 42 U.S.C. §1320a-7b
5. *United States v. Kats*, 871 F.2d 105 (9th Cir. 1989); *United States v. Greber*, 760 F.2d 68 (3d Cir.), *cert. denied*, 474 U.S. 988 (1985).

Chapter 30: Valuing Medical Director Services

6. Note that a wide variety of State legislation exists which is similar to Stark and FAKS, and some require additional considerations, depending on the particular State.

7. See the definition of fair market value in the *International Glossary of Business Valuation Terms* or in Revenue Ruling 59-60 for examples of the commonly accepted definition of FMV in the appraisal profession.

8. This is the Stark definition, set forth in 42 CFR §411.351. This definition is also consistent with similar fair market value guidance related to FAKS (codified at 42 U.S.C. §1320a-7b) and with the definition relied upon by the Internal Revenue Service (See, for example, Treas. Reg. 53.4958 et seq.)

9. CMS has stated, "...the definition of "fair market value" in the [Stark] statute... is qualified in ways that do not necessarily comport with the usage of the term in standard valuation techniques and methodologies. For example, the methodology must exclude valuations where the parties to the transactions are at arm's length but in a position to refer to one another." *69 FR 16107 (March 24, 2004)*.

10. *66 FR 876-77, 919, 941, 944 (January 4, 2001)*

11. *66 FR 876-77, 919, 944 (January 4, 2001)*

12. We should also note that some attorneys argue that the above limitation on the market approach is applicable only to the office space and equipment lease exception under Stark. They argue for this qualification because the limitation on the use of market comparables between referring physicians and DHS providers is discussed under the rubric of the space and equipment lease exception. On this exclusion, therefore, an appraiser may be given conflicting guidance from different clients. Appraisers should therefore obtain clarification from the client and/or the client's legal counsel as to the interpretation of Stark that is required for the particular appraisal assignment.

13. *72 F.R. 51016*

14. We have elected to treat medical director compensation surveys under the rubric of the market approach and the more general physician compensation surveys (e.g. MGMA, AMGA, SCA, etc.) under the cost approach for purposes of valuing medical director services. Some appraisers, on the other hand, place use of the general compensation surveys under the market approach and directorship surveys under the cost approach. Either categorization has merit and validity. Yet, such variations in categorization can be confusing to appraisal users and appraisers alike. It would be helpful for the healthcare valuation community to adopt a universal convention as to how the use of the surveys should be categorized relative to the approaches to value.

15. As explained elsewhere in this chapter, to comply with healthcare regulations, agreements and transactions between physicians and healthcare entities must generally be consistent with *fair market value*. Healthcare regulations also generally require such arrangements to be *commercially reasonable*. An arrangement or series of arrangements wherein a physician is compensated multiple times for performing a single function: (a) may result in the physician being paid an aggregate amount that exceeds fair market value for the overall bundle of services to be provided under the arrangement; (b) may fail the test of *commercial reasonableness* based on the definition of *commercially reasonable* provided in the applicable regulations.

16. One can also argue that the cost approach is derived from the principle of substitution in that the individual assets separately valued are substituted for the subject business. Conversely, it can be argued that the market approach illustrates the principle of alternatives: market comparables indicate the existence of alternatives to the subject in the marketplace. Such lines of reasoning illustrate the integral relationship among the fundamental principles of valuation and the three approaches to value. They also indicate the difficulty in assigning a given principle to only one approach to value. The principles may be found in more than one approach.

17. Under this adaptation of the income approach, future economic benefits are not intended to include the value or volume of referrals. Rather, the appraiser looks exclusively to the revenues, expenses, and resources investments related to the specific services and/or service lines provided for in the agreement. For example, in applying the income approach to physician employment arrangements, the appraiser would project future economic benefits deriving from the physician practice only. The value or volume or referrals to other business lines of the employer or the employer's parent or affiliated companies is not included in the projection. In some cases, future benefits may not be separately attributable to the subject agreement. In other cases, the future benefits may indirectly or unintentionally include certain ancillaries or other revenues that arise out of referral relationships. In these cases, the appraiser may be prevented from using the income approach to value the future benefits to one or both parties to a service arrangement.

Chapter 31

Valuing Management Services Contracts between Physicians and Hospitals

By Randy Biernat, CPA

This chapter presents a brief overview of the physician-hospital relationship present in management services contracts (MSCs) and then provides an analytical framework and some tools to prepare a credible fair market value appraisal.

Appraisers typically prepare an appraisal report at the request of a hospital or its counsel to analyze the contractual compensation and certify that the compensation component of a particular arrangement is consistent with fair market value. The resulting appraisal, or "Fair Market Value (FMV) Opinion," is then utilized in an attorney's legal opinion regarding the arrangement's compliance with the applicable laws and regulations governing the transaction.

This chapter briefly describes the "what" and "why" of management services contract appraisal and more extensively presents the "how" of executing the various analyses for this type of engagement.

PART ONE—BACKGROUND AND OVERVIEW

Management Services Contracts—The Basics

One non-scientific observation of the health care marketplace is an increasing tendency for hospitals to contract directly with physicians to provide management services, either exclusively or in combination with its internal managers, as an alternative to providing management services exclusively with employed non-physician staff. The result is management services contracts (MSCs) which require FMV Opinions to comply with the hospital's and physician's legal obligations.

MSCs come in all shapes and sizes. Some are little more than slightly expanded medical directorships, while others provide for the virtual outsourcing of nearly every permissible service required to run a department of a hospital. This chapter presumes that the MSC terms will call for a modest scope of services.

A discussion of appraisal techniques for MSCs that call for the provision of the majority of services necessary to provide the technical component of a hospital service is outside the scope of this chapter, although some of the techniques discussed in part three may be applicable. For instance, some management agreements will actually call for the MSC to provide the staffing, equipment, supplies, and management necessary to provide the technical component of

Chapter 31: Valuing Management Services Contracts between Physicians and Hospitals

outpatient surgery, cardiac catheterizations, imaging services, etc. These types of arrangements require the application of analyses not presented in this chapter.

Hospital Motivation for Purchase of Physician Management Services

The core purpose of engaging a physician or physician management company is to create operating synergies through the alignment of hospital and physician goals. Establishing an understanding of the background and genesis of the contemplated arrangement with management will help the appraiser clearly capture the expected mutual benefits and will likely result in a better FMV Opinion. Reasons that a hospital would enter into an agreement with a physician management company include the following:

- To obtain management expertise, including the integration of clinical leadership from the physician community to provide excellent patient care;

- To develop and implement "best practices" with respect to the delivery of clinical services; and

- To expand and improve the clinical services offered to patients and the community served by hospitals.

Motivation for Physicians Provision of Management Services

Physicians generally seek management opportunities for two reasons. First, engaging management services are a means to enhance personal income for physicians struggling in the present era of flat or declining reimbursement. Second, the ability to influence one's workplace entices a number of physicians to participate.

The intersection of the goals of hospitals and physicians often result in the formation of new physician–owned entities to contract with hospitals to provide management services. These entities are referred to in this chapter as MSCs, which can be presumed to be physician owned and operated unless otherwise stated.

PART TWO—MSC APPRAISAL CONSIDERATIONS

The task of an appraiser of an MSC is to provide a FMV Opinion regarding the proposed compensation. The appraiser balances the facts and circumstances surrounding an arrangement and determines whether the price to the hospital and the income to the physician(s) is reasonable and consistent with market levels of compensation for comparable services. The MSC appraisal process will result in a better end product if two questions are repeatedly considered: "Is it reasonable?" and "Can it be supported?" Every step along the path of analysis should be anchored by these two questions.

Chapter 31: Valuing Management Services Contracts between Physicians and Hospitals

Appraisal Objective

The fair market value analysis is intended to result in the appraiser gathering sufficient evidence to support a professional judgment as to whether or not the proposed compensation is consistent with "fair market value." Therefore, as with other arrangements between physicians and hospitals, the appraiser must systematically measure the expected benefits and costs to gather sufficient evidence to support an opinion regarding the contractual compensation.

Appraisal Process

It is important not to overlook the small details of a report. Very good financial analyses can be hindered by a poor explanation of the purpose of the agreement or confused by the reader due to too little narrative explaining the relationship of the parties. Therefore, this section starts with a summary of important considerations in preparing a strong MSC appraisal.

Overview—For purposes of determining if the MSC compensation is reasonable and within the range of fair market value, an appraiser should consider and document the following, when possible:

1. Identify the requirements for fair market value;

2. Discuss the jurisdictional exceptions to "fair market value" (Stark, etc.);

3. Identify the parties to the agreement;

4. Discuss the purpose of the agreement;

5. Discuss the method of compensation;

6. Present the valuation methodology(s) available and appropriate to the analysis of compensation;

7. Evaluate the transaction from the MSO's perspective;

8. Evaluate the transaction from the hospital's perspective;

9. Reconcile the findings from different methodologies; and

10. State a conclusion.

Depending on the engagement, appraisers may perform and/or present some or all of the steps identified above. However, the above list can serve as a starting point for the contents of a solid FMV Opinion.

Chapter 31: Valuing Management Services Contracts between Physicians and Hospitals

Gather Information—For many engagements, the art of the appraisal process is to maximize the utility of the information made available to the appraiser. Different circumstances and relationships among the parties yield differing mixtures of data available for analysis on a given project. Below is a short list of the items typically requested at the outset of a FMV Opinion engagement related to management services:

- The management services contract;

- Financial statements for the relevant department of the hospital for a representative period of time prior to the engagement of the physician management company;

- A financial forecast for the hospital department including the expected management fee;

- A written summary of the clinical and administrative benefits expected to be gained through the engagement of the physician management company; and

- A forecast of financial results for the physician management company.

Review Information—The information provided must be sufficient to perform one or more procedures that will provide the appraiser with a suitable basis for expressing a FMV Opinion. Appraisers would do well to be wary of accepting engagements where there is a very limited set of data. It may be necessary to expand the scope of the engagement or have the hospital or management company engage a third party to prepare the necessary projections or other relevant schedules.

Discussions with Management—It would be difficult to capture the intent of management without interviewing the parties responsible for the particular initiative under consideration. These individuals may be hospital executives, consultants to the hospital, hospital's counsel, or some combination thereof. Limited contact with the appropriate parties can impact the credibility of the FMV Opinion. Appraisers should clearly state their need to work with hospital management or their representatives very early in the appraisal process.

Management Approval of Facts and Data—Ultimately, management is responsible for reading, understanding, and accepting an appraiser's FMV Opinion, either on a standalone basis or in conjunction with a legal opinion. Therefore, before finalizing any project, management should be given sufficient opportunity to review draft report language and related exhibits. This allows management the opportunity to review and comment on the report's contents. This process can be an important quality measure as the key parties to the arrangement typically have additional insight into the analyses once presented in the context of an appraisal.

Chapter 31: Valuing Management Services Contracts between Physicians and Hospitals

PART THREE—APPRAISAL METHODOLOGIES

This section is devoted to the mechanics of preparing FMV Opinion analyses. These four subsections discuss the procedures often used to prepare FMV Opinions. However, there are other valid methodologies to determine whether MSC compensation is within the range of fair market value.

Salary Survey Benchmarking

In a basic management services agreement, the management company is paid for providing physician management services to a hospital department. In this arrangement, physician compensation represents virtually all of the management company's costs. Applying the cost approach in this case involves making a comparison between the proposed compensation and the range of compensation presented in market survey data.

The appraiser must study the agreement and work with management and counsel to ensure a good understanding of the expected efforts of the physicians. For example, the management company may commit to providing an average of 10 hours per week of physician management services every week of the year. In this case, the expected "physician management efforts" would be 520 hours (52 weeks x 10 hours per week). If, for example, the stated compensation for such service was $85,000, it can be inferred that the physician compensation is approximately $163 per hour, according to the terms of the agreement.

Once the contractual hourly compensation is identified, the appraiser must then analyze the available salary survey data to determine the market level compensation and whether the proposed compensation fits within the identified range.

Physician Management Market Data—Typically, medical director market data is utilized as a proxy for market levels of physician management compensation. Except in vary narrow circumstances, appraisers should avoid the use of compensation for medical services (e.g., vascular surgeon compensation data for a medical director whose training is in vascular surgery) for medical director compensation. Doing so can limit the validity of a FMV Opinion since the riskiness and expertise required for clinical services does not translate directly to management services.

Medical director market data for compensation can come from multiple sources. The following are three annual surveys often used: the Medical Group Management Association (MGMA) *Management Compensation Survey*, the American Medical Group Association (AMGA) *Compensation and Production Survey* and the Hospital & Healthcare Compensation Service (HHCS) *Physician Salary Survey Report*.

Based on the available set of relevant survey data, the appraiser must use professional judgment to determine a range of applicable market data. Typically, the data is presented in the surveys at the 25th, 50th (median), 75th, and 90th percentiles. The appraiser might also consider making an

Chapter 31: Valuing Management Services Contracts between Physicians and Hospitals

adjustment for the fact that the survey data is based on a prior year, while the contractual compensation under consideration is for work being performed in the present. How to make this adjustment is a matter of professional judgment. Options for making this adjustment include using an inflation benchmark, trends in historical data, or other observable market measures.

Conversion of Annual Salaries to Hourly Rates—The market data available is typically presented on an annual basis. To compare this annual data to the hourly data implied in the management services contract, the data must be converted to an equivalent basis. However, doing so presents a challenge since the surveys generally do not provide an "annual hours worked" metric. The compiled survey data is presented as a full-time equivalent (FTE) medical director, which is the number of hours "FTE" means to each organization submitting the data. That is, the FTE metric is not uniform but is instead defined according to each submitting organization's standards.

Therefore, the appraiser must estimate the number of hours worked per year to determine an effective hourly rate for a medical director. Again, reasonable estimates are in order. Options for appraisers include: estimating a 40 hour week for 48 weeks a year, considering the terms of full-time medical directorships in place for the hospital engaging the management company, or surveying hospitals to inquire about trends in relevant market data.

Once an annual hours commitment is assigned to a medical director FTE, an hourly management services rate can be calculated. However, this rate will likely not be suitable for comparison to the contractual rate since the services will, in virtually all cases, be provided on an independent contractor basis. Review of the survey instructions will likely indicate that the data is presented for employed medical directors.

Premium for Independent Contractor Status—Since most, if not all, market data for medical director compensation consists of gross W-2 wages, employment costs such as benefits are excluded. Also worthy of consideration is the cost an employer must bear to replace the productivity of vacationing employees. This is particularly true if management services are to be rendered continuously. A hospital will be financially indifferent to hiring a medical director versus contracting with a nonemployee medical director if the costs are equivalent. Therefore, the appraiser must identify and account for the "hidden" costs of employment to carefully compare the implied contractual compensation to the survey data.

An appraiser should consider applying a premium to the survey compensation to account for those items that are not included in the survey data but are standard costs of employment, including vacation pay, health insurance, retirement benefits, employer paid taxes, and other benefits. To calculate the premium, an appraiser can look to additional data in the identified surveys and other sources that will help validate the estimated costs of the foregone employee-type benefits. This data can be corroborated through an analysis of the benefit packages of local medical directors, if available. The adjustment for independent contractor status will create the "apples-to-apples" comparison necessary for analyzing the proposed management compensation.

Chapter 31: Valuing Management Services Contracts between Physicians and Hospitals

Salary Survey Benchmarking: Conclusion—By carefully analyzing and utilizing available market surveys, an appraiser can determine a range of physician management costs relevant for comparison to an implied hourly management fee in a subject contract. The key to a successful benchmarking analysis is to ensure that the market data and the proposed compensation are modified, as necessary, to be stated on an equivalent basis.

In some agreements, the management company will provide services to a hospital in addition to physician management. Even in these expanded arrangements, an analysis of the underlying compensation to physicians for their efforts can be an important component of the overall fair market value analysis.

Profit Margin Analysis

When a management services agreement calls for the physician management company to provide other services, such as non-physician staff, the purchasing and management of supplies, or billing and collections services, an entity-level application of the cost approach can be utilized when considering the compensation's fair market value status. In the case of this expanded arrangement, an appraiser can analyze the underlying costs in a similar manner to the benchmarking approach identified in the previous section. However, in most circumstances, an aggregate analysis of the expected revenue and expense should be undertaken to compare the physician management company to similar businesses. One indication that the aggregate compensation under a management services agreement is within the range of fair market value is when the overall profit margin of the management company is consistent with market data for similar businesses.

In order to determine the reasonableness of the compensation to be paid according to the subject agreement, an appraiser can compare the expected future profit margins of the physician management company to profit margins of other management services organizations. Unfortunately, there is not a great deal of reported data for small medical management services companies. However, one source appraisers can use is the data compiled by Risk Management Association (RMA). RMA reports profit margin data in a number of ways. Accordingly, the appraiser should work to gain a thorough understanding of the underlying data and use professional judgment to select an incisive metric for comparison to their subject.

Profit Margin Comparison Data—Although the RMA data is not specific to medical industry data, the included companies do provide management services. The appraiser should demonstrate that the service nature of the business is similar enough to management services specific to the healthcare industry to warrant a meaningful comparison.

RMA Statement Studies—The *RMA Annual Statement Studies: Financial Ratio Benchmarks 2007-2008* is a collection of financial information provided by RMA members including banks of all sizes as well as non-bank institutions. The "Valuation Edition" classifies the underlying data by asset size and revenue size and allows the appraiser to view the results in deciles, which is useful for presenting a range of values. The ability to access deciles is only available on CD-ROM.

Chapter 31: Valuing Management Services Contracts between Physicians and Hospitals

Appraisers can consider utilizing the data reported for "Administrative Management and General Management Consulting Services" which is comprised of businesses primarily engaged in providing operating advice and assistance to businesses and other organizations on administrative management, records management, office planning, strategic and organization planning, site selection, new business startup, and business process improvement.

While certainly not identical to the services to be provided by an MSO, the identified set of services provided by the companies included in the RMA data are similar in nature and may be suitable for comparison. Analyzing the RMA data is certainly a place to start, but there may be other sets of data that apply or better apply to the particular agreement being appraised.

Considerations for the Analysis of Profit Margin Data—Appraisers should be comfortable that the underlying data can be reasonably compared to the management company data. Issues such as the dates of published information, company asset and revenue size, as well as geography should be considered for reasonableness.

Profit Margin Comparison: Conclusion—The analysis of overall profit margins for physician management companies that provide expanded services to a hospital can assist in determining if the proposed compensation results in a profit margin consistent with similar firms in the marketplace. Profit margins within the identified range can be a useful determinant for a conclusion of fair market value.

Relative Profit Margin Comparison

This approach views the agreement from the hospital's perspective "before and after" implementation of the MSC. To complete this analysis, an appraiser can assess a hospital's historical income and expenses to determine if the additional costs associated with contracting with an MSO to provide management services have a material impact on a hospital's margin for that particular reporting unit.

By outsourcing management duties to an MSO, a hospital frequently acquires an increased scope of services but incurs higher labor costs due to a physician management company's use of physician managers. This drives an expectation of some type of financial impact to the hospital. The question then becomes whether a rational relationship exists between the margins of a hospital department before and after entering into the Agreement. If there is a material impact to a hospital's margins, it may be an indicator that compensation is excessive. That is, a comparison of "before-and-after" profit margins can help determine whether a hospital's payment to an MSO for services under the subject agreement is consistent with fair market value.

"Before and After" Analysis—A meaningful "before and after" analysis can provide valuable insight into the financial significance of entering into an outsourcing agreement for management services. An appraiser should prepare this type of analysis to measure the reasonableness of the financial impact of a hospital's decision to outsource services.

Chapter 31: Valuing Management Services Contracts between Physicians and Hospitals

Several different profitability measures can be used on a before and after basis, including EBIT, EBITDA, net income, etc. Because it is difficult and often subjective to assign indirect costs to hospital departments, appraisers might utilize a metric such as "contribution margin," which is generally defined as net revenue less direct expenses. This limits the appraiser's need to focus on whether or not the correct level of overhead is being allocated into the hospital department. This is irrelevant to the "before and after" analysis as long as the complete set of management costs are included in the analyzed expense data.

An appraiser should be able to work with hospital management to determine expected future margins for the hospital department by estimating the likely financial results on an "as is" basis. That is, the "before" scenario would be based on current conditions and expected trends for the hospital department. The "after" scenario is based on the expected financial results of entering into the management agreement.

The results of this analysis should be discussed with management to ensure a good understanding of the underlying differences between the two scenarios. The results of the appraiser's analysis coupled with management's input will help drive the report narrative critical in describing the value of the analysis as it relates to fair market value.

The "before and after" analysis is intended to detect unreasonable changes in the relative margins of a hospital department. If the expected difference in the contribution margin percentages under the "before and after" scenarios is relatively minor, this may indicate that the fee arrangement would not materially impact the hospitals ability to earn net margin or other comparison metric for the relevant department If there is a large variance in contribution margins, in the absence of extenuating circumstances, further scrutiny would be required to determine whether the services to be provided by the physician management company are necessary and reasonable.

Critical to the analysis of a MSC is a thorough analysis of the nonfinancial benefits of the proposed arrangement. Benefits to the hospital could include items such as: improved clinical quality through protocol review and development, improved patient satisfaction, and increased efficiencies with respect to supply usage and patient flow.

It is often unclear at the time of the appraisal the extent to which nonfinancial benefits of a proposed transaction will be realized. If a management company has been in place these values may be quantifiable. For example, the value of improved clinical quality could be measured through the reduction of "never events" (where the patient or insurer does not pay for complications). The associated savings could also be calculated through a documented reduction in the unit's average length of stay, etc.

When reconciling a "before and after" analysis, it is important for an appraiser to document all of the financial and nonfinancial benefits expected to be received in the engagement. There can be circumstances under which a hospital's contribution margin goes down significantly, but the payment per the contract is at fair market value due to the expected benefits of the arrangement which are not quantifiable at the time of appraisal.

Chapter 31: Valuing Management Services Contracts between Physicians and Hospitals

If, in considering all of the relevant facts and circumstances, an appraiser believes that a reasonable balance is maintained between contribution margins, the "before and after" analysis can provide an indication that the proposed compensation is consistent with fair market value. That is, if increased management costs associated with an arrangement are not unreasonable when considering the benefits expected to be accrued to a hospital, the appraiser's analysis can support the notion that the proposed compensation is within the range of fair market value.

Management Fee Benchmarking

As a secondary method to analyze the reasonableness of the fees to be paid by a hospital to a physician management company, appraisers can use a procedure consistent with the market approach. This procedure consists of comparing the fees to be paid to a physician management company as a percentage of a hospital's net revenue and comparing this percentage to the fees paid by other healthcare entities for management services.

There are only a limited number of sources for this type of data. Large national hospital management companies will not contract with a hospital to provide management services to a single department of a hospital. These companies, such as MedCath Corporation and Health Management Associates, Inc., typically own and operate hospitals and the level of detail in their public filings is insufficient to isolate the financial activity related specifically to management services. Therefore, as a substitute, an appraiser might consider turning to ambulatory surgery center (ASC) benchmarking information to analyze management services provided to a hospital surgery department.

While it is clear that a hospital's surgery department is not the same as an ASC, the skill set required of its managers is similar to that required by an ASC in terms of scheduling, personnel management, equipment selection, budgeting, marketing, quality assurance, utilization review, and general regulatory compliance. A fair number of surgery center managers also have hospital backgrounds. Therefore, an argument can be constructed that supports drawing a comparison between the management of an ASC versus the management of a surgery department of a hospital as a procedure to test the fair market value status of MSC compensation.

One of the available ASC surveys is published by MGMA, the *Ambulatory Surgery Center Performance Survey*. By using the different stratifications of data in this survey and potentially others, an appraiser can identify a relevant range of management services expense as a percentage of revenue. This particular survey has good information for benchmarking purposes but has historically not had high levels of participation. As always, appraisers should be cautious when applying and relying on surveys with small data sets. A second data source to consider is Intellimarker's *Ambulatory Surgical Center Financial and Operating Benchmarking Study*, which also presents management fee data.

The appraiser must be aware that a hospital's surgery department might generate net revenue in excess of the 90th percentile of ASC survey data. However, given that a hospital surgery department,

Chapter 31: Valuing Management Services Contracts between Physicians and Hospitals

in isolation from the rest of the hospital, may have a similar cost structure to an ASC with respect to management expenses, the appraiser must be cognizant of two limiting factors:

- Hospitals are more regulated than ASCs. The additional burdens of regulatory compliance are either the direct or indirect responsibility of management. This would tend to make management services to a hospital service line more costly and more valuable.

- Because net revenue may be high compared to ASC revenue, the appraiser must be sure that management fee percentages are congruent with the actual expenses of the physician management company. There is risk that a percentage applied to a hospital's surgery department revenue would overstate the amount that a management company would need to cover its costs and achieve a reasonable profit. Therefore, this analysis of survey data cannot be conducted without a corresponding analysis of the costs associated with providing the services, which would need to be included elsewhere in the report.

Management Fee Benchmarking: Conclusion—The market cost of acquiring management services can be determined either by securing comparative pricing for the desired services or by assessing the market for similar services through benchmark surveys. Because competitive market data may not available for management services provided to a single service line of a hospital, appraisers may consider the use of cost surveys for a variety of healthcare entities as a proxy for market level hospital expense. This can assist the appraiser in determining if the costs of purchasing management services are reasonable. It is not uncommon for appraisal reports to specifically state that a particular procedure was not relied upon as a primary means of analyzing the fair market value of the proposed compensation. Instead, reports often indicate the performance of this type of analysis is a secondary measure of the reasonableness of the conclusions drawn from the consideration of other methodologies. There are circumstances in which an appraiser may rely upon this methodology as a primary determinant of fair market value, but this, of course, should be decided by an appraiser on a case by case basis.

PART FOUR—SPECIAL TOPICS IN MSC APPRAISAL

'At Risk' Compensation

One of the variables seen in some MSC compensation formulas is the inclusion of an "at-risk" component. This creates a situation where MSC compensation is variable. From an appraisal point of view, appraisers must turn to management for guidance as to the expected outcome in terms of paid compensation to the MSO.

Once the expected compensation has been quantified, the appraiser can then consider the impact of volatility in compensation outcomes. In certain scenarios, compensation may be in excess of the appraiser's initial range of fair market value. In this situation, the appraiser should consult with

Chapter 31: Valuing Management Services Contracts between Physicians and Hospitals

management and legal counsel to determine whether this is an acceptable risk or if the agreement can be modified to include some type of cap at the high end of the range of fair market value.

Appraisers do not have the capacity to independently judge the likeliness of achieving a given performance benchmark. Therefore, the appraiser must rely on management to develop a sound understanding of the benchmarks and then consider whether or not management's estimates appear reasonable. The goal of the appraiser should be to collaborate with hospital management to ensure that the best possible estimates are used in the FMV Opinion. In some cases, there will be insufficient data to make a judgment. In these instances, there will often be contractual clauses that trigger a reassessment of fair market value when compensation falls outside of an expected range.

Return on Investment (ROI) Analysis

One topic worth considering is the use of return on investment analyses with respect to the appraisal of MSC's. The general theory is that a physician's investment in an MSO selling services to a hospital should produce a return on investment similar to the return of an arm's-length investment. While an analysis can be performed in which the MSO's expected ROI is compared to market data, its probative value may be limited.

General market theory provides that investors will invest in businesses that generate the highest return commensurate with their tolerable level of risk. As a corollary, the greater the risk of an investment, the greater the return an investor would require to invest in the business. When reviewing ROI market data for management companies, as compared to a projected return on investment for an MSC, it is very difficult to compare the risks of publicly traded companies to the risks of the management company under consideration. In addition, the capital investment required to run a publicly traded management company is significantly different than a one-off management company that may not even have its own separate office.

When the ROI definition of [Income/Investment] can change so significantly by the level of underlying investment, the usefulness of the entire ROI measure is suspect. For instance, if an appraiser determined a 10% - 75% ROI to be the range of fair market value, it seems unreasonable that investors of the management company (20, for example) could achieve "fair market value" status by each contributing an additional $5,000. The following two examples illustrate how unnecessary capital could distort the fair market value analysis:

Example 1:
Range of Fair Market Value—10% - 75%
Initial Expected Investment—$100,000
Initial Start-Up Costs and Working Capital Needs—$50,000
Capital Reserve—$50,000
Expected Annual Return—$85,000
Return on Investment = 85% ($85,000 ÷ $100,000)
Conclusion = not consistent with fair market value

Chapter 31: Valuing Management Services Contracts between Physicians and Hospitals

Example 2:
Range of Fair Market Value—10% - 75%
Initial Expected Investment—$200,000
Initial Start-Up Costs and Working Capital Needs—$50,000
Capital Reserve—$150,000
Expected Annual Return—$85,000
Return on Investment = 42.5% ($85,000 ÷ $200,000)
Conclusion = consistent with fair market value

It does not stand to reason that holding $150,000 in capital reserve versus $50,000 in capital reserve for a non-asset intensive firm is a good measure of fair market value. [Editor's Note: In a business valuation engagement, this would be considered "excess working capital" and a non-operating asset.] While analyzing the adequacy of the capitalization of a management company is certainly a reasonable inquiry for an appraiser, the ability to depress ROI to be within a given range does not lend much credence to an ROI analysis.

Also of concern with respect to an ROI analysis is the selection of market data and the development of a comprehensive framework upon which to benchmark the characteristics of the management company for indicators of where in the range of identified ROIs the subject company should fall. Limiting factors include differences in size, services provided, differences in capital structure (publicly traded companies typically carry more debt than private MSC's), which make comparisons more complicated.

While this type of analysis cannot be relied upon as a primary measure of the fair market value of this type of contractual arrangement, attorneys sometimes request that this procedure be considered by an appraiser.

CONCLUSION

This chapter was designed to provide appraisers with an introduction to physician– hospital relationships in the management services context, an overview of the appraisal process, detailed descriptions of fair market value analyses, and an introduction to select special topics related to MSCs.

The goal of the chapter is not to establish a right and wrong way of analyzing MSC compensation, but to provide a framework for analyzing fair market value in the context of these types of arrangements. Ultimately, an appraiser must collaborate with all of the interested parties to gather sufficient evidence to certify that the MSC compensation is reasonable and consistent with fair market value.

Chapter 32
Valuating Clinical Co-Management Arrangements

By Greg Anderson, CPA, ABV, CVA and Scott Safriet, AVA, MBA

Origin of the Co-Management Arrangement

As the healthcare landscape continues to mature, most healthcare organizations find themselves caught in an era of increasing competition, changing reimbursement structures and shifting operational paradigms. Nowhere is this more notable than amongst hospitals, whether an independent not-for-profit or one that is part of a large public for-profit system. Benchmarks and key clinical performance indicators have taken on increased importance as evidence-based medicine and pay-for-performance initiatives continue to evolve within the payer community. Technological advances allowing less invasive interventions and improved outcomes offer the promise of revolutionizing the way medicine is practiced. These market forces demand a shift in the health care industry toward collaborative care and aligned incentives, yet collaborative relationships among health care providers trigger compliance and business strategies that have not yet been fully played out in the marketplace and the health care regulatory environment. These market forces and compliance risks lead physicians and hospitals to create relationships that concentrate on patient outcomes, safety and satisfaction, while yielding incentives that reward positive behavioral changes by both parties.

Increasing competition

"Hospitals and physicians care for the same patients. Both feel squeezed by stagnating payment, rising expenses, proliferating regulations and rising consumer expectations."[1] Hospitals also face pressures from consumers for the latest technology, shortages of hospital personnel, increased regulation, rising cost of liability premiums, and the obligation to provide care to the uninsured.[2] Yet, the American Hospital Association recognizes that "the integration of clinical care across providers, across settings, and over time" is needed to reduce fragmentation in health care delivery and improve the quality and efficiency of care.[3]

Changing landscape of where services are performed

Advances in technology have transformed the delivery of health care in more ways than could have been imagined just a few decades ago. Many procedures that were exclusively performed in an inpatient setting are now furnished in hospital outpatient settings, specialty hospitals and ambulatory surgery centers, significantly altering the landscape in the industry and raising the

Chapter 32: Valuating Clinical Co-Management Arrangements

element of competition between physicians and hospitals. These surgical and diagnostic facilities represent viable alternatives to acute care hospitals, as patient and physician convenience, cost and comfort lure insured patients away, leaving hospitals with an ever increasing mix of indigent and low-pay patients. In some cases, hospitals have entered into clinical co-management arrangements (CCMAs) with physicians who operate competing facilities. The competitive environment leads hospitals to place even more emphasis on achieving better outcomes, higher patient satisfaction scores and more cost-effective care.

Difficulty in securing robust medical directorships

Health care regulatory enforcement activity by the Federal government continues to spotlight medical directorships as highly susceptible to abuse, with examples of arrangements alleged to be disguised payments for referrals of Federal health care program beneficiaries. Many of these suspect arrangements lack substantiation of duties and fail to implement appropriate systems for tracking and documenting hours worked in providing these services. Further, medical directorship arrangements can sometimes conflict with clinical duties and schedules, resulting in inattention to all but the most basic of administrative duties.

Need for increased efficiencies and quality in patient care

Responding to America's inefficient health care system, momentum is building for a shift to a pay-for-performance (P4P) system that correlates financial rewards with improved outcomes in patient care.[4] P4P systems reward providers with compensation for performance measured against a pre-defined set of targets or objectives that define what will be evaluated. In implementing such a system, it is important to identify performance standards for establishing the target criteria, as well as the rewards that are at risk, including the amount and the method for allocating the payments among those who meet or exceed the established thresholds.[5]

The Leapfrog Group[6] summarizes P4P programs containing incentives based on risk and rewards to providers. Various financial models exist in the marketplace, but while many models address quality-based measures, performance metrics could target any number of variables, including profitability, patient volume, or quality of care.

The nature and amount of bonuses and incentives play a significant role in determining how much providers will alter their current behaviors. For the P4P program to work, providers must be convinced of the benefits to investing in the necessary technology and in complying with the requirements of the program.

Although the P4P movement is gaining in popularity, several challenges still exist. First and foremost, providers, purchasers, and health plans have conflicting views on the funding of such programs. In addition, providers expect the program to be funded with new money, while

Chapter 32: Valuating Clinical Co-Management Arrangements

purchasers and health plans believe the incentives should be generated through savings or by replacing fee schedule increases with performance payments.

Consumer-directed health care empowers consumers by giving them a direct financial stake in the quality and cost of their own care and by providing information on the quality and price of health care so as to make informed decisions. Pressure by purchasers for transparent reporting is bringing about quality and efficiency improvements through hospital and physician collaborative and P4P arrangements. In addition, with Medicare and other payers, it is clear that data reporting on quality is a precursor to performance-based reimbursement.

There are other issues of fairness of such incentives due to the inherent differences among specialties, geographic limitations, and financial barriers faced by providers. Despite these issues, P4P arrangements are becoming increasingly popular throughout the United States.

Government and payer recognition of core measures of quality

Common measures of quality performance allow physicians to receive feedback and tie performance to financial and other incentives through P4P and public quality reporting. Performance measurements for physicians are not as fully mature as those for institutional providers; however, these programs have gained traction in the past few years, particularly with the introduction of quality-reporting initiatives by professional organizations, accrediting agencies, and Medicare. These programs contribute to physicians' acknowledgement that other stakeholders have the right to monitor their behavior and hold them accountable.[7]

Opportunities for increased hospital-physician alignment

Longstanding hospital-physician integration strategies that remain in the current market include employment of physicians by hospitals, creation of physician-owned or joint venture hospitals, development of clinically integrated hospital/physician entities, formation of community health information networks, and various hybrids and permutations of provider integration strategies. Physician engagement is essential for many cultural and behavioral changes to be successful at the hospital level. Compensation under these plans is increasingly tied to success with varying measurements that align financial incentives among the provider groups.

CCMAs represent a way to integrate hospital and physician management of clinical services and generally exist between physicians and hospitals. Physicians in a CCMA provide management services to a hospital that go beyond traditional medical director roles, and the CCMA involves physicians as participants in the day-to-day management of the hospital's clinical service line operations. The primary advantage of the CCMA is the significant operational input of the physicians and the alignment of physician and hospital interests to achieve improvements in the overall efficiency and quality of patient care.

Chapter 32: Valuating Clinical Co-Management Arrangements

Structure of Co-Management Arrangements

Rationale for formation

Competition. As described above, competitive market forces are primary drivers in the creation of the CCMA. Below is a hypothetical example of a community hospital's struggle to remain competitive by aligning with physicians:

> Healthy Regional Hospital (one of two hospitals in its community) and one of the local cardiology groups reached an impasse when the cardiology group announced its intent to open a cardiac catheterization lab (cath lab) in its own clinic facility. When the cath lab became operational, Healthy Regional saw a substantial decline in commercial patients in its own cath lab, and revenues immediately began a sharp downward trend. As tensions grew, the cardiology group began demanding payment for emergency department call coverage and one of the cardiologists—the medical director for cardiology at Healthy Regional—elected not to renew his administrative contract.
>
> Healthy Regional's new CEO entered into discussions with the cardiology group to form a CCMA. This endeavor would be in the form of a joint venture, which would acquire and operate the cardiologists' cath lab and enter into a management agreement with the Healthy Regional to manage the Healthy Regional's entire cardiology service line in the creation of a cardiovascular center of excellence. The end result was an immediate change in the competitive landscape in the community for cardiac care and an integration of the hospital and cardiology group in the operation of the joint venture CCMA.

Alignment with payer interests and participation in payer incentive programs. Many payers, including the Federal government, recognize the benefits to patients through enhanced quality care. The Centers for Medicare and Medicaid Services (CMS) sponsors various demonstration projects to encourage and reward improvements in quality health care. One such project is the Premier Hospital Quality Initiative demonstration project, which incorporates a P4P element that pays hospitals performance-based bonuses for quality measures associated with clinical conditions such as heart attack (acute myocardial infarction, or AMI), heart failure, pneumonia, coronary artery bypass graft (CABG) and hip and knee replacements.[8] The Joint Commission and CMS co-developed the Specifications Manual for National Hospital Quality Measures, which contains core measures of quality for AMI, heart failure, pneumonia, surgical care improvement, pregnancy and related conditions, and children's asthma care. Other payers, such as Blue Cross Blue Shield, have developed their own quality incentive projects, many of which reward providers with bonuses tied to achievement of quality targets. The Healthcare Effectiveness Data and Information Set (HEDIS)[9] is used by many such health plans to measure performance.

Chapter 32: Valuating Clinical Co-Management Arrangements

The following continues the hypothetical example of Healthy Regional Hospital and its cardiology CCMA:

> Healthy Regional and its cardiology group partner developed a set of quality measurements that paralleled those of a significant local payer. The payer's program resulted in bonuses to the hospital for attainment of the payer's targets in quality care. The CCMA agreement for Healthy Regional's cardiac service line included financial incentives for reaching these quality measures, which effectively aligned the interests of the joint venture and the hospital with those of the payer.

Consolidate medical directorship duties. With physicians as partners in clinical quality, the CCMA affords hospitals with opportunities to develop more robust duties and responsibilities for physician administrative positions over the managed service line. CCMA agreements provide for significant enhancements in administrative requirements for clinicians, to which a portion of the compensation is related, and often allows for a consolidation of multiple, and sometimes duplicative, directorships. The hypothetical example of Healthy Regional's CCMA continues below:

> In developing the CCMA, Healthy Regional's legal counsel recommended termination of the hospital's separate cardiology and cath lab medical directorship agreements, in favor of inclusion of the duties of both in the administrative responsibilities of the CCMA. The previous medical directorship agreements contained no requirements for contemporaneous documentation of physician administrative time and were paid in fixed monthly amounts, representing a significant compliance risk. Legal counsel also recommended additional requirements related to physician participation in quality assurance meetings, attendance at quality assurance training conferences, and additional duties as medical staff liaison to address quality concerns with staff physicians. As will be discussed in detail further in this chapter, such medical director duties were "folded into" the CCMA and were paid out of the negotiated management fee.

Consolidate other physician duties. With broader ties to physicians in hospital service line management, hospitals can use CCMAs to address other service deficiencies and staffing needs. The Healthy Regional Hospital example continues as follows:

> Prior to the CCMA joint venture, a rift developed between the hospital and cardiology group, and the hospital found itself in a position of seeking sporadic and expensive emergency department on-call coverage in the specialty of cardiology. Through negotiations with the cardiology group to enter into the CCMA with the hospital, Healthy Regional was able to gain physician commitment to cover emergency call on a 24/7/365 basis. This embedded call arrangement saved Healthy Regional nearly $200,000 in call coverage compensation paid to other local physicians and physician staffing companies and resulted in dependable cardiology coverage and improved patient quality outcomes.

Chapter 32: Valuating Clinical Co-Management Arrangements

Applicable specialties

CCMAs apply to many physician specialties, particularly when there is a relationship between the physician's administrative and clinical skills and the success of the hospital in meeting quality measures within the related service line. Some of the more common specialties, in no particular order, include the following:

- Cardiology / Cardiovascular Surgery
- Orthopedic Surgery
- General Surgery
- Oncology
- Sleep Lab

Ownership

Commonly, CCMAs are formed and operated as joint ventures between hospitals and physicians. While typically done on a 50/50 basis, it is not uncommon to see many different variations. For example, while a hospital may want to have good alignment with its physicians, it may still want to retain ultimate control, and therefore, may prefer a 60/40 split instead (*i.e.,* in favor of the hospital). The impact of this issue will be discussed in more detail later in this chapter. Because some CCMAs have ownership in health care facilities (*e.g.,* cardiac catheterization lab or outpatient imaging center), these are also structured as joint ventures, although usually with a significant requirement for capital infusion to accommodate the acquisition and/or operation of the outpatient facility, and subject to applicable fair market value analysis.

Organizational structure

The CCMA entity is typically established as a limited liability company. This entity enters into a management services arrangement with the hospital for purposes of managing the hospital's designated service line. This is often accomplished in a manner that meets the requirements of the Stark exception for personal service arrangements and the anti-kickback statute's safe harbor for personal services and management contracts.

Fee structure—base-plus-incentive

CCMAs ordinarily maintain management service agreements with the hospital for the service line management, with a multi-stage compensation structure. The first stage is a base

Chapter 32: Valuating Clinical Co-Management Arrangements

compensation associated with the day-to-day medical direction, management and administrative duties and responsibilities under the contract, and such services are paid for out of the base management fee, as further discussed in our chapter. This level of compensation is most often paid in the form of an hourly rate applied to the documented hours spent by the physicians furnishing the administrative services. This amount generally does not vary depending on the performance of the manager or the success in meeting the quality objectives of the arrangement.

The second component of compensation is the P4P incentive compensation, which is based on the attainment of clinical quality objectives and such other factors as patient satisfaction and budgetary compliance. There is a wide variety in the way P4P incentives are calculated and paid, the more common of which are described in the following section.

Incentive metrics and Pay-for-Performance

Core measures developed by CMS, The Joint Commission, and third-party payers are often referred to as organizations develop quality standards for incentive pay under CCMAs. Table 1 below summarizes core measures from CMS and the Joint Commission for heart failure:

Table 1: Heart Failure Core Measures

Medicare Short Name	Description
Discharge Instructions	Heart failure patients discharged home with written instructions or education material given to the patient or caregiver at discharge or during the hospital stay addressing all of the following: activity level, diet, discharge medications, follow-up appointment, weight monitoring, and what to do if symptoms worsen.
Evaluation of LVS Function	Heart failure patients with documentation in the hospital record that left ventricular systolic (LVS) function was evaluated before arrival, during hospitalization, or is planned for after discharge.
ACEI or ARB for LVSD	Heart failure patients with left ventricular systolic dysfunction (LVSD) and without both angiontensin converting enzyme inhibitor (ACEI) and angiontensin receptor blocker (ARB) contraindications who are prescribed an ACEI or ARB at hospital discharge. For purposes of this measure, LVSD is defined as chart documentation of a left ventricular ejection fraction (LVEF) less than 40% or a narrative of left ventricular systolic (LVS) function consistent with moderate or severe systolic dysfunction.
Adult Smoking Cessation Advice/Counseling	Heart failure patients with a history of smoking cigarettes, who are giving smoking cessation advice or counseling during the hospital stay. For purposes of this measure, a smoker is defined as someone who has smoked cigarettes anytime during the year prior to hospital arrival.

Chapter 32: Valuating Clinical Co-Management Arrangements

Quality measures like those above for heart failure are used as measurements in CCMAs to assess the level of quality attained through the management of the hospital service line. For example, a cardiac CCMA would likely measure quality for AMI, heart failure, and cardiac artery bypass graft (CABG), comparing the actual quality scores with expected or target scores. In the case of the Discharge Instructions core measure, the quality score is a fraction: the numerator of which is the number of patients discharged home that were given discharge instructions or educational materials that included all of the required instructions (i.e., activity level, diet, discharge medications, follow-up appointment, weight monitoring, and what to do if symptoms worsen), and the denominator of which is the total number of heart failure patients discharged home.

One of the key distinctions between a CCMA and a traditional management agreement is the P4P component, which provides for incentive compensation to the manager above and beyond the base compensation. The incentive compensation component is often based on attainment of quality scores like the one described above for heart failure. In the example of discharge instructions to heart failure patients, a score of 78 % may be the target score for discharge instructions. Reaching or exceeding this level would result in incentive bonus credit or payment to the CCMA manager. CCMAs vary in the application of bonus methodology, as some examples include specific amounts of bonus payment upon attainment of target scores or credit in the form of points to the manager, which are accumulated for purposes of determining payment under the CCMA incentive bonus formula.

Determination of FMV

In the context of a co-management arrangement, determining the fair market value (FMV) of management fees is critical not only for compliance with existing laws, but also to the ultimate success of the project. Therefore, before any hospital undertakes the implementation of a co-management arrangement, it is critical to determine the FMV of the management fee, including both the base and incentive components (these two components were discussed earlier in the chapter), in order to maintain compliance with existing laws and regulations.[10] However, there is little valuation theory for an appraiser to rely upon in assessing performance-based incentive or pay-for-performance programs, as these arrangements are still relatively new and, therefore, vary widely in their structure.

In theory, the FMV of the management fee could be established by assessing the required number of work hours needed to provide the management services, multiplied by a FMV hourly rate. However, as with most management services and/or service arrangements, the exact number of required work hours cannot reasonably be determined in advance. Most management arrangements observed in the marketplace are not based upon actual underlying time to establish the management fee.

Chapter 32: Valuating Clinical Co-Management Arrangements

Valuation theory applicable to CCMAs

The following three fundamental principles co-exist in the theory of business valuation: (i) the Principle of Substitution, (ii) the Principle of Alternatives, and (ii) the Principle of Future Benefits; each of these can be transferred into the context of valuing service agreements. For example, the Principle of Substitution states that an investor will pay no more for a service than for a substitute of equivalent economic utility. Under the Principle of Alternatives, each party to a contemplated contractual arrangement has alternatives to consummating the deal. The Principle of Future Benefits emphasizes that the value of an investment is based on the future benefits the investment will provide. These principles lay the foundation for the application of valuation methodology to developing a conclusion of fair market value in compensation arrangements as well, including CCMA compensation arrangements.

Valuation methodology

Several methods exist for determining value in a compensation arrangement. The justification for the use of a particular method or methods will often be dictated by the facts and circumstances of the contractual arrangement. These methods of valuation can be generally categorized into three broad approaches: Cost-based, Income-based and Market-based. Within the each valuation approach, one or more methods exist for determining value, with the relevance and applicability of each depending on the circumstances and the analyst's judgment.

In considering the value of payments under a CCMA, it is critically important to consider the value of the individual components of compensation (base compensation and incentive compensation), as well as aggregate compensation under the arrangement. A key consideration that must not be overlooked is that the methodology (and application thereof) that considers the fair market value of the individual components of compensation may differ from methodology that considers the value of aggregate compensation. The valuation analyst should consider the merits and applicability of all three valuation approaches in developing an appropriate FMV range.

Income-based approach

Valuation of a CCMA under the income-based approach considers the economic benefits enjoyed by the hospital from the management services furnished by the manager. The following examples demonstrate that quality care does indeed result in economic benefit, thus demonstrating that quality measures bring economic value to an organization:

- Use of beta blockers reduces 30-day readmission rates by 22 %.[11]

- Use of aspirin can result in savings of $209 per patient.[12]

Chapter 32: Valuating Clinical Co-Management Arrangements

- Use of smoking cessation advice results in a $15 savings per patient.[13]

- Use of a one-time 60 minute educational session prior to hospital discharge results in a 35 % reduction in hospital costs.[14]

The measurement of these and other benefits can represent a proxy for the fair market value of P4P arrangements, such as CCMAs. In two examples to follow, the FMV of physician management services are attributed in part to the reduction in costs associated with reduced hospital readmissions and reduced lengths of stay (LOS).

Reduced hospital readmissions

Valuation of a CCMA under the income-based approach may consider the value of management services as attributable in part to the reduction in costs associated with reduced readmissions. It is widely accepted that hospital readmissions increase the cost of care for patients by thousands of dollars. Therefore, an increase in quality that reduces readmission rates not only results in better patient care but is also accompanied by the potential of significant economic benefit to facilities.

The application of this method involves research and financial analysis regarding the link between pay-for-performance quality measures and the financial benefits of preventable patient readmissions. For example, a hospital managed under a CCMA for its cardiology service line found that its use of discharge instructions, prescription of ACE inhibitors and smoking cessation programs are associated with a reduction in readmissions for heart failure patients. These findings are consistent with research studies performed on heart failure quality core measures.

Measurement of the reduction of readmission rates resulting from the improvement of heart failure core measures begins with a study of research on the subject of reduced readmissions for this disease when the quality of care improves. Working directly with the hospital to determine the projected decrease in readmissions associated with these core measures results in expectations of hospital readmission rates for the managed facility under the CCMA.

Financial analysis of the implications associated with reduced readmissions involves work with the financial staff of the managed facility in projecting the changes in revenues, expenses and profitability resulting from the projected reduction in readmissions. The application of readmission methodology under the income-based approach to valuing CCMAs involves projections of the financial impact of changes resulting from improvements in quality, and this methodology requires experience in hospital reimbursement and costs. In some cases, market research and the valuation analyst's study of the applicable financial effects can be inconclusive or show that measurable cost savings are either negligible or nonexistent.

Chapter 32: Valuating Clinical Co-Management Arrangements

In the example of the hospital managed under the cardiac CCMA, findings linking reduced readmissions with core measures of quality resulted in a predictive analysis of reduced readmissions, and related cost savings could be projected from the anticipated decline in readmission rates.

It is important to consider under such an analysis that a portion of the benefits attributable to the management services under the CCMA can be a result of factors outside the manager's control. These must be factored into the analysis by the valuation analyst, lest an erroneous conclusion be reached. For example, in a hospital-physician CCMA in which no joint venture is established between the hospital and physicians and the physicians are designated as managers of the hospital service line, it is critical to determine the portions of management duties that are associated with the work of the physicians and the hospital. On the other hand, in cases in which a joint venture CCMA is in place, other environmental factors that contribute to patient readmission rates should be considered. Examples of these include changes in technology, pharmaceuticals, and clinical pathways associated with the managed disease.

It is also vitally important that the valuation analyst consider whether the methodology employed resulted in the value of the base compensation, the incentive compensation or the aggregate of both when considering the FMV of a CCMA. In the example of the hospital managed under a cardiac CCMA, the savings resulting from reduced readmission rates resulted in a proxy for FMV associated with the total administrative and management services under the CCMA; thus, the value conclusion reached was applicable to the aggregate compensation under the CCMA, because reaching the target core measures scores and the achievement of savings in this example was attributed to the entire scope of management under the CCMA. This becomes critical in the valuation of a CCMA because of the various components of compensation. For example, had the valuation analyst determined under the income approach that the resulting value was only applicable to the incentive compensation rate and not to the base component of compensation, the conclusion of value for the entire CCMA could have been significantly overstated.

This principle of properly matching the valuation methodology to the appropriate conclusion of value can be demonstrated in the use of market-based "inputs" into the income-, cost- or market-based approaches. For example, a conclusion of value based on a "build-up" of the value of physician administrative time (at market hourly rates) and a separate value for the P4P aspect of the agreement must be tested to ensure that the aggregate value conclusion is not overstated. In a simplistic sense, consider the fact that the administration of aspirin upon arrival in a myocardial infarction case yields value under the P4P aspect of the compensation arrangement. This compensation, in addition to compensation for the medical directorship element of the arrangement, is consistent with the proposition that meeting the core measure brings additional value to the patient, hospital, and insurer. However, methods that arrive at a conclusion of FMV for the aggregate service (including the medical directorship element), such as an income-based approach model that considers aggregate value to the hospital for the totality of services under the CCMA, should not then be added to the value of medical directorship compensation as separately computed.

Chapter 32: Valuating Clinical Co-Management Arrangements

Value of reduced hospital lengths of stay

Valuation of a CCMA under the income-based approach may also consider the value of management services as attributable in part to the reduction in costs associated with reduced hospital lengths of stay (LOS). Increases in quality that support reduced LOS data result in improved patient mortality, better care, and significant economic benefit to facilities.

Similar to the study of readmissions, the application of this method involves research and financial analysis regarding the link between pay-for-performance quality measures and the financial benefits of reductions in patient LOS. For example, studies have shown that a one-day improvement in LOS can significantly reduce the costs of caring for patients with pneumonia. Measurement of these reductions in LOS resulting from the improvement of core measures can be obtained with data from the managed facility and from market data on other facilities in the market, using such data as measurements from CMS on hospital quality incentives and data from the American Hospital Directory.

Financial analysis of the implications associated with reduced LOS involves analysis by the managed facility to projecting the changes in revenues and profitability associated with the projected decrease in LOS associated with the managed disease. Findings linking reduced LOS with improvements in core measures of quality can result in a study of reduced readmissions and related cost savings. As with readmission rates, market research and the valuation analyst's study of the applicable financial effects can be inconclusive or show that measurable cost savings are either negligible or non-existent.

Cost-based approach

Discussion of applicable service lines. While the income approach certainly has applicability in many instances, the two more prevalent valuation approaches utilized in the marketplace appear to be the cost and market approaches. In considering the cost approach (or "replacement cost" methodology), a possible alternative to the implementation of an agreement is a hospital's opportunity to engage various medical directors (either as employees or as independent contractors) to manage its identified service line offerings. As an example, were a valuation analyst engaged to determine the FMV of a cardiovascular co-management arrangement, such service line offerings for consideration would likely include, but not be limited to: medical cardiology, interventional cardiology, cardio/thoracic surgery, cardiac rehabilitation, cardiac intensive care and outpatient programs and services. Giving consideration to the number of medical directors that might reasonably be required to provide physician management to hospital's service lines, the valuation analyst could then consider the following key factors:

- What are the projected gross charges of the service line? Since most co-management arrangements are implemented for the management of existing service line offerings, looking at the most recent 12-month period of historical charges would be advisable.

Chapter 32: Valuating Clinical Co-Management Arrangements

Alternatively, if the service line in question is a new division of a hospital, for example, a cardiovascular center of excellence, it would be acceptable to rely on the hospital's annual projected gross charges for purposes of an analysis.

- How diverse are the service offerings? The diversity of service offerings in combination with the complexity of clinical operations and the volume of procedures, including both inpatient and outpatient services, require significant coordination among numerous physicians, associated hospital services, and a myriad of operational details. For example, for hospital- specific reasons, a proposed orthopedic co-management arrangement might exclude outpatient rehabilitation services. In this instance, all other things being equal, the resulting range from methodology employed under the cost approach would likely be significantly less than an arrangement that was all encompassing.

Determination of comparable positions. Once the scope of the service line is discussed and agreed upon, the determination of the particular physicians and the corresponding amount of time required to provide medical director services is dependent upon a variety of factors, including (i) the size of the hospital, (ii) the complexity of services being provided and (iii) the number of procedures performed. In consideration of these factors, the initial step would be to develop an expectation for the number of medical director positions that could have *reasonably* been supported in the absence of the co-management arrangement. The valuation analyst can either develop this guidance based on his or her own experience and informed judgment with similar arrangements, or can engage the services of an independent staffing expert (typically an independent physician with previous department head experience). By evaluating the applicable service lines, the valuation analyst should be in a good position to identify the relevant medical director positions, ensuring that there is no overlap and/or redundancy in the identification of such positions.

For example, if the valuation analyst were analyzing a co-management arrangement for a comprehensive cardiovascular center of excellence, by evaluating each potential service line component, it would not be unreasonable to conclude that the following Table 2 contains the six, part-time medical director positions that might have been engaged. Such positions would have been engaged on an independent contractor basis, in the absence of a co-management arrangement, to manage daily operations and provide needed oversight to hospital's service line.

Table 2 – Identified Service Line Medical Directorships

Medical Cardiology
Interventional/Invasive Cardiology
Cardiovascular and Cardiothoracic Surgery
Cardiac Rehabilitation & Recovery
Cardiac Intensive Care (CCU)
Outpatient Programs and Services

Chapter 32: Valuating Clinical Co-Management Arrangements

Determination of appropriate compensation rate. In order to determine the appropriate compensation for each identified medical director position, it is important to note that compensation earned by a physician in his specialty practice of medicine *may not* be directly comparable to the compensation for medical directorship duties. However, the valuation analyst should recognize that with regard to a medical director position, a hospital would need to identify not only an appropriately experienced clinician, but an individual with the skills and experience necessary to perform required administrative duties. At this point in the analysis, the valuation analyst should also give recognition to the size of the hospital. For example, a 500-bed, trauma facility, given its size and focus, would likely need the support for a more diverse community of both inpatients and outpatients as opposed to a 150-bed regional hospital. The implication here is that there is likely support for higher compensation and/or allowable monthly hours for the 500-bed trauma facility arrangement.

Given the above, the valuation analyst should review available compensation levels expected to be earned by a physician in his or her specialty practice of medicine as a reasonable starting point.[15] However, in most instances, such compensation values are likely *not* comparable to the FMV of compensation for medical directorship duties as described above. As stated above, in valuing administrative positions, a FMV analysis is not intended to establish an "opportunity cost" related to professional services. Therefore, to develop the most appropriate compensation range, the valuation analyst should review and consider available published sources of administrative compensation data. In developing compensation ranges, as *general* guidance, the valuation analyst should consider benchmark compensation values between the 50th (*i.e.,* the median) and 90th percentile values. However, as will be discussed below in detail, depending on the specific facts and circumstances of the arrangement, it may be reasonable to limit the upper end of the compensation range to the 75th percentile (*e.g.,* in those instances where there are multiple medical director positions, relatively low program revenue, etc.).

Determination of appropriate hours. Once a compensation range is identified, the next step in the cost approach is to identify the applicable hours attributable to each identified position. For ease of calculation, the typical convention would be to identify an annual number of hours, as this number would then be multiplied by the hourly compensation range identified above to determine the annual compensation attributable to the position. To identify the appropriate range of expected monthly hours, the valuation analyst should consider the following questions:

- How large is the hospital's service line to be managed (as measured by net revenue)?

- How large is the hospital, as measured by licensed bed count?

- Does the co-management arrangement contemplate the management of a single campus, or multiple campuses?[16]

Chapter 32: Valuating Clinical Co-Management Arrangements

As with the development of the compensation range, the valuation analyst should review and consider available published sources of administrative data regarding ranges of hours for respective administrative positions. The valuation analyst should view general guidance for annual hours as reasonably going up to the 75th percentile for most arrangements. However, as with the derivation of the hourly compensation, specific facts and circumstances might warrant exceeding this upper range. For example, using a hypothetical cardiovascular center of excellence, co-management arrangements relate to unique cardiovascular surgery services, in that these services are also provided to a hospital's patients that are transferred in from smaller regional hospitals where such services are not provided. In recognition of the added complexity of this relationship between hospitals, it would have been reasonable to utilize benchmark data for the 90th percentile to determine the number of hours required by the applicable cardiovascular surgery medical director positions. Such reasoning follows from our review of other comparable arrangements where either (i) the services are now more complex due to the varied parties involved, thus requiring a more experienced physician, or (ii) a physician would negotiate a higher reimbursement due to the additional burden of the second campus, etc.

Once these two market data points are identified, this data would then be used in conjunction with the appropriate staffing breakdown as detailed from Table 2 to determine the total FMV range as determined under a cost approach. Table 3 provides a simple summary of a hypothetical analysis used to determine the FMV range, under a cost approach, associated with the management of hospital's cardiovascular center of excellence:

Table 3: Summary of Cost Approach

Service Offering	Hours Worked Per Year	50th Percentile Hourly Rate	50th Percentile Annual Compensation[17]	90th Percentile Hourly Rate	90th Percentile Annual Compensation
Medical Cardiology	215	$134	$28,810	$174	$37,410
Interventional/Invasive Cardiology	150	$141	$21,150	$184	$27,600
Cardiovascular and Cardiothoracic Surgery	856	$186	$159,216	$256	$219,136
Cardiac Rehabilitation & Recovery	174	$150	$26,100	$173	$30,102
Cardiac Intensive Care (CCU)	220	$164	$36,080	$200	$44,000
Outpatient Programs and Services	220	$164	$36,080	$200	$44,000
TOTAL	1,835		≈ $308,000		≈ $402,000

Chapter 32: Valuating Clinical Co-Management Arrangements

Market based approach

The market approach to valuation provides an effective methodology to determine a FMV range while eliminating the constraints of a time-based analysis as required under a cost approach. However, the uniqueness of each co-management arrangement precludes *direct* market comparisons of the subject arrangement to other arrangements in the marketplace. Therefore, a critical part of the valuation process involves breaking down the co-management arrangement into its individual components. Once individual tasks, objectives, and performance metrics are identified, the arrangement can be compared to other arrangements with similar elements.[18] By comparing specific elements on an item-by-item basis, the valuation analyst is able to assess the relative worth of each metric[19], and determine the presence or absence of each metric in comparison to the comparable arrangements. Then, with reasonable objectivity, the valuation analyst is able to assess the overall relative value of the identified arrangement by comparing it to other available market arrangements.

Identification of services performed. In order to compare the management services to be provided by a manager against market comparables where the management fees are known (*i.e.,* a review of ASC management agreements), the valuation analyst should consider the creation of a "scoring grid," whereby a weighting factor and point value are assigned to each specific identified task contemplated under the arrangement. The services to be included in the arrangement can usually be found in the draft agreement provided by counsel (usually as an exhibit to the body of the agreement), but often times such services are also either contained within the body of the agreement or not addressed in detail at all. In these latter two examples, the valuation analyst should have a detailed discussion with counsel with regard to the detail and "breadth" of the contemplated management services, as the accurate identification of the specific services to be performed is the main driver within the market approach. For example, will the management company simply "assist" with the credentialing function by coordinating the necessary paperwork, or will the management company be responsible for handling the credentialing function? Once these services are identified, the valuation analyst will have a grid comprised of up to 35 specific services. This comprehensive listing of services typically provided by management companies will be a "baseline" listing from which the valuation analyst can then begin to make a series of "normalizing" adjustments to the available management fee percentages in developing a range applicable to the agreement.

Identification of baseline market comparables. One common type of management arrangement whereby significant market data is available involves the management of ambulatory surgery centers (ASC) by professional management companies. Generally, ASC management companies provide comprehensive management services, with recognition that the services do not include services that typically require the involvement of physicians.

Since there is a plethora of available data in the marketplace, the valuation analyst can conduct a survey of identified national or regional ASC management companies, identifying the management fee ranges, stated as a percentage of collections (or net revenue). In the authors' experience,

Chapter 32: Valuating Clinical Co-Management Arrangements

management fees range from approximately 3 % to 6 % of collections; however, the vast majority of such arrangements involve the existence of a full-time on-site manager who is compensated by the ASC, thereby effectively raising the total management fees to levels higher than 6 %. [Editor's Note: These arrangements are described in more detail in this Guide's chapter on Ambulatory Surgery Centers.] If there is not enough marketplace data available on such arrangements, the valuation analyst can also attempt to identify other management arrangements involving such programs as substance abuse, respiratory therapy, and physical therapy.[20] In considering the applicability of these arrangements to the agreement, however, the valuation analyst should be careful to ensure that such arrangements do not include clinical staffing services, as such arrangements would report a higher than expected management fee and result in a skewed analysis. As a result, a review of such arrangements may be helpful from a comparison perspective, but may not be as reliable as information gleaned from more "typical" management company arrangements.

Adjustments given scope of services. Armed with the data developed in steps 1 and 2 above, the valuation analyst is now in a position to utilize the developed grid to evaluate and score each task under the agreement. Some aspects to consider in the creation of a grid would be the following:

- Task Importance—Develop a point system that values the complexity and anticipated time commitment required by each identified task, possibly ranging from 1 to 5. For example, "arranging for the purchase of liability insurance, paid for by the hospital," is a much complicated and time intensive task as compared to the task of "develop community relationships that result in a satisfied referral base." As such, the scoring grid should be able to effectively distinguish between the two, and in this example, the latter task may be scored a 5, whereas the former task may be scored as a 3.

- Task Involvement—In management agreements, it is common to see tasks identified in an agreement that are meant to be more "supportive" in nature as compared to the management company having sole responsibility for the task. As referenced in the hypothetical example above, will the management company simply "assist" with the credentialing function by coordinating the necessary paperwork, or will the management company be responsible for handling the credentialing function? The grid should be able to delineate between the two, as the former task is certainly more limited in nature.

- Weighting Factor—A weighting factor is recommended to be developed and applied to each task based on the above identified categories. For example, a limited task may receive a weighting of 1.0, whereas a full task may receive a weighting of 3.0. Similarly, those tasks not included in the proposed agreement may receive a weighting of 0.0.

As a result of the above calculations, the analysis will yield a total point value, calculated as the sum of the various point values assigned in the above *task importance* section. In addition, the grid will produce a weighted point value, which would be the product of each specific point value, multiplied by the identified weighting factor. For example, if there were 30 tasks,

Chapter 32: Valuating Clinical Co-Management Arrangements

resulting in a total score of 110 possible points, the weighted score might have totaled 80 points, resulting in a final score of 73 % (*i.e.,* 80 / 110). In order to determine a comparable value for the management services, the results of the above-described scoring grid (*i.e.,* 73 %), would be applied to the identified market range for management fees. In this example, the result would be a *preliminary* fee range for the management services, under a market approach, of from 2.2 %[21] to 4.4 %[22] of net revenue.

Adjustments given revenue size. Depending on the specific facts and circumstances of the arrangement, the valuation analyst should also give consideration to the application of a *discount* of the preliminary range. While this may not appear to be intuitive, it is logical for a number of reasons. First, although the management services contemplated by the co-management agreement are likely comprehensive in nature, the hospital likely has the ability to rely upon many aspects of its infrastructure.[23] This is a significant point to consider, in that this reduces the hospital's required degree of dependence upon the management company. Second, in most instances, the revenue size of a service line subject to a co-management agreement is significantly higher than the typical ASC that is subject to an outside management arrangement, thereby warranting a lower fee as a percentage of net revenue.[24] Third, research indicates that as revenue sizes grow, there is an increased likelihood that a management organization would discount its normal management fees in recognition of the fact that it is able to achieve certain economies in the arrangement. Furthermore, once net revenue exceeds a certain threshold, the correlation between net revenue and the cost to manage the services is significantly reduced. Therefore, in recognition of this disconnect, and in order to apply a certain degree of conservatism to the analysis, the valuation analyst should consider the application of a discount to the initially calculated fee range, with a reasonable range of discounts being from 10 % to 30 %.

Reconciliation of the approaches. In considering the outcomes of the valuation approaches, the market approach is generally preferable in valuing management services. However, the market pproach can be subject to certain limitations since, as discussed above, there are no directly comparable market values. The income approach contains some element of speculation in the projection of LOS and readmission impact and may sometimes yield inconclusive results. Therefore, the valuation analyst must weigh these factors in determining the degree of reliance placed upon these methods. With respect to the cost approach, the buildup of the medical director time requirements does not necessarily value the services that will be contributed by a hospital partner in the management company (since the valuation of such services would result in significant subjectivity). As such, a common approach would be to give each methodology equal weighting, and take a simple average of the calculated values. In other instances, however, there may be a need to provide a double weighting of one approach or the other in recognition of additional arrangement dynamics. For example, if the valuation analyst were analyzing a relatively "light" management arrangement (*i.e.,* a small service line like ENT at a regional hospital), given the relatively scaled down services contemplated under that type of arrangement, an equal weighting may not necessarily accurately capture the essence of the arrangement.[25] In this instance, the valuation analyst might elect to normalize the valuation by giving a *double weighting* to the results of the cost approach.

Chapter 32: Valuating Clinical Co-Management Arrangements

Valuing the total fee

Within the framework of co-management arrangements, a reliable and comprehensive valuation approach should provide a FMV range that encompasses the total management fee (*i.e.,* both the base management fee *and* the incentive management fee). In addition, each co-management arrangement is unique and reflects specific market and operational factors which are singular to the specific setting. Therefore, by providing a broad range for the total management fee, the valuation analyst also provides the hospital with the opportunity to establish the proportion of the management fee payable as a base management fee versus the incentive management fee (which will be based upon achievement of the predetermined measures). That said, although the hospital should have significant discretion in establishing the relative value of the base management fee as compared to the incentive management fee, there are certain regulatory and market-based constraints that should be observed. In particular, regulatory considerations may affect the maximum percentage of the total fee that can be incentive based.[26]

However, within those constraints, it is not likely beneficial to set the incentive management fee at too low a percentage of the total management fee (since such an over-emphasis on the base fee would seem to diminish the ideals of achieving the pre-established performance objectives). As general guidance, the base management fee should generally be no higher than 60 % and no lower than 25 % of the total management fee. These constraints are based on observations of similar arrangements in the marketplace and, in the authors' opinion, preserve the general intent of the hospital with respect to the desired outcome of the co-managed services.

Issues impacting the FMV analysis

Once the FMV range of the management agreement is identified, it is important that the valuation analyst recognize that each management arrangement is completely unique, and as with most arrangements, these "unique" attributes can have a significant impact on the resulting FMV of the arrangement. This section of the chapter will focus on some of the common areas for discussion amongst the parties, each of which should be thoroughly explored by the valuation analyst.

The use of medical director positions. A very commonly used practice within co-management arrangements is to utilize medical directorships for select physician participants. While the intent of the arrangements are to typically have the management company perform all of the management services, it is not uncommon to find that certain of the management services are intended to be provided through a medical director arrangement provided by a qualified physician associated with the management company. While this is an acceptable practice, the valuation analyst should ensure the following:

- Such medical director arrangements are to be paid as an expense from the identified management fee. Since the FMV "build-up" of the management fee as discussed above in the Cost Approach section already contemplates the use of such positions, paying

Chapter 32: Valuating Clinical Co-Management Arrangements

for these positions outside of the management fee would be considered redundant. However, there are instances in which such positions would be allowed in a manner consistent with FMV, such as in a situation in which the medical directorship was for a specific subset service line, which was now going to be "carved out" from the management company (*e.g.,* in a cardiac co-management arrangement, the parties might agree to carve cardiac rehabilitation out of the arrangement). In this instance, the valuation analyst should ensure that the net revenue provided for the analysis specifically "excludes" any revenue attributable to the cardiac rehabilitation so as to not allow for redundancy of payment.

- If all parties agree on the treatment of revenues and positions, it is important that the valuation analyst ensure that such medical director arrangements will be for a number of monthly hours and rate that is *consistent with FMV*. As a good rule of thumb, the valuation analyst should ensure that the proposed hours and rate are equal to or below the upper end of the values provided in Table 3 above.

- Since the intent of a co-management arrangement is that there are no "passive investors," the valuation analyst should also give consideration to the magnitude of the total monies being allocated toward medical directorships. As discussed above, the base management fee is meant to compensate the management company for handling the day-to-day management services, which are expected to be handled in a proportional manner to each party's ownership. Therefore, assuming a 50/50 ownership (as is typical), it would not be reasonable to have a disproportionate share of the base management fee paid out as medical directorships. While there is latitude in the ultimate percentage "ceiling" that can be approved, another good rule of thumb is that *no more than* 50 % of the base fee should be allocated to medical director positions. By doing so, the valuation analyst can avoid any possible interpretation that this management company is simply a vehicle under which a hospital intends to distribute monies to the physicians while allowing the physicians to perform less than the required share of the overall duties. This is especially critical when the medical directorships are going to be with physician owners.

Provision/purchase of administrative services. It is not uncommon in many arrangements for the management company, whether jointly owned or not, to have a need for certain administrative services. In the case of a physician-owned management company, given the "loose" structure of the arrangement, and since there is no need for dedicated building space and/or staff, the physician owners simply do have the requisite infrastructure necessary to manage their operation. Such needed administrative support services may include, but not be limited to, the following: accounting, financial statement preparation; tax return preparation; payroll processing; legal support and clerical support, and in most instances, the hospital is more than willing to provide such services to the management company. By doing so, however, the hospital has just unintentionally (or intentionally as the case may be) created a fair market value implication by providing additional services that have a defined market worth.[27]

Chapter 32: Valuating Clinical Co-Management Arrangements

Ensuring equitable division of responsibilities. As has been stated numerous times throughout this chapter, the co-management structure is intended to be a vehicle that ensure that hospital and physician members both actively participate in the provision of the management services (i.e., there are no passive investors in a management company). Furthermore, a key representation in most management company analyses is that the resulting division of responsibilities within the management company (i.e., the management contribution of each party related to providing the management services), will be in approximate proportion to the ownership percentages determined. However, under most arrangements, assuming a 50/50 ownership structure, it would be virtually impossible to ensure that all of the required duties are handled on an "exact" 50/50 basis. That said, if the parties each own 50 % of the management company, and will thus receive 50 % of the management fee, the valuation analyst should ensure that (i) each party takes an active role in the management duties, and (ii) each party will manage efforts in approximate proportion to their ownership.

Summary

In summary, the emergence of incentive-based models for the delivery of healthcare services has contributed to the development of a broad range of new opportunities for hospital / physician partnerships. One of the most common forms of these partnerships involves the establishment of a hospital/physician-owned co-management company for the purpose of managing a specific hospital service line. This type of arrangement offers significant value propositions to *patients*, who have improved access to needed services; to *hospitals*, which realize improved patient satisfaction, operational efficiencies, financial controls and enhanced clinical quality; and to *physicians*, who are incented to effectively and efficiently manage the service line and facilitate the achievement of identified performance-based metrics.

However, the uniqueness of each co-management arrangement precludes *direct* market comparisons of the subject arrangement to other arrangements in the marketplace. Therefore, a critical part of the valuation process involves breaking down the co-management arrangement into its individual components. Once individual tasks, objectives and performance metrics are identified, the arrangement can be compared to other arrangements with similar elements, and/or analyzed by completing a "build-up" of comparable positions that would be required in the absence of such an arrangement. Regardless of the approach undertaken, determining the fair market value of these types of management agreements is of paramount importance, and by incorporating the above elements into a valuation repertoire, one can be assured that a thorough analysis will result.

Bibliography

Specifications Manual for National Hospital Quality Measures, The Joint Commission and Centers for Medicare and Medicaid Services.

Chapter 32: Valuating Clinical Co-Management Arrangements

Callender, Arianne N. et al., "Corporate Responsibility and Health Care Quality: A Resource for Health Care Boards of Directors", Office of Inspector General

http://oig.hhs.gov/fraud/docs/complianceguidance/CorporateResponsibilityFinal%209-4-07.pdf. (September 2007).

Lindenauer, Peter K. et al., "Public Reporting and Pay for Performance in Hospital Quality Improvement" New England Journal of Medicine Vol. 356, no. 5 (February 2007): 486-96.

Rosenthal, Meredith B. et al., "Paying For Quality: Providers' Incentives for Quality Improvement" Health Affairs Vol. 23, no. 2. (March /April 2004): 127.

Williams, Jeni. "Making the Grade with Pay for Performance: 7 Lessons from Best-performing Hospitals" Healthcare Financial Management (December 2006): 79.

"Improving Acute Myocardial Infarction Reliability and Outcomes", Institute for Healthcare Improvement http://www.ihi.org. [Internet accessed on January 24, 2008].

"Keeping 'Pay' In Pay-For-Performance (P4P) for Anesthesiologists: A Strategic Analysis of the Opportunities and Threats to Anesthesia Related to the Emerging P4P Trend" Smith Anderson Blount Dorsett Mitchell & Jernigan, LLP (September 2005).

"Testimony before House of Representatives Committee on Ways and Means, Subcommittee on Health: Promoting Quality and Efficiency of Care for Medicare Beneficiaries" Pacific Business Group on Health www.pbgh.org (March 2005).

---

1. Cohn, "Making Hospital-Physician Collaboration Work," Healthcare Financial Management Association, October 2005
2. "Improving Health Care: A Dose of Competition," U.S. Department of Justice and the Federal Trade Commission, July 2004
3. Am. Hosp. Ass'n., *Aligning Hospital and Physician Interests: Broadening the Concept of Gainsharing to Allow Care Improvement Incentives*, 2005
4. Med-Vantage, *Pay for Performance Incentive Programs in Healthcare: Market Dynamics and Business Process.*
5. Congressional Research Service, *Pay-for-Performance in Health Care.*
6. "Incentives and Rewards Compendium," http://www.leapfroggroup.org
7. Pham and Ginsburg, *Unhealthy Trends: The Future of Physician Services*, Health Affairs 26(6):1586-1598, November/December 2007
8. Accessed from http://www.cms.hhs.gov/ on June 13, 2008
9. National Committee for Quality Assurance
10. In addition, it should be noted that according to Rev. Proc. 97-13, certain not-for-profit entities with public bond financed property may also face additional Internal Revenue Service scrutiny regarding the split of the Management Fee. The authors would recommend that any hospital considering a co-management arrangement involve outside counsel in the process.

Chapter 32: Valuating Clinical Co-Management Arrangements

11. Accessed from http://www.cms.hhs.gov/ on November 13, 2007
12. Bridges to Excellence, *Cardiac Care Analysis – Savings Estimates*
13. Ibid
14. Centers for Health Care Strategies, Inc., *ROI Evidence Base: Studies on Congestive Heart Failure*
15. A good resource for cash compensation values can be obtained from the *MGMA Physician Compensation and Production Survey*, as this publication is a commonly used benchmark percentile in the determination of appropriate FMV compensation values.
16. In the authors' experience, it is not uncommon to see co-management arrangements covering multiple campuses for a hospital, particularly if certain services (*i.e.,* rehabilitation) are handled in a distinct location. This dynamic increases the complexity of the management arrangement, and would likely warrant an adjustment to the hourly and rate ranges.
17. Calculated by multiplying the number of hours worked per year by the hourly rate at the applicable percentile for each specialty (*i.e.,* 50th or 90th).
18. In the case of co-management arrangements, in the authors' experience, similar tasks and objectives might be found in ASC arrangements, which are readily available in the marketplace.
19. For example, metrics can be focused around tasks, objectives or performance outcomes.
20. Such arrangements may not be based upon designated percentages of net revenue. As such, to ensure an accurate comparison, it will be essential for the valuation analyst to convert each arrangement to a percentage of net revenue equivalent basis in order to facilitate comparisons.
21. .03 x 73%
22. .06 x 73%
23. Even if the agreement is not a traditional "co-management" agreement (*i.e.,* it is not uncommon to have such management companies solely owned by the physicians), the authors believe that the participating hospital will still be in a position to leverage aspects of its infrastructure.
24. In the authors' general experience, the "typical" revenue size of a co-managed service line might be in the $30-$70MM range, whereas the typical ASC has revenues in the range of $10MM or less.
25. In other words, the results of the Market Approach would likely understate the "value" of the services being provided by sole virtue of its reliance on the net revenue of the service line.
26. According to Rev. Proc. 97-13, certain not-for-profit entities with public bond financed property must ensure that the incentive portion of the management fee is not set too high as compared to the base fee, depending on the length of the contract term and other terms of the arrangement. Therefore, parties considering such arrangements are advised to seek the advice of experienced legal counsel prior to entering into any such arrangements.
27. In many instances, the valuation analyst is not asked to analyze and determine the FMV of such services. It is therefore acceptable to rely on the party's representation, and to list such as a governing assumption in the valuation report, that any such services will be subject to an appropriate FMV analysis.

Chapter 33

Fair Market Value: Ensuring Compliance within the Life Sciences Industry

By Ann S. Brandt, PhD, Jason Ruchaber, CFA, ASA, and Timothy R. Smith, CPA/ABV

OVERVIEW

The "life sciences industry," as it is frequently termed, encompasses a broad range of very different market sectors, including pharmaceutical, medical device, medical supplies/ equipment and biotechnology industries. Issues facing these sectors are similar in terms of escalating costs, increasing pressure from shareholders and a stringent regulatory environment. While these may be the best of times in terms of technological advances, companies within the life sciences industry are experiencing the same regulatory "wake up call" that the hospital sector experienced years earlier.

This chapter deals with the determination of fair market value (FMV) within the life sciences industry. In an effort to control health care costs and to maintain a level playing field within the healthcare industry, federal regulators are increasingly focusing their efforts on prosecuting violators of the anti-kickback and Stark laws as well as the False Claims Act. Resulting judgments to date have not been trivial, nor have they been isolated to any one particular segment of the life sciences industry. Numerous medical device and pharmaceutical companies have been targeted by the government, and all indications are that such compliance actions will increase for those companies that fail to comply with these laws, whether intentionally or not.

The determination of the FMV of most types of relationships between physicians and healthcare entities that compensate them, including pharmaceutical and medical device companies (as well as hospitals, clinics and clinical research entities), appears to be a significant issue for the government. As a result of recent action by the federal government, many pharmaceutical companies and medical device companies have been required to execute corporate integrity agreements (CIA) as part of their settlements.[1] CIAs are intended to cause the offending organization to develop a plan of self-improvement and self-monitoring, coupled with independent outside review to insure that the risk of future violations is minimized.

One element of a number of CIAs that have been executed with the government is the requirement that independent third party fair market value analyses be performed for all physician compensation arrangements over a certain dollar value threshold. For example, in the recent case of five of the country's largest medical device companies, this minimum threshold was identified to be compensation of $500 per hour. These specific requirements imposed by certain CIAs signal the government's concern when physicians receive "high" rates of compensation.

Chapter 33: Fair Market Value: Ensuring Compliance within the Life Sciences Industry

REGULATORY ISSUES IN THE LIFE SCIENCES SECTOR

Regulatory restrictions within the healthcare industry often prohibit marketing practices that are common in other less regulated industries. For example, the federal anti-kickback statute places significant constraint on the marketing and sales practices of healthcare-related companies. As a result, fraud and abuse enforcement activities tend to focus on areas the government believes offer the greatest potential for abusive arrangements, including arrangements between physicians and those entities that derive revenue from federal healthcare programs.

The Anti-Kickback Statutes

The federal anti-kickback statute places significant constraint on the marketing and sales practices of healthcare-related companies. This statute provides that *anyone who knowingly and willfully pays or receives anything of value to influence the referral of business, which is reimbursable in whole or in part by a federal healthcare program, can be charged with criminal penalties, civil monetary sanctions, and even exclusion from federal healthcare programs.*[2]

Clearly, relationships between medical device companies and physicians are encountering increased scrutiny from regulators. Questions are being raised with regard to the amount of money physician advisors and consultants are being paid, as well as possible conflicts of interest that may be inherent in these arrangements. The reality is that while relationships between physicians and medical device companies are not black and white, the relationships are often perfectly permissible provided they are appropriately structured.

With regard to the services being provided, experienced physicians offer a level of expertise that often cannot be duplicated by any other group of professionals. As a result, their input into product design and development, as well as their insight into market requirements, is invaluable. In fact, arrangements between medical device companies and physicians encompass a whole host of necessary services including product design, development, research and clinical trials, physician training and marketing. The government's concern with these types of arrangements revolves around the idea that they could be used as a vehicle to induce purchasing or prescribing of the company's products. Therefore, the government is focusing its attention on various types of *"consulting fee"* arrangements[3] to determine if they are tied to prescribing practices or to usage patterns involving the company's products. Of obvious importance in this scrutiny is whether the fees for these services appear to be in excess of FMV for actual services rendered. Similarly, medical device companies are being targeted for investigation when there is doubt as to the legitimate need for the particular consulting services, or when there is a lack of documentation of the services rendered.

By way of example, there have been several well-publicized enforcement actions for which the alleged illegal conduct included improper or sham consulting arrangements. In July, 2006, Medtronic reached a settlement agreement with the U.S. Department of Justice in which it agreed to pay $40 million to the United States and participating states to settle allegations

Chapter 33: Fair Market Value: Ensuring Compliance within the Life Sciences Industry

stemming from two *qui tam* lawsuits.[4] These lawsuits, which were brought under the federal False Claims Act (FCA), allege that Medtronic made illegal payments to physicians to promote its spinal products in violation of the federal healthcare program anti kickback statute. The alleged illegal payments included (i) consulting and royalty agreements for which little or no work was performed, as well as (ii) all expenses paid trips to lavish venues. In addition to the $40 million payment, Medtronic was required to enter into a five year CIA.

In another well-publicized case, to resolve allegations under the FCA, four major medical device manufacturers entered into civil settlement agreements with the government for a combined total of $311 million. The government alleged that the companies provided financial incentives to physicians including consulting agreements and lavish trips to persuade physicians to use their joint replacement products. The government alleged that by offering illegal inducements, the identified companies violated the FCA by causing hospitals to seek and obtain reimbursement from Medicare. To avoid criminal prosecution, each of the identified companies entered into an 18-month deferred prosecution agreement, under which they agreed to multiple remedies including the posting on their web sites of the names of consultants, along with the amount of payments to these consultants. In addition, each of the identified companies entered into a five year CIA.

Another case involves a physician who accepted kickbacks from a medical device company in return for using the company's products. Even though criminal prosecutors have rarely directly targeted physicians, a physician who accepts a kickback in return for using a product can be as culpable as the company that provided the kickback. Dr. Patrick Chan, a neurologist in Arkansas, paid a $1.5 million civil settlement in January, 2008, and pled guilty to soliciting and accepting kickbacks from Blackstone Medical. The kickbacks included gifts and payments for sham consulting agreements and fake research studies.

In another recent case, Lincare Holdings paid $10 million and entered into a five year CIA for allegedly providing kick-back payments to physicians in the form of sporting and entertainment tickets, rounds of golf, golf equipment, fishing trips, meals, office expenses and medical equipment, all of which were intended to induce the physicians to refer patients to the company. The government also alleged that Lincare provided kickbacks in the form of purported consulting arrangements that had no basis or foundation for payment. In addition the government alleged that Lincare violated the Stark Law by accepting referrals from parties to the consulting agreements.

The Stark Law

The federal physician self-referral ban (commonly referred to as the "Stark" law) prohibits referrals by a physician, or an immediate family member[5] to an entity for "designated health services"[6] if the physician has a "financial relationship"[7] with the entity receiving the referral. Within the framework of the Stark Law, (i) the physician may not make a referral to the entity for the furnishing of designated health services for which payment may be made

Chapter 33: Fair Market Value: Ensuring Compliance within the Life Sciences Industry

under Medicare or Medicaid, and (ii) the entity may not bill for designated health services furnished pursuant to such referral. It is also important to note that the Stark Law is not an intent based statute; therefore, receipt of a referral from a physician where a financial relationship exists results in a violation of the law, regardless of intent. Because it is not necessary to prove intent, a physician who has a financial relationship with an entity cannot make a referral to the entity for the furnishing of designated health services, unless it is demonstrated that the arrangement qualified for one of the identified personal services exemptions (or the so called "safe harbors").

In making the determination of whether the Stark statute applies to a particular arrangement, three questions must be answered. First, is the referral for a designated health service? Second, does this arrangement involve a referral of a Medicare or Medicaid patient by a physician or an immediate family member of a physician? Third, is there a financial relationship of any kind between the referring physician or family member and the entity to which the referral is being made? If the answer to any question is 'no', Stark does not apply. If the answers to all three questions are 'yes', then it is necessary to determine whether the arrangement falls within a statutory exception (*i.e.*, a safe harbor). Within Stark II Phase III regulations, which went into effect on December 5, 2007, CMS modifies and clarifies the Stark Law exceptions, particularly the regulations governing physician compensation arrangements. For the purposes of this chapter, we will discuss just one of these safe harbor changes …the one that deals with FMV.

Within the framework of Stark II Phase II, CMS created a voluntarily safe harbor provision within the definition of fair market value applicable to hourly payments to physicians for their personal services. Specifically, CMS identified two acceptable methodologies for calculating the FMV of physician services. The first method limited the hourly payment to the average hourly rate for emergency room physician services in the relevant market, provided there were at least three hospitals with emergency room services in the market. The second method was based on the average of the "50th percentile national compensation level for physicians in the same specialty" using at least four of six specified salary surveys, and dividing the result by 2,000 hours to establish an acceptable hourly rate.

In response to a broad range of negative industry comments concerning these methodologies, CMS eliminated specific reference to these methodologies in Phase III. CMS, however, indicated that it would continue to scrutinize fair market value arrangements as an essential component of many Stark Law safe harbors. CMS also addressed concerns regarding overreliance on independent appraisals, explaining that "while good faith reliance on an independent valuation (such as an appraisal) may be relevant to a party's intent, it does not establish the ultimate issue of the accuracy of the valuation figure itself."[8] CMS stated that "the appropriate method for determining fair market value for purposes of the physician self-referral law will depend on the nature of the transaction, its location, and other factors and that use of multiple, objective, independently published salary surveys remains a prudent practice for evaluating fair market value." It is also important to note that the regulations generally allow "any commercially reasonable methodology" for calculating fair market value.

Chapter 33: Fair Market Value: Ensuring Compliance within the Life Sciences Industry

Some recent Stark cases include the following:

- On March 17, 2008, Hardeman County Memorial Hospital, a 24-bed critical access hospital in rural Quanah, Texas, reached a settlement agreement with the OIG and the Department of Justice regarding an alleged 11 year long violation of the Stark law. In conjunction with the settlement agreement, Hardeman County Memorial Hospital was ordered to pay $398,231 and enter into a 3 year CIA.

- In May 2005, St. Joseph Mercy-Oakland Hospital in Pontiac, Michigan, paid a $4 million settlement related to a number of potential Stark Law violations that the hospital self-disclosed to the OIG. The hospital was not required to execute a CIA.

A common misconception is that the Stark law is the same as the anti-kickback statute. They are different laws, in different titles of the Social Security Act and different in scope. While the Stark statute pertains only to physician referrals under Medicare and Medicaid, the anti-kickback statute is much broader and affects anyone engaging in business with a federal health care program. The Stark statute does not require bad intent; a tainted financial relationship violates the Stark law regardless of good intentions. In contrast, the anti-kickback statute requires specific intent and violations may result in criminal actions.

The False Claims Act

The FCA is the federal government's primary civil remedy for improper or fraudulent claims. Originally enacted during the Civil War to reduce widespread fraud in government contracts, it applies to all federal programs, ranging from military procurement contracts to health care benefits. People who "knowingly" submit false claims may be found liable under the act for penalties of between $5,000 and $10,000 for each false claim plus up to three times the amount of the damages caused to the federal program. Specific intent to defraud the government is not required: the government need only establish that the claim submitted is false and that it was submitted knowingly, as defined in the statute. Therefore, the FCA covers activity that would not be included under the traditional definition of fraud, which requires actual knowledge and the intent to defraud. As with most other civil actions, the government must establish its case by presenting a preponderance of the evidence rather than by meeting the higher burden of proof that applies in criminal cases.

The FCA contains a *qui tam* provision that allows citizens, on behalf of the United States, to sue companies or individuals for false or fraudulent billings submitted to the government. While it applies to any false claim submitted to the United States government, the FCA has proven to be a one of the government's most potent weapons for combating Medicare and Medicaid billing fraud. The *qui tam* provision is a major reason for its success, because it encourages whistleblowers to expose fraud in return for a substantial percentage of money the government recovers. In general, a *qui tam* plaintiff can receive between 15% - 25% of the total amount recovered if the government prosecutes, and 25% - 30% if litigated by the *qui tam* plaintiff.

Chapter 33: Fair Market Value: Ensuring Compliance within the Life Sciences Industry

CMS reports that Medicare and Medicaid spending was over $500 billion for the 2006 fiscal year. In CMS' 2006 *Management's Discussion and Analysis*, it recognized that one of the best ways to cut Medicare and Medicaid spending and maintain the integrity of the programs was to reduce Medicare and Medicaid fraud and abuse. For example, the Department of Health and Human Services reports that it collected almost $2.3 billion in 2006 from false claims suits. By implementing and actively enforcing anti-fraud compliance laws, the government can recover more money and, thus, curb the amount of Medicare and Medicaid spending.

By way of example, since the FCA was revamped and strengthened in 1986, Department of Justice data indicates it has saved U.S. taxpayers more than $20 billion.[9] Estimates indicate that the federal government recovers $15 for every $1 invested in FCA health care investigations and prosecutions. In fact, the FCA is so effective that the 2005 Deficit Reduction Act included incentives for states to enact similar laws. Prior to this, state and federal government split any recovered funds on a 50/50 basis, but under the new law, states with qualifying false claims acts will get a 60/40 split of any recovered funds in their favor. This translates into approximately 20% more revenue from identified Medicaid fraud, not only by *qui tam* actions, but also by public agencies including the Attorney General's office and local District Attorneys.

Some recent FCA cases and their headlines include the following:

- **Walgreen's Pharmacy settles $35 Million Qui tam case**—The Illinois based Walgreen's Pharmacy has agreed to settle a *qui tam* case for $35 Million that involves drug switching of the following drugs: Ranitidine (or Zantac), which inhibits stomach acid production; Fluoxetine (or Prozac), an antidepressant; and Eldepryl, known generically as Selegiline, which is used with other medications to treat the symptoms of Parkinson's disease. Reports showed that Walgreens fraudulently increased reimbursement from Medicaid by switching the form of the drug dispensed to Medicaid patients while providing no additional medical benefit to patients.

- **Medtronic/ Kyphon Settle for $75 Million**—Medtronic Spine, formerly known as Kyphon Inc., has agreed to pay $75 million to settle a False Claims Act lawsuit which exposed the company's sales and pricing strategy which was designed to further fraud against Medicare. The case was filed by whistleblowers, who will receive $14.9 million of the settlement as an award for helping uncover and prosecute the fraud on behalf of the American government and its taxpayers.

- **Biovail to Pay $25 Million**—Biovail Corporation says it will pay $25 million to settle criminal allegations related to kickbacks paid to doctors in order to induce them to prescribe Cardizem. The probe began after reports in T*he Wall Street Journal* and *Barron's* revealed Biovail was paying doctors up to $1,000 each to write prescriptions for Cardizem LA and write reports on the drug as a Phase IV clinical trial marketing scam.

Chapter 33: Fair Market Value: Ensuring Compliance within the Life Sciences Industry

- **HealthSouth Pays $14.9 Million**—HealthSouth and two doctors have agreed to pay $14.9 million ($14.2 million to be paid by the company and $700,000 to be paid by the two doctors) to settle charges the company was submitting false claims to Medicare and paying illegal kickbacks to referring physicians. The settlement results from disclosures made by HealthSouth in 2004 and 2005 to the U.S. Attorney for the Northern District of Alabama.

Industry Perspectives and Issues

The Pharmaceutical Industry

As regulators hone in on the relatively symbiotic relationship between pharmaceutical companies and the physicians who write prescriptions, it is inevitable that there will be heightened scrutiny of industry marketing practices. One outcome of this intensified focus is that regulators are increasingly concerned that payments to healthcare professionals could easily result in conflicts of interest by influencing judgment and prescribing practices.

Pharmaceutical companies are dependent on their marketing organizations to increase sales and expand market share, and these marketing organizations have succeeded in raising awareness of some very profitable pharmaceuticals. However, as successful as this type of marketing has been, the reality is that physicians are still the keepers of the prescription pad; therefore, a significant amount of marketing dollars continue to be focused on persuading physicians to write prescriptions for certain branded drugs.

Since it is clear that physicians need to understand the indications, actions and contraindications of medications they prescribe, physician education is of paramount importance. As new drug discoveries are made, no one questions the fact that physicians and other healthcare providers need to be educated about the unique properties and medical efficacy of these newer, potentially more effective (and often more costly) medications. However, busy physicians who may treat increasing numbers of patients, due to decreases in reimbursement, may have little time to meet with pharmaceutical representatives who are often forced to compete with patients for the physician's limited time.

In an effort to inform physicians about newly developed medications, it is becoming increasingly common practice for pharmaceutical companies to engage the services of "physician leaders" who serve as advisors and consultants to other physicians practicing medicine in their targeted markets. Experience has shown that physicians are more willing to listen to and change their prescribing patterns after obtaining information regarding the therapeutic effectiveness of new medications from other well-credentialed physicians. As a result, pharmaceutical companies engage legions of physician consultants and advisors to conduct promotional meetings and advocate on behalf of their products. Payments to these physician advisors and consultants, which often total millions of dollars per year, have become routine marketing expenses for pharmaceutical companies.

Chapter 33: Fair Market Value: Ensuring Compliance within the Life Sciences Industry

The Medical Device Industry

The competitive medical device market is characterized by rapid technological advances, frequent new product introductions, evolving standards, growing demand and increased scrutiny. Therefore, as costs associated with developing and successfully bringing new medical devices to the marketplace continue to increase, medical device companies are also dependent upon their marketing organizations to expand market share, while simultaneously limiting many historically successful marketing practices. For example, providing certain "perks" to physicians who use or recommend a particular brand of knee or hip replacement, by paying for first class travel to conferences for physicians and their families may have a significant impact on which implants the physician uses. Clearly, physicians play a critical role in deciding or strongly influencing which medical devices are implanted or otherwise used in a hospital procedure or inpatient stay for which the hospital is reimbursed. As a result, medical device manufacturers have a vested interest in persuading physicians to use or recommend a particular device.

As government regulators hone in on the symbiotic relationship between medical device companies and the physicians who use or recommend these products, it is inevitable that industry marketing practices focusing on promoting the sale of newer and more costly devices will be subject to increasing regulatory scrutiny. One outcome of this intensified focus is that regulators, who are increasingly concerned that any type of payment to a healthcare professional could potentially result in a conflict of interest by influencing medical judgment and clinical practices, are investigating a broad spectrum of arrangements.

Fraud and abuse enforcement activities tend to focus on areas the government believes offer the potential for abusive arrangements, including arrangements between physicians and those entities that derive revenue from federal healthcare programs. As a result, relationships between medical device companies and physicians are encountering the results of increased scrutiny from regulators. In particular, a series of recent settlements between the government and medical device manufacturers, regarding payments to physician consultants, has triggered intensified efforts to ensure that physician relationships are fully compliant with the applicable laws.

Despite these intensified efforts, the reality is that medical device companies need physician input to ensure that their products are designed, implanted and used appropriately. Experienced physicians offer a level of expertise that often cannot be duplicated by any other group of professionals. As a result, their input into product design and development, as well as their insight into issues involving surgical implantation of the devices, is invaluable. In fact, arrangements between medical device companies and physicians encompass a whole host of necessary services including (i) product design, (ii) development, (iii) research and clinical trials, (iv) physician training and (v) marketing. Therefore, as with the pharmaceutical industry, the government has focused its attention on various types of consulting fee arrangements to determine if they are tied to prescribing practices or to use of the company's products. Similarly, medical device companies are being targeted for investigation when there is doubt as to the legitimate need for the particular consulting services, or when there is a lack of documentation of services rendered.

Chapter 33: Fair Market Value: Ensuring Compliance within the Life Sciences Industry

Mitigating Risk

Risk is not binary; rather it consists of an infinite number of points on a continuum ranging from *less* risk to *more* risk. Therefore, it is important to recognize that there is likely some degree of risk associated with every decision, although in some instances, especially those involving an area of increasing regulatory scrutiny, the risk level may be substantially greater. Figure 1 below provides a graphical depiction of the varying levels of risk:

Figure 1: The Healthcare Valuation Risk Continuum

More Risk ⟵⟶	Less Risk

• No formal valuation process;
• Payment rates based upon:
  · Market surveys
  · Physician "demands"
	• Use of independent credentialed appraiser;
	• Strict compliance with the FMV definition;
	• Formal documentation process;
	• Use of accepted valuation approaches;
	• Applicable market data is free from bias;
	• Conclusions are logical, defensible and reproducible.

As clearly described earlier in our chapter, relationships between life sciences companies and physicians are encountering increased scrutiny from regulators. Since it is routine for life sciences companies to engage physicians for the performance of multiple services, it is imperative to note that even if only one aspect of the remuneration for these services is to induce referrals, the anti-kickback statute is considered to be violated for the entire arrangement.[10] Therefore, key questions focus on determining *the best way to mitigate the apparent risk in relationships between life sciences companies and physicians.* Therefore, given the broad scope of the anti-kickback statute, the "personal services" safe harbor may provide an appropriate framework for structuring the arrangement.[11] The personal services safe harbor provides protection for arrangements with physicians as long as seven standards are met:

1. The agreement is set out in writing and signed by the parties;

2. The agreement identifies all the services to be provided by the physician as well as the term of the agreement;

3. If the agreement is intended to provide physician services on a sporadic or part-time basis, the agreement specifies the exact schedule of any intervals, their precise length and the exact charge for such intervals;

4. The term of the agreement is for not less than one year;

5. *The aggregate compensation paid to the physician over the term of the agreement is set in advance, is consistent with fair market value, and represents an arms-length transaction that is not determined in a manner that takes into consideration the volume or value of any referrals;*

Chapter 33: Fair Market Value: Ensuring Compliance within the Life Sciences Industry

6. The services performed under the agreement do not involve any activity that violates state or federal law; and

7. *The aggregate services contracted for under the agreement do not exceed those which are reasonably necessary to accomplish the commercially reasonable business purpose of the services.*

Of particular focus in the balance of this chapter are the requirements related to FMV and commercial reasonableness emphasized in italics above. Arguably, one of the most significant aspects of achieving the requirements of the personal services safe harbor involves establishing the FMV compensation associated with these arrangements. Fortunately, regulators agree that by basing compensation for legitimate services on a supportable FMV rate (assuming that the other requirements listed above generally have been met), the risk of payments being characterized as "in exchange for referrals" will largely be eliminated (*i.e.,* less risk as depicted above). However, defining FMV and developing methodologies to accurately determine FMV have proven to be a bit more elusive, as the government has historically provided little guidance on how FMV compensation should be calculated.

Valuing Thought Leader Compensation

Within the hospital sector, physicians who are compensated for administrative services are frequently referred to as medical directors. Within the life sciences sector, physicians who provide marketing/administrative services are frequently referred to as "thought leaders." In this chapter section, key aspects of establishing the FMV of thought leaders are discussed.

The term "fair market value" is generally defined in the Stark regulations as the value in arm's-length transactions, consistent with the general market value. In the context of consulting or advisory arrangements between medical device companies and physicians, "general market value" means the compensation that would be determined as the result of *bona fide* bargaining between well informed parties to the agreement who are not otherwise in a position to generate business for the other party.[12]

Determining the FMV of compensation paid by a life sciences company to a physician for advisory and/or consulting services is critical, but as indicated above, is not easily established. In particular, the volume or value of referrals cannot be considered in the determination (whether directly or indirectly), and market data cannot be considered to the extent that the data represents transactions between parties who are "in a position" to refer patients to one another. Therefore, compensation arrangements based on similar relationships should not be used as the sole determinant of FMV, as these arrangements may represent *tainted* values. This ultimately limits the techniques and data that healthcare valuators can use, and it makes FMV very difficult for life sciences companies and physicians to determine or even understand. Moreover, the consequences associated with failure to accurately determine the FMV of physician advisor and consultant compensation can be catastrophic to all of the involved parties.

Chapter 33: Fair Market Value: Ensuring Compliance within the Life Sciences Industry

The previously described series of government settlements with medical device and pharmaceutical manufacturers concerning payments to physician consultants provides some insight into the scope of the problem and likely solutions. While the settlements are not applicable to other companies and their physician consultant arrangements, they provide some helpful direction with respect to identifying potentially risky transactions. The settlement agreements reiterated that compensation for such arrangements must be within FMV, and further, certain settlements require the manufacturers to seek *independent third party opinions* to establish FMV for any physician consultant compensation in excess of $500 per hour.[13] In an interesting and perhaps confusing contrast, Hospital Corporation of America's (HCA) corporate integrity agreement from December 2000 required that HCA obtain an independent third party opinion for any physician consultant compensation in excess of $150 per hour.

Further confounding this analysis is that there is little valuation theory for an appraiser to rely upon in assessing these rather unique arrangements. The determination of the FMV of advisory and/or consulting relationships between physicians and medical device companies entails a significant amount of judgment. Unlike clinical compensation data for physicians, very little survey information exists related directly to these types of compensation arrangements, which, in many instances may significantly exceed the "proverbial" 90th percentile values provided by benchmark physician compensation surveys. Further, advisory and consulting arrangements can be quite diverse, making comparisons among arrangements difficult. Finally, a potential pitfall in looking to existing advisory and consulting arrangements as a basis for establishing FMV is that these relationships may be "tainted," as they may contain an overcompensation bias (*i.e.*, pharma and medical device companies and physicians may, willfully or otherwise, establish arrangements that tend towards providing compensation for business referrals).

One aspect of FMV guidance from the federal government was provided in the Stark Phase III regulations issued by CMS in September 2007. In response to comments it received, CMS stated in Phase III that an FMV hourly rate "may be used to compensate physicians for both administrative and clinical work, provided that the rate paid for clinical work is fair market value for the clinical work performed and the rate paid for administrative work is fair market value for the administrative work performed" (*72 F.R. 51016*). CMS then further explained, "*We note that the fair market value of administrative services may differ from the fair market value of clinical services* [Emphasis added]" (*72 F.R. 51016*). This commentary tends to suggest that a healthcare valuator may want to "dig deeper" than the commonly used "opportunity cost" approach that is the result of converting physician compensation survey data from Medical Group Management Association (MGMA) and other sources into hourly rates. In fact, within the life sciences sector, we note that hourly rates for a particular physician specialty may range from $150 per hour to $1,000 or more per hour.

Therefore, a reliable and comprehensive valuation approach should provide (i) an evaluation methodology that analyzes each parameter in an objective, consistent and repeatable way; (ii) an FMV outcome that encompasses all relevant parameters; and (iii) an FMV outcome that can be supported via *independent* market data. Such an approach to determine the FMV range for

Chapter 33: Fair Market Value: Ensuring Compliance within the Life Sciences Industry

physician consulting / development arrangements can be based upon consideration of certain parameters, including: the extent of the services (*i.e.,* the time requirement); the nature of the specialty; the credentials/qualifications of the advisor/consultant/presenter (*i.e.,* thought leader) and the specific services contemplated by the arrangement.

One available valuation approach entails the use of national and regional physician compensation survey data. Using the valuator's judgment, this compensation data, considered across multiple years and adjusted to reflect payroll-related taxes and benefits, can be adjusted based on (i) the extent of thought leader time required; (ii) the specific requirements of the position; and (iii) the skills/experience of the specifically identified physician thought leader, in terms of acknowledged leadership in his/her specialty.

More specifically, in valuing a potential advisory arrangement between a life sciences company and a physician, consideration can be given to the following factors based on the specific duties and responsibilities of the advisory position:

- Number of hours associated with each duty and/or responsibility.
- The specific duties and responsibilities of the position.
- The complexity of each duty and/or responsibility.
- Level of leadership required.
- Specific objectives and deliverables.
- Potential impact of Thought Leader on organizational and/or product success.

In addition, the following factors related to the physician's qualifications can be considered:

- Educational credentials and specialized training.
- Professional certifications.
- Leadership experience.
- Academic appointments.
- Research experience and funding history.
- Invited presentations.
- Publication history.
- Other professional leadership activities / reputation in the healthcare community.

Chapter 33: Fair Market Value: Ensuring Compliance within the Life Sciences Industry

Each of these factors should be considered and weighted, also giving consideration to any interdependencies among the factors (*e.g.*, if the requirements of the services are rather basic, it may be unnecessary to engage a particularly well qualified physician). Provided that these factors are evaluated in a logical and consistent manner, an objective valuation model can be developed to establish the FMV of physician consulting agreements applicable to the life sciences industry.

In addition to the approach described above, a *direct market approach* can be utilized, provided that the reference market data is free from potential referral bias. The surest ways of identifying reliable market data are to consider physician compensation arrangements in settings which are known to be free of referral bias (*e.g.*, a medical director for a managed care organization) or to "cross walk" the arrangement to non-healthcare settings (*e.g.*, rates paid to comparably qualified professionals providing comparable services in other industries). Physicians tend to be among the nation's most highly educated and experienced professionals, and the duties and activities that they are involved in have considerable financial (and non-financial) implications. When considering the FMV associated with a particular physician thought leader performing a known set of services, there are many possible market "benchmarks" that can be considered. Depending upon the circumstances, these benchmarks may involve, for example, comparably qualified consultants and specialists in various industries as well as attorneys and any other professionals which seem to have value in comparability. However, in considering such market data, it is important to distinguish between the value attributable to the professional, as opposed to the value that may be attributable to the combination of the professional and the professional's organization.

Valuing Clinical Trials Arrangements

In addition to consulting / development arrangements with physicians, life sciences companies frequently enter into compensated arrangements with physicians involving clinical trials or research studies. Clinical trials (or "studies") are treatment protocols that are coordinated by pharmaceutical companies, biotechnology companies or medical device manufacturers (commonly referred to as "sponsors") in order to obtain clinical data involving the use of its drugs or devices in the course of actual patient treatments. Clinical trials are classified as Phase I, II, III or IV. Briefly, Phase I and II trials are early stage studies that are intended to establish the safety and the apparent efficacy of a new drug or device which is not yet FDA-approved. Phase III clinical trials involve much larger groups of human subjects, and the results of Phase III testing are used by sponsors in support of their applications for FDA approval. Phase IV studies entail additional research that is conducted on a post-FDA approval basis. Sometimes referred to as "market studies," Phase IV trials are intended to establish additional information concerning a drug which may, for example, lead to new indications or improvements in dosing guidelines.

Phase I and II clinical trials generally do not implicate healthcare regulations related to the FMV of compensation since the studies tend to be performed in a strictly research setting. On the other hand, Phase III and Phase IV trials oftentimes involve compensation agreements by and among the sponsors, physicians and other third parties such as hospitals or ambulatory

Chapter 33: Fair Market Value: Ensuring Compliance within the Life Sciences Industry

treatment facilities. As these types of trials involve compensation payable to parties who are in a position to refer to one another, compliance with the FMV standard is required to demonstrate compliance with applicable federal and state healthcare regulations.

The clinical trials process is complex, and each trial requires the designation of a physician who serves as the principal investigator (PI) of the trial. There are a number of compensable arrangements inherent in clinical trials that must be consistent with FMV. First, the overall financial arrangement between the sponsor and the PI must be consistent with FMV. Typically, fees paid by a sponsor to a PI are based upon a study budget and include a fixed payment and variable payment based upon the number of patients. The fixed payment includes compensation for overall initiation of the study, as well as costs that may be assessed by third parties. For example, clinical studies involving hospital care must generally be approved by the hospital's governing body called the institutional review board, or the "IRB." The *per patient* fees can range from $1,000 per patient or less to $25,000 or more per patient. From the *per patient* fees, the PI may be responsible for purchasing certain services from third parties such as diagnostic imaging studies from a hospital or an imaging center. In some cases, the study budget may also contemplate payment to a study participant (*i.e.,* a patient).

When considering the FMV of a study budget between a sponsor and a PI, a valuator may want to give consideration to the PI's overall duties and responsibilities, including (i) the intellectual process of identifying desired clinical trials in which to participate; (ii) the investment in one or more research nurses and required research infrastructure; (iii) the assumption of the overall responsibility and liability for the conduct of such trials. As such, the conduct of clinical trials (and the profits related thereto) is more akin to an ancillary service as opposed to a physician's personally performed services. For example, a physician practice may offer in-house x-ray capabilities as a service to its patients, and the profits that the physician-owners may realize from such services generally do not bear any relationship to the physician's personal professional services.

As described above, many clinical studies reflect financial arrangements negotiated between sponsors and PIs. In other instances, organizations such as hospitals may be the party that attracts and negotiates the financial arrangement with the sponsor. Since a PI is still required for the study, a hospital may engage and compensate a physician to serve as the PI. Under this type of arrangement, the PI's services and involvement are significantly different than if the PI assumed the full risk for the study. Accordingly, the valuation methodology used in this case should focus more on the value of the physician's personally performed services.

A final valuation implication of clinical trials is that all trials are unique in both clinical structure and economics. Further, an active PI or a research-oriented hospital may be involved in dozens of trials each year. While it is critical to structure compensation arrangements that are consistent with FMV, it may be impractical from a cost and timing standpoint to value the individual payment streams associated with each and every clinical trial. Therefore, valuators and their clients may desire to develop compensation methodologies or guidelines that can be applied to a wide array of clinical trial arrangements as an approach similar to calculations of value.

Chapter 33: Fair Market Value: Ensuring Compliance within the Life Sciences Industry

Valuing Data Sets

Pharmaceutical companies, medical device manufacturers and other research entities require patient data in order to perform the clinical studies necessary to develop and successfully move potential drugs through the FDA's multi-phase approval process. Typically, researchers are not themselves providers of healthcare services, and accordingly, do not have the ability to capture the required data directly. Instead, they must commission clinical studies, either directly with providers or indirectly through outside researchers, universities, or clinical research organizations. However, regardless of which entity performs the actual research, the requirement for accurate and detailed patient data is essential.

Therefore, in addition to requiring the services of physicians, life sciences companies often need to acquire clinical data, outside of the clinical trial process, from direct service providers (*e.g.*, cancer clinics or dialysis centers). When determining the fair market value of a data purchase, the purchaser should have a legitimate need for the data and, within reasonable economic parameters, would seek to obtain the data by alternate means in the event that the data was not available from an initially identified source. It is also important to assume that the life sciences company reasonably expects that the expenditure for the data set will result in a future revenue stream or research/teaching benefit that will support the expenditure from a stand-alone economic perspective. Therefore, the purchaser should not contemplate deriving value from any reciprocal action of the seller.

In terms of approaches used to determine the fair market value of data acquisition, the use of an income approach is generally not appropriate as a valuation methodology for several reasons, including (i) if utilized within the framework of a clinical research project, no direct measurable income stream will be derived from the transaction; and (ii) the data most likely represents a by-product of patient services and not a revenue generating mechanism in and of itself. In other words, the clinical entity is not directly in the business of generating profits from its data, and no records reasonably exist to allow for an assessment of the results of operations from data licensure transactions. Further, applicable healthcare laws and regulations may prohibit the consideration of the value of possible referrals among the parties.

In addition, the utilization of a cost approach is generally impractical and/or impossible for either the seller or the purchaser, since it is almost impossible to replicate the broad scope of the elements captured by the clinical entity due to the "by-product" nature of the data. Under a market approach, an appraiser may be able to locate industry experts who can provide information related to similar transactions involving data sales and/or licensures since such transactions are generally not available in any databases or in the public domain.

Valuing Intellectual Property Within the Life Sciences Industry

The pharmaceutical industry was one of the first industries in the United States to routinely use licensing programs as a means for identifying and commercializing new drugs. Prior to the

Chapter 33: Fair Market Value: Ensuring Compliance within the Life Sciences Industry

rapid advances made over the last 30 to 40 years in computing and the development of sophisticated methods for mapping chemical paths, the process of finding and developing new drugs was arduous and exceptionally expensive, and the probability of successfully commercializing new pharmaceutical applications was extremely low. To combat these hurdles, pharmaceutical companies began licensing the right to screen the chemical libraries of industrial companies for pharmacological properties. This proved to be highly effective in reducing the cost of upfront research and development, and allowed existing discoveries to be further exploited through commercialization in previously unconsidered applications.

Today, intellectual capital has become a central focus of business strategy across all industries, and licensing activity for patents alone is estimated to account for more than $100 billion in revenue for U.S. firms. The healthcare industry continues to play a key role in this market, and an understanding of the basic tenets of licensing is critical to understanding value in the life sciences.

Definition of Licensing

Licensing is the act of granting another person or entity the right to make use of a particular asset in a specific context or application, for a specific length of time, and within a specific geographical area. A license does not typically carry the full rights of ownership, and therefore license agreements must be defined narrowly to prevent conflicts of interest between the owner of the asset (licensor) and the user of the asset (the licensee). This is particularly important when the licensor is exploiting the asset in other commercial uses such as in the licensor's own product(s) or through additional licenses.

Why do owners of property find it advantageous to enter licensing arrangements? The basic conceptual framework of the license is to create a symbiotic relationship whereby both the owner of the property and the licensee share in the commercial success of the end product. An example of this type of situation might include an inventor who does not have the resources to successfully commercialize the invention, or an owner of property who does not have the necessary expertise to commercialize the product in a new area.

Asset Types

A licensing arrangement can be entered into for virtually any type of asset, but licensing activity generally centers on intellectual property such as patents, trademarks, copyrights, and technologies.

Patents

The United States Patent & Trademark Office (USPTO) is the governing body that issues patents and trademarks in the United States. The USPTO defines a patent as "the right to

Chapter 33: Fair Market Value: Ensuring Compliance within the Life Sciences Industry

exclude others from making, using, offering for sale, or selling" the invention in the United States or "importing" the invention into the United States. Patent grants have a finite life typically defined as 20 years from the original date of the patent application. There are three distinct types of patents:

1) *Utility Patents* – granted for "the invention or discovery of a new and useful process, machine, article of manufacture, or composition of matter, or any new and useful improvement thereof."

2) *Design Patents* – granted for the invention of a "new, original, and ornamental design for an article of manufacture."

3) *Plant Patents* – granted "to anyone who invents or discovers and asexually reproduces any distinct and new variety of plant."

Within the life sciences industry, most patents fall under the category of utility patents, and include chemical compounds, medical devices, and medical equipment.

Trademarks

Trademarks, or servicemarks, were established by the Lanham Act, and are described by the USPTO as "a word, name, symbol, or device that is used in trade with goods to indicate the source of the goods and to distinguish them from the goods of others. A servicemark is the same as a trademark except that it identifies and distinguishes the source of a service rather than a product." Trademarks need not be registered to enjoy protection under the Act, however, most commercially used trademarks are registered with the USPTO. Trademarks registered after November 1989 are valid for a period of 10 years, and may be renewed for successive 10 year periods. Nearly every branded product with name recognition enjoys protection under the Lanham Act, but the most commonly observed trademarks in the life sciences are name brand pharmaceuticals and medical devices.

Copyrights

A copyright is a form of protection for original works of authorship (literary, artistic, musical, etc) established by the Copyright Act of 1976. A copyright generally establishes the exclusive right to print, publish, reproduce, perform in public, and/or create derivative works of the material. In the United States, copyrights are issued and registered with Copyright Office of the Library of Congress and have a term equal to the lifetime of the author plus 50 years. In some instances the copyright may be valid for a period of 75 years from the date of first publication. Within the life sciences copyrights may includes medical texts, manuals, research papers, articles, diagrams, photos and the like.

Chapter 33: Fair Market Value: Ensuring Compliance within the Life Sciences Industry

Royalties

Compensation under a licensing agreement typically includes the payment of a royalty by the licensee to the owner/licensor for the use of the property. Royalties can take many forms, but are most frequently set as an upfront lump-sum, an annual fee, a percentage of revenue on products sold, a dollar amount per unit sold, or a combination thereof. Royalties paid on ongoing revenue or units of sales are referred to as running royalties. It is also common to see royalty arrangements whereby an annual minimum and/or annual maximum fee applies, the royalty rate decreases with volumes in a stair-step pattern, or royalties decline over time. These types of arrangements are appealing to licensees because they attempt to match the economic life of the licensed asset with the commercial success of the end product.

Royalty rates vary significantly from one licensing arrangement to the next, and there are many factors that must be considered when attempting to establish a reasonable royalty rate within the context of a specific licensing agreement. Frequently there is no single right answer, and royalty rates for seemingly similar technologies may vary widely. In the landmark case *Georgia Pacific Corporation v. United States Plywood Corp.*[14], the court set out 15 factors that parties to a hypothetical negotiation would likely consider in determining a reasonable royalty. Though the case dealt specifically with reasonable royalties within the context of patent infringement damages, the context the court used was a hypothetical royalty arrangement that would have been negotiated had the parties negotiated immediately prior to the infringement. This is very similar to the hypothetical negotiation contemplated in the definition of fair market value[15], and the factors the court used are applicable in assessing reasonable royalties for licenses outside the construct of patent infringement.

The 15 factors identified by the court are listed (in generic form to remove the patent infringement context) and briefly discussed below:

1. The royalty rates received by the owner of the property in other licensing arrangements for the same property, proving or tending to prove an established royalty.

    Existing licensing arrangements for the subject property would tend to establish a reasonable royalty rate. However, it is important to consider relevance of prior licenses within the context of the contemplated license. Differences in the terms of the license (*such as factor #3 below*), the remaining life of the property (*such as factor #7 below*), and other factors presented in this list may limit the relevance of prior agreements.

2. The royalty rates paid by the licensee for the use of other property rights comparable to the property (for which a license is being contemplated).
    Established rates paid by the licensee for similar properties in agreements with comparable terms may serve to establish the reasonable royalty rate. As with #1 above, however, terms of the license agreements should be carefully examined for comparability to the contemplated arrangement.

Chapter 33: Fair Market Value: Ensuring Compliance within the Life Sciences Industry

3. The nature and scope of the license, as exclusive or non-exclusive; or as restricted or non-restricted in terms of territory or with respect to whom the manufactured product may be sold.

    Exclusivity – A license granting an exclusive right to use a property would generally demand a higher royalty rate than one which is non-exclusive (i.e. allows additional licenses to be granted)

    Geography – The geographical limitations of the license grant will influence the appropriate royalty rate. A worldwide license would typically demand a higher royalty rate than a license limiting use to a specific territory or boundary.

    Use – The use of the license may influence the royalty rate. A license granting unrestricted use of a property would generally demand a much higher royalty rate than one which is defined narrowly, for example, a chemical compound to be used only in drug-coated stents.

4. The licensor's established policy on licensing, either by not licensing to others the use of the property to maintain a monopoly, or by granting licenses under special conditions. An owner who is highly protective of their property rights, or who has an established policy of not licensing its properties, may justify a higher royalty rate. Such a rate would be necessary to induce the owner to deviate from their established policy. This is especially pertinent in infringement cases, but may be less so in the normal course of establishing a reasonable royalty rate between two willing parties. The absence of a history of licensing or policy restricting licensing should not be used as justification for a higher royalty rate in and of itself.

5. The commercial relationship between the licensor and licensee, such as, whether they are competitors in the same territory in the same line of business; or whether they are inventor and promoter.

    License agreements between competitors tend to justify higher royalty rates than those of non-competitors. Even when the license is structured to limit the use of the product or if the product's application is in a market where there is no competitive threat, licensors are reluctant to allow competitors to gain information or profits that would advance their competitive position.

6. The effect of selling the licensed property in promoting sales of other products of the licensee; the existing value of the invention to the licensor as a generator of sales of his non-patented items; and the extent of such derivative (or convoyed) sales.

    Licenses that allow the licensee to gain sales in other non-licensed products tend to justify higher royalty rates. For example, Bausch and Lomb may pay a higher royalty for new contact lens technology if they believe sales of the licensed product will lead to gains

Chapter 33: Fair Market Value: Ensuring Compliance within the Life Sciences Industry

in sales of related products such as saline solution, etc. Higher royalty rates may also be justified if the license agreement allows the licensee to gain access to new commercial channels, new customers, appeal to a new population demographic, or augment their current commercial presence.

7. The economic or functional life of the property (i.e. expiration date of a patent) and the term of the license.

   A product nearing the end of its life cycle will generally demand a lower royalty rate due to economic obsolescence, increased competition, and design around considerations. This may also be true for new technologies that are expected to have a short useful life.
   In some instances, the license is written as a perpetual license. This might be seen in the context of a trademark license agreement where the name brand is expected to continue indefinitely. In these situations additional analysis may be required to evaluate the life of the economic benefit associated with the licensed property.

8. The established profitability of the property or products embodying the property; its commercial success; and its current popularity.
   It follows logic that royalty rates for highly popular and/or highly profitable products are also high. As the popularity and profitability of the product diminishes so does the appropriate royalty rate.

9. The utility and advantages of the subject property over the old modes or devices, if any, that had been used previously for achieving similar results.
   Products that have significant advantages over currently existing technologies justify higher royalty rates. This is due to the simple fact that products with significant utility advantages also enjoy significant profit advantages.

10. The nature of the subject property; the character of the commercial embodiment of it as owned and produced by the licensor; and the benefits to others who have used the invention.

11. The extent to which the infringer has made use of the subject property; and any evidence probative of the value of that use. (*outside the context of infringement, the intended use of the subject property may be a substitute*)

12. The portion of the profit or of the selling price that may be customary in the particular business or in comparable businesses to allow for the use of the subject property or comparable properties.

    A common rule of thumb, referred to as the Goldscheider rule[16], suggests that a reasonable royalty represents 25% of the pre-profit expected to be made through the use of the licensed asset. There are also many databases that can be used to search for comparable license transactions within a given industry. In some cases, these databases can provide insight into the royalty rates being paid for similar properties. However, these should be referenced cautiously, as a truly comparable license transaction may be difficult to identify, and over-generalization may miss many of the nuances of the particular license arrangement.

13. The portion of the realizable profit that should be credited to the invention as distinguished from other elements of the end product, such as the manufacturing process, business risks, or significant features or improvements added by the infringer.

    Understanding the relative contribution of the licensed property to the overall utility of the end product may be helpful to the determination of a reasonable royalty. A license arrangement whereby both parties contribute technologies that equally support the end product may justify a profit split of 50/50. An example of this might be a owner of a medical laser device licensing sophisticated positioning and tracking software to control the movement of the laser.

14. The opinion of qualified experts.

    Frequently professionals in the licensing industry will have experience and expertise which can be helpful in establishing the reasonable royalty.

15. The amount that a licensor and a licensee would have agreed upon if both had been reasonably and voluntarily trying to reach an agreement; that is, the amount which a prudent licensee—who desired, as a business proposition, to obtain a license to manufacture and sell a particular article embodying the subject property—would have been willing to pay as a royalty and still be able to make a reasonable profit and which amount would have been acceptable by a prudent patentee who was willing to grant a license.

Though this list is fairly comprehensive, there are additional factors that should be considered in determining a reasonable royalty rate. These may include cost to design around the subject property (recreating the asset vs. licensing) and availability and preponderance of non-protected alternatives. It stands to reason that a licensee would not reasonably pay a royalty rate in excess of the cost to design or develop their own property with the same functionality (assuming it was possible to do so). Royalty rates will also be limited by the availability of acceptable alternatives. A licensee may prefer to have the subject property, but will not likely pay a high royalty rate if there are acceptable alternatives with the same or similar attributes available for license at a lower rate.

Valuation of Royalty Agreements

In some instances it may be necessary to determine the value of a license agreement. Situations where this might be necessary include purchase price allocations, formation of a new entity

Chapter 33: Fair Market Value: Ensuring Compliance within the Life Sciences Industry

(such as a joint venture) where the license agreement is assigned by one of the parties as its initial contribution, bankruptcy, termination of a licensing agreement, or sale of the licensing rights, among others. Though a complete discussion of valuation methodologies is beyond the scope of this chapter, the following is a high level overview of some of the more common methodologies to valuation and key considerations therein.

Income Approach

Any income producing asset can be valued with respect to its income generating capacity. Because royalty agreements have a fairly predictable royalty stream and a finite life, an income approach to valuation is generally used. Under the simplest variation of this approach expected future royalties over the remaining life of the agreement are discounted to their present value using a risk adjusted rate of return or discount rate. This rate of return is set at a level commensurate with the risk of realizing the projected royalty stream. Uncertain royalty streams will have a higher discount rate and reasonably certain royalty streams will have a lower discount rate.

To demonstrate the mechanics of this approach, assume a royalty arrangement calling for a royalty rate of 10% on sales of a specific product payable at year end over the next 3 years. Assume further that sales of the product are expected to total $1 million in each of the next three years. Based on the risk profile of the projected sales, a qualified appraiser has determined that a 25% rate of return is appropriate.

	Year 1	Year 2	Year 3
Expected Product Revenue (000s)	$1,000	$1,000	$1,000
Royalty Rate	10%	10%	10%
Royalty Income	100	100	100
Taxes @ 40%	(40)	(40)	(40)
After Tax Royalty Income	60	60	60
Present Value Factor @ 25%	0.800	0.640	0.512
Present Value of Royalty Income	48.00	38.40	30.70
Value of Royalty Agreement (sum of above)	**$117.10**		

In this example, the present value factor is calculated as $1 / (1+\text{rate of return})^{\text{time}}$, where time equals the number of years in the future (*i.e.,* year 2 = $1/(1.25)^2$). Excluding consideration of any additional factors, the value of the royalty agreement in this example is $117,100. As suggested, this is an oversimplified example, and each royalty agreement must be valued in context, giving proper consideration to all elements that contribute to value.

Chapter 33: Fair Market Value: Ensuring Compliance within the Life Sciences Industry

Market Approach

The market approach is premised on the idea that the value of an asset can be estimated by drawing reference to the prices paid for other assets with similar characteristics. The challenge to this approach, and especially with intellectual property assets, is finding truly comparable assets. Transactional data related to the prices paid for licensing agreements is somewhat limited, and even when a sufficient volume of data is available, it is highly unlikely that the underlying license agreement contains substantially all of the provisions of the subject agreement or an underlying asset of substantially the same nature.

Cost (or Asset Approach)

The cost approach is rooted in the concept of replication. Value under this approach is estimated with reference to the actual cost to create the asset or by estimating the cost of reproduction or replacement of the asset. For license agreements, the cost approach has limited application as the primary cost consideration pertains to the underlying asset subject to the license and not the license itself. Additionally, the rights associated with a license are generally less than those associated with full ownership of an asset, and the cost approach may significantly overstate value. However, there are circumstances where the value of the license may be determined in this manner. The question the appraiser must ask is "but for the license, what would it cost the licensee to develop their own non-infringing alternative to the licensed asset." Assuming a non-infringing alternative is feasible, the appraiser would then attempt to estimate the indirect costs (man-hours, overhead costs, etc), direct costs (materials, equipment, lab costs, etc), and the opportunity costs (time to recreate the asset vs. licensing it now).

Bibliography

Licensing Executive Society International, *The LESI Guide to Licensing Best Practices, Strategic Issues and Contemporary Realities*, Robert Goldscheider, Ed., May 2002.

Anson, Weston. *Intellectual Property Valuation Primer,* [DRAFT]. Available on www.lesi.org.

Reilly, Schweihs. *Valuing Intangible Assets*. McGraw-Hill, 1999.

Smith, Parr. *Valuation of Intellectual Property and Intangible Assets*, 3rd Edition. Wiley, March 31, 2000.

Sullivan and Fradkin, "A Primer on Benchmarking a Licensing Operation", September 2001, Available on www.lesi.org.

Chapter 33: Fair Market Value: Ensuring Compliance within the Life Sciences Industry

Porter, Mills and Weinstein, "Industry Norms and Reasonable Royalty Rate Determination", March 2008, Available on www.lesi.org.

Wendt, Jeffrey, "Medical Devices: New License Issues for Single Use Devices", *les Nouvelles*. September 2003.

---

1. A corporate integrity agreement, or CIA, is an agreement entered into between the OIG and the subject of an investigation typically as one component of a settlement agreement. A CIA stipulates certain actions and/or constraints which the subject company must comply with on a prospective basis.
2. Section 1128B(b) of the Act (42 U.S.C. 1320a–7b(b))(2003)
3. Commonly compared to "medical director" type arrangements in the hospital setting.
4. *Qui tam* lawsuits are initiated by a third party on behalf of the government. These actions are generally brought by whistleblowers under the federal False Claims Act.
5. The term "immediate family member" includes a husband or wife, birth or adoptive parent, child or sibling, father-in-law, mother-in-law, brother in-law, sister-in-law, grandparent or grandchild.
6. Designated health services include: radiology and other imaging services (MRI, CT and ultrasound); physical therapy; occupational therapy; radiation therapy; durable medical equipment; parenteral and enteral nutrients, equipment and supplies; prosthetics, orthotics and prosthetic devices and supplies; home health services; outpatient prescription drugs; and inpatient and outpatient hospital services. *Note that this listing of designated health services is not intended to be exhaustive, as the government has expanded the list on several occasions.*
7. Under the Phase III rule (2007), a physician "stands in the shoes" of his/her "physician organization" for purposes of analyzing financial relationships. A physician who "stands in the shoes" of his/her physician organization is deemed to have the same compensation arrangement (with the same parties and on the same terms) as the physician organization itself.
8. From CMS Phase III commentary (42 C.F.R. § 411.357(d)).
9. Department of Justice data is actually very conservative, as it does *not* include billions of dollars in civil recoveries returned to the states or criminal fines imposed as a direct consequence of False Claims Act filings and prosecutions.
10. The OIG has the authority to pursue violations of the anti-kickback statute under a provision of the Civil Monetary Penalties Law (CMP). In kickback cases, CMP remedies include monetary penalties of up to $50,000 for each act, including any offer, payment, solicitation or receipt of remuneration. In addition, under CMP, violators can be assessed up to three times the amount of remuneration, and face exclusion in federal healthcare programs.
11. Failure to comply with a safe harbor provision does not mean that an arrangement is illegal. Compliance with safe harbors is voluntary, and arrangements that do not comply with a safe harbor must be analyzed on a case-by-case basis for compliance with the anti-kickback statute. The reader should be sure to engage the advice of appropriate counsel before consummating a specific transaction.
12. 42 CFR §411.351 (as set forth by the Centers for Medicare and Medicaid Services with respect to physicians' referrals to health care entities with which they have financial relationships). Furthermore, this definition is consistent with similar fair market value guidance related to the Anti-Kickback Statute (42 U.S.C. §1320a-7b) and with the definition relied upon by the Internal Revenue Services. See, for example, Treas. Reg. 53.4958 et seq.
13. See article entitled *Artificial-Joint Makers Settle Kickback Case*, New York Times, September 28, 2007, and the agreements between the U.S. Department of Justice and Biomet, DePuy Orthopedics, Zimmer Holdings, Stryker Orthopedics, and Smith and Nephew.
14. *Georgia Pacific Corporation v. United States Plywood Corporation*, 318 F. Supp. 1116, 166 U.S.P.Q. 235, May 28, 1970.
15. Fair market value is defined in the International Glossary of Business Valuation Terms as *"the price, expressed in terms of cash equivalents, at which property would change hands between a hypothetical willing and able buyer and a hypothetical willing and able seller, acting at arms length in an open and unrestricted market, when neither is under compulsion to buy or sell and when both have reasonable knowledge of the relevant facts."*
16. Robert Goldscheider is a specialist & recognized authority on licensing. His calculations performed in the 1950s laid the ground work for the "25% rule" now frequently referred to as the Goldscheider rule.

Chapter 34

The Valuation of Hospitals

By Don Barbo, CPA/ABV, and Robbie Mundy, CPA/ABV, CVA

Editor's Note: The impact of the Healthcare Reform legislation is discussed in Chapter 1 and in the Appendix Teleconference Transcript.

Valuations of hospitals involve unique circumstances and nuances. It is imperative that an appraiser is mindful of and develops an understanding of these nuances in order to generate a sound opinion of value. This chapter will focus on these various distinctions from non-healthcare valuations and will also guide the professional in performing fair market valuations for general acute care hospitals in the context of transactions.

While this chapter will focus solely on general acute care hospitals, the appraiser should also recognize that there are various other "types" of hospitals present in the market, including:

1. Specialty surgical hospitals, such as heart hospitals

2. Critical Access Hospitals (CAH)

3. Rehabilitation hospitals

4. Long-term acute care hospitals (LTACs)

Valuations of these types of hospitals are somewhat similar in nature to general acute care hospital valuations, but each has its unique characteristics and trends that must be considered. The appraiser must be aware of the hospital industry, the challenges hospitals face, and trends affecting the values of hospitals.

Overview of the Hospital Industry

The hospital industry in the U.S. is highly fragmented. According to the American Hospital Association, there were 5,747 registered hospitals in the U.S. in 2006, with the overwhelming majority being community hospitals at 4,927. Of these community hospitals, over 59% were not-for-profit, 18% were for-profit, and almost 23% were state and local government hospitals.[1]

The industry is highly regulated at the federal level through the Centers for Medicare and Medicaid Services (CMS), and is also regulated by state and local governments. As such, the appraiser needs to be aware not only of the federal regulations affecting hospitals, but also the state and local regulations, which can vary by locality.

Chapter 34: The Valuation of Hospitals

Today, hospitals face a number of challenges that can have a significant impact on value. Some of the major challenges are presented below:

Growth in uninsured population

According to the U.S. Census Bureau, there were over 45 million uninsured in the U.S. as of 2007, up from just over 38 million uninsured in 2000. The uninsured population for 2007 was just over 15% of the total U.S. population.[2] This represents a great challenge to hospitals and their emergency rooms, which cannot refuse care based on insurance status or ability to pay. In fact, according to the American Hospital Association, the cost of uncompensated care has been rising dramatically from a cost of approximately $3.9 billion in 1980 to $31.2 billion in 2006.[3]

Shortage of Nurses

According to a 2007 survey of hospital leaders conducted by the American Hospital Association, hospitals had an estimated 116,000 registered nurse vacancies as of December 2006.[4] This shortage could also increase as demands for health care grow in the future with the aging baby boomer population. The nursing shortages impact the ability of hospitals to attract and retain nurses.

Difficulty in Maintaining Physician ED Coverage

Hospitals are finding increasing difficulty in providing and maintaining physician on-call coverage for their Emergency Departments. According to the AHA 2007 survey, over 55% of the hospital leader respondents experienced gaps in specialty coverage in the ED. Two of the specialties that have been increasingly difficult to staff are orthopedics and neurosurgery. In the past, physicians agreed to provide on-call coverage to hospitals without charging the hospitals as a way to build their practices (physicians would bill the patients/payers for their professional services rendered). However, with the growing number of uninsured patients visiting hospitals, declining reimbursement, and increasing medical malpractice insurance and operating costs, many physicians are now expecting some sort of payment for on-call coverage, which can be a strain on hospital profitability. In fact, more than a third of the hospital leader respondents reported some form of hospital payment for physician on-call coverage.[5]

Loss of Patients to ASCs

Ambulatory Surgery Centers (ASCs), also known as day surgery centers, are used by doctors to perform a variety of surgical procedures that do not require patients to stay overnight, including eye surgery, orthopedic and hand surgery, plastic surgery, pain management (spinal injections), podiatry, ear-nose-and-throat surgery, endoscopy, laparoscopy, and various other surgical specialties.

The number of ASC facilities has substantially increased in recent years. Between 1991 and 2001, the number of Medicare-certified ambulatory surgical centers increased from 1,460 centers to 3,371, representing an almost 9% compounded annual growth rate.[6] Growth in ASC

Chapter 34: The Valuation of Hospitals

facilities continues to remain strong. In 2005, there were 4,506 Medicare-certified ASC facilities, which represents a 7.5% compounded annual growth rate. [7]

Since ASCs only provide day surgery services, they are much smaller than general hospitals, which offer a much broader range of medical services. Because of their smaller size and focus on a considerably narrower medical service, they are able to operate with smaller staffs and lower overhead levels. This leads to lower operating costs than larger, full-size hospitals.

Additionally, since the ASC does not provide emergency room services and instead, schedules surgery cases in advance, physician-users prefer to use them. Because of its focus on selected types of surgeries, ASC's typically enjoy the following benefits over full-size hospitals:

- Patients are less at risk of being bumped or losing their scheduled surgery by more critical cases which can often occur in hospital settings; also, because of the lack of critical trauma cases being treated, the waiting room experience is typically less hectic and more pleasant than in full-service hospitals;

- Because of its lower operating cost structure and efficient operating environment, managed care companies and insurance companies look favorably to ASCs, and can often negotiate lower payments to ASCs for these medical services;

- Physicians are able to schedule their surgery cases in advance with less risk of being bumped. Also, the nursing staff is familiar and well trained in supporting the surgeries performed in the ASC. Physicians may also have a greater voice in the equipment and medical supplies being offered in the ASC.

Because of its focus on day surgeries, ASCs can also shift less urgent cases from the hospitals, and allow the hospitals to treat the more serious and traumatic cases. As a result, many outpatient cases are migrating out of the hospital setting and into ASCs, which can have a significant negative impact on hospital profitability.

Hospital Transaction Environment

The hospital transaction environment has been active, with a major trend in consolidation and "going-private" transactions. According to The Health Care Acquisition Report 2008, as published by Irving Levin Associates, Inc., the total number of hospital transactions for 2001 through 2007 were as follows:

Total transactions (annual for 2001 to 2007, including all transactions):

2001	2002	2003	2004	2005	2006	2007
118	101	56	236	88	249	149

Chapter 34: The Valuation of Hospitals

However, in 2004, 2006, and 2007, the transactions included deals for 3 major hospital entities. In 2004, the transaction information included 132 Tenet hospitals. In 2006, the total number of 249 transacted hospitals included 176 HCA hospitals (purchase of company to take to private equity). Total transactions for 2007 included the sale of 51 Triad hospitals to Community Health. Eliminating these transactions from the totals, the "adjusted" transaction totals are as follows:

2001	2002	2003	2004	2005	2006	2007
118	101	56	104	88	73	98

Even with these transactions eliminated, the transaction activity shows an active marketplace. Many of these transactions represent "portfolio shuffling" on the part of the publicly-traded and major hospital chain players. An emerging trend in hospital activity is whole-hospital syndication models, where physicians can purchase ownership interests in hospitals.

Knowledge of the hospital industry and its trends is essential for an appraiser. In addition, the appraiser must also have a working knowledge of the hospital value drivers. For general acute care hospitals, the key value drivers typically are (1) inpatient admissions, (2) outpatient visits, and (3) reimbursement factors affecting both inpatient and outpatient revenues.

Hospital Value Drivers

Inpatient Admissions and Inpatient Reimbursement

An inpatient is admitted to a hospital when the patient's medical procedure requires an overnight stay at the hospital. Inpatient admissions drive the amount of inpatient revenue that a hospital receives. The total number of days that a patient remains in the hospital after being admitted is called Patient Days. Patient Days also drive another important performance measure for hospitals known as Average Length of Stay (ALOS). ALOS is generally computed as Total Patient Days divided by Patient Admissions (or Patient Discharges).

Inpatient services are reimbursed for Medicare patients under the Medicare Inpatient Prospective Payment System (IPPS). Under the IPPS, patients are grouped into Medicare severity diagnosis-related groups (MS-DRGs) based upon the patient's diagnosis and the severity of the diagnosis assigned at the time of discharge. Reimbursement for an MS-DRG is based on the estimated hospital cost for a specific diagnosis. Medicare inpatient payment rates are updated annually based upon Market Basket updates. The market basket is designed to reflect price inflation by indexing the prices of a mix of goods and services for a certain time period to a base time period.[8]

It is important to note that the MS-DRG is a flat rate, meaning that a hospital is reimbursed the same amount regardless of a particular patient's cost. In other words, a hospital receives the same reimbursement for a diagnosis, whether the patient stays one day or three days. Accordingly, under the Medicare MS-DRG system, a hospital has the economic incentive to reduce its ALOS.

Chapter 34: The Valuation of Hospitals

A hospital's Medicare base reimbursement rate for inpatient services is divided into a labor and non-labor portion. The labor portion is adjusted by the hospital's local wage index and the non-labor portion is adjusted by a cost of living adjustment factor.[9] However, a hospital can receive various supplemental payments, for instance, if its costs for treating a patient exceed the usual Medicare reimbursement for that patient's treatment by a certain threshold (referred to as "outlier payments")[10] or if the hospital serves a disproportionately high percentage of low-income patients (referred to as "disproportionate share hospital payments")[11].

Some commercial insurance payers reimburse inpatient services on a per diem basis. Under this method, a hospital will receive reimbursement for an inpatient based on the number of days the patient is hospitalized. Since the first inpatient day is generally the most expensive in terms of the hospital's costs, some per diem structures pay more the first day than for subsequent days. Variations also occur in subsequent day's per diem amounts. This per diem rate can also fluctuate based upon the patient diagnosis and severity. Other payers can pay based upon negotiated rates, such as a percentage of charges billed, or under a capitation plan, which provides a fixed payment per member per month (PMPM) regardless of the hospital services actually provided.

Outpatient Visits and Outpatient Reimbursement

An outpatient visit is classified as any medical procedure performed in a hospital setting that does not require an overnight stay. Outpatient visits are the volume driver for a hospital's outpatient revenues, which can oftentimes be very profitable.

Outpatient services are generally reimbursed for Medicare patients under the Medicare Outpatient Prospective Payment System (OPPS). Under the OPPS, services are classified into ambulatory payment classifications (APCs) based on similar clinical procedures and required resources. Each APC has its own payment rate, which is adjusted based on geographic wage variations.[12]

For non-Medicare payers, reimbursement methods can vary widely from payer to payer (i.e., fee for service, percentage of charges billed, capitation, etc.).

Understanding these value drivers and how these drivers interact with each other is essential for hospital valuations. With these value drivers in mind, it is important for the appraiser to tailor the information request list to the client so that the data received can be useful in identifying trends in these value drivers.

Information Gathering

The information gathering phase for any valuation is important, and hospital valuations are certainly no exception. It is important to not only receive pertinent financial information, but to also receive the information in a format that allows the appraiser to identify trends and calculate ratios specific to a hospital. With the hospital "value drivers" in mind, the appraiser should

Chapter 34: The Valuation of Hospitals

ask for specific information from the client that will enable the appraiser to identify historical trends and provide a basis for reasonable future projections. Some of the specific items unique to hospitals to be requested might include the following:

1. For-profit vs. not-for-profit status

2. Number of patient beds, both licensed and in-use

3. Location of the facility

4. Current ownership of the hospital (i.e., community board, physician investors, corporate-owned, etc.)

5. Primary services provided and brief history of the hospital

6. Certificate of Need requirements

7. Detailed financial statements for the last 5 years, with revenues segregated by inpatient and outpatient revenue, and any other major service lines

8. Historical inpatient admissions, inpatient days and outpatient visits for the last 5 years

9. Other operating statistics of the hospital for the last 5 years, such as adjusted patient days, average length of stay, occupancy rate, etc.

10. Client-prepared operating budgets or projections

11. An often overlooked source of data and the hospital's position in a given market are the Prospectuses required for tax exempt bond financing by exempt hospitals. Federal tax law and underwriting standards require far more information in these documents than typically seen in a financial statement or even a Form 990.

Obviously, this list is not exhaustive, but will provide the appraiser a good starting point for recognizing and analyzing various trends present in the hospital being valued. It is important to be as specific as possible when requesting information, and is also a good idea to not request superfluous information so that the client will not be overloaded.

Analyzing Financial Ratios and Trends

After obtaining the necessary data from the client, the appraiser must now compile this data in a manner useful for identifying trends. An important part of identifying trends is calculating and analyzing various ratios. Hospitals have unique ratios and statistics that need to be considered.

Chapter 34: The Valuation of Hospitals

The main objective in analyzing ratios is to identify historical trends for projecting future cash flows, although this analysis is also useful in assessing the risks associated with the hospital, and potentially could be used as a basis for normalizing adjustments.

Obviously, the appraiser should consider the growth trends in both inpatient and outpatient revenues, inpatient admissions, and outpatient visits. Some other important statistics and ratios to consider are as follows:

1. *Patient Days*–the number of days the patient is in the hospital

2. *Adjusted patient days (APD)*–Patient Days plus the calculated Outpatient Days. The formula can vary, but may be:
   (Patient Days + (Outpatient Visits x 50%))

3. *Average length of stay (ALOS)*–calculated as the total inpatient days divided by total inpatient admissions

4. *Average daily census (ADC)*–calculated as inpatient days divided by 365 days per year

5. *Occupancy rate*–calculated as the ADC divided by the total number of hospital beds in service

6. *Gross and net inpatient revenue per inpatient day*

7. *Gross and net outpatient revenue per outpatient visit*

8. *Total gross and net patient revenue per APD*

9. *Medical supplies expense per APD*

10. *Bad debt expense as a percentage of net patient revenue*

11. *Staff full-time equivalents (FTEs) divided by APD*

12. *Salaries, wages & benefits divided by FTEs*

Trends in these statistics should be observed and understood, because these will contribute to developing reasonable projections of future cash flows. For example, the ALOS statistic is important in determining how efficiently a hospital is admitting and treating its patients. An increasing ALOS could be negative for a hospital, especially a hospital with a high Medicare patient mix, since Medicare reimburses on a DRG basis and not on a per diem basis. The occupancy rate can give an appraiser an idea of how well the hospital is utilizing its beds and whether the hospital may be facing capacity constraints regarding its future growth potential.

Chapter 34: The Valuation of Hospitals

The trends in gross and net patient revenues per APD can give some idea of the contracting strength of the hospital. Medical supplies expense per APD can provide insight on how efficiently a hospital is managing its medical supplies. The staffing ratios can also provide insights into how well the hospital is managing its employee costs. The more an appraiser can digest and decipher the reasons for the historical trends, the better basis he will have for developing future cash flow projections.

Normalizing Adjustments

After analyzing the financial trends of the hospital, normalizing adjustments should be made. The primary purpose of the normalizing adjustments is to produce a financial picture that will be used as a basis for future cash flow projections. Hospitals generally have more sophisticated accounting systems than other healthcare businesses. Therefore, normalizing adjustments for hospitals typically entail only eliminating non-recurring items or adjustments for income taxes. However, historical trends in expenses, especially as a percentage of revenues, should be considered to identify any unusual expenses. One of the largest expenses for a hospital is salaries and wages, so any abnormal trends in terms of salaries per FTE should be discussed with the client and normalized if necessary. Another large expense for hospitals is medical supplies expense. Any significant swings in terms of medical supplies as a percentage of revenue should be understood and, if the trend is not expected to continue in the future, should be normalized. Remember that the primary purpose of normalizing adjustments is to restate the financials in a manner that will be consistent with expected future operations.

Income Approach

In preparing the Income Approach value, the client's operating budget or financial projections (if available) should be reviewed for reasonableness by comparing it to observed historical financial trends. If, after review and discussion with the client, the projections appear reasonable, then they could be used as a guide for projecting future cash flows.

In projecting future revenues, growth factors for both volumes and net charges should be considered. For inpatient revenues, the volume driver will be inpatient admissions and days, while the volume driver for outpatient revenues will be outpatient visits. Typically, for a hospital, inpatient admissions are driven by a number of factors, including, but not limited to, the location and attractiveness of the facility, the types of services provided at the hospital, the key physicians practicing at the hospital, the key insurance payer contracts, the competitive environment in the community, the population demographics (including growth, affluence and age) and the strength of the hospital's medical staff. Outpatient visits will typically be driven by the types of surgeries performed at the hospital, any specialized services provided by the hospital (such as imaging services or cancer treatment), the key insurance payers, the hospital's relationship with area physicians, and the proximity and prevalence of competing physician-owned outpatient

Chapter 34: The Valuation of Hospitals

facilities (particularly ASCs). The appraiser should discuss these and any other items affecting volume growth with the client and should develop a good understanding of how the hospital is affected by these factors. Historical growth trends in inpatient admissions, inpatient days and outpatient visits should be analyzed and factored into any volume projections. Also, the occupancy rate should be calculated for each projected period to ensure that projected volume growth does not exceed the hospital's capacity.

For projections of the net charge rates of the hospital, analyzing the hospital's payer mix is crucial. For instance, if a hospital has a high Medicare patient mix, its reimbursement will be greatly affected by any reimbursement changes put forth by the Centers for Medicare & Medicaid Services (CMS). The Medicare reimbursement rates for the IPPS and the OPPS are updated annually and published on the CMS website. Likewise, a hospital with a large percentage of commercial payers will be more affected by any changes in negotiated rates or per diems. An appraiser should consider and discuss in detail with the client the contracting strength of the hospital, as well as expectations of any future changes in rates or commercial insurers.

Operating expenses should be projected based upon whether the expense is generally more fixed or variable in nature. For example, facility rent would typically be projected as a fixed expense, with inflationary increases each year. In contrast, bad debt expense or medical supplies expense should probably be projected as a percentage of projected net patient revenues or as a ratio to APD. However, some expenses contain both variable and fixed components, such as salaries & wages. One way to project salaries & wages could be to discuss with the client what level of full-time equivalent (FTE) staffing would be necessary to support any projected volume growth, and multiply the projected FTE's by an average salary per FTE employee, with inflationary increases to the average salary per FTE. Whatever method is employed, it is important to ensure that the growth trends in the operating expenses are reasonable compared to the growth trends in the projected volumes and revenues.

Capital expenditures of a hospital can be extremely important in the valuation. The appraiser should discuss with the client any current or planned facility expansions or large equipment purchases, such as highly specialized diagnostic imaging equipment or cancer treatment equipment. The appraiser should also keep in mind that significant capital equipment expenditures can greatly influence the projected inpatient and/or outpatient volumes. In addition to any planned capital expenditures, the appraiser should also make an allowance for the replacement of the hospital's current facility and equipment.

In developing the weighted average cost of capital (WACC), the appraiser should ensure that the WACC corresponds to the risks associated with the projected earnings stream. Specific company risk factors that either increase or decrease risk should be considered. Some of these factors may include the hospital's operating history (volatile vs. stable), status of payer contracts, strength of physician relationships, presence of any CON requirements, management depth, local competitive environment and the Medicare reimbursement outlook (particularly if the hospital has a high Medicare patient mix).

Chapter 34: The Valuation of Hospitals

Asset Approach

Under the Asset Approach, the hospital's assets and liabilities should be adjusted to Fair Market Value. One of the largest assets for a hospital is typically its real estate and related improvements. As with non-healthcare valuations, the appraiser should consider the need to have the real estate and improvements valued by a qualified real estate appraiser.

The Asset Approach for a hospital valuation has some unique characteristics that differentiate it from non-healthcare valuations. There are intangible assets for a hospital that need to be considered and valued that are not typically present for a non-healthcare valuation. One such intangible asset is a Certificate of Need (CON).

A CON is a state-regulated license to perform certain medical services. The purpose of the CON is to ensure that health providers and services are correctly matched to the needs for those specific health providers and services in a designated area. Not every state has CON requirements, so the appraiser should research whether the hospital being valued is located in a state that requires a CON. Obtaining a CON can be expensive and time-consuming, and in some cases, the granting of a CON can be uncertain or even impossible (due to an excess supply of providers, or a moratorium, etc). A CON is generally valued under one of two methods: (1) Cost to Recreate Method, or (2) Relief from Royalty Method.

Another unique intangible asset that the appraiser should consider is favorable or above-market payer contracts. This scenario may be present if the hospital has particular contracting power or exclusive contracts with payers and its experiencing above market profits. The appraiser should discuss with the client the nature of any above-market payer contracts, the likelihood of their future status, and the potential financial impact to the hospital.

As with other non-healthcare valuations, intangible assets such as Trade Name and Trained & Assembled Workforce should be considered for valuation. However, in assigning values to these intangible assets, the appraiser must remember that patient activity (and therefore, value) for a hospital is primarily driven by factors such as facility location, services provided, insurance coverage, and medical staff.

Typically, patient files are not valued in a hospital setting, since (unlike a medical practice) the likelihood of the patient returning to the hospital for future care is either unlikely or unknown. Also, the costs of maintaining, retrieving and being a custodian of the patient file may outweigh its future economic benefits (if any).

Market Approach

Like non-healthcare valuations, the Market Approach for a hospital is typically performed under two methods: (1) Comparable Transactions method and (2) Guideline Company method.

Chapter 34: The Valuation of Hospitals

The best place to find comparable transactions for hospitals is in the 10-K's or 10-Q's of publicly-traded hospital corporations. In addition, Irving Levin Associates, Inc. publishes an annual report titled *The Healthcare Acquisition Report*, which compiles transaction information for hospitals and other healthcare providers. The appraiser can compile and sort the data based on a number of factors, including, size in terms of revenues and number of beds, geographic location, for-profit vs. not-for-profit status, and number of hospital facilities.

The Guideline Company method can be used as a reasonableness check to the values calculated under the other valuation methods by comparing the pricing multiples (i.e., Total Invested Capital (TIC) to Revenue, TIC to EBITDA) for the publicly-traded hospitals to the subject hospital's valuation multiples. The reason that this method is generally not the primary indication of value is that the publicly-traded hospital corporations generally own dozens of hospitals throughout the U.S. and even internationally. Therefore, the publicly-traded hospitals have distinct advantages over smaller hospitals, including contracting power, geographic diversity, access to capital, and ability to purchase profitable hospitals and divest low-performing hospitals. The Guideline Company method can also be used to give an appraiser an idea of the hospital industry's growth, EBITDA margin and capital structure.

Some of the current publicly-traded hospital corporations are as follows:

- Health Management Associates, Inc. (HMA)

- Community Health Systems (CYH)

- LifePoint Hospital, Inc. (LPNT)

- Tenet Healthcare Corporation (THC)

Reconciliation of Values

In reconciling or selecting the final value outcome for a subject hospital, the appraiser, based on his research, needs to consider the current transaction environment. An important consideration is whether the transaction market is active with many participants and abundant capital. In this type of environment, the most likely buyer of a hospital is another hospital or hospital system that will continue its operations as a hospital. This fact needs to be remembered when reconciling the values under each valuation approach. There could be instances where the Asset Approach value is higher than the values under the Income or Market Approaches. For example, a hospital could have a large value under the Asset Approach if its facilities are large complexes that have a high cost to replace. For transaction purposes, the most likely buyer would be a hospital system that would continue to operate the facility as a hospital with the assets currently in place; therefore, more weight should be given to the Income Approach value, as that value encompasses the future cash flows available to an investor from the hospital's operations. While the Market Approach value is generally not relied upon as a primary indication of value, due to the lack of specific information regarding the transactions (i.e., payer mix, contracting strength, level of competition, etc.), it is important for the appraiser to understand where and why his valuation for the subject hospital falls in relation to the observed marketplace transactions.

Conclusion

Hospital valuations require a thorough understanding of the industry, the current hospital trends, and the various value drivers. The appraiser should stay abreast of the Medicare reimbursement environment, as this can have a significant impact on the profitability of hospitals. The more understanding an appraiser can develop of the hospital industry and its value drivers, the more sound opinion of value can be rendered.

Resource Materials

The following is a listing of some helpful resources to consider when undertaking a hospital valuation:

- *American Hospital Association – www.aha.org*

- *Centers for Medicare & Medicaid Services – www.cms.hhs.gov*

- *Hospital Benchmarking Information – www.hospitalbenchmarks.com (subscription site)*

- *Irving Levin Associates, Inc. – The Healthcare Acquisition Report*

- *Morningstar, Inc. – Cost of Capital Yearbook*

- *IRS Form 990 Finder – www.foundationcenter.org/findfunders/990finder*

- *Merritt Hawkins Physician Inpatient/Outpatient Revenue Survey—http://www.merritthawkins.com/compensation-surveys.aspx*

---

1. American Hospital Association website – www.aha.org/aha/resource-center/Statistics-and-Studies/fast-facts.html
2. U.S. Census Bureau website—http://www.census.gov/hhes/www/hlthins/historic/hihistt1.xls
3. Health Forum, AHA Annual Survey Data, 1980-2006
4. American Hospital Association website—http://www.aha.org/aha/content/2007/PowerPoint/StateofHospitalsChartPack2007.ppt
5. Ibid.

Chapter 34: The Valuation of Hospitals

6. Report to the Congress: Medicare Payment Policy, Section F; March 2003; MedPac
7. *"Ambulatory Surgery Centers A Positive Trend in Health Care."* http://www.ascassociation.org/advocacy/AmbulatorySurgeryCentersPositiveTrendHealthCare.pdf.
8. The Centers for Medicare and Medicaid Services website—http://www.cms.hhs.gov/MedicareProgramRatesStats/downloads/info.pdf
9. Centers for Medicare & Medicaid Services website – Overview of the IPPS
10. Centers for Medicare & Medicaid Services website – Press Releases: "CMS Announces Payment Reforms for Inpatient Hospital Services in 2008," August 1, 2007. www.cms.hhs.gov/apps/media/press_releases.asp
11. Centers for Medicare & Medicaid Services website – Overview of the IPPS
12. Centers for Medicare & Medicaid Services website – "Hospital Outpatient PPS Overview." www.cms.hhs.gov/HospitalOutpatientPPS

Chapter 35
Valuing Joint Ventures & 'Under Arrangements'

By Carol Carden, CPA/ABV, ASA, CFE

As a starting point for a discussion of the value drivers and typical valuation methodologies for joint ventures, it is important to understand the basic forms these joint ventures typically take. The specific characteristics, benefits and challenges of each structure will be discussed in greater detail later in the chapter, but typically hospital/physician joint ventures come in the form of: 1) equity joint ventures; 2) leases; 3) management agreements; and 4) a more comprehensive form of management agreement termed a clinical co-management agreement.

Reasons for valuation

The primary drivers for hospital/physician joint ventures are 1) physicians' desire to identify alternative revenue streams to supplement declining professional revenues; 2) regulations change which close old avenues of collaboration or open new ones; and 3) management has a desire to involve a higher level of clinical expertise in the management of a particular service.

Any collaboration that occurs between a hospital and physicians is subject to regulatory scrutiny. Therefore, as management contemplates one of the forms of joint venture discussed in this chapter, they will many times decide to enlist a valuation expert to ensure that they can demonstrate their attempt to transact the joint venture at terms that are both fair market value (as defined by both the IRS and for Stark/OIG purposes) and commercially reasonable (as required for regulatory purposes).

Regulatory Considerations

The following briefly discusses the five main areas of regulatory compliance consideration in contemplating a joint venture. The appraiser should have at least a cursory understanding of these issues to properly assess the risk of any contemplated joint venture. A detailed discussion of these regulations is beyond the scope of this chapter, however, it is critical that the client has competent legal counsel involved if contemplating a hospital/physician joint venture.

Stark

As discussed previously in this book, the Stark regulations govern referrals from a provider of designated health services (DHS) to an entity in which the provider has a financial

Chapter 35: Valuing Joint Ventures & 'Under Arrangements'

interest unless the transaction falls into a safe harbor. More often than not, the contemplated joint venture will involve one of the 11 DHS. Therefore, the Stark implications of a proposed transaction can have a tremendous impact on the valuation of the venture. It is critical when valuing these types of transactions to ensure the historical or anticipated referrals of business are not factored into the value of the venture. That is not to say that historical volume must be eliminated from the valuation analysis, just that the valuation analysis must be structured in such a way as to not specifically give recognition for previous referral patterns or anticipated referral patterns post-transaction.

For example, if after consummation of the joint venture, it is anticipated that, due to the stronger relationship with the hospital, the physicians will move procedures that they currently refer to competitor facilities to the newly joint-ventured facility, this anticipated volume should not be considered when determining the fair market value of the joint venture during formation. The value of the joint venture should be reflective of the cash flows and risk assessment as it currently exists absent the strengthened relationship that occurs as a result of the joint venture.

The OIG has recently re-focused its concern on the use of "referrals" in what are otherwise standard valuation methods under the income approach, such as the Discounted Cash Flow method, designed to produce an appropriate measure of fair market value. The so-called Thornton letter from 1993 has been reinvigorated. (See Chapter 12). Appraisers and legal counsel need to consider how best to conform to regulatory requirements while still achieving fair market value. One important consideration in using historical volume as the basis for forecasting future volume is to eliminate from both any volume based on a financial incentive to refer or utilize. This can be accomplished by analyzing and comparing referral sources having a financial interest and those not having a financial interest.

Additionally, Stark II Phase III became effective December 5, 2007.[1] Phase III eliminated the safe harbor for compensation arrangements. Now, the parties to the arrangement must be able to demonstrate that the contemplated compensation is stated at fair market value absent authoritative guidance. Phase III does not state that the previous safe harbor methodology cannot be used, just that use of that methodology no longer carries the added benefit of providing safe harbor protection. Compensation comes into play in valuation of management agreements.

Phase III also implemented new rules regarding leases for space and equipment which will be discussed in greater detail later in this chapter.

Anti-kickback regulations

It is not very likely that the proposed joint venture will fit squarely into one of the 13 AKS safe harbors.[2] Much like the discussion above regarding Stark implications, the valuation analyst must have an understanding of the AKS regulations sufficient to assess any undue risk of the contemplated transaction and the related impact on the value. Consideration of the AKS statute

Chapter 35: Valuing Joint Ventures & 'Under Arrangements'

was particularly important when a proposed leasing arrangement was stated on a per procedure or "per click" basis. CMS eliminated per click leases as discussed in a later section of this chapter.

Deficit Reduction Act (DRA)

The DRA of 2005 contained provisions that were far-reaching across many facets of the healthcare industry.[3] When providing business valuation services for a contemplated hospital/physician joint venture, it is critical to understand any reimbursement implications that resulted from provisions contained n the DRA. Imaging was the segment hardest hit by reductions implemented as a result of the DRA and, as a result, we saw an increase in divestitures of physician-owned imaging operations..

CMS proposed fee schedule changes

When CMS issued the Medicare Physician Fee Schedule for 2010, it included reductions in excess of 21% in physician fees across the board In-office imaging services, specifically those in the cardiology specialty, were particularly hard hit. In prior years, Congress has intervened in late December to eliminate proposed reductions of this magnitude across the board. However, as of this writing, the proposed reduction has only been postponed not eliminated.[4] It is important for the valuation analyst to understand proposed and monitor "final" changes such as this in light of the contemplated joint venture.

Private inurement/excess benefit

If the hospital involved in the joint venture is not-for-profit, the transaction must be consummated at fair market value as defined by the IRS (Revenue Ruling 59-60) in order to ensure no private inurement or excess benefit implications are triggered. In particular, the IRS is concerned that not-for-profit assets will be transferred in excess amounts to private individuals.[5] If a transaction is determined to contain private inurement or excess benefits, excise taxes can apply to both the hospital as well as the physician, if the latter is a Disqualified Person under the excess benefit transaction regulations.

Key Features and Typical Valuation Methodologies

It is important to understand the concept of value and, in particular, fair market value as defined by regulatory bodies when determining compensation related to any physician/hospital venture. There are valuation methodologies that are more commonly used for particular types of ventures and having a basic understanding of these will assist you in evaluating the transaction with your client. It is also important to understand the types of information to be considered and the

Chapter 35: Valuing Joint Ventures & 'Under Arrangements'

degree to which assumptions should be tested to ensure the valuation will withstand regulatory scrutiny in the event the transaction is selected for review. We will begin our discussion with the simplest form of joint venture and move toward more complex forms.

Equity joint ventures

Equity joint ventures occur when an existing company or, many times a service line of a hospital, is contributed into a new entity and an ownership interest in the new entity is offered to physicians. This type of venture is easily understood and has withstood the test of time. For plain "vanilla" equity joint ventures, an income approach is typically utilized. Generally speaking, equity joint ventures are chosen solely as an investment vehicle making anticipated cash flows the best indicator of value.

As discussed elsewhere in this book, if recent privately-held market transactions similar to the entity being joint ventured exist in sufficient number, there are still a number of hurdles to overcome before a market-based approach can be used for these joint ventures. Therefore, the market approach is not widely used for purposes of determining the value of equity joint ventures. Typically, the value of the entity to be included in the joint venture is determined from the income approach and the relevant ownership percentage is multiplied by that value. Given the level of ownership contemplated, consideration of discounts related to control and marketability may be warranted.

There are a few challenges to implementing the equity joint venture. Equity joint ventures are prohibited for services comprised of DHS for Stark purposes. The requirement of up-front capital or the incurrence of debt can also make this model less attractive dependent upon the financial goals and risk tolerance of the parties. Finally, equity joint ventures can result in a loss of reimbursement post-transaction due to the DRA discussed previously or other reimbursement differences between hospital-based reimbursement and free-standing entity reimbursement.

Leases

Leases typically involve access on a per block of time basis to a piece of equipment or the operations of a service line. Block leases have been commonly used for access to imaging equipment and cardiac cath labs. One of the more attractive features of the leasing option is that it gives access to the equipment/service line even if there is not sufficient volume to justify full-time provision of the service.

Typically, an income-based approach is used for leases. In general terms, total costs to be incurred through the lease are accumulated and a fair market return is added. The resulting total is divided by the hours of operation specific to the block desired to determine the lease rate. The rate of return should be commensurate with the risks being assumed and generally speaking ranges from 10% to 20%.

Chapter 35: Valuing Joint Ventures & 'Under Arrangements'

Alternatively, a market based approach can be used if the analyst has access to lease rates for similar services in the same geographic market. Given that these leases typically occur between unrelated private companies, this type of market information is not usually readily available.

Leasing arrangements are attractive as they do not require up-front capital and allow for the provision of a service when volume is not sufficient to support a full-time offering. However, leases can be tricky to structure from a regulatory standpoint and are fairly easy for competitors to duplicate.

Under the lease, the billing for the technical component of revenue is generally done by the entity purchasing access to the equipment/service line using their provider identification number.

Management agreements

Traditionally, management agreements have taken the form of physicians providing a stipulated number of hours per month to participate in a somewhat active manner in the management of a service line. Historically, these have been structured as medical directorships. The physician tracks the hours provided and is compensated on an hourly basis for services rendered. The current movement for management agreements is toward what are termed "co-management agreements." or "clinical co-management agreements." These agreements generally have an administrative component with a fixed fee and a quality incentive that allows a bonus payment if certain goals are met.

Editor's Note: Co-management agreements are described in chapter 32.

Typically, co-management agreements are valued using a blend of income and market approaches. The administrative component is generally calculated by multiplying an hourly rate by the number of anticipated hours. With the implementation of Stark Phase III, the safe harbor for determining an hourly rate has been eliminated. The elimination allows for additional flexibility in determining a fair market hourly rate. The flexibility has always been present (as compliance with the safe harbor was never a requirement), but hospitals that previously would have conservatively complied with the safe harbor methodology can now be more creative without stepping outside a comfort zone. The hourly rate analysis will likely now incorporate surveys not previously included in the safe harbor calculation as well as geographic specific compensation data.

The determination of the quality incentive is a more subjective determination with little or no regulatory guidance. Generally, the quality incentive is determined based upon either 1) other quality incentive programs which reward providers for good quality and reporting or penalizes them for bad outcomes or lack of reporting or 2) the cost the provider would incur absent the quality portion of the agreement. The current direction in the industry is moving away from paying for reporting and toward paying for outcomes. Therefore, it is important when using an existing quality incentive program criteria as guidance for valuation purposes, that the features of the agreement you are appraising match the features present in the existing quality incentive program.

Chapter 35: Valuing Joint Ventures & 'Under Arrangements'

To illustrate the concept of considering the costs the provider would incur absent the quality incentive consider that if, in the absence of the quality portion of the agreement, the hospital would have to hire a physician or other professional to administer its quality program, the cost of this hire can be used as one indication for the "value" of the quality incentive program.

The attractive features of a co-management agreement are that no change in ownership occurs and there is no up-front capital required. The original provider of care remains in place and the arrangement is virtually seamless to patients. However, the upside reward available to physicians can often be less than in other types of ventures and the payment of the quality incentive can be quite controversial. Additionally, in other industries, fees for management services are typically tied to profitability or performance, but in the healthcare industry, we must ensure that fees are as disconnected from the referral base as possible to ensure the transaction will withstand regulatory scrutiny.

'Under arrangements' management agreements

Much touted in prior years, these arrangements often were devices to allow a joint venture to provide a hospital with "soup to nuts services" (building, equipment, staffing, day to day management of a service) without giving the joint venture an equity stake in the hospital or service line. This type of management agreement is only permitted now for facilities which qualify for a rural exception under the Stark regulations or if the agreement involves non-referring physicians such as radiologists.

Under arrangements models were frequently used to maximize reimbursement so that services continue to be reimbursed by federal payors at hospital rates rather than free-standing rates. The hospital paid the joint venture (in which it might have been a participant) a monthly or per click fee covering all costs of the delivered services. The hospital maintained oversight, monitored quality standards (the hospital was the provider and remained responsible for service delivery), although on a day to day basis it may have provided very little.

Typically, a new entity was formed which was owned jointly by a hospital and a group of physicians. The physicians could be members of the same group or could have been unrelated physicians in the community normally practicing the same specialty. The new venture had to be capitalized as it typically purchased the equipment necessary to provide the service. Many times, the hospital retained a controlling interest in the new entity for regulatory purposes. "Under arrangements" joint ventures were used most commonly for outpatient surgery, cardiac catheterization labs and imaging.

Valuation determinations for "under arrangements" were generally a blend of the income and market approaches similar to co-management agreements. Some "under arrangements" were compensated based upon a flat monthly amount, but, more commonly, a fee schedule was developed that compensated the "under arrangements" service provider on a per procedure basis.

Chapter 35: Valuing Joint Ventures & 'Under Arrangements'

The attractive features of the "under arrangements" agreement were that it maintained hospital-based reimbursement, incorporated more in-depth clinical knowledge into management of the service and freed hospital management time. However, as mentioned previously, this is an option that is only available in very limited circumstances currently.

Types of Information Utilized and Testing Assumptions

Many of these ventures are complex to model from a valuation standpoint. The valuation analysis is made more difficult due to the fact that hospitals generally only track direct costs by service line so determining the total costs associated with a given service offering requires in-depth analysis and working closely with management to ensure all costs are captured. Once historical financial performance is developed, projected financial performance must be determined. Once more, it is important to keep the fair market value definitions in mind to ensure that assumptions do not incorporate changes that will come about due to the transaction.

A thorough understanding of historical and projected volumes must be obtained. Often, volume is tracked by hospitals on a per procedure basis while the new venture anticipates compensation on a per-case basis. Hospitals typically track volume based on individual charge codes for each procedure performed on a patient. The procedure based information is transferred electronically to the health information management (HIM) department of a hospital where it is grouped and summarized in a manner that facilitates billing. For outpatient procedures from Medicare and many commercial payors, the hospital receives reimbursement on a per case basis rather than a per procedure basis. However, absent the coding and grouping performed by the HIM department, it is difficult for the hospital to bridge the gap between procedures and cases. Therefore, the valuation analyst must work with management to ensure accurate adjustments are made to transition from one volume indicator to another.

An analysis of historical collections and reimbursement is necessary to ensure that the impact of potential changes post-transaction are understood and accounted for. This analysis can be quite challenging to perform particularly for inpatient volumes. Hospitals do not track inpatient reimbursement specific to particular departments or service lines as that reimbursement is more traditionally paid to them on a per admission basis. Therefore, many times outpatient reimbursement is used as a proxy for both inpatient and outpatient volume.

If the Medicare fee schedule is to be used as a proxy under a market-based approach, this will many times require the assistance of outside expertise in coding. To facilitate this analysis, the hospital must be able to produce historical procedure information including diagnosis codes.

When evaluating the thoroughness of the valuation analysis, it is important to understand how the assumptions provided by management are tested. When possible, historical and projected financial performance should be benchmarked against industry sources. The existence of benchmarking will strengthen the results should the transaction be reviewed.

Chapter 35: Valuing Joint Ventures & 'Under Arrangements'

It is also critical that upcoming changes in reimbursement and regulations be given appropriate consideration in the valuation analysis otherwise the results will be incorrect. The projected rates of return for the venture should be compared to alternative investment opportunities and should make sense relative to the risks being assumed. It is very difficult to balance investment goals, risks assumed and regulatory guidance, but documenting the thought process as much as possible will pay off if the results have to be supported to a regulatory body.

---

1. Department of Health and Human Services, Centers for Medicare & Medicaid Services, 42 CFR Parts 411 and 424, (CMS-1810-F), RIN 0938-AK67, *Medicare Program; Physicians' Referrals to Health Care Entities with Which They Have Financial Relationships (Phase III)*

2. *Federal Anti-Kickback Law and Regulatory Safe Harbors, Fact Sheet, November 1999,* Office of Inspector General, Office of Public Affairs.

3. Deficit Reduction Act of 2005, Pub. L. No. 109-171, 120 Stat. 4 (Feb. 8, 2006)

4. Shortly before press, CMS rolled back a portion of the cuts in myocardial perfusion imaging, cardiac CT and cardiac catheterization.

5. *Intermediate Sanctions – Excess Benefit Transactions,* Internal Revenue Service at www.irs.gov/charities/charitable/article/0,,id=123303,00.html and *Inurement – Section 501 (c) (4),* Internal Revenue Service at www.irs.gov/charities/nonprofits/article/0,,id=156404,00.html

Chapter 36

Ambulatory Surgery Centers

By Todd Sorensen, MBA, AVA

Editor's Note: The impact of the Healthcare Reform legislation is discussed in chapter 1 and in the Appendix Teleconference Transcript.

As patient care continues to migrate from an inpatient setting to an outpatient setting, surgery-center transactions have become one of the most popular joint-venture relationships involving both for-profit and not-for-profit healthcare providers and surgeons who perform outpatient surgery. Outside of engagements associated with physician practice transactions, valuation engagements associated with ambulatory surgery center (ASC) transactions have represented the highest volume healthcare segment for our firm. As with most healthcare segments, ensuring that transactions between potential referral source physician owners and healthcare systems occur within the range of fair market value is critical to compliance with the Stark Regulations, Federal Fraud and Abuse statutes and in some cases, state law.

Types of private ASC equity transactions include (1) controlling interests in stand-alone licensed free-standing surgery centers; (2) minority or non-controlling equity transactions in free-standing ASCs; and (3) controlling and non-controlling equity transactions in hospital outpatient departments re-licensed as free-standing ambulatory surgery centers. Each of these transactions typically has a different value.

Minority equity interests in private ASCs tend to trade at lower levels than controlling interests in those same ASCs. Surgery centers with little or no physician ownership tend to be valued lower than those with significant ownership. In general, valuations of any equity interest are based not only on external market factors but the facts and circumstances of the particular ASC being valued.

The ASC industry is highly fragmented, composed of several large publicly or privately owned companies and many small, independent operators. Of the 4,707 ASCs operating in the United States, only 969 facilities, or approximately 22%, are owned or managed by multi-facility chains. HealthSouth, AmSurg, USPI and HCA, Inc. are a few of the largest owners and operators.

The tides of change have come with an increasing market share of hospital-physician joint-venture ASCs. Healthcare systems have begun to recognize the role of such a business model within the industry, and what was once considered a competitive threat is now viewed as an intriguing avenue of partnership to increase profit margins and improve relations with physicians.

This chapter provides an overview of the ASC segment, typical ASC legal structures, ASC financial performance and primary value drivers, and the most common ASC valuation applications.

Chapter 36: Ambulatory Surgery Centers

Segment Overview

Ambulatory surgery refers to lower-acuity surgical procedures performed on an outpatient basis that do not require an overnight stay. These surgeries can occur in either a hospital outpatient (surgical) department (HOPD) or in a free-standing ASC.

ASCs offer a more productive and comfortable environment for both physicians and patients. A surgeon using an ASC can typically better maintain a schedule with more consistent weekly time blocked to schedule surgeries (block time) and quicker, more reliable turnaround times. Patients who receive treatment at an ASC benefit from a convenient, less-institutionalized environment, streamlined care, specialized services and proven lower infection rates.

ASCs provide the surgical equipment and supplies, specialized personnel, and other support services that enable their surgeon-users to perform surgeries. Physicians typically do not pay for these services. Instead, the ASC bills a technical fee, or facility fee, to the patient or payor. The physician bills a professional fee separately. The ASC neither employs nor pays compensation to the surgeon-users. Consequently, an ASC's success or failure relates directly to its ability to provide the necessary technical services to enable its surgeon-users to perform their surgical cases.

History of ASCs

The idea of performing outpatient surgery first materialized in 1966, in an article in the Journal of the American Medical Association (JAMA). Shortly thereafter, the health insurance industry began exploring alternatives to the high costs associated with procedures in hospitals, and the U.S. National Advisory Commission on Health Facilities began experimenting with ways to lower them. In 1970, the first ASC opened. In 1971, the American Medical Association (AMA) endorsed ASCs performing surgery under general and local anesthesia for selected procedures and patients. By 1976, 67 ASCs existed around the country.

Although the government, through Medicare, began collaborating with six ASCs in 1974, it wasn't until 1982 that the program approved payment for 200 selected procedures performed in ASCs. Today Medicare, Medicaid and private insurers allow and pay for more than 3,300 procedures performed in ASCs, and these numbers are expected to grow. Approved procedures generally are those offered in a hospital inpatient setting that also can be performed safely in outpatient facilities. ASC-approved procedures generally require less than 90 minutes of operating-room time, less than four hours of recovery-room time and no overnight stay.

Expanded acceptance by Medicare and other payors has led to large growth in the number of ASCs and total procedures performed. For example, the number of Medicare-certified ASCs grew at an average annual rate of 8% from 1999 to 2005. During that same period the Centers for Medicare & Medicaid Services (CMS) noted an annual average of 337 new

Chapter 36: Ambulatory Surgery Centers

Medicare-certified ASCs. There are currently close to 4,500 Medicare-certified facilities nationwide. There are an additional 500 ASCs that are not Medicare-certified.

Total Medicare payments for ASC services have continued to grow at a rapid pace. For example, data show that Medicare payments to ASCs more than quadrupled between 1992 and 2005. Payments increased by 15% per year, on average, from 1999 to 2005. Surgery case growth (as a percentage) peaked in 1996 and has slowed to a current rate of near 6%.

Certificate of need requirements

Some states require a certificate of need (CON) to operate an ASC. A CON is a regulatory review process that evaluates whether a proposed service or facility is actually needed in a specific market. Those subject to CON regulations include hospitals, nursing homes, outpatient surgery centers and anyone purchasing medical equipment valued above certain state-determined thresholds.

The CON mandate began in response to overwhelming requests for federal funding spurred by the 1946 Hill-Burton Program, which matched grants for the construction of hospitals in medically under-served areas. Congress needed to infuse effective measures to appropriately manage the billions of dollars in federal assistance being requested in response to the program.

In 1974, Congress passed the National Health Planning and Resources Development Act, offering states powerful incentives to enact laws implementing CON programs. By 1980, all states but Louisiana had one. Congress repealed the federal law in 1986 and many states have since relaxed or eliminated CON laws.

Exhibit 1 illustrates the states that require a CON, those that do not, and the number of Medicare-certified ASCs in the United States in 2005.

ASC growth

That healthcare costs have increased at rates in excess of inflation is considered the primary factor in the development and increased use of surgery centers. Procedures performed in an outpatient setting generally cost between 30 and 60% less than the same procedures performed in a hospital. As a result, Medicare, managed care and other payors have encouraged moving procedures to ASCs.

While cost containment was the initial driver in the growth of ASCs, current growth in the industry is also driven by advantages to both patients and physicians. In a survey completed by the Office of the Inspector General (OIG), part of the U.S. Department of Health and Human Services (HHS), Medicare beneficiaries who underwent procedures in ASCs strongly preferred

Chapter 36: Ambulatory Surgery Centers

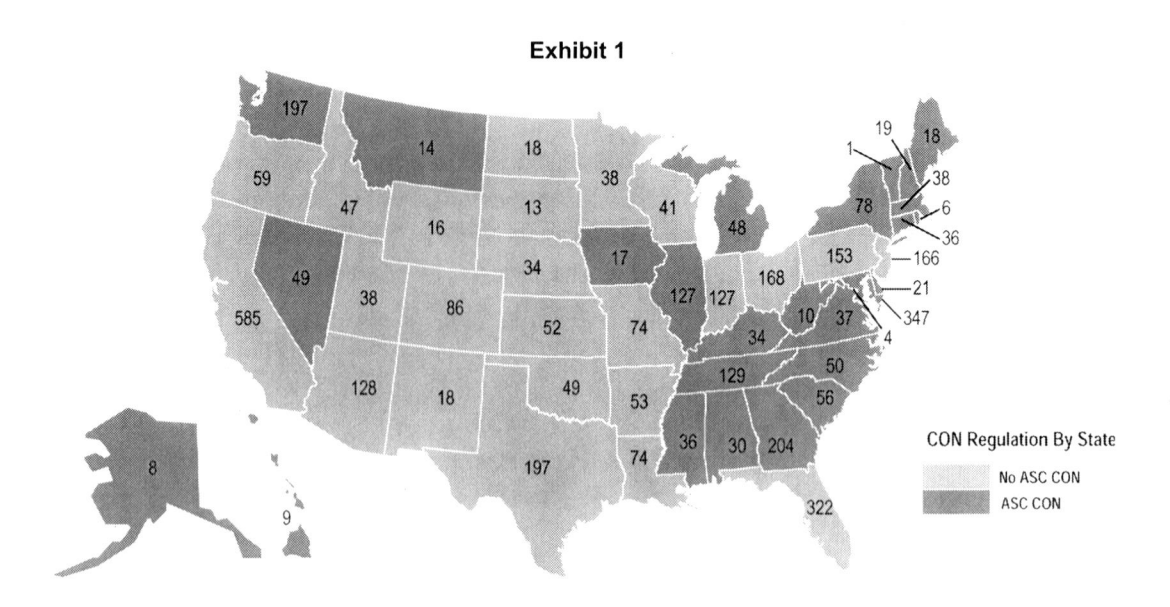

Exhibit 1

the facilities to hospitals.[1] Reasons included less paperwork, lower costs, more convenient locations, better parking, less wait time, better organization and friendlier staff. The study also determined that ASCs provided safety and post-operative care comparable to a hospital.

For physicians, the benefits of performing surgeries in ASCs go beyond increased patient satisfaction. Not only are their patients happier, but they can also achieve larger volumes and greater economies of scale. Unlike doctors at a hospital that provides a variety of surgical procedures and uses an array of supplies and equipment, doctors at free-standing surgery centers typically focus on a few select procedures. This increases patient turnaround time and decreases time between surgeries because the operating room needs minimal preparation for the next patient.

Physicians who act as partial owners or investors in the venture (by partnering with an ASC management chain like AmSurg or United Surgical Partners International (USPI), for example), have an additional incentive to prefer the ASC environment: they earn income for the procedures they perform. In other words, physicians capture a portion of a technical fee not accessible to them at a hospital.

Technological developments also have contributed to substantial growth in the ASC segment. Advances in laser, endoscopic and arthroscopic minimally invasive procedures have allowed for more variance in the array of procedures conducted at ASCs.

Demand for outpatient surgery will continue to increase during the next decade, driven by growth in the 55-plus population, as baby boomers shift into the senior-citizen bracket. This is largely because utilization rates for many outpatient surgical procedures appear to correlate directly with age. Population growth alone could drive a 2% annual increase in ambulatory surgical procedures through 2010.

Chapter 36: Ambulatory Surgery Centers

Changes in Medicare payment system for ASCs

The Medicare Prescription Drug, Improvement, and Modernization Act of 2003 (MMA) set in motion some much-anticipated changes to the ASC payment system. Through the MMA, CMS eliminated the update for ambulatory surgical center services for fiscal year 2005, changed the update cycle to a calendar year, and eliminated updates for calendar years 2006 through 2009. The MMA also removed the requirement that CMS survey ASCs' costs and charges every 5 years. It also asked the General Accounting Office (GAO) to study the relative cost of services in ASCs and HOPDs and determine whether the outpatient prospective payment system's (OPPS) procedure groups reflected ASC procedures. The results of this study formed the basis for the 2007 Proposed ASC Rule.

On August 8, 2006, CMS unveiled its proposal for a new ASC payment system. On January 1, 2008, CMS implemented the new system for payments to ASCs for the provision of medical services to Medicare beneficiaries. Exhibit 2 gives a brief description of the major events leading up to the implementation of the new system.

Exhibit 2

	NEW ASC PAYMENT SYSTEM TIMELINE
1998	CMS proposes a new ASC payment system and a new hospital outpatient department ("HOPD") payment system.
2000	CMS Begins paying HOPD using prospectively determined rates for bundles of services, called APCs. Congress prohibits CMS from implementing a new system for ASCs without a new cost survey.
2003	Congress requires CMS to implement a new ASC payment system by January 1, 2008, and freezes ASC payment rates through 2009.
2005	Introduction of Ambulatory Surgical Center Medicare Payment Modernization Act of 2005 (legislation) by Congressman Herger (R-CA) and Senator Crapo (R-ID).
2006	CMS issues proposed rule detailing its recommendations for a new payment system.
2007	On August 2, 2007, CMS issues a final rule establishing a new payment system for ASCs, including the methodology to be used in determining rates, and proposes rates for 2008. On November 27, 2007, CMS issues final rates for 2008.

The new payment system is similar to the old Medicare payment system in that CMS pays ASCs a facility fee intended to cover the non-professional costs associated with providing a surgical procedure. But instead of categorizing payments into one of nine groupers, the new payment is based on one of 201 ambulatory payment classifications (APCs). Medicare uses the same APCs for ASCs and HOPDs. Each procedure performed is assigned a common procedural terminology (CPT) code which in turn cross-walks to an APC, and each APC has a specific payment rate. But because CMS will continue to report payment rates by CPT code, ASCs will continue to bill and collect from Medicare using CPT codes.

Though ASCs and HOPDs both use APCs, payment rates vary between the two. The rate paid to an HOPD for each APC is based on relative weight, a measurement that ranks the costs to perform the procedures in one APC compared to the costs of those in another. CMS determines the relative weight for each APC using hospital cost reports. The relative weight is then multiplied by a uniform dollar conversion factor to get the national HOPD payment rate. ASCs payment is a percentage of the national HOPD rate. For 2008, ASCs received, on average, 65% of HOPD payments.

Chapter 36: Ambulatory Surgery Centers

Medicare reimbursed ASCs for providing 3,390 surgical procedures in 2008, 819 more than were reimbursable in 2007. Some of the new procedures will realize reimbursement significantly higher than 65% of HOPD rates. For example, procedures that requires use of a device estimated to cost more than 50% of the procedure's total APC reimbursement, the ASC payment rate includes the same dollar value that an HOPD receives for the device, without any discount. Forty-five ASC device-intensive procedures will be reimbursed in this fashion.

Approximately 44% of the new procedures have reimbursement rates lower than the 65% HOPD conversion factor. For procedures performed in physician offices more than 50% of the time, the ASC payment is the lesser of either the payment rate determined using the HOPD conversion factor or the amount Medicare typically pays the physician for performing the procedures in the office. This payment methodology only applies to new procedures introduced under the new payment system, not to procedures on the list in 2007.

When it comes to multiple procedures, the policy in effect prior to the implementation of the new payment system will remain. ASCs will earn 100% for the primary procedure (defined as the one with the highest reimbursement rate), and 50% for each additional procedure. Certain procedures are not subject to the multiple procedure discount; the classification of these procedures hasn't changed.

CMS established a four-year transition period for procedures already on the ASC list, to give individual ASCs more time to adjust to the new payment system. In 2008, Medicare ASC payment rates for these procedures will be based on a blended rate of 75% of the 2007 ASC payment rates and 25% of the amount Medicare would have paid in 2008 under the new system. In 2009, the ASC rate will be based 50% on the 2007 rate and 50% on the 2009 rate. In 2010, the payment will be made based on 25% and 75% of those respective payment rates, and in 2011, the transition will be complete.

The new payment methodology will affect surgical specialties differently. Using the 2008 rates, the Federated Ambulatory Surgery Association (FASA), which has since been merged with the American Association of Ambulatory Surgery Center (AAASC) to form the Ambulatory Surgery Center Association (ASCA) estimated a 5% decline for GI rates and a 23% increase for orthopedics. FASA estimates that once fully implemented, the new payment system will cause an overall decline of 19% for GI and an overall increase of 92% for orthopedics. FASA's analysis, detailed in the November/December *Update Magazine*, is summarized in Exhibit 3.

Under the new payment system, Medicare will reimburse nine of the 10 highest-volume procedures performed in ASCs at a lower rate. According to CMS, the overall lower payment rates, taking into consideration the 819 newly covered procedures, will result in the same total 2008 Medicare spending on ASCs than if a new payment system had not been adopted.

Chapter 36: Ambulatory Surgery Centers

Exhibit 3

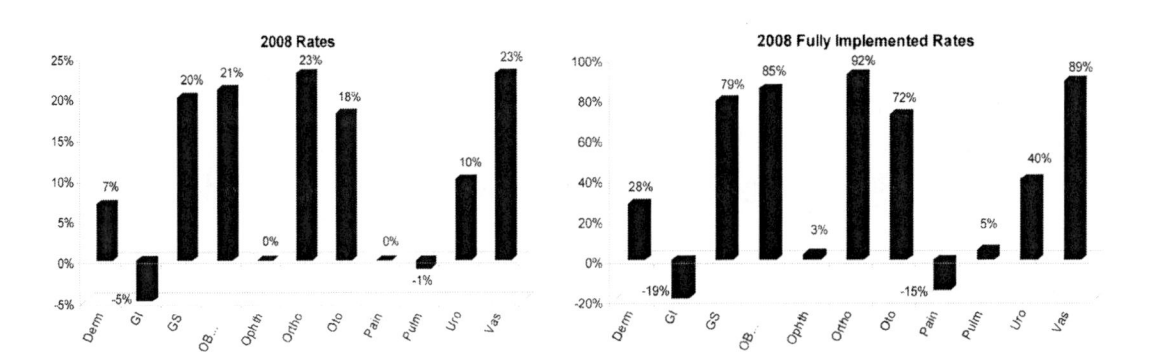

[Two bar charts shown side by side]

2008 Rates: Derm 7%, GI -5%, GS 20%, OB 21%, Ophth 0%, Ortho 23%, Oto 18%, Pain 0%, Pulm -1%, Uro 10%, Vas 23%

2008 Fully Implemented Rates: Derm 28%, GI -19%, GS 79%, OB 85%, Ophth 3%, Ortho 92%, Oto 72%, Pain -15%, Pulm 5%, Uro 40%, Vas 89%

Typical ASC Legal Structures

Typically, ASC entities are either structured as limited liability corporations (LLCs) or limited partnerships (LPs). In name and in legal form, these entities may differ, but they are similarly governed by the applicable agreement governing operations associated with ASCs, the operating agreement for LLCs and the partnership agreement for LPs.

The most critical elements that may affect the valuation of assets or an interest in an ASC include:

- Cash distributions

- Ownership restrictions

- Buy/sell provisions

In particular, these elements in turn have a direct or indirect impact on minority and marketability issues flowing from the valuation of an interest in an ASC.

Cash distributions

Most ASC operating or partnership agreements include detailed provisions that provide for the distribution of virtually all of the discretionary cash on at least a quarterly, and sometimes monthly, basis. Since the cash distributions are normally defined in this manner, this may reduce the impact of any applicable discounts for both lack of control and lack of marketability.

Chapter 36: Ambulatory Surgery Centers

Ownership restrictions

As previously discussed, federal regulations allow physicians who perform surgery in and refer patients to ASCs, to maintain ownership in an ASC. In order to fit in a safe harbor from the federal fraud and abuse statutes, physicians who maintain an ownership interest in an ASC must:

1. Derive one-third of their professional income from outpatient surgery; and

2. Perform one-third of their eligible cases in the ASC in which they invest.

Through the relevant operating or partnership agreement, some ASCs require that all physician owners meet both of these one-third tests to maintain ownership in the ASC while other ASCs are more flexible and the terms for maintaining ownership are less defined. Not all, but most ASCs require that physician owners be approved for admission to ownership and that they be redeemed upon their disability, retirement or move from their service area.

Buy/Sell

In either case (purchase or redemption), most ASC operating or partnership agreements require that physicians are redeemed or purchase shares at either fair market value or an amount based on a formula – often 3 to 4 times EBITDA less interest-bearing debt. While on occasion ASC operating or partnership agreements may in effect penalize owners selling an interest, more often than not the buy/sell provisions ensure that the amount received for a redemption is either at or similar to fair market value.

To summarize, the provisions for cash distributions, ownership and buy/sell arrangements typically included in ASC operating or partnership agreements reduce the impact of lack of control and marketability for non-controlling equity interests.

Typical ASC Financial Structure and Performance

All facilities are different. However, VMG HEALTH annually completes benchmarking studies. The *Endoscopy Intellimarker Study* and *Multi-Specialty Intellimarker Study* are based on analyses of actual detailed financial and operating performance information from more than 300 endoscopy and multi-specialty surgery centers across the United States. Exhibits 4 through 6 summarize the aggregate statistical analysis of the income statements from the *Multi-Specialty ASC Intellimarker 2007*.[2] Our observations on this data then follow.

Chapter 36: Ambulatory Surgery Centers

Exhibit 4 Income Statement

$ in thousands	Mean	Standard Dev.	25%	Median 50%	75%	90%
Patient Revenues						
Gross Charges	$ 20,233	$ 14,736	$ 9,921	$ 16,637	$ 27,454	$ 42,356
Adjustments	(13,914)	11,323	(17,998)	(10,781)	(6,211)	(3,086)
Net Revenue	6,768	5,461	3,638	5,647	8,945	11,940
Operating Expenses						
Employee Salary & Wages	1,491	936	884	1,305	1,869	2,677
Employee Taxes & Benefits	320	318	173	273	419	580
Occupancy Costs	429	319	221	393	540	769
Medical & Surgical Supplies	1,338	952	710	1,158	1,739	2,498
Other Medical Costs	335	930	30	99	262	721
Insurance	70	58	33	53	89	136
Depreciation & Amortization	305	219	152	252	401	575
General & Administrative						
Bad Debt	133	161	48	86	154	275
Management Fees	282	245	133	250	356	488
Other G & A	593	476	317	501	729	1,063
Total G & A	881	531	495	774	1,141	1,540
Total Operating Expenses	4,903	2,720	2,966	4,379	6,233	8,536
Operating Income	1,812	3,965	199	1,183	2,512	4,194
Other Expense (Income)	100	(550)	-	(3)	(13)	(75)
Net Interest Expense	73	128	3	43	107	195
Earnings Before Taxes	1,734	3,949	172	1,128	2,575	4,029
EBITDA	$ 2,117	$ 4,000	$ 417	$ 1,519	$ 2,797	$ 4,595

VMG HEALTH Multi-Specialty ASC Intellimarker 2007

Exhibit 5 Common Size Income Statement

	Mean	Standard Dev.	25%	Median 50%	75%	90%
Patient Revenues						
Gross Charges	298.9%	269.8%	272.7%	294.6%	306.9%	354.7%
Adjustments	-205.6%	207.3%	-494.7%	-190.9%	-69.4%	-25.8%
Net Revenue	100.0%	100.0%	100.0%	100.0%	100.0%	100.0%
Operating Expenses						
Employee Salary & Wages	24.9%	10.9%	19.0%	23.5%	29.0%	35.2%
Employee Taxes & Benefits	5.5%	6.7%	3.7%	4.8%	6.2%	7.5%
Occupancy Costs	8.5%	7.4%	3.9%	6.7%	10.3%	17.0%
Medical & Surgical Supplies	21.5%	10.1%	17.3%	20.9%	25.5%	30.7%
Other Medical Costs	4.6%	10.4%	0.6%	1.6%	3.7%	8.9%
Insurance	1.2%	1.1%	0.6%	1.0%	1.6%	2.4%
Depreciation & Amortization	5.9%	5.1%	2.9%	4.4%	7.1%	11.2%
General & Administrative						
Bad Debt	2.1%	1.9%	1.0%	1.9%	2.3%	4.0%
Management Fees	4.6%	2.8%	3.0%	4.8%	5.6%	6.6%
Other G & A	10.0%	6.7%	6.3%	8.5%	12.2%	18.1%
Total G & A	14.8%	7.9%	10.5%	13.1%	18.2%	23.9%
Total Operating Expenses	82.4%	36.0%	65.7%	77.8%	93.7%	113.8%
Operating Income	16.8%	35.4%	5.5%	22.1%	34.1%	44.5%
Other Expense (Income)	0.9%	-4.9%	0.0%	-0.1%	-0.3%	-1.2%
Net Interest Expense	3.0%	2.9%	0.1%	0.8%	2.1%	4.3%
Earnings Before Taxes	15.6%	36.5%	4.9%	20.3%	33.6%	43.4%
EBITDA	22.6%	32.5%	11.2%	26.4%	38.5%	48.8%

VMG HEALTH Multi-Specialty ASC Intellimarker 2007

Chapter 36: Ambulatory Surgery Centers

Exhibit 6 Operating Expense Analysis

as a % of Net Revenue	Mean	Standard Dev.	25%	Median 50%	75%	90%
Employee Salary & Wages	24.9%	10.9%	19.0%	23.5%	29.0%	35.2%
Employee Taxes & Benefits	5.5%	6.7%	3.7%	4.8%	6.2%	7.5%
Occupancy Costs	8.5%	7.4%	3.9%	6.7%	10.3%	17.0%
Medical & Surgical Supplies	21.5%	10.1%	17.3%	20.9%	25.5%	30.7%
Other Medical Costs	4.6%	10.4%	0.6%	1.6%	3.7%	8.9%
Insurance	1.2%	1.1%	0.6%	1.0%	1.6%	2.4%
General & Administrative	14.8%	7.9%	10.5%	13.1%	18.2%	23.9%
Total Operating Expenses	76.9%	32.9%	61.5%	73.3%	88.7%	104.4%

per Square Foot

Employee Salary & Wages	$ 117.70	$ 133.74	$ 74.41	$ 102.36	$ 127.58	$ 167.78
Employee Taxes & Benefits	24.41	28.38	15.29	20.98	26.87	35.22
Occupancy Costs	31.71	17.91	22.27	31.89	40.34	48.01
Medical & Surgical Supplies	110.74	180.46	63.08	88.42	119.09	149.91
Other Medical Costs	37.34	130.29	2.41	9.31	17.82	34.74
Insurance	5.55	6.06	2.52	4.17	6.36	10.45
General & Administrative	69.68	68.82	40.09	56.00	82.35	107.29
Total Operating Expenses	$ 368.20	$ 435.96	$ 244.20	$ 316.85	$ 389.64	$ 483.72

per OR ($'s in thousands)

Employee Salary & Wages	$ 358.9	$ 159.8	$ 257.7	$ 328.3	$ 448.2	$ 567.6
Employee Taxes & Benefits	79.4	73.7	48.7	69.4	98.3	126.4
Occupancy Costs	107.8	65.3	64.4	101.9	136.7	200.0
Medical & Surgical Supplies	324.4	164.2	204.3	310.3	425.3	531.5
Other Medical Costs	74.3	188.9	8.9	29.8	58.5	129.9
Insurance	17.8	13.7	8.9	13.8	22.6	32.5
General & Administrative	216.2	109.6	135.9	200.7	272.5	360.2
Total Operating Expenses	$ 1,121.4	$ 447.5	$ 800.0	$ 1,056.9	$ 1,426.2	$ 1,749.1

per Case

Employee Salary & Wages	$ 343.00	$ 132.97	$ 254.90	$ 318.58	$ 407.36	$ 525.57
Employee Taxes & Benefits	70.49	32.58	48.60	67.05	88.68	119.40
Occupancy Costs	117.55	107.72	47.55	91.01	148.03	226.98
Medical & Surgical Supplies	304.23	148.45	210.47	277.22	362.79	494.66
Other Medical Costs	52.06	112.45	6.59	20.08	47.09	81.87
Insurance	17.00	14.49	8.59	13.94	20.24	29.33
General & Administrative	205.95	115.39	128.62	182.49	254.15	348.50
Total Operating Expenses	$ 1,069.40	$ 437.13	$ 768.83	$ 995.39	$ 1,250.06	$ 1,641.77

VMG HEALTH Multi-Specialty ASC Intellimarker 2007

Income statement observations

Median net revenue, or reimbursement for ASCs participating in the *Multi-Specialty ASC Intellimarker 2007* is $5.6 million and median earnings before interest taxes depreciation and amortization (EBITDA) is $1.5 million. The single largest expense component is employee cost, including salaries, wages, taxes and benefits, representing 28% of net revenue. Median medical and surgical supplies costs represent 21% of net revenue. Median EBITDA is 26% of net revenue.

Net revenue for ASCs is driven by volume and specialty mix and varies widely across the spectrum of specialties. Exhibit 7 summarizes the median net revenue per case by specialty from the *Multi-Specialty ASC Intellimarker 2007*.

Chapter 36: Ambulatory Surgery Centers

Exhibit 7 Revenue per Case

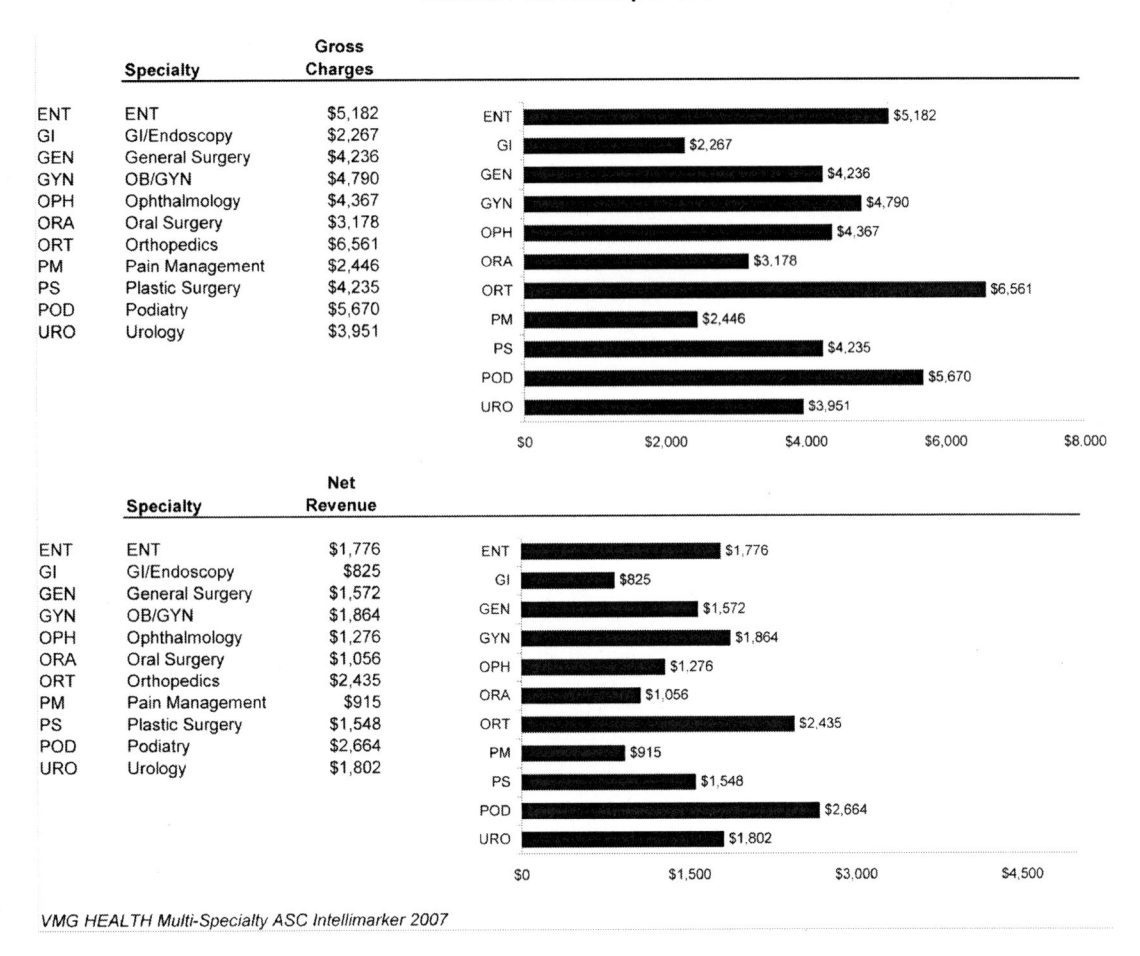

Specialty		Gross Charges
ENT	ENT	$5,182
GI	GI/Endoscopy	$2,267
GEN	General Surgery	$4,236
GYN	OB/GYN	$4,790
OPH	Ophthalmology	$4,367
ORA	Oral Surgery	$3,178
ORT	Orthopedics	$6,561
PM	Pain Management	$2,446
PS	Plastic Surgery	$4,235
POD	Podiatry	$5,670
URO	Urology	$3,951

Specialty		Net Revenue
ENT	ENT	$1,776
GI	GI/Endoscopy	$825
GEN	General Surgery	$1,572
GYN	OB/GYN	$1,864
OPH	Ophthalmology	$1,276
ORA	Oral Surgery	$1,056
ORT	Orthopedics	$2,435
PM	Pain Management	$915
PS	Plastic Surgery	$1,548
POD	Podiatry	$2,664
URO	Urology	$1,802

VMG HEALTH Multi-Specialty ASC Intellimarker 2007

From the *Multi-Specialty ASC Intellimarker 2007*, net revenue per case ranges from $825 for GI/Endoscopy and $915 for Pain Management on the low end, to $2,435 for Orthopedics and $2,664 for Podiatry on the high end.

While there is some variability in operating expenses from center to center, the largest components—employee costs and medical and surgical supplies—are both driven primarily by the case specialty mix in an ASC. Generally speaking, less complex cases such as those procedures for GI/Endoscopy and Pain require fewer staffing hours and supplies than more complex cases such as those in Orthopedics. Exhibit 8 contrasts costs per case for ASCs doing only GI/Endoscopy and ASCs with greater than 50% Orthopedics.

Chapter 36: Ambulatory Surgery Centers

Exhibit 8 Operating Expense Analysis Comparison

	Median		
as a % of Net Revenue	GI	All MS	MS > 50% Ortho
Employee Salary & Wages	22.3%	23.5%	23.3%
Employee Taxes & Benefits	5.2%	4.8%	4.4%
Occupancy Costs	4.3%	6.7%	6.9%
Medical & Surgical Supplies	7.6%	20.9%	22.5%
Other Medical Costs	1.8%	1.6%	1.1%
Insurance	1.2%	1.0%	0.9%
General & Administrative	13.8%	13.1%	11.9%
Total Operating Expenses	60.0%	73.3%	70.2%
per Case			
Employee Salary & Wages	$ 135.92	$ 318.58	$ 369.58
Employee Taxes & Benefits	36.86	67.05	64.98
Occupancy Costs	27.14	91.01	114.44
Medical & Surgical Supplies	44.63	277.22	372.91
Other Medical Costs	10.44	20.08	14.92
Insurance	5.94	13.94	15.69
General & Administrative	99.37	182.49	192.76
Total Operating Expenses	$ 368.60	$ 995.39	$ 1,147.94

VMG HEALTH Endoscopy Intellimarker 2007 and Multi-Specialty ASC Intellimarker 2007

Unlike employee costs and medical and surgical supplies per case, median employee costs and medical and surgical supplies as a percentage of net revenue are fairly consistent across the spectrum of case complexity from GI/Endoscopy to greater than 50% Orthopedics.

Since the most significant operating expense categories tend to vary somewhat consistently with revenue, the primary driver of surgery-center profitability is relative reimbursement levels. Relative reimbursement levels are, in turn, determined by both the payor mix and an individual center's commercial reimbursement. Government payors such as Medicare and Medicaid tend to reimburse ASCs less than commercial or managed care payors. Local market conditions and/or the strength of the ASC's commercial and managed care contracts may affect that ASC's relative commercial reimbursement.

Balance sheet observations

Median total assets for ASCs participating in the *Multi-Specialty ASC Intellimarker 2007* is $3.0 million and median long-term debt is $1.0 million. Median total current assets and net property, plant and equipment represent 44% and 48% of total assets, respectively. Median long-term debt is 32% of total assets. In comparison to the income-statement categories, the standard deviation for balance-sheet categories, and in particular, long-term debt, is much higher.

Exhibits 9 and 10 demonstrate the aggregate statistical analysis of the balance sheets from the *Multi-Specialty ASC Intellimarker 2007*.

Chapter 36: Ambulatory Surgery Centers

Exhibit 9 Balance Sheet

$'s in thousands	Mean	Standard Dev.	25%	Median 50%	75%	90%
ASSETS						
Cash & Equivalents	$ 463	$ 763	$ 50	$ 263	$ 735	$ 1,386
Net Accounts Receivable	674	1,007	379	645	1,062	1,555
Other Current Assets	471	1,187	146	261	452	1,096
Total Current Assets	1,608	1,383	735	1,428	2,179	3,099
Gross PP&E	2,817	2,363	1,063	2,122	4,050	5,716
Accumulated Depreciation	(1,684)	1,281	(2,465)	(1,698)	(574)	(198)
Net PP&E	1,464	1,599	732	1,163	2,210	3,467
Other Assets	930	2,041	22	209	881	2,518
Total Assets	$ 3,673	$ 3,545	$ 1,616	$ 3,023	$ 4,705	$ 7,647
LIABILITIES						
Current Liabilities	$ 504	$ 507	$ 218	$ 378	$ 651	$ 968
Current Portion of LTD	358	390	91	215	454	857
Total Current Liabilites	589	567	242	448	783	1,210
Total Long-Term Debt	1,504	1,731	328	977	2,057	3,674
Other LT Liabilities	186	588	3	15	86	333
Total Liabilities	1,836	1,963	604	1,336	2,426	3,974
EQUITY						
Total Shareholders' Equity	2,177	2,731	695	1,586	2,790	4,743
Total Liabilities & Equity	$ 3,673	$ 3,545	$ 1,616	$ 3,023	$ 4,705	$ 7,647

VMG HEALTH Multi-Specialty ASC Intellimarker 2007

Exhibit 10 Common Size Balance Sheet

	Mean	Standard Dev.	25%	Median 50%	75%	90%
ASSETS						
Cash & Equivalents	17.3%	37.3%	1.4%	9.0%	20.3%	36.6%
Net Accounts Receivable	20.5%	24.0%	13.0%	19.1%	33.3%	42.2%
Other Current Assets	12.0%	22.4%	4.5%	8.0%	15.0%	30.1%
Total Current Assets	46.3%	33.3%	27.7%	44.1%	62.1%	75.3%
Gross PP&E	58.3%	35.6%	32.6%	58.8%	80.2%	94.4%
Accumulated Depreciation	-43.1%	41.4%	-65.4%	-38.9%	-14.9%	-7.1%
Net PP&E	47.1%	23.7%	30.6%	47.9%	64.6%	77.0%
Other Assets	15.3%	22.7%	0.8%	5.8%	26.7%	46.6%
Total Assets	100.0%	0.0%	100.0%	100.0%	100.0%	100.0%
LIABILITIES						
Current Liabilities	15.1%	55.0%	6.8%	11.6%	20.9%	35.3%
Current Portion of LTD	17.3%	33.8%	3.3%	7.1%	13.5%	46.3%
Total Current Liabilites	19.6%	60.3%	7.2%	13.4%	27.1%	52.4%
Total Long-Term Debt	40.4%	57.2%	12.7%	32.4%	56.2%	82.5%
Other LT Liabilities	4.2%	11.8%	0.1%	0.3%	2.8%	8.4%
Total Liabilities	53.4%	93.5%	22.4%	43.3%	73.0%	118.3%
EQUITY						
Shareholders' Equity	49.5%	37.5%	31.6%	57.4%	77.9%	91.4%
Total Liabilities & Equity	100.0%	0.0%	100.0%	100.0%	100.0%	100.0%

VMG HEALTH Multi-Specialty ASC Intellimarker 2007

Chapter 36: Ambulatory Surgery Centers

Does the past tell us anything about the future?

Yes. No. Maybe. Maybe not. It depends. These all could be appropriate answers in a given situation. Whether an appraiser attempts to attach an appropriate market multiple to historical earnings or to develop "most likely case" projections, the future is much more important than the past. For ASCs with a substantial portion of Medicare revenue (and all other things equal), changes in the Medicare payment methodology over the next four years may affect revenue significantly. ASCs with a substantial portion of out-of-network revenue, (and all other things equal) the sustainability of maintaining relatively high out-of-network reimbursements, is in question. In other words, there is a substantial "risk" in relying on the past to project future performance.

ASC risk-assessment matrix

It's important to look at the inherent risks of investing in an ASC. To do so, we'll look at a tool developed by Jon O'Sullivan of VMG HEALTH that measures risk along the following lines:

- contracting
- service-area growth
- competition
- physician ownership
- non-owner utilization
- concentration by specialty
- out-of-network concentration
- staff and supplies efficiency
- location
- condition of the facility and equipment

See Exhibit 11 for the complete ASC Risk-Assessment Matrix.

The ASC Risk-Assessment Matrix produces a single score but gives different weights to different categories and sub-categories based on their relative importance to measuring risk. The weighting may be adjusted based on specific facts and circumstances, but typically, the highest weights are assigned to categories that directly affect volume and reimbursement expectations (e.g., the physician utilization profile, market reimbursement risk analysis and market competition).

Chapter 36: Ambulatory Surgery Centers

Exhibit 11 Risk Matrix

Risk Metric		Risk Metric: Sub-categories				
		1 (Highest Risk) to 5 (Lowest Risk)				
Description	Weight	Description	Weight	Rating	Grade	Total
Partnership Operating Agreement	3.0%					
		Buy/Sell Provisions: Voluntary/Involuntary (A1)	30.0%	5.0		0.05
		Covenants Not to Compete (A2)	30.0%	5.0		0.05
		Eligibility Rqmts: Safe Harbors, Active Staff (A3)	20.0%	5.0		0.03
		Governance Structure: GP/LP, LLC, LLP (A4)	10.0%	1.0		0.00
		Partnership Structure Sustainability/Legal Life (A5)	10.0%	5.0	84%	0.02
Partnership Distribution History	3.0%					
		Minority Distribution: Terms and History (A6)	40.0%	5.0		0.06
		5 year history of distributions (A7)	30.0%	5.0		0.05
		Percentage of Available Cash (A8)	30.0%	5.0	100%	0.05
Partnership Ownership	10.0%					
		Percent of Revenue Produced by Owners (B1)	30.0%	5.0		0.15
		Specialty Mix (B2)	25.0%	5.0		0.13
		Age Dispersion (B3)	25.0%	4.0		0.10
		Number of Physician Owners (B4)	20.0%	3.0	85%	0.06
Concentration of Surgical Specialty	5.0%					
		Volume Concentration by Specialty (D2)	50.0%	4.0		0.10
		Revenue Concentration by Specialty (D3)	50.0%	4.0	80%	0.10
Physician Utilization Profile	27.0%					
		Revenue Dispersion Among Owners (B5)	30.0%	2.0		0.16
		Revenue Dispersion Among Non Owners (C1)	15.0%	5.0		0.20
		Volume Growth History (D1)	12.5%	2.0		0.07
		Ownership by Utilizers in Competing Centers (B6)	12.5%	3.0		0.10
		Individual Physician Volume Retention (B7)	15.0%	3.0		0.12
		Physician Retention Risk (B8)	15.0%	2.0	57%	0.08
Market Reimbursement Risk Analysis	25.0%					
		Revenue Concentration by Payor (E1)	15.0%	4.0		0.15
		Percentage of out of network business (E2)	60.0%	2.0		0.30
		Commercial Reimbursement Relative to Medicare (E3)	10.0%	5.0		0.13
		Pending Legislation Impacting Reimbursement (E4)	15.0%	3.0	70%	0.11
Market Competition Profile	15.0%					
		Health system competition (A13)	20.0%	2.0		0.06
		Freestanding surgery center competition (A14)	25.0%	1.0		0.04
		Potential For New Centers (A15)	20.0%	2.0		0.06
		Market Demographic Growth (A16)	15.0%	2.0		0.05
		Percentage of Physicians with no ASC Investment (A17)	20.0%	1.0	32%	0.03
Barrier to Entry Analysis	5.0%					
		Existence of Certificate of Need (A11)	50.0%	5.0		0.13
		Managed Care Barriers (A12)	50.0%	5.0	100%	0.13
ASC Management/Expense Efficiency	2.0%					
		Relative Staff Efficiency (F1)	30.0%	5.0		0.03
		Relative Supply Cost Efficiency (F2)	30.0%	3.0		0.02
		Existence of Labor Unions (A9)	20.0%	5.0		0.02
		Geographic Cost Index (F3)	20.0%	3.0	80%	0.01
ASC Physical Attributes	5.0%					
		Location in Relation to Affiliated Acute Care Hospital (A10)	40.0%	1.0		0.02
		Age and Condition of Facility (G1)	20.0%	4.0		0.04
		Facility Location Sustainability (G2)	30.0%	4.0		0.06
		Capital Equipment Obsolescence (G3)	10.0%	4.0	65%	0.02
Total Risk Score	**100.0%**					**3.05**

Note: If any Risk Metric Category has a Grade of less than 60%, a FMV analysis should be conducted

Primary ASC Value Drivers

An ASC is an accumulation of the practices of the individual surgeons using the facility. Physician practices may be generally characterized as growing, mature or declining. To assess where an ASC falls on this continuum and the potential for its volume growth, it is critical to analyze the historical case volume by physician, by specialty. If, for example, the largest physician utilizers of an ASC are, for the most part, approaching the end of the mature stage of their respective practices, the current volumes and earnings may be relatively strong. However, this may not translate into expectations for growth or a strong future.

Remember, also, that 2008 is the first year of the transition from a payment system based on ASC groupers to one based on a percentage of HOPD APCs. While this move was designed to be neutral overall to Medicare payments, it will result in significant financial losses for GI/Endoscopy and Pain cases and significant gains for Orthopedics and General Surgery. For multi-specialty ASCs with a balanced case mix, this change may not affect overall revenues and earnings. However, ASCs with a concentration in one or more of the specialties significantly affected may win or lose big.

In addition, projected reimbursement should take into account out-of-network payments. In many states, large commercial/managed care payors such as Blue Cross have developed statewide fee schedules that apply to all contracted (in-network) ASCs. Rather than simply accepting the relatively low rates, which may range between 110 and 130% of Medicare, ASCs using an out-of-network strategy may collect significantly more based on the usual and customary rates. Because reimbursement may be higher out-of-network, a large number of ASCs contract with few or no commercial or managed care payors.

However, many commercial and managed care payors have taken steps to eliminate or reduce the level of out-of-network payments. In many markets, commercial and managed care payors have instituted measures in response to the increased costs of out-of-network payments. Examples of these include the following:

- Increased patient responsibility for payment for procedures performed in out-of-network facilities;

- Payment to patients rather than to facilities, requiring ASCs to seek payment for out-of-network services from the patient; and

- Requirement that physicians conduct procedures in contracted facilities in order to receive professional fees.

Though the efforts of the commercial and managed care payors to curb out-of-network payments have either not been attempted or have not been entirely successful, the industry appears to agree that high out-of-network payments are not likely sustainable over the long term. In some cases, the conversion from out-of-network to in-network rates could be immediate; in others, it could take several years.

Regardless of how long the transition takes, it's crucial to look at the potential outcome it will have on volumes. Requiring physicians to do procedures in contracted facilities in order to receive professional fees may result in movement of those surgeries to hospitals or in-network surgery centers. The increase in volume that often comes with converting an ASC from out-of-network to in-network may partially or entirely off-set the reduction in rates.

Chapter 36: Ambulatory Surgery Centers

ASC Valuation Purpose

As is the case with most valuations in the healthcare industry, the predominant overriding purpose for most ASC valuations is compliance with the fair market value requirements established by the Stark Regulations and the Federal Fraud and Abuse and Anti-Kickback statutes.

While the Federal Anti-Kickback statutes include a safe harbor for surgeons who wish to own an equity interest in an ASC to which they refer patients, pricing for any transaction involving a potential referral source physician must be consistent with fair market value. Whether they are buyers or sellers, hospital systems that have some level of ownership in an ASC are most concerned with ensuring that the purchase of an ownership interest from a physician does not exceed fair market value or the sale of an interest is not less than fair market value. Hence, most ASC valuation engagements happen at the request of a hospital or non-physician ASC owner/operator for either the hospital system or the ASC owner/operator. The most common specific applications involve:

1. Purchase or sale of controlling equity interest;

2. Purchase or sale of non-controlling equity interests; and

3. Conversion of a center operated as an HOPD to a free-standing joint venture and simultaneous offering of non-controlling equity interests in the free-standing joint venture.

Purchase or sale of controlling equity interest

The most common buyers of a controlling equity interest in an ASC are the national developers and operators of ASCs/hospital systems. Surveys have consistently found that the ASC owner/operators nearly unanimously analyze and price controlling equity interest transactions using a multiple of EBITDA less interest-bearing debt.[3] In light of their talent for recruiting additional physician owners and improving or maintaining efficient operations, ASC owner/operators are typically less concerned than non-controlling equity interest holders or hospital systems about the risks associated with potential volume loss.

ASC owner/operators often prefer to own a controlling equity interest in order to gain control over decisions typically associated with ASC entities such as:

- Deciding which physicians retain or receive equity in the ASC

- Maintaining the contractual relationship for management of the ASC

Unlike ASC owner/operators who typically price controlling equity interest transactions using a multiple of EBITDA, most hospital systems rely on the fair market value opinion provided by an independent appraiser to ensure that they meet Stark and Fraud and Abuse statute requirements, and private inurement concerns. Various professional standards require that business appraisers consider all relevant approaches and methods in developing an opinion of value. These other approaches and in particular, the income approach or discounted cash flow method, may provide a superior framework for measuring the impact of the individual facts and circumstances surrounding a subject ASC.

Cost approach. Some ASCs are either not profitable or are not expected to provide a return greater than the required return on the working capital and fixed assets employed in the operation of the ASC. The key is not historical earnings or cash flows, but instead projected earnings and cash flows under the control of a typical owner/operator.

In a transaction for a controlling interest, an ASC owner/operator is not likely to pay for all, or maybe even any, of the intangible value created through the ownership and management of an ASC. However, in the context of a "make or buy" decision typical of this type of transaction, the buyer may pay for the assembly of all tangible and some intangible assets (e.g., CON, an ASC license and payor contracts) under the premise of value in continued use, as part of a mass assemblage of assets.

This asset approach provides a "floor" or lowest minimum value related to a controlling interest in an ASC and may be appropriate when the market and income approaches (which are discussed later) produce lower values.

Surgery centers are an asset-intensive business. The median gross property and equipment plus working capital per operating room from VMG HEALTH's *Multi-Specialty ASC Intellimarker* is approximately $835,000. Depending on the age and condition of the furniture and equipment, the costs associated with these assets for an ASC may be substantial. Often, the application of the cost approach is important in situations in which an ASC has been over-built in terms of the space (e.g., number of operating and procedure rooms) and equipment required to accommodate the book of business.

Intangible assets. Even an ASC that has historically generated operating losses must consider the effect of intangible assets. The intangible assets in this case would be those that almost always have some legal title and are often separately marketable, including:

1. Certificate of Need (CON)

2. ASC license

3. Payor contracts

Certificate of need. Some states require a CON for an ASC to be licensed by the state and receive reimbursement from public payors such as Medicare and Medicaid. Again, in the context of the "make or buy" decision, a potential buyer will evaluate the probability of obtaining a CON. In

Chapter 36: Ambulatory Surgery Centers

states such as Georgia, Iowa, Kentucky and Tennessee, for example, many markets are saturated, making it extremely unlikely that a CON for a new surgery center could be obtained.

The valuation methodology for a CON may take the form of a cash-flow comparison under two scenarios: 1) the first assumes the CON is in place; and 2) the second assumes it is not. Using this "with and without" methodology, the value of the CON is quantified as the differential in the present value of the cash flows. In cases where it is likely that a CON might be obtained after legal and consulting costs are incurred and the passage of time, the incremental cash flows simply represent the present value of these incremental costs and cash flows foregone during the time required to obtain a CON. In extreme cases where the perceived probability of getting a CON seems remote, the present value of the incremental cash flows resulting from this analysis approaches the entire unidentified intangible value of the ASC. Since in this case the cash flows without a CON simply reflect the liquidation of the ASC's assets, the present value in the first scenario should be reduced by the value of the working capital, tangible assets and identified intangible assets. While the probability of getting a CON today may currently be near zero in many markets, the probability likely increases over time. As a result, some discount to the incremental cash flows may also be considered.

Another consideration in the application of the "with and without" methodology is the use of actual/expected versus typical financial performance in the cash-flow projections for the two scenarios. The volumes, reimbursement and operating expenses put into the model should consider whether the buyers' or sellers' expectations reflect their specific circumstances or those of a typical buyer. This assumption is of particular import when either historical operations or future reimbursement expectations reflect the operation of the ASC as a department of a hospital. In particular, if either the historical or projected financial statements provided reflect reimbursement at hospital rates rather than normalized free-standing rates, the rates utilized in the projections for this analysis should reflect normalized free-standing rates.

ASC license. An ASC is normally licensed by both the particular state in which it operates and by Medicare. It may take two or three months before an ASC receives licensure from both entities. This delay causes a delay in commencing the ramp-up period for operations, and in turn, a delay in reimbursement.

An ASC with a license in place can avoid this period of reduced cash flows. Like with a CON, the valuation methodology normally takes the form of a "with and without" analysis. The value of a CON exceeds that of a license because licenses are much easier to obtain. However, there is still uncertainty surrounding the licensing process. In California, for example, it's unclear how long it could take to obtain an ASC license. Some developers believe that it could take more than a year. In states requiring a CON, the value of an ASC license is generally not separated from the value of the CON.

Payor contracts. Recent experiences in California also point to the need to consider payor contracts as a potential source of significant value, particularly in cases in which the ASC has contracts with reimbursement in excess of market levels or in which large payors are threatening not to extend contracts to new ASCs. ASC payor contracts that cannot be terminated without cause and multi-year terms are uncommon, but there may be circumstances in which ASCs expect current reimbursement levels to extend beyond the legal term of the contract. Once again, the valuation methodology for payor contracts normally takes the form of a "with and without" analysis.

Market approach. ASC developers and operators generally rely on the market approach in pricing transactions. More specifically, they rely on the individual transactions method and use a multiple of EBITDA less interest-bearing debt in pricing a controlling equity interest in an ASC. Surveys have found that most respondents typically observed valuation multiples for controlling equity interests of 6 to 7 or more times EBITDA less interest-bearing debt.[4]

While ASC developers and operators often reference and use these general market guideline multiples, many factors may lead to an adjustment of the historical EBITDA or an ultimate transaction price that resides outside of this range.

In the discussion of the primary ASC value drivers, we detailed the need to consider changes in Medicare and out-of-network reimbursement when analyzing historical information and developing future projections. Based on our experience, the 6 to 7 or more times multiple used to price the purchase of a controlling interest is often applied to prospective or adjusted, rather than raw historical EBITDA. Accordingly, ASC developers and operators often adjust for changes in reimbursement to estimate the EBITDA to which that the multiple is applied. Due to expected changes in the practices of physician utilizers or competitive factors that historical performance might not reflect, prospective or adjusted EBITDA may also reflect case volume changes.

In addition to adjusting for potential reimbursement and volume changes, historical EBITDA may not reflect the payment of a management fee.

Valuation impact of management fees. Virtually all multi-center owner/operators of ASCs charge the centers a fee of between 4 and 7% of net revenues to provide management services. For this fee, the manager typically does the following:

- Manages the ASCs finances and annual operating budgets

- Administers all accounting, accounts payable and purchasing functions

- Manages human resources

- Oversees information technology

- Handles public relations

- Develops plans for facilities and services

Chapter 36: Ambulatory Surgery Centers

- Maintain all necessary licenses and regulatory compliance

- Designs, institutes, and supervises the physical and administrative operations of the ASC

- Prepares and submits all tax returns and cost reports

- Negotiates and consummates agreements and third-party contracts

Incremental costs associated with providing these services are generally fairly minimal. As a result, the contribution margin is very high. In addition, because the owner/operator receives the management fee off the revenue line before operating expenses, the risk associated with the fee are significantly less than the earnings generated by the owner/operator's equity investment in the ASC. Accordingly, when evaluating multiples from guideline transactions, it is particularly critical to understand whether the buyer received a management fee contract pursuant to the transaction.

To illustrate, suppose that an ASC owner/operator pays an amount equal to 7.0 times EBITDA less debt for a 60% interest in the ASC, and enters into a long-term management contract at 5% of net revenues. Assuming the subject ASC's revenues are $4 million, its EBITDA is $1 million and the contribution margin on the management fee is 50%, this 7.0 multiple becomes a 6.0 multiple after consideration of the additional $100,000 margin associated with the management contract. If the management fee is greater than 5% or if the assumed contribution margin is greater than 50%, the management contract could play an even greater role. There is a direct relationship between the level of the management fee and the assumed contribution (i.e. the higher the management fee, the higher the assumed contribution margin). We have not discovered any definitive data on the exact level of the contribution margins associated with management fees. While this question should certainly be posed to management for the subject ASC owner/operator, a definitive answer supported with any type of analysis would be the exception rather than the norm. Perhaps this is a function of the fact that many ASC owner/operators do not appear to make an attempt to isolate the costs or perhaps the ASC owner/operators do not simply wish to share this information. In any event, our experience with ASC owner/operators and review of transaction pricing would indicate that the contribution margin is likely in excess of 50% for management fees equal to 5% or higher of net revenues. Exhibit 12 demonstrates this analysis.

Though the existence of the management contract effectively lowers the multiple of EBITDA paid in the previous example, many hospitals and health systems purchasing a controlling interest in an ASC do not receive a management fee. This factor should be considered in utilizing guideline transactions.

Guideline public company method. The pricing of these companies, in terms multiples of revenues or earnings, provides little in the way of guidance regarding the pricing of either a controlling or non-controlling interest in an individual ASC.

Chapter 36: Ambulatory Surgery Centers

Exhibit 12 Management Fee Valuation Impact

Subject ASC				
Revenues				$ 4,000,000
Operating Expenses (Excluding Depreciation)				3,000,000
EBITDA				$ 1,000,000
	Management Fee	5.0%		$ 200,000
	Contribution Margin	50.0%		$ 100,000

Valuation of 60% Interest (assumes no Long-Term Debt)			
EBITDA (60% Interest)	$ 600,000	$ 100,000	$ 700,000
X	X		X
Invested Capital / EBITDA Multiple	7.0	---------->	6.0
Value Indication - 60% Interest	$ 4,200,000		$ 4,200,000

Three of the largest ASC owner/operators moved out of the public sector in the past two years when HealthSouth, USPI and Symbion sold to private equity groups. In addition, though HealthSouth and HCA, both had or have significant ASC operations, their primary operations fall outside of the ASC segment, in inpatient and outpatient rehabilitation and acute care hospitals, respectively.

The only pure-play, publicly traded ASC owner/operators are AmSurg and NovaMed. The larger of the two, AmSurg, operates 170 centers, with a majority of these being single-specialty GI/Endoscopy and Ophthalmology centers. NovaMed operates 34 single-specialty and multi-specialty centers, with some focus on Ophthalmology. Exhibit 13 summarizes the key valuation multiples for publicly traded ASC companies. Trailing twelve month EBITDA multiples are approximately 10.2x and 10.7x for AmSurg and NovaMed, respectively.

Exhibit 13 Public Company Multiples

$ in Millions — As of April 23, 2008

	Share Price	Shares Out	Market Cap	LTD	MVIC	MVIC / LTM Rev	MVIC / LTM EBITDA
AmSurg Corp (AMSG)	$ 25.45	31.38	$ 798.5	$ 222.6	$ 1,021.1	1.9x	10.2x
NovaMed Inc (NOVA)	$ 4.48	24.59	$ 110.2	$ 102.2	$ 212.4	1.7x	10.7x

Note: LTM EBITDA is less Minority Interest

Company Financial Statements

Companies such as AmSurg and NovaMed, and until they went private, Symbion and USPI, likely trade at much higher multiples than individual ASCs due to growth achieved through acquisition, access to and lower cost of capital, geographic diversification and size. There is a fairly substantial spread between acquisition prices and the public company multiples, thereby making it fairly easy for public companies to add substantial value from acquisitions.

Chapter 36: Ambulatory Surgery Centers

Accordingly, while it's necessary to consider the guideline company method, it rarely has a direct application to the valuation of either a controlling or non-controlling equity interest in an individual ASC.

Income approach/discounted cash flow method. In this method, the total equity value is calculated using equity cash flows. Whether the appraiser projects a number of scenarios with a range of applicable discount rates or develops a single most-likely case scenario with a single appropriate discount rate, the mechanics of the projections should be similar.

Volume is the first primary determinant of financial performance. Volume is typically analyzed and projected in terms of number of surgical cases. However, each case may consist of a number of individual procedures. As such, it is important to understand whether the information that has been provided is measured in cases or procedures. As previously discussed, reimbursement varies widely by specialty. In addition, volumes are driven by the sum of individual physician practice expectations. The combination of these factors makes it absolutely essential to analyze and develop volume projections by specialty, by physician.

Reimbursement levels are the second primary determinant of financial performance. Like most healthcare services, ASCs maintain a fee schedule consisting of gross charges, by procedure, for services performed and supplies utilized during surgery. Gross charges, though somewhat arbitrary, are often set as a percentage of the Medicare reimbursement for a procedure, say 300 to 400%.

Most governmental (including Medicare and Medicaid), commercial and managed care payors reimburse according to a set fee schedule (either their own or one negotiated during the contracting process). A large share of commercial and managed care payors either directly or indirectly base their fee schedules on Medicare rates, making Medicare reimbursement and reimbursement trends particularly important to future projections.

Except in the fairly rare event that an ASC has a substantial number of payors that reimburse based on a percentage of gross charges, gross charges are somewhat irrelevant.

In addition, employee costs and medical and surgical supplies vary significantly by specialty. To properly accommodate the largely variable component of employee costs, base projections on staffing hours per case and/or costs per case .Other expenses that typically vary based on volume, specialty mix or revenues may include contract services, insurance, office supplies and postage and management fees.

Capital Expenditures (CAPEX) are also significant to the discounted cash flow method for ASCs. A surgery center is typically an asset-intensive business. While the dangers of following rules of thumb have been subject to lively debate throughout the history of the valuation profession, we typically look at annual amounts ranging from $50,000 to $100,000 per operating room and slightly less per procedure room as a starting point for maintenance CAPEX. In addition to considering the age and condition of the existing furniture and equipment and the potential maintenance required, CAPEX assumptions should also consider possible growth in volume.

Chapter 36: Ambulatory Surgery Centers

Consistent with the tendencies of ASC owner/operators, we typically execute the indirect convention of the discounted cash flow method whereby the market value of invested capital (MVIC") is calculated using debt-free cash flows and book value of debt is deducted from MVIC to arrive at a Total Equity Value. Use of debt in the capital structure of ASCs varies widely based on the range of long-term debt to total assets from the *Multi-Specialty ASC Intellimarker 2007*. Based on our experience, use of substantial amounts of long-term debt is more prevalent for newer surgery centers and is almost entirely asset-based. While most ASCs typically use long-term debt to fund initial operations, many ASCs fund subsequent furniture and equipment purchases out of cash flows.

ASCs are generally located in either a medical office building or a separate freestanding facility. While it is certainly not uncommon for an ASC to own the land and building, particularly if the ASC is a separate facility, most lease their facilities. This comes into play in the ASC's valuation. If the ASC owns the real estate as well, the business appraiser should consider the potential difference in required returns on the real estate and ASC operations. The preferred solution is to engage a real estate appraiser to value the land and/or building and to then combine the values of the real estate and the ASC operations. This convention requires an adjustment for the rental rate from the real estate appraisal.

If a separate real estate appraisal cannot be obtained, adjust the discount rate utilized in the discount cash flows to reflect the generally lower expected returns associated with the real estate. An adjustment to account for real estate may be considered when using the market approach (discussed earlier) and is applicable in the valuation of either a controlling interest or non-controlling interest.

The valuation of a controlling equity interest approaching 100% requires an additional consideration. Under the income and market approaches, the pricing of most controlling interest transactions is for 51 to 60% interest. The same market multiples and rates of return may not apply to the incremental 40 to 49% interest of a 100% equity purchase. Generally the market multiples and implied rates of return reflect the buyer's assumption that the physician utilizers will maintain meaningful ownership. Buyers may not be willing to pay the same premium for ownership in excess of 60%.

Purchase or sale of non-controlling equity interests

Generally speaking, ASC owner/operators and healthcare systems are the typical buyers of controlling equity interests. Whether an ASC is a joint venture between a healthcare system and physicians; a three-way joint venture between ASC owner/operators, a healthcare system and physician utilizers; or wholly owned by physicians, individual physician utilizers are generally the non-controlling equity interest buyers.

Non-controlling equity interests in ASCs typically transact at relatively lower values compared to controlling equity interests. The same survey in which a large majority of respondents typically observed valuation multiples for controlling equity interests of 6.0 to 7.0 or more times EBITDA less interest-bearing debt found that a large majority of respondents typically observed valuation of non-controlling equity interest of 2.5 to 4.0 times EBITDA less interest-bearing debt.[5]

While the lower values associated with a non-controlling interest are consistent with the levels of value framework from general valuation theory, in which there may be discounts from the value associated with a controlling interest for both lack of marketability and lack of control, we generally prefer to view the differential outside of this framework. Because the continued success of an ASC depends so much on the continued support of its physician owners, most ASC operating or partnership agreements include provisions that

Provide liquidity to non-controlling equity interest holders through formulas or requirements for the completion of an independent fair market value opinion.

Clearly define discretionary cash flows, but require periodic distributions. ASC operating agreements or partnership agreements typically require cash distributions on a monthly or quarterly basis.

Within the levels of value framework from general valuation theory, a premium for control implies an inverse discount for lack of control. However, the difference in values for a controlling equity interest and a non-controlling equity interest may be more appropriately, and perhaps more specifically, attributed to ASC owner/operators, or the typical buyers of a controlling equity interest:

- obtaining a management fee;

- having better access to, and a lower cost of, capital; and

- having the ability to successfully manage and expand ownership.

Based on these factors and because ASC operating and partnership agreements provide some level of built-in liquidity, we prefer to simply view the valuation of a non-controlling equity interest as entirely separate rather than starting with a controlling equity interest valuation and applying marketability and lack-of-control discounts typically utilized in valuations.

Cost approach. Like for a controlling equity interest, the application of the cost approach for a non-controlling equity interest provides a "floor" or lowest minimum value. However, for a non-controlling equity interest, specific facts and circumstances may ultimately impair the value of any intangible assets.

Market approach. ASC owner/operators observed that transactions for non-controlling equity interests in ASCs occur at 2.5 to 4.0 times EBITDA less interest-bearing debt. Interestingly, for non-controlling interest buy-ins and buy-outs, more than half of the respondents (8 of 13) rely on a formula to determine pricing, while only 4 rely on independent fair market value opinions.[6]

This is not surprising considering that a large share of ASC operating or partnership agreements typically include formulas in the buy/sell provisions.

Based on our experience, a slightly smaller, but nonetheless large percentage of comprehensive valuations fall above or below the 2.5 to 4.0 times EBITDA range. In addition, the appropriate multiple to apply may vary widely within the range. Because the range is broad, and because of the lack of detailed information from both public and private sources, we typically use the market approach secondarily when valuing a non-controlling equity interest.

Discounted cash flow. The overriding distinguishing feature in the valuation of a non-controlling interest is that the projected volumes and revenues do not anticipate the change in ownership associated with the potential transaction. For example, if a non-controlling equity interest is being valued for the purposes of allowing a new physician buy-in, the projections would not include any consideration of the case volumes that the physician would likely perform following the purchase of an interest in the ASC.

Further, while an ASC owner/operator may take into account the potential loss of volumes to either existing or potential competitors, a non-controlling equity owner, on the other hand, is not in a position to do so. Plus, the typical buyer or seller of a non-controlling equity interest may have a higher cost of equity in comparison to the typical buyer or seller of a controlling equity interest.

Conversion of an HOPD

The purpose of the valuation of an ASC being converted from an HOPD to a free-standing center is generally to estimate the fair market value of a non-controlling equity interest. Though the application of the three approaches to value is generally the same as the application of the approaches to value for a non-controlling equity interest, modeling the expected financial performance of an ASC that has historically operated as a HOPD can be particularly challenging.

With this in mind, rather than explore the valuation of an ASC converting from a HOPD to a free-standing entity based on the application of the approaches to value, it seems appropriate to expand on the challenges an appraiser faces in modeling this type of center's expected financial performance.

There are three primary challenges, driven by the fact that the financial performance of a HOPD, as presented in the historical accounting for a department of a hospital, bears little resemblance to the financial performance of the operation of the unit as a free-standing entity:

- Proper volume assumptions

- Proper reimbursement assumptions

- Proper operating-expense assumptions

Chapter 36: Ambulatory Surgery Centers

While the cost accounting may be very complex, the historical accounting for a department of a hospital requires a maze of assumptions and allocations that cannot be used in estimating the performance of the business unit as a free-standing entity.

Volume assumptions. The level of difficulty in projecting volumes for this type of ASC depends on whether the volumes expected to transition come from the main operating rooms in the hospital or from a separate outpatient unit. As a result, the first consideration in estimating proper volume assumptions involves carving out the outpatient volumes expected to transition to the free-standing entity.

Historical financial and operating data provided by the hospital may include not only cases expected to transition, but the comingling of outpatient volumes not expected to transition to the free-standing ASC and inpatient volumes that have historically been performed in the hospital's main operating rooms or the separate facility. Estimating volumes expected to transition will require analyzing the case volumes by specialty by physician and interviewing the hospital staff, any outside parties assisting the hospital with the development of the free-standing ASC joint venture and the physicians currently performing surgery in the HOPD.

A second consideration in estimating proper volume assumptions involves evaluating the risk to the hospital of maintaining these volumes. Particularly in states that don't require a CON, a hospital may base its desire to transition an ASC to a free-standing entity entirely on the perception that the physicians currently performing cases in the HOPD have an opportunity to either develop a competitive ASC venture or join an existing one. The volumes assumed in the valuation should consider the probability that these cases will remain with the HOPD being converted to a free-standing entity, absent the anticipated change in ownership. In many cases, hospitals are converting the HOPD to a free-standing ASC joint venture in response to the competitive threat that the physicians currently performing surgeries in the HOPD are entertaining the potential to invest in and move all or a portion of their cases to a competitive ASC. Considering this potential risk may result in a much lower value for the HOPD than might be indicated by the current earnings levels.

Reimbursement assumptions. Generally speaking, hospital reimbursement is significantly higher than ASC reimbursement for the same outpatient procedures. As previously discussed, Medicare reimbursement is transitioning to a payment methodology that will ultimately result in hospitals receiving approximately 150% of the amount that ASCs will receive. In addition, while ASCs usually contract with commercial and managed care payors at rates from a negotiated fee schedule, hospitals usually receive a percentage of charges for outpatient surgery.

Due to this differential in reimbursement, net revenues from the historical data set provided by the hospital for an HOPD must shift to reflect the conversion of the HOPD to a free-standing ASC. Depending on the specialty mix and commercial and managed care reimbursement in the specific market, this could be a significant downward adjustment.

Operating-expense assumptions. Typically, expenses such as supplies and staffing are the only direct expenses that a hospital can identify in its departmental financial information. The remaining operating-expense information is not extremely useful in projecting the performance of an HOPD as a free-standing entity.

Fortunately, hospitals often include a developer or an ASC owner/operator in the joint-venture process who will work with the hospital to make financial projections to be included in the offering documents. Because the projections usually anticipate the change in ownership, they may include case volumes from physicians not currently doing cases in the HOPD and/or case volumes not adjusted for the potential risk of maintaining the case volumes if there is not a joint-venture opportunity. Operating-expense assumptions should be analyzed and/or developed specifically based on volume and specialty mix.

Data request

As we have discussed throughout this chapter, the analysis of volumes and revenue by specialty, by physician are critical to the valuation of any interest in an ASC. Since all ASCs bill for services on a per-procedure basis using CPT codes, all volumes and revenues should be readily available, though the ease with which the data can be prepared depends on the sophistication of the information system.

In any event, the nature of billing for ASC services puts all ASCs on a common framework for analysis of both revenues and expenses. Exhibit 14 is an example data request for the valuation of either a controlling or non-controlling equity interest.

Because hospital-based facilities often perform outpatient and inpatient procedures, the data request varies slightly. Exhibit 15 is an example data request for the valuation of either a controlling or non-controlling equity interest in an ASC being converted from an HOPD to a free-standing entity.

Conclusion

In this chapter, we provided an overview of the ASC segment, typical ASC legal structures, ASC financial performance and primary value drivers and the most common ASC valuation applications. The operations of an ASC and the framework for the valuation of an ASC are not complex. However, the myriad legal, competitive, reimbursement, out-of-network and other market and industry considerations complicate the analysis of historical data, the projection of future earnings and cash flows and the application of the approaches to value.

Chapter 36: Ambulatory Surgery Centers

Exhibit 14 Free-Standing ASC Data Request

1. Income statements and balance sheets for Fiscal Year (FY) 2004, FY 2005, FY 2006, FY 2007 and year-to-date (YTD) 2008 (including the same period YTD 2007).

2. Copies of any current budgets or projections for the ASC.

3. Data for FY 2004, FY 2005, FY 2006, FY 2007 and year-to-date (YTD) 2008 (including the same period YTD 2007) **_by physician_**, **_by specialty_** detailing the following:

   - Case Volume
   - Gross Charges
   - Contractual Adjustments
   - Net Revenues
   - Collections
   - Medical Supplies Costs (if available)

4. Top ten procedures (based on charges) **_by specialty_**.

5. For the ASC, Total FY 2007 and year-to-date 2008 data **_by payor type_** detailing the following:

   - Case Volume
   - Gross Charges
   - Contractual Adjustments
   - Net Revenues
   - Collections

6. Summary of managed care contracts for outpatient surgery. Please provide info regarding the average insurance reimbursement as a percentage of Medicare.

7. Copy of most recent Accounts Receivable Aging summary.

8. A listing of employees for the ASC: (a) name (may be omitted for confidentiality); (b) compensation; (c) average hours worked per week; (d) benefits; (e) responsibility/position description; and (f) tenure / date-of-hire.

9. Copies of facility leases and/or detailed information concerning square footage for the ASC.

10. Summary and/or copies of any furniture or equipment leases for the ASC.

11. A detailed listing of fixed assets for the ASC including the following: original acquisition cost, date of acquisition, and depreciation.

12. A copy of any market research or demographic data for the ASC's service area.

13. A copy of any organizational documents relating to the ASC, including the following:

    - Articles of Incorporation
    - Partnership Agreement
    - Operating Agreement
    - Management Agreement
    - Detailed Ownership Roster
    - Most recent Offering

14. For completed transactions or any offers to buy assets or equity in the ASC during the last 2 years, details regarding any completed transactions or offers to buy assets or equity in the ASC. If no transactions or offers in the last 2 years, please provide details regarding the most recent transaction(s) or offer(s).

Chapter 36: Ambulatory Surgery Centers

Exhibit 15 HOPD Data Request

1. Departmental income statements and balance sheets for Surgery for Fiscal Year (FY) 2004, FY 2005, FY 2006, FY 2007 and year-to-date (YTD) 2008 (including the same period YTD 2007).

2. Copies of any current budgets or projections for the subject Surgical Department.

3. For ***inpatient*** and ***outpatient*** cases currently being performed in the Hospital, FY 2004, FY 2005, FY 2006, FY 2007 and YTD 2008 (including the same period YTD 2007) data ***by physician***, ***by specialty*** detailing the following:

   - Case Volume
   - Gross Charges
   - Contractual Adjustments
   - Net Revenues
   - Collections
   - Medical Supplies Costs
   - Any additional Operating Expense Information Available

   Note: Please provide separate inpatient and outpatient data sets

4. Top ten ***outpatient*** procedures (based on charges) ***by specialty***.

5. For ***outpatient*** cases in the Hospital, FY 2007 and YTD 2008 (including the same period YTD 2007) data ***by payor type*** detailing the following:

   - Case Volume
   - Gross Charges
   - Contractual Adjustments
   - Net Revenues
   - Collections

6. Summary of managed care contracts for outpatient surgery. Please provide info regarding the average insurance reimbursement as a percentage of Medicare.

7. A listing of employees for the Hospital's ORs: (a) name (may be omitted for confidentiality); (b) compensation; (c) average hours worked per week; (d) benefits; (e) responsibility/position description; and (f) tenure / date-of-hire.

8. Copies of facility leases and/or detailed information concerning the space plan (square footage and estimated FMV rental rates) for the ASC JV.

9. Copies of any furniture or equipment leases for OP Surgery and/or the ASC JV.

10. A detailed listing of fixed assets for OP Surgery and/or the ASC JV including the following: original acquisition cost, date of acquisition, and depreciation (if available).

11. A copy of any market research or demographic data for the ASC JV's service area.

12. A copy of any organizational documents relating to the ASC JV, including the following:

    - Offering Documents
    - Partnership Agreement
    - Operating Agreement
    - Management Agreement
    - Detailed Ownership Roster

Chapter 36: Ambulatory Surgery Centers

Bibliography

CMS: National Health Expenditure Projections (2007-2017)

Avalere Health for American Hospital Association: Trendwatch Chartbook 2008 / Inpatient vs Outpatient Surgery 1981-2006

Avalere Health for American Hospital Association: Trendwatch Chartbook 2008 / Number of Freestanding Ambulatory Care Surgery Centers, 1996, 1998, and 2000-2007

Avalere Health for American Hospital Association: Trendwatch Chartbook 2008 / Percent of Outpatient Surgery by Facility Type, 1981-2005

Medpac: Healthcare Spending and the Medicare Program, June 2007

Verispan: 2007 Guide to Healthcare Market Segments.

Avalere Health: Analysis of American Hospital Association Annual Survey Data, 2006

Yahoo! Finance: NovaMed Inc. (NASDAQ: NOVA), Business Profile Summary

Yahoo! Finance, AmSurg Corp. (NASDAQ: AMSG), Business Profile Summary

Medical Facilities Corporation: Website, Company Profile; June 2008

NovaMed Incorporated (NASDAQ:NOVA): 10-Q; May 12, 2008

AmSurg Corporation (NASDAQ:AMSG): 10-Q; May 5, 2008

Medical Facilities Corporation (TSE:DR-UN-T): 2008 Q1 Financial Report; May 26, 2008

Northstar Healthcare Inc. (TSE:NHC) Q1 2008 Financial Statements; May 13, 2008

ASC Association: Changes to Conditions for Medicare Coverage; June 2008

Federated Ambulatory Surgery Association: Outpatient Prospective Payment System; FASA Update Magazine, November/December 2007

AmSurg Corporation (NASDAQ:AMSG): 10-K, February 27, 2008

MedPac: Ambulatory Surgical Centers Payment System, October 2007

---

1. Richard P. Kusserow, Inspector General: Patient Satisfaction with Outpatient Surgery, A National Survey of Medicare Beneficiaries; December 1989
2. The most recent *Intellimarker Survey* is available at www.vmghealth.com.
3. HealthCare Appraisers, Incorporated: 2008 ASC Valuation Survey and 2007 ASC Valuation Survey
4. HealthCare Appraisers, Incorporated: 2008 ASC Valuation Survey and 2007 ASC Valuation Survey
5. HealthCare Appraisers, Incorporated: 2008 ASC Valuation Survey and 2007 ASC Valuation Survey
6. HealthCare Appraisers, Incorporated: 2008 ASC Valuation Survey and 2007 ASC Valuation Survey

Chapter 37

Valuation Considerations Specific To Diagnostic Imaging Entities

By Doug Smith

Editor's Introduction: Appraisers and valuation analysts are often confronted with complex businesses or industries that require detailed study to understand or the retention of an industry expert for assistance. The Healthcare Industry is a broad example of such an area and the subset involving Imaging and particularly high-tech Imaging is more complex still. This Chapter is contributed by a leading Industry Consultant who "talks" to the valuation community about how to approach the development of revenue and expense forecasts which form the underlying basis for a conclusion of value under the Income Approach.

The content of this section of the publication is likely the only section to be authored by someone who is not a certified public accountant, certified valuation analyst, or any other licensed professional who was retained to perform a valuation. Rather, this section of the publication is being authored by a Diagnostic Imaging Consulting Specialist and Analyst who has been routinely retained to assist valuation professionals, or been retained by clients from a broad range of imaging settings to review and comment upon valuations performed on their facilities, or a facility in which they are about to invest or purchase.

In our experience there are a number of unique considerations related to diagnostic imaging facilities which may not be understood with sufficient specificity by many highly skilled valuation specialists who have not had the opportunity to routinely participate in the diagnostic imaging business space. Diagnostic Imaging is a business sector in which the old adage of see one—or perform one Diagnostic Imaging entity valuation— and the others following will be the same is definitely far from reality. The differences between one facility and another can be quite due to a number of variables in center content and local area influences on the business.

In this section we will provide a detailed understanding of the many unique considerations specific to Diagnostic Imaging Entities. Although many of the core elements of a medical practice valuation for other medical specialties can be directly applicable to Diagnostic Imaging entities, there are a number of unique elements of revenue and expense that require specific knowledge and experience to assure a valuation of these entities is an accurate representation of its value.

In this section we will discuss, explore and review:

1. The Unique Structure Of Diagnostic Imaging Services Requiring Analysis

Chapter 37: Valuation Considerations Specific To Diagnostic Imaging Entities

2. The Primary Unique Influences On Diagnostic Imaging Entity Revenue Streams; Factors For Consideration and Analysis of Historical Performance; Principal Considerations In Forecasting Future Streams Of Revenue In Specific Settings and Markets

3. Long-standing, Current, Recently Enacted, and Pending Regulatory Impacts Specific To Diagnostic Imaging Entities In Certain Settings and the Analysis Required To Accurately Understand Their Real and Potential Impacts to Valuations When Forecasting Future Revenue Streams

4. Existing and Emerging Third Party Payor Trends and Considerations When Forecasting Diagnostic Imaging Reimbursement

5. The Primary Influences and Considerations Required When Analyzing and Forecasting Diagnostic Imaging Infrastructure Expense.

6. Potential Landmines And Valuation Considerations That Can Come Back To Haunt You

To set the stage, and, to make sure we are all using the same language and references, I will list a rather universal set of diagnostic imaging entities you may be engaged to value. The list is not necessarily in any order of interest or importance. There are nuances within the construct of each entity type which need to be taken into consideration when valuing these entities. You should become familiar with each. However, in the interest of time and space available, we will not go into the nuances and subtleties of each entity type with any depth or specificity at this time. The core considerations for all imaging entities we will discuss will apply to all entity types mentioned here.

- Provider Entity - Hospital Owned Freestanding Imaging Center
- Radiology Group Owned "Office" Imaging Center
- Radiology Group/Hospital Owned Clinic Imaging Center
- Radiology Group/Hospital Independent Diagnostic Testing Facility (IDTF)
- Radiology Group/Physician Group/Hospital Freestanding Imaging Center (IDTF)
- Physician Office Imaging Entity
- Corporate Imaging Center(IDTF)
- Mobile Diagnostic Imaging Services
- Specialty Hospital Imaging Center
- OWA (other weird arrangements)

Chapter 37: Valuation Considerations Specific To Diagnostic Imaging Entities

I. The Unique Structure of Diagnostic Imaging Services Requiring Analysis

Diagnostic imaging services, unlike medicine, are billed to third party payors as **1. Global** services (technical component and professional component together); **2. Technical Component** services; **3. Professional Component only** services; or, for certain payors, a mix of Global, Technical and Professional services.

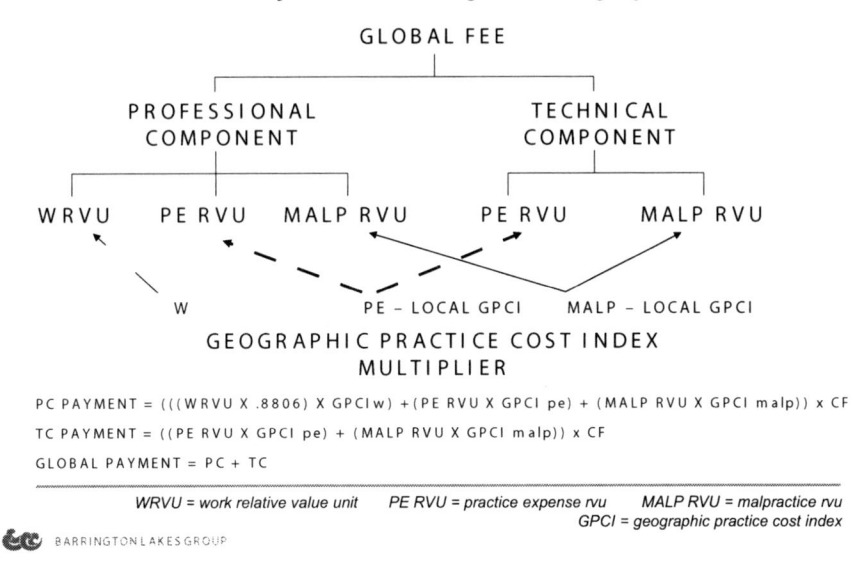

EXHIBIT 1: Payment Basis, Diagnostic Imaging Services

PC PAYMENT = (((WRVU X .8806) X GPCIw) + (PE RVU X GPCI pe) + (MALP RVU X GPCI malp)) x CF
TC PAYMENT = ((PE RVU X GPCI pe) + (MALP RVU X GPCI malp)) x CF
GLOBAL PAYMENT = PC + TC

WRVU = work relative value unit   PE RVU = practice expense rvu   MALP RVU = malpractice rvu
GPCI = geographic practice cost index

BARRINGTON LAKES GROUP

Generally, a diagnostic imaging entity will bill Global services and receive a Global payment from third party payors. The revenue line in the financial statement will include, by definition, payment for the professional interpretation of the studies performed at the facility as part of the Global fee. The entity will then pay a Radiologist, Radiology Group, or other Professional Services entity for the professional interpretation in accordance with a Professional Services Agreement and should appear as a line item of expense in the financial statement. The Technical Component Revenue is the principal source of net revenue. The exception to this rule is in the private practice radiology setting where the professional component is not later expressed as expense.

The importance of understanding the nuances of diagnostic imaging revenue elements is well known to those who have valued diagnostic imaging facilities pre- 2005 and post 2005. For those who have not had the experience of doing so, you are in for a real treat when performing an analysis of historical revenue streams, then trying to developing a base year with certain adjustments, and finally spring boarding off of this analysis to forecast revenue streams into the future to determine value.

At this point in the Chapter, the discussion transitions to the unique considerations and influences on diagnostic imaging revenue streams.

Chapter 37: Valuation Considerations Specific To Diagnostic Imaging Entities

II. The Primary Unique Influences On Diagnostic Imaging Entity Revenue Streams; Factors For Consideration and Analysis Of Historical Performance; Principal Considerations In Forecasting Future Streams Of Revenue In Specific Settings and Markets

A watershed event in the diagnostic imaging space occurred in 2005 with the introduction of the Deficit Reduction Act of 2005, which was effective January 1, 2006 (DRA 2005).

DRA 2005 contained two material changes in reimbursement implemented by the Centers for Medicare and Medicaid Services (CMS).

1. **Section 5104** of the Act froze the national Medicare Physician Fee Schedule (MPFS) conversion factor at the then current 2005 rate forgoing the forecast 4.4% decrease budgeted by CMS. That was the good news.

2. **Section 5102** of the Act introduced two provisions materially affecting reimbursement of the Technical Component, whether billed separately or Global (only the Technical component of the Global fee is effected – not the professional component)

    a. Section 5102(a) – the Multiple Procedure Discount

    b. Section 5102(b) payment of the lower of the MPFS or Outpatient Prospective Payment System (OPPS)

Section 5102(a) introduced the **Multiple Procedure Discount** on "11 Families" of procedures (CPT Codes). The 11 Families included Computed Tomography (CT), Magnetic Resonance Imaging (MRI) and Ultrasound modalities. The Act reduces reimbursement for subsequent procedures performed after the first procedure on contiguous body parts on the same patient at the same sitting by 25% of the base value of the procedure.

Section 5102(a) amounted to a decrease in reimbursement on the technical component of approximately 8% to 11% depending on the volume and mix of studies performed. However, the net effect on freestanding outpatient services has been, on the whole, less than 1% to 1.5% net decrease due to Section 5102(a) primarily because these combination of studies performed at the same sitting are more prevalent in the inpatient setting than the outpatient setting.

Section 5102(b) is another story altogether.

Section 5102(b) mandated reimbursement for the technical component, for Federal and State Programs to be restricted to the **lower of the Medicare Physician Fee Schedule (MPFS) or the Outpatient Prospective Payment System (OPPS)** level of payment. (the Hospital Outpatient Prospective Payment rate under Part A Medicare—HOPPS).

Chapter 37: Valuation Considerations Specific To Diagnostic Imaging Entities

EXHIBIT 2: DRA "11 Family" Discount Illstration 2006 & Beyond

	PROCEDURE 1 (CPT 74183) MRI ABDOMEN W/WO	PROCEDURE 2 (CPT 72196) MRI PELVIS W	CURRENT TOTAL PAY	2006 TOTAL PAY	2006 PAYMENT CALCULATION
PC	$ 114.22	$ 87.70	$ 201.92	$ 201.92	NO REDUCTION
TC	$ 857.57	$ 464.32	$ 1,321.89	$1,205.81	$857.57+ (.75 $464.32)
Global	$971.79	$ 552.02	$ 1,523.81	$1,407.73	$201.92+$857.57+(.75 $464.32)
TC VAR 2006 VS 2005				$ (116.08)	TV VAR 2007 VS 2006
GLOBAL VAR 2006 VS 2005				($116.08)	GLOBAL VAR 2007 VS 2006
				-8.8%	TC VAR 2007 VS 2005

*BASE RATES AT TEXAS RBRVS GPCI ADJUSTED

BARRINGTON LAKES GROUP

net effect of Section 5102(b) on revenue streams from Federal and State payors is yet to be fully understood as late as first quarter 2008. However, depending on the specific mix of billed codes per modality, we have seen payments decline, on a per unit of service basis, as follows: **(EXHIBIT 3)**

CT (12% to 21%), MRI (31% to 46%), Ultrasound (9% to 11%), X-Ray (6% to 10%), PET and PET/CT (45% to 50%) and Dexa Scans (23% to 34%).

At the time, Mammography and Nuclear Medicine were excluded from Section 5102(b). Today, Nuclear Medicine is now impacted by Section 5102(b), as is Breast MRI.

Why does the DRA remain important even in the third quarter of 2008? Ordinarily, the valuation analyst assumes the effects of DRA 2005 have already found their way into the revenue streams and stabilized to a degree that one can rely upon 2007 revenues to reflect the impact of DRA 2005. If this were the case, one could then rely upon the revenue streams in the 2007 base year to forecast revenue, along with certain additional assumptions. Can this be done?

The answer is – maybe. If a facility has a material revenue content based upon Nuclear Medicine, PET or PET/CT revenue, or Breast MRI revenue, the total impact will not yet be apparent. We

Chapter 37: Valuation Considerations Specific To Diagnostic Imaging Entities

will need to assess these revenues in detail, by payor, to determine if the revenue received is a commingling of pre-Section 5102(b) amended in 2007 to include Nuclear Medicine and PET and post Section 5102(b). We need to do the "homework" to assure ourselves we are properly assessing the revenue streams on a prospective basis.

EXHIBIT 3: Deficit Reduction Act 5202(b) Impact Example

MRI	8/DAY	2006	
TOTAL	2080		
WO	1664	$ 988,319.59	
W/WO	416	$ 617,699.75	
		$1,606,019.34	
-39.8%		$ (639,165.98)	VARIANCE TO 2006
		1,650	NUMBER OF PROC EQUIV
		~6	ADDITIONAL PER DAY REQUIRED
CT	**10/DAY**	**2006**	
TOTAL VOLUME	2600		
WITH CONTRAST	520	$ 366,109.19	
WO CONTRAST	2080	$ 585,774.70	
	20%	$ 951,883.89	
-28%		$ (266,527.49)	VARIANCE TO 2006
		1,213	NUMBER OF PROC EQUIV
		~5	ADDITIONAL PER DAY REQUIRED

$905,694

BARRINGTON LAKES GROUP

Keep in mind, Section 5102(a) and Section 5102(b) are only applicable to Federal and State programs. Therefore the analysis need only be performed definitively on studies performed for Medicare, Champus, Medicaid and other Federal Program secondary payors. (See further discussion below, however.)

Depending on the Medicare/Medicaid mix in the facility, the outcome may be either material to your forecasts or minimal. You need to find out with specificity. The only way to gain specificity is to obtain a report providing Count, Charges and Payments by CPT Code by Payor for 2005, 2006, 2007 and 2008 YTD June (what we call a CPT Frequency Report by Payor). In the absence of such data you are likely going to face a challenge on certain assumptions in your forecast which will quickly become a personality fight instead of a discussion on merit.

The aftershock of DRA 2005 has been further adjustments in payment by certain third party payor contractual arrangements with Diagnostic Imaging Centers. I found it interesting that certain national payors released new policies on payment for "Advanced Imaging" services before the ink was dry on DRA 2005 as posted in the Federal Register. Most national payors

Chapter 37: Valuation Considerations Specific To Diagnostic Imaging Entities

were quick to say "me too" in their fee schedules ratcheting down reimbursement for MRI, CT and PET progressively over the past two to three years. [Editor's Note: This "me too" or "piling on" phenomenon is common to healthcare fees.]

It is important to understand the influences of changes payor contract reimbursement over the retrospective 3 years and understand the contracting environment specific to the entity you are valuing. In many cases we have seen imaging centers maintain a level of "clout" resulting in attractive reimbursement for Advanced Imaging, while in other markets we have seen reimbursement follow Medicare in a proportional adjustment to prior contracts – all downward.

We strongly suggest you analyze reimbursement in 6 month increments rather than 12 month periods for the preceding year and current year to pick up any changes in contractual reimbursement.

Anecdotally, we recently were retained to analyze certain assumptions made by a valuator with respect to forecast payment for technical component services over the period of the valuation. We discovered a rather material variance between the valuator's payment per procedure assumptions for MRI and CT services forecast in year 1, and the actual current payment per procedure for MRI and CT services by an amount close to 35%—a material difference.

The difference was due to a lack of investigation into actual reimbursement in a defined recent 6 month period versus "average reimbursement" for a rolling historical 12 month period resulting in an overstatement of reimbursement. The valuator's analysis did not recognize a major recent shift in reimbursement from all principal payors with whom the facility was contracted for MRI, CT and Ultrasound procedures.

In contrast, we also reviewed a set of assumptions for another party in which the valuator understated current payments per procedure by close to 28% due to a lack of consideration and analysis of changes in payor mix and contract reimbursement following an intense period of contract renegotiations with certain payors in the area.

Another Important Note:

If the entity being valued is Radiologist owned, and the purchasing entity will not benefit from the Professional Component Revenue, the valuator will need to restate any Global revenue as technical component revenue only, or make accurate assumptions in the expense lines of the forecast to account for payment of the Professional Component. With respect to the determination of Professional Component, one needs to consider the change on ratio of PC to Global for DRA 2005 Technical Component impacts for all Federal and State program content. The ratio of PC to Global is material when the TC is reduced due to Section 5102(b).

Other considerations to be applied to revenue streams, on a prospective basis, include an understanding of a number of "environmental" or market-specific forces which may impact future streams of revenue, in addition to the DRA 2005 implications discussed previously.

Chapter 37: Valuation Considerations Specific To Diagnostic Imaging Entities

The major factors of influence specific to Diagnostic Imaging entities streams of revenue include, but are not limited to:

EXHIBIT 4: Primary Influences on Revenue Streams at Diagnostic Imaging Entities

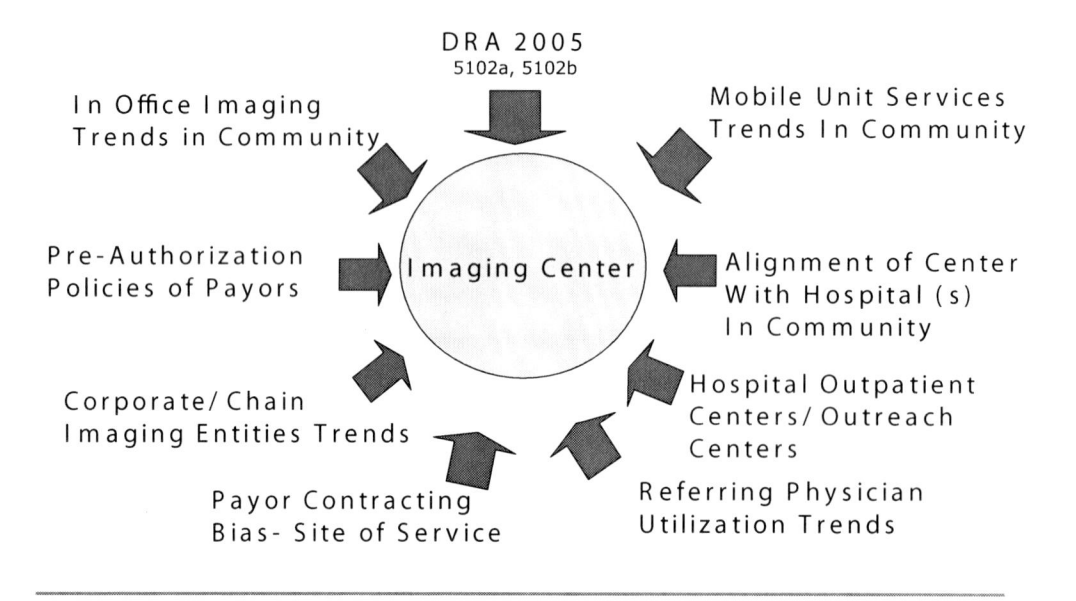

Influences on the Imaging Center:
- DRA 2005 (5102a, 5102b)
- In Office Imaging Trends in Community
- Mobile Unit Services Trends In Community
- Pre-Authorization Policies of Payors
- Alignment of Center With Hospital(s) In Community
- Corporate/Chain Imaging Entities Trends
- Hospital Outpatient Centers/Outreach Centers
- Payor Contracting Bias- Site of Service
- Referring Physician Utilization Trends

BARRINGTON LAKES GROUP

All, or some of the factors illustrated above can have a significant influence on determining and forecasting the value of future streams of revenue. These influences can be accounted for in "risk factors" applied to the determined value, or can be reflected through more conservative or aggressive assumptions of volume per modality, reimbursement per modality, or a combination of both in the forecast. Whichever methodology is employed, the valuator should clearly state the assumptions, bases and rationales used to create the assumptions used in the forecast.

Often, the buyer, or seller may attempt, either intentionally or unintentionally, to influence the valuator with respect to the potential effects of each of these factors of influence related to diagnostic imaging entities listed above.

It is important to understand, with as much specificity as is available at the time of the valuation, existing or emerging trends with respect to competition, regulatory changes effecting revenue and operations, referring physician pattern changes, center alignment in the community and the other factors listed above.

These are matters requiring a bit of homework to allow you to arrive at your own conclusions with respect to the degree to which the future will follow the documented history of the entity.

Chapter 37: Valuation Considerations Specific To Diagnostic Imaging Entities

For example—if the entity being valued is owned by a Radiology Group or Physician Group with a historical alignment relationship with a hospital and its medical staff in the community, and the relationship with the hospital has changed, then one needs to consider to what extent the change in relationship will affect future streams of revenue – positively or negatively.

Likewise, one needs to examine the historical sources of patients presented to the facility and competitive trends in the service area.

- Are there recent new entrants into the market?

- Is there evidence the new entrant is "stealing patients" from the entity?

- Is the new entrant a compliment to the entity or a competitor?

- Are the community's referring physicians taking imaging into their practices instead of referring to the entity?

- Are there emerging regulatory changes to the In-Office Ancillary Services Self Referral Prohibition Exceptions on the horizon which may change the market dynamics?

- Have certain in-office imagers found it financially unattractive to be in the imaging business and plan to return to the market as referring physicians?

- Have certain tightly managed third party payors entered the area or increased their subscriber populations at the expense of more liberal paying companies?

- Have any major employers in the area changed insurance carriers or covered services benefits for their employees?

You get the idea. Do the homework. Do not rely totally on input from either the buyer or seller.

In diagnostic imaging, due to the high fixed costs associated with the business, a change in volume of as little as 2 to 3 procedures per day (260 to 286 days per year) can make a material difference in net revenue. Once break-even is reached (a certain volume at a certain payment per procedure covers all fixed and variable costs), the lion's share of revenue per unit of service will drop straight to the bottom line. Conversely, the loss of 2 to 3 procedures per day (260 to 286 days per year) can turn the financial picture upside down in a hurry if your facility is dominated, as most are, by MRI and CT revenue.

Chapter 37: Valuation Considerations Specific To Diagnostic Imaging Entities

EXHIBIT 5: Revenue History Analysis Considerations

- ☐ **Retrospective** (2005 through YTD – 6 month intervals to assess seasonality impacts, if any)
  - ▪ **Volume**
    - ☐ By Modality (Total and Per Day)
    - ☐ By Payor
    - ☐ By Referring Physician (top 25)
  - ▪ **Charges and Receipts Trends**
    - ☐ By Modality
    - ☐ By Payor
    - ☐ By Referring Physician (top 25)
  - ▪ **Payments per Procedure Trend**
    - ☐ By Modality
    - ☐ By Payor
  - ▪ **Accounts Receivable Aging** (2005, 2006, 2007, 2008 YTD)
    - ☐ Special attention to "Self Pay" Patient Responsible

> **Watch For:**
> - Payor Mix Shift
> - Modality Shift
> - Referring Volume Shift

BARRINGTON LAKES GROUP

III. Recently Enacted, Current, and Pending Regulatory Impacts Specific To Diagnostic Imaging Entities In Certain Settings; and The Considerations Required To Accurately Understand Their Real and Potential Impacts When Forecasting Revenue Streams

We need to closely examine certain documents regarding the structure of the entity to determine what, if any existing, or pending regulatory or policy changes may impact future performance of the entity, or exact additional expense on the entity for which we must provision in the forecast of either revenue or expense if not already experienced by the entity.

Closely examine any existing Operating Agreements, contracts with outside providers of services, especially management services and professional services. We also urgently need to examine any contracts with third parties related to leasing of the entity infrastructure (Slot Leases, Per Unit of Service Leases, Under Arrangement Agreements with hospitals to provide technical component services to inpatients) which may need to be eliminated from revenue streams due to the nature of the transaction for which the valuation is being performed on behalf of the seller or buyer. New Federal or state policies on these matters may eliminate these streams of revenue. Currently IDTF sites of service are walking around with targets on their backs. (EXHIBIT 6)

Other pending matters for consideration with respect to revenue analysis and forecasts are included below. NOTE: These are matters either proposed by CMS or out for comment as of this writing. Some may have a material effect on revenue and others on operations. Stay tied into CMS over the next several months www.cms.gov as we all see what, if any of the proposed

Chapter 37: Valuation Considerations Specific To Diagnostic Imaging Entities

EXHIBIT 6: Regulatory and Industry Actions to Consider in Valuing Diagnostic Imaging Entities

- **Utilization Management Policies**
  - **Pre Authorization Policies**
    - Advanced Imaging Modalities
      - CT
        - CTA
      - MRI
        - MRA
      - PET & PET/CT
- **IDTF Classification** for all Office Based Imaging (all specialties)
  - Compliance with IDTF Rules
- **Slot Lease and Per Unit Lease Arrangement Legislation and recent actions**
- **Anti-Mark-up Legislation**
- **OIG and CMS Utilization Audits and Investigations**
- **Accreditation of Diagnostic Imaging Entities**.

BARRINGTON LAKES GROUP

changes actually find their way into the regulations, find their way into law, and then find their way into commercial payor policies effecting future reimbursement.

NOTE: Although the National Conversion factor appears to be on the rise (due to Congressional action only), an analysis of Radiology-specific CPT Codes in 2008 yielded, in many carrier localities, a net 1.8% decrease in the conversion factor due to a multitude of changes in the Radiology-specific CPT codes.

You are not done with the revenue side yet.

After collecting all of the historical material provided by the client, analyze it by modality, by site of service, by payor, by modality, by top 20 to 25 referring physicians, and by year. Then, step back and see if any metric stands out as unreasonable, or pops out as a red flag to future performance.

Items that scream out at you also demand you return to the client, or source of data and ask probing questions as to potential root causes for results you did not expect. Search for possible errors in data, and explanations for variances from expectations not available to you in your client interviews. It is important that you gain a full picture that meets the test of reason before you proceed on with a forecast of the future with all of the considerations mentioned herein.

Chapter 37: Valuation Considerations Specific To Diagnostic Imaging Entities

EXHIBIT 7: Current Considerations

- **2009 MPFS**
  - PROFESSIONAL COMPONENT
    - 1.0% Increase
  - TECHNICAL COMPONENT
    - EXPECT DECREASES IN PE RVU
    - DRA CONTINUES
      - MULTIPLE PROC DISCOUNT
      - LOWER OF OPPS VS MPFS

  > • IMPLEMENTS ANTI-MARKUP PROVISIONS
  > • NEW IDTF STANDARDS
  > • ELIMINATES CERTAIN "LEASE DEALS"
  > • SEVERAL NEW CARDIAC MRI AND CT CODES ADDED TO 5102(B)

- **COMMERCIAL PAYORS**
  - PROFESSIONAL COMPONENT
    - TIGHTENING EFFORTS
  - TECHNICAL COMPONENT/GLOBAL
    - "ME TOO" MEDICARE

  > EVER INCREASING PATIENT RESPONSIBLE PORTION OF PAYMENTS

- **OIG & CMS PLANNED EFFORTS**
  - INTENSE SCRUTINY OF OP "ADVANCED IMAGING" (CT, MRI, PET, ULTRASOUND – MEDICAL NECESSITY REVIEWS AND AUDITS
  - CODING PATTERN SCRUTINY (AUDITS)
  - HIGH POTENTIAL FOR "SURPRISE AUDITS"

2010 FORECAST = 21.5% DECREASE IN CONVERSION FACTOR

BARRINGTON LAKES GROUP

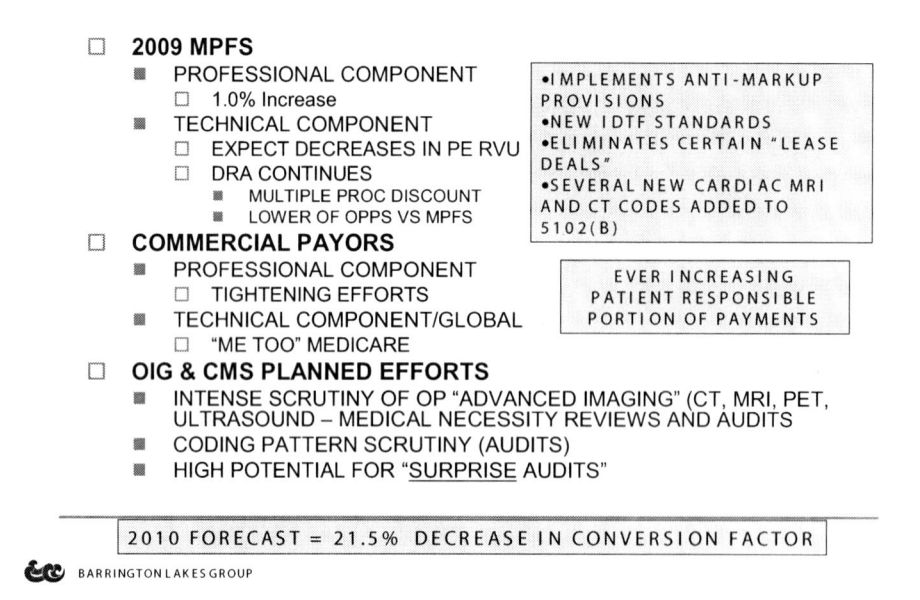

EXHIIBIT 7a: Medicare Physician Fee Schedule, Historical Trend (National)

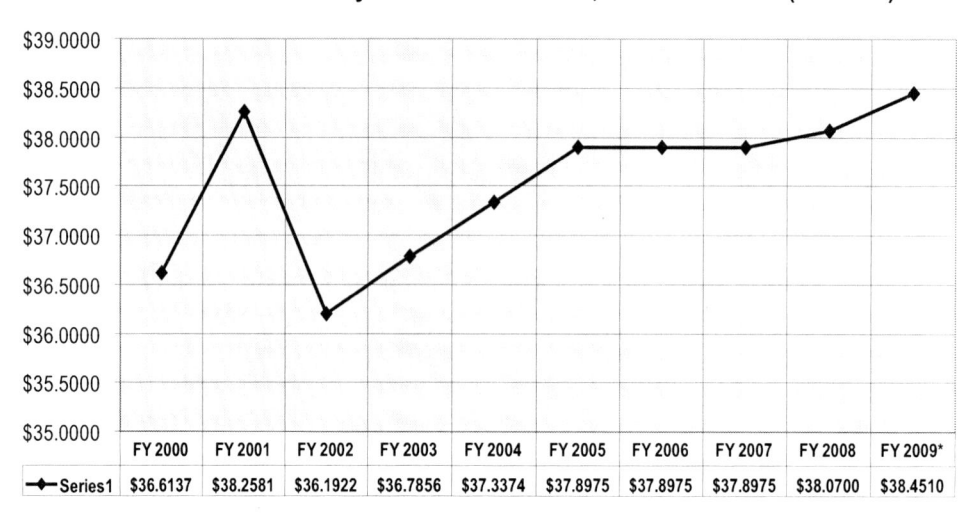

	FY 2000	FY 2001	FY 2002	FY 2003	FY 2004	FY 2005	FY 2006	FY 2007	FY 2008	FY 2009*
Series1	$36.6137	$38.2581	$36.1922	$36.7856	$37.3374	$37.8975	$37.8975	$37.8975	$38.0700	$38.4510

IV. The Primary Influences and Considerations Required When Analyzing and Forecasting Infrastructure *Expense* Unique To Diagnostic Imaging Entities

Now let's turn our attention to the expense side of valuation considerations. As with all medical practice settings, there are a number of unique matters to consider when forecasting entity expense. Diagnostic Imaging entities have especially unique elements of cost one needs to examine closely. The list provided here may not be totally exhaustive, but points to many material matters which need to be understood.

Chapter 37: Valuation Considerations Specific To Diagnostic Imaging Entities

EXHIBIT 8
Revenue Forecasting Considerations

- ☐ **Volume Assumptions**
  - By Modality (total and Per Day)
    - ☐ Calculate Total Market Demand (Utilization Per Thousand Population in Service Area)
      - Per Year over Forecast Period
    - ☐ Calculate Total Market Supply
    - ☐ Calculate Current Market Share
    - ☐ Calculate Available Market
    - ☐ Determine Assumptions for Market Share Growth/Decline
      - Competitive Landscape
      - Entity Leverage in Market – Specific Contributors

BARRINGTON LAKES GROUP

EXHIBIT 9
Revenue Forecasting Considerations

- ☐ **Revenue Per Procedure Assumptions**
  - By Modality
  - By Payor Category
  - Throughout Period of Forecast (reimbursement do not go up unless there is a significant rationale for Payor Mix Shift based upon evidence available at the time of the forecast)
- ☐ Test Forecast against History for Consistency
  - does the forecast make sense given the history and facts?
- ☐ Test Volume assumptions against throughput capacity of imaging equipment and staffing to determine:
  - what, if any additional provisions in the forecast need to be made for additional medical imaging equipment, maintenance and repair contracts and additional technician and administrative staff to accommodate additional volume forecast.

BARRINGTON LAKES GROUP

EXHIBIT 10
Primary Influences on Expense at Diagnostic Imaging Entities

- ☐ FMV of Existing Medical Imaging Equipment
- ☐ Medical Equipment Lease Cost
- ☐ Medical Equipment Depreciation Schedules and status
- ☐ FMV of non-medical imaging assets
- ☐ Medical Imaging Maintenance and Repair Contract Status
- ☐ Technician Staffing and Compensation

BARRINGTON LAKES GROUP

EXHIBIT 11
Primary Influences on Expense at Diagnostic Imaging Entities

- ☐ Technician Licensing Status
- ☐ PACS Status and Links to outside images
- ☐ RIS Status
- ☐ Medical Imaging Equipment Technology Relevance to Competitive Community Standard
- ☐ Additional Capacity Forecasts – Medical Imaging Equipment, Space, Personnel, Supply Costs
- ☐ Accreditation Status and investments required
- ☐ Marketing Expense Status and Forecast

BARRINGTON LAKES GROUP

We often find a certain facility has been "prepped" for sale by the owners. [Editor's Note: CPAs will recall from their audit training that this was termed "window dressing."] This means certain normal expense related to equipment maintenance and repair contracts have been deferred or eliminated in favor of "at risk" expense as required, or that certain critical technician and or administrative staff have been recently eliminated. It will be important to examine staffing ratios and credentials of certain technicians to determine what, if any additional adjustments need to be made to the base year and subsequent years.

Another often missing analysis, when creating a forecast of expense over the period of the valuation, is an analysis of assumptions of volume cross referenced to each modality of medical imaging equipment's throughput capacity, and cross referenced to staffing requirements to support the volume forecast – technical staff and administrative support staff.

It is very easy, and not unusual, to witness forecasts of volume that exceed the throughput capacity of the existing medical imaging equipment at some point in the out years of the forecast.

[Editor's Note: This is particularly critical not only for revenue but for terminal Capex and depreciation.] One must look at the viability of expanding operating hours to absorb the increase in volume in the specific market. But expanding hours of operation may not completely absorb the forecast volume. If throughput capacity is breached, then one must make a provision for the addition of additional equipment, maintenance and repair of the equipment, and additional Radiologic technicians, with their associated cost of employment to man the facility.

If the entity has a multi-slice CT unit (32 slice or 64 Slice), slot times may be shorter due to the increased scan speed of these devices thus increasing throughput capacity. Other modifications may need to be made to the times listed above based upon the unique characteristics of the medical imaging device in place.

In our consulting practice, we always request a document from the client describing their patient scheduling times for each modality. The "slot times" will include pre-scan preparation time, actual scan time, and post-scan time escorting the patient from the scanner room. In the case of procedures for which a contrast agent was administered, the total patient time will include the pre-scan injection time and post procedure "recovery" time. The actual "scan time" (time the patient is on the table) is not the true throughput determination – it is the total episode of care time.

EXHIBIT 12

	Assume 50% of 24 Hour Day								
Modality	**Time Slots/ hr.**	**% MIX**	**HRS/ DAY***	**MIX HRS/ DAY**	**DAYS/ WEEK****	**WKS/ YR**	**TOTAL MODALITY**	**PER UNIT**	**SCAN UNITS**
CT	0.33	X%							
CT W	0.50	X%							
CT W/WO	0.67	X%							
CTA	0.72	X%							
CTA WITH	2.56	X%							
MRI	0.50	X%							
MRI W	0.56	X%							
MRI W/WO	1.04	X%							
MRA	0.47	X%							
US	0.75								
DIAGNOSTIC	0.25								
SPECIALS	1.00								

For illustration only. "W" refers to With Contrast and "W/WO" refers to with *and* without contrast.

If the valuation results in the need for a Net Asset determination due to lack of excess net profit available to the owners, then the author recommends you retain the services of a qualified and experienced independent medical imaging equipment appraiser to perform a Fair Market Appraisal of

Chapter 37: Valuation Considerations Specific To Diagnostic Imaging Entities

the equipment, furniture and fixtures. To perform such an appraisal, the appraiser will require a comprehensive listing of all assets noting their purchase date and model number. [Editor's Note: I concur with the advice but there is a substantive question whether the hypothetical investor of the fair market value standard will pay for Net Asset Value when the value under the income approach is less.]

Other elements of expense that require examination include, general medical supply cost per unit of service (linens, gowns, and general medical supplies) as well as pharmaceutical costs per unit of service including contrast agents for CT and MRI services performed with and with and without contrast, as well as radiopharmaceutical costs per dose for PET and PET CT services.

As you forecast volume for these services you also need to forecast the associated costs for these items on a per unit of service basis. [Editor's Note: Note that per unit expense is not the same as using a percentage of collected revenue.]

V. Potential Landmines & Valuation Considerations That Can Come Back To Haunt You

As you enter the forecast stage of the engagement it is important to do a good deal of homework with respect to very specific conditions on the ground in the specific location of the entity being valued. Although the thought of going back to the basic supply and demand calculations which should have preceded the development of the imaging entity could make you lose sleep at night in anticipation, it is almost inevitable that the "fight" over the results of the valuation will rest primarily in the revenue forecast side and less so on the expense forecast side.

As discussed earlier, diagnostic imaging services are capital intensive services. Reimbursement for the technical component, on a per-unit-of-service basis, can either indicate substantial value, or certain impending financial death for the entity being valued. A diagnostic imaging entity has several key moving parts impacting revenue streams which examined individually may not indicate the true trajectory of the business. But taken altogether will definitely paint a brightly colored picture of the entity and its future capacity to generate excess revenue for the owner.

Volume projections will, by definition, be based upon the facts of recent history. If the entity has experienced an erosion of volume in key reimbursing modalities, one will need an impressive and quantitative rationale for a step function increase in volume in the forecast. Likewise, if recent history results in a per-unit-payment dollar amount, then any forecasts of improvement must be directly linked to quantitative explanations for any forecast increases in per-unit-of-service per modality.

We are often asked by an anxious buyer or seller to consider or ignore in forecasts past trends in reimbursement and/or known events such as the now planned 21.5% decrease in 2010 in the Medicare Physician Fee Schedule. The dilemma for us all is the representation we make as to the Fair market Value Determination. Can we ignore current facts in the forecast? Should we accommodate the probability of such an occurrence in the risk factors instead? That is a question for the valuator.

Chapter 37: Valuation Considerations Specific To Diagnostic Imaging Entities

A simple supply and demand analysis for the specific area may be required to test the assumptions of growth. If we know the population demographics of the primary and secondary service area of the entity, then we can, using current, available utilization-per-thousand-population by modality data, estimate the total demand for diagnostic imaging services in the area. If we then know the current market share of the entity, we can forecast with some degree of certainty the "available" population we should reasonably expect to capture. However, we also need to closely examine the age and sex mix to be more precise, and take into consideration known shifts, if any, in the construct of the medical staff in the area.

Are there more specialist physician high users of imaging services coming into the area? Are certain known high medical specialty users of imaging services fleeing the area? Do the population metrics support or deny the growth assumptions in the forecast?

If a particular geographic area population is flat or declining, does the natural increase in a certain imaging modality per population fit the forecast? One also needs to test the service area declared by the entity. A quick look at a historical patient population by zip code can either confirm or question the assertion of the reach of the entity. It is generally a good idea to at least perform a "back of the envelope" head check on these metrics.

Listed below are metrics published in 2008 by the American College of Radiology using 2005 data. Additional sources of diagnostic imaging utilization data include, but are not restricted to IMV Medical Information Division and GENESIS Medical Imaging. Data from each of these sources may provide slightly different results due to different data sets, but they are generally very close to one another. Slight variances will be insignificant to the purposes of your analysis.

You will note that utilization-per-thousand population is significantly different for the senior population (Medicare) and the General Population (non-Medicare). We suggest you segregate the population data for the service area of the entity using local demographic data for purposes of the analysis. I should also mention that there are noted differences in utilization by certain geographic areas of the country. However, for our purposes, we generally need not get into these subtle differences (see Table A).

It is important to recognize the source date of the data. Typically, utilization by modality data lags the real world by at least three years. The 2005 data, for example may not contain effects of utilization management controls put in place by certain national payors including pre-authorization policies and other utilization management policies for advanced imaging. As evidence, the most recent (April 2008) MEDPAC report to congress noted a slight decrease in utilization due to, in their opinion, DRA 2005, CMS policies related to in-office imaging services and utilization controls put in place by commercial insurance companies. There are no "point numbers" upon which we can rely with confidence. Rather we suggest using a range of utilization per thousand as a metric for the purposes described here. If we were performing a Feasibility Study to examine the viability of establishing an imaging center in a certain locality, then we would need to be significantly more precise.

Chapter 37: Valuation Considerations Specific To Diagnostic Imaging Entities

Both consultant and appraiser are often challenged on the forecast revenue per unit of service per modality – especially for entities with heavy CT and MRI content. The only way revenue per unit of service ever goes up over time is either a major payor mix shift to more highly paying third party payors versus historical payor mix data, or if the managed care portfolio has been recently renegotiated to higher than historical rates. In today's universe neither is probable, but the author has experienced situations in which it happens. If evidence can be provided in support of the contention, then we should by all means include the evidence and adjust the forecast accordingly.

If the client buyer desires a "higher number" it is their call to make a "management decision" to pay a higher price than the valuation results suggest. If the buyer has strategic reasons to pay a higher price than the valuation suggests, then they will need to document that reason, perhaps with a strategic value analysis that does not contain assumptions that violate the Stark law or AKS. Even if the purchaser is a hospital buying into or outright purchasing a diagnostic imaging entity from a referring physician or Radiology Group, which also maintains a Professional Services Agreement with the hospital, the ultimate transaction price may not necessarily trigger any anti-kickback statute violations.

Summary and Parting Comments:

Diagnostic Imaging entities, regardless of structure of setting, are in a state of change. Some recent transactions indicate material changes in historical multiples of EBITDA (a metric that drives the author crazy). Some recent transactions have been strategic purchases and sales. Others have been made on the merits. Some diagnostic imaging entities will prosper despite DRA 2005, in spite of downward pricing pressures and utilization management directives to reduce access to imaging services. Each transaction needs to be assessed at the local level. Valuing these unique entities requires a detailed understanding of the business unit in question.

1. **Get into the details. Make a detailed examination of past performance:**

    - By Modality

    - By Payor

    - By site of service

2. **Examine referral patterns** just as you examine then for other medical practices.

    - Who is coming, who is going and why?

3. **Understand the specifics** of certain modalities such as CT and MRI as well as other unique modalities.

Chapter 37: Valuation Considerations Specific To Diagnostic Imaging Entities

- How many studies with contrast are performed?

- How many Screening versus Diagnostic Mammograms are performed – not how many total Mammograms are performed?

- How many Mammography CAD (computer assisted detection) studies are performed?

4. **Does the data make sense** given the patient population demographics and referring physician demographics?

5. **Does reimbursement and payor mix** suggest the entity is capturing their fair share of better paying health plans, or have they been relegated the low-pay and "self-pay-no-pay" population?

6. **What events on the horizon do we need to accommodate** in the forecast build-up as known facts, and how many events on the horizon do we accommodate as risk factors?

Once you have the details and are comfortable that you understand the past with specificity. Then employ the same diligence in forecasting the future, based upon past trajectory and known or, reasonable, assumptions of local conditions and their likelihood of continuation, expansion or contraction. The answers will not come from financial statements and balance sheets alone. The answers will come through the tough drilling down into the details of each modality, payor trends, Accounts receivable analysis, payor analysis, denied services analysis, operational efficiency and expense by line item.

The diagnostic imaging sector is subject to very fast changes. Look for them, understand them, and assess their impact to the entity you are valuing. The devil is clearly in the details.

Do not get caught up in discussions of comparable EBITDA transactions. First, there are not many published sources upon which we can rely that provide us with any of the material facts we would need to know to assure ourselves the transactions are indeed "comparable". Many of the most noted transactions in the press have been strategic acquisitions having little to do with "Fair Market Value". The prices paid, and the multiple of earnings paid had little to do with the future stream of revenues any particular unit was expected to spin off to the owners, and more to do with the effects of the addition of the business to a larger picture. Many of these transactions have been structured with strings attached to the ultimate payout price based upon certain metrics being achieved in the future.

This is fun stuff.

Chapter 38

Valuing Dialysis Clinics

By Carol Carden, CPA/ABV, ASA, CFE

Reasons for valuation

There are two primary reasons for dialysis clinic valuations: 1) ownership buy in/buy out transactions, and 2) joint venture transactions between a physician and an operating partner. Although unique considerations apply for each of the above reasons, the underlying valuation approach is generally consistent.

When valuing a clinic for ownership buy in/buy-out purposes, it is critical to understand the control elements associated with the particular interest being transferred as well as any restrictions on transferring the subject interest which could limit the pool of potential future investors.

Non-competition agreements are often used to help protect the business from departing physicians who try to take part of the business with them. In some cases, non-competition agreements can have significant value; this value is part of the overall value of the business and represents that portion of the value that would be lost if the departing physician were to compete. However, in order to have value, the agreement must be enforceable[1] and the departing physician must actually be in a position to compete. For example, a non-competition agreement may not have much value in connection with physicians who are retiring or relocating to other geographic regions since they are less likely to compete with the clinic in the future. Even if the non-competition agreement doesn't have much value itself, the clinic as a whole may be just as valuable due to the reduced risk of competition. However, if there is an opportunity for the departing physician to compete and no such agreement exists, the potential impact should be considered when estimating the clinic's future cash flows.

The absence of a non-competition agreement can be particularly harmful to the value of a dialysis clinic as the life blood of the clinic revolves around its relationship with area nephrologists. Additionally, since dialysis clinics are not particularly capital intensive, it is fairly easy for a departing physician to start or join a competing clinic and attract the patients away.

Generally speaking, non-competition agreements will prohibit the departing physician from having a financial interest (defined as ownership or, more importantly, a compensation agreement such as a medical directorship) in a competing dialysis clinic within a specified geographic range for a specified time period following their departure from the clinic. Given the nature of dialysis services (patients should come three times per week for a 3 to 4 hour block of time) the geographic limitation tends to be more narrow for dialysis than it might be for other services. Generally speaking, the physician will be prohibited from competing within a 25 mile radius of the current center, a smaller radius for large, metropolitan areas. The rationale for this distance is that it becomes too inconvenient for current patients to follow the physician.

In addition to be prohibited from having a financial relationship, the physician is also generally prohibited from soliciting existing clinic employees for the same time period as the financial interest prohibition. Because patients spend such a significant amount of time at the clinic, they develop relationships with the staff that could be detrimental to patient satisfaction if the experienced staff is recruited away by a departing physician.

A valuation for joint venture purposes can be a much more complicated undertaking. It is critical to understand the nature of the joint venture to ensure that it does not contain unnecessary regulatory risks. In particular, it is important to ensure that the operating agreement does not reward incentives for referrals to the clinic. Also, it is important to understand any medical directorships that are attached to the operating agreement.

A medical directorship is typically awarded to a physician for clinical oversight of the center. If there are other physicians in the medical director's group, they will typically be included in any non-competition and non-solicitation provisions of the medical director agreement through a joinder. Under the medical director agreement, the physician agrees to head the governing body, provide the supervision of the clinic staff, oversee the safety of the clinic in regards to medical grade purified water, and give input into staffing and capital replenishment. In return, the physician generally receives a fixed amount per year paid on a monthly basis. Medical directorship fees can range from $50,000 to $75,000 annually, or more, depending on the size of the center. Payment of the medical directorship must be at fair market value to avoid the perception that the payment is being made in exchange for referrals to the clinic (AKS concern) or, if the clinic is not-for-profit, the payment must not appear excessive in nature (private inurement/excess benefit concern to the IRS). If a medical directorship exposes the clinic to undue regulatory risks, this factor must be considered when determining its value. This consideration is generally incorporated into the development of the discount rate. A higher discount rate would be attributed to the center resulting in a lower value than the center would otherwise have absent the risky medical director agreement.

Regulatory Considerations

The following briefly discusses the three main areas of regulatory compliance considerations when appraising a dialysis clinic. A detailed discussion of the myriad of regulatory complications that can arise with healthcare transactions is beyond the scope of this chapter but interested readers may want to do additional reading from the referenced materials.

Stark

In general, the Stark regulations govern referrals from a provider of Designated Health Services (DHS) to an entity in which the provider has a financial interest unless the arrangement falls

Chapter 38: Valuing Dialysis Clinics

into one of several safe harbor classifications. Dialysis services are not one of the 11 categories of DHS subject to the Stark requirements.[2] Therefore, the Stark restrictions do not generally have much of an impact on dialysis clinic valuations.

Anti-kickback regulations

The anti-kickback statute (AKS) prohibits the receipt or payment of anything of value to induce referrals of healthcare services.[3] There are 13 established safe harbors; however, even if the arrangement does not fit squarely into a safe harbor, that does not necessarily mean it will be per se illegal. In addition to treating patients at the dialysis clinic, any physicians involved in ownership of the clinic also admit patients for a variety of other kidney-related ailments. If a hospital is involved in the transaction, the parties must ensure that the remuneration paid is not impacted by past or future anticipated referral patterns to avoid AKS issues. Therefore, any analysis of the proposed dialysis transaction requires careful scrutiny to ensure the value of the interest is not negatively impacted by exposure to criminal, or alternatively, civil monetary penalties.

Private inurement/excess benefit

The third regulatory area to consider is private inurement and excess benefit transactions as defined by the Internal Revenue Service (IRS). In general, the IRS is concerned about financial or other arrangements that result in a benefit to private individuals in excess of the benefit supported by arms-length market transactions.[4] These concerns come into play most heavily when valuing joint venture transactions involving a not-for-profit clinic or venture partner. In particular, the IRS is concerned that not-for-profit assets will be transferred in excess amounts to private individuals. If a transaction is determined to contain private inurement or excess benefits, excise taxes may apply to both the organization making the payment as well as the individual receiving the benefit, if that individual is a Disqualified Person under the excess benefit regulations.

Reimbursement Models

Before undertaking a valuation of a dialysis clinic, it is important to understand the mechanics and any potential changes in the reimbursement methodology. Patients having end stage renal disease (ESRD) become eligible for Medicare four months after they begin dialysis treatments even if they have not reached the age of 65. Eligibility can begin sooner if the patient elects to train for home based dialysis. As a result, a significant portion of a dialysis clinic's patient base is covered by Medicare. Commercial insurance companies will cover dialysis services until the patient becomes eligible. Additionally, patients are not required to accept Medicare benefits and can elect to retain their commercial insurance benefits. Even though commercially insured patients do not typically comprise a significant number portion of the patient base, they can have a tremendous impact on the profitability of the clinic as the reimbursement from commercial insurance companies is generally significantly greater than Medicare.

Chapter 38: Valuing Dialysis Clinics

Since dialysis services are largely paid for by Medicare, the focus of our reimbursement discussion will be regarding Medicare's payment methodology and any forecasted changes. For outpatient maintenance dialysis treatments (typically done in the free-standing dialysis clinic setting), currently providers are paid on a per treatment basis using what is referred to as the composite payment rate. The composite payment rate is a partially bundled rate which covers dialysis treatment except for some drug and laboratory costs which are billed and paid for separately on a fee-for-service basis. The base Medicare composite payment rate for 2010 is $135.15.[5] The composite rate is adjusted specific to each patient's age, body surface index and body mass index.[6] Additionally, a wage index adjustment is applied. . The physician overseeing the patient is paid by Medicare Part B on a capitated basis referred to as the monthly capitation payment (MCP). The MCP covers dialysis-related services for the physician only. If additional services are required by the patient, the physician bills for these services separately.

Section 153(b) of the Medicare Improvements for Patients and Providers Act of 2008 (MIPPA) replaces the current case mix adjusted composite rate system with a bundled ESRD payment prospective payment system effective January 1, 2011. There is a four year transition period with full implementation by 2014. During the transition period, providers will be paid using a blend of the prospective payment rate and the current payment rate.[7] The MIPPA also mandated an overall decrease in spending for dialysis services of 2%.[8] It will obviously be important to understand how the bundled payment methodology is anticipated to impact specific clinics as it is anticipated that some clinics will see increases from the change while other will see declines in reimbursement.

Valuation Approaches

There are three basic approaches utilized for determining the value of any asset. Depending upon the facts and circumstances of the particular clinic being valued, some of the approaches may be more applicable than others.

Asset approach

This approach is generally not used for operating companies, such as dialysis clinics, unless the business is not generating sufficient cash flows to make its operations more valuable than the underlying net assets less any outstanding debt obligations. Because dialysis clinics are not capital-intensive in nature, the net asset value is generally not a good indicator of value for a clinic that is anticipated to produce future cash flows. The exception to this can be in regards to a new center under construction where the asset approach can be commonly used to value the clinic.

Market approach

The market approach values a business based upon publicly-traded guideline companies or sale transactions of other similar privately-held businesses. The challenges of applying this approach

Chapter 38: Valuing Dialysis Clinics

are two-fold. Due to merger and acquisition activity of recent years, there are only three remaining publicly-traded dialysis companies, Fresenius, Dialysis Corporation of America and DaVita. When utilizing the publicly-traded guideline method, it is critical to make the necessary adjustments to the public company information so that it is comparable to the private company being valued. These adjustments involve an analysis of the balance sheet differences such as levels of debt as well as differences in growth rates. This type of analysis can be quite time consuming and difficult to accomplish.

When utilizing merger and acquisition transaction data to develop valuation estimates for the subject company, it is important to gather and consider as much information about the sale transactions as possible. If possible, you should ascertain items about the sale such as: 1) was there a non-compete included in the transaction; 2) was the buyer a large, national player or smaller local or regional company; 3) what are the demographics of the market for the sold clinic; 4) the term of the medical director agreement and renewal options; 5) are other physicians in the group bound to the non-compete agreement by a joinder; and 6) are there any significant changes expected in the market demographics or competition in the short term. Unfortunately, these details can be difficult, if not impossible, to obtain. Additionally, sometimes the published transactions include assets (such as real estate) that may or may not be include in your transaction.

Market differences[9] must also be taken into consideration. However, dialysis clinics are typically dominated by Medicare patients (many times as high as 85% of patients), therefore, individual payor differences between markets do not have the same impact on the use of private transaction multiples for dialysis clinic valuation as they do for other segments of healthcare. There are, however, some reimbursement differences from market to market due to the wage index adjustment factor in the composite payment rate. Unfortunately, many times the transaction data is limited making application of the approach difficult.

Income approach

The income approach values a clinic based upon its ability to generate future cash flows and the anticipated risk associated with those cash flows. Depending upon the circumstances, the income approach can be a single period capitalization of earnings or a discounted cash flow analysis. Many times, an income approach will be stated as a multiple of earnings before interest, taxes, depreciation and amortization (EBITDA). Publicly-traded companies will generally state their acquisition prices as a multiple of EBITDA. The income approach is the most commonly used valuation approach for privately held businesses such as dialysis clinics.

In applying the income approach, the analyst will need to evaluate potential volume growth and capacity. Clinic volume is stated on a per patient basis. Dialysis clinics typically run two shifts per day although a third can be added and operate either three days per week or six days per week. Generally speaking, for a two shift clinic, there will be a morning shift that runs from approximately 6 a.m. to 10 a.m. and an afternoon shift that runs from 10 a.m. to

2 p.m. If the clinic runs a third shift, it will run from 2 p.m. to 6 p.m. To calculate capacity, determine the number of stations (each treatment is performed at a station comprised of a recliner and dialyzer machine) multiplied by the number of shifts being run. For volume and future growth to exceed capacity, additional stations or shifts must be added. If there is space in the physical location and the plumbing was planned in advance, adding additional stations is a relatively easy thing to do as the capital requirements are not extensive. However, if the current space is utilized, expansion will require a significant amount of leasehold improvements or build-out costs as the dialyzer machines require medical grade purified water and a substantial amount of plumbing.

In terms of projecting changes in the reimbursement, for the past few years, Medicare has increased the composite rate by amounts slightly less than 2%. However, as previously discussed, beginning in 2011 Medicare will move to a prospective payment system for dialysis treatment which will likely disrupt the normal level of payment adjustment at least until the four year transition period has ended.

Value Drivers

There are five primary drivers of value for any dialysis clinic. The following section discusses each of these drivers and their potential impact on value.

Demographics of the community

Senior adults, African-Americans and Native American adults use dialysis services more heavily than others.[10] Therefore, it is critical to understand the current demographics of the community where the clinic is located as well as the projections for future population growth in the area. Medicare patients often make up as much as 85% of the patient load for many dialysis clinics. As stated previously, patients can become eligible for Medicare without being seniors. However, generally, on average elderly patients comprise 23% to 28% of the total population.[11] Therefore, the composition of senior adults in the community as well as the projections for growth of this segment can have a tremendous impact on a clinic's ability to grow. It is also important to consider the geographic placement of the clinic. A location too far from the dominant patient base is vulnerable to competition from another clinic that's more conveniently located.

Relationship with area nephrologists

For any dialysis clinic to survive long term, it must secure and sustain relationships with area nephrologists. It is important to establish relationships with nephrology groups that have a good reputation in the community and that have a good mix of experienced physicians, preferably some of which are still early in their career. Many times, the dialysis clinic will formalize their relationship with a key nephrologist or group by negotiating a medical directorship contract.

Chapter 38: Valuing Dialysis Clinics

Medical directorships generally help build the physician's loyalty to the clinic which reduces the risk of losing revenues to a competing center. However, as stated previously, the terms and compensation of the medical directorship should be carefully evaluated to ensure the agreement does not unduly expose the clinic to regulatory risks.

Competition

The existence and aggressiveness of competitors can have a significant impact on the value of a dialysis clinic just as with any other business. When considering investing in a dialysis clinic, it is important to understand the competitive landscape in the community and any expansion plans that dominant groups may be considering. A community with one or two dominant nephrology groups will be a more difficult competitive environment than a community primarily comprised of many independent practices. The value of a clinic can be substantially eroded away if the dominant group in a community is planning a competing center in close proximity. Typically, certificate of need (CON) regulations do not govern the establishment of new dialysis clinics as the capital investment is not as significant as with some other healthcare ventures. However, the existence and extent of CON regulations is state specific so it is important to understand any limitations specific to your community.

Merger and acquisition activity

The dialysis industry has undergone extensive consolidation over the past few years. There are currently a small handful of companies that dominate the industry on a national basis with Fresenius and Davita being the largest players with a combined 60% market share[12]. When considering the value of a clinic for merger and acquisition purposes, it is critical to understand the status of current consolidation activity taking place, especially in your geographic area. These acquisition transactions could have a substantial impact on what a clinic could be worth in the market place.

Recent payor initiatives

A clinic's payor mix can have a substantial impact on its value. However, because dialysis clinics are typically dominated by governmental payors, specifically Medicare, it is very important to stay abreast of any upcoming changes in Medicare reimbursement rates. In March of each year, the Medicare Payment Advisory Committee (MedPac) issues their recommendations for changes in Medicare reimbursement rates for the upcoming year.

The most recent MedPac report (March 2010) did not include any recommendations that would have a significant impact on dialysis treatments specifically. MedPac recommended a payment update of .7% for 2011.[13] However, the MedPac reports generally include recommendations regarding outpatient reimbursements, so it is important to stay abreast of these developments and their potential impact on the clinic's revenues.

Chapter 38: Valuing Dialysis Clinics

Conclusion

Determining the value of a dialysis clinic is a complex undertaking. Therefore, it's important to ensure the valuation professional not only understands valuation techniques and methodologies, but also the regulatory issues of the healthcare industry. Additionally, a thorough analysis must be performed of the current and projected demographics of the community, the relationship with area nephrology groups and the state of merger and acquisition activity going on in the industry.

---

1. When determining the value of a noncompete agreement, it is necessary to be familiar with local law – both statute and court precedent – to determine the extent of enforceability. For example, Massachusetts General Law 112.12x precludes enforcement of geographic covenants not to compete among physicians.
2. Federal Register/Vol. 69 No. 59/Friday, March 26, 2004/Rules & Regulations, XI. Definitions (Section 1877(h) of the Act; Phase I-66 FR 922-49; §411.351)
3. *Federal Anti-Kickback Law and Regulatory Safe Harbors, Fact Sheet, November 1999,*Office of Inspector General, Office of Public Affairs
4. *Intermediate Sanctions – Excess Benefit Transactions,* Internal Revenue Service at www.irs.gov/charities/charitable/article/0,,id=123303,00.html and *Inurement – Section 501 (c)(4)*, Internal Revenue Service at www.irs.gov/charities/nonprofits/article/0,,id=156404,00.html
5. Federal Register/Vol. 74 No. 226/ Wednesday, November 25, 2009
6. For a detailed discussion of the payment mechanism, see http://www.medpac.gov/documents/MedPAC_Payment_Basics_07_dialysis.pdf
7. http://www.cms.gov/ESRDPayment/
8. *Report to Congress, Medicare Payment Policy, March 2010,* Medicare Payment Advisory Commission
9. For an extensive discussion of market differences, see Chapter 3, Healthcare Market Structure and its Implication for Valuation of Privately Held Provider Entities: An Empirical Analysis
10. 10*IBID*
11. *IBID.*
12. *IBID*
13. *IBID*

Chapter 39

Home Health Care Services

By Alan B. Simons, CPA/ABV, CMPE, DABFA

The valuation approaches and methods used to value home health care businesses are no different than any other business. However, in order to competently value these businesses, an appraiser must understand the industry and its associated risks. In addition, a number of home health care providers are also nonprofit organizations, or they may be sold to a nonprofit organization. Valuing transactions involving nonprofit organizations presents its own subset of issues. As a result, we will focus on what differentiates these businesses from others and what appraisers need to understand to develop a credible business valuation.

The Industry

Home health and hospice care is a subset of all health care providers (such as hospitals, physicians, senior care, etc.) that further breaks down into the following five major service lines:

- Home health – skilled nursing, physical therapy, occupational therapy, speech therapy, aide service, and medical social work provided to patients in their home

- Home hospice – care provided for terminally ill patients and their families in their homes (can also be provided in a hospice facility)

- Private duty and staffing services – home care that primarily provides home aide services

- Home medical and respiratory equipment – durable medical equipment such as walkers, beds, wheelchairs and oxygen concentrators

- Home infusion – intravenous therapies such as parenteral nutrition, antibiotics and chemotherapy

The goal of home health care is to provide a continuum of services designed to allow disabled or older individuals to stay in their homes for support and treatment as an alternative to assisted living, nursing homes and hospital facilities. Proponents of home health care believe that it is less expensive and a better care alternative for most people.

Chapter 39: Home Health Care Services

All together, these services, when combined, might represent a very comprehensive home health care business. But, more often than not, the appraiser will be valuing businesses with fewer service lines and many times the business may be comprised of only one service line.

The profitability and risks associated with each of these service lines is driven by a unique set of variables making it difficult to make global assumptions about the home health care business. The appraiser needs to develop an understanding of each service line and how these service lines interact if the subject business operates in two or more.

In some organizations, each service line can stand on its own as an independent, financially viable business. When this is the case, each business has a broad source of patient referrals independent of the other service lines. Under this scenario, each service line and the business as a whole would have more value than when service lines are interdependent upon each other for referrals.

For example, a service line might have no value to a potential buyer if all or most of its business was dependent on a previously related entity. If the service line is sold without the related entity there is no guarantee that referrals (and therefore the business) will continue. This can happen when a home health business or service line is a "captive" of a hospital or nursing home. It can also happen when a service line gets most or all of its referrals because of its relationship or proximity to one or more other related service lines. Generally a home health business will represent the core business or service line having a broad base of referrals, and the other service lines are then added to enhance the profitability of the core business. In this case, most or all of the value may be in the core business.

Appraisers need to understand the relationship among the service lines and referral sources to understand where the value resides. This is particularly important when the business is a captive or when not all of the service lines are being sold together.

Funding of Home Health Products and Services

Except for private duty services, most home care products and services are funded by governmental sources such as Medicare and Medicaid, commercial health care insurance and to a lesser extent payments from individuals (self pay or private pay).

Except for reimbursement by Medicare and individuals (because individuals or "self pay" would generally pay actual charges), the calculation and method of reimbursement for services can vary for each commercial insurance plan and for each state in the case of Medicaid. As a result, an explanation of each reimbursement system is beyond the scope of this book. However, since Medicare reimbursement is reasonably consistent and is frequently a significant percentage of a provider's total revenue, we will generally explain how Medicare reimbursement works and how it may change as of this writing.

Chapter 39: Home Health Care Services

For the calendar year 2006, Medicare paid home health agencies approximately $14.1 billion under part A and part B coverage for 103,980,865 visits, covering 3,302,649 patients, which means that for 2006 the average Medicare reimbursement was $135 per visit and $4,254 per patient. These are useful benchmarks in evaluating the relative performance of home health agencies.

It is incumbent upon appraisers to develop an understanding of reimbursement for the payors that drive each service line and those that drive the business being valued. While it is generally assumed that home health care services are provided to the elderly; that is not always the case. However, most services provided to the elderly and the disabled will be funded either directly by Medicare or through a commercial (private) payor that is being funded by Medicare Advantage plans. If and when Medicare coverage runs out, reimbursement may come directly from the individual or Medicaid for low income beneficiaries. Younger patients may be funded through commercial insurance, self pay or Medicaid if they meet the requirements. Like Medicare, some states may contract with commercial insurance plans such as a Blue Cross/Blue Shield Plan, Electronic Data Systems (EDS), or other third party payors to administer some or all of their Medicaid plans In such cases, the state retains administrative control of allowed services, fee schedules, and other costs, and the Administrator focuses on provider payment processing, claim denials and other administrative functions. In addition, many insurance plans require some contribution (or payment) from the beneficiary.

A general discussion of how Medicare reimburses home health services and products follows.

How home health care services and products are purchased

Home health care treatment plans are prescribed by a patient's physician and provided by a health care agency (the provider). Most home health care products and services are funded by Medicare, particularly for older or disabled patients. A portion of home health is funded by Medicaid, for lower income patients; commercial insurance, primarily for patients below Medicare age; and self (or private) pay, for either uninsured patients or for products or services that are not covered by Medicare, Medicaid or insurance.

During a valuation engagement, appraisers need to understand the mix of payors to evaluate risks and whether normalizing adjustments might be required.

For example, businesses funded primarily by Medicare are at risk for changes in reimbursement (rates and coverage criteria) and age demographics for the market. Businesses funded by commercial insurance may be at risk for the economy and employee layoffs, which would reduce the population covered by commercial insurance. Businesses reliant on payment from individuals (private or self pay) would also be dependent on the economy. Medicaid rules can be different in every state and are subject to changes in state regulations. Population growth or decline by age and income also need to be considered as it would impact the number of potential patients and how they might pay for these services in the future.

Chapter 39: Home Health Care Services

When valuing a controlling interest, the appraiser should consider whether typical normalizing adjustments (for example, owners' compensation and other perquisites; or nonrecurring revenues or expenses) need to be made. In addition, normalizing adjustments to revenue might be required if the payor mix being evaluated is not normal for the market, or if there are opportunities to add payors, or if the business is not billing properly or is not being reimbursed properly. Assuming these enhancements are available to most buyers in the marketplace, the adjustments would be consistent with the fair market value standard.

Home Health Funding

Medicare

Since October of 2000 Medicare funds the base payment for home heath care under a prospective payment system (PPS) *[Editor's Note: See Chapter 40 for discussion of* Caracci *case]*. Under PPS providers are reimbursed a fixed payment for services. Future reimbursement is determined by Congress and is influenced by historical industry results. Medicare pays for home health services in 60 day episodes. Most patients complete their care within 60 days. Additional 60 day episodes may be reimbursed until the patient recovers or moves to an alternative provider such as a hospital or nursing home, or dies. Often patients are discharged from a "skilled plan of care" and obtain in-home aide, chore and homemaker services paid for privately (private duty[1]) or possibly using Medicaid funds.

Providers (home health agencies or HHAs) are paid one fee for each 60 day episode. Medicare adjusts payments to reflect the level of care and services required based on home health resource groups (HHRGs), and the local wage differences. They will also increase the payment for the costliest patients (outliers) and reduce the payment for patients needing significantly less than 60 days of services. If there were less than five (5) visits in the sixty day episode (Low Utilization Patients—LUPAs) visits are paid on a per visit basis using a national standard rate that is wage adjusted based on the CBSA (core based statistical area) location of the patient.

Medicare implemented the HHRG-153 system on January 1, 2008 that utilizes 153 resource groups and replaces the prior system that used only 80 resource groups. These resource groups establish different payment rates based on patient need (acuity values) which are derived from a standardized national assessment instrument (called "OASIS"—Outcome And Assessment Information Set).

Appraisers need to be comfortable that historical and forecasted revenues are reasonable based upon the payment system in effect at the time or proposed changes being considered and the likelihood that they could become law (either Medicare or a state Medicaid program). *[Editor's Note: See Chapter 40 for discussion of* Caracci *case and the import of potential change to value]*. In addition, historical and forecasted revenues could be too high or too low if the level of care provided to patients is not properly determined. However, few appraisers could make this determination without using a specialist and most appraisers will consider this outside the scope of their work. Nonetheless, appraisers should become familiar enough with the industry to understand changes in reimbursement and the associated risks so that they can evaluate management's forecast assumptions for reasonableness. Industry surveys and/or articles that include historical data or assumptions about the impact of future reimbursement changes may be available. Benchmarking the business against similar businesses may help appraisers determine whether historical and forecasted revenue assumptions are reasonable.

Hospice Funding

Medicare

Hospice services are available to terminally ill patients with less than six months to live. A physician must certify a patient's terminal illness to qualify for the benefit. Benefits are provided in two 90 day increments and an unlimited number of 60 day increments, but payments are subject to the caps discussed below.

Hospice agencies are paid a CBSA wage adjusted daily rate based on the level of patient care required, which include:

- Routine home care

- Continuous home care

- Inpatient respite care

- General inpatient care

The daily rate includes a labor and a non-labor share and is intended to cover all services provided. The payment rates are adjusted annually by a Congressionally approved market basket inflation rate to account for both inflation and differences in market wage rates. Currently, the labor share is adjusted based on the hospice wage index that is derived from the hospital wage index and the non-labor share is adjusted based on the inflation factor approved by Congress.

Total payments to a provider are limited by two caps: 1) inpatient care (for example, in a facility, not home hospice) may not exceed 20% of total patient care days, and 2) an aggregate annual payment amount (an amount available to pay all Medicare hospice claims in a given year to control increasing Medicare costs) based on the number of patients electing the hospice benefit for the first time within the cap period. The hospice aggregate cap is adjusted annually by the consumer price index, but the base level of Medicare hospice funding stays constant.

Appraisers should research how these two caps might affect revenue forecasts. Longer average lengths of stay will cause the aggregate payment to be spread among more patients thereby reducing the benefit available on a per patient basis. If Medicare runs out of funds to reimburse hospice, providers could be liable for a repayment to Medicare for having exceeded the cap limit. If the payment system becomes inadequate to fund needed services, Medicare legislation may be proposed to change the aggregate base payment or could provide an alternate payment mechanism. The point is that this is a very tricky area and revenue forecasts and risk rates need to be evaluated based on the facts known at the time of the valuation.

Private Duty Funding

Private duty home care services are not funded by Medicare but may be funded through self pay, or government funded through Medicaid and/or Medicaid Waiver Community Alternative Programs (CAP) and long-term care insurance.

When valuing a private duty business appraisers need to consider patient demographics, particularly wealth factors, to determine the potential for services and profitability. Private duty businesses are generally more profitable in wealthier communities where patients can fund services through self pay and long-term care insurance. A provider that is heavily dependent on Medicaid funding for in-home aide services has an increased risk of losses or low margins on this service line.

Home Medical Equipment Funding[2] (HME)

Medicare

Generally, Medicare pays the lower of 1) the average of Medicare's allowed charges for 1986 and 1987 adjusted for the consumer price index for all urban consumers and further adjusted for geographic differences in equipment prices for each state; or 2) the provider's charge. State fee schedules are subject to a national floor and ceiling to limit variability. Prosthetics and orthotics are subject to regional limits. The fee is determined based upon where the beneficiary resides and not where the provider is located.

In addition, there are the following exceptions to the general Medicare payment rule:

- Customized equipment and medications are paid at rates that are determined item by item, by the regional carrier.

- Prices for most medications used in conjunction with HME are set at 106% of the average sales price (ASP). Drugs used with infusion equipment are paid at 95% of average wholesale price (AWP).

- Prices for home oxygen are based on the median 2002 Federal Employee Health Benefit plan price.

Chapter 39: Home Health Care Services

Some of these exceptions will be discussed in greater detail in other sections.

A competitive bidding process for HME is being phased in nationwide starting with 10 CBSAs on July 1, 2008 and expanding to 80 CBSAs by 2009 (unless delayed by Congress in a bill that is not otherwise vetoed by the President). In a demonstration project conducted between 2000 and 2002, competitive bidding lowered HME prices between 17 and 22% without serious quality or access issues. The prices from winning bidders in round one of the initial 10 CBSAs (the winning bidders for the July 1, 2008 effective date) actually averaged 23% lower than the existing Part B fee schedules for HME and respiratory providers in those locales.

Furthermore, Medicare follows a policy referred to as "Capped Rental" in that many rented items will only be reimbursed for 13 months and the beneficiary must be given a "purchase option" at 10 months. Currently, the capped rental period for oxygen is 36 months; however, there are CMS proposals to lower it to 13 months as with other equipment such as hospital beds and wheelchairs.

Appraisers will need to evaluate the effect competitive bidding will have on financial forecasts and how it may affect risk adjusted rates of return. Has management adequately incorporated these changes in their forecasts and, if not, how does that affect the appraiser's key assumptions? Also when using valuation methods under the market approach consider whether historical transactions are meaningful in evaluating businesses that are subject to a new reimbursement paradigm.

Home Infusion Therapy (HIT) Funding

This is a very specialized service line and is fraught with regulatory complexities governing coverage and reimbursement. Many infused drugs and biologicals must be "incident to physician services" meaning that the drugs and procedures are administered under the direct supervision of a physician (e.g., drugs administered through implantable pumps). Historically, profit margins in this service line have been the highest of all home care service lines but payment rates and margins are declining rather dramatically and driving industry consolidation even among large regional and national providers.

Increasingly, hospitals are discharging patients "sicker and quicker." In order to return home, some patients will require infused drugs or biologicals in their home. Many treatment regimens are of short duration (3-10 days) and due to this, patients may frequently be discharged from an acute care hospital bed to a skilled nursing facility bed to complete the therapy treatments before being sent home.

Home infusion therapy is covered by Medicare under Part B; however, unlike home health, hospice and home medical equipment service lines, private insurance (not Medicare) is the major payer of HIT services at this time. Private insurance companies have very competitive pricing and frequently select only a few suppliers in a geographic area for contracting (called

Chapter 39: Home Health Care Services

"closed panels."). Increasingly, providers must be large in size in order to compete on rates and many smaller independent providers have been exiting the market.

Medicare

Payment rates are established by each Medicare Part B Carrier based on a percentage of the average wholesale price for infusion drugs, related administration supplies and professional pharmacist fees. As such, these services are subject to Part B coinsurance and deductibles. The Part B benefit does not reimburse for any associated nursing visits for in-home infusion administration; however, there can be additional funding available for the administration of the drug by a nurse if covered under a home health plan of care by a Medicare-certified home health provider, or if covered under a state's Medicaid program or the patient's private insurance policy. If the nursing visits are not reimbursable through any of these sources, then the HIT provider can either absorb this cost or attempt to bill and collect from the patient. However, for smaller HIT providers, they may find that charging the patient for the nursing visits could put them at a competitive disadvantage if larger suppliers (especially national providers) do not charge for this as is their standard practice. Additionally, a patient may elect to complete the required infusion therapy in a SNF bed with the potential for less personal financial liability because third party coverage would be available. Often, HIT providers contract for HIT nursing services from a local home health agency.

Appraisers must be keenly aware of the service area's demographics and median incomes because collection of coinsurances and deductibles is a significant factor in supporting gross margins in this service line. Also the development, or proposed development, of other competing "locations of care" (such as a new outpatient cancer center operated by local oncologists, or the development of a hospital-based or physician-owned ambulatory infusion center) can dramatically reduce a HIT providers' revenue.

Home Health Industry Information

It is important for appraisers to compare the subject company being valued to industry benchmarks. The comparison can assist the appraiser in reaching a number of conclusions about the subject company. For example:

- Whether the subject company is being run effectively and efficiently relative to its peers.
- Whether the subject company has too much or too little debt.
- Whether the subject company has too much or too little working capital.
- Whether the subject company is growing faster or slower than other companies, and how growth is being financed.

Chapter 39: Home Health Care Services

In addition, it is important for appraisers to understand the outlook for the industry to evaluate growth, risks and other factors that might affect the subject company.

It's all about labor

As a service business, labor is the most important resource and cost component for most of the home health care service lines (home health, private duty and hospice). If you understand labor cost and efficiency, you can generally tell how a home health care business is performing relative to its peers. First, it's important to know how a company's labor cost per full time equivalent employee compares to other home health care businesses. Second, you need to know how productive those employees are relative to their peers. For example, according to the Homecare Salary & Benefits Report 2007-2008 (published by the National Association for Home Care, October 2007), a registered nurse should be compensated $25.50 per hour or $33.00 per visit (at the median) and average 5.02 visits in an 8 hour day.

It's also important to know the provider mix (for example, registered nurses, licensed practical nurses, home care aides, physical therapists, occupational therapists and social workers). Provider mix can tell you whether the company is too heavy or too light at various staffing levels and whether they may be missing opportunities to provide additional services.

There may be severe medical personnel labor shortages in many markets. As a result, maintaining low turnover rates is critical and should be carefully assessed during a valuation engagement. Many studies have shown that turnover costs (for example, recruitment, new employee training, and lost productivity) can increase the annual cost of an employee by 33%, or more, based on the nature of the position. High turnover rates may result from non-competitive wages and/or benefits, poor moral, lack of leadership, etc.

Except if they sell products

For those service lines that sell products (home medical and respiratory equipment, and home infusion), gross profit margins are the key benchmarks. Gross profit margins can be positively affected by payor mix on the revenue side or by cost of goods sold on the expense side. By understanding what revenue and margins should be, appraisers can evaluate whether or not there are opportunities available to a hypothetical buyer (under the fair market value standard).

Additional considerations for home hospice

For home hospice services where per diem (or daily) payments frequently represent the total amount available to care for the patient (that is, there are no separate payments for additional services), it is important to effectively manage the cost of drugs, HME, and continuous care nursing or home health aide expense. Hospice providers with abnormally high costs may be overpaying for these services and providers that have abnormally low costs may be missing out on necessary services that might attract a better mix of patients for financial success of the service line.

Chapter 39: Home Health Care Services

Data sources

There are a number of standard industry data sources (such as the Risk Management Association and Integra Information Systems) appraisers use and there may be industry specific sources such as surveys developed through trade associations or industry analyses complied by consultants and financial services companies. In addition, sometimes valuable information can be found in trade magazine articles.

For example, the National Association for Home Care & Hospice (www.nahc.org) has valuable industry resources but membership is required to access some of the more substantive information.

For highly regulated industries, like health care, there is a significant amount of information available from government agencies, think tanks, and advocacy groups.

MedPac

The Medicare Payment Advisory Commission (MedPAC) is an independent Congressional agency established by the Balanced Budget Act of 1997 (P.L. 105-33) to advise the U.S. Congress on issues affecting the Medicare program. The Commission's statutory mandate is quite broad: In addition to advising the Congress on payments to private health plans participating in Medicare and providers in Medicare's traditional fee-for-service program, MedPAC is also tasked with analyzing access to care, quality of care, and other issues affecting Medicare.[3]

MedPac, in its March 2008 report to Congress, projected home health agency margins of 15.4% in 2006 and 11.4% in 2008 However, all hospital-based agencies, which would have significantly lowered these reported margins, were excluded. The report also stated that agencies should be able to absorb cost increases without an increase in base (Medicare) payments. Agencies had profit margins of approximately 9.2% to 16.7% depending on the volume and type of episode mix.

Hospital-based agencies generally have lower profit margins (around 4.9%) because of the allocation of hospital-wide overhead costs. Hospitals usually do a good job allocating direct costs. However, hospital margins would be higher if overhead costs were normalized to reflect a non-hospital agency[4]. This is a critical consideration for the appraiser when valuing a hospital based agency. In most cases the appraiser will want to recast the agency as non-hospital based to reflect comparable overhead costs.

CMS plans to reduce Medicare payments to HHAs each year by 2.75% in 2008 through 2010 and by 2.71% in 2011. However, HHAs will receive a 3% "market basket" increase in 2008 resulting in a net increase of 0.25% for the year, *prior to wage adjusting the labor component of the market basket for each CBSA and rural area rate of each state. The labor component is approximately 77% of the total market basket.* A few CBSAs have wage adjustment rates above 1.0 while most CBSAs and state rural areas are far less than 1.0. Thus, many HHAs will actually "net" somewhat reduced payment rates based on the above two (2) regulatory actions. Complicating

Chapter 39: Home Health Care Services

revenue forecasting even more is that past changes in PPS coding has increased payments overall. MedPac is also assuming that the change from 80 HHRGs to 153 HHRGs will cause an overall increase in payments of 1.6% in 2008 and 2009. These changes need to be considered by appraisers when evaluating financial forecasts.

As a result, MedPac is not recommending increases in the Medicare reimbursement rate in the near term. However, Congress will make the ultimate decision on all Medicare home health rate adjustments.

Valuing Home Health Care Businesses

The income approach

The income approach, and more specifically the discounted cash flow method, is the valuation approach and method preferred by most appraisers to value profitable operating businesses. This method can be difficult to use for marginally profitable or unprofitable businesses if there is inadequate cash flow to provide a reasonable return on the business' assets. In that case, methods under the market or asset approach may be more appropriate.

Under an income approach it is important to determine whether the forecasted cash flows are reasonable and achievable. If the appraiser thoroughly understands the business and the industry (as previously discussed), he or she should be able to reasonably make this determination and factor this into the development of a discount rate applicable to the cash flows forecasted for the subject company.

When evaluating forecasted cash flow growth rates, the appraiser needs to consider imminent changes and proposed changes to reimbursement, opportunities for the subject company to expand, population growth, age demographics and age-cohort specific use rates where data might be available.

Looking at the specific operational issues affecting the company, its historical operations, and by making comparisons to industry data, the appraiser should be able to evaluate the reasonableness of future working capital needs and capital expenditures.

Care must be used in developing an equity discount rate that results in a risk adjusted rate of return necessary to attract buyers to invest in the subject company. Appraisers need to ensure that they understand the operating characteristics (for example, size, growth rates, margins, product and service mix) of the business or businesses from which discount rates and/or equity risk premiums are derived and make appropriate company specific risk adjustments to reflect differences between the subject company and the source of these rates or premiums. In addition, there could be other changes such as new legislation, proposed or enacted, that was unknown when the market derived discount rates or premiums were published.

Chapter 39: Home Health Care Services

Most home health care businesses are not capital intensive. (One exception would be a Hospice with an Inpatient and/or Residential facility.) As a result, they generally do not incur (or have a need to incur) significant long-term debt. The appraiser must consider this and other factors when determining a debt to equity ratio for a weighted average cost of capital (WACC) assumption. Caution should be used in automatically using debt to equity ratios derived from publicly traded companies because they may not be "pure plays"[5] and the subject company may have significantly different operating characteristics and growth opportunities. Under the fair market value standard, the debt to equity ratio should be one that is reasonably achievable by the subject company, and one that is likely to provide the returns anticipated to debt and equity investors, used in the WACC, from the anticipated cash flows used in the forecast

Appraisers need to ensure that risk adjusted rates of returns used match the earnings stream being valued. It is generally acknowledged that most discount rates are derived from public company transactions on an after-tax basis. When valuing health care businesses for regulatory purposes (for example, under the Anti-kickback Law and transactions involving nonprofit IRC 501(c)(3) entities), it is generally accepted that controlling interests must be valued on an after tax basis (including pass through entities) under the assumption that the most likely buyer is a commercial C corporation. One rationale for this is that, without having to pay taxes, nonprofit organizations could theoretically afford to pay more than a comparable for-profit organization for the same business. Valuing after-tax cash flows also keeps after-tax discount rates derived from public companies consistent with the subject company's earnings stream. Appraisers need to consider adjustments to the discount rate or methodology that might be required for non-regulatory valuation engagements and for engagements involving minority interests in pass-through entities to maintain consistency between the discount rate and the earnings stream.

The market approach

Methods under the market approach can be useful but difficult to use correctly when valuing home health care businesses because it is always hard to find publicly traded companies and sales transactions for companies that are truly comparable to the subject company. Unless the comparable company is publicly traded, it is almost impossible to adequately evaluate a comparable company's operating characteristics. Some comparable sales transactions may predate current reimbursement levels, economic changes, or not have anticipated proposed legislation, which might result in an erroneous conclusion about a current transaction. Furthermore, a significant number of comparable sales transactions represent acquisitions by existing health care companies that may realize economic synergies resulting in an investment or synergistic standard of value (not fair market value if that is the standard desired).

Despite these limitations, a thorough analysis of publicly traded companies and comparable sales transactions is extremely useful in developing an understanding of the marketplace, value drivers, who the most likely buyers are, and in determining a reasonable range (low to high) to test values indicated under other approaches.

Chapter 39: Home Health Care Services

The market approach can also be useful in situations where operating income and cash flows are indeterminable because of poor records or commingled operations; or in the case of the mismanagement of an otherwise sound company. In those cases, market derived valuation multiples that are not tied to earnings, can be useful. Assuming you have reliable revenues and/or daily census data for the subject company, price to revenue multiples or price to average daily census multiples from guideline publicly traded companies, or comparable sales transactions, are useful in estimating an indicated range of potential values.

For example, buyers within the industry will frequently use a multiple of patient average daily census (ADC) data to benchmark the value of these businesses. If the benchmark is $50,000 per ADC and the ADC is 200 patients, the business might be worth $10.0 million.

However, remember that when choosing a revenue multiple or census multiple you are implicitly assuming that the subject company has all of the operating characteristics from which the revenue or census multiple was derived. So appraisers must be extremely careful when relying primarily on market multiples.

Developing a significant understanding of the subject company and the industry can go a long way to overcoming the shortcomings inherent in the market approach. For example, if you can benchmark a company's revenue and direct labor costs relative to its peers, you may become more comfortable in choosing a revenue or daily census multiple.

Methods under the market approach appear simple and intuitive, and therefore have great appeal. But these methods need to be used judiciously and generally in conjunction with other approaches.

Aside from traditional public company research and general sales transaction databases, Irving Levin Associates, Inc. (www.levinassociates.com) publishes *The Senior Care Acquisition Report*, which includes information about publicly announced home health care transactions.

The asset approach

Methods under the asset approach are rarely used as the primary method to value operating companies like home health care unless the business is unprofitable or marginally profitable where cash flows do not produce an adequate return on assets. However, methods under the asset approach should still be considered to ensure that values under other approaches (primarily the income approach) exceed values that would be developed under an asset approach, which is usually viewed as the lowest or floor value.

Under an income or market approach, the premise of value is almost always a going concern. When using an asset approach, the premise of value is sometimes more difficult to determine but the valuation method(s) used must be applied consistent with the premise chosen.

Chapter 39: Home Health Care Services

Special Situations Affecting Home Health Care Value

Management's integrity

Health care is arguably the most highly regulated industry in the country. Many of the regulations facing providers today were enacted to address years of providers abusing the system and profiting illegally and unethically under government programs like Medicare and Medicaid and private insurance programs as well.

Today there are significant fines, penalties and the possibility of prison for violating federal and state regulations governing the health care industry and nonprofit organizations. While enforcement has helped to curb abuses, they still exist.

While appraisers generally are not performing due diligence, it is important for them to generally assess management's integrity. Appraisers who understand the home health care industry and the associated regulations also understand many of the illegal schemes and can evaluate management's integrity fairly effectively through benchmarking the company against its peers (looking for anomalies) and interviewing management (looking for inconsistencies).

The risk associated with management's integrity can impact whether revenue levels and profitability can be maintained by a hypothetical buyer who may not be willing or able to operate the business illegally or unethically. The appraiser should always require the organization being valued to disclose any and all correspondence and/or external audit findings that have been conducted by state licensure and Medicare certifying organizations, Medicare and Medicaid fiscal intermediaries, focused medical review audits and findings, as well as any past or ongoing notifications from the Office of the Inspector General (OIG) to include past or current corporate integrity agreements (CIAs). Other useful tools to test the operational integrity of the organization is whether there is a compliance plan in place that is modeled after the OIG's suggested format as well as internal audit committee reports and findings that would be a component of the compliance plan.

The appraiser's assessment of management's integrity may create the need for normalizing adjustments and/or should have a direct effect on risk adjusted rates of return used under an income approach as well as judgments made by the appraiser using methods under other approaches.

Certificate of need (CON) states

States may restrict or limit new home health businesses though certificate of need legislation. Typically, these states limit CON application to service lines that are "skilled in nature" and heavily dependent on Medicare and Medicaid certification and reimbursement such as home health and hospice. However, some states also have CON regulations that govern establishment of new "licensed-only" providers that will not be Medicare-certified but will obtain reimbursements from Medicaid.

Chapter 39: Home Health Care Services

In order to start a new home health care business in a CON state, you would need to demonstrate adequate demand and need. Depending on the state, the CON process can be time consuming and expensive. Generally, home health care businesses in CON states will be worth more compared to a similar business in a state without a CON. However, each state's CON rules may be more or less restrictive and the appraiser should research the state's current plan for home health care services to determine whether there is opportunity for new businesses to enter the market. Even if the business is no more profitable in the CON state, the lack of new competition will generally reduce risk compared to businesses in non-CON states.

In states where CONs are very restrictive, the CON alone can be worth a significant amount of money even without an operating business and, as a result, sometimes CONs are valued independent of the operating business.

Appraisers need to consider the effect on the discount rate when valuing home health care businesses in CON states versus non-CON states. When valuing a CON alone (without an operating business) appraisers should generally rely on the income approach (relief from royalty method) or possibly the cost approach unless comparable transaction data for the CONs in the state are available. If using a relief from royalty method, consider using 25% of the expected operating margin as the pre-tax royalty rate. For example, if agencies are expected to earn 12% in that market, the pre-tax royalty rate for the CON valuation calculation would be 3% of the forecasted revenues expected if the CON were used in an operating business.

Valuing provider-based home health care businesses

Home health care businesses owned by hospitals or nursing homes are unique because they generally will not have their own financial statements or tax returns; and will almost never have a balance sheet. They generally only track costs directly applicable to a department, like home health services (such as direct supplies, compensation and benefits) but allocate indirect overhead (such as telephone, security, maintenance, rent, utilities, human resource, and information systems) from the parent entity's total overhead. As a result, operations for provider-based owned home health care businesses are generally not comparable to stand alone businesses.

Without objective financial statements (and particularly balance sheets), it is usually impossible to develop meaningful financial ratios and analysis. However, a number of operational benchmarks, such as revenue per visit, average daily census, or visits per employee, can still be developed and compared to industry benchmarks to evaluate the quality of operations.

Another potential problem in valuing a provider-based home health care business is that sometimes they are not profit motivated. In some cases the lack of profit motivation may be due to a lack of focused attention on the part of the parent entity's management; particularly if the business is a very small part of overall operations. In other cases, the business may be viewed solely for its contribution to the parent entity's mission or as part of a continuum of care. While profitability is not inconsistent with these views of the business, management sometimes uses them to rationalize underperformance. Appraisers need to understand that marginal profitability or even losses in the hands of management doesn't necessarily mean these businesses cannot be run profitably in the hands of profit motivated management.

In order to value provider-based businesses, historical and forecasted operations need to be normalized and made comparable to non-provider-based or stand alone businesses. Great care must be exercised in doing this to ensure that only controllable costs are adjusted and uncontrollable costs, which may be unique to that marketplace, are not changed. Care must also be exercised to ensure that, under the fair market value standard, adjustments are not unique to a particular buyer.

Appraisers need to develop a reasonable understanding of industry benchmarks for home health care businesses in order to support or evaluate the assumptions that will be necessary to convert the hospital owned business into a non-hospital owned business.

Some questions typically asked during these assignments are:

- How much space (square footage) does the business really need?

- Is the rent too high and location too expensive for the needs of the business?

- Is the business sharing management with other departments and how are those costs allocated?

- Are the parent entity's labor costs and benefits comparable to a non-provider-based business?

- Are there cost and/or other administrative functions that are only required because they are part of the provider-based entity (for example, Joint Commission Accreditation)?

- How are patients referred for home health care services?

How referrals are made to a provider-based business can have a significant impact to its value—and, of course, referrals are a key regulatory risk area. For example, there is less risk of losing referrals if they come from a variety of physicians as opposed to only physicians employed by or on the staff of the parent entity. While this is a typical risk associated with a concentration of customers, it may be more prevalent for provider-based businesses. In valuing the business under a fair market value standard, the appraiser should evaluate what would change if the business were not part of, or reliant upon, the parent entity.

Real estate and non-operating assets

Most home health care businesses are not capital intensive (an exception might be a hospice that has an inpatient or residential facility). As a result, real estate and other non-operating assets can create special problems in determining value. In particular, cash flows from the operating business often will not provide an adequate return on the real estate and non-operating assets.

Generally, these assets should be excluded from the value of the operating business and valued separately if they are, in fact, going to be acquired as part of the transaction. These assets should be removed from the balance sheet and their historical costs should be removed from the income statements. For those assets, such as real estate, that are used in the business, fair market value rent expense (assuming a fair market value standard) should be substituted for the cost of owning and operating the real estate. Fair market value rent for the operating business should be consistent with rents that would be paid by other home care businesses for only the square footage needed to operate a similar business within the subject company's market. Fair market value rent could be more or less than rents paid historically or agreed to prospectively.

If the valuation is being done for regulatory purposes, rent that is below or above fair market value is a potential issue that should be evaluated by a health care attorney familiar with applicable regulations. The appraiser should either use the actual rent in the forecasts so that cash flows reflect the positive or negative impact; or, fair market value rents could be used in the forecast with the incremental increase or decrease in value related to the favorable or unfavorable lease added to or subtracted from the indicated value of the operating business.

Conclusion

Valuing home health care businesses is not unlike valuing other businesses except that appraisers should have a significant understanding of their operating characteristics and the industry. In addition, for any health care engagement, appraisers should have a reasonable understanding of regulations affecting health care providers and nonprofit organizations and a grasp of the current changes that may be enacted by Congress and state legislatures.

The author would like to thank Ron Clitherow, MPH and Gary R. Massey, CPA for their significant contributions to this chapter.

Acronyms & abbreviations used

ADC – average daily census
ASP – average sales price
AWP – average wholesale price
CAP – community alternative programs
CBSA – core based statistical area
CIA – corporate integrity agreement
CMS – Centers for Medicare and Medicaid Services
CON – certificate of need
HHA – home health agencies
HHRG – home health resource groups
HIT – home infusion therapy
HME – home medical equipment funding

Chapter 39: Home Health Care Services

LUPA – low utilization patients
MedPac – medicare payment advisory commission
OASIS – outcome and assessment information set
OIG – Office of the Inspector General
PPS – prospective payment system

---

1. It is generally paid by the individual or the individual might get reimbursed through private insurance like Long Term Care insurance
2. Payment basics, Durable Medical Equipment Payment System, Revised: October 2007, published by MedPac
3. From MedPac web site www.medpac.gov/about.cfm
4. MedPac Report to the Congress, March 2008
5. A pure play is a company that is only in one line of business. Many public companies are in multiple lines of business.

Chapter 40

What is to be Learned From Caracci?

By Mark O. Dietrich, CPA/ABV, and Kenneth W. Patton, ASA

This article first appeared in the Fall, 2007 Edition of CPA Expert. *Reprinted with permission.*

The appropriate use of the market approach in healthcare industry valuation is one of the most critical issues confronting the appraisal industry today. Many healthcare industry appraisers believe that market data is often unreliable or even misleading and must be used with abundant caution. Therefore, they focus primarily on the income approach. These appraisers cite such factors as local Medicaid coverage differences, the monopsonistic market power of local health insurers, the lack of sufficient data to determine comparability, and regulatory restrictions on the use of market data contained in the Stark regulations.

Appraisers who believe that the market approach, along with the income approach, should be given significant weight focus on the importance of actual transactions and not substituting one's judgment for that of the market. Where both groups agree is that use of market data in the healthcare industry requires significant skill and indepth analysis. In this article two leading experts, who have contrasting views on the topic, explore those issues in depth.

To illustrate our viewpoints, we discuss these issues in the context of the Fifth Circuit's reversal of the Tax Court's opinion in *Caracci*,[1] which poses a number of questions to business valuation professionals. With respect to the valuation issues only, Mark Dietrich believes that the Fifth Circuit's decision was more correct than the Tax Court's decision, while Ken Patton believes that the Tax Court's decision was more correct.[2] Ken Patton brings years of healthcare industry valuation expertise (although fewer years than Mark Dietrich), and more to the point, his knowledge of this specific market through his experience valuing other healthcare companies in the region during this time.[3]

The Key Valuation Issue and Valuation Experts

In *Caracci*, the key valuation issue was the value of the assets transferred from a not-for-profit entity to a for profit entity.

The valuation expert for the taxpayers, Sta-Home entities and the Caraccis, was Allen D. Hahn, a director in PricewaterhouseCoopers Northeast Region Corporation Valuation Consulting Group. The valuation expert for the IRS was Charles A. Wilhoite, a managing director of Willamette Management Associates and the national director of its health care industry services. In its opinion, the Tax Court recognized the experience and qualifications of the experts.

Chapter 40: What is to be Learned From Caracci?

History of Sta-Home

Sta-Home was a collection of entities that provided home health care services primarily paid for by Medicaid to residents of Mississippi. Reimbursements were limited to the cost of providing the service, which apparently precluded the possibility of profitability. Sta-Home completed a corporate reorganization in 1995, which ultimately led to the litigation with the IRS.

Sta-Home was approximately 20 years old at the time of the reorganization. According to the courts' decisions, it:

- Had a well-established brand name.

- Had well-documented intellectual capital (manuals, procedures).

- Had a "generally good reputation."

- Had a certificate of need and accreditation by the JCAHO (Joint Commission on the Accreditation of Healthcare Organizations).

- Was the largest provider of home healthcare services in Mississippi.

For perspective, as shown in Figure 1, Sta-Home's scale of operations had increased dramatically from 1991 to 1995. A question immediately comes to mind: Why would the owners grow the business to this extent if there were no chance of economic success?

Figure 1: Sta-Home's Revenues and Expenses (1991–1995)

Year	Revenue	Expenses	Net Income
1991	$11,736,061	$11,799,721	($63,660)
1992	$18,442,072	$18,414,315	$27,757
1993	$25,162,701	$25,208,255	($45,554)
1994	$36,882,957	$37,141,686	($258,729)
1995	$44,101,849	$44,535,239	($433,390)

Position of the Parties

This case involved the conversion of Mississippi's largest home health agency chain, Sta-Home, from tax exempt to for-profit status in 1995.[4] The entity had more than $44 million in revenues and a loss of $433,390 in that year, as well as a large share of the Mississippi market. Such conversions were common at this time. They took place against the expectation[5] of a prospective payment system (PPS)[6] replacing Medicare's cost-based system for paying for home healthcare.

Chapter 40: What is to be Learned From Caracci?

The PPS was ultimately adopted in the Balanced Budget Act of 1997. It paid agencies in 60-day episodes of care rather than on the basis of costs incurred. The cost-based system had led to the spending of excessive amounts on delivering care. Prior to the adoption of the PPS, home health agencies were often acquired by hospitals (and there was an active market in Mississippi). The hospitals, which were already paid by Medicare under a PPS, could therefore shift costs to the home health agency and obtain higher reimbursement for the same services.

The conversion was audited by the IRS, which found that the tax exempt entities had approximately $18.5 million in net equity value that had been improperly transferred to the subsequent owners. The new owners maintained that the liabilities assumed exceeded the value of the assets received. The IRS asserted that the net excess benefit of $18.5 million triggered excise taxes and penalties of more then $250 million. The Tax Court subsequently reduced this to $46 million.

Tax Court Opinion

According to Judge Laro's opinion, a valuation prepared contemporaneously with the transaction at the insistence of special tax counsel for Sta-Home was initially rejected by that counsel for failure to conform to Revenue Ruling 59-60[7] and to address the existence of intangible assets. A second appraisal found that the equity value of the entities was negative, although the Tax Court record indicates that special tax counsel remained concerned about the quality of the appraisal.

The Standard of Value

A key issue in the case was the conflict between the normalization of earnings adjustments available to a hypothetical willing buyer and those available only to a specific buyer or specific class of buyers, and whether the latter constituted fair market value. The following is quoted from the Tax Court's opinion:

> During 1995, the primary buyers of home health agencies were hospitals, nursing homes, and other home health agencies. They were able to take advantage of a mechanism known as 'cost-shifting.'

Cost shifting was commonly used in this time period by hospitals that were paid under a PPS. The PPS generated a fixed payment so that if costs could be transferred to the home health agency, additional revenue could be generated with no additional cost. The inclusion of this attribute by the Tax Court was critical in the determination of fair market value.

The taxpayer's expert, Hahn, valued the cost gap at $667,000 based upon his view that a buyer would have a one-year benefit from that strategy. The Tax Court disagreed:

Chapter 40: What is to be Learned From Caracci?

This value is too low. The cost gaps were available under the then-current reimbursement program. They would cease to exist under a PPS. Although there had been discussions of a PPS for several years, Congress had passed no such legislation at the time of the transfer, and there is no evidence that the prospect of such legislation had a negative effect upon the value of home health care agencies.

HAHN'S VALUATION APPROACHES

The Tax Court reviewed and critiqued each expert's use of the market approach. Hahn also relied primarily on an adjusted balance sheet methodology (a version of the cost approach), in which he valued the trained workforce and certificate of need. Hahn placed considerably less reliance on market comparables because purported comparables were "idiosyncratic" and lacked sufficient detail.

The Tax Court also noted Hahn's testimony that guideline public companies were not appropriate comparables because home health care was part of a broader service mix. In effect, there were no "pure-play" public companies.

WILHOITE'S VALUATION APPROACHES

Wilhoite relied primarily on the market approach utilizing both guideline public companies and guideline acquisitions. The Tax Court appeared to indicate a clear preference for this approach. Wilhoite derived revenue pricing multiples for MVIC, the use of which was a key issue in the Fifth Circuit's decision.[8]

The Tax Court discussed the two comparable acquired companies deemed most like Sta-Home according to Wilhoite. The Court then went on to develop its own view of the proper multiple.

There was no discussion by the Tax Court of differences in payor mix between the purported comparables and Sta-Home, which was 95% Medicare-based. The court did observe that Mississippi had the largest per capita spending on home health in the country under the Medicare program, but that speaks more to volume of services than rate per unit of service—and the latter drives profits. The court did allude to Hahn's testimony that successful home health agencies had non-government patients and more profitable lines of business, such as infusion therapy. These are all critical, and likely conclusive, differences as to comparability. Regardless of these concerns about the comparables, the Tax Court held that the taxpayers owed a crushing amount of excise taxes and penalties.

Chapter 40: What is to be Learned From Caracci?

APPELLATE COURT OPINION

The Fifth Circuit severely criticized the IRS for its numerous errors in the assessment process, Judge Laro for engaging in valuation, and Wilhoite for his failure to understand the Mississippi marketplace. The Fifth Circuit first observed that Sta-Home had looked for a hospital buyer unsuccessfully. Where Judge Laro had been dismissive of the taxpayer's expert, Hahn, the Fifth Circuit embraced him, observing that the IRS had also attempted to retain him and that he spent eight weeks in Mississippi working on the case[9] compared to Wilhoite's two days. Wilhoite's lack of experience in the home healthcare industry in particular, as opposed to his general valuation experience, was also cited. Significantly, the Fifth Circuit noted that: "Wilhoite used market-based and income-based approaches to assign values to all Sta-Home's assets in general, *without valuing any of Sta-Home's assets in particular*...." (Italics added for emphasis).

SYNONOMOUS STANDARD OF VALUE?

Caracci implicitly raises an issue regarding the standard of value. Without question, all of the parties believed that "fair market value" was applicable. The potential for sale of Sta-Home was discussed by the Tax Court and even more by the Fifth Circuit. Although fair market value is generally considered to refer to hypothetical willing buyers and sellers, it is evident that the very specific circumstances of potential buyers were considered.

Wilhoite used a method known as "cost shifting" in his analysis. Economic profits are created by charging a portion of the expense base to another business unit. Cost shifting was in frequent use in the region as a means of creating value for Medicare home health agencies. Because cost shifting incorporates business synergies, it raises the specter that the standard of value had really morphed into investment value, which is defined in the "International Glossary of Business Valuation Terms" as "the value to a particular investor based on individual requirements and expectations."[10] If virtually every market participant has the potential to use the cost shifting benefits, investment value might effectively become synonymous with fair market value.

The third standard of value, intrinsic value, is defined in the International Glossary as "the value that an investor considers, on the basis of an evaluation of available facts, to be the 'true' or 'real' value that will become the market value when other investors reach the same conclusion."

Why is intrinsic value important in this case? First there was great debate about the future of home health care as a business due to the implementation of PPS. Market participants in the geographical area had widely different views. Market transactions occurring contemporaneously and after the valuation date indicated that Medicare dependent home health agencies had value. Taking the opposite position with respect to Sta-Home clearly reflected a different view of the company's intrinsic prospects.

Second, the valuation of health care entities can be very volatile based on potential change in reimbursement rates. Note carefully the use of the word "potential." Medicare changes are often first rumored, followed by proposals that may not be implemented for a year or more, and then the actual implementation. The analyst is left to make key decisions about prospective economic conditions of a business in the face of both great and unique uncertainties. Without question, actual market transactions can differ from an individual analyst's belief about the future. The circumstances of Sta-Home reflect this conundrum. While hindsight may give comfort to an analyst's position, appraisers must look at the broader market and attempt to reconcile actual market activity with their expectations and the expectations of others.

KEY REGULATORY ISSUES IN HEALTHCARE

Certain regulatory structures discussed here were not in place or well-understood at the time of the Sta-Home conversion. However, they are critical to assessing the relevance of the *Caracci* decision to appraisals in today's marketplace.

The following are excerpts from a synopsis of the anti-kickback statute extracted from an advisory opinion of the Office of the Inspector General:

> The anti-kickback statute makes it a criminal offense knowingly and willfully to offer, pay, solicit, or receive any remuneration to induce or reward referrals of items or services payable by a federal health care program. See section 1128B(b) of the Act. Where remuneration is paid purposefully to induce or reward referrals of items or services paid for by a federal health care program, the anti-kickback statute is violated. By its terms, the statute ascribes criminal liability to parties on both sides of an impermissible 'kickback' transaction. For purposes of the anti-kickback statute, 'remuneration' includes the transfer of anything of value, directly or indirectly, overtly or covertly, in cash or in kind. [11]

A buyer paying a seller for the profits associated with the buyer's subsequent provision of new services to the seller's patients may well be seen as paying a prohibited kickback for future referrals, particularly when the sellers remain employed by or active in the business.[12]

VALUATION QUESTIONS RAISED BY THE CASE

At this point, the authors engage in some point-counterpoint by addressing valuation questions raised by the Tax Court and Fifth Circuit's decisions.

What is required for market comparability?

Dietrich: Payment mechanisms are one of the most fascinating things about health care. Most health care is covered by private insurance or government programs like Medicare (as in Sta-Home)

Chapter 40: What is to be Learned From Caracci?

or Medicaid. What is not widely understood is that the level of payment for those services varies radically from state to state and even market to market. Most urban markets are dominated by a few health insurers who hold significant influence over the fees paid to providers. Very few insurers have national market coverage, and those that do have significant market share in only a few states.[13] In order to use a guideline public company method or a guideline acquisition, the analyst would need to look at the payor mix for both the guideline and the subject and see if they were similar. In a poor state like Mississippi, the insurance market is unlikely to have been attractive because most patients would have had Medicaid, which pays the least. This would have made the out-of-market guideline transactions and public companies worthless.

Patton: The payment mechanism is clearly one of the most important factors in health care valuation. Reimbursement rates and sources vary by region and by state or even locality. Mississippi is a poor state that was experiencing a surge in home health visits, as compared with national activity. At the time, it shared these characteristics with the nearby states of Alabama, Louisiana, Arkansas, and portions of Tennessee and Kentucky. A market comparison to publicly traded companies or individual transactions outside the geographic region would likely be problematic. Nevertheless, there was acquisition activity in the aforementioned states in Medicare-based agencies, and demand for them was evident. Mercer Capital had observed market pricing in the range of $10 to $15 per visit for Medicare-based companies in the region.

Can appraisers differ reasonably about the implications of a foreseeable change?

Dietrich: Perhaps the most important issue raised in *Caracci* is the Tax Court's specific rejection of the impending change to a PPS, which was the basis of Hahn's position. Medicare had been converting various healthcare industry sectors from cost-based and other reimbursement systems to PPS in order to control rapidly expanding costs. There was no doubt PPS was coming and, therefore, the change was reasonably foreseeable on the valuation date.

Patton: Although there was little doubt that the change to PPS was coming, there was apparently considerable doubt as to the precise timing and the implications of its implementation. The prevailing temporary payment system (PIP) had placed considerable strain on the financial resources of Sta-Home and other home health care agencies. Yet, the company continued to grow the base of visits. Does this speak to a different view on the implication of the ultimate shift to PPS? Other companies were amassing size under a general theory that a well-operated company could prosper under PPS. Notwithstanding the ultimate wisdom of that position (based on a subsequent event), companies in the region were increasing their size in the belief that customer accumulation created value.

Does "market data" necessarily apply to the subject interest being valued?

Dietrich: Another problem is the conflict between the Fifth Circuit's view that Sta-Home had pursued buyers unsuccessfully and the Tax Court's apparent dismissal of this. It is important to understand that strategic buyers in a market do not need to buy every player in that market.

Chapter 40: What is to be Learned From Caracci?

Generally, they will buy only a sufficient mass to service the market area. There are antitrust implications to owning too much market share. If the hospitals in Sta-Home's service area had already acquired home health agencies, they would be unlikely to acquire another.

Patton: A market for Medicare dependent home health agencies clearly existed in the region. Yet, was there a market for this specific company based on conditions in Mississippi? As the geographical market shrinks, the analysis moves away from hypothetical buyers and sellers to a very specific list of each. In this case, Sta-Home would be the seller, and the list of buyers was thought to be very limited. At the same time, why was it appropriate to limit the list of likely buyers to Mississippi based entities? An analyst should not substitute his or her judgment for that of the marketplace and assume his or her analysis considers every reasonable type of buyer. In many respects, courts in these types of cases began to move toward an investment value standard that might well be reasonable in an industry highly influenced by regulations and dominated by a narrow payment structure.

When does data become "irrelevant history"?

Dietrich: Historical transactions would have been increasingly irrelevant measures as the PPS loomed ever closer, at least to the extent they were based on the cost gap. Comparability can be a function of time. If a major change in the reimbursement program occurs, comparability is lost. Therefore, one must be able to relate the reimbursement systems to the timing of the transaction.

Patton: My co-author should be given great credit for emphasizing this crucial point. The viability of any health care business is extremely exposed to the payment system. To the extent that payments are made by a government entity (Medicare, Medicaid, or local tax support), the prospects for that business can (and do) change greatly as reimbursement changes. Home health care literally exploded in the early 1990s. It was obvious that some reaction from the United States government would occur. Transactions that occurred during the time frame of growth may not be relevant to a specific valuation. The underlying conditions are just not comparable. Nevertheless, transactions for Medicare-based agencies continued to occur within the region for several years after 1995 at pre- 1995 levels. This was apparently due to the differences in outlook for the industry and the impact of PPS. The important point is, however, that allegedly comparable transactions can become dated literally overnight as the reimbursement rules change.

What does it mean to be reasonably informed of the relevant facts?

Dietrich: Knowledge of impending legislative changes in healthcare, even if several years in the future, is critical to developing a realistic cash flow forecast. Many of these changes are driven by the recommendation of the Medicare Payment Advisory Commission, established by Congress as part of the Balanced Budget Act of 1997 to advise it about needed changes. Equally important, extremely rapid growth in revenues in a particular industry sub-sector is compelling evidence that future growth is likely to be curtailed. For example, this happened in the summer of 2005 with respect to high tech imaging after four years of rapid growth, when payments for

Chapter 40: What is to be Learned From Caracci?

diagnostic exams, such as magnetic residence imaging (MRI) and computed tomography (CT) were curtailed and positron emission tomography (PET) was brought within the purview of the Stark Laws, which govern physician self-referral for Medicare and Medicaid patients.

As the present author noted in an article,[14] discussing the then just released Tax Court's decision in *Caracci*:

> Moreover, these cost shifting strategies have been the subject of numerous civil and criminal proceedings under the Medicare Fraud and Abuse Statute. In fact, MedPAC's current [2002] report[15] notes that:

> The new payment system's [The payment system was changed from a cost based system to an interim system with stricter payment limits in 1997, then changed again to the prospective payment system in October 2000.] adjustments to eligibility and fraud and abuse reduction efforts were intended to reduce spending and redirect the benefit toward briefer, more intense care. Changes in spending and use between 1997 and 1999 demonstrate that these changes had some dramatic effects (McCall et al. 2001): Total Medicare spending on home health fell 52%....

Allowing for the inherent distortions in reporting caused by the cost shifting strategy used by hospitals with respect to home health agencies, Figure 2 presents a graph that illustrates the four-year margin, from 1997–2000, on Medicare home health business for hospitals (the arguably strategic class of acquirer that was the basis for the Tax Court decision). This shows the decreased spending in those years, which occurred even though the PPS was not finally implemented due to delays until 2000. The bottom dropped out two years before the implementation.

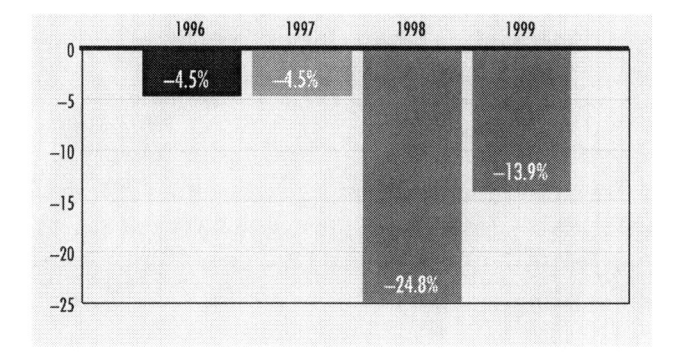

Figure 2: Four-Year Margin (1997–2000)

Year	Margin
1996	−4.5%
1997	−4.5%
1998	−24.8%
1999	−13.9%

What is astounding about the Tax Court decision is that this information was known at the time of the trial; the court either was unaware of it or ignored it. The information very clearly demonstrates that Hahn was correct. The court's rationale seemingly cannot be that the information came after the valuation date as can be seen clearly from the following statement by the court concerning post-valuation date data.[16]

Chapter 40: What is to be Learned From Caracci?

Home health agencies remained under a cost reimbursement system until September 30, 1999, when legislation passed by Congress in 1997 providing a PPS for home health agencies took full effect. The Health Care Financial Administration (HCFA) encountered problems implementing the system, and it was not finally implemented until October 1, 2000.

The requirement for regional market value evidence is now spelled out in the Stark Laws. Although implemented well after the Sta-Home transaction, abuses in valuing such transactions are a principal reason for the rule:

> Fair market value means the value in arm's-length transactions consistent with general market value. 'General market value' means the price that an asset would bring as the result of bona fide bargaining between well-informed buyers and sellers who are not otherwise in a position to generate business for the other party; or the compensation that would be included in a service agreement as a result of bona fide bargaining between well-informed parties to the agreement who are not otherwise in a position to generate business for the other party, on the date of acquisition or at the time of the service agreement. Usually the fair market price is the price at which bona fide sales have been consummated for assets of like type, quality, and quantity in a particular market at the time of acquisition.[17]

> Moreover, the definition of 'fair market value' in the statute and regulation is qualified in ways that do not necessarily comport with the usage of the term in standard valuation techniques and methodologies. For example, the methodology must exclude valuations where the parties to the transactions are at arm's length but in a position to refer to one another.[18]

The following clarifying statement should be included immediately following the standard definition of fair market value: *Reasonable knowledge of the relevant facts contemplates an understanding of the regulatory environment for health care entities.*

Patton: It is surely essential to understand the legal and regulatory structure. Once again, however, market data from relevant transactions appear to offer a different interpretation of the specific implications of the prospective changes in the home health care industry. Nevertheless, the comments above are extremely important in understanding the rules of valuation in a highly regulated industry such as healthcare.

How does the valuation analyst balance historical results with changes in the strategic position of the industry and varying views of the industry?

Dietrich: The single most powerful tool for differentiating "strategic" value inherent in acquisition prices from fair market value is a disciplined application of the income approach on a stand-alone basis. If the value indications under the market approach cannot be sustained on

Chapter 40: What is to be Learned From Caracci?

a stand-alone basis,[19] the analyst needs to perform an analysis to justify a crossover from strategic value to fair market value in the marketplace.[20] In other sectors of the economy, such as banking, most, if not all, buyers have "strategic" opportunities from things such as economies of scale. Because the definition of fair market value in health care is qualified by the regulatory environment, only certain types of otherwise strategic adjustments can be considered. Each category of "strategic" opportunity must be identified, evaluated for appropriateness under the statutes and regulations, and then, if appropriate, included in the valuation model (typically a discounted cash flow) to justify the value conclusion under the income approach. The value indications of the different approaches cannot be said to have been reconciled absent such an undertaking.

For example, it might be appropriate to value a subject in a sector that is being consolidated on the basis of consolidator transactions if the consolidators are active in the subject's service area. In that case, otherwise strategic adjustments such as a lower cost of capital, higher growth rates, and lower operating costs might be appropriate normalization adjustments in an income approach.[21]

At the same time, and more important, it is incumbent on the analyst to eliminate the possibility that market data may have included strategic considerations that violate the Stark laws, Anti-kickback Statute, or IRS regulations and rulings for exempt entities; *Caracci*, after all, was about excise taxes for an excess benefit transaction. In the two opinions, it is not clear whether there was testimony about the appropriateness from a regulatory standpoint of considering acquisition multiples based on agencies that included infusion or respiratory therapy. The Tax Court made it clear that Hahn, who was a leading expert in this area, eliminated them (appropriately):

> From these privately held transactions, Hahn excluded sales of privately held home health agencies that provided sophisticated 'infusion or respiratory therapy' because those could attract reimbursement at a higher rate than those available to the more traditional home health care agencies such as Sta-Home.

Patton: An analyst must consider the regulatory structure. Once again, this is a situation in which many of the prospective buyers are likely to view acquisition targets from the perspective of investment value. Hence, fair market value and investment value begin to merge.

Can a business that appears to be losing money in perpetuity have goodwill, or is there the potential for creating value even when there is no direct way to create profits?

Dietrich: This question is certainly one that often confronts appraisers. I believe the prevailing view among appraisers who limit themselves to the healthcare industry is that if one cannot generate a cash return, one generally cannot have intangible value. Because the definition of fair market value is constrained by what is legally permissible (for example, a cocaine dealership has no fair market value because it is illegal), one cannot ascribe fair market value to potential exit strategies from a losing business that are inconsistent with the law.

Chapter 40: What is to be Learned From Caracci?

Outside this regulatory constraint, a business that always loses money may have value to a larger entity due to economies of scale or other arguably strategic opportunities as discussed in the preceding section. A simple proscribed example would be a physician practice that earns the physician less than a reasonable salary, but generates significant revenues to a hospital through admissions and tests. The practice has a large value to the hospital, but the hospital cannot pay for that value since it violates both the Stark laws and the Anti-kickback Statute.

Value may exist on other than a stand-alone basis in such a circumstance as Sta-Home, but demonstrating that value to be consistent with fair market value is a required and significant burden on the appraiser and the parties to any transaction.

Patton: The Fifth Circuit places great reliance on a strain of thought that Sta-Home's operations could not have goodwill because the court could not identify a stream of profitability. Consider the following comment by the court:

> For Sta-Home, the overwhelming dependence on Medicare reimbursement meant that added revenue meant added reimbursement costs, which in turn, generated greater losses.

Given the growth in revenue of 276% evident in Figure 1 and the strategies of similar companies, why didn't Sta-Home just stop growing if the owners really believed that there was no hope of an economic return?

The Tax Court explained that it believed that this apparently illogical conclusion made sense: It found that Sta-Home had the potential to make a profit, which demonstrated that its assets had substantial fair market value.

There is a disconnect between the court's theory and the behavior of the owners of Sta-Home and the owners of other companies in the marketplace.

> To operate despite their perennial cash-flow problems, their lack of profitability, their increasing operating losses, and their increasing deficits.

> ...its patients—would only enable the agencies to lose money for the indefinite future.

Can a business that appears to be losing money in perpetuity have goodwill? Here again, the growth of the size of the business could indicate an alternative theory about the creation of value not linked to reported profitability.

Again, there is a disconnect between the business strategy of Sta-Home (and other similar companies in the region) and the observations of the Fifth Circuit. Rational people stop amassing assets when it continually increases their losses unless they believe that there is an economic return on some basis in the future.

Chapter 40: What is to be Learned From Caracci?

The Fifth Circuit posits the following argument that goodwill is derived from excess earnings; therefore, in this case, there can be no goodwill. It states:

> The Tax Court's mistaken belief that Sta-Home's intangible assets had substantial fair market value led it to ignore its own long-recognized position that unprofitable intangible assets do not contribute to fair market value unless those assets produce net income or earnings. Revenue Ruling 59-60 requires the IRS to assign zero value to unprofitable intangible assets. See Rev. Rule 59-60, 1959-1 C.B. 237 ('The presence of goodwill and its value, therefore, rests upon the excess of net earnings over and above a fair return on the net tangible assets.')

Putting aside the Fifth Circuit's legal position, the court's implicit economic position requires discussion. First and foremost, all value is a function of future benefits. The past may be instructive, but is not determinative of value. The core question for any asset or business value is "What benefits will it produce in the future?"

Most assets and businesses have the prospect of a visible positive return in the hands of its current owners. Value is most visible when net income is present. However, every valuation analyst has to be open to an alternative view of value creation that is not apparent until the ultimate sale of the assets. Appraisers often place virtually all of the value in a discounted cash flow analysis in the terminal value; therefore, interim profitability is not essential.

What happens, however, when profitability is never likely or even expected to occur in the hands of the current owner? Can goodwill exist? Of course it can, and it does. How could this be true? In one simple scenario, value in excess of cost can be created by accumulating a customer base. By selling the amassed base in bulk, there is value to the buyer, which is often a typical market participant. The seller realizes the value of its efforts to accumulate the customers.

Did the Tax Court and Wilhoite err by basing the valuation of the assets on the market value of invested capital?

Patton: The Tax Court and Wilhoite based the value of the assets, including the intangible assets, on the market value of invested capital. The Fifth Circuit said this was in error, and the value of the assets, including the intangible assets, should be based on a valuation of the direct value of the assets themselves. Was the Tax Court in error? From a valuation perspective, the answer is an emphatic "no."

The Fifth Circuit favors an approach to valuing goodwill by valuing the asset directly. Further, it seems not to accept the notion that the value of the assets must equal the value of the liabilities by referring to it as an accounting concept. This is incorrect. The value of the assets will, by definition, from a valuation perspective, be the value of the total invested capital plus other liabilities and non-operating assets. Additionally, the concept of direct valuation of goodwill will require the use of income methods that ultimately require the determination of total invested capital.

Chapter 40: What is to be Learned From Caracci?

Dietrich: Perhaps both courts got ahead of their knowledge in writing their opinions. The left-hand or asset side of the accounting equation must, of necessity, equal the right-hand or invested capital side. The Fifth Circuit thought a more meaningful result could be obtained from the left-hand side, while the Tax Court believed in the invested capital approach inherent in use of the guideline methods in which individual assets are not valued. It is a useful exercise to allocate value to the assets after making a preliminary determination of invested capital, and the present author often does so both analytically and in reports. Identifying the amount of intangible value is important in healthcare appraisal because this is where the regulatory risk is greatest.

LOOKING AHEAD

The opinions of the Tax Court and the Fifth Circuit in *Caracci* raise very interesting questions for business valuation professionals. The authors have attempted to address several of them. While they may not agree on every point, hopefully readers will find their insights helpful, and that this article furthers the discussion.

---

1. 118 TC 379 (2002), rev'd.: 456 F.3d 444, 98 AFTR2d 2006-5264: (CA-5, 2006).
2. The authors offer no opinion as to any of the legal aspects of this case.
3. Neither of the authors (or their firms) was involved in the case; therefore, they are relying solely on publicly available information.
4. The entities operated under state certificates of need.
5. A virtual certainty in the view of co-author Mark Dietrich. The Tax Court stated in its opinion that "Natl.expenditures for home nursing care grew from $3.8 billion in 1990 to $20.5 billion in 1997," a circumstance that guaranteed congressional action and always has.
6. A PPS pays for services on the basis of a fee set in advance.
7. 1959-1 CB 237.
8. Of particular note is the Service's expert's reliance on revenue multiples from *out of market* transactions and public companies. This is a notoriously bad multiple in the view of many healthcare valuation experts and one specifically banned by the later-issued Stark II regulations discussed below.
9. These facts do not appear in the Tax Court decision.
10. American Society of Appraisers Business Valuation Standards, Glossary, last revised June 2005. www.appraisers.org.
11. See Office of the Inspector General Advisory Opinion No. 03-12.
12. See, *McLeod Regional Medical Center to Pay U.S. Over $15 Million to Resolve False Claims Act Allegations*, U.S. Department of Justice Press Release, 11/1/02.
13. See, Government Accounting Office *Private Health Insurance: Number and Market Share of Carriers in the Small Group Health Insurance Market*.
14. "Valuation, Tax Exemption, 'Fair Market Value,' and The Tax Court (*Caracci, et al v. Commissioner*)", Medical Management Advisor, May, 2002.
15. *Report to the Congress: Medicare Payment Policy*, March 2002; see page 93 forward.
16. Later in the opinion, the court stated that Hahn's inclusion of a one-year "cost gap" should have been a two-year "cost gap," apparently because the PPS was, in fact, passed in 1997, two years after the Sta-Home transaction.
17. 420 CFR 411.351 (Emphasis added).
18. Medicare Program; Physicians' Referrals to Health Care Entities With Which They Have Financial Relationships (Phase II); Interim Final Rule; 69 Fed. Reg. 16053.
19. Damodoran describes stand-alone value in his writings on evaluating acquisitions. www.stern.nyu.edu/~adamodar/.
20. See Dietrich, "Understanding the Difference Between Strategic and Fair Market Value in Consolidating Industries," 21 Business Valuation Review 77 (June 2002).
21. *Ibid*.

Chapter 41

Quality Performance and Valuation: What's The Connection?

By Alice G. Gosfield, JD

When the Institute of Medicine (IOM) published "Crossing The Quality Chasm" in 2001[1], a new era in health care was launched. With no less a goal than the promulgation of a blueprint to drive healthcare delivery in the 21st Century, the report announced and explicated those values intended to determine how care is purchased, provided and evaluated for the foreseeable future. Later characterized as the STEEEP values, the IOM called for care to meet six explicit standards: Care should be:

- Safe—delivered in a manner which avoids injuries;

- Timely—explicitly organized to reduce waits and harmful delays;

- Effective—based on scientific knowledge avoiding underuse and overuse;

- Efficient—avoiding waste of equipment, supplies, ideas and energies and, although not articulated, economically efficient as well;

- Equitable—not variable in quality because of gender, ethnicity, location and socio-economic status; and

- Patient-centered—respectful and responsive to patient preferences, needs and values, and therefore subject to patient choice, which itself implies a more transparent, and publically reported healthcare system.

The report called for new payment models which would enhance the ability to render care in concordance with the values.

Quality problems in health care had long been identified as problems of overuse, misuse and underuse.[2] Overuse occurs where the patient gets too much of the proper treatment. Misuse is where the patient gets the wrong treatment. Underuse occurs when the patient does not get all the services he or she needs. All three have been found to be endemic in American healthcare. Overuse has led payors to impose blunt force control measures such as prior authorization of provider services, post-payment review and recoupment for medically unnecessary services. Misuse has gotten little attention in payment policy. But most of the pay-for-performance programs, which are burgeoning throughout the country, are focused on underuse because they

Chapter 41: Quality Performance and Valuation: What's The Connection?

pay physicians to do things they have not been doing enough of,[3] in part in response to studies which have demonstrated that Americans are receiving only about 55% of the services which evidence says should be used to treat them.[4]

Pay for Performance

With the call for better quality performance, we have seen a proliferation of pay-for-performance (P4P) programs; initiatives primarily sponsored by health plans to pay mostly physicians, but sometimes hospitals as well, additional monies on top of the capitation or fee for service or DRG payments they are already being paid, for performance as measured in enunciated metrics. The explosion of more measures themselves[5] has also been part of this changed environment with the National Quality Forum—a public-private partnership of multiple stakeholders (www.nqf.org)—providing consensus approval of measures created by others, to be applied nationally for a plethora of clinical conditions and services.

The data so far available about P4P programs, which began to appear around 2003, is neither robust nor compelling.[6] Many of these programs did not start with a threshold of performance against which to measure improved performance. There remain many questions about the extent to which they are improving the quality of health care services; yet there is a sense of inevitability about them and they are proliferating throughout the country.

All of them have added more money on top of the already existing payment systems. Sometimes these payments are a percentage of a shared pool of money (CMS-Premier Hospital program), an enhancement to the capitation rates (the most typical model), or a fixed stipend (the Bridges to Excellence model).[7] Most of them pay for physicians to do something they were not doing before—perform more tests, prescribe more drugs—to get better scores.

While the commercial payors have led the way in the development of these programs, Medicare is squarely in this business as well, with its demonstration projects[8], reduced payment to hospitals which do not report their quality results[9], and an incipient program for physicians, which pays them merely for reporting information, not for achieving specific scores[10]. The quality-payment nexus is more tightly joined with the refusal of payors, including Medicare, to pay hospitals at all for "never events"—errors and patient safety failures which never should have occurred in the first place, such as wrong site surgery, bed sores and hospital acquired pneumonia.[11]

Efficiency

The obverse of this pay-for-performance (or no pay for no performance) phenomenon is the parallel expansion of 'efficiency' based measurement, primarily in the form of tiered networks which exclude more expensive providers from eligibility to render care, when the health plan

Chapter 41: Quality Performance and Valuation: What's The Connection?

deems them too expensive[12]. Highly controversial, they have been characterized as "networks of the cheapest" by some[13], with allegations of defamatory and misguided characterization of the providers reported on. Tensions have run so high that, on one hand the New York State Attorney General has investigated the operation of these programs[14], while on the other a voluntary agreement among health plans and providers emerged regarding how these programs will be unfurled[15]. Still, the issue of the 'efficiency' of health care delivery is also in high relief as the quality mandates are also emphasized.

Crystallizing one side of the government's interest in quality performance, quality has now been cited by the Office of the Inspector General as a grounds for fraud and abuse enforcement.[16] Similarly the Department of Justice is paying attention to quality and its failures as the basis for enforcement[17]. Where providers exercise so much budgetary constraint that patients do not get appropriate care, criminal penalties have been imposed; and false claims have been assessed in still other contexts.

So the extent to which quality and payment are linked and made the basis for regulatory accountability is increasing. What does this quality/payment connection have to do with a book on valuation? As the implications of these connections are emerging, placing a value on what quality is will be an increasingly important challenge in a variety of ventures going forward.

The Legal Nexus with Valuation

Framed in terms which speak to the quality problems of overuse, misuse and underuse, the Stark statute is about overuse. The law was enacted because of data in the early 1990s which showed that physicians will refer patients to a provider entity in which they are invested, sometimes when those services are not medically necessary. The Stark statute[18] is a strict liability statute—no intent is required to find a violation. It affects physician referrals only, for a specified hit list of "designated health services" (DHS) and prohibits both the referral of Medicare patients to entities with which they have financial relationships for those services, and the entity's submission of claims pursuant to a tainted referral, unless the relationship complies with an exception.[19] Violations entail $15,000 civil money penalties for each claim submitted as a result of an improper referral, as well as the payment being deemed an overpayment.

There are many exceptions, including for personal services and rental of space and equipment. Many of them are particularly important for transactions between physicians and the hospitals to which they refer, because all inpatient and outpatient hospital services are DHS. There are a number of exceptions which require that payment reflect 'fair market value' and others that no payment directly reflect the 'volume or value of referrals' of DHS. In addition, because of the effort to forestall improper referrals wherever they might arise, the statute establishes that some of its exceptions are only available for application by a 'medical group' that meets specific standards, among which are standards regarding how the physicians in the group are compensated by the group.[20]

Chapter 41: Quality Performance and Valuation: What's The Connection?

An older, broader, but less rigid statute is often, today, included by non-lawyers under the rubric of Stark, but the "anti-kickback statute" (AKS) is entirely different and not even in the same title of the Social Security Act.[21] The AKS sweeps into its ambit all federal health payment programs and all parties to a violating transaction. Whoever solicits, pays, offers or receives, any remuneration, in cash or in kind, covertly or overtly, directly or indirectly, for the referral, to induce the referral, or for ordering, providing, leasing, furnishing, recommending, or arranging for the provision of any service, item or good payable under a federal program can be found to violate the law. Penalties are criminal—up to $25,000 fine, up to five years in jail, or both—but also can be punished by a $50,000 civil money penalty for each violation.

Unlike Stark, though, the AKS has an intent requirement. To violate it, one must knowingly and willfully engage in improper behavior. The AKS can also be said to reflect a desire to curb overuse of services which can result from a desire to realize the financial opportunities in business relationships involving patients whose care is paid for by the government. Unlike the regulations under Stark, which provide refinement to the strict prohibitions in the statute, the safe harbor regulations[22] under the AKS, report only what is explicitly safe. Arrangements which do not comply do not necessarily violate the statute, but will be evaluated on their facts and circumstances as reviewed with prosecutorial discretion. Like the Stark statute, the AKS also focuses heavily on the fair market value of the financial relationships involved.

While Stark targets leases of real estate and equipment, for a discussion of payment for quality, the fair market value of *services* is far more relevant. The definition of 'fair market value' for Stark purposes turns on 'general market value'.

> *Fair market value* means the value in arm's-length transactions, consistent with the general market value. "General market value" means the price an asset would bring as the result of *bona fide* bargaining between well-informed parties to the agreement who are not otherwise in a position to generate business for the other party, on the date of acquisition of the asset or at the time of the service agreement. Usually the fair market price is the price at which *bona fide* sales have been consummated for assets of like type, quality and quantity in a particular market at the time of acquisition or the compensation that has been included in *bona fide* service agreements with comparable terms at the time of the agreement, where the price or compensation has not been determined in any manner that takes into account the volume or value of anticipated or actual referrals.[23]

This definition was streamlined from an earlier version which created a safe harbor for hourly payments to physicians for services rendered. Payments for medical directorships, for example, were traditionally compensated on the basis of an hourly payment with documentation of time spent. The Stark regulations had taken this further with a safe harbor for hourly payments reflecting an average of the 50th percentile of four out of six compensation surveys, or the 50th percentile of what emergency department physicians were paid in the community as with at least three emergency departments. With the publication of the Stark III regulations, that aspect of

Chapter 41: Quality Performance and Valuation: What's The Connection?

the definition was removed, thereby enhancing the flexibility of the definition and opening the door to more creative ways of quantifying the value of physicians' personal services.

For AKS purposes, although there is a similar definition of 'fair market value' in the space and equipment lease safe harbor, there is no definition of 'fair market value' generally, or in the personal services and management contract exception, which is far more relevant to quality-based payments. The payment terms state that

> The aggregate compensation paid...over the term of the agreement is set in advance, is consistent with fair market value in arms-length transactions and is not calculated in a manner that takes into account the volume or value of any referrals or business otherwise generated between the parties for which payment may be made in whole or in part under Medicare or under a State health care program.[24]

Valuing Quality

Against this background of performance measurement, payment change, and fraud and abuse regulations, there are now emerging a range of initiatives, particularly where hospitals and physicians relate to each other, that are intended to improve quality of care. Because much of what occurs in a hospital is ultimately derivative of a physician order (even though a lot of what is being scored in hospital pay-for-performance programs involves team work in the institution among nurses, technicians, and others), for many scores, the collaboration between hospitals and physicians is essential for hospitals to succeed.[25] To pay physicians for their help, some measure of value becomes essential, especially in light of the impact of Stark and the AKS on these relationships.

As hospitals seek to improve their quality scores, for which they are at risk of reduced Medicare payments for reporting failures, they increasingly seek to engage physicians with them.[26] Paying the physicians for their activities in support of improvement can fall under the 'personal services arrangement' exception under the Stark regulations, but the payment must be based on fair market value. Some commentators now argue that lost opportunity time is a reasonable measure of fair market value when the job being performed by the physicians requires their special expertise.[27] Different specialties would be paid differently under this analysis. The types of activities for which this type of payment is relevant can include selection of clinical practice guidelines, pathways, protocols or other approaches to standardization of care, as well as medical staff leadership and service on medical staff committees, since the whole raison d'etre of the medical staff organization is to monitor and assure the quality of care in the institution and provide recommendations to the Board with respect to privileges, credentialing and corrective action.

Another approach to improving quality and efficiency has been through implementation of the modern versions of gainsharing which the Office of Inspector General (OIG) has approved. Gainsharing has been a basis for fraud enforcement against hospital in 1983 when DRGs were

Chapter 41: Quality Performance and Valuation: What's The Connection?

introduced. When gainsharing reemerged as a potential approach to bonding with physicians and saving money for the hospital, in July 1999, the OIG published a very critical statement that it would not approve programs that paid physicians to reduce services, even if they were from a baseline of overuse.[28] With six favorable opinions in 2005[29], and more in subsequent years, the OIG approved a revamped, time limited, surgical/procedure-focused approach to gainsharing, which turned in part on the valuation and payment methodologies. Under the gainsharing programs, which are intended to save money by standardizing supplies used, those explicitly approved get an OK because they have safeguards that prevent reduction of clinical services to patients. All of them are time limited to one year. They pay physicians half of the savings over thresholds currently achieved, so they reward actual improvement. The cost savings are calculated by subtracting the actual costs for the year of the supplies from historic costs associated with a set of recommended practices during specified procedures rendered. From these results are subtracted any inappropriate reductions that would fall afoul of the prohibition on a hospital paying physicians to reduce their services[30].

While the OIG was clear that the arrangements implicated the prohibition on payment to reduce services, the safeguards cited as supporting approval included, among the eight reasons cited: transparency and disclosure to patients; credible medical support that the arrangement wouldn't adversely affect patient care; all surgeries were included and not just those paid for by federal programs; the cost savings reflected actual costs and "not an accounting convention"; using clinical benchmarks of historical and current performance, any undue inducement to restrict care was mitigated.

Those reasons motivated the government to believe civil money penalties for reduction of services was inappropriate. In addition, addressing the compensation under the anti-kickback statute, because the program was limited to surgeons already on staff, the additional payment from the program, the OIG said, would not induce others to join the staff to get the money. Because only surgeons would benefit, referrals from other physicians, like cardiologists, would not be stimulated by the program. The payment reflected additional risk to the surgeons from changing their behaviors, which the OIG regarded as potentially not much more than "simple common sense", but a change in operating room practice based on standardized rules nonetheless. As a result of the analysis, in quality terms, the OIG postulated that the risks of underuse had been avoided by the safeguards against reduction of services, while the risks of overuse had been avoided by not encouraging additional referrals to obtain the additional, time-limited money the program would make available. While many would regard the analysis as purely financial, in fact, at its core, it reflects quality concerns.

Yet another tantalizing opportunity to improve quality was raised with the publication of the Stark III regulations. The regulators said compensation related to patient satisfaction goals or other quality measures unrelated to the volume or value of business generated by the referring physician and unrelated to reducing or limiting services would be permitted under the personal service arrangements exception.[31] This relatively open-ended recognition of the changing environment offers the opportunity to pay physicians not on a time basis, but on a

Chapter 41: Quality Performance and Valuation: What's The Connection?

value-of-contribution basis, now that the definition of fair market value no longer drives toward hourly payments. Of course, the protection would only pertain provided that all requirements of the exception are satisfied. The regulators have cited as a legitimate example compensation to reward physicians for providing appropriate preventive care services where the arrangement is otherwise structured to satisfy the requirements of the exception.

How physicians have contributed to improved performance could be valued by looking at each quality metric with a financial impact, and assessing the ratio of the physician contribution to its accomplishment, as distinct from the contributions of nurses, technicians, pharmacists and others. Similarly, payments which recognize physician contributions to commercial pay-for-performance enhancements to hospital reimbursement would also be permitted under this acknowledgement.

What likely is *not* proper under the definition, is looking at hospital payment on the DRG, and subtracting from it the fair market value of the hospital contributions (e.g., heat, light, staff, building, and license) and paying the remainder to the physicians.

In its co-authored guidance to hospital boards regarding trustee responsibilities for quality, with the American Health Lawyers Association, the OIG cited as a risk area the ways that incentive pools will be developed when otherwise independent providers seek to collaborate to achieve both improved efficiency and higher quality scores[32]. To set a value on the services rendered and results achieved, as contributed by each participant in an incentive pool, will present additional challenges to providers and those assisting them in constructing their arrangements within the boundaries of the law. Some have looked to commercial disease management companies as the analogues for valuation of the services rendered. These companies typically are paid performance bonuses for achieving specific targets or benchmarks. Given the definition of 'fair market value' under the Stark regulations, this is one general market source of comparison to support the legitimacy of the compensation that might be earned.

Selecting targets which do not reflect a shift to reduced services to patients is also important to avoid the potential for civil money penalties. Reduced length of stay measures would not be a good choice. Those measures which reflect correction of under use—use of beta blockers after heart attack, door to balloon time in providing angioplasty, timely administration of drugs—are less problematic.

While Medicare now pays for improved hospital mortality scores, paying physicians or hospitals or giving them bonuses for killing fewer of their patients is not an ideal page one story, if characterized inappropriately. So, valuation in this delicate arena may have public relations implications if the underpinnings of the financial model are made public. Worse yet are the risks from discovery requests and potential application in a lawsuit where a patient is harmed.

The likelihood that quality performance measures, particularly in combination with financial benefits to the participants, will become integral to malpractice actions is very high.[33]

Chapter 41: Quality Performance and Valuation: What's The Connection?

Conclusion

With the highly increased attention to quality performance in health care generally, business relationships where financial value attaches to that performance are proliferating. The law establishes significant restrictions on what is legitimate to take into account in valuations that support these new relationships; but it also offers new opportunities to connect the financial implications of improved quality of care, with financial consequences.

---

1. Corrigan et al., National Academy Press, Washington, D.C.
2. Chassin, Galvin and The National Roundtable for Health Care, "The urgent need to improve health care quality", JAMA, (Sept 16, 1998); 280; pp.1000-1005
3. Gosfield, "Pay for Performance: Transitional at Best," *Managed Care,* (Jan. 2005) http://www.managedcaremag.com/archives/0501/0501.p4p_gosfield.html
4. McGlynn et al, "The Quality of Health Care Delivered to Adults in the United States," 548 NEJM 2635 (Jan. 16, 2003)
5. Gosfield, "The Performance Measures Ball: Too Many Tunes, Too Many Dancers?", HEALTH LAW HANDBOOK (Gosfield. Ed) 2005 Edition, WestGroup a Thomson Company, pp. 227-283, http://www.gosfield.com/PDF/Ch4Gosfield.pdf
6. See, Gosfield, "Physician Compensation for Quality: Behind The Group's Green Door," HEALTH LAW HANDBOOK, (Gosfied ed) 2008 edition, pp. 3-7
7. www.bridgestoexcellence.org
8. http://www.cms.hhs.gov/HospitalQualityInits/35_HospitalPremier.asp#TopOfPage; http://www.cms.hhs.gov/DemoProjectsEvalRpts/downloads/MMA646_PGP_FactSheet.pdf
9. http://www.cms.hhs.gov/HospitalQualityInits/15_HospitalQualityAlliance.asp#TopOfPage
10. www.cms.hhs.gov/PQRI
11. Gabriel, "Medicare: Uncle Sam's New Scrutiny", *Physicians' Practice* (May 2008) http://www.physicianspractice.com/index/fuseaction/articles.details/articleID/1159.htm
12. See, Shay, "Transparency and The Law", HEALTH LAW HANDBOOK (Gosfield ed) 2008 edition, pp. 77-121
13. http://uft-a.com/latest_issues/issues.htm#netcheapest
14. http://www.oag.state.ny.us/press/2007/nov/nov13c_07.html
15. http://healthcaredisclosure.org/docs/files/PatientCharterDisclosureRelease040108.pdf
16. Co-authored with the American Health Lawyers Association, "Corporate Responsibility and Health Care Quality," http://oig.hhs.gov/fraud/docs/complianceguidance/CorporateResponsibilityFinal%209-4-07.pdf
17. http://www.gosfield.com/newissues.htm#pptjgs
18. 42 USC' 1395nn
19. For more information on the Stark statute see, Gosfield, Chapter 3, MEDICARE AND MEDICAID FRAUD AND ABUSE, 2008 ed., WestGroup, a Thomson Company, and www.gosfield.com/publications
20. Gosfield, "Physician Compensation for Quality: Behind The Group's Green Door", HEALTH LAW HANDBOOK, (Gosfield ed.) 2008 edition, WestGroup, a Thomson Company pp. 1-44, http://gosfield.com/PDF/gosfield.2008%20HLH.articlewithcoverpage.122807.pdf
21. 42 USC' 1320a-7b(b)(1) and (2)
22. 42 CFR §1001.952 et seq
23. 42 USC §411.351 (72 Fed Reg. 51081, Sept 5, 2007)
24. 42 CFR §1001.952(d)(5)
25. Gosfield, "In Common Cause for Quality", HEALTH LAW HANDBOOK, (Gosfield ed.) 2006 edition, WestGroup, a Thomson Company, pp. 177-222, http://www.gosfield.com/PDF/commoncausequalityCh5.pdf; Reinertsen, Gosfield, Rupp and Whittington, *"Engaging Physicians in a Shared Quality Agenda."* IHI Innovation Series

Chapter 41: Quality Performance and Valuation: What's The Connection?

white paper. Cambridge, MA: Institute for Healthcare Improvement; 2007. http://www.gosfield.com/PDF/IHIEngagingPhysiciansWhitePaper2007.pdf; and www.uft-a.com

26. Gosfield and Reinertsen, "Sharing The Quality Agenda with Physicians," *Trustee* (Oct. 2007) pp. 12-17.
27. Johnson, "Fair Market Value Support Required, " ALHA, *Health Law Weekly* (May 2008), http://www.healthlawyers.org/Template.cfm?Section=HLW_Archive&template=/ahlatestcode/google/g_articlelayout.cfm&ContentID=55890&IssueDate=2008-05-30%2000%3A00%3A00
28. http://oig.hhs.gov/fraud/docs/alertsandbulletins/gainsh.htm
29. Advisory Opinions 05-01 through 05-06, http://oig.hhs.gov/fraud/advisoryopinions/opinions0106.html
30. Advisory Opinion 07-21
31. 72 Federal Register 51046 (Sept 5, 2007)
32. http://oig.hhs.gov/fraud/docs/complianceguidance/CorporateResponsibilityFinal%209-4-07.pdf
33. Gosfield and Reinertsen, "The 100,000 Lives Campaign: Crystallizing Standards of Care for Hospitals", *Health Affairs* (Nov. 2005), pp. 1560-1570

Chapter 42

Fairness Opinions: Is the One You Receive Beyond Dispute?

By Cain Brothers

Copyright, 2005 by Cain Brothers and Company. Reprinted with permission.

Executive Summary

Recent trends have raised questions about the standard practice of using the investment bank that assists with an organization's merger and acquisition (M&A) transaction to also write the related fairness opinion. Overall attention to corporate responsibility as a result of the Sarbanes-Oxley legislation, recent interest in the general topic of fairness opinions by the National Association of Securities Dealers, and nonprofit regulatory cases are all signals that boards need to be careful in using and contracting for fairness opinions. Boards should review their organization's individual circumstances to match specific recommendations to their needs. In circumstances where the board is likely to be second-guessed about its ability to act on behalf of all stakeholders or in jurisdictions where regulatory review is more aggressive, boards should pay careful attention to process and err towards requiring more independence on the part of their financial experts and/or obtain a second opinion from another party otherwise unrelated to the transaction.

Board members have a fiduciary *duty of care* that requires them to be reasonably informed when making specific decisions on behalf of their stakeholders. This is never more important than when the organization is engaged in transactions involving change in control or the purchase or sale of significant assets. Since most governing boards are not constituted with experts in the M&A markets and attendant financial matters, they will often seek the opinion of an expert in business transactions and finance to assist them with their decision making. A formal opinion, most often referred to as a "fairness opinion," rendered by an expert also serves as evidence that a board and its members have conducted a process that was sufficient and consistent with meeting its fiduciary obligations.

Fairness opinions are appropriate for both investor owned companies, whether publicly owned or privately held, and nonprofit organizations. The fairness opinion itself is a short letter from a firm considered expert in the area of health care M&A and finance expressing the expert's opinion that the transaction is fair from a financial point of view. The opinion should be supported by, among other things, detailed analytic calculations using several standard industry valuation methodologies and be discussed with the board prior to the board making a final decision on a transaction.

Chapter 42: Fairness Opinions: Is the One You Receive Beyond Dispute?

Some health care transactions may also benefit from obtaining a valuation opinion instead of/or in addition to a fairness opinion because of anticipated regulatory review processes. A valuation opinion specifically estimates the fair market value of what is being considered, which might be the equity of a company, a line or lines of business, or an asset or group of assets, with or without related liabilities. Expert firms that can provide both quality fairness opinions and valuation opinions represent important contributors to board processes and deliberations.

Introduction

During 2004, the National Association of Securities Dealers (NASD) began an inquiry into fairness opinions that are used to support most corporate merger and acquisition targets' decisions to be acquired and, in many cases, the decisions of the acquiring companies. NASD is concerned about the possibility of conflicts of interest in rendering fairness opinions especially "when a transaction that is supported by management is also one in which the investment bank acted as the financial advisor to the company in recommending or structuring the transaction and/or where the investment bank will receive financial advisory fees upon successful completion of the transaction."[1] NASD will be looking to develop more thorough disclosure rules about the relationships that exist between the organization receiving the fairness opinion and the financial expert giving the opinion.

This NASD initiative is just the latest indication that companies engaged in mergers and acquisitions need to reconsider some traditional approaches to fairness opinions. The climate has begun to change. In the post-Sarbanes-Oxley (SOX) environment, there has been a nationwide increased focus on corporate responsibility and heightened awareness of conflicts of interest stemming from the securities analyst, mutual fund, and, more recently, insurance brokerage scandals.

In this *Strategies in Capital Finance* white paper, we focus on the challenge to boards of understanding and communicating about the value of a proposed M&A transaction.[2] In particular, we explore the role fairness opinions play in that process. The evolving post-SOX regulatory and legal environment will directly impact all publicly held companies. Medicare Fraud and Abuse regulation and Stark rules have caused all health care organizations to pay close attention to fair value in transactions involving physicians, especially in cases where physicians may also be shareholders. Nonprofit health care organizations engaged in M&A transactions have for some time been facing increased scrutiny from attorneys general and other regulators in many states concerning the level of value and consideration changing hands. The attention to corporate responsibility that started with public companies is increasingly creating an environment that must be attended to by all health care organizations regardless of ownership structure and tax status.

This white paper was written to help executives and board members of both for-profit and nonprofit health care organizations[3]

Chapter 42: Fairness Opinions: Is the One You Receive Beyond Dispute?

- understand what fairness opinions are and are not,

- identify the important fiduciary duties those individuals have to assure the realization of appropriate value in an M&A transaction,

- develop an expectation of what supports a quality fairness opinion, and

- consider options available to respond to current concerns of conflict of interest.

Recent Trends

Critics of the usefulness of fairness opinions note that when the same investment bank is engaged to both negotiate a M&A deal and render a fairness opinion it has an inherent conflict of interest. While the fee earned for rendering the fairness opinion is most often not contingent on a positive finding in the fairness opinion, critics point out that the bank typically stands to gain significant contingent fees from the completion of the transaction itself, and, of course, the fairness opinion provides justification to complete the deal. Since the purpose of a fairness opinion is to provide an independent credible source of expert information, a potential conflict of interest could render the fairness opinion less valuable.

Defenders of the current practice point to the fact that, in rendering a fairness opinion, investment banks put their reputations on the line in a business where reputation is vital for success. Defenders also note that in complicated transactions the investment bank that worked with management and the board in negotiating the terms of the transaction is often in the best position to understand and consider all of the facts and circumstances and render a fairness opinion.

A review of recent proxy statements issued by publicly-held companies could lead to the conclusion that not much has changed in the area of fairness opinions. The historic practice of engaging the investment bank responsible for completing the transaction to also render a fairness opinion for an additional fee continues to be standard practice. Despite the increasing number of voices beginning to question aspects of that historic model, it can be difficult for boards to know when it is important to go beyond a past industry practice. Recent experience with historically accepted practices in the mutual fund and insurance industries demonstrate that firms that wait until the implications become clear may find themselves with significant problems.

We believe that there is ample evidence that boards engaged in M&A transactions should carefully consider how they obtain and use fairness opinions and whether the opinions they receive add objectivity to the process undertaken to evaluate an M&A transaction. Fortunately there are a number of reasonable steps that can be taken in the current climate. Organizations engaged in transactions where minority interests are vulnerable or the public trust of a nonprofit mission is involved will need to be more attentive to these issues.

We review below a number of recent trends and their implications for fairness opinions.

Chapter 42: Fairness Opinions: Is the One You Receive Beyond Dispute?

■ Sarbanes Oxley

When Congress passed the Public Company Accounting Reform & Investor Protection Act of 2002 (better known as Sarbanes-Oxley, the names of the legislation's sponsors, or SOX), the legislation was not aimed at fairness opinions. The legislation relates to publicly traded companies, and its main thrust was to ensure the independence of directors, more effective board audit committees, auditor independence, more effective governance oversight of key decisions, and account-ability and timeliness for disclosure of financial information. The only direct reference to fairness opinions in the legislation is a prohibition against company auditors also performing non-audit services such as valuations or fairness opinions.

Since its passage, publicly traded companies have focused on the implications of compliance with the direct provisions of SOX; however, the passage of the bill has also created a climate of increased attention on the overall concept of corporate responsibility. Corporate responsibility can go beyond the direct provisions of SOX, and historic practices in other areas may need to be reexamined. Such provisions of SOX as focus on independent directors, importance of independent advisors to the board in the case of auditors, identification of the importance of "financial experts" on the board, and disclosure requirements are relevant issues for fairness opinions as well.

SOX also directed the Securities and Exchange Commission (SEC) to adopt rules that require disclosure of compensation arrangements for securities research analysts and investment bankers that may create inherent conflicts of interest. While this provision of SOX does not directly relate to fairness opinions, it does focus the spotlight on the practice of contingent compensation arrangements noted by critics of current fairness opinion practices. The post-SOX environment highlights the reality that acceptable business practices of today may not meet the needs that come with more transparency in transactions.

■ Sarbanes Oxley For Nonprofit Corporations

While SOX provisions apply only to publicly held companies, there are indications that some of the provisions of SOX are beginning to move into the nonprofit health care world.

In 2002, The Coalition for Nonprofit Health Care issued a white paper suggesting that it is only a matter of time until some of these corporate reforms get applied to nonprofit organizations. It recommended that its members voluntarily implement nine steps relating to audit committees, auditor independence, code of ethics for CFOs, financial statement certification, and review of compensation arrangements.

Some state legislatures and attorneys general have expressed interest in extending some SOX-like provisions to nonprofits. On September 2004 the California governor signed a new bill SB1262 that strengthened accountability for commercial fund-raisers and nonprofit organizations. The bill also requires larger non-profits to adopt some new SOX-like practices such as

Chapter 42: Fairness Opinions: Is the One You Receive Beyond Dispute?

auditor independence, separate and more independent audit committees, and board review of certain compensation arrangements.

Similarly, the New York State Attorney General's office has proposed substantial changes to the New York Not-For-Profit Corporation Law, reflecting the AG's desire that nonprofit organizations adhere to the principles contained in SOX.

■ Corporate Responsibility

Health care organizations need to also pay attention to the perspective of the Centers for Medicare & Medicaid Services (CMS) because of the importance of the Medicare and Medicaid programs to their operations. The post-SOX environment has led to some new attention on the concept of *corporate responsibility* for all health care organizations.

For example, a recent joint publication of the American Health Lawyers Association and the Office of the Inspector General[4] calls board members attention to their fiduciary responsibilities under the heading of corporate responsibility. The paper emphasizes the duty of care of directors for their decision making and oversight functions. It also points out that courts have generally interpreted that duty of care as identical for both for-profit and nonprofit corporations. The major focus of this publication is on the relationship of corporate responsibility to the compliance oversight responsibility of trustees.

While the CMS publication does not address fairness opinions, CMS interest in the corporate responsibility of boards is another indication that this area will change. Health care organizations that undertake transactions involving physician owner-ship or incentive arrangements have become familiar with the challenges of working through Medicare Fraud and Abuse implications. Expert valuations and fairness opinions can be an important part of the board's deliberations in some of these situations.

■ NASD

While the increased attention on corporate responsibility themes is important background, it does not directly relate to fairness opinions. On the other hand, the National Association of Securities Dealers (NASD) has the authority to propose rules that could directly govern fairness opinions. NASD is undertaking an investi-gation that may lead to proposals in the future.[5] NASD is currently focused on "whether it should propose a new rule to regulate the identification and disclosure of conflicts by members that provide fairness opinions in corporate control trans-actions."[6] This could lead to proposed rules about disclosure requirements in fairness opinions, increased documentation requirements, or more explicit evalua-tion of the relationship between compensation from a transaction and the fairness opinion. However, at the date of this writing, new rules have not been proposed.

Chapter 42: Fairness Opinions: Is the One You Receive Beyond Dispute?

■ New York's Attorney General

Mutual fund and insurance companies have begun adding a new word to Webster's as they describe being *spitzered*. New York's Attorney General, Eliot Spitzer, has been at the forefront of a campaign to use the state attorney general's platform to change longstanding business practices in several industries. In May of 2003, the New York Post reported that an AG's spokesman commented on fairness opinions: "The issue is intriguing to Spitzer and he thinks it ought to be looked at."[7]

Attorney General Spitzer has since been making headlines (and headaches) for executives in other industries and, to date, has not followed up on the speech that led to the article and quote mentioned above. Industry watchers conclude that he has found bigger fish to fry currently but may return to the question of fairness opinions if current practices continue.

■ Nonprofit Trends

A 1999 New York Supreme Court decision, *In re Manhattan Eye, Ear and Throat Hospital (MEETH)* criticizes a nonprofit board's process for deciding to abandon the traditional non-profit hospital mission of the corporation. One area of that criticism focused on whether the advice given by the investment bank in the transaction was independent. The fee arrangement for this proposed transaction was typical in investment banking with a success fee awarded only if the trans-action was completed and a substantially lower fee if the transaction was not competed. The court stated, "It is not necessary for me to conclude that this conflict of interest compromised the result; the fee arrangement certainly gives the appearance that the integrity of the process was flawed and that the Board had not obtained the assistance of a truly independent expert. Moreover, there does not appear to have been full disclosure to the Board of the potential for a conflict of interest in the expert."[8]

The more recent 2003 decision of the Maryland Insurance Commission (MIC) relating to the proposed conversion and sale of the CareFirst BlueCross BlueShield plan further illustrates this issue. In the decision, the MIC commented on the investment bank, Credit Suisse First Boston or "CSFB," that both negotiated the transaction and rendered the fairness opinion and valuation. "A question necessarily arises as to CSFB's ability to supply an independent and unbiased opinion as to the fairness of an agreement that it produced. There exists an inherent conflict in assessing the fairness of one's own product. The [CareFirst] Board, however, does not appear to have appreciated or acknowledged that inherent conflict and, thus, never considered the potential impact of such a conflict in accepting the CSFB Fairness Opinion." The MIC also criticized the success-fee arrangement with CSFB.[9]

While it is important to identify the most aggressive trends in this area, they currently do not set a standard to guide an organization's use of fairness opinions in many circumstances. There is considerable variability across states in their regulatory processes and standards for approving for-profit conversions. Organizations need to be aware of their local circumstances to identify

Chapter 42: Fairness Opinions: Is the One You Receive Beyond Dispute?

regulatory expectations. Additionally, in both of the state cases described above, the finding disapproving the transactions were based on substantive procedural or other issues that had nothing to do with the independence of the board's investment bank advisors. Although, the comments cited above were provided by regulators as additional evidence that the investment banks' processes may not have been dispassionate, they were not the sole basis of the findings.

The trends mentioned above highlight the need for all organizations to follow a rigorous process in M&A transactions. They suggest an independent review of the proposed transaction may be important in some circumstances to minimize the perception that the proposal was influenced by financial advice that was not entirely independent.

What Is A Fairness Opinion?

Board members weighing how to proceed in light of these recent trends should start by understanding more about fairness opinions.

A fairness opinion is a determination by an expert that a proposed business trans-action is "fair from a financial point of view" as of a specific date. The opinion is usually issued to the stakeholders[10] of an organization or those with governance responsibility and fiduciary duties owed to the stakeholders. Expert firms that deliver fairness opinions have experience in the M&A market and in related financial matters. A fairness opinion can serve as an important contributor to a board's decision making. It also shows evidence that a board followed a reasoned and deliberative process, and it can be used to defend board members against potential legal challenges by stakeholders.

In cases where shareholders are required to vote on pending transactions, fairness opinions and their associated descriptions and analyses are also routinely included as part of proxy statements filed with the SEC, and as such they are an important source of credible information for those voting on the transaction.

Typically investment bankers[11] with expertise in the market are hired as experts by the board of the corporation to render an official opinion as to whether the contemplated transaction is *fair* to the stakeholders of the corporation. To support the opinion that the proposed transaction is fair, the experts produce and present to boards detailed analyses that typically include valuation ranges for the business (and proposed consideration when the consideration includes something besides cash) using multiple valuation methodologies. The typical sections of a fairness opinion are described later in this paper in the section titled ANATOMY OF A FAIRNESS OPINION.

After reciting what was considered in the analysis process, fairness opinions typically rest on a one sentence conclusion that states the consideration received by stakeholders of the corporation in connection with the proposed transaction is *fair from a financial point of view*.

Chapter 42: Fairness Opinions: Is the One You Receive Beyond Dispute?

This conclusion depends on several important characteristics of fairness opinions. A determination of fairness *compares* the consideration offered in the proposed transaction in return for the value stakeholders currently hold in the equity in the organization. A fairness opinion is not a judgment that the *process* leading to the proposed transaction was necessarily fair. It does not comment on the fairness of the transaction from a legal perspective. It does not serve as a recommendation to the corporation in favor of the transaction. While these topics are very important for boards to consider, the fairness opinion limits itself to looking at the proposed transaction *from a financial point of view.*

When reaching the overall conclusion that the proposed transaction is fair, the writer of the opinion relies on a consideration of *all* of the relevant facts and circumstances. It is not customary, therefore to mathematically weight various components of the analytics to reach a fairness opinion conclusion. It is the overall consideration of the facts and circumstances combined with the opining firm's judgment based on experience in the industry that yields the finding of fairness.

WHAT A FAIRNESS OPINION IS NOT

What does the *fair* in fairness opinion mean? It is easiest to understand fair value or fair price by understanding what it is not. *Fair price* does not necessarily mean best price.

The valuation analytics that support the determination of fair price are aimed at estimating a range of values based on the standards of *fair value and/or fair market value* that apply to the particular circumstances of the fairness opinion. *Fair market value* is often defined as "the price at which the property would change hands between a willing buyer and a willing seller when the former is not under any compulsion to buy and the latter is not under any compulsion to sell, both parties having reasonable knowledge of relevant facts." This definition of fair market value comes from IRS Revenue Ruling 59-60, which was issued to define valuation of business interests for estate tax and gift tax purposes. Many of its principles, however, guide the analytical processes used in fairness opinions.[12]

While the fair market value definition provides an important underpinning of fairness opinions, its conditions can never exist in the real world. In every business there is always some compulsion to sell or buy and neither buyer nor seller can ever be fully informed of all facts. Boards, therefore, need to pay careful attention to assuring that the process that led to the proposed transaction was procedurally fair. Using market mechanisms to determine price where possible, avoiding conflicts of interest, and assuring transparency in the negotiating process that led to the proposed transaction terms are important elements of board responsibility to assure that the transaction best meets the needs of its stakeholders. A fairness opinion does not assure that the best possible price was obtained for the equity of the stakeholders.

Another important concept is that fair market value and best price say nothing about the form of the consideration being offered (e.g., cash, securities, or a combination) and its value, the

Chapter 42: Fairness Opinions: Is the One You Receive Beyond Dispute?

presence of any contingencies on the part of the acquirer, or the acquirer's ability to successfully close the proposed transaction. A fairness opinion, on the other hand will take into account important transaction terms and circumstances such as these.

To illustrate, imagine a situation where two potential buyers are competing for a property. Imagine further that one buyer offers to pay $X, all in cash, which is on hand, and the other buyer offers to pay $Y, which is a larger amount than $X, but has a debt financing contingency associated with it. If the buyer offering to pay $Y is a weak credit, an expert considering that buyer's offer may rightfully call into question the buyer's ability to close on the transaction in a timely manner or at all. In a case like this, and depending on the outcome of the analytical processes in evaluating the $X offer, an expert could conclude that the $X offer is fair from a financial point of view, even though the $X offer is not as high as the $Y offer and, therefore, not the best price.

A fairness opinion is also not a valuation. Both fairness opinions and valuation opinions rely on similar standard methodologies for estimating ranges of value, but unlike a valuation opinion, a fairness opinion does not reach a conclusion about what exactly is the fair market value of an asset or the consideration being paid.

WHEN AND WHY GET A FAIRNESS OPINION?

Most board members are not experts in M&A transactions and financial markets, knowledge of which is necessary to evaluate the appropriateness of certain material transactions such as an organization's change of control. However, these same board members have a fiduciary *duty of care* to their stakeholders that holds them responsible for the making decisions despite the lack of expertise. Fairness opinions have become a useful tool to inform boards about the financial aspects of proposed transactions and assist them with their deliberations. Fairness opinions can also serve as evidence that a board and its members have conducted a process that helped them fulfill their fiduciary obligations.[13]

Fairness opinions have become an expected part of board procedure for publicly-held companies engaging in change of control transactions and "going private" transactions, where a company's public shareholders are bought out by insider and management led groups. Fairness opinions are also sometimes used for other significant transactions such as the sale of equity to insiders or when a board wants more information or to mitigate being second-guessed by a group of shareholders or regulators. As a practical matter, fairness opinions are a routine part of these transactions for the target company and used less frequently by the acquiring company.

In health care, fairness opinions have also become important for some transactions that involve closely held private corporations. For example, board oversight of minority interests of physicians in closely held private corporations requires particular attention. Nonprofit health care boards have also relied on fairness opinions to assist them in fulfilling their fiduciary duty to

Chapter 42: Fairness Opinions: Is the One You Receive Beyond Dispute?

assure that any community assets transferred to or acquired from the private sector are done only with appropriate consideration. Regulatory approval of these transactions in some jurisdictions can also be supported by a well prepared fairness opinion.

WHAT IS A VALUATION?

A *valuation* is an estimate of value, expressed as a range or point, and usually an estimate of fair market value or fair value. In a *valuation opinion*, the issuing firm stakes its reputation on estimating the value of the business or the consideration offered. On the other hand, a valuation opinion does not comment on the *fairness of the transaction* from a financial point of view or how the proposed consideration relates to the value of the business. Valuations are routinely done for tax and estate purposes and there is an extensive body of literature and legal framework that guide the valuation process.

WHEN WOULD YOU GET A VALUATION?

In publicly owned companies, the uses of fairness opinions versus valuation opinions have been and remain fairly distinct. The investment banker associated with a proposed significant transaction, usually negotiating on the company's behalf, has typically been engaged to consider the terms of the transaction and write the fairness opinion. This is because of the importance of specific knowledge about transactions and financial markets and the particulars of the transaction. If a valuation was required for tax or estate purposes, a separate engagement with a firm specializing in valuations would usually be pursued. Separate valuation engagements are routinely done for M&A transactions to determine and allocate the value of specific assets for financial statement purposes. Valuations are routinely made on many business assets for which no fairness opinion is necessary.

Health care transactions can often require elements of both a fairness opinion and a valuation when there is concern about regulatory review, Medicare Fraud and Abuse regulations, or sale of a distressed asset. These needs can vary widely from state to state. Organizations need to assess the particular circumstances of the proposed transaction and the regulatory climate in which it is taking place to determine what kind of opinion will best serve. If California regulatory review for nonprofit conversion is anticipated, for example, state statute for hospital sale transactions uses the fair market value test. In this case, care should be taken to ensure that the engagement is structured in a way to provide the kind of valuation information required by the regulators.

In some cases an engagement that includes a valuation component, detailed description of the process leading to the proposed transaction, and factors involved in the decision may need to be linked to the fairness opinion. Firms that have the expertise to deliver both fairness opinions and valuation determinations can be useful resources in these situations.

Chapter 42: Fairness Opinions: Is the One You Receive Beyond Dispute?

RECOMMENDATIONS

We believe that awareness of the recent trends in fairness opinions is important for board members contemplating M&A transactions, but that they are not a cause for radical changes. Boards should secure the services of legal counsel with experience in similar transactions. Legal counsel can assist the board in identifying its needs in light of the organization's particular circumstances. Forging an open relationship with the investment bank negotiating the transaction is an important part of any major M&A transaction. When that process works well, the investment bank is in a position to help craft the deal in a way that reflects a favorable outcome for stakeholders. Obtaining a fairness opinion from the investment bank working on the transaction can provide value to the board and stakeholders.

Recent trends, however, also indicate that boards cannot take a business-as-usual attitude toward fairness opinions and the whole M&A process. Some specific recommendations for all transaction are:

1. Fees for the fairness opinion itself should be fully earned when the opinion is issued and not be contingent on completion of the transaction. (This has become fairly standard in the industry already.)

2. Increased disclosure of conflicts and potential conflicts in the communication of the fairness opinion to the board and public is helpful. Disclosure of the nature of the fee arrangement for both the fairness opinion and the M&A transaction, the nature and amount of other business between the fairness opinion provider and the recipient, and any other conflicts is becoming more common and should be emphasized.

3. Focus extra attention on the entire M&A process to ensure that the board as a whole has eliminated or disclosed any potential conflicts of interest. Whenever feasible the board should assure that the process has been open, with fair ways to expose the deal to competitive market forces, and that potential conflicts of interest such as an investment bank that is also an active market-maker in the acquirer's stock have been fully disclosed to board members and considered in the decision process.

Boards will need to make the difficult choice about whether these three recommendations are an adequate response to the current environment. Taking additional steps can add to time and expense. Judging the circumstances applicable in each case will be the best guide. In circumstances where the board is likely to be second-guessed about its ability to act on behalf of all stakeholders such as in "going private" transactions, sale of minority interests of physicians in closely held companies, or the sale or conversions of nonprofit assets to for-profit status, or in jurisdictions where regulatory review is more aggressive, three additional recommendations should be considered.

Chapter 42: Fairness Opinions: Is the One You Receive Beyond Dispute?

1. Form a special committee of the board consisting of independent board members to evaluate potential conflicts that may influence a transaction and having the authority to hire independent counsel and an independent financial advisor to render a fairness opinion.

2. Ask for a second fairness opinion by a qualified, independent party that has no financial interest in completing the proposed transaction.

3. Consider whether circumstances call for a valuation opinion in addition to a fairness opinion and engaging a firm with industry experience to deliver a combined/tailored opinion for the circumstances.

FIDUCIARY DUTY OF BOARD MEMBERS

Board members seeking to make decisions about the use of fairness opinions must start with an understanding of their fiduciary duty. In this section of the white paper, we describe those fiduciary duties and the way that fairness opinions have assisted boards in meeting those duties.

■ Duty of Care

Fairness opinions are directly aimed at assisting board members in meeting one of three important fiduciary obligations, the *duty of care*.

The *duty of care* relates to a director's obligation to be reasonably informed both in an oversight role over day-to-day operations and when making specific decisions. Specific decisions that involve change of control of a corporation or other significant ownership changes often involve specialized analytic skills that many board members do not directly have. Board members fulfill their fiduciary duty of care in these circumstances by relying on expert advice when it "has formed the basis of an informed board decision or an expert's report is assimilated and analyzed by the directors."[14] Fairness opinions are an important source of that expert advice to boards in this type of material decision.

Boards of publicly held companies began routinely asking for this expert advice to support change of control transactions following a January 1985 law suit that imposed personal liability on outside directors of the Trans Union Corporation. In that case, the Delaware court's *Van Gorkom* decision found the outside directors grossly negligent for failing to determine the company's value before selling it. The court's decision set the fairness opinion as a standard for boards with the implication that the directors could have avoided liability if they had obtained a fairness opinion.

A subsequent Delaware 1986 case established *The Revlon Standard* that board members of publicly-owned companies have a duty to get the highest price for its shareholders once it puts itself up for sale. While it is relatively easy to determine the highest price in an all-cash deal,

Chapter 42: Fairness Opinions: Is the One You Receive Beyond Dispute?

determining the highest price is not straight-forward when other types of consideration, such as stock, are involved. Factors such as the likelihood of a deal being consummated, a buyer's ongoing Fraud and Abuse investigation, or another buyer's need to obtain financing must be evaluated. The investment bankers' work to help the directors value the various bids in these situations is important in assuring the board can defend its actions in light of the Revlon Standard.

■ Duty of Loyalty

The *duty of loyalty* requires board members to exercise their powers in the interest of the corporation, not in their own interest or in the interest of another entity or person. By agreeing to serve on the board, the board member acknowledges that, with regard to any corporate activity, the best interest of the corporation and its stakeholders must prevail over the trustee's individual interests or the particular interests of any other outside group.

The duty of loyalty requires board member to maintain confidentiality when appropriate and to avoid conflicts of interest. A well designed process in all aspects of the proposed transaction is necessary in order to avoid conflicts of interest or perceived conflicts of interest with board members. The investment bank's opinion that the proposed transaction is *fair* relates directly to the *duty of care* of board members. Nevertheless, obtaining a credible fairness opinion can provide an indication that decisions did not result in advantage to individual interests.

Particular care in the merger and acquisition process must be paid to the *duty of loyalty* when one group of owners will continue owning the business and another group will not. This situation produces inherent conflicts of interest and the process must take this into account. Examples of this on the for-profit side include "going private" transactions (described below) and sale of physician minority ownership interests in a closely held company. Board members will also need to take special care when management has a conflict of interest, as for example with a promise of a continued position with one acquisition alternative as compared to another.

■ Duty to Mission

In health care it is important to identify a third fiduciary duty of nonprofit trustees, the *duty to mission*. While the best interests of shareholders can guide for-profit directors, nonprofit trustees must work to achieve the mission of their organization as defined in articles of incorporation and/or bylaws.

A 1999 New York Supreme Court decision, *In re Manhattan Eye, Ear and Throat Hospital (MEETH)* illustrates an aggressive application of this principle by the courts in some jurisdictions. The decision of the MEETH board of trustees to sell the hospital to a real estate purchaser and abandon the historic inpatient hospital mission was overturned. "In essence, the court in MEETH barred the board from abandoning the principal corporate purpose of operating a not-for-profit hospital absent a demonstration that the board had fully explored all possible options to preserve the corporate mission."[15]

Chapter 42: Fairness Opinions: Is the One You Receive Beyond Dispute?

The significance of the MEETH case to nonprofit boards is that the finding criticizing the board's process was made despite significant documentation that the board had undergone an extensive review process in reaching its decision. "On the surface at least, it appeared that the MEETH board had adopted a prudent, reason-able approach to dealing with substantial strategic and financial challenges. The board had retained a prominent, well-regarded investment bank pursuant to an industry-standard compensation arrangement, had delegated financial analysis to experts and to a board committee, and had relied on those delegates."[16] Despite this extensive process, the finding raised the bar for nonprofit boards to explore all available options to meet the mission of the organization in their decisions.[17]

Standards of Care

■ Business Standard of Care

In most states directors' actions to uphold their duty of care are judged based on a *business standard of care* that is similar for both for-profit and nonprofit directors. It "provides that a director fulfills his duty of care by acting (1) in good faith; (2) with the care an ordinarily prudent person in a like position would exercise under similar circumstances; and (3) in a manner the director reasonably believes to be in the best interests of the corporation."[18] As described in the previous section, this has generally led to the courts protecting board members who relied on expert advice such as fairness opinions as long as it was accompanied by a reasonable board process.

■ Entire Fairness Standard of Care

Delaware courts have imposed a higher standard of director liability on publicly-held companies engaged in "going private" (Rule 13e-3) transactions. In these transactions controlling stockholders are on both sides of a transaction such as when management buys shareholder's interests in the company. Instead of using the business standard of care described above, an *entire fairness standard of care* has been employed, raising the bar for director liability in these transactions.

Directors in these "going private" transactions must show both procedural fairness in conducting a fair process and substantive fairness in obtaining a fair price. The interests of minority shareholders should be protected by forming an independent committee to assure the transaction is fair. In these transactions, the fairness opinion is typically written on behalf of the special committee of minority share-holders rather than the board as a whole. While the Securities and Exchange Commission (SEC) can review and question fairness opinion analytics contained in proxy statements of all publicly-held companies, SEC scrutiny is virtually certain for these Rule 13e-3 transactions.

A recent Delaware Chancery Court case, *Emerging Communications Inc. Shareholders Litigation*, may complicate the traditional business judgment standard for directors. In the

Chapter 42: Fairness Opinions: Is the One You Receive Beyond Dispute?

Emerging Communications case, two directors were found liable for a total of $200 million in a going private transaction. Much of the finding in this case focused on flaws in both procedural fairness and substantive fairness of the price paid to minority shareholders under the *entire fairness standard*. The court found one director liable because he was "in a unique position to know that [the merger price was unfair]. He was a principal and general partner of an investment advising firm, with significant experience in finance and the telecommunications sector." The court judged the director's experience as equivalent or superior to that of the firm rendering the fairness opinion and therefore questioned his deferring to the opinion of the fairness opinion advisor.[19]

■ Business Standard of Care for Nonprofits

Board members of nonprofit organizations making merger and acquisition decisions are judged by the same *business standard of care* as their for-profit brethren when assessing negligence for their actions in most states. To impose liability, directors making these decisions must be found to have been grossly negligent rather than a higher standard of simple negligence applicable to the trustee of a nonprofit charitable trust. Courts have been reluctant to find board members of nonprofit corporations personally liable for their decisions in this area if they have conducted a well designed process and engaged in thoughtful review and reliance of experts in reaching their decision.

The recent Maryland opinion in the CareFirst conversion/sale, however, illustrates that the regulatory agencies in some states may make a distinction between the *business standard of care* that applies to a director's personal liability and a higher standard for regulatory approval of a conversion from nonprofit to for-profit status in some jurisdictions.[20] Nonprofit board members must uphold the fiduciary *duty to mission* to the nonprofit purpose of the organization. When the proposed trans-action involves changing that nonprofit purpose of an organization in a significant way, attorneys general and regulatory agencies in some states have signaled an increased willingness to second guess the decision making process of board members. In those circumstances, boards should expect to provide evidence that they have both conducted a diligent process and achieved substantive fairness in terms of price.

Because of their fiduciary *duty to mission*, nonprofit board members have not been subject to the Revlon Standard requiring boards to accept the proposal that offers the highest value. While citing a discussion of the legal arguments around applying the Revlon Standard to nonprofit organizations in the CareFirst case, Peregrine and Schwartz summarize this perspective. "We are...aware of no reported case in which any court has applied the Revlon duty to nonprofit charitable corporations. To the contrary, it appears that valid legal and policy reasons exist to distinguish nonprofit corporations from their for-profit brethren in this regard, particularly when non-cash consideration is offered and is deemed of material value to preserve or promote the nonprofit's charitable mission, or when other legitimate factors are present."[21]

Chapter 42: Fairness Opinions: Is the One You Receive Beyond Dispute?

ANATOMY OF A FAIRNESS OPINION

The essential elements of a fairness opinion are distilled into a short letter from the firm writing the fairness opinion to the board of the company involved in the proposed transaction. It contains a statement that, in the opinion of the issuing firm, the proposed transaction is fair from a financial point of view. Typical additional elements of the fairness opinion letter often include:

1. The effective date of the letter.

2. A reference to the parties in the proposed transaction.

3. A summary of the terms of the proposed transaction.

4. A summary of procedures performed including a list of documents reviewed and meetings held by the firm in reaching the fairness opinion.

5. A summary of assumptions and data or sources on which the firm relied in arriving at its opinion.

6. A reminder of the limitations of the fairness opinion as directed only at fairness from a financial point of view, which does not address the relative merits of the proposed merger as compared to other business strategies or transactions the company might pursue.

7. A statement that the opinion is not a recommendation to the board or share-holders about how to vote on the proposed transaction.

8. Disclosure of the issuing firm's business relationship with the firm for which it is rendering the fairness opinion including a disclosure of the fee arrangement for the fairness opinion. (More complete disclosure can include a list of other investment banking fee arrangements with the both the target and acquiring firms, including even stock trading revenues.)

9. Understandings about the confidentiality of the fairness opinion and how it may be used by the recipient.

■ Proposed Transaction Process Summary

Ensuring that the process used by the company to reach the proposed transaction was fair to stakeholders is an important part of the responsibility of board members. Boards therefore should expect to receive a thorough presentation including a process overview summarizing key events and dates. A chronology that documents the extent of market exposure undertaken in the transaction is also useful. The investment bank that assists with the M&A transaction is usually in the best position to provide this process summary to the board. When that bank also renders the fairness opinion, this proposed transaction summary is often included in the board presentation that also outlines the fairness opinion rationale.

The fairness opinion letter limits itself to fairness *from a financial point of view* and, therefore, does not make representations about the fairness of the process. Never the less, the process undertaken to reach the proposed transaction typically the fairness opinion. In commenting on this distinction, M. Mark Lee and Gilbert Matthews note: "A financial adviser should not render an opinion that the consideration is fair if he or she has reason to believe that the transaction taken as a whole is unfair."[22]

■ **Significant Valuation Factors**

Arriving at a fairness opinion conclusion is as much art as science. The conclusion is invariably based on the experience and judgment of the firm assessing the pro-posed transaction. That assessment includes understanding the significant factors that drive the value of the business involved in the proposed transaction and identifying similarities and differences between that business and others. In health care market segments that consist of both nonprofit and for-profit firms, the importance of industry knowledge to make those assessments becomes even more significant.

Boards often benefit when the implicit assessments are made explicit in such areas as market position, facility locations, regulatory environment, market share, size, physician climate, services, and earnings capacity. By understanding the judgment of whether these factors have positive or negative implications for valuing the proposed transaction, board members will be better able to exercise their duty of care.

Analytic Support

While there are typically multiple quantitative analyses that support the conclusion about the fairness of a proposed transaction, the analytics supporting the fairness opinion need to be taken and assessed as a whole. No one valuation factor is determinative in the fairness finding and there is no mathematical weighting of factors that yields an answer. The fairness opinion represents the judgment of the financial expert after weighing all of the analytic evidence as to how to assess the relevance of all the factors involved.

In the case of publicly traded companies, the analytic support for the fairness opinion typically starts by identifying a value for the equity of the target business based on the pre-merger value of the company's stock in the public trading market.

Since the current stock price of the equity is known and determined by the market, the analysis focuses on understanding the value of the consideration offered by the acquiring company and comparing the value of the equity to the value of the consideration offered.

Chapter 42: Fairness Opinions: Is the One You Receive Beyond Dispute?

The analysis then goes on to use several other valuation methodologies to estimate the value of the company (and in some cases the consideration offered). Results of these valuation methodologies are typically presented as ranges, not point estimates. The analytics finally conclude by returning to the question of how shareholders might expect their value to stand up over time if the consideration offered is in stock of another company.

In a fairness opinion of a publicly held company, the starting point is the value of shareholder equity as determined by the stock market. Since *equity* in a particular company cannot be compared directly to the results of standard valuation methodologies, the analysis adds debt and excess cash to the equity value to develop an *enterprise value*. That derived company enterprise value is then used to generate value indicators (e.g., multiple of EBITDA being offered in terms of the enterprise value) for comparison with similar value indicators present in the market place generally.

Analytic support for fairness opinions of closely-held companies and nonprofit organizations use the same analytic tools, but not in the same order. With no liquid stock to establish the current market price for equity in the business, fairness opinions for these organizations first estimate a range of enterprise values of the company. These enterprise values are estimated based on the same valuation methodologies[23] used in public companies and include discounted cash flow analysis, public stock market trading analysis, and comparable private sale trans-action analysis. Once a range of reasonable enterprise values is estimated, the value of the equity in the company is determined based on adjustments for debt and excess cash. The resulting estimated value of equity is compared to the value of the consideration offered for that equity.

While there is no standard for presentation of fairness opinion analytics, the remainder of this section presents some typical sections with a brief description. The analytic sections are listed in the order that is a typical presentation in proxy statements for publicly traded companies.

■ **Historical Stock Trading Analysis**

This section is presented to identify the historic pre-merger market value of the equity in the target company. It typically presents the trading history of the target company's price per share over time. It may also include comparisons with stock prices of the acquirer or stock price indices over time. This section also performs the important function of converting the *equity value* of the organization that is determined by starting with stock prices to *enterprise value*. To extend equity value to enterprise value, the value of debt is added and surplus cash (excess working capital) is subtracted. Determining enterprise value is important because it is necessary to determine the comparable value indicators to other companies used in the alternative valuation methodologies.

As described above, this step is not possible for closely-held or nonprofit organizations; therefore, target valuations usually look at several of the valuation methodologies described below to develop ranges of value.

Chapter 42: Fairness Opinions: Is the One You Receive Beyond Dispute?

■ Analysis of Implied Offer Price (or Merger Consideration)

This section is presented to estimate the value of the consideration offered. While the implications of an all-cash deal would be straightforward, more complex terms need to be analyzed and estimated. The analysis is typically presented by showing the premium in the price per share of the target company's stock implied by the consideration (stock of an acquiring company, cash or other instruments) offered. By expressing the consideration offered in a price per share and comparing that to the price of the target's stock, a premium over the current target's stock price is calculated. These premiums are either presented in price per share and/or percent using the proposed transaction closing date and historical (typically 1,3,6, and 12 month) comparisons.

■ Discounted Cash Flow Valuation Methodology

The Discounted Cash Flow Methodology or DCF is typically important in valuing closely-held companies or nonprofit organizations where no market price of stock is available. The DCF methodology is also used in valuation discussions of fairness opinions of publicly-held companies to support the future stock price analysis, accretion dilution analysis, and as a confirming valuation methodology.

DCF determines a range of values for an enterprise by estimating the present value of projected future *free cash flows* available to both debt and equity holders of the enterprise. Free cash flows represent the amount of cash projected to be generated by an enterprise equal to earnings before interest, taxes, depreciation, and amortization (EBITDA) plus or minus changes in working capital and other asset/liability changes resulting in changes to available cash, less capital expenditures to be made and less income taxes to be paid on taxable operating income, if any. Free cash flow is estimated first over a specific projected time horizon and then a terminal value multiple at the end of that time horizon is applied in order to "capitalize" the future free cash flow of the enterprise.

In practice, net cash flows are typically estimated for each year for 5 to 10 years in the future. Then the subject's value at the end of that projection period (the "terminal value") is estimated. The DCF estimate is very sensitive to this projected terminal value because the terminal value typically makes up a high percentage of the total DCF estimate. The terminal value is often estimated using a formula that projects the terminal year's cash flow into the future based on an expected growth rate for the entity.

The DCF methodology then uses an appropriate discount rate to express the free cash flows from each projection year and the terminal value in current terms. The discount rate is a very important assumption in the analysis. Although there are a variety of tools that can be utilized to estimate an appropriate discount rate, the

Weighted Average Cost of Capital (WACC) is often used. The WACC of an organization is generated by applying the Capital Asset Pricing Model (CAPM) along with key assumptions. Key WACC assumptions include the yield on "risk free" U.S. Treasury obligations, the organization's

Chapter 42: Fairness Opinions: Is the One You Receive Beyond Dispute?

tax rate (or tax-equivalency for nonprofit organizations), the cost of debt, the expectations of equity investors in this industry based on the organization's relative expected systematic risk (beta), independent company factors that affect risk, and the capital structure for the organization.

The DCF methodology is a basic component of finance theory. It takes into account expected earnings from the business and the risk associated with those earnings compared to other investment alternatives available in the market to estimate the price investors should be willing to pay. It is a very important tool for valuing businesses, especially in closely-held or nonprofit organizations that do not have stock prices to set a value on the equity. In the real world, however, its usefulness is dependent on the quality of the assumptions that go into the valuation. Particular attention should be paid to potential problems with DCF associated with the accuracy of projections of future financial performance, determination of the number of years to use in the projection, selection of the terminal value, and consideration of the appropriate capital structure to use in the WACC calculation of the discount rate.[24]

■ Public Market Valuation Methodology

The Public Market Valuation Methodology (also known as the Target or Guideline Company Methodology) estimates the enterprise value of a company by analyzing how selected comparable publicly traded companies are valued in the public market according to certain valuation multiples. These multiples are typically multiples of value related to operating revenues, enrollees, in the case of managed care organizations, net earnings, earnings before interest and taxes (EBIT), and EBITDA.

The valuation entails an analysis of publicly traded companies, to the extent possible, of comparable size and similar geographic, operating, and financial characteristics to that of the company being valued. This methodology, therefore, operates under the assumption that comparable companies should be valued similarly in the public market. Publicly available information including reports filed with the SEC or other regulatory bodies (e.g., Annual Reports on Form 10-K, Quarterly Reports on Form 10-Q, Current Reports on Form 8-K, proxy statements, and prospectuses) are analyzed in order to generate a set of defined operating and market statistics.

A group of comparable publicly traded guideline companies with similar characteristics is first identified. Then the most recent financial results available from those companies are used to derive comparable company multiples.

Careful attention to the data is necessary to identify adjustments that may be necessary to make the data of the guideline companies comparable to the company being valued. The particular circumstances of the company will also determine which of the indicators (EBITDA or EBIT for example) are most important to consider.

Because it uses stock prices of comparable companies as the starting point, the resulting public market valuation methodology yields the value of the company as expressed in the price of those stocks. This price represents the value of the company for a freely traded minority interest in the company.

Chapter 42: Fairness Opinions: Is the One You Receive Beyond Dispute?

Since investors have been shown to be willing to pay more for controlling interest in a company than a minority interest, the valuation should be adjusted by applying a *control premium* reflecting appropriate industry data, if applicable.

When the target does not have a publicly traded stock, an additional adjustment called a *marketability discount* may be necessary. According to various studies, the discounts for lack of marketability associated with private company transactions indicate a wide range of discounts with a central tendency in the range of 30% to 50%.[25] Studies have focused on two primary indicators of marketability discount: restricted stock studies and pre-initial public offering studies. Databases of both types are available enabling the analyst to select a marketability adjustment that is most appropriate to the circumstances of the particular organization.

■ Comparable Transaction Valuation Methodology

The Comparable Transactions Methodology attempts to determine a valuation range for the company based upon a range of values paid by buyers in completed merger and acquisition transactions involving comparable companies. While this valuation methodology is similar to the Public Market Valuation Methodology in its attempt to draw upon a universe of comparable companies in order to quantify certain valuation statistics, this methodology necessarily addresses valuation by detailing those valuation multiples paid to acquire similar businesses at some point in time.

It is seldom possible to find transactions that are exactly comparable to the pro-posed transaction. Variations between the comparable and proposed transaction can include size, geographic location, payment environment, physician and other provider market; competitive environment, programs and services provided, age of physical plants acquired, date on which the transaction will close, financial performance of business acquired, and the number of potential bidders.

Valuation multiples used in the Public Market Valuation Methology such as a revenue multiple, which reflects the underlying potential of the business, or EBITDA, which is a proxy for free cash flow, are also used for the Comparable Transaction Valuation Methodology. To select transaction multiples, the financial advisor must be familiar with the range of transactions in the industry segment. Since final financial terms of all transactions are not routinely published, industry experience can be particularly important for obtaining data on comparable transactions.

The need for additional adjustments to reflect control premiums and marketability discounts should also be assessed for this valuation methodology.

■ Premium Analysis

When analyzing the fairness of proposed transactions for publicly held companies, the stock price history provides another vehicle for understanding whether the change of control premium previously described is reasonable for a subject trans-action. The purpose of this analysis is to show that the consideration offered for majority control of the target company is fair relative to market comparables for that control premium.

This section first estimates the control premium associated with the proposed transaction by comparing the proposed transaction consideration to the pre-merger price of the stock for periods prior to the announcement of the proposed transaction (for example 1 day, 10 days and 30 days). By comparing this imputed control premium to data from other comparable transactions for control premium, the reasonableness of the proposed transaction can be further assessed.

- **Future Stock Price Analysis and Accretion/Dilution Analysis (or Pro Forma Analysis and Contribution Analysis)**

These sections can be presented in a number of ways but are designed to show that the value of any consideration received in stock of a publicly held company will hold up over time. The implied equity value of each company is determined as well as post-merger projections using discounted cash flow analysis. Depending on circumstances, the analysis can then determine if the transaction is expected to add value to the surviving company and therefore whether the consideration received in stock should be anticipated to hold value after the merger.

CONCLUSION

Fairness opinions can play an important role in providing support for board decisions in M&A and other material corporate transactions. We believe that board members need to review their particular circumstances in light of current trends for transparency, independence, and disclosure as they engage financial experts to provide fairness opinions. For many transactions involving publicly traded firms with no regulatory approvals required, a traditional fairness opinion with emphasis on appropriate disclosure may be adequate. Health care organizations that anticipate regulatory review of their transactions or where there is a question about the board's ability to represent the interests of minority owners without conflict of interest should pay particular attention to the fairness opinion engagement. Boards need to be careful about process and err towards requiring more independence on the part of their financial experts and/or obtain a second opinion from another party otherwise unrelated to the transaction. Firms with expertise in both health care M&A and valuations can be an important component of board decision-making.

1. "Request For Comment: Fairness Opinions Issued by Members," NASD Notice to Members, November 2004. p. 995.
2. M&A transactions are defined in this paper as sales, mergers, acquisitions, joint ventures, "going private" transactions, and other forms of transaction where meaningful assets are exchanged between parties.
3. The term *board members* is used generically in this paper to refer to the people responsible for an organization's governance, which are typically members of the board of directors in for-profit companies and members of a board of trustees in nonprofit health care corporations. Most of the material presented in this paper applies equally to health

Chapter 42: Fairness Opinions: Is the One You Receive Beyond Dispute?

care organizations regardless of ownership structure and tax status. Where there are important differences applicable to different ownership structures, the white paper identifies them.

4. "Corporate Responsibility and Corporate Compliance: A Resource for Health Care Boards of Directors," The Office of Inspector General Of The U.S. Department of Health and Human Services and The American Health Lawyers Association, 2003.

5. "NASD Scrutinizes Conflicts In Bankers' 'Fairness Opinions,'" *The Wall Street Journal*, June 11, 2004.

6. Ibid., "Request for Comment, Fairness Opinions Issued by Members," p. 998.

7. "New Eliot Target—'Fairness Opinion' Now Concern Spitzer," *The New York Post*, May 30, 2003.

8. Matter of the Manhattan Eye, Ear & Throat Hospital v. Spitzer, December 9, 1999, *New York Law Journal*, p. 30-31.

9. "Regarding the Proposed Conversion of CareFirst, Inc. To For-Profit Status And Acquisition By Wellpoint Health Networks, Inc., Exhibit A" *Report of the Maryland Insurance Administration, Steven B. Larsen, Commissioner*, pp. 148-149.

10. We use the word *stakeholders* in this paper to reflect those to whom boards owe their fiduciary duty. In public and private investor-owned corporations the primary stakeholders are the shareholders and owners; and in nonprofit organizations, primary stakeholders are those who benefit from the organization's mission.

11. Traditionally, investment bankers have written fairness opinions because of their expertise in the markets for M&A. Some independent valuation consultants have also begun writing fairness opinions.

12. While *fair market value* is a good starting point for interpreting many fairness opinions, terminology in state statutes can introduce confusion. Corporate statutes of some states allow minority shareholders in some circumstances to receive *fair value* for their shares. *Fair value* attempts to provide dissenting shareholders with "their proportionate share of fair value in the going concern on the date of the merger, rather than the value that is determined on a liquidation basis." (Lee and Matthews, "Fairness Opinions, Chapter 16," in *The Handbook of Advanced Business Valuation* by Reilly and Schweihs p. 313.) *Change* of control statutes in some states specify *fair value* as the standard when a public or charitable asset is converted to for-profit ownership. The challenge is that *fair value* is not defined in state statute, so is left to judicial interpretation. While courts determining *fair value* for minority shareholder have typically made a distinction between *fair value* and *fair market value*, the Maryland Insurance Commission found them to be equivalent concepts in the CareFirst decision: "The term fair value is not defined, but a reasonable approximation according to Blacks Law Dictionary is 'present market value.'" (Quotation from "Regarding the Proposed Conversion of CareFirst, Inc. To For-Profit Status And Acquisition By Wellpoint Health Networks, Inc., Exhibit A" *Report of the Maryland Insurance Administration, Steven B. Larsen, Commissioner*, p. 184).

13. We explore the concept of *duty of care* as it relates to fairness opinions in detail in a later section of this white paper.

14. Michael W. Peregrine and James R. Schwartz, "Revisiting the Duty of Care of the Nonprofit Director," *Journal of Health Law*, Spring 2003, Vol. 36, No. 2, pg 189.

15. Michael Peregrine and James Schwartz, "Nonprofit Corporations: The M&A Process and the Meaning of MEETH," *Health Law Digest*, May 2000, p. 4.

16. Ibid.

17. In MEETH the court also cited a success-based fee arrangement with the investment bank on the transaction as problematic in the board's process. We explored this issue in a previous section of this paper.

18. Ibid., Peregrine and Schwartz, "Revisiting the Duty of Care of the Nonprofit Director," pg 185. Quotes the ABA Revised Model Nonprofit Corporation Act.

19. In RE Emerging Communications, Inc. Shareholders Litigation, Consolidated Civil Action No. 16415, Court of Chancery of Delaware, New Castle, May 3, 2004 Decided, Section 144.

20. "The consolidated Application for the Conversion of CareFirst, Inc. and CareFirst of Maryland, Inc. to the For-Profit Status and the Acquisition of CarefFirst, Inc. by WellPoint Health Networks,," January 11, 2002, State of Maryland, Maryland Insurance Administration.

21. Ibid., Peregrine and Schwartz, "Revisiting the Duty of Care of the Nonprofit Director," p. 200.

22. Lee and Matthews, "Fairness Opinions, Chapter 16," in *The Handbook of Advanced Business Valuation* by Reilly and Schweihs p. 318.

23. From a valuation standpoint, IRS regulations do not permit nonprofit organizations to benefit from the tax shield in evaluating assets they acquire.

24. Ibid., Lee and Matthews, p. 331-332.

25. Shannon P. Pratt, *Cost of Capital Estimation and Applications*, John Wiley & Sons, Hoboken, NJ 2002, p. 166.

Chapter 43

Valuation of S Corporations

by Nancy Fannon, CPA/ABV, ASA, MCBA and Laura Pfeiffenberger

Editor's Note: S Corporation and other pass-through entities such as partnerships and LLCs are commonly encountered in the valuation of minority interests in Ambulatory Surgery Centers and Imaging Centers. This Chapter, taken from *BVR's Fannon's Guide to the Valuation of Subchapter S Corporations 2008 Edition*, by Nancy Fannon, CPA/ABV, ASA, MCBA and modified by Laura Pfeiffenberger of Fannon Valuation.

Valuation of S corporations, like so many practical applications in business valuation, is simplistic on its face but has been enormously complicated to convey to clients and the courts. The Simplified Model of S corporation valuation is a simple, transparent model intended to be effective for analysts to use and convey the issues that are unique to S corporation valuation, the most significant of which are:

1. Calculate the value of the S corporation "as if" it were a C corporation;

2. Calculate the benefit of the avoided dividend tax; and

3. Calculate (or consider) the benefit of retained net income (the ability to build up basis in one's stock).

The Simplified Model draws on the theoretical framework established by the pioneers of finance and investment and nearly a decade of collective wisdom that the entire valuation community has offered to the general discussion.[1] It renders abundantly clear the relevance of this specific application to other methods of valuation, as well as the cases in which this particular model may not apply.

Examples of the Simplified Method

The components of the Simplified Model are:

1. A traditional discounted cash flow (which can be expanded for any holding period or contracted to a single period capitalization);

2. Recognition of the benefit of the avoided dividend tax; and

3. Recognition of the capital gains tax benefit of the ability to build up basis.

Chapter 43: Valuation of S Corporations

What follows are four examples of the Simplified Model, each with slightly different assumptions to demonstrate the effect of changing variables. The highlighted areas of the tables below (in grey) are those the analyst must carefully consider in each valuation engagement. The areas to be considered include:

1. Annual distributions. These are calculated as a percent of net income before tax.

2. Holding period. The examples in this text assume two years purely for convenience, but in all cases the analyst should spread the period of cash flows as in any discounted cash flow calculation.

3. Likelihood of the buyer qualifying as pass-through buyer. In some cases, the majority of actual acquiring companies are C corporations; if empirical evidence supports this conclusion, the analyst should consider this evidence and weight it in the benefit conclusion. In most minority interest transfers, it is likely that the only buyer will be one who qualifies as an S corporation investor; in those cases, the benefit of continuing the single tax would be included in full, or slightly discounted.

4. Additions to the rate of return for ability to realize basis build-up. For some shareholders, this may be fully available; for others, such as small minority interests, there may be little opportunity to transfer their stock, thus affording no real ability to recognize the benefit of the retained net income. For these shareholders, an additional premium to the discount rate may be warranted. However, the analyst should be aware that there is no empirical way to determine the addition to the rate of return for this factor, similar to the dilemma analysts face when assessing specific company risk. Further, small changes to a rate of return can make a big difference in value. While the risks associated with the ability to realize the benefit of basis can be real, the analyst should be judicious with such additions, carefully considering the overall impact on value in the particular context.

Example 1 assumes the following facts, as displayed in Table 1.

Example 1: Simplified Model Assumptions	
Distributions as a percent of income	75%
Holding Period	2 years
Likelihood of buyer qualifying as pass-through buyer	100%
Additions to ROR (Rate of Return) for ability to realize basis build-up	0%

As stated previously, these assumptions are an integral part of the calculation, and merit careful consideration in each valuation.

We will use Example 1 to walk through the steps in the Simplified Model, as follows:

Chapter 43: Valuation of S Corporations

Table 1: Simplified Model

Simplified Model—Example 1

Assumptions:					
	Distributions		75%		
	Holding period		2	Years	
	Likelihood of buyer qualifying as pass-through buyer		100%		
	Additions to ROR for ability to realize basis build-up		0%		

PTE=Pass-through entity		Expand years as appropriate for DCF			
Indicated value of cash flows		Year 1	Year 2	Terminal Year	Sum net income— 2 years
Growth rate in earnings	5.0%				
Growth rate in terminal year	5.0%				
Net income before tax		100,000	105,000	110,250	205,000
Personal-level tax @	-41%	(41,000)	(43,050)	(45,203)	
Net income after tax		59,000	61,950	65,048	
Adjustments:					
Depreciation		10,000	10,000	10,000	
"Normal" capital additions		(10,000)	(10,000)	(10,000)	1. Basic DCF to equity at personal tax rates
Less: working capital (interim)					
Cash flow to equity		59,000	61,950	65,048	
				Terminal Value Cap Rate:	
Present value discount rate		25.0%	25.0%	20.0%	
Discounted cash flows		$47,200	$39,648	$325,238	
Sum of discounted cash flows	$86,848	Discount Rate		25.0%	
PV terminal value	$208,152	Present Value of Terminal Value		$208,152	
Indicated value of cash flows	$295,000				

Adjustment for dividend tax avoided		Year 1	Year 2	Year 3	
HIGHLIGHTED CELLS DENOTE SPECIFIC DECISION POINTS FOR THE PTE CALCULATIONS	Percent of income distributed annually			Assumed exit/terminal year	Sum of distributions—2 years
PTE Distributions (% of income in this example; percentage depends on expected distribution stream)	75%	75,000	78,750		153,750
Total entity taxes (from above)		(41,000)	(43,050)			2. Adjust for the benefit of the dividend tax avoided
Equivalent C corp dividends	Dividend tax rate	34,000	35,700	-	
State	5.0%	1,700	1,785	-	
Federal	15.0%	5,100	5,355	-	

Chapter 43: Valuation of S Corporations

Net PTE benefit (liability)	20%	6,800	7,140	-		
Terminal value cap rate				20.0%		
				-		
Present value discount rate		25.0%	25.0%	25.0%		
Present value		$5,440	$4,570	-	For hold into perpetuity, capitalize terminal year	
Sum of double taxation adjustment present values				$10,010		
Likelihood of buyer benefitting from pass-through benefits (could be ZERO to 100%)				100%		
Estimated benefit				10,010		
Benefit of build-up in basis (retained net income)						
HIGHLIGHTED CELLS DENOTE SPECIFIC DECISION POINTS FOR THE PTE CALCULATIONS		For limited holding period, sum of annual net income > distributions				
PTE net Income over period		100,000	$105,000	$205,000	For hold into perpetuity, capitalize representative year's retained net income > distribution	3. Calculate benefit of buildup in basis (retained net income)
PTE distributions over period		75,000	$78,750	$153,750		
Income over PTE distributions (sum net income before tax less sum PTE distributions)				51,250		
Capital gains tax (estimated combined federal & state)			20%	10,250		
PV (if limited hold) or cap rate (if perpetuity)	PV or cap rate	Additions to rate	Total rate			
Capitalization rate for basis	25.0%	0%	25.0%	$6,560		
Likelihood of buyer benefitting from pass-through benefits (could be ZERO to 100%)				100%		
Estimated benefit				$6,560		
Summary of recognized benefits						
Indicated value of cash flows	295,000					
Adjustment for dividend tax avoided	10,010					
Benefit of build-up in basis	6,560	16,570	6%	PTE premium/ (discount)		
Indicated value plus S Corp benefits— consider levels of value	311,570	Marketable, control or minority depending on cash flows				

© Fannon Valuation Group All Rights Reserved
As published in *Financial Valuation, Applications and Models*, Wiley Publishing 2006

Chapter 43: Valuation of S Corporations

1. First, the analyst performs a *typical discounted cash flow to equity analysis*. However, instead of using corporate tax rates, the analyst uses individual tax rates.[2] This avoids the step of calculating the value of an "otherwise identical C corporation" and then separately calculating the value of the differential of individual versus corporate income tax rates. The rate of return should also consider the additional risks of operating as an S Corp, relative to a publicly-traded C Corp.

2. Second, we calculate the *adjustment for dividend tax avoided* by the S corporation shareholder. We have assumed that the S corporation, both historically and in its projected business plans, distributes 75% of net income to its shareholders.[3] In this example, we have also assumed that the shareholders will receive the benefit of this distribution for two years (our holding period).[4]

Note that although it is possible to calculate dividends as less than the tax liability, such a strategy is unrealistic over the long-term, as the shareholder would likely demand payment or seek to break the S-election, unless there is a contractual prohibition.

Upon the third year, the company (or the shareholder) will exercise an exit strategy, at which time the distributions will cease. To the extent the distributions exceed the taxes on corporate income, the S corporation shareholder receives these funds free of dividend tax, a benefit over a shareholder in a publicly-traded C corporation. This is relevant, because we have used the publicly traded C corporation shareholder's rate of return, which includes an expectation of having to pay a dividend tax, when we calculated the value of the S corporation. Therefore, we must account for this dividend-tax-free benefit. To do so, we calculate the dividend tax that the S corporation shareholder has avoided and discount it at the firm's cost of capital.

We then apply the likelihood that the shareholder will realize this benefit—in our case, we have estimated 100%. Note that this may be an appropriate place to express issues relating to the buyer's ability to realize the S corporation benefits, and includes consideration of the pool of likely buyers. (A more complete discussion of the "pool of likely buyers" appears at the end of this chapter.)

The selection of a holding period and of an exit strategy following the holding period is an extremely important component that is built into the models (implicitly or explicitly), and has perhaps the single most significant impact on the amount of premium ascribed to the S corporation. Table 1 calculates the benefit of the avoided dividend tax for a limited holding period only, terminating the benefit upon an assumed exit strategy. This implies that the S corporation benefit of single taxation and avoidance of dividend tax will no longer be available following the holding period—presumably, because the subsequent buyer will be one who will not benefit from the single tax structure, such as a C corporation.[5] (In two of the later examples, we will work through an assumption that a subsequent buyer will qualify to retain the S corporation benefits.) An analyst must relate the decision regarding the term of the avoided dividend tax benefit to the specific facts and circumstances of each and every valuation engagement. As later examples demonstrate, if there is an expectation of a long-term holding period—or a reasonable expectation that the S corporation benefits will go on into perpetuity—it may be entirely appropriate to include a terminal value (as opposed to terminating the calculated benefit by assuming a sale to a C corporation).

Chapter 43: Valuation of S Corporations

> *Author's Note: Assuming a sale to a C corporation in the terminal year limits the benefit of the avoided dividend tax to a specific holding period only. This may be appropriate in an environment where all future buyers are expected to be C corporation buyers, but this is often not the case. A buyer following the holding period may be eligible to continue enjoying the benefits of the single tax structure, and a seller at that time would presumably take this into consideration.*
>
> *The analyst could modify either the limited holding period assumption or the perpetuity assumption in The Simplified Model.*

3. As a third step in the Simplified Model, we calculate the *Benefit of Build-Up in Basis* (retained net income) in the S corporation stock. For a limited holding period, at the very right hand side of the spreadsheet, from top to bottom, the model calculates the total net income and the total distributions for the holding period. The difference is the amount of earnings the corporation has retained. This amount adds to the basis of the shareholder's stock, saving capital gains taxes upon its sale. This benefit is present-valued from an assumed exit period—in this example, two years. Here, the analyst *may* wish to consider adding a premium to the discount rate to take account for the greater risk associated with realizing the benefit of the built-up basis. Compared to current distributions, the ability to benefit from these retained dollars may be far less certain. However, the analyst should take care not to "double count" this additional risk in assigning any discount for lack of control or marketability for the subject interest.

The analyst then sums the Indicated Value of the Cash Flow, the Adjustment for Dividend Tax Avoided, and the Benefit of the Build-Up in Basis.

Although not shown in this example, the final step is to consider the level of value. The cash flows used in the model would dictate control or minority level, as would the extent of any adjustments for the ability to realize the tax benefits. The Simplified Model produces a marketable value, so discounts for lack of marketability would usually apply for a non-controlling interest.

Tables 2 through 4 present Example 2 through 4 of the Simplified Model, each with different assumptions:

Example 2: Simplified Model Assumptions	
Distributions as a percent of income	41%
Holding Period	2 years
Likelihood of buyer qualifying as pass-through buyer	100%
Additions to ROR for ability to realize basis build-up	0%

Compared to Table 1, Tables 2 through 4 only modified the distributions, making them equal to the tax that must be paid on corporate earnings. While the premium is slightly less than the prior example (5% compared to 6%) there is still a premium because, to the extent that the

Chapter 43: Valuation of S Corporations

shareholder does not benefit from current distributions, he or she will benefit from the step-up to stock basis resulting from the retained net income. In other words, the company will either distribute the available earnings or retain them (contributing to the basis of the stock), but these earnings do not simply disappear. In this example, due to the expected two-year holding period, we are able to estimate the value of the additional basis with relative ease. In the real world, we seldom know exit strategies with such precision, as they are much more likely to be subject to additional risk or at the very least an unknown or longer term.

When the distribution is exactly equal to the income tax burden, there will be no dividend tax avoidance. This is because the dividend arises only to the extent that distributions are in excess of the amount of income tax. Since the entire dividend is being used to pay income taxes, the S corporation shareholder does not "benefit" from any avoided dividend. However, this does not mean that there is no benefit to the S corporation where dividends equal income taxes, as the balance of income is retained and increases the shareholder's basis in their stock. This benefit is reflected in the next section of the Simplified Model.

Note on the terminal benefit: In applying the Simplified Model, one could either terminate the benefit after an assigned holding period or calculate it into perpetuity. Examples 1 and 2 of the Simplified Model demonstrate a termination of the benefit; Examples 3 and 4, below, demonstrate a calculation of the benefit into perpetuity.

Example 3 of the Simplified Model assumes the following facts:

Example 3: Simplified Model Assumptions	
Distributions as a percent of income	95%
Holding Period	Unknown
Likelihood of buyer qualifying as pass-through buyer	100%
Additions to ROR for ability to realize basis build-up	5%

Under the same facts as Examples 1 and 2 but applying these assumptions to calculate value, the result is a much larger premium—20% compared to 5% and 6% in the earlier examples. The reason is primarily due to the holding period. As Chris Mercer, author of one of the S corporation models has observed, the longer the S corporation shareholder has to realize the benefit of the avoided dividend tax, the greater the potential benefit could be, simply because there is a longer period to realize the associated benefits. In his model, Chris Trehane has also noted that the holding periods for many minority interests are usually quite long, which could minimize the impact of their ability to realize the build-up in basis, by extending the holding period into perpetuity. However, it also maximizes the ability to realize the benefit of the avoided dividend tax.

Compared to Examples 1 and 2, which assumed a two-year holding period (and thus a very short time period to benefit from the avoided dividend tax), Example 3 involves a company with an unknown holding period. In this case, the analyst may want to consider the likelihood of

Chapter 43: Valuation of S Corporations

realizing the build-up in basis by adding a premium to the discount rate. In Example 3, we add an additional 5%. Here, the amount is not significant, as the company is currently distributing most of the earnings, leaving little income to retain.

The fourth and final example of the Simplified Model assumes the following facts:

Example 4: Simplified Model Assumptions	
Distributions as a percent of income	50%
Holding Period	Long-term
Likelihood of buyer qualifying as pass-through buyer	75%
Additions to ROR for ability to realize basis build-up	0%

Table2: Simplified Method					
		Example 2			
Assumptions:	Distributions as a percent of net income		41%		
	Holding period		2		Years
	Likelihood of buyer qualifying as pass-through buyer		100%		
	Additions to ROR for ability to realize basis build-up		0%		
PTE=Pass-through entity		Expand years as appropriate for DCF			
Indicated Value of Cash Flows		Year 1	Year 2	Terminal Year	
Growth rate in earnings	5.0%				
Growth rate in terminal year	5.0%				
Net income before tax		100,000	105,000	110,250	205,000
Personal-level tax @	-41%	(41,000)	(43,050)	(45,203)	Sum net income—2 years
Net income after tax		59,000	61,950	65,048	
Adjustments:					
Depreciation		10,000	10,000	10,000	
"Normal" capital additions		(10,000)	(10,000)	(10,000)	
Less: working capital (interim)					
Cash flow to equity		59,000	61,950	65,048	
				Terminal Value Cap Rate:	
Present value discount rate		25.0%	25.0%	20.0%	
Discounted cash flows		$47,200	$39,648	$325,238	
Sum of discounted cash flows	$86,848		Discount Rate	25.0%	
PV terminal value	$208,152		Present Value of Terminal Value	$208,152	
Indicated value of cash flows	$295,000				
Adjustment for dividend tax avoided		Year 1	Year 2	Year 3	

Chapter 43: Valuation of S Corporations

HIGHLIGHTED CELLS DENOTE SPECIFIC DECISION POINTS FOR THE PTE CALCULATIONS	Percent of income distributed annually			Assumed exit/terminal year	
PTE Distributions (% of income in this example; percentage depends on expected distribution stream)	41%	41,000	43,050		84,050
Total entity taxes (from above)		(41,000)	(43,050)		Sum of distributions—2 years
Equivalent C corp dividends	Dividend tax rate	-	-	-	
State	5.0%	-	-	-	
Federal	15.0%	-	-	-	
Net PTE benefit (liability)	20%	-	-	-	
Terminal value cap rate				20.0%	
				-	
Present value discount rate		25.0%	25.0%	25.0%	
Present value		$-	$-	$-	For hold into perpetuity, capitalize terminal year
Sum of double taxation adjustment present values				$-	
Likelihood of buyer benefitting from pass-through benefits (could be ZERO to 100%)				100%	
Estimated benefit				-	
Benefit of build-up in basis (retained net income)					
HIGHLIGHTED CELLS DENOTE SPECIFIC DECISION POINTS FOR THE PTE CALCULATIONS	For limited holding period, sum net income > distributions				
PTE net Income over period		$100,000	$105,000	$205,000	For hold into perpetuity, capitalize representative year's retained net income > distribution
PTE distributions over period		$41,000	$43,050	$84,050	
Income over PTE distributions (sum net income before tax less sum PTE distributions)				120,950	
Capital gains tax (estimated combined federal & state)			20%	24,190	
PV (if limited hold) or cap rate (if perpetuity)	PV or cap rate	Additions to rate	Total rate		
Capitalization rate for basis	25.0%	0%	25.0%	$15,482	
Likelihood of buyer benefitting from pass-through benefits (could be ZERO to 100%)				100%	
Estimated benefit				$15,482	
Summary of recognized benefits					
Indicated value of cash flows	295,000				
Adjustment for dividend tax avoided	-				
Benefit of build-up in basis	15,482	15,482	5%	PTE premium/(discount)	
Indicated value plus S Corp benefits—consider levels of value	310,482	Marketable, control or minority depending on cash flows			

© Fannon Valuation Group All Rights Reserved
As published in *Financial Valuation, Applications and Models*, Wiley Publishing 2006

Chapter 43: Valuation of S Corporations

Table3: Simplified Method					
	Example 3				
Assumptions:	Distributions as a percent of net income			95%	
	Holding period			Unknown	
	Likelihood of buyer qualifying as pass-through buyer			100%	
	Additions to ROR for ability to realize basis build-up			5%	
PTE=Pass-through entity			Expand years as appropriate for DCF		
Indicated Value of Cash Flows		Year 1	Year 2	Year 3	
Growth rate in earnings	5.0%				
Growth rate in terminal year	5.0%				
Net income before tax		100,000	105,000	110,250	
Personal-level tax @	-41%	(41,000)	(43,050)	(45,203)	
Net income after tax		59,000	61,950	65,048	
Adjustments:					
Depreciation		10,000	10,000	10,000	
"Normal" capital additions		(10,000)	(10,000)	(10,000)	
Less: working capital (interim)					
Cash flow to equity		59,000	61,950	65,048	
			Terminal Value Cap Rate:		
Present value discount rate		25.0%	25.0%	20.0%	
Discounted cash flows		$47,200	$39,648	$325,238	
Sum of discounted cash flows	$86,848		Discount Rate	25.0%	
PV terminal value	$208,152	Present Value of Terminal Value		$208,152	
Indicated value of cash flows	$295,000				
Adjustment for dividend tax avoided		Year 1	Year 2	Year 3	
HIGHLIGHTED CELLS DENOTE SPECIFIC DECISION POINTS FOR THE PTE CALCULATIONS	Percent of income distributed annually			Assumed exit/ terminal year	
PTE Distributions (% of income in this example; percentage depends on expected distribution stream)	95%	95,000	99,750	104,738	
Total entity taxes (from above)		(41,000)	(43,050)	(45,203)	
Equivalent C corp dividends	Dividend tax rate	54,000	56,700	59,535	

Chapter 43: Valuation of S Corporations

State	5.0%	2,700	2,835	2,977	
Federal	15.0%	8,100	8,505	8,930	
Net PTE benefit (liability)	20%	10,800	11,340	11,907	
Terminal value cap rate				20.0%	
				59,535	
Present value discount rate		25.0%	25.0%	25.0%	
Present value		$8,640	$7,258	$38,102	For hold into perpetuity, capitalize terminal year
Sum of double taxation adjustment present values				$54,000	
Likelihood of buyer benefitting from pass-through benefits (could be ZERO to 100%)				100%	
Estimated benefit				54,000	
Benefit of build-up in basis (retained net income)					
HIGHLIGHTED CELLS DENOTE SPECIFIC DECISION POINTS FOR THE PTE CALCULATIONS					
PTE net Income over period		$100,000		$100,000	For hold into perpetuity, capitalize representative year's retained net income > distribution
PTE distributions over period		$95,000		$95,000	
Income over PTE distributions (sum net income before tax less sum PTE distributions)				5,000	
Capital gains tax (estimated combined federal & state)			20%	1,000	
PV (if limited hold) or cap rate (if perpetuity)	PV or cap rate	Additions to rate	Total rate		
Capitalization rate for basis	20.0%	5%	25.0%	$4,000	
Likelihood of buyer benefitting from pass-through benefits (could be ZERO to 100%)				100%	
Estimated benefit				$4,000	
Summary of recognized benefits					
Indicated value of cash flows	295,000				
Adjustment for dividend tax avoided	54,000				
Benefit of build-up in basis	4,000	58,000	20%	PTE premium/ (discount)	
Indicated value plus S Corp benefits—consider levels of value	353,000	*Marketable, control or minority depending on cash flows*			

© Fannon Valuation Group All Rights Reserved
As published in *Financial Valuation, Applications and Models*, Wiley Publishing 2006

Chapter 43: Valuation of S Corporations

Table 4: Simplified Method

Example 4

Assumptions:					
	Distributions as a percent of net income			50%	
	Holding period			Long Term	
	Likelihood of buyer qualifying as pass-through buyer			75%	
	Additions to ROR for ability to realize basis build-up			0%	
PTE=Pass-through entity		\multicolumn{3}{c}{Expand years as appropriate for DCF}		
Indicated Value of Cash Flows		Year 1	Year 2	Terminal Year	
Growth rate in earnings	5.0%				
Growth rate in terminal year	5.0%				
Net income before tax		100,000	105,000	110,250	
Personal-level tax @	-41%	(41,000)	(43,050)	(45,203)	
Net income after tax		59,000	61,950	65,048	
Adjustments:					
Depreciation		10,000	10,000	10,000	
"Normal" capital additions		(10,000)	(10,000)	(10,000)	
Less: working capital (interim)					
Cash flow to equity		59,000	61,950	65,048	
				Terminal Value Cap Rate:	
Present value discount rate		25.0%	25.0%	20.0%	
Discounted cash flows		$47,200	$39,648	$325,238	
Sum of discounted cash flows	$86,848		Discount Rate	25.0%	
PV terminal value	$208,152	\multicolumn{2}{c}{Present Value of Terminal Value}	$208,152	
Indicated value of cash flows	$295,000				
Adjustment for dividend tax avoided		Year 1	Year 2	Year 3	
HIGHLIGHTED CELLS DENOTE SPECIFIC DECISION POINTS FOR THE PTE CALCULATIONS	Percent of income distributed annually			Assumed exit/ terminal year	
PTE Distributions (% of income in this example; percentage depends on expected distribution stream)	50%	50,000	52,500	55,125	
Total entity taxes (from above)		(41,000)	(43,050)	(45,203)	
Equivalent C corp dividends	Dividend tax rate	9,000	9,450	9,923	

Chapter 43: Valuation of S Corporations

State	5.0%	450	473	496	
Federal	15.0%	1,350	1,418	1,488	
Net PTE benefit (liability)	20%	1,800	1,890	1,985	
Terminal value cap rate				20.0%	
				9,923	
Present value discount rate		25.0%	25.0%	25.0%	
Present value		$1,440	$1,210	$6,350	
Sum of double taxation adjustment present values				$9,000	For hold into perpetuity, capitalize terminal year
Likelihood of buyer benefitting from pass-through benefits (could be ZERO to 100%)				75%	
Estimated benefit				6,750	
Benefit of build-up in basis (retained net income)					
HIGHLIGHTED CELLS DENOTE SPECIFIC DECISION POINTS FOR THE PTE CALCULATIONS					
PTE net Income over period		$100,000		$100,000	For hold into perpetuity, capitalize representative year's retained net income > distribution
PTE distributions over period		$50,000		$50,000	
Income over PTE distributions (sum net income before tax less sum PTE distributions)				50,000	
Capital gains tax (estimated combined federal & state)			20%	10,000	
PV (if limited hold) or cap rate (if perpetuity)	PV or cap rate	Additions to rate	Total rate		
Capitalization rate for basis	20.0%	0%	20.0%	$50,000	
Likelihood of buyer benefitting from pass-through benefits (could be ZERO to 100%)				75%	
Estimated benefit				$37,500	
Summary of recognized benefits					
Indicated value of cash flows	295,000				
Adjustment for dividend tax avoided	6,750				
Benefit of build-up in basis	37,500	44,250	15%	PTE premium/ (discount)	
Indicated value plus S Corp benefits—consider levels of value	339,250	*Marketable, control or minority depending on cash flows*			

© Fannon Valuation Group All Rights Reserved
As published in *Financial Valuation, Applications and Models*, Wiley Publishing 2006

Chapter 43: Valuation of S Corporations

In this example, the premium drops to 15%, largely because there is a tradeoff between the investor receiving additional current distributions, which is a present realizable benefit, compared to earnings that contribute to basis, which is a future benefit subject to greater risk. In addition, this application of the Simplified Model recognizes that the buyer may not be an individual or entity eligible to realize the pass-through benefits. To account for this distinction, we examine the pool of most likely buyers for the interest. This is an issue that is often neglected in valuation, not only when considering S corporation benefits, but in many contexts.

A note on the most likely buyer

The issue of the most likely buyer is important in divorce cases, because courts in some states will specifically consider the distinct context of the transfer or exchange; that is, those states consider that in a marital dissolution no real "purchase" of the interest takes place. Likewise, for courts considering equitable causes of action outside of divorce, the "likely buyer" is most certainly an issue, as in *Delaware Radiology*.[6] In that case, the Delaware Chancery Court (Vice Chancellor Strine) noted:

...I am trying to quantify the value of Delaware Radiology as a going concern with an S corporation structure and award the [minority shareholders] their pro rata share of that value.

In the Tax Court, the issue has arisen more frequently in the context of reasonable negotiation between a buyer and seller.[7]

Given these cases, when valuing pass-through entities in the estate and gift tax context, the analyst should consider whether a seller would be willing to sell the specific interest for less than the benefit received from the future cash flows; or at the very least, whether the seller would negotiate from this position. Thus, the buyers "pool" becomes relevant in virtually every context.

Evidence regarding the pool of potential buyers may arise from the specific facts of the case and also the company, such as restrictions set forth in a shareholder agreement or from the market, such as available transactional data. In some cases, the parties may contemplate the sale of the company within a known period of time. If the analyst searches market transactions and finds that many of the buyers in the subject industry are C corporations, then such buyers would not benefit from the continued pass-through benefits. In that instance, the analyst may find it appropriate to weight the S corporation benefits accordingly among actual market participants for the interest.

This approach first appeared in Hitchner, James R. (editor), *Financial Valuation Applications and Models*, John Wiley & Sons, Inc. (2d. ed. 2006), in the chapter by Nancy J. Fannon, "Valuation of Pass-Through Entities," pp. 569-623.

In its prior published version, the Simplified Model used corporate tax rates, noting that the differences between corporate and individual tax rates were not material to the calculation. By

Chapter 43: Valuation of S Corporations

using individual rates, as presented here, the Simplified Model directly calculates the benefit by deducting the tax burden that is actually incurred, at personal rates, thus avoiding any need to consider an adjustment. For those states where corporate income tax rates exist (i.e., S Corp status is not recognized), we calculate an effective rate to accomplish the end result of "cash to the investor's pockets."

In the review of a company's current and historic distributions, it does not matter if the analyst expresses distributions as a percent of net income or cash flow. However, the build-up in basis will always arise from the undistributed net income. Thus, if net income is $100, cash flow is $90, and distributions as a percent of cash flow are 50%, retained net income is calculated as net income of $100 minus $45 (50% of cash flow).

Some have suggested that a different rate of return be applied to the benefit of the avoided dividend tax than entity earnings. By applying the same rate of returns on earnings, we are merely accounting for the portion of income that our traditional application of the income approach failed to consider; the only additional risk factor (aside from minority versus control issues) would be those related to possible changes in tax policy.

In examples 1 and 2, we assume a sale to a C Corp as an exit strategy, thus terminating the benefits of dividend tax avoided and basis build-up. The analyst should correspondingly consider applying a corporate tax rate in the terminal year. However, when an assumed sale to a C Corp is made, this may be only one of many considerations of the differences between C and S corporations and their respective pricing in the market.

Delaware Open MRI Radiology Associates v. Kessler 898 A.2d 190, 314 (Del. Ch. 2006)

See, e.g., Mandelbaum v. Commissioner, T.C. Memo. 1995-255 (expert's disregard for the views of a willing seller may be fatal to the expert's opinion); *see also Estate of Cloutier v. Comm'r,* T.C. Memo. 1996-49; *Pabst Brewing Company v. Commissioner of Internal Revenue,* T.C. Memo 1996-506 (ignoring the views of the willing seller is contrary to this well-established test).

---

1. The models established today for the valuation of S corporations can be found in the work done by Roger J. Grabowski, Chris D. Treharne, Z. Christopher Mercer, and Daniel R. Van Vleet. While a discussion of each of their specific methodologies is beyond the scope of this chapter, their collective works form the core of the financial reality facing the S corporation owner that this chapter presents.

Chapter 44

Buy-Sell Agreements: An Overview

By Chris Mercer

Introduction

Buy-Sell agreements are some of the least discussed and most important of corporate agreements. This chapter is adapted from an in-depth treatment of the topic from valuation and business perspectives in *Buy-Sell Agreements: Ticking Time Bombs or Reasonable Resolutions?*

> *Editor's Note: Readers of this Guide are indeed fortunate to have a contribution from Chris Mercer on the issues involved in Buy-Sell Agreements, extracted form his Book on the same topic. In the Healthcare Industry, and particularly so with physician practices, conflicts arising from poorly drafted Buy-Sell agreements are commonplace. We have seen valuation formulas based on some entirely irrational measures such as charges (!), collected revenues without regard to outstanding debt, gross income (whatever that means), receivables valued on a basis of 70% collectability in a specialty practice where the collection rates was 30%. Many of these clauses were drafted by attorneys with no financial experience in healthcare or no experience in healthcare whatsoever. As can be seen in the frequency of litigation engagements involving buy outs agreements, they are a critical aspect of healthcare valuation.*

What Are Buy-Sell Agreements Designed To Accomplish?

Buy-sell agreements are designed to provide objective means of transferring ownership under anticipatable, but likely difficult circumstances. In the absence of a workable buy-sell agreement, the remaining shareholders and the corporation may be placed in the unenviable position of negotiating under adverse circumstances with former friends, their families, or their estates. At best, this can be difficult for all parties involved.

We use "QFRDD" to denote common trigger events for buy-sell agreements. The term "trigger" can have a benign connotation. If A happens, then B is triggered, or set in motion to happen. However, the majority of trigger events related to buy-sell agreements have less benign connotations. While it is easy to think of these events in personal terms, analogous situations also happen to companies. "Quits" equates to withdrawal from the venture; "disabled" could mean inability to answer a capital call; and, "dies" represents bankruptcy of a participant.

If you think about the events suggested by QFRDD, none of them are very pleasant to talk about, particularly to a group of shareholders who may have just come together for a common business purpose. In fact, circumstances could be such that the shareholder most affected by a trigger event has a proverbial gun to his or her head. In the alternative, the company may perceive that it has a gun to its head in order to fulfill the repurchase requirements of a buy-sell agreement.

Q – Quits. A buy-sell agreement may provide a mechanism for shareholders who leave a business to sell their shares to the corporation or other shareholders. From the corporation's viewpoint, the agreement may prevent the departing shareholder from retaining his shares. By requiring a shareholder who quits to sell his or her shares to the corporation upon departure, the corporation and remaining shareholders eliminate any potential for conflict over future corporate policies with the departed shareholder. They also eliminate the potential for the departed shareholder to benefit from future success of the business created by the remaining shareholders. Finally, the agreements prevent a shareholder (or his or her estate) from selling shares to "undesirable" parties, enabling the remaining shareholders to decide who will be the next shareholder, if any. These reasons for buy-sell provisions apply to virtually all trigger events.

F – Is Fired. When an employee-shareholder is terminated, most corporations desire to retain control over the shares. Terminations generally result in diverse, or more likely, adverse interests between the fired shareholder, the corporation, and remaining shareholders. From the employee's viewpoint, the buy-sell agreement assures that his or her shares can be sold at the buy-sell price and creates a market for the shares. From the corporation's viewpoint, buy-sell agreements create the right, or the obligation, to purchase the departing employee-shareholder's shares. They also eliminate the potential for the terminated shareholder to benefit from any future success of the business created by the remaining employees and shareholders. Some agreements call for a penalty to the valuation in cases of termination, particularly for cause.

R – Retires. The retirement of an employee-shareholder creates a potential divergence of interests between the shareholder and the corporation. The shareholder may desire current liquidity over the uncertain future performance of the corporation, and the corporation may desire not to have potential interference or disagreement with corporate policy, or to have the retired shareholder benefit from future appreciation in value.

D – Disabled. After a defined period of time, the corporation may have the right (from its viewpoint) or the obligation (perhaps, from the employee's viewpoint) to purchase the disabled employee's shares. The other features related to fired employees also relate to disabled ones.

D – Dies. The death of a shareholder creates issues that are often resolved by buy-sell agreements. If a shareholder dies owning a minority interest in a corporation for which there is no market for its shares, the illiquidity of the stock can create estate tax issues. The shares must be valued for estate tax purposes, and the appraisal amount will add to the estate's value. To the extent that the estate is taxable, there may be no liquidity to pay the estate taxes. Buy-sell agreements provide a mechanism for determining the value of shares for estate tax purposes and for monetizing that value for the estate, generally in cash or in a term note. Therefore, the shareholder's estate realizes liquidity and can pay taxes due and does not face the combination of uncertainty of independent valuation and

Chapter 44: Buy-Sell Agreements: An Overview

the certainty of payment of taxes in the absence of liquidity. From the corporation's viewpoint, the buy-sell agreement eliminates the need to address uncertain ownership dictated by the deceased shareholder's will and can create the requirement for funding.

If the parties agree, buy-sell agreements also operate in the event of the divorce, declaration of insolvency, or bankruptcy of one or more shareholders (or even the corporation). In the event of the divorce of an employee-shareholder, the buy-sell agreement will most likely be designed to prevent the non-employee spouse from realizing any ownership in the stock of the corporation. If an employee declares bankruptcy or becomes insolvent, the corporation may exercise its right to purchase the shares to prevent their dispersion to creditors.

It should be clear from the above that buy-sell agreements *can be* favorable from the viewpoints of employee-shareholders, non-employee shareholders, the corporation, and any remaining shareholders in many diverse situations. The emphasis is on "can be" because the operation of a buy-sell agreement can go awry despite the best intentions of its creators.

Categories of Buy-Sell Agreements

There are three general categories of buy-sell agreements which are defined by the relationships between the corporation and the shareholders who are subject to the agreements.

1. *Cross-Purchase Agreements*. Cross-purchase agreements are agreements between and among the shareholders of a corporation calling for the purchase by the other shareholder(s) of the shares subject to the buy-sell agreement. Cross-purchase agreements are often funded by life insurance owned by shareholder(s) on the lives of other shareholders. Cross-purchase agreements quickly become unworkable as the number of shareholders and market value increase. See Figure 1 for an illustration of the growing complexity of cross-purchase agreements.

2. *Entity-Purchase Agreements*. Entity-purchase agreements call for the corporation to purchase the shares upon the occurrence of trigger events. The entity is then responsible for defining or providing the funding mechanism. The funding mechanism may be the purchase of life insurance, financing by a third party or the selling shareholders, or cash on hand, or a combination.

3. *Hybrid Agreements*. Hybrid agreements generally call for the entity to have the right of first refusal to purchase shares upon the occurrence of trigger events. In the event that the corporation declines to purchase, it may have the right to offer the shares to the other shareholders pro rata, or to selected shareholders. Finally, hybrid agreements often give the corporation a "last look" if shares are first refused and other shareholders do not purchase the stock. For the hybrid agreement to be effective, the corporation's "last look" must be binding as to the purchase of the shares.

Chapter 44: Buy-Sell Agreements: An Overview

Hybrid agreements can be used to create non-pro rata changes in relative ownership if that result is desired for business reasons. Funding may be through a combination of self-financing by the corporation, notes from selling shareholders, and life insurance.

For larger corporations, most buy-sell agreements are entity-purchase agreements, or they are hybrid in nature if the corporation has the right to allow individual shareholders to stand in its place. For substantial corporations with more than a few shareholders, the preponderance of buy-sell agreements are entity-purchase agreements, some of which may allow the redirection of purchases to some or all shareholders.

Figure 1

Cross-Purchase Complexity		
Cross-purchase agreements are often used in relatively small businesses with two or three shareholders, although there are exceptions to this statement. On the first line of the table below, assume A and B each own 50% of the business: There are two shareholders There is one relationship If life insurance funds their buy-sell agreement, two policies will be required (A buys a policy on B's life and B buys a policy on A's life)		
# Shareholders	Shareholder Relationships	# Relationships / # Policies
2 (A and B)	AB	1 / 2
3 (A, B and C)	AB BC AC	3 / 6
4 (A, B, C and D)	AB AC AD BC BD CD	6 / 12
5 (A, B, C, D and E)	AB AC AD AE BC BD BE CD CE DE	10 / 20
6 (A, B, C, D, E and F)	You get the picture!	15 / 30
As the figire illustrates, the number of relationships increase as the number of shareholders increase. The number of required insurance policies increases even faster. At some point, cross-purchase agreements become too cumbersome for reasonable operation.		

Types of Buy-Sell Agreements

Buy-sell agreements can also be placed into five general types based on the nature of the valuation mechanism:

1. *Fixed Price Agreements.* These agreements fix the price of future purchases at a specific dollar amount by stating a value for the equity of the enterprise, either in dollars or a per share value.

2. *Formula Agreements.* Formula agreements establish value by providing a formula for determining value. Examples of formulas include a multiple of book value or earnings, or the agreement may call for an averaging of valuation indications developed using two or more formulas.

Chapter 44: Buy-Sell Agreements: An Overview

3. *Shotgun Agreements.* Shotgun agreements outline a process whereby one party offers to purchase (or sell) shares to another and the other party has the right (or the obligation) to sell (or purchase) the shares at the offered price.

4. *Rights of First Refusal.* Rights of first refusal (ROFRs) are sometimes considered to be a form of buy-sell agreement. More often, they are used in conjunction with buy-sell agreements.

5. *Process Agreements.* Process buy-sell agreements outline a process by which future transactions will be priced, i.e., they define valuation processes. In nearly all cases, process agreements call upon the use of one or more business appraisers in (the process of) determining the price at which contemplated future transactions will occur. We sub-divide process agreements into two categories, because of important differences in how they operate:

    a. *Multiple Appraiser Agreements.* Multiple appraiser buy-sell agreements outline processes by which two or more appraisers are employed to determine value.

    b. *Single Appraiser Agreements.* Single appraiser buy-sell agreements outline processes by which a single appraiser is employed to determine value.

In this chapter, we focus briefly on fixed price, formula, and process buy-sell agreements.

Fixed Price Buy-Sell Agreements

Fixed price buy-sell agreements do exactly what their name suggests. They fix a price today for transactions that will occur at future dates. Fixed price agreements are often found in smaller corporations, partnerships, and LLCs.

Fixed price agreements:

- **Require agreement** *at a point in time* between shareholders of a corporation and/or the corporation. With a fixed price agreement, the shareholders simply (or not so simply) agree on a price, which is memorialized in the agreement. The shareholders also agree on the other terms of its operation.

- **Relate to transactions** that may or will occur *at future points in time* between the shareholders, or between the shareholders and the corporation.

- **Define the conditions** that will cause the buy-sell provisions to be triggered. These are the business and/or personal events that will trigger the operation of the buy-sell agreement.

- **Determine the price** (for example, per share or per unit or per member interest) at which the identified future transactions will occur. Fixed price agreements often state that the agreed upon price will be updated periodically and that the agreed upon price will be determinative of value until the time of the next updating.

Advantages

There are advantages to fixed price agreements.

- *Easy to understand.* Once the price is agreed upon, everyone knows what the buy-sell price will be.

- *Easy to negotiate.* When fixed price agreements are installed, there is generally a common belief about the then-current value of the business (or business interest) among the shareholders.

- *Inexpensive.* Fixed price agreements require less legal documentation than more complex agreements and other professionals, such as accountants and business appraisers, are utilized less frequently.

Disadvantages

The primary disadvantage of fixed price agreements is that *they are out of date shortly after they are inked.* While the parties almost always intend to update the price, they seldom do.

It is often easy for the parties to agree on the initial price for a fixed price agreement; however, it can become increasingly difficult and confrontational to discuss price at later dates. Such discussions force shareholders to consider their potential disabilities, firings, retirements, and even deaths. Further, the range of shareholder characteristics tends to widen with the passage of time. Most business owners, at least in our experience, will go to extremes to avoid such discussions (see Figure 2 showing potential opposing characteristics which can relate to all types of buy-sell agreements).

FIGURE 2

Potential Opposing Shareholder Characteristics that Make Discussing Buy-Sell Agreements Difficult		
Characteristic	Shareholder 1	Shareholder 2
Age	Younger	Older
Ownership	Non-controlling	Controlling
Involvement	Active	Inactive
Investment Type	Sweat Equity	Real Money
Investment Amount	Smaller	Larger to Much Larger
Personal Guarantees	None	Substantial

Chapter 44: Buy-Sell Agreements: An Overview

If there is a controlling shareholder and the remaining shareholders hold minority interests, it can become awkward to discuss valuation. The minority shareholders are often thinking in terms of the value of the enterprise as a whole, and not in terms of illiquid, minority interests in the corporation. The controlling shareholder may consider the minority shares to be worth proportionately less than his shares.

We have seen agreements where the "out-of-date" problem is cured by calling for an appraisal in the event that an agreed-upon price is more than, say, one year old. This cure, however, just opens up the potential problems associated with process agreements, which we will discuss below.

At times, fixed price agreements become examples of potentially expensive bets on the part of shareholders. If the price is fixed and they know that price is substantially below the current value of the business, owners who do not update the value are making implicit or explicit bets that a trigger event will happen to the other shareholder(s) before it happens to them. In other words, there is bet that the other guy(s) will die first.

We think the point is clear, but a couple of real-life examples should drive it home.

Poster-Child Examples of Fixed Price Agreements

Bet and Lost. A friend of mine told me the true story of his family's experience. His father was an initial, minority shareholder and employee of a business during the early 1960s. At the outset of the enterprise, the shareholders implemented a buy-sell agreement with a fixed price. The father's shares were valued at his investment value of $250 thousand.

Fast forward to 1974. The business grew and was successful. My friend, who is quite knowledgeable about business valuation, said that his father's interest would have been worth more than $1.0 million by 1974—the year his father died.

Neither the corporation nor the other shareholders offered to update the price in the buy-sell agreement to purchase the shares from the father's estate, so the shares were purchased for $250 thousand. My friend noted that receiving $250 thousand in 1974, and not $1.0 million, made a significant difference in his mother's independence for the remaining 25 years of her life. In addition, it caused a great deal of bitterness towards his father's former partners.

My friend's father probably did not think in terms of making a bet on his company's buy-sell agreement, but the fact that it was not updated did indeed create a betting situation. He bet and, we don't mean this in any personal way, his family lost.

Bet and Did Not Lose. We have chosen our words carefully with this subtitle. You have heard the story about the cobbler's children having no shoes. This next example is illustrative of that expression. Sometimes, there is no better way to illustrate a point than with one's own mistakes.

Chapter 44: Buy-Sell Agreements: An Overview

Mercer Capital has had, throughout its history, several ownership structures. It began as a proprietorship which was followed by three shareholders, followed by an extended period of two shareholders, followed by its current form of ownership—one shareholder and an employee stock ownership plan.

There were times during this period when the company did not have a buy-sell agreement. At times, there was a fixed price agreement. Hindsight has brought a great deal of perspective. If anything, the focus on growing the business deflected attention from the buy-sell agreement. If, knowing better, we allowed this situation to perpetuate for so long; you have to believe that there are other situations that cry out for attention.

Conclusion Regarding Fixed Price Agreements

In our opinion, fixed price buy-sell agreements should be avoided like a contagious disease in most situations. However, if you have one, you must have the discipline to update the price periodically.

Take Away Thought
If you have a fixed price buy-sell agreement, first, determine whether the price is current or not. If it is not, update it immediately! And read on. Better alternatives are available to you.

Formula Buy-Sell Agreements

Companies (and their shareholders) with formula agreements may believe that these agreements are superior to fixed price agreements, but, as we will see, formula agreements have their own issues. They fix a *single formula* today for transactions that will occur at future dates. We examine formula agreements through four key aspects of buy-sell agreements. Formula agreements:

- **Require agreement** *at a point in time* between shareholders of a corporation and/or the corporation. With a formula agreement, the shareholders simply (or not so simply) agree on a formula to determine price, which is memorialized in the agreement.

- **Relate to transactions** that may or will occur *at future points in time* between the shareholders, or between the shareholders and the corporation.

- **Define the conditions** that will cause the buy-sell provisions to be triggered. These are the business conditions that will trigger the operation of the buy-sell agreement, and the obligation of the company (or the shareholders) to repurchase the shares.

- **Determine the price** (per share or per unit or per member interest) at which the identified future transactions will occur. Formula agreements state a formula, which is typically applied to the then-current balance sheet or income statement metrics, to determine value. Some agreements call for the averaging of two or more separate

Chapter 44: Buy-Sell Agreements: An Overview

calculations. Therefore, the series of calculations is the "formula" for those agreements. The formula can be changed over time by agreement of the parties, however, until such a change is made, the initial formula is determinative of value.

Advantages

As with other types of buy-sell agreements, formula agreements have certain advantages, including:

- *(Initially) Easy to understand.* Once the formula is selected, the specific calculations necessary to determine the buy-sell price are known. Some typical formulas include multiples of net income, pre-tax income, operating income, and earnings before interest, taxes, depreciation and amortization (EBITDA). These formulas refer to what is called the *capitalization of earnings.* Book value (or a multiple of book value) is sometimes used as well.

- *Easy to negotiate.* When a formula agreement is installed, there is generally a common belief among the shareholders about the then-current value of the business. The value is effectively converted into the formula.

- *Inexpensive.* Formula agreements require less legal documentation and typically less involvement of other professionals.

Disadvantages

Formula buy-sell agreements also have certain disadvantages. The primary disadvantage is that no formula selected at a given time can provide reasonable and realistic valuations over time. This is true because of the myriad changes that occur within individual companies, local or regional economies, the national economy, and within industries.

One summary representation of business value, i.e., a generalized formula, can be expressed as:

$$\text{Value} = \text{Earnings} \times \text{Multiple}$$

To develop a formula for a buy-sell agreement, "all one has to do" is to decide on the appropriate measure of earnings, and then, the appropriate multiple to be applied to that earnings measure (i.e., with which to *capitalize* the earnings). As we have said in many speeches, if valuation were that simple, appraisers would not be necessary. As Ken Patton, Mercer Capital's president, is fond of saying: "Whenever someone tells you that 'all you have to do is *it*,' [whatever *it* is], you know for sure that there is more to *it* than *it*!" And so it is with formula valuation.

Possible Formulas and Future Earnings Patterns

The purpose of the analysis and figures that follow is not to try to illustrate any particular formula. Rather, it is included to illustrate the complexity which underlies the use of formulas.

Chapter 44: Buy-Sell Agreements: An Overview

FIGURE 3

	Prior Year 4	Prior Year 3	Prior Year 2	Prior Year 1	Most Recent Year	Expected Next Year
Sustained Growth	600	700	800	900	1,000	1,100
Variable-Down	600	400	300	600	1,100	750
Variable-Up	600	400	300	600	1,100	1,400
Weights						
1					1	1
2				1	1	1
3					1	1
4				1	1	
5			1	1	1	
6		1	1	1	1	
7	1	1	1	1	1	
8					2	1
9				3	2	1
10			4	3	2	1
11		1	2	3	4	5
12	1	2	3	4	5	
13			1	2	3	4
14		1	2	3	4	
15				1	2	3
16			1	2	4	
17					1	2
18				1	2	

FIGURE 4

	Prior Year 4	Prior Year 3	Prior Year 2	Prior Year 1	Most Recent Year	Expected Next Year	Weighted Avg. Earnings	Values at Multiples 4.0	5.0	6.0
Sustained Growth	600	700	800	900	1,000	1,100				
Weights										
1					1	1	1,050	4,200	5,250	6,300
2				1	1	1	1,000	4,000	5,000	6,000
3					1	1	1,050	4,200	5,250	6,300
4				1	1		950	3,800	4,750	5,700
5			1	1	1		900	3,600	4,500	5,400
6		1	1	1	1		675	2,700	3,375	4,050
7	1	1	1	1	1		660	2,640	3,300	3,960
8					2	1	1,033	4,133	5,167	6,200
9				3	2	1	967	3,867	4,833	5,800
10			4	3	2	1	900	3,600	4,500	5,400
11		1	2	3	4	5	920	3,680	4,600	5,520
12	1	2	3	4	5		773	3,094	3,867	4,641
13			1	2	3	4	1,000	4,000	5,000	6,000
14		1	2	3	4		830	3,320	4,150	4,980
15				1	2	3	1,033	4,133	5,167	6,200
16			1	2	4		943	3,771	4,714	5,657
17					1	2	1,067	4,267	5,333	6,400
18				1	2		967	3,867	4,833	5,800
Minimums							660	2,640	3,300	3,960
Maximums							1,067	4,267	5,333	6,400

Chapter 44: Buy-Sell Agreements: An Overview

The analysis in Figures 3 and 4 considers different formulas based on earnings, and different earnings multiples, all of which could be, at a point in time, reasonably reflective of value for a given enterprise. In addition, three different earnings scenarios are considered; 1) sustained growth; 2) variable earnings, with expected earnings down; and 3) variable earnings, with expected earnings up. Assume we are discussing pre-tax earnings.

Examples of the three earnings scenarios noted above are illustrated in Figure 2, along with 18 possible weights to be assigned to combinations of historical or expected earnings.

If you use an earnings capitalization formula, chances are it will be something like one of the above weighting schemes applied to some measure of earnings.

Possible Multiples

If you use a formula method, you have to select a multiple. Multiples change over time in most industries based on industry conditions, interest rates, the economy, the stock market, and company-specific factors.

You be the judge. Assume for the moment that the appropriate earnings multiple is in the range of 4x to 6x the selected measure of earnings. Figure 4 illustrates the range of possible conclusions of value based on the 18 different weighting scenarios and the range of multiples from 4x to 6x earnings for steadily growing earnings (the "sustained growth" example in Figure 3).

We make the following observations from Figure 4:

- *Multiple.* The range of 4x to 6x for the selected measure of earnings (we use the EBITDA multiple here) indicates a 50% swing from low to high. Multiples change over time, so the selection of any single multiple for a formula today can be wrong, relative to the market, by 50% (or more) based solely on that selection.

- *Weighting.* The range of calculated values for any given multiple indicates a 62% swing from minimum to maximum.

- *Combination.* The combination of variations in multiples and weightings indicates a swing of 142% from the lowest value ($2.6 million) to the highest ($6.4 million).

Keep in mind, Figure 4 shows the range of weighted earnings and multiples based on steadily rising earnings. The range of value conclusions is even greater if expected earnings are variable.

If you have but one chance to select the appropriate valuation mechanism at a future date from the figures above, which would you pick? Might there not be a better way to decide the pricing mechanism for your buy-sell agreement?

Chapter 44: Buy-Sell Agreements: An Overview

Other Caveats Regarding Formula Agreements

It is one thing to think you understand a formula. It is quite another to write it down so that those who are called upon to calculate its intended value will understand exactly what the parties meant when the formula agreement was signed. As an example, review the following formula that might be found in a buy-sell agreement.

> a. The corporation's earnings before interest, taxes, depreciation and amortization (EBITDA) for the trailing twelve months ending the month-end prior to the event giving rise to the required transaction (the Determination Date) times a multiple of 5.0. The product of the calculated EBITDA and 5.0 will represent the market value of the total capital of the business (MVTC).
> b. From the MVTC of the business, the interest-bearing debt (IBD) outstanding on the balance sheet as of the month-end immediately prior to the event giving rise to the required transaction will be subtracted, with the difference representing the market value of the equity of the business (MVE).
> c. The MVE of the business will be divided by the number of shares outstanding as of the Determination Date (Shares Outstanding, or SO), with the result being MVE per share.
> d. MVE per share will be multiplied by the number of shares subject to the required transaction (Shares to be Purchased, or SP), with the result being the amount due to the selling shareholder (the Due Amount, or DA) from the corporation under the terms of Section 7.3 below.
> e. The Due Amount will therefore be calculated by the following formula:
> DA = (((EBITDA x 5.0) – IBD) / SO) x SP

Now assume the following as of the Determination Date:

- EBITDA, as calculated by the corporation's outside accountant is $10.0 million for the trailing twelve months ending closest to the Determination Date.

- Interest-bearing debt (IBD) totals $5.0 million as of the month-end prior to the Determination Date.

- Shares Outstanding, or SO, as of the Determination Date are 1,000,000 shares.

- The Shares to be Purchased, or SP, equals 10% of the Shares Outstanding, or 100,000 shares.

The corporation's outside accountant calculates the Due Amount as follows:

$$DA = ((($10,000,000 \times 5.0) - $5,000,000) / 1,000,000) \times 100,000$$

$$= (($50,000,000 - $5,000,000) / 1,000,000) \times 100,000$$

$$= $45 \text{ per share} \times 100,000 \text{ shares}$$

$$= $4,500,000$$

Chapter 44: Buy-Sell Agreements: An Overview

While the algebra may seem frightening to the math-impaired, it is actually fairly straightforward. Therein lies the attractiveness of formula buy-sell agreements. They are conceptually easy to understand and, supposedly, not difficult to implement.

Should the Selling Shareholder be happy with the resulting calculation? Let's dig a bit further. What if we learned that EBITDA, but for a one-time charge to write down stale inventory, would have been $12 million rather than $10 million? If an adjustment were made for this nonrecurring item, which would be fairly routine in most appraisals, the resulting value would have been $5.5 million.

What if the corporation had $5 million of excess cash on its balance sheet (with earnings of $10 million)? The Due Amount would have been $5 million.

Under these circumstances, the Selling Shareholder would likely be quite upset if he were offered only $4.5 million for his shares. However, given the language of the agreement, he might have no right to his pro rata share of excess assets accumulated (i.e., not distributed) during his tenure as a shareholder.

Situations like the above, where the application of formula pricing yields a conclusion obviously different from actual economic value will create the potential for litigation, unhappiness, anger, loss of friendships, and many other unfavorable results.

Conclusion Regarding Formula Agreements

Needless to say, we do not recommend the use of formulas in corporate buy-sell agreements.

Action Steps
a. Having noted the supposed ease of the formula calculations, formulas written by attorneys are seldom so clearly presented in the context of buy-sell agreements. There seems to be a tendency to put formulas (like the example above) in ponderous paragraphs and to omit the algebraic presentation of the actual formulas.
b. It is a good idea to be sure you know how your formula works and that the parties affected by the formula agree to how it is used.
c. It is an even better idea to calculate the formula value periodically so you will know what the buy-sell price would be if a trigger event occurred.
d. The changes you see in the price over time may cause you to reevaluate the use of the formula in your buy-sell agreement.

Chapter 44: Buy-Sell Agreements: An Overview

Process Buy-Sell Agreements

Process buy-sell agreements, or agreements where a *valuation process* is used to establish value, share certain commonalities. Process agreements:

- **Require agreement** *at a point in time* between shareholders of a corporation and/or the corporation. With a process agreement, the shareholders and the corporation reach agreement about the process that will determine the price (valuation) for future transactions, rather than stating a particular price or formula.

- **Relate to transactions** that may or will occur *at future points in time* between the shareholders, or between the shareholders and the corporation.

- **Define the conditions** that will cause the buy-sell provisions to be triggered. These are the business conditions that will trigger the operation of the buy-sell agreement and the obligation to purchase shares pursuant to the agreement.

- **Determine the price** (per share or per unit or per member interest) at which the identified future transactions will occur. The process, usually involving one or more appraisers, determines the price for future transactions.

We identify three groups of process agreements:

1. Multiple appraiser agreements

2. Single appraiser process agreements

3. Hybrid agreements[1]

In each process agreement group, we present different variations: four variations of the multiple appraiser process agreement and three variations of the single appraiser agreement. Each variation is discussed in this chapter.

Multiple Appraiser Agreements

Multiple appraiser agreements call for the selection of two or more appraisers to engage in a process that will develop one, two, or three appraisals whose conclusions form the basis for the prices. There are a number of variations that can be employed in multiple appraiser process agreements. We focus on three here and use non-technical, descriptive terms to differentiate between various types of processes.

Chapter 44: Buy-Sell Agreements: An Overview

Two and a Tie-Breaker

Two appraisers are retained initially to provide appraisals, and a third appraiser is selected if needed to resolve disparate valuation conclusions.

- The buying party typically retains one appraiser and the selling party another appraiser.

- Both appraisers then provide valuation opinions according to the time schedule specified in the agreement or agreed to by the parties.

- If the conclusions are within some percentage range (10% or 15%, or you pick the percentage) of each other, the buy-sell price is determined by the average of the two conclusions.

- If the conclusions are more than the selected percentage apart, the two appraisers are generally required to select a third appraiser who also provides a valuation conclusion.

- Typically, this third conclusion is averaged with the nearest of the first two, and that average becomes the price.

- Occasionally, if all three appraisal conclusions are sufficiently close together (you pick the percentage), the price for the agreement is the average of all three conclusions.

- Sometimes, the lower of the first two appraisals becomes a lower bound with the higher becoming the upper bound, regardless of the third appraiser's conclusion. For example, if the third appraiser's conclusion exceeded the upper bound, the higher of the first two appraisals would become the value.

Two and a Determiner

Two appraisers are hired initially, and their sole function is to mutually select a third appraiser who provides the sole and determinative appraisal.

- With this variation, the buying party retains one appraiser and the selling party another. These appraisers do not provide valuation opinions.

- Rather, they select a mutually agreeable third independent appraiser.

- The third appraiser provides the sole valuation opinion which determines the price. This process foreshadows the single appraiser processes discussed further on in this chapter.

Chapter 44: Buy-Sell Agreements: An Overview

Figure 5

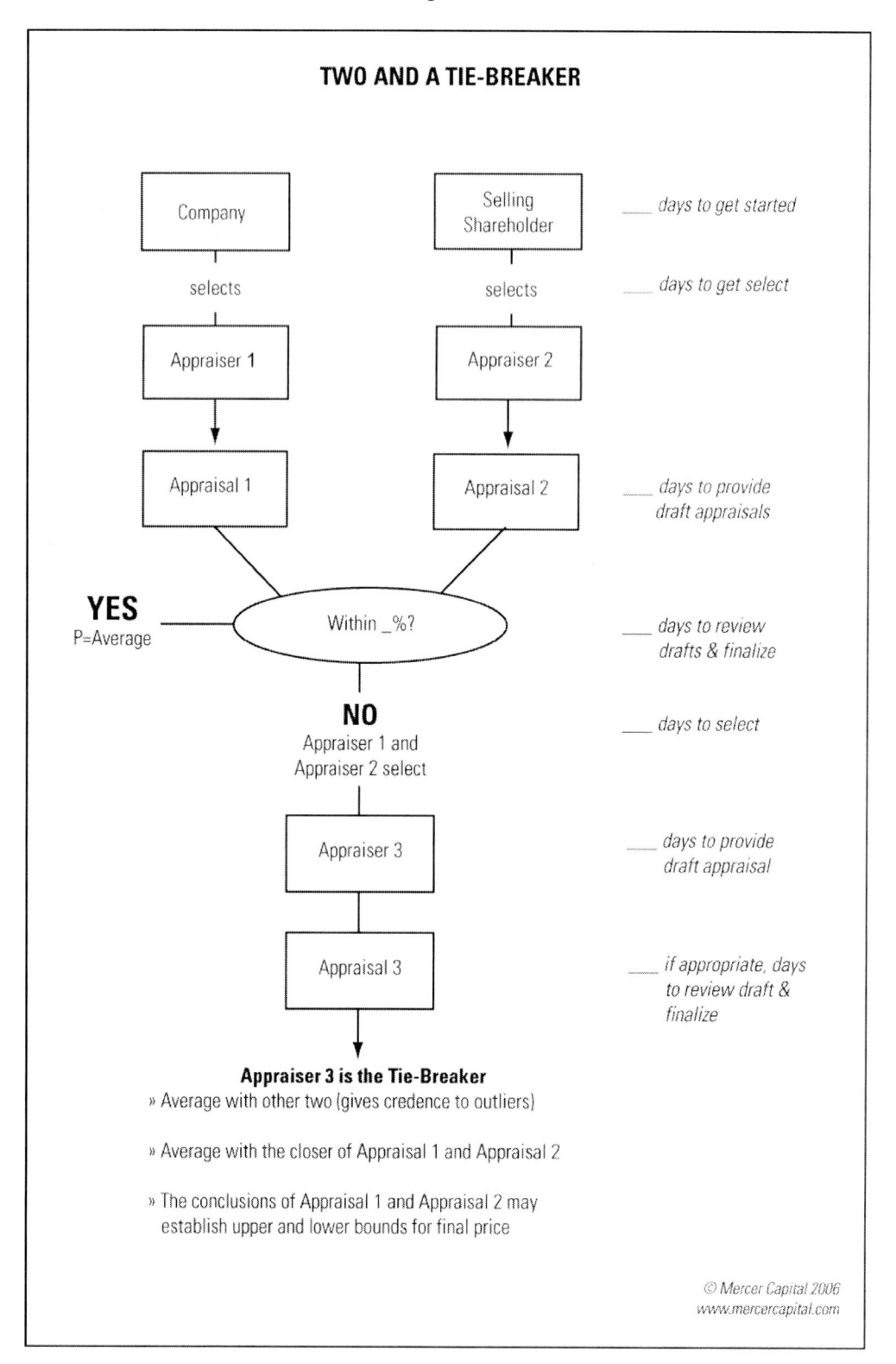

TWO AND A TIE-BREAKER

```
    ┌──────────┐              ┌──────────────┐
    │ Company  │              │   Selling    │       ____ days to get started
    └──────────┘              │ Shareholder  │
                              └──────────────┘
       selects                    selects            ____ days to get select
          │                          │
          ▼                          ▼
    ┌──────────┐              ┌──────────┐
    │Appraiser1│              │Appraiser2│
    └──────────┘              └──────────┘
          │                          │
          ▼                          ▼
    ┌──────────┐              ┌──────────┐
    │Appraisal1│              │Appraisal2│          ____ days to provide
    └──────────┘              └──────────┘               draft appraisals
           \                    /
            \                  /
   YES       ╲────────────────╱
 P=Average──(   Within __%?   )                     ____ days to review
             ╲────────────────╱                          drafts & finalize
                     │
                    NO                              ____ days to select
            Appraiser 1 and
            Appraiser 2 select
                     │
                     ▼
              ┌──────────┐
              │Appraiser3│                          ____ days to provide
              └──────────┘                               draft appraisal
                     │
                     ▼
              ┌──────────┐                          ____ if appropriate, days
              │Appraisal3│                               to review draft &
              └──────────┘                               finalize
                     │
                     ▼
```

Appraiser 3 is the Tie-Breaker

» Average with other two (gives credence to outliers)

» Average with the closer of Appraisal 1 and Appraisal 2

» The conclusions of Appraisal 1 and Appraisal 2 may establish upper and lower bounds for final price

© Mercer Capital 2006
www.mercercapital.com

Chapter 44: Buy-Sell Agreements: An Overview

Figure 6

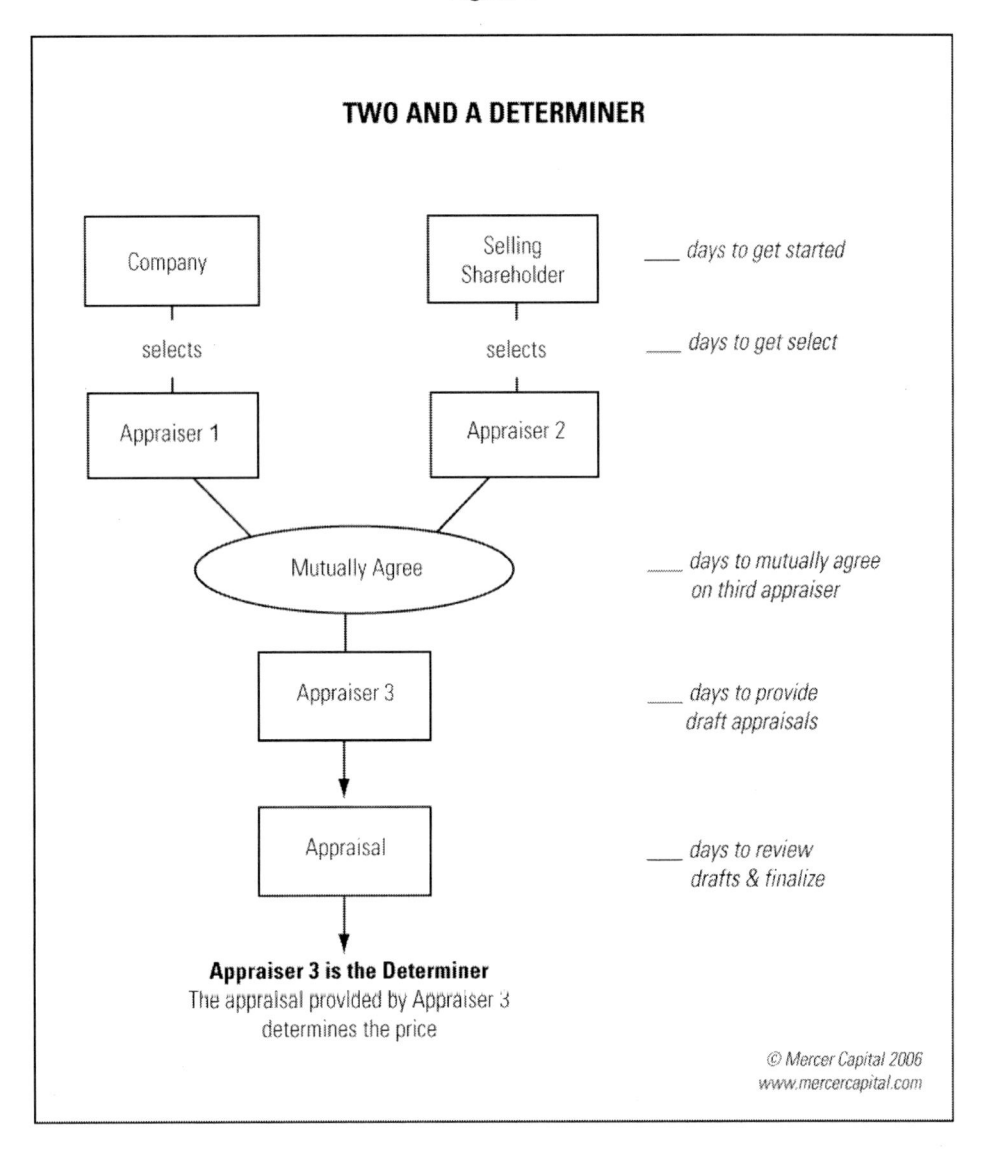

TWO AND A DETERMINER

- Company selects Appraiser 1
- Selling Shareholder selects Appraiser 2
- Appraiser 1 and Appraiser 2 Mutually Agree on Appraiser 3
- Appraiser 3 provides Appraisal

___ days to get started

___ days to get select

___ days to mutually agree on third appraiser

___ days to provide draft appraisals

___ days to review drafts & finalize

Appraiser 3 is the Determiner
The appraisal provided by Appraiser 3 determines the price

© Mercer Capital 2006
www.mercercapital.com

Chapter 44: Buy-Sell Agreements: An Overview

Figure 7

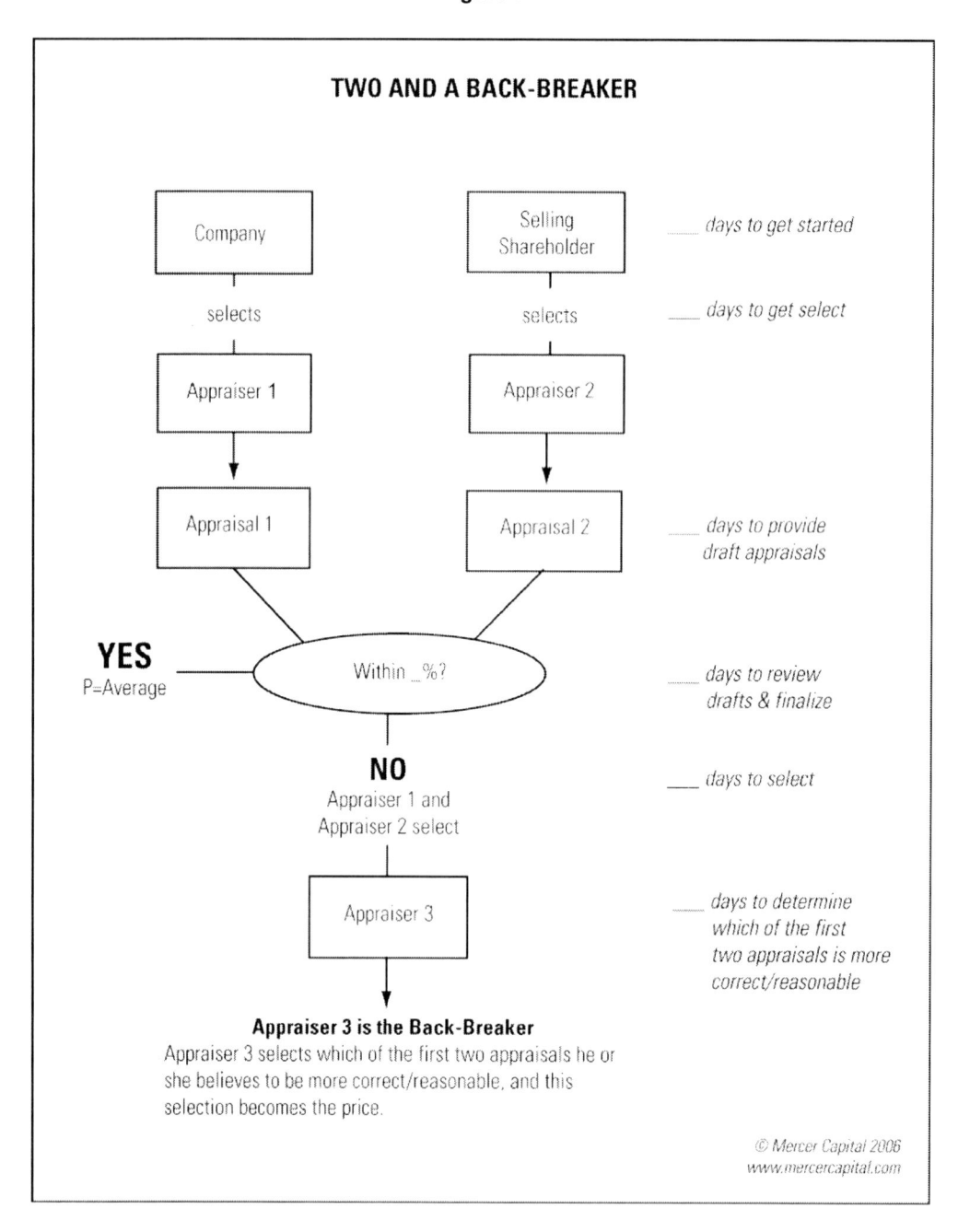

TWO AND A BACK-BREAKER

Company selects Appraiser 1 → Appraisal 1
Selling Shareholder selects Appraiser 2 → Appraisal 2

Within __%?

YES P=Average

NO Appraiser 1 and Appraiser 2 select Appraiser 3

Appraiser 3 is the Back-Breaker
Appraiser 3 selects which of the first two appraisals he or she believes to be more correct/reasonable, and this selection becomes the price.

_____ days to get started
_____ days to get select
_____ days to provide draft appraisals
_____ days to review drafts & finalize
_____ days to select
_____ days to determine which of the first two appraisals is more correct/reasonable

© Mercer Capital 2006
www.mercercapital.com

Chapter 44: Buy-Sell Agreements: An Overview

Two and a Back-Breaker

Two appraisers are selected to provide appraisals, and the third appraiser picks the "better" appraisal.

- The buying party retains one appraiser and the selling party selects another. Both provide valuation conclusions.

- If the appraisal conclusions are within a pre-determined percentage of each other, the price per the agreement is determined by the average of the two.

- If the conclusions are sufficiently apart, the two original appraisers must then select a third independent appraiser.

- The third appraiser must then select which of the first two appraisals he or she believes to be the more correct or reasonable valuation, and this selection becomes the price per the buy-sell agreement.

Multiple Appraiser Agreements Examined

The interests of shareholders (or former shareholders) and corporations (and remaining shareholders) often diverge when buy-sell agreements are triggered.

In the real world, motivations, whether actual or perceived, are embedded in many process agreements. These motivations are clear for buyers and sellers whose interests are obviously different. The motivations for the appraisers are less clear. Appraisers are supposed to be independent of the parties. Nevertheless, based on our experience, it is rare for the appraiser retained to represent a seller to reach a valuation conclusion that is lower than that reached by the appraiser for the buyer. This does not at all imply that both appraisers are biased. Consider the following possibilities:

- Valuation reflects both art and science and is the result of the exercise of judgment. It seems that many buy-sell agreements call for two appraisal conclusions to be within 10% of each other for the two to be averaged. Given the potential for differences in judgments, a range of 10% may be too small.[2] In other words, the process may create the appearance of bias by creating the expectation that two appraisers will reach conclusions so close to each other.[3]

- The buy-sell agreement may be unclear as to the engagement definition. In such cases, two independent appraisers who interpret the agreement differently from a valuation perspective may reach conclusions that are widely disparate.

Legal counsel for each side desires to protect the interests of their clients. As such, in the context of buy-sell agreements, the thinking may occur as follows:

> If my client is the seller, we need to be able to select 'our' appraiser, because the company will select its appraiser. Since I am concerned that the company will try to influence its appraiser on the downside, I want to be able to try to influence our appraiser on the upside. Since we are selling and they are buying, this is only natural.

For purposes of this discussion, if the two appraisals are not sufficiently close together, they can be viewed as advocating the positions of the seller and buyer, respectively. All the parties and their legal counsel may begin to think:

> What is needed now is a 'truly' independent appraiser to finalize the process.

Many process agreements call for the two appraisers to select a third appraiser who is mutually acceptable to them because:

> Surely, 'our' appraiser and 'their' appraiser, working together, can select a truly independent appraiser to break the log jam since neither side has been successful in influencing the outcome of the process. But, now that we have a third appraiser, what should his or her role be?

The role of the third appraiser will be determined by the agreement reached by the parties. Consider the following:

- Chances are, it is not a good idea for the third appraiser's conclusion to be averaged with the other two since the first two conclusions create a broader specified range than the range giving rise to the third appraisal. Averaging could provide too much influence to an outlier conclusion.

- Often, the third appraiser's conclusion will be averaged with that of the conclusion closest to his own. Since the first two appraisers often know this on the front end, they should be motivated to provide independent conclusions, since no one desires to have the outlier (ignored) conclusion.

- On the other hand, wouldn't the process be more independent if the third appraiser had to select, in his opinion, the more reasonable of the first two conclusions? Surely, that would tend to influence the first two appraisers to reach more similar conclusions. It would be embarrassing to have provided the conclusion that was not accepted.

- Still further, the first two appraisers would be under pressure if the third appraiser were to provide the defining conclusion. As discussed previously, some processes provide for the selection of the first two appraisers whose sole function is to mutually agree on the third appraiser, whose conclusion will be binding. Then all the pressure falls on the third appraiser.

We speak here from personal experience. Professionals at Mercer Capital have been the first, second, and third appraisers in numerous buy-sell agreement processes. Clients sometimes do attempt to influence the appraisers, either in blatant or subtle fashion. This is to be expected

Chapter 44: Buy-Sell Agreements: An Overview

and is not nefarious. Clients are naturally influenced by their desire for a conclusion favorable to them.[4] The purpose of process buy-sell agreements, however, regardless of their limitations, is to reach *reasonable* conclusions.

Advantages of Multiple Appraiser Agreements

Multiple appraiser buy-sell agreements have advantages.

- They provide a defined structure or process for determining the price at which future transactions will occur.

- All parties to the agreements know, at least generally, what the process will entail.

- Multiple appraiser agreements are fairly common and generally understood by attorneys. Many believe that process agreements are better than fixed price or formula agreements, particularly for substantial companies.

- Parties to such agreements may think that they are protected by the process since they will get to select "their" appraiser. This is an illusory benefit.

Disadvantages of Multiple Appraiser Agreements

There are several disadvantages to multiple appraiser buy-sell agreements:

- *The price is not determined now.* The actual value, or price, is left to be addressed at a future time, i.e., upon the occurrence of a trigger event. No one knows, until the end of an appraisal process, what the outcome will be.

- *There is potential for dissatisfaction with the process, the result, or both, for all parties.* Multiple appraiser process agreements are designed with the best of intentions, but as we have seen, they have a number of potential flaws. At best, they are time-consuming and expensive. At worst, they are fraught with potential for discord, disruption, and devastating emotional issues for one or all parties.

- *There is danger of advocacy with multiple appraiser agreements.* Even if there is no advocacy on the part of the appraisers, the *presumption of advocacy* may taint the process from the viewpoint of one or more participants.

- *There is considerable uncertainty regarding the process.* All parties to a multiple appraiser agreement experience uncertainty about how the process will work, even if they have seen another such process in the past. In our experience, the process, as it actually operates, is different in virtually every case, even with similar agreements. This is true because the parties, including the seller, company management and its directorate, and the appraisers are all different.

Chapter 44: Buy-Sell Agreements: An Overview

- *There is considerable uncertainty as to the final price.* The price is not determined until the end of the process. As a result, there is great and ongoing uncertainty regarding the price at which such future transactions will occur. First, before a trigger event occurs, no one has any idea what the price would be in the event that one did occur. Second, following a trigger event, there can be great uncertainty regarding the ultimate price for many, many months.

- *Process problems are not identified until the process is invoked.* We noted below that five defining elements are necessary to determine the price (value) at which shares are purchased pursuant to process agreements. Problems with agreements, such as a failure to identify the standard of value or the level of value, or the failure to define the qualifications of appraisers eligible to provide opinions or the appraisal standards they are to follow, are deferred until the occurrence of a trigger event. At this time, the interests of the parties are financially adverse and problems tend to be magnified. Based on our experience, the failure of multiple appraiser agreements to "pre-test" the process can be the most significant disadvantage on this list.

- *Multiple appraiser agreements can be expensive.* The cost of appraisals prepared in contentious, potentially litigious situations tends to be considerably higher than for appraisals conducted in the normal course of business.

- *Multiple appraiser agreements are time-consuming.* The typical appraisal process takes at least 60 to 90 days after appraisers are retained. The search for qualified appraisers can itself take considerable time. If a third appraiser is required, there will be additional time for his or her selection as well as for the preparation of the third appraisal. It is not unusual for multiple appraiser processes to drag on for six months to a year or more – perhaps much more.

- *Multiple appraiser agreements are distracting for management.* The appraisal process for a private company is intrusive. Appraisers require that substantial information be developed. They also visit with management, both in person and on the telephone, as part of the appraisal procedures. We worked with the CEO of a sizeable private company to determine the price for the purchase of a 50% interest of his family business. The selling shareholder hired another, very qualified business appraiser and we both provided appraisals, with the intention of negotiating a settlement rather than invoking the burdensome, formal procedures of the buy-sell agreement. Our appraisals were about 10% apart and the parties agreed to average them. During the nearly three months that this "less burdensome" process was underway, the CEO (and his CFO and his COO) could scarcely think about anything else.

- *Multiple appraiser agreements are potentially devastating for shareholders.* If the seller is the estate of a former shareholder, there is not only uncertainty regarding the value of the stock, but family members are involved in a valuation dispute (yes, that's pretty much what it is) with the friends and associates of their deceased loved one. Combine these issues with the fact that some agreements require that selling shareholders pay for their share (side) of the appraisal process and there is even more cause for distress.[5]

We summarize the disadvantages of multiple appraiser process agreements in Figure 8 for comparison with other options as the discussion progresses.

Figure 8

Disadvantages	Multiple Appraisers
1. Price not determined now	x
2. Potential for dissatisfaction with the process for all parties	x
3. Danger of advocacy	x
4. Uncertainty over what will happen when a trigger event occurs	x
5. Uncertainty over final price if the process is invoked	x
6. Problems or issues with definition of value, qualifications of appraisers, or any other aspects of the operation of the agreements are deferred until a trigger event – when the interests of the parties are adverse	x
7. Expensive	x
8. Time-consuming	x
9. Distracting for management	x
10. Potentially devastating for affected shareholders and their families	x

Further Observations

Based on our experience, multiple appraiser process agreements seem to be the norm for substantial private companies and in joint venture agreements among corporate venture partners. The standard forms or templates found for process agreements at many law firms include variations of multiple appraiser processes similar to those described previously.

As business appraisers, we participate in multiple appraiser buy-sell agreement processes with some frequency. Because of the reputation of our senior professionals and our firm, we are called into valuation processes around the country. Speaking personally, I have been the appraiser working on behalf of selling shareholders and companies, and I have been the third appraiser selected by the other two on other occasions. As the third appraiser, I have been required to provide opinions where the process called for the averaging of my conclusion with the other two as well as averaging with the conclusion nearest mine. I have also been asked to pick the better appraisal, in my opinion, given the definition of value in agreements. I have also been the third appraiser who provided the only appraisal. Others at Mercer Capital have also performed similar roles.

Chapter 44: Buy-Sell Agreements: An Overview

This experience is mentioned to emphasize that the disadvantages of multiple appraiser appraisal processes outlined here are quite real. We have seen or experienced first hand every disadvantage in the list above. We hope to provide alternatives with more advantages and fewer disadvantages based on our collective experience at Mercer Capital

Single Appraiser Agreements

Single appraiser agreements call for the selection of one appraiser who provides an appraisal for purposes of the agreement—the conclusion of which becomes the price. We use descriptive terms to differentiate between potential processes.

Select and Value at Trigger Event

The *Select and Value at Trigger Event* agreement calls for a single appraiser to be selected by the parties at the time of a trigger event. The selected appraiser then provides the valuation based on his interpretation of the language in the buy-sell agreement. The single appraiser's valuation conclusion then sets the price for purposes of the buy-sell agreement.

Figure 9
SELECT AND VALUE AT TRIGGER EVENT

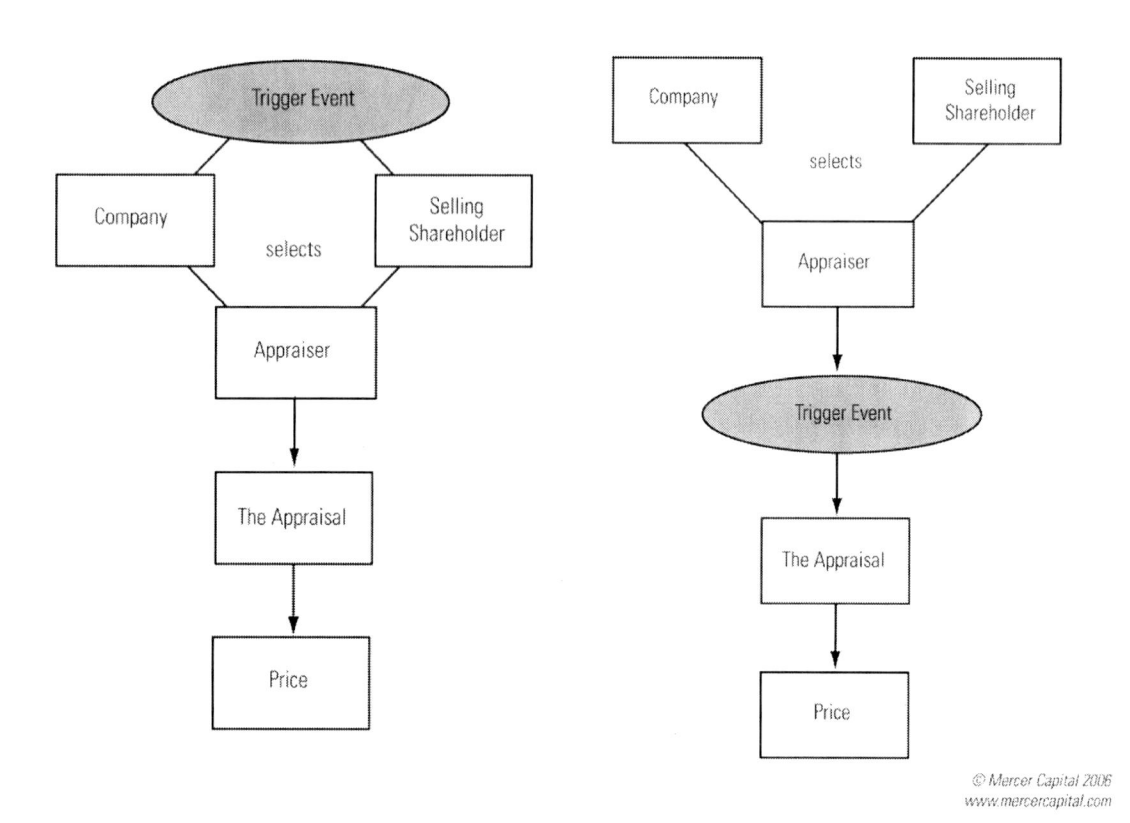

Figure 10
SELECT NOW AND VALUE AT TRIGGER EVENT

© Mercer Capital 2006
www.mercercapital.com

Chapter 44: Buy-Sell Agreements: An Overview

Select Now and Value at Trigger Event

The *Select Now and Value at Trigger Event* form of agreement eliminates the future uncertainty of selecting an appraiser, which is an improvement over *Select and Value at Trigger Event* agreements.

At the time the agreement is created (or an older agreement is revised), the parties discuss potential appraisers (appraisal firms), perhaps interview one or more firms, and select a mutually agreeable appraiser/firm. This appraiser provides the valuation called for at the time of a trigger event.

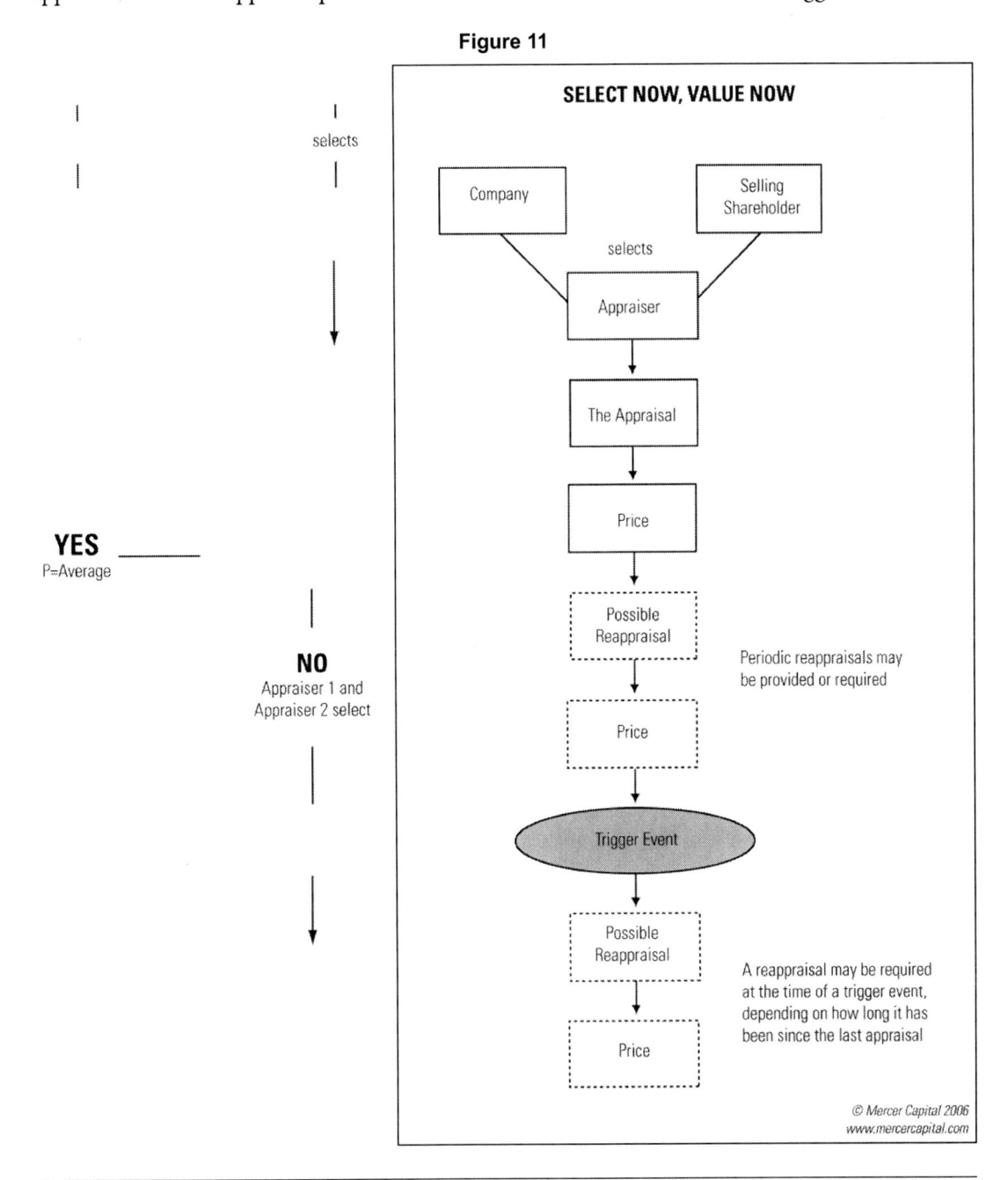

Figure 11

SELECT NOW, VALUE NOW

Company and Selling Shareholder select Appraiser → The Appraisal → Price → Possible Reappraisal (Periodic reappraisals may be provided or required) → Price → Trigger Event → Possible Reappraisal (A reappraisal may be required at the time of a trigger event, depending on how long it has been since the last appraisal) → Price

YES — P=Average

NO — Appraiser 1 and Appraiser 2 select

© Mercer Capital 2006
www.mercercapital.com

Chapter 44: Buy-Sell Agreements: An Overview

Select Now, Value Now

With the *Select Now, Value Now* process, the valuation process is invoked at the time the buy-sell agreement is signed. A baseline price is established and all parties are aware of the price and the process. The appraiser may provide periodic reappraisals. An additional appraisal may be required at the time of a trigger event, depending upon how long it has been since the last appraisal.

Single Appraiser Agreements Examined

As the readers can see, single appraiser agreements come in two general forms. The first calls for the appraiser to be mutually selected by the parties at the time of a trigger event. The second form calls for selection of the appraiser in advance of any trigger event, perhaps at the inception of the agreement. We examine the relative advantages and disadvantages of each form and relate them to multiple process agreements.

Single Appraiser – Select and Value at Trigger Event

In *Single Appraiser – Select and Value at Trigger Event* agreements, the selection of the single appraiser is called for at the time of a trigger event. The selected appraiser then provides the valuation based on his interpretation of the language in the buy-sell agreement. The single appraiser's valuation conclusion then sets the price for purposes of the buy-sell agreement.

The advantages of a single appraiser process are similar to those of the multiple appraiser processes previously outlined.

- It provides a defined structure or process for determining the price at which future transactions will occur.

- All parties to the agreement know in advance, at least generally, what the process will be.

- The cost of the process, if not known precisely in advance, is reasonably definable.

- The general process is fairly commonly known and understood by attorneys. The single appraiser process is simpler than multiple appraiser processes since only one appraiser must be selected.

- Parties to single appraiser agreements should believe they are protected by the process since they will have a voice in the selection of the appraiser. All sides have a role to ensure that an independent appraiser is selected, i.e., one who will provide a balanced analysis and a "fair" valuation, taking into account the interests of both sides during the appraisal process.[6]

There are, however, disadvantages specifically to the *Single Appraiser – Select and Value at Trigger Event* process as shown in Figure 12.

Chapter 44: Buy-Sell Agreements: An Overview

Figure 12

Disadvantages	Multiple Appraisers	Single Appraiser – Select & Value at Trigger Event
1. Price not determined now	x	x
2. Potential for dissatisfaction with the process for all parties	x	x
3. Danger of advocacy	x	x
4. Uncertainty over what will happen when a trigger event occurs	x	x
5. Uncertainty over final price if the process is invoked	x	x
6. Problems or issues with definition of value, qualifications of appraisers, or any other aspects of the operation of the agreements are deferred until a trigger event – when the interests of the parties are adverse	x	x
7. Expensive	x	
8. Time-consuming	x	
9. Distracting for management	x	
10. Potentially devastating for affected shareholders and their families	x	

1. *The price is not determined now.* The actual value, or price, is left to be determined upon the occurrence of a trigger event.

2. *There is potential for dissatisfaction with the ultimate result for all parties.* If one has no idea what the price for a transaction will be before it is determined by someone else, chances are that the appraiser's price will be exactly what one thought it should be only by chance. Hopefully, with a qualified, independent appraiser, both parties will be satisfied and consider that the process and the price are mutually fair.

3. *There can be danger of the perception of advocacy with single appraiser agreements.* The selected appraiser can be viewed by one side as more friendly to the other. Selling shareholders are more likely to have this perception because the appraiser is normally formally retained and paid by the corporation, and it can be thought that the selected appraiser would tend to favor the corporation in hopes of developing future business.

4. *There is some uncertainty regarding the process.* Generally, none of the parties to a single appraiser (select later) process have done business with the appraiser who is ultimately selected. As a result, none of the parties may be familiar with the appraiser and his or her work product.

5. *There is considerable uncertainty as to the final price.* Because there was no initial appraisal, there is great and ongoing uncertainty regarding the price at which future transactions will occur. First, prior to a trigger event, no one has any idea what the price would be in the event that one did occur. Second, following a trigger event, there is great uncertainty regarding the ultimate price for the duration of the single appraiser's engagement.

6. *Process problems are not identified until the process is invoked.* Once again, we cannot overemphasize the importance of this disadvantage. As with multiple appraiser

agreements, problems such as a failure to properly define the engagement, failure to define the qualifications of appraisers eligible to provide opinions, or the appraisal standards they are to follow, are deferred until the occurrence of a trigger event. Given the nature of the process, the appraiser who identifies problems with the definition of value, for example, may have to make a decision that is viewed by one or both parties as adverse to their respective interests.

On balance, the *Single Appraiser – Select and Value at Trigger Event* process eliminates a number of the disadvantages of multiple appraiser agreements, but still leaves room for perceptions of bias and has considerable uncertainty for both parties.

Single Appraiser – Select Now and Value at Trigger Event

The second single appraiser process is the *Single Appraiser – Select Now and Value at Trigger Event*. The appraiser is named in the agreement and will be called upon to provide the required appraisals at the time of future trigger events. At the time the agreement is created (or an older agreement is revised), the parties discuss potential appraisers (appraisal firms), perhaps interview one or more firms, and select a mutually agreeable appraiser/firm.

The *Single Appraiser – Select Now and Value at Trigger Event* form of agreement eliminates the future uncertainty of selecting an appraiser, which is an improvement over *Single Appraiser – Select and Value at Trigger Event* agreements, but the other uncertainties and disadvantages remain. However, concerns over the degree of perceived appraiser advocacy should be minimized since the parties have time to agree on the selected appraiser absent the pressure of a trigger event.

Single Appraiser – Select Now, Value Now

The third single appraiser process is *Single Appraiser – Select Now, Value Now*. The appraiser is not only named in the agreement, but he or she is engaged to provide an initial appraisal for purposes of the agreement. We at Mercer Capital have long recommended that parties creating buy-sell agreements with a named appraiser have the appraiser perform a baseline appraisal pursuant to the terms of the agreement. This option provides several distinct advantages relative to other process agreements, including:

- The structure and process, in addition to being defined in the agreement, will be known to all parties to the agreement in advance.

- The selected appraiser will be viewed as independent with respect to the process; otherwise, he or she would not have been named. At the very least, the suspicion of bias is minimized.

- The appraiser's valuation approaches and methodologies are seen first hand by the parties.

Chapter 44: Buy-Sell Agreements: An Overview

- The appraiser's valuation conclusion is known at the outset of the agreement by all parties and becomes the agreement's price until the next appraisal, or until a trigger event between recurring appraisals occurs.

- The process is observed at the outset; therefore, all parties know what will happen when a trigger event occurs.

- The appraiser must interpret the valuation terms of the agreement in conducting the initial appraisal. Any lack of clarity in the valuation-defining terms will be fleshed out and can be corrected to the parties' mutual satisfaction.

- Having provided an initial valuation opinion, the appraiser must maintain independence with respect to the process and render future valuations consistent with the instructions in the agreement.

- Because the appraisal process is exercised at least once, or on a recurring basis, it should go smoothly when employed at trigger events and be less time-consuming and less expensive than other alternatives.

One further element can improve the *Single Appraiser – Selection Now, Value Now* option even more – regular reappraisals. In our opinion, larger companies should have an annual revaluation for their agreements. By larger, we mean those for which the cost of the appraisal process is insignificant relative to the certainty provided by maintaining the pricing provisions on a current basis. Smaller companies should have reappraisals every two years, or at least, every three years.[7]

Additional benefits from annual or periodic reappraisal for buy-sell agreements include:

- *Confidence in the process.* The selected appraisal firm should provide valuations that are consistent with prior opinions, taking into account relevant changes in the company, the industry, the economy, and other relevant factors. Subsequent appraisals should be reconciled with prior appraisals so that all parties understand why value has changed.

- *Current value per the buy-sell agreement is known.* This can be beneficial for a company's planning purposes, for example, facilitating the maintenance of adequate life insurance on the appropriate shareholders. The periodic appraisal will also be helpful for the planning purposes of shareholders.

- *Knowledge* grows. Importantly, because the appraisals are recurring in nature, the appraisal firm's knowledge of a company's business and industry will grow over time, which should further enhance the confidence all parties have in the process and conclusion of value.

In all cases, if the most current appraisal is more than ___ months (you pick) old, then the agreements should provide for a reappraisal upon the occurrence of a trigger event.

Chapter 44: Buy-Sell Agreements: An Overview

Let's examine the remaining disadvantages (#2 to #6 in Figure 6) and see how the *Single Appraiser – Select Now, Value Now* process addresses these remaining disadvantages. Recall that disadvantage #1 regarding establishing the price is currently resolved by this process.

Figure 13

Disadvantages	Multiple Appraisers	Single Appraiser – Select & Value at Trigger Event	Single Appraiser – Select Now & Value at Trigger Event	Single Appraiser – Select Now, Value Now
1. Price not determined now	x	x	x	
2. Potential for dissatisfaction with the process for all parties	x	x	x	Minimized
3. Danger of advocacy	x	x	Minimized	Minimized
4. Uncertainty over what will happen when a trigger event occurs	x	x	x	Minimized
5. Uncertainty over final price if the process is invoked	x	x	x	Minimized
6. Problems or issues with definition of value, qualifications of appraisers, or any other aspects of the operation of the agreements are deferred until a trigger event – when the interests of the parties are adverse	x	x	x	Minimized
7. Expensive	x			
8. Time-consuming	x			
9. Distracting for management	x			
10. Potentially devastating for affected shareholders and their families	x			

1. *There is potential for dissatisfaction with the ultimate result for all parties.* There will always be potential for dissatisfaction. Buyers naturally want lower prices and sellers want higher prices. However, if the process works as it should, all parties are much more likely to believe that the prices created by the buy-sell process are *reasonable.*

2. *There can be danger of the perception of advocacy with single appraiser agreements.* At the outset, it is possible that one or more parties might believe that the selected single appraiser could be biased. Such perceptions would likely be mitigated over time as the appraiser provides subsequent appraisals and as all parties become more comfortable with the process.

3. *There is some uncertainty regarding the process.* With a single appraiser who is selected in advance providing recurring reappraisals, there should be little, if any, uncertainty about the process that will be invoked when trigger events occur. The process is seen on a recurring basis by all parties.

4. *There is considerable uncertainty as to the final price.* Given that there is a baseline appraisal and the potential for reappraisals over time, much of the uncertainty regarding the price at a trigger event should be eliminated. The price should be reasonably consistent with changes in the company's earnings, industry multiples, and other factors familiar to the parties, assuming that the selected appraiser continues to provide appraisals on a consistent basis.

5. *Process problems are not identified until the process is invoked.* Clearly, any issues with the process would be identified and fixed at the outset or along the way. The process should be clear and well-understood.

Chapter 44: Buy-Sell Agreements: An Overview

In summary, the *Single Appraiser – Select Now, Value Now* process eliminates one of the six remaining disadvantages applicable to multiple appraiser and other single appraiser processes. This process also minimizes the adverse impact of the remaining five disadvantages. This form of single appraiser process is, based on my experience over the last thirty years, the most reasonable valuation process for many privately owned businesses.

The Six Defining Valuation Elements of Process Buy-Sell Agreements

If appraisers are to determine price in a valuation process, they need instruction regarding the specific valuation the parties to a buy-sell agreement are seeking. The agreements must define five standard elements, in particular, for the appraiser(s) to provide the requested valuations. A sixth element is so important from a business perspective that it joins the list:

1. Standard of value
2. Level of value
3. The "as of" date
4. Qualifications of appraisers
5. Appraisal standards
6. Funding mechanism

Standard of Value

Will the pricing value be based on "fair market value" or "fair value" or some other standard? These words can have dramatically different interpretations. Some agreements simply specify "the value" of the company or interest.

The *standard of value* defines the value to be considered in an appraisal. In the case of buy-sell agreements, the document(s) must clearly specify the standard of value, and these provisions are normally binding on appraisers who prepare valuations pursuant to these agreements.

Value has many meanings. Like beauty, value may lie in the eye of the beholder. Confirming the confusion surrounding value, legal scholar James C. Bonbright writes:

> As long as common law and state law persist in using the 'value' as a legal jack-of-all-trades, judges are forced, willy-nilly, to reject the precedent of economists and instead to follow the precedent of Humpty Dumpty (from *Through a Looking Glass*): 'When I use a word, it means what I choose it to mean – neither more nor less.'[8]

Chapter 44: Buy-Sell Agreements: An Overview

If the standard of value provision in a buy-sell agreement are not clear, appraisers may be placed in the position of Humpty Dumpty, and have to decide what the written words mean—a decision they may prefer not to make. Or the parties, whose interests have already diverged, will have to agree on a standard of value to provide instructions to the appraiser(s).

Neither situation is ideal.

Level of Value

Interestingly, the term "level of value" is not a defined term in the ASA's *Glossary of the Business Valuation Standards*. So what are the so-called "levels of value," and why are they important in defining the value that appraisers must develop in buy-sell agreements? These are some of the most critical questions facing drafters of buy-sell agreements with built-in valuation processes.

The levels of value suggest a range of values, from the strategic controlling interest level of value of the enterprise as a whole, to the non-marketable minority interest level of value applicable to illiquid, minority interests.

Not surprisingly then, different assumptions regarding the appropriate level of value are, in our experience, the sources of some of the largest variations in valuation opinions by appraisers involved in process buy-sell agreements. These differences almost inevitably arise from absent or ambiguous specifications regarding the applicable level of value in particular agreements.

FIGURE 14

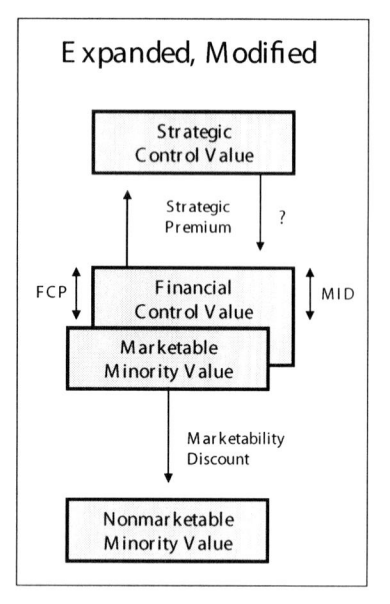

Expanded, Modified

- Strategic Control Value
- Strategic Premium / ?
- FCP / Financial Control Value / MID
- Marketable Minority Value
- Marketability Discount
- Nonmarketable Minority Value

But how can there be any confusion about the appropriate level of value in a buy-sell agreement? Isn't everyone familiar with these valuation concepts? The answer is no. Where there is a lack of understanding about valuation concepts, confusion will reign.

Recall the old expression: "A picture is worth a thousand words." Here's a picture, in words, and then in a picture.

The word picture. A buy-sell agreement is triggered, requiring the company to acquire a shareholder's shares per its terms. Unfortunately, the agreement has vague and confusing language regarding the level of value the parties selected.

The company retains a well-qualified business appraiser, as does the shareholder. Under the terms of the agreement, each is required to provide a valuation, and both do.

Chapter 44: Buy-Sell Agreements: An Overview

- Appraiser 1, for the company, interprets the level of value as the *non-marketable minority* level, citing specific language in the agreement for support. In developing her opinion, she concludes that the marketable minority level of value is $100 per share. She applies a 40% marketability discount, valuing the interest at $60 per share.

- Appraiser 2, for the shareholder, interprets the level of value as the *strategic control* level, citing specific language in the agreement for support. He also concludes that the marketable minority level of value is $100 per share. He applies a 40% control premium to value the interest at $140 per share.

The picture. The conclusions at each level of value appear below. Note that there is exact agreement on value at the marketable minority level. Further, note the dramatic difference in concluded values—$60 per share versus $140 per share.

The parties now have two appraisals. They are similar in many respects, but widely different in their conclusions of value. This illustration raises the immediate questions:

- How could this have happened?

- How will the mandatory third appraiser reconcile the (irreconcilable) differences in concluded values?

- Could this happen to you? Or to your client(s)?

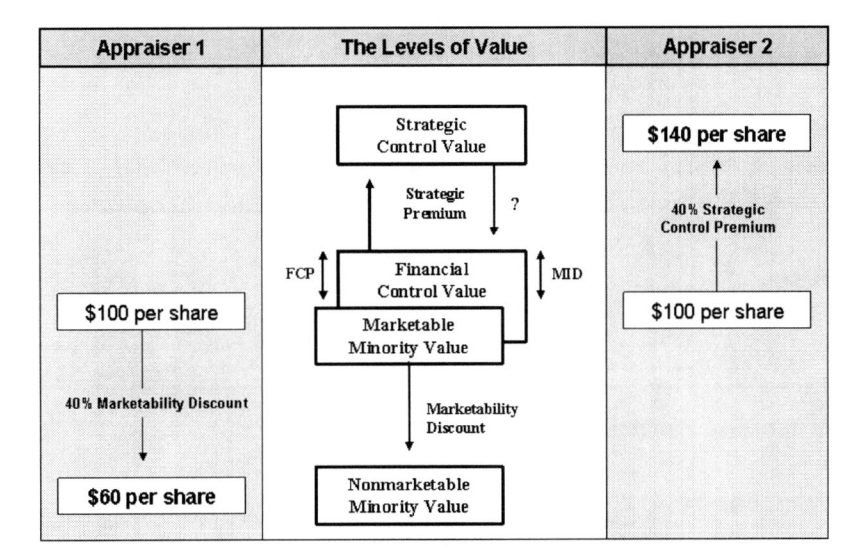

FIGURE 15

Situations like this can and do happen and they are never pretty in their resolution, nor are the parties generally satisfied with the ultimate results.

Chapter 44: Buy-Sell Agreements: An Overview

The 'as of' Date

The effective date of an appraisal is often called the "as of" date. It is the date "as of" which the appraisers should consider the available information pertaining to a buy-sell valuation. The effective date grounds the appraiser not only in the background and financial condition of a subject company, but in its local, regional, or national economy; its industry, in both operational and financial performance; and other relevant aspects.

Qualifications of Appraisers

Buy-sell agreements are often silent regarding the qualifications of appraisers. This is particularly true of agreements signed in the 1980s and 1990s, many of which have not yet been tested by trigger events.

Parties to buy-sell agreements should consider appraiser qualifications when agreeing on an appraisal process. The logical requirements become apparent as parties begin to reflect on individual appraisers and appraisal firms. Danger, in the form of future angst and uncertainty, arises when the parties have failed to conduct this selective review at the outset, or if they fail to specify qualifications in the agreements.

Qualifications of Appraisal Firms. When selecting an appraisal firm, it is desirable that the firm (or, at least, its legitimate successor) will be in business when future trigger events occur. For example, we recently reviewed a buy-sell agreement signed in the early 1980s. The agreement provided a list of fifteen accounting firms from which the parties could select their appraisers. At the time of the trigger event in 2005, only four of the firms still existed. Therefore, the qualifications of appraisal firms should be specified in the context of their size, the scope of their business, and perhaps, on their specific industry expertise.

Qualifications of Appraisers. Appraisal firms do not render appraisal reports—appraisers do. Appraiser qualifications can be examined through resumes, interviews, and professional references. Possible aspects of appraiser qualifications to consider include (in no order):

- Education

- Valuation training

- General appraisal experience

- Industry experience

- The firm employing the appraiser and the nature of its business

- Continuing valuation training

Chapter 44: Buy-Sell Agreements: An Overview

- Professional credentials

- Publications

- Expert testimony experience

Appraisal Standards

Some buy-sell agreements go so far as to name the specific business appraisal standards that any selected appraisers must follow. Professions are defined by the existence of entry-requirements as well as any applicable standards which govern the minimum requirements of the professional's operation and conduct.

The Funding Mechanism

Astute readers will recognize that this sixth, additional element is not actually necessary to define the kind of value that the parties desire in buy-sell agreements, and has nothing to do with appraisal standards or qualifications of appraisers. What the funding mechanism does, however, is insure that the agreed-upon value will first, be affordable to the company; and second, realizable by the selling shareholder or his family or estate. The funding mechanism, then, is an essential business element of buy-sell agreements.

Why Is It So Hard to Talk About These Six Elements?

Buy-sell agreements are important because they represent agreement between a corporation and its shareholders regarding how the future transactions contemplated by the agreements will occur. Remember that at the time most buy-sell agreements are initiated, either the interests of the corporation and the shareholders are aligned, or they are not sufficiently misaligned to prevent agreement from taking place. Perhaps, because of this, despite the best efforts of a corporation's counsel, the shareholders may not, prior to the initiation of a buy-sell agreement, take sufficient time to understand the exact nature of the agreement, how it will work in the future, and the implications for them (whether they will be a buyer or seller in future transactions). Focusing on these six defining elements is a good place to start.

Chapter 44: Buy-Sell Agreements: An Overview

CONCLUSION

This chapter has introduced the topic of buy-sell agreements from valuation and business perspectives. We have discussed fixed price and formula agreements and significant issues related to each of these forms.

In our experience, the largest number of buy-sell agreements using a valuation process employ multiple appraiser processes. We have discussed significant issues that can arise using these processes.

The number of companies using single appraiser buy-sell agreements is rising. For the reasons outlined above, we believe such processes are more appropriate and more likely to yield consistent and reasonable results over time.

Regardless of the form of buy-sell agreement your company—or your client's company—it is critical that you and the other shareholders understand what it is designed to do and how it will work when trigger events occur.

Buy-Sell Agreements: Ticking Time Bombs or Reasonable Resolutions? is available through BV Resources or at www.mercercapital.com. We have a dedicated website providing current information, including a blog on this important topic at www.buysellagreementsonline.com. Finally, Chapter 23 of *Buy-Sell Agreements*, is available in user-friendly 8 ½ x 11" size in PDF format at either of these sites.

1. See Chapter 4 of *Buy-Sell Agreements* for a discussion of hybrid agreements, which consider aspects of both single and multiple appraiser agreements.
2. See "How Close Should Appraisals Be Before Requiring a Third Appraiser?" in Chapter 11 of *Buy-Sell Agreements*.
3. Appraisers try to estimate the kind of value specified in buy-sell agreements. Consider the real world of actual transactions. In a typical auction process for a company, the range from the low bid to the high bid may be 50% to 100% or more, based on the varying interests and motivations of the group of buyers.
4. I have said many times to young appraisers, "Don't be surprised if a client tells you or hints at the appraisal result they desire." In most cases, our clients are parties with particular interests in appraisal outcomes. They cannot help that. What is important in these situations is our response, which must be to provide our independent conclusions of value – ones we can support and defend.
5. See Chapter 15 of *Buy-Sell Agreements* for a discussion of "Who Bears the Costs of the Appraisal Process?".
6. The company (its CEO or CFO) may be the primary driver in the process of selecting the appraiser. It is, therefore, important that the party(ies) subject to the agreement have an active role in the selection process (probably veto power). In other words, both sides must agree or there will almost definitely be a perception of bias.
7. If the buy-sell agreement calls for an enterprise level of value (marketable minority or financial control), the appraiser can provide a supplemental appraisal at the nonmarketable minority level for gift and estate tax purposes. This supplemental appraisal would have to consider the impact of the buy-sell agreement on the value of nonmarketable minority interests.
8. Bonbright, *Valuation of Property* (1937), as quoted in George D. McCarthy and Robert E. Healy, *Valuing a Company: Practices and Procedures* (New York: Ronald Press, 1971), p. 3.

Appendix

Teleconference Transcript: Healthcare Reform and Its Impact on Valuation

June 10, 2010

Presenters:
Mark O. Dietrich, CPA/ABV
Don Barbo, CPA/ABV
C. Elliott Jeter, CFA, CPA/ABV

Contents

Presenter Biographies . . . . page 836

Transcript . . . . page 839

Presentation Slides . . . . page 880

Appendix: Teleconference Transcript

Presenter Biographies

Mark O. Dietrich, CPA, ABV

Mark O. Dietrich, CPA/ABV is a *summa cum laude,* Beta Gamma Sigma graduate of Boston University where he also earned an MBA with high honors; he holds a Master in Taxation degree from Bentley College as well. Mark's web address, www.cpa.net, is the leader in medical practice valuation information. In addition to being Technical Editor and co-Editor of this Business Valuation Resources Guide to Healthcare Valuation, he is a contributor to other BVR publications including the Goodwill Guide and Lost Profits Guide. Mark is author of the Medical Practice Valuation Guidebook, co-author of PPC's Guide to Healthcare Consulting, a contributor to PPC's Guide to Business Valuation and author of more than 100 articles on valuation, taxation, managed care and the healthcare regulatory environment in the Journal of Accountancy, CPA Expert, Business Valuation Review and the ABA's Health Lawyer, among others. He is a member of the Editorial Board of CPA Expert as well as the Expert Panel of Financial Valuation and Litigation Expert, the American Society of Appraisers 2009 Business Valuation Conference Committee, the AICPA Healthcare Expert Panel (2007-2009) and the AICPA National Healthcare Industry Conference Committee (2008-2009). Mark was an AICPA Business Valuation Volunteer of the Year Award winner in 2006.

Mark is a frequent speaker at AICPA National Valuation and Healthcare Industry Conferences and has presented more than 120 self-authored seminars. In addition to a consulting practice that includes physician compensation, healthcare delivery network development and managed care contract negotiation, he has nearly 200 valuation engagements in the healthcare industry and his expertise includes reasonable compensation, healthcare markets, medical practices, imaging and surgery centers, regulatory planning and defense, personal goodwill and non-compete agreements.

Appendix: Teleconference Transcript

G. Don Barbo, CPA/ABV

Don Barbo is the Director of Healthcare Valuation Services for Mid America at Deloitte Financial Advisory Services LLP. Don has extensive experience in healthcare valuation engagements involving mergers and acquisitions, divestitures, partnership transactions, leasing arrangements, divorces, and commercial damages. His healthcare valuation experience includes hospitals, ambulatory surgery centers, imaging centers, cardiac catheter centers, and physician practices. He has also served as the chief financial officer for a physician practice management company.

Don has published numerous articles and is a frequent speaker regarding the valuation of healthcare businesses. He also serves on the Panel of Experts for the Healthcare Section of the Financial Valuation and Litigation Expert's Newsletter.

He holds an undergraduate degree in accounting from Texas Tech University and an MBA from the SMU Cox School of Business. He is also a Certified Public Accountant (CPA), and is Accredited in Business Valuations (CPA/ABV).

Don is actively involved in local community affairs and leadership positions. He is married to Judy Barbo, and they have a ten year old daughter, Lauren, and a seven year old son, Jordan.

Appendix: Teleconference Transcript

C. Elliott Jeter, CFA, CPA/ABV

Elliott Jeter is a Partner of the company. He specializes in providing valuation, transaction advisory, strategic and operational consulting services to the firm's healthcare clients. He has extensive experience working closely with ambulatory surgery centers, hospital systems, physician groups and other healthcare providers.

Prior to joining VMG Health, Mr. Jeter worked as the Director of Development for MedSynergies, Inc., a $50 million Ophthalmic Physician Practice Management Company. Mr. Jeter was responsible for in-market development efforts and oversaw many physician practice acquisitions. In addition to his development duties, Mr. Jeter supervised the centralized billing and collection department for the company on an interim basis.

Mr. Jeter also worked for the financial advisory services group of Ernst and Young. At Ernst and Young, Mr. Jeter worked on a wide range of healthcare clients, including hospital systems, physician practice management companies and other healthcare entities.

Mr. Jeter is a graduate of Texas A&M University and also earned a Masters of Business Administration from the University of Texas at Austin. Mr. Jeter is a Certified Public Accountant (CPA) and a Chartered Financial Analyst (CFA). Mr. Jeter is a frequent speaker at healthcare trade association meetings and has written numerous articles on healthcare valuation issues that have been published in industry magazines and journals. Mr. Jeter was named Who's Who in the Ambulatory Surgery Industry in 2007. Mr. Jeter is a member of the following organizations:

Healthcare Financial Management Association (HFMA)
Federated Ambulatory Surgery Association (FASA)
American Bar Association Health Law Section (ABA)
Association for Investment Management and Research (AIMR)
American Institute of Certified Public Accountants (AICPA)

Appendix: Teleconference Transcript

Transcript

Healthcare Reform and its Impact on Valuation
Business Valuation Resources
June 10, 2010/10:00 a.m. PT

Blake Lyman: Hello and welcome to *Healthcare Reform and its Impact on Valuation*, a BVR webinar featuring Mark Dietrich, Don Barbo and Elliott Jeter. My name is Blake Lyman, Professional Program Manager at BVR.

By now, you should all know that the federal government has passed a healthcare reform bill. Despite its uncertainties and regardless of how you feel about its scope and effect, its effect on the healthcare system in this country is due to have a major impact on valuations in that industry.

Joining us today to discuss these issues are three of the best in healthcare valuation.

Mark Dietrich, CPA/ABV is a leading expert in the field of healthcare valuation. Editor of *BVR's Guide to Healthcare Valuation* and *BVR's Guide to Physician Practice Valuation*, Mark is a contributor to other BVR publications including *Goodwill Guide* and *Lost Profits Guide*. He is also an author of more than 100 articles on valuation, taxation, managed care, and healthcare regulatory environment in the *Journal of Accountancy*, *CPA Expert*, *Business Valuation Review*, and the *ABA's Health Lawyer*, among others.

Elliott Jeter is a Partner at VMG Health where he specializes in providing valuation, transaction advisory, and strategic and operational consulting services to the firm's healthcare clients. He has extensive experience working closely with ambulatory surgery centers, hospital systems, physician groups, and other healthcare providers. Elliott's experience has seen him at such firms as MedSynergies, Inc., a $50 million Ophthalmic Physician Practice Management Company, and the accounting firm, Ernst & Young.

Don Barbo is the Director of health and valuation services for Mid-America at Deloitte Financial Advisory Services, LLP. Don has extensive experience in healthcare valuation engagements involving mergers and acquisitions, divestitures, partnership transactions, leasing arrangements, divorces, and commercial damages. His healthcare valuation experience includes hospitals, ambulatory surgical centers, imaging centers, cardiac catheter centers, and physician practices.

Appendix: Teleconference Transcript

	In the interest of time, I have abridged these three experts' impressive credentials and backgrounds about which you can read much more on our webpage for today's webinar.
	It is my pleasure to welcome them today and I'd also like to thank Accounting Web and Business Brokerage Press for their support today as co-presenters.
	With that, I'll turn it over to Mark Dietrich, Elliott Jeter and Don Barbo.
	Mark?
Mark Dietrich:	Good morning or good afternoon everyone. I welcome you all here today. I think we've got a pretty interesting program.
	In our preparatory conference calls Don and Elliott decided to throw me under the bus and give me credit for all these slides you've seen. I've been teaching several courses on the healthcare reform legislation.
	So the way the presentation is going to go today, I'm going to walk you through some of the background and then we'll pause periodically for the panel to comment on what's going on.
	You see the lead slide here. We have a picture of Elliott and Don. You can decide who is sitting at a table trying to decide what's going to happen in the future and me down on the bottom right here in the corner announcing that the reform legislation has flatlined the healthcare industry.
	Reform Overview – one of the things that I've seen is – and I probably have spent about 60 hours studying this legislation at this point in time – the scale of the changes is pretty traumatic.
	I think we've collectively felt, without at least getting some type of overview of the insurance provisions, the Medicaid changes, and then the Medicare provisions – the latter two of those which would be the traditional areas that you would think would affect those providers – that you really couldn't think through how to approach it from a valuation standpoint.
	We're going to look at some of the insurance provisions, which again, we're going to do it in very general terms because they're quite complex, and if you haven't had experience – some of us

Appendix: Teleconference Transcript

on the panel here have with frontline negotiations with insurance companies – it's fairly difficult to understand precisely what's going on in the insurance market.

More Medicare provisions, we'll be looking at the impact now in hospitals but also in skilled nursing facilities, ambulatory surgery centers, imaging centers, and then physician practices.

There are approximately 40 slides that we hope to get through during the presentation.

Beyond the 40th slide, there's a large quantity of supplemental material much of which comes from some of the other programs that I've prepared on this.

The last slides in that supplemental material also have a number of links to other material for those of you who are interested or find in the course of an engagement after this webinar that you need to do more research about a particular topic area. I believe that most of those links are also up on the BVR website and they're also up on my blog where you can link off my website which is *cpa.net*.

The three of us in preparing the presentation thought it would be best to get kind of a high level overview at the front end of the presentation about what we think reform means for the healthcare industry.

At this point, I'd ask Don and Elliott to comment on these bullet points that we developed.

Elliott Jeter: Hi, this is Elliott. I think from my healthcare valuation professional perspective, healthcare reform is going to be a very good thing. As you know, the healthcare debate dragged on for a very long time. So many of our clients in the healthcare transaction market were really sitting in their hands trying to figure out what was going to go on. Uncertainty, of course, in our business kills transaction activity.

Now our clients are assessing how they came out in the reform bill, whether they're winners or losers, and most of our clients are saying, "Tell me what it is. I can deal with it."

The winners are buying the losers. The hospitals are becoming much more active in buying physician competition around them.

The answer to the question when you get the question, "How does

Appendix: Teleconference Transcript

health reform affect my business?" is, "It depends," and "depends" is always good from a healthcare valuation perspective.

Don Barbo: Right, and this is Don Barbo, and Elliott, I think I agree with your observations in terms of we're seeing quite a bit of activity from our hospitals looking at various transactions and arrangements with medical practices to try to strengthen their relationships and alignment.

I also agree that this presents a wonderful opportunity to us on the healthcare valuation professional services not only because of the increase in activity but because of how we can help guide our clients through this.

Let's face it – we deal with uncertainty when we're doing a valuation whether it's trying to dodge just a health reform bill or if we're looking at what reimbursement is going to do in the future, or even trying to assess demographic trends and economic trends for a particular market area. Uncertainty isn't new to what we do in our appraisal arena.

I think as long as we keep our eyes on the ball when we're valuing a business and we're assessing things like what are the value drivers of this business, what's the impact on profitability and growth, what's the impact on risk, and what is the impact on marketability. That's what we do, that's what we do everyday.

With healthcare reform, the challenge is trying to arm ourselves with the best information we can in light of massiveness of the bill, in light of the fact that there's still a lot of things to be determined about it and there's still, frankly, a lot of uncertainty about it. You've got pilot programs to be rolled out. You've got a lot of rules to be made by the regulators as well as the secretary. That's the challenge that we're going to have.

Bottom line, what do we do as appraisers at the beginning of this presentation?

As Mark kind of walks you through his deck that he's prepared on health reform, look for things that might affect reimbursement for the company that you typically value, look for the things that might have fees that are specific to that industry such as payer. When I say "fees," I'm talking about penalties and taxes that this bill is going to now impose on certain sectors of healthcare.

Appendix: Teleconference Transcript

	It is a lot of information, so with that, Mark, I'm going to bow out and let you keep going.
Mark Dietrich:	All right. On the insurance provisions, you'll see there's a summary here, and again, this is my personal view of what they do. I again have spent quite a bit of time listening to industry commentators, former CMS heads, for example, in Health Affairs webcasts. I've listened to the Kaiser Family Foundation webcasts on it. I think that these views are reasonably well documented.
	"Aimed to preserve and forcibly expand employer-based insurance," so notwithstanding all the commentary, for example, during the run-up to the bill about there being a government plan or some such thing. Really in the end, we ended up with the same employer-based health insurance system.
	That "preserves the position of the health insurers," who, at least in my view, are one of the winners of the reform movement.
	Also to "force consumers to pay more for healthcare," this is something that I think in terms of the outer years of reform, and we have a timeline that I'll show momentarily about some of the provisions.
	A lot of these things don't take place for a long time and, therefore, as Don just indicated, there's a lot of uncertainty. Some of them may be legislatively repealed, and we, as valuation consultants, need to be cautious about how much of this stuff we attempt to quantify, for example, in a discounted cash flow analysis versus how much we account for in terms of increased risk in the discount rate.
	This business to "force consumers to pay more for healthcare" really goes into the outer years where you may recall having heard during the debate about the so called excise tax on Cadillac plans which could cause a fairly monumental decrease in the types of benefits that are provided through health insurance policies and ship the costs onto the consumer under the theory that it would cause the consumer to make better healthcare spending decisions.
	The underwriting rules, again, we'll look at these momentarily. As I said earlier, if you have never dealt frontline with insurance companies, this underwriting stuff may seem like it's coming out of left field.

Appendix: Teleconference Transcript

There are really significant changes in the legislation with respect to underwriting which will affect who pays how much for insurance. It will also affect the collection rate of providers which is a fairly significant issue that we have to consider in a valuation. For those of you who aren't full-time healthcare appraisers like the three of us who work in other industries, this legislation, I think, is very significant in the economy taken as a whole and you should at least have some awareness of it when you look at valuing businesses in any industry because obviously healthcare is one of the single largest costs and it runs about 17 percent of gross domestic product now.

Here's the timeline, and in the interest of space, I squeezed the changes in 2011 and 2010 onto a single slide and you'll see that this year children up to age 26 can be covered under their parents' policies which can be a fairly significant thing for those of you have post-college graduate children who haven't been able to find jobs or haven't been able to find jobs that provide benefits.

There's also a bar now on preventing children with preexisting conditions from being covered by insurance policies and that's effective September 23, 2010 which is six months after enactment.

There are some prohibitions on rescission of insurance contracts. Again, depending upon how much of this you follow in the news, there's been a lot of hoop-de-do about insurers in California, for example, canceling policies of women who develop breast cancer, so there's now a prohibition against that.

There's prohibitions against lifetime benefit caps in health insurance contracts which has been another big issue.

Also, medical loss ratio (MLR) limits are going to come into effect in 2011, and the MLR is the percentage of insurance premium that your insurance company spends on actual healthcare costs.

In 2014, we start to see most of the big changes taking place. This is where we will see the new rating rules which I'll describe briefly on the next slide.

There will now be only a 90-day limit per waiting period once you get insurance. For example, if you become sick, decide to go out and buy health insurance, you only have to wait 90 days until whatever that illness is is covered. There's now some considerable concern from actuarial analysis that that will permit people to opt in

Appendix: Teleconference Transcript

and opt out of insurance based upon sickness if they're willing to gamble 90 days.

Now there will be prohibitions in 2014 against annual benefit caps and health insurance contracts. Whereas the previous slide looked at lifetime limits, this 2014 is now annual limit prohibition.

Then there's some risk equalization which I'll look at in the slide after the next slide.

Now this is an interesting slide. This comes right out of the Centers for Medicare & Medicaid chief actuary's analysis of the legislation, and that's linked up on, I believe, the BVR's site as well as my blog, and on my blog, it's the lead post so you don't have to fish through it. I would say that any of you out there listening who are healthcare industry appraisers, who are a lot of healthcare industry appraisers, to take the time and read this. It's probably 25 or 30 pages. It's a very forthright analysis. The CMS chief actuary is a courier civil service employee. He's not a political employee. I assume he's got no political axe to grind. That individual points out a number of the weaknesses in the bill and the things that are likely not to take place or are likely to create a lot of difficulty in the industry and those are the ones, I think, that he points out that are likely to be repealed or modified at some point in the future.

What this slide shows is that of the people who are supposed to come into the system, approximately 20 million will go into Medicaid, and those – again, most of you are probably familiar with Medicaid which is a partly federal and partly state funded program – are for low income people. This brings 20 million people into Medicaid which we'll discuss in more detail later on.

The other coverage expansion you see on the right-hand side shows the individual market going from 26 million to approximately 42 million. The risk there is I say small premiums will explode.

This legislation is tightly modeled after the Massachusetts reform legislation where I presently sit, and what they did in Massachusetts was to merge the small group in individual markets. The individual market of health insurance is highly risky and that's why it's so expensive because from an actuarial standpoint – I think most of you are probably familiar with a bell curve – if you have a large population, the cost experience, for example, that population is reasonably predictable taken as an entire population.

Appendix: Teleconference Transcript

	Individual, if you look at the bell curve, you may have extremes at the right and left, but the bulk of your experience is going to fall in the center, and that's how an actuary would use it to set insurance premiums.
	If you take a single individual being insured as opposed to a large group, there's obviously an enormous amount of risk there.
	That risk in the Massachusetts legislation got dumped onto the small group market because the large group market generally self-insures and has an ERISA exemption from the states interfering with their self-insurance.
	The federal legislation permits states to merge the individual and small group markets which I suspect most of them will do because you can't make the individual market viable without merging it into something that spreads the risk more.
Elliott Jeter:	I think it's important, Mark, back on that slide that when you're valuing a business, you understand the shift and you understand how the shift from the uninsured to the individual market and to Medicaid affects the business that you're valuing.
	Many of our hospital clients who do have a significant amount of Medicaid are very concerned about taking additional Medicaid and what that would do to their financial performance.
	On the other hand, many of our urgent care clients or surgery center clients or imaging center clients are very excited about increased expansion of individual coverage because they don't take Medicaid for the most part anyway. That means additional patients with insurance.
	It very much depends on the business that you're valuing.
Mark Dietrich:	Okay. Here again, I'm going to kind of go through these briefly, but with the setup that I've made, I think it is important to have some general type of understanding on this.
	Health plan premiums – once these changes are effective which generally again take place in 2014, your insurance premium won't be able to vary by more than 3 to 1 based on age. So in effect, you can't charge a 55-year-old more than three time what you charge a 25-year-old for health insurance.

Appendix: Teleconference Transcript

There also will be permitted variations based upon geographic area.

Interestingly, you can't discriminate any more than by 1.5 to 1 against smokers which I think is a rather interesting provision that went into the legislation which I suspect has something to do with shifting cost for smoking-related illnesses back on to the private sector.

Health insurers again will be prohibited from imposing lifetime limits on coverage and prohibited from rescinding coverage except in cases of fraud.

I mentioned this one – young adults will be allowed to remain on their parents' health insurance up to age 26 which is actually, I think, one of the greater benefits of the legislation.

Waiting periods for coverage are going to be limited to 90 days. I've already discussed that one.

There is a grandfathering provision which, quite frankly, despite having read it numerous times, says what it says. It's not particularly clear to me actually what it means. There are policies that were in effect as of the date of enactment, March 23, 2010, including renewals. Those of you who may have been tax practitioners at some point know that this renewal language kind of has to be defined by regulation. Basically, these plans are grandfathered for many of the changes except that everybody is going to be required to extend dependent coverage to age 26, eliminate annual and lifetime limits on coverage, prohibit rescission of coverage, and eliminate waiting periods for coverage of greater than 90 days.

Those are global changes so that if you have contracts that were written before March 23, 2010, you'll be limited to those changes at least under the present legislation.

This I already introduced you to, the likely merger of the small group and individual markets. Those of you in the audience who are in small firms, which I suspect is many of you, this reform takes hold and the individual market is merged with the small group market, and that's something I encourage you as an employing unit to monitor in your state. I would expect to see your premiums skyrocket.

Appendix: Teleconference Transcript

Just from personal experience, in Massachusetts, my premium went up 64 percent this year. About half of that was due to crossing over an age rating threshold and the other half was due to general cost increases, which again have been exacerbated by this merger with the individual market.

Here's just a simplified example of why small group premiums go up, and this one I basically cooked up. I said if we have 9,510 insureds and 9,000 are standard risk and incur an annual cost of $2,000, that represents $18 million.

We have 500 individuals with preexisting conditions. However, those preexisting conditions aren't covered so that only $2,000 worth of cost is allowed.

Then we have ten individuals who would break through the annual limit in the policy but the annual limit in the policy is limited to $200,000 a year.

In the aggregate, they incur $21 million worth of cost or cost per insured of $2,207.

In a post-reform scenario, those with preexisting conditions are now entitled to be covered to much higher limits, and those with the very expensive illnesses who go up to $500,000 a year on average would have to get their cost covered as well.

You can see these few outliers here in terms of cost being that those with preexisting conditions and those who break through the annual limits cause a 33 percent increase in the cost per insured.

This is precisely what goes on and precisely what happened in Massachusetts.

There's also an individual mandate. You might have heard a lot of talk about this. The bottom line is that the penalties are negligible, and if you read the CMS chief actuary's report, his assessment was those penalties were insufficient to cause people to go out and buy insurance.

By contrast, if you look in the supplemental material and see what the penalties in Massachusetts are for not having insurance, they're much higher, and we have, I think, 97 percent coverage here.

Don Barbo: Mark, let me interject. This is Don. Before you move on to the

Appendix: Teleconference Transcript

Medicaid expansion, let me kind of get my arms around a little bit of what you just went over and perhaps the implications when we're valuing companies.

I think it's a necessary exercise to go through, perhaps the little mind-numbing exercise that we just went through, just again to get our arms around what this means to valuing a business.

For instance, if your payer mix has been predominantly Medicare/Medicaid or if you've been a not-for-profit system with high charity care and bad debt, if health reform is going to increase the number of insureds either through government payers or through small market and private, but if the impact is an increase in insureds, I think that might be helpful.

Also, if there's a phase-in of getting Medicaid rates up to Medicare, which I think you're going to get into a little bit later on in your slides, then one might say, "Well, why I am excited about getting more Medicaid coverage if that's traditionally been about the lowest payer out there?" Well, if the legislation has built in some increases in Medicaid, then perhaps that's not such an onerous deal.

I would also maybe throw out there if physician-owned entities generally have more discretion on patients that they treat at their centers, and if traditionally, charity care type patients are not treated there, then perhaps this might open up another revenue opportunity for physician-owned surgery centers particularly those that specialize in minimally invasive types of procedures that they can do efficiently and treat patients at a lower cost of care than in the hospital market.

Big picture – again, it kind of goes back to what Elliott said earlier, how does this impact your payer mix that your business that you're valuing has traditionally faced? Is it favorable or unfavorable?

That's my two cents on that.

Mark Dietrich: Okay. Elliott, did you want to chime in something?

Elliott Jeter: I think that's right. I would also add there's a static competitive landscape in each local market right now, so in many cases, the healthcare reform bill has changed that landscape. In most cases, the acute care hospital wins that battle.

Over the years, physician entrepreneurs have been taking out a lot

Appendix: Teleconference Transcript

of the profitable service lines from the acute care hospital.

I think the balance of power has changed here, whereas the healthcare reform bill was negative to hospitals on an absolute basis, but on a relative basis, compared to their physician-owned rivals, it really has tipped the scale.

To the extent the reform bill creates an advantageous competitive environment for the hospitals, that's something that should be considered when you're performing a valuation.

Mark Dietrich: Yeah, Elliott, I think that's an excellent point and probably the most well stated analysis of that particular factor that I've heard. I agree with you wholeheartedly. I think the competitive landscape in the near term has shifted to the hospitals for the moment.

All right, Medicaid expansion, now we're going to start looking more at the specifics of what changes affect providers.

If you think back to that graph I showed you earlier that showed about 20 million new Medicaid eligible individuals, more than half of the 33 to 35 million people that you hear about now having insurance are going in to Medicaid.

Traditionally, from the provider standpoint, this is an unprofitable line of business, and many physicians do not even accept Medicaid patients. Hospitals are required to accept Medicaid patients under a variety of legislative things like Emergency Medical Treatment and Active Labor Act (EMTALA).

You have to ask the question – are some revenue for these patients better than none at the margins? At least from my standpoint, I think that was to the extent that the drafters of the legislation managed to line up the provider community or the representative organizations of the provider community like the American Hospital Association to support the legislation. The idea was getting again some money for people who presently they treated for free in the emergency room or elsewhere was better than not getting any money.

Don or Elliott?

Elliott Jeter: I think the worry from the hospital community, at least the hospital community that depends upon disproportionate share payments, which is an annual payment that hospitals get based on their level

Appendix: Teleconference Transcript

of charity care as compared to other peer hospitals in their region or their state, is the reform bill states that those annual payments will go down significantly, and in exchange for that, new patients that can pay will come to the hospital.

The problem that we're hearing with that is there's a definite cut and there's a potential increase in payment, so the risk has definitely shifted away from the government providing that safety net to hospitals to the hospital itself where they have the impetus to go out and find those paying patients. There's a real concern especially in the rural hospital community about that dynamic.

Don Barbo: Let me give you my thoughts on the hospital side of this discussion. To some degree, it almost feels like you're taking money out of one pocket, sticking it into another, and then even perhaps moving it into a third, but at the end of the day, you're wondering, well, is it a zero net sum gain?

What I mean by that is that the hospital perhaps is going to benefit from having lower charity care and bad debt because now we've got more insureds. You would think that would be a good thing.

On the flip slide is, yeah, but if they're going to limit reimbursement increases to hospitals below what they normally have been, well, that's not such a good thing.

To Elliott's point, if the disproportionate share hospital (DSH) subsidies start getting slashed, then maybe that's not such a good thing.

The obvious challenge is trying to get your arms around all that, and to further complicate it, all these things are generally phased in over a period of time.

What are we doing at the moment? What are we advising our clients?

In essence, we're saying hospitals, get used to trying to operate profitably around a Medicare level of reimbursement, because if you can do that and you can lower your cost structure so that you can then be profitable at the level, then perhaps you're ahead of your weaker competitors and brothers in your market.

That's kind of a bottom line thing, in addition to pay attention to quality and pay definite attention to physician alignment strategies.

Appendix: Teleconference Transcript

Mark Dietrich: We'll look at what some of the Medicaid changes are. We have 17.1 million uninsured adults with income at or below 133 percent of poverty.

Generally speaking, the Medicaid expansion brings in low income adults who are childless. Most Medicaid programs, except for, I think, perhaps six or seven states generally did not cover childless adults.

The estimated price tag being the amount of money the federal and state governments will spend on bringing these individuals into Medicaid is around $450 billion, that being over the ten-year period used by the Congressional Budget Office for purposes of measuring the cost of the legislation. That $450 billion, the bulk of it is paid by the federal government. There's a phase-in schedule over the period of time. But something in excess of 90 percent of that $450 billion will be paid out of federal revenue or federal borrowing.

It also establishes a minimum uniform standard for Medicaid coverage in all states, which is a fairly dramatic change, because right now, the level of benefits that a Medicaid recipient gets in different states varies considerably. You could almost venue shop, so to speak, to get better benefits. Those costs of expanding or bringing up the Medicaid benefit coverage in states that presently have very low Medicaid benefits are also being born by the federal government. Those states that had better benefits already are, in effect, biting the bullet and they're not getting the same subsidy that the states with lower benefits are getting.

Some of these Medicaid changes will eliminate what I call cross-border differences that affect comparability of transactions under the Market Approach. There are a lot of other things that affect comparability of transactions under the Market Approach and these changes again phase in over a fairly long period of time.

I think that companies that specialize in Medicaid Managed Care are potential big winners because the only way that the states have found to even remotely successfully manage Medicaid cost is through hiring some of these Medicaid Managed Care contractors.

One of the changes, if you look at an actual provider level change, is that Medicaid payments in fee-for-service and managed care for primary care services provided by primary care doctors are increased to 100 percent of the Medicare payment rates for 2013

Appendix: Teleconference Transcript

and 2014. That change is only good for two years. I think in terms of the amount of money they could spend and the amount of offsets they could raise, they kind of ran out of money.

This slide tells you how significant the Medicaid problem actually is. This slide comes from the Kaiser Family Foundation. You'll see the citation down at the bottom left there. It shows those states where providers are paid less than 70 percent of what providers get from Medicare, and they're many of the largest states in the country – California, Florida, Illinois, New York, Maine. Maine is not one of the largest states but it happens to have the highest percentage of Medicaid covered individuals in the country.

Medicaid again pays providers, generally speaking, very poorly and it pays less than Medicare, and at least from a physician standpoint, Medicare is deemed to be a poor payer. So if you're getting 70 percent of Medicare or less for Medicaid, that's not a patient group that you want to treat.

It's not entirely clear to me, as I look at this, where we're going to find the non-hospital providers, meaning those who aren't compelled basically by force of law to treat Medicaid patients, where you're going to find the physicians to treat these patients for the kind of fees that the states are able to pay due to the costs associated with the program.

I don't know, Don and Elliott, whether you have any further comment on Medicaid before we look at the individual provider winners and losers in this segment of the program.

We're going to look at precisely the impact on providers – winners, losers, near-term and long-term, assuming the reform survives, and I think when Don made his introductory comments, he kind of hinted at this and then I followed up on it.

We don't know because many of the provisions in this legislation again don't take place until the outer years what ones will actually survive legislative challenge in the interim.

For example, the 40 percent excise tax on Cadillac insurance plans isn't effective until 2018. Well, 2018 is a long way off, almost eight years, I think.

Some of these other insurance changes aren't effective for a long period and there'll certainly be a lot of changes in the economy

Appendix: Teleconference Transcript

and perhaps a lot of changes in the government in that time that may impact whether or not there's an attempt made to change it or repeal it or what have you.

In overview, what the legislation does in order to pay for it is that there are reductions in payments to providers – hospitals, surgery centers, and what have you – in the Medicare program that are supposed to pay approximately $500 billion worth of the cost of this reform legislation.

Again, from the standpoint of the provider community, that money is supposed to be made up through expanding coverage in Medicaid, whereas I noted earlier there's approximately a $450 billion cost associated with the expansion of the Medicaid program, and through individuals newly being able to obtain health insurance, and there are a whole series of federal government subsidies to individuals to help them buy health insurance that apply to people up to 400 percent of the federal poverty limit on a phased-out basis.

Most of you doing this kind of stuff don't know the details of that but I kind of throw that out to you because if you're thinking, well, how is it these individuals who can't presently afford insurance are going to get insurance so that they can afford to pay for healthcare? The answer is the federal government is going to give them money in order to enable them to go out and buy health insurance.

Another thing I point out here is that I find that many individuals who don't work exclusively in this industry are unaware of how broad in scope the impact of the Medicare program is on what gets covered, so Medicare has National Coverage Decisions. Those are primary determinants of what new technologies and procedures get covered by all forms of insurance.

Basically, if you're looking to bring a new technology to the market and you can't get it approved by Medicare, the likelihood is you're not going to be able to bring it to the market because if Medicare doesn't approve it, the private health insurers are typically not going to pay for it either.

I can think of a couple of good examples of that. I think back around 1997 or so when they developed these drug-alluding stents that they use in interventional cardiology, in lieu of doing open heart surgery, the Medicare program was so impressed, I guess, with the potential to save cardiac surgery costs for lower expense of using interventional cardiology that they approved those drug-alluding

Appendix: Teleconference Transcript

stents ahead of the FDA approving them, and in effect, forced the FDA to move more quickly.

I think another good example on the technology side are PET scanners which, at least the last time I checked, the application of PET was limited to cancer treatment and planning even though PET arguably has a lot broader potential application.

Again, those are all driven by what Medicare is willing to pay for.

The last point I make here, because this is fairly significant for those of you who value physician practices, bringing all these new people into the system is going to create an incredible crunch on primary care physicians.

Those of you who may have seen my BV conference presentation, I think, two years ago, there was a health affairs study about the shortage in adult primary care doctors. It was already traumatic before the reform. It's going to get even worse so that now the federal government is going to try to shift residency training slots away from specialists and over to primary care, and those slots are paid for by the Medicare program. So when you look at the teaching hospitals, for example, and physician residents, all those residency slots are pretty much paid for by the federal government through the Medicare program by enhanced payments to teaching hospitals.

Here is a Medicare timeline and I'm not going to necessarily walk through all of these but these timelines, I think, are very important which is why I put them in here. If you're trying to forecast future cash flow in a DCF, for example, and trying to assess how a particular change in the reform legislation is going to impact your future cash flows, you really have to know when that change is effective, because again, they're effective at all kinds of different periods.

The provider update reductions really start immediately, and I've highlighted some of these in blue because there are other changes like the donut hole that we won't discuss today.

Medicare Advantage – if you're in Florida, Massachusetts, California, or probably Washington state – there are a handful of states – and Arizona as well – where these Medicare Advantage programs have fairly large enrollment and are very significant. Those reductions start in 2011.

Appendix: Teleconference Transcript

	The productivity offset, which we'll look in more detail, starts in 2012.
	Then we also have these Accountable Care Organizations (ACO) which we're going to discuss in some detail later.
	In 2013, there are changes in what hospitals get paid for based upon whether they make mistakes and there's something new called value-based purchasing (VBP).
	Elliott had alluded to these disproportionate share hospital (DSH) reductions which are a fairly big issue for hospitals with large Medicaid populations.
	We have an Independent Payment Advisory Board that's supposed to help rein in spending on healthcare, the idea here being to try to keep it from consuming the entire economy.
	Those are some of the things that we will look at.
	On the hospital side, I would encourage Elliott, maybe you'll comment on this point.
Elliott Jeter:	I think you can look at the hospital changes into buckets of positives and negatives. Obviously, a "market basket" reduction over time is a negative and that's primarily how Congress had decided to finance the bill.
Mark Dietrich:	Elliott, can you tell folks what the "market basket" is?
Elliott Jeter:	Hospitals, unless Congress or CMS intervenes, are going to get an inflation-based adjustment every year based on economic activity.
	The formula is you get the market basket adjustment, the increase, minus something that would be called a productivity decrease.
	It's usually a 25 to 30 percent reduction of the market basket.
	All it is, over time, hospitals are going to get lower increases in their Medicare rates.
Mark Dietrich:	As you can see from the slide, these changes, there's a little bit here, a little bit there over the course of the next ten years or so.
	Depending upon the sophistication of your forecasting model, if you

Appendix: Teleconference Transcript

looked at this market basket, which is, as Elliott said, an inflationary factor, traditionally, hospitals have been able to get an increase in their Medicare rates that generally tracks medial inflation or at least medical inflation as the Medicare program defines it. They're going to nip away at that over the next several years in an attempt to save money.

The hospitals, at least to the extent the American Hospital Association backed the legislation, were gambling that they pick it up someplace else.

The new productivity adjustment – we've been talking about this – this is something that those of you who are familiar with physician practice valuation in the Medicare physician conversion factor, that there is something called a Medical Economic Index (MEI) that goes into calculating the sustainable growth rate (SGR).

That economic index is one element of what drives the physician conversion factor and one element of why the physician conversion factor has to be legislatively overturned every year from dropping by 20, 25, and I think now they're talking in the out years 34 percent two years from now. So they're now taking this productivity adjustment, which is based upon economy-wide productivity changes, and applying it to hospitals.

I have a comment here that the CMS actuary says it's likely undoable.

Most of the increases in productivity in the economy come from technology.

I would say anecdotally or as an aside that a lot of it seems to come from back-loading what would otherwise be business responsibilities onto consumers like those of you who are trying to make an airline reservation other than the Internet and have to sit on the phone for an hour. That's very inefficient from the consumer's standpoint but probably efficient from the airline's standpoint.

That being said, the types of productivity changes we see in the economy are coming in the technology sector. They're not coming in the labor-intensive sector like a hospital.

The CMS actuary says this particular adjustment is unlikely to be achieved and, therefore, many hospitals would become marginal or

Appendix: Teleconference Transcript

unprofitable. If a hospital becomes unprofitable over a long term, that then makes it likely to go out of business which could drive consolidation of hospitals.

There are other changes here which include lower payment for preventable hospital readmissions, payment reduction for hospital-acquired conditions such as some of these drug-resistant infections that we see in hospitals.

Value-based purchasing – VBP is the new acronym you're going to see if you work in the industry.

You're going to see DSH reductions of 15 percent starting in 2014.

Don or Elliott, do you want to comment on these changes?

Elliott Jeter: I would add in totality, although you have significant areas in the negative column – and Don, you can add to this if need be – I think there's significant evidence that the market believes that hospitals have won in this area.

Two of the ten large transactions in 2010 were conducted by private equity firms. Private equity firms are a new entrance into the hospital acquisition field. I think it's pretty widely known. What the bet is that over time, due to healthcare reform and a large injection of capital, you can take a large, unprofitable system that's dependent on charity and Medicaid and, over time, create efficiencies with the help of the new healthcare reform bill with new paying patients and turn these into profitable businesses with the right capital allocation.

Don Barbo: Let me add this real quick, Elliott. I guess my thoughts on the hospital impact side is I would lean more towards it's a mixed impact.

What I mean is I think from a big picture perspective, I think this is an opportunity for stronger systems that can withstand the additional investment requirements, the additional quality of bars that's been set, along with digesting the changes in the payer market and the insureds. I think those are much better prepared to handle this and consequently acquire some of the weaker systems.

I think the weaker systems are going to struggle for numerous reasons. I think their access to capital is going to be questioned. I think their survival, in some instances, could be questioned.

Appendix: Teleconference Transcript

As a result, we've actually seen some transactions in which, in essence, there hasn't really been any upfront consideration paid for a system that's weak by a stronger system that's strong other than, "Hey, let us take over your operations and we'll assume your leases, and then on day two, we'll use our stronger payer contracts and better payer mix to, in essence, turn around your unprofitable cash flow fairly quickly but frankly without paying for that opportunity."

It's still a mixed situation in terms of doing valuations now, in terms of consulting with our hospital clients. It's pretty much a six-point plan around things like, "Focus on quality, focus on your market strategy, focus on your physician relationships, focus on your cost structure, and at the end of the day, can you operate profitability at Medicare?" That's, I think, the biggest challenge they face.

Elliott Jeter: Of course, physician-owned hospitals have been directly affected by the legislation. There are approximately 300 grandfathered physician-owned hospitals across the country. The legislation states there should be no new physician-owned hospitals. Those hospitals that are under development, approximately 65 around the country, have to have the facility completed and licensure in place by December 31, 2010.

Obviously, not all of the 65 of those are going to make it. There's a recently filed lawsuit in Tyler, Texas to try to ameliorate some of this language and we don't know how that will go, but there are significant efforts to get this language softened or changed.

How does it affect the 300 grandfathered hospitals? I think the answer to that, just like to any of these for our clients, is it depends.

If you can't grow beds, if you can't grow operating or procedure rooms, how do you expand?

Each individual hospital needs to be examined. There's a significant portion of hospitals that have plenty of bed capacity, plenty of operating room capacity and have no plans to expand, so that segment is really not very affected by the legislation.

But those small hospitals that have ultimate plans to expand, in order to create a strong competitive position in the marketplace, their hands are really tied. When you combine the growth restriction with the inability to add physicians as a percentage of the total ownership, it becomes a really onerous legislation that over

Appendix: Teleconference Transcript

	time, the financial performance of certain physician-owned hospitals will decline.
	You really have to understand the facts and circumstances of each grandfathered hospital.
Don Barbo:	Let me throw in to that discussion, Elliott, I would say probably another interesting dynamic is a situation where if you're a physician-owned hospital in a market that you've got a lot of large system competitors and your business model is capped, through legislation, you can't grow – you can't grow either beds or your physician level of ownership.
	Now you can turn that physician ownership as long as it maintains its current ownership percentage.
	But if you're a capped business model and you're competing in a market that has growth, I'm curious how much contracting leverage are you going to be able to have with the key payers in that market? I would probably say it's going to be a declining kind of a situation.
Elliott Jeter:	I think it's important to remember too that at least 100 of the 300 have large acute care hospital partners. That's ameliorated somewhat by the fact that they have a market-wide partner.
	Another thing, if you have a barrier with some of these physician owners of hospitals, they'll admit to you that in certain cases, this is a positive thing for their entity because it creates this huge barrier to entry because in many markets, Houston, for example, there are so many of these physician-owned hospitals and many times they compete against themselves. So to the extent no additional hospitals are allowed to build around you, that creates a competitive advantage, all else being equal.
Don Barbo:	In other words, you're in the market so legislation has prevented any new competitors from popping up, better lease physician-owned competitors.
Elliott Jeter;	That's right.
Don Barbo:	Real quick, have a permanent barrier to entry you would say.
Elliott Jeter:	That's right.
Mark Dietrich:	One thing I might ask either of you or both to comment on is why it

Appendix: Teleconference Transcript

was physician-owned hospitals were targeted and what, if anything, it might tell us about future targets of future legislation?

Don Barbo: I think the quick and dirty on that is you had a very strong hospital lobby that felt threatened by physician-owned hospitals.

Secondly, you had a constituency that wasn't all that big in terms of the political scene. In other words, how many toes am I really stepping on if I'm a politician, if I choose to kill physician-owned hospitals, versus how many toes am I stepping on with a 6,000 plus general hospital industry?

I think it was that and I think it was also just maybe trying to reduce the cost of healthcare.

In terms of how it might impact other types of entities, all the feedback I'm getting is that right now it appears that surgery centers are not necessarily threatened or really in the bull's eye, certainly not to the degree that physician-owned hospitals were for a number of factors.

One is there's already a bunch of them out there. They perform surgeries at a lower cost so Medicare kind of likes that.

Frankly, there's a lot of hospital ownership in those ambulatory surgery center (ASC) models.

Elliott, what are your thoughts on that?

Elliott Jeter: We're hearing the same thing and the ASC lobby has done a good job for now, and mark the concern about years in the future is relevant, but for now I think ASCs, imaging centers and other ancillary businesses are physician-owner safe.

From a legality perspective, you're always going to have reimbursement pressure.

Mark Dietrich: One other point I would make here is that for those of you who value hospitals, the assessment of the risk that the hospitals are under with respect to these changes are, by 2017, up to 6 percent of their diagnosis-related group (DRG) payments.

Those of you who are unfamiliar with the acronym, DRG is the basis upon which hospitals get paid under the Medicare system. Actually, under many insurances but not all insurances, a DRG is basically a payment per admission, only the D stands for discharge, so the hospital gets paid based upon the patient's diagnosis at the time they're discharged.

Okay, and again, I would encourage those of you out there who work in this healthcare appraisal industry to read that CMS analysis because I really think it's invaluable.

We do have one question here, and I'll toss it out to Don or Elliott, "With all the impending changes associated with healthcare reform, are historical valuation metrics like multiples relevant anymore and how do they need to be adjusted to reflect likely future conditions?

We had that slide at the opening, so do either of you two want to look into your crystal ball and give this participant some insight?

Don Barbo: Elliott, if you want to give it a shot and then I'm happy to jump in afterwards.

Elliott Jeter: I think you have to be careful when a lot of our physician clients especially call us and say, "XYZ has affected negatively my business so how has it affected the value of my business?"

The sustainable growth formula, the credit crisis, the physician employment trends, the economy – all of those things are very real factors in what's going on with the valuation of particularly physician owned ancillary businesses, but everybody seems to blame that on healthcare reform. So it really depends on what you're talking about.

The combination of factors, including healthcare reform, certainly has affected multiples for certain business segments.

For some segments like ambulatory surgery centers or imaging centers, healthcare reform, the legislation itself, really has a very minor negligible effect on the value of the business and inversely on multiples.

It's very important when you answer the question, "How does this affect our business?" that you clearly delineate and break out the bill itself compared to the other major significant factors that affect value and the business going on today.

Don Barbo: My personal view is on really the bottom line question, "What relevancy does the market transaction approach have to our

Appendix: Teleconference Transcript

valuations on a go-forward due to all this health reform uncertainty and major changes?" and I'll preface it with, "If I focus, let's say, on hospital surgery centers and maybe even medical practices."

But what I would probably say is using historical transaction multiples for current valuations, I would just be careful as we always are. We would want to say, "What is the range historically and how comparable are those identifiable transactions to my subject?"

But we also have to take into consideration even when those historical multiples were consummated. There's uncertainty even historically. What is reimbursement going to do? Specialty hospitals, what kind of impact are those industries facing? Physician fee schedule cuts – so on and so forth. So the air of uncertainty has always been in healthcare.

I will also say this, and this is just a real generality, particularly on medical practices where you have real sketchy market-based information, I generally use a transaction method really perhaps as a type of sanity check and also to understand the activity of the marketplace and maybe, "Why is my implied multiples, say from using an income approach, where does that fall in this range that I can observe and does it make sense to me?"

My response to this question is I would still consider historical multiples. To the degree I place any weight on them would probably be determined by where my other approach is to me.

Elliott Jeter: I'll give you an example – and I think this is a good segue to the next page on ASCs – ASC multiples in 2010 have picked up significantly from the last 18 months. There have been some trades going off that are publicly available information at much higher multiples than 2009 and 2008.

Of course, that's counterintuitive to the implementation of healthcare reform. Healthcare reform for ASCs over time will create negative Medicare productivity adjustments which will lower Medicare reimbursement over time.

But there are so many additional factors so important to ASCs. ASCs are typically 20, 25 percent of Medicare.

So the other 75 percent of reimbursement, commercial payments, what's going on there?

Appendix: Teleconference Transcript

	Then how are ASCs managing their cost structure?
	You go to these ASC conferences now, whereas ten years ago, everybody was developing new surgery centers. Now people are managing the surgery centers that they have in a very mature market and trying to operate them much more efficiently.
	Certainly, the ASC industry would have preferred large Medicare updates but the industry has not had a Medicare increase since 2003, if you can imagine that, flat Medicare rates for a very long period of time.
	So this is nothing new to the industry and certainly, you're not talking about something that's extremely negative, and compared to other segments, it's fairly neutral.
Mark Dietrich:	Elliott, do you want to mention your Intellimarker survey?
Elliott Jeter:	Yeah, in our firm, we value about 200 ambulatory surgery centers a year, so we coagulate the data and track about 80 statistics over time. We've just put out our 2010 survey that has data from 2008 and 2009.
	We track reimbursement margins, staffing levels, and over time, especially recently, you're seeing a significant improvement in efficiencies, not much increase in revenue per case, but you're seeing margins hold due to the fact that it's in a mature business and ASCs are really working with technology and managing their expenses.
	That's available on our website at *vmghealth.com*.
Mark Dietrich:	For those of you who haven't taken the time to download that, and I think all you've got to do is, in effect, register with your email address, and I've never gotten anything else from VMG after doing that, that is incredibly useful and it's still free, Elliott?
Elliott Jeter:	It's still free.
Mark Dietrich:	It's still free, and I mean for free, it's worth a whole heck of a lot more than nothing I can tell you that. It's really invaluable and something that I commend VMG for making that available to the valuation and healthcare industry community because it really is a wonderful tool. That kind of insight is very difficult to get even for money.

Appendix: Teleconference Transcript

Don Barbo: I agree that it's a wonderful resource and I commend VMG and my friends over there on that, and so speaking of free resources, I guess I just have to add at Deloitte, we have a health reform central war room that is, if you will, kind of depository of a lot of information that we've gathered as a firm regarding health reform, and that's for free if you go to *deloitte.com*.

There's some pieces out there that if you're valuing a hospital, if you're valuing a pharma company or whatever that looks at what the impact is by sector, then I encourage you to pull down our free information that's out their to the public as well.

Mark Dietrich: I would say Don got out ahead of me because when I started working on this reform stuff right after the legislation passed, I did, in fact, start out at the Deloitte website and they had some great stuff.

I always like to give a plug for the AICPA's National Healthcare Industry Conference where the Director of the Deloitte Center for Health Solutions, Paul Keckley, who some older folks may remember from the Phicore days in the 1990s, is our keynote speaker this year and something that those of us on that conference committee are really looking forward to.

Don Barbo: Dr. Keckley, he heads up our Deloitte Center for Health Solutions. That's a big think tank that we have also set up within the firm that is dedicated towards researching and preparing white papers and doing all kinds of research, not just on health reform, but on all different kinds of healthcare delivery models. Again, that's a free type of resource out there to our listeners as well.

Mark Dietrich: Now maybe we'll make a few brief comments on imaging because I think as we were preparing this, we kind of collectively decided that in the near term, other than one more nail in the coffin, there's really no near-term dramatic impact.

Elliott Jeter: I would say the Deficit Reduction Act (DRA) starting in 2007 really had a dramatic impact on the outpatient imaging segment. MRI and CT rates were cut fairly dramatically which caused a pretty large shakeout. A lot of the weak players failed or consolidated.

What you have now is an industry where the strong have survived and many of the weak have fallen off and that volume has been redistributed.

Appendix: Teleconference Transcript

	Something like a moderate decline in Medicare reimbursement – again, for most imaging centers, you talk about 20 to 30 percent Medicare – a moderate decline in that percentage of your payer mix, while it's not favorable, certainly none of these remaining imaging businesses that have survived the DRA are going to fail because of the healthcare reform bill.
	So it's again another negative factor to have to deal with on top of reimbursement cuts, increased regulatory constraints, new accreditation rules, and other regulatory factors.
	But what really matters for imaging centers is what happens to commercial rates and can I find the credit as an independent imaging center to update my equipment to be competitive in the marketplace.
Mark Dietrich:	This is one area that fascinates me and I'll just toss out an example. A friend of mine recently had a with and without contrast in a hospital outpatient setting which meant two CAT scans, with contrast and without contrast. The bill, excluding the physician side, was around $7,500 of which I think one of the larger insurance companies in the country who has some muscle paid about $6,000. I think on an outpatient basis, the Medicare program probably wouldn't have paid more than $1,000, if that, for it.
	So this just gives you some insight into the strength, if you will, of the hospitals with respect to the Medicare program and lobbying versus the free-standing physician imaging centers.
Don Barbo:	Let me just add that I can tell you that we've been involved in a number of imaging centers out of Dallas valuations and transactions over the last 12 months. Every one of them has been a scenario where the physician-owned imaging center is potentially being acquired by a hospital with the hospital potentially converting to an outpatient department to kind of play the arbitrage and the fee schedule.
Elliott Jeter:	It's important to remember when you're valuing the Part B target, that you can't give them credit for whatever the hospital will get post-transaction from Medicare and commercial payers.
Mark Dietrich:	Great point.
Don Barbo:	I agree 100 percent.

Appendix: Teleconference Transcript

Mark Dietrich: Let's move on to the next slide, and Elliott, I think you were going to give us some brief comments on the therapies, and then Don, you were going to give us some brief comments on home health.

Elliott Jeter: I think physical therapy, they really kicked the can down the road in the healthcare reform bill and they extended the exception to the therapy cap of about $1,860 to 2010 but no language about what's going to happen after that.

I think for physical therapy, they're going to benefit somewhat from the incentives for accountable care organizations and you'll see more volume on the physical therapy side if what is intended actually happens.

But there's always again that susceptibility in physical therapy to the physician fee schedule what happens to the SGR.

So those are some of the risks.

I think physical therapy in the healthcare reform bill is not a material event except that they did not fix the therapy cap problem.

Mark Dietrich: Right.

Don Barbo: The impact on home health, from a big picture, the reform measure is going to pull out about $40 billion over about a ten-year period of time through a variety of things where they're going to reduce reimbursement, they're going to go through this rebasing exercising, and so forth.

So I would say that it appears health reform is not necessarily favorable to home health.

Kind of the sister sector, which is hospice, health reform is expected to pull out about $7 billion in reimbursement over the next seven years. Again, it seems that hospice might be facing some challenges.

Mark Dietrich: Okay. We're starting to get some other questions in. I guess this is probably a good time before we get into accountable care organizations which I, myself, think are probably one of the potentially most significant things to come out of the legislation.

We have a compliment and a question, guys, very, very insightful. I always like compliments to read them on the air.

Appendix: Teleconference Transcript

"We are valuing a California senior assisted living facility. In order to bifurcate a recent sales transaction price between the real estate and operating entity – that is, general partner, owner of operations and limited partner who owns real estate – a dispute has arisen. What are some key value drivers for this sector arising from the legislation?"

Don Barbo: Well, let me just throw out and I'll just add this and then look for Elliott to chime in, from my understanding based on our Deloitte research, skilled nursing for 2010 to 2011, it looks like they're going to receive a full payment update for those years.

Beginning in 2012, it looks like that there will be a market basket update. Let me just read this out loud frankly on the fly. There will be a reduction to the skilled nursing facility market basket update by productivity factor based on a ten-year average of changes in productivity, so essentially about a 1 percent reduction in the estimated market basket update, which is an estimated total of about $14.6 billion over a ten-year period.

What's the takeaway? I think the takeaway is not any immediate cutbacks at least not until 2012. Then in 2012, it looks like the industry could be facing some reductions.

But please guys, chime in on your thoughts.

Elliott Jeter: My first thought is that site could benefit from the increase in Medicaid population, but generally, you're talking about people in retirement homes that have drained their bank accounts so they would qualify for Medicaid anyway.

Mark, what do you think?

I'm not sure the incremental effects would hit the senior segment.

Mark Dietrich: The question reads on to say, "51 percent of the units that are subject qualifies under California Assisted Living Waiver Program which allows qualified seniors to reside in specially selected care facilities in three California counties."

I don't think any of us are likely to know anything about there. It does have 89 percent occupancy.

I think it's in large part a payer mix driven question, and unfortunately, I don't know anything about the ALWP in California.

Appendix: Teleconference Transcript

Don Barbo: Yeah, I agree, Mark. I just happened to have done a recent valuation in that for letting you know it's facts and circumstances.

Mark Dietrich: We have another question about how healthcare reform will affect the value of dental practices, and I hadn't even though about that, but it's kind of an interesting question only because and really in large part depends upon what happens with Medicaid's defined benefits.

I know in Massachusetts, and we did the healthcare reform here, historically, adult dental benefits had kind of come and gone based upon the state budgeting process. So if the state was having a fat year, then they left the adult dental coverage in the Medicaid program, and if they weren't having a good year, then they took it out. The reform legislation, to a large extent, institutionalized it or left it in place.

The only comment I would make there is that depending upon what the Medicaid standard benefit package ends up being, that could look good for dental practices who treat Medicaid patients depending upon what the fees are.

Typically, in my limited experience cross-border, oral surgery tends to be covered by Medicaid. So if you were looking at an oral surgery practice rather than a general dentistry practice, you might find, because oral surgery is more likely to be covered, that if you're in a state that has poor Medicaid benefits for dentistry, once the Medicaid benefits are uniform across all states so there's a minimum required package, they'd do better.

Why don't we go now back to the accountable care organizations?

I will say that from the hospital systems I work with, this discussion is really all the rage. Whether or not it goes any place, one never knows. I think these are supposed to be start taking place in 2012. So if you want to have one in place, really two years to put one of these together is not a really long amount of time.

In my mind, now going through my second career phase with healthcare consolidation, the first being back in the 1990s, these look very much to me like newly named or newly acronymed integrated delivery systems (IDS).

Those of you who were around in the early and mid-1990s remember that the Friendly Hills transaction in California kind of

Appendix: Teleconference Transcript

started the wave of integrated delivery systems and I think it was about the same time that PhyCor formed down in Nashville and started going out and buying up physician practices and that kind of pushed the whole transaction market throughout the 1990s.

The integrated delivery systems, which started in California, there was a lot of and there probably still is a lot of capitated care in California where basically healthcare systems are paid a per member per month for having a member in the system. Generally, the amount of revenue is not a function of a fee for service type environment where the more you treat the more you get paid. You have a fixed amount of revenue and you're supposed to take care of the individual out of that fixed amount of money.

I think the accountable care organizations talk about bundled payments rather than capitation. Capitation kind of became a dirty word in healthcare particularly at the end of the 1990s when the consolidation wave collapsed and there was a big backlash against the managed care industry and tightly managed care, which is one of the reasons, quite frankly, as we sit here ten years later, healthcare spending has exploded again.

I don't know that anyone really knows what these ACOs are precisely and there'll be a lot of attempts to try to define them in the marketplace as well as define them in the forthcoming regulations. But again, "if it walks like a duck and quacks like a duck, it's unlikely to be a horse or a donkey," and I still think we're looking at an integrated delivery system. I'm not even sure if it's an IDS on steroids.

The way these things are supposed to be compensated is that you have to qualify as one and then you get an opportunity to share in any cost savings that they generate for the Medicare program. So that's kind of the motivation.

The legislative standards – and again, these are fairly fluid at this point pending regulatory definition – to qualify, you have to be accountable for the overall care of their Medicare beneficiaries – thus, the expression accountable care organization – you have to have adequate participation of primary care physicians. You see that I've emphasized this because as I alluded to earlier, I really think the potential biggest winners of the entire healthcare reform process on a supply and demand basis and, therefore, on a price basis are likely to be primary care doctors.

Appendix: Teleconference Transcript

ACOs also have to define processes to promote evidence-based medicine. There was a lot of talk in the legislation about this evidence-based medicine.

Then they have to report back to the Medicare program on quality and cost and coordinate the care of the people who are cared for by the accountable care organization.

Another new buzz phrase that comes out of the legislation is this idea of medical homes, and again, this is a primary care oriented approach where the primary care doctor, particularly for patients who have chronic conditions, is supposed to serve as the center point for that person's care, so everything gets funneled through the primary care doctor's office.

There's been a lot of work done on this in Massachusetts. I know Children's Hospital, for example, in Boston has been a leader in the development of medical homes for children with chronic conditions.

I think that this is probably the most significant element of reform with respect to transactions and what will be valuable.

Now I don't know that Elliott and Don share my view on that, and they'll comment momentarily, but I see a replay of the 1990s primary care craze in the offing.

I also think and I'm starting to think myself that new valuation models are required to account for the cash flows associated with risk sharing. Many of the integrated delivery system transactions in the 1990s were built around an expectation of converting a certain part of the underlying primary care population in the capitated contracts, both Medicare and commercial, and that required a particular type of a valuation model that we may have a need for again.

Finally, before I ask Elliott and Don to comment, there are a lot of antitrust implications associated with these accountable care organizations because of the sharing of revenue and sharing of fees and what have you that have yet to be addressed.

Again, for a plug for the AICPA's Healthcare Conference, I'm actually doing a session with an antitrust lawyer on the antitrust issues associated with some of the upcoming mergers that we're likely to see as a result of these accountable care organizations.

Appendix: Teleconference Transcript

With that, I'd ask Don and/or Elliott if they'd like to comment on this and either agree or disagree with my assessment.

Don Barbo: If you don't mind, let me jump in on that, Elliott, real quick.

A couple of things – one is we've got an excellent piece, a white paper on this specific topic. Paul Keckley is doing an outstanding job researching it. I'm going to email this to Blake so it'll be available to attendees at this webinar.

Secondly, I agree, Mark, this is a hot topic among our health system clients.

I will also say it's even a broader issue. The broader issue is physician alignment strategies. What should we be doing? Who should we be doing it with? What types of physicians should we be going after? Should they be specialists or primary care or a combination of the two? What types of physician personalities should we be focusing on because if you're going to have to play under comparative effectiveness rules and any medical home models where there are specific protocols to be followed and that require teamwork across the system, then clearly, you want physicians of like mind.

I agree that this is a very important current event topic for our health system clients.

I also agree to some degree that it is driving an interest in doing transactions.

Elliott, do you have any thoughts? Did we lose Elliott?

Mark Dietrich: I guess we did. Okay, well, hopefully, he'll get back in.

Let's now look at physician practices. I'm going to kind of take a more formal presentation approach here because there are a number of significant elements that come out of the reform legislation for primary care practices and also out of the so called high tech legislation which is several slides hence.

As I indicated earlier, there is already a serious shortage of primary care physicians, and in an attempt to make it more attractive for doctors to go into primary care, the reform legislation contains a 10 percent bonus that's 10 percent of the Medicare payment for office, skilled nursing facility, home, rest home, and other specified

Appendix: Teleconference Transcript

visits for primary care doctors who are defined as family medicine, internal medicine, geriatric medicine, and pediatric medicine.

In order to qualify for that 10 percent bonus, at least 60 percent of your Medicare allowed charges have to be for bonus-eligible services as specified by CPT code, and we'll look at that momentarily on the next slide.

This is effective for five years beginning January 1, 2011, and these need to be in your discounted cash flow analysis.

I can tell you I'm valuing three large primary care practices right now, and in one of those practices, this, along with the high tech payment that we'll discuss towards the end of the program, account for nearly $2 million of additional cash revenue between 2011 and 2015. You can imagine that $2 million of dumping right down to the bottom line has a fairly significant impact on the value of the practice.

The CPT codes that are covered – and again, these are statutory coverages – as many of you have heard me speak in the past and I've been maintaining for a long time, you really have to do a CPT analysis for a variety of reasons or you have to obtain one, I guess, from the target practice.

You have to know what the Medicare allowed charges are for these three sets of codes. 99201 through 99215 are the most common codes and account for a large slug of overall Medicare spending and I've seen these represent ofttimes as much as 75 to 85 percent of their revenue in a primary care practice.

The nursing facilities are less common. Many primary care doctors don't go to nursing facilities. The nursing facility visits, in my experience in a given geographic area, tend to devolve on to a few doctors who specialize in doing that.

And then home visits – I'm valuing a practice now that does about $15 million worth of revenue. I think it had five home visits. I don't know how common those are but they are covered by the legislation.

Your primary focus, if you will, if you're valuing one of these practices and trying to measure what the impact is going to be is on the first set, 99201 through 99215.

Appendix: Teleconference Transcript

This is a simplified calculation, and again, there are probably better ways to do it. If you can nail down the actual Medicare collections, obviously, then that would be the best way to do it but I've just done a simplified calculation here of total collected revenues of $10 million of which Medicare represents 25 percent or $2.5 million. The portion of the revenue coming from those CPT codes that are specified on the previous slide is 65 percent. The Medicare bonus percentage for these five years is 10 percent. So in this example, that would represent an additional $162,500 worth of revenue.

Again, for the eligible code percentage, you need to isolate actual Medicare allowed charges by CPT code by provider. So if you're valuing a multi-specialty group, this only applies to primary care doctors in that group, and, therefore, you'd have to isolate those primary care doctors from the non-primary care doctors.

For those of you who might not be familiar with the term "allowed charge," generally speaking, under Medicare Part B for physician practice, a Medicare allowed charge is defined by a fee schedule, the Medicare physician fee schedule we discussed briefly earlier.

Medicare pays 80 percent of the allowed charge and the patient co-pay is 20 percent of the allowed charge, and that affects really the way you want to go at obtaining this information.

Don Barbo: Mark, can I interject real quick?

Mark Dietrich: Sure.

Don Barbo: If you're encouraging the folks on the line to do that kind of an analysis – and I guess in your analogy, the bonus results in about a 1 to 2 percent overall increase in collections – but would you also increase physician compensation because assuming that that bonus wouldn't necessarily all flow to the bottom line, perhaps that would also increase your assumption regarding future physician compensation in your DCF model?

Mark Dietrich: It's certainly something you'd have to clarify.

As you probably know, Don, from us talking about this, one of the things that I do is before issuing an opinion on the valuation of a practice will be to get agreement on precisely what the physician compensation model is supposed to look like.

So if that Medicare bonus was going to flow right through to

Appendix: Teleconference Transcript

physician compensation and have no impact on the bottom line, then you'd want to know that.

On the other hand, if it's going to sit inside or some portion of it is going to go out, you'd want to know that as well.

Don Barbo: Right, okay.

Mark Dietrich: Now the "HITECH" Act, this is an earlier piece of legislation that basically provides a government grant for eligible providers and hospitals who "adopt and meaningfully use" certified electronic health record (EHR) technology.

The proposed regulations on this came out in January 2010 and I believe that those are linked up on the BVR website.

These things go on for hundreds and hundreds of pages, and I certainly haven't read them all, but I did go through them and extract tables that showed what the potential bonuses were for physician practices.

When you're doing a valuation of a physician practice, you need to ask whether they have implemented electronic health records and whether they're likely to qualify under this "meaningful use" standard which is yet to be formalized. It's contained in the proposed regulations but there was a lot of pushback, if you will, I think, particularly from the hospital industry about what qualified as "meaningful use." But you need to ask these questions.

As I say here, "For providers who have already incurred the expense, this is a windfall straight to the bottom line and to the value," and again, as Don suggested, there's going to be some bonusing out, if you will, or compensation element to this once the money comes in.

For those who are currently implementing EHR and qualify, this could be a reduction in their capital expense and, therefore, affects value as well with respect to a discounted cash flow model.

The HITECH Act makes "business associates" – and that means folks like us doing valuation work – directly responsible for complying with certain provisions of HIPAA's privacy rule and all of the HIPAA's security rules.

So one of the things that your data requests in this business should

Appendix: Teleconference Transcript

say is, "Do not give me any information containing HIPAA data," and that would be patient names, diagnosis codes, social security numbers, any of that kind of stuff.

If you end up getting it, and again, the client shouldn't be giving it to you without getting a business associate's agreement, but if you end up getting it, then you're now responsible. So the responsibility sits on both the provider of that information to you and on you with respect to complying with the privacy and security rules. I thought that was something well worth pointing out.

In this slide, I've extracted from those proposed regulations the potential recovery that a physician practice can receive again for meeting this "meaningful use" standard.

You see on the first table the first calendar year (CY) in which the enrolled provider receives an incentive payment assuming that they quality under the "meaningful use" standard.

In 2011, you get $18,000 if you qualify in 2011. In 2012, you get $12,000. In 2013, you get $8,000. In 2014, you get $4,000. In 2015, you get $2,000. So over the course of those five years, you get $44,000 per provider who's meaningfully using electronic health records.

If you're in a HPSA, which is a Health Provider Shortage Area, then there's a 10 percent bonus over and above that $44,000, so the aggregate payments would be $48,400.

Then if you implement and meet the "meaningful use" criteria in 2012, you can still get that same $44,000 over five years. Any year after that, you lose a year and you can see that the amounts of money drop significantly.

So I think this again is an important question to ask when you're doing a valuation of a physician practice or on the hospital side.

Don, I don't know whether you wanted to comment at all on the hospital potential but I know there it can be millions of dollars of potential recovery from this program.

Don Barbo: Yeah, just real quickly, there is kind of a similar type of reimbursement or subsidy, if you will, that the government will pay to hospitals. There's a fairly complicated formula that's involved which probably goes beyond the scope of our call and the small amount of time we have remaining.

Appendix: Teleconference Transcript

So I guess I just encourage our listeners that if you're valuing a hospital to ask questions similar to what Mark is encouraging you to ask about the medical practice and then do some research around it.

We've got a group that actually focuses on that area so by all means you can always send me an email.

Mark Dietrich: Other things out of the legislation, for physician practices, we have a serious shortage of general surgeons, so for any general surgeon practicing in a health provider shortage area, there's a 10 percent Medicare payment bonus for those individuals.

Funding for medical homes, which, as I said earlier, the leading edge is Massachusetts, there's going to be a voluntary pilot program for bundling for physician payments.

Then there's going to be a new physician quality incentive program that's supposed to be like a "you compare" website for physician quality and what have you.

There are already some analogous things for hospitals.

The last comment I want to make is on Medicare Advantage, and again, this applies to really a handful of states. You can see that of all Medicare enrollments in 2010, approximately 24 percent of Medicare beneficiaries were enrolled in Medicare Advantage plans, and 65 percent of that 24 percent were in HMOs and then the other types of things you see here.

This is where we saw Medicare capitation which still exists in some markets, particularly Florida, Massachusetts and California, which I'm familiar with, and I believe it's in Washington.

Some of these Medicare capitated programs are very lucrative.

Early on in the healthcare reform debate, there was talk about killing Medicare Advantage altogether and then there was a point where one of the senators from Florida managed to get it preserved in an early version of the bill for Florida only.

Then in the end, they actually did not hit this program anywhere near as hard as I expected or as fact as many of the early versions of the legislation will have suggested.

If you're valuing a practice in one of these states that has a

Appendix: Teleconference Transcript

Medicare Advantage contract, you need to be able to quantify the premium reductions and then use that to extrapolate what the reduction in the historical Medicare surplus bonuses is going to be.

I've already valued one of these practices and actually, the sponsoring health plan was fairly cooperative in quantifying for the practice and, therefore, for me what the likely reductions were going to be on a go-forward basis.

In summary, I think we probably hit most of this already, that it looks like hospitals generically are going to do better than most of the other provider groups which is not to say that there won't be a lot of individual hospitals who, because of their particular payer profile or particular underlying patient profile, will not do well.

In general, there will be expanded coverage, probably lower bad debts and more revenue going into the systems, and these accountable care organizations really shift or have the potential to shift a lot of power in the healthcare delivery system to hospitals along with primary care doctors.

Physician-owned hospitals are obviously big losers.

I think, and this is my view, that the specialists again were losers in the 1990s as there became this big focus on primary care. I think we may see that again, so you can be sure the specialists will fight it.

I don't know, Don, if you want to chime in.

Don Barbo: Yeah, again just to kind of wrap up, my personal thoughts are that I still think there's a lot of haze out there obviously. This is a highly partisan bill which makes it incredibly susceptible to challenges and amendments and repeals and so on and so forth.

In terms of advice to our appraisal friends, number one, you've got to stay current. Try to follow what's going on particularly with these pilot programs and legislative actions and so forth particularly for the sectors that you're focused on.

Stay current. Arm yourself with as much industry information as you possibly can. I think throughout the call we've thrown out some advice on really some free sources.

Then educate your clients, frankly, on how they may or may not be

Appendix: Teleconference Transcript

	impacted. There are lots of resources out there by sector that you can pull down and you can study and you can not only use that for your valuations but also use it for just giving good advice to your clients. Those are my thoughts, Mark.
Mark Dietrich:	All right, well, with that, I guess we'll end for the day and I thank you all for attending, and if you have any other questions, feel free to email me or Don directly.
Blake Lyman:	Thank you, Mark. This is Blake. I think we'll conclude today's presentation with that. BVR, of course, would like to thank Mark Dietrich, Elliott Jeter and Don Barbo for their expertise today and Accounting Web and Business Brokerage Press as well for their support as co-presenters and all of our listeners for attending. As we discussed throughout the conference, we've updated our reading page today with more materials from the Deloitte Center for Health Solutions along with a link to the VMG healthcare website where you can download their study. You may need to refresh that page to see those changes. If you'd like to order a transcript or a recording of this or any webinar, you can find those via our On-Demand Packs. More information on conference On-Demand Packs are available at *bvresources.com/training* where you can also find more information on upcoming BVR teleconferences, webinars and live events. Thank you. You may now disconnect.

Appendix: Teleconference Transcript

Presentation Slides

HEALTHCARE REFORM

and its Impact on Valuation
Mark Dietrich, Elliott Jeter, and Don Barbo

Reform Overview

- Insurance Provisions
  - Brief Overview
- Medicaid Changes
- Medicare Provisions
  - Hospitals
  - Physician-owned Hospitals

Appendix: Teleconference Transcript

Reform Overview

- **Medicare Provisions**
  - Skilled Nursing
  - Ambulatory Surgery Centers
  - Imaging Centers
  - Physician Practices
- **Supplemental Material**

The High Level Picture

- **Reform Means**
  - Consolidation
  - Higher Volumes at Lower Rates
  - Higher Emphasis on Payment for Quality
  - Lower Volume Providers at Risk
  - Cost shifts from older and sicker to younger and healthier
  - Cost shifts to Small Business
  - Cost shifts to individual from insurance

Appendix: Teleconference Transcript

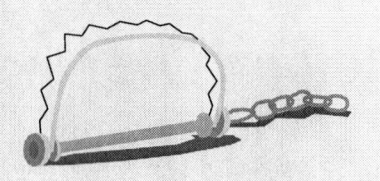

INSURANCE PROVISIONS

Aim to Preserve and Forcibly Expand Employer-based Insurance, Preserve Position of Health Insurers, Force Consumers to pay more for Healthcare

Source generally: "Summary of Coverage Provisions in the Patient Protection and Affordable Care Act", Kaiser Family Foundation, viewed 4/14/10, 5/22/10

Significance

- Underwriting rules affect:
  - What is covered by insurance versus out of pocket expense of patient
    - Affects collection rate of providers
  - How much insurance costs
    - Significant implications for cashflows of non-healthcare entities as well!

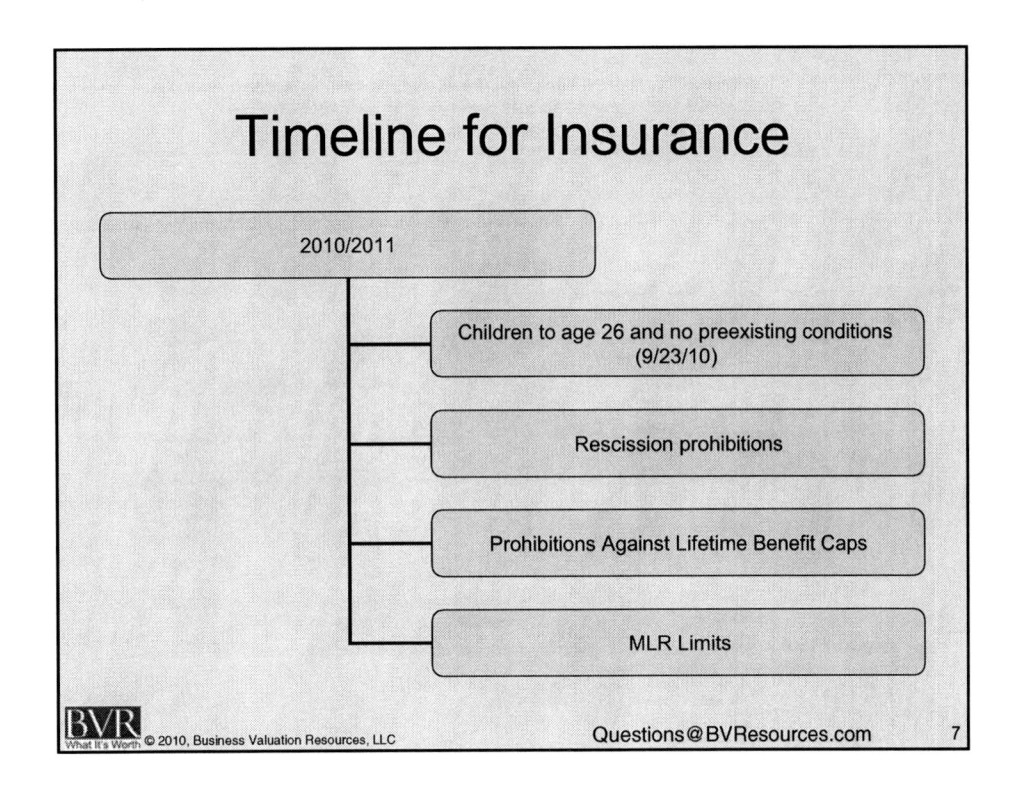

Appendix: Teleconference Transcript

Timeline for Insurance

2010/2011
- Children to age 26 and no preexisting conditions (9/23/10)
- Rescission prohibitions
- Prohibitions Against Lifetime Benefit Caps
- MLR Limits

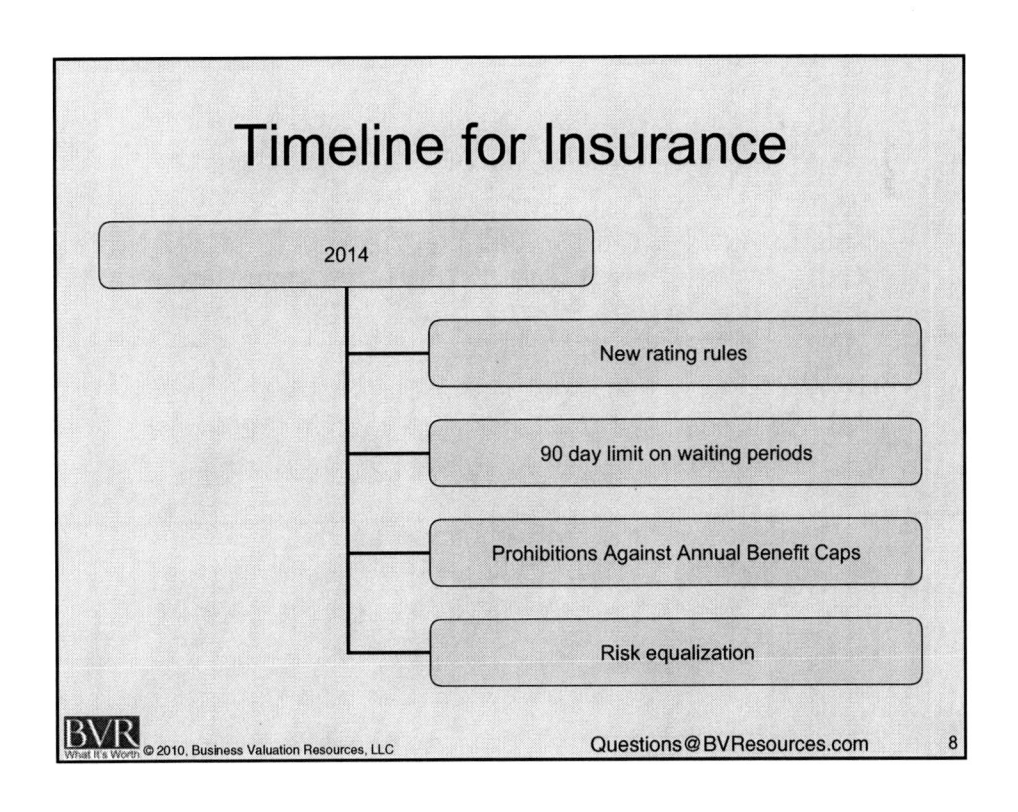

Timeline for Insurance

2014
- New rating rules
- 90 day limit on waiting periods
- Prohibitions Against Annual Benefit Caps
- Risk equalization

The AHLA/BVR Guide to Healthcare Valuation

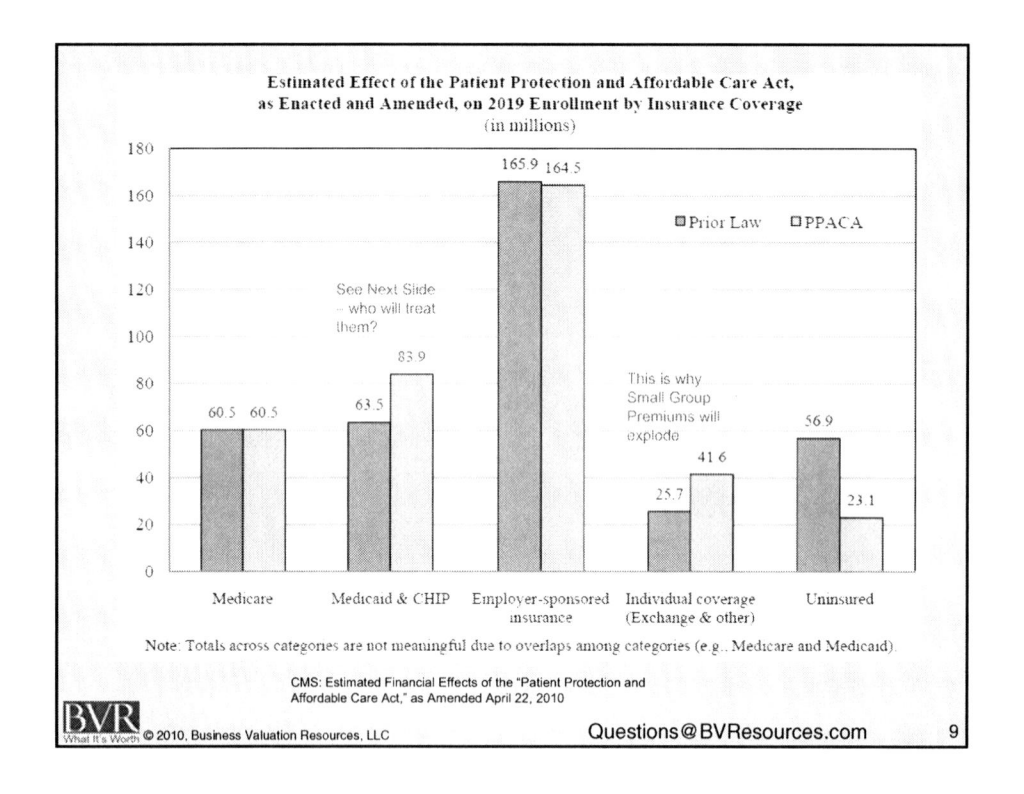

Appendix: Teleconference Transcript

Estimated Effect of the Patient Protection and Affordable Care Act, as Enacted and Amended, on 2019 Enrollment by Insurance Coverage
(in millions)

Category	Prior Law	PPACA
Medicare	60.5	60.5
Medicaid & CHIP	63.5	83.9
Employer-sponsored insurance	165.9	164.5
Individual coverage (Exchange & other)	25.7	41.6
Uninsured	56.9	23.1

Annotations:
- Medicaid & CHIP: "See Next Slide – who will treat them?"
- Individual coverage: "This is why Small Group Premiums will explode"

Note: Totals across categories are not meaningful due to overlaps among categories (e.g., Medicare and Medicaid).

CMS: Estimated Financial Effects of the "Patient Protection and Affordable Care Act," as Amended April 22, 2010

© 2010, Business Valuation Resources, LLC — Questions@BVResources.com

---

Insurance Underwriting

- Health plan premiums will be allowed to vary based on age (by a 3 to 1 ratio), geographic area, tobacco use (by a 1.5 to 1 ratio), and the number of family members.
- Health insurers will be prohibited from imposing lifetime limits on coverage and will be prohibited from rescinding coverage, except in cases of fraud.
  - Dramatic cost and premium implications
- Young adults will be allowed to remain on their parent's health insurance up to age 26. (Notice 2010-38)

© 2010, Business Valuation Resources, LLC — Questions@BVResources.com

Insurance Underwriting

- Waiting periods for coverage will be limited to 90 days.
  - [Observations:
    1. Dramatic cost implications
    2. Enables individuals to get insurance when needed then drop it]
- *Existing individual and employer-sponsored insurance plans* grandfathered as of March 23, 2010 including renewals,
  - except that they will be required to
    - extend dependent coverage to age 26,
    - eliminate annual and lifetime limits on coverage
    - prohibit rescissions of coverage
    - and eliminate waiting periods for coverage of greater than 90 days.

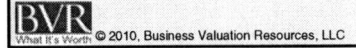

Likely Merger of Small Group and Individual Markets

- Small Group Premiums will go up
  - Benefit requirements
    - No pre-existing condition exclusions
    - No Lifetime limits
    - Deductibles limited: $2,000 individuals, $4,000 families
    - If merged w/ Individual Market, will be worse
  - HUGE increases at Age Crossover in Rating Scheme

Appendix: Teleconference Transcript

Small Group Premiums Will Go Up

PRE-REFORM

	Number	Cost	Total
Standard Insured	9,000	2,000	18,000,000
Pre-existing conditions	500	2,000	1,000,000
Annual limits	10	200,000	2,000,000
	9,510		21,000,000

Cost per Insured: 2,207

POST-REFORM

	Number	Cost	Total
Standard Insured	9,000	2,000	18,000,000
Pre-existing conditions	500	10,000	5,000,000
No Annual limits	10	500,000	5,000,000
	9,510		28,000,000

Cost per Insured: 2,944
Increase: 33.39%

ILLUSTRATIVE EXAMPLE

Individuals

- What – Individual "Mandate" for minimum insurance excluding
  - Those below income tax filing threshold
  - Non-residents, Native Americans, prisoners(!)
- Penalty is greater of (capped at actual cost of coverage):
  - $95 or 1% of income in 2014
  - $325 or 2% of income in 2015
  - $695 or 2.5% of income 2016+ (indexed for inflation)
- When – 2014

Medicaid Expansion

Where the Rubber Meets the Road – Most Newly Covered are Here

Facts Source generally: Financing New Medicaid Coverage Under Health Reform, Kaiser Family Foundation, May, 2010; commentary is my own

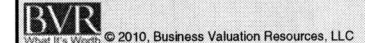

Significance

- More than half of newly covered go into Medicaid
  - Unprofitable line of business
  - Many physicians do not accept Medicaid patients
- Is some revenue for these patients better than none at the margins?

Medicaid Changes

- 17.1 million uninsured adults with incomes at or below 133 percent of poverty.
- Before Reform, adults without children generally ineligible for Medicaid unless they resided in one of a handful of states like Massachusetts
- Medicaid expansion is designed to fill these coverage gaps for
  - Low-income parents
  - Childless adults
- Estimated price tag is around $450 billion
  - New revenue in the system
  - Feds pay most of cost until 2020

Medicaid Changes

- Minimum uniform standard for Medicaid coverage in all states
- Eliminates *some* cross-border differences that affect comparability of transactions under the Market Approach
- Companies that specialize in Medicaid Managed Care potential big winners

Appendix: Teleconference Transcript

Medicaid Changes

- Medicaid payments in fee-for-service *and* managed care for Primary Care Services provided by Primary Care Doctors increased to 100% of the Medicare payment rates for 2013 and 2014.
  – Only two years

Medicaid-To-Medicare Provider Fee Ratios for All Services, 2008

U.S. Average = 72% of Medicare fees

- < 70% (11 states including DC)
- 70-99% (28 states)
- 100%+ (11 states)

Who will help me bake the bread?

NOTE: Tennessee does not have a fee-for-service component in its Medicaid program
SOURCE: S. Zuckerman, AF Williams, and KE Stockley, "Trends in Medicaid Physician Fees, 2003-2008," *Health Affairs*, 28 April 2009.

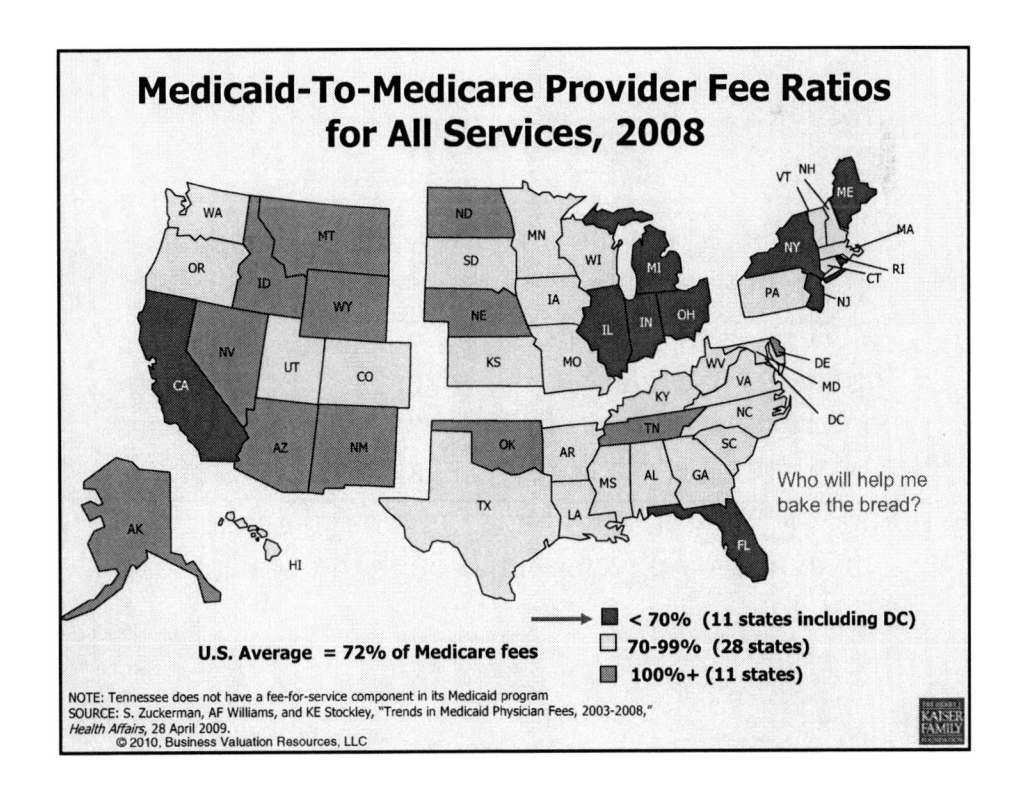

Appendix: Teleconference Transcript

Impact on Providers

Winners, Losers, Near-term and Long-term – assuming the Reform Survives

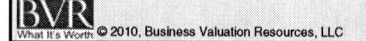

Overview

- Reductions in payments to providers – hospitals, surgi-centers, etc. – are supposed to pay $500 billion of reform's cost.
- Medicare NCDs (National Coverage Decisions) are primary determinant of what new technologies and procedures get covered by all forms of insurance.
- Federal government finances training/residency of almost all new physicians through the Medicare program.

Appendix: Teleconference Transcript

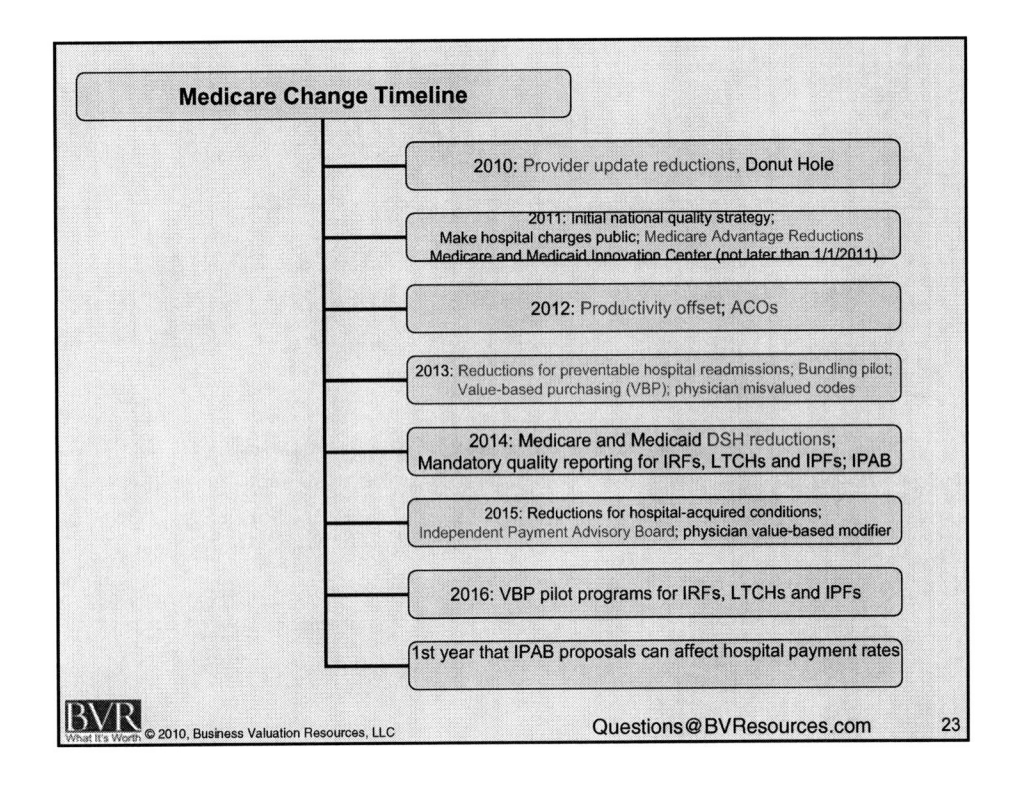

Medicare Change Timeline

- **2010:** Provider update reductions, **Donut Hole**
- **2011:** Initial national quality strategy; Make hospital charges public; Medicare Advantage Reductions Medicare and Medicaid Innovation Center (not later than 1/1/2011)
- **2012:** Productivity offset; ACOs
- **2013:** Reductions for preventable hospital readmissions; Bundling pilot; Value-based purchasing (VBP); physician misvalued codes
- **2014:** Medicare and Medicaid DSH reductions; Mandatory quality reporting for IRFs, LTCHs and IPFs; IPAB
- **2015:** Reductions for hospital-acquired conditions; Independent Payment Advisory Board; physician value-based modifier
- **2016:** VBP pilot programs for IRFs, LTCHs and IPFs
- 1st year that IPAB proposals can affect hospital payment rates

Hospital Changes

- "All in" purportedly saves $500 billion
- Reduction in hospital "Market Basket" updates
  - Historically, hospitals got medical inflation increase in their rates every year
  - Now, increases limited (also applies to Inpatient Rehab)
    - FY 2010-2011 market basket update reduced by 0.25 percent
    - (Effective April 1, 2010)
    - FY 2012-2013 market basket update reduced by 0.10 percent
    - FY 2014 market basket update reduced by 0.30 percent
    - FY 2015-2016 market basket update reduced by 0.20 percent
    - FY 2017-2019 market basket update reduced by 0.75 percent

Appendix: Teleconference Transcript

Hospital Changes

- New Productivity Adjustment
  - Based on economy-wide productivity changes and 10 year moving average in GDP
  - CMS Actuary says likely undoable
- Many More!
  - Lower payment for preventable hospital readmissions
  - Payment reduction for healthcare-acquired conditions
  - Value-Based Purchasing (VBP – new acronym)
  - DSH Reductions of 15% starting in 2014

Hospital Changes

- UP to 6% of DRG may be at risk by 2017!
- See Market Basket data at
  - http://www.cms.gov/MedicareProgramRatesStats/04_MarketBasketData.asp and
  - http://www.cms.gov/MedicareProgramRatesStats/downloads/mktbskt-economic-index.pdf
- Physician-owned Hospitals
  - Expansion of existing hospitals limited
  - Increased physician ownership limited
  - New ownership disclosure requirements
  - New facilities barred from Medicare after December 31, 2010

Other Providers

- **Ambulatory Surgical Centers**
  - **Productivity Adjustment** applied here as well
    - ASCs compete directly with Hospital Outpatient Dept.
    - If Adjustment of -1.3% in place, 2010 Rates would have gone down .1% rather than up by 1.2%
- **Imaging**
  - Utilization rate over which fixed overhead is recovered increased from 50% to 75%
  - DRA Caps limit near-term impact
  - One more nail in the coffin

Other Providers

- **Physical, Occupational and Speech therapy**
  - Suspension of limit on payments extended to 12/31/2010
- **Home Health**
  - Outlier payments cannot exceed 10% of overall revenues
  - 3.0% percent add-on payment for rural agencies, April 1, 2010 thru January 1, 2016

ACOs

- Accountable Care Organizations
  - 1990s style *capitated* Integrated Delivery Systems; Bundled Payments
  - Although no one really knows what these are yet, if it Walks like a Duck and Quacks like a Duck, it is unlikely to be a Horse or Donkey
    - Which is not to say ... never mind
  - Opportunity to share in the cost savings for Medicare program
  - Effective January 1, 2012.

ACOs

- To qualify
  - Be **Accountable** for the **Overall Care** of their Medicare beneficiaries,
  - "Adequate" **Participation** of **Primary Care Physicians**
  - **Define Processes** to promote evidence-based medicine,
  - **Report** on **Quality** and **Costs**, and Coordinate Care
    - Medical Homes

ACOs

- Probably THE most significant element of Reform with respect to Transactions and what will be Valuable
- A Replay of the 1990s Primary Care Craze is in the offing
- New Valuation Models required to account for cashflows associated with risk-sharing
- Antitrust and other implications

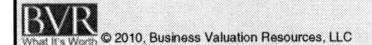

Physician Practices

- Higher payments for Primary Care Physicians (PCPs)
  - 10% bonus for Office, SNF, Home, Rest Home and other specified visits for Family Medicine, Internal Medicine, Geriatric Medicine, Pediatric Medicine if at least 60% of Medicare allowed charges are for Bonus-eligible Services by CPT
  - Effective for 5 years beginning January 1, 2011
  - Needs to be in your DCF!

Appendix: Teleconference Transcript

Physician Practices

- CPT Analysis MANDATORY! Bonus-Eligible Codes by PCPs
  - 99201 through 99215 (the most common codes)
    - Office - New and Established Patients visits
  - 99304 through 99340
    - Nursing facility visits
  - 99341 through 99350
    - Home visits

Simplified Sample Calculation

Total Collected Revenues	10,000,000
Medicare Percentage	25.00%
Eligible Code Percentage	65.00%
Bonus Percentage	10.00%
Bonus	162,500

- For Eligible Code Percentage, you need to isolate Actual Medicare **Allowed Charges** by CPT Code by Provider
- Appears calculation is done by Provider
- Appears bonus is 10% of Medicare Payment

"HITECH" Act

- Another, earlier piece of legislation that is creating quite a stir
- Provides government grant for eligible providers and hospitals who "adopt and meaningfully use" certified electronic health record (EHR) technology
- Proposed Regs issued in January 2010
  - Federal Register / Vol. 75, No. 8 / Wednesday, January 13, 2010 42 CFR Parts 412, 413, 422, and 495

"HITECH" Act

- YOU NEED TO ASK ABOUT THESE PAYMENTS!
  - For providers who have already incurred the expense, this is a windfall straight to the bottom line and to Value
  - For those who currently implement and qualify, could be a Capex reduction, which therefore affects value
- Heads UP! This Act makes "business associates" like you directly responsible for complying with certain provisions of HIPAA privacy rule and all of HIPAA security rules!

Appendix: Teleconference Transcript

Physician EHR Incentives

TABLE 22—MAXIMUM TOTAL AMOUNT OF EHR INCENTIVE PAYMENTS FOR A MEDICARE EP WHO DOES NOT PREDOMINANTLY FURNISH SERVICES IN A HPSA

Calendar year	First CY in which the EP receives an incentive payment				
	2011	2012	2013	2014	2015–subsequent years
2011	$18,000				
2012	12,000	$18,000			
2013	8,000	12,000	$15,000		
2014	4,000	8,000	12,000	$12,000	
2015	2,000	4,000	8,000	8,000	$0
2016		2,000	4,000	4,000	0
Total	44,000	44,000	39,000	24,000	0

TABLE 23—MAXIMUM TOTAL AMOUNT OF INCENTIVE PAYMENTS FOR A MEDICARE EP WHO PREDOMINANTLY PERFORMS SERVICES IN A HPSA

Calendar year	Year that EP becomes EHR user in a HPSA				
	2011	2012	2013	2014	2015 and subsequent years
2011	$19,800				
2012	13,200	$19,800			
2013	8,800	13,200	$16,500		
2014	4,400	8,800	13,200	$13,200	
2015	2,200	4,400	8,800	8,800	$0
2016		2,200	4,400	4,400	0
Total	48,400	48,400	42,900	26,400	0

Questions@BVResources.com

Physician Practices

- 10% bonus for major procedures furnished by general surgeons in HPSAs
- Medical Homes (leading edge is Massachusetts)
- Voluntary pilot program for bundling
- Physician Quality Incentive Program

Questions@BVResources.com

Appendix: Teleconference Transcript

Medicare Advantage

- Refers to things like private Medicare Plans

Exhibit 1
Distribution of Enrollment in Medicare Advantage Plans, by Plan Type, 2010

- Traditional Fee-for-service Medicare 76%
- Medicare Advantage 24%
  - HMO 65%
  - Local PPO 12%
  - Regional PPO 7%
  - PFFS 13%
  - Cost 3%
  - Other, 1%

Total Medicare Advantage Enrollment, 2010 = 11.1 Million

Source: MPR / KFF analysis of the Centers for Medicare and Medicaid Services (CMS) Medicare Advantage enrollment files.

Explaining Health Reform: Key Changes in the Medicare Advantage Program, Kaiser Family Fndn May, 2010; viewed 5/22/10

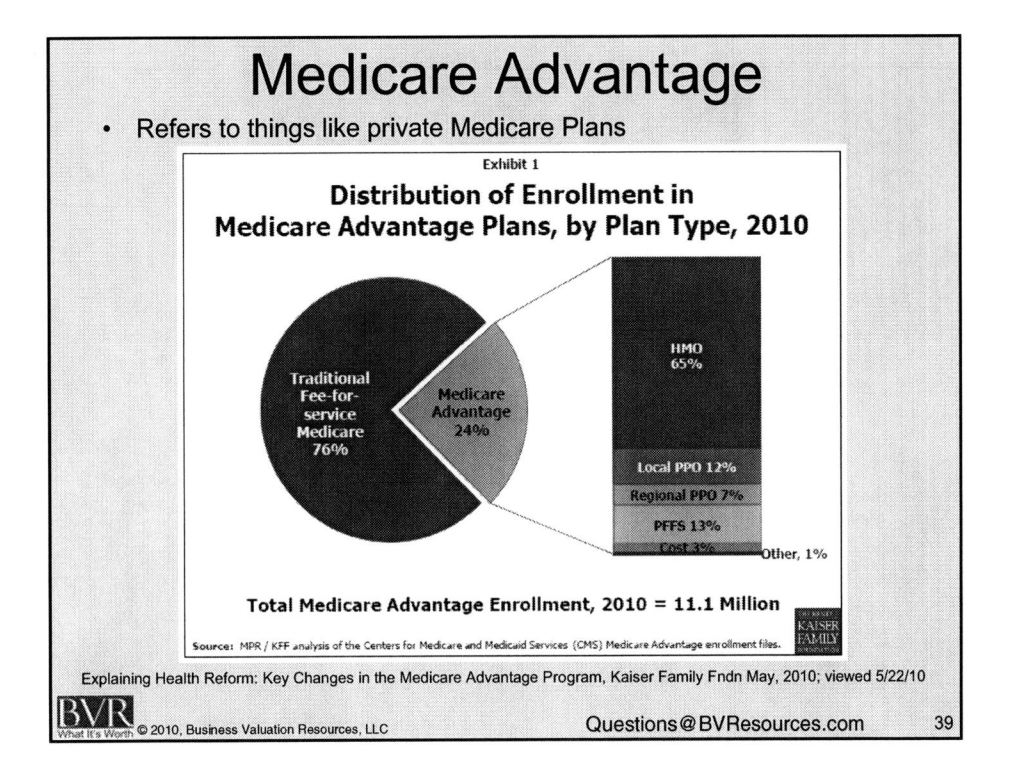

Medicare Advantage

- **Popular in states like Florida, Massachusetts, California, Washington**
  - Medicare beneficiaries like extra benefits
  - Providers and Insurers like big profits
- **Many in Congress wanted to eliminate**
  - *original* Senate bill continued only in Florida
- **Cutbacks in premiums from 2011 forward**
  - Likely to reduce availability and profit, as was the case between 1997 and 2003 when last reductions took place: BBA 1997 to Medicare Modernization Act 2003

Appendix: Teleconference Transcript

Provider Summary

- Winners
  - Hospitals (likely)
    - Already lobbying to undo reductions
    - Expanded coverage, lower bad debts
  - Integrated Delivery Systems
  - Primary Care
- Losers
  - Physician-owned Hospitals
  - Specialists

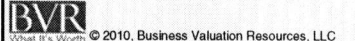

Supplemental Material

Tax-Exempt Hospital Changes
CMS Chief Actuary Analysis
Massachusetts: The Model for Federal Reform
Resources

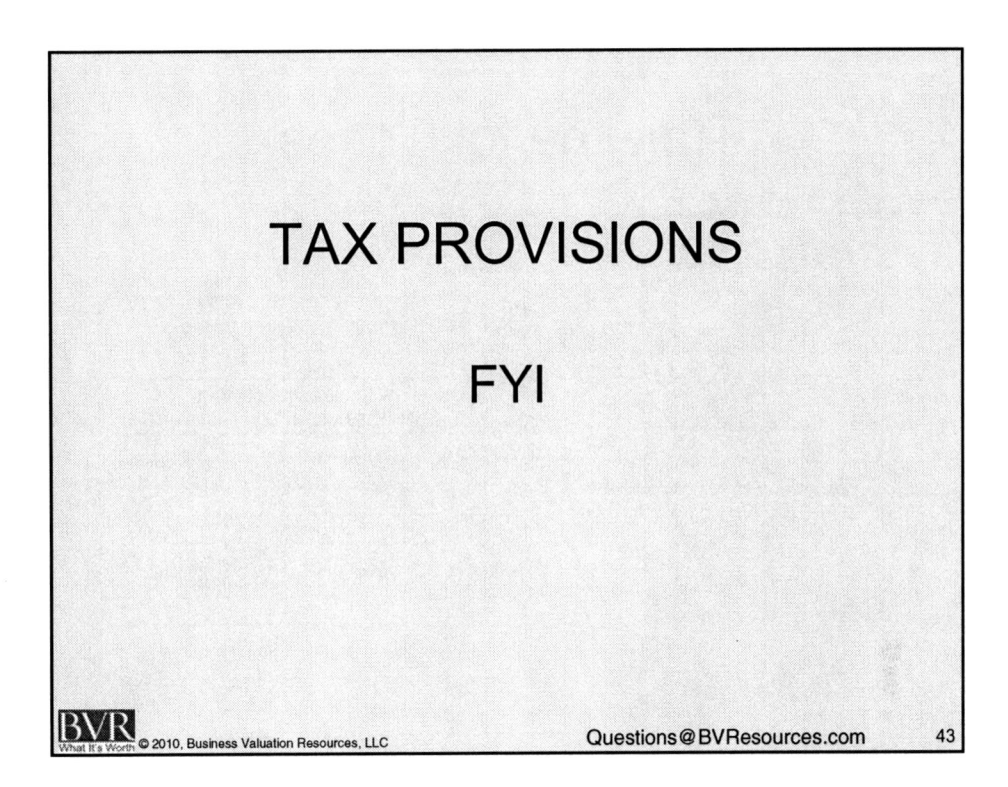

Appendix: Teleconference Transcript

TAX PROVISIONS

FYI

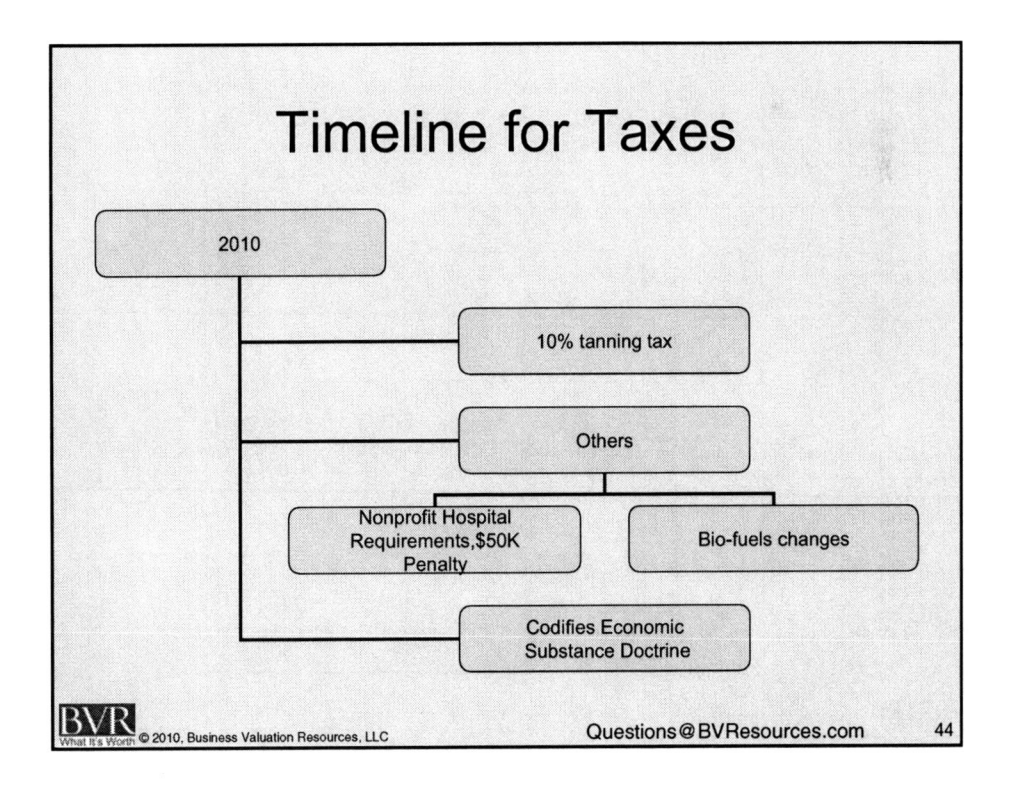

Timeline for Taxes

- 2010
  - 10% tanning tax
  - Others
    - Nonprofit Hospital Requirements, $50K Penalty
    - Bio-fuels changes
    - Codifies Economic Substance Doctrine

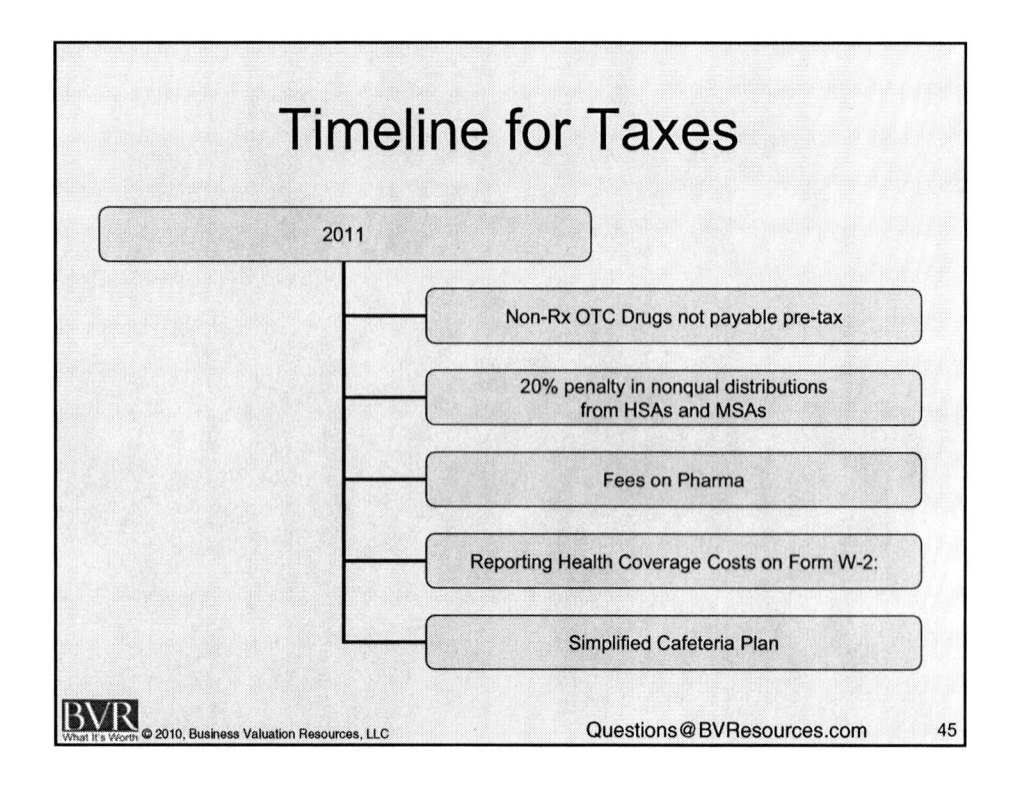

Appendix: Teleconference Transcript

Timeline for Taxes

2011
- Non-Rx OTC Drugs not payable pre-tax
- 20% penalty in nonqual distributions from HSAs and MSAs
- Fees on Pharma
- Reporting Health Coverage Costs on Form W-2:
- Simplified Cafeteria Plan

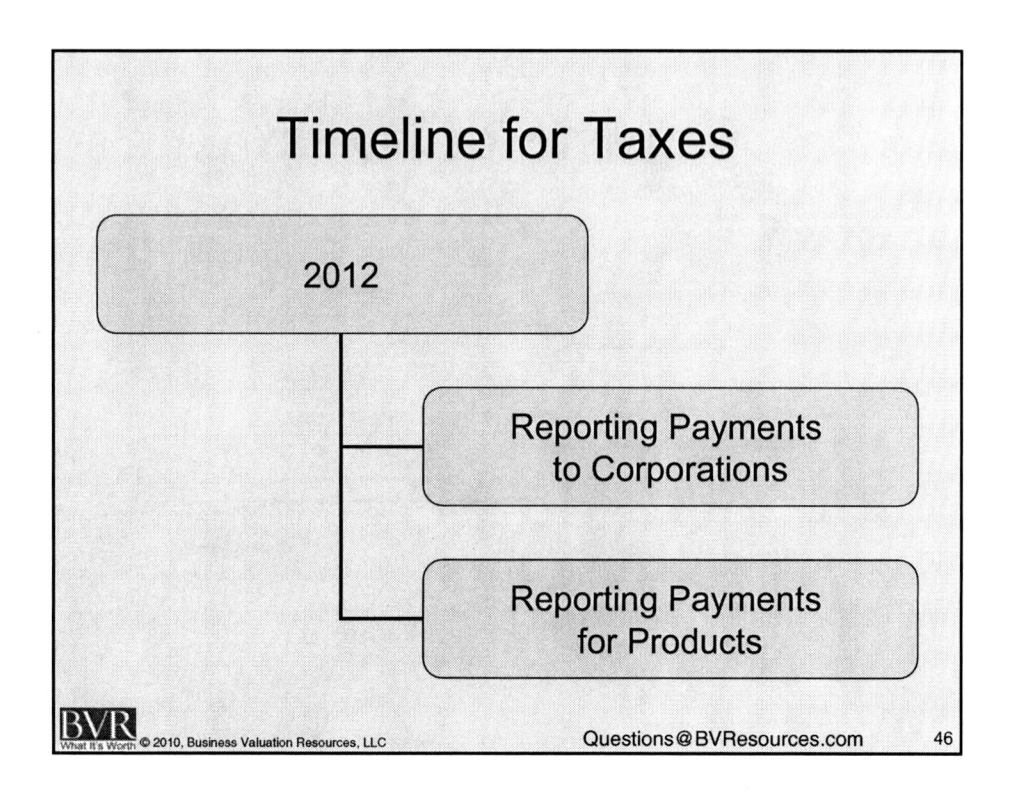

Timeline for Taxes

2012
- Reporting Payments to Corporations
- Reporting Payments for Products

902   The AHLA/BVR Guide to Healthcare Valuation

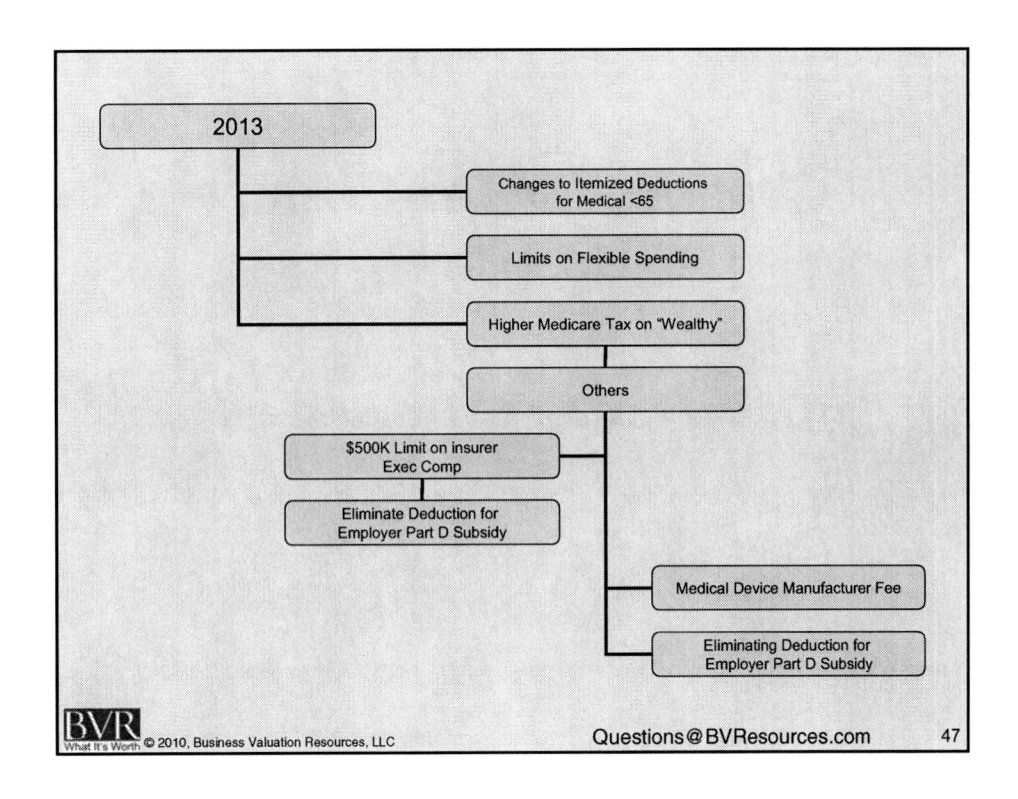

Appendix: Teleconference Transcript

2013
- Changes to Itemized Deductions for Medical <65
- Limits on Flexible Spending
- Higher Medicare Tax on "Wealthy"
- Others
  - $500K Limit on insurer Exec Comp
  - Eliminate Deduction for Employer Part D Subsidy
  - Medical Device Manufacturer Fee
  - Eliminating Deduction for Employer Part D Subsidy

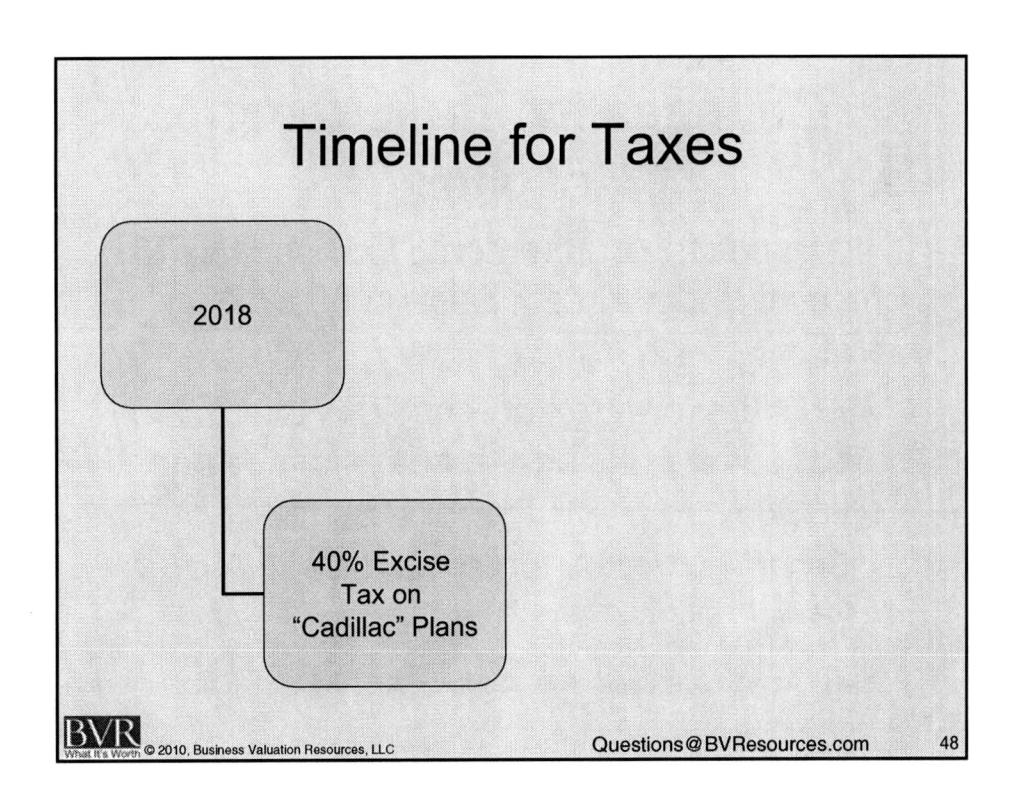

Timeline for Taxes

2018
- 40% Excise Tax on "Cadillac" Plans

Appendix: Teleconference Transcript

Changes for Tax-Exempt Hospitals

Closer Scrutiny, Codification of Community Benefit Requirement

Source generally: AHLA Tax and Finance Practice Group Members Briefing March 24, 2010

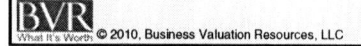

Changes for Tax-Exempt Hospitals

- Now specific requirements for hospitals to receive and maintain Section 501(c)(3) status.
- $50,000 excise tax on hospitals that fail to meet community health-needs assessment standard.
  - Generally effective for tax years beginning after the date of enactment

Source: AHLA Tax and Finance Practice Group Members Briefing March 24, 2010

Changes for Tax-Exempt Hospitals

- Codifies and elaborates on the "community benefit" standard for hospital tax exemption.
- Financial Assistance Policy
  - Amounts charged to eligible patients limited to not more than the lowest charge to patients who have insurance

Changes for Tax-Exempt Hospitals

- Billing and Collection Requirements
- "Extraordinary collection actions" prohibited until
  - "Reasonable efforts" made to determine whether a patient is eligible for Financial Assistance Policy.
  - "Reasonable efforts" to be determined

Appendix: Teleconference Transcript

Changes for Tax-Exempt Hospitals

- Tax-exempt hospitals must now include in Form 990 (tax return) two additional items:
  - (1) Report that describes on community needs assessment
  - (2) Their audited financial statements
- Implications on Goodwill Impairment for FASB purposes!

CMS CHIEF ACTUARY – WHAT TO EXPECT

Estimated Financial Effects of the "Patient Protection and Affordable Care Act," as Amended

April 22, 2010

Key Points From Actuary

1. "...the cost estimates shown in this memorandum do not represent a full 10-year cost for the new legislation."
2. "For many individuals, the penalty amounts for not having insurance coverage were not sufficiently large to have a sizable impact on the coverage decision."
3. "It is important to note that the estimated savings shown in this memorandum for one category of Medicare provisions may be unrealistic. .. While such payment update reductions will create a strong incentive for providers to maximize efficiency, it is doubtful that many will be able to improve their own productivity to the degree achieved by the economy at large."
4. "Simulations by the Office of the Actuary suggest that roughly 15 percent of Part A providers would become unprofitable within the 10-year projection period as a result of the productivity adjustments."
5. "In general, limiting cost growth to a level below medical price inflation alone would represent an exceedingly difficult challenge."
6. Because plan benefit values will generally increase faster than the threshold amounts for defining high-cost plans (which, after 2019, are indexed by the CPI), additional plans would become subject to the excise tax over time, prompting many of those employers to scale back coverage

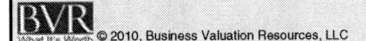

Costs & Savings

- "... we assume that employers and individuals would take roughly 3 to 5 years to fully adapt to the new insurance coverage options and that the enrollment of additional individuals under the Medicaid coverage expansion would be completed by the third year of implementation. Because of these transition effects and the fact that most of the coverage provisions would be in effect for only 6 of the 10 years of the budget period, *the cost estimates shown in this memorandum do not represent a full 10-year cost for the new legislation.*"

Appendix: Teleconference Transcript

Estimated Federal Costs (+) or Savings (−) under Selected Provisions of the Patient Protection and Affordable Care Act as Enacted and Amended
(in billions)

Provisions	2010	2011	2012	2013	2014	2015	2016	2017	2018	2019	Total 2010-19
Total*	$9.2	−$0.7	−$12.6	−$22.3	$16.8	$57.9	$63.1	$54.2	$47.2	$38.5	$251.3
Coverage†	3.3	4.6	4.9	5.2	82.9	119.2	138.2	146.6	157.6	165.8	828.2
Medicare	1.2	−4.7	−14.9	−26.3	−68.8	−60.8	−75.2	−92.1	−108.2	−125.2	−575.1
Medicaid/CHIP	−0.9	−0.9	0.8	4.5	8.6	5.1	4.6	3.4	1.3	1.7	28.3
Cost trend‡	—	—	—	—	−0.0	−0.1	−0.2	−0.4	−0.6	−0.9	−2.3
CLASS program	—	−2.8	−4.5	−5.6	−5.9	−6.0	−4.3	−3.4	−2.8	−2.4	−37.8
Immediate reforms	5.6	3.2	1.2	—	—	—	—	—	—	—	10.0

* Excludes Title IX revenue provisions except for sections 9008 and 9015, certain provisions with limited impacts, and Federal administrative costs
† Includes expansion of Medicaid eligibility and additional funding for CHIP.
‡ Includes estimated non-Medicare Federal savings from provisions for comparative effectiveness research, prevention and wellness, fraud and abuse, and administrative simplification. Excludes impacts of other provisions that would affect cost growth rates, such as the productivity adjustments to Medicare payment rates (which are reflected in the Medicare line) and the section 9001 excise tax on high-cost employer plans.

CMS Actuary Analysis, 4/22/2010

Costs & Savings

- "The Medicare, Medicaid, growth-trend, CLASS, and immediate reform provisions are estimated to result in net savings of about $577 billion, leaving a net overall cost for this period of $251 billion before consideration of additional Federal administrative expenses and the increase in Federal revenues that would result from the excise tax on high-cost employer-sponsored health insurance coverage and other revenue provisions. (The additional Supplementary Medical Insurance revenues from fees on brand-name prescription drugs under section 9008 of the PPACA, and the additional Hospital Insurance payroll tax income under section 9015, are included in the estimated Medicare savings shown here.)"

Appendix: Teleconference Transcript

Costs & Savings

- "The refundable premium tax credits in section 1401 of the PPACA (as amended by section 1001 of the Reconciliation Act) would limit the premiums paid by individuals with incomes up to 400 percent of the FPL to a range of 2.0 to 9.5 percent of their income and would cost an estimated $451 billion through 2019.
- We estimate that individual penalties would provide $33 billion in revenue to the Federal government in fiscal years 2014-2019
- Additionally, for firms that do not offer health insurance and are subject to the "play or pay" penalties, we estimate that the penalties would total $87 billion in 2014-2019."

Costs & Savings

- *"For many individuals, the penalty amounts for not having insurance coverage were not sufficiently large to have a sizable impact on the coverage decision.* Also, in this regard, individuals or families would not be subject to a penalty for failing to enroll in an Exchange plan if the "bronze" premium level (reduced by the premium tax credit, if applicable) would exceed 8 percent of income. We estimate that this provision would exempt individuals and families with incomes between about 400 percent and 542 percent of the FPL, representing about 16 percent of the nonaged population."

Appendix: Teleconference Transcript

Impact on Medicare and Medicaid

- "Net Medicare savings are estimated to total $575 billion for fiscal years 2010-2019. Substantial savings are attributable to provisions that would, among other changes, reduce Part A and Part B payment levels and adjust future "market basket" payment updates for productivity improvements ($233 billion); eliminate the Medicare Improvement Fund ($27 billion); reduce disproportionate share hospital (DSH) payments ($50 billion); reduce Medicare Advantage payment benchmarks and permanently extend the authority to adjust for coding intensity ($145 billion); freeze the income thresholds for the Part B income-related premium for 9 years ($8 billion); implement an Independent Payment Advisory Board together with strict Medicare expenditure growth rate targets ($24 billion); and increase the HI payroll tax rate by 0.9 percentage point for individuals with incomes above $200,000 and families above $250,000 ($63 billion)."

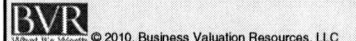

Impact on Medicare and Medicaid

- "Based on the estimated savings for Part A of Medicare, the assets of the Hospital Insurance trust fund would be exhausted in 2029 compared to 2017 under the prior law-an extension of 12 years. The combination of lower Part A costs and higher tax revenues results in a lower Federal deficit *based on budget accounting rules*. However, trust fund accounting considers the same lower expenditures and additional revenues as extending the exhaustion date of the HI trust fund. In practice, the improved HI financing cannot be simultaneously used to finance other Federal outlays (*such as the coverage expansions*) and to extend the trust fund, despite the appearance of this result from the respective accounting conventions." [!!!!]

- "Because plan benefit values will generally increase faster than the threshold amounts for defining high-cost plans (which, after 2019, are indexed by the CPI), *additional plans would become subject to the excise tax over time, prompting many of those employers to scale back coverage.*" [!!!!]

Appendix: Teleconference Transcript

Impact on Medicare and Medicaid

- *"It is important to note that the estimated savings shown in this memorandum for one category of Medicare provisions may be unrealistic.* The PPACA introduces permanent annual productivity adjustments to price updates for most providers (such as hospitals, skilled nursing facilities, and home health agencies), using a 10-year moving average of economy-wide private, non-farm productivity gains. While such payment update reductions will create a strong incentive for providers to maximize efficiency, it is doubtful that many will be able to improve their own productivity to the degree achieved by the economy at large.
- *Simulations by the Office of the Actuary suggest that roughly 15 percent of Part A providers would become unprofitable* within the 10-year projection period as a result of the productivity adjustments."

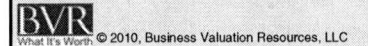

Impact on Medicare and Medicaid

- "The [Independent Payment Advisory] Board will be charged with recommending changes to certain Medicare payment categories in an effort to prevent per-beneficiary Medicare costs from increasing faster than the average of the CPI and the CPI-medical for "implementation years" 2015 through 2019.
- Average Medicare costs per beneficiary usually increase over time as a function of (i) medical specific price growth, (ii) more utilization of services by beneficiaries, and (iii) greater "intensity" or average complexity of these services. *In general, limiting cost growth to a level below medical price inflation alone would represent an exceedingly difficult challenge.*"

Impact of Provisions on the Rate of Growth in Health Care Costs

- "As discussed previously, however, the growth rate reductions from productivity adjustments are unlikely to be sustainable on a permanent annual basis, and meeting the CPI-based target growth rates prior to 2020 will be very challenging as well.
- The Independent Payment Advisory Board will also be required to periodically submit recommendations to Congress and the President regarding methods of slowing the growth of non-Federal health care programs. In many cases, Federal or State legislation would need to be enacted to implement these recommendations."

Impact of Provisions on the Rate of Growth in Health Care Costs

- "Because plan benefit values will generally increase faster than the threshold amounts for defining high-cost plans (which, after 2019, are indexed by the CPI), additional plans would become subject to the excise tax over time, prompting many of those employers to scale back coverage." [!!!!].

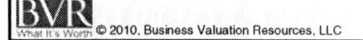

National Health Expenditure Impacts

- "[The] excise tax on employer-sponsored health insurance coverage with a benefit value above specified levels (generally $10,200 for individuals and $27,500 for families in 2018, adjusted in 2019 by growth in the CPI plus 1 percentage point and by growth in the CPI thereafter)
- *As mentioned earlier, the proportion of workers experiencing reductions in their employer-sponsored health coverage as a result of the excise tax is estimated to increase rapidly after 2019.*"

MASSACHUSETTS LEGISLATION vs FEDERAL

- Individual mandate - Yes
- Penalty for lack of coverage thru tax system - Yes
  - $52 each month, $624 for year for individuals aged 18-26.
  - $89 each month, $1068 for year for individuals 27 or older.
- No lifetime limits, waiting periods or barriers for pre-existing medical conditions - Yes
- Subsidies based on Federal Poverty Limit FPL – Yes
- State has own "Health Connector" Insurance Exchange – Yes
- Children eligible to age 26 – Yes
- Employer Penalty – Yes
- Benefit tiers (Platinum, gold, silver, bronze) – Yes

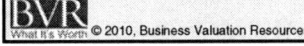

MASSACHUSETTS LEGISLATION vs FEDERAL

- Medicaid Expansion – Yes
- Merging the individual and small group markets – Allowed
- Targeted Primary Care Recruitment - Yes
- Insurance market and rating rules – Yes
- Rating variation in the individual and the small group market and the Exchanges based *only* on
  - age (limited to 3 to 1 ratio),
  - premium rating area,
  - family composition, and
  - tobacco use (limited to 1.5. to 1 ratio)
- No Antitrust Reform - Yes

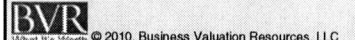

MASSACHUSETTS EXPERIENCE

- Highest rate of insured residents in the nation, 97.4%
- Highest premiums in nation
  - Many mandated benefits, e.g., IVF
- One of Highest rates of cost increase in nation
- Antitrust Issues - DOJ now investigating
- Second highest unemployment rate in New England
- **Self-insured** employers increasing to avoid merged Individual/Small Group Market premium increases
- Gap between Small Group Market and *Self-Insured* Large Group Market growing
- Tax Increases required in 2008 to cover costs
- Coverage for 30,000 legal immigrants terminated to cut costs
  - But transferred to Medicaid

Appendix: Teleconference Transcript

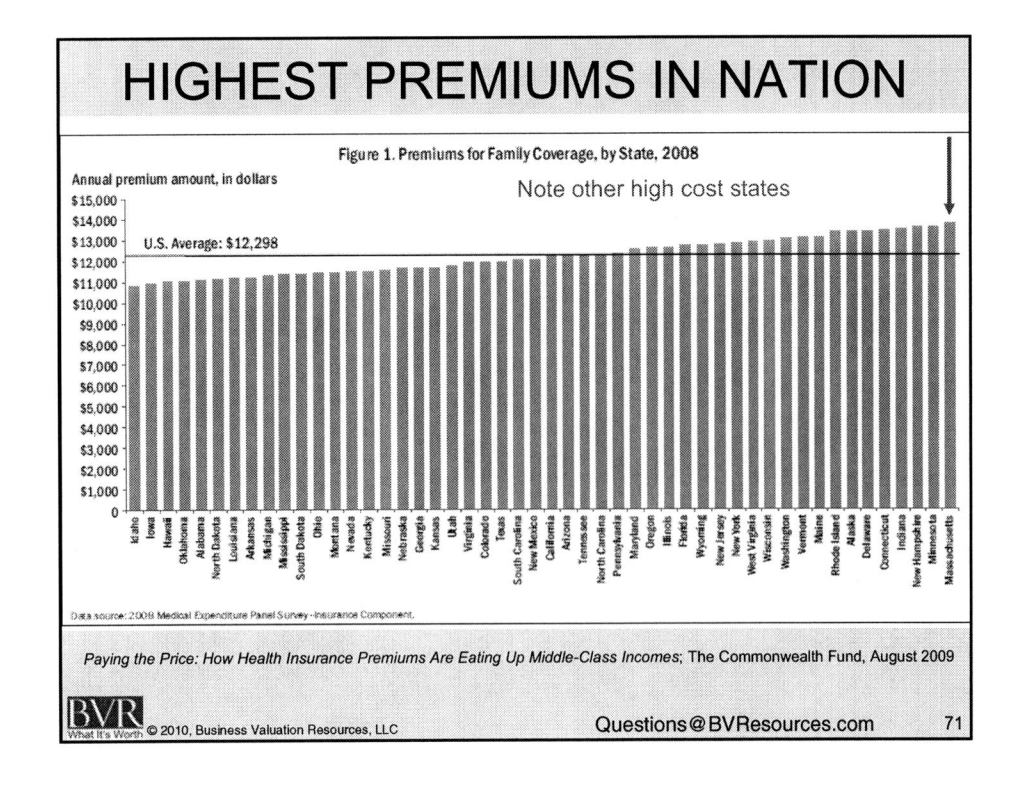

HIGHEST PREMIUMS IN NATION

Figure 1. Premiums for Family Coverage, by State, 2008

Note other high cost states

U.S. Average: $12,298

Data source: 2008 Medical Expenditure Panel Survey - Insurance Component.

Paying the Price: How Health Insurance Premiums Are Eating Up Middle-Class Incomes; The Commonwealth Fund, August 2009

DHCFP

Health Care in Massachusetts:

Key Indicators

February 2010

Deval L. Patrick, Governor
Commonwealth of Massachusetts

Timothy P. Murray
Lieutenant Governor

JudyAnn Bigby, Secretary
Executive Office of Health and Human Services

David Morales, Commissioner
Division of Health Care Finance and Policy

The AHLA/BVR Guide to Healthcare Valuation

Appendix: Teleconference Transcript

Insured Population by Type of Insurance
Excludes Medicare Enrollees

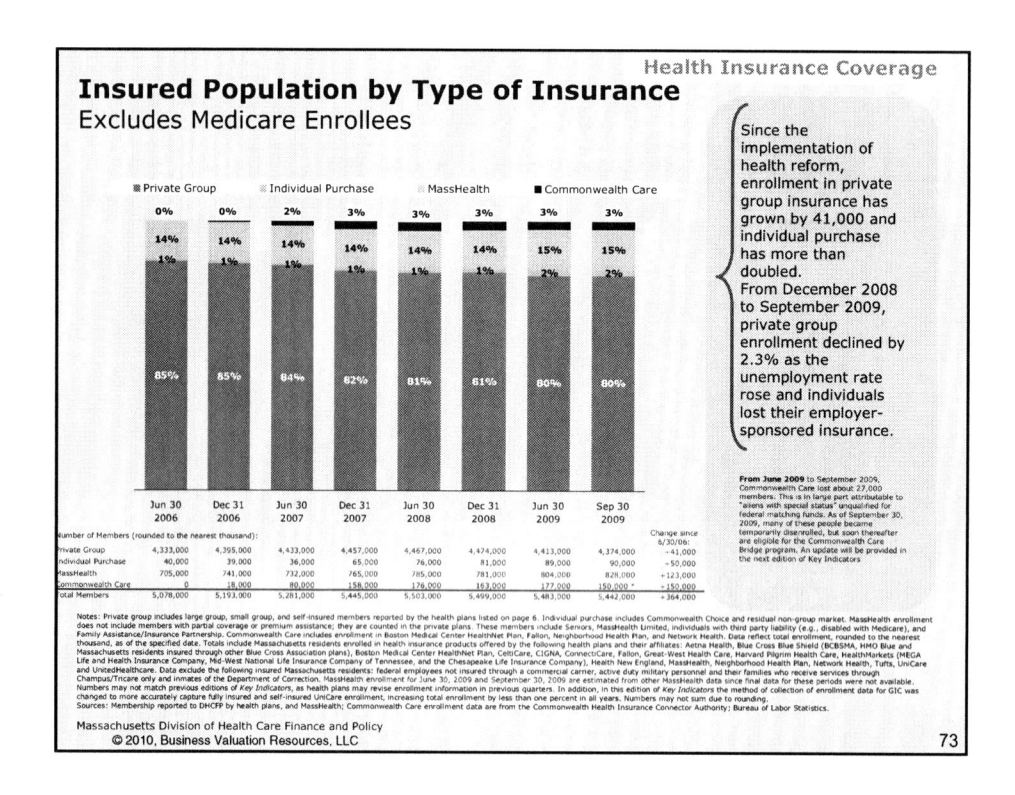

Legend: Private Group | Individual Purchase | MassHealth | Commonwealth Care

	Jun 30 2006	Dec 31 2006	Jun 30 2007	Dec 31 2007	Jun 30 2008	Dec 31 2008	Jun 30 2009	Sep 30 2009
Commonwealth Care	0%	0%	2%	3%	3%	3%	3%	3%
MassHealth	14%	14%	14%	14%	14%	14%	15%	15%
Individual Purchase	1%	1%	1%	1%	1%	1%	2%	2%
Private Group	85%	85%	84%	82%	81%	81%	80%	80%

Number of Members (rounded to the nearest thousand):

	Jun 30 2006	Dec 31 2006	Jun 30 2007	Dec 31 2007	Jun 30 2008	Dec 31 2008	Jun 30 2009	Sep 30 2009	Change since 6/30/06
Private Group	4,333,000	4,395,000	4,433,000	4,457,000	4,467,000	4,474,000	4,413,000	4,374,000	-41,000
Individual Purchase	40,000	39,000	36,000	65,000	76,000	81,000	89,000	90,000	+50,000
MassHealth	705,000	741,000	732,000	765,000	785,000	781,000	804,000	828,000	+123,000
Commonwealth Care	0	18,000	80,000	158,000	176,000	163,000	177,000	150,000*	+150,000
Total Members	5,078,000	5,193,000	5,281,000	5,445,000	5,503,000	5,499,000	5,483,000	5,442,000	+364,000

Since the implementation of health reform, enrollment in private group insurance has grown by 41,000 and individual purchase has more than doubled.

From December 2008 to September 2009, private group enrollment declined by 2.3% as the unemployment rate rose and individuals lost their employer-sponsored insurance.

From June 2009 to September 2009, Commonwealth Care lost about 27,000 members. This is in large part attributable to "aliens with special status" unqualified for federal matching funds. As of September 30, 2009, many of these people became temporarily disenrolled, but soon thereafter are eligible for the Commonwealth Care Bridge program. An update will be provided in the next edition of Key Indicators.

Notes: Private group includes large group, small group, and self-insured members reported by the health plans listed on page 6. Individual purchase includes Commonwealth Choice and residual non-group market. MassHealth enrollment does not include members with partial coverage or premium assistance; they are counted in the private plans. These members include Seniors, MassHealth Limited, individuals with third party liability (e.g., disabled with Medicare), and Family Assistance/Insurance Partnership. Commonwealth Care includes enrollment in Boston Medical Center HealthNet Plan, Fallon, Neighborhood Health Plan, and Network Health. Data reflect total enrollment, rounded to the nearest thousand, as of the specified date. Totals include Massachusetts residents enrolled in health insurance products offered by the following health plans and their affiliates: Aetna Health, Blue Cross Blue Shield (BCBSMA, HMO Blue and Massachusetts residents insured through other Blue Cross Association plans), Boston Medical Center HealthNet Plan, CeltiCare, CIGNA, ConnectiCare, Fallon, Great-West Health Care, Harvard Pilgrim Health Care, HealthMarkets (MEGA Life and Health Insurance Company, Mid-West National Life Insurance Company of Tennessee, and the Chesapeake Life Insurance Company), Health New England, MassHealth, Neighborhood Health Plan, Network Health, Tufts, UniCare and UnitedHealthcare. Data exclude the following insured Massachusetts residents: federal employees not insured through a commercial carrier, active duty military personnel and their families who receive services through Champus/Tricare only and inmates of the Department of Correction. MassHealth enrollment for June 30, 2009 and September 30, 2009 are estimated from other MassHealth data since final data for these periods were not available. Numbers may not match previous editions of Key Indicators, as health plans may revise enrollment information in previous quarters. In addition, in this edition of Key Indicators the method of collection of enrollment data for GIC was changed to more accurately capture fully insured and self-insured UniCare enrollment, increasing total enrollment by less than one percent in all years. Numbers may not sum due to rounding.
Sources: Membership reported to DHCFP by health plans, and MassHealth; Commonwealth Care enrollment data are from the Commonwealth Health Insurance Connector Authority; Bureau of Labor Statistics.

Massachusetts Division of Health Care Finance and Policy
© 2010, Business Valuation Resources, LLC

73

Private Group Enrollment
Excludes Medicare Advantage

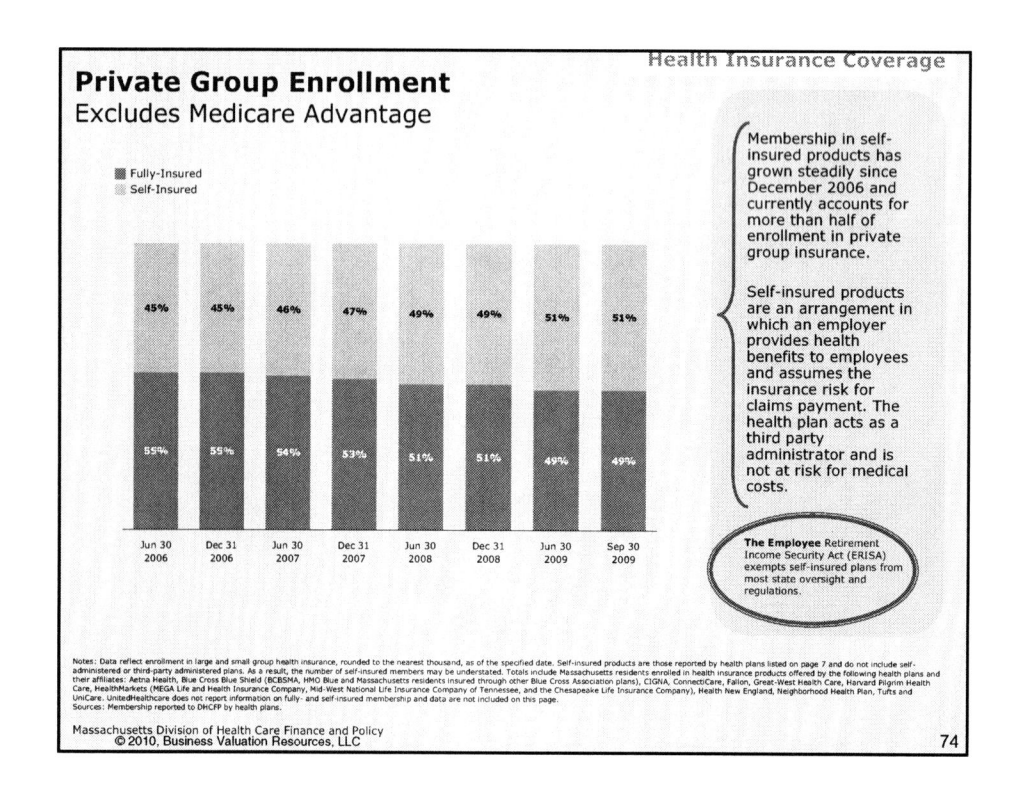

Legend: Fully-Insured | Self-Insured

	Jun 30 2006	Dec 31 2006	Jun 30 2007	Dec 31 2007	Jun 30 2008	Dec 31 2008	Jun 30 2009	Sep 30 2009
Self-Insured	45%	45%	46%	47%	49%	49%	51%	51%
Fully-Insured	55%	55%	54%	53%	51%	51%	49%	49%

Membership in self-insured products has grown steadily since December 2006 and currently accounts for more than half of enrollment in private group insurance.

Self-insured products are an arrangement in which an employer provides health benefits to employees and assumes the insurance risk for claims payment. The health plan acts as a third party administrator and is not at risk for medical costs.

The Employee Retirement Income Security Act (ERISA) exempts self-insured plans from most state oversight and regulations.

Notes: Data reflect enrollment in large and small group health insurance, rounded to the nearest thousand, as of the specified date. Self-insured products are those reported by health plans listed on page 7 and do not include self-administered or third-party administered plans. As a result, the number of self-insured members may be understated. Totals include Massachusetts residents enrolled in health insurance products offered by the following health plans and their affiliates: Aetna Health, Blue Cross Blue Shield (BCBSMA, HMO Blue and Massachusetts residents insured through other Blue Cross Association plans), CIGNA, ConnectiCare, Fallon, Great-West Health Care, Harvard Pilgrim Health Care, HealthMarkets (MEGA Life and Health Insurance Company, Mid-West National Life Insurance Company of Tennessee, and the Chesapeake Life Insurance Company), Health New England, Neighborhood Health Plan, Tufts and UniCare. UnitedHealthcare does not report information on fully- and self-insured membership and data are not included on this page.
Sources: Membership reported to DHCFP by health plans.

Massachusetts Division of Health Care Finance and Policy
© 2010, Business Valuation Resources, LLC

74

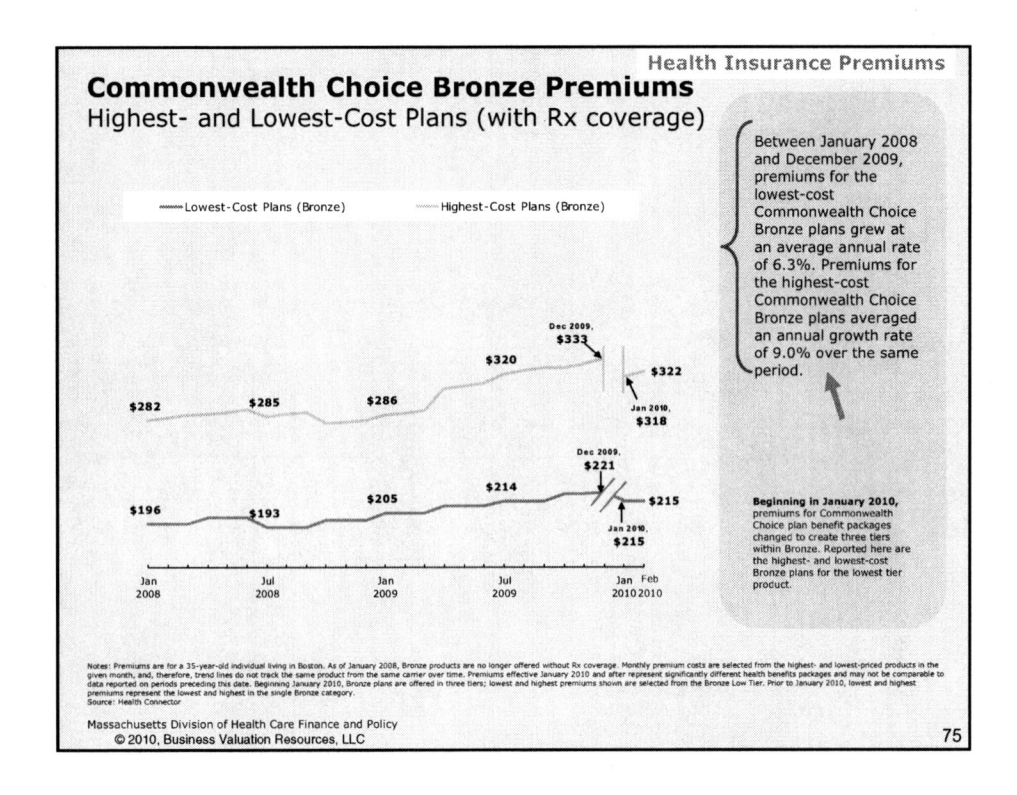

Appendix: Teleconference Transcript

Commonwealth Choice Bronze Premiums
Highest- and Lowest-Cost Plans (with Rx coverage)

Health Insurance Premiums

Between January 2008 and December 2009, premiums for the lowest-cost Commonwealth Choice Bronze plans grew at an average annual rate of 6.3%. Premiums for the highest-cost Commonwealth Choice Bronze plans averaged an annual growth rate of 9.0% over the same period.

Highest-Cost Plans (Bronze): $282 (Jan 2008), $285, $286, $320, Dec 2009 $333, Jan 2010 $318, $322 (Feb 2010)
Lowest-Cost Plans (Bronze): $196 (Jan 2008), $193, $205, $214, Dec 2009 $221, Jan 2010 $215, $215 (Feb 2010)

Beginning in January 2010, premiums for Commonwealth Choice plan benefit packages changed to create three tiers within Bronze. Reported here are the highest- and lowest-cost Bronze plans for the lowest tier product.

Notes: Premiums are for a 35-year-old individual living in Boston. As of January 2008, Bronze products are no longer offered without Rx coverage. Monthly premium costs are selected from the highest- and lowest-priced products in the given month, and, therefore, trend lines do not track the same product from the same carrier over time. Premiums effective January 2010 and after represent significantly different health benefits packages and may not be comparable to data reported on periods preceding this date. Beginning January 2010, Bronze plans are offered in three tiers; lowest and highest premiums shown are selected from the Bronze Low Tier. Prior to January 2010, lowest and highest premiums represent the lowest and highest in the single Bronze category.
Source: Health Connector
Massachusetts Division of Health Care Finance and Policy
© 2010, Business Valuation Resources, LLC

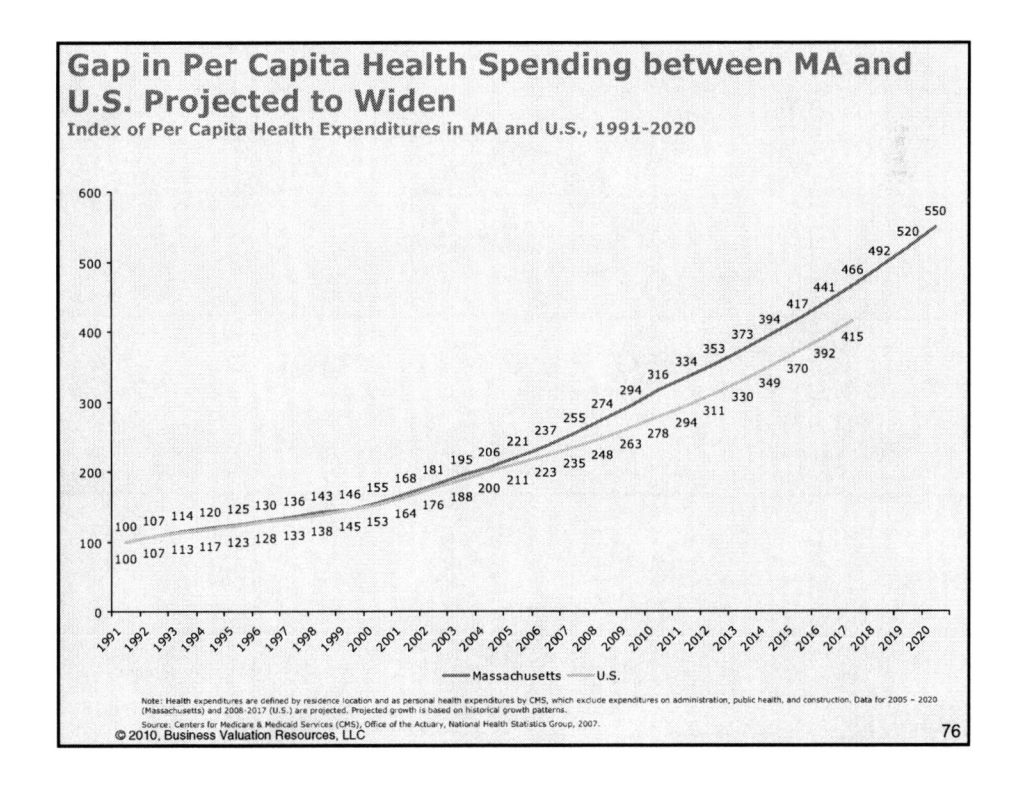

Gap in Per Capita Health Spending between MA and U.S. Projected to Widen
Index of Per Capita Health Expenditures in MA and U.S., 1991-2020

Massachusetts: 100, 107, 114, 120, 125, 130, 136, 143, 146, 155, 168, 181, 195, 206, 221, 237, 255, 274, 294, 316, 334, 353, 373, 394, 417, 441, 466, 492, 520, 550
U.S.: 100, 107, 113, 117, 123, 128, 133, 138, 145, 153, 164, 176, 188, 200, 211, 223, 235, 248, 263, 278, 294, 311, 330, 349, 370, 392, 415

Note: Health expenditures are defined by residence location and as personal health expenditures by CMS, which exclude expenditures on administration, public health, and construction. Data for 2005 – 2020 (Massachusetts) and 2008-2017 (U.S.) are projected. Projected growth is based on historical growth patterns.
Source: Centers for Medicare & Medicaid Services (CMS), Office of the Actuary, National Health Statistics Group, 2007.
© 2010, Business Valuation Resources, LLC

Appendix: Teleconference Transcript

Single and Family Premiums in MA Were 10% to 12% Higher than U.S. in 2008
Health Insurance Premiums in MA and U.S., 2000, 2006, 2008

Single Premiums

	Massachusetts	U.S.
2000	$2,719	$2,655
2006	$4,448	$4,118
2008	$4,836	$4,386

Family Premiums

	Massachusetts	U.S.
2000	$7,341	$6,772
2006	$12,290	$11,381
2008	$13,788	$12,298

The relative difference in premiums between Massachusetts and the U.S. tended to increase over time. The individual premium in Massachusetts was 2%, 8%, and 10% higher than in the U.S. and the family premium was 8%, 8%, and 12% higher in 2000, 2006, and 2008 respectively.

Sources: Agency for Healthcare Research and Quality (AHRQ), Medical Expenditure Panel Survey (MEPS)-insurance component.
© 2010, Business Valuation Resources, LLC

DHCFP

Premium Trends

March 2010

Deval L. Patrick, Governor
Commonwealth of Massachusetts
Timothy P. Murray
Lieutenant Governor

JudyAnn Bigby, Secretary
Executive Office of Health and Human Services
David Morales, Commissioner
Division of Health Care Finance and Policy

© 2010, Business Valuation Resources, LLC   Questions@BVResources.com

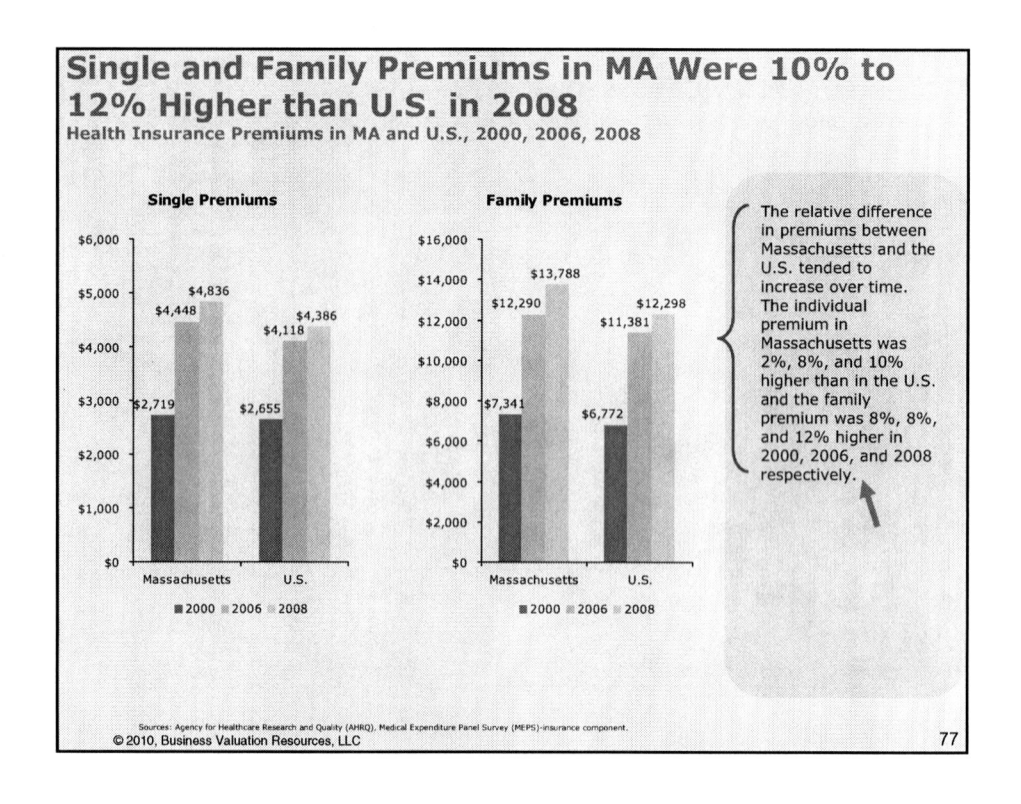

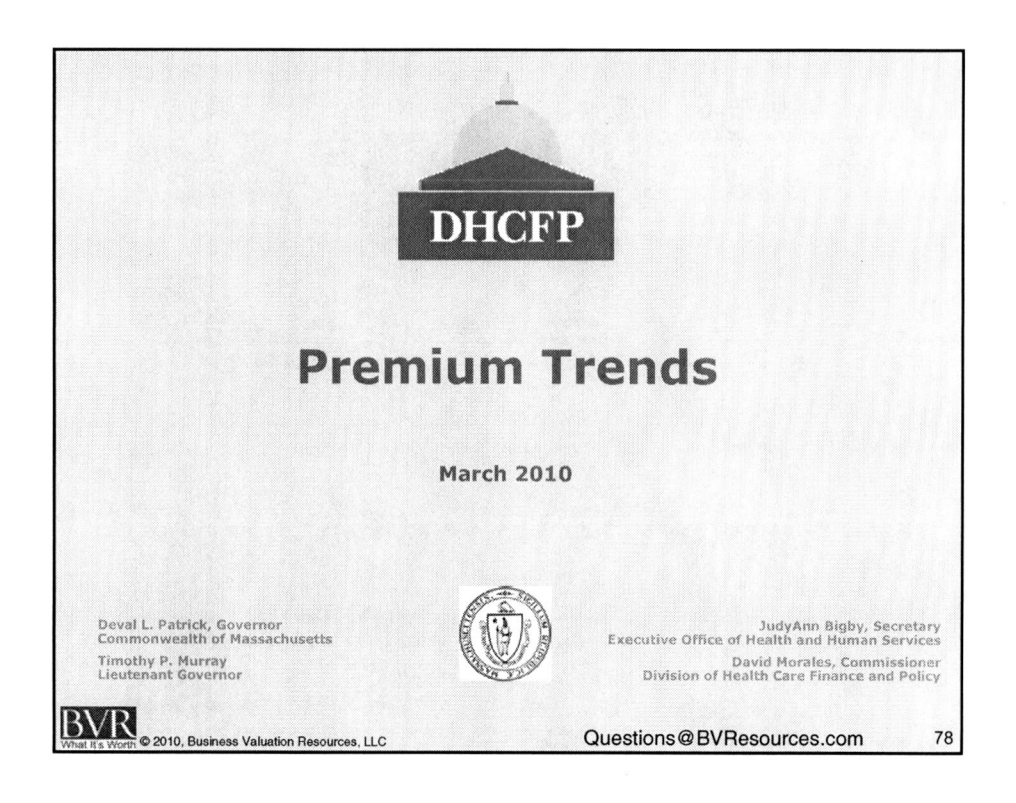

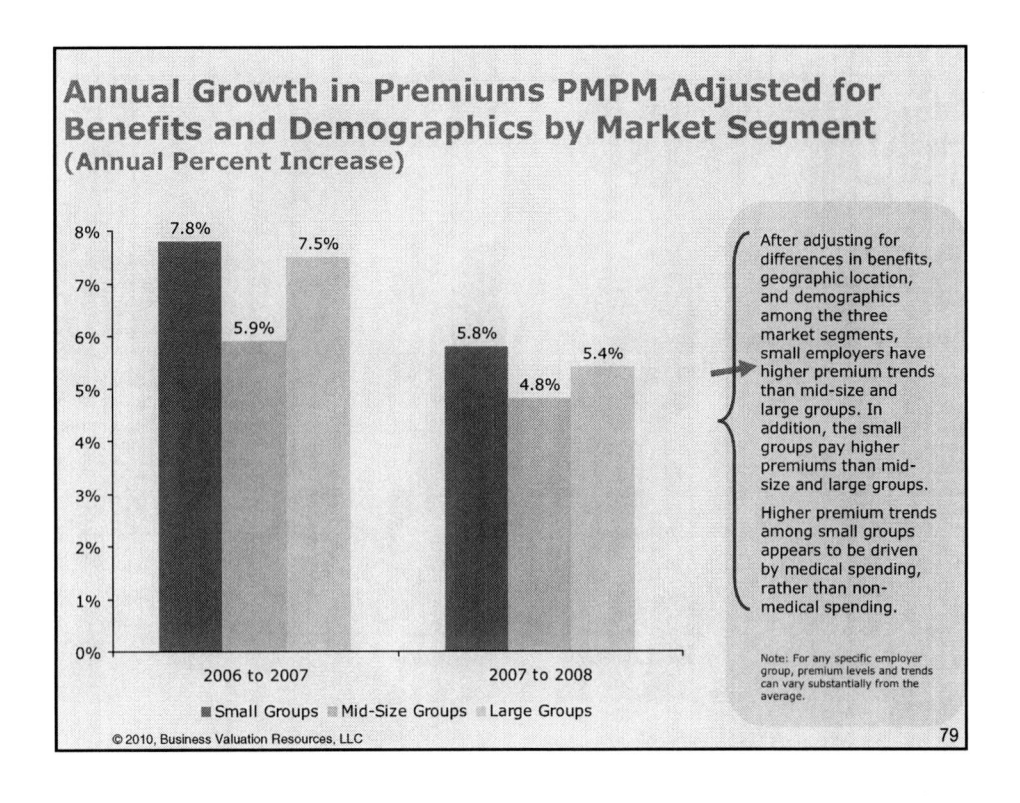

Appendix: Teleconference Transcript

Annual Growth in Premiums PMPM Adjusted for Benefits and Demographics by Market Segment
(Annual Percent Increase)

Period	Small Groups	Mid-Size Groups	Large Groups
2006 to 2007	7.8%	5.9%	7.5%
2007 to 2008	5.8%	4.8%	5.4%

After adjusting for differences in benefits, geographic location, and demographics among the three market segments, small employers have higher premium trends than mid-size and large groups. In addition, the small groups pay higher premiums than mid-size and large groups.

Higher premium trends among small groups appears to be driven by medical spending, rather than non-medical spending.

Note: For any specific employer group, premium levels and trends can vary substantially from the average.

© 2010, Business Valuation Resources, LLC

What To Expect
Written Testimony of Jon B. Hurst, President Retailers Association of Massachusetts Before the Division of Insurance December 28, 2009

- "For small employers across the Commonwealth no issue is of greater concern. Out of control premium increases continue to hamper any efforts made to promote new job growth and profitability for small businesses. While most have focused recently on the overall system cost increases, we feel that more immediate attention must be paid to the equally important issue of premium disparities and purchaser rights across all group sizes and types. Small employers are looking at prices of a family HMO plan this year often in excess of $23,000. On top of those unaffordable premiums are another year of forecasted double digit increases in 2010. Large employers, both big business and big government, have not seen increases anywhere near these levels. This creates an unfair competitive marketplace for small versus large companies. This is both troubling and ironic in an environment in which the law says you must have coverage."

- Unlike larger businesses and government entities, such as the Commonwealth's Group Insurance Commission (GIC) and cities and towns, small employers are not permitted under current law to group together to group buy and increase their buying clout.

Questions@BVResources.com

Appendix: Teleconference Transcript

Benefit Reductions Across All Market Segments' Most Popular Products
Median Actuarial Value by Market Segment

Market Segment	2006	2007	2008
Small Groups	0.907	0.898	0.882
Mid-Size Groups	0.917	0.907	0.882
Large Groups	0.944	0.928	0.915

All group segments have experienced decreases in benefits for the median **most popular product**.

However, on average **across all products**, mid-size and large groups have had very little change in benefits over this period. Small groups have reduced benefits more significantly.

Questions@BVResources.com

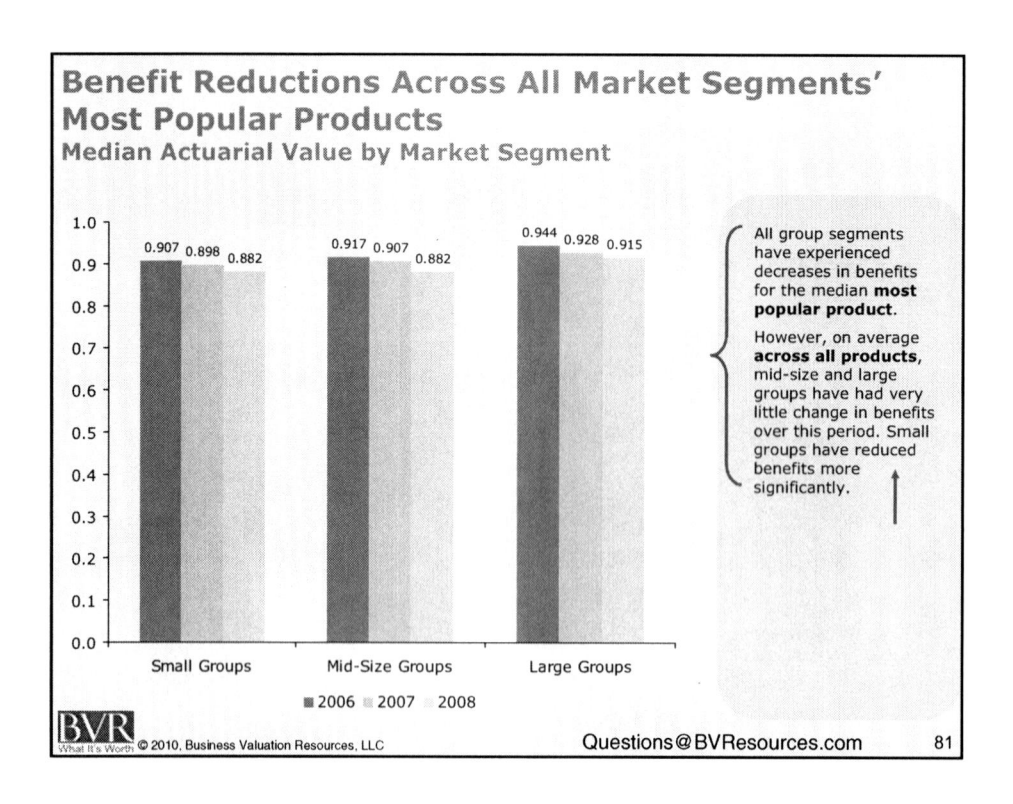

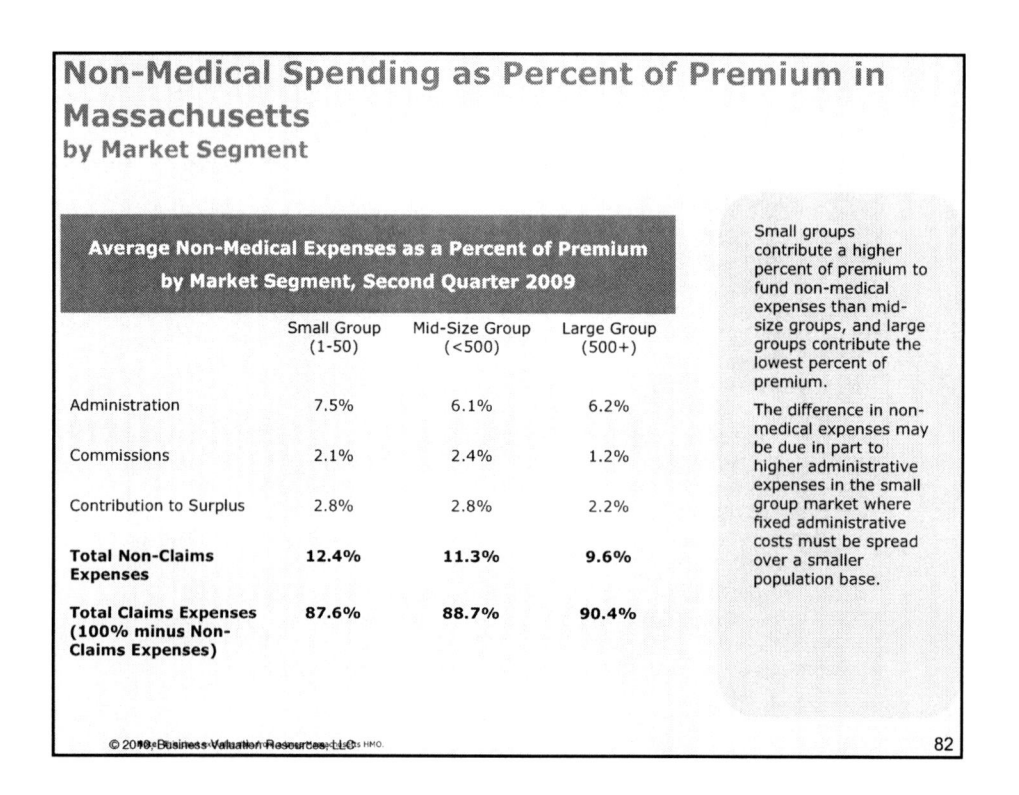

© 2010, Business Valuation Resources, LLC

Non-Medical Spending as Percent of Premium in Massachusetts
by Market Segment

Average Non-Medical Expenses as a Percent of Premium by Market Segment, Second Quarter 2009

	Small Group (1-50)	Mid-Size Group (<500)	Large Group (500+)
Administration	7.5%	6.1%	6.2%
Commissions	2.1%	2.4%	1.2%
Contribution to Surplus	2.8%	2.8%	2.2%
Total Non-Claims Expenses	**12.4%**	**11.3%**	**9.6%**
Total Claims Expenses (100% minus Non-Claims Expenses)	**87.6%**	**88.7%**	**90.4%**

Small groups contribute a higher percent of premium to fund non-medical expenses than mid-size groups, and large groups contribute the lowest percent of premium.

The difference in non-medical expenses may be due in part to higher administrative expenses in the small group market where fixed administrative costs must be spread over a smaller population base.

Appendix: Teleconference Transcript

Examples of Premium Growth Variability: Results of Aging of Employees or Changes in Group Size

Scenario 1 – Company with 6 Employees	Rate Increase	Scenario 2 – Company with 20 Employees	Rate Increase
Rate increase if no change in employee composition (no employees age into higher age bands – Note: not probable for the average employer)	6.0%	Rate increase if no change in employee composition (no employees age into higher age bands – Note: not probable for the average employer)	6.0%
Rate increase if there is no change in employees; two employees age into next five-year age band	10.2%	Rate increase if there is no change in employees; six employees age into next five-year age band	10.7%
Rate increase if one employee of average age leaves the group, leaving the group with 5 members.	15.8%	Rate increase if three employees of average age leave the group, leaving the group with 17 members.	6.1%
Rate increase if one employee of average age leaves the group, resulting in a group of 5 employees AND a current employee ages from 29 years to 30 years	17.6%	Rate increase if three employees of average age leave the group, AND three current employees age from 24 to 25 years, 44 to 45 years, and 54 to 55 years	9.2%
Rate increase if one employee in early 60s retires and a 40-year-old replacement is hired	-5.3%	Rate increase if one employee retires and a 40-year-old replacement is hired	1.5%

© 2010, Business Valuation Resources, LLC

Questions@BVResources.com

Sources Of Data

- **CMS Chief Actuary**
  - http://s3.amazonaws.com/thf_media/2010/pdf/OACT-Memo-FinImpactofPPACA-Enacted.pdf
- **MA Division Of Healthcare Finance & Policy**
  - http://www.mass.gov/Eeohhs2/docs/dhcfp/r/pubs/10/key_indicators_feb_10.ppt
  - http://www.mass.gov/Eeohhs2/docs/dhcfp/cost_trend_docs/presentations/2010_03_16_dianna_welch_trends.ppt
- **Commonwealth Fund**
  - Paying the Price: How Health Insurance Premiums Are Eating Up Middle-Class Incomes; August 2009
    - http://www.commonwealthfund.org/Content/Publications/Data-Briefs/2009/Aug/Paying-the-Price-How-Health-Insurance-Premiums-Are-Eating-Up-Middle-Class-Incomes.aspx
- **Kaiser Family Foundation**
  - Kaiser Fast Facts. Data Source: accessed on May 8, 2010; http://facts.kff.org/chartbook.aspx?cb=56

© 2010, Business Valuation Resources, LLC

Questions@BVResources.com

Appendix: Teleconference Transcript

Resources

- MedPAC 2010 *Report to Congress*
- AICPA *2010 National Healthcare Industry Conference*, Las Vegas: Nov 11 - Nov 12, Location: The Venetian
  https://www.cpa2biz.com/AST/Main/CPA2BIZ_Primary/FinancialManagement/Management/PRDOVR~PC-CARE/PC-CARE.jsp
- http://cpanet.typepad.com/ Mark Dietrich's BLOG
- American Health Lawyers Association
  - http://www.healthlawyers.org/Pages/Default.aspx

Resources

- Law Firm Sonnenschein Summary
  - http://www.sonnenschein.com/docs/Health_Care_Reform_Side-by-Side.pdf
- Kaiser Family Foundation on Reform
  - http://healthreform.kff.org/ (generally)
  - http://www.kff.org/healthreform/upload/8061.pdf
- Kaiser Family Foundation Subsidy Calculator
  - http://healthreform.kff.org/Subsidycalculator.aspx
- Kaiser Family/Alliance for Health Reform Podcast on Private Insurance Changes
  - http://www.kff.org/healthreform/ahr043010video.cfm

BVR
What It's Worth

www.BVResources.com

Bulletproof your valuation conclusions with BVR's comprehensive line of product offerings.

Every top firm depends on BVR for authoritative market data, continuing professional education, and expert opinion. So, turn to BVR whenever you need unimpeachable business valuation conclusions for any purpose. BVR's market databases, publications, and analysis have won in the courtroom—and the boardroom—for over a dozen years. All BVR products include a subscription to the profession's leading weekly eNewsletter, BVWire™, absolutely FREE!

Our expansive line of products include:

- Pratt's Stats®
- Public Stats™
- BIZCOMPS®
- Mergerstat®/BVR Control Premium Study™
- The FMV Restricted Stock Study™
- Valuation Advisors' Discount for Lack of Marketability Study™
- Integra 5-Year Industry Data Reports
- **NEW!** Duff & Phelps Risk Premium Reports
- Business Valuation Update™
- Deluxe BVUpdate™
- Annual Guides and Books
- Business Reference Guide Online Database

- Economic Outlook Update™
- BVLaw™
- BVResearch™
- Special reports, guides, and books
- Continuing Professional Education (CPE)
- BVNewsletter™ service
- BVBasics™ Seminar Package
- Teleconferences and Webinars
- Live Conferences
- BV Firm Marketing Services
- Butler Pinkerton Model™ - Total Cost of Equity (TCOE) and Public company Specific Risk Calculator

Learn more at www.BVResources.com

Business Valuation Resources, LLC . 1000 SW Broadway, Suite 1200 . Portland OR 97205
Phone: (503) 291-7963 . Fax: (503) 291-7955 . Email: CustomerService@BVResources.com